Lecture Notes in Computer Science 6012

Commenced Publication in 1973
Founding and Former Series Editors:
Gerhard Goos, Juris Hartmanis, and Jan van Leeuwen

Advanced Research in Computing and Software Science

Subline of Lectures Notes in Computer Science

Andrew D. Gordon (Ed.)

Programming Languages and Systems

19th European Symposium on Programming, ESOP 2010
Held as Part of the Joint European Conferences
on Theory and Practice of Software, ETAPS 2010
Paphos, Cyprus, March 20-28, 2010
Proceedings

 Springer

Volume Editor

Andrew D. Gordon
Microsoft Research
Roger Needham Building
7 J.J. Thomson Ave., Cambridge CB3 0FB, UK
E-mail: adg@microsoft.com

Library of Congress Control Number: 2010921912

CR Subject Classification (1998): D.2, F.3, C.2, D.3, H.4, D.1

LNCS Sublibrary: SL 1 – Theoretical Computer Science and General Issues

ISSN 0302-9743
ISBN 978-3-642-11956-9 Springer Berlin Heidelberg New York

Typesetting: Camera-ready by author, data conversion by Scientific Publishing Services, Chennai, India
Printed on acid-free paper   06/3180   5 4 3 2 1 0

Foreword

ETAPS 2010 was the 13th instance of the European Joint Conferences on Theory and Practice of Software. ETAPS is an annual federated conference that was established in 1998 by combining a number of existing and new conferences. This year it comprised the usual five sister conferences (CC, ESOP, FASE, FOSSACS, TACAS), 19 satellite workshops (ACCAT, ARSPA-WITS, Bytecode, CMCS, COCV, DCC, DICE, FBTC, FESCA, FOSS-AMA, GaLoP, GT-VMT, LDTA, MBT, PLACES, QAPL, SafeCert, WGT, and WRLA) and seven invited lectures (excluding those that were specific to the satellite events). The five main conferences this year received 497 submissions (including 31 tool demonstration papers), 130 of which were accepted (10 tool demos), giving an overall acceptance rate of 26%, with most of the conferences at around 24%. Congratulations therefore to all the authors who made it to the final programme! I hope that most of the other authors will still have found a way of participating in this exciting event, and that you will all continue submitting to ETAPS and contributing to make of it the best conference on software science and engineering.

The events that comprise ETAPS address various aspects of the system development process, including specification, design, implementation, analysis and improvement. The languages, methodologies and tools which support these activities are all well within its scope. Different blends of theory and practice are represented, with an inclination toward theory with a practical motivation on the one hand and soundly based practice on the other. Many of the issues involved in software design apply to systems in general, including hardware systems, and the emphasis on software is not intended to be exclusive.

ETAPS is a confederation in which each event retains its own identity, with a separate Programme Committee and proceedings. Its format is open-ended, allowing it to grow and evolve as time goes by. Contributed talks and system demonstrations are in synchronised parallel sessions, with invited lectures in plenary sessions. Two of the invited lectures are reserved for 'unifying' talks on topics of interest to the whole range of ETAPS attendees. The aim of cramming all this activity into a single one-week meeting is to create a strong magnet for academic and industrial researchers working on topics within its scope, giving them the opportunity to learn about research in related areas, and thereby to foster new and existing links between work in areas that were formerly addressed in separate meetings.

ETAPS 2010 was organised by the University of Cyprus in cooperation with:

▷ European Association for Theoretical Computer Science (EATCS)
▷ European Association for Programming Languages and Systems (EAPLS)
▷ European Association of Software Science and Technology (EASST)

and with support from the Cyprus Tourism Organisation.

The organising team comprised:

General Chairs: Tiziana Margaria and Anna Philippou
Local Chair: George Papadopoulos
Secretariat: Maria Kittira
Administration: Petros Stratis
Satellite Events: Anna Philippou
Website: Konstantinos Kakousis.

Overall planning for ETAPS conferences is the responsibility of its Steering Committee, whose current membership is:

Vladimiro Sassone (Southampton, Chair), Parosh Abdulla (Uppsala), Luca de Alfaro (Santa Cruz), Gilles Barthe (IMDEA-Software), Giuseppe Castagna (CNRS Paris), Marsha Chechik (Toronto), Sophia Drossopoulou (Imperial College London), Javier Esparza (TU Munich), Dimitra Giannakopoulou (CMU/NASA Ames), Andrew D. Gordon (MSR Cambridge), Rajiv Gupta (UC Riverside), Chris Hankin (Imperial College London), Holger Hermanns (Saarbrücken), Mike Hinchey (Lero, the Irish Software Engineering Research Centre), Martin Hofmann (LM Munich), Joost-Pieter Katoen (Aachen), Paul Klint (Amsterdam), Jens Knoop (Vienna), Shriram Krishnamurthi (Brown), Kim Larsen (Aalborg), Rustan Leino (MSR Redmond), Gerald Luettgen (Bamberg), Rupak Majumdar (Los Angeles), Tiziana Margaria (Potsdam), Ugo Montanari (Pisa), Oege de Moor (Oxford), Luke Ong (Oxford), Fernando Orejas (Barcelona) Catuscia Palamidessi (INRIA Paris), George Papadopoulos (Cyprus), David Rosenblum (UCL), Don Sannella (Edinburgh), João Saraiva (Minho), Michael Schwartzbach (Aarhus), Perdita Stevens (Edinburgh), Gabriele Taentzer (Marburg), and Martin Wirsing (LM Munich).

I would like to express my sincere gratitude to all of these people and organisations, the Programme Committee Chairs and members of the ETAPS conferences, the organizers of the satellite events, the speakers themselves, the many reviewers, all the participants, and Springer for agreeing to publish the ETAPS proceedings in the ARCoSS subline.

Finally, I would like to thank the Organising Chair of ETAPS 2010, George Papadopoulos, for arranging for us to have ETAPS in the most beautiful surroundings of Paphos.

January 2010   Vladimiro Sassone

Preface

This volume contains the papers presented at ESOP 2010, the 19th European Symposium on Programming held March 22–24, 2010 in Paphos (Cyprus).

ESOP is an annual conference devoted to fundamental issues in the specification, design, analysis, and implementation of programming languages and systems. The Programme Committee invited papers on all aspects of programming language research including, but not limited to, the following areas:

- Programming paradigms and styles: functional programming, object-oriented programming, aspect-oriented programming, logic programming, constraint programming, extensible programming languages, domain-specific languages, synchronous and real-time programming languages.
- Methods and tools to write and specify programs and languages: programming techniques, logical foundations, denotational semantics, operational semantics, meta programming, module systems, language-based security.
- Methods and tools for reasoning about programs: type systems, abstract interpretation, program verification, testing.
- Methods and tools for implementation: program transformations, rewriting systems, partial evaluation, experimental evaluations, virtual machines, intermediate languages, run-time environments.
- Concurrency and distribution: process algebras, concurrency theory, parallel programming, service-oriented computing, distributed and mobile languages.

After consultations within the programming language research community, we raised the page limit for ESOP 2010 to be 20 pages in LNCS format. We did so because research papers in programming languages tend to be longer than the 15 pages taken as the limit in previous editions of ESOP. This appears to be a successful change, and probably contributes to the healthy interest in ESOP as a publication venue; submissions to ESOP are up 20% year-on-year while the total of submissions to ETAPS conferences remains steady.

As for ESOP 2009, we included a rebuttal period as part of the selection procedure, when authors had the opportunity to respond to reviews. During that time, we obtained additional reviews on controversial papers, and on papers with only low-confidence reviews.

We received 149 abstracts and in the end got 121 full submissions, but one of these was rejected because it exceeded the page limit. Of the remaining 120 papers, each submission received at least 3, and on average 4, reviews from the Programme Committee members and their subreviewers. During a week-long electronic discussion, moderated by the wonderful EasyChair system, the committee selected 30 for publication. These proceedings consist of the 30 papers together with papers to accompany the invited lectures of Philip Wadler (ETAPS Unifying Speaker) and David Naumann (ESOP Invited Speaker).

I would like to thank the Programme Committee and our subreviewers for their hard work selecting papers for publication, and the authors of both accepted and rejected papers for their labours in research leading to submissions and to final papers. To those who were rejected I send our commiserations, with the hope that the reviews may be useful.

Finally, I would like to thank the local organizers, led by George Papadopoulos, without whom ETAPS would not take place, and last but not least Vladi Sassone, who does a superb job of herding the ETAPS cats.

January 2010   Andrew D. Gordon

Conference Organization

Programme Chair

Andrew D. Gordon   Microsoft Research (UK)

Programme Committee

Amal Ahmed	Indiana University (USA)
Anindya Banerjee	IMDEA Software (Spain)
Lars Birkedal	IT University of Copenhagen (Denmark)
Marzia Buscemi	IMT Lucca Institute for Advanced Studies (Italy)
Giuseppe Castagna	CNRS, Université Denis Diderot, Paris (France)
Patrick Cousot	ENS, Paris (France)
Dino Distefano	Queen Mary, University of London (UK)
Cormac Flanagan	UC Santa Cruz (USA)
Giorgio Ghelli	University of Pisa (Italy)
Sumit Gulwani	Microsoft Research, Redmond (USA)
Michael Hicks	University of Maryland, College Park (USA)
Naoki Kobayashi	Tohoku University (Japan)
Matteo Maffei	Saarland University (Germany)
Conor McBride	Strathclyde University (UK)
Anna Philippou	University of Cyprus (Cyprus)
Andreas Podelski	University of Freiburg (Germany)
Erik Poll	Radboud Universiteit Nijmegen (The Netherlands)
Julian Rathke	University of Southampton (UK)
Didier Rémy	INRIA Paris - Rocquencourt (France)
David Sands	Chalmers University of Technology (Sweden)
Helmut Seidl	TU Munich (Germany)
Greta Yorsh	IBM Research (USA)
Steve Zdancewic	University of Pennsylvania (USA)

External Reviewers

Acciai, Lucia	Baldan, Paolo
Adams, Michael	Barnett, Mike
Ahrendt, Wolfgang	Bartoletti, Massimo
Anderson, Austin	Beckman, Nels
Appel, Andrew	Berdine, Josh
Askarov, Aslan	Berg, Matthias
Atkey, Robert	Berger, Martin
Austin, Tom	Bettini, Lorenzo

Blume, Matthias
Bonchi, Filippo
Boreale, Michele
Brady, Edwin
Buisse, Alexandre
Burckhardt, Sebastian
Calcagno, Cristiano
Carbone, Marco
Carette, Jacques
Chadha, Rohit
Chang, Bor-Yuh Evan
Charguéraud, Arthur
Chaudhuri, Avik
Chaudhuri, Swarat
Chin, Wei-Ngan
Christ, Jürgen
Ciancia, Vincenzo
Ciobanu, Gabriel
Coleman, Joey
Cregut, Pierre
Danielsson, Nils Anders
Debois, Søren
de Vink, Erik
Demri, Stéphane
Dezani, Mariangiola
Dinsdale-Young, Thomas
Dodds, Mike
Dreyer, Derek
Dybvig, R. Kent
Escardo, Martin
Felty, Amy
Feng, Xinyu
Feret, Jérôme
Ferrara, Pietro
Filinski, Andrzej
Filipovic, Ivana
Flexeder, Andrea
Francalanza, Adrian
Freund, Stephen
Frisch, Alain
Garg, Deepak
Goethel, Thomas
Gorla, Daniele
Gotroff, Christian
Gotsman, Alexey

Hammon, Grégoire
Hancock, Peter
Harrison, John
Hasuo, Ichiro
Hoenicke, Jochen
Hoffmann, Jan
Horne, Ross
Hunt, Sebastian
Igarashi, Atsushi
Inaba, Kazuhiro
Jacobs, Bart
Jha, Somesh
Jones, Neil
Jost, Steffen
Kalvala, Sara
Kell, Stephen
Kennedy, Andrew
King, Andrew
Kiselyov, Oleg
Klein, Gerwin
Koopman, Pieter
Kreiker, Joerg
Lanese, Ivan
Lapadula, Alessandro
Lassen, Soren B.
Laud, Peeter
Laviron, Vincent
Le Botlan, Didier
Leconte, Jérémy
Leroy, Xavier
Lev-Ami, Tal
Licata, Daniel R
Lluch Lafuente, Alberto
Loreti, Michele
Lozes, Etiene
Müller-Olm, Markus
Magill, Stephen
Manzonetto, Giulio
Maranget, Luc
Massé, Damien
Mastroeni, Isabella
Mauborgne, Laurent
Mazza, Damiano
McCamant, Stephen
McKinna, James

Melgratti, Hernan
Miculan, Marino
Millstein, Todd
Miné, Antoine
Mitchell, Neil
Monniaux, David
Mostowski, Wojciech
Mu, Shin-Cheng
Mueller, Peter
Murawski, Andrzej
Myers, Andrew
Møgelberg, Rasmus
Nanevski, Aleksandar
Nanz, Sebastian
Neis, Georg
Norrish, Michael
O'Hearn, Peter
Ostermann, Klaus
Padovani, Luca
Parkinson, Matthew
Perez, Jorge A.
Petersen, Rasmus
Pitts, Andrew
Pottier, François
Pouillard, Nicolas
Pouzet, Marc
Ramalingam, G.
Raymond, Pascal
Régis-Gianas, Yann
Rensink, Arend
Reppy, John
Reus, Bernhard
Rinetzky, Noam
Rival, Xavier
Ross, Kyle
Rossberg, Andreas
Russo, Alejandro
Sankaranarayanan, Sriram
Saïdi, Hassen
Schack-Nielsen, Anders
Schmidt, Dave
Schöpp, Ulrich
Schwoon, Stefan
Serpette, Bernard

Sestoft, Peter
Sevcik, Jaroslav
Shao, Zhong
Shkaravska, Olha
Simon, Axel
Simpson, Alex
Singh, Rishabh
Souilah, Issam
Spitters, Bas
Spoto, Fausto
Sridharan, Manu
Srivastava, Saurabh
Staton, Sam
Støvring, Kristian
Sumii, Eijiro
Svendsen, Kasper
Svenningsson, Josef
Swamy, Nikhil
Tan, Gang
Terui, Kazushige
Thamsborg, Jacob
Thiemann, Peter
Tiwari, Ashish
Tiwary, Hans Raj
Torlak, Emina
Troina, Angelo
Unno, Hiroshi
Urban, Christian
van Eekelen, Marko
van Rossum, Peter
Varacca, Daniele
Veith, Helmut
Walker, David
Wehrheim, Heike
Wickerson, John
Wies, Thomas
Xu, Dana
Yang, Hongseok
Yuan, Hao
Zavattaro, Gianluigi
Zhai, Antonia
Zuleger, Florian
Zunino, Roberto

Table of Contents

The Audacity of Hope: Thoughts on Reclaiming the Database Dream
(ETAPS Invited Lecture) 1
  Sam Lindley and Philip Wadler

Dynamic Boundaries: Information Hiding by Second Order Framing
with First Order Assertions (ESOP Invited Lecture) 2
  David A. Naumann and Anindya Banerjee

Coupling Policy Iteration with Semi-definite Relaxation to Compute
Accurate Numerical Invariants in Static Analysis 23
  Assalé Adjé, Stéphane Gaubert, and Eric Goubault

Precise and Automated Contract-Based Reasoning for Verification
and Certification of Information Flow Properties of Programs with
Arrays 43
  Torben Amtoft, John Hatcliff, and Edwin Rodríguez

A Semantic Framework for Declassification and Endorsement 64
  Aslan Askarov and Andrew Myers

Amortised Resource Analysis with Separation Logic 85
  Robert Atkey

A PolyTime Functional Language from Light Linear Logic 104
  Patrick Baillot, Marco Gaboardi, and Virgile Mogbil

Testing Polymorphic Properties 125
  Jean-Philippe Bernardy, Patrik Jansson, and Koen Claessen

Formal Verification of Coalescing Graph-Coloring Register Allocation ... 145
  Sandrine Blazy, Benoît Robillard, and Andrew W. Appel

A Theory of Speculative Computation 165
  Gérard Boudol and Gustavo Petri

Propositional Interpolation and Abstract Interpretation 185
  Vijay D'Silva

Functional Programming in Sublinear Space 205
  Ugo Dal Lago and Ulrich Schöpp

Logical Concurrency Control from Sequential Proofs 226
  Jyotirmoy Deshmukh, G. Ramalingam,
  Venkatesh-Prasad Ranganath, and Kapil Vaswani

Fluid Updates: Beyond Strong vs.Weak Updates 246
   Isil Dillig, Thomas Dillig, and Alex Aiken

Parameterized Memory Models and Concurrent Separation Logic 267
   Rodrigo Ferreira, Xinyu Feng, and Zhong Shao

Amortized Resource Analysis with Polynomial Potential: A Static
Inference of Polynomial Bounds for Functional Programs.............. 287
   Jan Hoffmann and Martin Hofmann

Generative Operational Semantics for Relaxed Memory Models 307
   Radha Jagadeesan, Corin Pitcher, and James Riely

Automating Security Mediation Placement 327
   Dave King, Susmit Jha, Divya Muthukumaran, Trent Jaeger,
   Somesh Jha, and Sanjit A. Seshia

TRX: A Formally Verified Parser Interpreter 345
   Adam Koprowski and Henri Binsztok

On the Expressive Power of Primitives for Compensation Handling 366
   Ivan Lanese, Cátia Vaz, and Carla Ferreira

Separating Shape Graphs 387
   Vincent Laviron, Bor-Yuh Evan Chang, and Xavier Rival

Deadlock-Free Channels and Locks 407
   K. Rustan M. Leino, Peter Müller, and Jan Smans

Verifying a Compiler for Java Threads 427
   Andreas Lochbihler

A Grammar-Based Approach to Invertible Programs 448
   Kazutaka Matsuda, Shin-Cheng Mu, Zhenjiang Hu, and
   Masato Takeichi

Faulty Logic: Reasoning about Fault Tolerant Programs 468
   Matthew L. Meola and David Walker

A Hoare Logic for the Coinductive Trace-Based Big-Step Semantics of
While 488
   Keiko Nakata and Tarmo Uustalu

A Universal Calculus for Stream Processing Languages 507
   Robert Soulé, Martin Hirzel, Robert Grimm, Buğra Gedik,
   Henrique Andrade, Vibhore Kumar, and Kun-Lung Wu

Enforcing Stateful Authorization and Information Flow Policies in
FINE 529
   Nikhil Swamy, Juan Chen, and Ravi Chugh

Stateful Contracts for Affine Types 550
    Jesse A. Tov and Riccardo Pucella

CFA2: A Context-Free Approach to Control-Flow Analysis 570
    Dimitrios Vardoulakis and Olin Shivers

Weighted Dynamic Pushdown Networks 590
    Alexander Wenner

Explicit Stabilisation for Modular Rely-Guarantee Reasoning 610
    John Wickerson, Mike Dodds, and Matthew Parkinson

Author Index 631

The Audacity of Hope:
Thoughts on Reclaiming the Database Dream*

Sam Lindley and Philip Wadler

University of Edinburgh

Abstract. A venerable line of research aims to provide a general-purpose programming language with a well-defined subset that compiles into efficient queries, perhaps by translation into SQL or some other suitable query language. This talk discusses some older and more recent advances in this direction, including the languages Kleisli, LINQ, Ferry, M, and Links.

Twenty-five years ago, Copeland and Maier decried the "impedance mismatch" between databases and progamming languages, and Atkinson and Buneman observed "Databases and programming languages have developed almost independently of one another for the past twenty years", a situation that has not greatly changed in the intervening time, and spoke of "The need for a *uniform* language" (their emphasis).

The problem is simple: two languages are more than twice as difficult to use as one language. Most programming languages support data abstraction and nested data, while most relational databases support tables over a few fixed scalar types. Any task involving both requires that the programmer keep in mind two representations of the same underlying data, converting between them and synchronizing updates to either. This persistent bookkeeping adds to the mental burden on the programmer and adds to the complexity of the code.

The solution is equally simple: provide a single language with a well-defined subset that compiles into efficient queries, perhaps by translation into SQL or some other suitable query language. It is important that the subset support the abstraction mechanisms of the language, for example allowing one to lambda abstract over a predicate used in a query, where instantiating the abstraction with a specific predicate should result in an efficient query. In the simplest case, only flat data (such as bags of records) can be translated into the database. In a more sophisticated system, nested data (such as records of bags) can be represented in the database via a suitable encoding, the details of which need not concern the programmer. While easy to envision, practical implementation of such languages has proved elusive in practice.

This talk discusses some older and more recent advances in this direction, including the languages Kleisli, LINQ, Ferry, M, and Links.

---

* With apologies to Barack Obama and David August.

A.D. Gordon (Ed.): ESOP 2010, LNCS 6012, p. 1, 2010.

Dynamic Boundaries: Information Hiding by Second Order Framing with First Order Assertions

David A. Naumann[1],* and Anindya Banerjee[2],**

[1] Stevens Institute of Technology, Hoboken NJ, USA
[2] IMDEA Software, Madrid, Spain

Abstract. The hiding of internal invariants creates a mismatch between procedure specifications in an interface and proof obligations on the implementations of those procedures. The mismatch is sound if the invariants depend only on encapsulated state, but encapsulation is problematic in contemporary software due to the many uses of shared mutable objects. The mismatch is formalized here in a proof rule that achieves flexibility via explicit restrictions on client effects, expressed using ghost state and ordinary first order assertions.

1 Introduction

From the simplest collection class to the most complex application framework, software modules provide useful abstractions by hiding the complexity of efficient implementations. Many abstractions and most representations involve state, so the information to be hidden includes invariants on internal data structures. Hoare described the hiding of invariants as a mismatch between the procedure specifications in a module interface, used for reasoning about client code, and the specifications with respect to which implementations of those procedures are verified. The latter assume the invariant and are obliged to maintain it [17]. The justification is simple: A hidden invariant should depend only on encapsulated state, in which case it is necessarily maintained by client code. Hoare's formalization was set in a high level object-oriented language (Simula 67), which is remarkable because for such languages the encapsulation problem has far too many recent published solutions to be considered definitively solved.

For reasoning about shared, dynamically allocated objects, the last decade has seen major advances, especially the emergence of Separation Logic, which helped reduce what O'Hearn et al. aptly called a "mismatch between the simple intuitions about the way pointer operations work and the complexity of their axiomatic treatments" [29, Sect. 1]. For encapsulation, there remains a gap between the simple idea of hiding an invariant and the profusion of complex encapsulation techniques and methodologies. The profusion is a result of tensions between

- The need to prevent violations of encapsulation due to misuse of shared references.
- The need to encompass useful designs including overlapping and non-regular data structures, callbacks, and the deliberate use of shared references that cross encapsulation boundaries. Illustrative examples are the topic of Sect. 2.

* Partially supported by US NSF awards CNS-0627338, CRI-0708330, CCF-0915611.
** Partially supported by US NSF awards CNS-0627748.

A.D. Gordon (Ed.): ESOP 2010, LNCS 6012, pp. 2–22, 2010.

- The need for effective, modular reasoning on both sides of an interface: for clients and for the module implementation.
- The hope to achieve high automation through mature techniques including types and static analyses as well as theorem proving.
- The need to encompass language features such as parametric polymorphism and code pointers for which semantics is difficult.

This paper seeks to reconcile all but the last of these and to bridge the gap using a simple but flexible idea that complements scope-based encapsulation. The idea is to include in an interface specification an explicit description of the key intuition, the internal state or "heap footprint" on which an invariant rests. This set of locations, called the *dynamic boundary*, is designated by an expression that may depend on ordinary and ghost state.

We formalize the idea using first order assertions in a Hoare logic for object based programs called Region Logic (Sect. 3); it is adapted from a previous paper in which we briefly sketched the idea and approach [2]. Our approach is based on correctness judgements with hypotheses, to account for linking of client code to the modules used, and a frame rule to capture hiding. These two ingredients data back to the 1970's (e.g., [15]) but we build directly on their novel combination in the second order frame rule of separation logic [30]. Our version of the rule is the topic of Sect. 4.

Owing to the explicit expression of footprints, region logic for first order programs and specifications has an elementary semantics and is amenable to automation with SMT solvers [21]. One price to pay is verbosity, but the foundation explored in this paper supports syntactic sugars for common cases while avoiding the need to hard-code those cases. Another price is an additional proof obligation on clients, to respect the dynamic boundaries of modules used. In many cases this can be discharged by type checking. But our main goal is to account for hiding in a way that is sufficiently flexible to encompass ad hoc disciplines for encapsulation; even more, to let the formalization of such a discipline be a matter of program annotation, with its adequacy checked by a verification tool, rather than being fodder for research papers.

The main result is soundness of our second order frame and boundary introduction rules, whose range of applicability is indicated by application, in Sect. 5, to the examples in Sect. 2. For lack of space, technical details are only skimmed, as is related work (Sect. 6). An appendix with the soundness proof can be found online.

2 The Challenge of Hiding Invariants on Shared Mutable Objects

2.1 A Collection Implemented by a List

We begin with a textbook example of encapsulation and information hiding, the toy program in Fig. 1.[1] Annotations include method postconditions that refer to a global variable, *pool*, marked as ghost state. Ghost variables and fields are auxiliary state used

---

[1] The programming notation is similar to sequential Java. A value of a class type like *Node* is either null or a reference to an allocated object with the fields declared in its class. Methods have an implicit parameter, self, which may be elided in field updates; e.g., the assignment *lst* := null in the body of the *Set* constructor is short for self.*lst* := null.

ghost *pool* : rgn;

class *Set* { *lst* : *Node*; ghost *rep* : rgn;
  model *elements* = *elts*(*lst*)
      where *elts*(*n* : *Node*) = (if *n* = null then $\varnothing$ else {*n.val*} $\cup$ *elts*(*n.nxt*))

  Set() ensures *elements* = $\varnothing$ $\wedge$ *pool* = old(*pool*) $\cup$ {self}
  { *lst* := null; *rep* := $\varnothing$; *pool* := *pool* $\cup$ {self}; }

  add(*i* : int) ensures *elements* = old(*elements*) $\cup$ {*i*}
  { if ¬*contains*(*i*) then var *n* : *Node* := new *Node*; *n.val* := *i*; *n.nxt* := *lst*; *lst* := *n*;
                        n.own := self; *rep* := *rep* $\cup$ {*n*}; endif }

  contains(*i* : int) : boolean ensures result = (*i* $\in$ *elements*) { "linear search for *i*" }
  remove(*i* : int) ensures *elements* = old(*elements*) − {*i*} { "remove first *i*, if any" } }

class *Node* { *val* : int; *nxt* : *Node*; ghost *own* : Object; }   //library code, not part of *SET*

Fig. 1. Module *SET*, together with class *Node*. Variable result is the returned result.

in reasoning, but not mentioned in branch conditions or expressions assigned to ordinary state. Assignments to ghost state can be removed from a program without altering its observable behavior, so ghosts support reasoning about that behavior. A *region* is a set of object references (which may include the improper reference, null). Type rgn, which denotes regions, is used only for ghost state.

The specifications are expressed in terms of an integer set, *elements*. Abstraction of this sort is commonplace and plays a role in Hoare's paper [17], but it is included here only to flesh out the example. Our concern is with other aspects so we content ourselves with a recursive definition (of *elts*) that may seem naïve in not addressing the possibility of cyclic references.

Suppose the implementation of *remove* only removes the first occurrence of *i*, if any. That is, it relies on the invariant that no integer value is duplicated in the singly linked list rooted at *lst*. To cater for effective automated verification, especially using SMT solvers, we want to avoid using reachability or other recursively defined notions in the invariant. The ghost field *rep* is intended to refer to the set of nodes reachable from field *lst* via *nxt*. The invariant is expressed using elementary set theoretic notions including the image of a region under a field. The expression *s.rep*ʻ*nxt* denotes the region consisting of *nxt* values of objects in region *s.rep*. It is used in this definition:[2]

$$SetI(s : Set): \quad (\forall n, m : Node \in s.rep \mid n = m \vee n.val \neq m.val)$$
$$\wedge \; s.lst \in s.rep \wedge s.rep\text{ʻ}nxt \subseteq s.rep \wedge s.rep\text{ʻ}own \subseteq \{s\}$$

The first conjunct says there are no duplicates among elements of *s.rep*. The next says that *s.rep* contains the first node, if any (or else null). The inclusion *s.rep*ʻ*nxt* $\subseteq$ *s.rep*

[2] The range condition "*n* $\in$ *s.rep*" is false in case *s* is null, because *n* $\in$ *s.rep* is shorthand for *n* $\in$ {*s*}ʻ*rep* and {null}ʻ*rep* is empty. Our assertion logic is 2-valued and avoids undefined expressions. We do not use sets of regions. The image operator flattens, for region fields: For any region expression *G*, the image region *G*ʻ*rep* is the union of *rep* images whereas *G*ʻ*nxt* is the set of *nxt* images, because *rep* has type rgn and *nxt* has class type.

says that $s.rep$ is nxt-closed; this is equivalent to $\forall o \mid o \in s.rep \Rightarrow o.nxt \in s.rep$.[3] One can show by induction that these conditions imply there are no duplicates; so the invariant says what we want, though not itself using induction. However, $s.rep$ could be nxt-closed even if $s.rep$ contained extraneous objects, in particular nodes reached from other instances of Set. This is prevented by the inclusion $s.rep`own \subseteq \{s\}$; or rather, by requiring the inclusion for every instance of Set. So we adopt an invariant to be associated with module SET:

$$I_{set}: \quad \text{null} \notin pool \land \forall s: Set \in pool \mid SetI(s)$$

As used here, variable $pool$ is superfluous, but we are hinting at examples where an invariant is not maintained for all instances of a class but, e.g., only those created by a factory method. The need for null $\notin pool$ is minor and discussed later. A bigger concern is the global nature of I_{set}, which is addressed in Sect. 3.2.

Consider this client code, acting on boolean variable b, under precondition $true$:

$$\text{var } s: Set := \text{ new } Set; \text{ var } n: Node := \text{ new } Node;$$
$$s.add(1); \; s.add(2); \; n.val := 1; \; s.remove(1); \; b := s.contains(1); \tag{1}$$

The implementation of $remove$ relies on the invariant $SetI(s)$, but this is not included as a precondition in Fig. 1 and the client is thus not responsible to establish it before the invocation of $remove$. As articulated by Hoare [17], the justification is that the invariant appears as both pre- and post-condition for verification of the methods add, $remove$, $contains$, and should be established by the Set constructor. And the invariant should depend only on state that is encapsulated. So it is not falsified by the initialization of n and still holds following $s.add(2)$; again by encapsulation it is not falsified by the update $n.val := 1$ so it holds as assumed by $s.remove$.

We call this *Hoare's mismatch*: the specifications used in reasoning about invocations in client code, i.e. code outside the encapsulation boundary, differ from those used to verify the implementations of the invoked methods. By contrast, ordinary procedure call rules in program logic use the same specification at the call site and to verify the procedure implementation. Automated, modular verifiers are often based on an intermediate language using assert and assume statements: At a call site the method precondition is asserted and this same precondition is assumed for the method's implementation; so the assumption is justified by the semantics of assert and assume. Hoare's mismatch asserts the public precondition but assumes an added conjunct, the invariant.

The mismatch is unsound if encapsulation is faulty, which can easily happen due to shared references, e.g., if in place of $n.val := 1$ the client code had $s.lst.val := 1$. Lexical scope and typing can provide encapsulation, e.g., field lst should have module scope. (We gloss over scope in the examples.) However, scope does not prevent that references can be leaked to clients, e.g., via a global variable of type Object. Moreover, code within the module, acting on one instance of Set, could violate the invariant of another instance. Besides scope and typing, a popular technique to deal with encapsulation in the presence of pointers is "ownership" (e.g., [9,11]). Ownership systems restrict the form of invariants and the use of references, to support modular reasoning

---

[3] Quantified variables range over non-null, allocated references.

ghost *freed* : rgn;
var *flist* : *Node*; *count* : int;
alloc() : *Node*
    ensures result $\neq$ null $\wedge$ *freed* = old(*freed*) − {result} $\wedge$ (result $\in$ old(*freed*) $\vee$ fresh(result))
{ if *count* = 0 then result : = new *Node*;
    else result : = *flist*; *flist* : = *flist*.*nxt*; *count* : = *count* − 1; *freed* : = *freed* − {result}; endif}
free(*n* : *Node*) requires *n* $\neq$ null $\wedge$ *n* $\notin$ *freed*   ensures *freed* = old(*freed*) $\cup$ {*n*}
{ *n*.*nxt* : = *flist*; *flist* : = *n*; *count* : = *count* − 1; *freed* : = *freed* $\cup$ {*n*}; }

Fig. 2. Module *MM*

at the granularity of a single instance and its representation. Ownership works well for *SetI* and indeed for invariants in many programs.

2.2 A Toy Memory Manager

It is difficult to find a single notion of ownership that is sufficiently flexible yet sound for invariant hiding. Fig. 2 presents a module that is static in the sense that there is a single memory manager, not a class of them. Instances of class *Node* (from Fig. 1) are treated as a resource. The instances currently "owned" by the module are tracked using variable *freed*. The hidden invariant, I_{mm}, is defined to be $FC(flist, freed, count)$ where $FC(f : Node, r : \text{rgn}, c : \text{int})$ is defined, by induction on the size of r, as

$$(f = \text{null} \Rightarrow r = \varnothing \wedge c = 0) \wedge (f \neq \text{null} \Rightarrow f \in r \wedge c > 0 \wedge FC(f.nxt, r - \{f\}, c - 1))$$

The invariant says *freed* is the nodes reached from *flist* and *count* is the size. The implementation of *alloc* relies on accuracy of *count*. It relies directly on *count* $\neq 0 \Rightarrow$ *flist* $\neq$ null, as otherwise the dereference *flist*.*nxt* could fault, but for this to hold on subsequent calls the stronger condition I_{mm} needs to be maintained as invariant.

Consider this strange client that both reads and writes data in the free list —but not in a way that interferes with the module.

var x, y : *Node*; x : = new *Node*; y : = *alloc*(); *free*(x); *free*(y);
while $y \neq$ null do y.*val* : = 7; y : = y.*nxt*; od

The loop updates *val* fields of freed objects, but it does not write the *nxt* fields, on which the invariant depends; the client never causes a fault. Suppose we replaced the loop by the assignment y.*nxt* : = null. This falsifies the invariant I_{mm}, if initially *count* is sufficiently high, and then subsequent invocations of *alloc* break.

The strange client is rejected by most ownership systems. But there is an encapsulation boundary here: clients must not write the *nxt* field of objects in *freed* (nor write variables *flist* and *count*). The strange client respects this boundary.

Sharing of references across encapsulation boundaries is common in system code, at the C level of abstraction. But it also occurs with notional resources such as database connections in programs at the level of abstraction we consider here, where references are abstract values susceptible only to equality test and field dereference.

class *Subject* { *obs*: *Observer*; *val*:int; ghost O:rgn;

  Subject() { *obs*:= null; *val*:= 0; O:= $\varnothing$; }

  update(n:int) ensures $\forall b$: *Observer* $\in O$ | $Obs(b,\text{self},n)$
  { *val*:= n; var b: *Observer*:= *obs*; while $b \neq$ null do $b.notify()$; b:= $b.nxto$; od }

  get():int { result:= *val*; }

  register(b: *Observer*) { $b.nxto$:= *obs*; *obs*:= b; O:= $O \cup \{b\}$; $b.notify()$; } }

class *Observer* { *sub*: *Subject*; *cache*:int; *nxto*: *Observer*;

  Observer(s: *Subject*) requires $\forall b$: *Observer* $\in s.O$ | $Obs(b,s,s.val)$
              ensures self $\in s.O \wedge \forall b$: *Observer* $\in s.O$ | $Obs(b,s,s.val)$
  { *sub*:= s; $s.register$(self); }

  notify() { *cache*:= *sub.get*(); } }

Fig. 3. Module OB. We define $Obs(b,s,v)$ as $b.sub = s \wedge b.cache = v$.

2.3 Observer Pattern: Cluster Invariants

Fig. 3 is a simple version of the Observer design pattern in which an observer only tracks a single subject. Parkinson [31] used the example to argue against instance-oriented notions of invariant. We address that issue using a single invariant predicate that in effect quantifies over clusters of client-visible objects. Classes *Subject* and *Observer* are together in a module, in which methods *register* and *notify* should have module scope. The implementation maintains the elements of O in the *nxto*-linked list threaded through the observers themselves, and it relies on the hidden invariant

$$I_{ob}: \quad (\forall s: Subject \mid List(s.obs, s.O)) \wedge (\forall o: Observer \mid o.sub \neq \text{null} \Rightarrow o \in o.sub.O)$$

where $List(o, r)$ says the list beginning at o lies in region r (compare FC in Sect. 2.2). The second conjunct of I_{ob} says that any observer tracking a subject lies in that subject's O region. As with I_{set}, the instantiations of I_{ob} are local in that they depend on nearby objects, but here a subject and its observers form a cooperating cluster of objects not in an ownership relation. Clients may rely on separation between clusters. As an example, consider a state in which there are two subjects s, t with $s.val = 0$ and $t.val = 5$. Consider this client: $o:=$ new $Observer(s); p:=$ new $Observer(t); s.update(2)$. Owing to separation, $t.val = 5$ holds in the final state.

2.4 Overlapping Data Structures and Nested Modules

One feature of the preceding example is that there is an overlapping data structure because a list structure is threaded through observer objects that are client visible. We now consider another example which further illustrates overlapping data structures and also hiding in the presence of nested modules. The module in Fig. 4 consists of a class, *ObsSet*, that extends *Observer*. Instances of *ObsSet* are in two overlapping data structures. First, these objects are arranged in a cyclic doubly-linked list, traversed using *next* and *prev* pointers, whose elements may be observing the same or different subjects. Second, each *ObsSet* is in the *nxto*-linked list of observers of its subject.

```
class ObsSet extends Observer { next : ObsSet; prev : ObsSet;
  ObsSet(s : Subject, os : ObsSet)
    requires ∀b : Observer ∈ s.O | Obs(b, s, s.val)
    ensures self ∈ s.O ∧ ∀b : Observer ∈ s.O | Obs(b, s, s.val)
  { super(s);
    if os = null then prev := self; next := self;
    else next := os; prev := os.prev; os.prev.next := self; os.prev := self; endif } }
```

Fig. 4. Module OS

The constructor of $ObsSet$ first calls the superclass constructor, $Observer$, with subject s. This call adds the newly allocated object to the front of the list of observers of s. The newly allocated object is then added to the cyclic doubly-linked list by manipulating $next$ and $prev$ pointers.

Module OS is defined in the context of module OB, because $ObsSet$ is a subclass of $Observer$. The verification of the implementation of $ObsSet$ will require its module invariant, but not I_{ob}. The invariant I_{os} expresses a simple property of cyclic doubly-linked lists: $os.prev.next = os \land os.next.prev = os$ for all allocated os of type $ObsSet$. Despite the overlapping structure, there is no interference between the code and invariants of modules OB and OS because different locations are involved.

Interesting variations on the example include observers that track multiple subjects, and observers that are also in the role of subject (cf. [19]). Of particular interest are callbacks between modules (as opposed to the $notify/get$ callback within module OB), which are within reach of our approach but not formalized in this paper.

3   Region Logic Background: Effects and First Order Framing

3.1   Preliminaries: Programming Language, States, Assertions

Our formal results are given for an idealized object-based language with syntax sketched in Fig. 5. Programs are considered in the context of a fixed collection of class declarations, of the form class $K \{ \bar{f} : \bar{T} \}$, where field types may make mutually recursive reference to other classes. We write Fields(K) for $\bar{f} : \bar{T}$ and for simplicity let names in the list $\bar{f}$ have global scope. Ordinary expressions do not depend on the heap: $y.f$ is not an expression but rather part of the command $x := y.f$ for reading a field, as in separation logic. Instead of methods associated with classes, we formalize simple

$$
\begin{array}{llr}
T & ::= \text{int} \mid K \mid \text{rgn} \quad \text{where } K \text{ is in } DeclaredClassName & \text{data types} \\
E & ::= x \mid c \mid \text{null} \mid E \oplus E \quad \text{where } c \text{ is in } \mathbb{Z}, \oplus \text{ in } \{=, +, >, \ldots\} & \text{ordinary expressions} \\
G & ::= x \mid \{E\} \mid \varnothing \mid G`f \mid G \otimes G \quad \text{where } \otimes \text{ is in } \{\cup, \cap, -\} & \text{region expressions} \\
F & ::= E \mid G & \text{expressions} \\
C & ::= m(x) \mid x := F \mid x := \text{new } K \mid x := x.f \mid x.f := F & \text{primitive commands} \\
  & \mid \text{let } m(x : T) \text{ be } C \text{ in } C \mid \text{var } x : T \text{ in } C \text{ end} \mid C ; C \mid \ldots & \text{binding, control struct.}
\end{array}
$$

Fig. 5. Program syntax, where $x \in VarName$, $f \in FieldName$, $m \in ProcName$

procedures without an implicit self parameter. The typing judgement for commands is written as $\Pi \vdash^\Gamma C$ where Γ is a variable context and Π is a list of procedure signatures of the form $m(x:T)$. The form "let $m(x:T)$ be B in C" is typable in context Π and Γ if $\Pi, m:(x:T) \vdash^{\Gamma, x:T} B$ and $\Pi, m:(x:T) \vdash^\Gamma C$. The generalization to multiple parameters and mutually recursive procedures is straightforward and left to the reader. Typing rules enforce that type int is separated from reference types: there is no pointer arithmetic, but pointers can be tested for equality. The variable alloc, being of type rgn, cannot occur in non-ghost code.

The semantics is based on conventional program states. We assume given a set Ref of reference values including a distinguished value, null. A Γ-*state* has a global heap and a store. The store assigns values to the variables in Γ and to the variable alloc:rgn which is special in that its updates are built in to the semantics of the language: newly allocated references are added and there are no other updates, so it holds the set of allocated references. The heap maps each allocated reference to its type (which is immutable) and field values. The values of a class type K are null and allocated references of type K. We assume the usual operations are available for a state σ. For example, $\sigma(x)$ is the value of variable x, $\sigma(F)$ is the value of expression F, Type(o, σ) is the type of an allocated reference o, Update($\sigma, o.f, v$) overrides σ to map field f of o to v (for $o \in \sigma(\text{alloc})$), Extend($\sigma, x, v$) extends σ to map x to value v (for $x \notin \text{Dom}(\sigma)$). Heaps have no dangling references; we do not model garbage collection or deallocation.

In a given state the region expression $G^\iota f$ (read "G's image under f") denotes one of two things. If f has class type then $G^\iota f$ is the set of values $o.f$ where o ranges over (non-null) elements of G that have field f. If f has region type, like rep in our example, then $G^\iota f$ is the union of the values of f.

Assertions are interpreted with respect to a single state, e.g., the semantics of the primitive $x.f = E$ that reads a field is defined: $\sigma \models x.f = E$ iff $\sigma(x) \neq$ null and $\sigma(x.f) = \sigma(E)$. The operator "old" used in specifications can be desugared using auxiliaries quantified over specifications (omitted from this version of the paper). We do not use quantified variables of type rgn. Quantified variables of class type range over non-null, currently allocated references: $\sigma \models^\Gamma (\forall x:K \mid P)$ iff Extend(σ, x, o) $\models^{\Gamma, x:K} P$ for all $o \in \sigma(\text{alloc})$ such that Type(o, σ) $= K$. In a richer language with subclassing, this would be $\leq K$.

3.2 Effect Specifications and the Framing of Commands and Formulas

Let us augment the specifications in Fig. 1 with the effect specifications in Fig. 6. Effects are given by the grammar $\varepsilon ::= \text{wr } x \mid \text{rd } x \mid \text{wr } G^\iota f \mid \text{rd } G^\iota f \mid \text{fr } G$. We omit tags wr and rd in lists of effects of the same kind. In this paper, read effects are used for formulas and write effects as frame conditions for commands and methods; commands are allowed to read anything. Freshness effect fr G is used for commands; it says that the value of G in

$Set()$	wr *pool*
$add(i:int)$	wr alloc, self.any, self.rep^ιany
$remove(i:int)$	wr self.any, self.rep^ιany

Fig. 6. Effect specifications for methods in Fig. 1. For *contains* the specification has no effects.

the final state contains only (but not necessarily all) references that were not allocated in the initial state.

The effect specification for the constructor method, $Set()$, says variable *pool* may be updated. For *add*, the effect wr alloc means that new objects may be allocated. The effect wr self.any says that any fields of self may be written. The effect wr self.*rep*'any says that any field of any object in self.*rep* may be written; in fact none are written in our implementation, but this caters for other implementations. The effect wr self.*rep*'any is state dependent, because *rep* is a mutable field.

In general, let G be a region expression and f be a field name. The effect wr G'f refers to l-values: the locations of the f fields of objects in G —where G is interpreted in the initial state. A location is merely a reference paired with a field name.

An effect of the form wr $x.f$ abbreviates wr $\{x\}$'f. In case x is null, this is well defined and designates the empty set of locations. We also allow f to be a data group [26], e.g., the built-in data group "any" that stands for all fields of an object.

We say effect list $\bar{\varepsilon}$ *allows transition from* σ *to* σ', written $\sigma \rightsquigarrow \sigma' \models \bar{\varepsilon}$, if and only if σ' succeeds[4] σ and

(a) for every y in $\mathrm{Dom}(\Gamma) \cup \{\mathrm{alloc}\}$, either $\sigma(y) = \sigma'(y)$ or wr y is in $\bar{\varepsilon}$
(b) for every o in $\sigma(\mathrm{alloc})$ and every f in Fields(Type(o,σ)), either $\sigma(o.f) = \sigma'(o.f)$
    or there is G such that wr G'f is in $\bar{\varepsilon}$ and o is in $\sigma(G)$
(c) for each fr G in $\bar{\varepsilon}$, we have $\sigma'(G) \subseteq \sigma'(\mathrm{alloc}) - \sigma(\mathrm{alloc})$.

Formulas are framed by read effects. We aim to make explicit the footprint of I_{set}, which will serve as a dynamic boundary expressing the state-dependent aspect of the encapsulation that will allow I_{set} to be hidden from clients. First we frame the object invariant $SetI(s)$, which will be used for "local reasoning" [29] at the granularity of a single instance of Set. We choose to frame[5] it by

$$\bar{\delta}_0: \quad \mathrm{rd}\ s,\ s.(rep, lst),\ s.rep\text{'}(nxt, val, own) \qquad \text{(abbreviating } s.rep, s.lst, \text{ etc.)}$$

A read effect designates l-values. Here, $\bar{\delta}_0$ allows to read variable s, fields *rep* and *lst* of the object currently referenced by s if any, and the fields *nxt*, *val*, and *own* of any objects in the current value of *s.rep*.

We use a judgement for framing of formulas, e.g., $true \vdash \bar{\delta}_0$ frames $SetI(s)$ says that if two states agree on the locations designated by $\bar{\delta}_0$ then they agree on the value of $SetI(s)$. The judgement involves a formula, here $true$, because framing by state-dependent effects may hold only under some conditions on that state. For example we have $s \in pool \vdash \mathrm{rd}\, pool$'$(rep, lst)$ frames $s.lst \in s.rep$.

The semantics of judgement $P \vdash \bar{\delta}$ frames P' is specified by the following: If $\sigma \models P$ and Agree($\sigma, \sigma', \bar{\delta}$) then $\sigma \models P'$ implies $\sigma' \models P'$. Here Agree($\sigma, \sigma', \bar{\delta}$) is defined to mean: σ' succeeds σ, $\sigma(x) = \sigma'(x)$ for all rd x in $\bar{\delta}$, and $\sigma(o.f) = \sigma'(o.f)$ for all rd G'f in $\bar{\delta}$ and all $o \in \sigma(G)$ with $f \in$ Fields(o, σ).

There are two ways to establish a framing judgement. One is to directly check the semantics, which is straightforward but incomplete using an SMT prover, provided the

---

[4] σ' *succeeds* σ iff $\sigma(\mathrm{alloc}) \subseteq \sigma'(\mathrm{alloc})$ and Type(o,σ) = Type(o,σ') for all $o \in \sigma(\mathrm{alloc})$.
[5] The term "frame" traditionally refers to that which does not change, but frame conditions specify what may change. To avoid confusion we refrain from using "frame" as a noun.

heap model admits quantification over field names (to express agreement). The other way is to use inference rules for the judgement [2]. These include syntax-directed rules together with first-order provability and subsumption. As an example, the rule for $P \vdash \overline{\eta}$ frames $(\forall x : K \mid x \in G \Rightarrow P')$ has antecedent of the form $P \wedge x \in G \vdash \overline{\eta}'$ frames P' and requires $\overline{\eta}$ to subsume the footprint of G. Our rules are proved to yield a stronger property than the specification: $\sigma \models P'$ iff $\sigma' \models P'$ when $\sigma \models P$ and $\text{Agree}(\sigma, \sigma', \overline{\eta})$.

For I_{set}, we can use the specific judgements above to derive $true \vdash \overline{\delta}_{set}$ frames I_{set}, where $\overline{\delta}_{set}$ is rd $pool, pool^{\mathsf{c}}(rep, lst), pool^{\mathsf{c}}rep^{\mathsf{c}}(nxt, val, own)$. This is subsumed by

$\overline{\theta}_{set}$: rd $pool, pool^{\mathsf{c}}$any$, pool^{\mathsf{c}}rep^{\mathsf{c}}$any

A frame rule. To verify the implementations in Fig. 1 we would like to reason in terms of a single instance of *Set*. Let B_{add} be the body of method *add*. By ordinary means we can verify that B_{add} satisfies the frame conditions wr alloc, self.any and thus those for *add* in Fig. 6. Moreover we can verify the following Hoare triple:

$$\{SetI(\mathsf{self})\} \ B_{add} \ \{SetI(\mathsf{self}) \wedge elements = \text{old}(elements) \cup \{i\}\} \qquad (2)$$

From this local property we aim to derive that B_{add} preserves the global invariant I_{set}. It is for this reason that $SetI(s)$ includes ownership conditions. These yield a confinement property: $I_{set} \Rightarrow (\forall s, t : Set \in pool \mid s = t \vee s.rep \# t.rep)$, because if $n \neq$ null, and n is in $s.rep \cap t.rep$ then $n.own = s$ and $n.own = t$. Here # denotes disjointness of sets; more precisely, $G \# G'$ means $G \cap G' \subseteq \{\text{null}\}$. Now I_{set} is logically equivalent to $SetI(\mathsf{self}) \wedge Iexcept$, with $\overline{\delta}_x$ framing $Iexcept$, defined as

$Iexcept$: null $\notin pool \wedge \forall s \in pool - \{\mathsf{self}\} \mid SetI(s)$

$\overline{\delta}_x$: rd self, $pool, (pool - \{\mathsf{self}\})^{\mathsf{c}}(rep, lst), (pool - \{\mathsf{self}\})^{\mathsf{c}}rep^{\mathsf{c}}(nxt, val, own)$

We aim to conjoin $Iexcept$ to the pre and post conditions of (2). To make this precise we use an operator $\star$, called the *separator*. If $\overline{\delta}$ is a set of read effects and $\overline{\varepsilon}$ is a set of write effects then $\overline{\delta} \star \overline{\varepsilon}$ is a conjunction of disjointness formulas, describing states in which writes allowed by $\overline{\varepsilon}$ cannot affect the value of a formula with footprint $\overline{\delta}$. The formula $\overline{\delta} \star \overline{\varepsilon}$ can be defined by induction on the syntax of effects [2]. Its meaning is specified by this property: If $\sigma \rightsquigarrow \sigma' \models \overline{\varepsilon}$ and $\sigma \models \overline{\delta} \star \overline{\varepsilon}$ then $\text{Agree}(\sigma, \sigma', \overline{\delta})$.

It happens that $\overline{\delta}_x \star (\text{wr self.any}, \text{wr alloc})$ is *true*. So, to complete the proof of $\{I_{set}\} B_{add} \{elements = \text{old}(elements) \cup \{i\} \wedge I_{set}\}$ we can take Q to be $Iexcept$ and $\overline{\delta}$ to be $\overline{\delta}_x$ in this rule which uses notations explained in Sect. 3.3:

$$\text{FRAME} \ \frac{\Delta \vdash \{P\} \ C \ \{P'\} \ [\overline{\varepsilon}] \qquad P \vdash \overline{\delta} \text{ frames } Q \qquad P \Rightarrow \overline{\delta} \star \overline{\varepsilon}}{\Delta \vdash \{P \wedge Q\} \ C \ \{P' \wedge Q\} \ [\overline{\varepsilon}]}$$

Similar reasoning verifies the implementation of *remove*. Note that its effects include wr self.rep^{c}any. Moreover $\overline{\delta}_x \star$ wr self.rep^{c}any yields nontrivial disjointnesses: self.$rep \# (pool - \{\mathsf{self}\}) \wedge$ self.$rep \# (pool - \{\mathsf{self}\})^{\mathsf{c}}rep$. The first conjunct holds because elements of self.rep have type *Node* and those of $pool - \{\mathsf{self}\}$ have type *Set* (details left to reader). The second conjunct is a consequence of the ownership confinement property mentioned earlier, which follows from I_{set}. For verifying *remove*, the precondition P in FRAME will be $true \wedge I_{set}$ because $true$ is the precondition of *remove* in Fig. 1.

$$\langle \text{let } m(x:T) \text{ be } B \text{ in } C, \sigma, \mu \rangle \longmapsto \langle (C;\text{end}(m)), \sigma, \text{Extend}(\mu, m, (\lambda x:T.B)) \rangle$$

$$\frac{\mu(m) = \lambda x:T.B \qquad x' \notin \text{Dom}(\sigma) \qquad x' \notin params(\Delta) \qquad B' = B_{x'}^x}{\langle m(z), \sigma, \mu \rangle \longmapsto \langle (B';\text{end}(x')), \text{Extend}(\sigma, x', \sigma(z)), \mu \rangle}$$

$$\frac{\Delta \text{ contains } \{P\}m(x:T)\{P'\}[\bar{\varepsilon}]}{\langle m(z), \sigma, \mu \rangle \longmapsto \langle \text{skip}, \sigma', \mu \rangle} \qquad \frac{\sigma \rightsquigarrow \sigma' \models \bar{\varepsilon} \qquad \text{Extend}(\sigma, x, \sigma(z)) \models P \qquad \text{Extend}(\sigma', x, \sigma(z)) \models P'}{}$$

$$\frac{\Delta \text{ contains } \{P\}m(x:T)\{P'\}[\bar{\varepsilon}] \qquad \text{Extend}(\sigma, x, \sigma(z)) \not\models P}{\langle m(z), \sigma, \mu \rangle \longmapsto \langle \text{skip}, \sigma', \mu \rangle \quad \text{and also} \quad \langle m(z), \sigma, \mu \rangle \longmapsto \text{fault}}$$

Fig. 7. The transition relation $\stackrel{\Delta}{\longmapsto}$. Here Δ is the same throughout and omitted.

3.3   Correctness Judgements and Program Semantics

A *procedure context*, Δ, is a comma-separated list of specifications, each of the form $\{Q\}m(x:T)\{Q'\}[\bar{\varepsilon}]$. For the specification to be well formed in a variable context Γ, all of $Q, Q', \bar{\varepsilon}$ should be well formed in $\Gamma, x:T$. Moreover the frame condition $\bar{\varepsilon}$ must not contain wr x, so the use of x in Q' and $\bar{\varepsilon}$ refers to its initial value. A correctness judgement takes roughly the form $\Delta \vdash^\Gamma \{P\} C \{P'\} [\bar{\varepsilon}]$ and is well formed if $\Delta, P, P', \bar{\varepsilon}$ are well formed in Γ and $signatures(\Delta) \vdash^\Gamma C$. In Sect. 4 we partition Δ into modules (see Def. 1). A correctness judgement is intended to mean that from any initial state that satisfies P, C does not fault (due to null dereference) and if it terminates then the final state satisfies P'. Moreover, any transition from initial state to final is allowed by $\bar{\varepsilon}$.

The hypothesis Δ is taken into account as well. One semantics would quantify over all implementations of Δ. Instead, we use a mixed-step semantics in which a call $m(z)$ for m in Δ takes a single step to an arbitrary outcome allowed by the specification of m.[6] A configuration has the form $\langle C, \sigma, \mu \rangle$ where C is a command, σ is a state, and the *procedure environment* μ is a partial function from procedure names to parameterized commands of the form $(\lambda x:T.C)$. By assuming that in a well formed program no procedure names are shadowed, we can use this simple representation, together with a special command end(m) to mark the end of the scope of a let-bound procedure m. Renaming is used for a parameter or local variable x, together with end marker end(x).

The transition relation $\stackrel{\Delta}{\longmapsto}$ is defined in Fig. 7. The procedures in Δ are to be distinct from those in the procedure environment. A terminating computation ends in a configuration of the form $\langle \text{skip}, \sigma, \mu \rangle$, or else "fault" which results from null dereference. The cases omitted from Fig. 7 are quite standard. We note only that the semantics of new K, which updates alloc, is parameterized on a function which, given a state, returns a non-empty set of fresh references. Thus our results encompass deterministic allocators as well as the maximally nondeterministic one on which some separation logics rely.

---

[6] Such semantics is popular in work on program refinement; see also O'Hearn et al [30].

4 Dynamic Boundaries and Second Order Framing

Rule FRAME is useful for reasoning about a predicate that a command is explicitly responsible for preserving, like I_{except} and B_{add} in Sect. 3.2. For the client (1), we want I_{set} to be preserved; semantically, the rationale amounts to framing, but rule FRAME is not helpful because our goal is to hide I_{set} from clients. A client command in a context Δ is second order in that the behavior of the command is a function of the procedures provided by Δ, as is evident in the transition semantics (Fig. 7). Second order framing is about a rely-guarantee relationship: the module relies on good behavior by the client, such that the client unwittingly preserves the hidden invariant, and in return the module guarantees the behavior specified in Δ.

Our rely condition is list of read effects, called the *dynamic boundary*, that must be respected by the client in the sense that it does not write the locations designated by those effects. A dynamic boundary $\overline{\delta}$ is associated with a list Δ of procedure specifications using notation $\Delta\langle\overline{\delta}\rangle$. The general form for correctness judgement would have a sequence $\Delta_1\langle\overline{\delta}_1\rangle;\ldots;\Delta_n\langle\overline{\delta}_n\rangle$ of hypotheses, for n modules, $n \geq 0$. In an attempt to improve readability, we will state the rules for the case of just two modules, typically using name Θ for Δ_n. So a correctness judgement has the form

$$\Delta\langle\overline{\delta}\rangle;\Theta\langle\overline{\theta}\rangle \vdash^{\Gamma} \{P\}\ C\ \{P'\}\,[\overline{\varepsilon}] \tag{3}$$

where $\overline{\delta}$ and $\overline{\theta}$ are lists of read effects that are well formed in Γ. The order of modules is significant: the implementation of Θ may use procedures from Δ and is obliged to respect dynamic boundary $\overline{\delta}$. For a dynamic boundary to be useful it should frame the invariant to be hidden, e.g., $\overline{\theta}_{set}$ frames I_{set}. That proof obligation is on the module.

The following derived rule embodies Hoare's mismatch in the case where module Θ is a single procedure specification $\{Q\}m(x\colon T)\{Q'\}[\overline{\eta}]$.

$$\text{MISMATCH}\ \ \frac{\Delta\langle\overline{\delta}\rangle;\Theta\langle\overline{\theta}\rangle \vdash \{P\}\ C\ \{P'\}\,[\overline{\varepsilon}] \qquad I \vdash \overline{\theta}\ \text{frames}\ I}{\Delta\langle\overline{\delta}\rangle;(\Theta\otimes I)\langle\rangle \vdash \{Q\wedge I\}\ B\ \{Q'\wedge I\}\,[\overline{\eta}] \qquad Init \Rightarrow I}{\Delta\langle\overline{\delta}\rangle \vdash \{P\wedge Init\}\ \text{let}\ m\ \text{be}\ B\ \text{in}\ C\ \{P'\}\,[\overline{\varepsilon}]}$$

The client C is obliged to respect $\overline{\theta}$ (and also $\overline{\delta}$) but does not see the hidden invariant. The implementation B is verified under additional precondition I and has additional obligation to reestablish I. (In the general case there is a list of bodies B_i, each verified in the same context against the specification for m_i.) The context Δ is another module that may be used both by C and by the implementation B of m. So B must respect $\overline{\delta}$, but note that it is not required (or likely) to respect $\overline{\theta}$. The obligation on B refers to context $\Theta \otimes I$, not Θ; this is only relevant if B recursively invokes m (or, in general, other methods of the same module). The operation $\otimes I$ conjoins a formula I to pre- and post-conditions of specifications: $(\{Q\}m(x\colon T)\{Q'\}[\overline{\eta}])\otimes I = \{Q\wedge I\}m(x\colon T)\{Q'\wedge I\}[\overline{\eta}]$.

Typical formalizations of data abstraction include a command for initialization, so a closed client program takes the form let m be B in $(init;C)$. With dynamic allocation, it is constructors that do much of the work to establish invariants. In order to avoid the need to formalize constructors, we use an initial condition. For the *Set* example, take

$Init_{set}$ to be the condition $pool = \varnothing$ which is suitable to be declared in the module interface. Note that $Init_{set} \Rightarrow I_{set}$ is valid.

Remarkably, there is a simple interpretation of judgement (3) that captures the idea that C respects the boundaries $\overline{\delta}$ and $\overline{\theta}$: No step of C's execution may write locations designated by $\overline{\delta}$ —interpreted in the pre-state of that step— unless it is a step of a procedure of Δ; *mutatis mutandis* for $\overline{\theta}$ and Θ. Before turning to the formal details, we discuss this proof obligation.

Verifying a client of SET. Using the public specifications of the four methods of Set, it is straightforward to prove that the client (1) establishes $b = false$. But there is an additional obligation, that every step respects the dynamic boundary $\overline{\theta}_{set}$. Consider the assignment $n.val := 1$ in (1), which is critical because I_{set} depends on field val. The effect of $n.val := 1$ is wr $n.val$ and it must be shown to be outside the boundary $\overline{\theta}_{set}$. By definition of $\star$, we have that $\overline{\theta}_{set} \star$ wr $n.val$ is $\{n\} \# pool \wedge \{n\} \# pool'rep$, which simplifies to $n \notin pool \wedge n \notin pool'rep$. We have $n \notin pool$ because n is fresh and variable $pool$ is not updated by the client. The condition $n \notin pool'rep$ is more interesting. Note that I_{set} implies

$$R: \quad pool'rep'own \subseteq pool \wedge null \notin pool$$

Unlike I_{set}, this is suitable to appear in the module interface, as a public invariant [23] or explicitly conjoined to the procedure specifications of SET. The client does not update the default value, null, of $n.own$. Together, R and $n.own = null$ imply $n \notin pool'rep$.

One point of this example is that "package confinement" [14] applies here: references to the instances of $Node$ used by the Set implementation are never made available to client code. Thus a lightweight, type-based confinement analysis of the module could be used together with simple syntactic checks on the client to verify that the boundary is respected. The results of an analysis could be expressed in first order assertions like R and thus be checked rather than trusted by a verifier.

As in rule FRAME, the separator can be used to express that a primitive command respects a dynamic boundary, allowing precise reasoning in cases like module MM (Sect. 5) that are not amenable to general purpose static analyses. A dynamic boundary is expressed in terms of state potentially mutated by the module implementation, e.g., the effect of add in Fig. 1 allows writing state on which $\overline{\theta}_{set}$ depends.[7] So interface specifications need to provide clients with sufficient information to reason about the boundary. For MM, it is not an invariant like R but rather the individual method specifications that facilitate such reasoning (see Sect. 5).

Formalization. The beauty of the second order frame rule, the form of which is due to O'Hearn et al [29], is that it distills the essence of Hoare's mismatch. Rule MISMATCH is derived in Fig.8 from our rule SOF together with two unsurprising rules which are among those given in Fig. 9. Before turning to the rules we define the semantics.

The current command in a configuration can always be written as a sequence of one or more commands that are not themselves sequences; the first is the *active command*, the one that is rewritten in the next step. We define $\text{Active}(C_1; C_2) = \text{Active}(C_1)$ and $\text{Active}(C) = C$ if there are no C_1, C_2 such that C is $C_1; C_2$.

---

[7] State-dependent effects may interfere, which is handled by the sequence rule [2].

$$\dfrac{\Delta\langle\overline{\delta}\rangle;(\Theta\otimes I)\langle\rangle\vdash\{Q\cdot I\}\ B\ \{Q'\cdot I\}\,[\overline{\eta}] \qquad \dfrac{\Delta\langle\overline{\delta}\rangle;\Theta\langle\overline{\theta}\rangle\vdash\{P\}\ C\ \{P'\}\,[\overline{\varepsilon}]}{\Delta\langle\overline{\delta}\rangle;(\Theta\otimes I)\langle\overline{\theta}\rangle\vdash\{P\cdot I\}\ C\ \{P'\cdot I\}\,[\overline{\varepsilon}]}\ \text{\scriptsize SOF}}{\Delta\langle\overline{\delta}\rangle\vdash\{P\cdot I\}\ \text{let }m\text{ be }B\text{ in }C\ \{P'\cdot I\}\,[\overline{\varepsilon}]}$$

$$\dfrac{}{\Delta\langle\overline{\delta}\rangle\vdash\{P\cdot Init\}\ \text{let }m\text{ be }B\text{ in }C\ \{P'\}\,[\overline{\varepsilon}]}$$

Fig. 8. Derivation of rule MISMATCH, where Θ is a single specification $\{Q\}m(x\colon T)\{Q'\}\,[\overline{\eta}]$ and we write $\cdot$ for $\wedge$ to save space. The side condition for SOF is $I\vdash(\overline{\theta},\mathrm{rd\,alloc})$ frames I. The next step is by rule LINK, followed by CONSEQ with side condition $Init\Rightarrow I$.

$$\text{SOF}\ \ \dfrac{\Delta\langle\overline{\delta}\rangle;\Theta\langle\overline{\theta}\rangle\vdash\{P\}\ C\ \{P'\}\,[\overline{\varepsilon}] \qquad I\vdash(\overline{\theta},\mathrm{rd\,alloc})\text{ frames }I \qquad \mathrm{Admiss}(I,\Theta)}{\Delta\langle\overline{\delta}\rangle;(\Theta\otimes I)\langle\overline{\theta}\rangle\vdash\{P\wedge I\}\ C\ \{P'\wedge I\}\,[\overline{\varepsilon}]}$$

$$\text{CTXINTRO}\ \ \dfrac{\Delta\langle\overline{\delta}\rangle\vdash\{P\}\ C\ \{P'\}\,[\overline{\varepsilon}] \qquad C\text{ is primitive} \qquad P\Rightarrow\overline{\theta}\star\overline{\varepsilon}}{\Delta\langle\overline{\delta}\rangle;\Theta\langle\overline{\theta}\rangle\vdash\{P\}\ C\ \{P'\}\,[\overline{\varepsilon}]}$$

$$\text{CALL}\ \ \dfrac{\{P\}m(x\colon T)\{P'\}\,[\overline{\varepsilon}]\text{ is in }\Theta \qquad P_z^x\Rightarrow\overline{\delta}\star\overline{\varepsilon}_z^x}{\Delta\langle\overline{\delta}\rangle;\Theta\langle\overline{\theta}\rangle\vdash\{P_z^x\}\ m(z)\ \{P'^x_z\}\,[\overline{\varepsilon}_z^x]}$$

$$\text{LINK}\ \ \dfrac{\Theta\text{ is }\{Q\}m(x\colon T)\{Q'\}\,[\overline{\eta}]}{\Delta\langle\overline{\delta}\rangle;\Theta\langle\overline{\theta}\rangle\vdash^\Gamma\{P\}\ C\ \{P'\}\,[\overline{\varepsilon}] \qquad \Delta\langle\overline{\delta}\rangle;\Theta\langle\rangle\vdash^{\Gamma,x\colon T}\{Q\}\ B\ \{Q'\}\,[\overline{\eta}]}{\Delta\langle\overline{\delta}\rangle\vdash^\Gamma\{P\}\ \text{let }m(x\colon T)\text{ be }B\text{ in }C\ \{P'\}\,[\overline{\varepsilon}]}$$

Fig. 9. Selected proof rules

Definition 1. *A correctness judgement $\Delta\langle\overline{\delta}\rangle;\Theta\langle\overline{\theta}\rangle\vdash^\Gamma\{P\}\ C\ \{P'\}\,[\overline{\varepsilon}]$ is valid iff the following holds. Let Δ' be the catenated list (Δ,Θ), let C_0 be C, and let μ_0 be an arbitrary procedure environment disjoint from the procedures bound within C or present in Δ,Θ. Then for all Γ-states σ_0 such that $\sigma_0\models P$.*

(i) *It is not the case that $\langle C_0,\sigma_0,\mu_0\rangle\overset{\Delta'}{\longmapsto}{}^*$ fault.*

(ii) *Every terminating computation $\langle C_0,\sigma_0,\mu_0\rangle\overset{\Delta'}{\longmapsto}{}^*\langle\mathrm{skip},\sigma_n,\mu_n\rangle$ satisfies $\sigma_n\models P'$ and $\sigma_0\leadsto\sigma_n\models\overline{\varepsilon}$.*

(iii) *For any reachable computation step, i.e. $\langle C_0,\sigma_0,\mu_0\rangle\overset{\Delta'}{\longmapsto}{}^*\langle C_{i-1},\sigma_{i-1},\mu_{i-1}\rangle\overset{\Delta'}{\longmapsto}\langle C_i,\sigma_i,\mu_i\rangle$, either $\mathrm{Active}(C_{i-1})$ is a call to some m in Δ (respectively, in Θ) or else $\mathrm{Agree}(\sigma_{i-1},\sigma_i,\overline{\delta})$ (respectively, $\mathrm{Agree}(\sigma_{i-1},\sigma_i,\overline{\theta})$).*

Let us paraphrase (iii) in a way that makes clear the generalization to contexts with more modules: Every dynamic encapsulation bound must be respected by every step of computation (terminating or not), with the exception that a call of a context procedure is exempt from the bound of its module.

Selected proof rules are given in Fig. 9. An implicit side condition on all proof rules is that both the consequent and the antecedents are well formed. We omit standard rules for control structures, and structural rules like consequence, which do not manipulate the procedure context. Rule FRAME also leaves its context unchanged. For the assignment commands we can use "small axioms" inspired by [29]. The axioms have empty context; rule CTXINTRO is used to add hypotheses.

Rule CTXINTRO is restricted to primitive commands (Fig. 5), because the side condition $P \Rightarrow \overline{\theta} \star \overline{\varepsilon}$ only enforces the dynamic encapsulation boundary $\overline{\theta}$ for the initial and final states —there are no intermediate steps in the semantics of these commands. Note that CTXINTRO introduces a dynamic boundary $\overline{\theta}$ that will not be imposed on the implementations of the procedures of the outer module Δ. This works because, due to nesting, those implementations cannot invoke procedures of Θ at all. The implementation of a procedure m in Θ may invoke a procedure p of enclosing module Δ. The effect of that invocation might even violate the dynamic boundary $\overline{\theta}$, but there is no harm —indeed, the implementation of m is likely to temporarily falsify the invariant for Θ but is explicitly obliged to restore it.

The implementation of an inner module is required (by rule LINK) to respect the encapsulation boundaries of enclosing modules. That is why it is sound for procedure m in rule CALL to be in the scope of the dynamic effect bound $\overline{\delta}$ with only the obligation that the end-to-end effect $\overline{\varepsilon}_z^x$ is separate from $\overline{\delta}$. The general form of CALL has n contexts and the called procedure is in the innermost. Additional context can subsequently be introduced on the inside, e.g., CALL can be used for a procedure of Θ and then the context extended to $\Delta \langle \overline{\delta} \rangle ; \Theta \langle \overline{\theta} \rangle ; \Upsilon \langle \overline{\upsilon} \rangle$ using rule CTXINTRO. In case there is only a single module, rule CALL can be used with Δ and $\overline{\delta}$ empty.

Rule SOF imposes an admissibility condition on I. In this paper, Admiss is defined to say I must not be falsifiable by allocation (i.e. $\sigma \models I$ implies $\sigma' \models I$, if σ' is just σ extended with a new object). The issue is that some useful invariants include alloc in their footprint, especially if the footprint is derived using our rules for framing [2].[8] Typical clients do allocation, and thus write alloc, which would conflict with a dynamic boundary containing rd alloc (cf. [33]). The rule explicitly allows this conflict: by condition $P \vdash (\overline{\delta}, \text{rd alloc})$ frames Q, it appears that Q depends on alloc, but by condition Admiss(Q, Θ) it does not. We include Θ in the notation, even though it is not used in the definition, because in a richer language with constructor methods there is a more practical definition of Admiss that allows the conflict. We can allow a module invariant I to have subformulas $\forall x : K \in \text{alloc} \mid P(x)$ that do depend on alloc, and yet not include alloc in the dynamic bound, because the constructor will be obliged to maintain I.

Theorem 1. *Each of the rules is sound. Hence any derivable correctness judgement is valid.*

5   Specification and Verification of the Examples

For the toy memory manager of Sect. 2.2, we specify the effects for procedure $alloc$ to be wr result, $freed, flist, count$, alloc, $freed`nxt$. For $free(n: Node)$ the effects are wr $freed, flist, count, freed`nxt$. Ordinary scoping could be used to hide effects on the module variables $flist$ and $count$, and the ghost $freed$ could be "spec-public", i.e.

---

[8] An example such I is $\forall x : K \in \text{alloc} \mid x.init \Rightarrow P(x)$ with $init$ a boolean field, initially false. Such a formula would be suitable as an invariant in a program where $x.init$ only gets truthified by procedures that also establish $P(x)$.

not writeable outside module MM. To frame I_{mm} we choose as dynamic boundary rd $freed, flist, count, freed`nxt$. The interesting part is $freed`nxt$, as $flist$ and $count$ should be scoped within the module and $freed$ should be spec-public. Using the specifications in Sect. 2.2 together with these effect specifications, it is straightforward to verify the client given there. The client writes $freed`val$ but it does not write $freed`nxt$, nor variable $freed$ itself, and thus it respects the dynamic boundary. So it can be linked with $alloc$ and $free$ using rule MISMATCH. By contrast with the use of an invariant, R, to verify that client (1) respects the dynamic boundary $\overline{\theta}_{set}$, here it is the procedure specifications themselves that support reasoning about the dynamic boundary. Suppose we add the assignment $y.nxt := null$ just after $y := alloc()$; although this writes a nxt field, the object is outside $freed$ according to the specification of $alloc$.

Recall the example of Sect. 2.3. For method $update$ we choose effects wr $self.val, self.O`cache$. The effects for $Observer(u)$ are wr $u.O`nxto, u.(O, dg)$. Here dg is a data group that abstracts the private field obs. These suffice to verify the client in Sect. 2.3 which relies on separation between subjects. The dynamic boundary, $\overline{\delta}_{ob}$, is rd $alloc`(O, dg), alloc`O`nxto$. Region $alloc$ is very coarse, but fields $O, dg, nxto$ could be protected from clients by scoping; indeed, we might simply use $alloc`nxto$.[9] Verification of the implementations uses rule FRAME to exploit per-subject separation, similar to the Set example in Sect. 4. Then rule MISMATCH links the client.

Finally, recall the example of nested modules and overlapping data structures in Sect. 2.4. Let the dynamic boundary be rd $alloc, alloc`(next, prev)$, which frames I_{os}. Consider a client that constructs a new $ObsSet$. The implementation of the $ObsSet$ constructor can be verified, assuming and maintaining I_{os}, including the obligation to respect the dynamic boundary $\overline{\delta}_{ob}$ of module OB. The client can be linked to OS using rule MISMATCH and then that rule is used again to link with module OB.

6 Related Work

It is notoriously difficult to achieve encapsulation in the presence of shared, dynamically allocated mutable objects [22,30]. Current tools for automated software verification either do not support hiding of invariants (e.g., Jahob [39], jStar [10], Krakatoa [12]), do not treat object invariants soundly (e.g., ESC/Java [13]) or at best offer soundness for restricted situations where a hierarchical structure can be imposed on the heap (e.g. Spec# [3]). Some of these tools do achieve significant automation, especially by using SMT solvers [21].

The use of ghost state to encode inductive properties without induction has been fruitful in verifications using SMT solvers (e.g., [8,16,39]). Our use of ghost state for frame conditions and separation reasoning was directly inspired by the state-dependent effects of Kassios [18] (who calls them dynamic frames, whence our term "dynamic boundary"). Variations on state-dependent effects have been explored in SMT-based verifiers, e.g., Smans et al implemented a verifier that abstracts footprints using location sets and pure method calls in assertions and in frame conditions [37]. Another verifier uses novel assertions for an implicit encoding (inspired by separation logic) of frame

---
[9] In fact $nxto$ should be abstracted by a data group, but we report here on the version for which we did a detailed proof.

conditions by preconditions [36]. Leino's Dafny tool [24] features effects in the form we write as $G^{\text{'}}$any. The Boogie tool [3] has been used for experiments with region logic specifications of the Observer [1] and Composite [34] patterns.

Hiding is easy to encode in an axiomatic semantics —it is just Hoare's mismatch, phrased in terms of assert and assume statements. The verifiers above which provide hiding enforce specific encapsulation disciplines through some combination of type checking and extra verification conditions. For example, the Boogie methodology [25] used by Spec# stipulates intermediate assertions (in all code) that guarantees an all-states ownership invariant. Another version of Spec# [37] generates verification conditions at intermediate steps to approximate read footprints, in addition to the usual end-to-end check for modifies specifications of methed bodies. One way to enforce our requirement for respecting dynamic boundaries would be to generate verification conditions for writes at intermediate steps, which could be optimized away in cases where their validity is ensured by a static analysis.

A number of methodologies have been proposed for ownership-based hiding of invariants (e.g., [28]). Drossopoulou et al. [11] introduce a general framework to describe verification techniques for invariants. A number of ownership disciplines from the literature are studied as instances of the framework. The framework encompasses variations on the idea that invariants hold exactly when control crosses module boundaries, e.g., *visible state semantics* requires all invariants to hold on all public method call/return boundaries; other proposals require invariants to hold more often [25] or less [38]. The difficulty of generalizing ownership to fit important design patterns led Parkinson and Bierman [5,31] to pursue abstraction instead of hiding, via second order assertions in separation logic; this has been implemented [10].

Separation logic (SL) is a major influence on our work. Our SOF rule is adapted from [30], as is the example in Sect. 2.2. The SOF rule of SL relies on two critical features: the separating conjunction and the *tight interpretation* of a correctness judgement $\{P\}C\{Q\}$ which requires that C neither reads nor writes outside the footprint of P. These features yield great economy of expression, but conflating read and write has consequences. To get shared reads, the semantics of separating conjunction can embody some notion of permissions [7] which adds complication but is useful for concurrent programs (and to our knowledge has not been combined with SOF). The SOF rule of SL also hides effects on encapsulated state whereas our SOF rule hides only the invariant. By disentangling the footprint from the state condition we enable shared reads (retaining a simple semantics), but that means we cannot hide effects within the dynamic encapsulation boundary —the effects can be visible to clients.

Both our FRAME rule and our SOF rule use ordinary conjunction to introduce an invariant, together with side conditions that designate a footprint of the invariant which is separated from the write effect of a command. In SL these rules use the separating conjunction which expresses the existence of such footprints for the command's precondition and for the invariant. Reynolds gave a derivation using the rule of conjunction[10] that shows the SOF rule of SL is not sound without restriction to predicates that are

---

[10] From $\{P\}C\{P'\}$ and $\{Q\}C\{Q'\}$ infer $\{P \land Q\}C\{P' \land Q'\}$.

"precise" in the sense of determining a unique footprint [30].[11] The semantic analysis in [30] shows that the need for a unique footprint applies to region logic as well. However, region logic separates the footprint from the formula, allowing the invariant formula to denote an imprecise predicate while framing the formula by effects that in a given state determines a unique set of locations.

The restriction to precise predicates for SOF in SL can be dropped using a semantics that does not validate the rule of conjunction [6]. This was eschewed by the authors of [30] because the rule is patently sound in ordinary readings of Hoare triples. Dropping the rule facilitates the modeling of higher order framing rules that capture visible state semantics for invariants even in programs using code pointers (e.g., [35]). The metatheory underlying the Ynot tool for interactive verification [27] uses a model that does not validate the conjunction rule [32]. Higher order separation logics offer elegant means to achieve data abstraction and strong functional specifications of interesting design patterns [20,19,27]. The ability to explicitly quantify over invariants would seem to lessen the importance of hiding, but it requires considerable sophistication on the part of the user and their reasoning tools.

7 Conclusion

In this paper we explore a novel interface specification feature: the *dynamic boundary* which must be respected by clients. The dynamic boundary is designated by read effects that approximate, in a way suitable to appear in the interface, the footprint of an invariant which is hidden, i.e. does not appear in the interface specifications. Explicit description of footprints is complementary to syntactic mechanisms that encapsulate state named by identifiers. The expressions whose l-values constitute the dynamic boundary are state-dependent and thus denote different sets of locations over time.

Hiding is formalized in a second order frame rule that is proved sound for a simple operational semantics of sequential programs. We show by examples that our SOF handles not only invariants that pertain to several objects with a single owner but also design patterns in which several client-reachable peers cooperate and in which data structures may be overlapping or irregular. These are incompatible with ownership and remain as challenge problems in the current literature [4,22,27]. A program may link together multiple modules, each with its own hidden invariant and dynamic boundary. Our approach encompasses alias confinement disciplines that are enforceable by static analysis [9] as well as less restrictive disciplines that impose proof obligations on clients, e.g., ownership transfers that are "in the eye of the asserter" [30].

One of our aims is to provide a logical foundation that can justify the axiomatic semantics used in automated verifiers. Even more, we want a framework in which encapsulation disciplines, both specialized and general-purpose, can be specified in program annotations and perhaps "specification schemas" or aspects —so that soundness for hiding becomes a verification condition rather than a meta-theorem. This could improve usability and applicability of verifiers, e.g., by deploying disciplines on a per-module

---

[11] A predicate I is *precise* iff $(I * \_)$ distributes over $\wedge$. In this paper our invariants are all precise, but not all useful ones are, e.g., "there exists a non-full queue".

basis. It could also facilitate foundational program proofs, by factoring methodological considerations apart from the underlying program model embodied in axiomatic semantics. Our approach does not rely on inductive predicates, much less higher order ones, but on the other hand it does not preclude the use of more expressive assertions (such as the inductive FC in the example in Sect. 2.2).

It remains to be seen how the approach explored here extends to more advanced programming features such as code pointers and concurrency. There are a number of more immediate issues such as integration with a proper module system, inference of ghost annotations based on static analysis, and full encapsulation for representation independence and for hiding of effects.

Acknowledgements. Many people helped with advice and encouragement, including Lennart Beringer, Lars Birkedal, Sophia Drossopoulou, Bart Jacobs, Gary Leavens, Peter Müller, Peter O'Hearn, Matthew Parkinson, Jan Smans, Stan Rosenberg, Jacob Thamsborg, Hongseok Yang, organizers and participants of Dagstuhl seminars 08061 and 09301.

References

1. Banerjee, A., Barnett, M., Naumann, D.A.: Boogie meets regions: A verification experience report. In: Shankar, N., Woodcock, J. (eds.) VSTTE 2008. LNCS, vol. 5295, pp. 177–191. Springer, Heidelberg (2008)
2. Banerjee, A., Naumann, D.A., Rosenberg, S.: Regional logic for local reasoning about global invariants. In: Vitek, J. (ed.) ECOOP 2008. LNCS, vol. 5142, pp. 387–411. Springer, Heidelberg (2008); Draft journal version available at authors' web sites
3. Barnett, M., Leino, K.R.M., Schulte, W.: The Spec# programming system: An overview. In: Barthe, G., Burdy, L., Huisman, M., Lanet, J.-L., Muntean, T. (eds.) CASSIS 2004. LNCS, vol. 3362, pp. 49–69. Springer, Heidelberg (2005)
4. Berdine, J., Calcagno, C., Cook, B., Distefano, D., O'Hearn, P.W., Wies, T., Yang, H.: Shape analysis for composite data structures. In: Damm, W., Hermanns, H. (eds.) CAV 2007. LNCS, vol. 4590, pp. 178–192. Springer, Heidelberg (2007)
5. Bierman, G., Parkinson, M.: Separation logic and abstraction. In: POPL, pp. 247–258 (2005)
6. Birkedal, L., Torp-Smith, N., Yang, H.: Semantics of separation-logic typing and higher-order frame rules for Algol-like languages. Logical Methods in Computer Science 2(5) (2006)
7. Bornat, R., Calcagno, C., O'Hearn, P., Parkinson, M.: Permission accounting in separation logic. In: POPL, pp. 259–270 (2005)
8. Cohen, E., Dahlweid, M., Hillebrand, M.A., Leinenbach, D., Moskal, M., Santen, T., Schulte, W., Tobies, S.: VCC: a practical system for verifying concurrent C. In: TPHOLs, pp. 23–42 (2009)
9. Dietl, W., Müller, P.: Universes: Lightweight ownership for JML. Journal of Object Technology 4, 5–32 (2005)
10. Distefano, D., Parkinson, M.J.: jStar: Towards practical verification for Java. In: OOPSLA, pp. 213–226 (2008)
11. Drossopoulou, S., Francalanza, A., Müller, P., Summers, A.J.: A unified framework for verification techniques for object invariants. In: Vitek, J. (ed.) ECOOP 2008. LNCS, vol. 5142, pp. 412–437. Springer, Heidelberg (2008)

12. Filliâtre, J.-C., Marché, C.: The Why/Krakatoa/Caduceus platform for deductive program verification (tool paper). In: Damm, W., Hermanns, H. (eds.) CAV 2007. LNCS, vol. 4590, pp. 173–177. Springer, Heidelberg (2007)
13. Flanagan, C., Leino, K.R.M., Lillibridge, M., Nelson, G., Saxe, J.B., Stata, R.: Extended static checking for Java. In: PLDI, pp. 234–245 (2002)
14. Grothoff, C., Palsberg, J., Vitek, J.: Encapsulating objects with confined types. ACM TOPLAS 29(6) (2007)
15. Harel, D., Pnueli, A., Stavi, J.: A complete axiomatic system for proving deductions about recursive programs. In: STOC, pp. 249–260 (1977)
16. Hawblitzel, C., Petrank, E.: Automated verification of practical garbage collectors. In: POPL, pp. 441–453 (2009)
17. Hoare, C.A.R.: Proofs of correctness of data representations. Acta Inf. 1, 271–281 (1972)
18. Kassios, I.T.: Dynamic framing: Support for framing, dependencies and sharing without restriction. In: Misra, J., Nipkow, T., Sekerinski, E. (eds.) FM 2006. LNCS, vol. 4085, pp. 268–283. Springer, Heidelberg (2006)
19. Krishnaswami, N.R., Aldrich, J., Birkedal, L.: Verifying event-driven programs using ramified frame properties. In: TLDI (2010)
20. Krishnaswami, N.R., Aldrich, J., Birkedal, L., Svendsen, K., Buisse, A.: Design patterns in separation logic. In: TLDI (2009)
21. Kroening, D., Strichman, O.: Decision Procedures: An Algorithmic Point of View. Springer, Heidelberg (2008)
22. Leavens, G.T., Leino, K.R.M., Müller, P.: Specification and verification challenges for sequential object-oriented programs. Formal Aspects of Computing 19(2), 159–189 (2007)
23. Leavens, G.T., Müller, P.: Information hiding and visibility in interface specifications. In: ICSE, pp. 385–395 (2007)
24. Leino, K.R.M.: Specification and verification in object-oriented software. Marktoberdorf lecture notes (2008)
25. Rustan, K., Leino, M., Müller, P.: Object invariants in dynamic contexts. In: Odersky, M. (ed.) ECOOP 2004. LNCS, vol. 3086, pp. 491–515. Springer, Heidelberg (2004)
26. Leino, K.R.M., Poetzsch-Heffter, A., Zhou, Y.: Using data groups to specify and check side effects. In: PLDI, pp. 246–257 (2002)
27. Malecha, G., Morrisett, G., Shinnar, A., Wisnesky, R.: Toward a verified relational database management system. In: POPL (2010)
28. Müller, P., Poetzsch-Heffter, A., Leavens, G.T.: Modular invariants for layered object structures. Sci. Comput. Programming 62(3), 253–286 (2006)
29. O'Hearn, P.W., Reynolds, J.C., Yang, H.: Local reasoning about programs that alter data structures. In: Fribourg, L. (ed.) CSL 2001 and EACSL 2001. LNCS, vol. 2142, pp. 1–19. Springer, Heidelberg (2001)
30. O'Hearn, P.W., Yang, H., Reynolds, J.C.: Separation and information hiding. ACM TOPLAS 31(3), 1–50 (2009); Extended version of POPL 2004
31. Parkinson, M.: Class invariants: The end of the road. In: IWACO (2007)
32. Petersen, R.L., Birkedal, L., Nanevski, A., Morrisett, G.: A realizability model for impredicative Hoare type theory. In: Drossopoulou, S. (ed.) ESOP 2008. LNCS, vol. 4960, pp. 337–352. Springer, Heidelberg (2008)
33. Pierik, C., Clarke, D., de Boer, F.S.: Controlling object allocation using creation guards. In: Fitzgerald, J.S., Hayes, I.J., Tarlecki, A. (eds.) FM 2005. LNCS, vol. 3582, pp. 59–74. Springer, Heidelberg (2005)
34. Rosenberg, S., Banerjee, A., Naumann, D.A.: Local reasoning and dynamic framing for the composite pattern and its clients (submitted, 2009)

35. Schwinghammer, J., Yang, H., Birkedal, L., Pottier, F., Reus, B.: A semantic foundation for hidden state. In: Ong, L. (ed.) FOSSACS 2010. LNCS, vol. 6014, pp. 2–17. Springer, Heidelberg (2010)
36. Smans, J., Jacobs, B., Piessens, F.: Implicit dynamic frames: Combining dynamic frames and separation logic. In: Drossopoulou, S. (ed.) ECOOP 2009. LNCS, vol. 5653, pp. 148–172. Springer, Heidelberg (2009)
37. Smans, J., Jacobs, B., Piessens, F., Schulte, W.: An automatic verifier for Java-like programs based on dynamic frames. In: Fiadeiro, J.L., Inverardi, P. (eds.) FASE 2008. LNCS, vol. 4961, pp. 261–275. Springer, Heidelberg (2008)
38. Summers, A.J., Drossopoulou, S.: Considerate reasoning and the composite design pattern. In: Barthe, G., Hermenegildo (eds.) VMCAI 2010. LNCS, vol. 5944, pp. 328–344. Springer, Heidelberg (2010)
39. Zee, K., Kuncak, V., Rinard, M.C.: Full functional verification of linked data structures. In: PLDI, pp. 349–361 (2008)

Coupling Policy Iteration with Semi-definite Relaxation to Compute Accurate Numerical Invariants in Static Analysis*

Assalé Adjé[1], Stéphane Gaubert[2], and Eric Goubault[3]

[1] CEA, LIST and LIX, Ecole Polytechnique (MeASI),
F-91128 Palaiseau Cedex, France
Assale.Adje@cea.fr
[2] INRIA Saclay and CMAP, Ecole Polytechnique,
F-91128 Palaiseau Cedex, France
Stephane.Gaubert@inria.fr
[3] CEA, LIST (MeASI),
F-91191 Gif-sur-Yvette Cedex, France
Eric.Goubault@cea.fr

Abstract. We introduce a new domain for finding precise numerical invariants of programs by abstract interpretation. This domain, which consists of level sets of non-linear functions, generalizes the domain of linear "templates" introduced by Manna, Sankaranarayanan, and Sipma. In the case of quadratic templates, we use Shor's semi-definite relaxation to derive computable yet precise abstractions of semantic functionals, and we show that the abstract fixpoint equation can be solved accurately by coupling policy iteration and semi-definite programming. We demonstrate the interest of our approach on a series of examples (filters, integration schemes) including a degenerate one (symplectic scheme).

1 Introduction

We introduce a complete lattice consisting of level sets of (possibly non-convex) functions, which we use as an abstract domain in the sense of abstract interpretation [CC77] for precisely over-approximating numerical program invariants. This abstract domain is parametrized by a basis of functions, akin to the approach set forward by Manna, Sankaranarayanan, and Sipma (the template abstract domain [SSM05, SCSM06]), except that the basis functions or "templates" which we use here need not be linear. The domains obtained in this way encompass the classical abstract domains of intervals, octagons and (linear) templates.

To illustrate the interest of this generalization, let us consider an harmonic oscillator: $\ddot{x} + c\dot{x} + x = 0$. By taking an explicit Euler scheme, and for $c = 1$ we get the program shown at the left of Figure 1.

The invariant found with our method is shown right of Figure 1. For this, we have considered the "template" based on functions $\{x, -x, v, -v, 2x^2 + 3v^2 + 2xv\}$,

---

* The first author has been supported by a fellowship from the Région Île-de-France. This work has been partially supported by the ANR project ASOPT.

A.D. Gordon (Ed.): ESOP 2010, LNCS 6012, pp. 23–42, 2010.

```
x = [0,1];
v: = [0,1];
h = 0.01;
while (true) { [2]
    w = v;
    v = v*(1-h)-h*x;
    x = x+h*w; [3] }
```
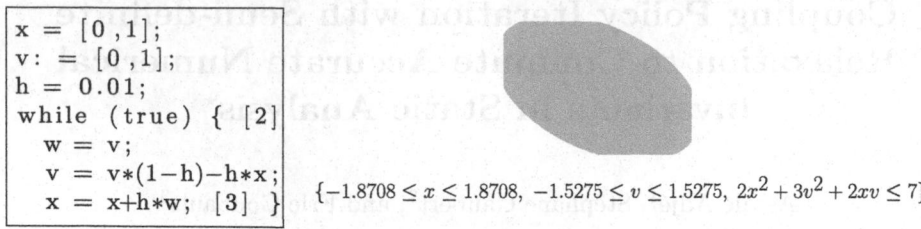
$\{-1.8708 \leq x \leq 1.8708, -1.5275 \leq v \leq 1.5275, 2x^2 + 3v^2 + 2xv \leq 7\}$

Fig. 1. An harmonic oscillator, its Euler integration scheme and the loop invariant found at control point 2

i.e. we consider a domain where we are looking for upper bounds of these quantities. This means that we consider the linear templates based on $\{x, -x, v, -v\}$, i.e. intervals for each variable of the program, together with the *non-linear* template $2x^2 + 3v^2 + 2xv$. The last template comes from the Lyapunov function that the designer of the *algorithm* may have considered to prove the stability of his scheme, *before it has been implemented*. In view of *proving the implementation correct*, one is naturally led to considering such templates[1]. Last but not least, it is to be noted that the loop invariant using intervals, zones, octagons or even polyhedra (hence with any linear template) is the very disappointing invariant $h = 0.01$ (the variables v and x cannot be bounded.) However, the main interest of the present method is to carry over to the non-linear setting. For instance, we include in our benchmarks a computation of invariants (of the same quality) for an implementation of the Arrow-Hurwicz algorithm, which is essentially an harmonic oscillator limited by a non-linear saturation term (a projection on the positive cone), or a highly degenerate example (a symplectic integration scheme, for which alternative methods fail due to the absence of stability margin).

Contributions of the paper. We describe the lattice theoretical operations in terms of Galois connections and generalized convexity in Section 2. We also show that in the case of a basis of quadratic functions, good over-approximations $F^{\mathcal{R}}$ of abstractions $F^{\sharp}$ of semantic functionals can be computed in polynomial time (Section 3). Such over-approximations are obtained using Shor's relaxation, which is based on semi-definite programming. Moreover, we show in Subsection 4.3 that the multipliers produced by this relaxation are naturally "policies", in a policy iteration technique for finding the fixpoints of $F^{\mathcal{R}}$, precisely over-approximating the fixpoints of $F^{\sharp}$. Finally, we illustrate on examples (linear recursive filters, numerical integration schemes) that policy iteration on such quadratic templates is extremely efficient and precise in practice, compared with Kleene iteration with widenings/narrowings. The fact that quadratic templates are efficient on such algorithms is generally due to the existence of (quadratic)

---

[1] Of course, as for the templates of [SSM05, SCSM06], we can be interested in automatically finding or refining the set of templates considered to achieve a good precision of the abstract analysis, but this is outside the scope of this article.

Lyapunov functions that prove their stability. The method has been implemented as a set of Matlab programs.

Related work. This work is to be considered as a generalization of [SSM05], [SCSM06] because it extends the notion of template to non-linear functions, and of [CGG+05], [GGTZ07], [AGG08], [GS07a] and [GS07b] since it also generalizes the use of policy iteration for better and faster resolution of abstract semantic equations. Polynomial inequalities (of bounded degree) were used in [BRCZ05] in the abstract interpretation framework but the method relies on a reduction to linear inequalities (the polyhedra domain), hence is more abstract than our domain. Particular quadratic inequalities (involving two variables - i.e. ellipsoidal methods) were used for order 2 linear recursive filters invariant generation in [Fer05][2]. Polynomial *equalities* (and not general functional inequalities as we consider here) were considered in [MOS04, RCK07]. The use of optimization techniques and relaxation for program analysis has also been proposed in [Cou05], mostly for synthetizing variants for proving termination, but invariant synthesis was also briefly sketched, with different methods than ours (concerning the abstract semantics and the fixpoint algorithm). Finally, the interest of using quadratic invariants and in particular Lyapunov functions for proving control programs correct (mostly in the context of Hoare-like program proofs) has also been advocated very recently by E. Féron et al. in [FF08, FA08].

2   Lattices of Level Sets and Abstract Support Functions

We introduce a new abstract domain, parametrized by a basis of functions (P below). The idea is that an abstract value will be a vector of bounds for each of these functions, hence the name of "level sets", with some abstract convexity condition, Definition 3.

2.1 P-Level Sets, and Their Galois Connection with $\mathcal{P}(\mathbb{R}^d)$

Let P denote a set of functions from $\mathbb{R}^d$ to $\mathbb{R}$, which is going to be the basis of our templates. We denote $\mathcal{F}(P, \overline{\mathbb{R}})$ the set of functions v from P to $\overline{\mathbb{R}} = \mathbb{R} \cup \{\pm\infty\}$. We define a Galois connection (Proposition 1) between $\mathcal{F}(P, \overline{\mathbb{R}})$ and the set of subsets of $\mathbb{R}^d$ (made of a concretization operator $v \mapsto v^\star$, Definition 1 and an abstraction operator $C \mapsto C^\dagger$, Definition 2). This will give the formal background for constructing abstract semantics using P-level sets using abstract interpretation [CC77], in Section 3.

Definition 1 (P-level sets). *To a function $v \in \mathcal{F}(P, \overline{\mathbb{R}})$, we associate the P-level set denoted by $v^\star$ and defined as:*

$$v^\star = \{x \in \mathbb{R}^d \mid p(x) \le v(p), \ \forall p \in P\}$$

---

[2] A generalization to order n linear recursive filters is also sketched in this article.

When P is a set of convex functions, the P-level sets are the intersection of classical level sets known in convex analysis. In our case, P can contain non-convex functions so P-level sets are not necessarily convex in the usual sense.

Example 1. We come back to the first example and we are focusing on its representation in term of P-level set. Let us write, for $(x, v) \in \mathbb{R}^2$, $p_1 : (x, v) \mapsto x$, $p_2 : (x, v) \mapsto v$ and $p_3 : (x, v) \mapsto 2x^2 + 3v^2 + 2xv$. Let us take $P = \{p_1, -p_1, p_2, -p_2, p_3\}$, $v(p_1) = 1.8708$, $v(-p_1) = 1.8708$, $v(p_2) = 1.5275$, $v(-p_2) = 1.5275$, and $v(p_3) = 7$. The set $v^\star$ is precisely the one shown right of Figure 1.

Example 2. We next show some P-level sets which are not convex in the usual sense. Let us write, for $(x, y) \in \mathbb{R}^2$, $p_1 : (x, y) \mapsto -y^2 - (x + 2)^2$, $p_2 : (x, y) \mapsto -y^2 - (x - 2)^2$ and $p_3 : (x, y) \mapsto -(y - 2)^2 - x^2$, $p_4 : (x, y) \mapsto -(y + 2)^2 - x^2$. Let us take $P = \{p_1, p_2, p_3, p_4\}$ and $v(p_1) = v(p_2) = v(p_3) = v(p_4) = -2$. The set $v^\star$ is shown Figure 2.

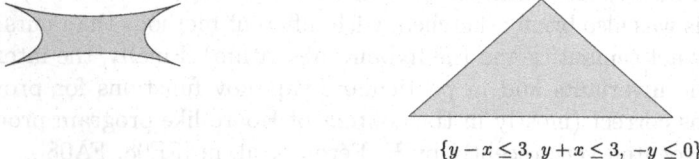

$\{y - x \leq 3,\ y + x \leq 3,\ -y \leq 0\}$

Fig. 2. A P-level set arising from non-convex quadratic functions

Fig. 3. A P-level set arising from linear forms

In our case, P is a set of functions from $\mathbb{R}^d$ to $\mathbb{R}$ not necessarily linear, so we generalize the concept of support functions (e.g see Section 13 of [Roc96]).

Definition 2 (Abstract support functions). *To $X \subset \mathbb{R}^d$, we associate the abstract support function denoted by $X^\dagger$ and defined as:*

$$X^\dagger(p) = \sup_{x \in X} p(x)$$

Proposition 1. *The pair of maps $v \mapsto v^\star$ and $X \mapsto X^\dagger$ defines a Galois connection between $\mathcal{F}(P, \overline{\mathbb{R}})$ and the set of subsets of $\mathbb{R}^d$.*

In the terminology of abstract interpretation, $(.)^\dagger$ is the abstraction function, and $(.)^\star$ is the concretization function.

2.2 The Lattices of P-Convex Sets and P-Convex Functions

The sets of points in $\mathbb{R}^d$ which are exactly represented by their corresponding P-level sets are called P-convex sets, as in the definition below. These can be identified to the set of *abstract elements* we are considering[3]. We show in Theorem 1 that they constitute a complete lattice.

---

[3] Formally, this is the upper-closure in $\mathcal{P}(\mathbb{R}^d)$ of the set of abstract elements.

Definition 3 (P-convexity). *Let $v \in \mathcal{F}(P, \overline{\mathbb{R}})$, we say that v is a P-convex function if $v = (v^*)^\dagger$. A set $X \subset \mathbb{R}^d$ is a P-convex set if $X = (X^\dagger)^*$.*

Example 3. Let us consider a triangle, depicted in Figure 3. If P is the set of linear forms defined by the faces of this triangle i.e P consists of the maps $(x, y) \mapsto y - x$, $(x, y) \mapsto y + x$ and $(x, y) \mapsto -y$, then it is an abstract convex set. But if P is, for example, linear forms defined by orthogonal vectors to the faces of the triangle, the previous triangle is no longer an abstract convex set.

Definition 4. *We respectively denote by* $\mathrm{Vex_P}(P \mapsto \overline{\mathbb{R}})$ *and* $\mathrm{Vex_P}(\mathbb{R}^d)$ *the set of P-convex function of $\mathcal{F}(P, \overline{\mathbb{R}})$ and the set of P-convex sets of $\mathbb{R}^d$.*

Definition 5 (The meet and join). *Let v and w be in $\mathcal{F}(P, \overline{\mathbb{R}})$. We denote by $\inf(v, w)$ and $\sup(v, w)$ the functions defined respectively by, $p \mapsto \inf(v(p), w(p))$ and $p \mapsto \sup(v(p), w(p))$. We equip* $\mathrm{Vex_P}(P \mapsto \overline{\mathbb{R}})$ *with the meet (respectively join) operator:*

$$v \vee w = \sup(v, w) \tag{1}$$

$$v \wedge w = (\inf(v, w)^*)^\dagger \tag{2}$$

Similarly, we equip $\mathrm{Vex_P}(\mathbb{R}^d)$ *with the two following operators: $X \sqcup Y = ((X \cup Y)^\dagger)^*$, $X \sqcap Y = X \cap Y$.*

The family of functions $\mathrm{Vex_P}(P \mapsto \overline{\mathbb{R}})$ is ordered by the partial order of real-valued functions i.e $v \leq w \iff v(p) \leq w(p) \; \forall p \in P$. The family of set $\mathrm{Vex_P}(\mathbb{R}^d)$ is ordered by the inclusion order denoted by $\subseteq$.

Theorem 1. $(\mathrm{Vex_P}(P \mapsto \overline{\mathbb{R}}), \wedge, \vee)$ *and* $(\mathrm{Vex_P}(\mathbb{R}^d), \sqcap, \sqcup)$ *are isomorphic complete lattices.*

Definition 6. *For $v \in \mathcal{F}(P, \overline{\mathbb{R}})$, we denote by $\mathrm{vex_P}(v)$ the P-convex hull of v which is the greatest P-convex function smaller than v.*
Similarly, we denote by the set $\mathrm{vex_P}(X)$ the P-convex hull of a subset X which is the smallest P-convex set greater than X.

Example 4. Let us come back to the Example 3. Let us take $P = \{(x, y) \mapsto y + x, \; (x, y) \mapsto x - y, \; (x, y) \mapsto -x\}$. Its P-convex hull is the one depicted Figure 4. If we take instead $P = \{(x, y) \mapsto y^2 - x^2, \; (x, y) \mapsto x, \; (x, y) \mapsto -x\}$, its P-convex hull is shown in Figure 5.

Proposition 2 (P-convex hull characterization). *Let v be in $\mathcal{F}(P, \overline{\mathbb{R}})$ and X be a subset of $\mathbb{R}^d$.*

1. *For $p \in P$, $(\mathrm{vex_P}(v))(p) = \sup\{p(x) \mid x \in \mathbb{R}^d, \; q(x) \leq v(q), \; \forall q \in P\}$*
2. *$\mathrm{vex_P}(X) = \bigcap\{Y \mid Y \in \mathrm{Vex_P}(\mathbb{R}^d), \; X \subseteq Y\}$*

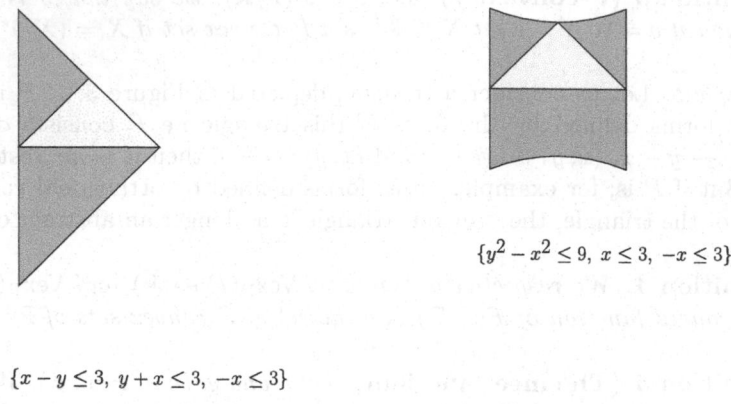

$$\{y^2 - x^2 \leq 9,\ x \leq 3,\ -x \leq 3\}$$

$$\{x - y \leq 3,\ y + x \leq 3,\ -x \leq 3\}$$

Fig. 4. A convex hull of the triangle   **Fig. 5.** Another convex hull of the same triangle, with a different set of templates

2.3 Intervals, Zones, Octagons and Manna et al's Templates

The interval domain is naturally subsumed by our abstract convex sets: take as basis $P = \{x_1, -x_1, \ldots, x_n, -x_n\}$ where x_i $(i = 1, \ldots, n)$ are the program variables. And abstract value v in our domain thus naturally corresponds to the supremum of the interval for x_i: $v(x_i)$ and its infimum: $-v(-x_i)$.

Zones and octagons are treated in a similar manner. For instance, for zones, take $P = \{x_i - x_j \mid i, j = 0, \ldots, n, i \neq j\}$, adding a slack variable x_0 (always equal to 0), as customary, to subsume intervals. Of course, (linear) templates as defined in [SSM05] are particular abstract convex sets, for which P is given by a set of linear functionals.

We remark that in the case of zones, $v(x_i - x_j)$ is exactly the entry i, j of the DBM (Difference Bound Matrix) representing the corresponding zone. Also, elements of $\mathrm{Vex_P}(P \mapsto \overline{\mathbb{R}})$ corresponding naturally to *closed* DBMs, that is, canonical forms of DBMs. As well known [Min04b], the union of two zones preserves closure whereas the intersection does not necessarily preserve closure. This is reflected in our domain by (1) and (2).

3   Quadratic Zones

In this section, we instantiate the set P to linear and quadratic functions. This allows us to give a systematic way to derive the abstract semantics of a program. The main result is that the abstract semantics for an assignment for instance, can be approximated precisely in polynomial time by Shor's relaxation scheme, Fact 1.

Definition 7. *We say that P is a quadratic zone if every element (template) $p \in P$ can be written as:*

$$x \mapsto p(x) = x^T A_p x + b_p^T x + c_p,$$

where A_p is a $d \times d$ symmetric matrix (so A can be a zero matrix), x^T denotes the transpose of a vector x, b_p is a $\mathbb{R}^d$ vector and c_p a scalar.

Now, we suppose that P is finite and we suppose that for all q, $v(q) > -\infty$. We denote by $\mathcal{F}(P, \mathbb{R} \cup \{+\infty\})$ the set of functions from P to $\mathbb{R} \cup \{+\infty\}$ and $\mathcal{F}(P, \mathbb{R}_+)$, the set of functions from P to $\mathbb{R}_+$.

Suppose now we are given a program with d variables $(x_1, \ldots, x_d)$ and n control points numbered from 1 to n. We suppose this program is written in a simple toy version of a C-like imperative language, comprising global variables, no procedures, assignments of variables using only *parallel affine assignments*[4] $(x_1, \ldots, x_d) = T(x_1, \ldots, x_d)$ (i.e. T is an affine map), tests of the form $(x_1, \ldots, x_d) \in C$, where C is some shape in $\mathcal{P}(\mathbb{R}^d)$, and while loops with similar entry tests. We do not recap the standard collecting semantics that associates to this program a monotone map $F : (\mathcal{P}(\mathbb{R}^d))^n \to (\mathcal{P}(\mathbb{R}^d))^n$ whose least fixed points $lfp\, F$ has as ith component ($i = 1, \ldots, n$) the subset of $\mathbb{R}^d$ of values that the d variables $x_1, \ldots, x_d$ can take at control point i.

The aim of this section is to compute, inductively on the syntax, the abstraction (or a good over-approximation of it) $F^\sharp$ of F from $\mathcal{F}(P, \mathbb{R} \cup \{+\infty\})^n$ to itself defined as usual as:

$$F^\sharp(v) = (F(v^\star)^\dagger) \tag{3}$$

The notation $v^\star$ is in fact the vector of sets $(v_1^\star, \cdots, v_n^\star)$ and $(F(v^\star)^\dagger)$ is also interpreted component-wise. The notation $\text{vex}_P(v)$ will be also understood component-wise.

3.1 Shor's Semi-definite Relaxation Scheme

Shor's relaxation scheme (see Section 4.3.1 of [TN01] or Shor's original article [Sho87] for details) consists of over-approximating the value of a general quadratic optimization problem by the optimal value of a semi-definite programming (SDP) problem. We know, if a dual feasibility condition holds, that the SDP problems are solvable in polynomial time by an interior point method, see e.g [Ali95].

Let p, $\{q_i\}_{i=1,\ldots,m}$ be quadratic functions on $\mathbb{R}^d$. Let us consider the following constrained maximization problem:

$$\sup\{p(x) \mid q_i(x) \le 0, \forall i = 1, \ldots, m\} \tag{4}$$

The first step is to relax the latter optimization problem by Lagrange duality techniques see e.g Section 5.3 of [AT03]. The relaxed problem is:

$$\inf_{\lambda \in \mathbb{R}_+^m} \sup_{x \in \mathbb{R}^d} p(x) + \sum_{i=1}^m \lambda_i q_i(x)$$

---

[4] The abstraction of non-linear assignments is outside the scope of this article. Easy ways to deal with them from the material given in this paper include: getting back, locally, to an interval semantics in case of non-linear assignments, or using the linearization methods of [Min04a].

where $\lambda \in \mathbb{R}_+^m$ are called Lagrange multipliers. Its optimal value is always greater or equal than the optimal value of the problem (4) and is, even, in well-known cases equal (this will be used Proposition 3).

Then, we introduce the matrix $M(p)$, for a quadratic function as in Definition 7 p and the matrix $N(y)$ for a real y defined as:

$$M(p) = \begin{pmatrix} c_p & \frac{1}{2}b_p^T \\ \frac{1}{2}b_p & A_p \end{pmatrix}, \text{ and } N_{1,1}(y) = y, \ N_{i,j}(y) = 0 \text{ if } (i,j) \neq (1,1) \quad (5)$$

Let $\preceq$ denotes the Loewner ordering of symmetric matrices, so that $A \preceq B$ if all eigenvalues of $B - A$ are non-negative.

Shor's relaxation scheme consists of solving the following SDP problem:

$$\inf_{\substack{\lambda \in \mathbb{R}_+^m \\ \eta \in \mathbb{R}}} \{\eta \text{ s.t } M(p) + \eta N(-1) - \sum_{i=1}^{m} \lambda_i M(q)] \preceq 0\}$$

which is the optimal value of the relaxed problem, hence an over-approximation of the optimal value of the problem (4).

3.2   Abstraction of Assignments

In this subsection, we focus on assignments $(x_1, \ldots, x_d) = T(x_1, \ldots, x_d)$ at control point i. Equation 3 translates in that case to (given that v_{i-1} defines the abstract value at control point $i - 1$, i.e. immediately before the assignment):

$$(F_i^\sharp(v))(p) = \sup\{p \circ T(x) \mid q(x) \leq v_{i-1}(q), \forall q \in P\} \quad (6)$$

We recognize the constrained optimization problem 4 and we use Lagrange duality as in the first step of Subsection 3.1. In our case, the Lagrange multipliers are some non-negative functions λ from P to $\mathbb{R}$. We thus consider the transformed optimization problem:

$$\inf_{\lambda \in \mathcal{F}(P, \mathbb{R}_+)} \sup_{x \in \mathbb{R}^d} p \circ T(x) + \sum_{q \in P} \lambda(q)[v_{i-1}(q) - q(x)] \quad (7)$$

We write $F_i^{\mathcal{R}}(v)(p)$ for the value of Equation 7. It is called the relaxed function of $F_i^\sharp$. In general, $F_i^{\mathcal{R}}$ is more abstract than $F_i^\sharp$, in other words:

Theorem 2. *For all* $v \in \mathcal{F}(P, \mathbb{R} \cup \{+\infty\})^n$, *for all* $p \in P$,

$$(F_i^\sharp(v))(p) \leq (F_i^{\mathcal{R}}(v))(p)$$

Moreover, if a constraint qualification, called Slater condition, is satisfied, there exists some λ which achieves the minimum in (7); and the over-approximation we make is not in general that big; in some cases even, the inequality above is an equality:

Proposition 3 (Selection Property). *If the set $\{x \in \mathbb{R}^d \mid q(x) - v_{i-1}(q) < 0, \forall q \in P\}$ is nonempty, there exists $\lambda^* \in \mathcal{F}(P, \mathbb{R}_+)$ such that:*

$$F_i^{\mathcal{R}}(v)(p) = \sup_{x \in \mathbb{R}^d} p \circ T(x) + \sum_{q \in P} \lambda^*(q)[v_{i-1}(q) - q(x)]$$

Furthermore, if p is a concave quadratic form and if $v_{i-1}(q) < \infty$ only when q is a convex quadratic form, then, we get: $(F_i^{\mathcal{R}}(v))(p) = (F_i^{\sharp}(v))(p)$.

The second part of Proposition 3 follows from the strong duality theorem for convex optimization problems, see e.g. Proposition 5.3.2 of [AT03].

From now on, we write, for a map w from P to $\mathbb{R} \cup \{+\infty\}$,

$$w^\circ = \{x \in \mathbb{R}^d \mid q(x) - w(q) < 0, \forall q \in P\}.$$

Let us suppose that $v_{i-1}^\circ \neq \emptyset$, let us fix $\lambda \in \mathcal{F}(P, \mathbb{R}_+)$, and observe that the sum $\sum_{q \in P} \lambda(q)v_{i-1}(q)$ does not depend on the variable x in (7). We now define $F_i^\lambda(v)$ by :

$$(F_i^\lambda(v))(p) = \sum_{q \in P} \lambda(q)v_{i-1}(q) + V_i^\lambda(p) \tag{8}$$

$$\text{where } V_i^\lambda(p) = \sup_{x \in \mathbb{R}^d} p \circ T(x) - \sum_{q \in P} \lambda(q)q(x) \tag{9}$$

So that, $(F_i^{\mathcal{R}}(v))(p) = \inf_{\lambda \in \mathcal{F}(P, \mathbb{R}_+)}(F^\lambda(v))(p)$.

By applying the so-called "Simple Lemma" of Section 4.3.1 of [TN01], we can write (9) as the following SDP problem:

$$V_i^\lambda(p) = \inf\{\eta \in \mathbb{R} \mid M(p \circ T) + \eta N(-1) - \sum_{q \in P} \lambda(q)M(q) \preceq 0\}$$

where $M(p \circ T)$, $N(-1)$ and $M(q)$ are the matrices defined in (5).

So, by applying Shor's relaxation scheme of Subsection 3.1, we get:

$$(F_i^{\mathcal{R}}(v))(p) = \inf_{\substack{\lambda \in \mathcal{F}(P, \mathbb{R}_+) \\ \eta \in \mathbb{R}}} \eta \text{ s.t } M(p \circ T) + \eta N(-1) + \sum_{q \in P} \lambda(q)[N(v_{i-1}(q)) - M(q)] \preceq 0$$

$$\tag{10}$$

which can be solved by a SDP solver.

To get a safe optimal value of (10), we can use a verified SDP solver as VSDP [JCK07].

We remark that we can apply the Shor's relaxation scheme for over-approximating the P-convex hull of a given function $w \in \mathcal{F}(P, \overline{\mathbb{R}})$, which will be useful in the next section.

Corollary 1. *Let w be in $\mathcal{F}(P, \overline{\mathbb{R}})$ and p in P we have:*

$$(\text{vex}_P(w))(p) \leq \inf_{\substack{\lambda \in \mathcal{F}(P, \mathbb{R}_+) \\ \eta \in \mathbb{R}}} \eta \text{ s.t } M(p) + \eta N(-1) + \sum_{q \in P} \lambda(q)[N(w(q)) - M(q)] \preceq 0$$

Finally, we conclude that we can compute over-approximations of (6) as well as over-approximations of the P-convex hull of an element of $\mathcal{F}(P, \overline{\mathbb{R}})$ by solving a SDP problem, which can be done in polynomial time [TN01]. We sum up what we achieved in the following fact:

Fact 1. *In the case of quadratic templates, the relaxed functional $F^{\mathcal{R}}$ and a sound over-approximation of the P-convex hull operation can be evaluated using Shor's semi-definite relaxation.*

Example 5. We analyze the following parallel affine assignment T that implements a rotation of angle ϕ on the unit sphere S^1 of $\mathbb{R}^2$:

$$T\begin{pmatrix} x \\ y \end{pmatrix} = \begin{pmatrix} \cos\phi & -\sin\phi \\ \sin\phi & \cos\phi \end{pmatrix}\begin{pmatrix} x \\ y \end{pmatrix}$$

where $x^2 + y^2 = 1$.

Let us take $P = \{p_1(x, y) \mapsto x^2 + y^2, \; p_2(x, y) \mapsto -(x^2 + y^2)\}$ and we set $v_1(p_1) = 1$ and $v_1(p_2) = -1$. Equation (10) translates into:

$$v_2(p_1) = T(v_1^\star)^\dagger(p_1) = \sup\{p_1(T(x, y)) \mid p_1(x, y) \le 1, \; p_2(x, y) \le -1\}$$
$$v_2(p_2) = T(v_1^\star)^\dagger(p_2) = \sup\{p_2(T(x, y)) \mid p_1(x, y) \le 1, \; p_2(x, y) \le -1\}$$

$$v_2(p_1) =$$

$$\inf_{\substack{\lambda(p_1)\ge 0 \\ \lambda(p_2)\ge 0 \\ \eta\in\mathbb{R}}} \eta \text{ s.t } \begin{pmatrix} -\eta + \lambda(p_1) - \lambda(p_2) & 0 & 0 \\ 0 & 1 - \lambda(p_1) + \lambda(p_2) & 0 \\ 0 & 0 & 1 - \lambda(p_1) + \lambda(p_2) \end{pmatrix} \preceq 0$$

and
$$v_2(p_2) =$$

$$\inf_{\substack{\lambda(p_1)\ge 0 \\ \lambda(p_2)\ge 0 \\ \eta\in\mathbb{R}}} \eta \text{ s.t } \begin{pmatrix} -\eta + \lambda(p_1) - \lambda(p_2) & 0 & 0 \\ 0 & -1 - \lambda(p_1) + \lambda(p_2) & 0 \\ 0 & 0 & -1 - \lambda(p_1) + \lambda(p_2) \end{pmatrix} \preceq 0$$

To solve these optimization problems, we could call an SDP solver, but in this case, it suffices to solve a system of inequalities: all the diagonal elements must be non-positive, for example, for the first problem, this implies that $\eta \ge 1$ and since we minimize η we get $\eta = 1$.

Hence, we find $v_2(p_1) = 1$ and $v_2(p_2) = -1$. This simple analysis finds automatically that the circle is invariant by a rotation.

3.3   Abstraction of Simple Tests

We assume here that a test $(x_1, \ldots, x_d) \in C$ is translated on three control points $j-2$, $j-1$, j and $j+1$ as follows: $F_{j-1}(X) = C$, $F_j(X) = X_{j-2} \cap X_{j-1}$, for the "`then`" branch. For the "`else`" branch, beginning at control point k, we have similarly $F_k(X) = X_{j-2} \cap \neg X_{j-1}$. As we deal with arbitrary $C \in \mathcal{P}(\mathbb{R}^d)$, it is sufficient to show here how to deal with the equations on control points $j - 2$, $j - 1$ and j.

By using Equation (3), we get, for $v \in \mathcal{F}(P, \mathbb{R} \cup \{+\infty\})^n$, and $p \in P$, $(F_j^\sharp(v))(p) = ((v_{j-2}^\star \sqcap v_{j-1}^\star)^\dagger(p)$ then, by a simple calculus,

$$(F_j^\sharp(v))(p) = (v_{j-2} \wedge v_{j-1})(p).$$

As for the abstraction of assignments, we calculate $F_j^\mathcal{R}$ instead of $F_j^\sharp$. We can compute $F_j^\mathcal{R}$ in two ways. The first one consists in using the fact that $(v_{j-2} \wedge v_{j-1})(p) = \mathrm{vex}_P(\inf(v_{j-2}, v_{j-1}))(p)$. Hence we can apply Proposition 1 to $\inf(v_{j-2}, v_{j-1})$ as a practical means to compute $F_j^\mathcal{R}$, using a SDP solver. This method can be used during Kleene iteration, since at any iteration, we know the values taken by v_{j-2} and v_{j-1}. Unfortunately, this method cannot be used in policy iteration, hence we use the following method in that case.

The second method consists in noticing that $x \in v_{j-2}^\star \sqcap v_{j-1}^\star \Rightarrow \forall q \in P, q(x) \leq v_{j-2}(q)$ and $q(x) \leq v_{j-1}(q)$ so:

$$(F_j^\sharp(v))(p) = \sup\{p(x) \mid q(x) \leq v_{j-2}(q), \ q(x) \leq v_{j-1}(q) \ \forall q \in P\}$$

Then, supposing the Slater condition is satisfied, it suffices to apply the same techniques as for the abstraction of assignments. The only difference is that we have now a couple (λ, μ) of $\mathcal{F}(P, \mathbb{R}_+)$ as Lagrange multipliers, the first one is associated to v_{j-1} and the second one to v_{j-2}. The function (9) becomes a function which depends on the two parameters (λ, μ), this new function is written $V_j^{(\lambda, \mu)}$, its evaluation is reduced once again to a SDP problem.

Thus, as for (8), we have the following affine form $F_j^{(\lambda, \mu)}$ on $\mathcal{F}(P, \mathbb{R} \cup \{+\infty\})$:

$$(F_j^{(\lambda, \mu)}(v))(p) = \sum_{q \in P} \lambda(q) v_{j-1}(q) + \sum_{q \in P} \mu(q) v_{j-2}(q) + V_j^{(\lambda, \mu)}(p) \qquad (11)$$

The latter affine form is used for computing by linear programming the smallest fixpoint of a map associated to a policy (that, we will see in Section 4.3 corresponds to the Lagrange multipliers (λ, μ)).

Then, the relaxed function of $F_j^\sharp$ is evaluated by solving the same kind of SDP problem as in Equation (10).

3.4 Abstraction of Loops

The only thing that we do not know yet how to interpret in the collecting semantics equations is the equation at control point i where we collect the values of the variables before the entry in the body of the loop, at control point $i - 1$, with the values of the variables at the end of the body of the loop, at control point j: $F_i(X) = X_{i-1} \cup X_j$, since we know now how to deal with the interpretation of tests.

By using Equation (3), for $v \in \mathcal{F}(P, \mathbb{R} \cup \{+\infty\})^n$ and $p \in P$, $(F_i^\sharp(v))(p) = (v_{i-1}^\star \sqcup v_j^\star)^\dagger(p)$, by a simple calculus, the latter equality becomes:

$$(F_i^\sharp(v))(p) = \mathrm{vex}_P(\sup(v_{i-1}, v_j))(p).$$

Hence, the calculus of the union can be reduced to a P-convex hull computation, see Proposition 1.

During a fixpoint iteration (as in Section 4), we only have to deal with "closed" abstract values, that is, elements v in $\mathrm{Vex}_P(P \mapsto \overline{\mathbb{R}})^n$. As for zones, we notice that the union of two such "closed" abstract values v_{i-1} and v_j is directly given by taking their maximum on each element of the basis of quadratic functions P, without having to take its closure.

4   Solving the Semantic Equation

4.1   Fixpoint Equations in Quadratic Zones

We recall that P is a finite set of quadratic templates and F is a monotone map which interprets a program with d variables and n labels in $(\mathcal{P}(\mathbb{R}^d))^n$. We want to find the smallest vector in $(\mathcal{P}(\mathbb{R}^d))^n$ such that $F(X) = X$. This fixpoint equation is generally unsolvable algorithmically. So as customary in abstract interpretation, we solve instead the abstract equation:

$$\inf\{v \in \mathrm{Vex}_P(P \mapsto \overline{\mathbb{R}})^n \mid v = F^{\mathcal{R}}(v)\} \tag{12}$$

where v belongs to $\mathrm{Vex}_P(P \mapsto \overline{\mathbb{R}})^n$.

We recall that $v^\star$ denotes the vector of sets $((v_1)^\star, \cdots, (v_n)^\star)$ and $F^\sharp(v) = (F(v^\star))^\dagger$ i.e $\forall i$, $F_i^\sharp(v) = (F_i(v^\star))^\dagger$ and $F^{\mathcal{R}}$ is the map, the components of which are the relaxed functions of $F^\sharp$.

We define and compare two ways of solving the fixpoint equation: Kleene iteration in Section 4.2, and policy iteration in Section 4.3.

4.2   Kleene Iteration

We note by $\bot$ the smallest element of $\mathrm{Vex}_P(P \mapsto \overline{\mathbb{R}})^n$ i.e for all $i = 1, \cdots, n$ and for all $p \in P$, $\bot_i(p) = -\infty$. The Kleene iteration sequence in $\mathrm{Vex}_P(P \mapsto \overline{\mathbb{R}})^n$ is thus as follows:

1. $v^0 = \bot$
2. for $k \geq 0$, $v^{k+1} = \mathrm{vex}_P(\sup(v^k, F^{\mathcal{R}}(v^k)))$

This sequence converges to the smallest fixpoint of $\mathrm{vex}_P(F^{\mathcal{R}})$. But, the computation of it can be very slow or can never end so we use an acceleration technique to over-approximate it rapidly. After a certain number of iterations and during some iterations, we round bounds outwards with a decreasing precision (akin to the widening used in [GPBG08]). The closure we use, after each widening step during Kleene iteration, might end up not being a widening (as is the case in zones). So we extrapolate the result to $\top$ ($\top_i(p) = \infty$ for all $i = 1, \cdots, n$ and all $p \in P$) after a fixed number of steps.

4.3   Policy Iteration Algorithm

Selection property and policy iteration algorithm. To define a policy iteration algorithm, we need policies. Here, our policies are given by the Lagrange multipliers introduced by the relaxation in the interpretation of assignments, Section 3.2, and in the interpretation of tests, Section 3.3. Hence the set of policies is the union of the sets of Lagrange multipliers for each assignment of the program and couple of Lagrange multipliers for each test of the program.

To define a policy iteration algorithm, we also need a selection property, as in e.g [GGTZ07]. We saw in Proposition 3 that the selection property is given by a constraint qualification argument. We thus introduce $\mathcal{FS}(P, \overline{\mathbb{R}})^n$, the set of elements of $\mathcal{F}(P, \overline{\mathbb{R}})$ which satisfy the Slater condition:

- when the component F_i of F corresponds to an assignment, the set of policies at i is the union of the sets of Lagrange multipliers,
- when the component F_j of F corresponds to a test, the set of policies at j is the union of the sets of couple of Lagrange multipliers.

We saw that for other coordinates, the set of policy is a singleton. We denote by Π the set of all policies π and by π_i a policy at i.

Algorithm 1. Policy Iteration in Quadratic Templates

---

1 Choose $\pi^0 \in \Pi$ such that $V^{\pi^0} < +\infty$, $k = 0$.
2 Compute $V^{\pi_i^k} = \{V^{\pi_i^k}(q)\}_{q \in P}$.
3 Compute the smallest fixpoint v^k in $\mathcal{F}(P, \overline{\mathbb{R}})^n$ of F^{π^k}.
4 Compute $w^k = \mathrm{vex}_P(v^k)$.
5 If $w^k \in \mathcal{FS}(P, \overline{\mathbb{R}})^n$ continue otherwise return w^k.
6 Evaluate $F^{\mathcal{R}}(w^k)$, if $F^{\mathcal{R}}(w^k) = w^k$ return w^k otherwise take π^{k+1} s.t $F^{\mathcal{R}}(w^k) = F^{\pi^{k+1}}(w^k)$ and go to 2.

Remark 1. The initial policy is given after few Kleene iterations: this gives us a vector $v \in \mathrm{Vex}_P(P \mapsto \overline{\mathbb{R}})^n$, then we compute, by solving Equation (10) and its equivalent for the abstraction of tests, a policy π^0.

For the third step of Algorithm 1, since P is finite and using (8) and (11), F^{π^l} is monotone and affine $\mathcal{F}(P, \overline{\mathbb{R}})^n$, we compute the smallest fixpoint of F^{π^l} by solving the following linear program see Section 4 of [GGTZ07]:

$$\min \sum_{i=1}^{n} \sum_{q \in P} v^i(q) \text{ s.t } (F_k^{\pi^l}(v))(q) \leq v_k(q), \; \forall k = 1, \cdots, n, \; \forall q \in P \qquad (13)$$

Remark 2. To ensure the feasibility of the solution of (13) computed by the LP solver, we replace, when possible, the constraint set by $F^{\pi^l}(v) + \epsilon \leq v$, where ϵ is a small constant (typically of the order of several $ulp(v)$).

To obtain safe bounds even though we run our algorithm on machine which uses finite-precision arithmetic, we should use a guaranteed LP solver (e.g LU-RUPA see [Kei05]) to check that the solution obtained verifies $F^{\pi^l}(v) \leq v$.

We can only prove that policy iteration on quadratic templates converges (maybe in infinite time) towards a post-fixed point of our abstract functional and that under some technical conditions, it converges towards a fixed point. One interest in policy iteration for static analysis is that we can always terminate the iteration after a finite time, and ends up with a post-fixed point.

Theorem 3. *The sequence v^l computed by Algorithm 1 is non-increasing.*

Remark 3. In the case of intervals, zones and templates, at least for programs containing only linear or concave quadratic expressions in assignments, Proposition 3 implies that $F^\sharp = F^\mathcal{R}$. Therefore, we are giving a policy iteration algorithm in this paper, computing the same least fixpoints as the policy iteration algorithms described in papers [CGG+05, AGG08, GGTZ07].

4.4 A Detailed Calculation on the Running Example

Now we give details on the harmonic oscillator of Example 1. The program of this example implements an Euler explicit scheme with a small step h, that is, which simulates the linear system $(x, v)^T \leftarrow T(x, v)^T$ with $T = \begin{pmatrix} 1 & h \\ -h & 1-h \end{pmatrix}$.

The function $(x, v) :\mapsto (x, v)L(x, v)^T$ is a Lyapunov function of the new linear system with $L = \begin{pmatrix} 2 & 1 \\ 1 & 3 \end{pmatrix}$.

We write $\underline{x} : (x, v) \mapsto x$, $\underline{v} : (x, v) \mapsto v$, $\underline{L} : (x, v) \mapsto (x, v)L(x, v)^T$ and finally $P = \{\underline{x}, -\underline{x}, \underline{v}, -\underline{v}, \underline{L}\}$. For $p = \underline{x}$, $-\underline{x}$, $\underline{v}$, $-\underline{v}$, $\underline{L}$ and $w \in \mathcal{F}(P, \mathbb{R})$, we get the semantic equations described below the corresponding C code, at Figure 6, for all three control points.

Now we are going to focus on the third coordinate of $(F^\mathcal{R}(v))(p)$. Let us consider, for example, $p = \underline{x}$, we get: $(F_3^\mathcal{R}(v))(\underline{x}) =$

$$\inf_{\lambda \in \mathcal{F}(P, \mathbb{R}_+)} \sum_{q \in P} \lambda(q)v_2(q) + \sup_{(x,v)}(x, v)(\lambda(\underline{L})(x, v)^T + \begin{pmatrix} 1 + \lambda(-\underline{x}) - \lambda(\underline{x}) \\ h + \lambda(-\underline{v}) - \lambda(\underline{v}) \end{pmatrix}(x, v)^T + 0.$$

(14)

By introducing the following symmetric matrices, we can rewrite (14) as (8): $M(\underline{x})(1, 2) = M(\underline{x})(2, 1) = \frac{1}{2}$ and 0 otherwise. $M(\underline{v})(1, 3) = M(-\underline{v})(3, 1) = \frac{1}{2}$ and 0 otherwise. $M(\underline{L})(2, 2) = 2$, $M(\underline{L})(3, 3) = 3$, $M(\underline{L})(2, 3) = M(\underline{L})(3, 2) = 1$ and 0 otherwise. Furthermore, $M(-\underline{x}) = M(\underline{x})$ and $M(-\underline{v}) = M(\underline{v})$.

$$M(\underline{x} \circ T) = \begin{pmatrix} 0 & \frac{1}{2} & \frac{h}{2} \\ \frac{1}{2} & 0 & 0 \\ \frac{h}{2} & 0 & 0 \end{pmatrix}$$

To initialize Algorithm 1, we choose a policy π^0. For the third coordinate of $F^\mathcal{R}$, we have to choose a policy π_3^0 such that $V_3^{\pi_3^0}(p)$ is finite. We can start,

```
x = [0,1];
v = [0,1]; [1]
h = 0.01;
while (true) { [2]
  u = v;
  v = v*(1-h)-h*x;
  x = x+h*u; [3] }
```

$$F_1^\sharp(w)(p) = \{\underline{x}(x,v) \leq 1, -\underline{x}(x,v) \leq 0, \underline{v}(x,v) \leq 1, -\underline{v}(x,v) \leq 0, \underline{L}(x,v) \leq 7\}$$
$$F_2^\sharp(w)(p) = \sup\{w_1(p), w_3(p)\}$$
$$F_3^\sharp(w)(p) = \sup_{(x,v)\in(w_2)^*} (p \circ T)(x,v)$$

Fig. 6. Implementation of the harmonic oscillator and its semantics in $\mathcal{F}(P,\overline{\mathbb{R}})^3$

for example, by $\pi_3^0(p) = (0,0,0,0,1)$ for all $p \in P$. This consists, for $p = \underline{x}$, in taking $\lambda(\underline{x}) = \lambda(-\underline{x}) = \lambda(\underline{v}) = \lambda(-\underline{v}) = 0$ and $\lambda(\underline{L}) = 1$ in (14). By a Matlab[5] implementation, using Yalmip [L04] and SeDuMi [Stu99], we find:

$$V_3^{\pi_3^0}(\underline{x} \circ F) = V_3^{\pi_3^0}(-\underline{x}) = 0.149, \; V_3^{\pi_3^0}(\underline{v}) = V_3^{\pi_3^0}(-\underline{v}) = 0.099 \text{ and } V_3^{\pi_3^0}(\underline{L}) = 0.$$

We solve the following linear program (see (13)):

$$\min \sum_{i=1}^{3} \sum_{p\in P} \beta_i(p)$$

$$\beta_2(\underline{L}) + V^{\pi_3^0}(p\circ F) \leq \beta_3(p) \; \forall p$$
$$\beta_3(p) \leq \beta_2(p), \; \forall p$$
$$1 \leq \beta_2(\underline{x}), \; 0 \leq \beta_2(-\underline{x}), 1 \leq \beta_2(\underline{v}), \; 0 \leq \beta_2(-\underline{v}), \; 7 \leq \beta_2(\underline{L})$$
$$1 \leq \beta_1(\underline{x}), \; 0 \leq \beta_1(-\underline{x}), 1 \leq \beta_1(\underline{v}), \; 0 \leq \beta_1(-\underline{v}), \; 7 \leq \beta_1(\underline{L})$$

Using solver Linprog, we find:

$w_1^0(\underline{x}) = 1.0000$	$w_2^0(\underline{x}) = 7.1490$	$w_3^0(\underline{x}) = 7.1490$
$w_1^0(-\underline{x}) = 0$	$w_2^0(-\underline{x}) = 7.1490$	$w_3^0(-\underline{x}) = 7.1490$
$w_1^0(\underline{v}) = 1.0000$	$w_2^0(\underline{v}) = 7.0990$	$w_3^0(\underline{v}) = 7.0990$
$w_1^0(-\underline{v}) = 0$	$w_2^0(-\underline{v}) = 7.0990$	$w_3^0(-\underline{v}) = 7.0990$
$w_1^0(\underline{L}) = 7.0000$	$w_2^0(\underline{L}) = 7.0000$	$w_3^0(\underline{L}) = 7.0000$

The calculus of $u = \text{vexp}(w^1)$ returns:

$u_1^0(\underline{x}) = 1.0000$	$u_2^0(\underline{x}) = 2.0493$	$u_3^0(\underline{x}) = 2.0493$
$u_1^0(-\underline{x}) = 0$	$u_2^0(-\underline{x}) = 2.0493$	$u_3^0(-\underline{x}) = 2.0493$
$u_1^0(\underline{v}) = 1.0000$	$u_2^0(\underline{v}) = 1.6733$	$u_3^0(\underline{v}) = 1.6733$
$u_1^0(-\underline{v}) = 0$	$u_2^0(-\underline{v}) = 1.6733$	$u_3^0(-\underline{v}) = 1.6733$
$u_1^0(\underline{L}) = 7.0000$	$u_2^0(\underline{L}) = 7.0000$	$u_3^0(\underline{L}) = 7.0000$

Using again Yalmip with the solver SeDuMi, the vector u is not a fixpoint of $F^{\mathcal{R}}$, so we get the new following new policy: $\pi_3^1(\underline{x}) = (0.9035, 0, 0, 0, 0.0134)$,

---

[5] Matlab is a registered trademark of the MathWorks,Inc.

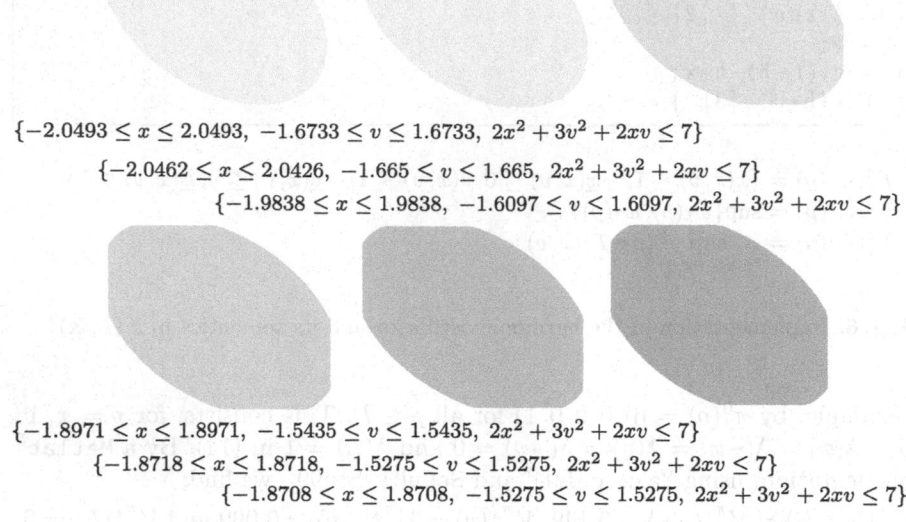

$$\{-2.0493 \leq x \leq 2.0493, \; -1.6733 \leq v \leq 1.6733, \; 2x^2 + 3v^2 + 2xv \leq 7\}$$
$$\{-2.0462 \leq x \leq 2.0426, \; -1.665 \leq v \leq 1.665, \; 2x^2 + 3v^2 + 2xv \leq 7\}$$
$$\{-1.9838 \leq x \leq 1.9838, \; -1.6097 \leq v \leq 1.6097, \; 2x^2 + 3v^2 + 2xv \leq 7\}$$

$$\{-1.8971 \leq x \leq 1.8971, \; -1.5435 \leq v \leq 1.5435, \; 2x^2 + 3v^2 + 2xv \leq 7\}$$
$$\{-1.8718 \leq x \leq 1.8718, \; -1.5275 \leq v \leq 1.5275, \; 2x^2 + 3v^2 + 2xv \leq 7\}$$
$$\{-1.8708 \leq x \leq 1.8708, \; -1.5275 \leq v \leq 1.5275, \; 2x^2 + 3v^2 + 2xv \leq 7\}$$

Fig. 7. Successive templates along policy iteration, at control point 2, for the harmonic oscillator

$\pi_3^1(-\underline{x}) = (0, 0.9035, 0, 0, 0.0134)$, $\pi_3^1(\underline{v}) = (0, 0, 0.8830, 0, 0.0135)$, $\pi_3^1(-\underline{v}) = (0, 0, 0, 0.8830, 0.0135)$, $\pi_3^1(\underline{L}) = (0, 0, 0, 0, 0.9946)$. The invariant of the loop i.e. $w_2^\star$ at control point 2 is $\{-1.8708 \leq x \leq 1.8708, \; -1.5275 \leq v \leq 1.5275, \; 2x^2 + 3v^2 + 2xv \leq 7\}$ and is computed in 14 seconds. We draw $w_2^\star$ at each iteration of Algorithm 1 in Figure 7.

This method is to be compared with the classical Kleene iteration with widening. On this example, we find without widening $x \in [-1.87078, 1.87083]$, $v \in [-1.52753, 1.52752]$ and $2x^2 + 3v^2 + 2xv \leq 7$ in 1360 iterations (for an overall time, under Matlab of 69 minutes).

4.5   Benchmarks

We implemented an analyzer for the quadratic template domain we presented, written in Matlab version 7.7(R2008b). This analyzer takes a text file in argument, this text file corresponds to the abstract equation $v = F^\sharp(v)$ where $F^\sharp$ is defined by Equation (2). The quadratic template can be loaded from a dat file by the analyzer. The affine maps are treated in the same manner.

In this analyzer, we can choose to use the Kleene iteration method or policy iteration. For the Kleene iteration method, the user gives as an argument a maximal number of iteration and the iteration number at which the acceleration method is applied. For the policy iteration method, the user gives the dat file defining the initial policy or chooses to make Kleene iterations before determining the initial policy.

Table 1. Benchmarks results

Programs	Method	#P	#lines	#var	#loops	#Iter.	Inv. quality	Time
Rotation2	Policy	2	2	2	0	0	Fixpoint	0.72
Rotation2	Kleene	2	2	2	0	1	Fixpoint	1.07
Rotation10	Policy	2	2	10	0	0	Fixpoint	1.17
Rotation10	Kleene	2	2	10	0	1	Fixpoint	1.82
Filter	Policy	5	3	2	1	2	Fixpoint	9.35
Filter	Kleene	5	3	2	1	2	Fixpoint	19.7
Oscillator	Policy	5	3	2	1	5	Fixpoint	12
Oscillator	Kleene	5	3	2	1	15	Fixpoint	18.8
Symplectic	Policy	5	3	2	1	0	Fixpoint	3
Symplectic	Kleene	5	3	2	1	15	Fixpoint	18.3
SymplecticSeu	Policy	5	5	2	1	30	Postfixpoint	125.3
SymplecticSeu	Kleene	5	5	2	1	30	Postfixpoint	78.9
Arrow-Hurwicz	Policy	2	14	4	3	10	Postfixpoint	44.6
Arrow-Hurwicz	Kleene	2	14	4	3	26	Postfixpoint	81.7

Each ten steps during policy iteration, the user can decide to stop the analysis and so a postfixpoint is reached (as in policy iteration the least fixed point is always reached from above). Similarly, the Kleene iteration with acceleration provides a postfixpoint after acceleration and widening to top, if the iteration does not converge after a given number of iterations. The analyzer writes, in a text file, information about time, quality of the invariants found and number of iterations.

For the benchmarks, we used a PC equipped with a quad core AMD Phenom(tm) II X4 920 Processor at 2.8 Ghz and a memory of 4 Gb. We indicate in the Table 1, the name of the program analyzed, the method used (policy iteration or Kleene iteration) for solving the fixpoint equation, the cardinality of the basis of quadratic templates used, the number of lines of C code the program has, the number of variables it manipulates, the number of loops. Then we indicate the number of iterations made, whether it reaches a fixpoint or (strictly) a postfixpoint, and the time it took with our Matlab prototype.

The file Rotation10 is the problem of Example 5 in dimension 10. By the fixpoint computation, we prove automatically that the unit sphere in dimension 10 is invariant by rotation. Both Kleene iteration and policy iteration find the unit sphere as invariant.

The program Oscillator is the problem 1. The invariant depicted Figure 1 in Section 1 is found by policy iteration whereas Kleene iteration after applying acceleration techniques from the iteration 5 to iteration 15 finds the less precise invariant $\{-2.44949 \leq x \leq 2.44949, -2 \leq v \leq 2, 2x^2 + 3v^2 + 2xv \leq 10\}$, in more time.

Symplectic is the implementation of a discretization of $\ddot{x} + c\dot{x} + x = 0$ with $c = 0$ by a symplectic method. In the case of $c = 0$, the dynamical system has imaginary eigenvalues (its orbits are circle), and the Euler scheme diverges, so we use a symplectic discretization scheme (preserving the symplectic form, see [HLW03]), which is an interesting highly degenerate numerical example from the point of view of static analysis (because there is no "stability margin", methods not exploiting the Lyapunov function are likely to produce trivial invariants when $c = 0$). As in Oscillator, we start from a position $x \in [0,1]$ and a speed $v \in [0,1]$. The discretization of $\ddot{x} + x = 0$ with the symplectic method and a step $\tau = 0.1$ gives us the matrix T such that $T_{1,1} = 1 - \frac{\tau}{2}$, $T_{1,2} = \tau - \frac{\tau^3}{4}$, $T_{2,1} = -\tau$ and $T_{2,2} = 1 - \frac{\tau}{2}$. We use the Lyapunov function L such that $L(x,v) = (x,v)Q(x,v)^T$ with $Q = \begin{pmatrix} 1 & 0 \\ 0 & 1 - \frac{\tau^2}{4} \end{pmatrix}$. The symplectic method ensures that $L(T(x,v)) = L(x,v)$. Our method takes advantage of this conservation law, since L is embedded as a template. The policy iteration returns: $\{-1.41333 \leq x \leq 1.41333, -1.4151 \leq v \leq 1.4151, x^2 + 0.9975v^2 \leq 1.9975\}$. The Kleene iteration returns: $\{-3.16624 \leq x \leq 3.16624, -3.16628 \leq v \leq 3.16628, x^2 + 0.9975v^2 \leq 10\}$, which is less precise. In particular, the Kleene algorithm misses the invariance of the Lyapunov function.

SymplecticSeu is a symplectic method with a threshold on $v = \dot{x}$. We iterate the Symplectic method while $v \geq \frac{1}{2}$, which gives the following code:

```
x = [0,1];
v = [0,1];
tau = 0.1 [1]
while [2] ((v>=1/2) [3]) { [4]
  x = (1-tau/2)*x+(tau-(tau^3)/4)*v;
  v = -tau*x+(1-tau/2)*v; [5]
};
```

Arrow-Hurwicz is an algorithm to compute both primal and dual solutions for convex constrained optimization problems. Arrow-Hurwicz ends when a fixpoint for the algorithm is reached, by our techniques, we prove that, if the last line of the program which implements the Arrow-Hurwicz method is attained, a fixpoint is reached. Our analysis also permits to find bounds at each control points. As pointed out in the introduction, the interest of the analysis resides in the appearance of saturations (non-linear projections) in the scheme. For both Kleene iteration and policy iteration, the invariant set of last line is $\{0 \leq \frac{11}{16}(u-x)^2 + (v-y)^2 \leq 1e-9\}$. The difference between the two final invariants comes from other lines where the invariant found by policy iteration is always smaller than the set found by Kleene, for example, when policy iteration returns, for example at line 11, $\{0 \leq \frac{11}{16}(u-x)^2 + (v-y)^2 \leq 3.18292\}$, Kleene returns $\{0 \leq \frac{11}{16}(u-x)^2 + (v-y)^2 \leq 10\}$.

The example files are available at:

http://www.lix.polytechnique.fr/~adje/publi-presentations.html.

5   Conclusion and Future Work

We have presented in this paper a generalization of the linear templates of Manna et al. [SSM05, SCSM06] that can also deal with non-linear templates. We showed that in the case of quadratic templates, we could efficiently abstract the semantic functionals using Shor's relaxation, and compute the resulting fixpoint using policy iteration. Future work include the use of more tight relaxations for quadratic problems. The use of SOS relaxation (see for instance [Las07] and [Par03]) for dealing with more general polynomial templates will be also considered. An other problem is to extend of the minimality result of [AGG08] which is currently only available for the interval domain, to our template domain. Finally, we wish to study more in-depth the complexity issues raised by our general policy iteration algorithm.

Acknowledgement. We thank Thomas Gawlitza and David Monniaux for their remarks on an earlier version of this paper.

References

[AGG08]   Adje, A., Gaubert, S., Goubault, E.: Computing the smallest fixed point of nonexpansive mappings arising in game theory and static analysis of programs. Technical report, arXiv:0806.1160. In: Proceedings of MTNS 2008, Blacksburg, Virginia (July 2008)

[Ali95]   Alizadeh, F.: Interior point methods in semidefinite programming with applications to combinatorial optimization. SIAM Journal on Optimization 5, 13–51 (1995)

[AT03]   Auslender, A., Teboulle, M.: Asymptotic Cones and Functions in Optimization and Variational Inequalities. Springer, Heidelberg (2003)

[BRCZ05]   Bagnara, R., Rodríguez-Carbonell, E., Zaffanella, E.: Generation of basic semi-algebraic invariants using convex polyhedra. In: Hankin, C., Siveroni, I. (eds.) SAS 2005. LNCS, vol. 3672, pp. 19–34. Springer, Heidelberg (2005)

[CC77]   Cousot, P., Cousot, R.: Abstract interpretation: a unified lattice model for static analysis of programs by construction or approximation of fixpoints. In: Conference Record of the Fourth Annual ACM SIGPLAN-SIGACT Symposium on Principles of Programming Languages, Los Angeles, California, pp. 238–252. ACM Press, New York (1977)

[CGG+05]   Costan, A., Gaubert, S., Goubault, E., Martel, M., Putot, S.: A policy iteration algorithm for computing fixed points in static analysis of programs. In: Etessami, K., Rajamani, S.K. (eds.) CAV 2005. LNCS, vol. 3576, pp. 462–475. Springer, Heidelberg (2005)

[Cou05]   Cousot, P.: Proving program invariance and termination by parametric abstraction, lagrangian relaxation and semidefinite programming. In: Cousot, R. (ed.) VMCAI 2005. LNCS, vol. 3385, pp. 1–24. Springer, Heidelberg (2005)

[FA08]   Feron, E., Alegre, F.: Control software analysis, part II: Closed-loop analysis. Technical report, arXiv:0812.1986 (2008)

[Fer05]   Feret, J.: Numerical abstract domains for digital filters. In: International workshop on Numerical and Symbolic Abstract Domains, NSAD 2005 (2005)

[FF08]   Feron, E., Alegre, F.: Control software analysis, part I: Open-loop properties. Technical report, arXiv:0809.4812 (2008)

[GGTZ07]   Gaubert, S., Goubault, E., Taly, A., Zennou, S.: Static analysis by policy iteration on relational domains. In: De Nicola, R. (ed.) ESOP 2007. LNCS, vol. 4421, pp. 237–252. Springer, Heidelberg (2007)

[GPBG08]   Goubault, E., Putot, S., Baufreton, P., Gassino, J.: Static analysis of
            the accuracy in control systems: Principles and experiments. In: Leue,
            S., Merino, P. (eds.) FMICS 2007. LNCS, vol. 4916, pp. 3–20. Springer,
            Heidelberg (2008)
[GS07a]   Gawlitza, T., Seidl, H.: Precise fixpoint computation through strategy
            iteration. In: De Nicola, R. (ed.) ESOP 2007. LNCS, vol. 4421, pp. 300–
            315. Springer, Heidelberg (2007)
[GS07b]   Gawlitza, T., Seidl, H.: Precise relational invariants through strategy iter-
            ation. In: Duparc, J., Henzinger, T.A. (eds.) CSL 2007. LNCS, vol. 4646,
            pp. 23–40. Springer, Heidelberg (2007)
[HLW03]   Hairer, E., Lubich, C., Wanner, G.: Geometric numerical integration illus-
            trated by the Störmer/Verlet method. Acta Numerica 12, 399–450 (2003)
[JCK07]   Jansson, C., Chaykin, D., Keil, C.: Rigorous error bounds for the optimal
            value in semidefinite programming. SIAM J. Numer. Anal. 46(1), 180–200
            (2007)
[Kei05]   Keil, C.: Lurupa - rigorous error bounds in linear programming. Alge-
            braic and Numerical Algorithms and Computer-assisted Proofs (2005),
            http://drops.dagstuhl.de/opus/volltexte/2006/445
[Las07]   Lasserre, J.-B.: A sum of squares approximations of nonnegative polyno-
            mials. SIAM Review 49(4), 651–669 (2007)
[L04]   Lfberg, J.: Yalmip: A toolbox for modeling and optimization in MAT-
            LAB. In: Proceedings of the CACSD Conference, Taipei, Taiwan (2004),
            http://control.ee.ethz.ch/~joloef/yalmip.php
[Min04a]   Miné, A.: Relational abstract domains for the detection of floating-point
            run-time errors. In: Schmidt, D. (ed.) ESOP 2004. LNCS, vol. 2986, pp.
            3–17. Springer, Heidelberg (2004)
[Min04b]   Miné, A.: Weakly Relational Numerical Abstract Domains. PhD
            thesis, École Polytechnique, Palaiseau, France (December 2004),
            http://www.di.ens.fr/~mine/these/these-color.pdf
[MOS04]   Müller-Olm, M., Seidl, H.: Computing polynomial program invariants.
            Inf. Process. Lett. 91(5), 233–244 (2004)
[Par03]   Parillo, P.: Semidefinite programming relaxations for semialgebraic prob-
            lems. Math. Prog. 96(2, series B), 293–320 (2003)
[RCK07]   Rodríguez-Carbonell, E., Kapur, D.: Automatic generation of polynomial
            invariants of bounded degree using abstract interpretation. Sci. Comput.
            Program. 64(1), 54–75 (2007)
[Roc96]   Rockafellar, R.T.: Convex Analysis. Princeton University Press, Princeton
            (1996)
[SCSM06]   Sankaranarayanan, S., Colon, M., Sipma, H., Manna, Z.: Efficient strongly
            relational polyhedral analysis. In: Emerson, E.A., Namjoshi, K.S. (eds.)
            VMCAI 2006. LNCS, vol. 3855, pp. 111–125. Springer, Heidelberg (2005)
[Sho87]   Shor, N.: Quadratic optimization problems. Soviet J. of Computer and
            Systems Science 25(6), 1–11 (1987)
[SSM05]   Sankaranarayanan, S., Sipma, H.B., Manna, Z.: Scalable analysis of linear
            systems using mathematical programming. In: Cousot, R. (ed.) VMCAI
            2005. LNCS, vol. 3385, pp. 25–41. Springer, Heidelberg (2005)
[Stu99]   Sturm, J.F.: Using sedumi 1.02, a matlab toolbox for optimization over
            symmetric cones. Optimization Methods and Software 11-12, 625–653
            (1999)
[TN01]   Ben Tal, A., Nemirowski, A.: Lecture on Modern Convex Optimization:
            Analysis, Algorithm and Engineering Applications. SIAM, Philadelphia
            (2001)

Precise and Automated Contract-Based Reasoning for Verification and Certification of Information Flow Properties of Programs with Arrays

Torben Amtoft, John Hatcliff, and Edwin Rodríguez

SAnToS Laboratory
Kansas State University
{tamtoft,hatcliff,edwin}@cis.k-state.edu

Abstract. Embedded information assurance applications that are critical to national and international infrastructures, must often adhere to certification regimes that require information flow properties to be specified and verified. SPARK, a subset of Ada for engineering safety critical systems, is being used to develop multiple certified information assurance systems. While SPARK provides information flow annotations and associated automated checking mechanisms, industrial experience has revealed that these annotations are not precise enough to specify many desired information flow policies. One key problem is that arrays are treated as indivisible entities – flows that involve only particular locations of an array have to be abstracted into flows on the whole array. This has substantial practical impact since SPARK does not allow dynamic allocation of memory, and hence makes heavy use of arrays to implement complex data structures.

In this paper, we present a Hoare logic for information flow that enables precise compositional specification of information flow in programs with arrays, and automated deduction algorithms for checking and inferring contracts in an enhanced SPARK information flow contract language. We demonstrate the expressiveness of the enhanced contracts and effectiveness of the automated verification algorithm on realistic embedded applications.

1 Introduction

Much effort has been spent on developing techniques to analyze information flow in computer programs [27] – leading to several languages such as Myers' JFlow [21], and FlowCaml [28], that include language-level specifications (often in the form of "security types") and automated checking mechanisms that establish that a program's information flow conforms to supplied specifications. SPARK, a safety-critical subset of Ada, is being used by various organizations, including Rockwell Collins [23] and the US National Security Agency (NSA) [7], to engineer information assurance systems including cryptographic controllers, network guards, and key management systems. SPARK provides automatically checked procedure annotations that specify information flows between procedure inputs and outputs. In the certification process, these annotations play a key role justifying conformance to information flow requirements and separation policies relevant to architectures such as MILS (Multiple Independent

A.D. Gordon (Ed.): ESOP 2010, LNCS 6012, pp. 43–63, 2010.

Levels of Security) [10]. However, experience in these industrial/government development efforts has shown that the annotations of SPARK, as well as those of other language-based information flow specification frameworks, are not precise enough to specify many important information flow policies. In such situations, policy adherence arguments are often reduced to informal claims substantiated by manual inspections that are time-consuming, tedious, and error-prone.

Inability to specify desired information flow policies in realistic applications, using existing language annotation frameworks, often stems from two issues: a) Coarse treatment of information channels, where information flowing between two variables is regarded as creating a channel without regard to the conditions under which that channel is active; and b) Coarse treatment of structured data, such as arrays, where information can only be specified as flowing into/from an array as a whole, instead of its constituent cells. Our previous work [5] gives one approach for addressing the first issue by providing inference and checking of conditional information flow contracts, allowing the specification of conditions that determine when the information flow channels are active, using a precondition generation algorithm and an extension to the logic previously developed by Amtoft and Banerjee [2,3]. This paper builds on this earlier work to address the second problem: precise information flow analysis for arrays.

Support for precise reasoning about information flow in arrays is especially important in resource-bounded embedded high-assurance security applications, because storage for data structures such as buffers, rule tables, *etc.*, must often be statically allocated and accessed via offset calculations. Motivated by the need to guarantee analyzability and conformance to resource bounds, SPARK does not include pointers and heap-based data. Thus, complex data structures must be implemented in terms of arrays whose size is fixed at compile time.

This paper presents a novel approach for automated contract-based reasoning about information flow within arrays – targeted to applications that require high assurance and certification. The specific contributions of this work are as follows:

- A language-independent Hoare-like logic for secure information flow that can be used to reason precisely about information flow between array components,
- An extension of the SPARK information flow contract language (with semantics provided by the Hoare logic) that supports specification of information flow policies about array components,
- An algorithm for automatically checking and inferring enhanced SPARK contracts against code,
- A novel approach for computing universally-quantified information flow properties for arrays,
- The study of an information assurance application that shows the importance of precise information flow analysis for arrays, based on the MILS Message Router specification given in [25], and
- An empirical evaluation of the performance and verification effectiveness of our approach against a collection of SPARK programs.

The logical/algorithmic foundations of our work are language independent, and could be applied to array-based data structures in other languages. However, our implementation in the context of SPARK is especially relevant because SPARK is the only commercially supported framework that we know of for specifying and checking information flows. Indeed, this work has been inspired by challenge problems provided by our industrial collaborators at Rockwell Collins who are using SPARK on multiple information assurance development projects.

2   Information Flow Contracts in SPARK

SPARK is a safety critical subset of Ada developed and supported by Praxis High Integrity Systems that provides (a) an annotation language for writing both functional and information flow software contracts, and (b) automated static analyses and semi-automated proof assistants for proving absence of run-time exceptions, and conformance of code to contracts. SPARK has been used to build a number of high-assurance systems including the UK's iFACTS next generation air traffic control system.

Figure 1 (a) shows a collection of very simple procedures with SPARK information flow annotations. SPARK demands that all procedures explicitly declare all the global variables that they read and/or write. As illustrated in the SinglePositionAssign procedure, this is done via a global annotation that lists global variables with each variable prefixed by a modifier that indicates the *mode* of the variable, *i.e.*, whether the variable is read (in), written (out), or both (in out). Parameters to the procedures must also be annotated with in and out modifiers indicating their mode. In addition, all out variables (*i.e.*, all variables that are modified by the procedures) must declare a derives clause. A derives clause for out variable X specifies the in parameters/globals whose initial values were used to derive the final value of variable X. In SinglePositionAssign, the derives clause states that the out variable Flags is derived from itself (*), Flag and Value. SPARK also provides other annotation

```
procedure SinglePositionAssign
(Flag : in Int; Value : in Types.Flagvalue)
--# global in out Flags;
--# derives Flags from *, Flag, Value;
is
begin
  Flags(Flag) := Value;
end SinglePositionAssign;
```

```
procedure SinglePositionAssign
(Flag : in Int; Value : in Types.Flagvalue)
--# global out Flags(Flag);
--# derives Flags(Flag) from Value;
is
begin
  Flags(Flag) := Value;
end SinglePositionAssign;
```

```
procedure Scrub_Cache (cache : in out Sensor_Cache_Type)
--# derives cache from *;
is
  begin
    for I in Sensor_Ids loop
      cache(I) := 0;
    end loop;
end Scrub_Cache;
```

```
procedure Scrub_Cache (cache : out Sensor_Cache_Type)
--# derives for all J in Sensor_Ids => (cache(J) from {});
is
  begin
    for I in Sensor_Ids loop
      cache(I) := 0;
    end loop;
end Scrub_Cache;
```

```
procedure Copy_Keys (inkeys : in Key_Table_Type,
                     outkeys : in out Key_Table_Type)
--# derives outkeys from *, inkeys;
is
  begin
    for I in Key_Table_Entries loop
      outkeys(I) := inkeys(I);
    end loop;
end Scrub_Cache;
```

```
procedure Copy_Keys (inkeys : in Key_Table_Type,
                     outkeys : out Key_Table_Type)
--# derives for all J in Key_Table_Entries
--#                => (outkeys(J) from inkeys(J));
is
  begin
    for I in Key_Table_Entries loop
      outkeys(I) := inkeys(I);
    end loop;
end Copy_Keys;
```

(a)   (b)

Fig. 1. (a) Limitations of SPARK annotations and (b) proposed enhancements

mechanisms to specify pre- and postconditions, but for this discussion we will focus on those directly related to information flow analysis.

While the semantics of existing SPARK contracts, as presented in Figure 1 (a), can be captured using conventional slicing and data/control-dependence, we have developed a more powerful and flexible theory of information flow contracts backed by a Hoare-style logic, and a precondition generation algorithm [5] that is able to provide additional analysis precision and contract expressiveness not found in conventional static-analysis-based approaches. Moreover, in the context of embedded applications and languages like SPARK, which eschew complicated language features, we have been able to achieve this power while maintaining a very high degree of automation and low computational costs. In our previous work [5], we demonstrated how this logical framework could support extensions to SPARK contracts that allow developers to specify that information flows from inputs to an output only under certain conditions, *i.e.*, *conditional information flow*. This provides the ability to state information flow policies that are typical of *network guard applications*, where a message on an input port may flow to a certain output in one state, but may flow to a different output in another state.

In this paper, we overcome other limitations of conventional dependence/information flow frameworks by adding additional capabilities to the logic, and associated automated deduction algorithms that enable precise reasoning about array-based data structures. Figure 1 (a) presents a series of micro-examples that illustrate the deficiencies of current SPARK annotations for arrays, and Fig. 1 (b) shows our proposed enhancements. These examples are concise representations of common idioms that occur in the embedded information assurance applications of our industrial partners.

Procedure `SinglePositionAssign` assigns a value to a particular index position (the value of `Flag`) in the array `Flags`. However, the SPARK information flow contract states that (a) the whole array is modified (*i.e.*, `global out flags`), and (b) the new value of the array is derived from its old value, the `Value` parameter, and the `Flag` index parameter. This is an over-approximation of the true frame-condition and information flow, but the contract cannot be made more precise in the current SPARK annotation language. To remedy this, Figure 1 (b) illustrates that our enhanced language provides the ability to specify properties of particular array cells. The `global out` declaration now indicates that the only array cell modified is `Flags(Flag)` (which currently is a disallowed `global` expression in SPARK) while the contents of other cells remain unchanged. The enhanced `derives` indicates that the modified cell derives its value only from the parameter `Value`. To support this more precise reasoning, the underlying analysis algorithm must be able to reason symbolically about array index values.

`Scrub_Cache` in Fig. 1 (a) presents a code idiom often used when initializing an array or scrubbing the contents of a message buffer; all positions of the array are initialized to a constant value. The SPARK annotations required for this example exhibit several forms of imprecision. First, the `cache` array parameter must be declared with mode `in` even though no array element value is read during execution of the procedure. Second, the information flow specification captured in the `derives` clause is the antithesis of what we desire: it states that the final value of `cache` depends on the initial value of `cache`, whereas we desire a specification that captures the fact that the final value of cache *does not* depend on the initial value of cache, *i.e.*, all values in the input cache have been erased.

This imprecision stems from the fact that on each iteration of the loop, the entire array is treated as a single entity in the information flow analysis: the updated value of the array depends on a constant value at position I and on its previous value at all positions other than I. Since flow from constants is not indicated in SPARK contracts, the information flow analysis indicates that the new value of the array depends on the old value at every iteration. There is no way to indicate that the loop has carried out an exhaustive processing of each position of the array in which the old value at each position is overwritten with a new value not based on the array's previous contents. Figure 1 (b) illustrates that we address this problem by extending the specification language with a notion of universal quantification (using syntax based on SPARK's universal quantification allowed in assertions) to specify schematically the information flow for each array cell. We also add the capability to indicate that the source of the information flow is some constant (represented by {}). Together, these additions allow us to formalize the higher level security policy: the array contents are indeed scrubbed – cache's final value does not depend in any way on its initial value, nor does information from any other piece of the program state flows into it.

To support this more precise reasoning, the underlying analysis algorithm must be able to perform a logical *universal generalization* step to introduce the quantified flow specification. In general, this is quite difficult to do, but we have found that loops that manipulate arrays often follow a structure that admits an automated solution. When an automated solution is not possible, the developer may supply an information flow loop invariant (which are simpler than functional invariants) that enables the rest of the checking to be completed automatically.

The Copy_Keys example of Fig. 1 (a) illustrates a common idiom in which the contents of a table are copied, or where a portion of a database is moved from a central database to a copy for a client. In essence, this creates multiple channels of information flow – one channel for each index position of the arrays. In such cases, one often seeks to verify a separation policy that states that information flow between the different channels is not confused or merged. The SPARK derives clause for Copy_Keys simply states that information flows from the inkeys array to the outkeys array and cannot capture the separation property that information only flows between corresponding entries of the arrays. Fig. 1 (b) illustrates that, using the universal quantification introduced in the previous paragraph, one formalizes the policy that information only flows between entries at the same index position. Notice also that this enables us to specify flow between different regions of the array, by having the quantified variables take values from more restricted ranges of the possible index values.

3 Syntax and Semantics Background

We now present the foundations of our approach using a simple imperative language that can be considered an "idealized core language" for SPARK. Since SPARK omits constructs that are difficult to reason about, such as dynamically allocated data, pointers, and exceptions, its semantics is very close to that of this language.

Expressions:

arithmetic
$$A ::= x \mid u \mid c \mid A \text{ op } A \mid H[A]$$
array
$$H ::= h \mid Z \mid H\{A : A\}$$
boolean
$$\phi, B ::= A \text{ bop } A \mid \phi \wedge \phi \mid \phi \vee \phi \mid \neg\phi$$

Commands:

$$S ::= \textbf{skip} \mid S\,;S \mid x := A \mid \textbf{assert}(\phi)$$
$$\mid \quad \textbf{call } p$$
$$\mid \quad \textbf{if } B \textbf{ then } S \textbf{ else } S$$
$$\mid \quad \textbf{for } q \leftarrow 1 \textbf{ to } y \textbf{ do } S$$
$$\mid \quad \textbf{while } B \textbf{ do } S \textbf{ od}$$
$$\mid \quad h := \textbf{new} \mid h[A] := A$$

Fig. 2. Syntax of a simple imperative language

In Fig. 2, we present the syntax of the simple imperative language. For commands, procedures are parameterless; this simplifies our exposition but our implementation supports procedures with parameters (there are no conceptual challenges in this extended functionality). In **for** loops, following similar restrictions in SPARK, we require that the index variable q is not modified by S, and does not occur anywhere except in S. Arrays are restricted to a single dimension with integer contents. Array assignment has two forms: $h := \textbf{new}$ creates an array with all elements set to 0, and $h[A_0] := A_1$ assigns the integer value of A_1 to array h at the index position given by A_0. For convenience of presentation, we omit some SPARK features such as records and package structure since these do not present conceptual challenges.

We use E to range over expressions which include arithmetic, boolean, and array expressions. Boolean expressions are also used as assertions. We use x to range over integer (scalar) variables (but q to range over such when used as counters in **for** loops), h to range over array variables, u to range over universally quantified variables; we shall use w, z to range over all kind of variables. We use c to range over integer constants, op to range over arithmetic operators in $\{+, \times, \text{mod}, \ldots\}$, and bop to range over comparison operators in $\{=, <, \ldots\}$.

To enable convenient reasoning about individual array elements, in particular the computation of preconditions, we follow Gries [18] and allow, in intermediate forms of assertions manipulated by the automated reasoning engine, the construct $H\{A_0 : A_1\}$, which represents the value of array H except that index A_0 now has value A_1. We also use Z to denote an initial array as created by the command $h := \textbf{new}$. We require a program (command) submitted for verification to be *pure* in the sense that it does not contain these additional array constructs. Thus, in a pure entity, all array accesses are of the form $h[A]$ with h a variable. Similarly, universal variables u are used only in specifications; *programs* submitted for verification cannot contain universal variables.

The use of programmer assertions is optional, but often helps to improve the precision of our analysis. We refer to the assertions of Fig. 2 as *1-assertions* since they represent predicates on a single program state; they can be contrasted with *2-assertions* that we introduce later for reasoning about information flow in terms of a *pair* of program states. For an expression E, we write fv(E) for the variables in E and write $E[A/x]$ for the result of substituting in E all occurrences of x by A (similarly for $E[H/h]$).

Expressions:

$$[\![x]\!]_s = s(x) \quad \text{similarly for } u$$
$$[\![H[A]]\!]_s = [\![H]\!]_s([\![A]\!]_s)$$

$$[\![h]\!]_s = s(h)$$
$$[\![Z]\!]_s = \lambda n.0$$
$$[\![H\{A_0 : A\}]\!]_s = [\![H]\!]_s \mid [\![A_0]\!]_s \mapsto [\![A]\!]_s]$$

Commands:

$$s [\![x := A]\!]\ s' \text{ iff } \exists v : v = [\![A]\!]_s \text{ and } s' = [s \mid x \mapsto v]$$
$$s [\![\mathbf{assert}(\phi)]\!]\ s' \text{ iff } s \models \phi \text{ and } s' = s$$
$$s [\![\mathbf{call}\ p]\!]\ s' \text{ iff } s\ \mathcal{P}(p)\ s'$$
$$s [\![\mathbf{for}\ q \leftarrow 1\ \mathbf{to}\ y\ \mathbf{do}\ S]\!]\ s' \text{ iff } \exists n \geq 1 : n = s(y) \text{ and } \forall i \in \{0 \dots n\}\ \exists s_i : s_0 = s \text{ and }$$
$$s' = [s_n \mid q \mapsto n+1] \text{ and } \forall j \in \{1 \dots n\} : [s_{j-1} \mid q \mapsto j]\ [\![S]\!]\ s_j$$
$$s [\![h[A_0] := A]\!]\ s' \text{ iff } \exists n, v : n = [\![A_0]\!]_s,\ v = [\![A]\!]_s \text{ and } s' = [s \mid h(n) \mapsto v]$$
$$s [\![h := \mathbf{new}]\!]\ s' \text{ iff } s' = [s \mid h \mapsto \lambda n.0]$$

Fig. 3. Semantics of the Simple Programming Language (excerpts)

Fig. 3 gives excerpts of the language semantics definition (the definitions for conditionals and while loops are standard and omitted). In the expression semantics, we model an array as a mapping ($a \in Array$) from integers to values, where a value ($v \in Val$) is an integer n; we write $[a \mid n \mapsto v]$ for the array that is like a except that it maps n into v. We shall ignore bounds and range checks (unlike [15] where array length may be revealed separately from array content) and assume that an array reference $a(n)$ is always well-defined (the typical SPARK development process will prove statically that array-out-of-bounds exceptions cannot occur).

A *store* $s \in Store$ (we shall also use σ to range over stores) maps scalar and universal variables to values, and array variables to arrays; we write $dom(s)$ for the domain of s and write $[s \mid x \mapsto v]$ ($[s \mid h \mapsto a]$) for the store that is like s except that it maps x into v (maps h into a), and write $[s \mid h(n) \mapsto v]$ for $[s \mid h \mapsto [s(h) \mid n \mapsto v]]$. We write $s \models \phi$ for $[\![\phi]\!]_s = $ True. We define ϕ and ϕ' to be 1-equivalent, written $\phi \equiv_1 \phi'$, if for all s it holds that $s \models \phi$ iff $s \models \phi'$. Similarly, we write $\phi \rhd_1 \phi'$ if whenever $s \models \phi$ then also $s \models \phi'$.

In the definition of the **call** command, we assume a global procedure environment $\mathcal{P}$ that for each p returns a relation between input and output stores; we expect that if $s\ \mathcal{P}(p)\ s'$ then, with S_p the body of p, we have $s\ [\![S_p]\!]\ s'$. For some S and s, there may not exist any s' such that $s\ [\![S]\!]\ s'$; this can happen if a while loop does not terminate, a for loop has a non-positive upper bound, or an **assert** fails.

4 Information Flow Contracts for Arrays

To motivate our treatment of information flow, consider the code

```
procedure p begin x := a+1; y := b * 2; end p;
```

where there are two "channels" of information flow associated with x and y: (1) from a to x, and (2) from b to y Using SPARK to specify these flows, we would write:

```
derives x from a & y from b;
```

We may express the "non-interference" [16] of the assignment to y with channel (1) via the following semantic property: for any pair of states s_1 and s_2, if $s_1(a) = s_2(a)$

then $s'_1(x) = s'_2(x)$ where s'_1, s'_2 are the states that result from executing the procedure body on s_1 and s_2, respectively. Thus x depends on a but on no other variables, cf. Cohen[12]. We desire to state such properties (which would provide a semantic foundation for derives contracts), using program level assertions. However, the property requires reasoning about *two* states at method pre/postcondition (cf. s_1 and s_2). Thus, it cannot be stated using traditional assertions, because such assertions are interpreted in terms of *one* state at a particular program point.

The innovation of the logic developed in [1,2] lies in the introduction of a novel *agreement assertion* $x\Join$ that is satisfied by a *pair* of states, s_1 and s_2, if $s_1(x) = s_2(x)$. Using this assertion, the non-interference property above is phrased $\{a\Join\} \ S \ \{x\Join\}$. In general, triples are of the form $\{x_1\Join, \ldots, x_n\Join\} \ P \ \{y_1\Join, \ldots, y_m\Join\}$ which is interpreted as follows: *given two runs of P that initially agree on variables $x_1 \ldots x_n$, at the end of both runs, they agree on variables $y_1 \ldots y_m$.* Such a specification says that the variables y_j may depend *only* on the variables x_i, and not on any other variables. In situations as above where we want to reason about multiple separated channels of information flow simultaneously (*e.g.*, a to x and b to y), we would *not* write $\{a\Join, b\Join\} \ S \ \{x\Join, y\Join\}$ since this would imply that y may depend on a and x depend on b. Instead, *channel-indexed agreement assertions* would be used to distinguish the separate channels for x and y: $\{a\Join_x, b\Join_y\} \ S \ \{x\Join_x, y\Join_y\}$. This is equivalent to requiring both $\{a\Join\} \ S \ \{x\Join\}$ and $\{b\Join\} \ S \ \{y\Join\}$ to hold in the unindexed version of the logic. Our implementation uses the indexed assertions to deal with multiple channels, but to simplify the formalization, in this document we shall deal with one channel at a time.

One advantage of this logical approach over traditional data/control-flow based approaches to reasoning about information flow and program dependencies, is that the assertion primitive can be enhanced to reason about additional properties of the state – leading to greater precision and flexibility. For example, to capture conditional information flow, we use *conditional* agreement assertions $\phi \Rightarrow E\Join$, also called *2-assertions*, introduced by Banerjee and the first author [3]. Such assertions are satisfied by a pair of stores if either at least one of them does not satisfy ϕ, or they agree on the value of E: $s \ \& \ \sigma \models \phi \Rightarrow E\Join$ iff whenever $s \models \phi$ and $\sigma \models \phi$ then $[\![E]\!]_s = [\![E]\!]_\sigma$.

We use $\theta \in \mathbf{2Assert}$ to range over 2-assertions. For $\theta = (\phi \Rightarrow E\Join)$, we call ϕ the antecedent of θ and write $\phi = ant(\theta)$, and we call E the consequent of θ and write $E = con(\theta)$. We often write $E\Join$ for $true \Rightarrow E\Join$. We use $\Theta \in \mathcal{P}(\mathbf{2Assert})$ to range over sets of 2-assertions (where we often write θ for the singleton set $\{\theta\}$), with conjunction implicit. Thus, $s\&\sigma \models \Theta$ iff $\forall\theta \in \Theta : s\&\sigma \models \theta$.

For the semantics of command triples, we write $\{\Theta\}S\{\Theta'\}$ iff for all s, s', σ, σ', if $s \ [\![S]\!] \ s'$ and $\sigma \ [\![S]\!] \ \sigma'$, and also $s\&\sigma \models \Theta$, then $s'\&\sigma' \models \Theta'$.

We define $\Theta \vartriangleright_2 \Theta'$, pronounced "$\Theta$ 2-implies Θ'", to hold iff for all s, σ: whenever $s\&\sigma \models \Theta$ then also $s\&\sigma \models \Theta'$. In development terms, when $\Theta \vartriangleright_2 \Theta'$ holds we can think of Θ as a *refinement* of of Θ', and Θ' an *abstraction* of Θ. Intuitively, Θ requires agreement in more cases than Θ' (Θ is a strengthening of Θ'). For example, $\{x\Join, y\Join\}$ refines $x\Join$ by adding an (unconditional) agreement requirement on y, and $y < 10 \Rightarrow x\Join$ refines $y < 7 \Rightarrow x\Join$ by weakening the antecedent of a 2-assertion so that agreement on x is required for more values of y.

$\{\Theta\} \Longleftarrow \textbf{skip} \{\Theta'\}$ iff $\Theta = \Theta'$ $\{\Theta\} \Longleftarrow x := A \{\Theta'\}$ iff $\Theta = \Theta'[A/x]$

$\{\Theta\} \Longleftarrow h := \textbf{new} \{\Theta'\}$ iff $\Theta = \Theta'[Z/h]$ $\{\Theta\} \Longleftarrow h[A_0] := A_1 \{\Theta'\}$ iff $\Theta = \Theta'[h\{A_0 : A_1\}/h]$

$\{\Theta\} \Longleftarrow \textbf{assert}(\phi_0) \{\Theta'\}$ iff $\Theta = \{(\phi \wedge \phi_0) \Rightarrow E\ltimes \mid \phi \Rightarrow E\ltimes \in \Theta'\}$

$\{\Theta\} \Longleftarrow S_1 ; S_2 \{\Theta'\}$ iff $\{\Theta''\} \Longleftarrow S_2 \{\Theta'\}$ and $\{\Theta\} \Longleftarrow S_1 \{\Theta''\}$

$\{\Theta\} \Longleftarrow \textbf{if } B \textbf{ then } S_1 \textbf{ else } S_2 \{\Theta'\}$ iff $\Theta = \bigcup_{\theta \in \Theta'} \text{Pre}_{\text{if}}(\theta)$ where
$\quad \text{Pre}_{\text{if}}(\phi' \Rightarrow E\ltimes) =$
$\qquad \text{let } \{\Theta_i\} \Longleftarrow S_i \{\phi' \Rightarrow E\ltimes\} \text{ for } i = 1, 2$
$\qquad \text{in if } S_1 \text{ preserves } E \text{ and } S_2 \text{ preserves } E$
$\qquad \text{then } \{(\phi_1 \wedge B) \vee (\phi_2 \wedge \neg B) \Rightarrow E\ltimes \mid \phi_i \Rightarrow \_\ltimes \in \Theta_i \ (i = 1, 2)\}$
$\qquad \text{else } \{\phi_1 \wedge B \Rightarrow E_1\ltimes \mid \phi_1 \Rightarrow E_1\ltimes \in \Theta_1\} \cup \{\phi_2 \wedge \neg B \Rightarrow E_2\ltimes \mid \phi_2 \Rightarrow E_2\ltimes \in \Theta_2\} \cup$
$\qquad\quad \{(\phi_1 \wedge B) \vee (\phi_2 \wedge \neg B) \Rightarrow B\ltimes \mid \phi_i \Rightarrow \_\ltimes \in \Theta_i \ (i = 1, 2)\}$

$\{\Theta\} \Longleftarrow \textbf{call } p \ (= S) \{\Theta'\}$ iff $\Theta = R \cup \bigcup_{\theta \in T} \text{Pre}_{\text{call}}(\theta)$ where
$\quad (R, T) = \text{PreProc}(S, \Theta') \text{ and}$
$\quad \text{Pre}_{\text{call}}(\phi' \Rightarrow E\ltimes) = \text{let } \phi_0 = NPC(S, \phi') \text{ in case } E \text{ of}$
$\qquad w : \{\phi_0 \wedge \phi_w \Rightarrow E_w\ltimes \mid \phi_w \Rightarrow E_w\ltimes \in 2PC_w^p\}$
$\qquad h[A] : \text{let } 2PC_{h[\_]}^p = \forall u. \Theta_h \quad /\!/ S \text{ preserves } A$
$\qquad\quad \text{in } \{\phi_0 \Rightarrow A\ltimes\} \cup \{\phi_0 \wedge \phi_h[A/u] \Rightarrow E_h[A/u]\ltimes \mid \phi_h \Rightarrow E_h\ltimes \in \Theta_h\}$

$\{\Theta\} \Longleftarrow \textbf{while } B \textbf{ do } S_0 \textbf{ od } (= S) \{\Theta'\}$ iff $\Theta = R \cup \Theta_A \cup \Theta_W$ where
$\quad (R, T) = \text{PreProc}(S, \Theta') \qquad\qquad \Theta_A = \{NPC(S, \phi) \Rightarrow A\ltimes \mid \phi \Rightarrow h[A]\ltimes \in T\}$
$\quad \Theta_W = \text{Pre}_{\text{while}}(S_0, B, T_w) \qquad\quad T_w = \{\phi \Rightarrow w\ltimes \in T\} \cup \{\phi \Rightarrow h\ltimes \mid \phi \Rightarrow h[A]\ltimes \in T\}$

$\{\Theta\} \Longleftarrow \textbf{for } q \leftarrow 1 \textbf{ to } m \textbf{ do } S_0 \ (= S) \{\Theta'\}$ iff $\Theta = R \cup \Theta_A \cup \Theta_W \cup \Theta_F$ where
$\quad (R, T) = \text{PreProc}(S, \Theta') \quad u \text{ is fresh} \quad \Theta_A = \{NPC(S, \phi) \Rightarrow A\ltimes \mid \phi \Rightarrow h[A]\ltimes \in T\}$
$\quad \Theta_W = \text{Pre}_{\text{while}}((S_0 ; q := q + 1), q \leq m, T_w)[1/q]$
$\quad \Theta_F = \{NPC(S, \phi) \wedge \phi_1[A/u] \Rightarrow E_1[A/u]\ltimes \mid \phi_1 \Rightarrow E_1\ltimes \in \Theta_h, \phi \Rightarrow h[A]\ltimes \in T, \Theta_h \neq \textbf{fail}\}$
$\quad T_w = \{\phi \Rightarrow w\ltimes \in T\} \cup \{\phi \Rightarrow h\ltimes \mid \phi \Rightarrow h[A]\ltimes \in T, \Theta_h = \textbf{fail}\}$
$\quad \Theta_h = \text{Pre}_{\text{for}}(S_0, q, m, h[u]\ltimes) \quad (\text{for all } h)$

Fig. 4. The Precondition Generator

5   Computing Preconditions

Figure 4, selected parts of which will be explained later, presents a rule-based precondition generation algorithm inductively defined over the language syntax. The definition uses rules of the form $\{\Theta\} \Longleftarrow S \{\Theta'\}$ to specify that, given command S and postcondition Θ', the algorithm computes precondition Θ. The algorithm uses some auxiliary functions, defined in Fig. 5, as well as some other functions that will be sketched below but for whose complete definitions we refer to [4].

The algorithm *does not* always compute the weakest precondition; main sources of imprecision are: on loops, approximations have to be made to ensure termination of the analysis; on procedure calls, the analysis (for the sake of modularity) uses the procedure's specification rather than its actual code. As a result, antecedents may be too weak, yielding too strong 2-assertions.

This algorithm extends our earlier work [5] by adding the notion of universal quantification for reasoning about arrays, and a method for inferring universally quantified preconditions for certain **for**-loop structures. The following theorem summarizes the correctness of the algorithm:

Theorem 1. *For all S, Θ, Θ', if $\{\Theta\} \Longleftarrow S \{\Theta'\}$ holds, then $\{\Theta\}S\{\Theta'\}$ holds.*

For a detailed proof of this theorem, we refer the reader to [4]. The main structure of the proof is quite similar to our earlier work [3,5] though a main difference is that we

$\text{PreProc}(S, \Theta') =$
    $P \leftarrow Purify(\Theta');\quad R \leftarrow \emptyset;\quad T \leftarrow \emptyset$
    while $P \neq \emptyset$ do: remove $(\phi \Rightarrow E\kappa)$ from P, and
        if S $preserves$ E then $R \leftarrow R \cup \{NPC(S,\phi) \Rightarrow E\kappa\}$
        else case E of
            E_1 op E_2 or E_1 bop E_2 or $E_1 \wedge E_2$ or $E_1 \vee E_2$ or $\neg E_1$: $P \leftarrow P \cup \{\phi \Rightarrow E_1\kappa, \phi \Rightarrow E_2\kappa\}$
            $w : T \leftarrow T \cup \{\phi \Rightarrow w\kappa\}$
            $h[A]$: if S $preserves$ A and not S $preserves$ h then $T \leftarrow T \cup \{\phi \Rightarrow h[A]\kappa\}$
                else if S $preserves$ h and not (S $preserves$ A)
                then $P \leftarrow P \cup \{\phi \Rightarrow A\kappa\};\quad R \leftarrow R \cup \{NPC(S,\phi) \Rightarrow h\kappa\}$
                else if not (S $preserves$ h) and not (S $preserves$ A)
                then $T \leftarrow T \cup \{\phi \Rightarrow h\kappa\};\quad P \leftarrow P \cup \{\phi \Rightarrow A\kappa\}$
    return (R, T)

$\text{Pre}_{\text{for}}(S_0, q, m, h[u]\kappa) =$
    let $\{A_j \mid j \in J\}$ be all occurrences such that $h[A_j] := \_$ is a subcommand of S_0
    let $\{\Theta_j\} \Longleftarrow S_0 \{h[A_j]\kappa\}$ (for all $j \in J$)
    in if 1. $\mathbf{call}$ p $preserves$ h for all $\mathbf{call}$ p occurring in S_0, and for all $j \in J$ it holds that
        2. S_0 $preserves$ A_j
        3. there exists A'_j with $\mathrm{fv}(A'_j) \subseteq \{u\} \cup \mathrm{fv}(A_j) \setminus \{q\}$ where for all s,n with $dom(s) \subseteq \mathrm{fv}(A_j)$,
            $[\![n = A_j]\!]_s = [\![q = A'_j[n/u]]\!]_s$
        4. there exists ϕ_j with $\mathrm{fv}(\phi_j) \subseteq \{u\} \cup \mathrm{fv}(A_j) \setminus \{q\}$ where for all s,n with $dom(s) \subseteq \mathrm{fv}(A_j)$,
            $n \in \{[\![A_j]\!]_{[s|q \to i]} \mid 1 \leq i \leq s(m)\}$ iff $s \models \phi_j[n/u]$
        5. if $w \in \mathrm{fv}(\Theta_j)$ with $w \neq h$ then S_0 $preserves$ w
        6. if h occurs in Θ_j it is in the context $h[A]$ where for all $j_1 \in J$, all s, all $i, i' \in \{1 \ldots s(m)\}$:
            if $[\![A]\!]_{[s|q \to i']} = [\![A_{j_1}]\!]_{[s|q \to i]}$ then $i' \leq i$
        then $\mathbf{succeed}$ and return $\{\phi_j \Rightarrow \Theta_j[A'_j/q]\kappa \mid j \in J\} \cup$
            $\{\wedge_{j \in J}\neg\phi_j \Rightarrow h[u]\kappa\} \cup \{x\kappa \mid \exists j \in J : x \in \mathrm{fv}(A_j) \setminus \{q\}\} \cup \{m\kappa\}$
        else $\mathbf{fail}$

$\text{Pre}_{\text{while}}(S_0, B, \Theta') =$
    $\psi_w \leftarrow \emptyset$ for all variables w (including a dummy variable d)
    for $\phi \Rightarrow w\kappa \in \Theta'$ do
        $\psi_w \leftarrow \psi_w \vee (\phi \wedge \neg B)$; if $w \notin \mathrm{fv}(B)$ and not (S_0 $preserves$ w) then $\psi_d \leftarrow \psi_d \vee (\phi \wedge \neg B)$
    repeat
        for each variable w do $\{\Theta_w\} \Longleftarrow S_0 \{\psi_w \Rightarrow w\kappa\}$;
            for each $\phi \Rightarrow E\kappa \in \Theta_w$ do
                for each $z \in \mathrm{fv}(E)$ do $\psi_z \leftarrow \psi_z \vee (\phi \wedge B)$;
                if $w \in \mathrm{fv}(B)$ or S_0 $preserves$ w then $\psi_w \leftarrow \psi_w \vee (\phi \wedge B)$
        for all $w \in \mathrm{fv}(B)$, for all z with not (S_0 $preserves$ z) do $\psi_w \leftarrow \psi_w \vee \psi_z$
    until each ψ_w stabilizes (through $widening$) into Ψ_w
    return $\Theta = \{\Psi_w \Rightarrow w\kappa \mid w$ is variable$\}$

Fig. 5. The Precondition Generator, Helper functions

have disposed with the "R-component"; this allows for a more streamlined presentation. Quite similar to those earlier works, we need the following lemma:

Lemma 1. *Assume that* $\{\Theta\} \Longleftarrow S \{\Theta'\}$. *For all* $\phi' \Rightarrow \_\kappa \in \Theta'$, *there exists* $\phi \Rightarrow \_\kappa \in \Theta$ *such that whenever* s $[\![S]\!]$ s' *and* $s' \models \phi'$ *then* $s \models \phi$.

Observe that it is easy to modify Fig. 4 so that Lemma 1 trivially holds, for example by adding $true \Rightarrow 0\kappa$ to all preconditions, but the analysis of a command may become less precise if the analysis of a subcommand is augmented in that way.

The algorithm can be applied to automatically check or infer information flow contracts. For implementing checking, the algorithm would be used to compute a candidate precondition from the stated postcondition, and then a supplementary algorithm would check that the stated precondition entails the computed precondition (this functionality is present in our implementation using theorem-prover technology). We focus on contract inference in the remainder of our discussion.

As with conventional forms of compositional contract-based reasoning, when processing the body of some procedure p, our algorithm assumes that any procedure called by p already has an associated contract: for each w that may be modified by p, the contract contains a precondition $2PC_w^p$ (at least one assertion in which must be unconditional) such that $\{2PC_w^p\}p\{w\ltimes\}$; for each h that may be modified by p, the contract contains a precondition $2PC_{h[\_]}^p$ which is a *quantified set of 2-assertions* of the form $\forall u.\Theta$ where we demand that $\{\Theta\}p\{h[u]\ltimes\}$. Since SPARK does not include recursion, contract inference for all procedures in the program can be carried out via a bottom up traversal of the call graph.

Concerning the roles of universal variables, they are introduced in two situations: when analyzing a **for** loop (the output of $\mathrm{Pre_{for}}$), and when looking up $2PC_{h[\_]}^p$ for procedure calls. In both cases, they are instantiated immediately afterwards. When we *compute* summaries, however, universal variables are present throughout the derivation.

For most language constructs, the corresponding rule in Fig. 4 is straightforward. Assignments, to variables as well as array elements, are handled by syntactic replacement, as in classical Hoare logic.

For a conditional if B then S_1 else S_2, if E is such that neither S_1 nor S_2 modifies E, the the precondition for $\phi \Rightarrow E\ltimes$ does not need to involve $B\ltimes$. There are several other instances where the generation of the precondition for S from its post-condition $\phi \Rightarrow E\ltimes$ can be simplified if S preserves the semantics of E. Accordingly, we utilize a predicate S *preserves* E such that if S *preserves* E holds then whenever s $[\![S]\!]$ s' we have $[\![E]\!]_s = [\![E]\!]_{s'}$. S *preserves* E can be computed in a straightforward manner by detecting if S modifies variables occuring in E either directly via an assignment or indirectly via updates in a procedure call (in which case, the procedure's contract is consulted).

The NPC Function: When generating a precondition for S for post-condition $\phi' \Rightarrow E\ltimes$ where S *preserves* E holds, but S may affect the antecedent ϕ', we must compute a new antecedent ϕ so that $\{\phi \Rightarrow E\ltimes\}S\{\phi' \Rightarrow E\ltimes\}$. For this to be the case, we must ensure that if two post-states satisfy ϕ' then the pre-states satisfy ϕ and hence $E\ltimes$.

Accordingly, we utilize a function NPC computing a "necessary precondition" for ϕ' to hold after S. That is, with $\phi = NPC(S, \phi')$ (we can assume ϕ' to be pure) it holds that if s $[\![S]\!]$ s' and $s' \models \phi'$ then $s \models \phi$. It may seem counterintuitive that we are talking about *necessary* precondition instead of *weakest* precondition, but this stems from the contravariant nature of the antecedent component of 2-assertions.

Note that if S *preserves* ϕ then we can pick $\phi_0 = \phi$, and that we can always pick $\phi_0 = true$, but often we can compute something stronger. Our implementation, which assumes that each procedure p is equipped with a function that computes $NPC(p, \_)$, contains rules such as $NPC(x := A, \phi) = \phi[A/x]$ and
$NPC(\text{if } B \text{ then } S_1 \text{ else } S_2, \phi) = (NPC(S_1, \phi) \wedge B) \vee (NPC(S_2, \phi) \wedge \neg B)$.

The *Purify* Function: As noted earlier, the rules for array update (creation) may generate a precondition that include impure expressions of the form $H_0\{A_0 : A_1\}$ (or Z) that we would not like to see in contracts. We therefore employ a function *Purify* with the following properties:

1. given ϕ, with $\phi_0 = Purify(\phi)$ we have $\phi \equiv_1 \phi_0$ with ϕ_0 pure.
2. given A, $Purify$ returns pure $\phi_1 \ldots \phi_k$, and pure $A_1 \ldots A_k$, such that for all $i \in 1..k$: if $s \models \phi_i$ then $[\![A]\!]_s = [\![A_i]\!]_s$.
3. given Θ, with $\Theta_0 = Purify(\Theta)$ we have $\Theta_0 \rhd_2 \Theta$ with Θ_0 pure, and for all $\phi \Rightarrow \_\ltimes \in \Theta$ there exists $\phi_0 \Rightarrow \_\ltimes \in \Theta_0$ with $\phi \rhd_1 \phi_0$.

As an example of case 2, if A is given by $h\{x : y\}[z]$ then $Purify$ returns ϕ_1, ϕ_2 given by $z = x$ and $z \neq x$, and A_1, A_2 given by y and $h[z]$. As an example of case 3, with A as above then $Purify(y > 0 \Rightarrow A\ltimes)$ is given by

$$\{y > 0 \wedge z = x \Rightarrow y\ltimes, \ y > 0 \wedge z \neq x \Rightarrow h[z]\ltimes, \ y > 0 \Rightarrow (z = x)\ltimes\}.$$

The PreProc Function: The computation of preconditions for procedure calls and loops shares certain steps that can be broken out into a preprocessing phase realized by a common function, called PreProc and listed in Fig. 5. Preprocessing includes two main ideas: (1) strengthening 2-assertions to a canonical form $\phi \Rightarrow E_{con}\ltimes$ where E_{con} must be a variable name or array access expression (but not an operation), and (2) the immediate construction of preconditions, which is possible for 2-assertions whose consequents are not modified by the command under consideration. Point (1) is required for, e.g., the identification of dependence connections between a calling context and the contract of the called procedure. Formally, we have: $PreProc(S, \Theta')$ always terminates and returns R,T such that

1. for all Θ, if $\{\Theta\}S\{T\}$ then $\{\Theta \cup R\}S\{\Theta'\}$.
2. T is pure, and if $\phi \Rightarrow E\ltimes \in T$ then either $E = w$ where S *preserves* w does not hold, or $E = h[A]$ where S *preserves* A holds but S *preserves* h does not hold.

To prove this result, we observe that an invariant for the loop inside PreProc is: for all Θ, if $\{\Theta\}S\{T \cup P\}$ then $\{\Theta \cup R\}S\{\Theta'\}$.

The Pre$_{for}$ Function: The rule (Fig. 4) for for-loops, with associated helper function Pre$_{for}$ (Fig. 5), generates universally quantified information flow assertions for arrays, and is one of the main innovations of this paper. The idea behind this function is to identify and exploit a common pattern: for-loops are often used to traverse arrays to perform updates or other processing on a per-location basis *and* the processing is often done in a manner in which the current iteration does not depend on previous iterations, *i.e.*, there are no *loop-carried-dependencies* [20]. Consider the following procedure body

$$\textbf{for } q \leftarrow 1 \textbf{ to } m \textbf{ do } (t := h[q] \ ; h[q] := h[q + m] \ ; h[q + m] := t) \qquad (1)$$

that flips the values between the upper and lower halves of an array, resulting in information flow between the two halves. However, if we apply the approach to loop processing from our previous work [5], we obtain a contract that merely says that the final value of the array is derived from its original value (h $\texttt{from}$ $*$), but nothing more precise.

Still, this procedure possesses no loop-carried-dependencies: changes made in the current iteration do not depend on previous ones. So, we should be able to reason about the flows in all iterations of this loop (and analogously, flows related to all index positions of array h) using a single "schematic" iteration (and analogously, a single "schematic" index position $h[u]$). And indeed, replacing the **for** loop by its body (thus being iterated once only) will result in a contract showing the flow between the two locations on the separate halves of the array. What we want is a quantified version of that specification.

The definition of Pre_{for} given in Fig. 5 implements the above intuition, for a given array h. (If multiple arrays are updated in the same loop, Pre_{for} must be called separately on each array.) To handle also multiple updates, none of which can happen indirectly through procedure calls (condition 1), we let J range over all occurrences of such updates. Thus each array update is of the form $h[A_j] := \_$ where (condition 2) we can not allow A_j to be modified by the loop body (but we certainly expect A_j to contain the loop counter). Condition 3 states that each A_j must have an "inverse" A'_j. For example, if $A_j = q + 1$, then $A'_j = u - 1$. Condition 4 states that the range of each A_j can be expressed. For example, if q ranges from 1 to 10, and $A_j = q + 1$, then the range of A_j is determined by the predicate ϕ_j given by $1 + 1 \leq u \leq 10 + 1$. Condition 5 states that nothing in the precondition is modified except possibly h; that is, there are no loop carried dependencies between scalar variables. Condition 6 states that there are no loop-carried dependencies between array locations. That is, an array location is not read *after* it has been updated.

Thus conditions 3 and 4 ensure that contracts can be expressed, whereas the absence of loop-carried dependencies, as formalized in conditions 5 and 6, ensures the soundness of quantification: we can reason about a single run of the loop and generalize the result, because there is no interdependence among the different iterations. If any of the conditions is not satisfied, then the loop is treated as a **while** loop, in effect smashing together all array entries without obtaining a quantified information flow precondition.

The following lemma is a key step in the proof of Theorem 1.

Lemma 2. *Let S be* **for** $q \leftarrow 1$ **to** m **do** S_0. *Assume* $\text{Pre}_{\text{for}}(S_0, q, m, h[u]\ltimes)$ *succeeds, with result Θ. Then for all integer constants c we have* $\{\Theta[c/u]\}S\{h[c]\ltimes\}$.

Example 1. Consider the **for**-loop from (1). With $J = \{1, 2\}$ we have $A_1 = q$, $A_2 = q + m$. Our algorithm then computes: $A'_1 = u$, $A'_2 = u - m$ which satisfies Condition 3 since $(n = q) \equiv_1 (q = n)$ and $(n = q + m) \equiv_1 (q = n - m)$.

Next, we compute the ranges for expressions: $\phi_1 = 1 \leq u \leq m$, $\phi_2 = m + 1 \leq u \leq m + m$. This satisfies Condition 4 since for all s and for all n,

$$n \in \{[\![q]\!]_{[s|q \rightarrow i]} \mid 1 \leq i \leq s(m)\} \text{ iff } s \models 1 \leq n \leq m$$

$$n \in \{[\![q + m]\!]_{[s|q \rightarrow i]} \mid 1 \leq i \leq s(m)\} \text{ iff } s \models m + 1 \leq n \leq m + m.$$

With S_0 the body of the **for** loop we now compute

$$\{\Theta_1\} \Longleftarrow S_0 \{h[q]\ltimes\}, \{\Theta_2\} \Longleftarrow S_0 \{h[q + m]\ltimes\}$$

where it is easy to see that Θ_2 simplifies to $h[q]\ltimes$, and that Θ_1 simplifies – assuming we know that $m \geq 1$ – to $h[q + m]\ltimes$.

The only non-trivial requirement which is left to check is condition 6 which splits into 4 equations that *each* should imply $i' \leq i$ (given s and i, i' with $i, i' \in \{1 \ldots s(m)\}$):

(1) $[\![q + m]\!]_{[s|q \rightarrow i']} = [\![q]\!]_{[s|q \rightarrow i]}$ (3) $[\![q]\!]_{[s|q \rightarrow i']} = [\![q]\!]_{[s|q \rightarrow i]}$

(2) $[\![q + m]\!]_{[s|q \rightarrow i']} = [\![q + m]\!]_{[s|q \rightarrow i]}$ (4) $[\![q]\!]_{[s|q \rightarrow i']} = [\![q + m]\!]_{[s|q \rightarrow i]}$

Here (2) and (3) trivially imply $i' \leq i$ since they reduce to $i' + s(m) = i + s(m)$ and to $i' = i$; (1) and (4) vacuously imply $i' \leq i$ since they reduce to $i' + s(m) = i$ and to $i' = i + s(m)$ which both are impossible given $1 \leq i, i' \leq s(m)$. As all requirements are fulfilled, we see that $\mathsf{Pre_{for}}$ succeeds for the given program. After some simplifications, we end up with the expected preconditions

$$1 \leq u \leq m \Rightarrow h[u + m]\bowtie, \quad m + 1 \leq u \leq (m + m) \Rightarrow h[u - m]\bowtie,$$
$$(1 > u) \vee (u > m + m) \Rightarrow h[u]\bowtie, \quad m\bowtie.$$

The $\mathsf{Pre_{while}}$ Function For the analysis of while loops (or for loops with loop-carried dependencies), we employ the function $\mathsf{Pre_{while}}$ (Fig. 5) which expects a postcondition Θ' where each $\theta' \in \Theta'$ is of the form $\phi \Rightarrow w\bowtie$ (w a scalar or array variable).

The idea is to consider assertions of the form $\phi_w \Rightarrow w\bowtie$ and then repeatedly analyze the loop body so as to iteratively weaken the antecedents until a fixed point is reached.

To ensure termination, we need a "widening operator" [13] on 1-assertions. A trivial widening operator is the one that always returns *true*, in effect converting conditional agreement assertions into unconditional. Our implementation uses disjunction as a widening operator but returns *true* if convergence is not achieved after a certain number of iterations. Space constraints prevent us from further explaining the algorithm (a variant of which was presented in [5]); we refer the reader to [4].

6   Experimental Assessment

To assess the ideas presented in this paper, we have developed an implementation that checks and infers information flow contracts for SPARK using our more precise enhanced contract language. The algorithm extends our implementation for conditional contracts described in [5] to support arrays, universally quantified flow contracts, and precise processing of `for` loops as detailed in previous sections.

We tested this implementation on an information assurance application (a MILS Message Router) that presents a number of challenges due to its extensive use of arrays, a collection of embedded applications (an Autopilot, a Minepump, a Water Boiler monitor, and a Missile Guidance system – all developed outside of our research group), and a collection of small programs that we developed ourselves to highlight common array idioms that we discovered in information assurance applications. We provide a more detailed assessment of the MMR example after summarizing the results of the experiments and illustrating the following array idiom examples (see Fig. 6).

- **ArrayInit:** A procedure that initializes all elements of an array to a particular value.
- **ArrayScrub:** A procedure that replaces the elements of an array that satisfy a predetermined condition, with a particular value.
- **ArrayTransfer:** A procedure that transfer the elements from one array to another.
- **ArrayPartitionedTransfer:** Similar to the previous one except that the transfer from one array to the other is done only within certain partitions (ranges) defined in each array.

In each of these examples, using original SPARK contracts/analysis would have allowed us to specify only that information is flowing from one entire array to another. Fig. 6

```
procedure ArrayInit
—# global out A(*);
—# derives for all I in A.Range => (A(I) from {});
is
begin
  for I in A.Range loop
    A(I) := 0;
  end loop;
end ArrayInit;



procedure ArrayScrub
—# global in Scrub_Constant,
—#        out A(*);
—# derives for all I in A.Range =>
—#        (A(I) from Scrub_Constant
—#         when should_scrub(A(I)));
is
  begin
    for I in A.Range loop
      if should_scrub(A(I)) then
        A(I) := Scrub_Constant;
      end if;
    end loop;
end ArrayScrub;
```

```
procedure ArrayTransfer
—# global in B(*),
—#        out A(*);
—# derives for all I in A.Range => (A(I) from B(I));
is
begin
  for I in A.Range loop
    A(I) := B(I);
  end loop;
end ArrayTransfer;

procedure ArrayPartitionedTransfer
—# global in B(*), C(*), K,
—#        out A(*);
—# derives for all I in range
—#        A'First .. K => (A(I) from B(I)) &
—#        for all I in range
—#        K+1 .. A'Last => (A(I) from C(I-K));
is
begin
    for I in range A'First .. K loop
      A(I) := B(I);
    end loop;

    for I in range k+1 .. A'Last loop
      A(I) := C(I-K);
    end loop;
end ArrayPartitionedTransfer;
```

Fig. 6. Information flow contracts inferred by our implementation for a selection of examples

illustrates how our conditional and quantified contracts allow a much more precise verified specification of the flows.

A total of **66 procedures** were analyzed, and information flow contracts were inferred for all of them, taking **less than two seconds for each** to run on a Core 2 Duo 2.2GHz processor and 3 GB of RAM. Of these procedures, ten included array manipulations that tested our new extensions to the logic. In all of these cases, our implementation generates a quantified information flow specification showing the dependence dynamics in the arrays.

The MMR Example: The MMR (MILS Message Router) is an idealized version of a MILS infrastructure component (first proposed by researchers at the University of Idaho [25]) designed to mediate communication between partitions in a *separation kernel* [26] – the foundation of specialized real-time platforms used in security contexts to provide strong data and temporal separation.

Fig. 7 illustrates a set of partition processes that execute in a static round-robin schedule. During each schedule cycle, each process is allowed to post up to one bounded-size message to each of the other partitions and receive messages from partitions sent during the previous cycle. Different partitions do not communicate directly. Instead, they post messages to the MMR, which only propagates a message if it conforms to a static security policy represented by a two dimensional boolean array *Policy* indexed by process IDs. In Fig. 7, a shaded square (representing the value *True*) in the *Policy* array indicates that the row process (*e.g.*, B) is allowed to send messages to the column process (*e.g.*, D). The figure illustrates that unidirectional communication can be enforced (*e.g.*, D is not allowed to send messages to B).

During the posting, the infrastructure attaches an unspoofable header to the message indicating the ID of the sender process and the ID of the destination process. The MMR places each posted message in a pool of shared *Memory* slots (represented as an array of messages), and updates *Pointers* (represented as a two-dimensional array of indices

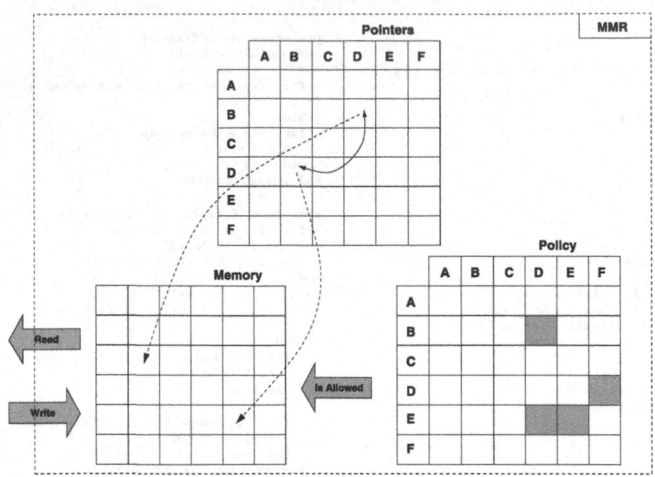

Fig. 7. Diagram of the MILS Message Router

into *Memory*) that organizes incoming/outgoing messages. During posting, a *Memory* cell indexed by row *A*, column *B* holding pointer *X* indicates that the memory location pointed to by *X* is "owned" by process *A* and holds a message from process *A* destined for process *B*. Entries in Flags (an array of boolean values with the same dimensions as *Pointers*) indicate if the corresponding entry in *Pointers* represents a valid message or a "place holder" default message that will not be propagated by the MMR.

Fig. 8 (a) displays the SPARK code for procedure Route that implements part of the MMR routing phase. Conceptually, messages are routed by swapping Pointers entries. Before Route is executed, the array of pointers points to *outgoing* messages, whereas after routing it points to *incoming* messages. After routing, a Memory cell indexed by Pointers row *A*, column *B* holding pointer *X* indicates that the memory location pointed to by *X* is "owned" by process *A* and holds a message from process *B* sent to process *A*. For any two processes *A* and *B*, the first two conditional blocks in Route determine if messages from *A* and *B* (and vice versa) are allowed by the security policy. If a message is not allowed, then the memory location holding it is cleared with a default message and the corresponding Flags entry is set to *false*. Then, if there remains a valid message flowing in either direction, Route swaps the Memory cell indices in Pointers so that the ownership between the memory locations is exchanged among the processes (note that if a message is allowed in one direction but not the other, the swap will propagate a default message in the "disallowed" direction).

There are multiple reasons why it is very difficult to verify statically that the MMR conforms to the end-to-end information flow policy as captured by the *Policy* matrix. First, the examples of Section 2 illustrated the difficulties of statically reasoning about individual cells of an array, and, in the MMR, invalid message channels are "squelched" by clearing out (with a default message) individual cells within a large array. Second, the information flow path between two partitions is not implemented via direct reference to source and destination memory cells, but instead involves a level of indirection via

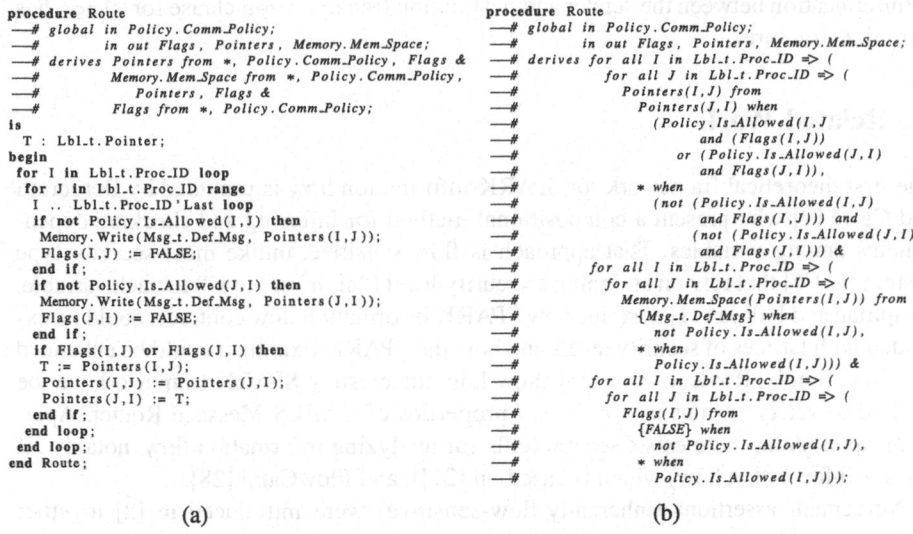

```
procedure Route
—# global in Policy.Comm_Policy;
—#        in out Flags, Pointers, Memory.Mem_Space;
—# derives Pointers from *, Policy.Comm_Policy, Flags &
—#         Memory.Mem_Space from *, Policy.Comm_Policy,
—#         Pointers, Flags &
—#         Flags from *, Policy.Comm_Policy;
is
   T : Lbl_t.Pointer;
begin
   for I in Lbl_t.Proc_ID loop
     for J in Lbl_t.Proc_ID range
        I .. Lbl_t.Proc_ID'Last loop
        if not Policy.Is_Allowed(I,J) then
           Memory.Write(Msg_t.Def_Msg, Pointers(I,J));
           Flags(I,J) := FALSE;
        end if;
        if not Policy.Is_Allowed(J,I) then
           Memory.Write(Msg_t.Def_Msg, Pointers(J,I));
           Flags(J,I) := FALSE;
        end if;
        if Flags(I,J) or Flags(J,I) then
           T := Pointers(I,J);
           Pointers(I,J) := Pointers(J,I);
           Pointers(J,I) := T;
        end if;
     end loop;
   end loop;
end Route;
```

```
procedure Route
—# global in Policy.Comm_Policy;
—#        in out Flags, Pointers, Memory.Mem_Space;
—# derives for all I in Lbl_t.Proc_ID => (
—#   for all J in Lbl_t.Proc_ID => (
—#     Pointers(I,J) from
—#     Pointers(J,I) when
—#     (Policy.Is_Allowed(I,J
—#       and (Flags(I,J))
—#       or (Policy.Is_Allowed(J,I)
—#       and Flags(J,I)),
—#   * when
—#   (not (Policy.Is_Allowed(I,J)
—#     and Flags(I,J))) and
—#   (not (Policy.Is_Allowed(J,I)
—#     and Flags(J,I))) &
—#   for all I in Lbl_t.Proc_ID => (
—#   for all J in Lbl_t.Proc_ID => (
—#     Memory.Mem_Space(Pointers(I,J)) from
—#     {Msg_t.Def_Msg} when
—#     not Policy.Is_Allowed(I,J),
—#   * when
—#     Policy.Is_Allowed(I,J))) &
—#   for all I in Lbl_t.Proc_ID => (
—#   for all J in Lbl_t.Proc_ID => (
—#     Flags(I,J) from
—#     {FALSE} when
—#     not Policy.Is_Allowed(I,J),
—#   * when
—#     Policy.Is_Allowed(I,J)));
```

(a)   (b)

Fig. 8. Source code and initial specification for procedure Routing of the MILS Message Router (a), and information flow specification for the same procedure using extended specification and analysis techniques for arrays (b)

the *Pointers* array. Third, the information flow path through the MMR between two partitions is not static (*e.g.*, as is the case for information flow between two variables of scalar type), but it is changing – information for the same conceptual path flows through different *Memory* cells whose "ownership" changes on different iterations.

As anticipated, Figure 8 (a) illustrates that the original SPARK annotations for Route are far too imprecise to support verification of the desired end-to-end policy. For example, the derives clause for Pointers states that the final value of the array is derived from its initial value (*), from the communication policy (Policy.Comm_Policy), and from the array of flags (Flags). The problem here is that the forced abstraction of Pointers array cells into a single atomic entity collapses the individual *allowed* inter-partition information flow channels (where we needed to verify *separation of channels*) and does not capture the fact that some inter-partition flows are *disallowed*. Furthermore, we have lost information about the specific conditions of the Policy that enable or disable corresponding flows in Pointers. Finally, without precise accounting of flows for Pointers, it is impossible to get a handle on what we are most interested in: flows of the actual messages through Memory.

Figure 8 (b) displays a contract in our extended contract language that is automatically inferred using the precondition generation algorithm of the preceding section. The derives clause for Pointers uses nested quantification (derived from the nested loop structure) to capture the "swapping" action of Route. Moreover, it includes the conditions under which the swapping occurs or under which Pointers(I,J) retains its value. The Memory derives clause correctly captures the fact that the cell holding an outgoing message is "cleared" with the default message when the policy disallows communication between the sender and destination (the `derives` clause for `Flags` has a similar structure).

7 Related Work

The first theoretical framework for SPARK information flow is provided by Bergeretti and Carré [9] who present a compositional method for inferring and checking dependencies among variables. That approach is flow-sensitive, unlike most security type systems [31,6] that rely on assigning a security level ("high" or "low") to each variable. Chapman and Hilton [11] describe how SPARK information flow contracts could be extended with lattices of security levels and how the SPARK Examiner could be enhanced correspondingly. Rossebo *et al.*[25] show how the existing SPARK framework can be applied to verify various *unconditional* properties of a MILS Message Router. Apart from Spark Ada, there exists several tools for analyzing information flow, notably Jif (Java + information flow) which is based on [21]), and FlowCaml [28].

Agreement assertions (inherently flow-sensitive) were introduced in [2] together with an algorithm for computing (weakest) preconditions, but the approach does not integrate with programmer assertions. To address that, and to analyze heap-manipulating languages, the logic of [1] employs *three* kinds of primitive assertions: agreement, programmer, and region (for a simple alias analysis). But, since those can be combined only through conjunction, programmer assertions are not smoothly integrated, and one cannot capture *conditional* information flows. This motivated Amtoft & Banerjee [3] to introduce conditional agreement assertions (for a heap-manipulating language); in [5] that approach was applied to the (heap-free) SPARK setting and worked out extensively, with an algorithm for computing loop invariants and with reports from an implementation. All of these works treat arrays as indivisible entities.

Reasoning about individual array elements is desirable for the precise analysis of a loop that traverses an array. We have established syntactic and semantic conditions for when we can allow such fine-grained analysis; these conditions include what is essentially the absence of loop-carried dependencies. This suggests a relationship to the body of work, with [24] as a seminal paper, addressing when loops can be parallelized. Our conditions are more permissive though since they allow a location to be read *before* it is written, as for the loop body $h[q] := h[q+1]$ (whereas we do not allow $h[q+1] := h[q]$). Even though our focus is on the flow between between array elements, not their actual content, we might look into the body of work on static analysis of array content to see if some techniques may improve the precision of our analysis.

Rather than designing a specific logic for information flow, one can employ general logic as does the recently popular self-composition technique. Here the information flow property which we encode as $\{x\bowtie\}$ S $\{y\bowtie\}$ is encoded as $\{x = x'\}$ $S; S'$ $\{y = y'\}$ where S' is a copy of S with all variables renamed (primed); such a property can be checked using existing static verifiers. This is the approach by Barthe et al. [8] that was extended by, e.g., Terauchi and Aiken [30] and Naumann [22]. The effect of self-composition can also be obtained through dynamic logic, as done by Darvas et al [14].

When it comes to *conditional* information flow, the most noteworthy existing tool is the slicer by Snelting et al [29] which generates *path conditions* in program dependence graphs for reasoning about end-to-end flows between specified program points/variables. In contrast, we provide a contract-based approach for *compositional* reasoning about conditions on flows with an underlying logic representation that can provide external evidence for conformance to conditional flow properties. We plan to investigate the deeper technical connections between the two approaches.

Ground-breaking efforts in certification of MILS infrastructure [17,19] have used approaches in which source code has been hand-translated into executable models in theorem provers such as ACL2 and PVS. While the direct theorem-proving approach followed in these efforts enables proofs of very strong properties beyond what our framework can currently handle, our aim is to dramatically reduce the labor required, and the potential for error, by integrating automated techniques directly on code, models, and developer workflows to allow many information flow verification obligations to be discharged earlier in the life cycle.

8   Conclusions and Future Work

We believe that the results of this paper provide another demonstration that information flow logic as introduced in [2] provides a powerful and flexible framework for precise compositional reasoning about information flow. The logic seems particularly well-suited for SPARK because (a) it naturally provides a semantics for SPARK's original flow contracts, and (b) SPARK's simplicity means that extensive use of the more complicated aspects of the logic (e.g., *object invariants* required to handle the heap[3]) can be avoided while still yielding significant increases in precision compared to the original SPARK contract language.

Several challenges remain as we transition this work into an environment that will be used by industrial engineers. First, the contracts that we infer can be so precise that they become large and unwieldy. The complexity of the contracts in these cases often results when the contract makes distinctions between different conditional flows that are unnecessary for establishing the desired end-to-end flow policy of a system or subsystem. We are developing tool-supported methodologies that guide programmers in writing more abstract specifications that capture distinctions required for end-to-end policies. Second, although our treatment of arrays using quantification works well for buffer manipulations often seen in information assurance applications, it works less well when trying to describe flows between elements of data structures such as trees implemented using arrays. We are investigating how separation logic might be able to provide a solution for this.

Acknowledgements. This work is funded in part by the Air Force Office of Scientific Research (FA9550-09-1-0138) and Rockwell Collins. We would like to thank Andrew Cousino for reading a draft of this paper, catching a subtle error, and assisting with some of the correctness proofs. We would also like to thank the anonymous referees for constructive comments and suggestions.

References

1. Amtoft, T., Bandhakavi, S., Banerjee, A.: A logic for information flow in object-oriented programs. In: Proceedings of the 33rd ACM SIGPLAN-SIGACT symposium on Principles of programming languages (POPL 2006). ACM Press, New York (2006)
2. Amtoft, T., Banerjee, A.: Information flow analysis in logical form. In: Giacobazzi, R. (ed.) SAS 2004. LNCS, vol. 3148, pp. 100–115. Springer, Heidelberg (2004)
3. Amtoft, T., Banerjee, A.: Verification condition generation for conditional information flow. In: 5th ACM Workshop on Formal Methods in Security Engineering (FMSE 2007), George Mason University, pp. 2–11. ACM, New York (2007); The full paper appears as Technical report 2007-2, Department of Computing and Information Sciences, Kansas State University (August 2007)
4. Amtoft, T., Hatcliff, J., Rodríguez, E.: Precise and automated contract-based reasoning for verification and certification of information flow properties of programs with arrays. Technical report, Kansas State University (October 2009),
http://www.cis.ksu.edu/~edwin/papers/TR-esop10.pdf
5. Amtoft, T., Hatcliff, J., Rodríguez, E., Robby, Hoag, J., Greve, D.: Specification and checking of software contracts for conditional information flow. In: Cuellar, J., Maibaum, T., Sere, K. (eds.) FM 2008. LNCS, vol. 5014, pp. 229–245. Springer, Heidelberg (2008)
6. Banerjee, A., Naumann, D.A.: History-based access control and secure information flow. In: Barthe, G., Burdy, L., Huisman, M., Lanet, J.-L., Muntean, T. (eds.) CASSIS 2004. LNCS, vol. 3362, pp. 27–48. Springer, Heidelberg (2005)
7. Barnes, J., Chapman, R., Johnson, R., Widmaier, J., Cooper, D., Everett, B.: Engineering the Tokeneer enclave protection software. In: Proceedings of the IEEE International Symposium on Secure Software Engineering (ISSSE 2006). IEEE Press, Los Alamitos (2006)
8. Barthe, G., D'Argenio, P., Rezk, T.: Secure information flow by self-composition. In: Proceedings of the 17th IEEE Computer Security Foundations Workshop, Pacific Grove, California, USA, June 28 - 30, pp. 100–114. IEEE Computer Society Press, Los Alamitos (2004)
9. Bergeretti, J.-F., Carré, B.A.: Information-flow and data-flow analysis of while-programs. ACM Transactions on Programming Languages and Systems 7(1), 37–61 (1985)
10. Boettcher, C., Delong, R., Rushby, J., Sifre, W.: The MILS component integration approach to secure information sharing. In: 27th IEEE/AIAA Digital Avionics Systems Conference (DASC 2008). IEEE, Los Alamitos (2008)
11. Chapman, R., Hilton, A.: Enforcing security and safety models with an information flow analysis tool. ACM SIGAda Ada Letters XXIV(4), 39–46 (2004)
12. Cohen, E.S.: Information transmission in sequential programs. In: DeMillo, R.A., Dobkin, D.P., Jones, A.K., Lipton, R.J. (eds.) Foundations of Secure Computation, pp. 297–335. Academic Press, London (1978)
13. Cousot, P., Cousot, R.: Abstract interpretation: A unified lattice model for static analysis of programs by construction or approximation of fixpoints. In: Conference Record of the Fourth Annual ACM Symposium on Principles of Programming Languages, pp. 238–252 (1977)
14. Darvas, A., Hähnle, R., Sands, D.: A theorem proving approach to analysis of secure information flow. In: Hutter, D., Ullmann, M. (eds.) SPC 2005. LNCS, vol. 3450, pp. 193–209. Springer, Heidelberg (2005)
15. Deng, Z., Smith, G.: Lenient array operations for practical secure information flow. In: 17th IEEE Computer Security Foundations Workshop, Pacific Grove, California, June 2004, pp. 115–124 (2004)
16. Goguen, J., Meseguer, J.: Security policies and security models. In: Proceedings of the 1982 Symposium on Security and Privacy, pp. 11–20. IEEE, Los Alamitos (1982)

17. Greve, D., Wilding, M., Vanfleet, W.M.: A separation kernel formal security policy. In: 4th International Workshop on the ACL2 Theorem Prover and its Applications (2003)
18. Gries, D.: The Science of programming. Springer, New York (1981)
19. Heitmeyer, C.L., Archer, M., Leonard, E.I., McLean, J.: Formal specification and verification of data separation in a separation kernel for an embedded system. In: Proceedings of the 13th ACM Conference on Computer and Communications Security (CCS 2006), pp. 346–355. ACM, New York (2006)
20. Muchnick, S.: Advanced Compiler Design and Implementation. Morgan Kaufmann Publishers, San Francisco (1997)
21. Myers, A.C.: JFlow: practical mostly-static information flow control. In: Proceedings of the 26th ACM SIGPLAN-SIGACT symposium on Principles of programming languages (POPL 1999), pp. 228–241. ACM Press, New York (1999)
22. Naumann, D.A.: From coupling relations to mated invariants for checking information flow. In: Gollmann, D., Meier, J., Sabelfeld, A. (eds.) ESORICS 2006. LNCS, vol. 4189, pp. 279–296. Springer, Heidelberg (2006)
23. Praxis High Integrity Systems. Rockwell Collins selects SPARK Ada for high-grade programmable cryptographic engine. Press Release (2006), http://www.praxis-his.com/sparkada/pdfs/praxis_rockwell_final_pr.pdf
24. Pugh, W.: A practical algorithm for exact array dependence analysis. Commun. ACM 35(8), 102–114 (1992)
25. Rossebo, B., Oman, P., Alves-Foss, J., Blue, R., Jaszkowiak, P.: Using Spark-Ada to model and verify a MILS message router. In: Proceedings of the 2006 IEEE International Symposium on Secure Software Engineering, pp. 7–14. IEEE, Los Alamitos (2006)
26. Rushby, J.: The design and verification of secure systems. In: Proceedings of the 8th ACM Symposium on Operating System Principles (SOSP 1981), Asilomar, CA, pp. 12–21. ACM Press, New York (1981); ACM Operating Systems Review 15(5)
27. Sabelfeld, A., Myers, A.C.: Language-based information-flow security. IEEE Journal On Selected Areas in Communications 21(1), 5–19 (2003)
28. Simonet, V., Rocquencourt, I.: Flow Caml in a nutshell. In: Proceedings of the first APPSEM-II workshop, pp. 152–165 (2003)
29. Snelting, G., Robschink, T., Krinke, J.: Efficient path conditions in dependence graphs for software safety analysis. ACM Transactions on Software Engineering and Methodology 15(4), 410–457 (2006)
30. Terauchi, T., Aiken, A.: Secure information flow as a safety problem. In: Hankin, C., Siveroni, I. (eds.) SAS 2005. LNCS, vol. 3672, pp. 352–367. Springer, Heidelberg (2005)
31. Volpano, D.M., Smith, G.: A type-based approach to program security. In: Bidoit, M., Dauchet, M. (eds.) CAAP 1997, FASE 1997, and TAPSOFT 1997. LNCS, vol. 1214, pp. 607–621. Springer, Heidelberg (1997)

A Semantic Framework for Declassification and Endorsement

Aslan Askarov and Andrew Myers

Department of Computer Science, Cornell University

Abstract. Language-based information flow methods offer a principled way to enforce strong security properties, but enforcing noninterference is too inflexible for realistic applications. Security-typed languages have therefore introduced declassification mechanisms for relaxing confidentiality policies, and endorsement mechanisms for relaxing integrity policies. However, a continuing challenge has been to define what security is guaranteed when such mechanisms are used. This paper presents a new semantic framework for expressing security policies for declassification and endorsement in a language-based setting. The key insight is that security can be described in terms of the power that declassification and endorsement give the attacker. The new framework specifies how attacker-controlled code affects program execution and what the attacker is able to learn from observable effects of this code. This approach yields novel security conditions for checked endorsements and robust integrity. The framework is flexible enough to recover and to improve on the previously introduced notions of robustness and qualified robustness. Further, the new security conditions can be soundly enforced by a security type system. The applicability and enforcement of the new policies is illustrated through various examples, including data sanitization and authentication.

1 Introduction

Many common security vulnerabilities can be seen as violations of either confidentiality or integrity. As a general way to prevent these information security vulnerabilities, information flow control has become a popular subject of study, both at the language level [17] and at the operating-system level. The language-based approach holds the appeal that the security property of noninterference [11], can be provably enforced using a type system [19]. In practice, however, noninterference is too rigid: many programs considered secure need to violate noninterference in limited ways.

Using language-based downgrading mechanisms such as *declassification* [14] and *endorsement* [16,21], programs can be written in which information is intentionally released, and in which untrusted information is intentionally used to affect trusted information or decisions. Declassification relaxes confidentiality policies, and endorsement relaxes integrity policies. Both endorsement and declassification have been essential for building realistic applications: for example, the various applications built with Jif [12,15], including games [4], a voting system [10], and web applications [8].

A continuing challenge is to understand what security is obtained when code uses downgrading. The contribution of this paper is providing a more precise and satisfactory

A.D. Gordon (Ed.): ESOP 2010, LNCS 6012, pp. 64–84, 2010.

answer to this question. Much prior work on declassification is usefully summarized by Sands and Sabelfeld [18]. However, there is comparatively little work on characterizing the security of declassification in the presence of endorsement. Because confidentiality and integrity are not independent, it is important to understand how endorsement weakens confidentiality.

To see an interaction between endorsement and confidentiality, consider the following notional code example, in which a service holds both old data (old_data) and new data (new_data), but the new data is not to be released until time embargo_time. The variable new_data is considered confidential, and must be declassified to be released:

```
if request_time >= embargo_time
  then return declassify(new_data)
  else return old_data
```

Because the requester is not trusted, the requester must be treated as a possible attacker. Suppose the requester has control over the variable request_time, which we can model by considering that variable to be low-integrity. Because the intended security policy depends on request_time, that means the attacker controls the policy that is being enforced, and can obtain the confidential new data earlier than intended. This example shows that the integrity of request_time affects the confidentiality of new_data. Therefore, the program should be considered secure only when the guard expression, request_time >= embargo_time, is high-integrity.

A different but reasonable security policy is that the requester may specify the request time as long as the request time is in the past. This policy could be enforced in a language with endorsement by first checking the low-integrity request time to ensure it is in the past; then, if the check succeeds, endorsing it to be high-integrity and proceeding with the information release. The explicit endorsement is justifiable because the attacker's actions are permitted to affect the release of confidential information as long as adversarial inputs have been properly sanitized. This is a common pattern in servers that process possibly adversarial inputs.

Robust declassification has been introduced in prior work [20,13,9] as a semantic condition for secure interactions between integrity and confidentiality. The prior work also develops type systems for enforcing robust declassification, which are implemented as part of Jif [15]. However, the security conditions for robustness are not satisfactory. First, they largely ignore the possibility of endorsement, with the exception of *qualified robustness* [13], which works by giving the endorse operation a somewhat ad-hoc, nondeterministic semantics. Second, prior conditions only characterize information security for programs that terminate. A program that does not terminate is automatically considered to satisfy robust declassification, even if it releases information improperly during execution. Therefore the security of programs that do not terminate (such as servers) cannot be described.

The main contribution of this paper is a general, language-based semantic framework for expressing information flow security. This semantically captures the ability of the attacker to influence knowledge. The robust interaction of integrity and confidentiality can then be captured cleanly as a constraint on attacker control. Endorsement is naturally represented in this framework as a form of attacker control, and a more

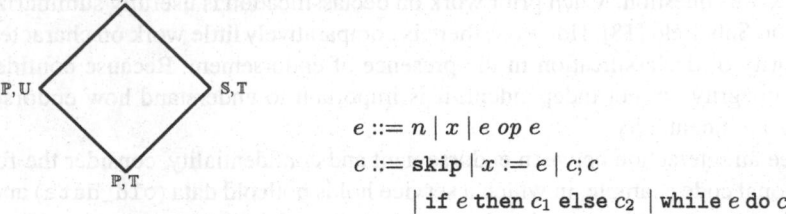

$$e ::= n \mid x \mid e \ op \ e$$
$$c ::= \texttt{skip} \mid x := e \mid c; c$$
$$\mid \texttt{if } e \texttt{ then } c_1 \texttt{ else } c_2 \mid \texttt{while } e \texttt{ do } c$$

Fig. 1. Information flow lattice   **Fig. 2.** Syntax of the language

satisfactory version of qualified robustness can be defined. All these security conditions can be formalized in both *progress-sensitive* and *progress-insensitive* variants.

We show that the progress-insensitive variants of these improved security conditions can be enforced soundly by a simple security type system. Recent versions of Jif have added a *checked endorsement* construct that is useful for expressing complex security policies [8], but whose semantics were not precisely defined; this paper gives semantics, typing rules and a semantic security condition for checked endorsement, and shows that checked endorsement can be translated faithfully into simple endorsement at both the language and the semantic level.

The rest of this paper is structured as follows. Section 2 shows how to define information security in terms of attacker knowledge. Section 3 introduces attacker control. Section 4 defines progress-sensitive and progress-insensitive robustness using the new framework. Section 5 extends this to improved definitions of robustness that allow endorsements, generalizing qualified robustness. A type system for enforcing these robustness conditions is presented in Section 6. The checked endorsement construct appears in Section 7, which introduces a new notion of robustness that allows checked endorsements, and shows that it can be understood in terms of robustness extended with simple endorsements. Section 8 introduces attacker power. Additional examples are presented in Section 9, related work is discussed in Section 10, and Section 11 concludes.

2   Semantics

Information flow levels. We assume two security levels for confidentiality—*public* and *secret*—and two security levels for integrity—*trusted* and *untrusted*. These levels are denoted respectively $\mathbb{P}, \mathbb{S}$ and $\mathbb{T}, \mathbb{U}$. We define information flow ordering $\sqsubseteq$ between these two levels: $\mathbb{P} \sqsubseteq \mathbb{S}$, and $\mathbb{T} \sqsubseteq \mathbb{U}$. The four levels define a security lattice, as shown on Figure 1. Every point on this lattice has two security components: one for confidentiality, and one for integrity. We extend information flow ordering to elements on this lattice: $\ell_1 \sqsubseteq \ell_2$ if the ordering holds between the corresponding components. As standard, we define *join* $\ell_1 \sqcup \ell_2$ as the least upper bound of ℓ_1 and ℓ_2, and *meet* $\ell_1 \sqcap \ell_2$ as the greatest upper bound of ℓ_1 and ℓ_2.

Language and semantics. We consider a simple imperative language with syntax presented on Figure 2. The semantics of the language is fairly standard. For expressions we define big-step evaluation of the form $\langle e, m \rangle \downarrow v$, where v is the result of evaluating expression e in memory m.

For commands we define a small-step operational semantics. For a single transition, we write $\langle c, m \rangle \longrightarrow_t \langle c', m' \rangle$, where c and m are the initial command and memory, c' and m' are the resulting command and memory. The transitions defined by the semantics are fully standard, and are described in detail in the associated technical report. The only unusual feature is the annotation t on each transition, which we call an *event*. Events record assignments: an assignment to variable x of value v is recorded by an event (x, v). We write $\langle c, m \rangle \longrightarrow^*_{\vec{t}}$ to mean that trace $\vec{t}$ is produced starting from $\langle c, m \rangle$ using zero or more transitions. Each trace $\vec{t}$ is composed of individual events $t_1 \ldots t_k \ldots$, and a *prefix* of $\vec{t}$ up to the i-th event is denoted as $\vec{t_i}$. If a transition does not affect memory, its event is *empty*, which is either written as ϵ or is omitted, e.g.: $\langle c, m \rangle \longrightarrow \langle c', m' \rangle$.

Finally, we assume that the *security environment* Γ maps program variables to their security levels. Given a memory m we write $m_\mathbb{P}$ for the public part of the memory.

2.1 Attacker Knowledge

This section provides background on the attacker-centric model for information flow security [2]. We recall definitions of attacker knowledge, progress knowledge, and divergence knowledge, and introduce progress-(in)sensitive *release events*.

Low events. Among the events that are generated during a trace, we distinguish a set of low (or public) events. Low events correspond to observations that an attacker can make during a run of the program. We assume that attacker may observe individual assignments to public variables. Furthermore, if the program terminates, we assume that a termination event $\Downarrow$ may also be observed by the attacker.

Given a trace $\vec{t}$, low events in that trace are denoted as $\vec{t}_\mathbb{P}$. A single low event is often denoted as ℓ, and a sequence of low events is denoted as $\vec{\ell}$. We overload the notation for semantic transitions, writing $\langle c, m \rangle \longrightarrow^*_{\vec{\ell}}$ if only low events produced from configuration $\langle c, m \rangle$ are relevant, that is there is a trace $\vec{t}$ such that $\langle c, m \rangle \longrightarrow^*_{\vec{t}} \wedge \vec{t}_\mathbb{P} = \vec{\ell}$. Low events are the key element in the definition of *attacker knowledge* [2].

The knowledge of the attacker is described by the set of initial memories compatible with low observations. Any reduction in this set means the attacker has learned something about secret parts of the initial memory.

Definition 1 (Attacker knowledge). *Given a sequence of low events $\vec{\ell}$, initial low memory $m_\mathbb{P}$, and program c, attacker knowledge is*

$$k(c, m_\mathbb{P}, \vec{\ell}) \triangleq \{m' \mid m_\mathbb{P} = m'_\mathbb{P} \wedge \langle c, m' \rangle \longrightarrow^*_{\vec{\ell}} \}$$

Attacker knowledge gives a handle on what information attacker learns with every low event. The smaller the knowledge set, the more precise is the attacker's information about secrets. Knowledge is monotonic in the number of low events: as the program produces low events, the attacker may learn more about secrets.

Two extensions of attacker knowledge are useful: *progress knowledge* [1,3] and *divergence knowledge* [1].

Definition 2 (Progress knowledge). *Given a sequence of low events $\vec{\ell}$, initial low memory $m_{\mathbb{P}}$, and a program c, define progress knowledge $k_{\rightarrow}(c, m_{\mathbb{P}}, \vec{\ell})$ as*

$$k_{\rightarrow}(c, m_{\mathbb{P}}, \vec{\ell}) \triangleq \{m' \mid m_{\mathbb{P}}' = m_{\mathbb{P}} \wedge \langle c, m' \rangle \longrightarrow^{*}_{\vec{\ell}} \langle c'', m'' \rangle \longrightarrow^{*}_{\ell'} \}$$

Progress knowledge represents the information the attacker obtains by seeing public events $\vec{\ell}$ followed by one more public event. Progress knowledge and attacker knowledge are related as follows: given a program c, memory m and a sequence of low events $\ell_1 \ldots \ell_n$ obtained from $\langle c, m \rangle$ we have that for all $i < n$,

$$k(c, m_{\mathbb{P}}, \vec{\ell_i}) \supseteq k_{\rightarrow}(c, m_{\mathbb{P}}, \vec{\ell_i}) \supseteq k(c, m_{\mathbb{P}}, \vec{\ell_{i+1}})$$

To illustrate this, consider program $l := 0; \mathtt{while}\ h = 0\ \mathtt{do}\ \mathtt{skip}; l := h$ with initial memory $m(h) = 7$. This program produces a sequence of two low events $(l, 0)(l, 7)$. The knowledge after the first event $k(c, m_{\mathbb{P}}, (l, 0))$ is a set of all possible memories. Note that no low events are possible after the first assignment unless h is non-zero. Progress knowledge reflects this: $k_{\rightarrow}(c, m_{\mathbb{P}}, (l, 0))$ is a set of memories such that $h \neq 0$. Finally, the knowledge after two events $k(c, m_{\mathbb{P}}, (l, 0)(l, 7))$ is a set of memories where $h = 7$.

Using attacker knowledge, one can express many confidentiality policies [6,3,7]. For example, a strong notion of *progress-sensitive noninterference* [11] can be expressed by demanding that knowledge between low events does not change:

$$k(c, m_{\mathbb{P}}, \vec{\ell_i}) = k(c, m_{\mathbb{P}}, \vec{\ell_{i+1}})$$

Progress knowledge enables expressing more permissive policies, such as *progress-insensitive noninterference* (in [1] it is called *termination-insensitive*), which allows leakage of information, but only via termination channels. This is expressed by requiring equivalence of progress knowledge after seeing i events with the knowledge obtained after $i + 1$-th event:

$$k_{\rightarrow}(c, m_{\mathbb{P}}, \vec{\ell_i}) = k(c, m_{\mathbb{P}}, \vec{\ell_{i+1}})$$

In the example $l := 0; \mathtt{while}\ h = 0\ \mathtt{do}\ \mathtt{skip}; l := 1$, the knowledge inclusion between the two events is strict: $k(c, m_{\mathbb{P}}, (l, 0)) \supset k(c, m_{\mathbb{P}}, (l, 0)(l, 1))$. Therefore, the example does not satisfy progress-sensitive noninterference. On the other hand, the low event that follows the while loop does not reveal more information than the knowledge about the existence of that event. Formally, $k_{\rightarrow}(c, m_{\mathbb{P}}, (l, 0)) = k(c, m_{\mathbb{P}}, (l, 0)(l, 1))$, hence the program satisfies progress-insensitive noninterference.

These definitions also allow us to reason about knowledge changes along *parts of the traces*. We say that knowledge is preserved in a progress-(in)sensitive way along a part of a trace, assuming that the respective knowledge equality holds for the low events that correspond to that part.

Next, we extend possible observations to a divergence event $\Uparrow$. For attackers that may observe program divergence $\Uparrow$, we define knowledge on the sequence of low events that includes divergence (we write $\langle c, m \rangle \Uparrow$ to mean configuration $\langle c, m \rangle$ diverges):

Definition 3 (Divergence knowledge)

$$k(c, m_{\mathbb{P}}, \vec{\ell} \Uparrow) \triangleq \{m' \mid m_{\mathbb{P}}' = m_{\mathbb{P}} \wedge \langle c, m' \rangle \longrightarrow^{*}_{\vec{\ell}} \langle c'', m'' \rangle \wedge \langle c'', m'' \rangle \Uparrow \}$$

Note that the above definition does not require divergence immediately after $\vec{\ell}$ — it allows for more low events to be produced after $\vec{\ell}$. Divergence knowledge is used in Section 4.

Let us consider events at which knowledge preservation is broken. We call these events *release events*.

Definition 4 (Release events). *Given a program c and a memory m, such that*

$$\langle c, m \rangle \longrightarrow^*_{\vec{\ell}} \langle c', m' \rangle \longrightarrow^*_r$$

- *r is a* progress-sensitive release event, *if* $k(c, m_{\mathbb{P}}, \vec{\ell}) \supset k(c, m_{\mathbb{P}}, \vec{\ell} r)$
- *r is a* progress-insensitive release event, *if* $k_{\rightarrow}(c, m_{\mathbb{P}}, \vec{\ell}) \supset k(c, m_{\mathbb{P}}, \vec{\ell} r)$

For example, in the program *low* := 1; *low'* := h, the second assignment is both a progress-sensitive and a progress-insensitive release event. In the program while $h = 0$ do skip; *low* := 1 the assignment to *low* is a progress-sensitive release event, but is not a progress-insensitive release event.

3 Attacks

To reason about security of program in the presence of active attacks, we introduce a formal model of the attacker. Our formalization follows the one in [13], where attacker-provided code can be injected into the program. This section provides examples of how attacker-injected code may affect attacker knowledge, followed by a semantic characterization of the attacker's influence on knowledge.

We extend the syntax to allow execution of attacker-controlled code:

$$c[\bullet] ::= \dots \mid [\bullet]$$

We limit attacks that can be substituted into the holes to so-called *fair attacks* — attacks that do not read confidential information and do not modify trusted variables.

Definition 5 (Fair attacks). *An attack is a vector of commands $\vec{a}$ that are substituted in place of holes in $c[\vec{\bullet}]$. Fair attacks are defined by the following grammar where for all variables y in e we have $\Gamma(y) \sqsubseteq (\mathbb{P}, \mathbb{U})$ and for variable x in assignments we have $(\mathbb{P}, \mathbb{U}) \sqsubseteq \Gamma(x)$.*

$$a ::= \text{skip} \mid x := e \mid a; a \mid \text{if } e \text{ then } a \text{ else } a \mid \text{while } e \text{ do } a$$

3.1 Examples of Attacker Influence

In the examples below, we use notation $[(u, v)]$ when a low event (u, v) is generated by attacker-injected code.

Consider program $[\bullet]$; *low* := $u > h$; where h is a secret variable, and u is an untrusted public variable. The attacker's code is executed before the low assignment and may change the value of u. Consider memory m, where $m(h) = 7$ and the two attacks $a_1 = u := 0$ and $a_2 = u := 10$. These attacks result in different values being assigned to variable *low*. The first trace results in low events $[(u, 0)](low, 0)$, while the second trace results in low events $[(u, 10)](low, 1)$. This also means that the knowledge about the secret is different in each trace. We have

$$k(c[a_1], m_\mathbb{P}, [(u, 0)](low, 0)) = \{m' \mid m'(h) \geq 0\}$$
$$k(c[a_2], m_\mathbb{P}, [(u, 10)](low, 1)) = \{m' \mid m'(h) < 10\}$$

Clearly, in this program the attacker has some control over what information about secrets he learns. Observe that it is not necessary for the last assignment to differ in order for the knowledge to be different. For this, consider attack $a_3 = u := 5$. This attack results in low events $[(u, 5)](low, 0)$, that do the same assignment to *low* as a_1 does. Attacker knowledge, however, is different from that obtained by a_1:

$$k(c[a_3], m_\mathbb{P}, [(u, 5)](low, 0)) = \{m' \mid m'(h) \geq 5\}$$

Next, consider program $[\bullet]; low := h$. This program gives away knowledge about the value of h independently of untrusted variables. The only way for the attacker to influence what information he learns is to prevent that assignment from happening at all, which, as a result, will prevent him from learning that information. This can be done by an attack such as $a = \texttt{while true do skip}$, which makes the program diverge before the assignment is reached. We call attacks like this *pure availability attacks*. Another example of a pure availability attack is in the program $[\bullet]; \texttt{while } u = 0 \texttt{ do skip}; low := h$. In this program, any attack that sets u to 0 prevents the assignment from happening.

Consider another example $[\bullet]; \texttt{while } u < h' \texttt{ do skip}; low := 1$. As in the previous example, the value of u may change the reachability of $low := 1$. However, this is not a pure availability attack, because (assuming the attacker can observe divergence) diverging before the last assignment gives the attacker additional information about secrets, namely that $u < h'$. New information is also obtained if the attacker sees the low assignment. We name attacks like this *progress attacks*. In general, a progress attack is an attack that leads to program divergence in a way that observing that divergence (i.e., detecting there is no progress) gives new knowledge to the attacker.

3.2 Attacker Control

We represent attacker control as a set of attacks that are similar in their influence on knowledge. Intuitively, if a program leaks no information to the attacker, the control corresponds to all possible attacks. In general, the more attacks are similar, the less influence the attacker has. Moreover, the control is a temporal property and depends on the trace that has been currently produced. Here, the longer a trace is, the more influence an attack may have, and the smaller the control set is.

Similar attacks. The key element in the definition of control is specifying when two attacks are similar. Given a program $c[\bullet]$, memory m, consider two attacks $\vec{a}$, and $\vec{b}$ that produce traces $\vec{t}$ and $\vec{q}$ respectively:

$$\langle c[\vec{a}], m \rangle \longrightarrow^*_{\vec{t}} \quad \text{and} \quad \langle c[\vec{b}], m \rangle \longrightarrow^*_{\vec{q}}$$

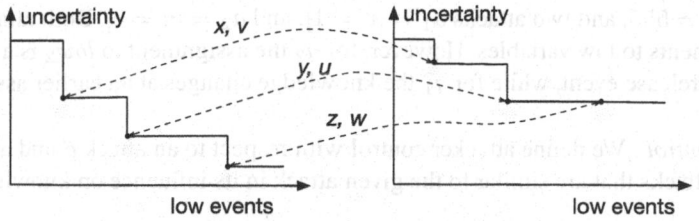

Fig. 3. Similar attacks and traces

We compare $\vec{a}$ and $\vec{b}$ based on how they change attacker knowledge along their respective traces. First, if knowledge is preserved along one of the traces, say $\vec{t}$, it must be preserved along $\vec{q}$ as well. Second, if at some point in $\vec{t}$ there is a release event (x, v), there must be a matching low event (x, v) in $\vec{q}$, and the attacks are similar along the rest of the traces.

Visually, this requirement is described by the two diagrams in Figure 3. Each diagram shows the change of knowledge as more low events are produced. Here the x-axis corresponds to low events, and the y-axis reflects the attacker's uncertainty about initial secrets. Whenever one of traces reaches a release event, depicted by vertical drops, there must be a corresponding low event in the other trace, such that the two events agree. This is depicted by the dashed lines between the two diagrams.

Formally, these requirements are stated using the following definitions.

Definition 6 (Knowledge segmentation). *Given a program* c, *memory* m, *and a trace* $\vec{t}$, *a sequence of indexes* $p_1, \ldots p_N$ *such that* $p_1 < p_2 \cdots < p_N$ *and* $\vec{t}_{\mathbb{P}} = \ell_{1 \ldots p_1} \ell_{p_1 + 1 \ldots p_2} \cdots \ell_{p_{N-1} + 1 \ldots p_N}$ *is called*

- *progress-sensitive knowledge segmentation of size* N, *if* $\forall j \leq N, \forall i . p_{j-1} + 1 \leq i < p_j . k(c, m_{\mathbb{P}}, \vec{\ell_i}) = k(c, m_{\mathbb{P}}, \vec{\ell}_{i+1})$, *denoted by* $Seg(c, m, \vec{t}, p_1 \ldots p_N)$.
- *progress-insensitive knowledge segmentation of size* N *if* $\forall j \leq N, \forall i . p_{j-1} + 1 \leq i < p_j . k_{\rightarrow}(c, m_{\mathbb{P}}, \vec{\ell_i}) = k(c, m_{\mathbb{P}}, \vec{\ell}_{i+1})$, *denoted by* $Seg_{\rightarrow}(c, m, \vec{t}, p_1 \ldots p_N)$.

Low events $p_i + 1$ *for* $1 \leq i < N$ *are called* segmentation events.

Note that given a trace there can be more than one way to segment it, and for every trace consisting of n low events this can be trivially achieved by a segmentation of size n.

Definition 7 (Similar attacks and traces $\sim^{c[\bullet], m}$). *Given a program* $c[\bullet]$, *memory* m, *and two attacks* $\vec{a}$ *and* $\vec{b}$ *that produce traces* $\vec{t}$ *and* $\vec{q}$, *define* $\vec{a}$ *and* $\vec{b}$ *as* similar *along* $\vec{t}$ *and* $\vec{q}$ *for the progress-sensitive attacker, if there are two segmentations* $p_1 \ldots p_N$ *and* $p'_1 \ldots p'_N$ *(for some* N*) such that* $Seg(c[\vec{a}], m, \vec{t}, p_1 \ldots p_N)$, $Seg(c[\vec{b}], m, \vec{q}, p'_1 \ldots p'_N)$, *and* $\forall i . 1 \leq i < N . t_{\mathbb{P}p_i + 1} = q_{\mathbb{P}p'_i + 1}$.

For the progress-insensitive attacker, the definition is similar except that it uses progress-insensitive segmentation $Seg_{\rightarrow}$. *If two attack–trace pairs are similar, we write* $(\vec{a}, \vec{t}) \sim^{c[\bullet], m} (\vec{b}, \vec{q})$ *(for progress-insensitive similarity,* $(\vec{a}, \vec{t}) \sim^{c[\bullet], m}_{\rightarrow} (\vec{b}, \vec{q})$*)*.

The construction of Definitions 6 and 7 can be exemplified by program $[\bullet]$; if u then (while $h \leq 100$ do skip) else skip; $low_1 := 0$; $low_2 := h > 100$. Consider memory with $m(h) = 555$, and two attacks $a_1 = [u = 1]$, and $a_2 = [u = 0]$. Both attacks reach the assignments to low variables. However, for a_2 the assignment to low_2 is a progress-insensitive release event, while for a_1 the knowledge changes at an earlier assignment.

Attacker control. We define attacker control with respect to an attack $\vec{a}$ and a trace $\vec{t}$ as the set of attacks that are similar to the given attack in its influence on knowledge.

Definition 8 (Attacker control (progress-sensitive))

$$R(c[\bullet], m, \vec{a}, \vec{t}) \triangleq \{\vec{b} \mid \exists \vec{q} . (\vec{a}, \vec{t}) \sim^{c[\bullet], m} (\vec{b}, \vec{q})\}$$

To illustrate how attacker control changes, consider example program $[\bullet]; low := u < h; low' := h$ where u is an untrusted variable and h is a secret variable. To understand attacker control of this program, we consider an initial memory $m(h) = 7$ and attack $a = u := 5$. The low event $(low, 1)$ in this trace is a release event. The attacker control is a set of all attacks that are similar to a and trace $[(u := 5)], (low, 1)$ in its influence on knowledge. This corresponds to attacks that set u to values such that $u < 7$. The assignment to low' changes attacker knowledge as well, but the information that the attacker gets does not depend on the attack: any trace starting in m and reaching the second assignment produces the low event $(low', 7)$; hence the attacker control does not change at that event.

Consider the same example but with the two assignments swapped: $[\bullet]; low' := h; low := u < h$. The assignment to low' is a release event that the attacker cannot affect. Hence the control includes all attacks that reach this assignment. The result of the assignment to low depends on u. However, this result does not change attacker knowledge. Indeed, in this program, the second assignment is not a release event at all. Therefore, the attacker control is simply all attacks that reach the first assignment.

Progress-insensitive control. For progress-insensitive security, attacker control is defined similarly using the progress-insensitive comparison of attacks.

Definition 9 (Attacker control (progress-insensitive))

$$R_\rightarrow(c[\bullet], m, \vec{a}, \vec{t}) \triangleq \{\vec{b} \mid \exists \vec{q} . (\vec{a}, \vec{t}) \sim^{c[\bullet], m}_\rightarrow (\vec{b}, \vec{q})\}$$

Consider program $[\bullet]; \text{while } u < h \text{ do skip}; low := 1$. Here, any attack produces a trace that preserves progress-insensitive noninterference. If the loop is taken, the program produces no low events, hence, it gives no new knowledge to the attacker. If the loop is not taken, and the low assignment is reached, this assignment preserves attacker knowledge in a progress-insensitive way. Therefore, the attacker control is all attacks.

4   Robustness

Release control. Next, we define *release control* $R^\triangleright$, which captures the attacker's influence on release events. Intuitively, release control expresses the extent to which an attacker can affect the *decision* to produce some release event.

Definition 10 (Release control (progress-sensitive))

$$R^{\triangleright}(c[\vec{\bullet}], m, \vec{a}, \vec{t}) \triangleq \{\vec{b} \mid \exists \vec{q} . (\vec{a}, \vec{t}) \sim^{c[\vec{\bullet}],m} (\vec{b}, \vec{q}) \wedge$$
$$(\exists \vec{r^j} . k(c[\vec{b}], m_{\mathbb{P}}, \vec{q}_{\mathbb{P}}) \supset k(c[\vec{b}], m_{\mathbb{P}}, \vec{q}_{\mathbb{P}} \vec{r^j}_{\mathbb{P}})$$
$$\vee k(c[\vec{b}], m_{\mathbb{P}}, \vec{q}_{\mathbb{P}}) \supset k(c[\vec{b}], m_{\mathbb{P}}, \vec{q}_{\mathbb{P}} \Uparrow)$$
$$\vee \langle c[\vec{b}], m \rangle \Downarrow)\}$$

The definition for release control is based on the one for attacker control with the three additional clauses, explained below. These clauses restrict the set of attacks to those that either terminate or produce a release event. Because the progress-sensitive attacker can also learn new information by observing divergence, the definition contains additional clause (on the third line) that uses divergence knowledge to reflect that.

Figure 4a depicts the relationship between release control and attacker control, where the x-axis corresponds to low events, and the y-axis corresponds to attacks. The top line depicts attacker control R, where vertical lines correspond to release events. The gray area denotes release control $R^{\triangleright}$. In general, for a given attack $\vec{a}$ and a corresponding trace $\vec{tr}$, where $\vec{r}$ contains a release event, we have the following relation between release control and attacker control:

$$R(c[\vec{\bullet}], m, \vec{a}, \vec{t}) \supseteq R^{\triangleright}(c[\vec{\bullet}], m, \vec{a}, \vec{t}) \supseteq R(c[\vec{\bullet}], m, \vec{a}, \vec{tr})$$

Note the white gaps and the gray release control above the dotted lines on Figure 4a. The white gaps correspond to difference $R(c[\vec{\bullet}], m, \vec{a}, \vec{t}) \setminus R^{\triangleright}(c[\vec{\bullet}], m, \vec{a}, \vec{t})$. This is a set of attacks that do not produce further release events and diverge without giving any new information to the attacker—pure availability attacks. The gray zones above the dotted lines are more interesting. Every such zone corresponds to the difference $R^{\triangleright}(c[\vec{\bullet}], m, \vec{a}, \vec{t}) \setminus R(c[\vec{\bullet}], m, \vec{a}, \vec{tr})$. In particular, when this set is non-empty, the attacker can launch attacks corresponding to each of the last three lines of Definition 10:

1. either trigger a different release event $\vec{r^j}$, or
2. cause program to diverge in a way that also releases information, or
3. prevent a release event from happening in a way that leads to program termination

Absence of such attacks constitutes the basis for our security conditions in Definitions 12 and 13. Before moving on to these definitions, we introduce the progress-insensitive variant of release control.

Definition 11 (Release control (progress-insensitive))

$$R^{\triangleright}_{\rightarrow}(c[\vec{\bullet}], m, \vec{a}, \vec{t}) \triangleq \{\vec{b} \mid \exists \vec{q} . (\vec{a}, \vec{t}) \sim^{c[\vec{\bullet}],m}_{\rightarrow} (\vec{b}, \vec{q}) \wedge$$
$$(\exists \vec{r^j} . k_{\rightarrow}(c[\vec{b}], m_{\mathbb{P}}, \vec{q}_{\mathbb{P}}) \supset k(c[\vec{b}], m_{\mathbb{P}}, \vec{q}_{\mathbb{P}} \vec{r^j}_{\mathbb{P}}) \vee \langle c[\vec{b}], m \rangle \Downarrow)\}$$

This definition uses the progress-insensitive variants of similar attacks and release events. It also does not account for knowledge obtained from divergence.

With the definition of release control at hand we can now define semantic conditions for robustness. The intuition is that all attacks leading to release events should lead

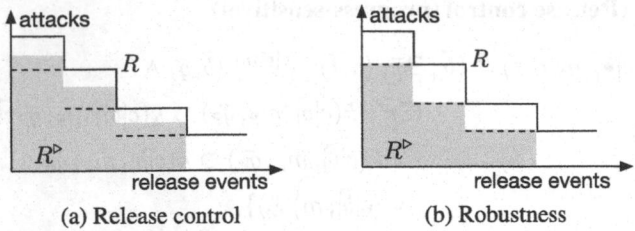

Fig. 4. Release control and robustness

to the same release event. Formally, this is defined as inclusion of release control into attacker control, where release control is computed on the prefix of the trace without a release event.

Definition 12 (Progress-sensitive robustness). *Program $c[\bullet]$ satisfies progress-sensitive robustness if for all memories m and attacks $\vec{a}$, s.t. $\langle c[\vec{a}], m \rangle \longrightarrow^*_{\vec{a}} \langle c', m' \rangle \longrightarrow^*_{\vec{r}}$, and $\vec{r}$ contains a release event, i.e., $k(c[\vec{a}], m_{\mathbb{P}}, \vec{t}_{\mathbb{P}}) \supset k(c[\vec{a}], m_{\mathbb{P}}, \vec{t}_{\mathbb{P}}\vec{r}_{\mathbb{P}})$, we have*

$$R^{\triangleright}(c[\bullet], m, \vec{a}, \vec{t}) \subseteq R(c[\bullet], m, \vec{a}, \vec{t}\vec{r})$$

Note that set inclusion in the above definition could be replaced with strict equality, but we use $\subseteq$ for compatibility with future definitions. Figure 4b illustrates the relation between release control and attacker control for robust programs. Note how release control is bounded by the attacker control at the next release event.

Examples. We illustrate the definition of robustness with a few examples.

Consider program $[\bullet]; low := u < h$, and memory such that $m(h) = 7$. This program is rejected by Definition 12. To see this, pick an $a = u := 5$, and consider the part of the trace preceding the low assignment. Release control $R^{\triangleright}(c[\bullet], m, a, [(u, 5)])$ is all attacks that reach the assignment to low. On the other hand, the attacker control $R(c[\bullet], m, a, [(u, 5)](low, 1))$ is a set of all attacks where $u < 7$, which is smaller than $R^{\triangleright}$. Therefore this program does not satisfy the condition.

Program $[\bullet]; low := h; low' := u < h$ satisfies robustness. The only release event here corresponds to the first assignment. However, because the knowledge given by that assignment does not depend on untrusted variables, the release control includes all attacks that reach the assignment.

Program $[\bullet];$ if $u > 0$ then $low := h$ else skip is rejected. Consider memory $m(h) = 7$, and attack $a = u := 1$ that leads to low trace $[(u, 1)], (low, 7)$. The attacker control for this attack and trace is a set of all attacks such that $u > 0$. On the other hand, release control $R^{\triangleright}(c[\bullet], m, \vec{a}, [(u, 1)])$ is the set of all attacks that lead to termination, which includes attacks such that $u \leq 0$. Therefore, the release control corresponds to a bigger set than the attacker control.

Program $[\bullet];$ while $u > 0$ do skip; $low := h$ is accepted. Depending on the attacker controlled variable the release event is reached. However, this is an example of availability attack, which is ignored by Definition 12.

Program $[\bullet]$; while $u > h$ do skip; $low := 1$ is rejected. Any attack leading to the low assignment restricts the control to attacks such that $u \leq h$. However, release control includes attacks $u > h$, because the attacker learns information from divergence.

The definition of progress-insensitive robustness is similar to Definition 12, but uses progress-insensitive variants of release events, control, and release control. As a result, program $[\bullet]$; while $u > h$ do skip; $low := 1$ is accepted: attacker control is all attacks.

Definition 13 (Progress-insensitive robustness). *Program* $c[\vec{\bullet}]$ *satisfies* progress-insensitive robustness *if for all memories* m *and attacks* $\vec{a}$, *s.t.* $\langle c[\vec{a}], m \rangle \longrightarrow^*_{\vec{a}} \langle c', m' \rangle \longrightarrow^*_{\vec{r}}$, *and* $\vec{r}$ *contains a release event, i.e.,* $k_{\rightarrow}(c[\vec{a}], m_{\mathbb{P}}, \vec{t}_{\mathbb{P}}) \supset k(c[\vec{a}], m_{\mathbb{P}}, \vec{t}_{\mathbb{P}} \vec{r}_{\mathbb{P}})$, *we have*

$$R^{\triangleright}_{\rightarrow}(c[\vec{\bullet}], m, \vec{a}, \vec{t}) \subseteq R_{\rightarrow}(c[\vec{\bullet}], m, \vec{a}, \vec{t}\vec{r})$$

5 Endorsement

This section extends the semantic policies for robustness in a way that allows *endorsing* attacker-provided values.

Syntax and semantics. We extend the language syntax with endorsement:

$$c[\vec{\bullet}] ::= \dots \mid x := \mathtt{endorse}_\eta(e)$$

We assume that every endorsement in the program source has a unique *endorsement label* η. Semantically, endorsements produce *endorsement events* which record the label of the endorsement statement together with the value that is endorsed. Whenever the endorsement label is unimportant we omit it from the examples.

$$\frac{\langle e, m \rangle \downarrow v}{\langle x := \mathtt{endorse}_{\eta_i}(e), m \rangle \longrightarrow_{endorse(\eta_i, v)} \langle stop, m[x \mapsto v] \rangle}$$

Note that $endorse(\eta_i, v)$ events need not mention variable name x since that information is implied by the unique label η_i.

Irrelevant attacks. Given a trace $\vec{t}$, we introduce *irrelevant attacks* $\Phi(\vec{t})$ as the attacks that lead to the same sequence of endorsement events as in $\vec{t}$, until they necessarily disagree on one of the endorsements. Because the influence of these attacks is reflected at endorsement events, we exclude them from consideration when comparing with attacker control. We start by defining *irrelevant traces*. Given a trace $\vec{t}$, irrelevant traces for $\vec{t}$ are all traces $\vec{t'}$ that agree with $\vec{t}$ on all endorsements but the last one. We define this set as follows.

Definition 14 (Irrelevant traces). *Given a trace* $\vec{t}$, *where endorsements are marked as* $endorse(\eta_j, v_j)$, *define a set of irrelevant traces based on the number of endorsements in* $\vec{t}$ *as* $\phi_i(\vec{t})$: $\phi_0(\vec{t}) = \emptyset$, *and*

$$\phi_i(\vec{t}) = \{\vec{t'} \mid \vec{t'} = \dots endorse(\eta_{i-1}, v_{i-1}) \dots endorse(\eta_i, v'_i) \dots \} \text{ s.t. } v_i \neq v'_i$$

Define $\phi(\vec{t}) \triangleq \bigcup_i \phi_i(\vec{t})$ *as a set of* irrelevant traces *w.r.t.* $\vec{t}$.

Definition 15 (Irrelevant attacks). $\Phi(c[\vec{\bullet}], m, \vec{t}) \triangleq \{\vec{a} \mid \langle c[\vec{a}], m \rangle \longrightarrow^*_{\vec{t'}} \wedge \vec{t'} \in \phi(\vec{t})\}$

Security. The security conditions for robustness can be adjusted now to accommodate endorsements that happen along the trace. The idea is to exclude irrelevant attacks from the left-hand side of Definitions 12 and 13. This security condition, which has both progress-sensitive and progress-insensitive versions, expresses roughly the same idea as *qualified robustness* [13], but in a more natural and direct way.

Definition 16 (Progress-sensitive robustness with endorsements). *Program $c[\bullet]$ satisfies* progress-sensitive robustness with endorsement *if for all memories m and attacks $\vec{a}$, such that $\langle c[\vec{a}], m \rangle \longrightarrow^*_{\vec{t}} \langle c', m' \rangle \longrightarrow^*_{\vec{r}}$, and $\vec{r}$ contains a release event, i.e., $k(c[\vec{a}], m_{\mathbb{P}}, \vec{t}_{\mathbb{P}}) \supset k(c[\vec{a}], m_{\mathbb{P}}, \vec{t}_{\mathbb{P}}\vec{r}_{\mathbb{P}})$, we have*

$$R^{\triangleright}(c[\vec{\bullet}], m, \vec{a}, \vec{t}) \setminus \Phi(c[\vec{\bullet}], m, \vec{tr}) \subseteq R(c[\vec{\bullet}], m, \vec{a}, \vec{tr})$$

We refer to the set $R^{\triangleright}(c[\vec{\bullet}], m, \vec{a}, \vec{t}) \setminus \Phi(c[\vec{\bullet}], m, \vec{tr})$ as a set of *relevant attacks*.

Examples. Program $[\bullet]$; $low := \text{endorse}_{\eta_1}(u < h)$ is accepted. Consider initial memory $m(h) = 7$, and an attack $u := 1$; this produces a trace $[(u, 1)]\,endorse(\eta_1, 1)$. The endorsed assignment also produces a release event. We have that

- Release control $R^{\triangleright}$ is a set of all attacks that reach the low assignment.
- Irrelevant traces $\phi([\bullet]$; $low := \text{endorse}_{\eta_1}(u < h), m, [(u, 1)]\,endorse(\eta_1, 0))$ is a set of traces that end in endorsement event $endorse(\eta_1, v)$ such that $v \neq 0$. Thus, irrelevant attacks $\Phi([\bullet]$; $low := \text{endorse}_{\eta_1}(u < h), m, [(u, 1)]\,endorse(\eta_1, 0))$ must consist of attacks that reach the low assignment and set u to values $u \geq 7$.
- The left-hand side of Definition 16 is therefore the set of attacks that reach the endorsement and set u to $u < 7$.
- As for the attacker control on the right-hand side, it consists of attacks that set $u < 7$. Hence, the set inclusion of Definition 16 holds and the program is accepted.

Program $[\bullet]$; $low := \text{endorse}_{\eta_1}(u)$; $low' := u < h''$ is accepted. The endorsement in the first assignment implies that all relevant attacks must agree on the value of u, and, consequently, they agree on the value of $u < h''$, which gets assigned to low'. This also means that relevant attacks belong to the attacker control (which contains all attacks that agree on $u < h''$).

Program $[\bullet]$; $low := \text{endorse}_{\eta_1}(u < h)$; $low' := u < h''$ is rejected. Take initial memory such that $m(h) \neq m(h')$. The set of relevant attacks after the second assignment contains attacks that agree on $u < h$ (due to the endorsement), but not necessarily on $u < h''$. The latter, however, is the requirement for the attacks that belong to the attacker control.

Program $[\bullet]$; if $u > 0$ then $h' := endorse(u)$ else skip; $low := h' < h$ is rejected. Assume initial memory where $m(h) = m(h') = 7$. Consider attack a_1 that sets $u := 1$ and consider trace $\vec{t}_1$ which it gives. This trace endorses u in the then branch, overwrites the value of h' with 1, and produces a release event $(low, 1)$. Consider another attack a_2 which sets $u := 0$, and consider the corresponding trace $\vec{t}_2$. This trace contains release event $(low, 0)$ without any endorsements. Now, attacker control $R(c[\vec{\bullet}], m, a_2, \vec{t}_2)$ excludes a_1, because of the disagreement at the release event. At the same time, a_1 is a relevant attack for a_2, because no endorsements happen along $\vec{t}_2$.

We can also define robustness with endorsement in a progress-insensitive way:

Definition 17 (Progress-insensitive robustness with endorsement). *Program* $c[\vec{\bullet}]$ *satisfies* progress-insensitive robustness with endorsement *if for all memories* m *and attacks* $\vec{a}$, *such that* $\langle c[\vec{a}], m \rangle \longrightarrow^*_{\vec{t}} \langle c', m' \rangle \longrightarrow^*_{\vec{r}}$, *and* $\vec{r}$ *contains a release event, i.e.,* $k_{\rightarrow}(c[\vec{a}], m_{\mathbb{P}}, \vec{t}_{\mathbb{P}}) \supset k(c[\vec{a}], m_{\mathbb{P}}, \vec{t}_{\mathbb{P}}\vec{r}_{\mathbb{P}})$, *we have*

$$R^{\triangleright}_{\rightarrow}(c[\vec{\bullet}], m, \vec{a}, \vec{t}) \setminus \Phi(c[\vec{\bullet}], m, \vec{t}\vec{r}) \subseteq R_{\rightarrow}(c[\vec{\bullet}], m, \vec{a}, \vec{t}\vec{r})$$

6 Enforcement

This section shows the enforcement of robustness using a security type system. While this section focuses on progress-insensitive enforcement, it is possible to refine the type system to deal with progress-sensitivity (modulo availability attacks). Figure 5 displays type rules for expressions and commands. This type system is based on the one of [13] and is similar to many standard security type systems.

Declassification. We extend the language with a language construct for *declassification* of expressions declassify(e). Whereas in earlier examples, we considered an assignment $l := h$ to be secure if it did not violate robustness, we now require information flows from public to secret to be mediated by declassification. While declassification has no additional semantics and can be inferred automatically, its use has the following motivations:

1. On the enforcement level, the type system conveniently ensures that a non-progress release event may happen only at declassification. All other assignments preserve progress-insensitive knowledge.
2. Much of the related work on language-based declassification policies uses similar type systems. Showing our security policies can be enforced using such systems makes the results more general.

Typing of expressions. Type rules for expressions have form $\Gamma \vdash e : \ell, D$ where ℓ is the level of the expression, and D is a set of variables that may be declassified. The declassification is the most interesting rule among expressions. It downgrades the confidentiality level of the expression by returning $\ell \sqcap (\mathbb{P}, \mathbb{U})$, and counts all variables in e as declassified.

Typing of commands. Type rule for commands have form $\Gamma, pc \vdash c$. The rules are standard for a security type system. We highlight typing of assignments, endorsement, and holes.

Assignments have two extra clauses for when expression contains declassification ($D \neq \emptyset$). It requires all variables that can be declassified have high integrity, and bounds the pc-label by $(\mathbb{P}, \mathbb{T})$. This enforces that no declassification happens in untrusted or secret contexts. These requirements guarantee that the information released by the declassification does not directly depend on the attacker-controlled variables.

$$\Gamma \vdash n : \ell, \emptyset \qquad \Gamma \vdash x : \Gamma(x), \emptyset \qquad \frac{\Gamma \vdash e_1 : \ell_1, D_1 \qquad \Gamma \vdash e_2 : \ell_2, D_2}{\Gamma \vdash e_1 \ op \ e_2 : \ell_1 \sqcup \ell_2, D_1 \cup D_2}$$

$$\frac{\Gamma \vdash e : \ell, D}{\Gamma \vdash \texttt{declassify}(e) : \ell \sqcap (\mathbb{P}, \mathbb{U}), \mathit{vars}(e)} \qquad \Gamma, pc \vdash \texttt{skip} \qquad \frac{\Gamma, pc \vdash c_1 \qquad \Gamma, pc \vdash c_2}{\Gamma, pc \vdash c_1; c_2}$$

$$\frac{\Gamma \vdash e : \ell, D \qquad \ell \sqcup pc \sqsubseteq \Gamma(x) \qquad \forall y \in D \,.\, \Gamma(y) \sqsubseteq (\mathbb{S}, \mathbb{T}) \qquad D \neq \emptyset \implies pc \sqsubseteq (\mathbb{P}, \mathbb{T})}{\Gamma, pc \vdash x := e}$$

$$\frac{\Gamma \vdash e : \ell, \emptyset \qquad \Gamma, pc \sqcup \ell \vdash c_1 \qquad \Gamma, pc \sqcup \ell \vdash c_2}{\Gamma, pc \vdash \texttt{if } e \texttt{ then } c_1 \texttt{ else } c_2} \qquad \frac{\Gamma \vdash e : \ell, \emptyset \qquad \Gamma, pc \sqcup \ell \vdash c}{\Gamma, pc \vdash \texttt{while } e \texttt{ do } c}$$

$$\frac{pc \sqsubseteq (\mathbb{P}, \mathbb{U})}{\Gamma, pc \vdash \bullet} \qquad \frac{pc \sqsubseteq (\mathbb{S}, \mathbb{T}) \qquad pc \sqsubseteq \Gamma(x) \qquad \Gamma \vdash e : \ell \qquad \ell \sqcap (\mathbb{S}, \mathbb{T}) \sqsubseteq \Gamma(x)}{\Gamma, pc \vdash x := \texttt{endorse}(e)}$$

Fig. 5. Type system: expressions and commands

Typing rule for endorsement requires that pc-label is trusted: $pc \sqsubseteq (\mathbb{S}, \mathbb{T})$. Because endorsed expressions preserve their confidentiality level we also check that x has the right security level to store the result of the expression. This is done by demanding that $\ell \sqcap (\mathbb{S}, \mathbb{T}) \sqsubseteq \Gamma(x)$, where taking meet of ℓ and $(\mathbb{S}, \mathbb{T})$ boosts integrity, but keeps the confidentiality level of ℓ.

The rule for holes forbids placing attacker-provided code in high confidentiality contexts. For simplicity, we disallow declassification in the guards of if and while.

Soundness. Soundness of the type system is stated by the following proposition.

Proposition 1. *If $\Gamma, pc \vdash c[\vec{\bullet}]$ then for all attacks $\vec{a}$, memories m, and traces $\vec{tr}$ produced by $\langle c[\vec{a}], m \rangle$, where $k_{\rightarrow}(c[\vec{a}], m_\mathbb{P}, \vec{t}_\mathbb{P}) \supset k(c[\vec{a}], m_\mathbb{P}, \vec{t}_\mathbb{P}\vec{r}_\mathbb{P})$, we have that*

$$R^\triangleright_{\rightarrow}(c[\vec{\bullet}], m, \vec{a}, \vec{t}) \setminus \Phi(c[\vec{\bullet}], m, \vec{tr}) \subseteq R_{\rightarrow}(c[\vec{\bullet}], m, \vec{a}, \vec{tr})$$

The proof of this and following propositions are given in the associated technical report.

7 Checked Endorsement

Realistic applications endorse attacker-provided data based on certain conditions. For instance, an SQL string that depends on user-provided input is executed if it passes sanitization, a new password is accepted if the user can provide an old one, and a secret key is accepted if nonces match. Because this is a recurring pattern in security-critical applications, we argue for language support in the form of *checked endorsements*.

This section extends the language with checked endorsements and derives both security conditions and a typing rule for them. Moreover, we show checked endorsements can be decomposed into a sequence of direct endorsements, and prove that for well-typed programs the semantic conditions for robustness with checked endorsements and with unchecked endorsements are the same.

Syntax and semantics. In the scope of this section, we assume checked endorsements are the only endorsement mechanism in the language. We introduce a syntax for checked endorsements:

$$c[\vec{\bullet}] ::= \ldots \mid \text{endorse}_\eta(x) \text{ if } e \text{ then } c \text{ else } c$$

The semantics of this command is that a variable x is endorsed if the expression e evaluates to true. If the check succeeds, the then branch is taken, and x is assumed to have high integrity there. If the check fails, the else branch is taken. As with direct endorsements, we assume checked endorsements in program text have unique labels η. These labels may be omitted from the examples, but they are explicit in the semantics.

Endorsement events. Checked endorsement events $checked(\eta, v, b)$, record the unique label of the endorsement command η, the value of variable that can potentially be endorsed v, and a result of the check b, which can be either 0 or 1.

$$\frac{m(e) \downarrow v \qquad v \neq 0}{\langle \text{endorse}_\eta(x) \text{ if } e \text{ then } c_1 \text{ else } c_2, m \rangle \xrightarrow{checked(\eta, m(x), 1)} \langle c_1, m \rangle}$$

$$\frac{m(e) \downarrow v \qquad v = 0}{\langle \text{endorse}_\eta(x) \text{ if } e \text{ then } c_1 \text{ else } c_2, m \rangle \xrightarrow{checked(\eta, m(x), 0)} \langle c_2, m \rangle}$$

Irrelevant attacks. For checked endorsement we define a suitable notion of irrelevant attacks. The reasoning behind this is the following.

1. Both $\vec{t}$ and $\vec{t'}$ reach the same endorsement statement: $\eta_i = \eta_i'$.
2. At least one of them results in the positive endorsement: $b_i + b_i' \geq 1$. This ensures that if both traces do not take the branch then none of the attacks are ignored.
3. The endorsed values are different: $v_i \neq v_i'$. Otherwise, there should be no further difference in what the attacker can influence along the trace.

The following definitions formalize the above construction.

Definition 18 (Irrelevant traces). *Given a trace $\vec{t}$, where endorsements are labeled as $checked(\eta_j, v_j, b_j)$, define a set of irrelevant traces based on the number of checked endorsements in $\vec{t}$ as $\psi_i(\vec{t})$. Then $\psi_0(\vec{t}) = \emptyset$, and*

$$\psi_i(\vec{t}) = \{\vec{t'} \mid \vec{t'} = \ldots checked(\eta_{i-1}, v_{i-1}, b_{i-1}) \ldots checked(\eta_i, v_i', b_i') \ldots \}$$
$$such \ that \ (b_i + b_i' \geq 1) \wedge (v_i \neq v_i')$$

Define $\psi(\vec{t}) \triangleq \bigcup_i \psi_i(\vec{t})$ as a set of irrelevant traces *w.r.t. $\vec{t}$.*

Definition 19 (Irrelevant attacks). $\Psi(c[\vec{\bullet}], m, \vec{t}) \triangleq \{\vec{a} \mid \langle c[\vec{a}], m \rangle \longrightarrow^*_{\vec{t'}} \wedge \vec{t'} \in \psi(\vec{t})\}$

Using this definition, we can define security conditions for checked robustness.

Definition 20 (Progress-sensitive robustness with checked endorsement). *Program* $c[\bullet]$ *satisfies* progress-sensitive robustness with checked endorsement *if for all memories* m *and attacks* $\vec{a}$, *such that* $\langle c[\vec{a}], m\rangle \longrightarrow^*_{\vec{a}} \langle c', m'\rangle \longrightarrow^*_{\vec{r}}$, *and* $\vec{r}$ *contains a release event, i.e.,* $k(c[\vec{a}], m_{\mathbb{P}}, \vec{t_{\mathbb{P}}}) \supset k(c[\vec{a}], m_{\mathbb{P}}, \vec{t_{\mathbb{P}}}\vec{r_{\mathbb{P}}})$, *we have*

$$R^{\triangleright}(c[\bullet], m, \vec{a}, \vec{t}) \setminus \Psi(c[\bullet], m, \vec{tr}) \subseteq R(c[\bullet], m, \vec{a}, \vec{tr})$$

The progress-insensitive version is defined similarly, using progress-insensitive definition for release events and progress-insensitive versions of control and release control.

Example. In program $[\bullet]; \text{endorse}_{\eta_1}(u)$ if $u = u'$ then *low* $:= u < h$ else skip, the attacker can modify u and u'. This program is insecure because the unendorsed, attacker-controlled variable u' influences the decision to declassify. To see that Definition 20 rejects this program, consider running it in memory with $m(h) = 7$, and two attacks: a_1, where attacker sets $u := 5; u' := 0$, and a_2, where attacker sets $u := 5; u' = 5$. Denote the corresponding traces up to endorsement by $\vec{t_1}$ and $\vec{t_2}$. We have $\vec{t_1} = [(u, 5)(u', 0)]$ *checked* $(\eta_1, 5, 0)$ and $\vec{t_2} = [(u, 5)(u', 5)]$ *checked* $(\eta_1, 5, 1)$. Because endorsement in the second trace succeeds, this trace also continues with a low event $(low, 1)$. Following Definition 18 we have that $t_1 \notin \psi(\vec{t_2}(low, 1))$, implying $a_1 \notin \Psi(c[\bullet], m, \vec{t_2}(low, 1))$. Therefore, $a_1 \in R^{\triangleright}(c[\bullet], m, \vec{a_2}, \vec{t_2}) \setminus \Psi(c[\bullet], m, \vec{t_2}(low, 1))$. On the other hand, $a_1 \notin R(c[\bullet], m, \vec{a_2}, \vec{t_2}(low, 1))$ because a_1 can produce no low events corresponding to $(low, 1)$.

Endorsing multiple variables. The syntax for checked endorsements can be extended to multiple variables with the following syntactic sugar, where η_i is an endorsement label corresponding to variable x_i:

$$\text{endorse}(x_1, \ldots x_n) \text{ if } e \text{ then } c_1 \text{ else } c_2 \Longrightarrow \text{endorse}_{\eta_1}(x_1) \text{ if } e \text{ then}$$
$$\text{endorse}_{\eta_2}(x_2) \text{ if true then } \ldots c_1 \text{ else skip} \ldots \text{ else } c_2$$

This is a semantically faithful encoding: the condition is checked as early as possible.

Typing checked endorsements To enforce programs with checked endorsements, we extend the type system with the following general rule:

$$\frac{\begin{array}{ccc} \Gamma' \triangleq \Gamma[x_i \mapsto x_i \sqcap (\mathbb{S}, \mathbb{T})] & \Gamma' \vdash e : \ell', D' & pc' \triangleq pc \sqcup \ell' \\ pc' \sqsubseteq (\mathbb{S}, \mathbb{T}) & \Gamma', pc' \vdash c_1 & \Gamma, pc' \vdash c_2 \end{array}}{\Gamma, pc \vdash \text{endorse}(x_1, \ldots, x_n) \text{ if } e \text{ then } c_1 \text{ else } c_2}$$

The expression e is type-checked in an environment Γ' in which endorsed variables $x_1, \ldots x_n$ have trusted integrity; its label ℓ' is joined to form auxiliary pc-label pc'. The level of pc' must be trusted, ensuring that endorsements happen in a trusted context, and that no declassification in e depends on untrusted variables other than the x_i (this effectively subsumes the need to check individual variables in D'). Each of the branches is type-checked with the program label set to pc'; however, for c_1 we use the auxiliary typing environment Γ', since the x_i are trusted there.

Program $[\bullet]; \text{endorse}(u)$ if $u = u'$ then *low* $:= \text{declassify}(u < h)$ else skip is rejected by this type system. Because variable u' is not endorsed, the auxiliary pc-label has untrusted integrity.

Relation to direct endorsements. Finally, for well-typed programs we can safely translate checked endorsements to direct endorsements using a translation in which a checked endorsement of n variables is translated to $n + 1$ direct endorsements. First, we unconditionally endorse the result of the check. The rest of the endorsements happen in the then branch, before translation of c_1. We save the results of the endorsements in temporary variables $t_1 \ldots t_n$ and replace all occurrences of $x_1 \ldots x_n$ within c_1 with the temporary ones. All other commands are translated to themselves.

$$\llbracket \text{endorse}(x_1, \ldots x_n) \text{ if } e \text{ then } c_1 \text{ else } c_2 \rrbracket \implies t_0 := \text{endorse}_{\eta_0}(e); \text{if } t_0$$
$$\text{then } t_1 := \text{endorse}_{\eta_1}(x_1); \ldots t_n := \text{endorse}_{\eta_n}(x_n); \llbracket c_1[t_i/x_i] \rrbracket \text{ else } \llbracket c_2 \rrbracket$$

The following proposition relates the security of the original and translated programs.

Proposition 2 (Relation of checked and direct endorsements). *Given a program $c[\bullet]$ that only uses checked endorsements such that $\Gamma, pc \vdash c[\bullet]$, then $c[\bullet]$ satisfies progress-(in)sensitive robustness for checked endorsements if and only if $\llbracket c[\bullet] \rrbracket$ satisfies progress-(in)sensitive robustness for direct endorsements.*

For non-typed programs, the relation does not hold. For instance, a program like $[\bullet]$; endorse(u) if $u = u'$ then c_1 else c_2 satisfies Defn. 20, but not Defn. 16.

8 Attacker Power

In prior work, robustness controls the attacker's ability to cause information release. In the presence of endorsement, the attacker's ability to influence trusted locations also becomes an important security issue. To capture this influence, we introduce an integrity dual to attacker knowledge, called *attacker power*. Similarly to low events, we define *trusted events* as assignments to trusted variables and termination. Given a trace $\vec{t}$, we denote the trusted events in the trace as $\vec{t}_\mathrm{T}$. We use notation $t_\star$ for a single trusted event, and $\vec{t}_\star$ for a sequence of trusted events.

Definition 21 (Attacker power). *Given a program $c[\bullet]$, memory m, and trusted events $\vec{t}_\star$, define $p(c[\bullet], m, \vec{t}_\star)$ to be a set of attacks $\vec{a}$ which match trusted events $\vec{t}_\star$:*

$$p(c[\bullet], m, \vec{t}_\star) \triangleq \{\vec{a} \mid \langle c[\vec{a}], m \rangle \longrightarrow^*_{\vec{t}'} \wedge \vec{t}_\star = \vec{t}'_\mathrm{T}\}$$

Attacker power is defined with respect to a given sequence of trusted events $\vec{t}_\star$, starting in memory m, and program $c[\bullet]$. The power returns the set of all attacks that agree with $\vec{t}_\star$ in their footprint on trusted variables.

Intuitively, a smaller set for attacker power means that the attacker has greater power to influence trusted events. Similarly to progress knowledge, we define *progress power*, characterizing which attacks lead to one more trusted event. This then allows us to define robustness conditions for *integrity*, which have not previously been identified.

Definition 22 (Progress power). *Given a program $c[\bullet]$, memory m, and sequence of trusted $\vec{t}_\star$, define progress power $p_\rightarrow(c[\bullet], m, \vec{t}_\star)$ as*

$$p_\rightarrow(c[\bullet], m, \vec{t}_\star) \triangleq \{\vec{a} \mid \langle c[\vec{a}], m \rangle \longrightarrow^*_{\vec{t}'} \langle c', m' \rangle \wedge \vec{t}_\star = \vec{t}'_\mathrm{T} \wedge \langle c', m' \rangle \longrightarrow^*_{t''_\star}\}$$

Definition 23 (Progress-insensitive integrity robustness with endorsements). *A program* $c[\vec{\bullet}]$ *satisfies progress-insensitive robustness for integrity if for all memories* m, *and for all traces* $\vec{tt}_\star$ *where* $t_\star$ *is a trusted event, we have*

$$p_\to(c[\vec{\bullet}], m, \vec{t}_T) \setminus \Phi(c[\vec{\bullet}], m, \vec{tt}_\star) \subseteq p(c[\vec{\bullet}], m, \vec{t}_T t_\star)$$

Irrelevant attacks are defined precisely as in Section 5. We omit the corresponding definitions for programs without endorsements and with checked endorsements.

The type system of Section 6 also enforces integrity robustness with endorsements, rejecting insecure programs such as $t := u$ and if (u_1) then $t := \texttt{endorse}(u_2)$, but accepting $t := \texttt{endorse}(u)$. Moreover, a connection between checked and direct endorsements, analogous to Proposition 2, holds for integrity robustness too.

9   Examples

Password update. Figure 6 shows code for updating a password. The attacker controls variables `guess` of level $(\mathbb{P}, \mathbb{U})$ and `new_password` of level $(\mathbb{S}, \mathbb{U})$. The variable `password` has level $(\mathbb{S}, \mathbb{T})$ and variables `nfailed` and `ok` have level $(\mathbb{P}, \mathbb{T})$. The declassification on line 3 uses the untrusted variable `guess`. This variable, however, is listed in the `endorse` clause on line 2; therefore, the declassification is accepted. The initially untrusted variable `new_password` has to be endorsed to update the password on line 5. The example also shows how other trusted variables—`nfailed` and `ok`—can be updated in the `then` and `else` branches.

Data sanitization. Figure 7 shows an annotated version of the code from the introduction, in which some information (`new_data`) is not allowed to be released until time `embargo_time`. The attacker-controlled variable is `req_time` of level $(\mathbb{P}, \mathbb{U})$, and `new_data` has level $(\mathbb{S}, \mathbb{T})$. The checked endorse ensures that the attacker cannot violate the integrity of the test `req_time >= embargo_time`. (Variable `now` is high-integrity and contains the current time). Without the checked endorse, the release of `new_data` would not be permitted either semantically or by the type system.

```
1   [•]
2   endorse(guess, new_password)
3   if (declassify(guess==password))
4   then
5       password = new_password;
6       nfailed = 0;
7       ok = true;
8   else
9       nfailed  = nfailed + 1;
10      ok = false;
```

```
1   [•]
2   endorse(req_time)
3   if (req_time <= now)
4   then
5       if (req_time >= embargo_time)
6       then return declassify(new_data)
7       else return old_data
8   else
9       return old_data
```

Fig. 6. Password update   **Fig. 7.** Accessing embargoed information

10 Related Work

Prior robustness definitions [13,9], based on equivalence of low traces, do not differentiate programs such as $[\bullet]$; $low := u < h$; $low' := h$ and $[\bullet]$; $low' := h$; $low := u < h$; Per dimensions of information release [18], the new security conditions cover not only the "who" dimension, but are also sensitive to "where" information release happens. Also, the security condition of robustness with endorsement does not suffer from the occlusion problems of qualified robustness. Balliu and Mastroeni [5] derive sufficient conditions for robustness using weakest precondition semantics. These conditions are not precise enough for distinguishing the examples above, and, moreover, do not support endorsement.

Prior work on robustness semantics defines termination-insensitive security conditions [13,5]. Because the new framework is powerful enough to capture the security of programs with intermediate observable events, it can describe the robustness of nonterminating programs. Prior work on qualified robustness [13] uses a non-standard *scrambling* semantics in which qualified robustness unfortunately becomes a *possibilistic* condition, leading to anomalies such as reachability of dead code. The new framework avoids such artifacts because it uses a standard, deterministic semantics.

Checked endorsement was introduced informally in the Swift framework [8] as a convenient way to implement complex security policies. The current paper is the first to formalize and to study the properties of checked endorsement.

Our semantic framework is based on the definition of attacker knowledge, developed in prior work introducing *gradual release* [2]. Attacker knowledge is used for expressing confidentiality policies in recent work [6,1,3,7]. However, none of this work considers integrity; applying attacker-centric reasoning to integrity policies is novel.

11 Conclusion

We have introduced a new knowledge-based framework for semantic security conditions for information security with declassification and endorsement. A key technical idea is to characterize the power and control of the attacker over information in terms of sets of similar attacks. Using this framework, we can express semantic conditions that more precisely characterize the security offered by a security type system, and derive a satisfactory account of new language features such as checked endorsement.

References

1. Askarov, A., Hunt, S., Sabelfeld, A., Sands, D.: Termination-insensitive noninterference leaks more than just a bit. In: Jajodia, S., Lopez, J. (eds.) ESORICS 2008. LNCS, vol. 5283, pp. 333–348. Springer, Heidelberg (2008)
2. Askarov, A., Sabelfeld, A.: Gradual release: Unifying declassification, encryption and key release policies. In: Proc. IEEE Symp. on Security and Privacy, May 2007, pp. 207–221 (2007)
3. Askarov, A., Sabelfeld, A.: Tight enforcement of information-release policies for dynamic languages. In: Proc. IEEE Computer Security Foundations Symposium (July 2009)

4. Askarov, A., Sabelfeld, A.: Security-typed languages for implementation of cryptographic protocols: A case study. In: di Vimercati, S.d.C., Syverson, P.F., Gollmann, D. (eds.) ESORICS 2005. LNCS, vol. 3679, pp. 197–221. Springer, Heidelberg (2005)
5. Balliu, M., Mastroeni, I.: A weakest precondition approach to active attacks analysis. In: PLAS 2009: Proc. of the ACM SIGPLAN Fourth Workshop on Programming Languages and Analysis for Security, pp. 59–71. ACM, New York (2009)
6. Banerjee, A., Naumann, D., Rosenberg, S.: Expressive declassification policies and modular static enforcement. In: Proc. IEEE Symp. on Security and Privacy, May 2008, pp. 339–353 (2008)
7. Broberg, N., Sands, D.: Flow-sensitive semantics for dynamic information flow policies. In: Chong, S., Naumann, D. (eds.) ACM SIGPLAN Fourth Workshop on Programming Languages and Analysis for Security (PLAS 2009), Dublin, June 15. ACM, New York (2009)
8. Chong, S., Liu, J., Myers, A.C., Qi, X., Vikram, K., Zheng, L., Zheng, X.: Secure web applications via automatic partitioning. In: Proc. SOSP 2007, October 2007, pp. 31–44 (2007)
9. Chong, S., Myers, A.C.: Decentralized robustness. In: CSFW 2006: Proc. of the 19th IEEE workshop on Computer Security Foundations, Washington, DC, USA, pp. 242–256. IEEE Computer Society, Los Alamitos (2006)
10. Clarkson, M.R., Chong, S., Myers, A.C.: Civitas: Toward a secure voting system. In: Proc. IEEE Symp. on Security and Privacy, May 2008, pp. 354–368 (2008)
11. Goguen, J.A., Meseguer, J.: Security policies and security models. In: Proc. IEEE Symp. on Security and Privacy, April 1982, pp. 11–20 (1982)
12. Myers, A.C.: JFlow: Practical mostly-static information flow control. In: Proc. ACM Symp. on Principles of Programming Languages, January 1999, pp. 228–241 (1999)
13. Myers, A.C., Sabelfeld, A., Zdancewic, S.: Enforcing robust declassification and qualified robustness. J. Computer Security 14(2), 157–196 (2006)
14. Myers, A.C., Liskov, B.: A decentralized model for information flow control. In: Proc. 17th ACM Symp. on Operating System Principles (SOSP), Saint-Malo, France, pp. 129–142 (1997)
15. Myers, A.C., Zheng, L., Zdancewic, S., Chong, S., Nystrom, N.: Jif 3.0: Java information flow. Software release (July 2006), http://www.cs.cornell.edu/jif
16. Ørbæk, P., Palsberg, J.: Trust in the λ-calculus. J. Functional Programming 7(6), 557–591 (1997)
17. Sabelfeld, A., Myers, A.C.: Language-based information-flow security. IEEE J. Selected Areas in Communications 21(1), 5–19 (2003)
18. Sabelfeld, A., Sands, D.: Declassification: Dimensions and principles. J. Computer Security 17(5), 517–548 (2009)
19. Volpano, D., Smith, G., Irvine, C.: A sound type system for secure flow analysis. J. Computer Security 4(3), 167–187 (1996)
20. Zdancewic, S., Myers, A.C.: Robust declassification. In: Proc. 14th IEEE Computer Security Foundations Workshop, June 2001, pp. 15–23 (2001)
21. Zdancewic, S., Zheng, L., Nystrom, N., Myers, A.C.: Secure program partitioning. ACM Transactions on Computer Systems 20(3), 283–328 (2002)

Amortised Resource Analysis with Separation Logic

Robert Atkey

LFCS, School of Informatics, University of Edinburgh
bob.atkey@ed.ac.uk

Abstract. Type-based amortised resource analysis following Hofmann and Jost—where resources are associated with individual elements of data structures and doled out to the programmer under a linear typing discipline—have been successful in providing concrete resource bounds for functional programs, with good support for inference. In this work we translate the idea of amortised resource analysis to imperative languages by embedding a logic of resources, based on Bunched Implications, within Separation Logic. The Separation Logic component allows us to assert the presence and shape of mutable data structures on the heap, while the resource component allows us to state the resources associated with each member of the structure.

We present the logic on a small imperative language with procedures and mutable heap, based on Java bytecode. We have formalised the logic within the Coq proof assistant and extracted a certified verification condition generator. We demonstrate the logic on some examples, including proving termination of in-place list reversal on lists with cyclic tails.

1 Introduction

Tarjan, in his paper introducing the concept of amortised complexity analysis [15], noted that the statement and proof of complexity bounds for operations on some data structures can be simplified if we can conceptually think of the data structure as being able to store "credits" that are used up by later operations. By setting aside credit inside a data structure to be used by later operations we amortise the cost of the operation over time. In this paper, we propose a way to merge amortised complexity analysis with Separation Logic [12,14] to formalise some of these arguments.

Separation Logic is built upon a notion of resources and their separation. The assertion $A * B$ holds for a resource if it can be split into two resources that make A true and B true respectively. Resource separation enables local reasoning about mutation of resources; if the program mutates the resource associated with A, then we know that B is still true on its separate resource.

For the purposes of complexity analysis, we want to consider resource consumption as well as resource mutation, e.g. the consumption of time as a program executes. To see how Separation Logic-style reasoning about resources helps in

A.D. Gordon (Ed.): ESOP 2010, LNCS 6012, pp. 85–103, 2010.
© Springer-Verlag Berlin Heidelberg 2010

this case, consider the standard inductively defined list predicate from Separation Logic, augmented with an additional proposition R denoting the presence of a consumable resource for every element of the list:

$$\text{list}_R(x) \equiv \quad x = \text{null} \land \text{emp}$$
$$\lor \exists y, z. \ [x \stackrel{\text{data}}{\mapsto} y] * [x \stackrel{\text{next}}{\mapsto} z] * R * \text{list}_R(z)$$

We will introduce the assertion logic properly in Section 4 below. We can represent a heap H and a consumable resource r that satisfy this predicate graphically:

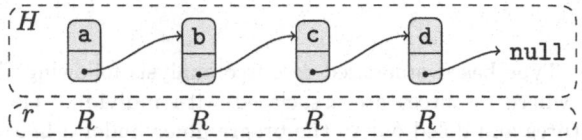

So we have $r, H \models \text{list}_R(x)$, assuming x points to the head of the list. Here $r = R \cdot R \cdot R \cdot R$—we assume that consumable resources form a commutative monoid—and r represents the resource that is available for the program to use in the future. We can split H and r to separate out the head of the list with its associated resource:

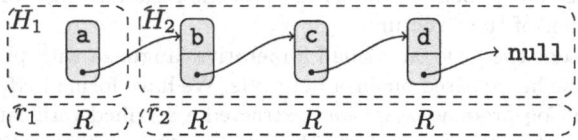

This heap and resource satisfy $r_1 \cdot r_2, H_1 \uplus H_2 \models [x \stackrel{\text{data}}{\mapsto} \text{a}] * [x \stackrel{\text{next}}{\mapsto} y] * R * \text{list}_R(y)$, where $H_1 \uplus H_2 = H$, $r_1 \cdot r_2 = r$ and we assume that y points to the b element. Now that we have separated out the head of the list and its associated consumable resource, we are free to mutate the heap H_1 and consume the resource r_1 without it affecting the tail of the list, so the program can move to a state:

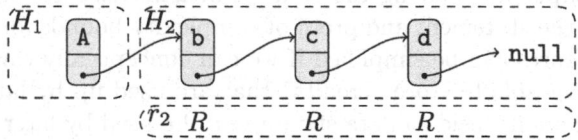

where the head of the list has been mutated to A and the associated resource has been consumed; we do not need to do anything special to reason that the tail of the list and its associated consumable resource are unaffected.

The combined assertion about heap and consumable resource describes the current shape and contents of the heap and also the available resource that the program may consume in the future. By ensuring that, for every state in the program's execution, the resource consumed plus the resource available for consumption in the future is less than or equal to a predefined bound, we can ensure that the entire execution is resource bounded. This is the main assertion of soundness for our program logic in Section 3.4.

By intermixing resource assertions with Separation Logic assertions about the shapes of data structures, as we have done with the resource carrying list$_R$ predicate above, we can specify amounts of resource that depend on the shape of data structures in memory. By the definition of list$_R$, we know that the amount of resource available to the program is proportional to the length of the list, without having to do any arithmetic reasoning about lengths of lists.

The association of resources with parts of a data structure is exactly the banker's approach to amortised complexity analysis proposed by Tarjan [15].

Our original inspiration for this work came from the work of Hofmann and Jost [9] on the automatic heap-space analysis of functional programs. Their analysis associates with every element of a data structure a permission to use a piece of resource (in their case, heap space). This resource is made available to the program when the data structure is decomposed using pattern matching. When constructing part of a data structure, the required resources must be available. A linear type system is used to ensure that data structures carrying resources are not duplicated: this would entail duplication of consumable resource. This scheme was later extended to imperative object-oriented languages [10,11], but still using a type-based analysis.

Contributions We summarise the content and contributions of this work:

- In Section 3, we define a program logic that allows mixing of assertions about heap shapes, in the tradition of separation logic, and assertions about future consumable resources. Tying these together allows us to easily state resource properties in terms of the shapes of heap-based data structures, rather than extensional properties such as their size or contents. We have also formalised the soundness proof of our program logic in Coq, along with a verified verification condition generator.
- In Section 5, we define a restricted subset of the assertion logic that allows us to perform effective proof search and inference of resource annotations. A particular feature of the way this is set up is that, given loop invariants that talk only about the the shape of data structures, we can infer necessary resource bounds.
- In Sections 2 and 6, we demonstrate the logic on two small examples, showing how a mixture of amortised resource analysis and Separation Logic can be used to simplify resource-aware specifications, and how it can be used to prove termination in the presence of cyclic structures in the heap.

2 Motivating Example: Functional Queues

Before defining our program logic, we give another example to demonstrate how amortised reasoning is easier than the traditional approach of keeping a global counter for consumed resources as an auxiliary "ghost" variable in the proof. This example is a standard one for introducing amortised complexity analysis, but here we look at the specifications of operations on an imperative data structure taking into account their resource consumption.

We consider functional queues, where a queue is represented by a pair of lists:

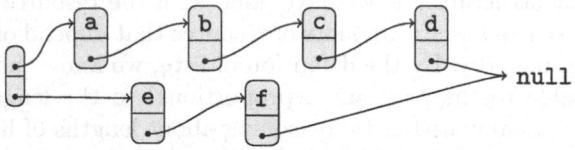

The top list represents the head of the queue, while the bottom list represents the tail of the queue in reverse; thus this structure represents the queue $[a, b, c, d, f, e]$. When we enqueue a new element, we add it to the head of the bottom list. To dequeue an element, we remove it from the head of the top list. If the top list is empty, then we reverse the bottom list and change the top pointer to point to it, changing the bottom pointer to point to null.

When determining the complexity of these operations, it is obvious that the enqueue operation is constant time, but the dequeue operation either takes constant time if the top list is empty, or time linear in the size of the bottom list, in order to perform the reversal. If we were to account for resource usage by maintaining a global counter then we would have to expose the lengths of the two lists in specification of the enqueue and dequeue instructions. So we would need a predicate $queue(x, h, t)$ to state that x points to a queue with a head and tail lists of lengths h and t respectively. The operations would have the specifications:

$$\{queue(x, h, t) \land r_c = r_1\}\text{enqueue}\{queue(x, h, t + 1) \land r_c = r_1 + R\}$$

$$\{queue(x, 0, 0) \land r_c = r_1\}\text{dequeue}\{queue(x, 0, 0) \land r_c = r_1\}$$

$$\{queue(x, 0, t + 1) \land r_c = r_1\}\text{dequeue}\{queue(x, t, 0) \land r_c = r_1 + (1 + t)R\}$$

$$\{queue(x, h + 1, t) \land r_c = r_1\}\text{dequeue}\{queue(x, h, t) \land r_c = r_1 + R\}$$

where r_c is a ghost variable counting the total amount of resource (time, in this case) consumed by the program, and R is the amount of resource required to perform a single list node manipulation. Note that we have had to give three specifications for dequeue for the cases when the queue is empty, when the head list is empty and when the head list has an element. The accounting for the sizes of the internals of the queue data structure is of no interest to clients of this data structure, these specifications will complicate reasoning that must be done by clients in order to use these queues.

Using amortised analysis, this specification can be drastically simplified. We associate a single piece of resource with each element of the tail list so that when we come to reverse the list we have the necessary resource available to reverse each list element. The queue predicate is therefore:

$$queue(x) \equiv \exists y, z. [x \stackrel{head}{\mapsto} y] * [x \stackrel{tail}{\mapsto} z] * list(y) * list_R(z)$$

where list is the standard Separation Logic list predicate, and list$_R$ is the resource-carrying list predicate given above. The specifications of the operations now become straightforward:

$$\{queue(x) * R * R\}enqueue\{queue(x)\} \qquad \{queue(x) * R\}dequeue\{queue(x)\}$$

To enqueue an element, we require two resources: one to add the new element to the tail list, and one to "store" in the list so that we may use it for a future reversal operation. To dequeue an element, we require a single resource to remove an element from a list. If a list reversal is required then it is paid for by the resources required by the enqueue operation.

Once we have set the specification of queues to store one element of resource for every node in the tail list, we can use the resource annotation inference procedure presented in Section 5 to generate the resource parts of the specifications for the enqueue and dequeue operations.

3   A Program Logic for Heap and Resources

We define a logic that is capable of asserting facts about both the mutable heap and the consumable resources that a program has access to. Assertions about resources available to a program are intimately connected to the shapes of the data structures that it is manipulating. In this section, we introduce a simple programming language and a resource-aware program logic for it. We define a "shallow" program logic where we treat pre- and post-conditions and program assertions as arbitrary predicates over heaps and consumable resources. In the next section, we will layer on top a "deep" assertion logic where predicates are actually Separation Logic formulae augmented with resource assertions.

3.1   Semantic Domains

Assume an infinite set $\mathbb{A}$ of memory addresses. We model heaps as finite partial maps $\mathbb{H} = (\mathbb{A} \times \mathbb{F}) \rightharpoonup_{fin} \mathbb{V}$, where $\mathbb{F}$ ranges over field names and $\mathbb{V} = \mathbb{A}_\perp + \mathbb{Z}$ represents the values that programs can directly manipulate: possibly null addresses and integers. We write $dom(H)$ for the domain of a heap and $H_1 \# H_2$ for heaps with separate domains; $H_1 \uplus H_2$ denotes union of heaps with disjoint domains.

Consumable resources are represented as elements of an ordered monoid $(\mathbb{R}, \sqsubseteq, \cdot, e)$, where e is the least element. Example consumable resources include $(\mathbb{N}, \leq, +, 0)$ or $(\mathbb{Q}^{\geq 0}, \leq, +, 0)$ for representing a single resource that is consumed (e.g. time or space), or multisets for representing multiple named resources that may be consumed independently. The ordering on consumable resources is used to allow weakening in our assertion logic: we allow the asserter to assert that more resources are required by the program than are actually needed.

To talk about separated combinations of heaps and resources, we make use of a ternary relation on pairs of heaps and consumable resources, as is standard in the semantics of substructural logics [13]:

$$Rxyz \Leftrightarrow H_1 \# H_2 \wedge H_1 \uplus H_2 = H_3 \wedge r_1 \cdot r_2 \sqsubseteq r_3$$
$$\text{where } x = (H_1, r_1), y = (H_2, r_2), z = (H_3, r_3)$$

We extend the order on resources to pairs of heaps and resources by $(H_1, r_1) \sqsubseteq (H_2, r_2)$ iff $H_1 = H_2$ and $r_1 \sqsubseteq r_2$.

3.2   A Little Virtual Machine

The programming language we treat is a simple stack-based virtual machine, similar to Java bytecode without objects or virtual methods, but with mutable heap and procedures. There are two types: int and ref, corresponding to the two kinds of values in $\mathbb{V}$. We assume a set $\mathbb{P}$ of procedure names, where a procedure's name determines its list of argument types and its return type. Programs are organised into a finite set of procedures, indexed by their name and individually consisting of lists of instructions from the following collection:

$$\iota ::= \text{iconst } z \mid \text{ibinop } op \mid \text{pop} \mid \text{load } n \mid \text{store } n \mid \text{aconst\_null}$$
$$\mid \text{binarycmp } cmp \; offset \mid \text{unarycmp } cmp \; offset \mid \text{ifnull } offset \mid \text{goto } offset$$
$$\mid \text{new } desc \mid \text{getfield } fnm \mid \text{putfield } fnm \mid \text{free } desc \mid \text{consume } r$$
$$\mid \text{return} \mid \text{call } pname$$

These instructions—apart from consume—are standard, so we only briefly explain them. Inside each activation frame, the virtual machine maintains an operand stack and a collection of local variables, both of which contain values from the semantic domain $\mathbb{V}$. Local variables are indexed by natural numbers. The instructions in the first two lines of the list perform the standard operations with the operand stack, local variables and program counter. The third line includes instructions that allocate, free and manipulate structures stored in the heap. The instruction consume r consumes the resource r. The $desc$ argument to new and free describe the structure to be created on the heap by the fields and their types. The fourth line has the procedure call and return instructions that manipulate the stack of activation frames.

Individual activation frames are tuples $\langle code, S, L, pc \rangle \in \text{Frm}$ consisting of the list of instructions from the procedure being executed, the operand stack and local variables, and the program counter. The first two lines of instructions that we gave above only operate within a single activation frame, so we give their semantics as a small-step relation between frames: $\xrightarrow{frm} \subseteq \text{Frm} \times \text{Frm}$. This accounts for the bulk of instructions.

The third line of instructions includes those that manipulate the heap and consume resources. Their small-step operational semantics is modelled by a relation $\xrightarrow{mut} \subseteq \text{Frm} \times \mathbb{H} \times \text{Frm} \times \mathbb{H} \times \mathbb{R}$, which relates the before and after activation frames and heaps, and states the consumable resource consumed by this step.

A state of the full virtual machine is a tuple $\langle r, H, fs \rangle \in \text{State}$, where r is the resource consumed to this point, h is the current heap, and fs is a list of activation frames. The small-step operational semantics of the full machine for some program prg is given by a relation $\longrightarrow_{prg} \subseteq \text{State} \times \text{State}$ which incorporates the $\xrightarrow{frm}$ and $\xrightarrow{mut}$ relations and also describes how the call and return instructions manipulate the stack of activation frames.

Finally, we use the predicate $s \downarrow H, r, v$ to indicate when the last activation frame is popped and the machine halts. The H, r and v are the final heap, the consumed resources and the return value respectively.

3.3   Program Logic

We annotate every procedure *pname* in the program with a pre-condition P_{pname} and a post-condition Q_{pname}. Pre-conditions are predicates over $\mathbb{V}^* \times \mathbb{H} \times \mathbb{R}$: lists of arguments to the procedure and the heap and available resource at the start of the procedure's execution. Post-conditions are predicates over $\mathbb{V}^* \times \mathbb{H} \times \mathbb{R} \times \mathbb{V}$: argument lists and the heap, remaining consumable resource and return value. Intermediate assertions in our program logic are predicates over $\mathbb{V}^* \times \mathbb{H} \times \mathbb{R} \times \mathbb{V}^* \times (\mathbb{N} \rightharpoonup \mathbb{V})$: argument lists, the heap, remaining consumable resource and the current operand stack and local variable store.

For our program logic, a proof that a given procedure's implementation *code* matches its specification (P, Q) consists of a map C from instruction offsets in *code* to assertions such that:

1. Every instruction's assertion is suitable for that instruction: for every instruction offset i in *code*, there exists an assertion A such that $C, Q \vdash i{:}code[i] : A$ and $C[i]$ implies A. Figure 1 gives the definition of $C, Q \vdash i{:}\iota : A$ for a selected subset of the instructions ι. The post-condition Q is used for the case of the return instruction.
2. The precondition implies the assertion for the first instruction: for all arguments *args*, heaps H and consumable resources r, $P(args, H, r)$ implies $C[0](args, H, r, [], \ulcorner args \urcorner)$, where $[]$ denotes the empty operand stack, and $\ulcorner \cdot \urcorner$ maps lists of values to finite maps from naturals to values in the obvious way.

When condition 1 holds, we write this as $C \vdash code : Q$, indicating that the procedure implementation *code* has a valid proof C for the post-condition Q.

3.4   Soundness

We say that an activation frame is safe if there is a proof for the code being executed in the frame such that the requirements of the next instruction to be executed are satisfied. Formally, a frame $f = \langle code, S, L, pc \rangle$ is safe for arguments *args*, heap H, resource r and post-condition Q, written $safeFrame(f, H, r, args, Q)$ if[1]:

1. There exists a certificate C such that $C \vdash code : Q$;
2. $C[pc]$ exists and $C[pc](args, r, H, S, L)$ holds.

---

[1] In this definition, and all the later ones in this section, we have omitted necessary assertions about well-typedness of the stack, local variables and the heap because they would only clutter our presentation.

$C, Q \vdash i{:}\mathsf{consume}\ r_c : \lambda(args, r, H, S, L).\exists r'.r_c \cdot r' \sqsubseteq r \wedge C[i+1](args, r', H, S, L)$

$C, Q \vdash i{:}\mathsf{ifnull}\ n : \lambda(args, r, H, S, L).\forall a\ S'.S = a :: S' \Rightarrow$
$$(a \neq \mathtt{null} \Rightarrow C[i+1](args, r, H, S', L)) \wedge$$
$$(a = \mathtt{null} \Rightarrow C[n](args, r, H, S', L))$$

$$C, Q \vdash i{:}\mathsf{call}\ pname :$$

$\lambda(args, r, H, S, L).\forall args'\ S'.S = args'@S' \Rightarrow$
$$\exists (H_1, r_1)\ (H_2, r_2).$$
$$R(H_1, r_1)(H_2, r_2)(H, r) \wedge$$
$$P_{pname}(args', H_1, r_1) \wedge$$
$$\forall v\ (H_1', r_1').$$
$$H_1' \# H_2 \Rightarrow$$
$$Q_{pname}(args', H_1', r_1', v) \Rightarrow$$
$$C[i+1](args', r_1' \cdot r_2, H_1' \uplus H_2, v :: S', L)$$

Fig. 1. Program Logic Rules (Extract)

Safety of activation frames is preserved by steps in the virtual machine:

Lemma 1 (Intra-frame safety preservation)

1. *If safeFrame$(f, H, r, args, Q)$ and $f \xrightarrow{frm} f'$, then safeFrame$(f', H, r, args, Q)$.*
2. *If safeFrame$(f, H_1, r, args, Q)$ and $H_1 \# H_2$ and $H_1 \uplus H_2 = H$ and $f, H \xrightarrow{mut} f', H', r_c$, then there exists H_1' and r' such that $H_1' \# H_2$ and $H_1' \uplus H_2 = H'$, $r_c \cdot r' \sqsubseteq r$ and safeFrame$(f', H_1', r', args, Q)$.*

Remark 1. We pause for a moment to consider the relationship between our program logic and traditional Separation Logic. The second part of the previous lemma effectively states that execution steps for mutating instructions are *local*: for any other piece of heap that is present but not mentioned in its precondition, the execution of a mutating instruction will not affect it. This is usually expressed in Separation Logic by the Frame rule that states if we know that $\{P\}C\{Q\}$ holds, then $\{P * R\}C\{Q * R\}$ holds for any other resource assertion R. We do not have an explicit Frame rule in our program logic; application of the rule is implicit in the rule for the call instruction (so, conflatingly, the Frame rule is applied when we create a new activation frame). We do not have access to the Frame rule in order to modularly reason about the internals of each procedure, e.g. local reasoning about individual loops. This is partially a consequence of the unstructured nature of the bytecode that we are working with. It has not been a hindrance in the small examples that we have verified so far, but may well become so in larger procedures with multiple loops that need invariants. In such a case it may be useful to layer a hierarchical structure, matching the loops or other sub-program structure, on top of the unstructured bytecode that we have considered here in order to apply Frame rules and facilitate local reasoning inside procedures.

We have now handled all the instructions except the call and return instructions that create and destroy activation frames. To state soundness of our program logic for these we need to define what it means for a stack of activation frames to be safe. Intuitively, a stack of activation frames is a bridge between the overall arguments $args_{top}$ and post-condition Q_{top} for the program and the arguments $args_{cur}$ and post-condition Q_{cur} for the current activation frame, with respect to the current heap H and available consumable resources r, such that, when the current activation frame finishes, its calling frame on the top of the stack is safe. We write this as $safeStack(fs, H, r, args_{cur}, Q_{cur}, args_{top}, Q_{top})$.

Accordingly, we say that the empty frame stack is safe when $r = e$, $H = \mathsf{emp}$, $args_{cur} = args_{top}$ and $Q_{cur} = Q_{top}$. A frame stack $fs = \langle code, S, L, pc \rangle :: fs'$ is safe when there exists (H_1, r_1), (H_2, r_2), $args$, Q and C, A such that:

1. $R(H_1, r_1)(H_2, r_2)(H, r)$;
2. The code is certified: $C, Q \vdash code$;
3. The next instruction has pre-condition A: $C[pc] = A$;
4. When the callee returns, the instruction's pre-condition will be satisfied: for all $v \in \mathbb{V}, H_2', r_2'$ such that $H_2' \# H_1$ and $Q_{cur}(args_{cur}, H_2', r_2', v)$ holds, then $A(args, r_2' \cdot r_1, H_2' \uplus H_1, v :: S, L)$ holds.
5. The rest of the frame stack fs is safe when this activation frame returns: $safeStack(fs, H_2, r_2, args, Q, args_{top}, Q_{top})$.

Note how the $safeStack$ predicate divides up the heap and consumable resource between the activation frames on the call stack; each frame hands a piece of its heap and consumable resource off to its callees to use.

Finally, we say that a state $s = \langle r_c, H, fs \rangle$ is safe for arguments $args$, post-condition Q and maximum resource r_{max}, written $safeState(s, args, Q, r_{max})$, if:

1. there exists an r_{future} such that $r_c \cdot r_{future} \sqsubseteq r_{max}$; and also
2. r_{future} and H split into (H_1, r_1) and (H_2, r_2), i.e. $R(H_1, r_1)(H_2, r_2)(H, r_{future})$;
3. there exists at least one activation frame: $fs = f :: fs'$ and arguments $args_{cur}$ and post-condition Q_{cur}; such that
4. $safeFrame(f, H_1, r_1, args_{cur}, Q_{cur})$; and
5. $safeStack(fs, H_2, r_2, args_{cur}, Q_{cur}, args, Q)$.

The key point in the definition of $safeState$ is that the assertions of the program logic talk about the resources that will be consumed in the $future$ of the program's execution. Safety for a state says that when we combine the future resource requirements with resources that have been consumed in the past, r_c, then the total is less than the total resources r_{max} that are allowed for the execution.

Theorem 1 (Soundness)

1. *Assume that all the procedures in prg match their specifications. Then if $safeState(s, args, Q, r_{max})$ and $s \longrightarrow_{prg} s'$ then $safeState(s', args, Q, r_{max})$.*
2. *If $safeState(s, args, Q, r_{max})$ and $s \downarrow H, r, v$, then there exists an r' such that $Q(args, H, r', v)$ and $r \sqsubseteq r_{max}$.*

In the halting case in this theorem, the existentially quantified resource r' indicates the resources that the program still had available at the end of its execution. We are also guaranteed that when the program halts, the total resource that it has consumed will be less than the fixed maximum r_{max} that we have set, and moreover, by part 1 of the theorem, this bound has been observed at every step of the computation.

4   Deep Assertion Logic

In the previous section we described a program logic but remained agnostic as to the exact form of the assertions save that they must be predicates over certain domains. The shallow approach to stating makes the statement and soundness proof easier, but inhibits discussion of actual specifications and proofs in the logic. In this section we show that the logic of Bunched Implications, in its Separation Logic guise, can be used as a language for assertions in the program logic.

We defined three different types of assertion in the previous section: procedure pre- and post-conditions and intermediate assertions in methods. These all operate on heaps and consumable resources and the arguments to the current procedure, but differ in whether they talk about return values or the operand stack and local variables. To deal with these differences we assume that we have a set of terms in our logic, ranged over by $t, t_1, t_2, ...$, that at least includes logical variables and a constant *null* for representing the null reference, and also variables for representing the current procedure arguments, the return value and the operand stack and local variables as appropriate.

Formulae are built from at least the following constructors:

$$\phi ::= t_1 \bowtie t_2 \mid \phi_1 \wedge \phi_2 \mid \phi_1 \vee \phi_2 \mid \phi_1 \rightarrow \phi_2 \mid \mathsf{emp} \mid \phi_1 * \phi_2 \mid \phi_1 -\!\!* \phi_2 \mid \forall x.\phi \mid \exists x.\phi$$
$$\mid [t_1 \overset{\mathsf{f}}{\mapsto} t_2] \mid R_r \mid ...$$

Where $\bowtie \in \{=, \neq\}$. We can also add inductively defined predicates for lists and list segments as needed. The only non-standard formula with respect to Separation Logic is R_r which represents the presence of some consumable resource r. The semantics of the assertion logic is given in Figure 2 as a relation $\models$ between environments and heap/consumable resource pairs and formulae. We assume a sensible semantics $[\![\cdot]\!]_\eta$ for terms in a given environment.

As a consequence of having an ordering on consumable resources, and our chosen semantics of emp, $*$ and $-\!\!*$, our logic contains affine Bunched Implications as a sub-logic for reasoning about pure consumable resources.

Proposition 1. *If ϕ is a propositional BI formula with only R_r as atoms, then $r \models_{\mathsf{bi}} \phi$ iff $\eta, (r, h) \models \phi$.*

We have only considered a single separating connective, $\phi_1 * \phi_2$, which states that both the heap and consumable resources must be separated. Evidently, there

$$\eta, x \models \top \qquad\qquad \text{iff always}$$
$$\eta, x \models t_1 \bowtie t_2 \quad\ \text{iff } [\![t_1]\!]_\eta \bowtie [\![t_2]\!]_\eta$$
$$\eta, x \models \mathsf{emp} \qquad\ \text{iff } x = (h, r) \text{ and } h = \{\}$$
$$\eta, x \models [t_1 \overset{f}{\mapsto} t_2] \text{ iff } x = (h, r) \text{ and } h = \{([\![t_1]\!]_\eta, f) \mapsto [\![t_2]\!]_\eta\}$$
$$\eta, x \models R_{r_i} \qquad\ \text{iff } x = (h, r) \text{ and } r_i \sqsubseteq r \text{ and } h = \{\}$$
$$\eta, x \models \phi_1 \wedge \phi_2 \ \text{ iff } \eta, x \models \phi_1 \text{ and } \eta, x \models \phi_2$$
$$\eta, x \models \phi_1 \vee \phi_2 \ \text{ iff } \eta, x \models \phi_1 \text{ or } \eta, x \models \phi_2$$
$$\eta, x \models \phi_1 * \phi_2 \ \text{ iff exists } y, z. \text{ st. } Ryzx \text{ and } \eta, y \models \phi_1 \text{ and } \eta, z \models \phi_2$$
$$\eta, x \models \phi_1 \rightarrow \phi_2 \text{ iff for all } y. \text{ if } x \sqsubseteq y \text{ and } \eta, y \models \phi_1 \text{ then } \eta, y \models \phi_2$$
$$\eta, x \models \phi_1 \mathbin{-\!\!*} \phi_2 \text{ iff for all } y, z. \text{ if } Rxyz \text{ and } \eta, y \models \phi_1 \text{ then } \eta, z \models \phi_2$$
$$\eta, x \models \forall v.\phi \qquad \text{iff for all } a, \eta[v \mapsto a], x \models \phi$$
$$\eta, x \models \exists v.\phi \qquad \text{iff exists } a, \eta[v \mapsto a], x \models \phi$$

Fig. 2. Semantics of assertions

are two other possible combinations that allow sharing of heap or resources. Separation of resources, but sharing of heap:

$$\eta, x \models \phi_1 *_R \phi_2 \text{ iff } \ x = (H, r) \text{ and exists } r_1, r_2. \text{ st.}$$
$$r_1 \cdot r_2 \sqsubseteq r$$
$$\text{and } \eta, (H, r_1) \models \phi_1 \text{ and } \eta, (H, r_2) \models \phi_2$$

may be useful to specify that we have a single data structure in memory, but two resource views on it. However, we leave such investigation of alternative assertions to future work.

5   Automated Verification

In this section we describe an verification condition generation and proof search procedure for automated proving of programs against programs against specifications in our program logic, as long as procedures have been annotated with loop invariants. The restricted subset of separation logic that we use in this section is similar to the subset used by Berdine et al [3], though instead of performing a forwards analysis of the program, we generate verification conditions by backwards analysis and then attempt to solve them using proof search. As we demonstrate below, the proof search procedure is mainly guided by the structure of the program and the shape of the data structures that it manipulates. The resource annotations that are required can be inferred by linear programming.

5.1   Restricted Assertion Logic

Following Berdine et al, the restricted subset of the assertion logic that we use segregates assertions into pure data, heap and consumable resource sections.

Data: $P := t_1 = t_2 \mid t_1 \neq t_2 \mid \top$

Heap: $X := [t_1 \overset{f}{\mapsto} t_2] \mid \mathsf{lseg}(\Theta, t_1, t_2) \mid \mathsf{emp}$

Resource: $R := R_r \mid \top$

The terms that we allow in the data and heap assertions are either variables, or the constant null. The list segment predicate that we use here is defined inductively as:

$$\mathsf{lseg}(\Theta, x, y) \equiv (x = y \land \mathsf{emp}) \lor (\exists z, z'. \ [x \overset{\mathsf{data}}{\mapsto} z] * [x \overset{\mathsf{next}}{\mapsto} z'] * \Theta * \mathsf{lseg}(\Theta, z', y))$$

We restrict the pre- and post-conditions of each procedure to be of the form $\bigvee_i (\Pi_i \land (\Sigma_i * \Theta_i))$ and we use S to range over such formulae. The three components of each disjunct are lists of data, heap and resource assertions, with interpretations as in the following table.

Data: $\Pi := P_1, ..., P_n$ $(P_1 \land ... \land P_n)$
Heap: $\Sigma := X_1, ..., X_n$ $(X_1 * ... * X_n)$
Resource: $\Theta := R_1, ..., R_n$ $(R_1 * ... * R_n)$

Note that, due to the presence of resource assertions in the lseg predicate, heap assertions may also describe consumable resources, even if the resource part of a disjunct is empty.

Finally, we have the set of goal formulae that the verification condition generator will produce and the proof search will solve.

$$G := S * G \mid S \twoheadrightarrow G \mid S \mid G_1 \land G_2 \mid P \to G \mid \forall x.G \mid \exists x.G$$

Note that we only allow implications ($\to$ and $\twoheadrightarrow$) to appear in positive positions. This means that we can interpret them in our proof search as adding extra information to the context.

5.2   Verification Condition Generation

Verification condition generation is performed for each procedure individually by computing weakest preconditions for each instruction, working backwards from the last instruction in the method. To resolve loops, we require that the targets of all backwards jumps have been annotated with loop invariants S that are of the same form as the pre- and post-condition formulae from the previous section. We omit the rules that we use for weakest precondition generation since they are very similar to the rules for the shallowly embedded logic in Figure 1. The verification condition generator will always produce a VC for the required entailment of the computed pre-condition of the first instruction and the procedure's pre-condition, plus a VC for each annotated instruction, being the entailment between the annotation and the computed precondition. All VCs will have a formula of the form $\bigvee_i (\Pi_i \land (\Sigma_i * \Theta_i))$ as the antecedent and a goal formula as the conclusion.

5.3   Proof Search

The output of the verification condition generation phase is a collection of problems of the form $\Pi|\Sigma|\Theta \vdash G$. We define a proof search procedure by a set of rules shown in Figures 3, 4, 6 and 5. The key idea here is to use the I/O model of proof search as defined for intuitionistic linear logic by Cervesato, Hodas and Pfenning [5], and also the use of heuristic rules for unfolding the inductive list segment predicate.

As well as the main proof search judgement $\Pi|\Sigma|\Theta \vdash G$, we make use of several auxiliary judgements:

$$\begin{array}{ll} \Pi|\Sigma|\Theta \vdash \Sigma_1\backslash\Sigma_2, \Theta' & \text{Heap assertion matching} \\ \Theta \vdash \Theta_1\backslash\Theta_2 & \text{Resource matching} \\ \Pi \vdash \bot & \text{Contradiction spotting} \\ \Pi \vdash \Pi' & \text{Data entailment} \end{array}$$

The backslash notation used in these rules follows the I/O model of Cervesato et al, where in the judgement $\Theta \vdash \Theta_1\backslash\Theta_2$, the proof context Θ denotes the facts used as input and Θ_2 denotes the facts that are left over (the output) from proving Θ_1. A similar interpretation is used for the heap assertion matching judgement. We do not define the data entailment or contradiction spotting judgement explicitly here; we intend that these judgements satisfy the basic axioms of equalities and disequalities.

The rules in Figure 3 are the goal driven search rules. There is an individual rule for each possible kind of goal formula. The first two rules are matching rules that match a formula S against the context, altering the context to remove the heap and resource assertions that S requires, as dictated by the semantics of the assertion logic. We must search for a disjunct i that matches the current context. There may be multiple such i, and in this case the search may have to backtrack. When the goal is a formula S, then we check that the left-over heap is empty, in order to detect memory leaks.

$$\text{exists } i. \quad \frac{\Pi|\Sigma|\Theta \vdash \Sigma_i\backslash\Sigma', \Theta' \quad \Pi \vdash \Pi_i \quad \Theta' \vdash \Theta_i\backslash\Theta'' \quad \Pi|\Sigma'|\Theta'' \vdash G}{\Pi|\Sigma|\Theta \vdash \bigvee_i (\Pi_i \wedge (\Sigma_i * \Theta_i)) * G}$$

$$\text{exists } i. \quad \frac{\Pi|\Sigma|\Theta \vdash \Sigma_i\backslash\text{emp}, \Theta' \quad \Pi \vdash \Pi_i \quad \Theta' \vdash \Theta_i\backslash\Theta''}{\Pi|\Sigma|\Theta \vdash \bigvee_i (\Pi_i \wedge (\Sigma_i * \Theta_i))}$$

$$\text{forall } i. \quad \frac{\Pi, \Pi_i|\Sigma, \Sigma_i|\Theta, \Theta_i \vdash G}{\Pi|\Sigma|\Theta \vdash \bigvee_i (\Pi_i \wedge (\Sigma_i * \Theta_i)) \mathbin{-\!\!*} G} \qquad \frac{\Pi, P|\Sigma|\Theta \vdash G}{\Pi|\Sigma|\Theta \vdash P \rightarrow G}$$

$$\frac{\Pi|\Sigma|\Theta \vdash G_1 \quad \Pi|\Sigma|\Theta \vdash G_2}{\Pi|\Sigma|\Theta \vdash G_1 \wedge G_2} \qquad \frac{\Pi|\Sigma|\Theta \vdash G \quad x \notin \mathsf{fv}(\Pi) \cup \mathsf{fv}(\Sigma)}{\Pi|\Sigma|\Theta \vdash \forall x.G}$$

$$\frac{\Pi|\Sigma|\Theta \vdash G[t/x]}{\Pi|\Sigma|\Theta \vdash \exists x.G}$$

Fig. 3. Goal Driven Search Rules

Heap Matching Rules:

$$\frac{}{\Pi|\Sigma|\Theta \vdash \mathsf{emp}\backslash\Sigma,\Theta} \qquad \frac{\Pi \vdash t_1 = t_1' \qquad \Pi \vdash t_2 = t_2'}{\Pi|\Sigma,[t_1 \overset{\mathsf{f}}{\mapsto} t_2]|\Theta \vdash [t_1' \overset{\mathsf{f}}{\mapsto} t_2']\backslash\Sigma,\Theta}$$

$$\frac{\Pi|\Sigma|\Theta \vdash \Sigma_1\backslash\Sigma',\Theta' \qquad \Pi|\Sigma'|\Theta' \vdash \Sigma_2\backslash\Sigma'',\Theta''}{\Pi|\Sigma|\Theta \vdash \Sigma_1 * \Sigma_2\backslash\Sigma'',\Theta''} \qquad \frac{\Pi \vdash t_1 = t_2}{\Pi|\Sigma|\Theta \vdash \mathsf{lseg}(\Theta_l,t_1,t_2)\backslash\Sigma,\Theta}$$

$$\frac{\Pi \vdash t_1 = t_1' \qquad \Theta \vdash \Theta_l\backslash\Theta' \qquad \Pi|\Sigma|\Theta' \vdash \mathsf{lseg}(\Theta_l,t_n,t_2)\backslash\Sigma',\Theta''}{\Pi|\Sigma,[t_1 \overset{\mathsf{n}}{\mapsto} t_n],[t_1 \overset{\mathsf{d}}{\mapsto} t_d]|\Theta \vdash \mathsf{lseg}(\Theta_l,t_1',t_2)\backslash\Sigma',\Theta''}$$

$$\frac{\Pi \vdash t_1' = t_1 \qquad \Pi|\Sigma|\Theta \vdash \mathsf{lseg}(\Theta_l,t_2,t_3)\backslash\Sigma',\Theta'}{\Pi|\Sigma,\mathsf{lseg}(\Theta_l,t_1,t_2)|\Theta \vdash \mathsf{lseg}(\Theta_l,t_1',t_3)\backslash\Sigma',\Theta'}$$

Resource Matching Rules:

$$\frac{}{\Theta,R^\rho \vdash R^\rho\backslash\Theta} \qquad \frac{}{\Theta \vdash \top\backslash\Theta} \qquad \frac{\Theta \vdash \Theta_1\backslash\Theta' \qquad \Theta' \vdash \Theta_2\backslash\Theta''}{\Theta \vdash \Theta_1 * \Theta_2\backslash\Theta''}$$

Fig. 4. Matching Rules

The matching rules make use of the heap and resource matching judgements defined in Figure 4. The heap matching judgements take a data, heap and resource context and attempt to match a list of heap assertions against them, returning the left over heap and resource contexts. The first three rules are straightforward: the empty heap assertion is always matchable, points-to relations are looked up in the context directly and pairs of heap assertions are split, threading the contexts through. For the list segment rules, there are three cases. Either the two pointers involved in the list are equal, in which case we are immediately done; or we have a single list cell in the context that matches the start pointer of the predicate we are trying to satisfy, and we have the required resources for an element of this list, so we can reduce the goal by one step; or we have a whole list segment in the context and we can reduce the goal accordingly. The resource matching rules are straightforward.

The final two sets of rules operate on the proof search context . The first set, shown in Figure 5, describe how information flows from the heap part of the context to the data part. If we know that two variables both have a points-to relation involving a field f, then we know that these locations must not be equal. Similarly, if we know that a variable does point to something, then it cannot be null. If any contradictions are found using these rules, then the proof search can terminate immediately for the current goal. This is provided for by the first rule in Figure 5.

The final set of rules performs heuristic unfolding of the inductive lseg predicate. These rules are shown in Figure 6. These rules take information from the data context and use it to unfold lseg predicates that occur in the heap context. The first rule is triggered when the proof search learns that there is a list

$$\frac{\Pi \vdash \bot}{\Pi|\Sigma|\Theta \vdash G}$$

$$\frac{\Sigma = [t_1 \overset{f}{\mapsto} t], [t_2 \overset{f}{\mapsto} t'], \Sigma' \qquad \Pi, t_1 \neq t_2|\Sigma|\Theta \vdash G}{\Pi|\Sigma|\Theta \vdash G}$$

$$\frac{\Sigma = [t \overset{f}{\mapsto} t'], \Sigma' \qquad \Pi, t \neq \mathsf{null}|\Sigma|\Theta \vdash G}{\Pi|\Sigma|\Theta \vdash G}$$

Fig. 5. Contradiction Flushing

$$\frac{\Pi \vdash t_1 \neq \mathsf{null}}{\Pi, t_1 = t_2|\Sigma|\Theta \vdash G \qquad \Pi|\Sigma, [t_1 \overset{n}{\mapsto} x], [t_1 \overset{d}{\mapsto} y], \mathsf{lseg}(R, x, t_2)|\Theta, R \vdash G}{\Pi|\Sigma, \mathsf{lseg}(R, t_1, t_2)|\Theta \vdash G}$$

$$\frac{\Pi \vdash t_1 = \mathsf{null} \qquad \Pi, t_2 = \mathsf{null}|\Sigma|\Theta \vdash G}{\Pi|\Sigma, \mathsf{lseg}(R, t_1, t_2)|\Theta \vdash G} \qquad \frac{\Pi \vdash t_1 = t_2 \qquad \Pi|\Sigma|\Theta \vdash G}{\Pi|\Sigma, \mathsf{lseg}(R, t_1, t_2)|\Theta \vdash G}$$

$$\frac{\Pi \vdash t_1 \neq t_2 \qquad \Pi|\Sigma, [t_1 \overset{n}{\mapsto} x], [t_1 \overset{d}{\mapsto} y], \mathsf{lseg}(R, x, t_2)|\Theta, R \vdash G}{\Pi|\Sigma, \mathsf{lseg}(R, t_1, t_2)|\Theta \vdash G}$$

Fig. 6. List Unfolding Rules

segment where the head pointer of the list is not equal to null. In this case, two proof search goals are produced, one for the case that the list segment is empty and one for when it isn't. The other rules are similar; taking information from the data context and using it to refine the heap context.

The proof search strategy that we employ works by first saturating the context by repeatedly applying the rules in Figures 5 and 6 to move information from the data context into the heap context and vice versa. This process terminates because there are a finite number of points-to relations and list segment predicates to generate rule applications, and when new predicates are introduced via list segment unfolding they either do not trigger any new inequalities or are over fresh variables about which nothing is yet known. Once the context is fully saturated, the proof search reduces the goal by using the goal-driven search rules and the process begins again.

Theorem 2. *The proof search procedure is sound and terminating.*

5.4 Integration with Linear Programming

A key feature of Hofmann and Jost's system for inference of resource bounds of functional programs [9] is the use of linear programming. In this section, we sketch how to extend the procedure of the previous section with linear constraint generation. Using this technique, as long as the resource bounds are linear, we can simply state our specifications in terms of the shapes of the data structures that the program manipulates and infer the necessary resource annotations.

For simplicity, we assume that we are dealing with resources that are positive rational numbers, so we can replace the resource contexts Θ in the proof search procedure of the previous section with linear expressions over the rationals. The resource matching judgement is altered to take and output linear expressions over rationals, while producing linear constraints over the variables mentioned in the resource expression, and we have the single rule:

$$e_1 \vdash e_2 \backslash e_1 - e_2, e_2 \leq e_1$$

The proof search judgement is altered to generate a set of constraints over the variables mentioned in the resource expression $e: \Pi|\Sigma|e \vdash G\backslash\mathcal{C}$. The goal driven search rules are then modified to accumulate the generated constraints. The heap matching rules are similarly modified.

Given a collection of verification conditions and a successful proof search over them that has generated a set of linear constraints, we input these into a linear solver, along with the constraint that every variable is positive and an objective function that attempts to minimise variables appearing in the pre-condition.

6   Example: Frying Pan List Reversal

We demonstrate the use of the proof search procedure coupled with linear constraint generation to the standard imperative in-place list reversal algorithm on lists with cyclic tails (also known as "frying pan" lists). This example was used by Brotherston, Bornat and Calcagno [4] to demonstrate the use of cyclic proofs to prove program termination. Here we show how our amortised resource logic can be used to infer bounds on the complexity of this procedure.

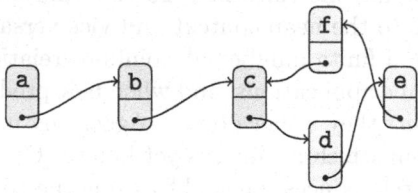

The "handle" of the structure consists of the nodes a, b, c and the "pan" consists of the nodes d, e and f. When the in-place list-reversal procedure is run upon a structure of this shape, it will proceed up the handle, reversing it, around the pan, reversing it, and then back down the handle, restoring it to its original order. For the purposes of this example, we assume that it takes one element of resource to handle the reversal of one node. Following Brotherston, Bornat and Calcagno, we can specify a cyclic list in Separation Logic by the following formula, where v_0 points to the head of the list and v_1 points to the join between the handle and the pan.

$$\exists k.\mathsf{lseg}(x_1, v_0, v_1) * [v_1 \overset{\mathsf{next}}{\mapsto} k] * \mathsf{lseg}(x_2, k, v_1) * R^{x_3}$$

We have annotated the list segments involved with resource annotation variables x_1 and x_2 that we will instantiate using linear programming. The predicate R^{x_3} denotes any extra resource we may require. Similarly, we have annotated the required loop invariant (adapted from Brotherston et al):

$$(\exists k.\mathsf{lseg}(a_1, l_0, v_1) * \mathsf{lseg}(a_2, l_1, \mathtt{null}) * [v_1 \overset{\mathsf{next}}{\mapsto} k] * \mathsf{lseg}(a_3, k, v_1) * R^{a_4})$$
$$\vee (\exists k.\mathsf{lseg}(b_1, k, \mathtt{null}) * [j \overset{\mathsf{next}}{\mapsto} k] * \mathsf{lseg}(b_2, l_0, v_1) * \mathsf{lseg}(b_3, l_1, j) * R^{b_4})$$
$$\vee (\exists k.\mathsf{lseg}(c_1, l_0, \mathtt{null}) * \mathsf{lseg}(c_2, l_1, v_1) * [v_1 \overset{\mathsf{next}}{\mapsto} k] * \mathsf{lseg}(c_3, k, v_1) * R^{c_4})$$

Each disjunct of the loop invariant corresponds to a different phase of the procedure's progress. Brotherston et al note that it is possible to infer the shape part of this loop invariant using current Separation Logic tools. Here, we are adding the ability to infer resource bounds. Running our tool on this example produces the following instantiation of the variables:

Pre-condition	$x_1 = 2$	$x_2 = 1$	$x_3 = 2$	
Loop invariant, phase 1	$a_1 = 2$	$a_2 = 1$	$a_3 = 1$	$a_4 = 2$
Loop invariant, phase 2	$b_1 = 1$	$b_2 = 1$	$b_3 = 0$	$b_4 = 1$
Loop invariant, phase 3	$c_1 = 1$	$c_2 = 0$	$c_3 = 0$	$c_4 = 0$
Post-condition	$x_1' = 0$	$x_2' = 0$	$x_3' = 0$	

Pictorially, the inference has associated the following amount of resource with each part of the input structure:

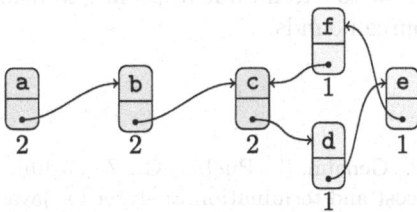

Each node of the handle has 2 associated elements of resource, to handle the two passes of the handle that the procedure takes, while the pan has one element of resource for each node. The inferred annotations for the loop invariant track how the resources on each node are consumed by the procedure, gradually all reducing to zero. Since we have added a consume instruction to be executed every time the procedure starts a loop, the resource inference process has also verified the termination of this procedure, and given us a bound on the number of times the loop will execute in terms of the shape of the input.

7   Conclusions

The main limitation of our proof search procedure is that it only supports the statement and inference of bounds that are linear in the size of lists that are mentioned in a procedure's precondition. This is a limitation shared with the work of Hofmann and Jost [9]. We note that this is not a limitation of the program logic that we have presented, only of the automated verification procedure that we have layered on top. We have demonstrated that the use of mixed shape and resource assertions can simplify the complexity of specifications that talk about resources, and this should extend to extensions of the proof search procedure, or to interactive systems based on this program logic. The resource aware program logic of Aspinall et al [2] also uses the same layering: a general program logic for resources (which is proved complete in their case) is used as a base for a specialised logic for reasoning about the output of the Hofmann-Jost system.

A possible direction for future work is to consider different assertion logics and their expressiveness in terms of the magnitude of resources they can express. We conjecture that the deep assertion logic we have presented here, extended with the lseg predicate can express resources linear in the size of the heap. It would be interesting to consider more expressive logics and evaluate them from the point of view of implicit computational complexity; the amount of resource that one can express in an assertion dictates the amount of resource that is available for the future execution of the program.

Other resource inference procedures that are able to deal with non-linear bounds include those of Chin et al [6,7], Albert et al [1] and Gulwani et al [8]. When dealing with heap-based data structures, all of these techniques use a method of attaching size information to assertions about data structures. As we demonstrated in Section 2, this can lead to additional unwanted complexity in specifications. However, all of these techniques deal with numerically bounded loops better than our current prototype automated procedure can, and we are currently investigating how to extend our approach to deal with non-linear and numerically-driven resource bounds.

References

1. Albert, E., Arenas, P., Genaim, S., Puebla, G., Zanardini, D.: Costa: Design and implementation of a cost and termination analyzer for java bytecode. In: de Boer, F.S., Bonsangue, M.M., Graf, S., de Roever, W.-P. (eds.) FMCO 2007. LNCS, vol. 5382, pp. 113–132. Springer, Heidelberg (2008)
2. Aspinall, D., Beringer, L., Hofmann, M., Loidl, H.-W., Momigliano, A.: A program logic for resources. Theor. Comput. Sci. 389(3), 411–445 (2007)
3. Berdine, J., Calcagno, C., O'Hearn, P.W.: Symbolic execution with separation logic. In: Yi, K. (ed.) APLAS 2005. LNCS, vol. 3780, pp. 52–68. Springer, Heidelberg (2005)
4. Brotherston, J., Bornat, R., Calcagno, C.: Cyclic proofs of program termination in separation logic. In: Necula, G.C., Wadler, P. (eds.) POPL, pp. 101–112. ACM, New York (2008)
5. Cervesato, I., Hodas, J.S., Pfenning, F.: Efficient resource management for linear logic proof search. Theor. Comput. Sci. 232(1-2), 133–163 (2000)
6. Chin, W.-N., Nguyen, H.H., Popeea, C., Qin, S.: Analysing memory resource bounds for low-level programs. In: Jones, R., Blackburn, S.M. (eds.) ISMM, pp. 151–160. ACM, New York (2008)

7. Chin, W.-N., Nguyen, H.H., Qin, S., Rinard, M.C.: Memory usage verification for oo programs. In: Hankin, C., Siveroni, I. (eds.) SAS 2005. LNCS, vol. 3672, pp. 70–86. Springer, Heidelberg (2005)
8. Gulwani, S., Mehra, K.K., Chilimbi, T.M.: Speed: precise and efficient static estimation of program computational complexity. In: Shao, Z., Pierce, B.C. (eds.) POPL, pp. 127–139. ACM, New York (2009)
9. Hofmann, M., Jost, S.: Static prediction of heap space usage for first-order functional programs. In: POPL, pp. 185–197 (2003)
10. Hofmann, M., Jost, S.: Type-based amortised heap-space analysis. In: Sestoft, P. (ed.) ESOP 2006. LNCS, vol. 3924, pp. 22–37. Springer, Heidelberg (2006)
11. Hofmann, M., Rodriguez, D.: Efficient type-checking for amortised heap-space analysis. In: Grädel, E., Kahle, R. (eds.) CSL 2009. LNCS, vol. 5771, pp. 317–331. Springer, Heidelberg (2009)
12. Ishtiaq, S., O'Hearn, P.W.: Bi as an assertion language for mutable data structures. In: Proceedings of the 28th Symposium on Principles of Programming Languages, January 2001, pp. 14–26 (2001)
13. Restall, G.: An Introduction to Substructural Logics. Routledge (2000)
14. Reynolds, J.C.: Separation logic: A logic for shared mutable data structures. In: Proceedings of 17th Annual IEEE Symposium on Logic in Computer Science (2002)
15. Tarjan, R.E.: Amortized computational complexity. SIAM Journal on Algebraic and Discrete Methods 6(2), 306–318 (1985)

A PolyTime Functional Language from Light Linear Logic*

Patrick Baillot[1], Marco Gaboardi[2], and Virgile Mogbil[3]

[1] LIP - UMR 5668 CNRS ENS-Lyon UCBL INRIA - Université de Lyon
patrick.baillot@ens-lyon.fr
[2] Dipartimento di Informatica, Università degli studi di Torino
gaboardi@di.unito.it
[3] LIPN - UMR 7030, CNRS - Université Paris 13
virgile.mogbil@lipn.univ-paris13.fr

Abstract. We introduce a typed functional programming language LPL (acronym for Light linear Programming Language) in which all valid programs run in polynomial time, and which is complete for polynomial time functions. LPL is based on lambda-calculus, with constructors for algebraic data-types, pattern matching and recursive definitions, and thus allows for a natural programming style. The validity of LPL programs is checked through typing and a syntactic criterion on recursive definitions. The higher order type system is designed from the ideas of Light linear logic: stratification, to control recursive calls, and weak exponential connectives §, !, to control duplication of arguments.

1 Introduction

Implicit computational complexity (ICC). This line of research aims at characterizing complexity classes not by external measuring conditions on a machine model, but instead by investigating restrictions on programming languages or calculi which imply a complexity bound. So for instance characterizing the class PTIME in such a framework means that all the programs of the framework considered can be evaluated in polynomial time (*soundness*), and that conversely all polynomial time *functions* can be represented by a program of the framework (*extensional completeness*).

The initial motivation was to provide new characterizations of complexity classes of functions to bring some insight on their nature [1,2,3,4]. In a second step, e.g. [5,6], the issue was raised of using these techniques to design some ways of statically verifying the complexity of concrete programs. Some efforts in this direction have been done also following other approaches, e.g. [7,8,9]. For this point of view it is quite convenient to consider a general programming language or calculus, and to state the ICC condition as a *criterion* on programs, which can be checked statically, and which ensures on the validated programs a time or space complexity bound. In this respect the previous extensional completeness is of limited interest, and one is interested in designing criteria which are *intensionally expressive*, that is to say which validate as many interesting programs as possible. Note that for a Turing-complete language the class

---

* Partially supported by project ANR-08-BLANC-0211-01 "COMPLICE".

A.D. Gordon (Ed.): ESOP 2010, LNCS 6012, pp. 104–124, 2010.

of PTIME programs is non recursively enumerable, and so an intensionally complete criterion would not be decidable. Actually we think that three aspects should be taken into consideration for discussing intensional expressivity:

1. what are the algorithmic schemes that can be validated by the criterion,
2. what are the features of the programming language: e.g. higher-order functional language, polymorphism, exceptions handling . . .
3. how effective is the criterion: what is the complexity of the corresponding decision problem.

Results and methodology. The main contribution of the present work is the definition of LPL (acronym for Light linear Programming Language), a typed functional programming language inspired by Light linear logic satisfying an ICC criterion ensuring a PTIME bound. LPL improves with respect to previous PTIME linear logic inspired languages in aspects 1 and 2 above, since it combines the advantages of a user-friendly and expressive language and of modular programming. The distinguishing feature of LPL is the combination of

- higher-order types by means of a typed λ-calculus,
- pattern-matching and recursive definitions by means of a LetRec construction,
- a syntactic restriction avoiding intrinsically exponential recursive definitions and a light type system ensuring duplication control,

in such a way that all valid typed programs run in polynomial time, and all polynomial time functions can be programmed by valid typed programs.

A difficulty in dealing with λ-calculus and recursion is that we can easily combine apparently harmless terms to obtain exponential time programs like the following one

$$\lambda x.x(\lambda y. \text{mul } 2 \text{ y})1$$

where mul is the usual recursive definition for multiplication. Such a term is apparently harmless, but for each Church numeral $\underline{n} = \lambda s.\lambda z.s^n z$ this program returns the (standard) numeral 2^n. In order to prevent this kind of programs, to achieve polynomial time soundness, a strict control over both the numbers of recursive calls and beta-reduction steps is needed. Moreover, the extension to higher order in the context of polynomial time bounded computations is not trivial. Consider the classical foldr higher order function; its unrestricted use leads to exponential time programs. E.g. let ListOf2 be a program that given a natural number n returns a list of 2 of length n. Then, the following program is exponential in its argument:

$$\lambda x.\text{foldr mul } 1 \text{ (ListOf2 x)}$$

For these reasons, besides the syntactic restriction avoiding intrinsically exponential recursive definitions, we impose a strict typing discipline inspired by the ideas of Light linear logic. In λ-calculus, Light linear logic allows to bound the number of beta-steps, using weak exponential connectives ! and § in order to control duplication of arguments and term stratification in order to control the size. The syntactic restriction of function definitions limits the number of recursive steps for *one* function call. But this is not enough since function calls appear at run time and the size of values can increase during the computation. Our type system addresses these issues, and a key point for that is the typing rule for recursive definition. In particular, a function of type $\mathbb{N} \multimap \mathbb{N}$ can increase the size of its input by at most a constant, while a function of type $\mathbb{N} \multimap \S\mathbb{N}$ can increase it by a (fixed) polynomial bound. For a recursive definition of the shape $f\ t = M\{f\ t'\}$, the typing rule ensures that the context M does not *increase the size too much*, and it types the function f accordingly. In this way the type system allows to bound both the number of beta-steps and the size of values, and together with the syntactic restriction this results in a PTIME bound on execution.

The typing restrictions on higher order functions are not too severe. Indeed, we can write in a natural way some interesting programs using higher order functions without exponential blow up. For instance consider again the foldr function, we can type a term representing one of its classical uses as

$$\lambda x.\text{foldr add 0 } x$$

About the methodology we use, we stress that we do not aim at proving the properties of LPL by encoding it into Light linear logic. Instead, we take inspiration from it and we adapt the *abstract* structure of its PTIME soundness proof to our new setting. Moreover, our guideline is to follow a gradual approach: we propose here a strict criterion, that has the advantage of handling naturally higher-order. We hope that once this step has been established we might study how the criterion can be relaxed in various ways.

Indeed, the choice of using a *combined criterion*, i.e. a first condition ensuring termination, and a second one dealing with controlling the size, will be an advantage for future works. In particular, by relaxing either one of the two conditions one can explore generalizations, as well as different criteria to characterize other complexity classes. Finally we think that the ICC criterion we give can be effectively checked since this is the case for λ-calculus [10], but we leave the development of this point for future work.

Related works. *Higher-order calculi: linear logic and linear type systems.* Linear logic [11] was introduced to control in proof theory the operations of duplication and erasing, thanks to specific modalities !, ?. Through the proofs-as-programs correspondence it provided a way to analyze typed λ-calculus. The idea of designing alternative *weak versions* of the modalities implying a PTIME bound on normalization was proposed in [12] and led to *Light Linear Logic* (LLL) in [4] and *Soft Linear Logic* (SLL) in [13]. Starting from the principles underlying these logics different PTIME term languages have been proposed [14,15]. In a second step [16] type systems as criteria for λ-calculus were designed out of these logics, like DLAL [17] and STA [18]. This approach completely fits in the proofs-as-programs paradigm, thereby offering some advantages from the programming language point of view (point 2 above): it encompasses higher-order and polymorphism. The drawback is that data are represented in λ-calculus and so one is handling encodings of data-types analogous to Church integers. Moreover the kinds of algorithms one can represent is very limited (point 1). However testing the criterion can be done efficiently (point 3) thanks to some polynomial time type inference algorithms [10,19].

In [20] the authors propose a language for PTIME extending to higher-order the characterizations based on *ramification* [1,2]. The language is a *ramified* variant of Gödel's system T where higher-order arguments cannot be duplicated, which is quite a strong restriction. Moreover, the system T style does not make it as easy to program in this system as one would like. Another characterization of PTIME by means of a restriction of System T in a linear setting has been studied in [21,22].

In [5], Hofmann proposed a typed λ-calculus with recursor (essentially a variant of system T), LFPL, overcoming the problems of ramification, which allows to represent *non-size-increasing* programs and enjoys a PTIME bound. This improves on point 1 by allowing to represent more algorithms and by featuring higher-order types. However, the restriction on higher-order arguments similar to the one in [20] and the system T programming style make it quite far from ordinary functional languages.

First-order calculi and interpretations. Starting from works on *ramification* [1,2], Marion and collaborators have generalized them progressively by first replacing primitive recursion by termination orderings [23], and then ramification by notions of *quasi-interpretation* [6,24,25] and *sup-interpretation* [26,27] on a first-order functional language with recursion and pattern-matching. These latter notions are semantic, inspired from polynomial interpretations, and essentially statically provide a bound on the size of the values computed during the evaluation. If a program admits both a termination ordering *and* a quasi-interpretation or sup-interpretation of a certain shape, then it admits a complexity bound. The main benefit of this method is that more algorithms are validated (point 1) than in the ramification-based frameworks. An advantage of our present contribution however is that it handles higher-order and that type checking is easier than checking of quasi-interpretations .

Outline. We introduce in Section 2 the language LPL, its type system and the syntactic criterion required on programs, and then provide some programming examples. In Section 3 we define an extended language, eLPL, where a stratification is explicit in the term syntax, and which is meant for translating and executing LPL typed programs. We then show that all PTIME functions can be computed in LPL (Section 4). Finally, Section 5 establishes our main result, that all LPL programs can be executed in polynomial time w.r.t. the size of the input.

2 LPL

We introduce the language LPL, an extension of λ-calculus with constructors for algebraic data types, pattern matching and recursive function definitions. In order to limit the computational complexity of programs we need to impose some restrictions. To achieve polynomial time properties two key ingredients are used: a syntactic criterion and a type system.

The syntactic criterion imposes restrictions to recursive schemes in order to avoid the ones which are intrinsically exponential. The type system allows through a stratification over terms to avoid the dangerous nesting of recursive definition.

2.1 The Syntax

Let the denumerable sets Var, PVar, Cst and Fct be respectively a set of *variables*, a set of *pattern variables*, a set of *constructors* and a set of *function symbols*. Each constructor $c \in$ Cst and each function symbol $F \in$ Fct has an *arity* $n \geq 0$: the number of arguments that it expects. In particular a constructor c of arity 0 is a *base constant*.

The program syntax is given in Table 1 where $x \in$ Var, $X \in$ PVar, $c \in$ Cst and $F \in$ Fct. Among function symbols we distinguish a subset of symbols which we will call

Table 1. LPL term language definition

p ::= M | LetRec d_F in p	program definition
v ::= c $v_1 \cdots v_n$	value definition
t ::= X | c $t_1 \ldots t_n$	pattern definition
d_F ::= F $t_1 \ldots t_n$ = N | d_F, d_F	function definition
M, N ::= x | c $M_1 \ldots M_n$ | X | F $M_1 \ldots M_n$ | λx.M | MM	term definition

basic functions and denote as $\underline{F}, \underline{G}, \ldots$ We use the symbol $\varkappa$ to denote either a variable or a pattern variable. Observe that values and patterns are subsets of terms.

The size |M| of a term M is the number of symbols occurring in it. The size of patterns and programs are defined similarly. We denote by $n_o(\varkappa, M)$ the number of occurrences of $\varkappa$ in M. Let $s \in$ Cst $\cup$ Fct be a symbol of arity n, then we will often write $s(M_1, \ldots, M_n)$ or $s(\overrightarrow{M})$ instead of $s\ M_1 \ldots M_n$.

The set Cst includes the usual constructors s of arity one and the base constant 0 for natural numbers, the constructor : of arity two and the base constant nil for lists of natural numbers, node of arity three and the base constant ϵ for binary trees with node natural numbers.

A *function definition* d_F for the function symbol F of arity n is a sequence of *definition cases* of the shape $F(t_1, \cdots, t_n) = N$ where F is applied to *patterns* $t_1, \ldots, t_n$, the free variables of N are a subset of the free variables of $t_1, \ldots, t_n$ (thus pattern variables), and N is normal for the reduction (which will be given in Def. 4). Besides in a definition case:

1. if F is a basic function $\underline{G}$, then N does not contain any function symbol,
2. if F is not a basic function, then (i) N does not contain any basic function symbol, and (ii) every occurrence of F in N appears in subterms of the form $F(t_1^1, \ldots, t_n^1)$, $\ldots, F(t_1^k, \ldots, t_n^k)$; these subterms are called the *recursive calls* of F in N.

Patterns are *linear* in the sense that a pattern variable X cannot appear several times in a given pattern. Moreover we assume that patterns $t_1, \ldots, t_n$ in the l.h.s. of a definition case have distinct sets of pattern variables. The notion of sub-term is adapted to patterns: we denote by $t' \prec t$ the fact that t' is a strict sub-pattern of t. As usual $\preceq$ is the reflexive closure of $\prec$. Patterns t and t' such that $t \not\preceq t'$ and $t' \not\preceq t$ are *incomparable*.

A *program* is a term M without free pattern variables preceded by a sequence of function definitions $d_{F_1}, \ldots, d_{F_n}$ defining all the function symbols occurring in M. We ask that every function definition d_{F_i} uses only the function symbols $F_1, \ldots, F_i$. We write a program of the shape LetRec d_{F_1} in $\cdots$ LetRec d_{F_n} in M simply as LetRec $d_{F_1}, \ldots, d_{F_n}$ in M. As usual we consider programs up to renaming of bound variables.

A *substitution* σ is a mapping replacing variables by terms. This is used to define the notion of matching which is essential for the reduction mechanism of our language.

Let t be a pattern. We say the term M *matches t* if and only if there exists a substitution σ such that $M = \sigma(t)$. Analogously, given a definition case $F(t_1, \ldots, t_n) = N$, the term M *matches* it if and only if there exists a substitution σ such that $M = F(\sigma(\overrightarrow{t}))$.

We say a sequence $d_1, \ldots, d_n$ of function definition cases for the function symbol F of arity n is *exhaustive* if for every sequence of values $V_1, \ldots, V_n$ such that $F(\overrightarrow{V})$ is typable, there exists a unique $1 \leq i \leq n$ such that $F(\overrightarrow{V})$ matches the l.h.s. of d_i.

A program p is *well defined* if and only if all the function definitions in it are exhaustive.

2.2 Syntactic Criterion

As we have already stressed, the first ingredient to ensure the intended complexity properties for LPL programs is a *syntactic criterion*.

Consider a definition case $F(t_1, \ldots, t_n) = M$. We say t is *recursive* if it contains some recursive calls $F(t_1^1, \ldots, t_n^1), \ldots, F(t_1^m, \ldots, t_n^m)$ $(m \geq 1)$ in M, and *base* otherwise. Note that basic functions by definition only have base definition cases. We now need the following notion of safe definition cases.

Definition 1 (Safe definition case). *Let* $F(t_1, \ldots, t_n) = M$ *be a definition case. It is safe if for every recursive call* $F(t_1^1, \ldots, t_n^1), \ldots, F(t_1^m, \ldots, t_n^m)$ *of F in M, we have:*

(i) $\forall k, \forall i : t_i^k \preceq t_i,$ *(ii)* $\forall k, \exists j : t_j^k \prec t_j,$ *(iii)* $\forall j, \forall k \neq l, t_j^k \npreceq t_j^l$ *and* $t_j^l \npreceq t_j^k.$

Note that this condition is trivially satisfied by base definition cases, and thus by basic functions. The syntactic criterion for LPL program can now be defined:

Definition 2 (Syntactic Criterion). *An* LPL *program* M *satisfies the* syntactic criterion *if and only if every definition case in it is safe.*

We now state some definitions and properties that will be useful in the sequel.

Definition 3 (Matching argument). *Let* $F(t_1, \ldots, t_n) = M$ *be a definition case. Every position of index j such that* t_j *is not a pattern variable X is a* matching position.

The set $\mathcal{R}(F)$ *is the set of all positions j for which there exists a definition case of F where j is in matching position. The* matching arguments *of a function symbol F are the arguments in a matching position of* $\mathcal{R}(F)$.

Note that in Definition 1 the condition (ii) asks that for every recursive call there exists at least one *recurrence argument*. Every such recurrence argument is a matching argument. Moreover conditions (iii) and (ii) imply that in safe definition cases making recursion over integer or list there is at most one recursive call. This to avoid exponential functions like the following: $\exp(s\,X) = (\exp X) + (\exp X)$. Nevertheless, we have functions with more recursive calls over trees, for example:

Tadd (node X Y Z) (node X' Y' Z') = node (X + X') (Tadd Y Y') (Tadd Z Z').

Safe definition cases have the following remarkable property.

Lemma 1. *Let* $F(t_1, \ldots, t_n) = M$ *be a safe definition case and let the recursive calls of F in M be* $F(t_1^1, .., t_n^1), \ldots, F(t_1^m, .., t_n^m)$. *Then* $\sum_{i=1}^n |t_i| > \sum_{k=1}^m (\sum_{i=1}^n |t_i^k|)$.

2.3 Reduction

The computational mechanism of LPL will be the reduction relation obtained by extending the usual β-reduction with rewriting rules for the LetRec construct.

We denote by M{} a *context*, that is to say a term with a hole, and by M{N} the result of substituting the term N for the hole.

Definition 4. *The reduction relation* $\to_L$ *is the contextual closure of:*

- *the relation* $\to_\beta$ *defined as:* $(\lambda x.M)N \to_\beta M[N/x]$,
- *the relation* $\to_\gamma$ *defined for basic functions* $\underline{F}$ *by: if* $\exists i\ \sigma(\vec{t_i}) = \vec{N}$ *then*

$$\text{LetRec } \underline{F}(t_1) = M_1, \ldots, \underline{F}(t_n) = M_n \text{ in } M\{\underline{F}(\vec{N})\} \to_\gamma$$
$$\text{LetRec } \underline{F}(t_1) = M_1, \ldots, \underline{F}(t_n) = M_n \text{ in } M\{\sigma(M_i)\}$$

- *and of the relation* $\to_{Rec}$ *defined as* $\to_\gamma$ *but for non-basic functions.*

We write $\to_{\gamma_{\underline{F}_i}}$ *(resp.* $\to_{Rec_{F_i}}$*) instead of* $\to_\gamma$ *(resp.* $\to_{Rec}$*) when we want to stress which function* $\underline{F}_i$ *(resp.* F_i*) has been triggered. As usual* $\to_L^*$ *denotes the reflexive and transitive closure of* $\to_L$.

We remark that the syntactic criterion alone implies that a program satisfying it cannot have an infinite $\to_{Rec}$ reduction sequence.

2.4   Type System

The fundamental ingredient to ensure the complexity properties of LPL is the type system. It allows to derive different kinds of typing judgments. One assigns types to terms, another one assigns types to programs and the last one assigns types to function definitions. We start with a set of *ground* types containing $\mathbb{B}_n, \mathbb{N}, \mathbb{L}_n, \mathbb{L}, \mathbb{T}$ representing respectively finite types with $n \geq 1$ elements, unary integers (natural numbers), lists over $\mathbb{B}_n$, lists of unary integers and binary trees with unary integers at the nodes. Ground types can also be constructed using products $\mathbb{D}_1 \times \mathbb{D}_2$ whose elements are of the form $(p\ d_1\ d_2)$ where d_i is an element of $\mathbb{D}_i$ $(i = \{1,2\})$. The constructor p has type $\mathbb{D}_1 \multimap \mathbb{D}_2 \multimap \mathbb{D}_1 \times \mathbb{D}_2$. This set of ground types could easily be extended to all the usual standard data types. Types are defined by the following grammars:

$$\mathbb{D} ::= \mathbb{B}_n \mid \mathbb{N} \mid \mathbb{L}_n \mid \mathbb{L} \mid \mathbb{T} \mid \mathbb{D} \times \mathbb{D} \qquad \text{and} \qquad A ::= \mathbb{D} \mid A \multimap B \mid !A \multimap B \mid \S A$$

The type $!A \multimap B$ is the translation of the intuitionistic implication $A \Rightarrow B$ in linear logic. It uses the modality ! to manage typing of non-linear variable in a program. In particular, $!A \multimap B$ is a type for functions that can use their argument several times, while $A \multimap B$ (when A is not of the form $!A'$) is a type of functions that use their argument at most once. It is worth noting that the modality ! here cannot be nested, i.e. $!!A$ does not occur in types since ! is used only in combination with $\multimap$, on its left hand side. The other modality $\S A$ is used in Light linear logic [4] (and in DLAL) to guarantee a PTIME bound normalization. A possible intuition is that it marks different levels of computation, like in ramified type systems: a function defined by recursion over an argument of type D (a data type) will produce a result at higher level, so of type $\S A$, for some A. A formula A is *modal* if it is of the form $A = \S B$ or $!B$. We write $\dagger$ for modalities in $\{!, \S\}$, and $\dagger^n A = \dagger(\dagger^{n-1}A), \dagger^0 A = A$.

Now we give types to constructors and functions:

Definition 5. *To each constructor or function symbol* s, *of arity* n, *a fixed type is associated, denoted* $\mathcal{T}(s)$:

- *If* $s = c$ *or* $\underline{F}$ *then* $\mathcal{T}(s) = \mathbb{D}_1 \multimap \cdots \multimap \mathbb{D}_n \multimap \mathbb{D}_{n+1}$,
- *If* $s = F$ *a non-basic function then* $\mathcal{T}(F) = !^{i_1}\S^{j_1}A_1 \multimap \cdots \multimap !^{i_n}\S^{j_n}A_n \multimap \S^j A$ *with:*

i) $j \geq 1$ and $0 \leq i_r \leq 1$ for any $1 \leq r \leq n$,

ii) for $1 \leq r \leq n$, if $r \in \mathcal{R}(\mathrm{F})$ then A_r is a ground type $\mathbb{D}$ and $i_r = j_r = 0$; otherwise $i_r + j_r \geq 1$.

Where for $1 \leq i \leq n+1$, the $\mathbb{D}_i$ are ground types, and the A_i and A are non-modal.

Example 1. For the ground type $\mathbb{N}$ of natural numbers we have: $\mathcal{T}(0) = \mathbb{N}, \mathcal{T}(\mathbf{s}) = \mathbb{N} \multimap \mathbb{N}$. For the ground type $\mathbb{L}$ of finite lists of natural numbers we have: $\mathcal{T}(\mathtt{nil}) = \mathbb{L}$, $\mathcal{T}(:) = \mathbb{N} \multimap \mathbb{L} \multimap \mathbb{L}$. For the ground type $\mathbb{T}$ of finite binary trees with natural numbers as node we have: $\mathcal{T}(\epsilon) = \mathbb{T}, \mathcal{T}(\mathtt{node}) = \mathbb{N} \multimap \mathbb{T} \multimap \mathbb{T} \multimap \mathbb{T}$.

We design a declarative type assignment system (Table 2) to favor simplicity rather than to make type inference easy. So the typing rules will not be syntax-directed but they could be. Contexts, denoted $\Gamma, \Delta, \ldots$ are sets of assignments of the shape $\mathrm{x} : A$ or $\mathrm{X} : A$ where A is a type. Note that there are no symbols of function or constructor in contexts.

The *type judgments for terms and programs* have the shape $\Gamma; \Delta \vdash \mathrm{M} : A$ and $\Gamma; \Delta \vdash \mathrm{p} : A$ respectively, where Γ and Δ are two distinct contexts, M is a term and p is a program, while A is a type. The context Γ is called *non-linear*, while Δ is *linear* (in fact *affine*): the type system will ensure that variables from Δ occur at most once in the term M or the program p. If Δ is $\varkappa_1 : A_1, \ldots, \varkappa_n : A_n$ then $\S\Delta$ will stand for $\varkappa_1 : \S A_1, \ldots, \varkappa_n : \S A_n$.

The *type judgments for function definitions* have the shape $\triangleright \mathrm{d_F} : A$, where $\mathrm{d_F}$ is a definition of F (possibly not completed yet) and A is a type.

We now explain some rules. In binary rules, like $(\Rightarrow E)$, the contexts of the two premises have disjoint sets of variables. The typing rules for terms in Table 2.2 are essentially those of the type system DLAL [17] for λ-calculus but extended to pattern variables. Note that the linear application $(\multimap E)$ is unrestricted, while in the non-linear

Table 2. LPL Typing rules

$$\frac{}{\vdash \mathrm{c} : \mathcal{T}(\mathrm{c})} \qquad \frac{}{\vdash \mathrm{F} : \mathcal{T}(\mathrm{F})}$$

1: Constructors and functions

$$\frac{}{; \varkappa : A \vdash \varkappa : A} \ (Ax) \qquad \frac{\Gamma_1; \Delta_1 \vdash \mathrm{M} : B}{\Gamma_1, \Gamma_2; \Delta_1, \Delta_2 \vdash \mathrm{M} : B} \ (W) \qquad \frac{\Gamma, \varkappa_1 : A, \varkappa_2 : A; \Delta \vdash \mathrm{M} : B}{\Gamma, \varkappa : A; \Delta \vdash \mathrm{M}[\varkappa/\varkappa_1, \varkappa/\varkappa_2] : B} \ (C)$$

$$\frac{\Gamma; \Delta, \mathrm{x} : A \vdash \mathrm{M} : B}{\Gamma; \Delta \vdash \lambda \mathrm{x}.\mathrm{M} : A \multimap B} \ (\multimap I) \qquad \frac{\Gamma_1; \Delta_1 \vdash \mathrm{M} : A \multimap B \quad \Gamma_2; \Delta_2 \vdash \mathrm{N} : A}{\Gamma_1, \Gamma_2; \Delta_1, \Delta_2 \vdash \mathrm{MN} : B} \ (\multimap E)$$

$$\frac{\Gamma, \mathrm{x} : A; \Delta \vdash \mathrm{M} : B}{\Gamma; \Delta \vdash \lambda \mathrm{x}.\mathrm{M} :! A \multimap B} \ (\Rightarrow I) \qquad \frac{\Gamma_1; \Delta \vdash \mathrm{M} :! A \multimap B \quad ; \Gamma_2 \vdash \mathrm{N} : A \quad \Gamma_2 \subseteq \{\varkappa : C\}}{\Gamma_1, \Gamma_2; \Delta \vdash \mathrm{MN} : B} \ (\Rightarrow E)$$

$$\frac{; \Gamma, \Delta \vdash \mathrm{M} : A}{\Gamma; \S\Delta \vdash \mathrm{M} : \S A} \ (\S I) \qquad \frac{\Gamma_1; \Delta_1 \vdash \mathrm{N} : \S A \quad \Gamma_2; \mathrm{x} : \S A, \Delta_2 \vdash \mathrm{M} : B}{\Gamma_1, \Gamma_2; \Delta_1, \Delta_2, \vdash \mathrm{M}[\mathrm{N}/\mathrm{x}] : B} \ (\S E)$$

2: Terms

$$\frac{\Gamma; \Delta \vdash \mathrm{F}(\overrightarrow{t_i}) : B \quad \Gamma; \Delta \vdash \mathrm{N}_i : B \quad \triangleright \mathrm{d_F} : B}{\triangleright (\mathrm{F}(\overrightarrow{t_i}) = \mathrm{N}_i), \mathrm{d_F} : B} \ (D) \qquad \frac{\Gamma; \Delta \vdash \mathrm{p} : A \quad \triangleright \mathrm{d_F} : B}{\Gamma; \Delta \vdash \mathtt{LetRec}\ \mathrm{d_F}\ \mathtt{in}\ \mathrm{p} : A} \ (R)$$

3: Recursive definitions and programs

one ($\Rightarrow E$): the argument N should have at most one free variable x, which is linear; in the conclusion, x then has a non-linear status. This is a key to bound β-reduction steps.

The typing rules for definitions are presented in Table 2.3 and together with those for function symbols, are the main novelty of the present system. They need some comments. The rule (D) serves to add a definition case to a partial definition d_F of F. The new definition typed is then $d'_F = (F(\overrightarrow{t_i}) = N_i), d_F$. Whereas the rule (R) then serves to form a new program from a program and a definition of a function.

By a straightforward adaptation of DLAL subject reduction we have:

Theorem 1 (Subject Reduction). *Let* p *be a LPL program such that* $\Gamma; \Delta \vdash$ p $: A$. *Then,* p $\rightarrow_L^*$ q *implies* $\Gamma; \Delta \vdash$ q $: A$.

2.5 Some Examples

We give here some hints on how to program in LPL. More information about the typing can be found in Section 3.1. Addition can be defined by a standard definition d_A as:

$$\text{Add} \, (\text{s X}) \, Y = \text{s} \, (\text{Add X Y}) \, , \, \text{Add} \, 0 \, Y = Y$$

the first is a matching arguments, so d_A is typable for example by taking Add : $N \multimap \S N \multimap \S N$. Multiplication can be given by a function definition d_M as:

$$\text{Mul} \, (\text{s X}) \, Y = \text{Add} \, Y \, (\text{Mul X Y}) \, , \, \text{Mul} \, 0 \, Y = 0$$

the first is a matching argument and since Add : $N \multimap \S N \multimap \S N$ we can type d_M using Mul : $N \multimap !N \multimap \S\S N$ and by means of rule ($\S I$) and ($\S E$). We have a type coercion program for every data type, e.g on numerals we have d_C as:

$$\text{Coer} \, (\text{s X}) = \text{s} \, (\text{Coer X}) \, , \, \text{Coer} \, 0 = 0$$

typable with Coer : $N \multimap \S N$. This can be used in d_P to define the usual Map program:

$$\text{Map} \, Y \, (X : XS) = (Y \, (\text{Coer X})) : (\text{Map} \, Y \, XS) \, , \, \text{Map} \, Y \, \text{nil} = \text{nil}$$

typable with Map :$!(N \multimap N) \multimap L \multimap \S L$. Note that we have also a typing for non linear function argument of Map. Using this we can write a program Map $(\times 2) \, (1 : 2 : 3 : 4)$ that doubles all the elements of $(1 : 2 : 3 : 4)$ as

$$\text{LetRec } d_A, d_M, d_C, d_P \text{ in Map } (\lambda x.\text{Mul } x \, 2) \, (1 : 2 : 3 : 4)$$

typable with type $\S\S\S L$ using Map :$!(N \multimap \S\S N) \multimap L \multimap \S\S\S L$. Using again the coercions we have a definition d_R for the Foldr program:

$$\text{Foldr } Y \, Z \, (X : XS) = Y \, (\text{Coer X}) \, (\text{Foldr } Y \, Z \, XS) \, , \, \text{Foldr } Y \, Z \, \text{nil} = Z$$

typable with Foldr :$!(N \multimap N \multimap N) \multimap \S N \multimap L \multimap \S N$. Note that we have also a typing Foldr :$!(N \multimap \S N \multimap \S N) \multimap \S\S N \multimap L \multimap \S\S N$, we can use it to write the program Foldr $(+) \, 0 \, (1 : 2 : 3)$ that sums the values in the list $(1 : 2 : 3)$. We have

$$\text{LetRec } d_A, d_C, d_R \text{ in Foldr } (\lambda x.\lambda y.\text{Add } x \, y) \, 0 \, (1 : 2 : 3)$$

typable with type $\S\S N$. Finally have also some interesting programs over trees. For example we have d_T defining addition Tadd : $T \multimap T \multimap \S T$ as:

$$\text{Tadd} \, (\text{node X Y Z}) \, (\text{node X' Y' Z'}) = \text{node} \, (\text{Add X X'}) \, (\text{Tadd Y Y'}) \, (\text{Tadd Z Z'}) \, ,$$
$$\text{Tadd} \, \epsilon \, X = \text{Coer}_T \, X \, , \, \text{Tadd X} \, \epsilon = \text{Coer}_T \, X$$

where Coer_T is a coercion for the T data type (defined analogously to the one for natural numbers). It should be stressed that even though in LLL one can define a type for binary trees (as in system F) there is no simple way in this system to program Tadd. Moreover, we here can program some more examples that would be awkward to program in LLL. For example division by 2 on unary integers.

$\text{Div}\,(\text{s}\,(\text{s}\,\text{X})) = \text{s}\,(\text{Div}\,\text{X}),\ \text{Div}\,(\text{s}\,0) = 0\,,\ \text{Div}\,0 = 0\,,$

that gets type $\mathbb{N} \multimap \S\mathbb{N}$. The problem for typing DIV in LLL is that this kind of recursion scheme (using the pattern $\text{s}(\text{s}\,\text{X})$) cannot be implemented directly on Church integers, by using their iteration scheme. Similarly functions that are defined by pattern matching over two arguments, like for example Tadd above and the minimum function:

$\text{Min}\,(\text{s}\,\text{X})\,(\text{s}\,\text{Y}) = \text{s}\,(\text{Min}\,\text{X}\,\text{Y}),\ \text{Min}\,(\text{s}\,\text{X})\,0 = 0\,,\ \text{Min}\,0\,(\text{s}\,\text{Y}) = 0\,,$

that is typable as $\text{Min} : \mathbb{N} \multimap \mathbb{N} \multimap \S\mathbb{N}$ cannot be programmed naturally in LLL.

3 Translating LPL in eLPL

The proof of the polynomial time complexity bound for light linear logic [4] and light λ-calculus [14] uses a notion of *stratification* of the proofs or λ-terms by *depths*. To adapt this methodology to LPL we need to make the stratification explicit in the programs. For that we introduce an intermediate language called eLPL, adapted from light λ-calculus [14], and where the stratification is managed by new constructions (corresponding to the modality rules). Note that the user is not expected to program directly in eLPL, but instead he will write typed LPL programs, which will then be *compiled* in eLPL. The polynomial bound on execution will then be proved for a certain strategy of evaluation of eLPL programs.

The syntax of eLPL is given in Table 3. An eLPL term $\lambda x.\text{let } x \text{ be } !y \text{ in } M[y/x]$, where y is fresh, is abbreviated by $\lambda^! x.M$. Moreover, we write $\text{let } M \text{ be } \dagger^n x \text{ in } N$ to denote terms as $\text{let } M \text{ be } \dagger x_1 \text{ in } (\text{let } x_1 \text{ be } \dagger x_2 \text{ in } (\ldots (\text{let } x_{n-1} \text{ be } \dagger x_n \text{ in } N) \cdots))$. We will give a translation of type derivations of LPL programs to type derivations of eLPL programs, which will leave almost unchanged the typing part, and act only on the term part of LPL programs.

The contexts of typing judgments for eLPL terms and programs can contain a new kind of type declaration, denoted $x : [A]_\S$, where A is a type, which corresponds to a kind of intermediary status for variables with type $\S A$. In particular, $[A]_\S$ does not belong to the type grammar and these variables cannot be λ-abstracted, the only possibility is to bind them by means of a let. This kind of declarations is made necessary by the fact that eLPL is handling explicitly stratification. If $\Delta = x_1 : A_1, \ldots, x_n : A_n$ then $[\Delta]_\S$ is $x_1 : [A_1]_\S, \ldots, x_n : [A_n]_\S$. The typing rules are given in Table 4. Note that declarations $x : [A]_\S$ are introduced by (§ I) rules, and eliminated by (§ E) rules. Intuitively, a variable $x : [A]_\S$ is a kind of special pattern for $\S x$, and only a term of the

Table 3. eLPL term language definition

program definition	$p ::= M \mid \text{LetRec } d_F \text{ in } p$
value definition	$v ::= c(v_1, \cdots, v_n)$
pattern definition	$t ::= X \mid c(t_1, \ldots, t_n)$
function definition	$d_F ::= F(t_1, \ldots, t_n) = N \mid d_F, d_F$
term definition	$M, N ::= x \mid c \mid X \mid F \mid \lambda x.M \mid MM \mid \,!M \mid \S M \mid \text{let } M \text{ be } !x \text{ in } M \mid \text{let } M \text{ be } \S x \text{ in } M$

Table 4. eLPL type system

---

constructors and functions rules, $(Ax), (W), (C), (-\circ\ I), (-\circ\ E), (D), (R)$: as in Table 2

$$\frac{;\Gamma, \Delta \vdash \texttt{M} : A}{\Gamma; [\Delta]_\S \vdash \S\texttt{M} : \S A}\ (\S I) \qquad \frac{\Gamma, \texttt{x} : A; \Delta \vdash \texttt{M} : B}{\Gamma; \Delta \vdash \lambda^! \texttt{x.M} : !A -\circ B}\ (\Rightarrow I) \qquad \frac{\Gamma, \varkappa : A; \Delta \vdash \texttt{M} : B \quad \texttt{x fresh}}{\Gamma, \varkappa : A; \Delta \vdash \texttt{let } \varkappa \texttt{ be !x in M}[\texttt{x}/\varkappa] : B}\ (l!)$$

$$\frac{\Gamma_1; \Delta_1 \vdash \texttt{N} : \S A \quad \Gamma_2; \texttt{x} : [A]_\S, \Delta_2 \vdash \texttt{M} : B}{\Gamma_1, \Gamma_2, \Delta_1; \Delta_2, \vdash \texttt{let N be }\S\texttt{x in M} : B}\ (\S E) \qquad \frac{\Gamma_1; \Delta \vdash \texttt{M} : (!A) -\circ B \ ; \Gamma_2 \vdash \texttt{N} : A \quad \Gamma_2 \subseteq \{\varkappa : C\}}{\Gamma_1, \Gamma_2; \Delta \vdash \texttt{M!N} : B}\ (\Rightarrow E)$$

---

shape $\S\texttt{M}$ will be able to trigger the reduction of the `let`. Observe that if $\lambda\texttt{x.M}$ is a well typed eLPL term, then $n_o(\texttt{x}, \texttt{M}) \leq 1$.

Note that all the rules in Table 4, but the rule $(l!)$, are the same rules as in Table 2 but for the terms being the subjects of each rule and for the distinction between $\S A$ and $[A]_\S$. This suggests that we can give a translation on type derivation inducing a translation on typable terms. From this observation we have the following:

Definition 6. *Let* M *be an LPL term and* Π *be a type derivation proving* $\Gamma; \Delta \vdash \texttt{M} : B$. *Then,* Π^* *is the type derivation in eLPL proving* $\Gamma; \Delta \vdash \texttt{M}^* : B$ *obtained by:*

- *substituting to each rule* (X) *of LPL in* Π *the corresponding rule* (X) *in eLPL and changing accordingly the subject,*
- *adding at the end: for each variable* $\varkappa \in \Gamma$ *(resp.* x $: [A]_\S \in \Delta$) *an occurrence of the rule* $(l!)$ *(resp.* $(\S E)$ *with a l.h.s. premise of the form* ; y $: \S A \vdash$ y $: \S A$).

The above translation leaves the contexts Γ and Δ and the type B, the same as in the source derivation. The translation can be easily extended to function definitions:

Definition 7. *Let* $\texttt{F}(\overrightarrow{t_i}) = \texttt{N}_i, \texttt{d}_\texttt{F}$ *be an LPL function definition and* Π *be its type derivation in LPL ending as:*

$$\frac{\Sigma_1 : \Gamma; \Delta \vdash \texttt{F}(\overrightarrow{t_i}) : B \quad \Sigma_2 : \Gamma; \Delta \vdash \texttt{N}_i : B \quad \Sigma_3 : \triangleright\texttt{d}_\texttt{F} : B}{\triangleright\texttt{F}(\overrightarrow{t_i}) = \texttt{N}_i, \texttt{d}_\texttt{F} : B}\ (D)$$

Then, Π^* *is the type derivation in eLPL ending as:*

$$\frac{\Sigma_1 : \Gamma; \Delta \vdash \texttt{F}(\overrightarrow{t_i}) : B \quad \Sigma_2^* : \Gamma; \Delta \vdash \texttt{N}_i^* : B \quad \Sigma_3^* : \triangleright\texttt{d}_\texttt{F}^* : B}{\triangleright\texttt{F}(\overrightarrow{t_i}) = \texttt{N}_i^*, \texttt{d}_\texttt{F}^* : B}\ (D)$$

Note that in the translation we do not translate the left hand-side of a definition case, we keep it to be exactly the same as in LPL. We can now extend the translation to programs.

Definition 8. *Let* p $=$ $\texttt{LetRec } \texttt{d}_{\texttt{F}_1}, \ldots, \texttt{d}_{\texttt{F}_n} \texttt{ in } \texttt{M}$ *be an LPL program and let* Π *be a type derivation in LPL proving* $\Gamma; \Delta \vdash \texttt{LetRec } \texttt{d}_{\texttt{F}_1}, \ldots, \texttt{d}_{\texttt{F}_n} \texttt{ in } \texttt{M} : B$. *Then,* Π^* *is the derivation in eLPL proving* $\Gamma; \Delta \vdash \texttt{LetRec } \texttt{d}_{\texttt{F}_1}^*, \ldots, \texttt{d}_{\texttt{F}_n}^* \texttt{ in } \texttt{M}^* : B$ *obtained by replacing every derivation* $\Sigma_i : \triangleright\texttt{d}_{\texttt{F}_i} : \S B$ *in* Π *by the derivation* $\Sigma_i^* \triangleright \texttt{d}_{\texttt{F}_i}^* : \S B$ *and by replacing the derivation* $\Sigma : \Gamma; \Delta \vdash \texttt{M} : B$ *by the derivation* $\Sigma^* : \Gamma; \Delta \vdash \texttt{M}^* : B$.

The above translation is not exactly syntax directed; the reason is that we want the following remarkable property:

Lemma 2. *Let* M *be an* LPL *term and* Π *be a type derivation for it. Then the term* M* *obtained by the derivation* Π^* *is such that* $n_o(\varkappa, M^*) \leq 1$ *for each* $\varkappa \in FV(M^*)$.

Because of the new let constructions, the reduction rules are extended as follows:

Definition 9. *The reduction relation* $\to_I$ *is the contextual closure of the relations* $\to_{Rec}$, $\to_\gamma$ *(as in Def. 4) and of the reductions* $\to_\beta$, $\to_!$, $\to_\S$, $\to_{com_1}$, $\to_{com_2}$ *and* $\to_{com_3}$ *for* $\dagger \in \{!, \S\}$ *defined as:*

$$(\lambda x.M)N \to_\beta M[N/x], \quad \text{let } !N \text{ be } !x \text{ in } M \to_! M[N/x], \quad \text{let } \S N \text{ be } \S x \text{ in } M \to_\S M[N/x],$$

$$M(\text{let } U \text{ be } \dagger x \text{ in } V) \to_{com_1} \text{let } U \text{ be } \dagger x \text{ in } (MV),$$

$$(\text{let } U \text{ be } \dagger x \text{ in } V)M \to_{com_2} \text{let } U \text{ be } \dagger x \text{ in } (VM),$$

$$\text{let } (\text{let } U \text{ be } \dagger x \text{ in } V) \text{ be } \dagger y \text{ in } W \to_{com_3} \text{let } U \text{ be } \dagger x \text{ in } (\text{let } V \text{ be } \dagger y \text{ in } W).$$

As usual $\to_I^*$ *denotes the reflexive and transitive closure of* $\to_I$.

We write $\to_{com}$ for any one of the three *commutation reductions* $\to_{com_i}$. Note that:

– in $\to_\beta$ and $\to_\S$ *at most one occurrence* of x is substituted in M (linear substitution),
– the reduction $\to_!$, $\to_{Rec}$, $\to_\gamma$ are the only ones inducing non-linear substitutions.

In fact, a β-step in LPL corresponds in eLPL to a (linear) β step followed by a ! step. Now, to reason about the stratification we define the notion of *depth*.

Definition 10. *Let* M *be an eLPL term and* N *be an occurrence of a subterm in it. The depth of* N *in* M, *denoted* $d(N, M)$ *is the number of* $\S$ *or* ! *symbols encountered in the syntax tree of* M *when going from the root of* M *to the root of* N. *The degree of an eLPL term* M, *denoted by* $d(M)$, *is the maximal depth of any subterm in it.*

E.g. Take M as N!(let y be !x in$\S$(F x)). Then $d(N, M) = 0$, $d(y, M) = 1$ and $d(x, M) = 2$. In what follows we write $N \in_i M$ to denote the fact that N is a subterm of M at depth i, i.e. $d(N, M) = i$. We write $n_o^i(\varkappa, M)$ (respectively $|M|_i$, $FV(M)^i$ and $FO(M)^i$) to denote the restriction of $n_o(\varkappa, M)$ (respectively $|M|$, $FV(M)$ and $FO(M)$) at depth i.
Now we can state some important properties of typing on eLPL terms.

Lemma 3 (Variable occurrences). *Let* $\Gamma; \Delta \vdash M : A$. *Then:*

i) *if* $\varkappa \in dom(\Delta)$ *then* $n_o(\varkappa, M) \leq 1$.
ii) *if* $n_o(\varkappa, M) > 1$ *then* $\varkappa \in dom(\Gamma)$ *and* $d(\varkappa, M) = 1$.
iii) *if* $\varkappa \in dom(\Gamma \cup \Delta)$ *we have* $n_o^0(\varkappa, M) \leq 1$.

Lemma 4. *Let* $F(t_1, \ldots, t_n) = N$ *and let* $F(t_1^1, \ldots, t_n^1), \ldots, F(t_1^m, \ldots, t_n^m)$ *be the recursive calls of* F *in* N. *Then,* $d(F(t_1^i, \ldots, t_n^i), N) = 0$.

These properties will be useful when studying the bounds on the reductions in eLPL.

3.1 Revisiting the Examples

We now come back to the examples of Section 2.5 in order to clarify the way such programs can be typed by giving the translations in eLPL. The function definitions d_C, d_A and d_M for the programs $\text{Coer} : \mathbb{N} \multimap \S\mathbb{N}$, $\text{Add} : \mathbb{N} \multimap \S\mathbb{N} \multimap \S\mathbb{N}$ and $\text{Mul} : \mathbb{N} \multimap !\mathbb{N} \multimap \S\S\mathbb{N}$ respectively, can be translated in eLPL as

Coer (s X) = let (Coer X) be §z in §(sz) , Coer 0 = §0
Add (s X) Y = let (Add X Y) be §z in §(sz) , Add 0 Y = Y
Mul (s X) Y = let Y be !r in let (Mul X !r) be §z in §(Add r z) , Mul 0 Y = §§0

Similarly, the definition d_P for $\text{Map} : !(\mathbb{N} \multimap \S\S\mathbb{N}) \multimap \mathbb{L} \multimap \S\S\S\mathbb{L}$ can be translated as:

Map Y (X : XS) = let Y be !y in let Map !y XS be §§§z in let Coer X be §x in
§(let y x be §§r in r : z) , Map Y nil = §§§nil

Then the program $\text{LetRec } d_A, d_M, d_C, d_P$ in $\text{Map } (\lambda x.\text{Mul } x \, 2) \, (1:2:3:4)$ can be translated in eLPL as $\text{LetRec } d_A^*, d_M^*, d_C^*, d_P^*$ in $\text{Map } !(\lambda x.\text{Mul } x \, !2) \, (1:2:3:4)$. Analogously, the definition d_R for $\text{Foldr} : !(\mathbb{N} \multimap \S\mathbb{N} \multimap \S\mathbb{N}) \multimap \S\S\mathbb{N} \multimap \mathbb{L} \multimap \S\S\mathbb{N}$ can be translated as:

Foldr Y Z (X : XS) = let Y be !y in let Coer X be §x in let Foldr !y Z XS
be §r in §(yxr) , Foldr Y Z nil = Z

Then the program $\text{LetRec } d_A, d_C, d_R$ in $\text{Foldr } (\lambda x.\lambda y.\text{Add } x \, y) \, 0 \, (1:2:3)$ can be translated as $\text{LetRec } d_A^*, d_C^*, d_R^*$ in $\text{Foldr } !(\lambda x.\lambda y.\text{Add } x \, y) \, \S\S0 \, (1:2:3)$.

Finally the definition d_T for $\text{Tadd} : \mathbb{T} \multimap \mathbb{T} \multimap \S\mathbb{T}$ can be translated using a coercion $\text{Coer}_\mathbb{T}$ for the $\mathbb{T}$ data type (defined analogously to the one for natural numbers) as:

Tadd (node X Y Z) (node X' Y' Z') = let Add X X' be §x in let Tadd Y Y' be §y in
let Tadd Z Z' be §z in §(node x y z) , Tadd X ε = Coer_T X , Tadd ε X = Coer_T X

4   PTIME Completeness

The proof that LPL is complete for polynomial time functions is rather standard: we can simulate any polynomial time (one tape) Turing machine in the language. In LPL we can represent all the polynomials in $\mathbb{N}[X]$, but here it is sufficient to use:

Lemma 5. *For any $K, k \in \mathbb{N}$, there exists an integer l and an LPL program of type $\mathbb{N} \multimap \S^l\mathbb{N}$ representing the polynomial $K \times x^{2^k}$.*

We consider a polytime Turing machine $\mathcal{M}$ with witness time polynomial P, n states, and a 3 symbol alphabet (0,1 and blank). We encode the configurations with the type $\text{config} = (\mathbb{L}_3 \times \mathbb{L}_3) \times \mathbb{B}_n$ where the first $\mathbb{L}_3$ type corresponds to the left part of the tape, the second one corresponds to the right part, starting from the scanned symbol.

Lemma 6. *For any transition function δ, there exists an   LPL basic function* conf2conf : config $\multimap$ config *representing the corresponding action on configurations.*

We easily check that conf2conf can be defined by a case analysis, using the pattern-matching, and does not need recursion; so it is a basic function, hence its type. We will also use an iterator of type $\mathbb{N} \multimap !(A \multimap A) \multimap \S A \multimap \S A$ with $A = \text{config}$ defined by:

Iter (s X) f base = f Iter X f base , Iter 0 f base = base

Theorem 2 (Ptime Completeness). *For any polynomial time function f on $\{0,1\}^*$, there exists an integer j and an LPL program of type $\mathbb{L}_2 \multimap \S^j \mathbb{L}_2$, representing f.*

Proof. We simulate the machine $\mathcal{M}$ computing f. By Lemma 5 we represent in LPL the polynomial P, with a term t of type $\mathbb{N} \multimap \S^m \mathbb{N}$, for some m. It is also easy to define a Length : $\mathbb{L}_2 \multimap \S\mathbb{N}$ and a Init : $\mathbb{L}_2 \multimap$ config which maps a word to the corresponding initial configuration. The simulation is then obtained by iterating conf2conf for $(t\ (\text{Length w}))$ steps, starting from the base (Init w), and then extracting the result by using projection maps. This can be suitably typed, using some coercions on $\mathbb{L}_2$. $\square$

5   Polynomial Time Soundness

We here show that well-typed LPL programs satisfying the syntactic criterion can be evaluated in polynomial time in the size of the input (with the degree of the polynomial given by the type derivation). For that we work on the eLPL translated programs. For simplicity we do not consider basic functions, but the proof can be easily extended to the whole LPL. From now on we only consider eLPL programs obtained by translation from well-typed LPL programs satisfying the syntactic criterion.

Similarly to the polynomial soundness proof for LLL, we prove that the evaluation of eLPL programs can be done in polynomial time using a specific depth-by-depth stratified strategy. The polynomial bound for this strategy in LLL relies on:

1. reducing a redex at depth i does not affect the size at depth $j < i$
2. a reduction at depth i strictly decreases the size at depth i
3. a reduction at depth i increases the size at depth $j > i$ at most quadratically
4. the reduction does not increase the degree of a term

Unfortunately for eLPL facts 2, 3 and 4 above do not hold due to the presence of LetRec, hence some adaptations are needed.

In order to adapt these facts we need to impose a rigid structure on the reductions at a fixed depth. We consider a notion of *standard reduction round* at a fixed depth i, denoted $\Rightarrow^i$ and a notion of *standard reduction step* at a fixed depth i denoted $\twoheadrightarrow^i_{\text{Rec}_F}$ for each function symbol F of the program. A *standard reduction step* $\twoheadrightarrow^i_{\text{Rec}_F}$ is an alternating maximal sequence of $\rightarrow_{\text{Rec}_F}$ and $\rightarrow^*_{\text{com}}$ steps at depth i as represented in Figure 1.(i). It is maximal in the sense that in the step $\rightarrow^*_{\text{com}}$ all the possible commutations are done. Note that, during a standard reduction step the size of the term at depth i might grow as

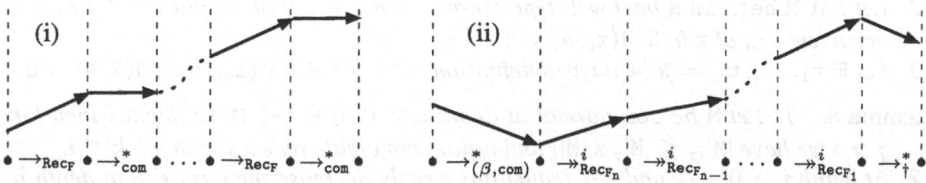

Fig. 1. Term size variations at fixed depth i by a standard reduction step and round at same depth.

depicted in Figure 1.(i), i.e. $\rightarrow^*_{\text{com}}$ steps leave the size unchanged while $\rightarrow_{\text{Rec}_F}$ steps can grow the size at depth i. We introduce some new measures on matching arguments to show that this growth is polynomial in the size of the initial term i.e. Lemma 20.

A *standard reduction round* $\Rightarrow^i$ is a sequence of maximal reduction steps as represented in Figure 1.(ii). Every reduction step is maximal in the sense that it reduces all the possible redexes of the intended kind. Note that, also during a standard reduction round the size of the term at depth i might grow as depicted in Figure 1.(ii), i.e. $\rightarrow^*_{\beta,\text{com}}$ and $\rightarrow^*_{\dagger}$ steps make the size decrease while $\twoheadrightarrow^i_{\text{Rec}_{F_j}}$ steps can make the size grow as discussed above. So, by using the bound on a standard reduction step and by the fact that the number of standard reduction steps depends on the shape of the program, we adapt fact 2 above by showing that this growth is polynomial in the size of the initial term, i.e. Theorem 3. Moreover, by similar arguments we adapt fact 3 above by showing that a standard reduction round at depth i can increase the size at depth $j > i$ at most polynomially, Lemma 21.

Finally, in order to adapt fact 4 to our framework, we introduce the notion of *potential degree*. This is the maximal degree a term can have during the reduction and it can be statically determinated. We show that a *standard reduction*, i.e. a sequence of standard reduction rounds of increasing depth, does not increase the potential degree, Lemma 23. Summarizing, what we obtain can be reformulated for eLPL as:

1. reducing a redex at depth i does not affect depth $j < i$
2. a *standard reduction round* at depth i strictly decreases *some measures on matching arguments* and increases the size at depth i at most *polynomially*
3. a *standard reduction round* at depth i increases the size at depth $j > i$ at most *polynomially*
4. the *standard reduction* does not increase the *potential degree* of a term

Now, from these new key facts, the polynomial soundness, Theorem 4, will follow.

5.1 Preliminary Properties

For a given a program $p = \text{LetRec } d_{F_1}, \ldots, d_{F_n}$ in M it is convenient to introduce the following static constants:

$$K_{F_i} = \max\{|N|_j \mid F_i(t_1, \ldots, t_n) = N \in d_{F_i}\} \quad \text{and} \quad K = \max\{K_{F_i} \mid 1 \le i \le n\}$$

We now show some simple properties about eLPL term depths. Recall that eLPL has been designed in such a way to preserve the good LLL properties. Indeed, the following lemmas can be directly adapted from the arguments in [14].

Lemma 7. *1. Let $\lambda x.M$ be a well typed term. Then $n_o(x, M) \le 1$ and $d(x, M) = 0$.*
2. Let let M be$\dagger$x in N be a well typed term. Then $x \in FV(N)$ implies that for each occurrence x_i of x in N, $d(x_i, N) = 1$.
3. Let $F(t_1, \ldots, t_n) = N$ be a typed definition case: if $X \in FV(t_i)$, then $d(X, N) = 0$.

Lemma 8. *1. Let M be com-normal at depth $i \ge 0$. If $M \rightarrow^*_{\dagger} M'$ at depth i then for $j > i$ we have $|M'|_j \le |M|_j \times |M|_i$ and it does not create redexes at depth $k \le i$.*
2. At depth $i \ge 0$, $\rightarrow_\beta$ and $\rightarrow_\dagger$ reductions strictly decrease the term size at depth i. The number of com-reductions in $M \rightarrow^*_{\text{com}} M'$ is bounded by $(|M|_i)^2$. The number of $(\beta, \dagger)$-reductions in $M \rightarrow^*_{\beta, \dagger} M'$ is bounded by $|M|_i$.

5.2   Bound the Number of Steps at a Fixed Depth

We need to define a measure, denoted $\mathrm{SA}_j^F(M)$, that will be used to bound the number of rec-reduction steps at depth j. For that we will first introduce an intermediary notion:

Definition 11 (External constructor size). *The* external constructor size *of a term* M *at depth* j, *denoted* $\|M\|_j$, *is the number of constructors of* M *at depth* j *which are not in an argument of a function, of a* let *or of a variable at depth* j.

The external constructor size measure enjoys the following remarkable property.

Lemma 9. *Let* $F(t_1, \ldots, t_n) = N$ *be safe and let the recursive calls of* F *in* N *be* $F(t_1^1, .., t_n^1), \ldots, F(t_1^m, .., t_n^m)$. *Then* $\sum_{r \in \mathcal{R}(F)} \|t_r\|_0 > \sum_{k=1}^m \sum_{r \in \mathcal{R}(F)} \|t_r^k\|_0$.

Proof. By induction on m by using Lemma 4 and Definition 1.   □

Lemma 10.   *1. If* $\Gamma; \Delta \vdash M : \dagger A$ *and* M *is* (β, com)-*normal at depth* 0, *then* $\|M\|_0 = 0$.
  2. If $\Gamma; \Delta \vdash M : A$ *and* M *is* (β, com)-*normal at depth* 0 *and* $M \to_{\mathrm{Rec}_F} M'$ *at depth* 0,
  then $\|M'\|_0 = \|M\|_0$.

Proof. 1. By induction on M. 2. By induction on M using point 1.   □

Note that the above lemma applies on each typable term. This means that for each (β, com)-normal term M the measure $\|M\|_0$ is invariant under Rec_F function calls.

Definition 12. *We call* $\mathrm{SA}_j^F(M)$ *the sum of the external constructor sizes of the matching arguments at depth* j *of the function* F *in* M. *It is inductively defined as:*

$$\mathrm{SA}_0^F(\dagger M') = 0 \quad \mathrm{SA}_{j+1}^F(\dagger M') = \mathrm{SA}_j^F(M') \quad \mathrm{SA}_{j+1}^F(F(M_1, \ldots, M_n)) = \sum_{i=1}^n \mathrm{SA}_{j+1}^F(M_i)$$

$$\mathrm{SA}_0^F(F(M_1, \ldots, M_n)) = \sum_{i=1}^n \mathrm{SA}_0^F(M_i) + \sum_{r \in \mathcal{R}(F)} \|M_r\|_0$$

$$\mathrm{SA}_j^F(sM_1 \cdots M_n) = \mathrm{SA}_j^F(G(M_1, \ldots, M_n)) = \sum_{i=1}^n \mathrm{SA}_j^F(M_i) \qquad if\ s \in \{y, c\}$$

$$\mathrm{SA}_j^F((\lambda x.M')M_1 \cdots M_n) = \mathrm{SA}_j^F(M') + \sum_{i=1}^n \mathrm{SA}_j^F(M_i)$$

$$\mathrm{SA}_j^F((\mathrm{let}\ N_1\ \mathrm{be}\ \dagger x\ \mathrm{in}\ N_2)M_1 \cdots M_n) = \mathrm{SA}_j^F(N_1) + \mathrm{SA}_j^F(N_2) + \sum_{i=1}^n \mathrm{SA}_j^F(M_i)$$

The following Lemma follows by the above definition.

Lemma 11. *We have* $\|M\|_0 + \sum\{\mathrm{SA}_0^G(M) \mid G \in M\} \leqslant |M|_0$. *Moreover for* $i \geq 0$ *we have* $\sum\{\mathrm{SA}_i^G(M) \mid G \in M\} \leq |M|_i$.

We remark that the above lemma gives a bound for all the function symbols of the program, but often we use it to give a bound only for one function symbol: $\mathrm{SA}_i^F(M) \leqslant |M|_i$. The following key lemma is the reason for which we have introduced $\mathrm{SA}_i^F(M)$:

Lemma 12. *If* M *is* (β, com)-*normal and* $M \to_{\mathrm{Rec}_F} M'$ *at depth* i *then* $\mathrm{SA}_i^F(M') < \mathrm{SA}_i^F(M)$.

Proof. Let $M = Q\{F(\sigma(t_1), \ldots, \sigma(t_n))\} \to_{\mathrm{Rec}_F} Q\{\sigma(N)\} = M'$. It follows by induction on the shape of $Q\{\}$ and on the depth i by using Definition 12 and Lemma 10.2.   □

The above lemma will be useful to show that the number of Rec-reductions is bounded. Before, we need some properties on Rec-redexes w.r.t. other redexes.

Lemma 13. *1. Reducing a* Rec-*redex at depth i cannot introduce a β-redex at depth i.*
2. Reducing a com-*redex at depth i cannot introduce a* Rec-*redex at depth i.*

Proof. 1. By typing constraints and since the r.h.s. of a definition case is normal.
2. Easy, by the shape of the reduct in a com-reduction.   □

Note that from the above lemma follows that if M is β-normal at depth i and M $\rightarrow_{\mathtt{Rec}}$ M'
at depth i then M' is β-normal at depth i and analogously, if M is $\mathtt{Rec_F}$-normal at depth i
and M $\rightarrow_{\mathtt{com}}$ M' at depth i then M' is $\mathtt{Rec_F}$-normal at depth i.
In order to show that the number of Rec-reductions is bounded, we now need to consider
the behaviour of Rec-reductions on Rec-redexes of other function symbols.

Lemma 14. *Consider* p = LetRec $d_{F_1}, \ldots, d_{F_n}$ *in* M.

1. A $\mathtt{Rec_{F_i}}$-*reduction in* M *at depth d can introduce only* F_j *for $j \leq i$ function symbols*
at a depth less or equal to $d + \max\{d(N_j) \mid N_j$ body in a definition case of $F_i\}$.
2. If M *is* (β, com)-*normal, a* $\mathtt{Rec_{F_i}}$-*reduction in* M *at depth d cannot introduce a* $\mathtt{rec_{F_j}}$-
redex for $n \geq j > i$ at depth d.

Proof. 1. Substitutions are done at depth d of terms with degree at most $\max d(N_j)$.
2. Easy, blocked symbols remain blocked by point 1 and Lemma 10.2.   □

From the above lemmas and Lemma 12 we have the following.

Corollary 15 (Rec$_\mathsf{F}$-**reductions bound**). *Let* M *be* (β, com)-*normal at depth i. If*
M $\rightarrow_{\mathtt{Rec_F}}^k$ M' *at depth i then $k \leq SA_i^F(M)$.*

Now we also need to control the term's size increase during a Rec-reduction step.

Lemma 16 (**Size lemma**). *If* M $\rightarrow_{\mathtt{Rec_F}}$ M' *at depth i then for all $j \geq i$ we have* $|M'|_j \leq$
$|M|_j + K_\mathsf{F}$.

Proof. Let M = $M_1\{F(\sigma(t_1), \ldots, \sigma(t_n))\}$ $\rightarrow_{\mathtt{Rec_F}}$ $M_1\{\sigma(N)\}$ = M'. By definition we
have $|M'|_j = |M_1\{\}|_j + |\sigma(N)|_{j-i}$ and $|M|_j + K_\mathsf{F} = |M_1\{\}|_j + K_\mathsf{F} + |F(\sigma(t_1),$
$\ldots, \sigma(t_n))|_{j-i}$.
What we need to show is that $|\sigma(N)|_{j-i} \leq K_\mathsf{F} + |F(\sigma(t_1), \ldots, \sigma(t_n))|_{j-i}$. We
consider the following two cases: $j - i = 0$ or $j - i > 0$. In the case $j - i = 0$
we have $|\sigma(N)|_0 = |N|_0 + \sum_{X \in_0 FO(N)}(|\sigma(X)|_0 - 1)$ and $|F(\sigma(t_1), \ldots, \sigma(t_n))|_0 =$
$1 + \sum_{k=1}^n |t_k|_0 + \sum_{X \in_0 FO(\overrightarrow{t})}(|\sigma(X)|_0 - 1)$. By definition $|N|_0 \leq K_\mathsf{F}$, moreover by
definition $FV(N) \subseteq FV(\overrightarrow{t})$ and by Lemma 2 every $X \in FV(\overrightarrow{t})$ occurs at most once
in N at depth 0. So we have $\sum_{X \in_0 FO(N)}(|\sigma(X)|_0 - 1) \leq \sum_{X \in_0 FO(\overrightarrow{t})}(|\sigma(X)|_0 - 1)$. So
the conclusion follows for this case. In the case $j - i = h > 0$ we have the same by
Lemma 2: the pattern variables of $\overrightarrow{t}$ occur linearly in N at depth 0.   □

It remains to observe that com-reductions preserve our term measures.

Lemma 17. *Let* M $\rightarrow_{com}$ M' *then we have: (i)* $d(M) = d(M')$, *(ii)* $|M'|_i = |M|_i$ *for each*
$i \leq d(M)$, *and (iii)* $SA_i^F(M) = SA_i^F(M')$ *for every* F *and every $i \leq d(M)$.*

The above properties justify the next definition. We describe the reduction strategy *at a
fixed depth* that we will use to bound the number of reduction steps of eLPL programs.

Definition 13 (standard reduction round). *Let* $p = \text{LetRec } d_{F_1}, \ldots, d_{F_n} \text{ in } M$ *be a program. Then:*

- *a* standard reduction step *at depth* i, *denoted* $R \twoheadrightarrow^i_{\text{Rec}_F} R'$, *is a sequence of reductions at depth* i *of the shape:*

$$R \to_{\text{Rec}_F} T \to^*_{\text{com}} R_1 \to_{\text{Rec}_F} T_1 \to^*_{\text{com}} \cdots \to_{\text{Rec}_F} T_k \to^*_{\text{com}} R_k \equiv R'$$

  such that every R_j *is* com*-normal and* R_k *is* Rec_F*-normal at depth* i.
- *a* standard reduction round *at depth* i, *denoted* $M \Rightarrow^i M'$, *is the following sequence of reductions at depth* i:

$$M \to^*_{(\beta, \text{com})} M_0 \twoheadrightarrow^i_{\text{Rec}_{F_n}} M_1 \twoheadrightarrow^i_{\text{Rec}_{F_{n-1}}} \cdots \twoheadrightarrow^i_{\text{Rec}_{F_1}} M_n \to^*_{\dagger} M'$$

  such that M_0 *is* (β, com)*-normal and* M' *is normal at depth* i.

When we need to stress the number k *of reduction steps in a standard reduction round we simply write it as* $M \Rightarrow^i_k M'$.

In order to show that the relation $\twoheadrightarrow^i$ is well defined for every term we need to prove that all the reductions are finite. First we need the following in order to have its direct corollary.

Lemma 18. *A sequence of reductions* $\to_{\text{Rec}_F} \to^*_{\text{com}}$ *at depth* i *cannot introduce a* β*-redex at depth* i.

Proof. By typing constraints and by cases on Definition 9.   □

Corollary 19. *If* M *is* β*-normal at depth* i *and* $M \to_{\text{Rec}_F} \to^*_{\text{com}} M'$ *at depth* i *then* M' *is* β*-normal at depth* i.

Now we can prove that the relation $\twoheadrightarrow^i$ is well defined.

Lemma 20 (Bound on standard reduction step at depth i**).** *Let* M *be* (β, com)*-normal at depth* i. *If* $M \twoheadrightarrow^i_{\text{Rec}_F} M'$ *then* M' *is* $(\beta, \text{com}, \text{Rec}_F)$*-normal at depth* i, *the number of reductions is bounded by*

$$2 \times (|M|_i)^3 \times (K_F + 1)^2 \quad \text{and for } j \geq i, \quad |M'|_j \leq |M|_j + |M|_i \times K_F.$$

Proof. By a detailed analysis of the standard reduction step $M \twoheadrightarrow^i_{\text{Rec}_F} M'$ and by using Lemma 12, Lemma 8.2, Lemma 17.ii-iii, Corollary 19, Lemma 16 and Lemma 11.   □

With this bound on standard reduction steps at fixed depth, we now state what we obtain whenever a standard round is done at fixed depth.

Theorem 3 (Bound on standard round at depth i **).** *Let* $p = \text{LetRec } d_{F_1}, \ldots, d_{F_n} \text{ in } M$ *be a program. Let* $M \Rightarrow^i_k M'$ *be a standard reduction round at depth* $i \geq 0$. *Then* M' *is normal at depth* i *and we have*

$$|M'|_i \leq |M|_i \times (K+1)^n \quad \text{and} \quad k \leq 3 \times (|M|_i)^3 \times (K+1)^{3n+2}$$

Proof. By analyzing the standard reduction round $M \Rightarrow^i_k M'$ and by using Lemma 8.1-2, Lemma 20, Lemma 14.1-2, Lemma 13.2, Lemma 12 and Lemma 17.ii   □

Now we have a bound on a term size at fixed depth when we apply our strategy at the same depth. In order to bound the whole program execution we need next to examine what happens to the sizes at higher depth during the standard reduction round.

Lemma 21 (Size bound at depth greater than i, for a standard reduction round)
Let $p = \text{LetRec } d_{F_1}, \ldots, d_{F_n}$ *in* M *be a program. Let* $M \Rightarrow^i_k M'$ *be a standard reduction round at depth* $i \geq 0$. *Then we have*

$$|M'|_{i+1} \leq |M|_{i+1}|M|_i \times (K+1)^n + (|M|_i)^2 \times (K+1)^{2n+1}$$

Proof. By an analysis of the shape of the standard reduction round $M \Rightarrow^i_k M'$ and by using Lemma 8.1-2, Lemma 20 and Lemma 17. ☐

Corollary 22. *Let* $p = \text{LetRec } d_{F_1}, \ldots, d_{F_n}$ *in* M *be a program. Let* $M \Rightarrow^i M'$ *be a standard reduction round at depth* $i \geq 0$. *Then we have* $|M'| \leq 2(|M|)^2 \times (K+1)^{2n+1}$.

5.3 Bound on a Program Normalization

We apply our reduction strategy by standard rounds progressively at depths $0, 1, 2 \ldots$

Definition 14 (standard reduction). *Let* $p = \text{LetRec } d_{F_1}, \ldots, d_{F_n}$ *in* M *be a program. A standard reduction, denoted* $M \Rightarrow M'$, *is a sequence of standard reduction rounds of increasing depths of the shape:*

$$M \Rightarrow^0 M_0 \Rightarrow^1 \cdots \Rightarrow^{d-1} M_{d-1} \Rightarrow^d M'$$

To stress the number k of total reduction steps we simply write it as $M \Rightarrow_k M'$.

Every standard reduction can be summarized as follows

$$M \quad \to^*_{\beta,com} M^0_{k_0} \twoheadrightarrow^0_{\text{Rec}_{F_n}} M^0_{k_1} \twoheadrightarrow^0_{\text{Rec}_{F_{n-1}}} \cdots \twoheadrightarrow^0_{\text{Rec}_{F_1}} M^0_{k_n} \to^*_\dagger M_0$$

$$M_0 \quad \to^*_{\beta,com} M^1_0 \twoheadrightarrow^1_{\text{Rec}_{F_n}} M^1_1 \twoheadrightarrow^1_{\text{Rec}_{F_{n-1}}} \cdots \twoheadrightarrow^1_{\text{Rec}_{F_1}} M^1_n \to^*_\dagger M_1$$

$$\vdots$$

$$M_{m-1} \to^*_{\beta,com} M^m_0 \twoheadrightarrow^m_{\text{Rec}_{F_n}} M^m_1 \twoheadrightarrow^m_{\text{Rec}_{F_{n-1}}} \cdots \twoheadrightarrow^m_{\text{Rec}_{F_1}} M^m_n \to^*_\dagger M_m$$

To give an upper bound on standard reductions we need the notion of *potential depth*.

Definition 15 (Potential Depth). *Consider* $p = \text{LetRec } d_{F_1}, \ldots, d_{F_n}$ *in* M *and an occurrence* N *of a subterm in* M. *The* potential depth, $\text{pt}_d(N, p)$, *of* N *in* p, *is defined as*

$$\text{pt}_d(N, p) = d(N, M) + \sum_{i=1}^n \max_j \{ d(N^j_i) \mid F_i(t^j_1, .., t^j_n) = N^j_i \in d_{F_i} \}$$

The potential degree, $\text{pt}_d(p)$, *of* p *is the maximal potential depth of any subterm in* M.

Even if standard reductions can increase the depth of a term, we have the following:

Lemma 23. *Let* $p = \text{LetRec } d_{F_1}, .., d_{F_n}$ *in* M *be a program and* $M \Rightarrow^0 M_0 \Rightarrow^1 \cdots \Rightarrow^m M_m$ *be a standard reduction. Then* $m < \text{pt}_d(p)$.

Proof. By double induction using Lemma 14. ☐

In the previous subsection we gave a bound on the number of program reduction steps at fixed depth when we apply a standard reduction round. In the previous lemma we stated that the potential depth is a bound on the possible depths to apply such standard reduction rounds. So our standard reduction normalizes a given program as follows:

Theorem 4. *Let* $p = \text{LetRec } d_{F_1}, \ldots, d_{F_n}$ *in* M *be an eLPL translated program satisfying the syntactic criterion and* $d = \text{pt}_d(p)$ *be its potential degree. Let* M $\Rightarrow_k$ M' *be a standard reduction. Then,* M' *is normal, and* $|M'| \in \mathcal{O}(|M|^{2^{d+1}})$ *and* $k \in \mathcal{O}(|M|^{3 \times 2^d})$.

Proof. Looking at the shape of the standard reduction M $\Rightarrow_k$ M' and by using Theorem 3, Lemma 23, Corollary 22.   □

Corollary 24. *If* p *is is a closed LPL program which satisfies the syntactic criterion and with type* $\mathbb{D}_1 \multimap \S^i \mathbb{D}_2$, *where* i *is an integer and* $\mathbb{D}_1$, $\mathbb{D}_2$ *are ground types, then* p *represents a polynomial time function.*

Proof. If v is value of type $\mathbb{D}_1$ we consider the translation of (p v) in eLPL, and use the fact that its potential degree only depends on the type derivation of p. Therefore using Theorem 4 the evaluation can be done in eLPL a polynomial number of steps, hence in polynomial time since the cost of each step can be polynomially bounded.

6   Conclusion and Future Developments

In this work we have introduced Light linear Programming Language (LPL), a typed functional programming language with pattern-matching, recursive definitions and higher-order types. The main feature of LPL is to give an implicit complexity characterization of PTIME where programming is more natural than in previous proposals. In order to ensure the PTIME soundness we have given a combined criterion composed of a syntactic restriction and a type system inspired by the one of Dual Light Affine Logic.

As future developments we consider the following directions:

- Verifying the effectiveness of our criterion and study the exact complexity of its checking. This study should lead to an efficient type inference procedure.
- Studying different ways of relaxing our criterion in order to improve the intensional expressiveness of LPL. One interesting direction is to include, in analogy with [5], recursive definitions of non-size increasing functions with a special status.
- Analyzing the relation between the strategy proposed here to prove the PTIME soundness and some standard evaluation strategies, e.g. lazy evaluation.

References

1. Bellantoni, S., Cook, S.: A new recursion-theoretic characterization of the polytime functions. Computational Complexity 2(2), 97–110 (1992)
2. Leivant, D.: A foundational delineation of computational feasibility. In: Meyer, A.R. (ed.) LICS 1991, pp. 2–11. IEEE Computer Society, Los Alamitos (1991)
3. Leivant, D., Marion, J.Y.: Lambda calculus characterizations of poly-time. In: Bezem, M., Groote, J.F. (eds.) TLCA 1993. LNCS, vol. 664, pp. 274–288. Springer, Heidelberg (1993)

4. Girard, J.Y.: Light linear logic. Information and Computation 143(2), 175–204 (1998)
5. Hofmann, M.: Linear types and non-size-increasing polynomial time computation. In: LICS 1999, pp. 464–473 (1999)
6. Marion, J.Y., Moyen, J.Y.: Efficient first order functional program interpreter with time bound certifications. In: Parigot, M., Voronkov, A. (eds.) LPAR 2000. LNCS (LNAI), vol. 1955, pp. 25–42. Springer, Heidelberg (2000)
7. Hughes, J., Pareto, L.: Recursion and dynamic data-structures in bounded space: Towards embedded ML programming. In: ACM ICFP 1999, pp. 70–81 (1999)
8. Hofmann, M., Jost, S.: Static prediction of heap usage for first-order functional programs. In: ACM POPL 2003, New Orleans, LA, USA (2003)
9. Crary, K., Weirich, S.: Resource bound certification. In: ACM POPL 2000, pp. 184–198 (2000)
10. Atassi, V., Baillot, P., Terui, K.: Verification of ptime reducibility for system F terms via dual light affine logic. In: Ésik, Z. (ed.) CSL 2006. LNCS, vol. 4207, pp. 150–166. Springer, Heidelberg (2006)
11. Girard, J.Y.: Linear logic. TCS 50, 1–102 (1987)
12. Girard, J.Y., Scedrov, A., Scott, P.J.: Bounded linear logic: a modular approach to polynomial-time computability. TCS 97(1), 1–66 (1992)
13. Lafont, Y.: Soft linear logic and polynomial time. TCS 318(1-2), 163–180 (2004)
14. Terui, K.: Light affine lambda calculus and polytime strong normalization. In: LICS 2001, pp. 209–220. IEEE Computer Society, Los Alamitos (2001)
15. Baillot, P., Mogbil, V.: Soft lambda-calculus: a language for polynomial time computation. In: Walukiewicz, I. (ed.) FOSSACS 2004. LNCS, vol. 2987, pp. 27–41. Springer, Heidelberg (2004)
16. Baillot, P.: Checking polynomial time complexity with types. In: Proceedings of the 2nd IFIP International Conference on TCS, pp. 370–382 (2002)
17. Baillot, P., Terui, K.: Light types for polynomial time computation in lambda calculus. Information and Computation 207(1), 41–62 (2009)
18. Gaboardi, M., Ronchi Della Rocca, S.: A soft type assignment system for λ-calculus. In: Duparc, J., Henzinger, T.A. (eds.) CSL 2007. LNCS, vol. 4646, pp. 253–267. Springer, Heidelberg (2007)
19. Gaboardi, M., Ronchi Della Rocca, S.: Type inference for a polynomial lambda calculus. In: Berardi, S., Damiani, F., de'Liguoro, U. (eds.) TYPES 2008. LNCS, vol. 5497, pp. 136–152. Springer, Heidelberg (2009)
20. Bellantoni, S., Niggl, K.H., Schwichtenberg, H.: Higher type recursion, ramification and polynomial time. APAL 104, 17–30 (2000)
21. Dal Lago, U., Martini, S., Roversi, L.: Higher order linear ramified recurrence. In: Berardi, S., Coppo, M., Damiani, F. (eds.) TYPES 2003. LNCS, vol. 3085, pp. 178–193. Springer, Heidelberg (2004)
22. Dal Lago, U.: The geometry of linear higher-order recursion. ACM TOCL 10(2) (2009)
23. Marion, J.Y.: Analysing the implicit complexity of programs. Information and Computation 183(1), 2–18 (2003)
24. Bonfante, G., Marion, J.Y., Moyen, J.Y.: On lexicographic termination ordering with space bound certifications. In: Bjørner, D., Broy, M., Zamulin, A.V. (eds.) PSI 2001. LNCS, vol. 2244, pp. 482–493. Springer, Heidelberg (2001)
25. Amadio, R.M.: Synthesis of max-plus quasi-interpretations. Fundamenta Informaticae 65(1-2), 29–60 (2005)
26. Marion, J.Y., Péchoux, R.: Characterizations of polynomial complexity classes with a better intensionality. In: ACM-PPDP 2008, pp. 79–88 (2008)
27. Marion, J.Y., Péchoux, R.: Sup-interpretations, a semantic method for static analysis of program resources. ACM TOCL 10(4) (2009)

Testing Polymorphic Properties

Jean-Philippe Bernardy, Patrik Jansson, and Koen Claessen

Chalmers University of Technology
{bernardy,patrikj,koen}@chalmers.se

Abstract. This paper is concerned with testing properties of polymorphic functions. The problem is that testing can only be performed on specific monomorphic instances, whereas parametrically polymorphic functions are expected to work for any type. We present a schema for constructing a monomorphic instance for a polymorphic property, such that correctness of that single instance implies correctness for all other instances. We also give a formal definition of the class of polymorphic properties the schema can be used for. Compared to the standard method of testing such properties, our schema leads to a significant reduction of necessary test cases.

Keywords: polymorphism, parametricity, initiality, testing.

1   Introduction

How should one test a polymorphic function?

A modern and convenient approach to testing is to write specifications as properties, and let a tool generate test cases. Such tools have been implemented for many programming languages, such as Ada, C++, Curry, Erlang, Haskell, Java, .NET and Scala [2, 3, 6, 7, 16, 20, 24, 27]. But how should one generate test cases for polymorphic functions? Parametrically polymorphic functions, by their very nature, work uniformly on values of any type, whereas in order to run a concrete test, one must pick values from a specific monomorphic type.

As an example, suppose we have two different implementations of the standard function *reverse* that reverses a list:

$reverse1, reverse2 : \forall a. [a] \rightarrow [a]$

In order to test that they do the same thing, what monomorphic type should we pick for the type variable a? Standard praxis, as for example used by QuickCheck [7], suggests to simply use a type with a large enough domain, such as natural numbers, resulting in the following property:

$\forall xs : [\mathbb{N}]. \ reverse1 \ xs == reverse2 \ xs$

Intuitively, testing the functions only on the type $\mathbb{N}$ is "enough"; if the original polymorphic property has a counter example (in this case a monomorphic type T and a concrete list $xs : [T]$), there also exists a counter example to the monomorphic property (in this case a concrete list $xs' : [\mathbb{N}]$).

However, how do we *know* this is enough? And, can we do better than this? This paper aims to provide an answer to these questions for a large class of

A.D. Gordon (Ed.): ESOP 2010, LNCS 6012, pp. 125–144, 2010.

properties of polymorphic functions. We give a systematic way of computing the monomorphic type that a polymorphic property should be tested on. Perhaps surprisingly, we do this by only inspecting the type of the functions that are being tested, not their definition. Moreover, our method significantly improves on the standard testing praxis by making the monomorphic domains over which we quantify even more precise. For example, to check that *reverse1* and *reverse2* implement the same function, it turns out to be enough to test:

$$\forall\, n : \mathbb{N}.\; reverse1\,[1\,..\,n] \mathrel{==} reverse2\,[1\,..\,n]$$

In other words, we only need to quantify over the *length* of the argument list, and not its elements! This is a big improvement over the previous property; for each list length n, only *one* test suffices, whereas previously, we had an unbounded number of lists to test for each length. This significantly increases test efficiency.

Related Work. There are a few cases in the literature where it has been shown that, for a specific polymorphic function, testing it on a particular monomorphic type is enough. For example, Knuth's classical result that verifying a sorting network only has to be done on booleans [19, sec. 5.3.4], can be cast into a question about polymorphic testing [11]. The network can be represented as a polymorphic function parametrised over a comparator (a 2-element sorter):

$$sort : \forall a.\; (a \times a \to a \times a) \to [a] \to [a]$$

Knuth has shown that, in order to check whether such a function really sorts, it is enough to show that it works for booleans; in other words checking if the following function is a sorting function:

$$sort\_Bool : [Bool] \to [Bool]$$
$$sort\_Bool = sort\,(\lambda(x, y) \to (x \wedge y, x \vee y))$$

Another example is a result by [28], which says that in order to check that a given function is a scan function, it is enough to check it for all possible combinations on a domain of three elements.

The result we present in this paper has the same motivation as these earlier results, but the concrete details are not exactly the same. In section 4, we compare our general result with Knuth's and Voigtländer's specific results.

Contributions and outlook. Our main contribution is a schema for testing polymorphic properties effectively and efficiently. We explain the schema both from a theoretical and practical point of view. Our examples are aimed at giving practitioners a good intuition of the method (section 2) and demonstrate some of its applications (section 4). A more formal exposition is provided in section 3. We cover related and future work in sections 5 and 6 and we conclude in section 7.

2   Examples

In this section, we discuss a number of examples illustrating the idea behind our method in preparation for the more formal treatment in the next section. We are using Haskell-like notation and QuickCheck-like properties here, but our result can be used in the context of other languages and other property-testing frameworks.

Example 1. Let us first compare two implementations of the function *filter*:

$filter1, filter2 : \forall a. (a \to Bool) \to [a] \to [a]$

A parametric polymorphic function knows nothing about the type it is being used on. So, the only way an element of type a can appear in the result, is if it was produced somehow by the argument of the function. We can analyse the type of the arguments of the functions under test, in order to see in what way the arguments can be used to produce an element of type a. The monomorphic type A we are going to construct to test the functions on will represent all such ways in which the arguments can be used to produce an a.

In the case of *filter*, the only way we can produce elements of type a, is by using an element from its argument list (the predicate $(a \to Bool)$ can only inspect elements). So, a natural choice for A is to be the index of the element from the argument list it used:

data $A = X\,\mathbb{N}$

In other words, $X\,i$ stands for the ith element (of type a) from the input list. Now, we have not only fixed a type to use for a, but also decided which elements the list xs should be filled with, once we know the length. Thus, the final monomorphic property becomes:

$$\forall\, n : \mathbb{N}, p : A \to Bool.\ \mathbf{let}\ xs = [X\,1\,..\,X\,n]$$
$$\mathbf{in}\ filter1\ p\ xs == filter2\ p\ xs$$

The construction we apply here can be seen as a kind of *symbolic simulation*: we feed the function with symbolic variables (here represented by naturals), and examine the output. This becomes more clear in the next example.

Example 2. Let us take a look at a typical polymorphic property, relating the functions *reverse* and append ($+\!\!+$)

$$\forall\, a: \star, \forall xs, ys : [a].\ reverse\,(xs +\!\!+ ys) == reverse\ ys +\!\!+ reverse\ xs$$

We can view the left- and right-hand sides of the property as two different polymorphic functions that are supposed to deliver the same result. Where can elements in the result list come from? Either from the list xs, or the list ys. Thus, the monomorphic type A becomes:

data $A = X\,\mathbb{N}\ |\ Y\,\mathbb{N}$

And in the property, we not only instantiate the type, but also the elements of the lists:

$$\forall\, n, m : \mathbb{N}.\ \mathbf{let}\ xs = [X\,1\,..\,X\,n]$$
$$ys = [Y\,1\,..\,Y\,m]$$
$$\mathbf{in}\ reverse\,(xs +\!\!+ ys) == reverse\ ys +\!\!+ reverse\ xs$$

Finally, an example of a property that does not hold.

Example 3. Take a look at the following property which claims that *map* and *filter* commute (which is incorrect as formulated).

$$\forall\, a: \star, \forall p : a \to Bool, f : a \to a, xs : [a].$$
$$map\ f\ (filter\ p\ xs) == filter\ p\ (map\ f\ xs)$$

A typical QuickCheck user may pick a to be $\mathbb{N}$, and running QuickCheck might produce the following counterexample[1]:

$$p = \{1 \to True, \_ \to False\}; f = \{\_ \to 1\}; xs = [3]$$

In other words, if p is a predicate that holds only for 1, and f is the constant function 1, and if we start with a list $[3]$, the property does not hold.

Investigating the left- and right-hand sides as functions from p, f, and xs to lists, we see that an element of type a may either directly come from the list xs, or be the result of applying f. Expressing this in terms of a datatype, we get:

data $A = X\,\mathbb{N} \mid F\,A$

And the property turns into:

$$\forall\, p : A \to Bool, n : \mathbb{N}.\ \textbf{let}\ xs = [X\,1 .. X\,n]$$
$$\textbf{in}\ map\ F\ (filter\ p\ xs) == filter\ p\ (map\ F\ xs)$$

The only arguments we need to quantify over are the predicate p and the length of the list xs: the function f is fixed to the constructor F. But there is one more advantage; the counterexample that is produced is more descriptive:

$$p = \{F\,(X\,1) \to True, \_ \to False\}; f = F; xs = [X\,1]$$

We clearly see that p holds only for the result of applying f to the (only) element in the list xs.

3   Generalisation

In this section we present a systematic formulation of our schema to test polymorphic functions. Additionally we expose the main theoretical results that back up the method and argue for their correctness. We assume familiarity with basic notions of category theory, notably the interpretation of data types as initial algebras [4, ch. 2].

3.1   Revisiting *Reverse*

We start by going through all the necessary steps for one particular concrete example, namely testing two implementations of *reverse* against each other:

$$reverse1, reverse2 : \forall a.\ [a] \to [a]$$

The method we use makes a clear distinction between *arguments* (values that are passed to the function) and *results* (values which are delivered by the function, and should be compared with other results). Furthermore, the arguments are divided up into two kinds; arguments that can be used by the function to *construct* elements of type a, and arguments that can only be used to *observe* arguments of type a.

The first step we take in order to compute the monomorphic instance is to transform the function under test into a function that makes these three parts of the function type explicit. The final type we are looking for is of the form:

$$\forall\, a.\ (F\,a \to a) \times (G\,a \to X) \to H\,a$$

for functors F, G, H and a monomorphic type X. The argument of type $F\,a \to a$ can be used to construct elements of type a, the argument of type $G\,a \to X$ can

---

[1] Using a recent QuickCheck extension to show functions.

be used to observe arguments of type a (by transforming them into a known type X), and $H\ a$ is the result of the function. We call the type above the *canonical testing type*; all polymorphic functions of the above type can be tested using our method, if there exists an initial F-algebra.

How do we transform functions like *reverse* into functions with a canonical testing type? We start by "dissecting" arguments that can produce *a*s into functions that produce exactly one a. For *reverse*, the one argument that contains *a*s is of type $[a]$. We now make use of the fact that all lists can be represented by a pair of its length and its indexing function, and we thus replace the list argument with an argument of type $\mathbb{N} \times (\mathbb{N} \rightarrow a)$ (we will say more about this transformation in section 3.5). After re-ordering the arguments the new type is:

$\forall\ a.\ (\mathbb{N} \rightarrow a) \times \mathbb{N} \rightarrow [a]$

which fits the requirement, with $F\ a = \mathbb{N}$, $G\ a = ()$, $X = \mathbb{N}$, and $H\ a = [a]$.

For the original function *reverse1* (and similarly for *reverse2*), we can define a corresponding function with a canonical testing type as follows:

    reverse1' : $\forall a.\ (\mathbb{N} \rightarrow a) \times \mathbb{N} \rightarrow [a]$

    reverse1' = *reverse1* ∘ *project*

This uses an auxiliary function to project the arguments of the new function to the initial arguments:

    project : $(\mathbb{N} \rightarrow a) \times \mathbb{N} \rightarrow [a]$

    project (x, obs) = *map* $x\ [1\ ..\ obs]$

Observe that if the new arguments properly cover the domain $(\mathbb{N} \rightarrow a) \times \mathbb{N}$, then the original arguments also properly cover the domain $[a]$. It means that the transformations that we have performed to fit the canonical testing type do not weaken the verification procedure.

What have we gained by this rewriting? Our main result says: to test whether two polymorphic functions with a canonical testing type are equal, it is enough to test for equality on the monomorphic type A, where A is the least fixpoint of the functor F, and to use the initial algebra $\alpha : F\ A \rightarrow A$ as the first argument.

For the *reverse* example, the least fixpoint of F is simply $\mathbb{N}$ and the initial algebra is the identity function. Thus, to check if *reverse1'* and *reverse2'* are equal, we merely have to check

    $\forall\ obs : \mathbb{N}.$ *reverse1'* (id, obs) == *reverse2'* (id, obs)

Writing the transformation explicitly is cumbersome, and indeed we can avoid it, by picking arguments directly from the image of the partially applied projection function, that is, from the set $\{$ *project* $(id, obs)\ |\ obs \in \mathbb{N}\}$. By doing so, we obtain the property given in the introduction.

    $\forall\ n : \mathbb{N}.$ *reverse1* $[1\ ..\ n]$ == *reverse2* $[1\ ..\ n]$

3.2   Overview

In general, given a function of type $\forall a.\ \sigma[a] \rightarrow H\ a$, the objective is to construct a type A, and identify a set of arguments of type $\sigma[a := A]$ to test it against. To do so, we proceed with the following three steps.

1. Transform the function to test and its type $(\forall a.\ \sigma[a] \rightarrow H\ a)$ into a function with its type in the canonical form $(\forall a.\ (F\ a \rightarrow a) \times (G\ a \rightarrow X) \rightarrow H\ a)$, where

F, G, H are functors. This must be done through an embedding-projection pair $((e, p) : \sigma[a] \subseteq (F\,a \to a) \times (G\,a \to X))$. The purpose is to identify all the ways (for the function) to construct values of type a, and express them as an algebra of the functor F. (Sect. 3.5).

2. Calculate the initial algebra $(\mu F, \alpha)$ of the functor F. Parametricity and initiality implies that fixing the algebra to α and a to μF still covers all cases. Note that the type argument has now been removed. (Sect. 3.3)

3. Re-interpret the fixing of the algebra to α in step 2 in the context of the original type, using the projection produced in step 1. The arguments to test the function on are picked in the set $\{p\,(\alpha, s) \mid s \in G\,(\mu F) \to X\}$. (Sect. 3.4)

After these steps the type argument is gone, and testing can proceed as usual. We detail the procedure and argue for its validity in the following sections.

3.3   The Initial View

In this section we expose and justify the crucial step of our approach: the removal of polymorphism itself. We begin with showing that applications of (some) polymorphic functions can be expressed in terms of a monomorphic case.

Suppose that the polymorphic function has the type $(\forall a.\,(F\,a \to a) \times (G\,a \to X) \to H\,a)$, that is, its only way to construct values of type a are given by an algebra of functor F, (X is a constant type where a cannot appear). Then, instead of passing a given algebra to a polymorphic function, one can pass the initial algebra, and use the catamorphism of the algebra (often called *fold* and denoted $([\_])$ in the sequel) to translate the results. If the function can also observe the values of the polymorphic parameter, then the observation functions passed as argument must be composed with the catamorphism.

By passing the initial algebra, the type parameter is fixed to μF. The applications of the catamorphism handle the polymorphism, effectively hiding it from the function under test. The following theorem expresses the idea formally. Our proof relies on parametricity [29] and properties of initial algebras [4, ch. 2]

Theorem 1. *Let F, G, H be functors and let $f : (\forall a{:}\star.(F\,a \to a) \times (G\,a \to X) \to H\,a)$. If there is an initial F-algebra $(\mu F, \alpha)$, then*
$$\forall\,t{:}\star, p : F\,t \to t, r : G\,t \to X.$$
$$f_t\,(p, r) = H\,([p])\,(f_{\mu F}\,(\alpha, r \circ G\,([p])))$$

Proof. We apply the parametricity theorem (restricted to functions) on the type of f, following mechanically the rules given by [12], theorem 1. After simplification we obtain:
$$\forall f : (\forall a{:}\star.(F\,a \to a) \times (G\,a \to X) \to H\,a),$$
$$t_1, t_2{:}\star, \quad \varrho : t_2 \to t_1,$$
$$p_1 : F\,t_1 \to t_1, p_2 : F\,t_2 \to t_2. \quad r : G\,t_1 \to X,$$
$$p_1 \circ F\,\varrho = \varrho \circ p_2 \;\Rightarrow\; f_{t_1}\,(p_1, r) = H\,\varrho\,(f_{t_2}\,(p_2, r \circ G\,\varrho))$$
This equation expresses a general case $(f_{t_1}\,(p_1, r))$ in terms of a specific case $(H\,\varrho\,(f_{t_2}\,(p_2, r \circ G\,\varrho)))$, under the assumption $p_1 \circ F\,\varrho = \varrho \circ p_2$. Here, we hope to find specific values for t_2, q and ϱ which verify the assumption, and obtain a characterisation of the polymorphic case in terms of a monomorphic case.

Satisfying the assumption $(p_1 \circ F\, \varrho = \varrho \circ p_2)$ is equivalent to making the diagram on the right commute. Let us pick the following values for t_2, p_2 and ϱ:

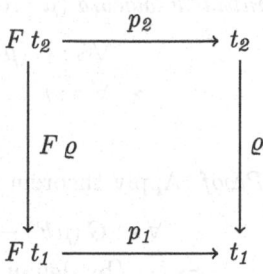

- $t_2 = \mu F$, the least fixpoint of F;
- $p_2 = \alpha$, the initial F-algebra;
- $\varrho = (\![p_1]\!)$, the catamorphism of p_1.

We know from properties of initial algebras and catamorphisms that these choices make the diagram commute. Thus, the assumption is verified, and the proof is complete.

Theorem 1 shows that we can express a polymorphic function in terms of a particular monomorphic instance, but the expressions still involve applying (polymorphic) catamorphisms. In the case where we have a function to test (f) and a model (g) to compare against, we can apply theorem 1 to both sides and simplify away the catamorphisms.

Theorem 2. *Let F, G, H be functors, let $f, g : \forall a:\star.(F\, a \to a) \times (G\, a \to X) \to H\, a$. If there is an initial F-algebra $(\mu F, \alpha)$, then*

$$\forall s : G\,(\mu F) \to X.$$
$$\Rightarrow \forall a : \star, p : F\, a \to a, r : G\, a \to X.$$

$$f_{\mu F}\,(\alpha, s) = g_{\mu F}\,(\alpha, s)$$
$$f_a\,(p, r) = g_a\,(p, r)$$

Proof. If $f_{\mu F}\,(\alpha, s) = g_{\mu F}\,(\alpha, s)$ holds for any s, then in particular the equality $f_{\mu F}\,(\alpha, r \circ G\,(\![p]\!)) = g_{\mu F}\,(\alpha, r \circ G\,(\![p]\!))$ holds. Applying $H\,(\![p]\!)$ to both sides of the equality preserves it, and then we can use theorem 1 to transform both sides and obtain that $f_a\,(p, r) = g_a\,(p, r)$ holds for any choice of a, p and r.

3.4   General Form of Arguments

The results of the previous section apply only to functions of type $(\forall a.\, (F\, a \to a) \times (G\, a \to X) \to H\, a)$. In this section we show that we can extend these results to any argument types which can be *embedded* in $(F\, a \to a) \times (G\, a \to X)$.

Definition 1. *An embedding-projection pair (an EP) is a pair of functions $e : A \to B$, $p : B \to A$ satisfying $p \circ e = id$. Because it constitutes evidence that covering B is enough to cover A, we write $(e, p) : A \subseteq B$ to denote such a pair.*

Given an EP[2] $(e, p) : \sigma[a] \subseteq (F\, a \to a) \times (G\, a \to X)$, one can transform the arguments calculated in the previous section (α paired with any function of type $G\,(\mu F) \to X$) into $\sigma[a]$ by using the projection component, p. The existence of the embedding guarantees that the domain of the original function is properly covered. This idea is expressed formally in the following theorem.

---

[2] Strictly speaking, this is a polymorphic EP — one EP for each type a.

Theorem 3. *Let F, G, H be functors and let $f, g : \forall a.\ \sigma[a] \to H\ a$. If there is an initial F-algebra $(\mu F, \alpha)$ and an EP $(e, p) : \sigma[a] \subseteq (F\ a \to a) \times (G\ a \to X)$, then*

$$\forall s : G\,(\mu F) \to X. \qquad f_{\mu F}\,(p\,(\alpha, s)) = g_{\mu F}\,(p\,(\alpha, s))$$
$$\Rightarrow \quad \forall a : \star, l : \sigma[a]. \qquad f_a\,l = g_a\,l$$

Proof. Apply theorem 2 to $f' = f \circ p$ and $g' = g \circ p$ as follows:

$$\forall s : G\,(\mu F) \to X. \qquad f_{\mu F}\,(p\,(\alpha, s)) = g_{\mu F}\,(p\,(\alpha, s))$$
$\Leftrightarrow$ {by definition of $\circ$, f' and g'}
$$\forall s : G\,(\mu F) \to X. \qquad f'_{\mu F}\,(\alpha, s) = g'_{\mu F}\,(\alpha, s)$$
$\Rightarrow$ {by theorem 2}
$$\forall a : \star, q : (F\ a \to a) \times (G\ a \to X). \qquad f'_a\,q = g'_a\,q$$
$\Rightarrow$ {by $e\ l$ being a special case of q}
$$\forall a : \star, l : \sigma[a]. \qquad f'_a\,(e\ l) = g'_a\,(e\ l)$$
$\Leftrightarrow$ {by definition of $\circ$, f' and g'}
$$\forall a : \star, l : \sigma[a]. \qquad f_a\,((p \circ e)\ l) = g_a\,((p \circ e)\ l)$$
$\Leftrightarrow$ {by the EP law: $p \circ e \equiv id$}
$$\forall a : \star, l : \sigma[a]. \qquad f_a\,l = g_a\,l$$

Properties used for testing are not always expressed in terms of a model, but very often directly as a predicate: they are merely Boolean-valued functions. We can specialise the above result to that case: given a polymorphic predicate, it is enough to verify it for the initial algebra.

Theorem 4. *Let F, G be functors, let $f : \forall a.\ \sigma[a] \to Bool$. If there is an EP $(e, p) : \sigma[a] \subseteq (F\ a \to a) \times (G\ a \to X)$ and an initial F-algebra $(\mu F, \alpha)$, then*

$$\forall s : G\,(\mu F) \to X. \qquad f_{\mu F}\,(p\,(\alpha, s))$$
$$\Rightarrow \quad \forall a : \star, l : \sigma[a]. \qquad f_a\,l$$

Proof. Substitute *const True* for g in theorem 3.

One might think that theorem 3, about models, follows from theorem 4, about properties, using $f\,(p, r) = test\,(p, r) \mathbin{==} model\,(p, r)$. This is in fact invalid in general, because one cannot assume that equality ($==$) is available for arbitrary types. Indeed, our usage of parametricity in the proof assumes the opposite.

The above results show that it is enough to test on arguments picked from the set $I = \{p\,(\alpha, s) \mid s : G\,(\mu F) \to X\}$. This could be done by picking elements s in $G(\mu F) \to X$ and testing on $p(\alpha, s)$. However, for the efficiency of testing, it is important *not* to proceed as such, because it can cause redundant tests to be performed. This is because the projection can map different inputs into a single element in I. A better way to proceed is to generate elements of I directly.

3.5 Embedding Construction

The previous section shows that our technique can handle arguments that can be embedded in $(F\,a \to a) \times (G\,a \to X)$. In this section we show that all first-order polymorphic arguments can be embedded. Our proof is constructive: it is also a method to build the EP. It is important to construct the embedding because it is used in computing the set of arguments to test the property on.

The general form of a first order argument is a function of type $C\,a \to D\,a$, where C and D are functors and D is polynomial. Note that non-functional values can be represented by adding a dummy argument. Similarly, the above form includes n-ary functions, as long as they are written in an uncurried form. We structure the proof as a series of embedding steps between the most general form and the canonical form. EPs for each step are composed into the final EP. The overall plan is to split all complex arguments into observations or constructors, then group each class together. Lemmas detailing these important steps are given after the top-level proof outline.

Theorem 5. *Let C_i and D_i be functors. If D_i are constructed by sum, products and fixpoints $(0, 1, +, \times, \mu)$, and none of the $C_i\,a$ are empty, then there exist functors F, G and an EP $(e, p) : \forall a : \star. \times_i (C_i\,a \to D_i\,a) \subseteq (F\,a \to a) \times (G\,a \to X)$.*

Proof.

$\times_i (C_i\,a \to D_i\,a)$

$\subseteq$ {by lemma 2}

$\times_i (C_i\,a \to (S_i \times (P_i \to a)))$

$\equiv$ {by distributing $\to$ over $\times$}

$\times_i (C_i\,a \to S_i) \times (C_i\,a \times P_i \to a)$

$\equiv$ {by letting $F_i\,a = G_i\,a \times P_i$}

$\times_i (C_i\,a \to S_i) \times (F_i\,a \to a)$

$\equiv$ {by commutativity and associativity of $\times$}

$\times_i (C_i\,a \to S_i) \times \times_i (F_i\,a \to a)$

$\subseteq$ {by lemma 1}

$(G\,a \to X) \times \times_i (F_i\,a \to a)$

$\equiv$ {by $(\tau_1 \to a) \times (\tau_2 \to a) \equiv (\tau_1 + \tau_2) \to a$}

$(G\,a \to X) \times (F\,a \to a)$

where $G\,a = \times_i (C_i\,a)$; $X = \times_i X_i$ and $F\,a = +_i (F_i\,a)$.

Lemma 1. *For all types σ_1, σ_2 and non-empty types τ_1, τ_2 (witness$_1 : \tau_1$ and witness$_2 : \tau_2$) then there exists $(e, p) : (\tau_1 \to \sigma_1) \times (\tau_2 \to \sigma_2) \subseteq \tau_1 \times \tau_2 \to \sigma_1 \times \sigma_2$.*

Proof. The embedding applies the embedded functions pair-wise.

$e\,(f_1, f_2) = \lambda(t_1, t_2) \to (f_1\,t_1, f_2\,t_2)$

The projection can be constructed by providing dummy arguments (*witness*) to missing parts of the pair. It is safe to do so, because that part of the pair is ultimately ignored anyway.

$$p\,h = (\lambda t_1 \rightarrow \mathit{fst}\ (h\,(t_1 \qquad , \mathit{witness}_2)),$$
$$\lambda t_2 \rightarrow \mathit{snd}\,(h\,(\mathit{witness}_1, t_2 \qquad)))$$

Lemma 2. *Let D be a functor constructed by sum, products and fixpoints. Then there exist types S, P and $(e, p) : D\,a \subseteq S \times (P \rightarrow a)$*

Proof. D represents a data structure, which can be decomposed into a shape (S) and a function from positions inside that shape to elements ($P \rightarrow a$). ([1] provide a detailed explanation). The shape can be obtained by using trivial elements ($S = D\,1$). For testing purposes, only structures with a finite number of elements can be generated, and therefore one can use natural numbers for positions ($P = \mathbb{N}$). The projection can traverse the data structure in pre-order and use the second component of the pair ($\mathbb{N} \rightarrow a$) to look up the element to put at each position. The corresponding embedding is easy to build.

3.6   Correctness in Practice

We have reasoned in a fast-and-loose fashion: our proofs rely on the strongest version of parametricity, which holds only in the polymorphic lambda-calculus.

Applying them to real-world languages (like Ada, Haskell, Java, ML, etc.) is merely "morally correct" [8]. We assume that the functions under test are well-behaved with respect to parametricity: they should not make use of side-effects, infinite data structures, bottoms, etc. In the context of random or exhaustive testing, these assumptions are generally valid. Therefore, our results are readily applicable in practice with a very high level of confidence.

Still, we could extend the result by using a more precise version of parametricity, as for example [18] expose it.

4   More Examples

4.1   Multiple Type Parameters

While the theoretical development assumes a single type parameter, we can apply our schema to functions with multiple type parameters. The basic idea is to treat parameters one at a time, assuming the others constant. We do not justify this formally, but merely show how to proceed on a couple of examples.

Example 4 (map). Consider the ubiquitous function *map*, which applies a function to each element in a list.
$$map : \forall a\,b.\,(a \rightarrow b) \rightarrow [a] \rightarrow [b]$$
As usual, we are interested in testing a candidate *map* function against a known-working model.

We first aim to remove the type parameter a. To do so, we isolate the constructors for a by embedding the list argument into a shape (the length of the list) and a function giving the element at each position (see lemma 2). We obtain the type $\forall a\,b.\,(a \rightarrow b) \rightarrow \mathbb{N} \rightarrow (\mathbb{N} \rightarrow a) \rightarrow [b]$. We see from the type that the only constructor is an algebra of the functor $F\,a = \mathbb{N}$. The initial F-algebra is
data $A = X\,\mathbb{N}$

After substitution, we have the type $\forall b.\ (A \to b) \to \mathbb{N} \to (\mathbb{N} \to A) \to [b]$, and we know that the third argument is fixed to X.

We can proceed and remove the type parameter b. There is only one constructor for b, which is already isolated, so the initial algebra is easy to compute:

data $B = F\,A$

After substitution, we have the type $(A \to B) \to \mathbb{N} \to (\mathbb{N} \to A) \to [B]$, and we know that the first argument is fixed to F. The second and third arguments can be projected back into a list, so we get the final property:

$\forall\, n : \mathbb{N}.$ **let** $xs = [X\,1 \mathinner{\ldotp\ldotp} X\,n]$
  in $map1\ F\ xs \mathrel{==} map2\ F\ xs$

Note that the function to pass to map is fixed: again, only testing for various lengths is enough!

Example 5 (prefix). In Haskell, the standard function *isPrefixOf* tests whether its first argument is a prefix list of its second argument. *isPrefixOf* normally uses the overloaded equality $((\mathop{==}) : a \to a \to Bool)$ to compare elements in the first list to elements in the second one. Instead we consider a more general version that explicitly takes a comparison function as parameter. In that case, the types of elements in input lists do not have to match. This generalisation is captured in a type as follows:

$isPrefixOf : \forall a\,b.\ (a \to b \to Bool) \to [a] \to [b] \to Bool$

In this example, the type arguments are completely independent, so we can remove both at once. Both lists can be embedded into a shape ($\mathbb{N}$) and a function from positions ($\mathbb{N} \to a$) in the familiar way. We get the type: $\forall a\,b.\ (a \to b \to Bool) \to \mathbb{N} \to (\mathbb{N} \to a) \to \mathbb{N} \to (\mathbb{N} \to b) \to Bool$.

Computing the initial algebras offers no surprise. We obtain:

data $A = X\,\mathbb{N}$
data $B = Y\,\mathbb{N}$

We have to test functions of type $(A \to B \to Bool) \to \mathbb{N} \to (\mathbb{N} \to A) \to \mathbb{N} \to (\mathbb{N} \to B) \to Bool$, with the third argument fixed to X and the fifth fixed to Y. Again, by using the projection, we know that we can instead generate lists of $X\,i$ and $Y\,j$ to pass directly to the polymorphic function.

Thus, a property to check that two implementations of *isPrefixOf* have the same behaviour is written as follows:

$\forall\, eq : A \to B \to Bool, m : \mathbb{N}, n : \mathbb{N}.$
  let $xs = [X\,1 \mathinner{\ldotp\ldotp} X\,m]$
    $ys = [Y\,1 \mathinner{\ldotp\ldotp} Y\,n]$
  in $isPrefixOf1\ eq\ xs\ ys \mathrel{==} isPrefixOf2\ eq\ xs\ ys$

What if we had used the less general type $\forall a.\ (a \to a \to Bool) \to [a] \to [a] \to Bool$ (which is isomorphic to the standard type $\forall a.\ Eq\ a \Rightarrow [a] \to [a] \to Bool$)? In that case, the initial algebra would be

data $A = X\,\mathbb{N} \mid Y\,\mathbb{N}$

and the property would look exactly the same. The difference is that the function eq would be quantified over a larger set. It would only be passed values of the form $X\,i$ for the first argument, and $Y\,i$ for the second argument, but the generator of random values does not "know" it. Therefore, it might generate redundant test cases, where eq only differs in its results for argument-pairs that are not in the form $X\,i$, $Y\,i$. As we have seen in the above example, this redundancy is avoided by using the most general type. This is another example where more polymorphism makes testing more efficient.

4.2   Assumptions on Arguments

It can be quite challenging to write properties for functions whose arguments must satisfy non-trivial properties. For example, generating associative functions or total orders is not obvious. A naive solution is to generate unrestricted arguments and then condition the final property on the arguments being well behaved. This can be highly inefficient if the probability to generate a well-behaved argument is small. Since our technique fixes some parameters, it is sometimes easier to find (or more efficient to generate) arguments with a complex structure. We give examples in the following sections.

Example 6 (Parallel Prefix). A parallel-prefix computation computes the list $[x_1, x_1 \oplus x_2, \ldots, x_1 \oplus \ldots \oplus x_n]$, given an associative operation $\oplus$ and a list of inputs $x_1, \ldots, x_n$. How can we test that two given parallel-prefix computations have equivalent outputs?

We start with the type $\forall a.(a \to a \to a) \to [a] \to [a]$. To isolate the constructors, we rewrite the list type as usual and get $\forall a.(a \to a \to a) \to \mathbb{N} \to (\mathbb{N} \to a) \to [a]$. We can group the constructors to make the algebra more apparent: $\forall a.((a \times a + \mathbb{N}) \to a) \to \mathbb{N} \to [a]$. The next step is to pick the initial algebra.

One might be tempted to use the following datatype and its constructors for the initial algebra.

   data $A = OPlus\ A\ A \mid X\ \mathbb{N}$

However, we must take into account that the operation passed to the prefix computation must be associative. The *OPlus* constructor retains too much information: one can recover how the applications of $\oplus$ were associated by examining the structure of A. In order to reflect associativity, a "flat" structure is required. Thus, one should work with lists, as follows:

   type $A = [\mathbb{N}]$
   $x\ n = [n]$
   $oplus = (+\!\!+)$

The final property is therefore:

   $\forall\, n : \mathbb{N}.\ \textbf{let}\ xs = map\ x\ [1\mathbin{..} n]$
       in *prefix1 oplus xs* == *prefix2 oplus xs*

The problem of testing parallel prefix networks has been studied before, notably by Sheeran, who has presented a preliminary version of our result in an invited talk in Hardware Design and Functional Languages [25]. [28] presents another monomorphic instance: he shows that it is enough to test over a 3-value type (**3**). At first sight, it might seem that testing over **3** is better than over $\mathbb{N}$. However, merely substituting the type-variable with **3** still requires testing all combinations of the other arguments, yielding 113×3^n tests[3] to cover the lists of length n, while by our method a single test is enough for a given length. Again, the efficiency of our method comes from the fixing of more arguments than the type variable.

The above explanation to deal with associativity relies very much on intuition, but it can be generalised. One must always take in account the laws restricting the input when computing the initial algebra: that is, one must find the initial object of the category of algebras that respect those laws. We direct the interested reader to [13] for details.

Example 7 (Insertion in sorted list). Consider testing an insertion function which assumes that its input list is strictly ascending. That is, its type is $\forall a.\ (a \to a \to Bool) \to a \to [a] \to [a]$, but the list argument is restricted to lists that are strictly ascending according to the first argument, which in turn must be a strict total order. After breaking down the list as usual one must handle the type $\forall a.\ (a \to a \to Bool) \to a \to \mathbb{N} \to (\mathbb{N} \to a) \to [a]$.

Forcing the list to be sorted can be tricky to encode as a property of an algebra. So, instead of constraining the lists, we put all the burden on the first argument (an observation): it must be a strict total order that also makes the list ascending. This change of perspective lets us calculate the initial algebra without limitation. We obtain

data $A = Y \mid X\,\mathbb{N}$

The element to insert is Y, and as in many preceding examples, the function receives lists of the form $[X\,1\,..\,X\,n]$. This makes generating suitable orders $(A \to A \to Bool)$ easy. Indeed, for such an order (ord) to respect the order of the list, it must satisfy the equation:

$ord\,(X\,i)\,(X\,j) = i < j$

Therefore, we only need to decide on how to order Y with respect to $X\,i$. That is, decide where to position Y in the list. For an input list of length n, there are exactly $n+1$ possible positions to insert an element. The final property shows how to define the order given a position k for Y.

$\forall\,n : \mathbb{N}, k : \{0\,..\,n\}.\ \textbf{let}\ xs = [X\,1\,..\,X\,n]$
$\qquad\qquad\quad \textbf{in}\ insert1\,(ord\,k)\,Y\,xs\ \text{==}\ insert2\,(ord\,k)\,Y\,xs$
$\quad \textbf{where}\ ord\,k\,(X\,i)\,(X\,j) = i < j$
$\qquad\qquad ord\,k\,Y \qquad Y \quad = False$
$\qquad\qquad ord\,k\,(X\,i)\,Y \quad\; = i \leqslant k$
$\qquad\qquad ord\,k\,Y \qquad (X\,j) = k < j$

Example 8 (Sorting network). A generator of sorting networks can be represented as a polymorphic function of type $\forall a.\ (a \times a \to a \times a) \to [a] \to [a]$. The first argument is a two-element comparator. Note that, by parametricity, the function cannot check whether the comparator swaps its inputs or not. It is restricted to merely compose instances of the comparator.

---

[3] [28] shows that only some combinations are relevant, but the number of tests is still quadratic in the length of the input list. 113 is the number of associative functions in $\textbf{3} \to \textbf{3} \to \textbf{3}$.

Let us apply our schema on the above type. We use the isomorphism $\tau \rightarrow a \times b \cong (\tau \rightarrow a) \times (\tau \rightarrow b)$ to split the first argument, and handle the list as usual. We obtain the following type.

$$\forall\, a.\ (a \times a \rightarrow a) \rightarrow (a \times a \rightarrow a) \rightarrow \mathbb{N} \rightarrow (\mathbb{N} \rightarrow a) \rightarrow [a]$$

If we overlook the restrictions on the constructors, the initial algebra is

data $A = Min\ A\ A \mid Max\ A\ A \mid X\ Int$

As usual, the sorting function is to be run on $[X\,1\,..\,X\,n]$. The comparator is built out of *Min* and *Max*. Therefore, to fully test the sorting function, it suffices to test the following function.

$$sort\_Lat : \mathbb{N} \rightarrow [A]$$
$$sort\_Lat\ n = sort\ (\lambda(x, y) \rightarrow (Min\ x\ y, Max\ x\ y))\,[X\,1\,..\,X\,n]$$

The output is a list where each element is a comparison tree: a description of how to compute the element by taking minimums and maximums of some elements of the input. In order to verify that the function works, we are left with checking that the output trees are those of a correct sorting function.

Note that this must be checked modulo the laws which restrict our initial algebra. *Min* and *Max* must faithfully represent 2-element comparators which can be passed to the polymorphic function. Therefore, the type A must be understood as a free distributive lattice [10] where *Min* and *Max* are meet ($\wedge$) and join ($\vee$) and Xi are generators.

The correctness of the function can then be expressed as checking each element of the output (o_k) against the output of a known sorting function. Formally:

$$o_k = \bigvee_{M \subseteq \{1...n\}, \#M = n-k} \left(\bigwedge_{i \in M} Xi \right)$$

There are (at least) two possible approaches to proceed with the verification.

1. Verify the equivalence symbolically, using the laws of the distributive lattice. This is known as the word problem for distributive lattices. One way to do this is to test for syntactical equivalence after transformation to normal form.
2. Check the equivalence for all possible assignments of booleans to the variables $X\,i$, meet and join being interpreted as Boolean conjunction and disjunction. This is valid because truth tables are a complete interpretation of free distributive lattices. In effect, proceeding as such is equivalent to testing the sorting function on all lists of booleans.

   This second way to test equivalence shows that our technique is essentially (at least) as efficient as that of [19], provided that properties of the distributive lattice structure are cleverly exploited.

5   Related Work

Universe-bound polymorphism. [17] have studied the testing of datatype-generic functions: polymorphic functions where the type parameter is bound to a given universe. This restriction allows them to proceed by case analysis on the shape of the type. In contrast, our method makes the assumption that type parameters are *universally* quantified, taking advantage of parametricity. Since universal quantification and shape analysis are mutually exclusive, Jansson's method and ours complement each other very well.

Shortcut Fusion. Shortcut deforestation [14] is a technique to remove intermediate lists. A pre-requisite to shortcut deforestation is that producers of lists are written on the form g (:) [], or essentially, $g\,\alpha$ where α is the initial algebra of the list functor. In general, functions that are normally written in terms of the initial algebra must be parametrised over any algebra, thereby adding a level of polymorphism. This is the exact opposite of the transformation we perform.

Similarity with our work does not stop here, as the correctness argument for shortcut deforestation also relies heavily on polymorphism and parametricity.

Church Encodings. The purpose of Church encodings is to encode data types in the pure lambda calculus. Church encodings can also target the polymorphic lambda calculus [5], and the resulting types are polymorphic. In essence, the Church encoding of a data type is the type of its fold (catamorphism). [15] provides an illuminating example.

Theorem 1 describes (almost) an inverse of Church-encoding: we aim at recovering the datatype underlying polymorphic types. It is not exactly an inverse though: the church-encoded type might be encapsulated in a polymorphic function, which may expose only some of its constructors. Therefore we target these constructors instead of directly targeting the datatype.

Defunctionalisation. [22] describes defunctionalisation: a transformation technique to remove higher-order functions. Each lambda-abstraction is replaced by a distinctive constructor, whose argument holds the free variables. Applications are implemented via case-analysis: the tag of the constructor tells which which abstraction is entered.

[9] have shown that defunctionalisation works as an inverse to church encoding. Thus, theorem 1 can be seen as a special case of defunctionalisation, targeted at the constructors of a polymorphic type. However, our main focus is not the removal of function parameters, but of type parameters. Indeed, our embedding step, which *introduces* function parameters, is often crucial for the removal of polymorphism. Note also that we do not transform the function under test. In fact, only the arguments passed to the function are defunctionalised. The constructing functions are transformed to constructors of a datatype, and the observations have to perform case-analysis on this datatype.

Concretisation. [21] introduce *concretisation*: a generalisation of defunctionalisation that can target any source language construct by translating its introduction form into an injection, and its elimination form into case analysis. They apply concretisation to Rémy-style polymorphic records and Haskell type classes, but not removal of polymorphism altogether.

QuickCheck. As explained in the introduction, the standard way to test polymorphic functions in QuickCheck [7] is to substitute $\mathbb{N}$ for polymorphic parameters.

In the first runs, QuickCheck assigns only small values to parameters of this type, effectively testing small subsets of $\mathbb{N}$. As testing progresses, the size is increased. This strategy is already very difficult to beat! Indeed, we observe that, thanks to parametricity, if one verifies correctness for a type of size n, the function works for all types of size n or less. Additionally, because of the inherent nature of testing, it is only possible to run a finite number of test cases. Therefore, the standard QuickCheck strategy of type instantiation is already very good. We can do better because, in addition to fixing the type, we also fix some (components of) parameters passed to the function. In effect, meaningless tests (tests that are isomorphic to other already run tests, or tests that are unnecessarily specific) are avoided.

Table 1. Comparison of the traditional QuickCheck praxis to the new method

criterion	traditional	new
type	$\mathbb{N}$	μF
constructors	$F\mathbb{N} \to \mathbb{N}$	$\{\alpha\}$
observations	$G\mathbb{N} \to X$	$G(\mu F) \to X$

The situation is summarised in table 1. By fixing the constructors, a whole dimension is removed from the testing space. Even though the space of observations is enlarged when $\mu F > \mathbb{N}$ (from $G\mathbb{N} \to X$ to $G(\mu F) \to X$), the trade-off is still beneficial in most cases. We argue informally as follows: if $\mu F > \mathbb{N}$, then F is a "big" functor, such as $F\ a = 1 + a \times a$. This means that the set $F\mathbb{N} \to \mathbb{N}$ is big, and as we replace that by a singleton set, this gain dwarfs the ratio between $G(\mu F) \to X$ and $G\mathbb{N} \to X$, for any polynomial functor G.

Besides efficiency, another benefit to the new method is that the generated counter examples are more informative, as seen on an example in section 2.

In Haskell, there is another pitfall to substituting the polymorphic parameter by $\mathbb{N}$: type classes. Imagine for example that the type parameter is constrained to be an instance of the Eq typeclass. Because $\mathbb{N}$ is such an instance, it *is* possible to use it for the type parameter, but this badly skews the distribution of inputs. Indeed, on average, the probability that $a == b$, for generated a and b tends to be very small. A better strategy would be to have a different instance of Eq for each run, each with a probability of equality close to $1/2$. Our method does not suffer from this problem: we insist that the methods of classes are explicitly taken into account when identifying the constructors and the observations.

Exhaustive Checking. We argue in the previous section that using $\mathbb{N}$ for type parameters is a sensible approach for random testing. However, as [23] remark, this does not work as well for depth-bound exhaustive testing: the dimension of the test space for constructors ($F\mathbb{N} \to \mathbb{N}$) grows exponentially as the depth of the search increases. They suggest to use smaller types to test on (such as the unit or Boolean), but the user of the library is left to guess which size is suitable. Our method kills two birds with one stone: we conjure up a suitable type parameter to use, and prevent the exponential explosion of the search for constructors by fixing them. Therefore, we believe that our method is an essential improvement for exhaustive testing of polymorphic functions.

Symbolic execution [27] generate test cases by symbolic execution of the property to check. As we have mentioned in section 2, our technique can be understood as symbolic execution, therefore, generating test cases by symbolic execution potentially subsumes our method. The advantage of our approach is that it is purely type-based: the monomorphic instance is independent of the actual definition of the property. Therefore, it can work with an underlying black-box tester for monomorphic code.

6   Future Work

While the scope of this paper is the testing of polymorphic functions, our technique to remove polymorphism is not specific to testing: any kind of verification technique can be applied on the produced monomorphic instance. This suggests that it has applications outside the domain of testing, maybe in automated theorem proving. This remains to be investigated.

Automated test-case generation libraries typically address the problem of generating random values for monomorphic arguments. We have addressed the problem of calculating values for type arguments. A natural development would be to unify both approaches in the framework of a dependently-typed programming language. A first step towards this goal would be to give a detailed account of parametricity in presence of dependent types.

With the exception of computing initial algebras with laws, the technique described here is completely algorithmic. Therefore, one can assume that it is easy to automate it and build a QuickCheck-like library to test polymorphic properties. However, such a tool would need to analyse the type structure of the functions it is given, and languages based on the polymorphic lambda calculus typically lack such a feature. Moreover, this very feature would invalidate the parametricity theorem, since it relies on universally quantified types being opaque, thereby invalidating our "monomorphisation" transformation. A long term area of research would be to design a programming language where parametricity and type-analysis can be specified on a case-by-case basis. As a short-term goal, we propose to mechanise the technique as an external tool rather than a library, or require the programmer to explicitly inform the polymorphic test generator about the type structure.

We have shown how to get rid of polymorphism using the "initial view" of the type parameters. As there exists a dual to shortcut fusion [26], we conjecture that there exists a dual to our method, using the "final view". That is, the function should be transformed to isolate a co-algebra and fix it to the final element of the category. Is is unclear at this point what would be the outcome of this dual in terms of testing behaviour.

The technique that we present requires a specific form for the type of the function to test. While our examples show that this form covers a wide range of polymorphic functions that are commonly tested, one can still aspire for a larger applicability. We hope to improve this aspect, either by showing that more types can be embedded, or by amending the core theory. In particular, we address only rank-1 polymorphism: extending to rank-n would be useful. Also, the restriction that F must be a functor in $(F\, a \to a) \times (G\, a \to X)$ seems too specific. Indeed, Church-encoding some types may lead to F being a type-function that is not a functor, and there is *a-priori* no reason that the encoding cannot be reverted. An example is given by [30]: **data** $T = Lam\,(T \to T) \mid App\,T\,T$ is encoded as $\forall a.\ ((a \to a) \to a) \to (a \to a \to a) \to a$, and $F\,a = (a \to a) + (a \times a)$, which is not a functor. We hope to achieve this by fully explaining our technique in a defunctionalisation setting.

7 Conclusion

We have presented a schema for efficient testing of polymorphic properties. The idea is to substitute polymorphic values by a faithful symbolic representation. This symbolic representation is obtained by type analysis, in two steps:

1. isolation of the constructors (yielding a functor F); and
2. restriction to the initial F-algebra.

We suspect that neither of these steps is original, but we could not find them spelt out as such, and therefore we believe that bringing them to the attention of the programming languages community is worthwhile. Furthermore, the testing of polymorphic properties is a novel application for these theoretical ideas.

We have shown on numerous examples, and informally argued that applying our technique not only *enables* testing polymorphic properties by removing polymorphism, but yields good efficiency compared to the standard praxis of substituting N for the polymorphic argument. In some cases, this improvement is so dramatic that it makes the difference between testing being useful or not. As another evidence of the value of the method, we have applied it to classical problems and have recovered or improved on the corresponding specific results.

Giving a more polymorphic type to a given function enlarges its domain, so one might think that this can increase the amount of testing necessary to verify properties about that function. If our technique is applied, the opposite is true.

You love polymorphism, but you were afraid that it would complicate testing? Fear no more! On the contrary, polymorphism can facilitate testing if approached from the right angle.

Acknowledgments. We would like to give special thanks to Marcin Zalewski, whose repeated interest for the topic and early results gave us the motivation to pursue the ideas presented in this paper. Josef Svenningson and Ulf Norell provided counter examples to our technique. Peter Dybjer gave useful references about Church encodings. Anonymous reviewers gave useful comments and helped improve the presentation of the paper. This work is partially funded by the Swedish Research Council.

References

[1] Abbott, M., Altenkirch, T., Ghani, N.: Categories of containers. In: Gordon, A.D. (ed.) FOSSACS 2003. LNCS, vol. 2620, pp. 23–38. Springer, Heidelberg (2003)

[2] Arts, T., Hughes, J., Johansson, J., Wiger, U.: Testing telecoms software with quviq QuickCheck. In: Proc. of the 2006 ACM SIGPLAN workshop on Erlang, pp. 2–10. ACM, New York (2006)

[3] Bagge, A.H., David, V., Haveraaen, M.: Axiom-based testing for C++. In: Companion to the 23rd ACM SIGPLAN conference on Object-oriented programming systems languages and applications, pp. 721–722. ACM, New York (2008)

[4] Bird, R., de Moor, O.: Algebra of programming. Prentice-Hall, Englewood Cliffs (1997)

[5] Böhm, C., Berarducci, A.: Automatic synthesis of typed lambda-programs on term algebras. Theoretical Computer Science 39(2-3), 135–154 (1985)

[6] Christiansen, J., Fischer, S.: EasyCheck — test data for free. In: Garrigue, J., Hermenegildo, M.V. (eds.) FLOPS 2008. LNCS, vol. 4989, pp. 322–336. Springer, Heidelberg (2008)

[7] Claessen, K., Hughes, J.: QuickCheck: a lightweight tool for random testing of Haskell programs. In: Proc. of the fifth ACM SIGPLAN international conference on Functional programming, pp. 268–279. ACM, New York (2000)

[8] Danielsson, N.A., Gibbons, J., Hughes, J., Jansson, P.: Fast and loose reasoning is morally correct. In: POPL 2006, pp. 206–217. ACM Press, New York (2006)

[9] Danvy, O., Nielsen, L.R.: Defunctionalization at work. In: Proc. of the 3rd ACM SIGPLAN international conference on Principles and practice of declarative programming, pp. 162–174. ACM, New York (2001)

[10] Davey, B.A., Priestley, H.A.: Introduction to lattices and order. Cambridge University Press, Cambridge (2002)

[11] Day, N.A., Launchbury, J., Lewis, J.: Logical abstractions in Haskell. In: Proc. of the 1999 Haskell Workshop (1999)

[12] Fegaras, L., Sheard, T.: Revisiting catamorphisms over datatypes with embedded functions (or, programs from outer space). In: Proc. of the 23rd ACM SIGPLAN-SIGACT symposium on Principles of programming languages, pp. 284–294. ACM, New York (1996)

[13] Fokkinga, M.M.: Datatype laws without signatures. Mathematical Structures in Computer Science 6(01), 1–32 (1996)

[14] Gill, A., Launchbury, J., Peyton Jones, S.L.: A short cut to deforestation. In: Proc. of the conference on Functional programming languages and computer architecture, pp. 223–232. ACM, New York (1993)

[15] Hinze, R.: Church numerals, twice! J. of Funct. Program 15(01), 1–13 (2005)

[16] Hoffman, D., Nair, J., Strooper, P.: Testing generic Ada packages with APE. Ada Lett. XVIII(6), 255–262 (1998)

[17] Jansson, P., Jeuring, J., Cabenda, L., Engels, G., Kleerekoper, J., Mak, S., Overeem, M., Visser, K.: Testing properties of generic functions. In: Horváth, Z., Zsók, V., Butterfield, A. (eds.) IFL 2006. LNCS, vol. 4449, pp. 217–234. Springer, Heidelberg (2007)

[18] Johann, P., Voigtländer, J.: Free theorems in the presence of seq. In: Proc. of the 31st ACM SIGPLAN-SIGACT symposium on Principles of programming languages, pp. 99–110. ACM, New York (2004)

[19] Knuth, D.E.: The Art of Computer Programming, 2nd edn. Sorting and Searching, vol. 3. Addison-Wesley Professional, Reading (1998)

[20] Nilsson, R.: ScalaCheck (2009), http://code.google.com/p/scalacheck/
[21] Pottier, F., Gauthier, N.: Polymorphic typed defunctionalization and concretization. Higher-Order Symbol. Comput. 19(1), 125–162 (2006)
[22] Reynolds, J.C.: Definitional interpreters for Higher-Order programming languages. Higher Order Symbol. Comput. 11(4), 363–397 (1998)
[23] Runciman, C., Naylor, M., Lindblad, F.: Smallcheck and lazy smallcheck: automatic exhaustive testing for small values. In: Proc. of the first ACM SIGPLAN symposium on Haskell, pp. 37–48. ACM, New York (2008)
[24] Saff, D.: Theory-infected: or how i learned to stop worrying and love universal quantification. In: Companion to the 22nd ACM SIGPLAN conference on Object-oriented programming systems and applications companion, pp. 846–847. ACM, New York (2007)
[25] Sheeran, M.: Hardware design and functional programming: a perfect match. Talk at Hardware Design and Functional Languages (2007)
[26] Svenningsson, J.: Shortcut fusion for accumulating parameters & zip-like functions. In: Proc. of the seventh ACM SIGPLAN international conference on Functional programming, vol. 37, pp. 124–132. ACM, New York (2002)
[27] Tillmann, N., Schulte, W.: Parameterized unit tests. SIGSOFT Softw. Eng. Notes 30(5), 253–262 (2005)
[28] Voigtländer, J.: Much ado about two (pearl): a pearl on parallel prefix computation. SIGPLAN Not. 43(1), 29–35 (2008)
[29] Wadler, P.: Theorems for free! In: Proc. of the fourth international conference on Functional programming languages and computer architecture, pp. 347–359. ACM, New York (1989)
[30] Washburn, G., Weirich, S.: Boxes go bananas: encoding higher-order abstract syntax with parametric polymorphism. In: Proc. of the eighth ACM SIGPLAN international conference on Functional programming, pp. 249–262. ACM, New York (2003)

Formal Verification of Coalescing Graph-Coloring Register Allocation

Sandrine Blazy[1], Benoît Robillard[2], and Andrew W. Appel[3]

[1] IRISA - Université Rennes 1
[2] CEDRIC - ENSIIE
[3] Princeton University

Abstract. Iterated Register Coalescing (IRC) is a widely used heuristic for performing register allocation via graph coloring. Many implementations in existing compilers follow (more or less faithfully) the imperative algorithm published in 1996. Several mistakes have been found in some of these implementations.

In this paper, we present a formal verification (in Coq) of the whole IRC algorithm. We detail a specification that can be used as a reference for IRC. We also define the theory of register-interference graphs; we implement a purely functional version of the IRC algorithm, and we prove the total correctness of our implementation. The automatic extraction of our IRC algorithm into Caml yields a program with competitive performance. This work has been integrated into the CompCert verified compiler.

1 Introduction: Iterated Register Coalescing

Register allocation via graph coloring was invented by Chaitin et al. [9]. The variables of the program are treated as vertices in an interference graph. If two program variables are live at the same time[1] then they must not be assigned to the same register: this situation is indicated by placing an edge in the interference graph. If the target machine architecture has K registers, then a K-coloring of the graph corresponds to a good register allocation.

Kempe's 1879 graph-coloring algorithm works as follows. Find a vertex x of degree $< K$ from the graph. (Call such a vertex a *low-degree* vertex.) Remove x from the graph. Recursively K-color the rest of the graph. Now put x back in the graph, assigning it a color. Because (when x was removed) its degree was $< K$, there must be an available color for x. Kempe's algorithm is easy to implement and has a good running time.

But some K-colorable graphs have no low-degree vertices (i.e. Kempe's algorithm is incomplete); not only that, some source programs are not K-colorable. Chaitin augmented Kempe's algorithm to handle *spills*—that is, some vertices are not colored at all, and the corresponding program variables are kept in memory instead of in registers. Spills are costly, because memory-resident variables

---

[1] Except in specific cases where the variables are known to contain the same value.

A.D. Gordon (Ed.): ESOP 2010, LNCS 6012, pp. 145–164, 2010.

must be loaded and stored. Chaitin's algorithm also chooses the set of variables to spill, based on interference properties of the graph and on cost heuristics.

Briggs *et al.* [8] improve the algorithm by adding *coalescing:* if the program contains a move instruction from variable a to variable b, then these two variables should be colored the same (assigned to the same register) if possible. Briggs's algorithm works by adding *preference* edges to the interference graph in addition to interference edges. The problem is now, "K-color the graph subject to all interference constraints, with the least-cost-possible set of uncolored vertices, and with the fewest possible preference edges that connect differently colored vertices." Because overeager coalescing can lead to uncolorable graphs, Briggs coalesces preference-related vertices together only when it would not change a low-degree ($< K$) vertex to a vertex having more than K high-degree neighbors.

George and Appel [13] improve on Briggs's algorithm by interleaving graph simplification with Briggs's coalescing heuristic, and by adding a second coalescing heuristic. The result is that the coalescing is significantly better than in Briggs's version, and the algorithm runs no slower. George and Appel's "Iterated Register Coalescing" (IRC) algorithm is widely used in both academic and industrial settings, and many implementations follow the imperative pseudocode given in their paper.

Graph coloring is NP-hard; IRC (like Chaitin's algorithm) is subquadratic, but does not find optimal solutions. In practice IRC performs well in optimizing compilers, especially for machines with many registers (16 or more). When there are few registers available (8 or fewer) *and* when register allocation is preceded by aggressive live-range splitting, the IRC algorithm is too conservative: it does not coalesce enough, and spills excessively. In such cases, algorithms that use integer linear programming [3] or the properties of chordal graphs [15] are sometimes used to compute an optimal solution.

The CompCert compiler is a formally verified optimizing compiler for the C language [7,17]. Almost all of CompCert is written in the purely functional Gallina programming language within the Coq theorem prover. That part of CompCert is formally verified with a machine-checked correctness proof, and automatically translated to executable Caml code using Coq's extraction facility.

As CompCert targets PowerPC, 32 registers are available. Register allocation in CompCert thus uses an imperative implementation of IRC implemented in Caml, closely following George and Appel's pseudocode. The result of (each run of) the Caml register-allocator is checked for consistency by a Gallina program, whose correctness is formally verified. This is *translation validation* [20,19], meaning that CompCert will (provably) never produce an incorrect translation of the source program, but if the Caml program produces an incorrect coloring (or fails to terminate) then CompCert will fail to produce a result at all.

In this new work we have written Iterated Register Coalescing as a pure functional program, expressed in Gallina (and easily expressible in pure ML or Haskell). We have proved the total correctness of the algorithm with a machine-checked proof in Coq, as well as its termination. Register allocation is widely recognized as complex by compiler writers, and IRC itself has sometimes been incompletely or incorrectly described and implemented. In the years since publication of a description of IRC as detailed imperative pseudocode [2], the third author has received several (correct) reports of minor errata in that presentation of the algorithm. Thus, a verified description and implementation of IRC is valuable. One contribution of our formalization work is to provide a correct reference description of IRC. We believe this is the first formal verification of an optimizing register allocation algorithm that is used in industrial practice.

All results presented in this paper have been mechanically verified using the Coq proof assistant [12,6]. The complete Coq development is available online at http://www.ensiie.fr/~robillard/IRC/. A technical-report version of this paper with extensive proofs is also available at http://www.ensiie.fr/~robillard/IRC/techreport.pdf. Consequently, the paper only sketches the proofs of some of its results; the reader is referred to the Coq development and the report for the full proofs.

The remainder of this paper is organized as follows. Section 2 introduces the IRC algorithm. Then, section 3 details this algorithm, as well as the worklists it computes incrementally. Section 4 defines the interference graphs and their main properties. Section 5 describes some properties that are useful for updating incrementally the worklists. Section 6 summarizes the termination proof of the IRC algorithm. Section 7 explains the soundness of the IRC algorithm. Section 8 is devoted to the experimental evaluation of our implementation. Related work is discussed in section 9, followed by concluding remarks.

2 Specification of the IRC Algorithm

The input to IRC is an interference *graph* and a *palette* of colors. The vertices of the graph are program variables. Some program variables must be assigned to specific machine registers, because they are used in calling conventions and for other reasons; these vertices are called *precolored*. The *palette* represents the set of all the machine registers, which corresponds to the precolored variables. The (undirected) edges of the graph are *interference* edges, which are unweighted, and *preference* edges, which are weighted.

There is just one data type Vertex.t representing all of these concepts: variable, graph vertex, register, color. A color is just a register; a register is simply one of the variables from the set of precolored vertices. We require nothing of the Vertex.t type except that it be provided with a computable total ordering (for fast search-tree lookups). An edge is (isomorphic to) a pair of vertices with an optional weight. The equality over edges considers the edge $a \rightarrow b$ equal to the edge $b \rightarrow a$ and we denote the edge by (a, b).

The output of IRC is a *coloring*, that is, a partial mapping from variables to colors. The range of the coloring must be a subset of the precolored variables (i.e. machine registers). Whenever the graph contains an interference edge between a and b, the coloring must map a and b to different colors.

The cost of a coloring is the sum of move-cost and spill-cost. Move-cost w occurs when there is a preference edge of weight w between a and b, and the coloring maps a and b to different colors. Spill-cost occurs when the coloring fails to map a variable. IRC does not in general produce optimum-cost colorings, so we will not reason formally about costs: we will not formalize move-cost and spill-cost, nor specify the properties of the weight type.

The next section details a Gallina program that is equivalent to the IRC algorithm. *Informally* we will see that this Gallina program is equivalent to the IRC algorithm that performs well in the real world, *formally* we prove that the algorithm always terminates with a valid coloring, and *empirically* we measure the run time of the program (as extracted from Gallina to ML and compiled with the Caml compiler).

3   Sketch of the IRC Algorithm

Recall that a *low-degree* vertex is incident on $< K$ interference edges. A *high-degree* vertex has $\geq K$ interference edges. A *move-related* vertex is mentioned in at least one preference edge. To run faster, IRC uses worklists which classify vertices according to their degree and their move-relationship. The worklists are the following ones.

1. spillWL is defined as the set of high-degree, nonprecolored vertices.
2. freezeWL is defined as the set of low-degree, move-related, nonprecolored vertices.
3. simplifyWL is defined as the set of low-degree, nonmove-related, nonprecolored vertices.
4. movesWL is defined as the set of preference edges.

The properties of the four worklists can be seen as an invariant, that we call WL_invariant. The efficiency of IRC and its proof rely on this invariant.

Given a graph g, the worklists can be computed straightforwardly by examining the set of edges incident on each vertex. George and Appel's IRC algorithm incrementally updates these worklists. Thus, there is no need to search for low-degree vertices and move-related vertices in the whole graph after each step, but only at their initialization.

IRC usually takes as argument the interference graph g and the *palette* of colors (or K which is the cardinality of *palette* since *palette* is isomorphic to $1..K$). The first step is then to initialize the worklists wl that we define as the quadruple (spillWL, freezeWL, simplifyWL, movesWL). The only argument we give to the IRC algorithm is a record (called irc_graph) consisting of g, wl, pal, K, a proof that (WL_invariant g pal wl) is preserved, and a proof that K is the cardinality of *pal*. Maintaining K in the irc_graph record avoids computing it at each recursive call to IRC. This record is defined in Fig. 1 as well as its construction.

The IRC algorithm as we write it in Gallina[2] is given in Fig. 2. Option types are used to represent partial functions. A value of type option t is either $\emptyset$ (pronounced "none"), denoting failure, or $\lfloor x \rfloor$ (pronounced "some x"), denoting success with result $x : t$.

---

[2] Modulo some notation, but otherwise unchanged.

```
Record irc_graph := Make_IRC_Graph {
  gph : Graph.t;
  wl : WL,
  pal : VertexSet.t;
  k : nat;
  Hwl : WL_invariant gph pal wl;
  Hk : VertexSet.cardinal pal = k }.

Definition graph_to_IRC_graph g palette :=
  let K := VertexSet.cardinal palette in
  let wl := init_WL g K in
  Make_IRC_Graph g wl palette K
                 (WL_invariant_init g K wl) (refl_equal K).

Definition Iterated_Register_Coalescing g palette :=
  let g' := graph_to_IRC_graph g palette in (IRC g').
```

Fig. 1. The irc_graph record and the initialization of IRC. The record is built from an interference graph and a palette. This irc_graph is given as argument to IRC.

```
 1 : Algorithm IRC g : Coloring :=
 2 : match simplify g with
 3 : |⌊(r,g')⌋ => available_coloring g r (IRC g')
 4 : | ∅      => match coalesce g with
 5 :   |⌊(e,g')⌋ => complete_coloring e (IRC g')
 6 :   | ∅ => match freeze g with
 7 :     |⌊g'⌋ => IRC g'
 8 :     | ∅  => match spill g with
 9 :       |⌊r,g'⌋ => available_coloring g r (IRC g')
10:       | ∅ => precoloring g
11:      end
12:     end
13:   end
14: end.
```

Fig. 2. Implementation of the IRC algorithm in Coq

The IRC algorithm is as follows. If there is a low-degree, nonmove-related vertex, then *simplify* (lines 2 and 3): remove a low-degree vertex, color the rest of the graph, put back the vertex. Otherwise, if there is a coalescible move (i.e. vertices a and b related by a preference edge, such that the combined vertex ab has less than K high-degree neighbors), then *coalesce* (lines 4 and 5). Otherwise, if there is a low-degree vertex, then *freeze* (lines 6 and 7): mark the low-degree vertex for simplification, even though it is related by a preference edge, and even though this could cause the move-related vertices to be colored differently. Otherwise, if there are only high-degree vertices, then *spill* (lines 8 and 9): remove a vertex, color the rest of the graph, then attempt to put this vertex back into the graph. This attempt may succeed, but is not guaranteed to; there may be no color available for it. Finally, if there are neither low-degree nor high-degree nonprecolored vertices, the graph contains only precolored vertices, and the recursion bottoms out (line 10).

Our different data structures are represented using the Coq library for finite sets (and finite maps) of elements from a totally ordered type, implemented as AVL trees. We take advantage of not only the library implementations (with $O(\log N)$ operations for nondestructive insert, membership, etc.) but also the library proofs of correctness of these operations. Thus we can write the algorithm in a purely functional style with only an asymptotic cost penalty of $\log N$.

Our formally verified implementation of IRC abstracts interference graphs, so that several implementations of the graph abstraction can be plugged to the algorithm. We have built one such graph implementation, and proved it correct. The extraction (automatic translation into Caml) of our implementation runs competitively with the standard IRC algorithm as implemented imperatively in Caml.

3.1   Functions Updating the Graph

Four auxiliary functions called by IRC update the irc_graph g and yield a new irc_graph. These functions are:

(simplify g) simplifies a vertex v and returns $\lfloor (v, g') \rfloor$ where g' is the result from the removal of v from g. If no vertex is candidate for the simplification, then $\emptyset$ is returned.

(freeze g) deletes the preference edges incident on a low-degree, nonprecolored, move-related vertex v, and returns $\lfloor g' \rfloor$. If no vertex can be frozen, then $\emptyset$ is returned.

(coalesce g) looks for a coalescible edge e of g and merges its endpoints, leading to a graph g', and returns $\lfloor (e, g') \rfloor$. If there is no coalescible edge in the graph, $\emptyset$ is returned.

(spill g) spills a vertex v having the lowest spill cost and returns $\lfloor (v, g') \rfloor$ where g' is the result from the removal of v from g. If no nonprecolored vertex remains in the graph, then $\emptyset$ is returned.

Each of these functions is divided into two parts : first it determines whether the operation is possible or not (e.g. if there exists a coalescible move); then if it is, it updates the irc_graph by calling another function, postnamed with _irc. These latter functions call operations of the graph abstract data type, reuse directly the palette (as well as K and the proof of Hk), and update the worklists. Moreover, the proof of the worklist invariant is incrementally updated in order to prove the invariant for the new graph.

Fig. 3 shows how the simplify_irc function calls the remove_vertex function. The (nontrivial) specification of the function updating the graph is defined in the graph interface. Inv_simplify_wl is the lemma stating that the invariant is preserved by the simplify_wl function. Its proof is hard and needs to be done separately for each function. It is required to build the record.

```
Definition simplify_irc r ircg H :=
Make_IRC_Graph (remove_vertex r (gph ircg))
               (simplify_wl r ircg (k ircg))
               (pal ircg)
               (k ircg)
               (Inv_simplify_wl r ircg H)
               (Hk ircg).
```

Fig. 3. Definition of the `simplify_irc` function. It takes a vertex `r` to simplify and an `irc_graph` as input and calls the function `remove_vertex` acting on a `graph`. The hypothesis called `H` states that `r` belongs to the simplify worklist of (`wl ircg`).

3.2 Functions Updating the Coloring

The algorithm starts from a nonempty coloring (i.e. with precolored vertices). Then, IRC colors at most one vertex per recursive call until all the nonprecolored vertices are colored or marked for spilling. This process uses the three following functions.

(`precoloring g`) is a mapping containing just $x \mapsto x$ for every x such that $x \in$ vertices (gph g) $\cap$ *palette*. When we use this function, it should be the case that vertices (gph g) $\subseteq$ *palette*, that is, g contains only precolored nodes.

(`available_coloring g v m`) is defined as $m[v \mapsto c]$, where c is any element of $((pal\ g) - (\text{forbidden } v\ m\ g))$. Informally, this function assigns to v a color c such that no interference neighbor of v is colored with c, if such a color exists (it may not be the case when a variable is spilled). The forbidden set is the union of all the colors (in the range of m) of the interference neighbors of v in g.

(`complete_coloring e m`), with $e = (x, y)$, is defined as $m[y \mapsto m(x)]$ if $x \in$ dom (m), otherwise just m. It is used to assign the same color to the endpoints of a coalesced edge.

4 Interference Graphs

The Coq standard library does not contain any general library on graphs yet. Indeed, formalizing graph theory requires many application-specific choices. We have defined a generic interface for *interference graphs* (i.e. the type called graph), as well as an implementation of them. Our interface is voluntarily minimal: it consists only of definitions and properties that are needed by the IRC algorithm. Such a minimal interface could be reused and extended in a further development. This section presents this interface and focuses on the specification of the functions updating the graph. The implementation of the interface as well as the proofs of the properties are not detailed in this paper, but can be consulted online.

4.1   Vertices and Edges

An interference graph is a graph with two kinds of edges. Thus, we have chosen to describe interference graphs as a set of vertices and two sets of edges, since this representation is very expressive and is commonly used in graph theory. However, these sets are only used for the specification. The underlying implementation of our interface uses adjacency maps. Both vertices and edges are required to be ordered types in order to use efficient data structures of the Coq standard library.

The type of edges generalizes interference and preference edges. The edges are classically specified as triples (v_1, v_2, w) where v_1 and v_2 are the extremities of the edge, and w is the optional weight of the edge. For convenience, weights will be omitted when they do not matter. In addition, edges are provided with accessors to their first endpoint (fst_end), their second endpoint (snd_end) and their weight (get_weight). We also define that an edge e is incident to a vertex v iff v is an endpoint of e:

$$\text{incident } e\,v =_{\text{def}} \text{fst\_end } e = v \ \lor \ \text{snd\_end } e = v$$

The two kinds of edges can be discriminated by their weight : interference edges are unweighted edges, their weight is $\emptyset$, preference edges are weighted edges, their weight is $\lfloor x \rfloor$. Moreover, two predicates pref_edge and interf_edge are used to specify whether an edge is a preference edge or an interference edge, and a predicate same_type which holds for two edges iff they are of the same type. We also define an equality over edges (denoted by $=$) as the commutative equality of their endpoints, and the equality of their weight.

Interference graphs are updated through accessors (to vertices and edges) and predicates that test the belonging of a vertex or an edge to the graph. More precisely:

 - V g is the set of vertices of g.
 - IE g is the set of interference edges of g.
 - PE g is the set of preference edges of the g.
 - $v_1 \in_v g$ holds iff the vertex v_1 belongs to g.
 - $e_1 \in_e g$ holds iff the edge e_1 belongs to g.

From this basis we derive two other key predicates, representing neighborhood relations.

 - interfere $x\,y\,g =_{\text{def}} (x, y, \emptyset) \in_e g$
 - prefere $x\,y\,g =_{\text{def}} \exists w, (x, y, \lfloor w \rfloor) \in_e g$

4.2   Properties of Interference Graphs

An interference graph g must be a simple graph, that is, there is at most one edge between each pair of vertices. This is not restrictive and avoids conflicts between preference and interference edges. Indeed, two edges of the same type linking the same vertices are equivalent to one edge of this type, and two edges of different types linking the same vertices are equivalent to an interference edge. Formally specifying this property requires some intermediate definitions.

We define an equivalence (denoted by $\simeq$) between edges that does not take weights into account.

$$e \simeq e' =_{\text{def}} (\texttt{fst\_end } e = \texttt{fst\_end } e' \wedge \texttt{snd\_end } e = \texttt{snd\_end } e') \vee$$
$$(\texttt{fst\_end } e = \texttt{snd\_end } e' \wedge \texttt{snd\_end } e = \texttt{fst\_end } e')$$

In a simple graph, this equivalence implies equality.

Theorem 1. *If* $e_1 \in_e g \wedge e_2 \in_e g \wedge e_1 \simeq e_2$, *then* $e_1 = e_2$.

An interference graph must be loop-free: no edge goes from a vertex to itself.
Theorem 2. *If* $e_1 \in_e g$, *then* $\texttt{fst\_end } e_1 \neq \texttt{snd\_end } e_1$.

The endpoints of any edge of g must belong to g.

Theorem 3. *If* $e_1 \in_e g$, *then* $(\texttt{fst\_end } e_1) \in_v g \wedge (\texttt{snd\_end } e_1) \in_v g$.

4.3 Specification of the `remove_vertex` Function

We characterize $g' = \texttt{remove\_vertex } v\, g$ with the three following properties.
(RM1) $Vg' = (Vg) - \{v\}$
(RM2) $\texttt{precolored } g' = (\texttt{precolored } g) - \{v\}$
(RM3) $e_1 \in_e g' \Leftrightarrow (e_1 \in_e g \wedge \neg\texttt{incident } e_1 v)$

4.4 Specification of the `delete_preference_edges` Function

Given $g' = \texttt{delete\_preference\_edges } v$, all the preference edges incident to v in g are deleted in g'. We axiomatize this function as follows.
(DP1) $Vg' = Vg$
(DP2) $\texttt{precolored } g' = \texttt{precolored } g$
(DP3) $\texttt{IE } g' = \texttt{IE } g$
(DP4) $\texttt{PE } g' = \texttt{PE } g - \{e \mid \texttt{incident } e\, v\}$

4.5 Specification of the `merge` Function

The hardest function of the interface to specify is the `merge` function. Given an edge $e = (x, y)$ of g, $(\texttt{merge } e\, g)$ yields the graph g' such that x and y have been merged into a single vertex. This operation requires to define the redirection of an edge. Intuitively, when an edge is merged, it is transformed into its redirection in g'.

Let $e' = (a, b)$ be an edge. The redirection of e' from c to d (denoted by $e'_{[c \to d]}$) is the edge such that each occurrence of c in the endpoints of e' is replaced with d. We do not consider the case where $e' = (c, c)$ since, interference graphs are loop-free. $e'_{[c \to d]}$ is defined as follows.

1. $(a, b)_{[a \to d]} =_{\text{def}} (d, b)$ if $a \neq b$
2. $(a, b)_{[b \to d]} =_{\text{def}} (a, d)$ if $a \neq b$
3. $(a, b)_{[c \to d]} =_{\text{def}} (a, b)$ if $a \neq c \wedge b \neq c$

For $g' = \mathtt{merge}\ (x, y)\ g$, we consider that x is the merged vertex. Thus, the vertices of g' are those of g minus y. Any interference edge e of g is transformed into the edge $e_{[y \to x]}$ in g'. Any preference edge e of g is transformed into the edge $e_{[y \to x]}$ in g' if the extremities of $e_{[y \to x]}$ are not linked with an interference edge in g'. The merge function is axiomatized as follows.

(ME1) $V g' = (V g) - \{y\}$

(ME2) $\mathtt{precolored}\ g' = (\mathtt{precolored}\ g) - \{y\}$

(ME3) If $e' \in (\mathtt{IE}\ g)$, then $e'_{[y \to x]} \in (\mathtt{IE}\ g')$.

(ME4) If $e' \in (\mathtt{PE}\ g) \wedge \neg \mathtt{interfere}\ (\mathtt{fst\_end}\ e'_{[y \to x]})(\mathtt{snd\_end}\ e'_{[y \to x]})\ g' \wedge e \neq e'$, then $\mathtt{prefere}\ (\mathtt{fst\_end}\ e'_{[y \to x]})\ (\mathtt{snd\_end}\ e'_{[y \to x]})\ g'$.

(ME5) If $e' \in_e g'$, then $\exists e'' \in_e g$ such that $e' \simeq e''_{[y \to x]} \wedge (\mathtt{same\_type}\ e'\ e'')$.

This specification of merge is under restrictive since there is no constraint on weights. It simplifies both the specification and the implementation of merge. It allows the user not to take care about possible weights of preference edges.

4.6   Basic Interference Graph Functions

The specification of IRC also requires a few other functions and predicates, that are used for instance to determine the neighbors of a vertex.

The interference (resp. preference) neighborhood of a vertex v in a graph g, denoted by $N(v, g)$ (resp. $N_p(v, g)$) is the set containing the vertices x such that there exists an interference edge (resp. a preference edge) between v and x.

$$x \in N(v, g) =_{\mathrm{def}} \mathtt{interfere}\ \mathtt{x}\ \mathtt{v}\ \mathtt{g}$$

$$x \in N_p(v, g) =_{\mathrm{def}} \mathtt{prefere}\ \mathtt{x}\ \mathtt{v}\ \mathtt{g}$$

The interference (resp. preference) degree of a vertex v in a graph g, denoted by $\delta(v, g)$ (resp. $\delta_p(v, g)$), is the cardinality of $N(v, g)$ (resp. $N_p(v, g)$).

$$\delta(v, g) =_{\mathrm{def}} \mathtt{card}(N(v, g))$$

$$\delta_p(v, g) =_{\mathrm{def}} \mathtt{card}(N_p(v, g))$$

The IRC algorithm heavily relies on move-relationship and interference degrees of the vertices. Hence, we have to define move-related and low-degree vertices. Both of them are defined as functions yielding booleans, in order to be computable.

A vertex v is move_related in a graph g iff the preference neighborhood of v in g is not empty.

$$\mathtt{move\_related}\ g\ v =_{\mathrm{def}} \neg\ \mathtt{is\_empty}\ N_p(v, g)$$

A vertex v is of low-degree in a graph g if its interference degree is strictly lower than K.

$$\text{has\_low\_degree } g\, K\, v =_{\text{def}} \delta(v, g) < K$$

5 Incremental Update of Worklists

The core of the IRC algorithm is the incremental update of the worklists and the preservation of the associated invariant. Our IRC algorithm handles the worklists efficiently and updates, for each recursive call, the minimal sets of vertices that must be updated. Due to a lack of space, only the main properties are given in this paper. For each kind of update (vertex removal, coalescing of vertices, and deletion of a preference edge), this section details the main lemmas that are required to prove that the WL_invariant holds on the updated graph and worklists.

This section only provides the key lemmas sketching in which conditions vertices have to be moved from a worklist to another one (i.e. how move-related and low-degree vertices evolve through the updates and the way the worklists have to be updated).

5.1 Vertex Removal

Removing a vertex generalizes both simplification and spill. Given a vertex v and a graph g, the following properties hold for $g' = \text{remove\_vertex } v\, g$.

Theorem 4. *Any nonmove-related vertex $x \neq v$ of g is also nonmove-related in g'.*

Theorem 5. *Any move-related vertex $x \neq v$ of g is nonmove-related in g' iff $x \in N_p(v, g) \; \wedge \; \delta_p(x, g) = 1$.*

Theorem 6. *Any low-degree vertex $x \neq v$ of g is also a low-degree vertex of g'.*

Theorem 7. *Any high-degree vertex $x \neq v$ of g is of low-degree in g' iff $x \in N(v, g) \; \wedge \; \delta(x, g) = K$.*

Let $wl = (\text{spillWL}, \text{freezeWL}, \text{simplifyWL}, \text{movesWL})$ such that the invariant (WL_invariant $g\, palette\, wl$) holds. We denote by $IN(v, g)$ the set of nonprecolored interference neighbors of v in g having an interference degree equal to K. These vertices are of high-degree in g and will be of low-degree in g'. Thus, we need to know if they will be move-related of not in g' to classify them in the appropriate worklist. To that purpose, $IN_{mr}(v, g)$ and $IN_{nmr}(v, g)$ are respectively defined as the set of move-related vertices of $IN(v, g)$ in g and of nonmove-related vertices of $IN(v, g)$ in g. Similarly, we denote by $PN(v, g)$ the set of nonprecolored, low-degree preference neighbors of v in g having a preference degree equal to 1 in g. These low-degree vertices will not be move-related anymore and have to be moved from the freeze worklist to the simplify one.

Let $wl' = (\text{spillWL}', \text{freezeWL}', \text{simplifyWL}', \text{movesWL}')$ the four worklists that result from the following updates of wl.

1. Vertices of $IN(v,g)$ are removed from spillWL, with $IN(v,g)$ defined as follows. $IN(v,g) =_{\text{def}} \{x \in N(v,g) \mid x \notin \text{precolored}(g) \land \delta(x,g) = K\}$.
2. Vertices of IN_{mr} are added to freezeWL, with IN_{mr} defined as follows. $IN_{mr}(v,g) =_{\text{def}} \{x \in IN(v,g) \mid \text{move\_related } g\, x\}$
3. Vertices of IN_{nmr} are added to simplifyWL, with IN_{nmr} defined as follows. $IN_{nmr}(v,g) =_{\text{def}} \{x \in IN(v,g) \mid \neg\, \text{move\_related } g\, x\}$
4. Vertices of $PN(v,g)$ are removed from the freeze worklist resulting from 2 and added to the simplify worklist resulting from 3. $PN(v,g)$ is defined as follows.
   $PN(v,g) =_{\text{def}} \{x \in N_p(v,g) \mid x \notin \text{precolored}(g) \land \delta_p(x,g) = 1 \land (\text{has\_low\_degree } g\, K\, x)\}$
5. Preference edges incident to v are removed from movesWL.
6. The vertex v is removed from the worklist it belongs to.

Theorem 8. WL_invariant g' *palette wl'.*

The accurate update of worklists for the the simplify and spill cases can be simply derived from the general theorem about vertex removal above : a spill is a vertex removal of a vertex belonging to spillWL and the simplify case is a vertex removal of a vertex v belonging to simplifyWL (and hence such that $PN(v,g)$ is empty by definition of simplifyWL).

5.2   Coalescing Two Vertices

The coalescing case is the hardest one to deal with. We consider here a graph g and an edge (x,y) to be coalesced. In other words, x and y are merged in order to assign the same color to both of them. The resulting graph is called g'. Classically, there are two coalescing criteria :

1. George's criterion states that x and y can be coalesced if $N(x,v) \subseteq N(y,v)$. This criterion is not yet implemented, but represents no real difficulty.
2. Briggs's criterion states that x and y can be coalesced if the vertex resulting from the merge has less than K high-degree neighbors, that is $\text{card}(N(x,g) \cup N(y,g)) \cap H < K$, where H is the set of high-degree vertices of g. This criterion is simpler and performs usually as well as the previous one.

The proof of correctness of the algorithm only requires that the vertices to be merged are not both precolored. The other conditions only ensure the conservability of the coalescing, that is g' remains K-colorable if g is K-colorable. Intuitively, the vertices to be updated in the worklists are the neighbors of the coalesced edge endpoints. Actually, only a small subset of them needs to be updated.

Let $e = (x,y)$ and $g' = \text{merge } e\, g$. The key lemmas are the following.

Theorem 9. *Any nonmove-related vertex of g is also nonmove-related in g'.*

Theorem 10. *Any move-related vertex v different from x and y is nonmove-related in g' iff $v \in (N_p(x,g) \cap N(y,g)) \cup (N_p(y,g) \cap N(x,g)) \land \delta_p(v,g) = 1$.*

Theorem 11. *Any low-degree vertex v different from x and y of g is also a low-degree vertex of g'.*

Theorem 12. *Any high-degree vertex v different from x and y of g is of low-degree in g' iff $v \in N(x,g) \cap N(y,g) \wedge \delta(v,g) = K$.*

Let $wl = (\text{spillWL}, \text{freezeWL}, \text{simplifyWL}, \text{movesWL})$ such that the invariant $(\text{WL\_invariant } g \text{ palette } wl)$ holds. We introduce notations that are similar to those defined in the previous section. We denote by $L(x,y,g)$ the set of non-precolored interference neighbors of both x and y having an interference degree equal to K in g. These high-degree vertices of g will be low-degree vertices of g'. We reason as in the vertex removal case and respectively define $L_{mr}(x,y,g)$ and $L_{nmr}(x,y,g)$ as the set of move-related vertices of $L(x,y,g)$ and of nonmove-related vertices of $L(x,y,g)$. Last, we denote by $M(x,y,g)$ the set of nonpre-colored low-degree vertices of $(N(x,g) \cap N_p(y,g)) \cup (N_p(x,g) \cap N(y,g))$ having a preference degree equal to 1 in g. These vertices will not be move-related anymore and have to be transfered to the simplify worklist.

Let $wl' = (\text{spillWL}', \text{freezeWL}', \text{simplifyWL}', \text{movesWL}')$ the four worklists that result from the following updates of wl.

1. Vertices of $L(x,y,g)$ are removed from spillWL, with $L(x,y,g)$ defined as follows. $L(x,y,g) =_{\text{def}} IN(x,g) \cap IN(y,g)$.
2. Vertices of $M(x,y,g)$ are removed from freezeWL, with $M(x,y,g)$ defined as follows. $M(x,y,g) =_{\text{def}} \{x \in (N(x,g) \cap N_p(y,g)) \cup (N_p(x,g) \cap N(y,g)) \mid x \notin \text{precolored}(g) \wedge \delta_p(x,g) = 1 \wedge (\text{has\_low\_degree } g \, K \, x)\}$.
3. Vertices of $L_{mr}(x,y,g)$ are added to the freeze worklist resulting from 2, with $L_{mr}(x,y,g)$ defined as follows. $L_{mr}(x,y,g) =_{\text{def}} \{x \in L(x,y,g) \mid \text{move\_related } g \, x\}$.
4. Vertices of $L_{nmr}(x,y,g)$ and $M(x,y,g)$ are added to the simplify worklist resulting from 1, where L_{nmr} is defined as follows. $L_{nmr}(x,y,g) =_{\text{def}} \{x \in L(x,y,g) \mid \neg \text{move\_related } g \, x\}$
5. For every vertex v of $N_p(x,g) \cap N(y,g)$ the preference edge (v,x) is removed from movesWL.
6. For every vertex v of $N_p(y,g) - N(x,g)$ a preference edge (v,x) is added to the move worklist resulting from 5.
7. Every preference edge incident to y is removed from the move worklist resulting from 6.
8. If x is not precolored, x is classified in the appropriate worklist, depending on its preference and interference degrees.
9. x (and similarly y) is removed from the spill worklist resulting from 1 if it is of high-degree in g or from the freeze worklist resulting from 3 if it is of low-degree in g.

Theorem 13. $\text{WL\_invariant } g' \text{ palette } wl'$.

5.3   Deletion of Preference Edges

Let $g' = \text{delete\_preference\_edges } v \, g$. The key lemmas are the following.

Theorem 14. *Any nonmove-related vertex of g is also nonmove-related in g'.*

Theorem 15. *Any move-related vertex $x \neq v$ of g is nonmove-related in g' iff $x \in N_p(v, g) \wedge \delta_p(x, g) = 1$.*

Theorem 16. *Any vertex is of low-degree in g' iff it is of low-degree in g.*

Let $wl = (\texttt{spillWL}, \texttt{freezeWL}, \texttt{simplifyWL}, \texttt{movesWL})$ such that the invariant $(\texttt{WL\_invariant } g \texttt{ palette } wl)$ holds. We denote by D the set of nonprecolored preference neighbors of v having a degree equal to 1 in g, that are also low-degree vertices. These vertices have to be moved from the freeze worklist to the simplify one. D is formally defined as follows.

$$D(v, g) =_{\text{def}} \{x \in N_p(v, g) \mid x \notin \texttt{precolored}(g) \wedge \delta_p(x, g) = 1$$
$$\wedge \texttt{ has\_low\_degree } g \, K \, x\}$$

Let $wl' = (\texttt{spillWL'}, \texttt{freezeWL'}, \texttt{simplifyWL'}, \texttt{movesWL'})$ the four worklists that result from the following updates of wl and g' the updated graph.

1. The vertex v is removed from `freezeWL` and added to `simplifyWL`.
2. Vertices of D are removed from the freeze worklist resulting from 1.
3. Vertices of D are added to the simplify worklist resulting from 1.
4. Preference edges incident to v are removed from `movesWL`.

Theorem 17. $\texttt{WL\_invariant } g' \texttt{ palette } wl'$.

6   Termination Proof

When looking at the IRC algorithm, it is not straightforward to realize that it terminates. Thus, we have proved the termination of IRC. As 1) IRC is not structurally recursive (there is no argument that decreases along the recursive calls) and 2) we aim at extracting automatically a Caml code from our IRC algorithm, a termination proof is required by Coq.

Our termination argument is a linear measure that gives an accurate bound of the number of recursive calls. Our bound is $\mathcal{B}(g) = (2 \times n(g)) - p(g)$ where $n(g)$ is the number of nonprecolored vertices of the graph g, and $p(g)$ is the number of nonprecolored, low-degree, nonmove-related vertices of the graph g. $p(g)$ can also be seen as the number of candidates to the simplification in g. The proof that $\mathcal{B}(g)$ decreases at each recursive call heavily relies on the theorems 4 to 17 related to the update of the worklists. The termination proof also ensures that the number of calls to IRC is linear in the size of the graph.

Theorem 18. *Let v be a nonprecolored vertex of g and $g' = \texttt{remove\_vertex } v \, g$. Then, $\mathcal{B}(g') < \mathcal{B}(g)$.*

Proof. First, we show that $n(g') = n(g) - 1$. This proof is trivial, since the vertices of g are the same as the vertices of g', minus v (which is nonprecolored). Second, we show that $p(g) \leq p(g') + 1$. Indeed, according to theorem 8, the number of candidates for the simplification cannot decrease by more than 1. Thus, $2n(g') - p(g') < 2n(g) - p(g)$.

Theorem 19. *Let e be a coalescible edge of g and g' the graph resulting from the coalescing of e in g. Then, $\mathcal{B}(g') < \mathcal{B}(g)$.*

Proof. First, we show that $n(g') = n(g) - 1$. This proof is trivial, since the vertices of g are the same as the vertices of g', minus the second endpoint of e (which is nonprecolored). Second, we show that $p(g) \leq p(g')$. This proof is trivial too, since, according to theorem 13, the simplify worklist can only grow during the coalescing. Hence we obtain $\mathcal{B}(g') < \mathcal{B}(g)$.

Theorem 20. *Let v be a freeze candidate to g and g' the graph resulting from the freeze of v in g. Then, $\mathcal{B}(g') < \mathcal{B}(g)$.*

Proof. First, we show that $n(g') = n(g)$. This proof is trivial, since the vertices of g are the same as the vertices of g'. Second, we show that $p(g) \leq p(g')$. This proof is trivial too, since, according to theorem 17, the simplify worklist can only grow during the freeze. Hence we obtain $\mathcal{B}(g') < \mathcal{B}(g)$.

Theorem 21. *If IRC g calls recursively IRC g', then $\mathcal{B}(g') < \mathcal{B}(g)$. Consequently, the number of recursive calls of IRC g is bounded by $\mathcal{B}(g)$ and IRC g terminates.*

Proof. The proof is done by induction on the recursive calls. Each case is discharged thanks to one of the above lemmas.

7   Soundness

A *coloring*, w.r.t. a *palette* maps vertices to colors such that 1) two vertices linked with an interference edge have different colors, 2) any vertex to which a color is assigned belongs to the graph, and 3) any assigned color belongs to *palette*. A coloring is a partial mapping since the variables that are spilled are not colored.

A *coloring* of an interference graph g w.r.t a palette *palette* is a function f from **Vertex.t** to **option Vertex.t** such that :

(C1). $\forall e = (x, y) \in \text{IE}(g), f(x) \neq f(y)$
(C2). $\forall x, f(x) = \lfloor y \rfloor \Rightarrow x \in V(g)$
(C3). $\forall x \in V(g), f(x) = \lfloor y \rfloor \Rightarrow y \in palette$

The soundness proof of IRC states that IRC returns a valid coloring of the graph when the precoloring of the graph (defined in section 3.2) is valid.

Theorem 22. *If precoloring (g) is a coloring of g w.r.t. palette, then IRC g returns a coloring of g w.r.t. palette.*

Proof. The proof is done by induction on the recursive calls. There are five proof obligations to consider (one for each recursive call (PO1 to PO4), and one for the terminal call (PO5))[3].

---

[3] For convenience, we present the proof obligations once the **irc_graph** record has been unfolded.

(PO1). *If col* = IRC *(*remove_vertex *r g) is a coloring of (*remove_vertex *r g) w.r.t. palette, then (*available_coloring *g r col) is a coloring of g w.r.t. palette.*

(PO2). *If col* = IRC *(*merge *e g) is a coloring of (*merge *e g) w.r.t. palette and e is a coalescible edge, then (*complete_coloring *e col) is a coloring of g w.r.t. palette.*

(PO3). *If col* = IRC *(*delete_preference_edges *r g) is a coloring of (*delete_preference_edges *r g) w.r.t. palette, then* col *is a coloring of g w.r.t. palette.*

(PO4). *Same proof obligation as (PO1).*

(PO5). *(*precoloring *g) is a coloring of g w.r.t. palette.*

The proof of each of the four cases is almost straightforward using the soundness lemmas of precoloring, available_coloring *and* complete_coloring *that are not detailed in this paper. The last case is true by assumption.*

8   Experimental Evaluation

The source code of IRC is 600 lines of Coq functions and definitions. 1000 lines of Coq define generic data structures (and modules) that are not used directly by IRC. The whole proof represents approximately 4800 lines of Coq statements and proof scripts (excluding comments and blank lines), including 3300 lines

benchmark	graphs	variables	interferences	preferences
AES cipher	7	113	586	166
Almabench	10	53	310	22
Binary trees	6	23	42	14
Fannkuch	2	50	332	27
FFT	4	72	391	37
Fibonacci	2	17	18	9
Integral	7	12	12	5
K-nucleotide	17	24	74	14
Lists	5	18	33	11
Mandelbrot	2	45	117	17
N-body	9	28	73	10
Number sieve	2	25	53	12
Number sieve bits	3	76	58	12
Quicksort	3	28	116	16
SHA1 hash	8	34	107	15
Spectral test	9	14	35	6
Virtual machine	2	73	214	38
Arithmetic coding	37	31	85	15
Lempel-Ziv-Welch	32	32	127	16
Lempel-Ziv	33	29	92	15

Fig. 4. Benchmark characteristics

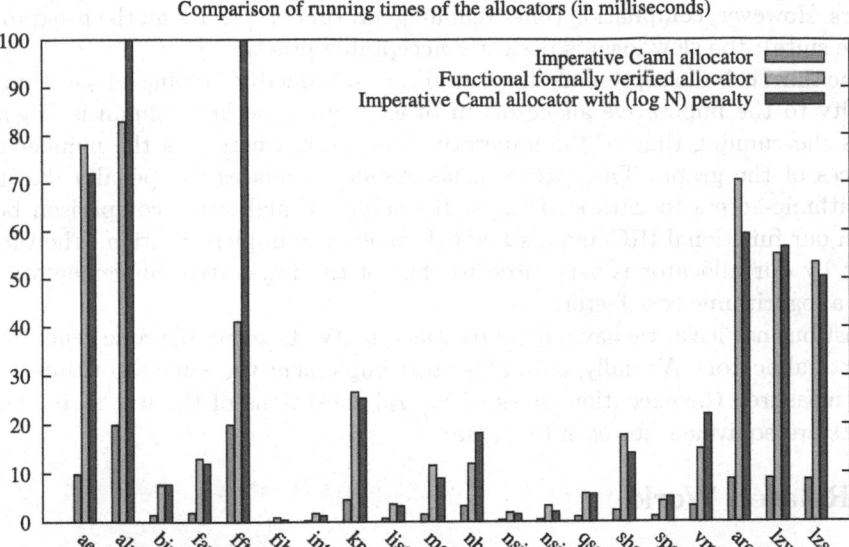

Comparison of running times of the allocators (in milliseconds)

Fig. 5. Comparison of the running times of our register allocator and the Caml one. To improve readability, results for the third column of almabench and fft are bounded by 100 though they are actually respectively 131 and 120.

(110 lemmas) for the properties of incremental update of worklists, 300 lines (17 lemmas) for the termination proof, 650 lines (22 lemmas) for the soundness proof and 550 lines (55 lemmas) for the properties of interference graphs. The proof is therefore 8 times bigger than the code it proves, which is a common ratio in the CompCert development [17].

We have integrated our IRC in the CompCert compiler. Thus, we can compare our Caml implementation of IRC (that is automatically generated from our Gallina program) with the Caml imperative one of CompCert. This comparison is done on the CompCert benchmark, whose characteristics are given in Fig. 4. The test programs range from 50 to 3000 lines of C code. Classically, for each program, the compiler generates at most two graphs for each function, one for integer variables and one for float variables. IRC is applied separately to each graph. Each line of Fig. 4 represents a program. The columns show the number of nonempty graphs to color, as well as the average numbers of vertices, interference edges and preference edges of these graphs.

Integrating our IRC in the CompCert compiler allows us to compare the running times of both register allocations. The results on the CompCert benchmark are shown in Fig. 5. Measurements were performed on an Apple PowerMac workstation with two 2.0 GHz PowerPC 970 processors and 6Gb of RAM, running MacOS 10.4.11. The first two columns of the histogram show the running times of both allocators in milliseconds. Our allocator does not run as fast as the imperative one : a logarithmic penalty arising from operations on data structures occurs. However, compilation times remain good (under $\frac{1}{10}$s. for all the programs of the suite); the slowdown is perfectly acceptable practically.

The third column represents the virtual time obtained by adding a logarithmic penalty to the imperative allocator. In other words, the last column is $(\log n)$ times the running time of the imperative allocator, where n is the number of vertices of the graph. This virtual measurement emulates the penalty due to logarithmic-access to data structures. It enables a qualitative comparison between our functional IRC and a standard imperative implementation. The time spent by our allocator is very close to that of the imperative implementation with a logarithmic cost factor.

Last but not least, we have compared the quality of executable code generated by both allocators. Actually, both allocators implement the same algorithm. We have measured the execution times of several executions of the test suite. The results are equivalent for each test case.

9   Related Work

Despite their wide use in computer science and the maturity of their theory, graphs are the subject of only a few works in the theorem-proving literature. Only a small part of graph theory has been represented in proof assistants.

A few works on graphs are devoted to the specification of graph theory basics. In 1994, Chou formalized in HOL some usual notions of graph theory [11], e.g. graphs, digraphs, acyclic graphs, trees. Works of Chou were followed by formalizations of planar graphs [21] and of graph search algorithms [22] in HOL. In 2001, Duprat formalized the same notions as Chou and directed graphs in Coq, using inductive definitions. Unfortunately, these definitions cannot be extracted using the Coq mechanism for extraction. Hence our work does not use this library. Mizar is probably the theorem prover in which graph theory has been studied the most. It provides a large library on graphs including previous-cited basics and more elaborated formalizations as the one of chordal graphs.

Other work naturally focuses on polynomial graph problems and their algorithms. More precisely, the most studied problem is the (very classical) problem of the shortest path in a positive-weighted graph. In 1998, Paulin and Filliâtre proved Floyd's algorithm using Coq and a tool for verifying imperative programs that will become Caduceus later. To fit this tool, their algorithm is written in an imperative style where graphs are simply represented as matrices. Another algorithm for the same problem, Dijkstra's algorithm, has been formalized and proved correct in both Mizar [10] and ACL2 [18]. Again, Mizar is in advance with the formalizations of other algorithms as the Ford-Fulkerson algorithm for flows, LexBFS for chordal graph recognition, or Prim's algorithm for minimum spanning tree. The latter algorithm has also been proved correct using B [1].

Kempe proved the five-color theorem for planar graphs in 1879 using a variation of the simple algorithm described in the second paragraph of this paper. Alas, he had no mechanical proof assistant; his "proof" of the four-color theorem [16] had an error that was not caught by mathematicians for 11 years. Appel and Haken proved the four-color theorem 97 years later [4]; this was the first use of a computer to prove a major open problem that was unsolved without mechanization. But major parts of that proof were unmechanized.

Recently, the theoretical problems of reasoning about planar graph coloring have been tackled in modern proof assistants. Bauer and Nipkow formalized undirected planar graphs and discussed a proof of the five-color theorem in Isabelle/HOL [5]. Gonthier and Werner produced the first fully mechanized proof of the four-color theorem, using a formalization of hypergraphs which are a generalization of graphs [14]. Gonthier and Werner's proof includes graph algorithms implemented in Gallina and reasoned about in Coq.

Our work is significant for many reasons. It constitutes the first machine-checked proof of a nontrivial register allocation algorithm and a reference implementation of IRC. In addition, using a functional language, such as Gallina, and a recursive definition of an algorithm, requires hard work on the termination proof. Furthermore, the algorithm we prove is an optimizing algorithm working on interference graphs. These graphs have specific properties that must be kept in mind along the specification of the algorithm. Finally, we took a special care of the algorithmic complexity of the generated code since it deals with a real and concrete problem, register allocation that has been integrated to the CompCert compiler.

10 Conclusion

We have presented, formalized and implemented an optimizing register allocation algorithm based on graph coloring. The specification of this algorithm raises difficult programming issues, such as the proof of termination, the specification of interference graphs, the care of algorithmic complexity and the functional translation of an imperative algorithm. In particular, we provided a very accurate way to adjust worklists incrementally, even better than the ones usually implemented. We also provided a correct reference description of IRC.

Technically, this work required the use of advanced features of the Coq system: mainly automatic generation of induction principles for non-structural recursive functions, but also dependent types for factoring development and proofs, generic modules, and efficient data structures.

The automatic extraction of our implementation leads to a Caml code that has been embedded in CompCert and whose results are equivalent to the one of the current release version of CompCert. The execution times (of the graph coloring phase of the CompCert compiler) are competitive with the ones of the release version of CompCert. Only a very little slowdown that cannot be avoided appears, due to logarithmic data structures operations of purely functional programming.

References

1. Abrial, J.-R., Cansell, D., Méry, D.: Formal derivation of spanning trees algorithms. In: Bert, D., Bowen, J.P., King, S. (eds.) ZB 2003. LNCS, vol. 2651, pp. 457–476. Springer, Heidelberg (2003)
2. Appel, A.W.: Modern Compiler Implementation in ML. Cambridge University Press, Cambridge (1998)

3. Appel, A.W., George, L.: Optimal spilling for CISC machines with few registers. In: PLDI. ACM, New York (2001)
4. Appel, K., Haken, W.: Every planar map is four colorable. Bulletin of the American Mathematical Society 82, 711–712 (1976)
5. Bauer, G., Nipkow, T.: The 5 colour theorem in Isabelle/Isar. In: Carreño, V.A., Muñoz, C.A., Tahar, S. (eds.) TPHOLs 2002. LNCS, vol. 2410, pp. 67–82. Springer, Heidelberg (2002)
6. Bertot, Y., Castéran, P.: Interactive Theorem Proving and Program Development. Coq'Art: The Calculus of Inductive Constructions. Texts in Theoretical Computer Science. Springer, Heidelberg (2004)
7. Blazy, S., Dargaye, Z., Leroy, X.: Formal verification of a C compiler front-end. In: Misra, J., Nipkow, T., Sekerinski, E. (eds.) FM 2006. LNCS, vol. 4085, pp. 460–475. Springer, Heidelberg (2006)
8. Briggs, P., Cooper, K.D., Torczon, L.: Improvements to graph coloring register allocation. TOPLAS 16(3), 428–455 (1994)
9. Chaitin, G.J., Auslander, M.A., Chandra, A.K., Cocke, J., Hopkins, M.E., Markstein, P.W.: Register allocation via coloring. Computer Languages 6, 47–57 (1981)
10. Chen, J.-C.: Dijkstra's shortest path algorithm. Journal of Formalized Mathematics 15 (2003)
11. Chou, C.-T.: A formal theory of undirected graphs in higher-order logic. In: Melham, T.F., Camilleri, J. (eds.) HUG 1994. LNCS, vol. 859, pp. 144–157. Springer, Heidelberg (1994)
12. Coq. The coq proof assistant, http://coq.inria.fr
13. George, L., Appel, A.W.: Iterated register coalescing. TOPLAS 18(3), 300–324 (1996)
14. Gonthier, G.: Formal proof – the four-color theorem. Notices of the American Mathematical Society 55(11), 1382–1393 (2008)
15. Hack, S., Goos, G.: Copy coalescing by graph recoloring. In: PLDI. ACM, New York (2008)
16. Kempe, A.B.: On the geographical problem of the four colors. American Journal of Mathematics 2, 193–200 (1879)
17. Leroy, X.: Formal certification of a compiler back-end or: Programming a compiler with a proof assistant. In: POPL, pp. 42–54. ACM, New York (2006)
18. Moore, J.S., Zhang, Q.: Proof pearl: Dijkstra's shortest path algorithm verified with ACL2. In: Hurd, J., Melham, T. (eds.) TPHOLs 2005. LNCS, vol. 3603, pp. 373–384. Springer, Heidelberg (2005)
19. Necula, G.C.: Translation validation for an optimizing compiler. SIGPLAN Not. 35(5), 83–94 (2000)
20. Pnueli, A., Siegel, M., Singerman, E.: Translation validation. In: Steffen, B. (ed.) TACAS 1998. LNCS, vol. 1384, pp. 151–166. Springer, Heidelberg (1998)
21. Yamamoto, M., Nishizaki, S.-y., Hagiya, M., Toda, Y.: Formalization of planar graphs. In: Workshop on Higher Order Logic Theorem Proving and Its Applications, pp. 369–384 (1995)
22. Yamamoto, M., Takahashi, K., Hagiya, M., Nishizaki, S.-y., Tamai, T.: Formalization of graph search algorithms and its applications. In: Grundy, J., Newey, M. (eds.) TPHOLs 1998. LNCS, vol. 1479, pp. 479–496. Springer, Heidelberg (1998)

A Theory of Speculative Computation*

Gérard Boudol and Gustavo Petri

INRIA, 06902 Sophia Antipolis, France

Abstract. We propose a formal definition for (valid) speculative computations, which is independent of any implementation technique. By speculative computations we mean optimization mechanisms that rely on relaxing the flow of execution in a given program, and on guessing the values read from pointers in the memory. Our framework for formalizing these computations is the standard operational one that is used to describe the semantics of programming languages. In particular, we introduce speculation contexts, that generalize classical evaluation contexts, and allow us to deal with out of order computations. Regarding concurrent programs, we show that the standard DRF guarantee, asserting that data race free programs are correctly implemented in a relaxed semantics, fails with speculative computations, but that a similar guarantee holds for programs that are free of data races in the speculative semantics.

1 Introduction

Speculative computation [8,16] is an implementation technique that aims at speeding up the execution of programs, by computing pieces of code in advance, possibly in parallel with the rest of the program, without being sure that these computations are actually needed. We shall actually use the terminology *"speculative computation"* in a very broad sense here: we try to capture the optimization techniques that rely on executing the code as it is, but relaxing the flow of control, not necessarily following the order prescribed by the reference operational semantics. Some keywords here are: pipelining, instruction level parallelism, out-of-order execution, branch prediction, thread level speculation, etc. – we shall not cite any particular paper from the huge literature on these classical topics. By considering parallel composition of speculations, we also include relaxed memory models [1] into this picture – though not those that try to capture compiler optimizations, that transform the code on the basis of semantical reasoning (see [4,20,24]).

Let us see some examples of speculative computations. In these examples, we use ML's notation $!p$ for dereferencing a pointer, and $()$ to mean termination, and we present the speculation as a sequence of transitions, each labelled by an action to be performed. More specifically, $\mathsf{rd}_{p,v}$ is the action of reading the value v for pointer p, $\mathsf{wr}_{p,v}$ means the action of writing the value v for p in the

---

* Work partially supported by the ANR-SETI-06-010 grant.

A.D. Gordon (Ed.): ESOP 2010, LNCS 6012, pp. 165–184, 2010.

memory, and $\checkmark$ is taking the first branch in a conditional branching. In our first example, the write to pointer q is reordered with respect to the read of p, which predicts the value tt – regardless of the actual value found in the memory, which is ignored at this stage:

$$(r := \,!\,p)\,;(q := tt) \xrightarrow{\mathsf{wr}_{q,tt}} (r := \,!\,p)\,;() \xrightarrow{\mathsf{rd}_{p,tt}} (r := tt)\,;() \qquad (1)$$

In our second example

$$(\text{if } !\,p \text{ then } q := tt \text{ else } ()) \xrightarrow{\mathsf{wr}_{q,tt}} (\text{if } !\,p \text{ then } () \text{ else } ())$$

$$\xrightarrow{\mathsf{rd}_{p,tt}} (\text{if } tt \text{ then } () \text{ else } ()) \qquad (2)$$

$$\xrightarrow{\checkmark} ()$$

the assignment in the first branch is issued speculatively, and the value tt is guessed for p. In both cases, the write to q could be issued to run in parallel with the rest of the code.

The idea of optimizing by computing in parallel is quite old, but the work that has been done so far on this topic is almost exclusively concerned with implementation techniques, either from the hardware or the software point of view, optimizing the execution of sequential code. These implementations are quite often complex, as speculations are not always correct, and need to be aborted or undone is some cases. For instance, the two speculations above are intuitively correct, provided that the predicted values coincide with the actual ones, but it would be wrong, in Example (2), to perform the write for q if the value eventually read for $!\,p$ is $f\!f$. Due to the complexity of implementing speculations perhaps, the notion of a *valid speculation* does not seem to have been formally defined before, except in some particular cases that we will mention below. Nevertheless, the various implementations of speculative techniques are generally considered correct, as regards the semantics of sequential programs.

Our first and main aim in this work is to design a semantical framework to formalize in a comprehensive manner the notion of a speculative computation, and to characterize the ones that are valid for sequential programs. We adopt and extend the approach presented in [7], that is, we define, using a pretty standard operational style, the speculative semantics of an expressive language, namely a call-by-value λ-calculus with mutable state and threads. Our formalization relies on extending the usual notion of an evaluation context [9], and using *value prediction* [11,19] as regards the values read from the memory. By introducing *speculation contexts*, we are able to formalize out of order executions, as in relaxed memory models, and also *branch prediction* [26], allowing to compute in the alternatives of a conditional branching construct. A particular case of out of order computation is provided by the future construct of Multilisp [14]. Our model therefore encompasses many speculative techniques.

The central definition in this paper is the one of a *valid* speculative computation. Roughly speaking, a thread's speculation is valid if it can be proved equivalent to a normal order computation. Our criterion here is that a thread's speculation is only valid if it preserves the sequential semantics. The equivalence of computations we use is the *permutation of transitions equivalence* introduced, for a purely functional language, by Borry and Lévy in [5], stating that independent steps can be performed in any order (or in parallel) without essentially changing the computation. One can see, for instance, that the two speculations (1) and (2) above are valid, by executing the same operations in normal order. In an implementation setting we would say that a speculation is allowed to *commit* in the case it is valid, but one should notice that our formulation is fully independent from any implementation mechanism. One could therefore use our formal model to assess the correctness of an implementation, showing that the latter only allows valid speculations to be performed.

As we shall see, valid speculations indeed preserve the semantics of sequential programs. This is no longer the case for *multithreaded* applications running on multiprocessor architectures. This is not surprising, since most optimizations found in relaxed memory models do not preserve the standard interleaving semantics – also known as "sequential consistency" [17] in the area of memory models –, see the survey [1]. For instance, continuing with Example (1), one can see that with the thread system

$$(r := \,! \, p)\,;(q := tt) \; \| \; (r' := \,! \, q)\,;(p := tt)$$

and starting with a state where $!\,p = f\!\!f = \,!\,q$, one can get a state where $!\,r = tt = \,!\,r'$ as an outcome of a valid speculative computation, that first issues the writes to q and p. This cannot be obtained by a standard interleaving execution, but is allowed in memory models where reads can be reordered with respect to subsequent memory operations, a property symbolically called $\mathbf{R \rightarrow RW}$, according to the terminology of [1]. One could check that most of the allowed behaviors (the so called "litmus tests") in weak memory models can also be obtained by speculative computations, thus stressing the generality of our framework, which offers a very relaxed semantical model.

Since the interleaving semantics of thread systems is not preserved by optimizing platforms, such as parallelized hardware, and since the latter are unlikely to be changed for the purpose of running concurrent programs, some conditions must be found for multithreaded applications to be executed correctly on these platforms. For instance, most memory models support the well-known "DRF guarantee," that asserts that programs free of data races, with respect to the interleaving semantics, are correctly executed in the optimized semantics [2,12,20]. However, with speculative computations, this guarantee fails. For instance, extending the second example given above, one can see that with the thread system

$$\begin{array}{ll} p := f\!\!f\,; & q := f\!\!f\,; \\ (\text{if } !\,p \text{ then } q := tt \text{ else } ()) & \| \; (\text{if } !\,q \text{ then } p := tt \text{ else } ()) \end{array}$$

one can get the outcome $!\,p = tt = \,!\,q$, by speculatively performing, after the initial assignments, the two assignments $q := tt$ and $p := tt$, thus justifying the branch prediction made in the other thread (see [13] Section 17.4.8, and [6] for similar examples). This example, though not very interesting from a programming point of view, exhibits the failure of the DRF guarantee. Let us see another example, which looks more like a standard idiom, for a producer-consumer scenario. In this example, we use a construct (with ℓ do e) to ensure mutual exclusion, by acquiring a lock ℓ, computing e and, upon termination, releasing ℓ. Then with the two threads

$$
\begin{array}{l}
\text{data} := 1; \\
\text{(with } \ell \text{ do flag} := tt)
\end{array}
\;\Big\|\;
\begin{array}{l}
\text{while not (with } \ell \text{ do !flag) do skip;} \\
r := \text{!data}
\end{array}
$$

if initially !data $= 0$ and !flag $= ff$, we can speculate that !data in the second thread returns 0, and therefore get an unexpected value for r (the other instructions being processed in the normal way). Since speculating ahead of synchronization (unlock) is permitted in our model, this is, according to our definition, a valid speculation, and this provides another example of the failure of the DRF guarantee in the speculative semantics.

Now a question is: what kind of property should concurrent programs possess to be "robust" against aggressive optimizations – and more precisely: speculations – found in optimized execution platforms, and how to ensure such robustness? In this paper we address the first part of this question[1]. We have seen that data race free concurrent programs are not necessarily robust – where "robust" means that the speculative semantics does not introduce unexpected behaviors (w.r.t. the normal order semantics) for the program under consideration. In this paper we show that *speculatively* data race free programs *are* robust – this is our main technical result. Here speculatively DRF means that there is no data race occurring in the speculative semantics, where a data race is, as usual, the possibility of performing – according to the speculative semantics – concurrent accesses, one of them being a write, to the same memory location. Then sequential programs in particular are robust, that is, speculative computation is a correct implementation for these programs.

Related work

To the best of our knowledge, the notion of a (valid) speculation has not been previously stated in a formal way. In this respect, the work that is the closest to ours is the one on the mathematical semantics of Multilisp's future construct, starting with the work [10] of Flanagan and Felleisen. This was later extended by Moreau in [22] to deal with mutable state and continuations (extending the work in [15] as regards the latter). A similar work regarding JAVA has been done by Jagannathan and colleagues, dealing with mutable state [27] and exceptions [23]. However, all these works on the future construct aim at preserving the sequential semantics, but they are not concerned with shared memory concurrency. Moreover, they do not include branch prediction and value prediction.

---

[1] For an answer to the second part we refer to the forthcoming extended version of this paper.

2   The Language

The language supporting speculative computations is an imperative call-by-value λ-calculus, with boolean values and conditional branching, enriched with thread creation and a construct for ensuring mutual exclusion. The syntax is:

$$e ::= v \mid (e_0 e_1) \mid (\text{if } e \text{ then } e_0 \text{ else } e_1) \mid (\text{ref } e) \qquad \textit{expressions}$$
$$\mid (!\, e) \mid (e_0 := e_1) \mid (\text{thread } e) \mid (\text{with } \ell \text{ do } e)$$
$$v ::= x \mid \lambda x e \mid tt \mid f\!f \mid () \qquad\qquad\qquad \textit{values}$$

where ℓ is a *lock*, that is a name from a given infinite set *Locks*. As usual, λ is a binder for the variable x in $\lambda x e$, and we shall consider expressions up to α-conversion, that is up to the renaming of bound variables. The capture-avoiding substitution of e_0 for the free occurrences of x in e_1 is denoted $\{x \mapsto e_0\} e_1$. We shall use some standard abbreviations like $(\text{let } x = e_0 \text{ in } e_1)$ for $(\lambda x e_1 e_0)$, which is also denoted $e_0 \,;\, e_1$ whenever x does not occur free in e_1.

To state the operational semantics of the language, we have to extend it with run-time constructs, in two ways. First, we introduce *references* (sometimes also referred to as memory locations, memory addresses, or pointers) $p, q, \dots$ that are names from a given infinite set $\mathcal{Ref}$. These are (run-time) values. Then we use the construct $(e \backslash \ell)$ to hold a lock for e. As it is standard with languages involving concurrency with shared variables, we follow a *small-step* style to describe the operational semantics, where an atomic transition consists in reducing a *redex* (reducible expression) within an *evaluation context*, while possibly performing a side effect. The syntax is then extended and enriched as follows:

$$p, q \dots \in \mathcal{Ref} \qquad\qquad\qquad\qquad\qquad\qquad\qquad\qquad \textit{references}$$
$$v ::= \cdots \mid p \qquad\qquad\qquad\qquad\qquad\qquad\qquad \textit{run-time values}$$
$$e ::= \cdots \mid (e \backslash \ell) \qquad\qquad\qquad\qquad\qquad \textit{run-time expressions}$$
$$u ::= (\lambda x e v) \mid (\text{if } tt \text{ then } e_0 \text{ else } e_1) \mid (\text{if } f\!f \text{ then } e_0 \text{ else } e_1) \qquad \textit{redexes}$$
$$\mid (\text{ref } v) \mid (!\, p) \mid (p := v) \mid (\text{thread } e) \mid (\text{with } \ell \text{ do } e) \mid (v \backslash \ell)$$
$$\mathbf{E} ::= [\,] \mid \mathbf{E}[\mathbf{F}] \qquad\qquad\qquad\qquad\qquad \textit{evaluation contexts}$$
$$\mathbf{F} = ([\,]\, e) \mid (v\, [\,]) \mid (\text{if } [\,] \text{ then } e_0 \text{ else } e_1) \qquad\qquad\qquad \textit{frames}$$
$$\mid (\text{ref } [\,]) \mid (!\, [\,]) \mid ([\,] := e) \mid (v := [\,]) \mid ([\,] \backslash \ell)$$

As usual, we denote by $\mathbf{E}[e]$ the expression resulting from filling the hole in $\mathbf{E}$ by e. Every expression of the (run-time) language is either a value, or a redex in a position to be reduced, or faulty. More precisely, let us say that an expression is *faulty* if it has one of the following forms:

- (ve) where the value v is not a function $\lambda x e'$;
- $(\text{if } v \text{ then } e_0 \text{ else } e_1)$ where the value v is not a boolean value, tt or $f\!f$;
- $(!\, v)$ or $v := v'$ where the value v is not a reference.

Then we have:

LEMMA 2.1.   *For any expression e of the run-time language, either e is a value, or there is a unique evaluation context $\mathbf{E}$ and a unique expression e' which either is a redex, or is faulty, such that $e = \mathbf{E}[e']$.*

To define speculative computations, we extend the class of standard evaluation contexts by introducing *speculation contexts*, defined as follows:

$$\Sigma ::= [] \mid \Sigma[\Phi] \qquad\qquad\qquad \textit{speculation contexts}$$

$$\Phi ::= \mathbf{F} \mid (e\,[]) \mid (\lambda x[]\,e) \mid (\text{if } e \text{ then } [] \text{ else } e_1) \qquad \textit{speculation frames}$$
$$\mid (\text{if } e \text{ then } e_0 \text{ else } []) \mid (e := [])$$

Let us comment briefly on the speculation contexts. With frames of the shape $(\lambda x[]\,e)$, one can for instance compute e_1 in the expression $(\lambda x e_1 e_0)$ – hence in $(\text{let } x = e_0 \text{ in } e_1)$ and $e_0 \,; e_1$ in particular –, whereas in a normal order computation one has to compute e_0 first. This is similar to a *future* expression $(\text{let } x = \text{future } e_0 \text{ in } e_1)$ [10], where e_1 is computed *in advance*, or *in parallel* with e_0. With the frames (if e then $[]$ else e_1) and (if e then e_0 else $[]$), one is allowed to compute in a branch (or in both branches) of a conditional construct, without knowing the value of the condition, again computing in advance (or in parallel) with respect to the normal order. This is known as "*branch prediction*" [26]. Notice that, by contrast, the construct (with ℓ do e) acts as a "speculation barrier," that is, (with ℓ do $[]$) is not a speculation frame. Indeed, the purpose of acquiring a lock is to separate side-effecting operations. We could allow pure (i.e. without side effect) speculations inside such a construct[2], but this would complicate the technical developments, with no added value, since, as we shall see, we can always speculatively acquire a lock (but not speculatively release it).

To define the semantics of locking, which allows for *reentrant* locks, we shall use the set, denoted $\lceil \Sigma \rceil$, of locks held in the context Σ, defined as follows:

$$\begin{aligned} \lceil [] \rceil &= \emptyset \\ \lceil \Sigma[\Phi] \rceil &= \lceil \Sigma \rceil \cup \lceil \Phi \rceil \end{aligned} \qquad \text{where} \qquad \lceil \Phi \rceil = \begin{cases} \{\ell\} & \text{if } \Phi = ([]\backslash\ell) \\ \emptyset & \text{otherwise} \end{cases}$$

Speculative computations are defined in two stages: first we define *speculations*, that are abstract computations of a given thread – abstract in the sense that the state, made of a memory, a set of busy locks, and a multiset of threads, is ignored at this stage. We can regard these as attempts to perform some computation, with no real side effect. Then we shall compose such speculations by interleaving them, now taking at this stage the global state into account. In order to do so, it is convenient to formalize speculations as labeled transitions, explicitly indicating *what* reduction occurs, that is what is the *action* performed at each step. There are several kinds of actions, namely performing a β-reduction, denoted β, choosing a branch in a conditional construct ($\checkmark$ and $\searrow$), creating a new reference p in the store with some initial (closed) value ($\nu_{p,v}$), reading ($\mathsf{rd}_{p,v}$) or writing ($\mathsf{wr}_{p,v}$) a reference, spawning a new thread (spw_e), acquiring ($\widehat{\ell}$) or releasing ($\overset{\frown}{\ell}$) a lock ℓ. Then the syntax of actions is as follows:

$$a ::= \beta \mid \checkmark \mid \searrow \mid \nu_{p,v} \mid \mathsf{rd}_{p,v} \mid \mathsf{wr}_{p,v} \mid \mu \mid \widehat{\ell} \mid b$$
$$b := \mathsf{spw}_e \mid \overset{\frown}{\ell}$$

---

[2] By enriching the conflict relation, see below.

where v and e are closed. The action μ stands for taking a lock that is already held. We denote by $\mathcal{A}ct$ the set of actions, and by $\mathcal{B}$ the subset of b actions.

In order to define *valid* speculations, we shall also need to explicitly indicate in the semantics *where* actions are performed. To this end, we introduce the notion of an *occurrence*, which is a sequence over a set of symbols, each associated with a frame, denoting a path from the root of the expression to the redex that is evaluated at some step. In the case of a frame $(e\,[])$, it is convenient to distinguish the case where this is a "normal" frame, that is, when e is a value, from the case where this is a true speculation frame. Then an occurrence is a sequence o over the set $\mathcal{SO}cc$ below:

$$\mathcal{O}cc = \{([]\,\_), (\bullet\,[]), (\text{if } [] \text{ then } \_ \text{ else } \_), (\text{ref } []), (!\,[]), ([] := \_), (v := []), ([]\backslash\ell)\}$$

$$\mathcal{SO}cc = \mathcal{O}cc \cup \{(\_[]), (\lambda x[]\,\_), (\text{if } \_ \text{ then } [] \text{ else } \_), (\text{if } \_ \text{ then } \_ \text{ else } []), (\_ := [])\}$$

The occurrences $o \in \mathcal{O}cc^*$ are called *normal*. Notice that we do not consider $\lambda x[]$ as an occurrence. This corresponds to the fact that speculating inside a value is forbidden, except in the case of a function applied to an argument, that is $(\lambda x e_1 e_0)$ where speculatively computing e_1 is allowed (again we could relax this as regards pure speculations, but this would involve heavy technical complications). One then defines the occurrence $@\Sigma$, as the sequence of frames that points to the hole in Σ, that is:

$$@[] = \varepsilon$$

$$@\Sigma[\Phi] = @\Sigma \cdot @\Phi$$

where

$$@([]\,e) = ([]\,\_)$$

$$@(e\,[]) = \begin{cases} (\bullet\,[]) & \text{if } e \in \mathcal{V}al \\ (\_[]) & \text{otherwise} \end{cases}$$

$$@(e := []) = \begin{cases} (v := []) & \text{if } e = v \in \mathcal{V}al \\ (\_ := []) & \text{otherwise} \end{cases}$$

and so on. We denote by $o \cdot o'$ the concatenation of the two sequences o and o', and we say that o is a prefix of o', denoted $o \leq o'$, if $o' = o \cdot o''$ for some o''. If $o \not\leq o'$ and $o' \not\leq o$ then we say that o and o' are disjoint occurrences.

We can now define the "local" speculations, for a given (sequential) thread. This is determined independently of any context (memory or other threads), and without any real side effect. Speculations are defined as a small step semantics, namely labeled transitions

$$e \xrightarrow[o]{a} e'$$

where a is the action performed at this step and o is the occurrence at which the action is performed (in the given thread). These are defined in Figure 1. Speculating here means not only computing "in advance" (or "out-of-order"), but also *guessing* the values from the global context (the memory and the lock context). More precisely, the speculative character of this semantics is twofold. On the one hand, some computations are allowed to occur in speculation contexts Σ, like with future computations or branch prediction. On the other hand, the

$$\Sigma[(\lambda x e v)] \xrightarrow[\text{@}\Sigma]{\beta} \Sigma[\{x \mapsto v\}e] \qquad \Sigma[(p := v)] \xrightarrow[\text{@}\Sigma]{\text{wr}_{p,v}} \Sigma[()]$$

$$\Sigma[(\text{if } tt \text{ then } e_0 \text{ else } e_1)] \xrightarrow[\text{@}\Sigma]{\checkmark} \Sigma[e_0] \qquad \mathbf{E}[(\text{thread } e)] \xrightarrow[\text{@E}]{\text{spw}_e} \mathbf{E}[()]$$

$$\Sigma[(\text{if } ff \text{ then } e_0 \text{ else } e_1)] \xrightarrow[\text{@}\Sigma]{\searrow} \Sigma[e_1] \qquad \Sigma[(\text{with } \ell \text{ do } e)] \xrightarrow[\text{@}\Sigma]{\mu} \Sigma[e] \qquad \ell \in \lceil \Sigma \rceil$$

$$\Sigma[(\text{ref } v)] \xrightarrow[\text{@}\Sigma]{\nu_{p,v}} \Sigma[p] \qquad \Sigma[(\text{with } \ell \text{ do } e)] \xrightarrow[\text{@}\Sigma]{\widehat{\ell}} \Sigma[(e\backslash \ell)] \quad \ell \notin \lceil \Sigma \rceil$$

$$\Sigma[(!\,p)] \xrightarrow[\text{@}\Sigma]{\text{rd}_{p,v}} \Sigma[v] \qquad \mathbf{E}[(v\backslash \ell)] \xrightarrow[\text{@E}]{\widehat{\ell}} \mathbf{E}[v]$$

Fig. 1. Speculations

value resulting from a dereference operation ($!\,p$), or the status of the lock in the case of a locking construct (with ℓ do e), is "guessed", or "predicted" – as regards loads from the memory, this is known as *value prediction*, and was introduced in [11,19]. These guessed values may be written by other threads, which are ignored at this stage. One should notice that the b actions are only allowed to occur from within an evaluation context, not a speculation context. However, one should also observe that an evaluation context can be modified by a speculation, while still being an evaluation context. This is typically the case of ($[]\,e$) and ($\lambda x e\,[]$) – hence in particular (let $x = []$ in e) and $[]\,;e$ –, where one is allowed to speculate the execution of e; this is also the case with (if $[]$ then e_0 else e_1) where one can speculate in a branch, that is in e_0 or e_1. Then for instance with an expression of the form ($e_0\backslash \ell$)$\,;e_1$, one can speculatively compute in e_1 before trying to release the lock ℓ and proceed with e_0 (a special case of this is the so-called "roach motel semantics," see [3]). The following is a standard property:

LEMMA 2.2.   *If $e \xrightarrow[o]{a} e'$ then $\{x \mapsto v\}e \xrightarrow[o]{a} \{x \mapsto v\}e'$ for any v.*

DEFINITION (SPECULATIONS) 2.3.   *A speculation from an expression e to an expression e' is a (possibly empty) sequence $\sigma = \left(e_i \xrightarrow[o_i]{a_i} e_{i+1}\right)_{0 \leqslant i \leqslant n}$ of speculation steps such that $e_0 = e$ and $e_n = e'$. This is written $\sigma : e \xrightarrow{*} e'$. The empty speculation (with $e' = e$) is denoted ε. The sequence σ is normal iff for all i the occurrence o_i is normal. The concatenation $\sigma \cdot \sigma' : e \xrightarrow{*} e'$ of σ and σ' is only defined (in the obvious way) if σ ends on the expression e'' where σ' originates.*

Notice that a normal speculation proceeds in program order, evaluating redexes inside evaluation contexts – not speculation contexts; still it may involve guessing some values that have to be read from the memory. Let us see two examples of speculations – omitting some labels, just mentioning the actions:

EXAMPLE 2.4

$$r := !\,p\,;q := tt \xrightarrow{\text{wr}_{q,tt}} r := !\,p\,;() \xrightarrow{\text{rd}_{p,tt}} r := tt\,;() \xrightarrow{\text{wr}_{r,tt}} ()\,;() \xrightarrow{\beta} ()$$

Here we speculate in two ways: first, the assignment $q := tt$, which would normally take place after reading p and updating r, is performed, or rather, issued, out of order; second, we guess a value read from memory location p.

EXAMPLE 2.5

(if ! p then $q := tt$ else $()$) $\xrightarrow{\text{wr}_{q,tt}}$ (if ! p then $()$ else $()$) $\xrightarrow{\text{rd}_{p,tt}}$ (if tt then $()$ else $()$) $\xrightarrow{\quad}$ $()$

Here we speculate by predicting that we will have to compute in the first branch, while guessing that the value pointed to by p is tt. Obviously this guessed value may not be the correct one, and in this case the computation made in the "then" branch has to be invalidated. We shall define valid speculations in the next section.

The concurrent speculative semantics is again a small step semantics, consisting in transitions between *configurations* $C = (S, L, T)$ where the store S, also called here the memory, is a mapping from a finite set dom(S) of references to values, the lock context L is a finite set of locks, those that are currently held by some thread, and T, the thread system, is a mapping from a finite set dom(T) of thread names (or thread identifiers), subset of $\mathcal{N}ames$, to expressions. If dom(T) = $\{t_1, \ldots, t_n\}$ and $T(t_i) = e_i$ we also write T as

$$(t_1, e_1) \| \cdots \| (t_n, e_n)$$

As usual, we shall assume we consider only *well-formed* configurations, meaning that any reference that occurs somewhere in the configuration belongs to the domain of the store, that is, it is bound to a value in the memory – we shall not define this property, which is preserved in the operational semantics, more formally. For instance, if e is an expression of the source language, any initial configuration $(\emptyset, \emptyset, (t, e))$ is well-formed. The speculative computations are made of transitions that have the form

$$C \xrightarrow[t,o]{a} C'$$

indicating the action a that is performed, the thread t that performs it, and the occurrence o where it is performed in the thread (these labels are just annotations, introduced for technical convenience, but they do not entail any constraint on the semantics). At each step, a speculation attempted by one thread is recorded, provided that *the global state agrees* with the action that is issued. That is, the value guessed by a thread for a pointer must be the value of that pointer in the memory (but notice that the store itself is speculative, being speculatively updated), and similarly acquiring a lock can only be done if the lock is free. We distinguish two cases, depending on whether the action spawns a new thread or not. The corresponding two rules are given in Figure 2, where

$$(*) \begin{cases} a = \beta, \checkmark, \searrow, \mu \Rightarrow S' = S \ \& \ L' = L \\ a = \nu_{p,v} \Rightarrow p \notin \text{dom}(S) \ \& \ S' = S \cup \{p \mapsto v\} \\ \qquad \& \ L' = L \\ a = \text{rd}_{p,v} \Rightarrow v = S(p) \ \& \ S' = S \ \& \ L' = L \\ a = \text{wr}_{p,v} \Rightarrow S' = S[p := v] \ \& \ L' = L \\ a = \widehat{\ell} \Rightarrow S' = S \ \& \ \ell \notin L \ \& \ L' = L \cup \{\ell\} \\ a = \widecheck{\ell} \Rightarrow S' = S \ \& \ L' = L - \{\ell\} \end{cases}$$

$$\frac{e \xrightarrow[o]{a} e' \qquad a \neq \mathsf{spw}_{e''}}{(S, L, (t, e) \parallel T) \xrightarrow[t,o]{a} (S', L', (t, e') \parallel T)} \quad (*)$$

$$\frac{e \xrightarrow[o]{\mathsf{spw}_{e'}} e''}{(S, L, (t, e) \parallel T) \xrightarrow[t,o]{\mathsf{spw}_{e'}} (S, L, (t, e'') \parallel (t', e') \parallel T)} \quad t' \notin \mathrm{dom}(T) \cup \{t\}$$

Fig. 2. Speculative Computations

DEFINITION (COMPUTATIONS) 2.6. *A speculative computation from a configuration C to a configuration C' is a (possibly empty) sequence γ of steps $\left(C_i \xrightarrow[t_i,o_i]{a_i} C_{i+1}\right)_{0 \leqslant i \leqslant n}$ in the speculative operational semantics such that $C_0 = C$ and $C_n = C'$. This is written $\gamma : C \xrightarrow{*} C'$. The empty computation is denoted ε. The concatenation $\gamma \cdot \gamma' : C \xrightarrow{*} C'$ is only defined (in the obvious way) if γ ends on the configuration C'' where γ' originates, that is $\gamma : C \xrightarrow{*} C''$ and $\gamma' : C'' \xrightarrow{*} C'$. The computation $\gamma = \left(C_i \xrightarrow[t_i,o_i]{a_i} C_{i+1}\right)_{0 \leqslant i \leqslant n}$ is normal if for all i the occurrence o_i is normal.*

One can see that normal computations correspond to computations in the standard *interleaving semantics*, that we regard as the reference semantics from the programmer's point of view. Even though our definition of speculative computations ensures that the values read from the memory are correctly guessed, some speculation sequences are still wrong, like – omitting the occurrences

$$(\{p \mapsto f\!f\}, \emptyset, (t, (\text{if } !p \text{ then } p := tt \text{ else } ()))) \xrightarrow{\mathsf{wr}_{p,tt}} (\{p \mapsto tt\}, \emptyset, (t, (\text{if } !p \text{ then } () \text{ else } ())))$$
$$\xrightarrow{\mathsf{rd}_{p,tt}} (\{p \mapsto tt\}, \emptyset, (t, (\text{if } tt \text{ then } () \text{ else } ())))$$

Here the normal *data dependency* between the read and write on p is broken, and the branch prediction is therefore wrong. Similarly, the computation

$$(\{p \mapsto f\!f\}, \emptyset, (t, (\text{if } f\!f \text{ then } p := tt \text{ else } ()))) \xrightarrow{\mathsf{wr}_{p,tt}} (\{p \mapsto tt\}, \emptyset, (t, (\text{if } f\!f \text{ then } () \text{ else } ())))$$
$$\xrightarrow{\mathsf{rd}_{p,tt}} (\{p \mapsto tt\}, \emptyset, (t, ()))$$

is wrong because it violates the normal *control dependency* between the predicate and the branches of the conditional branching. In the next section we shall define which are the correct speculative computations. To this end, we shall need the following technical definition, which formalizes the contribution of each thread to a speculative computation:

DEFINITION (PROJECTION) 2.7. *Given a thread identifier t, the projection $\gamma|_t$ of a speculative computation γ on thread t is defined as follows, by induction on γ:*

$$\varepsilon|_t = \varepsilon$$

$$(C \xrightarrow[t',o]{a} C' \cdot \gamma)|_t = \begin{cases} e \xrightarrow[o]{a} e' \cdot (\gamma|_t) & \text{if } t' = t \text{ \&} \\ & \quad C = (S, L, (t, e) \, \| \, T) \text{ \&} \\ & \quad C' = (S', L', (t, e') \, \| \, T) \\ \gamma|_t & \text{otherwise} \end{cases}$$

It is easy to check that this is indeed well-defined, that is:

REMARK 2.8. *For any speculative computation γ and name t, the projection $\gamma|_t$ is a speculation.*

3   Valid Speculations

We shall qualify a speculative computation as *valid* in the case where each of its projections is *equivalent* in some sense to a normal evaluation. That is, a speculative computation is valid if it only involves thread speculations that correctly guess the values read from the memory, and preserves, up to some equivalence, the normal program order. In other words, the validity criterion is local to the threads, namely, each thread's speculation should be equivalent to a sequential execution.[3] The equivalence we use is the *permutation of transitions equivalence* introduced by Berry and Lévy [5,18], that we also used in our previous work on memory models [7]. Intuitively, this equivalence says that permuting independent steps in a speculation results in "the same" speculation, and that such independent steps could actually be performed in parallel. It is clear, for instance, that actions performed at disjoint occurrences can be done in any order, provided that they are not conflicting accesses to the same memory location (the conflict relation will be defined below). This applies for instance to

$$r := \,! p \,; q := tt \xrightarrow{\mathsf{wr}_{q,tt}} r := \,! p \,; () \xrightarrow{\mathsf{rd}_{p,tt}} r := tt \,; ()$$

from Example 2.4. Similarly, we can commute two steps such as

$$(\text{if } tt \text{ then } q := tt \text{ else } ()) \xrightarrow{\mathsf{wr}_{q,tt}} (\text{if } tt \text{ then } () \text{ else } ()) \xrightarrow{\checkmark} ()$$

(see Example 2.5), although in this case we first need to say that the first step in this sequence is indeed "the same" as the second one in

$$(\text{if } tt \text{ then } q := tt \text{ else } ()) \xrightarrow{\checkmark} q := tt \xrightarrow{\mathsf{wr}_{q,tt}} ()$$

To this end, given a speculation step $e \xrightarrow[o]{a} e'$ and an occurrence o' in e, we define the *residual* of o' after this step, that is the occurrence, if any, that points to the same subterm (if any) as o' pointed to in e. For instance, if the step is

$$(\text{if } tt \text{ then } e_0 \text{ else } e_1) \xrightarrow{\checkmark} e_0$$

then for $o' = \varepsilon$ or $o' = (\text{if } [] \text{ then } \_ \text{ else } \_)$ there is not residual, because the occurrence has been consumed in reducing the expression. The residual of any

---

[3] This appears to be the standard – though implicit – validity criterion in the literature on speculative execution of sequential programs.

occurrence pointing into e_0, i.e. of the form $(\text{if } \_ \text{ then } [] \text{ else } \_) \cdot o'$, is o', whereas an occurrence of the form $(\text{if } \_ \text{ then } \_ \text{ else } []) \cdot o'$, pointing into e_1, has no residual, since the subexpression e_1 is discarded by reducing to the first branch of the conditional expression. This is the way we deal with control dependencies. The notion of a residual here is much simpler than in the λ-calculus (see [18]), because an occurrence is never duplicated, since we do not compute inside a value (except in a function applied to an argument). Here the residual of an occurrence after a speculation step will be either undefined, whenever it is discarded by a conditional branching, or a single occurrence. We actually only need to know the action a that is performed and the occurrence o where it is performed in order to define the residual of o' after such a step. We therefore define $o'/(a, o)$ as follows:

$$o'/(a,o) = \begin{cases} o' & \text{if } o \not\leq o' \\ o \cdot o'' & \text{if } o' = o \cdot (\lambda x[] \_) \cdot o'' \ \& \ a = \beta \\ & \text{or } o' = o \cdot (\text{if } \_ \text{ then } [] \text{ else } \_) \cdot o'' \ \& \ a = \checkmark \\ & \text{or } o' = o \cdot (\text{if } \_ \text{ then } \_ \text{ else } []) \cdot o'' \ \& \ a = \searrow \\ \text{undefined} & \text{otherwise} \end{cases}$$

In the following we write $o'/(a, o) \equiv o''$ to mean that the residual of o' after (a, o) is defined, and is o''. Notice that if $o'/(a, o) \equiv o''$ with $o' \in \mathcal{O}cc^*$ then $o'' = o'$ and $o \not\leq o'$.

Speculation enjoys a partial confluence property, namely that if an occurrence of an action has a residual after another one, then one can still perform the action from the resulting expression. This property is known as the Diamond Lemma. For lack of space, the proof of this Lemma is omitted (as well as the proofs of other statements below).

LEMMA (DIAMOND LEMMA) 3.1. *If* $e \xrightarrow[o_0]{a_0} e_0$ *and* $e \xrightarrow[o_1]{a_1} e_1$ *with* $o_1/(a_0, o_0) \equiv o_1'$ *and* $o_0/(a_1, o_1) \equiv o_0'$ *then there exists* e' *such that* $e_0 \xrightarrow[o_1']{a_1} e'$ *and* $e_1 \xrightarrow[o_0']{a_0} e'$.

One should notice that the e', the existence of which is asserted in this lemma, is actually unique, up to α-conversion. Let us see an example: with the expression of Example 2.4, we have – recall that $e_0 \, ; e_1$ stands for $(\lambda x e_1 e_0)$ where x is not free in e_1:

$$r := \, !\, p \, ; q := tt \xrightarrow[(\lambda x[] \_)]{\mathsf{wr}_{q,tt}} r := \, !\, p \, ; ()$$

and

$$r := \, !\, p \, ; q := tt \xrightarrow[(\bullet,[]) \cdot (r:=[])]{\mathsf{rd}_{p,tt}} r := tt \, ; q := tt$$

Then we can close the diagram, ending up with the expression $r := tt \, ; ()$. This confluence property is the basis for the definition of the equivalence by permutation of computing steps: with the hypotheses of the Diamond Lemma, we shall regard the two speculations

$$e \xrightarrow[o_0]{a_0} e_0 \xrightarrow[o_1']{a_1} e' \quad \text{and} \quad e \xrightarrow[o_1]{a_1} e_1 \xrightarrow[o_0']{a_0} e'$$

as equivalent. However, this cannot be so simple, because we have to ensure that the program order is preserved as regards accesses to a given memory

location (unless these accesses are all reads). For instance, the speculation –
again, omitting the occurrences:

$$p := tt \,; r := \,! p \xrightarrow{\mathsf{rd}_{p,ff}} p := tt \,; r := ff \xrightarrow{\mathsf{wr}_{p,tt}} () \,; r := ff$$

should not be considered as valid, because it breaks the data dependency between
the write and the read on p. To take this into account, we introduce the *conflict*
relation between actions, as follows[4]:

DEFINITION (CONFLICTING ACTIONS) 3.2.   *The conflict relation $\#$ between
actions is given by*

$$\# = \bigcup_{p\in\mathcal{R}ef,v,w\in\mathcal{V}al} \left\{ (\mathsf{wr}_{p,v},\mathsf{wr}_{p,w}),(\mathsf{wr}_{p,v},\mathsf{rd}_{p,w}),(\mathsf{rd}_{p,v},\mathsf{wr}_{p,w}) \right\}$$

We can now define the permutation equivalence, which is the congruence (with
respect to concatenation) on speculations generated by the conflict-free Diamond
property.

DEFINITION (PERMUTATION EQUIVALENCE) 3.3.   *The* equivalence by permuta-
tion of transitions *is the least equivalence $\simeq$ on speculations such that if $e \xrightarrow[o_0]{a_0} e_0$
and $e \xrightarrow[o_1]{a_1} e_1$ with $o_1/(a_0,o_0) \equiv o_1'$ and $o_0/(a_1,o_1) \equiv o_0'$ and $\neg(a_0 \# a_1)$ then*

$$\sigma_0 \cdot e \xrightarrow[o_0]{a_0} e_0 \xrightarrow[o_1']{a_1} e' \cdot \sigma_1 \simeq \sigma_0 \cdot e \xrightarrow[o_1]{a_1} e_1 \xrightarrow[o_0']{a_0} e' \cdot \sigma_1$$

where e' is determined as in the Diamond Lemma.

Notice that two equivalent speculations have the same length. Let us see some
examples. The speculation given in Example 2.4 is equivalent to the normal
speculation

$$r := \,! p \,; q := tt \xrightarrow{\mathsf{rd}_{p,tt}} r := tt \,; q := tt$$

$$\xrightarrow{\mathsf{wr}_{r,tt}} () \,; q := tt \xrightarrow{\beta} q := tt$$

$$\xrightarrow{\mathsf{wr}_{q,tt}} ()$$

Similarly, the speculation given in Example 2.5 is equivalent to the normal speculation

$$(\text{if } !p \text{ then } q := tt \text{ else } ()) \xrightarrow{\mathsf{rd}_{p,tt}} (\text{if } tt \text{ then } q := tt \text{ else } ())$$

$$\xrightarrow{} q := tt \xrightarrow{\mathsf{wr}_{q,tt}} ()$$

We are now ready to give the definition that is central to our work, characterizing
what is a *valid* speculative computation.

DEFINITION (VALID SPECULATIVE COMPUTATION) 3.4.   *A speculation is* valid
*if it is equivalent by permutation to a normal speculation. A speculative com-
putation γ is* valid *if all its thread projections $\gamma|_t$ are valid speculations.*

---

[4] We notice that in some (extremely, or even excessively) relaxed memory model (such
as the one of the Alpha architecture, see [21]) the data dependencies are not maintained. To deal with such models, we would adopt an empty conflict relation, and a
different notion of data race free program (see below).

It is clear for instance that the speculations given above that do not preserve the normal data dependencies are not valid. Similarly, regarding control dependencies, one can see that the following speculation

$$(\text{if } !p \text{ then } () \text{ else } q := tt) \xrightarrow{\text{wr}_{q},tt} (\text{if } !p \text{ then } () \text{ else } ()) \xrightarrow{\text{rd}_{p},tt} (\text{if } tt \text{ then } () \text{ else } ()) \xrightarrow{\;\;} ()$$

which is an example of wrong branch prediction, is invalid, since the occurrence of the first action has no residual after the last one, and cannot therefore by permuted with it. We have already seen that the speculations from Examples 2.4 and 2.5 are valid. (Notice that, obviously, any normal computation is valid.) Then the reader can observe that from the thread system – where we omit the thread identifiers

$$r := !p\,;q := tt \parallel r' := !q\,;p := tt$$

and an initial memory S such that $S(p) = f\!\!f = S(q)$, we can, by a valid speculative computation, get as an outcome a state where the memory S' is such that $S'(r) = tt = S'(r')$, something that cannot be obtained with the standard, non-speculative interleaving semantics. This is typical of a memory model where the reads can be reordered with respect to subsequent memory operations – a property symbolically called $\mathbf{R{\rightarrow}RW}$, according to the terminology of [1], that was not captured in our previous work [7] on write-buffering memory models. We conjecture that our operational model of speculative computations is more general (for static thread systems) than the weak memory model of [7], in the sense that for any configuration, there are more outcomes following (valid) speculative computations than with write buffering. We also believe, although this would have to be more formally stated, that speculative computations are more general than most hardware memory models, which deal with access memory, but do not transform programs using some semantical reasoning as optimizing compilers do. For instance, let us examine the case of the amd6 example (see [25]), that is

$$p := tt \parallel q := tt \parallel \begin{array}{l} r_0 := !p; \\ r_1 := !q \end{array} \parallel \begin{array}{l} r_2 := !q; \\ r_3 := !p \end{array}$$

If we start from a configuration where the memory S is such that $S(p) = f\!\!f = S(q)$, we may speculate in the third thread that $!q$ returns $f\!\!f$ (which is indeed the initial value of q), and similarly in the fourth thread that $!p$ returns $f\!\!f$, and then proceed with the assignments $p := tt$ and $q := tt$, and so on. Then we can reach, by a valid speculative computation, a state where the memory S' is such that $S'(r_0) = tt = S'(r_2)$ and $S'(r_1) = f\!\!f = S'(r_3)$, an outcome which cannot be obtained with the interleaving semantics.

Another unusual example is based on Example 2.5. Let us consider the following system made of two threads

$$\begin{array}{l} p := f\!\!f\,; \\ (\text{if } !p \text{ then } q := tt \text{ else } ()) \end{array} \parallel \begin{array}{l} q := f\!\!f\,; \\ (\text{if } !q \text{ then } p := tt \text{ else } ()) \end{array}$$

Then by a valid speculative computation we can reach, after having performed the two initial assignments, a state where $S(p) = tt = S(q)$. What is unusual with this example, with respect to what is generally expected from relaxed memory models for instance [2,12], is that this is, with respect to the interleaving semantics, a data race free thread system, which still has an "unwanted" outcome in the optimizing framework of speculative computations (see [6] for a similar example). This indicates that we have to assume a stronger property than DRF (data-race freeness) to ensure that a program is "robust" with respect to speculations.

DEFINITION (ROBUST PROGRAMS) 3.5. *A closed expression e is robust iff for any t and γ such that $\gamma : (\emptyset, \emptyset, (t, e)) \xrightarrow{*} (S, L, T)$ there exists a normal computation $\bar{\gamma}$ such that $\bar{\gamma} : (\emptyset, \emptyset, (t, e)) \xrightarrow{*} (S, L, T)$.*

In other words, for a robust expression the speculative and interleaving semantics coincide, or: the robust programs are the ones for which the speculative semantics is correct (with respect to the interleaving semantics).

4   Robustness

Our main result is that *speculatively* data-race free programs are robust.

DEFINITION (SPECULATIVELY DRF PROGRAM) 4.1. *A configuration C has a speculative data race iff there exist t_i, o_i, a_i and C_i $(i = 0, 1)$ such that $C' \xrightarrow[t_0, o_0]{a_0} C_0$ and $C' \xrightarrow[t_1, o_1]{a_1} C_1$ with $t_0 \neq t_1$ & $a_0 \# a_1$. A valid speculative computation $(C_i \xrightarrow[t_i, o_i]{a_i} C_{i+1})_{0 \leqslant i \leqslant n}$ is speculatively date race free iff for all i, C_i has no speculative data race. A configuration C is speculatively date race free (speculatively DRF, or SDRF) iff any valid speculative computation originating in C is data race free. An expression e is speculatively DRF iff for any t the configuration $(\emptyset, \emptyset, (t, e))$ is speculatively DRF.*

It is obvious that this is a safety property, in the sense that if C is speculatively DRF and C' is reachable from C by a normal computation, then C' is speculatively DRF. We could have formulated this property directly, without resorting to the conflict relation, saying that there are no reachable concurrent accesses to the same location in the memory. In this way we could deal with optimizing architectures (such as the Alpha memory model, see [21]) that allow to reorder such accesses, by including the case where these concurrent accesses can occur (in the speculative semantics) from within the same thread, like for instance in $p := f\!f ; r := \,!\,p$. We do not follow this way here, since such a model requires unnatural synchronizations from the programmer.

In order to establish our main result, we need a number of preliminary lemmas, regarding both speculations and speculative computations. First, we extend the notion of residual by defining o/σ where o is an occurrence and σ a speculation. This is defined by induction on the length of σ, where the notation $o' \equiv o/\sigma$ means that o/σ is defined and is o'.

$$o/\varepsilon \equiv o$$
$$o/(e \xrightarrow[o']{a} e') \cdot \sigma \equiv (o/(a, o'))/\sigma$$

In the following we shall often omit the expressions in a speculation, writing $\sigma_0 \cdot \xrightarrow[o]{a} \cdot \sigma_1$ instead of $\sigma_0 \cdot (e_0 \xrightarrow[o]{a} e_1) \cdot \sigma_1$. Indeed, e_0 is determined by σ_0, and, given e_0, the expression e_1 is determined by the pair (a, o). Now we introduce the notion of a *step*, called "redex-with-history" in [5,18], and of steps being in the same *family*, a property introduced in [5].

DEFINITION (STEPS) 4.2.   *A step is a pair $[\sigma, (a, o)]$ of a speculation $\sigma : e \xrightarrow{*} e'$ and an action a at occurrence o such that $e' \xrightarrow{a}_{o} e''$ for some expression e''. Given a speculation σ, the set $\mathsf{Step}(\sigma)$ is the set of steps $[\varsigma, (a, o)]$ such that $\varsigma \cdot \xrightarrow{a}_{o} \leq \sigma$. The binary relation $\sim$ on steps, meaning that two steps are in the same family, is the equivalence relation generated by the rule*

$$\frac{\exists \sigma''. \; \sigma' \simeq \sigma \cdot \sigma'' \; \& \; o' \equiv o/\sigma''}{[\sigma, (a, o)] \sim [\sigma', (a, o')]}$$

Equivalent speculations have similar steps:

LEMMA 4.3.   *If $[\varsigma, (a, o)] \in \mathsf{Step}(\sigma)$ and $\sigma' \simeq \sigma$ then there exists $[\varsigma', (a, o')] \in \mathsf{Step}(\sigma')$ such that $[\varsigma, (a, o)] \sim [\varsigma', (a, o')]$.*

Proof: by induction on the definition of $\sigma' \simeq \sigma$.   ◻

A property that should be intuitively clear is that if a step in a speculation is in the same family as the initial step of an equivalent speculation, then it can be commuted with all the steps that precede it:

LEMMA 4.4.   *Let $\sigma = \sigma_0 \cdot \xrightarrow{a}_{o} \cdot \sigma_1$ be such that $\sigma \simeq \xrightarrow{a}_{o'} \cdot \varsigma$ with $[\varepsilon, (a, o')] \sim [\sigma_0, (a, o)]$. If $\sigma_0 = \varsigma_0 \cdot (e \xrightarrow{\bar{a}}_{\bar{o}} e') \cdot \varsigma_1$ then there exist o'', e'', $\bar{o}'$ and σ_1' such that $\varsigma_0 \cdot (e \xrightarrow{a}_{o''} e'' \xrightarrow{\bar{a}}_{\bar{o}'} \bar{e}) \cdot \sigma_1' \simeq \sigma$ where $o \equiv o''/\xrightarrow{\bar{a}}_{\bar{o}'} \cdot \sigma_1'$ and $\bar{o}' \equiv \bar{o}/(a, o'')$.*

Next, we can show that, in a speculation, the unlock actions, and also spawning a new thread, act as *barriers* with respect to other actions that occur in an evaluation context: these actions cannot be permuted with unlock (or spawn) actions. This is expressed by the following lemma:

LEMMA 4.5.   *Let $\sigma = \sigma_0 \cdot \xrightarrow{a}_{o} \cdot \sigma_1$ where $a \in \mathcal{B}$, and $\sigma \simeq \sigma'$ with $\sigma' = \sigma_0' \cdot \xrightarrow{a}_{o} \cdot \sigma_1'$ where $[\sigma_0, (a, o)] \sim [\sigma_0', (a, o)]$. If $[\varsigma, (a', o')] \in \mathsf{Step}(\sigma_0)$ with $o' \in \mathcal{O}cc^*$ then there exist ς' and o'' such that $[\varsigma', (a', o'')] \in \mathsf{Step}(\sigma_0')$ and $[\varsigma, (a', o')] \sim [\varsigma', (a', o'')]$.*

An immediate consequence of this property is:

COROLLARY 4.6.   *If σ is a valid speculation, that is $\sigma \simeq \bar{\sigma}$ for some normal speculation $\bar{\sigma}$, and if $\bar{\sigma} = \bar{\sigma}_0 \cdot \xrightarrow{a}_{o} \cdot \bar{\sigma}_1$ with $a \in \mathcal{B}$, then $\sigma = \sigma_0 \cdot \xrightarrow{a}_{o} \cdot \sigma_1$ with $[\sigma_0, (a, o)] \sim [\bar{\sigma}_0, (a, o)]$, such that for any step $[\bar{\varsigma}, (a', o')]$ of $\bar{\sigma}_0$ there exists a step $[\varsigma, (a', o'')]$ in the same family which is in σ_0.*

This is to say that, in order for a speculation to be valid, all the operations that normally precede a $\mathcal{B}$ action, and in particular an unlocking action, must be performed before this action in the speculation.

From now on, we shall consider *regular* configurations, where at most one thread can hold a given lock, and where a lock held by some thread is indeed in the lock context. This is defined as follows:

DEFINITION (REGULAR CONFIGURATION) 4.7.   *A configuration $C = (S, L, T)$ is regular if and only if it satisfies*

(i) *if* $T = (t_i, \Sigma_i[(e_i \backslash \ell)]) \| T_i$ *for* $i = 0, 1$ *then* $t_0 = t_1$ *&* $\Sigma_0 = \Sigma_1$ *&* $e_0 = e_1$ *&* $T_0 = T_1$

(ii) $T = (t, \Sigma[(e \backslash \ell)]) \| T' \Rightarrow \ell \in L$

For instance, any configuration of the form $(\emptyset, \emptyset, (t, e))$ where e is an expression is regular. The following should be obvious:

REMARK 4.8.   *If C is regular and $C \xrightarrow[t,o]{a} C'$ then C' is regular.*

The following lemma (for a different notion of computation) was called the "Asynchrony Lemma" in [7]. There it was used as the basis to define the equivalence by permutation of computations. We could also introduce such an equivalence here, generalizing the one for speculations, but this is actually not necessary.

LEMMA 4.9.   *Let C be a (well-formed) regular configuration. If $C \xrightarrow[t_0,o_0]{a_0} C_0 \xrightarrow[t_1,o_1]{a_1} C'$ with $t_0 \neq t_1$, $\neg(a_0 \# a_1)$ and $a_0 = \widehat{\ell} \Rightarrow a_1 \neq \widehat{\ell}$, then there exists C_1 such that $C \xrightarrow[t_1,o_1]{a_1} C_1 \xrightarrow[t_0,o_0]{a_0} C'$.*

We have a similar property regarding "local" computations, that occur in the same thread:

LEMMA 4.10.   *Let C be a (well-formed) regular configuration. If $C \xrightarrow[t,o_0]{a_0} C_0 \xrightarrow[t,o_1']{a_1} C'$ with $C = (S, L, (t, e) \| T)$, $C_0 = (S_0, L_0, (t, e_0) \| T_0) =$, $C' = (S', L', (t, e') \| T')$ and*

$$e \xrightarrow[o_0]{a_0} e_0 \xrightarrow[o_1']{a_1} e' \simeq e \xrightarrow[o_1]{a_1} e_1 \xrightarrow[o_0']{a_0} e'$$

then $C \xrightarrow[t,o_1]{a_1} (S_1, L_1, (t, e_1) \| T_1) \xrightarrow[t,o_0']{a_0} C'$ for some S_1, L_1 and T_1.

PROPOSITION 4.11.   *Let C be a well-formed, closed, regular configuration. If $\gamma : C \xrightarrow{*} C'$ is a valid data race free speculative computation, then there exists a normal computation $\bar{\gamma}$ from C to C'.*

Proof: by induction on the length of γ. This is trivial if $\gamma = \varepsilon$. Otherwise, let $\gamma = \left(C_i \xrightarrow[t_i,o_i]{a_i} C_{i+1} \right)_{0 \leqslant i \leqslant n}$ with $n > 0$. Notice that for any i, the configuration C_i is well-formed, regular and has no data race. The set $\{ t \mid \gamma|_t \neq \varepsilon \}$ is nonempty. For any t there exists a normal speculation σ^t such that $\sigma^t \simeq \gamma|_t$. Let j be the first index $(0 \leqslant j < n)$ such that $\gamma|_{t_j} = \sigma_0 \cdot \xrightarrow[o_j]{a_j} \cdot \sigma_1$ and $\sigma^{t_j} = \xrightarrow[o]{a_j} \cdot \sigma'$ with $[\varepsilon, (o, a_j)] \sim [\sigma_0, (a_j, o_j)]$. Now we proceed by induction on j. If $j = 0$

then $o = o_j \in \mathcal{O}cc^*$, and we use the induction hypothesis (on the length n) to conclude. Otherwise, we have $C_{j-1} \xrightarrow[t_{j-1},o_{j-1}]{a_{j-1}} C_j \xrightarrow[t_j,o_j]{a_j} C_{j+1}$. We distinguish two cases.

• If $t_{j-1} \neq t_j$ then we have $\neg(a_{j-1} \# a_j)$ since γ is speculatively data-race free. We show that $i < j \Rightarrow a_i \notin \mathcal{B}$. Assume the contrary, that is $a_i \in \mathcal{B}$ for some $i < j$. Then $\gamma|_{t_i} = \varsigma_0 \cdot \xrightarrow[o_i]{a_i} \cdot \varsigma_1$, and by Lemma 4.3 we have $\sigma^{t_i} = \bar{\varsigma}_0 \cdot \xrightarrow[o']{a_i} \cdot \bar{\varsigma}_1$ with $[\varsigma_0, (o_i, a_i)] \sim [\bar{\varsigma}_0, (o', a_i)]$. Then by Corollary 4.6 the first step of $\bar{\varsigma}_0 \cdot \xrightarrow[o']{a_i}$ is in the family of a step in $\varsigma_0 \cdot \xrightarrow[o_i]{a_i}$, contradicting the minimality of j. We therefore have $a_{j-1} \neq \hat{\ell}$ in particular. By Lemma 4.9 we can commute the two steps $\xrightarrow[o_{j-1}]{a_{j-1}}$ and $\xrightarrow[o_j]{a_j}$, and we conclude using the induction hypothesis (on j).

• If $t_{j-1} = t_j$, we have $\sigma_0 = \varsigma_0 \cdot \xrightarrow[o_{j-1}]{a_{j-1}}$, and by Lemma 4.4 there exist o', o'' and σ'_1 such that $\gamma|_{t_j} \simeq \varsigma_0 \cdot \xrightarrow[o']{a_j} \cdot \xrightarrow[o'']{a_{j-1}} \cdot \sigma'_1$ with $o \equiv o'/(a_{j-1}, o_{j-1})$. We conclude using Lemma 4.10 and the induction hypothesis (on j). □

Notice that we proved a property that is actually more precise than stated in the proposition, since the $\bar{\gamma}$ that is constructed is equivalent, by permutations, to γ – but we decided not to introduce explicitly this equivalence as regards speculative computations. An immediate consequence of this property is the announced robustness result:

THEOREM (ROBUSTNESS) 4.12. *Any speculatively data race free closed expression is robust.*

We observe that if an expression is purely sequential, that is, it does not spawn any thread, then it is speculatively data race free, and therefore robust, that is, all the valid speculations for it are correct with respect to its standard semantics.

Our result holds with synchronization mechanisms other than acquiring and releasing locks. We could have considered simpler memory barrier operations than the mutual exclusion construct (with ℓ do e), such as fence. This is a programming constant (but not a value), the semantics of which is given by

$$\mathbf{E}[\text{fence}] \to \mathbf{E}[()]$$

with no side effect. Performing a fence should be categorized as a $\mathcal{B}$ action, so that the Corollary 4.6 holds for such an action, since it is only performed from within a normal evaluation context. Then our Theorem 4.12, which, as far as the $\mathcal{B}$ actions are concerned, relies on this property 4.6, still holds with this construct. However when speculation is allowed this construct is rather weak, and in particular it does not help very much in preventing data races, or even to separate the accesses to the memory from a given thread. We let the reader check for instance that with the IRIW example (see [6]), that is

$$p := tt \parallel q := tt \parallel r_0 := \,! p; \parallel r_2 := \,! q\,;$$
$$\text{fence}\,; \qquad \text{fence}\,;$$
$$r_1 := \,! q \qquad r_3 := \,! p$$

starting from a configuration where the memory S is such that $S(p) = f\!f = S(q)$ we may, as with the amd6 example above, get by a valid speculative computation a state where the memory S' is such that $S'(r_0) = tt = S'(r_2)$ and $S'(r_1) = f\!f = S'(r_3)$. This is because the assignments to r_1 and r_3 can be speculatively performed first (after having read pointers p and q), and, in the projections over their respective threads, be commuted with the assignments to r_0 and r_2 (since there is no data dependency), and the fence, thus checking that local normal order evaluations with the same actions is possible.

5 Conclusion

We have given a formal definition for speculative computations which, we believe, is quite general. We have, in particular, checked the classical "litmus tests" that are considered when dealing with memory models, and we have seen that most of these are correctly described in our setting (except in the cases relying on code transformations, which are beyond the scope of our theory of speculations). This means that our semantics is quite permissive as regards the allowed optimizations, while being correct for sequential programs, but also that it is very easy to use for justifying that a particular outcome is allowed or forbidden. This is clearly a benefit from using a standard operational style. We think that our model of speculative computation could be used to justify implementation techniques, and to design formal analysis and verification methods for checking concurrent programs, as well as developing programming styles for safe multi-threading. Our model could also be made less permissive, either by restricting the class of speculation contexts, or by extending the conflict relation, to forbid some commutations (regarding synchronization actions in particular), in order to capture more precisely actual optimized execution platforms. Obviously, our robustness result still holds, but in some cases one could hope to get a more liberal robustness property, like the DRF guarantee for instance. We plan to explore the variety of such speculation scenarios in future work.

References

1. Adve, S.A., Gharachorloo, K.: Shared memory consistency models: a tutorial. IEEE Computer 29(12), 66–76 (1996)
2. Adve, S., Hill, M.D.: Weak ordering – A new definition. In: ISCA 1990, pp. 2–14 (1990)
3. Aspinall, D., Ševčík, J.: Java memory model examples: good, bad and ugly. In: VAMP 2007 (2007)
4. Ševčík, J., Aspinall, D.: On validity of program transformations in the JAVA memory model. In: Vitek, J. (ed.) ECOOP 2008. LNCS, vol. 5142, pp. 27–51. Springer, Heidelberg (2008)
5. Berry, G., Lévy, J.-J.: Minimal and optimal computations of recursive programs. J. of ACM 26, 148–175 (1979)

6. Boehm, H.-J., Adve, S.V.: Foundations of the C++ concurrency model. In: PLDI 2008, pp. 68–78 (2008)
7. Boudol, G., Petri, G.: Relaxed memory models: an operational approach. In: POPL 2009, pp. 392–403 (2009)
8. Burton, F.W.: Speculative computation, parallelism, and functional programming. IEEE Trans. on Computers C-34(12), 1190–1193 (1985)
9. Felleisen, M., Friedman, D.P.: Control operators, the SECD-machine and the λ-calculus. In: Wirsing, M. (ed.) Formal Description of Programming Concepts III, pp. 193–217. Elsevier, Amsterdam (1986)
10. Flanagan, C., Felleisen, M.: The semantics of future and its use in program optimization. In: POPL 1995, pp. 209–220 (1995)
11. Gabbay, F., Mendelson, A.: Using value prediction to increase the power of speculative execution hardware. ACM Trans. on Computer Systems 16(3), 234–270 (1998)
12. Gharachorloo, K., Lenoski, D., Laudon, J., Gibbons, P., Gupta, A., Hennessy, J.: Memory consistency and event ordering in scalable sharedmemory multiprocessors. ACM SIGARCH Computer Architecture News 18(3a), 15–26 (1990)
13. Gosling, J., Joy, B., Steele, G.L., Bracha, G.: The JAVA Language Specification, 3rd edn. Prentice Hall, Englewood Cliffs (2005)
14. Halstead, R.H.: Multilisp: a language for concurrent symbolic computation. ACM TOPLAS 7(4), 501–538 (1985)
15. Katz, M., Weise, D.: Continuing into the future: on the interaction of futures and first-class continuations. In: ACM Conf. on Lisp and Functional Programming, pp. 176–184 (1990)
16. Knight, T.: An architecture for mostly functional languages. In: ACM Conf. on Lisp and Functional Programming, pp. 105–112 (1986)
17. Lamport, L.: How to make a multiprocessor computer that correctly executes multiprocess programs. IEEE Trans. on Computers 28(9), 690–691 (1979)
18. Lévy, J.-J.: Optimal reductions in the lambda calculus. In: To, H.B.C., Seldin, J.P., Hindley, J.R. (eds.) Essays on Combinatory Logic, Lambda Calculus and Formalism, pp. 159–191. Academic Press, London (1980)
19. Lipasti, M.H., Wilkerson, C.B., Shen, J.P.: Value locality and load value prediction. In: ASPLOS 1996, pp. 138–147 (1996)
20. Manson, J., Pugh, W., Adve, S.A.: The Java memory model. In: POPL 2005, pp. 378–391 (2005)
21. Martin, M.K., Sorin, D.J., Cain, H.W., Hill, M.D., Lipasti, M.H.: Correctly implementing value prediction in microprocessors that support multithreading or multiprocessing. In: 34th International Symp. on Microarchitecture, pp. 328–337 (2001)
22. Moreau, L.: The semantics of Scheme with futures. In: ICFP 1996, pp. 146–156 (1996)
23. Navabi, A., Jagannathan, S.: Exceptionally safe futures. In: Field, J., Vasconcelos, V.T. (eds.) COORDINATION 2009. LNCS, vol. 5521, pp. 47–65. Springer, Heidelberg (2009)
24. Saraswat, V., Jagadeesan, R., Michael, M., von Praun, C.: A theory of memorymodels. In: PPoPP 2007, pp. 161–172 (2007)
25. Sarkar, S., Sewell, P., Zappa Nardelli, F., Owens, S., Ridge, T., Braibant, T., Myreen, M.O., Alglave, J.: The semantics of x86-CC multiprocessor machine code. In: POPL 2009, pp. 379–391 (2009)
26. Smith, J.E.: A study of branch prediction strategies. In: ISCA 1981, pp. 135–148 (1981)
27. Welc, A., Jagannathan, S., Hosking, A.: Safe futures for JAVA. In: OOPSLA 2005, pp. 439–453 (2005)

Propositional Interpolation and Abstract Interpretation

Vijay D'Silva*

Computing Laboratory, Oxford University
vijay.dsilva@comlab.ox.ac.uk

Abstract. Algorithms for computing Craig interpolants have several applications in program verification. Though different algorithms exist, the relationship between them and the properties of the interpolants they generate are not well understood. This paper is a study of interpolation algorithms for propositional resolution proofs. We show that existing interpolation algorithms are abstractions of a more general, parametrised algorithm. Further, existing algorithms reside in the coarsest abstraction that admits correct interpolation algorithms. The strength of interpolants constructed by existing interpolation algorithms and the variables they eliminate are analysed. The algorithms and their properties are formulated and analysed using abstract interpretation.

1 Introduction

Interpolation theorems provide insights about what can be expressed in a logic or derived in a proof system. An interpolation theorem states that if A and B are logical formulae such that A implies B, there is a formula I defined only over the symbols occurring in both A and B such that A implies I and I implies B. This statement was proved by Craig [8] for first order logic and has since been shown to hold for several other logics and logical theories. Consult [18] for a survey of the history and consequences of this theorem in mathematical logic. This paper is concerned with constructing interpolants from propositional resolution proofs.

An *interpolation system* is an algorithm for computing interpolants from proofs. We briefly review the use of interpolation systems for propositional resolution proofs in verification. Consider the formulae $S(x)$ encoding a set of states S, $T(x, x')$ encoding a transition relation T and $\varphi(x')$ encoding a correctness property φ. The *image* of S under the relation T is given by the formula $\exists x.S(x) \wedge T(x, x')$. The standard approach to determine if the states reachable from S satisfy the property φ is to iteratively compute images until a fixed point is reached. However, image computation and fixed point detection both involve quantifier elimination and are computationally expensive.

Consider the formula $S(x) \wedge T(x, x') \Rightarrow \varphi(x')$. If this formula is valid, the states reachable from S by a transition in T satisfy φ. Let A be the formula $S(x) \wedge T(x, x')$ and let B be the formula $\varphi(x')$ and I be an interpolant for

---

* Supported by Microsoft Research's European PhD Scholarship Programme.

A.D. Gordon (Ed.): ESOP 2010, LNCS 6012, pp. 185–204, 2010.

$A \Rightarrow B$. The formula I represents a set of states that contains the image of S and satisfies the property φ. Thus, as shown by McMillan [19], one can implement a property-preserving, approximate image operator with an interpolation system. Contemporary SAT solvers are capable of generating resolution proofs, so an interpolation system for such proofs yields a verification algorithm for finite-state systems that uses only a SAT solver. The efficiency and precision of such a verification algorithm is contingent on the size and logical strength of the interpolants used. Hence, it is important to understand the properties of interpolants generated by different interpolation systems.

We are aware of three interpolation systems for propositional resolution proofs. The first, which we call the HKP-system, was discovered independently by Huang [14], Krajíček [16] and Pudlák [21]. Another was proposed by McMillan [19] and a third *parametrised* system was proposed by the author and his collaborators [10] as a generalisation of the other systems. One may however ask if the HKP-algorithm and McMillan's algorithm have properties that distinguish them from other instances of the parametrised algorithm. We answer this question in this paper and study other properties of these systems.

Contents and Organisation. In this paper, we study the family of propositional interpolation systems proposed in [10]. We ask two questions about these systems: (1) What is the structure of this space of interpolation systems and how does it relate to the HKP-system and McMillan's system? (2) How are the strength and size of interpolants generated by these systems related? Our contributions to answering these questions are the following results.

- The set of interpolation systems forms a lattice. Interpolation systems that partition variables are abstractions of this lattice. The HKP-system and McMillan's system are two of three systems in the coarsest abstraction that admits correct interpolation systems.
- The set of clauses equipped with interpolants (called extended clauses or e-clauses) is a complete lattice. An interpolation system Int defines a concrete interpretation on this lattice. The lattice of CNF formulae is an abstraction of the lattice of e-clauses and the resolution proof system is a complete abstract interpretation of Int.
- Interpolation systems and e-clauses are ordered by logical strength of interpolants giving rise to a precision order on the lattice of interpolation systems and the lattice of e-clauses. Interpolation systems that eliminate the largest and smallest set of variables from a formula are identified and shown to be different from the most abstract interpolation systems.

The paper is organised as follows: The background on propositional logic and resolution is covered in § 2. Existing interpolation systems are formalised and illustrated with examples in § 3. Some background on abstract interpretation is introduced in § 4 and applied to study the space of interpolation systems and its abstractions in § 4.1 and § 4.2. The logical strength of interpolants and the variables they contain are analysed in § 5. We discuss related work in § 6 and conclude in § 7.

2 Propositional Logic and Interpolation

Propositional logic, resolution and interpolation are introduced in this section.

Sets and functions. Let $\wp(X)$ denote the powerset of X, $X \to Y$ be the set of functions from X to Y and $f \circ g$ denote functional composition. Given $f : X \to Y$ and $S \subseteq X$, we write $f(S)$ for the set $\{f(x) \in Y | x \in S\}$.

Propositional Logic. Fix a finite set Prop of variables (propositions) for this paper. Let T and F denote true and false, respectively. The set of propositional formulae, $\mathbb{B}$, is defined as usual over the basis $\{\neg, \wedge, \vee, \Rightarrow\}$. The set of variables occurring in a formula $F \in \mathbb{B}$ is denoted $\mathrm{Var}(F)$. An *assignment* $\sigma : \mathrm{Prop} \to \{\mathsf{T}, \mathsf{F}\}$ is a function that maps variables to truth values. Let F be a formula. The *evaluation* of F under an assignment σ, written $eval(F, \sigma)$, is defined as usual. F is a *tautology* if $eval(F, \sigma) = \mathsf{T}$ for every assignment σ and F is *unsatisfiable* if $eval(F, \sigma) = \mathsf{F}$ for every assignment σ.

Resolution. A *literal* is a variable $x \in \mathrm{Prop}$ or its negation, denoted $\neg x$ or $\overline{x}$. For a literal t being x or $\overline{x}$, we write $\mathrm{var}(t)$ for x. A *clause* is a disjunction of literals $t_1 \vee \cdots t_k$ represented as a set $\{t_1, \ldots, t_k\}$. Let $\mathbb{C}$ be the set of all clauses. The disjunction of two clauses is denoted $C \vee D$, further simplified to $C \vee t$ if D is the singleton $\{t\}$. The *restriction* of a clause C by a formula F, $C|_F \overset{\text{def}}{=} C \cap \{x, \overline{x} | x \in \mathrm{Var}(F)\}$ is the set of literals in C over variables in F. A formula in Conjunctive Normal Form (CNF) is a conjunction of clauses, also represented as a set of clauses. A clause containing t and $\overline{t}$ is a tautology as is the empty formula $\emptyset$. The empty clause, denoted $\square$, is unsatisfiable.

The *resolution principle* states that an assignment satisfying the clauses $C \vee x$ and $D \vee \overline{x}$ also satisfies $C \vee D$. It is given by the inference rule below.

$$\frac{C \vee x \qquad D \vee \overline{x}}{C \vee D} \quad [\text{Res}]$$

The clauses $C \vee x$ and $D \vee \overline{x}$ are the *antecedents*, x is the *pivot*, and $C \vee D$ is the *resolvent*. A clause C is derived from a CNF formula F by resolution if it is the resolvent of two clauses that either occur in F or have been derived from F by resolution. The resolvent of C and D with a pivot x is denoted $Res(x, C, D)$. A *proof* is a sequence of resolution deductions. A *refutation* is a proof of $\square$.

Interpolation. Consider two formulae A and B such that A implies B. Take for example $x \wedge y \Rightarrow y \vee z$. Since B does not involve x, whatever A asserts about y should be enough to imply B. Theorem 1 codifies this intuition and the proof (from [1]) gives a simple but infeasible method for interpolant construction.

Theorem 1. *For propositional formulae A and B, if $A \Rightarrow B$ is a tautology, there exists a propositional formula I, called an interpolant, such that (a) $A \Rightarrow I$ and (b) $I \Rightarrow B$ and (c) $\mathrm{Var}(I) \subseteq \mathrm{Var}(A) \cap \mathrm{Var}(B)$.*

Proof. We proceed in two steps. We first construct a formula I from A and then show that I has the requisite properties. For any set $X \subseteq \mathrm{Prop}$ and assignment σ, let $\mathrm{Pos}(X, \sigma) = \{x \in X | \sigma(x) = \mathsf{T}\}$ be the set of variables in X assigned T and let $\mathrm{Neg}(X, \sigma)$ be $X \setminus \mathrm{Pos}(X, \sigma)$. Let Y be $\mathrm{Var}(A) \cap \mathrm{Var}(B)$. Define:

$$I \stackrel{\mathrm{def}}{=} \bigvee_{\sigma \in \mathrm{Mod}(A)} \left(\bigwedge_{x \in \mathrm{Pos}(Y, \sigma)} x \wedge \bigwedge_{z \in \mathrm{Neg}(Y, \sigma)} \neg z \right)$$

We show that I is an interpolant.

(a) By construction, if $\sigma \models A$, then $\sigma \models I$, so $A \Rightarrow I$ is a tautology.

(b) If $\sigma \models I$, there exists an assignment σ' such that $\sigma' \models A$ and for all $x \in \mathrm{Var}(B)$, $\sigma(x) = \sigma'(x)$. As σ and σ' agree on $\mathrm{Var}(B)$, $eval(B, \sigma) = \mathsf{T}$ iff $eval(B, \sigma') = \mathsf{T}$. From the assumption that $A \Rightarrow B$, we have that $\sigma \models B$. It follows that $I \Rightarrow B$.

(c) $\mathrm{Var}(I) \subseteq \mathrm{Var}(A) \cap \mathrm{Var}(B)$ by construction.   ∎

The interpolant in the proof above is constructed by existentially eliminating some variables in A. Another possibility is to universally eliminate some variables in B. A tautology $A \Rightarrow B$ can have several interpolants and the set of all interpolants forms a complete lattice [11]. The construction above examines the models of A, hence it requires time exponential in $|Y|$ and can produce exponentially large interpolants. Complexity issues aside, the design of an interpolation algorithm follows the same steps. One must provide a procedure for constructing a formula and then prove that the formula is an interpolant. In this paper, we generalise these two steps in the context of resolution.

3   Interpolation Systems

Interpolation systems are introduced in this section. No new results are presented but existing systems are formally defined and explained with examples.

A *CNF pair* $\langle A, B \rangle$ is a pair of disjoint CNF formulae (that is, $A \cap B = \emptyset$). A CNF pair $\langle A, B \rangle$ is unsatisfiable if $A \wedge B$ is unsatisfiable. Given $\langle A, B \rangle$, let V_A denote $\mathrm{Var}(A) \setminus \mathrm{Var}(B)$, V_B denote $\mathrm{Var}(B) \setminus \mathrm{Var}(A)$ and $V_{\langle A, B \rangle}$ denote $\mathrm{Var}(A) \cap \mathrm{Var}(B)$. An interpolant for an unsatisfiable CNF pair is defined below.

Definition 1 (Interpolant). *An interpolant for an unsatisfiable CNF pair $\langle A, B \rangle$, is a formula I such that $A \Rightarrow I$, $I \Rightarrow \neg B$, and $\mathrm{Var}(I) \subseteq \mathrm{Var}(A) \cap \mathrm{Var}(B)$.*

An interpolant is not necessarily symmetric with respect to $\langle A, B \rangle$. If I is an interpolant for $\langle A, B \rangle$, then, $\neg I$ is an interpolant for $\langle B, A \rangle$. Interpolants are constructed inductively over the structure of a refutation. Figure 1 illustrates interpolant construction for the CNF pair $\langle A, B \rangle$, where $A = (a_1 \vee \bar{a}_2) \wedge (\bar{a}_1 \vee \bar{a}_3) \wedge a_2$ and $B = (\bar{a}_2 \vee a_3) \wedge (a_2 \vee a_4) \wedge \bar{a}_4$. McMillan's construction [19] is shown on the left and that of Huang [14], Krajíček [16] and Pudlák [21] is on the right. The formula labelling the empty clause is the interpolant for $\langle A, B \rangle$. Observe that the two methods produce different interpolants.

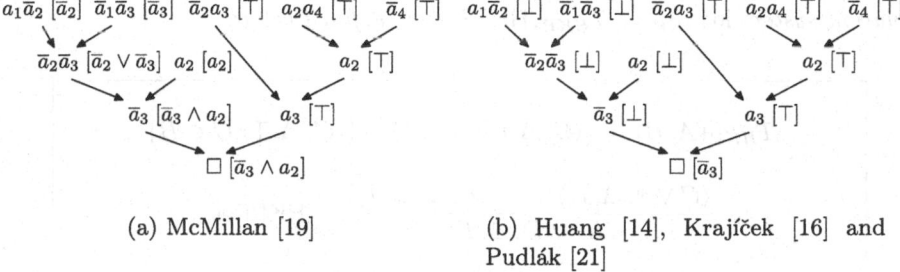

(a) McMillan [19]

(b) Huang [14], Krajíček [16] and Pudlák [21]

Fig. 1. Interpolant construction using systems in the literature

We formalise these constructions as *interpolation systems*. Recall that $\mathbb{B}$ is the set of all formulae and $\mathbb{C}$ is the set of all clauses. Let $S \stackrel{\text{def}}{=} \wp(\{A, B\})$ be a set of symbols. To reduce notation, we write A for $\{A\}$, B for $\{B\}$ and AB for $\{A, B\}$. A *distinction function* is an element of $\mathbb{D} \stackrel{\text{def}}{=} \text{Prop} \to S$. An *extended clause* (e-clause) is an element of $\mathbb{C} \times \mathbb{D} \times \mathbb{B}$. In an e-clause $E = \langle C, \Delta, I \rangle$, $cl(E) = C$ is a clause, $df(E) = \Delta$ is a distinction function and $int(E) = I$ is a *partial interpolant*. An interpolation system extends resolution to e-clauses.

Definition 2 (Interpolation System). *Let $\mathbb{E} = \mathbb{C} \times \mathbb{D} \times \mathbb{B}$ be a set of* extended *clauses. An interpolation system for $\mathbb{E}$ is a tuple* $\mathsf{Int} = \langle T, \mathsf{ERes} \rangle$*, where* $T :$ $\wp(\mathbb{C}) \times \wp(\mathbb{C}) \to \wp(\mathbb{E})$ *is a translation function and* ERes *is an inference rule. The function T satisfies that for all disjoint $A, B \in \wp(\mathbb{C})$, a clause $C \in A \cup B$ iff there exists a unique $\Delta \in \mathbb{D}$ and $I \in \mathbb{B}$ such that $\langle C, \Delta, I \rangle \in T(A, B)$. The inference rule is of the form:*

$$\frac{\langle C_1 \vee x, \Delta_1, I_1 \rangle \qquad \langle C_2 \vee \bar{x}, \Delta_2, I_1 \rangle}{\langle C_1 \vee C_2, \Delta, I \rangle} \quad \text{[ERes]}$$

The variable x is called the pivot.

An e-clause derived from E_1 and E_2 by applying ERes with a pivot x is an *e-resolvent* and is denoted $ERes(x, E_1, E_2)$. For C derived from $\langle A, B \rangle$ by resolution, the *corresponding e-clause* E is defined as:

- If $C \in A \cup B$, then E is the unique e-clause in $T(A, B)$ such that $cl(E) = C$.
- If $C = Res(x, C_1, C_2)$, then $E = ERes(x, E_1, E_2)$, where E_1 and E_2 are the corresponding e-clauses for C_1 and C_2 respectively.

Given a derivation of a clause C, the corresponding e-clause is uniquely defined. In general, there may be multiple derivations of C, and consequently, multiple e-clauses E with $cl(E) = C$. An interpolation system Int is *correct* if for every derivation of the empty clause $\square$, the corresponding e-clause $E_\square$ satisfies that $int(E_\square)$ is an interpolant for $\langle A, B \rangle$. We introduce existing interpolation systems next. The first two systems do not modify the inference rule but the parametrised system does. This difference leads to the abstraction we identify in § 4.2.

Definition 3 (HKP System [14,16,21]). *The Huang-Krajíček-Pudlák interpolation system* $\mathsf{Int}_{HKP} = \langle T_{HKP}, \mathsf{HKPRes} \rangle$ *is defined below.*

$$T_{HKP}(A,B) \overset{\text{def}}{=} \{\langle C, \Delta, \mathsf{F}\rangle | C \in A\} \cup \{\langle C, \Delta, \mathsf{T}\rangle | C \in B\}$$

$$\frac{\langle C \vee x, \Delta, I_1 \rangle \qquad \langle D \vee \bar{x}, \Delta, I_2 \rangle}{\langle C \vee D, \Delta, I \rangle} \quad \text{[HKPRes]}$$

$$\Delta(x) \overset{\text{def}}{=} \begin{matrix} \text{A} & \textit{if } x \in V_A \\ \text{AB} & \textit{if } x \in V_{\langle A,B \rangle} \\ \text{B} & \textit{if } x \in V_B \end{matrix} \quad \textit{and } I \overset{\text{def}}{=} (x \vee I_1) \wedge (\bar{x} \vee I_2) \quad \begin{matrix} I_1 \vee I_2 & \textit{if } \Delta(x) = \text{A} \\ & \textit{if } \Delta(x) = \text{AB} \\ I_1 \wedge I_2 & \textit{if } \Delta(x) = \text{B} \end{matrix}$$

The system above distinguishes between variables appearing only in A, variables appearing in A and B and variables appearing only in B. McMillan's system, defined below, has a different translation function and ERes rule.

Definition 4 (McMillan's System [19]). *McMillan's interpolation system* $\mathsf{Int}_M = \langle T_M, \mathsf{MRes} \rangle$ *is defined below with Δ as in Definition 3.*

$$T_M(A,B) \overset{\text{def}}{=} \{\langle C, \Delta, C|_B \rangle | C \in A\} \cup \{\langle C, \Delta, \mathsf{T}\rangle | C \in B\}$$

$$\frac{\langle C \vee x, \Delta, I_1 \rangle \qquad \langle D \vee \bar{x}, \Delta, I_2 \rangle}{\langle C \vee D, \Delta, I \rangle} \quad \text{[MRes]}$$

$$I \overset{\text{def}}{=} \begin{matrix} I_1 \vee I_2 & \textit{if } \Delta(x) = \text{A} \\ I_1 \wedge I_2 & \textit{if } \Delta(x) = \text{AB} \\ I_1 \wedge I_2 & \textit{if } \Delta(x) = \text{B} \end{matrix}$$

Note that the AB and B cases above are identical. Example 1 below shows that the two systems produce different interpolants and that different interpolants can be obtained by interchanging A and B. Example 2 shows that there are interpolants not obtained in either system.

Example 1. Let A be $(a_1 \vee \bar{a}_2) \wedge (\bar{a}_1 \vee \bar{a}_3) \wedge a_2$ and B be $(\bar{a}_2 \vee a_3) \wedge (a_2 \vee a_4) \wedge \bar{a}_4$. The e-clauses in McMillan's system are shown on the left of Figure 1 and those in the other system are on the right. The partial interpolants in both systems are shown in square brackets. The interpolants are different. The interpolant for $\langle B, A \rangle$ in McMillan's system is $a_2 \wedge a_3$. By negating it, we obtain $\bar{a}_2 \vee \bar{a}_3$, which is also an interpolant for $\langle A, B \rangle$ but is not the interpolant obtained from McMillan's system. In contrast, the interpolant for $\langle B, A \rangle$ in the HKP system is a_3, which when negated yields the same interpolant as before.   ◁

Example 2. Let A be the formula $\bar{a}_1 \wedge (a_1 \vee \bar{a}_2)$ and B be the formula $(\bar{a}_1 \vee a_2) \wedge$ a_1. A refutation for $A \wedge B$ is shown alongside. The interpolant obtained in both systems is $\bar{a}_1 \wedge \bar{a}_2$. The interpolant for $\langle B, A \rangle$ obtained from Int_{HKP} is $a_1 \vee a_2$ and that obtained from Int_M is $a_1 \wedge a_2$. By negating these, we get the additional interpolant $\bar{a}_1 \vee \bar{a}_2$. The pair $\langle A, B \rangle$ has two more interpolants, namely $\bar{a}_1$ and $\bar{a}_2$. These interpolants can be obtained with Int_{HKP} and Int_M from different proofs. ◁

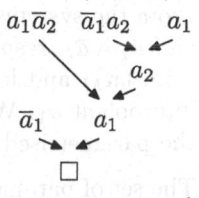

A third, *parametrised* interpolation system that generalises the other two systems was defined in [10]. Unlike Int_{HKP} and Int_M, this system manipulates distinction functions. A parameter to this system associates a distinction function with each clause in a pair $\langle A, B \rangle$. Formally, a *parameter* is a function $\mathcal{D} : \mathbb{C} \to \mathbb{D}$. For simplicity, we write $\mathcal{D}(C)(t)$ for $\mathcal{D}(C)(\mathrm{var}(t))$, where C is a clause and $t \in C$. The resolution of two distinction functions $\Delta_1, \Delta_2 \in \mathbb{D}$ with respect to a pivot x is the distinction function Δ, denoted $DRes(x, \Delta_1, \Delta_2)$, defined as follows: for $y \in \mathrm{Prop}$, $\Delta(y) \overset{\mathrm{def}}{=} \emptyset$ if $y = x$ and $\Delta(y) \overset{\mathrm{def}}{=} \Delta_1(y) \cup \Delta_2(y)$, if $y \neq x$. The parametrised interpolation system is defined below.

Definition 5 (Parametrised Interpolation System [10]). *Let $\mathcal{D}$ be a parameter. The interpolation system $\mathsf{Int}_{\mathcal{D}} \overset{\mathrm{def}}{=} \langle T_{\mathcal{D}}, \mathsf{PRes} \rangle$ is defined below.*

$$T_{\mathcal{D}}(A, B) \overset{\mathrm{def}}{=} \{\langle C, \mathcal{D}(C), I \rangle \mid C \in A \cup B\},$$
where I is defined below.

For $C \in A$	*For $C \in B$*
$I \overset{\mathrm{def}}{=} \{t \in C \mid \mathcal{D}(C)(t) = \mathrm{B}\}$	$I \overset{\mathrm{def}}{=} \neg\{t \in C \mid \mathcal{D}(C)(t) = \mathrm{A}\}$

$$\frac{\langle C \vee x, \Delta_1, I_1 \rangle \quad \langle D \vee \bar{x}, \Delta_2, I_2 \rangle}{\langle C \vee D, DRes(x, \Delta_1, \Delta_2), I \rangle} \ \ [\mathsf{PRes}]$$

The partial interpolant I in the e-resolvent is defined below.

$$I \overset{\mathrm{def}}{=} \begin{array}{ll} I_1 \vee I_2 & \text{if } \Delta_1(x) \cup \Delta_2(x) = \mathrm{A} \\ (x \vee I_1) \wedge (\bar{x} \vee I_2) & \text{if } \Delta_1(x) \cup \Delta_2(x) = \mathrm{AB} \\ I_1 \wedge I_2 & \text{if } \Delta_1(x) \cup \Delta_2(x) = \mathrm{B} \end{array}$$

Example 3. Recall the CNF pair $\langle A, B \rangle$ from Example 2. Written as sets, A is $\{\{\bar{a}_1\}, \{a_1, \bar{a}_2\}\}$ and B is $\{\{\bar{a}_1, a_2\}, \{a_1\}\}$. Define two distinction functions $\Delta_{\mathrm{A}} \overset{\mathrm{def}}{=} \{a_1 \mapsto \mathrm{A}, a_2 \mapsto \mathrm{A}\}$ and $\Delta_{\mathrm{B}} \overset{\mathrm{def}}{=} \{a_1 \mapsto \mathrm{B}, a_2 \mapsto \mathrm{B}\}$. Three parameters are defined below (all mappings not shown go to the empty set):

- $\mathcal{D}_1(C) \overset{\mathrm{def}}{=} \Delta_{\mathrm{A}}$ for all $C \in A \cup B$.
- $\mathcal{D}_2(C) \overset{\mathrm{def}}{=} \Delta_{\mathrm{A}}$ for all $C \in A$ and is Δ_{B} for $C \in B$.
- $\mathcal{D}_3(C) \overset{\mathrm{def}}{=} \Delta_{\mathrm{B}}$ for all $C \in A \cup B$.

We apply the parametrised interpolation system to the refutation in Example 2. From the systems $\mathsf{Int}_{\mathcal{D}_1}$, $\mathsf{Int}_{\mathcal{D}_2}$ and $\mathsf{Int}_{\mathcal{D}_3}$, we obtain the interpolants $\bar{a}_1 \vee \bar{a}_2$, $\bar{a}_2$ and $\bar{a}_1 \wedge \bar{a}_2$, respectively. Recall that the interpolant $\bar{a}_2$ could not be obtained from Int_M and Int_{HKP} for the given refutation. The pair $\langle A, B \rangle$ has one more interpolant $\bar{a}_1$. We show in § 5 that this interpolant cannot be obtained from the parametrised system. ◁

The set of parameters defines a set of interpolation systems. However, not all of these interpolation systems are correct. An interpolant I for $\langle A, B \rangle$ must satisfy that $\mathrm{Var}(I) \subseteq V_{\langle A,B \rangle}$. Specifically, if $x \notin V_{\langle A,B \rangle}$, x must not be added to the interpolant by $T_{\mathcal{D}}$ or the PRes rule. Observe that if for every clause $C \in A$ and literal $t \in C$ with $\mathrm{var}(t) \in V_A$, it holds that $\mathcal{D}(C)(t) = \textsc{a}$, then t will not appear in the interpolant. The same applies for $C \in B$ and $\mathrm{var}(t) \in V_B$. *Locality preserving parameters* make this intuition precise and yield correct interpolation systems. Let $\Lambda_{\langle A,B \rangle}$ be the set of locality preserving parameters for $\langle A, B \rangle$.

Definition 6 (Locality [10]). *A parameter $\mathcal{D}$ is locality preserving for a CNF pair $\langle A, B \rangle$ if it satisfies the following conditions.*

- *For all $C \in A \cup B$ and $x \in \mathrm{Var}(C)$, $\mathcal{D}(C)(x) \neq \emptyset$.*
- *For any $C \in \mathbb{C}$ and $x \in V_A$, $\mathcal{D}(C)(x) \subseteq \textsc{a}$.*
- *For any $C \in \mathbb{C}$ and $x \in V_B$, $\mathcal{D}(C)(x) \subseteq \textsc{b}$.*

Theorem 2 ([10]). *Let $\mathcal{D}$ be locality preserving for a CNF pair $\langle A, B \rangle$. If $\square$ is derived from $\langle A, B \rangle$ by resolution and $E_{\square}$ is the corresponding e-clause derived with $\mathsf{Int}_{\mathcal{D}}$, then $int(E_{\square})$ is an interpolant for $\langle A, B \rangle$.*

The theorem is proved by showing that for every clause C derived by resolution, the corresponding e-clause $E = \langle C, \Delta, I \rangle$ satisfies the following conditions:

- $A \wedge \neg\{t \in C | \{\textsc{a}\} \subseteq \Delta(\mathrm{var}(t))\} \Rightarrow I$
- $B \wedge \neg\{t \in C | \{\textsc{b}\} \subseteq \Delta(\mathrm{var}(t))\} \Rightarrow \neg I$
- $\mathrm{Var}(I) \subseteq \mathrm{Var}(A) \cap \mathrm{Var}(B)$.

4   Interpolation Systems and Abstract Interpretation

In this section, the parametrised interpolation system is related to the other systems and the resolution proof system by abstract interpretation.

Lattices. A *lattice*, $\langle S, \sqsubseteq, \sqcup, \sqcap \rangle$ (abbreviated to $\langle S, \sqsubseteq \rangle$), is a set S equipped with a partial order $\sqsubseteq$ and two binary operators; a least upper bound, $\sqcup$, called the *join*, and a greatest lower bound, $\sqcap$, called the *meet*. A lattice is complete if for every $X \subseteq S$, the join $\bigsqcup X$ and meet $\bigsqcap X$ are defined and exist in S. A function $F : S \rightarrow S$ is *monotone* if for any $x, y \in S$, $x \sqsubseteq y$ implies that $F(x) \sqsubseteq F(y)$. It follows from the Knaster-Tarski theorem that a monotone function on a complete lattice has unique least fixed point, denoted $\mu x.F(x)$.

Consider a set P. A *powerset lattice* is the complete lattice $\langle \wp(P), \subseteq, \cup, \cap \rangle$. Given the set $P \rightarrow S$, where S is the lattice above, the structure of S can be *lifted pointwise* to obtain the lattice $\langle P \rightarrow S, \dot{\sqsubseteq}, \dot{\sqcup}, \dot{\sqcap} \rangle$ defined below.

- For $f, g \in P \to S$, $f \dot{\sqsubseteq} g$ iff for all $x \in S$, $f(x) \sqsubseteq g(x)$.
- For $f, g \in P \to S$, $f \dot{\sqcup} g$ is the function that maps $x \in S$ to $f(x) \sqcup g(x)$. The pointwise meet operation is similarly defined.

Consult [9] for more details on lattice theory.

Abstract Interpretation. Abstract interpretation is a framework for reasoning about approximation. Only limited aspects of the framework required for the paper are covered here. See [3,4] for an in-depth treatment.

Elements in one lattice, $\langle C, \sqsubseteq_C \rangle$ called the *concrete domain*, are approximated by elements in another $\langle A, \sqsubseteq_A \rangle$, called the *abstract domain*. The notion of approximation is formalised by an *abstraction function* $\alpha : C \to A$ and a *concretisation function* $\gamma : A \to C$ which form a *Galois connection*. The functions satisfy that for all $c \in C, a \in A$, $c \sqsubseteq_C \gamma(\alpha(c))$ and $\alpha(\gamma(a)) \sqsubseteq_A a$. If in addition $\alpha \circ \gamma$ is the identity map on A, the pair is called a *Galois insertion*. A monotone function $F : C \to C$ is approximated in A by the function $F^A : A \to A$, defined as $(\alpha \circ F \circ \gamma)$ and called the *best approximation*. The structure $\langle C, \sqsubseteq_C, F \rangle$ is the *concrete interpretation* and $\langle A, \sqsubseteq_A, F^A \rangle$ is the *abstract interpretation*. In general, the concrete and abstract interpretations may involve several functions.

The approximation F^A is *sound*, meaning that for any $c \in C$ and $a \in A$, $F(\gamma(a)) \sqsubseteq_C \gamma(F^A(a))$ and $\alpha(F(c)) \sqsubseteq_A F^A(\alpha(c))$. Soundness further implies fixed point soundness. That is, $\mu X.F(X) \sqsubseteq_C \gamma(\mu Y.F^A(Y))$ and $\alpha(\mu X.F(X)) \sqsubseteq_A \mu Y.F^A(Y)$. Thus, to compute sound approximations of concrete fixed points it suffices to compute abstract fixed points. The approximation is *complete* if $\alpha(F(c)) = F^A(\alpha(C)$. An abstract interpretation is not necessarily complete [12].

Domains connected by Galois insertions can be formalised in several other ways, in particular by closure operators [5]. An *upper closure operator* is a function $\rho : C \to C$ that is (a) *extensive*: $c \sqsubseteq_C \rho(c)$, (b) *idempotent*: $\rho(c) = \rho(\rho(c))$, and (c) *monotone*: if $c_1 \sqsubseteq_C c_2$, then $\rho(c_1) \sqsubseteq_C \rho(c_2)$. To show that an operator on a lattice defines an abstraction, it suffices to show that it is a closure operator. Closure operators are convenient because one can deal with abstractions without introducing two different lattices. Both Galois insertions and closure operators are used in this paper, as per convenience.

4.1 The Concrete Domain of Parameters

We introduce the lattice of parameters and show that locality preserving parameters are closed under certain operations on this lattice. Recall from § 3 that S is the powerset lattice $\langle \wp(\{A, B\}), \subseteq, \cup, \cap \rangle$. Further, define the *dual* of an element of S as follows: $\widehat{A} \stackrel{def}{=} B$, $\widehat{B} \stackrel{def}{=} A$, $\widehat{AB} \stackrel{def}{=} AB$ and $\widehat{\emptyset} \stackrel{def}{=} \emptyset$. That is, the dual of A is B and vice versa, but AB and $\emptyset$ are self-duals. The term *dual* is due to Huang [14] who defined the dual of Int_{HKP}. The lattice of distinction functions, $\langle \mathbb{D}, \sqsubseteq^{\mathbb{D}}, \sqcup^{\mathbb{D}}, \sqcap^{\mathbb{D}} \rangle$, where $\mathbb{D} = \mathsf{Prop} \to S$, is derived from S by pointwise lifting. The lattice of parameters, $\langle \mathbb{C} \to \mathbb{D}, \sqsubseteq, \sqcup, \sqcap \rangle$, is derived from $\mathbb{D}$, also by pointwise lifting. The dual of a distinction function and a parameter are similarly defined by pointwise lifting. In addition, define the function $\delta_{\langle A, B \rangle}$ that maps a parameter $\mathcal{D}$ to one that agrees with $\mathcal{D}$ on $x \in V_A \cup V_B$ but maps all other variables to their duals. Formally, $\delta_{\langle A,B \rangle}(\mathcal{D}) \stackrel{\text{def}}{=} \mathcal{D}'$, where for $C \in \mathbb{C}$ and $x \in \text{Prop}$, $\mathcal{D}'(C)(x)$ is $\mathcal{D}(C)(x)$ if $x \in V_A \cup V_B$ and is $\widehat{\mathcal{D}}(C)(x)$ if $x \in V_{\langle A,B \rangle}$.

Locality preserving parameters define correct interpolation systems, so operations on parameters that preserve locality are of particular interest. Such operations are illustrated in Example 4 and formally identified in Lemma 1.

Example 4. Consider again the CNF pair $\langle A, B \rangle$ in Example 1, where $A = \{\{a_1, \bar{a}_2\}, \{\bar{a}_1, \bar{a}_3\}, \{a_2\}\}$ and $B = \{\{\bar{a}_2, \bar{a}_3\}, \{a_2, a_4\}, \{\bar{a}_4\}\}$. Define the $\mathcal{D}_4, \mathcal{D}_5$ and $\mathcal{D}_6$ as below. Let $C \in \mathbb{C}$ be a clause.

– $\mathcal{D}_4(C)(x)$ is A for $x \in V_A$, and is B for $x \notin V_A$.
– $\mathcal{D}_5(C)(x)$ is A for $x \notin V_B$, and is B for $x \in V_B$.
– $\mathcal{D}_6(C)(x)$ is A for $x \in V_A$, is AB for $x \in V_{\langle A,B \rangle}$, and is B for $x \in V_B$.

These parameters are locality preserving for $\langle A, B \rangle$ and that their duals are locality preserving for $\langle B, A \rangle$. Further, we have that $\delta_{\langle A,B \rangle}(\mathcal{D}_4) = \mathcal{D}_5$ and $\mathcal{D}_4 \sqcup \mathcal{D}_5 = \mathcal{D}_6$, so $\delta_{\langle A,B \rangle}$ and $\sqcup$ preserve locality. In contrast, $\mathcal{D}_4 \sqcap \mathcal{D}_5$ is not locality preserving for $\langle A, B \rangle$.   ◁

Lemma 1. *Let $\langle A, B \rangle$ be a CNF pair.*

1. *If $\mathcal{D}_1$ and $\mathcal{D}_2$ are locality preserving for $\langle A, B \rangle$, then so is $\mathcal{D}_1 \sqcup \mathcal{D}_2$.*
2. *If $\mathcal{D}$ is locality preserving for $\langle A, B \rangle$, then $\widehat{\mathcal{D}}$ is locality preserving for $\langle B, A \rangle$. Further, if C is derived by resolution and E and F are the corresponding clauses in $\mathsf{Int}_{\mathcal{D}}$ and $\mathsf{Int}_{\widehat{\mathcal{D}}}$ respectively, then $int(E) = \neg int(F)$.*
3. *If $\mathcal{D}$ is locality preserving for $\langle A, B \rangle$, so is $\delta_{\langle A,B \rangle}(\mathcal{D})$.*

Proof. (1) Consider each condition in Definition 6. Observe that $\mathcal{D}_1 \sqcup \mathcal{D}_2$ is the pointwise join of the two parameters. It follows that for any $C \in \mathbb{C}$ and $x \in \text{Var}(C)$, if $\mathcal{D}_1(C)(t) \neq \emptyset$ and $\mathcal{D}_2(C)(t) \neq \emptyset$, then $(\mathcal{D}_1 \sqcup \mathcal{D}_2)(C)(t) \neq \emptyset$. The same argument applies for the other two locality conditions.

(2) The sets $\text{Var}(A) \setminus \text{Var}(B)$ and $\text{Var}(B) \setminus \text{Var}(A)$ are identical in both $\langle A, B \rangle$ and $\langle B, A \rangle$. To preserve locality, any $x \in \text{Var}(A) \setminus \text{Var}(B)$ must be labelled B by $\widehat{\mathcal{D}}$. As $\mathcal{D}$ is locality preserving, these variables are labelled A and by the definition of $\widehat{\mathcal{D}}$, will be labelled B. A symmetric argument applies for $x \in \text{Var}(B) \setminus \text{Var}(A)$.

The second property is shown by structural induction.

Base case. Consider $C \in A \cup B$, and the corresponding e-clauses $E \in T_{\mathcal{D}}(A, B)$ and $F \in T_{\widehat{\mathcal{D}}}(B, A)$. For any $t \in C$, if $\mathcal{D}(C)(x) = \text{A}$, then $\widehat{\mathcal{D}}(C)(x) = \text{B}$. It follows from the definition of $T_{\mathcal{D}}$ and $T_{\widehat{\mathcal{D}}}$ that $int(E) = \neg int(F)$. Observe in addition that $df(E) = \widehat{df(F)}$.

Induction step. For a derived clause $C = Res(x, C_1, C_2)$ and consider the corresponding e-clauses $E = ERes(x, E_1, E_2)$ and $F = ERes(x, F_1, F_2)$ derived in $\mathsf{Int}_{\mathcal{D}}$ and $\mathsf{Int}_{\widehat{\mathcal{D}}}$, respectively. For the induction hypothesis, assume that $int(E_1) = \neg int(F_1)$ and $df(E_1) = \widehat{df(F_1)}$ and likewise for E_2 and F_2. For the induction step, consider the PRes rule in Definition 5. There are three cases for defining $int(E)$. If case A applies in $\mathsf{Int}_{\mathcal{D}}$, then, by the induction hypothesis, case B applies for $\mathsf{Int}_{\widehat{\mathcal{D}}}$. That is, $int(E) = I_1 \vee I_2$ and $int(F) = \neg I_1 \wedge \neg I_2$, so $int(E) = \neg(int(F))$ as required. The other cases are similar.

(3) Holds as $\mathcal{D}(C)(x) = (\delta_{\langle A,B \rangle}(\mathcal{D}))(C)(x)$ for $C \in A \cup B$ and $x \in V_A \cup V_B$. ∎

4.2 Abstract Domains of Parameters

Algorithms derived from Int_{HKP}, Int_M and the parametrised system have a running time that is linear in proof size, however Int_{HKP} and Int_M are more space efficient because they do not modify the distinction function. Intuitively, an interpolation system is space efficient if the value of the distinction function at a pivot variable does not change in a proof. Formally, a parameter $\mathcal{D}$ is *derivation invariant* with respect to $\langle A, B \rangle$ if for any e-clause E derived from $\langle A, B \rangle$ in $\mathsf{Int}_{\mathcal{D}}$ and any $C \in A \cup B$, if $x \in \mathrm{Var}(cl(E)) \cap \mathrm{Var}(C)$, then $df(E)(x) = \mathcal{D}(C)(x)$.

Example 5. Consider the pair $\langle A, B \rangle$ and the parameters $\mathcal{D}_1$ and $\mathcal{D}_3$ in Example 2. For any clause C derived from $\langle A, B \rangle$ and corresponding e-clause E in the example, $df(E)(x)$ is the same as $\mathcal{D}(C')(x)$, where $C' \in \langle A, B \rangle$. The parameters in Example 4 are also derivation invariant. In contrast, the parameter $\mathcal{D}_2$ in Example 2 is not derivation invariant because the value of the distinction function at a_2 changes in the proof. ◁

We identify a family of abstractions that give rise to derivation invariant parameters. These abstractions are defined over partitions of Prop. A *partition* π of a set S is a set of disjoint subsets of S, called *blocks*, that are pairwise disjoint and whose disjoint union is S. Let $[x]_\pi$ denote the block containing $x \in S$. A partition π is *coarser than* a partition π', denoted $\pi \preceq \pi'$, if for every block $\beta \in \pi$, there is a block $\beta' \in \pi'$ such that $\beta \subseteq \beta'$. It is known that the set of partitions forms a complete lattice. Let $\langle \mathrm{Part}(\mathrm{Prop}), \preceq, \sqcup, \sqcap \rangle$ be the lattice of partitions of Prop. For a CNF pair $\langle A, B \rangle$, define the partition $\pi^{\langle A,B \rangle} \stackrel{\text{def}}{=} \{\{x | x \in V_A\}, \{x | x \in V_{\langle A,B \rangle}\}, \{x | x \in V_B\}, \{x | x \notin \mathrm{Var}(A) \cup \mathrm{Var}(B)\}\}$. Given a partition $\pi \in \mathrm{Part}(\mathrm{Prop})$ we define a function Υ_π that maps a parameter to another one, assigning the same symbol in S to variables in the same block.

$$\Upsilon_\pi(\mathcal{D}) \stackrel{\text{def}}{=} \mathcal{D}' \text{ where } \mathcal{D}'(C)(x) \stackrel{\text{def}}{=} \bigcup_{C' \in \mathbb{C}} \bigcup_{y \in [x]_\pi} \mathcal{D}(C')(y) \text{ for } C \in \mathbb{C} \text{ and } x \in \mathrm{Prop}.$$

A parameter $\mathcal{D}$ is *partitioning* if $\Upsilon_\pi(\mathcal{D}) = \mathcal{D}$ for some $\pi \in \mathrm{Part}(\mathrm{Prop})$. In Theorem 3, we show that each function Υ_π defines an abstract domain of parameters and relate such parameters to derivation invariance and locality preservation.

Example 6. Consider the CNF pair $\langle A, B \rangle$ in Example 4 and the partitions $\pi_A = \{\{x | x \in V_A\}, \{x | x \notin V_A\}\}$, $\pi_B = \{\{x | x \in V_B\}, \{x | x \notin V_B\}\}$, and $\pi^{\langle A,B \rangle}$. Assume that $\mathrm{Var}(A \cup B) = \mathrm{Prop}$. The parameters $\mathcal{D}_4, \mathcal{D}_5$ and $\mathcal{D}_6$ are partitioning, as witnessed by the partitions π_A, π_B and $\pi^{\langle A,B \rangle}$ respectively.

Consider the CNF pair $\langle A, B \rangle$, the parameters $\mathcal{D}_1, \mathcal{D}_2$ and $\mathcal{D}_3$ in Example 3 and the partition $\pi = \{\text{Prop}\}$. Observe that $V_A = V_B = \emptyset$, so $\mathcal{D}_1$ and $\mathcal{D}_3$ are partitioning with respect to π. However, $\mathcal{D}_2$ is not partitioning.   ◁

Theorem 3. *1. The function Υ_π is a closure operator.*
2. A partitioning parameter is derivation invariant.
3. If $\mathcal{D}_1$ and $\mathcal{D}_2$ are partitioning, so are $\mathcal{D}_1 \sqcup \mathcal{D}_2$, $\widehat{\mathcal{D}}_1$ and $\delta_{\langle A, B \rangle}(\mathcal{D}_1)$
4. If $\mathcal{D}$ is locality preserving and $\pi \preceq \pi^{\langle A, B \rangle}$, then $\Upsilon_\pi(\mathcal{D})$ is locality preserving.
5. The coarsest π for which $\Upsilon_\pi(\Lambda_{\langle A, B \rangle}) \subseteq \Lambda_{\langle A, B \rangle}$, for any $\langle A, B \rangle$, is $\pi = \pi^{\langle A, B \rangle}$.

Proof. (1) We show that Υ_π is a closure operator. The function is extensive because for all $C \in \mathbb{C}$ and $x \in \text{Prop}$, $\mathcal{D}(C)(x) \subseteq \Upsilon_\pi(\mathcal{D})(C)(x)$. For any $C \in \mathbb{C}$ and $y \in [x]_\pi$, $\Upsilon_\pi(\mathcal{D})(C)(x) = \Upsilon_\pi(\mathcal{D})(C)(y)$, so the function is idempotent. If $\mathcal{D}_1 \sqsubseteq \mathcal{D}_2$, then for all $C \in \mathbb{C}$ and $x \in \text{Prop}$, $\mathcal{D}_1(C)(x) \subseteq \mathcal{D}_2(C)(x)$. The values $\Upsilon_\pi(\mathcal{D}_1)(C)(x)$ and $\Upsilon_\pi(\mathcal{D}_2)(C)(x)$ are defined as the union over a set of variables of $\mathcal{D}_1$ and $\mathcal{D}_2$ respectively. Monotonicity follows because union is monotone.
(2) Let E be an e-clause derived with $\text{Int}_\mathcal{D}$ from $\langle A, B \rangle$. We show that $\mathcal{D}$ is derivation invariant by induction on the structure of the derivation.

Base Case. If $E \in T_\mathcal{D}(A, B)$, as $\mathcal{D}$ is partitioning, $\mathcal{D}(C)(x) = df(E)(x)$ for any clause $C \in \mathbb{C}$ and variable $x \in \text{Prop}$.

Induction Step. Consider $E = ERes(x, E_1, E_2)$ for e-clauses E_1 and E_2. For the induction hypothesis, assume that for any $C \in A \cup B$ and $x \in \text{Var}(cl(E_1)) \cap \text{Var}(C)$, $df(E_1)(x) = \mathcal{D}(C)(x)$ and the same for E_2. Consider $C \in A \cup B$ and $x \in \text{Var}(cl(E)) \cap \text{Var}(C)$. Now, x must be in $\text{Var}(cl(E_1))$ only, $\text{Var}(cl(E_2))$ only or both. If $x \in \text{Var}(cl(E_1))$ only, $df(E)(x) = df(E_1)(x)$ and by the induction hypothesis, $df(E)(x) = \mathcal{D}(C)(x)$. The remaining cases are similar.

(3) Consider $\mathcal{D}_1$ and $\mathcal{D}_2$ which are partitioning. That is, there exist π_1 and π_2 such that $\Upsilon_{\pi_1}(\mathcal{D}_1) = \mathcal{D}_1$ and $\Upsilon_{\pi_2}(\mathcal{D}_2) = \mathcal{D}_2$. Let $\mathcal{D} = \mathcal{D}_1 \sqcup \mathcal{D}_2$ and $\pi = \pi_1 \sqcap \pi_2$. and $\mathcal{D} = \mathcal{D}_1 \sqcup \mathcal{D}_2$. Because $\mathcal{D}_1$ and $\mathcal{D}_2$ are partitioning, it follows that for all x and $y \in [x]_\pi$, $\mathcal{D}(C)(x) = \mathcal{D}(C)(y)$. Thus, $\Upsilon_\pi(\mathcal{D}) = \mathcal{D}$ and $\mathcal{D}$ is partitioning. The other cases hold because the dual and $\delta_{\langle A, B \rangle}$ are defined pointwise on variables, so the partition for $\mathcal{D}_1$ is the partition for $\widehat{\mathcal{D}}_1$ and $\delta_{\langle A, B \rangle}(\mathcal{D})$.
(4) If $\pi \preceq \pi^{\langle A, B \rangle}$, for any $x \in V_A$, if $y \in [x]_\pi$, then $y \in V_A$. For a locality preserving $\mathcal{D}$ and $C \in A \cup B$, it holds that $\mathcal{D}(C)(y) \subseteq \text{A}$. Hence, $\bigcup_{C \in \mathbb{C}} \bigcup_{y \in [x]_\pi} \mathcal{D}(C)(y) \subseteq \text{A}$. The same applies for $x \in V_B$, so $\Upsilon_\pi(\mathcal{D})$ is locality preserving.
(5) It follows from the previous part that $\Upsilon_{\pi^{\langle A, B \rangle}}(\Lambda_{\langle A, B \rangle}) \subseteq \Lambda_{\langle A, B \rangle}$. It suffices to show that there is no $\pi^{\langle A, B \rangle} \prec \pi$ such that $\Upsilon_\pi(\Lambda_{\langle A, B \rangle}) \subseteq \Lambda_{\langle A, B \rangle}$ for all $\langle A, B \rangle$. We prove it by contradiction. It suffices to find a pair $\langle A, B \rangle$ and $\mathcal{D} \in \Lambda_{\langle A, B \rangle}$ such that $\Upsilon_\pi(\mathcal{D}) \notin \Lambda_{\langle A, B \rangle}$. Consider $\langle A, B \rangle$ with $V_A, V_{\langle A, B \rangle}$ and V_B being non-empty. Let $\mathcal{D}$ map $x \in V_A$ to A, $x \in V_B$ to B and $x \in V_{\langle A, B \rangle}$ to AB. Consider variables $x \in V_A, y \in V_{\langle A, B \rangle}$ and $z \in V_B$. As $\pi^{\langle A, B \rangle} \prec \pi$, either $[x]_\pi = [y]_\pi$, or $[y]_\pi = [z]_\pi$, or $[x]_\pi = [z]_\pi$. If $[x]_\pi = [y]_\pi$, then $\mathcal{D}(C)(x) = \text{AB}$, violating the condition $\mathcal{D}(C)(x) \subseteq \text{A}$ in Definition 6. Thus, $\Upsilon_\pi(\Lambda_{\langle A, B \rangle}) \not\subseteq \Lambda_{\langle A, B \rangle}$. The other two cases are similar, leading to a contradiction as required.   ∎

We highlight that part 5 of Theorem 3 applies to all $\langle A, B \rangle$ and all parameters $\mathcal{D} \in \Lambda_{\langle A,B \rangle}$. For a specific parameter $\mathcal{D} \in \Lambda_{\langle A,B \rangle}$ and a specific pair $\langle A, B \rangle$, there may exist $\pi^{\langle A,B \rangle} \prec \pi$ such that $\Upsilon_\pi(\mathcal{D})$ is locality preserving.

4.3   Existing Systems as Abstractions

The setting of the previous section is now applied to study existing systems. We define two parameters that were shown in [10] to correspond to McMillan's system and the HKP system. Let $\langle A, B \rangle$ be a CNF pair. Define the value of the parameters $\mathcal{D}_M$ and $\mathcal{D}_{HKP}$ for $C \in \mathbb{C}$ and $x \in \text{Prop}$ as below.

- $\mathcal{D}_M(C)(x)$ is A if $x \in V_A$ and is B otherwise.
- $\mathcal{D}_{HKP}(C)(x)$ is A if $x \in V_A$ B if $x \in V_B$ and is AB for $x \in V_{\langle A,B \rangle}$.

Lemma 2 shows that the parameters above are two of three that exist in the coarsest partitioning abstraction defined by $\pi^{\langle A,B \rangle}$. The third system, $\delta_{\langle A,B \rangle}$ $(\mathcal{D}_M)$, was also identified in [10] but the connections presented here were not.

Lemma 2. *Let $\langle A, B \rangle$ be a CNF pair. The image of $\Lambda_{\langle A,B \rangle}$ under $\Upsilon_{\pi^{\langle A,B \rangle}}$ is $\{\mathcal{D}_M, \mathcal{D}_{HKP}, \delta_{\langle A,B \rangle}(\mathcal{D}_M)\}$.*

Proof. There are two steps. The first step is to show that each parameter in the lemma is a fixed point of $\Upsilon_{\pi^{\langle A,B \rangle}}$. We skip this step. The second is to show that no other such fixed points exist. As only elements of $\Lambda_{\langle A,B \rangle}$ are considered, assume that $\mathcal{D}$ is locality preserving. By definition of the closure operator we have that $\Upsilon_{\pi^{\langle A,B \rangle}}(\mathcal{D}) = \mathcal{D}$ only if for any $C_1, C_2 \in \mathbb{C}$ and $x, y \in V_{\langle A,B \rangle}$, $\mathcal{D}(C_1)(x) = \mathcal{D}(C_2)(y)$. It follows that for all C and $x \in V_{\langle A,B \rangle}$, $\mathcal{D}(C)(x)$ must be either A, AB or B. Thus, the only three possible parameters are the ones above.   ∎

The parameter $\mathcal{D}_{HKP}$ has several properties. It is the greatest locality preserving parameter with respect to $\sqsubseteq$, is symmetric in the sense that $\delta_{\langle A,B \rangle}(\mathcal{D}_{HKP}) = \mathcal{D}_{HKP}$ and can be derived from McMillan's system. These properties, summarised below, may explain why Int_{HKP} has been repeatedly discovered.

$$\mathcal{D}_{HKP} = \bigsqcup_{\mathcal{D} \in \Lambda_{\langle A,B \rangle}} \mathcal{D} \quad \text{and} \quad \mathcal{D}_M \sqcup \delta_{\langle A,B \rangle}(\mathcal{D}_M) = \mathcal{D}_{HKP}$$

4.4   The Domains of E-Clauses and Clauses

We remarked earlier that an interpolation system is an extension of resolution. This intuition is now made precise using the method in [7]. E-clauses constitute a concrete domain and interpolation systems define concrete interpretations. We show that sets of clauses form an abstract domain and that the resolution rule defines a complete abstract interpretation of an interpolation system.

Recall that $\mathbb{E}$ is the set of e-clauses and that for $E = \langle C, \Delta, I \rangle$, $cl(E) = C$. The powerset of e-clauses forms the concrete domain $\langle \wp(\mathbb{E}), \subseteq, \cup, \cap \rangle$. A parameter $\mathcal{D}$

defines an interpolation system $\mathsf{Int}_\mathcal{D} = \langle T_\mathcal{D}, \mathsf{PRes} \rangle$, which gives rise to a concrete interpretation consisting of two functions. The translation function $T_\mathcal{D} : \wp(\mathbb{C}) \times \wp(\mathbb{C}) \to \wp(\mathbb{E})$ and a function $PRes : \wp(\mathbb{E}) \to \wp(\mathbb{E})$ encoding the effect of the PRes rule. The function $PRes$ is defined in a sequence of steps.

- $PRes : \mathrm{Prop} \times \mathbb{E} \times \mathbb{E} \to \mathbb{E}$ is defined as follows. If $E_1, E_2 \in \mathbb{E}$ with $cl(E_1) = x \vee C$ and $cl(E_2) = D \vee \overline{x}$, then $PRes(x, E_1, E_2)$ is given by the PRes rule in Definition 5. $PRes(x, E_1, E_2)$ is defined as $\langle \emptyset, \emptyset, \mathsf{F} \rangle$ otherwise.
- Let $PRes : \mathbb{E} \times \mathbb{E} \to \mathbb{E}$ be $PRes(E_1, E_2) \stackrel{\text{def}}{=} \{PRes(x, E_1, E_2) | x \in \mathrm{Prop}\}$.
- Finally, $PRes : \wp(\mathbb{E}) \to \wp(\mathbb{E})$ maps $X \in \wp(\mathbb{E})$ to $\bigcup_{E_1, E_2 \in X} PRes(E_1, E_2)$.

The concrete semantic object of interest is the set of e-clauses that can be derived in an interpolation system $\mathsf{Int}_\mathcal{D}$ and the interpolants obtained from these e-clauses. These sets are defined below.

$$\mathcal{E}_\mathcal{D} \stackrel{\text{def}}{=} \mu X.(T_\mathcal{D}(A, B) \cup PRes(X)) \text{ and } \mathcal{I}_\mathcal{D} \stackrel{\text{def}}{=} \{int(E) | E \in \mathcal{E}_\mathcal{D} \text{ and } cl(E) = \square\}.$$

The set $\mathcal{I}_\mathcal{D}$ contains all interpolants that can be derived with $\mathsf{Int}_\mathcal{D}$ from $\langle A, B \rangle$. Observe that each interpolation system $\mathsf{Int}_\mathcal{D}$ defines a different concrete interpretation and a different set of interpolants $\mathcal{I}_\mathcal{D}$. Note also that the definition of $PRes$ is independent of the parameter $\mathcal{D}$. Hence, to analyse the properties of the set $\mathcal{I}_\mathcal{D}$, we only have to analyse $T_\mathcal{D}$. We exploit this observation in § 5.1.

We now relate resolution with interpolation systems. Define the domain $\langle \wp(\mathbb{C}), \subseteq, \cup, \cap \rangle$ of CNF formulae. The function Res corresponding to the resolution rule is first defined as $Res : \mathrm{Prop} \times \mathbb{C} \times \mathbb{C} \to \mathbb{C}$ and then lifted to a function $Res : \wp(\mathbb{C}) \to \wp(\mathbb{C})$, in a manner similar to $PRes$.

Abstraction and concretisation functions between $\langle \wp\mathbb{E}, \subseteq \rangle$ and $\langle \wp\mathbb{C}, \subseteq \rangle$ are defined next. Let $\alpha : \wp(\mathbb{E}) \to \wp(\mathbb{C})$ be a function that maps $X \in \wp(\mathbb{E})$ to the set of clauses $cl(X)$. The concretisation function $\gamma : \wp(\mathbb{C}) \to \wp(\mathbb{E})$ maps a set of clauses $Y \in \wp(\mathbb{C})$ to the set of e-clauses $\{\langle C, \Delta, I \rangle | C \in Y, \Delta \in \mathbb{D}, I \in \mathbb{B}\}$. Lemma 3 states that α and γ define a Galois insertion and that Res is the best approximation of $PRes$.

What do soundness and completeness mean in this setting? If $\alpha(PRes(X)) \subseteq Res(\alpha(X))$, every clause that can be derived with the inference rule PRes can also be derived with Res. However, we also want that the interpolation system can derive all clauses that can be derived by resolution. That is, as an inference rule, PRes should be as powerful as Res. In abstract interpretation terms, the function Res should be a complete abstraction of $PRes$.

Lemma 3. *The functions α and γ define a Galois insertion between $\wp(\mathbb{E})$ and $\wp(\mathbb{C})$. Further, $Res = (\alpha \circ PRes \circ \gamma)$, and $(Res \circ \alpha) = (\alpha \circ PRes)$.*

The best approximation of $T_\mathcal{D}$ is union: $(\alpha \circ T_\mathcal{D} \circ \gamma) = \cup$. The abstract semantic object corresponding to $\mathcal{E}_\mathcal{D}$ is the set of clauses that can be derived by resolution from $\langle A, B \rangle$. The viewpoint presented here is summarised below.

$$\mathcal{C} \stackrel{\text{def}}{=} \mu X.((A \cup B) \cup Res(X)) = \alpha(\mathcal{E}_\mathcal{D})$$

$\langle \wp(\mathbb{C}), \subseteq, \cup, Res \rangle$ is a complete abstract interpretation of $\langle \wp(\mathbb{E}), \subseteq, T_\mathcal{D}, PRes \rangle$.

5   Logical Strength and Variable Elimination

Interpolation systems are used in verification tools. The performance of such a tool depends on the logical strength and size of the interpolants obtained. The influence of interpolant strength on the termination of a verification tool is discussed in [10]. Interpolant size affects the memory requirements of a verification tool. The set of variables in an interpolant gives an upper bound on its size, so we study the smallest and largest sets of variables that can occur in an interpolant. We now analyse the logical strength of and variables occurring in interpolants.

5.1   Logical Strength as a Precision Order

The subset ordering on the domain $\wp(\mathbb{E})$ is a *computational order*. Meaning, it is the order with respect to which fixed points are defined. The elements of $\wp(\mathbb{E})$ can moreover be ordered by *precision*, where the notion of precision is application dependent. Cousot and Cousot have emphasised that though the computational and precision orders often coincide, this is not necessary [6]. To understand the logical strength of interpolants, we use a precision order based on implication.

Given X and Y in $\wp(\mathbb{E})$, the set X is more precise than Y if for every interpolant in Y, there is a logically stronger interpolant in X. Formally, define the relation $\preceq_{\mathbb{E}}$ on $\wp(\mathbb{E}) \times \wp(\mathbb{E})$ as $X \preceq_{\mathbb{E}} Y$ iff for all $E_1 \in Y$ with $cl(E_1) = \Box$, there exists $E_2 \in X$ with $cl(E_2) = \Box$ and $int(E_2) \Rightarrow int(E_1)$. Let $\langle A, B \rangle$ be a CNF pair, $\mathcal{D}_1$ and $\mathcal{D}_2$ be two parameters and $\mathcal{E}_1$ and $\mathcal{E}_2$ be the sets of e-clauses derived in these two systems. The system $\mathsf{Int}_{\mathcal{D}_1}$ is *more precise* or *stronger* than $\mathsf{Int}_{\mathcal{D}_2}$ if $\mathcal{E}_1 \preceq_{\mathbb{E}} \mathcal{E}_2$. If *PRes* is monotone with respect to $\preceq_{\mathbb{E}}$, the problem of computing logically stronger interpolants can be reduced to that of ordering translation functions by precision. However, *PRes* is not monotone with respect to $\preceq_{\mathbb{E}}$ because $\preceq_{\mathbb{E}}$ does not take distinction functions into account.

We now derive an order for $\wp(\mathbb{E})$ that is stronger than $\preceq_{\mathbb{E}}$ and with respect to which *PRes* is monotone. The order from [10] is adapted to our setting. We define an order on $\mathcal{S}$ and lift it pointwise. Define the order $\preceq_{\mathcal{S}}$ on $\mathcal{S}$ as $\mathrm{B} \preceq_{\mathcal{S}}$ $\mathrm{AB} \preceq_{\mathcal{S}} \mathrm{A} \preceq_{\mathcal{S}} \emptyset$. The set $\mathcal{S}$ with this order forms the lattice $\langle \mathcal{S}, \preceq_{\mathcal{S}}, \max, \min \rangle$. By pointwise lifting, we obtain the lattice $\langle \mathbb{D}, \preceq_{\mathbb{D}}, \Uparrow_{\mathbb{D}}, \Downarrow_{\mathbb{D}} \rangle$. We use the symbols $\Uparrow_{\mathbb{D}}$ and $\Downarrow_{\mathbb{D}}$ to distinguish them from the computational meet and join, $\sqcup^{\mathbb{D}}$ and $\sqcap^{\mathbb{D}}$, and to emphasise the connection to logical implication.

Recall from § 2 that $C|_A$ is the restriction of C to variables in A. Define a relation $\sqsubseteq_{\mathbb{E}}$ on $\wp(\mathbb{E}) \times \wp(\mathbb{E})$ as: $X \sqsubseteq_{\mathbb{E}} Y$ if for each $E_1 \in Y$ there is an $E_2 \in X$ such that $cl(E_1) = cl(E_2)$, $df(E_1) \preceq_{\mathbb{D}} df(E_2)$ and $int(E_2) \Rightarrow int(E_1) \vee (cl(E_1)|_A \cap cl(E_1)|_B)$. Intuitively, in a strong interpolant, literals are added to the partial interpolant by the translation function whereas in a weaker interpolant, literals are added in the resolution step. The partial interpolant $int(E_1)$ in the definition of $\sqsubseteq_{\mathbb{E}}$ is weakened with $(cl(E_1)|_A \cap cl(E_1)|_B)$ to account for this difference. Nonetheless, if $X \sqsubseteq_{\mathbb{E}} Y$ and $cl(E_1) = \Box$ for $E_1 \in Y$, there exists $E_2 \in X$ such that $cl(E_2) = \Box$ and $int(E_2) \Rightarrow int(E_1)$. Thus, $X \sqsubseteq_{\mathbb{E}} Y$ implies that $X \preceq_{\mathbb{E}} Y$. Theorem 4 shows that *PRes* is monotone with respect to $\sqsubseteq_{\mathbb{E}}$. To order interpolation systems by precision, the precision order on distinction functions is lifted pointwise to parameters to obtain the lattice $\langle \mathbb{C} \to \mathbb{D}, \preceq, \Uparrow, \Downarrow \rangle$.

Example 7. Revisit the functions $\mathcal{D}_1, \mathcal{D}_2$ and $\mathcal{D}_3$ in Example 3. It holds that $\mathcal{D}_3 \preceq \mathcal{D}_2 \preceq \mathcal{D}_1$ and the corresponding interpolants imply each other.   ◁

Theorem 4. *Let $\langle A, B \rangle$ be a CNF pair, and $\mathcal{D}_1$ and $\mathcal{D}_2$ be locality preserving parameters for $\langle A, B \rangle$.*

1. *If $\mathcal{D}_1 \preceq \mathcal{D}_2$, then $T_{\mathcal{D}_1}(A, B) \sqsubseteq_\mathbb{E} T_{\mathcal{D}_2}(A, B)$.*
2. *If $X \sqsubseteq_\mathbb{E} Y$ for $X, Y \in \wp(\mathbb{E})$, then $PRes(X) \sqsubseteq_\mathbb{E} PRes(Y)$.*
3. *The structure $\langle \Lambda_{\langle A, B \rangle}, \preceq, \Uparrow, \Downarrow \rangle$ is a complete lattice [10].*

Proof. (1) Consider $T_{\mathcal{D}_1}(A, B)$, $T_{\mathcal{D}_2}(A, B)$, and $F \in T_{\mathcal{D}_2}(A, B)$. It follows from the definition of a translation function that there exists $E \in T_{\mathcal{D}_1}(A, B)$ such that $cl(E) = cl(F)$. If $C \in A$, we further have that $int(E) \subseteq (cl(F)|_A \cap cl(F)|_B)$, and so $int(E) \Rightarrow int(F) \vee (cl(F)|_A \cap cl(F)|_B)$. If $C \in B$, then by definition, $\neg int(F) = \{t \in cl(F) | \mathcal{D}_2(cl(F))(t) = \mathtt{A}\}$. Because $\mathcal{D}_2$ is locality preserving, $\neg int(F) \subseteq (cl(F)|_A \cap cl(F)|_B)$ and we can conclude that $\neg int(F) \subseteq \neg(int(E)) \vee (cl(F)|_A \cap cl(F)|_B)$ and so $int(E) \subseteq int(F) \vee (cl(F)|_A \cap cl(F)|_B)$.
(2) Consider $X \sqsubseteq_\mathbb{E} Y$ and $F \in PRes(Y)$. There exists $x \in \mathrm{Prop}$ and $F_1, F_2 \in X$ such that $F = PRes(x, F_1, F_2)$. By the monotony hypothesis, there exist E_1 and E_2 in X such that $E_1 \sqsubseteq_\mathbb{E} F_1$ and $E_2 \sqsubseteq_\mathbb{E} F_2$. From the definition of $\sqsubseteq_\mathbb{E}$ we conclude that $E = PRes(x, E_1, E_2)$ satisfies that $cl(E) = cl(F)$. It remains to show that $int(E) \Rightarrow int(F) \vee (cl(E)|_A \cap cl(E)|_B)$. This can be shown by a straightforward case analysis.   ∎

The following corollary of Theorem 4 formally states that if $\mathcal{D}_1 \preceq \mathcal{D}_2$, then the interpolants obtained from $\mathsf{Int}_{\mathcal{D}_1}$ imply the interpolants obtained from $\mathsf{Int}_{\mathcal{D}_2}$.

Corollary 1. *If $\mathcal{D}_1$ and $\mathcal{D}_2$ are locality preserving parameters for the CNF pair $\langle A, B \rangle$, then $\mu X.(T_{\mathcal{D}_1}(A, B) \cup PRes(X)) \preceq_\mathbb{E} \mu X.(T_{\mathcal{D}_2}(A, B) \cup PRes(X))$.*

5.2   Variable Elimination

Any interpolant I for an unsatisfiable CNF pair $\langle A, B \rangle$ satisfies that $\mathrm{Var}(I) \subseteq V_{\langle A, B \rangle}$. We ask what the largest and smallest possible sets V are such that $\mathrm{Var}(I) \subseteq V$. To develop some intuition for this question, we visualise the *flow* of literals in a proof. Flow graphs have been used by Carbone to study interpolant size in the sequent calculus [2]. We only use them informally.

Example 8. The flow of literals in the refutation from Example 2 is shown in Figure 2. Dashed edges connect antecedents with resolvents and solid edges depict flows. Each literal is a vertex in the flow graph. Positive literals flow upwards and negative literals flow downwards. Observe that a_1 appears in multiple cycles connecting literals in A, literals in B and literals in A and B. In contrast, a_2 appears in only cycle which connects an A and a B literal. Recall that every interpolant constructed from this refutation contained a_2.   ◁

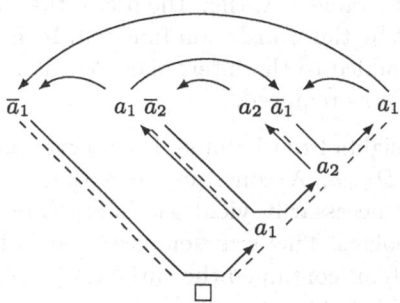

Fig. 2. A resolution proof and its logical flow graph. Dashed edges represent resolution and solid edges represent flows. Every occurrence of a literal is in a cycle.

Informally, a refutation defines a set of may and must variables. Any literal flowing from the A to the B part, like a_1 above, *may* be added to the interpolant. A literal that only flows from an A literal to a B literal, like a_2, *must* be added to the interpolant. To obtain the interpolant with the smallest set of variables, we need a parameter that adds only those literals to the interpolant that flow between A and B. We define two parameters for $\langle A, B \rangle$ as follows.

- $\mathcal{D}_{\min}(C)(x)$ is A for $C \in A$ and $x \in$ Prop and is B for $C \in B$ and $x \in$ Prop.
- $\mathcal{D}_{\max} \stackrel{\text{def}}{=} \delta_{\langle A,B \rangle}(\mathcal{D}_{\min})$.

Observe that both these parameters are locality preserving. Lemma 4 states that the parameters above determine the smallest and largest sets of variables that occur syntactically in an interpolant.

Lemma 4. *Let $\square$ be derived from $\langle A, B \rangle$ and $E_{\min}$ and $E_{\max}$ be the corresponding e-clauses derived in $\mathsf{Int}_{\mathcal{D}_{\min}}$ and $\mathsf{Int}_{\mathcal{D}_{\max}}$ respectively. Let E be the corresponding e-clause in $\mathsf{Int}_{\mathcal{D}}$ for a locality preserving parameter $\mathcal{D}$. It holds that $\mathrm{Var}(int(E_{\min})) \subseteq \mathrm{Var}(int(E)) \subseteq \mathrm{Var}(int(E_{\max}))$.*

Proof. We first show that if $x \in \mathrm{Var}(int(E))$, then $x \in \mathrm{Var}(int(E_{\max}))$. Observe that if $x \in \mathrm{Var}(int(E))$, then $x \in V_{\langle A,B \rangle}$ and either x or $\overline{x}$ must occur in some $C \in A \cup B$. Let F be the clause corresponding to C in $\mathsf{Int}_{\mathcal{D}_{\max}}$. If $C \in A$, $\mathcal{D}_{\max}(C)(x) = $ B and if $C \in B$, $\mathcal{D}_{\max}(C)(x) = $ A. In both cases, by the definition of $T_{\mathcal{D}_{\max}}$ it holds that $x \in \mathrm{Var}(int(F))$.

We show that if $x \in \mathrm{Var}(int(E_{\min}))$, then $x \in \mathrm{Var}(int(E))$. We proceed by induction on the structure of the derivation and consider the step in which x was added to the partial interpolant. Let F be the e-clause derived by the PRes rule in $\mathsf{Int}_{\mathcal{D}_{\min}}$, given as $F = PRes(x, F_1, F_2)$ where F_1 and F_2 are antecedents. It must be that $df(F_1)(x) \cup df(F_2)(x) = $ AB. Further, it must be that $x \in cl(F_1)$ and $\overline{x} \in cl(F_2)$ originated in A and B respectively, or vice versa, or are derived from two literals that originated from these two parts of the formulae. Let G, G_1, G_2 be the corresponding e-clauses derived in $\mathsf{Int}_{\mathcal{D}}$. There are three possibilities for $df(G_1)(x) \cup df(G_2)(x)$. If the value is AB, then x is added to the interpolant in this derivation step. If the value is A, then the literal that originated from B was added to the interpolant by the translation function. If the value is B, the literal originating from A was added to the interpolant by the translation function. In all cases, $x \in \text{Var}(int(G))$ as required. ∎

We draw two further insights from Lemma 4. Observe that $\mathcal{D}_{\min}$ and $\mathcal{D}_{\max}$ are distinct from $\mathcal{D}_M$ and $\mathcal{D}_{HKP}$. A consequence is that McMillan's system and the HKP-system do not necessarily yield the interpolant with the smallest set of variables in an interpolant. This was demonstrated in Example 2, where the interpolants in these systems contained the variables $\{a_1, a_2\}$, but an interpolant over $\{a_2\}$ could be obtained.

A more general insight is a way to determine if specific interpolants cannot be obtained from a refutation. To revisit Example 2 (for the last time), observe that $\text{Var}(int(E_{\min})) = \{a_2\}$ and that $\text{Var}(int(E_{\max})) = \{a_1, a_2\}$. It follows that the interpolant $\bar{a}_1$ for this pair cannot be obtained by any interpolation system $\text{Int}_{\mathcal{D}}$ in the family we consider.

6 Related Work

Though Craig's interpolation theorem was published in 1957 [8], the independent study of interpolation systems is relatively recent. Constructive proofs of Craig's theorem implicitly define interpolation systems. The first such proof is due to Maehara who introduced *split sequents* to capture the contribution of the A and B formulae in a sequent calculus proof [17]. Carbone generalised this construction to flow graphs to study the effect of cut-elimination on interpolant size [2].

Interpolant size was first studied by Mundici [20], Krajíček observed that lower bounds on interpolation systems for propositional proofs have implications for separating complexity classes and gave an interpolation system for resolution [16]. Pudlák published the same system simultaneously [21].

Huang gave an interpolation system for resolution and its dual [14] but his work appears to have gone unnoticed. McMillan proposed an propositional interpolation system and applied it to obtain a purely SAT-based finite-state model checker [19]. These systems were generalised in [10] and the system in that paper was studied here. Yorsh and Musuvathi [24] study interpolation for first-order theories, but also gave a new and elaborate correctness proof for the HKP-system. The invariant for proving Theorem 2 is generalises the induction hypothesis in their proof. The precision order $\sqsubseteq_E$ is a modification of their induction hypothesis to relate interpolants by strength rather than correctness.

The study of variables that can be eliminated from a formula is an issue of gaining interest [13,15]. Several researchers have noticed that an interpolant can contain fewer variables than $V_{\langle A,B \rangle}$. Related observations have been made by Simmonds and others [23] and have often featured in personal communication. We have shown that studying variables that cannot be eliminated from a proof can provide insights into the limitations of a family of interpolation systems.

Abstract interpretation, due to Cousot and Cousot [4] is a standard framework for reasoning about abstractions of a program's semantics. They have also applied the framework to inference rules in [7]. In program verification, the framework is typically applied to design abstract domains. In contrast, our application of abstract interpretation has been concerned with identifying concrete interpretations corresponding to existing interpolation systems and resolution. Our work was in part inspired by that Ranzato and Tapparo's application of abstract interpretation to analyse state minimisation algorithms [22].

7   Conclusion

Interpolation algorithms have several applications in program verification and several interpolation algorithms exist. In this paper, we applied abstract interpretation to study a family of interpolation algorithms for propositional resolution proofs. We showed that existing interpolation algorithms can be derived by abstraction from a general, parametrised algorithm. In abstract interpretation terms, sets of clauses and the resolution proof system define an abstract domain and an abstract interpretation. The set of clauses annotated with interpolants and an interpolation system define a concrete domain and a concrete interpretation. We have also shown analysed these domains gain insights about interpolant strength and about variables that are eliminated by an interpolation system.

However, the analysis in this paper has focused on propositional interpolation systems. Software verification methods based on interpolation require interpolation systems for first order theories. The design and analysis of interpolation algorithms for such theories is the topic of much current research. An open question is whether the kind of analysis in this paper is applicable to these settings. Another question is whether the approach here extends to a comparative analysis of interpolation in different propositional proof systems. Answering these questions is left as future work.

Acknowledgements. Mitra Purandare's observation triggered the logical flows leading to this paper. Leopold Haller interpolated the flow diagrams from my sketches and discussions with Philipp Ruemmer proved useful. A great debt is to my fellow interpolator Georg Weissenbacher; I hope I have refuted his resolution against my abstract interpretation of our propositions. I am grateful to Greta Yorsh for her encouragement and comments.

References

1. Buss, S.R.: Propositional proof complexity: An introduction. In: Berger, U., Schwichtenberg, H. (eds.) Computational Logic. NATO ASI Series F: Computer and Systems Sciences, vol. 165, pp. 127–178. Springer, Heidelberg (1999)
2. Carbone, A.: Interpolants, cut elimination and flow graphs for the propositional calculus. Annals of Pure and Applied Logic 83(3), 249–299 (1997)
3. Cousot, P.: Abstract interpretation. MIT course 16.399 (February–May 2005)
4. Cousot, P., Cousot, R.: Abstract interpretation: a unified lattice model for static analysis of programs by construction or approximation of fixpoints. In: Principles of Programming Languages, pp. 238–252. ACM Press, New York (1977)

5. Cousot, P., Cousot, R.: Systematic design of program analysis frameworks. In: Principles of Programming Languages, pp. 269–282. ACM Press, New York (1979)
6. Cousot, P., Cousot, R.: Abstract interpretation frameworks. Journal of Logic and Computation 2(4), 511–547 (1992)
7. Cousot, P., Cousot, R.: Inductive definitions, semantics and abstract interpretations. In: Principles of Programming Languages, pp. 83–94. ACM Press, New York (1992)
8. Craig, W.: Linear reasoning. A new form of the Herbrand-Gentzen theorem. Journal of Symbolic Logic 22(3), 250–268 (1957)
9. Davey, B.A., Priestley, H.A.: Introduction to Lattices and Order. Cambridge University Press, Cambridge (1990)
10. D'Silva, V., Kroening, D., Purandare, M., Weissenbacher, G.: Interpolant strength. In: Barthe, G., Hermenegildo, M. (eds.) Verification, Model Checking and Abstract Interpretation. LNCS. Springer, Heidelberg (2010)
11. Esparza, J., Kiefer, S., Schwoon, S.: Abstraction refinement with Craig interpolation and symbolic pushdown systems. Journal on Satisfiability, Boolean Modeling and Computation 5, 27–56 (2008); Special Issue on Constraints to Formal Verification
12. Giacobazzi, R., Ranzato, F., Scozzari, F.: Making abstract interpretations complete. Journal of the ACM 47(2), 361–416 (2000)
13. Gulwani, S., Musuvathi, M.: Cover algorithms and their combination. In: Drossopoulou, S. (ed.) ESOP 2008. LNCS, vol. 4960, pp. 193–207. Springer, Heidelberg (2008)
14. Huang, G.: Constructing Craig interpolation formulas. In: Li, M., Du, D.-Z. (eds.) COCOON 1995. LNCS, vol. 959, pp. 181–190. Springer, Heidelberg (1995)
15. Kovács, L., Voronkov, A.: Interpolation and symbol elimination. In: Schmidt, R.A. (ed.) Automated Deduction – CADE-22. LNCS, vol. 5663, pp. 199–213. Springer, Heidelberg (2009)
16. Krajíček, J.: Interpolation theorems, lower bounds for proof systems, and independence results for bounded arithmetic. The Journal of Symbolic Logic 62(2), 457–486 (1997)
17. Maehara, S.: On the interpolation theorem of Craig (in Japanese). Sûgaku 12, 235–237 (1961)
18. Mancosu, P. (ed.): Interpolations. Essays in Honor of William Craig. Synthese, vol. 164(3). Springer, Heidelberg (2008)
19. McMillan, K.L.: Interpolation and SAT-based model checking. In: Hunt Jr., W.A., Somenzi, F. (eds.) CAV 2003. LNCS, vol. 2725, pp. 1–13. Springer, Heidelberg (2003)
20. Mundici, D.: Complexity of Craig's interpolation. Fundamenta Informaticae 5, 261–278 (1982)
21. Pudlák, P.: Lower bounds for resolution and cutting plane proofs and monotone computations. The Journal of Symbolic Logic 62(3), 981–998 (1997)
22. Ranzato, F., Tapparo, F.: Generalizing the Paige-Tarjan algorithm by abstract interpretation. Information and Computation 206(5), 620–651 (2008)
23. Simmonds, J., Davies, J., Gurfinkel, A., Chechik, M.: Exploiting resolution proofs to speed up LTL vacuity detection for BMC. In: Formal Methods in Computer-Aided Design, pp. 3–12. IEEE Computer Society, Los Alamitos (2007)
24. Yorsh, G., Musuvathi, M.: A combination method for generating interpolants. In: Nieuwenhuis, R. (ed.) CADE 2005. LNCS (LNAI), vol. 3632, pp. 353–368. Springer, Heidelberg (2005)

Functional Programming in Sublinear Space

Ugo Dal Lago[1] and Ulrich Schöpp[2,*]

[1] University of Bologna, Italy
[2] University of Munich, Germany

Abstract. We consider the problem of functional programming with data in external memory, in particular as it appears in sublinear space computation. Writing programs with sublinear space usage often requires one to use special implementation techniques for otherwise easy tasks, e.g. one cannot compose functions directly for lack of space for the intermediate result, but must instead compute and recompute small parts of the intermediate result on demand. In this paper, we study how the implementation of such techniques can be supported by functional programming languages.

Our approach is based on modeling computation by interaction using the Int construction of Joyal, Street & Verity. We derive functional programming constructs from the structure obtained by applying the Int construction to a term model of a given functional language. The thus derived functional language is formulated by means of a type system inspired by Baillot & Terui's Dual Light Affine Logic. We assess its expressiveness by showing that it captures LOGSPACE.

1 Introduction

A central goal in programming language theory is to design programming languages that allow a programmer to express efficient algorithms in a convenient way. The programmer should be able to focus on algorithmic issues as much as possible and the programming language should give him the means to delegate inessential implementation details to the computer.

In this paper we study programming language constructs that are useful for expressing sublinear space algorithms. Sublinear space algorithms use less memory space than would be needed to store their input. They are useful for computing with large inputs that do not fit into memory.

When writing programs with sublinear space usage, one must often use special techniques for tasks that would normally be simple. A typical example is the composition of two algorithms. In order to remain in sublinear space, one cannot run them one after the other, as there may not be enough space to store the intermediate result. Instead, one can implement composition by storing at any time only a small part of the intermediate value and by (re)computing small parts only as they are needed.

Since it is easy to make mistakes in the implementation of such on-demand recomputation of intermediate values, we believe that programming language support should be very useful for such tasks. Instead of implementing composition with on-demand

---

* This work was carried out while Ulrich Schöpp was supported by a fellowship of the Institute of Advanced Studies at the University of Bologna.

A.D. Gordon (Ed.): ESOP 2010, LNCS 6012, pp. 205–225, 2010.

recomputation by hand, the programmer should be able to write function composition in the usual way and have a compiler generate the complicated program.

The possibilities of doing this have been explored in work on implicit characterisations of LOGSPACE. A number of characterisations of this complexity class have been explored in terms of function algebras [14] and linear logics [15] (there is more work for LOGSPACE-predicates, e.g. [10,5], but we focus on functions here). However, these characterisations are still far away from being real programming languages.

Here we work towards the goal of making the abstractions explored in this line of work usable in programming. In contrast to previous work [14,15], we aim to enrich the language with constructs for working with on-demand recomputation conveniently, rather than hiding it completely. This is in line with the fact that sublinear space algorithms are usually not used in isolation and will generally appear within larger programs. Language support for writing sublinear space algorithms should not become a hindrance in other parts of the program that do not operate on large data.

In this paper we present the functional programming language INTML for programming with sublinear space. This language is derived from an instance of the Int construction [7]. Our thesis is that the Int construction naturally captures space bounded computation and thus exposes mathematical structure that is useful for writing space bounded programs. Even though the type system of INTML is quite simple when compared to earlier higher-order type systems for LOGSPACE [15], INTML allows LOGSPACE algorithms to be written in a natural way, as is discussed in Sec. 3.2.

2 Space-Bounded Computation

Our approach to representing sublinear space computation in a functional programming language is best explained by analysing the definition of space complexity classes.

In the definition of space complexity classes, in particular sublinear space complexity classes, one uses *Offline Turing Machines* (OTMs) instead of standard Turing Machines. Offline Turing Machines are multi-tape Turing Machines that differ from the standard ones in that the input tape is read-only, the output tape is write-only and the output head may be moved in one direction only; finally the input and output tapes do not count towards the space usage of an Offline Turing Machine.

The definition of Offline Turing Machine captures a special class of Turing Machines that do not store their input or output in memory, but instead have (random) access to some externally stored input, and that give their output as a stream of characters. Since neither input nor output must be stored in memory, it is justified to count only the work tape towards the space usage of an Offline Turing Machine.

More formally, while a normal Turing Machine computes a function $\Sigma^* \to \Sigma^*$ on words over an alphabet Σ, an Offline Turing Machine may be seen as a function of type

$$(State \times \Sigma) + \mathbb{N} \longrightarrow (State \times \mathbb{N}) + \Sigma \ ,$$

where $A + B$ denotes the (tagged) disjoint union $\{inl(x) \mid x \in A\} \cup \{inr(y) \mid y \in B\}$. An input $n \in \mathbb{N}$ stands for the request to compute the n-th character on the OTM's output tape. An output in Σ is a response to this request. Whenever the OTM wants to read a character from its input tape, it outputs a pair $\langle s, n \rangle \in State \times \mathbb{N}$, where n is the number of the input character it wants to read and s is its machine state, comprising finite control state, work tape contents, etc. Receiving this request, the environment looks up the n-th input character i_n and restarts the machine with input $\langle s, i_n \rangle \in State \times \Sigma$. It supplies the machine state s that was part of the input request, so that the machine can resume its computation from the point where it requested an input.

In this way, we can consider each Offline Turing Machine as a normal Turing Machine with the special input/output interface given by the type above. This special machine needs space only to store the work tape(s) of the OTM and the positions of the OTM's input and output heads. This view justifies the exclusion of the input and output tapes in the definition of the space usage of OTMs, as long as the space usage is at least logarithmic. We will not consider OTMs with sublogarithmic space usage here and indeed 'Classes of languages accepted within sublogarithmic space depend heavily on the machine models and the mode of space complexity' [16].

While at first sight, the step from Turing Machines to Offline Turing Machines appears to be just a technicality, it is a step from unidirectional to bidirectional computation. For example, while standard Turing Machines are composed just by running them one after the other, composition of Offline Turing Machines involves bidirectional data flow. This composition is implemented as a dialogue between the machines: one starts by requesting an output character from the second machine and every time this machine queries a character of its input, the first machine is started to compute this character.

Bidirectional computation is thus an integral feature of space-bounded computation, which must be accounted for in a programming language for space-bounded functions. We argue that a good way of accounting for this bidirectionality is to study space-bounded computation in terms of the Int construction of Joyal, Street & Verity [7,6]. The Int construction is a general algebraic method of constructing a bidirectional universe from a unidirectional one. It appears in categorical formulations of the Geometry of Interaction [1,2] and has many applications, e.g. to Attribute Grammars [8].

2.1 Structuring Space Bounded Computation

In this section we observe that the step from Turing Machines to Offline Turing Machines can be understood in terms of the Int construction. This simple observation gives us guidance for structuring space-bounded computation, since it allows us to draw on existing work on the structure obtained by the Int construction.

The idea is to start from a computational model, e.g. the partial computable functions as formalised by Turing Machines, and then apply the Int construction to this model. The result is a model that still contains the original one, but in addition also captures bidirectional (or interactive) computation in the style of Offline Turing Machines.

In general, the Int construction starts with a traced monoidal category $\mathbf{B}$ and yields a category $Int(\mathbf{B})$ that represents bidirectional computation in $\mathbf{B}$. For the argument in this paper, it suffices to describe just one particular instance of $Int(\mathbf{B})$, that where $\mathbf{B}$ is the category $\mathbf{Pfn}$ of sets and partial functions. In this example we drop computability for the sake of simplicity and assume that our 'computational' model consists just of partial functions between arbitrary sets.

If we apply the Int construction to $\mathbf{Pfn}$ with respect to tagged disjoint union as monoidal structure, then we obtain the following category $Int(\mathbf{Pfn})$. Its objects are pairs (X^-, X^+) of sets X^- and X^+. A morphism f from $X = (X^-, X^+)$ to $Y = (Y^-, Y^+)$ is a partial function $\underline{f} \colon X^+ + Y^- \to Y^+ + X^-$.

Morphisms capture bidirectional computation. Let us think of the partial function $\underline{f}$ as a message-passing node with two input wires and two output wires as drawn on the right. When an input value arrives on an input wire then the function $\underline{f}$ is applied to it and the resulting value is passed along the corresponding output wire.

We will combine the two edges for X^- and X^+ into a single edge in which messages may be passed both ways (and likewise for Y). Thus we obtain the node on the right, whose edges are bidirectional in the sense that an edge with label X allows any message from X^+ to be passed in the forward direction and any message from X^- to be passed in the backwards direction.

Composition in $\mathrm{Int}(\mathbf{Pfn})$ allows one to build message passing networks out of such nodes. The composition $g \circ f \colon X \to Z$ of $f \colon X \to Y$ and $g \colon Y \to Z$ is obtained simply by connecting the two nodes. The underlying partial function $\underline{g \circ f} \colon X^+ + Z^- \to Z^+ + X^-$ is most easily described in terms of message passing. An input in X^+ is given to $\underline{f}$ and one in Z^- to $\underline{g}$. If either $\underline{f}$ or $\underline{g}$ give an output in X^- or Z^+ then this is the output of $g \circ f$. If, however, $\underline{f}$ (resp. $\underline{g}$) outputs a message on Y^+ (resp. Y^-), this message is given as an input to $\underline{g}$ (resp. $\underline{f}$). This may lead to a looping computation and $g \circ f$ may be partial even if g and f are both total.

Offline Turing Machines appear as morphisms of type $(State \times \mathbb{N}, State \times \Sigma) \to (\mathbb{N}, \Sigma)$ in $\mathrm{Int}(\mathbf{Pfn})$. This follows immediately from the definition of morphisms and the discussion in Sec. 2. What we gain from viewing OTMs as morphisms in $\mathrm{Int}(\mathbf{Pfn})$ is that we can use the well-known structure of this category for constructing and manipulating them. For example, $\mathrm{Int}(\mathbf{Pfn})$ is compact closed and therefore allows us to use linear lambda calculus and higher-order functions for the manipulation of OTMs.

We list the structure in $\mathrm{Int}(\mathbf{Pfn})$ that we use in the definition of INTML.

Partial Functions. First we note that inside $\mathrm{Int}(\mathbf{Pfn})$ we still find $\mathbf{Pfn}$. For any set A we have an object $\mathcal{I}A = (\emptyset, A)$. A morphism from $\mathcal{I}A$ to $\mathcal{I}B$ is a partial function of type $A + \emptyset \to \emptyset + B$, so that the morphisms of that type are in one-to-one correspondence with the partial functions from A to B.

Thunks. Also useful is the object $[A] = (\{*\}, A)$, where a singleton replaces the empty set. We will use $*$ as question that signals an explicit request for a value of type A. Thus, one may think of $[A]$ as a type of thunks that are evaluated on demand.

Higher-order Functions. $\mathrm{Int}(\mathbf{Pfn})$ has a monoidal structure $\otimes$ that on objects is defined by $X \otimes Y = (X^- + Y^-, X^+ + Y^+)$. In addition, there is a dualising operation $(-)^*$ that exchanges question and answer sets, i.e. $(X^-, X^+)^* = (X^+, X^-)$. Together, $\otimes$ and $(-)^*$ make $\mathrm{Int}(\mathbf{Pfn})$ a compact closed category. As a consequence, we obtain a linear function space by letting $X \multimap Y = X^* \otimes Y$.

Indexed Tensor. Of further use is an indexed tensor product $\bigotimes_A X$. The object $\bigotimes_A X$ is isomorphic to $X \otimes \cdots \otimes X$ ($|A|$ times). It is defined by $(\bigotimes_A X)^- = A \times X^-$ and $(\bigotimes_A X)^+ = A \times X^+$. The first component in the messages indicates which component of the tensor product we are communicating with.

To see how this structure is useful for working with OTMs, consider a morphism of type

$$\bigotimes_{State} (\mathcal{IN} \multimap \mathcal{I\Sigma}) \longrightarrow (\mathcal{IN} \multimap \mathcal{I\Sigma}) \tag{1}$$

in $\mathrm{Int}(\mathbf{Pfn})$. By definition, it is a partial function from $(State \times (\emptyset + \Sigma)) + (\mathbb{N} + \emptyset)$ to $(State \times (\mathbb{N} + \emptyset)) + (\emptyset + \Sigma)$, which, if we remove the superfluous empty sets, is the same as the type of an Offline Turing Machine, as described in Sec. 2.

As a morphism of type (1), an Offline Turing Machine is modelled simply as a map from inputs to outputs, which are both modelled as (linear) functions $\mathcal{IN} \multimap \mathcal{I\Sigma}$. This encoding of words as functions reflects the fact that Offline Turing Machines do not have access to the whole input at once, but rather can read only a single character at a time. Reading the n-th character just corresponds to applying the input function of type $\mathcal{IN} \multimap \mathcal{I\Sigma}$ to the natural number n. In $\mathrm{Int}(\mathbf{Pfn})$ we may therefore use the input as if it were a single function from natural numbers to characters, even though in reality the input can only be queried character by character. We argue that this is more convenient than the access to the input by means of explicit questions as in the direct implementation of Offline Turing Machines. For example we can use λ-calculus to manipulate the input functions.

3 A Functional Language for Logarithmic Space

In the rest of this paper we develop a functional programming language INTML that is based on understanding space-bounded computation in terms of the Int construction. For the definition of INTML we start with a standard functional programming language. In order to program sublinear space algorithms in this language, we would like to implement message passing networks in it and we would like to manipulate these networks using the structure that we have found in the Int construction. We obtain INTML by extending the original programming language with primitives for constructing and manipulating such message passing networks.

INTML provides a syntax for the structure that one obtains from applying the Int construction to a *term model* of the standard functional programming that we start with. In terms of the outline above, one should replace all the partial functions in **Pfn** with terms in the functional programming language. That means that the message passing networks caputred by the Int construction are now not just partial functions but partial functions implemented in the functional programming language.

INTML is thus a typed functional programming language with two classes of terms and types: one for the functional language that we start with and one for the structure that we obtain by applying the Int construction to a term model of this language. We call the former the *working class* and the latter the *upper class*. The upper class part can be seen as a definitional extension of the working class part. Upper class terms do not compute themselves, but rather represent message passing networks that are implemented by working class terms.

In this paper, we choose for the working class part of INTML a simple first order functional language with finite types. We have chosen such a simple language because the main novelty of INTML is the upper class calculus. We stress that the working class calculus may be replaced by a more expressive language, like PCF for example.

The upper class provides constructs for space-bounded programming. It is a linear type system inspired by Dual Light Affine Logic (DLAL) [4]. INTML treats the indexed tensor $\bigotimes_A$ much like exponential modality ! is treated in DLAL. Just as the exponential modality may only appear in negative positions in DLAL, i.e. one can have $!X \multimap Y$ but not $X \multimap !Y$, INTML only accounts for types of the form $\bigotimes_A X \multimap Y$. In the syntax we write $A \cdot X \multimap Y$ for them. The restriction to negative occurrences of $\bigotimes_A$ simplifies the type system without being too limiting in applications. In fact, we do not know of an example where $\bigotimes_A$ in a positive position would be useful.

3.1 Type System

Working class types are first-order types with type variables. They may appear in the upper class types, which represent structure obtained from the Int construction.

$$\text{Working class} \qquad A, B ::= \alpha \mid 1 \mid A \times B \mid A + B$$
$$\text{Upper class} \qquad X, Y ::= [A] \mid X \otimes Y \mid A \cdot X \multimap Y$$

Instead of $1 \cdot X \multimap Y$ we write just $X \multimap Y$. For working class types we define coherent type isomorphism to be the least congruence generated by $1 \times A \cong A \times 1 \cong A$ and $A \times (B + C) \cong (A \times B) + (A \times C)$ and $(B + C) \times A \cong (B \times A) + (C \times A)$.

The terms of INTML are formed by the grammars below. We write c, d for working class variables and use f, g, h to range over working class terms. Upper class variables are ranged over by x, y and upper class terms by s, t. The terms $\text{loop}(c.f)(g)$ and $\text{hack}(c.f)$ bind the variable c in f.

$$\text{Working class} \quad f, g, h ::= c \mid min_A \mid succ_A(f) \mid eq_A(f, g)$$
$$\mid \text{inl}(f) \mid \text{inr}(f) \mid \text{case } f \text{ of inl}(c) \Rightarrow g \mid \text{inr}(d) \Rightarrow h$$
$$\mid * \mid \langle f, g \rangle \mid \text{fst}(f) \mid \text{snd}(f) \mid \text{loop}(c.f)(g) \mid \text{unbox}(t)$$
$$\text{Upper class} \quad s, t ::= x \mid \langle t, t \rangle \mid \text{let } s \text{ be } \langle x, y \rangle \text{ in } t \mid \lambda x.t \mid s\,t$$
$$\mid [f] \mid \text{let } s \text{ be } [c] \text{ in } t \mid \text{case } f \text{ of inl}(c) \Rightarrow s \mid \text{inr}(d) \Rightarrow t$$
$$\mid \text{copy } t \text{ as } x, y \text{ in } t \mid \text{hack}(c.f)$$

The working class terms include the standard terms for 1, $\times$ and $+$. In addition there are constants min_A, $succ_A$ and eq_A for any type A. These constants provide a total ordering and decidable equality on any type A. For example, the values of the type $(1+1) \times (1+1)$ can be ordered as $\langle inl(*), inl(*) \rangle$, $\langle inr(*), inl(*) \rangle$, $\langle inl(*), inr(*) \rangle$, $\langle inr(*), inr(*) \rangle$ and with min and $succ$ we can access such an ordering generically for any type without having to define it by hand. Finally, there is a term $\text{loop}(c.f)$ for iteration. It is a simple syntax for a trace operator with respect to $+$. The intendet operational semantics of loop is $\text{loop}(c.f)(\text{inl}(v)) \longrightarrow \text{loop}(c.f)(f[\text{inl}(v)/c]))$ and $\text{loop}(c.f)(\text{inr}(v)) \longrightarrow v$, where in both cases v has already been reduced to a value (see Section 4.1).

The typing rules for working class terms appear in Fig. 1. They derive working class sequents of the form $\Sigma \vdash f : A$ asserting that f has type A in context Σ. The context Σ assigns working class types to a finite number of working class variables. As usual, the comma in contexts corresponds to $\times$, even though loop corresponds to a trace with respect to $+$. The typing rules should be unsurprising, except perhaps that for unbox. One may think of a term $t:[A]$ as a thunk that can be evaluated with unbox.

$$\Sigma, c{:}A \vdash c : A \qquad \Sigma \vdash min_A : A \qquad \frac{\Sigma \vdash f : A}{\Sigma \vdash succ_A(f) : A} \qquad \frac{\Sigma \vdash f : A \quad \Sigma \vdash g : A}{\Sigma \vdash eq_A(f,g) : 1+1}$$

$$\frac{}{\Sigma \vdash * : 1} \qquad \frac{\Sigma \vdash f : A \quad \Sigma \vdash g : B}{\Sigma \vdash \langle f,g\rangle : A \times B} \qquad \frac{\Sigma \vdash f : A \times B}{\Sigma \vdash \mathsf{fst}(f) : A} \qquad \frac{\Sigma \vdash f : A \times B}{\Sigma \vdash \mathsf{snd}(g) : B}$$

$$\frac{\Sigma \vdash f : A}{\Sigma \vdash \mathsf{inl}(f) : A + B} \qquad \frac{\Sigma \vdash f : A + B \quad \Sigma, c{:}A \vdash g : C \quad \Sigma, d{:}B \vdash h : C}{\Sigma \vdash \mathsf{case}\ f\ \mathsf{of}\ \mathsf{inl}(c) \Rightarrow g \mid \mathsf{inr}(d) \Rightarrow h : C}$$

$$\frac{\Sigma \vdash f : B}{\Sigma \vdash \mathsf{inr}(f) : A + B} \qquad \frac{\Sigma, c{:}A + B \vdash f : C + B \quad \Sigma \vdash g : A + B}{\Sigma \vdash \mathsf{loop}(c.\,f)(g) : C} \qquad \frac{\Sigma \mid\, \vdash t : [A]}{\Sigma \vdash \mathsf{unbox}(t) : A}$$

Fig. 1. Working Class Typing Rules

Upper class terms denote message passing networks that will be implemented by working class terms. An upper class typing sequent has the form $\Sigma \mid \Gamma \vdash t : X$, where Σ is a working class context. The context Γ is a finite list of declarations of the form $x_1 : A_1 {\cdot} X_1, \ldots, x_k : A_k {\cdot} X_k$. As usual, we assume that no variable is declared more than once in Γ. The term t denotes a network with a single (bidirectional) output edge of type X and (bidirectional) input edges of types $\bigotimes_{A_1} X_1, \ldots, \bigotimes_{A_k} X_k$. Informally, one may think of a declaration $x : A{\cdot}X$ as a declaration of A-many copies of a value in X, i.e. one copy for each value $v{:}A$. Having multiple copies is useful because our message passing networks are stateless. When we send a query to X and later receive an answer, then we may not know what to do with that answer, since we have forgotten all that was computed earlier. However, we can use $A \cdot X$ instead of X in order to remember a value of type A. If we want to remember a value $v{:}A$ then we simply query the v-th copy of X.

For any upper class context Γ and any working class type A, we define an upper class context $A \cdot \Gamma$ by $A \cdot \langle\rangle = \langle\rangle$ and $A \cdot (\Delta, x{:}B{\cdot}X) = (A \cdot \Delta), x{:}(A \times B){\cdot}X$.

The upper class typing rules appear in Fig. 2. While upper class terms denote message passing networks, at a first reading they may be understood without knowing precisely the networks they denote. In particular, the reader may wish to look at the reduction rules in Fig. 5, which are soundly implemented by the translation of terms to message passing networks. In Sec. 4 we describe which networks the terms denote.

The upper class rules represent a choice of the structure that the Int construction adds to the working class calculus. It does not capture this rich structure completely, however. Therefore we add the 'hacking' rule below that allows one to implement message passing nodes directly, much like one can use inline assembler in C.

$$\text{(HACK)} \quad \frac{\Sigma, c{:}X^- \vdash f : X^+}{\Sigma \mid \Gamma \vdash \mathsf{hack}(c.f) : X}$$

In this rule, X^- and X^+ denote the negative and positive parts of X defined by:

$$
\begin{aligned}
[A]^- &= 1 & [A]^+ &= A \\
(X \otimes Y)^- &= X^- + Y^- & (X \otimes Y)^+ &= X^+ + Y^+ \\
(A \cdot X \multimap Y)^- &= A \times X^+ + Y^- & (A \cdot X \multimap Y)^+ &= A \times X^- + Y^+
\end{aligned}
$$

$$(\text{WEAK}) \quad \frac{\Sigma \mid \Gamma \vdash s : Y}{\Sigma \mid \Gamma, x : A \cdot X \vdash s : Y} \qquad (\text{EXCH}) \quad \frac{\Sigma \mid \Gamma, x : A \cdot X, y : B \cdot Y, \Delta \vdash s : Z}{\Sigma \mid \Gamma, y : B \cdot Y, x : A \cdot X, \Delta \vdash s : Z}$$

$$(\text{LWEAK}) \quad \frac{\Sigma \mid \Gamma, x : A \cdot X \vdash s : Y}{\Sigma \mid \Gamma, x : (B \times A) \cdot X \vdash s : Y} \qquad (\text{CONGR}) \quad \frac{\Sigma \mid \Gamma, x : A \cdot X \vdash s : Y}{\Sigma \mid \Gamma, x : B \cdot X \vdash s : Y} \; A \cong B$$

$$(\text{VAR}) \quad \frac{}{\Sigma \mid \Gamma, x : A \cdot X \vdash x : X} \qquad (\otimes \text{I}) \quad \frac{\Sigma \mid \Gamma \vdash s : X \qquad \Sigma \mid \Delta \vdash t : Y}{\Sigma \mid \Gamma, \Delta \vdash \langle s, t \rangle : X \otimes Y}$$

$$(\otimes \text{E}) \quad \frac{\Sigma \mid \Gamma \vdash s : X \otimes Y \qquad \Sigma \mid \Delta, x : A \cdot X, y : A \cdot Y \vdash t : Z}{\Sigma \mid \Delta, A \cdot \Gamma \vdash \text{let } s \text{ be } \langle x, y \rangle \text{ in } t : Z}$$

$$(\multimap \text{I}) \quad \frac{\Sigma \mid \Gamma, x : A \cdot X \vdash s : Y}{\Sigma \mid \Gamma \vdash \lambda x. s : A \cdot X \multimap Y} \qquad (\multimap \text{E}) \quad \frac{\Sigma \mid \Gamma \vdash s : A \cdot X \multimap Y \qquad \Sigma \mid \Delta \vdash t : X}{\Sigma \mid \Gamma, A \cdot \Delta \vdash s\,t : Y}$$

$$(\text{CONTR}) \quad \frac{\Sigma \mid \Gamma \vdash s : X \qquad \Sigma \mid \Delta, x : A \cdot X, y : B \cdot X \vdash t : Y}{\Sigma \mid \Delta, (A + B) \cdot \Gamma \vdash \text{copy } s \text{ as } x, y \text{ in } t : Y}$$

$$(\text{CASE}) \quad \frac{\Sigma \vdash f : A + B \qquad \Sigma, c{:}A \mid \Gamma \vdash s : X \qquad \Sigma, d{:}B \mid \Gamma \vdash t : X}{\Sigma \mid \Gamma \vdash \text{case } f \text{ of inl}(c) \Rightarrow s \mid \text{inr}(d) \Rightarrow t : X}$$

$$([\,]\text{I}) \quad \frac{\Sigma \vdash f : A}{\Sigma \mid \Gamma \vdash [f] : [A]} \qquad ([\,]\text{E}) \quad \frac{\Sigma \mid \Gamma \vdash s : [A] \qquad \Sigma, c{:}A \mid \Delta \vdash t : [B]}{\Sigma \mid \Gamma, A \cdot \Delta \vdash \text{let } s \text{ be } [c] \text{ in } t : [B]}$$

Fig. 2. Upper Class Typing Rules

Examples. We give an example derivation to illustrate that while the upper class type system is linear, working-class variables can be copied arbitrarily:

$$\frac{\dfrac{\mid x{:}1{\cdot}[\alpha] \vdash x : [\alpha] \qquad \dfrac{\vdots \qquad \dfrac{c{:}\alpha \mid f{:}1{\cdot}([\alpha] \multimap [\alpha] \multimap [\beta]) \vdash f\,[c] : [\alpha] \multimap [\beta] \qquad \dfrac{c{:}\alpha \vdash c : \alpha}{c{:}\alpha \mid \vdash [c] : [\alpha]}}{c{:}\alpha \mid f{:}1{\cdot}([\alpha] \multimap [\alpha] \multimap [\beta]) \vdash f\,[c]\,[c] : [\beta]}}}{f{:}(\alpha \times 1){\cdot}([\alpha] \multimap [\alpha] \multimap [\beta]), x{:}1{\cdot}[\alpha] \vdash \text{let } x \text{ be } [c] \text{ in } f\,[c]\,[c] : [\beta]}}{\dfrac{f{:}\alpha{\cdot}([\alpha] \multimap [\alpha] \multimap [\beta]) \vdash \lambda x. \text{let } x \text{ be } [c] \text{ in } f\,[c]\,[c] : [\alpha] \multimap [\beta]}{\vdash \lambda f. \lambda x. \text{let } x \text{ be } [c] \text{ in } f\,[c]\,[c] : \alpha \cdot ([\alpha] \multimap [\alpha] \multimap [\beta]) \multimap [\alpha] \multimap [\beta]}}}$$

$$([\,]\text{E})$$
$$(\text{CONGR}), (\multimap \text{I})$$
$$(\multimap \text{I})$$

Even though upper class terms can be understood as if they were implemented by the reduction rules in Fig. 5, it is important to understand that they will be (in Sec. 4) compiled down to (large) working class terms that implement certain message passing networks. The network for the upper class term in the conclusion of the above derivation, for example, represents a message passing network with a single (bidirectional) output wire. It behaves as follows: if it receives a request for the value of the result in $[\beta]$, it first requests the value of x. Upon receipt of this value, the network will then ask the function f for its return value. Since f has a type of the form $\alpha \cdot X$, the network has access to α-many copies of f. It chooses the copy indexed by the value of x, so that, even though the network is stateless, the value of x will be available once an answer from f arrives. If f answers with a value in $[\beta]$, then this answer is forwarded as the final answer of the whole network. If f answers with a request for one of its arguments, then the network gives the value of x as reply to f.

That being able to copy working class variables does not make copy superfluous can be seen in the following terms for conversion between $[\alpha \times \beta]$ and $[\alpha] \otimes [\beta]$.

$$\lambda y. \text{ copy } y \text{ as } y_1, y_2 \text{ in} \qquad\qquad\qquad : (\gamma + \delta) \cdot [\alpha \times \beta] \multimap [\alpha] \otimes [\beta]$$
$$\langle \text{let } y_1 \text{ be } [c] \text{ in } [\text{fst}(c)], \text{let } y_2 \text{ be } [c] \text{ in } [\text{snd}(c)] \rangle$$

$$\lambda z. \text{let } z \text{ be } \langle x, y \rangle \text{ in let } x \text{ be } [c] \text{ in let } y \text{ be } [d] \text{ in } [\langle c, d \rangle] : \quad \alpha \cdot ([\alpha] \otimes [\beta]) \multimap [\alpha \times \beta]$$

Useful Combinators. The upper class calculus is a simple linear lambda calculus for constructing message passing networks. It appears to be missing many constructs, such as loops, that are required to make it an expressive programming language. Such constructs can be defined as higher-order combinators using hack.

The most important example of such a combinator is a loop iterator that informally satisfies $\text{loop } f \, v = w$ if $f \, v = \text{inr}(w)$ and $\text{loop } f \, v = \text{loop } f \, w$ if $f \, v = \text{inl}(w)$.

$$\text{loop: } \alpha \cdot (\gamma \cdot [\alpha] \multimap [\alpha + \beta]) \multimap [\alpha] \multimap [\beta]$$

Before we define loop, we give a typical example for its use. We define fold_α, such that $\text{fold}_\alpha \, f \, y$ computes $f \, x_n \, (\dots (f \, x_1 \, (f \, x_0 \, y)))$, where $x_0 = \min_\alpha$ and $x_{i+1} = \text{succ}_\alpha(x_i)$ and x_n is the maximum element of α, i.e. the element with $x_n = \text{succ}_\alpha(x_n)$.

$$\text{fold}_\alpha : (\alpha \times \beta \times \alpha \times \beta) \cdot ([\alpha] \multimap [\beta] \multimap [\beta]) \multimap [\beta] \multimap [\beta]$$
$$\text{fold}_\alpha = \lambda f. \lambda y. \text{loop } (\lambda w. \text{let } w \text{ be } [e] \text{ in let } f \, [\text{fst}(e)] \, [\text{snd}(e)] \text{ be } [z] \text{ in}$$
$$\text{case } eq_\alpha(\text{fst}(e), \text{succ}_\alpha(\text{fst}(e))) \text{ of inl}(\textit{true}) \Rightarrow [\text{inr}(z)]$$
$$| \text{ inr}(\textit{false}) \Rightarrow [\text{inl}(\langle \text{succ}_\alpha(\text{fst}(e)), z \rangle)])$$
$$(\text{let } y \text{ be } [z] \text{ in } [\langle \min_\alpha, z \rangle])$$

The definition of loop uses hack and therefore makes explicit reference to the translation of upper class terms to message passing networks, which we describe in detail in Sec 4. The loop-combinator is defined by $\text{loop} = \text{hack}(c.l)$, where l is a working class term of type $c{:}\alpha \times (\gamma \times 1 + (\alpha + \beta)) + (\alpha + 1) \vdash l{:} \alpha \times (\gamma \times \alpha + 1) + (1 + \beta)$ that implements the following mappings using a nested case expression: (i) $inr(inr(*)) \mapsto inl(inr(*))$; (ii) $inr(inl(a)) \mapsto inl(a, inr(*))$; (iii) $inl(a, inr(inl(b))) \mapsto inr(inr(b))$; (iv) $inl(a, inr(inl(a'))) \mapsto inl(a', inr(*))$; and (v) $inl(a, inl(g, *)) \mapsto inl(a, inl(g, a))$. These assignments can be interpreted as follows: Mapping (i) says that when we get a request for the final value, we start by asking the base case for its value. When an answer from the base cases arrives, we put it in a memory cell (corresponding to $\alpha \cdot -$ in the type) and ask the step function for its result (ii). Whenever the step function asks for its argument, we supply the value from the memory cell (v). If the step function answers $inr(b)$, then we are done and give b as output (iii). If the step function answers $inl(a')$, then we overwrite the memory cell content with a' and restart the step function by asking for its result (iv).

A second useful combinator is a simple version of callcc. It can be given the following type for any upper class type X.

$$\text{callcc: } \left(\gamma \cdot ([\alpha] \multimap X) \multimap [\alpha] \right) \multimap [\alpha]$$

This combinator is defined by $\texttt{callcc} = \text{hack}(c.l)$, where l is a working-class term of type $c{:}(\gamma \times (\alpha + X^-) + \alpha) + 1 \vdash l{:} (\gamma \times (1 + X^+) + 1) + \alpha$ that implements the following mappings: (i) $inr(*) \mapsto inl(inr(*))$; (ii) $inl(inr(a)) \mapsto inr(a)$; (iii) $inl(inl(g, inr(x))) \mapsto inl(inl(g, inl(*)))$; and (iv) $inl(inl(g, inl(a))) \mapsto inr(a)$. These assignments implement $\texttt{callcc}$ as follows: a request for the result becomes a request for the result of the argument function (i); When the argument function produces a result value, we forward it as the final result (ii). If the argument function ever uses its argument, i.e. calls the continuation, then the value passed to the continuation should be returned as the final result. This is done by assignments (iii) and (iv). Whenever the result of the continuation is requested, this request is turned into a request for the argument of the continuation (iii). Upon supply of the argument to the continuation, the computation is aborted and this argument is returned as the end result (iv).

3.2 Programming in INTML

We have introduced the upper class in INTML with the intention of helping the programmer to implement functions with sublinear space usage. Let us give a few examples of how we think the upper class features will be useful.

Consider for example binary words. For sublinear space computation, they are suitably modelled as functions of type $A \cdot [B] \multimap [3]$. With the constants *min* and *succ*, we can regard B as a type of numbers. We interpret 3 as a type containing characters '0', '1' and a blank symbol. Then, $A \cdot [B] \multimap [3]$ can represent words by functions that map the n-th element of B to the n-th character of the word (see Sec. 5 for a precise definition). Being a higher-order language, INTML allows the programmer both to define such words directly, but also to write higher-order combinators to manipulate them.

When working with $A \cdot X \multimap Y$, we have found that often we are not interested in the particular type A, only that some such type exists. Let us therefore in the following hide all such annotations and write just $X \to Y$ to mean $A \cdot X \multimap Y$ for some A.

Useful combinators for words encoded as functions are, e.g. $\texttt{zero}\colon ([\alpha] \to [3])$ for the empty word, $\texttt{succ}_0\colon ([\alpha] \to [3]) \to ([\alpha] \to [3])$ for appending the character 0 or $\texttt{if}\colon ([\alpha] \to [3]) \to ([\alpha] \to [3]) \to ([\alpha] \to [3]) \to ([\alpha] \to [3])$ for case distinction on the last character of a word. They allow one to work with words encoded as functions as if they were normal strings, even though these words do not even necessarily fit into memory. The combinators themselves can be implemented easily in INTML.

$$\texttt{succ}_0 := \lambda w.\, \lambda i.\ \text{let } i \text{ be } [c] \text{ in case } eq(c, min) \text{ of } \ \textsf{inl}(true) \Rightarrow [min]$$
$$| \ \textsf{inr}(false) \Rightarrow w\, [pred\ c]$$

Here *pred* denotes a working class predecessor term, which is easy to define.

$$\texttt{if} := \lambda w.\, \lambda w_0.\, \lambda w_1.\, \lambda i.\ \text{let } w\, [min] \text{ be } [c] \text{ in}$$
$$\text{case } c \text{ of } \ \textsf{inl}(blank) \Rightarrow w_0\, i$$
$$| \ \textsf{inr}(z) \Rightarrow \text{case } z \text{ of } \ \textsf{inl}(zero) \Rightarrow w_0\, i$$
$$| \ \textsf{inr}(one) \Rightarrow w_1\, i$$

These are simple examples, of course. We believe that nontrivial combinators can also be implemented. For example, Møller-Neergaard gives a LOGSPACE implementation of safe recursion on notation by computational amnesia [14]. We believe that using loop and callcc a similar program can be implemented in INTML as a combinator saferec taking as arguments a base case $g \colon [\alpha] \to [3]$, two step functions $h_0, h_1 \colon ([\alpha] \to [3]) \to ([\alpha] \to [3])$ and a word $w \colon [\alpha] \to [3]$ to recurse on and giving a word as output.

In this way the higher-order features of INTML can be used to abstract away details of a message-passing implementation of functions on words and to write LOGSPACE functions just like in BC_ε^- [14]. Moreover, INTML gives access to the implementation details, should the abstraction not be expressive enough. For instance, the proof of LOGSPACE completeness in Thm. 3 below goes by a straightforward encoding of a OTM. It is much simpler than the corresponding encoding in BC_ε^- [14] because INTML allows us to manipulate working class values directly.

The higher order approach also works for data types other than strings. For example, graphs can be represented by a type of the form $([\alpha] \to [2]) \otimes ([\alpha \times \alpha] \to [2])$, where the first component is a predicate that indicates which elements of α count as graph nodes and the second component is the edge relation.

4 Evaluation

In this section we present the evaluation mechanism for INTML. Evaluation of upper class terms is closely related to evaluation in [15], but also to Mackie's Interaction Abstract Machine [11] and to read-back from optimal reduction [12,3]. Indeed, in his 1995 paper [11] Mackie speculates that this form of evaluation could have applications where space usage is important. With INTML we present a calculus that makes space usage analysis possible. INTML differs from the work in loc. cit. in that one can mix working class and upper class terms. Previously only the upper class part was considered.

4.1 Reduction of Working-Class Terms

The evaluation of INTML programs is done by reduction of working class terms. Before evaluation of an INTML program, all upper class terms are compiled into working class terms. Since, in particular, any occurrence of unbox will be removed, it suffices to define reduction only for unbox-free working class terms.

Working class values are defined by:

$$v, w := c \mid * \mid \langle v, w \rangle \mid \mathsf{inl}(v) \mid \mathsf{inr}(v)$$

The reduction of working class terms is explained by a small step reduction relation $\longrightarrow$ between closed unbox-free terms. Closedness here means the absence of both term variables and type variables (which could appear in the type annotations of constants like min_A). The relation $\longrightarrow$ formalises standard *eager* reduction, see e.g. [17]. We omit standard reduction rules and just explain here how loop and the constants min_A and $succ_A$ are treated. Loops are unfolded by the rules $\mathsf{loop}(c.f)(\mathsf{inr}(v)) \longrightarrow v$ and $\mathsf{loop}(c.f)(\mathsf{inl}(v)) \longrightarrow \mathsf{loop}(c.f)(f[\mathsf{inl}(v)/c])$, in both of which v must be a value. Constants are unfolded on demand, guided by their type annotation. The minimum elements of all closed types are defined by:

$$min_1 \longrightarrow * \qquad min_{A+B} \longrightarrow \mathsf{inl}(min_A) \qquad min_{A \times B} \longrightarrow \langle min_A, min_B \rangle$$

In the implementation of $succ_A$, we must be a little careful that reducts do not become too large. We implement $succ$ using a new constant $succmin$ that informally denotes a function $succmin_A\colon A \to A + A$ with the following meaning: $succmin_A(x) = \mathsf{inl}(y)$ means that y is the successor of x; $succmin_A(x) = \mathsf{inr}(y)$ means that x has no successor and y is the minimum element of A. We use the following rules for $succmin$.

$$succmin_1(*) \longrightarrow \mathsf{inr}(*)$$
$$succmin_{A+B}(\mathsf{inl}(v)) \longrightarrow \mathsf{case}\ succmin_A(v)\ \mathsf{of}\ \mathsf{inl}(x) \Rightarrow \mathsf{inl}(\mathsf{inl}(x))$$
$$\mid\ \mathsf{inr}(y) \Rightarrow \mathsf{inl}(\mathsf{inr}(min_B))$$
$$succmin_{A+B}(\mathsf{inr}(v)) \longrightarrow \mathsf{case}\ succmin_B(v)\ \mathsf{of}\ \mathsf{inl}(x) \Rightarrow \mathsf{inl}(\mathsf{inr}(x))$$
$$\mid\ \mathsf{inr}(y) \Rightarrow \mathsf{inr}(\mathsf{inl}(min_A))$$
$$succmin_{A\times B}(\langle v, w\rangle) \longrightarrow \mathsf{case}\ succmin_A(v)\ \mathsf{of}\ \mathsf{inl}(x) \Rightarrow \mathsf{inl}(\langle x, w\rangle)$$
$$\mid\ \mathsf{inr}(x) \Rightarrow \mathsf{case}\ succmin_B(w)\ \mathsf{of}\ \mathsf{inl}(y) \Rightarrow \mathsf{inl}(\langle x, y\rangle)$$
$$\mid\ \mathsf{inr}(y) \Rightarrow \mathsf{inr}(\langle x, y\rangle)$$

We use these rules instead of the evident rules for $succ$ because they are linear in v, w, A and B, which is important for the proof of Prop. 1 below.

Because of the simplicity of the working class calculus, it is possible to give useful upper bounds on how large a term can become during the course of eager reduction directly by induction on the term structure. Essentially, we can bound the size of values in terms of their types and use this to derive a bound on the potential size of a term under reduction by looking at its variables and their types. We state this result in the following proposition, in which $|g|$ and $|C|$ denote the size of the abstract syntax trees of g and C respectively.

Proposition 1. *If $c{:}A \vdash f\colon B$ is derivable then there are constants n and m such that $(f[C/\alpha])[v/c] \longrightarrow^* g$ implies $|g| \leq n + m \cdot |C|$ for every closed type C and every closed value v of type $A[C/\alpha]$.*

We will use for C types of the form $2 \times \cdots \times 2$ (k times), where 2 denotes $1 + 1$. This type represents the numbers from 0 to $2^k - 1$ in binary and we have $|C| \in O(k)$. A unary encoding is also possible with $C = 1 + \cdots + 1$ (2^k times), but we have $|C| \geq 2^k$ and values can indeed become as large as this.

4.2 Reducing Upper Class to Working Class

Now we explain how closed upper class terms are compiled down to working class terms, so that they can be reduced with the relation $\longrightarrow$ from the previous section. The compilation works by interpreting upper class terms as message passing circuits as in Sec. 2 and then implementing these circuits by working class terms.

We start by defining the message passing circuits we use in the compilation. These circuits may be understood as a particular instance of string diagrams for monoidal categories [13]. The are also related to proof nets, see [13] for a discussion. Circuits are directed graphs that represent networks in which messages are passed along edges. A node labelling allows us to use nodes with different message passing behaviour. Edges are labelled with types that tell which kind of messages can be passed along them. Edge labels are formed by the grammar below, in which A ranges over working class types.

$$X, Y ::= [A] \mid [A]^* \mid X \otimes Y \mid \bigotimes_A X$$

We define an operation $(-)^*$ on edge labels as follows. It maps $[A]$ to $[A]^*$ and $[A]^*$ to $[A]$ and is defined on compound expressions by $(X \otimes Y)^* = X^* \otimes Y^*$ and $(\bigotimes_A X)^* = \bigotimes_A X^*$. Note in particular that we have $X^{**} = X$ for any type label X.

Circuits are labelled directed graphs that are in addition equipped with a *two-way local ordering*. A two-way local ordering for a graph $G = (V, E)$ specifies for each node $v \in V$ a total ordering on both the set $(\{v\} \times V) \cap E$ of outgoing edges from v and on the set $(V \times \{v\}) \cap E$ of incoming edges to v. The need for a local ordering arises in the treatment of nodes such as $\otimes E$ below. This node has an incoming edge labelled with $X \otimes Y$ and two outgoing edges labelled with X and Y and we want to distinguish the two outgoing edges even if X and Y are the same.

Furthermore, circuits have a number of input and output ports. We capture input and output edges by means of two distinguished nodes: a source and a sink. Edges from the distinguished source are input edges and edges to the sink are output edges. We write $D: (X_1, \ldots, X_n) \to (Y_1, \ldots, Y_m)$ for such a graph D with input edges of type $X_1, \ldots, X_n$ and output edges of type $Y_1, \ldots, Y_m$ (note that they are ordered because of the local ordering for source and sink). We usually draw D as shown on the right.

Given two graphs $D: (X) \to (Y)$ and $E: (Y) \to (Z)$, their sequential composition $E \circ D: (X) \to (Z)$ is defined as depicted below: the i-th incoming edge to the sink of D and the i-th outgoing edge from the source of E are joined to a single edge. The sink of D and the source of E are removed. Furthermore, given $F: (X) \to (Y)$ and $G: (U) \to (V)$, we write $F \otimes G$ for the graph of type $(X, U) \to (Y, V)$ obtained by putting F and G in parallel.

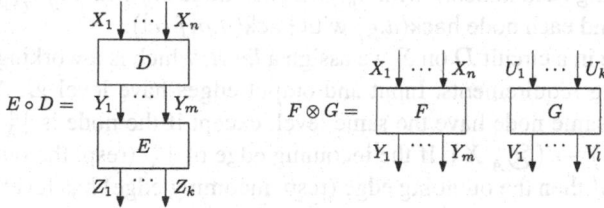

Notice that in a composition the local ordering on the edges labelled with Y disappears. For example, if we let $swap_{X,Y}: (X, Y) \to (Y, X)$ be the graph on the right, then $swap_{Y,X} \circ swap_{X,Y}$ is $id_X \otimes id_Y: (X, Y) \to (X, Y)$, where $id_X: (X) \to (X)$ is a single edge labelled X from input to output.

Definition 1 (Circuit on Σ). For any working class context Σ, we define the set of *circuits on Σ* to be the smallest set of two-way locally ordered graphs with input and output edges that satisfies the following conditions.

- For all X and Y both id_X and $swap_{X,Y}$ are are circuits on Σ.
- Each of the following single-node graphs is a circuit on Σ, where X and Y may be arbitrary type labels, A and B may be arbitrary working class types and f and g may be arbitrary terms with $\Sigma \vdash f \colon A$ and $\Sigma, c{:}X^- \vdash g \colon X^+$.

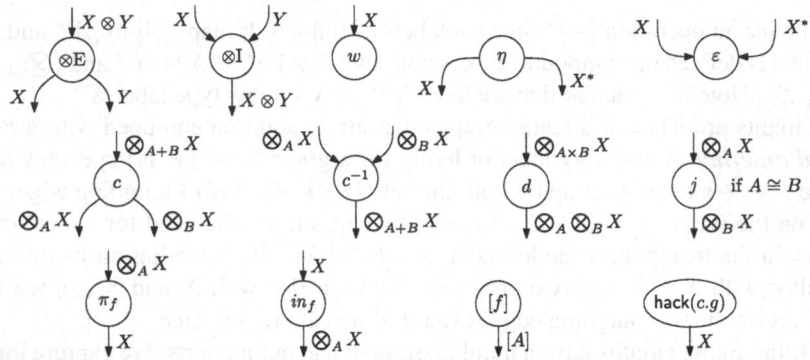

- If $D \colon (\boldsymbol{X}) \to (\boldsymbol{Y})$ and $E \colon (\boldsymbol{Y}) \to (\boldsymbol{Z})$ are circuits on Σ then so is $E \circ D$.
- If $D \colon (\boldsymbol{X}) \to (\boldsymbol{Y})$ and $E \colon (\boldsymbol{U}) \to (\boldsymbol{V})$ are circuits on Σ then so is $D \otimes E$.
- If $D \colon (X_1, \ldots, X_n) \to (Y_1, \ldots, Y_m)$ is a circuit on Σ, $c{:}A$ then the graph $\bigotimes_{c:A} D \colon (\bigotimes_A X_1, \ldots, \bigotimes_A X_n) \to (\bigotimes_A Y_1, \ldots, \bigotimes_A Y_m)$ constructed as follows is a circuit on Σ: each incoming edge of D is prepended with a node $\downarrow^c_{X_i} \colon (\bigotimes_A X_i) \to (X_i)$ and to each outgoing edge of D a node $\uparrow^c_{Y_i} \colon (Y_i) \to (\bigotimes_A Y_i)$ is appended. For better readability, we do not draw these nodes explicitly and draw a box around D instead, as depicted on the right.

Given a circuit D on $(\Sigma, c{:}A)$ and a term $\Sigma \vdash f : A$, we can form a circuit $D[f/c]$ on Σ by replacing each node π_g with $\pi_{g[f/c]}$, each node in_g with $in_{g[f/c]}$, each node $[g]$ with $[g[f/c]]$, and each node $\mathsf{hack}(d.g)$ with $\mathsf{hack}(d.g[f/c])$.

To each edge in a circuit D on Σ we assign a *level*, which is a working class context, by the following requirements. Input and output edges have level Σ. Any two edges incident to the same node have the same level, except if the node is $\downarrow^c_X \colon (\bigotimes_A X) \to (X)$ or $\uparrow^c_X \colon (X) \to (\bigotimes_A X)$. If the incoming edge of $\downarrow^c_X$ (resp. the outgoing edge of $\uparrow^c_X$) has level Σ' then the outgoing edge (resp. incoming edge) has level Σ', $c{:}A$.

Message Passing. Write $\mathcal{V}_A$ for the set of all closed working class values of type A. Write $\mathcal{E}_\Sigma$ for the set of Σ-*environments* consisting of all functions that map the variables in Σ to closed values of their declared types. The set $M_{\Sigma,X}$ of messages that can be passed along an edge labelled with X at level Σ is then defined by $M_{\Sigma,X} = \mathcal{E}_\Sigma \times (\mathcal{V}_{X^+} \times \{+\} \cup \mathcal{V}_{X^-} \times \{-\})$. A message $m \in M_{\Sigma,X}$ is either a *question* or an *answer* depending on whether its third component is '$-$' or '$+$'. Answers travel in the direction of the edge while questions travel in the opposite direction. Messages are essentially the same as the contexts in context semantics [12].

To define message passing for a circuit $D \colon (\boldsymbol{X}) \to (\boldsymbol{Y})$ on Σ, let the set M_D of messages on D consist of all pairs (e, m) of an edge e in D and a message

$m \in M_{\Sigma(e),X(e)}$, where $\Sigma(e)$ is the level of e and $X(e)$ is its label. Now we define how each node in D locally reacts to arriving messages. To this end we define for each node v a partial function φ_v by the assignments in Fig. 3. For example φ_π implements the behaviour of the term in ([ ]E), as sketched in Sec. 3.1. An initial question on edge o becomes a request for the value of type $[A]$ on edge i_1. Upon receipt of an answer $w{:}A$ from there, this answer is put into the memory cell provided by $\bigotimes_A$ and the value of type $[B]$ is queried on edge i_2. An answer to this request is then passed as final answer along edge o. In Fig. 3 we have omitted the cases for φ_ε and $\varphi_{c^{-1}}$, which are just like those for φ_η and φ_c. Notice that for different nodes v and w in D, the domains of φ_v and φ_w do not overlap.

The message passing behaviour of the whole circuit is then the partial function $\varphi_D : M_D \to M_D$ defined by repeatedly applying the local functions φ_v:

$$\varphi_D = Tr\left(\bigcup_{v \in V(D)} \varphi_v\right) \qquad Tr(f)(m) = \begin{cases} Tr(f)(f(m)) & \text{if } f(m) \text{ defined} \\ m & \text{if } f(m) \text{ undefined} \end{cases}$$

It is not hard to see that messages cannot get stuck inside the circuit, i.e. $\varphi_D(e,m) = (e',m')$ implies that e' is an input or an output edge. In fact, we will forget about the internal structure of D and consider just the restriction of φ_D to messages on input or output edges of D. This restriction corresponds to a partial function Φ_D of type $\left(X_1^+ + \cdots + X_n^+ + Y_1^- + \cdots + Y_m^-\right) \times \mathcal{E}_\Sigma \longrightarrow Y_1^+ + \cdots + Y_m^+ + X_1^- + \cdots + X_n^-$. We call Φ_D *the behaviour of* D and consider circuits with the same behaviour to be equal. We write $D \sim E$ if D and E are circuits with the same interface and $\Phi_D = \Phi_E$.

Upper Class to Circuits. We now interpret upper class terms by circuits. To each derivation δ ending with sequent $\Sigma \mid x_1 : A_1 {\cdot} X_1, \ldots, x_n : A_n {\cdot} X_n \vdash s : Y$ we assign $[\![\delta]\!]$, a circuit on Σ with one output wire of type Y and n input wires of type $(\bigotimes_{A_1} X_1, \ldots, \bigotimes_{A_n} X_n)$, where we identify $A \cdot X \multimap Y$ with $(\bigotimes_A X)^* \otimes Y$. That is, each variable declaration in Γ becomes an input wire of the translated circuit. Abusing notation slightly, we will write Γ also for the list of input types of this circuit.

The definition goes by induction on derivations and is given in the table in Fig. 4. In this table we denote the premises of δ by δ_s and δ_t depending on the term in the premise. We write just $\bigotimes_A$ for $\bigotimes_{c:A}$ if c does not appear anywhere. Given an upper class context Γ we write w_Γ for $w \otimes \cdots \otimes w : (\Gamma) \to ()$. Similarly, we write $id_\Gamma : (\Gamma) \to (\Gamma)$, $d_{A \cdot \Gamma} : (A \cdot \Gamma) \to (\bigotimes_A \Gamma)$, $(in_f)_\Gamma : (\Gamma) \to (\bigotimes_A \Gamma)$ and $c_\Gamma : (\Gamma) \to (\Gamma, \Gamma)$ for the analogous tensorings of id, d, in_f and c (the definition of c_Γ involves evident permutations of the outputs to arrive at the indicated type).

Implementing Message Passing. The compilation of upper class terms to message passing circuits almost completes the translation from upper class to working class. It just remains to implement message passing in the working class calculus.

That is, for any circuit D we construct a closed working class term that implements its behaviour Φ_D. In essence, the construction works in the same way as the definition of Φ_D above. First note that we can represent the set of messages $M_{\Sigma,X}$ by the working class type $(A_1 \times \cdots \times A_n) \times (X^- + X^+)$, where $\Sigma = x_1{:}A_1, \ldots, x_n{:}A_n$. With this we can represent M_D in the working class calculus in the form of a big sum type. Then,

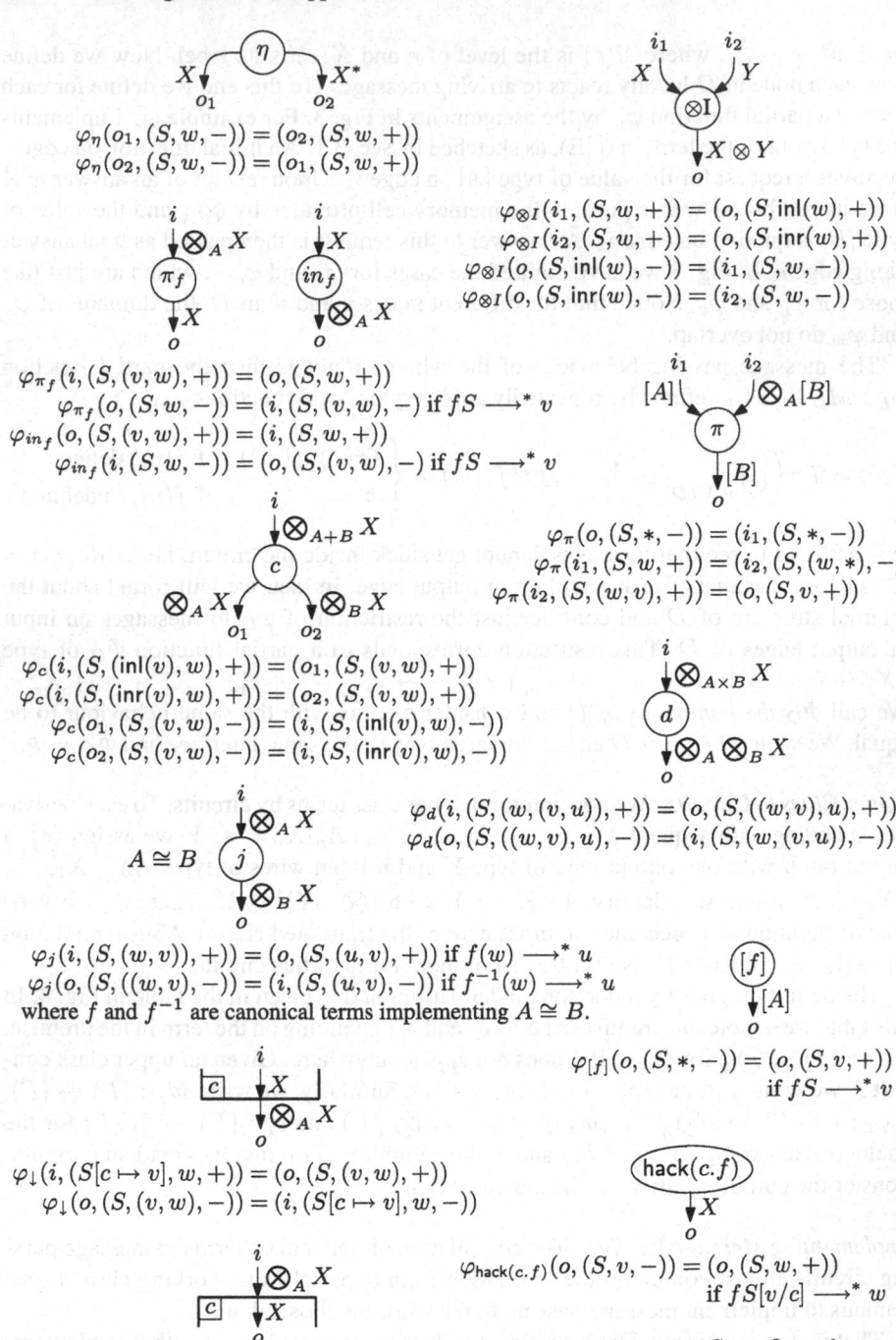

Fig. 3. Local message passing

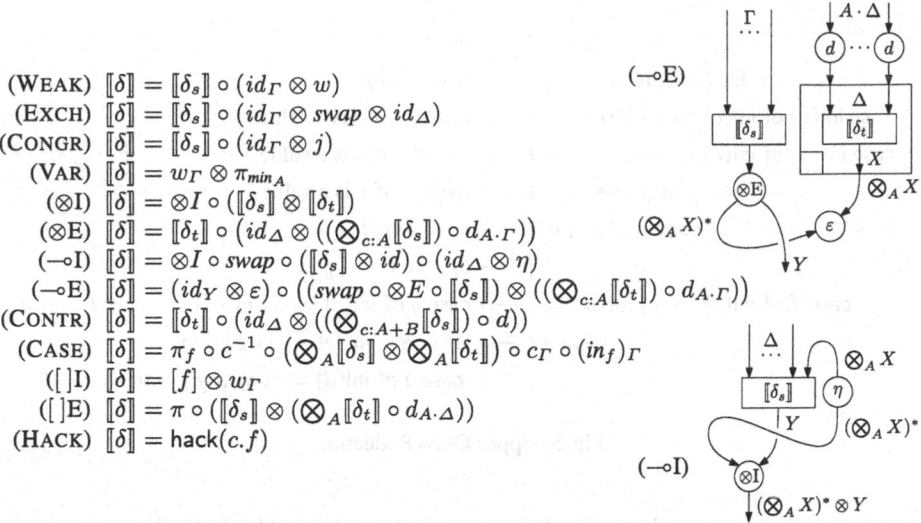

$$
\begin{aligned}
\text{(WEAK)} \quad & [\![\delta]\!] = [\![\delta_s]\!] \circ (id_\Gamma \otimes w) \\
\text{(EXCH)} \quad & [\![\delta]\!] = [\![\delta_s]\!] \circ (id_\Gamma \otimes swap \otimes id_\Delta) \\
\text{(CONGR)} \quad & [\![\delta]\!] = [\![\delta_s]\!] \circ (id_\Gamma \otimes j) \\
\text{(VAR)} \quad & [\![\delta]\!] = w_\Gamma \otimes \pi_{min\,A} \\
\text{($\otimes$I)} \quad & [\![\delta]\!] = \otimes I \circ ([\![\delta_s]\!] \otimes [\![\delta_t]\!]) \\
\text{($\otimes$E)} \quad & [\![\delta]\!] = [\![\delta_t]\!] \circ (id_\Delta \otimes ((\bigotimes_{c:A} [\![\delta_s]\!]) \circ d_{A.\Gamma})) \\
\text{($\multimap$I)} \quad & [\![\delta]\!] = \otimes I \circ swap \circ ([\![\delta_s]\!] \otimes id) \circ (id_\Delta \otimes \eta) \\
\text{($\multimap$E)} \quad & [\![\delta]\!] = (id_Y \otimes \varepsilon) \circ ((swap \circ \otimes E \circ [\![\delta_s]\!]) \otimes ((\bigotimes_{c:A} [\![\delta_t]\!]) \circ d_{A.\Gamma})) \\
\text{(CONTR)} \quad & [\![\delta]\!] = [\![\delta_t]\!] \circ (id_\Delta \otimes ((\bigotimes_{c:A+B} [\![\delta_s]\!]) \circ d)) \\
\text{(CASE)} \quad & [\![\delta]\!] = \pi_f \circ c^{-1} \circ (\bigotimes_A [\![\delta_s]\!] \otimes \bigotimes_A [\![\delta_t]\!]) \circ c_\Gamma \circ (in_f)_\Gamma \\
\text{([\,]I)} \quad & [\![\delta]\!] = [f] \otimes w_\Gamma \\
\text{([\,]E)} \quad & [\![\delta]\!] = \pi \circ ([\![\delta_s]\!] \otimes (\bigotimes_A [\![\delta_t]\!] \circ d_{A.\Delta})) \\
\text{(HACK)} \quad & [\![\delta]\!] = \mathsf{hack}(c.f)
\end{aligned}
$$

Fig. 4. Compilation to Circuits

$\bigcup_{v \in V(D)} \varphi_v \colon M_D \to M_D$ can be implemented easily by a big case distinction and it is easy to obtain φ_D from this using a single loop. From this, finally, we obtain Φ_D.

We have thus explained how each upper class term can be translated to a working class term. It remains to say how we deal with terms of the form $\Sigma \vdash \mathsf{unbox}(s) \colon A$ where $\Sigma \mid \vdash s \colon [A]$. Note that s is translated to a circuit $[\![\delta_s]\!]$ whose behaviour is a function of type $\Phi_{[\![\delta_s]\!]} \colon 1 \times \mathcal{E}_\Sigma \to A$. The working class term implementing this function is just what we need to interpret the term unbox.

4.3 Soundness

We have defined the evaluation of INTML by translation of upper class to working class, since this allows us to obtain sublinear space bounds (cf. Sec. 5). However, the translation is somewhat complicated and it is does not make it obvious just what it is that the upper class terms compute. In this section, we show that one may also consider the upper class as a functional programming language with standard reduction rules, which are then soundly implemented by the translation.

A notion of reduction can be formulated by the rules in Fig. 5. We include a rule for loop but note that we cannot give rules for hack in general. When we write $s \longrightarrow t$ we assume $\vdash s \colon X$ and $\vdash t \colon X$ for some X. We close these rules under evaluation contexts.

$$
\begin{aligned}
E, F ::= &[\cdot] \mid \langle E, t \rangle \mid \langle t, E \rangle \mid \mathsf{let}\ E\ \mathsf{be}\ \langle x, y \rangle\ \mathsf{in}\ t \mid \\
& E\ t \mid t\ E \mid \mathsf{let}\ E\ \mathsf{be}\ [c]\ \mathsf{in}\ t \mid \mathsf{copy}\ E\ \mathsf{as}\ x, y\ \mathsf{in}\ t
\end{aligned}
$$

As usual, $E[s]$ is the term obtained by substituting s for the only occurrence of $[\cdot]$ in E.

The translation to working class terms is invariant under reduction:

Theorem 1 (Soundness). *If δ derives $\vdash s \colon X$ and $s \longrightarrow t$, then there exists a derivation ρ of $\vdash t \colon X$ that satisfies $[\![\delta]\!] \sim [\![\rho]\!]$.*

$$(\lambda x.s)t \longrightarrow s[t/x]$$

$$\text{let } \langle s,t \rangle \text{ be } \langle x,y \rangle \text{ in } u \longrightarrow u[s/x][t/y]$$

$$\text{case inl}(v) \text{ of inl}(c) \Rightarrow s \mid \text{inr}(d) \Rightarrow t \longrightarrow s[v/c] \quad \text{if } v \text{ is a value}$$

$$\text{case inr}(v) \text{ of inl}(c) \Rightarrow s \mid \text{inr}(d) \Rightarrow t \longrightarrow t[v/d] \quad \text{if } v \text{ is a value}$$

$$\text{let } [v] \text{ be } [c] \text{ in } t \longrightarrow t[v/c] \quad \text{if } v \text{ is a value}$$

$$\text{copy } s \text{ as } x,y \text{ in } t \longrightarrow t[s/x][s/y]$$

$$[f] \longrightarrow [g] \quad \text{if } f \longrightarrow g$$

$$\text{case } f \text{ of inl}(c) \Rightarrow s \mid \text{inr}(d) \Rightarrow t \longrightarrow \text{case } g \text{ of inl}(c) \Rightarrow s \mid \text{inr}(d) \Rightarrow t \quad \text{if } f \longrightarrow g$$

$$\text{loop } s \, t \longrightarrow \text{let } t \text{ be } [c] \text{ in let } s \, [c] \text{ be } [d] \text{ in}$$

$$\text{case } d \text{ of inl}(d) \Rightarrow \text{loop } s \, [d] \mid \text{inr}(d) \Rightarrow [d]$$

Fig. 5. Upper Class Reduction

For the proof we need substitution lemmas, which are proved by induction on ρ.

Lemma 1. *If $v \in \mathcal{V}_A$ and ρ derives $\Sigma, c{:}A \mid \Gamma \vdash t{:} X$, then there is a derivation $\rho[v/c]$ of $\Sigma \mid \Gamma \vdash t[v/c]{:} X$ such that $[\![\rho[v/c]]\!] \sim [\![\rho]\!][v/c]$ holds.*

Lemma 2. *If δ derives $\Sigma \mid \vdash s{:} X$ and ρ derives $\Sigma \mid \Gamma, x{:}A{\cdot}X, \Delta \vdash t{:} Y$, then there exists a derivation $\rho[\delta/x]$ of $\Sigma \mid \Gamma, \Delta \vdash t[s/x]{:} Y$ that satisfies $[\![\rho[\delta/x]]\!] \sim [\![\rho]\!] \circ (id_\Gamma \otimes \bigotimes_A [\![\delta]\!] \otimes id_\Delta)$.*

Proof (of Theorem 1). For any reduction $s \longrightarrow t$ there exist decompositions $s = E[s']$ and $t = E[t']$ such that $s' \longrightarrow t'$ is an instance of one of the reductions in Fig 5.

The proof then goes by induction on the structure of E. The base case where E is empty, amounts to showing the assertion for the basic reductions. For lack of space, we just spell out the first case where $s \longrightarrow t$ has the form $(\lambda x.\, q)\, p \longrightarrow q[p/x]$.

Since δ ends in a sequent with empty context, it cannot end with a structural rule. Hence, the last two rules in δ must be $(\multimap E)$ after $(\multimap I)$. Let σ and τ be the derivations of $x{:}B \cdot Z \vdash q{:} Y$ and $\vdash p{:} Z$ that derive the premises of these rules. Then we can use $\otimes E \circ \otimes I \sim id$ and $(id \otimes \varepsilon) \circ (\eta \otimes id) \sim id$, which are both easy to show directly, and the substitution lemma to calculate:

$$[\![\delta]\!] = (id_Y \otimes \varepsilon) \circ ((swap \circ \otimes E \circ \otimes I \circ swap \circ ([\![\sigma]\!] \otimes id_{\otimes_B Z}) \circ \eta) \otimes \bigotimes\nolimits_B [\![\tau]\!])$$

$$\sim (id_Y \otimes \varepsilon) \circ (((\![\![\sigma]\!] \otimes id_{\otimes_B Z}) \circ \eta) \otimes \bigotimes\nolimits_B [\![\tau]\!])$$

$$\sim [\![\sigma]\!] \circ ((id_{\otimes_B Z} \otimes \varepsilon) \circ (\eta \otimes id_{\otimes_B Z})) \circ \bigotimes\nolimits_B [\![\tau]\!]$$

$$\sim [\![\sigma]\!] \circ \bigotimes\nolimits_B [\![\tau]\!] \sim [\![\sigma[\tau/y]]\!]$$

Since $\sigma[\tau/y]$ derives $\vdash q[p/x]{:} Y$, this concludes this case.

The induction step follows straightforwardly from the induction hypothesis. If, for example, E is $\langle F, u \rangle$, then δ must end in rule $(\otimes I)$ with two premises $\vdash F[s']{:} Y$ and $\vdash u{:} Z$, derived by σ and τ. We apply the induction hypothesis to σ to obtain σ'. Then we note that replacing σ with σ' in δ gives us a derivation ρ of the required term. The assertion then follows: $[\![\delta]\!] = \otimes I \circ ([\![\sigma]\!] \otimes [\![\tau]\!]) \sim \otimes I \circ ([\![\sigma']\!] \otimes [\![\tau]\!]) = [\![\rho]\!]$. □

We can conclude that the compilation in the previous section computes the same results as the standard reduction introduced here.

Corollary 1. *If δ derives $\vdash s\colon [A]$ and $s \longrightarrow^* [v]$ for some $v \in \mathcal{V}_A$, then $\Phi_{[\![\delta]\!]}$ is the function of type $\mathcal{V}_1 \times 1 \to \mathcal{V}_A$ that maps the unique element of its domain to v.*

This corollary follows by observing that $\vdash [v]\colon [A]$ must be derived by some ρ with $([\,]\mathrm{I})$ as last rule, that $\Phi_{[\![\rho]\!]}$ is by definition the function in the corollary and that $\Phi_{[\![\rho]\!]} \sim \Phi_{[\![\delta]\!]}$ follows from the theorem.

5 Logarithmic Space

In this section we describe a precise correspondence between the class of functions representable in INTML and the class of functions computable in logarithmic space.

First we must define how to represent functions from binary strings to binary strings in INTML. In principle, such functions can be programmed directly as terms of type $A \cdot [B] \multimap [B]$, where B is a working class type of binary strings. However, this would lead to linear space usage, so we use a more interactive type as discussed in Sec. 2.

With the constants *min* and *succ*, we can view any closed type $[A]$ as a type of natural numbers that can represent the numbers from 0 to $|\mathcal{V}_A| - 1$: the number i is encoded by the normal form of $[succ_A^i(min_A)]$, for which we write $\langle i \rangle_A$.

Then, for every closed type B, binary strings of length at most $|\mathcal{V}_B|$ can be represented as terms of type $\mathbb{B}_A(B) = A \cdot [B] \multimap [3]$: a binary string s is encoded by a function that when applied to $\langle i \rangle_B$ returns: b if the i-th symbol in s is b and 2 if i exceeds the length of s. Write $\langle s \rangle_{A,B}$ for the encoding of $s \in \{0,1\}^{\leq |\mathcal{V}_B|}$ in $\mathbb{B}_A(B)$.

Functions that take as inputs strings of arbitrary length can be represented using type variables. Let X be the upper class type $A \cdot \mathbb{B}_B(\alpha) \multimap \mathbb{B}_C(D)$, where α is a type variable and where A, B, C and D are arbitrary types that may also contain α, but not other type variables. If E is a closed type then $X[E/\alpha]$ is a type of functions from strings of length at most $|\mathcal{V}_E|$ to strings of length at most $|\mathcal{V}_{D[E/\alpha]}|$. We say that a term $\vdash t\colon X$ *represents* a function $\phi\colon \{0,1\}^* \to \{0,1\}^*$ if and only if:

- For every n and every $x \in \{0,1\}^n$, $|\phi(x)| \leq |\mathcal{V}_{D[n/\alpha]}|$;
- For every n, every $x \in \{0,1\}^n$ and every E with $|\mathcal{V}_E| \geq n$, if $\phi(x) = b_1 \ldots b_m$ then for every $i \leq |\mathcal{V}_{D[n/\alpha]}|$, the term $t[E/\alpha]\langle s \rangle_{B[E/\alpha],E}\langle i \rangle_{D[E/\alpha]}$ reduces to $\langle b_i \rangle_3$ if $i \leq m$ and to $\langle 2 \rangle_3$ if $i > m$.

We remark that one may also use an alternate definition, for which the following theorems are also valid, but which does not refer to upper class reduction: instead of requiring $t[E/\alpha]\langle s \rangle_{B[E/\alpha],E}\langle i \rangle_{D[E/\alpha]}$ to reduce to one of $\langle b_i \rangle_3$ or $\langle 2 \rangle_3$, one may ask that the circuit for this term have the same behaviour as either $\langle b_i \rangle_3$ or $\langle 2 \rangle_3$, depending on i.

Theorem 2 (Logspace Soundness). *If $\phi\colon \{0,1\}^* \to \{0,1\}^*$ is represented by t, then ϕ is computable in logarithmic space. Moreover, a LOGSPACE algorithm computing ϕ is given by INTML-evaluation of t.*

Proof. Compiling t to a working class term yields a term $x\colon X^- \vdash f\colon X^+$. We now choose $E_n = 2^{\lceil \log n \rceil}$ to substitute for α. Clearly, $|\mathcal{V}_{E_n}| \geq n$, but $|E_n| \leq 2(\log n + 1)$. By Prop. 1, evaluation of $f[E_n/\alpha]$ (i.e. computation of ϕ on strings of length up to n) can be implemented using space linear in $|2^{\lceil \log n \rceil}|$, thus logarithmic in n.

Theorem 3 (Logspace Completeness). *Any function* $\phi\colon \{0,1\}^* \to \{0,1\}^*$ *computable in logarithmic space is represented by some upper class term* t_ϕ.

The proof goes by an easy encoding of Offline Turing Machines in INTML. The step function of a given LOGSPACE OTM M can be mimicked by an upper class term $\mid x{:}[\alpha] \multimap [3] \vdash \mathrm{step}_M\colon [S(\alpha)] \multimap [S(\alpha) + S(\alpha)]$, where x represents the input string and where $S(\alpha)$ is a type with free variable α that can encode the state of M. The term t_M can be obtained by passing step_M to the loop combinator.

6   Conclusion

We have found that the Int construction is a good way of structuring space bounded computation that can help us to understand the principles of space bounded functional programming. This view has guided the design of INTML, a simple language capturing LOGSPACE. Initial experience with an experimental implementation of INTML suggests that, with suitable type inference, INTML can be made to be quite usable.

We hope that our systematic approach will be helpful for developing INTML further. For instance, recent results on capturing non-deterministic token machines by the Int construction [9] may perhaps be used to develop a NLOGSPACE-version of INTML.

References

1. Abramsky, S., Jagadeesan, R.: New Foundations for the Geometry of Interaction. Inf. Comput. 111(1), 53–119 (1994)
2. Abramsky, S., Haghverdi, E., Scott, P.J.: Geometry of interaction and linear combinatory algebras. Math. Struct. in Comput. Sci. 12(5), 625–665 (2002)
3. Asperti, A., Guerrini, S.: The optimal implementation of functional programming languages. Cambridge University Press, Cambridge (1998)
4. Baillot, P., Terui, K.: Light types for polynomial time computation in lambda calculus. Inf. Comput. 207(1), 41–62 (2009)
5. Bonfante, G.: Some programming languages for Logspace and Ptime. In: Johnson, M., Vene, V. (eds.) AMAST 2006. LNCS, vol. 4019, pp. 66–80. Springer, Heidelberg (2006)
6. Hasegawa, M.: On traced monoidal closed categories. Math. Struct. in Comput. Sci. 19(2), 217–244 (2009)
7. Joyal, A., Street, R., Verity, D.: Traced monoidal categories. Math. Proc. Cambridge Philos. Soc. 119(3), 447–468 (1996)
8. Katsumata, S.: Attribute grammars and categorical semantics. In: Aceto, L., Damgård, I., Goldberg, L.A., Halldórsson, M.M., Ingólfsdóttir, A., Walukiewicz, I. (eds.) ICALP 2008, Part II. LNCS, vol. 5126, pp. 271–282. Springer, Heidelberg (2008)
9. Katsumata, S., Hoshino, N.: Int construction and semibiproducts. RIMS-Technical Report 1676 (2009)
10. Kristiansen, L.: Neat function algebraic characterizations of LOGSPACE and LINSPACE. Computational Complexity 14, 72–88 (2005)
11. Mackie, I.: The geometry of interaction machine. In: POPL, pp. 198–208 (1995)

12. Mairson, H.G.: From hilbert spaces to dilbert spaces: Context semantics made simple. In: Agrawal, M., Seth, A.K. (eds.) FSTTCS 2002. LNCS, vol. 2556, pp. 2–17. Springer, Heidelberg (2002)
13. Melliès, P.A.: Functorial boxes in string diagrams. In: Ésik, Z. (ed.) CSL 2006. LNCS, vol. 4207, pp. 1–30. Springer, Heidelberg (2006)
14. Neergaard, P.M.: A functional language for logarithmic space. In: Chin, W.-N. (ed.) APLAS 2004. LNCS, vol. 3302, pp. 311–326. Springer, Heidelberg (2004)
15. Schöpp, U.: Stratified bounded affine logic for logarithmic space. In: LICS, pp. 411–420 (2007)
16. Szepietowski, A.: Turing Machines with Sublogarithmic Space. LNCS, vol. 843. Springer, Heidelberg (1994)
17. Winskel, G.: The Formal Semantics of Programming Languages. MIT Press, Cambridge (1993)

Logical Concurrency Control
from Sequential Proofs

Jyotirmoy Deshmukh[1], G. Ramalingam[2], Venkatesh-Prasad Ranganath[2],
and Kapil Vaswani[2]

[1] Univeristy of Texas at Austin
jyotirmoy@cerc.utexas.edu
[2] Microsoft Research, India
{grama,rvprasad,kapilv}@microsoft.com

Abstract. We are interested in identifying and enforcing the *isolation requirements* of a concurrent program, i.e., concurrency control that ensures that the program meets its specification. The thesis of this paper is that this can be done systematically starting from a sequential proof, i.e., a proof of correctness of the program in the absence of concurrent interleavings. We illustrate our thesis by presenting a solution to the problem of making a sequential library thread-safe for concurrent clients. We consider a sequential library annotated with assertions along with a proof that these assertions hold in a sequential execution. We show how we can use the proof to derive concurrency control that ensures that any execution of the library methods, when invoked by concurrent clients, satisfies the same assertions. We also present an extension to guarantee that the library is linearizable with respect to its sequential specification.

1   Introduction

A key challenge in concurrent programming is identifying and enforcing the *isolation requirements* of a program: determining what constitutes undesirable interference between different threads and implementing concurrency control mechanisms that prevent this. In this paper, we show how a solution to this problem can be obtained systematically from a *sequential proof*: a proof that the program satisfies a specification in the absence of concurrent interleaving.

Problem Setting. We illustrate our thesis by considering the concrete problem of making a sequential library safe for concurrent clients. Informally, given a sequential library that works correctly when invoked by any sequential client, we show how to synthesize concurrency control code for the library that ensures that it will work correctly when invoked by any concurrent client.

Consider the example in Fig. 1(a). The library consists of one procedure Compute, which applies an expensive function f to an input variable num. As a performance optimization, the implementation caches the last input and result. If the current input matches the last input, the last computed result is returned.

A.D. Gordon (Ed.): ESOP 2010, LNCS 6012, pp. 226–245, 2010.

```
1:  int lastNum = 0;
2:  int lastRes = f(0);
3:  /* @returns f(num) */
4:  Compute(num) {
5:      /* acquire (1); */
6:      if(lastNum==num) {
7:          res = lastRes;
8:      } else {
9:          /* release (1); */
10:         res = f(num);
11:         /* acquire (1); */
12:         lastNum = num;
13:         lastRes = res;
14:     }
15:     /* release (1); */
16:     return res;
17: }
```

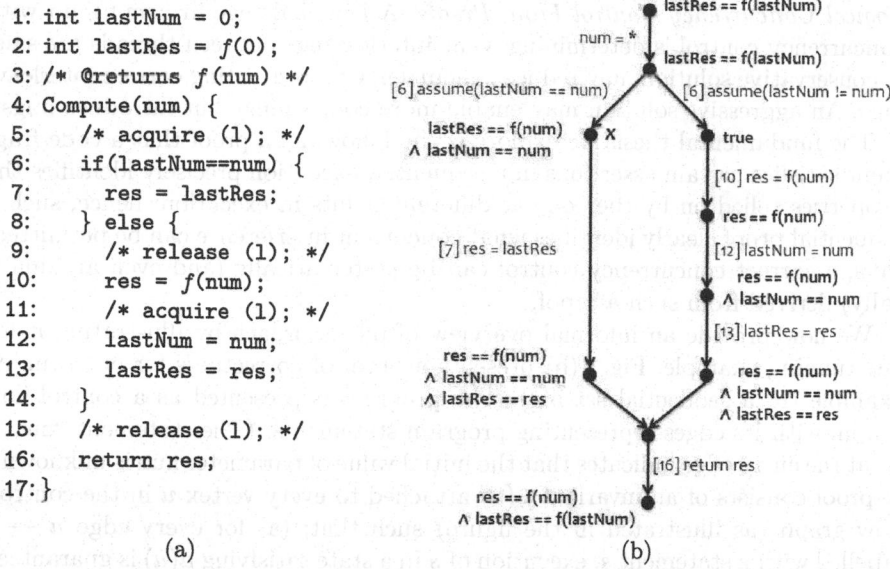

(a)   (b)

Fig. 1. (a) (excluding Lines 5,9,11,15) shows a procedure Compute that applies a (side-effect free) function f to a parameter num and caches the result for later invocations. Lines 5,9,11,15 contain a lock-based concurrency control generated by our technique. (b) shows the control-flow graph of Compute, its edges labeled by statements of Compute and nodes labeled by proof assertions.

This procedure works correctly when used by a sequential client, but not in the presence of concurrent procedure invocations. E.g., consider an invocation of Compute(5) followed by concurrent invocations of Compute(5) and Compute(7). Assume that the second invocation of Compute(5) evaluates the condition in Line 6, and proceeds to Line 7. Assume a context switch occurs at this point, and the invocation of Compute(7) executes completely, overwriting lastRes in Line 13. Now, when the invocation of Compute(5) resumes, it will erroneously return the (changed) value of lastRes.

In this paper, we present a technique that can detect the potential for such interference and synthesize concurrency control to prevent the same. The (lock-based) solution synthesized by our technique for the above example is shown (as comments) in Lines 5, 9, 11, and 15 in Fig. 1(a). With this concurrency control, the example works correctly even for concurrent procedure invocations while permitting threads to perform the expensive function f concurrently.

The Formal Problem. Formally, we assume that the correctness criterion for the library is specified as a set of assertions and that the library satisfies these assertions in any execution of any sequential client. *Our goal is to ensure that any execution of the library with any concurrent client also satisfies the given assertions.* For our running example in Fig. 1(a), Line 3 specifies the desired functionality for procedure Compute: Compute returns the value $f(\text{num})$.

Logical Concurrency Control From Proofs. A key challenge in coming up with concurrency control is determining what interleavings between threads are safe. A conservative solution may reduce concurrency by preventing correct interleavings. An aggressive solution may enable more concurrency but introduce bugs.

The fundamental thesis we explore is the following: a proof that a code fragment satisfies certain assertions in a sequential execution precisely identifies the properties relied on by the code at different points in execution; hence, such a sequential proof clearly identifies what concurrent interference can be permitted; thus, a correct concurrency control can be systematically (and even automatically) derived from such a proof.

We now provide an informal overview of our approach by illustrating it for our running example. Fig. 1(b) presents a proof of correctness for our running example (in a sequential setting). The program is presented as a control-flow graph, with its edges representing program statements. (The statement "num = *" at the entry edge indicates that the initial value of parameter num is unknown.) A proof consists of an invariant $\mu(u)$ attached to every vertex u in the control-flow graph (as illustrated in the figure) such that: (a) for every edge $u \rightarrow v$ labelled with a statement s, execution of s in a state satisfying $\mu(u)$ is guaranteed to produce a state satisfying $\mu(v)$, (b) The invariant $\mu(entry)$ attached to the entry vertex is satisfied by the initial state and is implied by the invariant $\mu(exit)$ attached to the exit vertex, and (c) for every edge $u \rightarrow v$ annotated with an assertion φ, we have $\mu(u) \Rightarrow \varphi$. Condition (b) ensures that the proof is valid over any *sequence of* executions of the procedure.

The invariant $\mu(u)$ at vertex u indicates the property required (by the proof) to hold at u to ensure that a sequential execution satisfies all assertions of the library. We can reinterpret this in a concurrent setting as follows: when a thread t_1 is at point u, it can tolerate changes to the state by another thread t_2 as long as the invariant $\mu(u)$ continues to hold from t_1's perspective; however, if another thread t_2 were to change the state such that t_1's invariant $\mu(u)$ is broken, then the continued execution by t_1 may fail to satisfy the desired assertions.

Consider the proof in Fig. 1(b). The vertex labeled x in the figure corresponds to the point before the execution of Line 7. The invariant attached to x indicates that the proof of correctness depends on the condition $lastRes == f(num)$ being true at x. The execution of Line 10 by another thread will not invalidate this condition. But, the execution of Line 13 by another thread can potentially invalidate this condition. Thus, we infer that, when one thread is at point x, an execution of Line 13 by another thread should be avoided.

We prevent the execution of a statement s by one thread when another thread is at a program point u (if s might invalidate a predicate p that is required at u) as follows. We introduce a lock ℓ_p corresponding to p, and ensure that every thread holds ℓ_p at u and ensure that every thread holds ℓ_p when executing s.

Our algorithm does this as follows. From the invariant $\mu(u)$ at vertex u, we compute a set of predicates $\mathfrak{pm}(u)$. (For now, think of $\mu(u)$ as the conjunction of predicates in $\mathfrak{pm}(u)$.) $\mathfrak{pm}(u)$ represents the set of predicates required at u. For any edge $u \rightarrow v$, any predicate p that is in $\mathfrak{pm}(v) \setminus \mathfrak{pm}(u)$ is required at v

but not at u. Hence, we acquire the lock for p along this edge. Dually, for any predicate that is required at u but not at v, we release the lock along the edge. As a special case, we acquire (release) the locks for all predicates in $\mathbf{pm}(u)$ at procedure entry (exit) when u is the procedure entry (exit) vertex. Finally, if the execution of the statement on edge $u \rightarrow v$ can invalidate a predicate p that is required at some vertex, we acquire and release the corresponding lock before and after the statement (unless it is already a required predicate at u or v).

Our algorithm ensures that the locking scheme does not lead to deadlocks by merging locks when necessary, as described later. Finally, we optimize the synthesized solution using a few simple techniques. E.g., in our example whenever the lock corresponding to `lastRes == res` is held, the lock for `lastNum == num` is also held. Hence, the first lock is redundant and can be eliminated.

Fig. 1 shows the resulting library with the concurrency control we synthesize. This implementation satisfies its specification even in a concurrrent setting. The synthesized solution permits a high degree to concurrency since it allows multiple threads to compute f concurrently. A more conservative but correct locking scheme would hold the lock during the entire procedure execution.

A distinguishing aspect of our algorithm is that it requires only local reasoning and not reasoning about interleaved executions, as is common with many analyses of concurrent programs. Note that the synthesized solution depends on the proof used. Different proofs can potentially yield different concurrency control solutions (all correct, but with potentially different performance).

Linearizability. The above approach can be used to ensure that concurrent executions guarantee desired safety properties, preserve data-structure invariants, and meet specifications (e.g., given as a precondition/postcondition pair). Library implementors may, however, wish to provide the stronger guarantee of linearizability with respect to the sequential specification: *any concurrent execution of a procedure is guaranteed to satisfy its specification and appears to take effect instantaneously at some point during its execution.* In this paper, we show how the techniques sketched above can be extended to guarantee linearizability.

Implementation. We have implemented our algorithm, using an existing software model checker to generate the sequential proofs. We used the tool to successfully synthesize concurrency control for several small examples. The synthesized solutions are equivalent to those an expert programmer would use.

Contributions

We present a technique for synthesizing concurrency control for a library (e.g., developed for use by a single-threaded client) to make it safe for use by concurrent clients. However, we believe that the key idea we present – a technique for identifying and realizing isolation requirements from a sequential proof – can be used in other contexts as well (e.g., in the context of a whole program consisting of multiple threads, each with its own assertions and sequential proofs).

Sometimes, a library designer may choose to delegate the responsibility for concurrency control to the clients of the library and not make the library thread-safe[1]. Alternatively, library implementers could choose to make the execution of a library method appear atomic by wrapping it in a transaction and executing it in an STM (assuming this is feasible). These are valid options but orthogonal to the point of this paper. Typically, a program is a software stack, with each level serving as a library. Passing the buck, with regards to concurrency control, has to stop somewhere. Somewhere in the stack, the developer needs to decide what degree of isolation is required by the program; otherwise, we would end up with a program consisting of multiple threads where we require every thread's execution to appear atomic, which could be rather severe and restrict concurrency needlessly. The ideas in this paper provide a systematic method for determining the isolation requirements. While we illustrate the idea in a simplified setting, it should ideally be used at the appropriate level of the software stack.

In practice, full specifications are rarely available. We believe that our technique can be used even with lightweight specifications or in the absence of specifications. Consider our example in Fig. 1. A symbolic analysis of this library, with a harness representing a sequential client making an arbitrary sequence of calls to the library, can, in principle, infer that the returned value equals f(num). As the returned value is the only observable value, this is the strongest functional specification a user can write. Our tool can be used with such an inferred specification as well.

Logical interference. Existing concurrency control mechanisms (both pessimistic as well as optimistic) rely on a data-access based notion of interference: concurrent accesses to the same data, where at least one access is a write, is conservatively treated as interference. A contribution of this paper is that it introduces a more logical/semantic notion of interference that can be used to achieve more permissive, yet safe, concurrency control. Specifically, concurrency control based on this approach permits interleavings that existing schemes based on stricter notion of interference will disallow. Hand-crafted concurrent code often permits "benign interference" for performance reasons, suggesting that programmers do rely on such a logical notion of interference.

2 The Problem

In this section, we introduce required terminology and formally define the problem. Rather than restrict ourselves to a specific syntax for programs and assertions, we will treat them abstractly, assuming only that they can be given a semantics as indicated below, which is fairly standard.

2.1 The Sequential Setting

Sequential Libraries. A library $\mathcal{L}$ is a pair $(\mathcal{P}, V_G)$, where $\mathcal{P}$ is a set of procedures (defined below), and V_G is a set of variables, termed *global* variables, accessible

---

[1] This may be a valid design option in some cases. However, in examples such as our running example, this could be a bad idea.

to all and only procedures in $\mathcal{P}$. A procedure P is a pair (G_P, V_P), where G_P is a control-flow graph with each edge labeled by a primitive statement, and V_P is a set of variables, referred to as *local* variables, restricted to the scope of P. (Note that V_P includes the formal parameters of P as well.) To simplify the semantics, we will assume that the set V_P is the same for all procedures and denote it V_L.

Every control-flow graph has a unique entry vertex N_P (with no predecessors) and a unique exit vertex X_P (with no successors). Primitive statements are either skip statements, assignment statements, assume statements, return statements, or assert statements. An assume statement is used to implement conditional control flow as usual. Given control-flow graph nodes u and v, we denote an edge from u to v, labeled with a primitive statement s, by $u \xrightarrow{s} v$.

To reason about all possible sequences of invocations of the library's procedures, we define the *control graph* of a library to be the union of the control-flow graphs of all the procedures, augmented by a new vertex w, as well as an edge from every procedure exit vertex to w and an edge from w to every procedure entry vertex. We refer to w as the *quiescent* vertex. Note that a one-to-one correspondence exists between a path in the control graph of the library, starting from w, and the execution of a sequence of procedure calls. The edge $w \to N_P$ from the quiescent vertex to the entry vertex of a procedure P models an arbitrary call to procedure P. We refer to these as *call edges*.

Sequential States. A procedure-local state $\sigma_\ell \in \Sigma_\ell^s$ is a pair (pc, σ_d) where pc, the program counter, is a vertex in the control graph and σ_d is a map from the local variables V_L to their values. A global state $\sigma_g \in \Sigma_g^s$ is a map from global variables V_G to their values. A library state σ is a pair $(\sigma_\ell, \sigma_g) \in \Sigma_\ell^s \times \Sigma_g^s$. We say that a state is a *quiescent state* if its pc value is w and that it is a *entry state* if its pc value equals the entry vertex of some procedure.

Sequential Executions. We assume a standard semantics for primitive statements that can be captured as a transition relation $\leadsto_s \subseteq \Sigma^s \times \Sigma^s$ as follows. Every control-flow edge e induces a transition relation $\overset{e}{\leadsto}_s$, where $\sigma \overset{e}{\leadsto}_s \sigma'$ iff the execution of (the statement labeling) edge e transforms state σ to σ'. The edge $w \to N_P$ from the quiescent vertex to the entry vertex of a procedure P models an arbitrary call to procedure P. Hence, in defining the transition relation, such edges are treated as statements that assign a non-deterministically chosen value to every formal parameter of P and the default initial value to every local variable of P. Similarly, the edge $X_P \to w$ is treated as a skip statement. We say $\sigma \leadsto_s \sigma'$ if there exists some edge e such that $\sigma \overset{e}{\leadsto}_s \sigma'$.

A *sequential execution* is a sequence of states $\sigma_0 \sigma_1 \cdots \sigma_k$ where σ_0 is the initial state of the library and we have $\sigma_i \leadsto_s \sigma_{i+1}$ for $0 \le i < k$. A sequential execution represents the execution of a sequence of calls to the library's procedures (where the last call's execution may be incomplete). Given a sequential execution $\sigma_0 \sigma_1 \cdots \sigma_k$, we say that σ_i is the *corresponding entry state* of σ_j if σ_i is an entry state and no state σ_h is an entry state for $i < h \le j$.

Sequential Assertions. We use assert statements to specify desired correctness properties of the library. Assert statements have no effect on the execution semantics and are equivalent to `skip` statements in the semantics. Assertions are used only to define the notion of *well-behaved* executions as follows.

An `assert` statement is of the form `assert` θ where, θ is a 1-state assertion φ or a 2-state assertion Φ. A 1-state assertion, which we also refer to as a predicate, makes an assertion about a single library state. Rather than define a specific syntax for assertions, we assume that the semantics of assertions are defined by a relation $\sigma \models_s \varphi$ denoting that a state σ satisfies the assertion φ.

1-state assertions can be used to specify the invariants expected at certain program points. In general, specifications for procedures take the form of two-state assertions, which relate the input state to output state. We use 2-state assertions for this purpose. The semantics of a 2-state assertion Φ is assumed to be defined by a relation $(\sigma_{in}, \sigma_{out}) \models_s \Phi$ (meaning that state σ_{out} satisfies assertion Φ with respect to state σ_{in}). In our examples, we use special input variables v^{in} to refer to the value of the variable v in the first state. E.g., the specification "$x == x^{in} + 1$" asserts that the value of x in the second state is one more than its value in the first state.

Definition 1. *A sequential execution is said to satisfy the library's assertions if for any transition $\sigma_i \overset{assert\ \theta}{\leadsto}_s \sigma_{i+1}$ in the execution, we have (a) $\sigma_i \models_s \theta$ if θ is a 1-state assertion, and (b) $(\sigma_{in}, \sigma_i) \models_s \theta$ where σ_{in} is the corresponding entry state of σ_i, otherwise. A sequential library satisfies its specifications if every execution of the library satisfies its specifications.*

2.2   The Concurrent Setting

Concurrent Libraries. A concurrent library $\mathcal{L}$ is a triple $(\mathcal{P}, V_G, Lk)$, where $\mathcal{P}$ is a set of concurrent procedures, V_G is a set of global variables, and Lk is a set of global locks. A concurrent procedure is like a sequential procedure, with the extension that a primitive statement is either a sequential primitive statement or a locking statement of the form `acquire`(ℓ) or `release`(ℓ) where ℓ is a lock.

Concurrent States. A concurrent library permits concurrent invocations of procedures. We associate each procedure invocation with a thread (representing the client thread that invoked the procedure). Let T denote an infinite set of thread-ids, which are used as unique identifiers for threads. In a concurrent execution, every thread has a private copy of local variables, but all threads share a single copy of the global variables. Hence, the local-state in a concurrent execution is represented by a map from T to Σ_ℓ^s. (A thread whose local-state's pc value is the quiescent point represents an idle thread, i.e., a thread not processing any procedure invocation.) Let $\Sigma_\ell^c = T \to \Sigma_\ell^s$ denote the set of all local states.

At any point during execution, a lock lk is either free or held by one thread. We represent the state of locks by a partial function from Lk to T indicating which thread, if any, holds any given lock. Let $\Sigma_{lk}^c = Lk \hookrightarrow T$ represent the set of all lock-states. Let $\Sigma_g^c = \Sigma_g^s \times \Sigma_{lk}^c$ denote the set of all global states. Let $\Sigma^c = \Sigma_\ell^c \times \Sigma_g^c$ denote the set of all states. Given a concurrent state $\sigma = (\sigma_\ell, (\sigma_g, \sigma_{lk}))$ and thread t, we define $\sigma[t]$ to be the sequential state $(\sigma_\ell(t), \sigma_g)$.

Concurrent Executions. The concurrent semantics is induced by the sequential semantics as follows. Let e be any control-flow edge labelled with a sequential primitive statement, and t be any thread. We say that $(\sigma_\ell, (\sigma_g, \sigma_{lk})) \overset{(t,e)}{\leadsto}_c (\sigma'_\ell, (\sigma'_g, \sigma_{lk}))$ iff $(\sigma_t, \sigma_g) \overset{e}{\leadsto}_s (\sigma'_t, \sigma'_g)$ where $\sigma_t = \sigma_\ell(t)$ and $\sigma'_\ell = \sigma_\ell[t \mapsto \sigma'_t]$. The transitions corresponding to lock acquire/release are defined in the obvious way. We say that $\sigma \leadsto_c \sigma'$ iff there exists some (t, e) such that $\sigma \overset{(t,e)}{\leadsto}_c \sigma'$.

A *concurrent execution* is a sequence $\sigma_0 \sigma_1 \cdots \sigma_k$, where σ_0 is the initial state of the library and $\sigma_i \overset{\ell_i}{\leadsto}_c \sigma_{i+1}$ for $0 \le i < k$. We say that $\ell_0 \cdots \ell_{k-1}$ is the *schedule* of this execution. A sequence $\ell_0 \cdots \ell_m$ is a *feasible schedule* if it is the schedule of some concurrent execution. Consider a concurrent execution $\sigma_0 \sigma_1 \cdots \sigma_k$. We say that a state σ_i is a t-entry-state if it is generated from a quiescent state by thread t executing a call edge. We say that σ_i is the *corresponding t-entry state* of σ_j if σ_i is a t-entry-state and no state σ_h is a t-entry-state for $i < h \le j$.

We note that our semantics uses sequential consistency. Extending our results to support weaker memory models is future work.

Interpreting Assertions In Concurrent Executions. In a concurrent setting, assertions are evaluated in the context of the thread that executes the corresponding **assert** statement. We say that state σ satisfies a 1-state assertion φ in the context of thread t_i (denoted by $(\sigma, t_i) \models_c \varphi$) iff $\sigma[t_i] \models_s \varphi$. For any 2-state assertion Φ, we say that a given pair of states $(\sigma_{in}, \sigma_{out})$ satisfies Φ in the context of thread t (denoted by $((\sigma_{in}, \sigma_{out}), t) \models_c \Phi)$ iff $(\sigma_{in}[t], \sigma_{out}[t]) \models_s \Phi$.

Definition 2. *A concurrent execution π is said to satisfy the library's assertions if for any transition $\sigma_i \overset{(t, \mathit{assert}\ \theta)}{\leadsto}_c \sigma_{i+1}$ in the execution we have (a) $(\sigma_i, t) \models_c \theta$, if θ is a 1-state assertion, and (b) $((\sigma_{in}, \sigma_i), t) \models_c \theta$ where σ_{in} is the corresponding t-entry state of σ_i, otherwise. A concurrent library satisfies its specifications if every execution of the library satisfies its specifications.*

Frame Conditions. Consider a library with two global variables x and y and a procedure IncX that increments x by 1. A possible specification for IncX is $(x == x^{in} + 1)$ && $(y == y^{in})$. The condition $y == y^{in}$ is IncX's frame condition, which says that it will not modify y. Explicitly stating such frame conditions is unnecessarily restrictive, as a concurrent update to y by another procedure, when IncX is executing, would be considered a violation of IncX's specification. Frame conditions can be handled better by treating a specification as a pair (S, Φ) where S is the set of all global variables referenced by the procedure, and Φ is a specification that does not refer to any global variables outside S. For our above example, the specification will be $(\{x\}, x == x^{in} + 1))$. In the sequel, however, we will restrict ourselves to the simpler setting and ignore this issue.

2.3   Goals

Our goal is: Given a sequential library $\mathcal{L}$ with assertions satisfied in every sequential execution, construct $\hat{\mathcal{L}}$, by augmenting $\mathcal{L}$ with concurrency control, such that every concurrent execution of $\hat{\mathcal{L}}$ satisfies all assertions. In Section 5, we extend this goal to construct $\hat{\mathcal{L}}$ such that every concurrent execution of $\hat{\mathcal{L}}$ is linearizable.

3   Preserving Single-State Assertions

In this section we describe our algorithm for synthesizing concurrency control, but restrict our attention to single-state assertions.

3.1   Algorithm Overview

A *sequential proof* is a mapping μ from vertices of the control graph to predicates such that (a) for every edge $e = u \xrightarrow{t} v$, $\{\mu(u)\}t\{\mu(v)\}$ is a valid Hoare triple (i.e., $\sigma_1 \models_s \mu(u)$ and $\sigma_1 \overset{e}{\leadsto}_s \sigma_2$ implies $\sigma_2 \models_s \mu(v)$), and (b) for every edge $u \xrightarrow{assert\ \varphi} v$, we have $\mu(u) \Rightarrow \varphi$.

Note that the invariant $\mu(u)$ attached to a vertex u by a proof indicates two things: (i) any sequential execution reaching point u will produce a state satisfying $\mu(u)$, and (ii) any sequential execution from point u, starting from a state satisfying $\mu(u)$ will satisfy the invariants labelling other program points (and satisfy all assertions encountered during the execution).

A procedure that satisfies its assertions in a sequential execution may fail to do so in a concurrent execution due to interference. The preceding paragraph, however, hints at the interference we must avoid to ensure correctness: when a thread t_1 is at point u, we should ensure that no other thread t_2 changes the state to one where t_1's invariant $\mu(u)$ fails to hold. Any change to the state by another thread t_2 can be tolerated by t_1 *as long as the invariant* $\mu(u)$ *continues to hold*. We can achieve this by associating a lock with the invariant $\mu(u)$, ensuring that t_1 holds this lock when it is at program point u, and ensuring that any thread t_2 acquires this lock before executing a statement that may break this invariant. An invariant $\mu(u)$, in general, may be a boolean formula over simpler predicates. We could potentially get different locking solutions by associating different locks with different sub-formulae of the invariant. We elaborate on this idea below.

A *predicate mapping* is a mapping $\mathfrak{pm}$ from the vertices of the control graph to a set of predicates. A predicate mapping $\mathfrak{pm}$ is said to be a *basis* for a proof μ if every $\mu(u)$ can be expressed as a boolean formula (involving conjunctions, disjunctions, and negation) over $\mathfrak{pm}(u)$. A basis $\mathfrak{pm}$ for proof μ is *positive* if every $\mu(u)$ can be expressed as a boolean formula involving only conjunctions and disjunctions over $\mathfrak{pm}(u)$.

Given a proof μ, we say that an edge $u \xrightarrow{s} v$ *sequentially positively preserves* a predicate φ if $\{\mu(u) \wedge \varphi\}s\{\varphi\}$ is a valid Hoare triple. Otherwise, we say that the edge *may sequentially falsify* the predicate φ. Note that the above definition is in terms of the Hoare logic for our sequential language. However, we want to formalize the notion of a thread t_2's execution of an edge falsifying a predicate φ in a thread t_1's scope. Given a predicate φ, let $\hat{\varphi}$ denote the predicate obtained by replacing every local variable x with a new unique variable $\hat{x}$. We say that an edge $u \xrightarrow{s} v$ *may falsify* φ iff the edge may sequentially falsify $\hat{\varphi}$. (Note that this reasoning requires working with formulas with free variables, such as $\hat{x}$. This is straightforward as these can be handled just like extra program variables.)

E.g., consider Line 13 in Fig. 1. Consider predicate $lastRes==f(num)$. By renaming local variable num to avoid naming conflicts, we obtain predicate lastRes ==f(nûm). We say that Line 13 *may falsify* this predicate because the triple $\{res == f(num) \wedge lastNum == num \wedge lastRes == f(n\hat{u}m)\}$ lastRes = res $\{lastRes == f(n\hat{u}m)\}$ is not a valid Hoare triple.

Let $\mathfrak{pm}$ be a positive basis for a proof μ and $\mathcal{R} = \cup_u \mathfrak{pm}(u)$. If a predicate φ is in $\mathfrak{pm}(u)$, we say that φ is *relevant* at program point u. In a concurrent execution, we say that a predicate φ is relevant to a thread t in a given state if t is at a program point u in the given state and $\varphi \in \mathfrak{pm}(u)$. Our locking scheme associates a lock with every predicate φ in $\mathcal{R}$. The invariant it establishes is that a thread, in any state, will hold the locks corresponding to precisely the predicates that are relevant to it. We will simplify the initial description of our algorithm by assuming that distinct predicates are associated with distinct locks and later relax this requirement.

Consider any control-flow edge $e = u \xrightarrow{s} v$. Consider any predicate φ in $\mathfrak{pm}(v) \setminus \mathfrak{pm}(u)$. We say that predicate φ *becomes relevant* at edge e. In the motivating example, the predicate lastNum == num becomes relevant at Line 12

We ensure the desired invariant by acquiring the locks corresponding to every predicate that becomes relevant at edge e *prior to statement s in the edge.* (Acquiring the lock after s may be too late, as some other thread could intervene between s and the acquire and falsify predicate φ.)

Now consider any predicate φ in $\mathfrak{pm}(u) \setminus \mathfrak{pm}(v)$. We say that φ *becomes irrelevant* at edge e. E.g., predicate lastres == f(lastNum) becomes irrelevant once the false branch at Line 8 is taken. For every p that becomes irrelevant at edge e, we release the lock corresponding to p *after* statement s.

The above steps ensure that in a concurrent execution a thread will hold a lock on all predicates relevant to it. The second component of the concurrency control mechanism is to ensure that any thread that acquires a lock on any predicate before it falsifies the predicate. Consider an edge $e = u \xrightarrow{s} v$ in the control-flow graph. Consider any predicate $\varphi \in \mathcal{R}$ that may be falsified by edge e. We add an acquire of the lock corresponding to this predicate before s (unless $\varphi \in \mathfrak{pm}(u)$), and add a release of the same lock after s (unless $\varphi \in \mathfrak{pm}(v)$).

Managing locks at procedure entry/exit. We will need to acquire/release locks at procedure entry and exit differently from the scheme above. Our algorithm works with the control graph defined in Section 2. Recall that we use a quiescent vertex w in the control graph. The invariant $\mu(w)$ attached to this quiescent vertex describes invariants maintained by the library (in between procedure calls). Any return edge $u \xrightarrow{return} v$ must be augmented to release all locks corresponding to predicates in $\mathfrak{pm}(u)$ before returning. Dually, any procedure entry edge $w \rightarrow u$ must be augmented to acquire all locks corresponding to predicates in $\mathfrak{pm}(u)$.

However, this is not enough. Let $w \rightarrow u$ be a procedure p's entry edge. The invariant $\mu(u)$ is part of the library invariant that procedure p depends upon.

It is important to ensure that when p executes the entry edge (and acquires locks corresponding to the basis of $\mu(u)$) the invariant $\mu(u)$ holds. We achieve this by ensuring that any procedure that invalidates the invariant $\mu(u)$ holds the locks on the corresponding basis predicates until it reestablishes $\mu(u)$. We now describe how this can be done in a simplified setting where the invariant $\mu(u)$ can be expressed as the conjunction of the predicates in the basis $\mathfrak{pm}(u)$ for every procedure entry vertex u. (Disjunction can be handled at the cost of extra notational complexity.) We will refer to the predicates that occur in the basis $\mathfrak{pm}(u)$ of some procedure entry vertex u as *library invariant predicates*.

We use an *obligation* mapping $\mathfrak{om}(v)$ that maps each vertex v to a set of library invariant predicates to track the invariant predicates that may be invalid at v and need to be reestablished before the procedure exit. We say a function $\mathfrak{om}$ is a valid obligation mapping if it satisfies the following constraints for any edge $e = u \to v$: (a) if e may falsify a library invariant φ, then φ must be in $\mathfrak{om}(v)$, and (b) if $\varphi \in \mathfrak{om}(u)$, then φ must be in $\mathfrak{om}(v)$ unless e *establishes* φ. Here, we say that an edge $u \xrightarrow{s} v$ *establishes* a predicate φ if $\{\mu(u)\}s\{\varphi\}$ is a valid Hoare triple. Define $\mathfrak{m}(u)$ to be $\mathfrak{pm}(u) \cup \mathfrak{om}(u)$. Now, the scheme described earlier can be used, except that we use $\mathfrak{m}$ in place of $\mathfrak{pm}$.

Locking along assume *edges.* Any lock to be acquired along an assume edge will need to be acquired before the condition is evaluated. If the lock is not required along all assume edges out of a vertex, then we will have to release the lock along the edges where it is not required.

Deadlock Prevention. The locking scheme synthesized above may potentially lead to a deadlock. We now show how to modify the locking scheme to avoid this possibility. For any edge e, let $\mathfrak{mbf}(e)$ be (a conservative approximation of) the set of all predicates that may be falsified by the execution of edge e. We first define a binary relation $\rightarrowtail$ on the predicates used (i.e., the set $\mathcal{R}$) as follows: we say that $p \rightarrowtail r$ iff there exists a control-flow edge $u \xrightarrow{s} v$ such that $p \in \mathfrak{m}(u) \wedge r \in (\mathfrak{m}(v) \cup \mathfrak{mbf}(u \xrightarrow{s} v)) \setminus \mathfrak{m}(u)$. Note that $p \rightarrowtail r$ holds iff it is possible for some thread to try to acquire a lock on r while it holds a lock on p. Let $\rightarrowtail^*$ denote the transitive closure of $\rightarrowtail$.

We define an equivalence relation $\rightleftarrows$ on $\mathcal{R}$ as follows: $p \rightleftarrows r$ iff $p \rightarrowtail^* r \wedge r \rightarrowtail^* p$. Note that any possible deadlock must involve an equivalence class of this relation. We map all predicates in an equivalence class to the same lock to avoid deadlocks. In addition to the above, we establish a total ordering on all the locks, and ensure that all lock acquisitions we add to a single edge are done in an order consistent with the established ordering.

Optimizations. Our scheme can sometimes introduce *redundant* locking. E.g., assume that in the generated solution a lock ℓ_1 is always held whenever a lock ℓ_2 is acquired. Then, the lock ℓ_2 is redundant and can be eliminated. Similarly, if we have a predicate φ that is never falsified by any statement in the library, then we do not need to acquire a lock for this predicate. We can eliminate such redundant locks as a final optimization pass over the generated solution.

Note that it is safe for multiple threads to simultaneously hold a lock on the same predicate φ if they want to "preserve" it, but a thread that wants to "break" φ needs an exclusive lock. Thus, reader-writer locks can be used to improve concurrency, but space constraints prevent a discussion of this extension.

Generating Proofs. The sequential proof required by our scheme can be generated using verification tools such as SLAM [2], BLAST [10,11] and Yogi [9]. Since a minimal proof can lead to better concurrency control, approaches that produce a "parsimonious proof" (e.g., see [11]) are preferable. A parsimonious proof is one that avoids the use of unnecessary predicates at any program point.

3.2 Complete Schema

We now present a complete outline of our schema for synthesizing concurrency control.

1. Construct a sequential proof μ that the library satisfies the given assertions in any sequential execution.
2. Construct positive basis $\mathfrak{pm}$ and an obligation mapping $\mathfrak{om}$ for the proof μ.
3. Compute a map $\mathfrak{mbf}$ from the edges of the control graph to $\mathcal{R}$, the range of $\mathfrak{pm}$, such that $\mathfrak{mbf}(e)$ (conservatively) includes all predicates in $\mathcal{R}$ that may be falsified by the execution of e.
4. Compute the equivalence relation $\rightleftarrows$ on $\mathcal{R}$.
5. Generate a predicate lock allocation map $\mathfrak{lm} : \mathcal{R} \rightarrow \mathcal{L}$ such that for any $\varphi_1 \rightleftarrows \varphi_2$, we have $\mathfrak{lm}(\varphi_1) = \mathfrak{lm}(\varphi_2)$.
6. Compute the following quantities for every edge $e = u \xrightarrow{s} v$, where we use $\mathfrak{lm}(X)$ as shorthand for $\{\, \mathfrak{lm}(p) \mid p \in X \,\}$ and $\mathfrak{m}(u) = \mathfrak{pm}(u) \cup \mathfrak{om}(u)$:

$$BasisLocksAcq(e) = \mathfrak{lm}(\mathfrak{m}(v)) \setminus \mathfrak{lm}(\mathfrak{m}(u))$$
$$BasisLocksRel(e) = \mathfrak{lm}(\mathfrak{m}(u)) \setminus \mathfrak{lm}(\mathfrak{m}(v))$$
$$BreakLocks(e) = \mathfrak{lm}(\mathfrak{mbf}(e)) \setminus \mathfrak{lm}(\mathfrak{m}(u)) \setminus \mathfrak{lm}(\mathfrak{m}(v))$$

7. We obtain the concurrency-safe library $\widehat{\mathcal{L}}$ by transforming every edge $u \xrightarrow{s} v$ in the library $\mathcal{L}$ as follows:
   (a) $\forall\, p \in BasisLocksAcq(u \xrightarrow{s} v)$, add an `acquire(`$\mathfrak{lm}(p)$`)` before s;
   (b) $\forall\, p \in BasisLocksRel(u \xrightarrow{s} v)$, add a `release(`$\mathfrak{lm}(p)$`)` after s;
   (c) $\forall\, p \in BreakLocks(u \xrightarrow{s} v)$, add an `acquire(`$\mathfrak{lm}(p)$`)` before s and a `release(`$\mathfrak{lm}(p)$`)` after s.
   All lock acquisitions along a given edge are added in an order consistent with a total order established on all locks.

3.3 Correctness

Let $\mathcal{L}$ be a given library with a set of embedded assertions satisfied by all sequential executions of $\mathcal{L}$. Let $\widehat{\mathcal{L}}$ be the library obtained by augmenting $\mathcal{L}$ with concurrency control using the algorithm presented in Section 3.2.

Theorem 1. *(a) Any concurrent execution of $\widehat{\mathcal{L}}$ satisfies every assertion of $\mathcal{L}$. (b) The library $\widehat{\mathcal{L}}$ is deadlock-free.*

See [5] for all proofs.

4   Extensions for 2-State Assertions

The algorithm presented in the previous section can be extended to handle 2-state assertions via a simple program transformation that allows us to treat 2-state assertions (in the original program) as single-state assertions (in the transformed program). We augment the set of local variables with a new variable $\tilde{v}$ for every (local or shared) variable v in the original program and add a primitive statement $\mathcal{LP}$ at the entry of every procedure, whose execution essentially copies the value of every original variable v to the corresponding new variable $\tilde{v}$.

Let $\underline{\sigma'}$ denote the projection of a transformed program state σ' to a state of the original program obtained by forgetting the values of the new variables. Given a 2-state assertion Φ, let $\tilde{\Phi}$ denote the single-state assertion obtained by replacing every v^{in} by $\tilde{v}$. As formalized by the claim below, the satisfaction of a 2-state assertion Φ by executions in the original program corresponds to satisfaction of the single-state assertion $\tilde{\Phi}$ in the transformed program.

Lemma 1. *(a) A schedule ξ is feasible in the transformed program iff it is feasible in the original program. (b) Let σ' and σ be the states produced by a particular schedule with the transformed and original programs, respectively. Then, $\sigma = \underline{\sigma'}$. (c) Let π' and π be the executions produced by a particular schedule with the transformed and original program, respectively. Then, π satisfies a single-state assertion φ iff π' satisfies it. Furthermore, π satisfies a 2-state assertion Φ iff π' satisfies the corresponding one-state assertion $\tilde{\Phi}$.*

Synthesizing concurrency control. We now apply the technique discussed in Section 3 to the transformed program to synthesize concurrency control that preserves the assertions transformed as discussed above. It follows from the above Lemma that this concurrency control, used with the original program, preserves both single-state and two-state assertions.

5   Guaranteeing Linearizability

In the previous section, we showed how to derive concurrency control to ensure that each procedure satisfies its sequential specification even in a concurrent execution. However, this may still be too permissive, allowing interleaved executions that produce counter-intuitive results and preventing compositional reasoning in clients of the library. E.g., consider the procedure Increment shown in Fig. 2, which increments a shared variable x by 1. The figure shows the concurrency control derived using our approach to ensure specification correctness. Now consider a multi-threaded client that initializes x to 0 and invokes Increment concurrently in two threads. It would be natural to expect that the value of x would be 2 at the end of any execution of this client. However, this implementation permits an interleaving in which the value of x at the end of the execution is 1: the problem is that both invocations of Increment individually meet their specifications, but the cumulative effect is unexpected. (We note that such concerns do not arise

```
1 int x = 0;
2 //@ensures x == x^{in} + 1 ∧ returns x
3 Increment () {
4     int tmp;
5     acquire(l_{(x==x^{in})}); tmp = x; release(l_{(x==x^{in})});
6     tmp = tmp + 1;
7     acquire(l_{(x==x^{in})}); x = tmp; release(l_{(x==x^{in})});
8     return tmp;
9 }
```

Fig. 2. A non-linearizable implementation of the procedure `Increment`

when the specification does not refer to shared variables. For instance, the specification for our example in Fig. 1 does not refer to shared variables, even though the implementation uses shared variables.)

One solution to this problem is to apply concurrency control synthesis to the code (library) that calls `Increment`. The synthesis can then detect the potential for interference between the calls to `Increment` and prevent them from happening concurrently. Another possible solution, which we explore in this section, is for the library to guarantee a stronger correctness criteria called *linearizability* [12]. Linearizability gives the illusion that in any concurrent execution, (the sequential specification of) every procedure of the library appears to execute *instantaneously* at some point between its call and return. This illusion allows clients to reason about the behavior of concurrent library compositionally using its sequential specifications.

In this section, we extend our approach to derive concurrency control that guarantees linearizability. Due to space constraints, we show how to ensure that every procedure appears to execute instantaneously along its entry edge, while satisfying its sequential specification. The technique can be generalized to permit linearization points (i.e., the point at which the procedure'appears to execute instantaneously) other than the procedure entry, subject to some constraints (see [5]). Recall that we adapt the control-flow graph representation of each procedure by labelling the procedure entry edge with the statement $\mathcal{LP}$ defined in Section 4 to handle 2-state assertions. Without loss of generality, we assume that each procedure P_j returns the value of a special local variable ret_j.

We start by characterizing non-linearizable interleavings permitted by our earlier approach. We classify the interleavings based on the nature of linearizability violations they cause. For each class of interleavings, we describe an extension to our approach to generate additional concurrency control to prohibit these interleavings.

Delayed Falsification. Informally, the problem with the `Increment` example can be characterized as "dirty reads" and "lost updates": the second procedure invocation executes its linearization point later than the first procedure invocation but reads the original value of x, instead of the value produced by the the first invocation. Dually, the update done by the first procedure invocation is lost, when the second procedure invocation updates x. From a logical perspective, the second invocation relies on the invariant $x == x^{in}$ early on, and the first invocation breaks this invariant later on when it assigns to x (at a point when the second invocation no longer relies on the invariant). This prevents us from reordering the execution to construct an equivalent sequential execution (while preserving the proof).

The extension we now describe prevents such interference by ensuring that instructions that may falsify predicates and occur after the linearization point appear to execute atomically at the linearization point. We achieve this by modifying the strategy to acquire locks as follows.

- We generalize the earlier notion of *may-falsify*. We say that a path *may-falsify* a predicate φ if some edge in the path may-falsify φ. We say that a predicate φ *may-be-falsified-after* vertex u if there exists some path from u to the exit vertex of the procedure that does not contain any linearization point and may-falsify φ.
- Let mf be a predicate map such that for any vertex u, $\mathsf{mf}(u)$ includes any predicate that may-be-falsified-after u.
- We generalize the original scheme for acquiring locks. We augment every edge $e = u \xrightarrow{S} v$ as follows:
    1. $\forall\, \ell \in \mathsf{lm}(\mathsf{mf}(v))\backslash\mathsf{lm}(\mathsf{mf}(u))$, add an "acquire($\ell$)" before S
    2. $\forall\, \ell \in \mathsf{lm}(\mathsf{mf}(u))\backslash\mathsf{lm}(\mathsf{mf}(v))$, add an "release($\ell$)" after S

This extension suffices to produce a linearizable implementation of the example in Fig. 2.

Return Value Interference. We now focus on interference that can affect *the actual value returned by a procedure invocation*, leading to non-linearizable executions.

Consider procedures IncX and IncY in Fig. 5, which increment variables x and y respectively. Both procedures return the values of x *and* y. However, the postconditions of IncX (and IncY) do not *specify anything about the final value of* y (and x respectively). Let us assume that the linearization points of the procedures are their entry points. Initially, we have $x = y = 0$. Consider the following interleaving of a concurrent execution of the two procedures. The two procedures execute the increments in some order, producing the state with $x = y = 1$. Then, both procedures return $(1, 1)$. This execution is non-linearizable because in any legal sequential execution, the procedure executing second is obliged to return a value that differs from the value returned by the procedure executing first. The left column in Fig. 5 shows the concurrency control derived using our approach with previously described extensions. This is insufficient to prevent the above interleaving. This interference is allowed because the specification for IncX allows it to change the value of y arbitrarily; hence, a concurrent modification to y by any other procedure is not seen as a hindrance to IncX.

To prohibit such interferences within our framework, we need to determine whether the execution of a statement s can potentially affect the return-value of another procedure invocation. We do this by computing a predicate $\phi(ret')$ at

```
int x, y;                    int x, y;                         int x, y;
IncX() {                     @ensures x = xin + 1              IncX() {
  acquire(lx==xin);          @returns (x, y)                     acquire(lmerged);
  x = x + 1;                 IncX() {                            x = x+1;
  (ret11,ret12)=(x,y);         [ret'11==x+1 ∧ ret'12==y]          (ret11,ret12)=(x,y);
  release(lx==xin);            LP : x = xin                       release(lmerged);
}                              [x==xin ∧ ret'11==x+1 ∧ ret'12=y]  }
IncY() {                       x = x + 1;                       IncY() {
  acquire(ly==yin);            [x==xin+1 ∧ ret'11==x ∧ ret'12= y]  acquire(lmerged);
  y = y + 1;                   (ret11,ret12)=(x,y);               y = y+1;
  (ret21,ret22)=(x,y);         [x==xin+1 ∧ ret11==ret'11          (ret21,ret22)=(x,y);
  release(ly==yin);            ∧ ret12==ret'12]                   release(lmerged);
}                            }                                  }

        (a)                          (b)                              (c)
```

Fig. 3. An example illustrating return value interference. Both procedures return (x,y). ret_{ij} refers to the jth return variable of the ith procedure. Figure 3(a) is a non-linearizable implementation synthesized using the approach described in Section 3. Figure 3(b) shows the extended proof of correctness of the procedure IncX and Figure 3(c) shows the linearizable implementation.

every program point u that captures the relation between the program state at point u and the value returned by the procedure invocation eventually (denoted by ret'). We then check if the execution of a statement s will break predicate $\phi(ret')$, treating ret' as a free variable, to determine if the statement could affect the return value of some other procedure invocation.

Formally, we assume that each procedure returns the value of a special variable ret. (Thus, "return exp" is shorthand for "$ret = exp$".) We introduce a special primed variable ret'. We compute a predicate $\phi(u)$ at every program point u such that (a) $\phi(u) = ret' == ret$ for the exit vertex u, and (b) for every edge $u \xrightarrow{s} v$, $\{\phi(u)\}s\{\phi(v)\}$ is a valid Hoare triple. In this computation, ret' is treated as a free variable. In effect, this is a weakest-precondition computation of the predicate $ret' == ret$ from the exit vertex.

Next, we augment the basis at every vertex u so that it includes a basis for $\phi(u)$ as well. We now apply our earlier algorithm using this enriched basis set.

The middle column in Fig. 5 shows the augmented sequential proof of correctness of IncX. The concurrency control derived using our approach starting with this proof is shown in the third column of Fig. 5. The lock l_{merged} denotes a lock obtained by merging locks corresponding to multiple predicates simultaneously acquired/released. It is easy to see that this implementation is linearizable. Also note that if the shared variables y and x were *not* returned by procedures IncX and IncY respectively, we will derive a locking scheme in which accesses to x and y are protected by different locks, allowing these procedures to execute concurrently.

Control Flow Interference. An interesting aspect of our scheme is that it permits interference that alters the control flow of a procedure invocation if it does not

```
1 int x, y;
2 //@ensures y = y^in + 1
3 IncY() {
4       [true] LP : y^in = y
5       [y == y^in] y = y + 1;
6       [y == y^in + 1]
7 }
```

```
1 //@ensures x < y
2 ReduceX() {
3       [true] LP
4       [true] if (x ≥ y) {
5       [true] x = y - 1;
6                  }
7       [x < y]
8 }
```

Fig. 4. An example illustrating interference in control flow. Each line is annotated (in square braces) with a predicate the holds at that program point.

cause the invocation to violate its specification. Consider procedures ReduceX and IncY shown in Fig. 4. The specification of ReduceX is that it will produce a final state where $x < y$, while the specification of IncY is that it will increment the value of y by 1. ReduceX meets its specification by setting x to be $y - 1$, but does so *only if* $x \geq y$.

Now consider a client that invokes ReduceX and IncY concurrently from a state where $x = y = 0$. Assume that the ReduceX invocation enters the procedure. Then, the invocation of IncY executes completely. The ReduceX invocation continues, and does nothing since $x < y$ at this point.

Fig. 4 shows a sequential proof and the concurrency control derived by the scheme so far, assuming that the linearization points are at the procedure entry. A key point to note is that ReduceX's proof needs only the single predicate $x < y$. The statement $y = y + 1$ in IncY does *not falsify* the predicate $x < y$; hence, IncY does not acquire the lock for this predicate. This locking scheme permits IncY to execute concurrently with ReduceX and affect its control flow. While our approach guarantees that this control flow interference will not cause assertion violations, proving linearizability in the presence of such control flow interference, in the general case, is challenging (and an open problem). Therefore, we conservatively extend our scheme to prevent control flow interference, which suffices to guarantee linearizability.

We ensure that interference by one thread does not affect the execution path another thread takes. We achieve this by strengthening the notion of positive basis as follows: (a) The set of basis predicates at a branch node must be sufficient to express the assume conditions on outgoing edges using disjunctions and conjunctions over the basis predicates, and (b) The set of basis predicates at neighbouring vertices must be positively consistent with each other: for any edge $u \xrightarrow{s} v$, and any predicate φ in the basis at v, the weakest-pre-condition of φ with respect to s must be expressible using disjunctions and conjunctions of the basis predicates at u.

In the current example, this requires predicate $x \geq y$ to be added to the basis for ReduceX. As a result, ReduceX will acquire lock $l_{x \geq y}$ at entry, while IncY will acquire the same lock at its linearization point and release the lock after the statement $y = y + 1$. It is easy to see that this implementation is linearizable.

Correctness. The extensions described above to the algorithm of Sections 3 and 4 for synthesizing concurrency control are sufficient to guarantee linearizability, as stated in the theorem below.

Theorem 2. *Given a library* $\mathcal{L}$ *that is totally correct with respect to a given sequential specification, the library* $\widehat{\mathcal{L}}$ *generated by our algorithm is linearizable with respect to the given specification.*

6   Implementation

We have built a prototype implementation of our algorithm that uses a predicate-abstraction based software verification tool [9] to generate the required proofs. Our implementation takes a sequential library and its assertions as input. It uses a pre-processing phase to combine the library with a harness (that simulates the execution of any possible sequence of library calls) to get a valid C program. It then use the verification tool to generate a proof of correctness for this program. It then uses the algorithm presented in this paper to synthesize concurrency control for the library.

We used a set of benchmark programs to evaluate our approach. The programs include examples shown in Figure 1, 5 and 4. We also used two real world libraries, a device cache library [6] that reads data from a device and caches the data for subsequent reads, and a C implementation of the Simple Authentication and Security Layer (SASL). This library is a generic server side library that manages security context objects for user sessions. We applied our technique manually to the device cache library and the SASL library because the model checker we used does not permit quantifiers in specifications. For these libraries, we wrote full specifications (which required using quantified predicates) and manually generated proofs of correctness.

Starting with these (manually and automatically generated) proofs, the concurrency control scheme we synthesized was identical to what an experienced programmer would generate (in terms of the number and scope of locks). Our solutions permit more concurrency as compared to naive solutions that use one global lock or an atomic section around the body of each procedure. In all cases, the concurrency control scheme we synthesize are the same or better than the concurrency control defined by developers of the library. For example, in case of the server store library, our scheme generates smaller critical sections and identifies a larger number of critical sections that acquire different locks as compared to the default implementation. The source code for all our examples and their concurrent versions are available online at [1]. We leave a more detailed evaluation of our approach as future work.

7   Related Work

Synthesizing Concurrency Control. Most existing work [8,3,7,15,13,19] on synthesizing concurrency control focuses on inferring lock-based synchronization for atomic sections to guarantee atomicity. Our work differs in expoiting a (sequential) specification to derive concurrency control. We also present an extension to guarantee linearizability with respect to a sequential specification, which is a weaker requirement that permits greater concurrency than the notion of atomic sections. Furthermore, existing lock inference schemes identify potential conflicts between atomic sections at the granularity of data items and acquire locks to prevent these conflicts, either all at once or using a two-phase locking approach. Our approach is novel in using a logical notion of interference (based on predicates), which can permit more concurrency. Finally, the locking disciplines we infer do not necessarily follow two-phase locking, yet guarantee linearizability.

[18] describes a sketching technique to add missing synchronization by iteratively exploring the space of candidate programs for a given thread schedule, and pruning the search space based on counterexample candidates. [14] uses model-checking to repair errors in a concurrent program by pruning erroneous paths from the control-flow graph of the interleaved program execution. In [21], the key goal is to obtain a maximally concurrent program for a given cost. This is achieved by deleting transitions from the state-space based on observational equivalence between states, and inspecting if the resulting program satisfies the specification and is implementable. [4] allows users to specify synchronization patterns for critical sections, which are used to infer appropriate synchronization for each of the user-identified region. Vechev *et al.* [20] address the problem of automatically deriving linearizable objects with fine-grained concurrency, using hardware primitives to achieve atomicity. The approach is semi-automated, and requires the developer to provide algorithm schema and insightful manual transformations. Our approach differs from all of these techniques in exploiting a proof of correctness (for a sequential computation) to synthesize concurrency control that guarantees thread-safety.

Verifying Concurrent Programs. Our proposed style of reasoning is closely related to the axiomatic approach for proving concurrent programs of Owicki & Gries [17]. While they focus on proving a concurrent program correct, we focus on synthesizing concurrency control. They observe that if two statements *do not interfere*, the Hoare triple for their parallel composition can be obtained from the sequential Hoare triples. Our approach identifies statements that *may interfere* and violate the sequential Hoare triples, and then synthesizes concurrency control to ensure that sequential assertions are preserved by parallel composition.

Prior work on verifying concurrent programs [16] has also shown that attaching invariants to resources (such as locks and semaphores) can enable modular reasoning about concurrent programs. Our paper turns this around: we use sequential proofs (which are modular proofs, but valid only for sequential executions) to identify critical invariants and create locks corresponding to such invariants and augment the program with concurrency control that enables us to lift the sequential proof into a valid proof for the concurrent program.

References

1. WYPIWYG examples (June 2009),
   http://research.microsoft.com/en-us/projects/wypiwyg/wypiwyg_examples.zip
2. Ball, T., Rajamani, S.K.: Bebop: A symbolic model checker for Boolean programs. In: Havelund, K., Penix, J., Visser, W. (eds.) SPIN 2000. LNCS, vol. 1885, pp. 113–130. Springer, Heidelberg (2000)
3. Cherem, S., Chilimbi, T., Gulwani, S.: Inferring locks for atomic sections. In: Proc. of PLDI (2008)
4. Deng, X., Dwyer, M.B., Hatcliff, J., Mizuno, M.: Invariant-based specification, synthesis, and verification of synchronization in concurrent programs. In: Proc. of ICSE, pp. 442–452 (2002)
5. Deshmukh, J., Ramalingam, G., Ranganath, V.P., Vaswani, K.: Logical concurrency control from sequential proofs. Tech. Rep. MSR-TR-2009-81, Microsoft Research (2009)
6. Elmas, T., Tasiran, S., Qadeer, S.: A calculus of atomic sections. In: Proc. of POPL (2009)
7. Emmi, M., Fischer, J., Jhala, R., Majumdar, R.: Lock allocation. In: Proc. of POPL (2007)
8. Flanagan, C., Freund, S.N.: Automatic synchronization correction. In: Proc. of SCOOL (2005)
9. Gulavani, B.S., Henzinger, T.A., Kannan, Y., Nori, A.V., Rajamani, S.K.: Synergy: A new algorithm for property checking. In: Proc. of FSE (November 2006)
10. Henzinger, T.A., Jhala, R., Majumdar, R., Sutre, G.: Lazy abstraction. In: Proc. of POPL, pp. 58–70 (2002)
11. Henzinger, T.A., Jhala, R., Majumdar, R., McMillan, K.L.: Abstractions from proofs. In: Proc. of POPL, pp. 232–244 (2004)
12. Herlihy, M.P., Wing, J.M.: Linearizability: a correctness condition for concurrent objects. Proc. of ACM TOPLAS 12(3), 463–492 (1990)
13. Hicks, M., Foster, J.S., Pratikakis, P.: Lock inference for atomic sections. In: First Workshop on Languages, Compilers, and Hardware Support for Transactional Computing (2006)
14. Janjua, M.U., Mycroft, A.: Automatic correcting transformations for safety property violations. In: Proc. of Thread Verification, pp. 111–116 (2006)
15. McCloskey, B., Zhou, F., Gay, D., Brewer, E.A.: Autolocker: Synchronization inference for atomic sections. In: Proc. of POPL (2006)
16. O'Hearn, P.W.: Resources, concurrency, and local reasoning. Theor. Comput. Sci. 375(1-3), 271–307 (2007)
17. Owicki, S., Gries, D.: Verifying properties of parallel programs: An axiomatic approach. In: Proc. of CACM (1976)
18. Solar-Lezama, A., Jones, C.G., Bodik, R.: Sketching concurrent data structures. In: Proc. of PLDI, pp. 136–148 (2008)
19. Vaziri, M., Tip, F., Dolby, J.: Associating synchronization constraints with data in an object-oriented language. In: Proc. of POPL, pp. 334–345 (2006)
20. Vechev, M., Yahav, E.: Deriving linearizable fine-grained concurrent objects. In: Proc. of PLDI, pp. 125–135 (2008)
21. Vechev, M., Yahav, E., Yorsh, G.: Inferring synchronization under limited observability. In: Kowalewski, S., Philippou, A. (eds.) TACAS 2009. LNCS, vol. 5505, pp. 139–154. Springer, Heidelberg (2009)

Fluid Updates: Beyond Strong vs. Weak Updates*

Isil Dillig**, Thomas Dillig***, and Alex Aiken

Department of Computer Science, Stanford University
{isil,tdillig,aiken}@cs.stanford.edu

Abstract. We describe a *symbolic heap abstraction* that unifies reasoning about arrays, pointers, and scalars, and we define a *fluid update* operation on this symbolic heap that relaxes the dichotomy between strong and weak updates. Our technique is fully automatic, does not suffer from the kind of state-space explosion problem partition-based approaches are prone to, and can naturally express properties that hold for non-contiguous array elements. We demonstrate the effectiveness of this technique by evaluating it on challenging array benchmarks and by automatically verifying buffer accesses and dereferences in five Unix Coreutils applications with no annotations or false alarms.

1 Introduction

In existing work on pointer and shape analysis, there is a fundamental distinction between two kinds of updates to memory locations: *weak updates* and *strong updates* [1–4]. A strong update overwrites the old content of an abstract memory location l with a new value, whereas a weak update adds new values to the existing set of values associated with l. Whenever safe, it is preferable to apply strong updates to achieve better precision.

Applying strong updates to abstract location l requires that l correspond to exactly one concrete location. This requirement poses a difficulty for applying strong updates to (potentially) unbounded data structures, such as arrays and lists, since the number of elements may be unknown at analysis time. Many techniques combine all elements of an unbounded data structure into a single *summary location* and only allow weak updates [2, 5, 6]. More sophisticated techniques, such as analyses based on 3-valued logic [3], first isolate individual elements of an unbounded data structure via a *focus* operation to apply a strong update, and the isolated element is folded back into the summary location via a dual *blur* operation to avoid creating an unbounded number of locations. While such an approach allows precise reasoning about unbounded data structures, finding the right focus and blur strategies can be challenging and hard to automate [3].

---

* This work was supported by grants from NSF (CNS-050955 and CCF-0430378) with additional support from DARPA.
** Supported by a Stanford Graduate Fellowship.
*** Supported by a Siebel Fellowship.

A.D. Gordon (Ed.): ESOP 2010, LNCS 6012, pp. 246–266, 2010.

In this paper, we propose a way of relaxing the dichotomy between applying weak vs. strong updates to a particular kind of unbounded data structure, arrays, by introducing *fluid updates*. Fluid updates can always be safely applied regardless of whether a given abstract memory location represents a single concrete location or an array. Three key ideas underpin fluid updates:

1. Arrays are modeled as abstract locations qualified by *index variables*; constraints on index variables specify which concrete elements are referred to by a points-to edge.
2. In general, we may not know the exact subset of concrete elements updated by a statement. To deal with this uncertainty, each points-to edge is qualified by a pair of constraints $\langle \phi_{NC}, \phi_{SC} \rangle$, called *bracketing constraints*, over- and underapproximating the subset of concrete elements selected by this edge.
3. To apply a fluid update, we compute a bracketing constraint $\langle \phi_{NC}, \phi_{SC} \rangle$ representing over- and underapproximations for the set of concrete elements updated by a statement. A fluid update preserves all existing points-to edges under the negation of the update condition, i.e., $\neg \langle \phi_{NC}, \phi_{SC} \rangle = \langle \neg \phi_{SC}, \neg \phi_{NC} \rangle$, while applying the update under $\langle \phi_{NC}, \phi_{SC} \rangle$.

An important property of bracketing constraints is that the intersection of a bracketing constraint B and its negation $\neg B$ is not necessarily empty (see Section 2.1). For array elements in the intersection, both the new value is added and the old values are retained—i.e., a weak update is performed. Because fluid updates rely on negation, having both over- and underapproximations (or equivalently, necessary and sufficient conditions) is crucial for the correctness of our approach.

If the concrete elements updated by a statement s are known exactly, i.e., ϕ_{NC} and ϕ_{SC} are the same, the fluid update represents a strong update to some set of elements in the array. On the other hand, if nothing is known about the update condition, i.e., $\langle \phi_{NC}, \phi_{SC} \rangle = \langle true, false \rangle$, the fluid update is equivalent to a weak update to all elements in the array. Otherwise, if only partial information is available about the concrete elements modified by s, the fluid update encodes this partial information soundly and precisely. Consider the following example:

```
void send_packets(struct packet** buf, int c, int size) {
    assert(2*c <= size);
    for(int j=0; j< 2*c; j+=2)
        if(transmit_packet(buf[j]) == SUCCESS) {free(buf[j]); buf[j] = NULL;}
}
```

The function send_packets takes an array buf of packet*'s, an integer c representing the number of high-priority packets to be sent, and an integer size, denoting the number of elements in buf. All even indices in buf correspond to high-priority packets whereas all odd indices are low-priority.[1] This function submits one high-priority packet at a time; if the transfer is successful (which may

---

[1] The distinction between even and odd-numbered elements in a network buffer arises in many real network applications, for example in packet scheduling [7] and p2p video streaming [8] .

depend on network traffic), it sets the corresponding element in buf to NULL to indicate the packet has been processed.

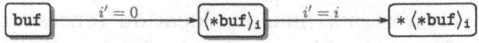

The figure above shows the *symbolic heap abstraction* at the entry of send_packets. Here, nodes represent abstract locations named by *access paths* [9], and edges denote points-to relations. Because either the source or target of an edge may be a set, we write constraints on edges to indicate which elements of the source point to which elements of the target. In the figure, the dereference of buf is an array, hence, it is qualified by an *index variable* i; the location named $\langle *\text{buf} \rangle_i$ represents all elements of array *buf. By convention, primed index variables on an edge qualify the edge's target, and unprimed index variables qualify the source. If the over- and underapproximations on an edge are the same, we write a single constraint instead of a pair. In this graph, the edge from buf to $\langle *\text{buf} \rangle_i$ is qualified by $i' = 0$ because buf points to the first element of array $\langle *\text{buf} \rangle_i$. The constraint $i = i'$ on the edge from $\langle *\text{buf} \rangle_i$ to $*\langle *\text{buf} \rangle_i$ indicates that the i'th element of array *buf points to some corresponding target called $*\langle *\text{buf} \rangle_i$.

The concrete elements modified by the statement buf[j] = NULL cannot be specified exactly at analysis time since the success of transmit_packet depends on an environment choice (i.e., network state). The loop may, but does not have to, set all even elements between 0 and $2c$ to NULL. Hence, the best over-approximation of the indices of *buf modified by this statement is $0 \leq i < 2c \land i\%2 = 0$. On the other hand, the best underapproximation of the set of indices updated in the loop is the empty set (indicated by the constraint *false*) since no element is guaranteed to be updated by the statement buf[j] = NULL.

Figure 1 shows the symbolic heap abstraction at the end of send_packets. Since the set of concrete elements that may be updated by buf[j] = NULL is given by $\langle 0 \leq i < 2c \land i\%2 = 0,\ false \rangle$, the fluid update adds an edge from $\langle *\text{buf} \rangle_i$ to *NULL under this bracketing constraint. The existing edge from $\langle *\text{buf} \rangle_i$ to $*\langle *\text{buf} \rangle_i$ is preserved under $\neg \langle 0 \leq i < 2c \land i\%2 = 0,\ false \rangle$. Now, the complement (negation) of an overapproximation is an underapproximation of the complement; similarly the complement of an underapproximation is an overapproximation of the complement. Thus, assuming $i \geq 0$, this is equivalent to $\langle true,\ i \geq 2c \lor i\%2 \neq 0 \rangle$. Since the initial constraint on the edge stipulates $i = i'$, the edge constraint after the fluid update becomes $\langle i = i',\ (i \geq 2c \lor i\%2 \neq 0) \land i = i' \rangle$. The new edge condition correctly and precisely states that any element of *buf may still point to its original target when the function exits, but only those elements whose index satisfies the constraint $i \geq 2c$ or $i\%2 \neq 0$ *must* point to their original target. As this example illustrates, fluid updates have the following characteristics:

- Fluid updates do not require concretizing individual elements of an array to perform updates, making operations such as focus and blur unnecessary.
- Fluid updates never construct explicit partitions of an array, making this approach less vulnerable to the kind of state space explosion problem that partition-based approaches, such as [3], are prone to.

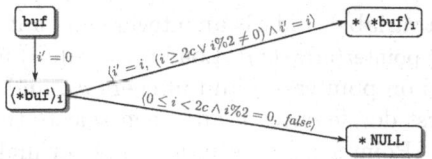

Fig. 1. The points-to graph at the end of function send_packets

- Fluid updates preserve partial information despite imprecision and uncertainty. In the above example, although the result of transmit_packet is unknown, the analysis can still determine that no odd packet is set to NULL.
- Fluid updates separate the problem of determining *which* concrete elements are updated from *how* the update is performed. Fluid updates are oblivious to the precision of the over- and underapproximations, and retain the best possible information with respect to these approximations. In the above example, a less precise overapproximation, such as $0 \leq i < 2c$, would not affect the way updates are performed.

This paper is organized as follows: Section 2 defines a simple language and introduces basic concepts. Section 3 formalizes the symbolic heap abstraction, Section 4 presents the basic pointer and value analysis based on fluid updates, and Section 5 discusses treatment of loops. Section 6 discusses a prototype implementation, Section 7 presents our experimental results, and Section 8 surveys related work. To summarize, this paper makes the following key contributions:

- We introduce *fluid updates* as a viable alternative to the dichotomy between weak vs. strong updates, and we describe an expressive memory analysis based on *symbolic heap abstraction* that unifies reasoning about arrays, pointers, and scalars. (We do not, however, address recursive pointer-based data structures in this paper.)
- We propose *bracketing constraints* to allow a sound negation operation when performing updates in the presence of imprecision and uncertainty.
- We demonstrate our technique is precise and efficient for reasoning about values and points-to targets of array elements. Furthermore, our technique is fully automatic, requiring no annotations or user-provided predicates.
- We show the effectiveness of our approach by verifying the safety of buffer accesses and dereferences fully automatically in five Unix Coreutils applications that manipulate arrays and pointers in intricate ways.

2   Language and Preliminaries

We first define a small imperative language in which we formalize our technique:

$$\text{Program } P \; := F^+$$
$$\text{Function } F \; := \text{define } f(v_1, \ldots, v_n) = S$$
$$\text{Statement } S := S_1; S_2 \mid v_1 = v_2 \mid v_1 = c \mid v_1 = alloc(v_2) \mid v_1 = v_2[v_3] \mid v_2[v_3] = v_1$$
$$\mid v_1 = v_2 \oplus v_3 \mid v_1 = v_2 \text{ intop } v_3 \mid v_1 = v_2 \text{ predop } v_3 \mid$$
$$\text{if } v \neq 0 \text{ then } S_1 \text{ else } S_2 \mid \text{while } v \neq 0 \text{ do } S \text{ end}$$

In this grammar, v is a variable, and c is an integer constant. Types are defined by the grammar $\tau := \text{int} \mid \text{pointer}(\text{array}(\tau))$. Load $(v_1 = v_2[v_3])$ and store $(v_2[v_3] = v_1)$ statements are defined on pointers v_2 and integers v_3, and we assume programs are well-typed. $v[i]$ first dereferences v and then selects the i'th element of the array pointed to by v. Pointer arithmetic $v_1 = v_2 \oplus v_3$ makes v_1 point to offset v_3 in the array pointed to by v_2. Integer operations (intop) include $+, -,$ and $\times$. Predicate operators (predop) are $=, \neq$ and $<$, and predicates evaluate to 0 (false) or 1 (true). The $alloc(v_2)$ statement allocates an array with v_2 elements.

An operational semantics for this language is given in the extended version of this paper [30]. In the concrete semantics, a concrete location l_c is a pair (s, i) where s is a start address for a block of memory and i is an offset from s. An environment E maps program variables to concrete locations, and a store S maps locations to other locations or integer values. Due to space limitations, we omit function calls from our formal discussion; Section 6 discusses how we treat function calls in the implementation.

2.1   Constraint Language

The constraints used in the analysis are defined by:

$$
\begin{array}{ll}
Term\ T & := c \mid v \mid T_1 \text{ intop } T_2 \mid select(T_1, T_2) \mid deref(T) \\
Literal\ L & := true \mid false \mid T_1 \text{ predop } T_2 \mid T\%c = 0 \\
Atom\ A & := L \mid \neg A \mid A_1 \wedge A_2 \mid A_1 \vee A_2 \\
Constraint\ C & := \langle A_{NC}, A_{SC} \rangle
\end{array}
$$

Terms are constants, variables, arithmetic terms, and the uninterpreted function terms $select(T_1, T_2)$, and $deref(T)$. Terms are used to represent scalars, pointers, and arrays; the uninterpreted function term $select(T_1, T_2)$ represents the result of selecting element at index T_2 of array T_1, and the term $deref(T)$ represents the result of dereferencing T.

Literals are $true$, $false$, comparisons $(=, \neq, <)$ between two terms, and divisibility checks on terms. Atomic constraints A are arbitrary boolean combinations of literals. Satisfiability and validity of atomic constraints are decided over the combined theory of uninterpreted functions and linear integer arithmetic extended with divisibility (mod) predicates. Bracketing constraints C are pairs of atomic constraints of the form $\langle A_{NC}, A_{SC} \rangle$ representing necessary and sufficient conditions for some fact. A bracketing constraint is well-formed if and only if $A_{SC} \Rightarrow A_{NC}$. We write $\lceil \phi \rceil$ to denote the necessary condition of a bracketing constraint ϕ and $\lfloor \phi \rfloor$ to denote the sufficient condition of ϕ.

Example 1. Consider an edge from location $\langle *a \rangle_i$ to *NULL qualified by $\langle 0 \leq i < size, 0 \leq i < size \rangle$. This constraint expresses that *all* elements of the array with indices between 0 and $size$ are NULL. Since it is sufficient that i is between 0 and $size$ for $\langle *a \rangle_i$ to point to *NULL, it follows that all elements in this range are NULL. On the other hand, if the constraint on the edge is $\langle 0 \leq i < size, false \rangle$, any element in the array may be NULL, but no element must be NULL.

Boolean operators $\neg, \wedge,$ and $\vee$ on bracketing constraints are defined as:

$$\neg\langle A_{NC}, A_{SC}\rangle = \langle\neg A_{SC}, \neg A_{NC}\rangle$$
$$\langle A_{NC1}, A_{SC1}\rangle \star \langle A_{NC2}, A_{SC2}\rangle = \langle A_{NC1} \star A_{NC2}, A_{SC1} \star A_{SC2}\rangle \quad (\star \in \{\wedge, \vee\})$$

Since the negation of the overapproximation for some set S is an underapproximation for the complement of S, necessary and sufficient conditions are swapped under negation. The following lemma is easy to show:

Lemma 1. *Bracketing constraints preserve the well-formedness property $A_{SC} \Rightarrow A_{NC}$ under boolean operations.*

Satisfiability and validity are defined in the following natural way:

$$SAT(\langle A_{NC}, A_{SC}\rangle) \equiv SAT(A_{NC}) \qquad VALID(\langle A_{NC}, A_{SC}\rangle) \equiv VALID(A_{SC})$$

Lemma 2. *Bracketing constraints do not obey the law of the excluded middle and non-contradiction, but they satisfy the following weaker properties:*

$$VALID(\lceil\langle A_{NC}, A_{SC}\rangle \vee \neg\langle A_{NC}, A_{SC}\rangle\rceil) \qquad UNSAT(\lfloor\langle A_{NC}, A_{SC}\rangle \wedge \neg\langle A_{NC}, A_{SC}\rangle\rfloor)$$

Proof. $\lceil\langle A_{NC}, A_{SC}\rangle \vee \neg\langle A_{NC}, A_{SC}\rangle\rceil$ is $(A_{NC} \vee \neg A_{SC}) \Leftrightarrow (A_{SC} \Rightarrow A_{NC}) \Leftrightarrow true$, where the last equivalence follows from well-formedness. Similarly, $\lfloor\langle A_{NC}, A_{SC}\rangle \wedge \neg\langle A_{NC}, A_{SC}\rangle\rfloor$ is $(A_{SC} \wedge \neg A_{NC}) \Leftrightarrow false$, where the last step follows from the well-formedness property.

3 Symbolic Heap Abstraction

Abstract locations are named by *access paths* [9] and defined by the grammar:

$$Access\ Path\ \pi := \mathfrak{L}_v \mid alloc_{id} \mid \langle\pi\rangle_i \mid *\pi \mid c \mid \pi_1 \text{ intop } \pi_2 \mid \top$$

Here, $\mathfrak{L}_v$ denotes the abstract location corresponding to variable v, and $alloc_{id}$ denotes locations allocated at program point id. Any array location is represented by an access path $\langle\pi\rangle_i$, where π represents the array and i is an *index variable* ranging over the indices of π (similar to [22]). The location $*\pi$ represents the dereference of π. The access path c denotes constants, π_1 intop π_2 represents the result of performing intop on π_1 and π_2, and $\top$ denotes any possible value.

A *memory access path*, denoted π_{mem}, is any access path that does not involve c, π_1 intop π_2, and $\top$. We differentiate memory access paths because only locations that are identified by memory access paths may be written to; other kinds of access paths are only used for encoding values of scalars.

Given a concrete store S and an environment E mapping program variables to concrete locations, a function γ maps abstract memory locations to a set of concrete locations $(s_1, i_1) \ldots (s_k, i_k)$:

$$\gamma(E, S, \mathfrak{L}_v) = \{E(v)\}$$
$$\gamma(E, S, alloc_{id}) = \{(l, 0) \mid l \text{ is the result of allocation at program point } id\}$$
$$\gamma(E, S, \langle\pi\rangle_i) = \{(l, index_j) \mid (l, index_j) \in S \wedge (l, 0) \in \gamma(E, S, \pi))\}$$
$$\gamma(E, S, *\pi) = \bigcup_{l_i \in \gamma(E, S, \pi)} S(l_i)$$

Since we will concretize abstract memory locations under a certain assumption about their index variables, we define another function γ_c, similar to γ but qualified by constraint ϕ. The only interesting modification is for $\langle \pi \rangle_i$:

$$\gamma_c(E, S, \langle \pi \rangle_i, \phi) = \{(l, index_j) \mid (l, index_j) \in S \wedge (l, 0) \in \gamma_c(E, S, \pi, \phi) \wedge \mathrm{SAT}(\phi[index_j/i])\}$$

As is standard in points-to graphs, we enforce that for any two memory access paths, either $\pi_{mem} = \pi'_{mem}$ or $\gamma(E, S, \pi_{mem}) \cap \gamma(E, S, \pi'_{mem}) = \emptyset$.

A *symbolic heap abstraction* is a directed graph where nodes denote abstract locations identified by access paths and edges qualified by bracketing constraints denote points-to relations. Since we want to uniformly encode points-to and value information, we extend the notion of points-to relations to scalars. For example, if an integer **a** has value 3, the symbolic heap abstraction contains a "points-to" edge from **a**'s location to some location named *3, thereby encoding that the value of **a** is 3. Hence, the symbolic heap encodes the value of each scalar.

Formally, a symbolic heap abstraction is defined by

$$\Gamma : \pi_{mem} \rightarrow 2^{(\pi, \phi)}$$

mapping a source location to a set of (target location, constraint) pairs. The edge constraint ϕ may constrain program variables to encode the condition under which this points-to relation holds. More interestingly, ϕ may also qualify the source and the target location's index variables, thereby specifying which elements of the source may (and must) point to which elements of the target.

The combination of indexed locations and edge constraints parametric over these index variables makes the symbolic heap abstraction both very expressive but also non-trivial to interpret. In particular, if the source location is an array, we might want to determine the points-to targets of a specific element (or some of the elements) in this array. However, the symbolic heap abstraction does not directly provide this information since edge constraints are parametric over the source and the target's index variables. Consider the following points-to relation:

Suppose we want to know which location(s) the fourth element of array $\langle *a \rangle_{i_1}$ points to. Intuitively, we can determine the target of the fourth element of $\langle *a \rangle_{i_1}$ by substituting the index variable i_1 by value 3 in the edge constraint $0 \leq i_1 < 5 \wedge i'_2 = i_1 + 1$. This would yield $i'_2 = 4$, indicating that the fourth element of $\langle *a \rangle_i$ points to the target of the fifth element of $\langle *b \rangle_{i_2}$.

While a simple substitution allows us to determine the target of a specific array element as in the above example, in general, we need to determine the targets of those array elements whose indices satisfy a certain constraint. Since this constraint may not limit the index variable to a single value, determining points-to targets from an indexed symbolic heap abstraction requires existential quantifier elimination in general. In the above example, we can determine the possible targets of elements of $\langle *a \rangle_{i_1}$ whose indices are in the range $[0, 3]$ (i.e., satisfy the constraint $0 \leq i_1 \leq 3$) by eliminating i_1 from the following formula:

$$\exists i_1.(0 \leq i_1 \leq 3 \wedge (0 \leq i_1 < 5 \wedge i'_2 = i_1 + 1))$$

This yields $1 \le i_2' \le 4$, indicating that the target's index must lie in the range $[1, 4]$. To formalize this intuition, we define an operation $\phi_1 \downarrow_I \phi_2$, which yields the result of restricting constraint ϕ_1 to only those values of the index variables I that are consistent with ϕ_2.

Definition 1. ($\phi_1 \downarrow_I \phi_2$) Let ϕ_1 be a constraint qualifying a points-to edge and let ϕ_2 be a constraint restricting the values of index variables I. Then,

$$\phi_1 \downarrow_I \phi_2 \equiv Eliminate(\exists I. \ \phi_1 \wedge \phi_2)$$

where the function *Eliminate* performs existential quantifier elimination.

The quantifier elimination performed in this definition is exact because index variables qualifying the source or the target never appear in uninterpreted functions in a valid symbolic heap abstraction; thus the elimination can be performed using [10].

4 Pointer and Value Analysis Using Fluid Updates

In this section, we give deductive rules describing the basic pointer and value analysis using fluid updates. An invariant mapping $\Sigma : Var \to \pi_{mem}$ maps program variables to abstract locations, and the environment Γ defining the symbolic heap abstraction maps memory access paths to a set of (access path, constraint) pairs. Judgments $\Sigma \vdash \mathbf{a} : \mathcal{L}_a$ indicate that variable $\mathbf{a}$ has abstract location $\mathcal{L}_a$, and judgments $\Gamma \vdash_j \pi_s : \langle \pi_{t_j, \phi_j} \rangle$ state that $\langle \pi_{t_j}, \phi_j \rangle \in \Gamma(\pi_s)$. Note that there may be many $\langle \pi_{t_j}, \phi_j \rangle$ pairs in $\Gamma(\pi_s)$, and this form of judgment is used in the rules to refer to each of them without needing to use sets.

We first explain some notation used in Figure 2. The function $U(\phi)$ replaces the primed index variables in constraint ϕ with their unprimed counterparts, e.g., $U(i_1' = 2)$ is $(i_1 = 2)$; this is necessary when traversing the points-to graph because the target location of an incoming edge becomes the source of the outgoing edge from this location. We use the notation $\Gamma \wedge \phi$ as shorthand for:

$$\Gamma'(\pi) = \{ \langle \pi_l, \phi_l \wedge \phi \rangle \mid \langle \pi_l, \phi_l \rangle \in \Gamma(\pi) \}$$

A union operation $\Gamma = \Gamma' \cup \Gamma''$ on symbolic heap abstractions is defined as:

$$\langle \pi', \phi' \vee \phi'' \rangle \in \Gamma(\pi) \ \Leftrightarrow \ \langle \pi', \phi' \rangle \in \Gamma'(\pi) \ \wedge \ \langle \pi', \phi'' \rangle \in \Gamma''(\pi).$$

We write $\Im(\pi)$ to denote the set of all index variables used in π, and we say "i is index of π" if i is the outermost index variable in π.

The basic rules of the pointer and value analysis using fluid updates are presented in Figure 2. We focus mainly on the inference rules involving arrays, since these rules either directly perform fluid updates (Array Store) or rely on the constraint and index-based representation that is key for fluid updates.

We start by explaining the Array Load rule. In this inference rule, each π_{2_j} represents one possible points-to target of v_2 under constraint ϕ_{2_j}. Because π_{2_j} is an array, the constraint ϕ_{2_j} qualifies π_{2_j}'s index variables. Each π_{3_k} represents one possible (scalar) value of v_3. Since we want to access the element

Assign

$$\frac{\Sigma \vdash v_1 : \mathcal{L}_{v_1}, \ v_2 : \mathcal{L}_{v_2}}{\Sigma, \Gamma \vdash v_1 = v_2 \ : \ \Gamma'} \quad \Gamma' = \Gamma[\mathcal{L}_{v_1} \leftarrow \Gamma(\mathcal{L}_{v_2})]$$

Alloc

$$\frac{\Sigma \vdash v_1 : \mathcal{L}_{v_1}}{\Sigma, \Gamma \vdash v_1 = alloc(v_2) \ : \ \Gamma'} \quad \Gamma' = \Gamma[\mathcal{L}_{v_1} \leftarrow \langle alloc_{id}\rangle_i] \wedge i' = 0 \ \ (i \ \text{fresh})$$

Array Load

$$\begin{array}{c} \Sigma \vdash v_1 : \mathcal{L}_{v_1}, \ v_2 : \mathcal{L}_{v_2}, v_3 : \mathcal{L}_{v_3} \\ \Gamma \vdash_j \mathcal{L}_{v_2} : \langle \pi_{2_j}, \phi_{2_j}\rangle \ \ (i \ \text{index of} \ \pi_{2_j}) \\ \Gamma \vdash_k \mathcal{L}_{v_3} : \langle *\pi_{3_k}, \phi_{3_k}\rangle \\ \Gamma \vdash_l \pi_{2_j} : \langle \pi_{t_{jl}}, \phi_{t_{jl}}\rangle \\ \phi'_{2_{jk}} = U(\phi_{2_j}[i' - \pi_{3_k}/i']) \\ \phi'_{t_{jkl}} = \phi_{t_{jl}} \downarrow_{\Im(\pi_{2_j})} \phi'_{2_{jk}} \\ \Gamma' = \Gamma[\mathcal{L}_{v_1} \leftarrow (\bigcup_{jkl}\langle \pi_{t_{jl}}, \phi'_{t_{jkl}} \wedge \phi_{3_k}\rangle)] \\ \hline \Sigma, \Gamma \vdash v_1 = v_2[v_3] \ : \ \Gamma' \end{array}$$

Array Store (Fluid Update)

$$\begin{array}{c} \Sigma \vdash v_1 : \mathcal{L}_{v_1}, \ v_2 : \mathcal{L}_{v_2}, v_3 : \mathcal{L}_{v_3} \\ \Gamma \vdash_j \mathcal{L}_{v_1} : \langle \pi_{1_j}, \phi_{1_j}\rangle \\ \Gamma \vdash \mathcal{L}_{v_2} : \{\langle \pi_{2_1}, \phi_{2_1}\rangle \ldots \langle \pi_{2_n}, \phi_{2_n}\rangle\} \ (i_k \ \text{index of} \ \pi_{2_k}) \\ \Gamma \vdash_l \mathcal{L}_{v_3} : \langle *\pi_{3_l}, \phi_{3_l}\rangle \end{array}$$

$$\Gamma' = \begin{cases} \pi \leftarrow \Gamma(\pi) \ \text{if} \ \pi \notin \{\pi_{2_1}, \ldots \pi_{2_n}\} \\ \pi \leftarrow \{\langle \pi'_k, \phi'_k \wedge \neg \bigvee_{kl}(U(\phi_{2_k}[i'_k - \pi_{3_l}/i'_k]) \wedge \phi_{3_l})\rangle \\ \quad | \ \langle \pi'_k, \phi'_k\rangle \in \Gamma(\pi_{2_k})\} \ \text{if} \ \pi = \pi_{2_k} \in \{\pi_{2_1}, \ldots \pi_{2_n}\} \end{cases}$$

$$\Gamma'' = \begin{cases} \pi_{2_1} \leftarrow (\bigcup_{jl}\langle \pi_{1_j}, U(\phi_{2_1}[i'_1 - \pi_{3_l}/i'_1]) \wedge \phi_{3_l} \wedge \phi_{1_j})\rangle \\ \cdots \\ \pi_{2_n} \leftarrow (\bigcup_{jl}\langle \pi_{1_j}, U(\phi_{2_n}[i'_n - \pi_{3_l}/i'_n]) \wedge \phi_{3_l} \wedge \phi_{1_j})\rangle \end{cases}$$

$$\Sigma, \Gamma \vdash v_2[v_3] = v_1 \ : \ \Gamma' \cup \Gamma''$$

Pointer Arithmetic

$$\begin{array}{c} \Sigma \vdash v_1 : \mathcal{L}_{v_1}, \ v_2 : \mathcal{L}_{v_2}, v_3 : \mathcal{L}_{v_3} \\ \Gamma \vdash_j \mathcal{L}_{v_2} : \langle \pi_{2_j}, \phi_{2_j}\rangle \\ \Gamma \vdash_k \mathcal{L}_{v_3} : \langle *\pi_{3_k}, \phi_{3_k}\rangle \\ \phi'_{2_{jk}} = \phi_{2_j}[(i' - \pi_{3_k})/i'] \ \ (i \ \text{index of} \ \pi_{2_j}) \\ \Gamma' = \Gamma[\mathcal{L}_{v_1} \leftarrow (\bigcup_{jk}\langle \pi_{2_j}, \phi'_{2_{jk}} \wedge \phi_{3_k}\rangle)] \\ \hline \Sigma, \Gamma \vdash v_1 = v_2 \oplus v_3 \ : \ \Gamma' \end{array}$$

Predop

$$\begin{array}{c} \Sigma \vdash v_1 : \mathcal{L}_{v_1}, v_2 : \mathcal{L}_{v_2}, v_3 : \mathcal{L}_{v_3} \\ \Gamma \vdash_j \mathcal{L}_{v_2} : \langle *\pi_{2_j}, \phi_{2_k}\rangle \ (\text{rename all index variables to fresh} \ f_2) \\ \Gamma \vdash_k \mathcal{L}_{v_3} : \langle *\pi_{3_k}, \phi_{3_k}\rangle \ (\text{rename all index variables to fresh} \ f_3) \\ \phi_{jk} = (\overline{\pi_{2_j}} \ predop \ \overline{\pi_{3_k}}) \wedge \phi_{2_j} \wedge \phi_{3_k} \\ \phi^{true}_{jk} = Eliminate(\exists f_2, f_3. \ \phi_{jk}) \\ \Gamma' = \Gamma[\mathcal{L}_{v_1} \leftarrow (\bigcup_{jk}\langle *1, \phi^{true}_{jk}\rangle \cup \langle *0, \neg\phi^{true}_{jk}\rangle)] \\ \hline \Sigma, \Gamma \vdash v_1 = v_2 \ predop \ v_3 : \Gamma' \end{array}$$

If Statement

$$\begin{array}{c} \Sigma \vdash v : \mathcal{L}_v \\ \Gamma \vdash \mathcal{L}_v : \{\langle *1, \phi_{true}\rangle, \langle *0, \phi_{false}\rangle\} \\ \Sigma, \Gamma \vdash S_1 : \Gamma'' \\ \Sigma, \Gamma \vdash S_2 : \Gamma'' \\ \Gamma_T = \Gamma' \wedge \phi_{true} \\ \Gamma_F = \Gamma'' \wedge \phi_{false} \\ \hline \Sigma, \Gamma \vdash if \ v \neq 0 \ then \ S_1 \ else \ S_2 : \Gamma_T \cup \Gamma_F \end{array}$$

While Loop

$$\begin{array}{c} \Gamma_P = Parametrize(\Gamma) \\ \Sigma \vdash v : \mathcal{L}_v \\ \Gamma_P \vdash \mathcal{L}_v : \{\langle *1, \phi_{true}\rangle, \langle *0, \phi_{false}\rangle\} \\ \Sigma, \Gamma_P \vdash S : \Gamma''' \quad \Gamma''' = \Gamma'' \wedge \phi_{true} \\ \Delta = \Gamma''' - \Gamma_P \quad \Delta_n = fix(\Delta) \\ \Delta_{gen} = Generalize(\Delta_n) \\ \Gamma_{final} = \Gamma \circ \Delta_{gen} \ (\text{Generalized Fluid Update}) \\ \hline \Sigma, \Gamma \vdash while \ v \neq 0 \ do \ S \ end : \Gamma_{final} \end{array}$$

Fig. 2. Rules describing the basic analysis

at offset v_3 of v_2's target, we select the element at offset v_3 by substituting i' with $i' - \pi_{3_k}$ in the constraint ϕ_{2_j}, which effectively increments the value of i' by π_{3_k}. Now, we need to determine the targets of those elements of π_{2_j} whose indices are consistent with $\phi'_{2_{jk}}$; hence, we compute $\phi_{t_{jl}} \downarrow_{\Im(\pi_{2_j})} \phi'_{2_{jk}}$ (recall Section 3) for each target $\pi_{t_{jl}}$ of π_{2_j}. The following example illustrates this rule.

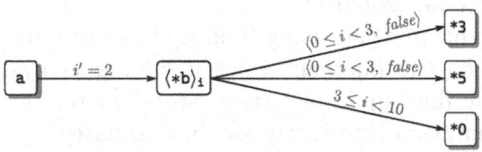

Fig. 3. Here, a points to the third element of an array of size 10, whose first three elements have the value 3 or 5, and the remaining elements are 0

Example 2. Consider performing t = a[1] on the symbolic heap abstraction shown in Figure 3. Here, $\mathcal{L}_{v_2}$ is the memory location labeled a, the only target π_{2_j} of $\mathcal{L}_{v_2}$ is $\langle *b\rangle_i$, and the only π_{3_k} is 1. The constraint $\phi'_{2_{jk}}$ is $U((i' = 2)[i'/i' - 1])$, which is $i = 3$. Thus, we need to determine the target(s) of the fourth element in array $\langle *\mathtt{b}\rangle_i$. There are three targets $\pi_{t_{jl}}$ of $\langle *\mathtt{b}\rangle_i$: $*3, *5, *0$; hence, we compute $\phi'_{t_{jkl}}$ once for each $\pi_{t_{jkl}}$. The only satisfiable edge under constraint $i = 3$ is the edge to $*0$ and we compute $Eliminate(\exists i.\ 3 \leq i < 10 \wedge i = 3)$, which is *true*. Thus, the value of $\mathtt{t}$ is guaranteed to be 0 after this statement.

The Array Store rule performs a fluid update on an abstract memory location associated with an array. In this rule, each $\pi_{2_k} \in \{\pi_{2_1} \dots \pi_{2_n}\}$ represents an array location, a subset of whose elements may be written to as a result of this store. Γ' represents the symbolic heap abstraction after removing the points-to edges from array elements that are written to by this store while preserving all other edges, and Γ''' represents all edges added by this store. Hence, Γ' and Γ''' are unioned to obtain the symbolic heap abstraction after the store. Note that Γ' preserves the existing targets of any access path $\pi \notin \{\pi_{2_1} \dots \pi_{2_n}\}$. The points-to targets of those elements of $\pi_{2_1}, \dots \pi_{2_n}$ that are not affected by this store are also preserved in Γ' while elements that are written to by the store are killed in Γ'. This is because elements that are updated by the store *must* satisfy $U(\phi_{2_k}[i'_k - \pi_{3_l}/i'_k]) \wedge \phi_{3_l}$ for some k, l such that the edge to π'_k is effectively killed for those elements updated by the store. On the other hand, elements that are *not* affected by the store are guaranteed not to satisfy $U(\phi_{2_k}[i'_k - \pi_{3_l}/i'_k]) \wedge \phi_{3_l}$ for any k, l, i.e., $\neg \bigvee_{kl}(U(\phi_{2_k}[i'_k - \pi_{3_l}/i'_k]) \wedge \phi_{3_l}) = false$, and the existing edge to π'_k is therefore preserved. Note that negation is only used in the Fluid Update rule; the soundness of negation, and therefore the correctness of fluid updates, relies on using bracketing constraints.

Example 3. Consider the effect of the following store instructions
$$\mathtt{a[k]} = 7; \quad \mathtt{a[m]} = 3;$$
on Figure 3. Suppose $\mathtt{k}$ and $\mathtt{m}$ are symbolic, i.e., their values are unknown. When processing the statement $\mathtt{a[k]} = 7$, the only location stored into, i.e., π_{2_k}, is $\langle *\mathtt{b}\rangle_i$. The only π_{3_l} is $\mathtt{k}$ under *true*, and the only π_{1_j} is $*7$ under *true*. The elements of $\langle *\mathtt{b}\rangle_i$ updated by the store are determined from $U((i' = 2)[i' - \mathtt{k}/i']) = (i = \mathtt{k}+2)$. Thus, a new edge is added from $\langle *\mathtt{b}\rangle_i$ to $*7$ under $i = \mathtt{k}+2$ but all outgoing edges from $\langle *\mathtt{b}\rangle_i$ are preserved under the constraint $i \neq \mathtt{k}+2$. Thus, after this statement, the edge from $\langle *\mathtt{b}\rangle_i$ to $*3$ and $*5$ are qualified by the constraint $\langle 0 \leq i < 3 \wedge i \neq \mathtt{k}+2,\ false\rangle$, and the edge to $*0$ is qualified by $3 \leq i < 10 \wedge i \neq \mathtt{k}+2$. The instruction $\mathtt{a[m]} = 3$ is processed similarly; Figure 4 shows the resulting

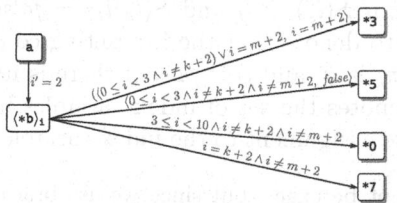

Fig. 4. Graph after processing the statements in Example 3

Fig. 5. Colored rectangles illustrates the partitions in Example 3; equations on the left describe the ordering between variables

symbolic heap abstraction after these store instructions. Note that if $k = m$, the graph correctly reflects a[k] must be 3. This is because if $k = m$, the constraint on the edge from $\langle *b \rangle_i$ to $*7$ is unsatisfiable. Since the only other feasible edge under the constraint $i = k + 2$ is the one to $*3$, $k = m$ implies a[k] must be 3.

As Example 3 illustrates, fluid updates do not construct explicit partitions of the heap when different symbolic values are used to store into an array. Instead, all "partitions" are implicitly encoded in the constraints, and while the constraint solver may eventually need to analyze all of the cases, in many cases it will not because a query is more easily shown satisfiable or unsatisfiable for other reasons. As a comparison, in Example 3, approaches that eagerly construct explicit partitions may be forced to enumerate all partitions created due to stores using symbolic indices. Figure 5 shows that eight different heap configurations arise after performing the updates in Example 3. In fact, only one more store using a symbolic index could create over 50 different heap configurations.

In the Pointer Arithmetic rule, the index variable i' is replaced by $i' - \pi_{3_k}$ in the index constraint ϕ_{2_j}, effectively incrementing the value of i' by v_3. We also discuss the Predop rule, since some complications arise when array elements are used in predicates. In this rule, we make use of an operation $\overline{\pi}$ which converts an access path to a term in the constraint language:

$$\overline{\pi_R} = \pi_R \quad \text{if } \pi_R \in \{c, \mathcal{L}_v, alloc_{id}\} \qquad \overline{*\pi} = deref(\overline{\pi})$$
$$\overline{\langle \pi \rangle_i} = select(\overline{\pi}, i) \qquad\qquad\qquad \overline{\pi_1 \ intop \ \pi_2} = \overline{\pi_1} \ intop \ \overline{\pi_2}$$

In this rule, notice that index variables used in the targets of $\mathcal{L}_{v_2}$ and $\mathcal{L}_{v_3}$ are first renamed to fresh variables f_2 and f_3 to avoid naming conflicts and are then existentially quantified and eliminated similar to computing $\phi_1 \downarrow_I \phi_2$. The renaming of index variables is necessary since naming conflicts arise when $\langle *\pi_{2_j}, \phi_{2_j} \rangle$ and $\langle *\pi_{3_k}, \phi_{3_k} \rangle$ refer to different elements of the same array.[2]

In the If Statement rule, observe that the constraint under which $v \neq 0$ evaluates to true (resp. false) is conjoined with all the edge constraints in Γ' (resp. Γ''); hence, the analysis is path-sensitive. We defer discussion of the While Loop rule until Section 5.

4.1   Soundness of the Memory Abstraction

We now state the soundness theorem for our memory abstraction. For a concrete store S, we use the notation $S(l_s, l_t) = true$ if $S(l_s) = l_t$ and $S(l_s, l_t) = false$ otherwise. Similarly, we write $\Gamma(\pi_s, \pi_t) = \phi$ to denote that the bracketing constraint associated with the edge from π_s to π_t is ϕ, and ϕ is $false$ if there is no edge between π_s and π_t. Recall that $\mathfrak{I}(\pi)$ denotes the set of index variables in π, and we write $\sigma_{\mathfrak{I}(\pi)}$ to denote some concrete assignment to the index variables

---

[2] Quantifier elimination performed here may not be exact; but since we use bracketing constraints, we compute quantifier-free over- and underapproximations. For instance, [11] presents a technique for computing covers of existentially quantified formulas in combined theories involving uninterpreted functions. Another alternative is to allow quantification in our constraint language.

in $\Im(n)$; $\sigma'_{\Im(\pi)}$ is an assignment to $\Im(\pi)$ with all index variables primed. The notation $\sigma(\phi)$ applies substitution σ to ϕ. Finally, we use a function $eval^\star(\phi, E, S)$ for $\star \in \{+, -\}$ which evaluates the truth value of the necessary and sufficient conditions of constraint ϕ for some concrete environment E and concrete store S; this function is precisely defined in [30].

Definition 2 (Agreement). We say a concrete environment and concrete store (E, S) *agrees with* abstract environment and abstract store (Σ, Γ) (written $(E, S) \sim (\Sigma, \Gamma)$) if and only if the following conditions hold:

1. E and Σ have the same domain
2. If $S(l_s, l_t) = b$ and $\Gamma(\pi_s, \pi_t) = \langle \phi^+, \phi^- \rangle$, then for all substitutions $\sigma_{\Im(\pi_s)}$, $\sigma'_{\Im(\pi_t)}$ such that $l_s \in \gamma_c(E, S, \pi_s, \sigma_{\Im(\pi_s)})$ and $l_t \in \gamma_c(E, S, \pi_t, \sigma'_{\Im(\pi_t)})$, we have:

$$eval^-(\sigma'(\sigma(\phi^-)), E, S) \Rightarrow b \Rightarrow eval^+(\sigma'(\sigma(\phi^+)), E, S)$$

Theorem 1 (Soundness). Let P be any program. If $(E, S) \sim (\Sigma, \Gamma)$, then

$$E, S \vdash P : S' \Rightarrow (\Sigma, \Gamma \vdash P : \Gamma' \wedge (E, S') \sim (\Sigma, \Gamma'))$$

We sketch the proof of Theorem 1 in the extended version [30].

5 Fluid Updates in Loops

In loop-free code, a store modifies one array element, but stores inside a loop often update many elements. In this section, we describe a technique to over- and underapproximate the set of concrete elements updated in loops. The main idea of our approach is to analyze the loop body and perform a fixed-point computation parametric over an *iteration counter*. Once a fixed-point is reached, we use quantifier elimination to infer elements that may and must be modified by the loop.[3]

5.1 Parametrizing the Symbolic Heap Abstraction

When analyzing loops, our analysis first identifies the set of scalars modified by the loop; we call such values *loop-dependent* scalars. We then infer equalities relating each loop-dependent scalar to the unique iteration counter k for that loop. The iteration counter k is assumed to be initialized to 0 at loop entry and is incremented by one along the back edge of the loop. We say that a loop-dependent value i is *linear* with respect to the loop if $i - i_0 = c * k$ for some constant $c \neq 0$. We compute a set of equalities relating loop-dependent scalars to the iteration counter using standard linear invariant generation techniques [12, 13]. At loop entry, we use these linear equalities to modify Γ as follows:

---

[3] In this section, we assume no pointer arithmetic occurs in loops; our implementation, however, does not make this restriction.

- Let π be a linear loop-dependent scalar with the linear relation $\pi = \pi_0 + c * k$, and let $\langle *\pi_t, c_t \rangle \in \Gamma(\pi)$. Then, replace π_t by $\pi_t + c * k$.
- Let π be a loop-dependent value not linear in k. Then, $\Gamma(\pi) \leftarrow \{\langle \top, true \rangle\}$.

Thus, all loop-dependent scalars are expressed in terms of their value at iteration k or $\top$; analysis of the loop body proceeds as described in Section 4.

Example 4. Consider the `send_packets` function from Section 1. Here, we infer the equality $j = j_0 + 2k$, and Γ initially contains an edge from j to $*(j_0 + 2k)$.

5.2   Fixed-Point Computation

Next, we perform a fixed-point computation (parametric on k) over the loop's net effect on the symbolic heap abstraction. This is necessary because there may be loop carried dependencies through heap reads and writes. We define the net effect of the loop on the symbolic heap abstraction during some iteration k as the *effect set*:

Definition 3. (Effect Set Δ) Let Γ' be a symbolic heap obtained by performing fluid updates on Γ. Let $\Delta = \Gamma' - \Gamma$ be the set of edges such that if ϕ qualifies edge e in Γ and ϕ' qualifies e in Γ', then Δ includes e under constraint $\phi' \wedge \neg\phi$ (where $\phi = false$ if $e \notin \Gamma$). We call Δ the *effect set* of Γ' with respect to Γ.

Example 5. Figure 6 shows the effect set of the loop in `send_packets` after analyzing its body once. (Edges with *false* constraints are not shown.) Note that the constraints qualifying edges in this figure are parametric over k.

We define $\Gamma \circ \Delta$ as the generalized fluid update that applies Δ to Γ:

Definition 4. ($\Gamma \circ \Delta$) Let π be a location in Γ and let S_π denote the edges in Δ whose source is π. Let $\delta(S_\pi)$ be the disjunction of constraints qualifying edges in S_π, and let I be the set of index variables used in the target locations in S_π but not the source. Let $Update(\pi) = Eliminate(\exists I.\delta(S_\pi))$. Then, for each $\pi \in \Gamma$:

$$(\Gamma \circ \Delta)[\pi] = (\Gamma(\pi) \wedge \neg Update(\pi)) \cup S_\pi$$

The above definition is a straightforward generalization of the fluid update operation given in the Store rule of Figure 2. Instead of processing a single store, it reflects the overall effect on Γ of a set of updates defined by Δ. The fixed-point computation is performed on Δ. We denote an edge from location π_s to π_t qualified by constraint ϕ as $\langle \pi_s, \pi_t \rangle \backslash \phi$. Since we compute a least fixed point, $\langle \pi_s, \pi_t \rangle \backslash \langle false, true \rangle \in \perp$ for all legal combinations (i.e., obeying type restrictions)

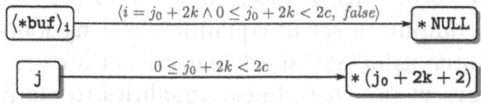

Fig. 6. The effect set after analyzing the loop body once in function `send_packets`

of all $\langle \pi_s, \pi_t \rangle$ pairs. Note that the edge constraints in $\bot$ are the inconsistent bounds $\langle false, true \rangle$ representing the strongest over- and underapproximations. We define a $\sqcup$ and $\sqsubseteq$ on effect sets as follows:

$$\langle \pi_s, \pi_t \rangle \backslash \langle (\phi_{nc1} \vee \phi_{nc2}), (\phi_{sc1} \wedge \phi_{sc2}) \rangle \in \Delta_1 \sqcup \Delta_2 \qquad \Delta_1 \sqsubseteq \Delta_2$$
$$\Longleftrightarrow \qquad\qquad\qquad\qquad\qquad\qquad \Longleftrightarrow$$

$$(\langle \pi_s, \pi_t \rangle \backslash \langle \phi_{nc1}, \phi_{sc1} \rangle \in \Delta_1 \wedge \qquad ((\phi_{nc1} \Rightarrow \phi_{nc2} \wedge \phi_{sc2} \Rightarrow \phi_{sc1})$$
$$\langle \pi_s, \pi_t \rangle \backslash \langle \phi_{nc2}, \phi_{sc2} \rangle \in \Delta_2) \qquad \forall \langle \pi_s, \pi_t \rangle \backslash \langle \phi_{nc1}, \phi_{sc1} \rangle \in \Delta_1 \wedge$$
$$\forall \langle \pi_s, \pi_t \rangle \backslash \langle \phi_{nc2}, \phi_{sc2} \rangle \in \Delta_2)$$

Let Γ_0 be the initial symbolic heap abstraction before the loop. We compute Γ^n_{entry} representing the symbolic heap on entry to the n'th iteration of the loop:

$$\Gamma^n_{entry} = \begin{cases} \Gamma_0 & if \quad n = 1 \\ \Gamma_0 \circ (\Delta_{n-1}[k - 1/k]) & if \quad n > 1 \end{cases}$$

Γ^n_{exit} is obtained by analyzing the body of the loop using Γ^n_{entry} at the entry point of the loop. In the definition of Γ^n_{entry}, the substitution $[k - 1/k]$ normalizes the effect set with respect to the iteration counter so that values of loop-dependent scalars always remain in terms of their value at iteration k. We define Δ_n representing the total effect of the loop in n iterations as follows:

$$\Delta_n = \begin{cases} \bot & if \, n = 0 \\ (\Gamma^n_{exit} - \Gamma^n_{entry}) \sqcup \Delta_{n-1} & if \, n > 0 \end{cases}$$

First, observe that $\Delta_{n-1} \sqsubseteq \Delta_n$ by construction (monotonicity). Second, observe the analysis cannot create an infinite number of abstract locations because (i) arrays are represented as indexed locations, (ii) pointers can be dereferenced only as many times as their types permit, (iii) all allocations are named by their allocation site, and (iv) scalars are represented in terms of their linear relation to k. However, our constraint domain does not have finite ascending chains, hence, we define a widening operator on bracketing constraints (although widening was never required in our experiments). Let β denote the unshared literals between any constraint ϕ_1 and ϕ_2. Then, we widen bracketing constraints as follows:

$$\phi_1 \triangledown \phi_2 = \langle (\lceil \phi_1 \rceil \vee \lceil \phi_2 \rceil)[true/\beta] \vee (\lceil \phi_1 \rceil \vee \lceil \phi_2 \rceil)[false/\beta],$$
$$(\lfloor \phi_1 \rfloor \wedge \lfloor \phi_2 \rfloor)[true/\beta] \wedge (\lfloor \phi_1 \rfloor \wedge \lfloor \phi_2 \rfloor)[false/\beta] \rangle$$

Example 6. The effect set obtained in Example 5 does not change in the second iteration; therefore the fixed-point computation terminates after two iterations.

5.3 Generalization

In this section, we describe how to *generalize* the final effect set after a fixed-point is reached. This last step allows the analysis to extrapolate from the elements modified in the k'th iteration to the set of elements modified across all iterations and is based on existential quantifier elimination.

Definition 5. (Generalizable Location) We say a location identified by π is *generalizable* in a loop if (i) π is an array, (ii) if π_i is used as an index in a store to π, then π_i must be a linear function of the iteration counter, and (iii) if two distinct indices π_i and π_j may be used to store into π, then either only π_i, or only π_j (or neither) is used to index π across all iterations.

Intuitively, if a location π is generalizable, then all writes to π at different iterations of the loop must refer to distinct concrete elements. Clearly, if π is not an array, different iterations of the loop cannot refer to distinct concrete elements. If an index used to store into π is not a linear function of k, then the loop may update the same concrete element in different iterations. Furthermore, if two values that do not have the same relation with respect to k are used to store into π, then they may update the same element in different iterations.

In order to generalize the effect set, we make use of a variable N unique for each loop that represents the number of times the loop body executes. If the value of N can be determined precisely, we use this exact value instead of introducing N. For instance, if a loop increments i by 1 until $i \geq size$, then it is easy to determine that $N = size - i_0$, assuming the loop executes at least once.[4] Finally, we generalize the effect set as follows:

- If an edge qualified by ϕ has a generalizable source whose target does not mention k, the generalized constraint is $\phi' = Eliminate(\exists k. (\phi \wedge 0 \leq k < N))$.
- If an edge qualified by ϕ does not have a generalizable source, the generalized constraint is $\phi' = Eliminate\langle \exists k. \phi \wedge 0 \leq k < N, \forall k. 0 \leq k < N \Rightarrow \phi \rangle$[5].
- If π is a loop-dependent scalar, then $\Delta[\pi] \leftarrow \Delta[\pi][N/k]$.

We now briefly explain these generalization rules. If the source of an edge is generalizable, for each iteration of the loop, there exists a corresponding concrete element of the array that is updated during this iteration; thus, k is existentially quantified in both the over- and underapproximation. The constraint after the existential quantifier elimination specifies the set of concrete elements updated by the loop. If the source is not generalizable, it is unsafe to existentially quantify k in the underapproximation since the same concrete element may be overwritten in future iterations. One way to obtain an underapproximation is to universally quantify k because if the update happens in all iterations, then the update must happen after the loop terminates. According to the last rule, loop-dependent scalar values are assigned to their value on termination. Once the effect set is generalized, we apply it to Γ_0 to obtain the final symbolic heap abstraction after the loop.

Example 7. Consider the effect set given in Figure 6. In the send_packets function, $\langle *\texttt{buf} \rangle_i$ is generalizable since j is linear in k and no other value is used to index $\langle *\texttt{buf} \rangle_i$. Furthermore, if the loop executes, it executes exactly c times; thus $N = c$. To generalize the edge from $\langle *\texttt{buf} \rangle_i$ to *NULL, we perform quantifier elimination on $\langle \exists k.i = j_0 + 2k \wedge 0 \leq j_0 + 2k < 2c \wedge 0 \leq k < c, false \rangle$, which yields $\langle j_0 \leq i \wedge i < j_0 + 2c \wedge (i - j_0)\%2 = 0, false \rangle$. Since j_0 is 0 at loop entry, after applying the generalized effect set to Γ_0, we obtain the graph from Figure 1.

---

[4] Even though it is often not possible to determine the exact value of N, our analysis utilizes the constraint $(\forall k.0 \leq k < N \Rightarrow \neg\phi_{term}(k)) \wedge \phi_{term}(N)$ stating that the termination condition ϕ_{term} does not hold on iterations before N but holds at the N'th iteration. Our analysis takes this "background axiom" into account when determining satisfiability and validity.

[5] We can eliminate a universally quantified variable k from $\forall k.\phi$ by eliminating existentially quantified k in the formula $\neg\exists k.\neg\phi$.

6   Implementation and Extensions

We have implemented the ideas presented in this paper in the Compass program verification framework for analyzing C programs. For solving constraints, Compass utilizes a custom SMT solver called Mistral [14], which also provides support for simplifying constraints. Compass does not assume type safety and handles casts soundly using a technique based on physical subtyping [15]. Compass supports most features of the C language, including structs, unions, multi-dimensional arrays, dynamic memory allocation, and pointer arithmetic. To check buffer overruns, Compass also tracks buffer and allocation sizes. For inter-procedural analysis, Compass performs a path- and context-sensitive summary-based analysis. Loop bodies are analyzed in isolation before the function or loop in which they are defined; thus techniques from Section 5 extend to nested loops.

While the language defined in Section 2 only allows loops with a single exit point, techniques described in this paper can be extended to loops with multiple break points by introducing different iteration counters for each backedge, similar to the technique used in [16] for complexity analysis.

Compass allows checking arbitrary assertions using a static_assert(...) primitive, which can be either manually or automatically inserted (e.g., for memory safety properties). The static_assert primitive also allows for checking quantified properties, such as "all elements of arrays a and b are equal" by writing:

```
static_assert(buffer_size(b) == buffer_size(a));
for(i=0; i<buffer_size(a); i++) static_assert(a[i] == b[i]);
```

7   Experiments

7.1   Case Study on Example Benchmarks

To demonstrate the expressiveness of our technique, we evaluate it on 28 challenging array benchmarks available at http://www.stanford.edu/~tdillig/array.tar.gz and shown in Figure 7. The functions init and init_noncost initialize all elements of an array to a constant and an iteration-dependent value respectively. init_partial initializes part of the array, and init_even initializes even positions. 2D_array_init initializes a 2-dimensional array using a nested loop. The programs labeled _buggy exhibit subtle bugs, such as off-by-one errors. Various versions of copy copy all, some, or odd elements of an array to another array. reverse reverses elements, while swap (shown in Figure 8) swaps the contents of two arrays. double_swap invokes swap twice and checks that both arrays are back in their initial state. strcpy, strlen, and memcpy implement the functionality of the standard C library functions and assert their correctness. find (resp. find_first_nonnull) looks for a specified (resp. non-null) element and returns its index (or -1 if element is not found). append appends the contents of one array to another, and merge_interleave interleaves odd and even-numbered elements of two arrays into a result array. The function alloc_fixed_size initializes all elements of a double array to a freshly allocated array of fixed size, and then checks that buffer

Program	Time	Memory	#Sat queries	Solve time
init	0.01s	< 1 MB	172	0s
init_nonconst	0.02s	< 1 MB	184	0.01s
init_partial	0.01s	< 1MB	166	0.01s
init_partial_buggy	0.02s	< 1 MB	168	0s
init_even	0.04s	< 1 MB	146	0.04s
init_even_buggy	0.04s	< 1 MB	166	0.03s
2D_array_init	0.04s	< 1 MB	311	0.04s
copy	0.01s	< 1 MB	209	0.01s
copy_partial	0.01s	< 1 MB	220	0.01s
copy_odd	0.04s	< 1 MB	243	0.02s
copy_odd_buggy	0.05s	< 1 MB	246	0.05s
reverse	0.03s	< 1 MB	273	0.01s
reverse_buggy	0.04s	< 1 MB	281	0.02s
swap	0.12s	2 MB	590	0.11s
swap_buggy	0.11s	2 MB	557	0.06s
double_swap	0.16s	2 MB	601	0.1s
strcpy	0.07s	< 1 MB	355	0.04s
strlen	0.02s	< 1 MB	165	0.01s
strlen_buggy	0.01s	< 1 MB	89	0.01s
memcpy	0.04s	< 1 MB	225	0.04s
find	0.02s	< 1 MB	119	0.02s
find_first_nonnull	0.02s	< 1 MB	183	0.02s
append	0.02s	< 1 MB	183	0.01s
merge_interleave	0.09s	< 1 MB	296	0.07s
merge_interleave _buggy	0.11s	< 1 MB	305	0.09s
alloc_fixed_size	0.02s	< 1 MB	176	0.02s
alloc_fixed_size_buggy	0.02s	< 1 MB	172	0.02s
alloc_nonfixed_size	0.03s	< 1 MB	214	0.02

Fig. 7. Case Study

```
void swap(int* a, int* b, int size) {
  for(int i=0; i<size; i++) {
    int t = a[i]; a[i] = b[i]; b[i] = t; }
}
void check_swap(int size, int* a, int* b) {
  int* a_copy = malloc(sizeof(int)*size);
  int* b_copy = malloc(sizeof(int)*size);
  for(int i=0; i<size; i++)  a_copy[i] = a[i];
  for(int i=0; i<size; i++)  b_copy[i] = b[i];
  swap(a, b, size);
  for(i=0; i<size; i++) {
    static_assert(a[i] == b_copy[i]);
    static_assert(b[i] == a_copy[i]);
  }
  free(a_copy); free(b_copy);
}
```

Fig. 8. Swap Function from Figure 7. The static assertions check that all elements of a and b are indeed swapped after the call to the swap function. Compass verifies these assertions automatically in 0.12 seconds.

accesses to the element arrays are safe. The function alloc_nonfixed_size initializes elements of the double array a to freshly allocated arrays of different size, encoded by the elements of another array b and checks that accessing indices $[0, b[i] - 1]]$ of array a[i] is safe. Compass can automatically verify the full functional correctness of all of the correct programs without any annotations and reports all errors present in buggy programs. To check functional correctness, we add static assertions as described in Section 6 and as shown in Figure 8.

Figure 7 reports for each program the total running time, memory usage (including the constraint solver), number of queries to the SMT solver, and constraint solving time. All experiments were performed on a 2.66 GHz Xeon workstation. We believe these experiments demonstrate that Compass reasons precisely and efficiently about array contents despite being fully automatic. As a comparison, while Compass takes 0.01 seconds to verify the full correctness of copy, the approach described in [4] reports a running time of 338.1 seconds, and the counterexample-guided abstraction refinement based approach described in [17] takes 3.65 seconds. Furthermore, our technique is naturally able to verify the correctness of programs that manipulate non-contiguous array elements (e.g., copy_odd), as well as programs that require reasoning about arrays inside other arrays (e.g., alloc_nonfixed_size). Figure 7 also shows that the analysis is memory efficient since none of the programs require more than 2 MB. We believe this to be the case because fluid updates do not create explicit partitions.

Observe that the choice of benchmarks in Figure 7 sheds light on both what our technique is good at and what it is *not* meant for. In particular, notice these benchmarks do not include sorting routines. While sorting is an interesting problem for invariant generation techniques, the focus of this work is improving static analysis of updates to aggregate data structures, such as arrays, through fluid

Program	Lines	Total Time	Memory	#Sat queries	Solve Time
hostname	304	0.13s	5 MB	1533	0.12s
chroot	371	0.13s	3 MB	1821	0.10s
rmdir	483	1.05s	12 MB	3401	1.02s
su	1047	1.86s	32 MB	6088	1.69s
mv	1151	0.70s	21 MB	7427	0.68s
Total	3356	3.87s	73 MB	20330	3.61

Fig. 9. Experimental results on Unix Coreutils applications

updates. As shown in Section 5, fluid updates can be combined with invariant generation techniques to analyze loops, but we do not claim that this particular invariant generation approach is the best possible. We leave as future work the combination of fluid updates and more powerful invariant generation techniques.

7.2   Checking Memory Safety on Unix Coreutils Applications

To evaluate the usefulness of our technique on real programs, we also check for memory safety errors on five Unix Coreutils applications [20] that manipulate arrays and pointers in complex ways. In particular, we verify the safety of buffer accesses (both buffer overruns and underruns) and pointer dereferences. However, since Compass treats integers as mathematical integers, the soundness of the buffer analysis assumes lack of integer overflow errors, which can be verified by a separate analysis. In the experiments, Compass reports zero false positives, only requiring two annotations describing inputs to main: assume(buffer_size(argv) == argc) and assume(argv! = NULL)). Compass is even able to discharge some arbitrary assertions inserted by the original programmers. Some of the buffer accesses that Compass can discharge rely on complex dependencies that are difficult even for experienced programmers to track; an interesting example is given in [30].

The chosen benchmarks are challenging for static analysis tools for multiple reasons: First, these applications heavily use arrays and string buffers, making them difficult for techniques that do not track array contents. Second, they heavily rely on path conditions and correlations between scalars used to index buffers. Finally, the behavior of these applications depends on environment choice, such as user input. Our technique is powerful enough to deal with these challenges because it is capable of reasoning about array elements, is path-sensitive, and uses bracketing constraints to capture uncertainty. To give the reader some idea about the importance of these components, 85.4% of the assertions fail if array contents are smashed and 98.2% fail if path-sensitivity is disabled.

As Figure 9 illustrates, Compass is able to analyze all applications in under 2 seconds, and the maximum memory used both for the program verification and constraint solving combined is less than 35 MB. We believe these running times and memory requirements demonstrate that the current state of Compass is useful and practical for verifying memory safety in real modest-sized C applications manipulating arrays, pointers, and scalars in complex ways.

8   Related Work

Reasoning about unbounded data structures has a long history. Jones et al. first propose *summary nodes* to finitely represent lists in LISP [21], and [1] extends this work to languages with updates and introduces strong and weak updates. Representation of access paths qualified by indices is first introduced in Deutsch [22], which uses a combination of *symbolic access paths* and numeric abstract domains to represent may-alias pairs for recursive data structures. This technique does not address arrays, and since it does not reason about updates, negation is not a consideration. Deutsch's technique does not allow disjunctive constraints, is not path-sensitive, and does not address underapproximations.

The most basic technique for reasoning about array contents is *array smashing*, which represents all elements with one summary node and only allows weak updates [2]. Gopan et al. propose a 3-valued logic based framework to discover relationships about values of array elements [4]. This technique isolates individual elements to perform strong updates and places elements that share a common property into a partition (usually a contiguous range), and relevant partitions are heuristically inferred. In contrast, our approach does not need to distinguish between strong and weak updates or concretize individual elements; it can also naturally express invariants about non-contiguous array elements. Furthermore, our approach obviates the need for explicit partitioning, and effectively delays decisions about partitions until constraint solving. While many factors contribute to the overall performance of program analysis systems, we believe our tool's significantly better performance over [4] is largely due to avoiding the construction of explicit partitions. Jhala and McMillan propose a technique similar to [4] for reasoning about arrays, but their technique is based on counterexample guided abstraction refinement and interpolation [17]. This approach also only reasons about contiguous ranges and constructs explicit partitions. Furthermore, the predicates used in the abstraction belong to a finite language to guarantee convergence.

Many techniques have been proposed for generating invariants about elements of unbounded data structures [18, 19, 23–26]. Some of these techniques can reason about complex data invariants, such as sortedness, which is orthogonal to the ability to perform fluid updates. Unlike these approaches whose goal is to discover complex invariants about array elements, our goal is to design an expressive pointer and value analysis that unifies reasoning about pointers, scalars, and arrays. However, we believe these techniques can be gainfully combined.

Concepts similar to the *iteration counter* from Section 5 have been previously proposed. For example, Gulwani et al. [16] use an iteration counter for performing complexity analysis. The invariant generation technique described in [19] also uses a combination of an iteration counter combined with quantifier elimination.

Our technique uses bracketing constraints to represent both over- and underapproximations to naturally handle imprecision and uncertainty. Furthermore, bracketing constraints allow for a sound negation operation in the presence of approximations. The idea of over- and underapproximations has been proposed previously in the context of abstract interpretation by Schmidt [27]; however, the techniques presented there are not concerned with negation. In this paper, we share the goal of gracefully handling imprecision when analyzing unbounded data structures with [28], which presents a compositional shape analysis based on separation logic. In contrast to [28] which focuses exclusively on recursive pointer data structures, such as linked lists, this paper focuses on arrays. We believe our approach can be extended to at least some useful recursive data structures, such as lists, and we leave this extension as future work.

References

1. Chase, D.R., Wegman, M., Zadeck, F.K.: Analysis of pointers and structures. In: PLDI, pp. 296–310. ACM, New York (1990)
2. Blanchet, B., Cousot, P., Cousot, R., Feret, J., Mauborgne, L., Miné, A., Monniaux, D., Rival, X.: Design and implementation of a special-purpose static program analyzer for safety-critical real-time embedded software (2002)
3. Reps, T.W., Sagiv, S., Wilhelm, R.: Static program analysis via 3-valued logic. In: Alur, R., Peled, D.A. (eds.) CAV 2004. LNCS, vol. 3114, pp. 15–30. Springer, Heidelberg (2004)
4. Gopan, D., Reps, T., Sagiv, M.: A framework for numeric analysis of array operations. In: POPL, pp. 338–350. ACM, New York (2005)
5. Aiken, A., Bugrara, S., Dillig, I., Dillig, T., Hackett, B., Hawkins, P.: An overview of the saturn project. In: PASTE, pp. 43–48. ACM, New York (2007)
6. Ball, T., Rajamani, S.: The slam project: debugging system software via static analysis. In: POPL, NY, USA, pp. 1–3 (2002)
7. Lee, S., Cho, D.: Packet-scheduling algorithm based on priority of separate buffers for unicast and multicast services. Electronics Letters 39(2), 259–260 (2003)
8. Nguyen, K., Nguyen, T., Cheung, S.: P2p streaming with hierarchical network coding (July 2007)
9. Landi, W., Ryder, B.G.: A safe approximate algorithm for interprocedural aliasing. SIGPLAN Not. 27(7), 235–248 (1992)
10. Cooper, D.: Theorem proving in arithmetic without multiplication. Machine Intelligence 7, 91–100 (1972)
11. Gulwani, S., Musuvathi, M.: Cover algorithms. In: Drossopoulou, S. (ed.) ESOP 2008. LNCS, vol. 4960, pp. 193–207. Springer, Heidelberg (2008)
12. Karr, M.: Affine relationships among variables of a program. A.I., 133–151 (1976)
13. Cousot, P., Halbwachs, N.: Automatic discovery of linear restraints among variables of a program. In: POPL, pp. 84–96. ACM, New York (1978)
14. Dillig, I., Dillig, T., Aiken, A.: Cuts from proofs: A complete and practical technique for solving linear inequalities over integers. In: Bouajjani, A., Maler, O. (eds.) CAV 2009. LNCS, vol. 5643, pp. 233–247. Springer, Heidelberg (2009)
15. Chandra, S., Reps, T.: Physical type checking for c. SIGSOFT 24(5), 66–75 (1999)
16. Gulwani, S., Mehra, K., Chilimbi, T.: SPEED: precise and efficient static estimation of program computational complexity. In: POPL, pp. 127–139 (2009)
17. Jhala, R., Mcmillan, K.L.: Array abstractions from proofs. In: Damm, W., Hermanns, H. (eds.) CAV 2007. LNCS, vol. 4590, pp. 193–206. Springer, Heidelberg (2007)
18. Halbwachs, N., Péron, M.: Discovering properties about arrays in simple programs. In: PLDI, pp. 339–348. ACM, New York (2008)

19. Kovacs, L., Voronkov, A.: Finding loop invariants for programs over arrays using a theorem prover. In: Chechik, M., Wirsing, M. (eds.) FASE 2009. LNCS, vol. 5503, pp. 470–485. Springer, Heidelberg (2009)
20. http://www.gnu.org/software/coreutils/ Unix coreutils
21. Jones, N., Muchnick, S.: Flow analysis and optimization of LISP-like structures. In: POPL, pp. 244–256. ACM, New York (1979)
22. Deutsch, A.: Interprocedural may-alias analysis for pointers: Beyond k-limiting. In: PLDI, pp. 230–241. ACM, New York (1994)
23. Allamigeon, X.: Non-disjunctive numerical domain for array predicate abstraction. In: Drossopoulou, S. (ed.) ESOP 2008. LNCS, vol. 4960, pp. 163–177. Springer, Heidelberg (2008)
24. Gulwani, S., McCloskey, B., Tiwari, A.: Lifting abstract interpreters to quantified logical domains. In: POPL, pp. 235–246. ACM, New York (2008)
25. Seghir, M., Podelski, A., Wies, T.: Abstraction Refinement for Quantified Array Assertions. In: Palsberg, J., Su, Z. (eds.) SAS 2009. LNCS, vol. 5673, pp. 3–18. Springer, Heidelberg (2009)
26. Flanagan, C., Qadeer, S.: Predicate abstraction for software verification. In: POPL, pp. 191–202. ACM, New York (2002)
27. Schmidt, D.A.: A calculus of logical relations for over- and underapproximating static analyses. Sci. Comput. Program. 64(1), 29–53 (2007)
28. Calcagno, C., Distefano, D., O'Hearn, P., Yang, H.: Compositional shape analysis by means of bi-abduction. In: POPL, pp. 289–300. ACM, New York (2009)
29. Cousot, P.: Verification by abstract interpretation. In: Dershowitz, N. (ed.) Verification: Theory and Practice. LNCS, vol. 2772, pp. 243–268. Springer, Heidelberg (2004)
30. Dillig, I., Dillig, T., Aiken, A.: Fluid updates: Beyond strong vs. weak updates (extended version), http://www.stanford.edu/~isil/esop-extended.pdf

Parameterized Memory Models and Concurrent Separation Logic

Rodrigo Ferreira[1], Xinyu Feng[2], and Zhong Shao[1]

[1] Yale University
{rodrigo.ferreira,zhong.shao}@yale.edu
[2] Toyota Technological Institute at Chicago
feng@ttic.edu

Abstract. In this paper, we formalize relaxed memory models by giving a parameterized operational semantics to a concurrent programming language. Behaviors of a program under a relaxed memory model are defined as behaviors of a set of *related* programs under the *sequentially consistent model*. This semantics is parameterized in the sense that different memory models can be obtained by using different relations between programs. We present one particular relation that is weaker than many memory models and accounts for the majority of sequential optimizations. We then show that the derived semantics has the DRF-guarantee, using a notion of race-freedom captured by an operational grainless semantics. Our grainless semantics bridges concurrent separation logic (CSL) and relaxed memory models naturally, which allows us to finally prove the folklore theorem that CSL is sound with relaxed memory models.

1 Introduction

For many years, optimizations of sequential code — by both compilers and architectures — have been the major source of performance improvement for computing systems. However, they were designed to preserve only the sequential semantics of the code. When placed in a concurrent context, many of them violate the so-called sequential consistency [19], which requires that the instructions in each thread be executed following the program order.

A classic example to demonstrate this problem is Dekker's mutual exclusion algorithm [12] as shown below:

Initially $[x] = [y] = 0$ and $x \neq y$

$[x] := 1;$		$[y] := 1;$
$v_1 := [y];$	$\parallel$	$v_2 := [x];$
if $v_1 = 0$ **then** *critical section*		**if** $v_2 = 0$ **then** *critical section*

where $[e]$ refers to the memory cell at the location e. Its correctness in the sequentially consistent memory model is ensured by the invariant that we would never have $v_1 = v_2 = 0$ when the conditional statements are reached. However, memory models in reality often relax the ordering of memory accesses and their

A.D. Gordon (Ed.): ESOP 2010, LNCS 6012, pp. 267–286, 2010.

visibility to other threads to create room for optimizations. Many of them allow reordering of the first two statements in each thread above, thus breaking the invariant. Other synchronization algorithms are susceptible to failure in a similar fashion, which is a well-known problem [5, 1].

The semantics of concurrent programming languages rely on a formal memory model to rigorously define how threads interact through a shared memory system. Many relaxed memory models have been proposed in the computer architecture community. A tutorial about the subject is given by Adve and Gharachorloo [1], and a detailed survey is given by Mosberger [22]. Formalization of memory models for languages such as Java [21, 11], C++ [4] and x86 multiprocessor machine code [24] were also developed recently. These models typically allow some relaxation of the program order and provide mechanisms for enforcing ordering when necessary. These mechanisms are commonly referred to as barriers, fences, or strong/ordered operations at the machine level, and locks, synchronization blocks and volatile operations at the high level. The majority of the models provide the so-called DRF-guarantee [2], in which data-race-free programs (i.e. well-synchronized programs) behave in a sequentially consistent manner. The DRF-guarantee is also known as the fundamental property [26] of a memory model. It is desirable because it frees the programmer from reasoning about idiosyncrasies of memory models when the program is well-synchronized.

However, as Boudol and Petri [7] pointed out, most memory models are defined axiomatically by giving partial orders of events in the execution traces of programs. These are more abstract than operational semantics of languages that are normally used to model the execution of programs and also to reason about them. Also, they *"only establish a very abstract version of the DRF-guarantee, from which the notion of a program, in the sense of programming languages, is actually absent"* [7]. This gap, we believe, partly explains why most program logics for concurrency verification are proved sound only in a sequentially consistent model, and their soundness in relaxed memory models is rarely discussed.

For instance, the soundness of concurrent separation logic (CSL) [23] in sequentially consistent models has been proved in various ways [9, 10, 14, 18], which all show directly or indirectly that CSL-verified programs are race-free. So it seems quite obvious that CSL is sound with any memory model that gives the DRF-guarantee, as Hobor et al. [18] argued that it *"permits only well-synchronized programs to execute, so we can [...] execute in an interleaving semantics or even a weakly consistent memory model"*. However, to our best knowledge, this folklore theorem has never been formally proved. Actually proving it is non-trivial, and is especially difficult in an operational setting, because the two sides (CSL and memory models) use different semantics of languages and different notions of data-race-freedom (as shown in Fig. 1 (a)).

In this paper, we propose a new approach to formalizing relaxed memory models by giving a parameterized operational semantics to a concurrent programming language. Behaviors of a program under a relaxed memory model are defined as behaviors of a set of *related* programs under the *sequentially consistent model*. This semantics is parameterized in that different relations between

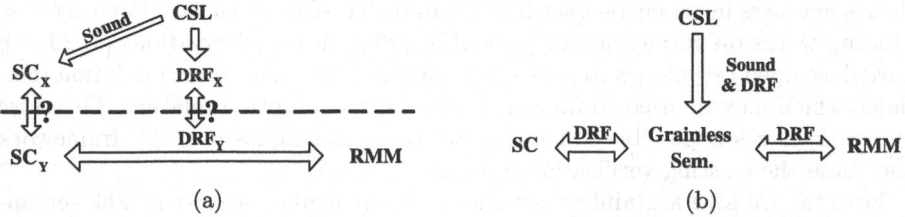

Fig. 1. (a) the gap between the language-side (above the dashed line) and the memory-model-side (below the line); we use subscripts X and Y to represent the different formulations in the two sides; (b) our solution: a new RMM and a grainless semantics. Here single arrows represent (informally) logical implications. Double arrows represent logical equivalence, with premises annotated on top. The single arrow and the double arrows on the left and right in (b) correspond to Lemmas 6.2, 5.3 and 5.4 respectively.

programs yield different memory models. We present one particular relation that is weaker than many memory models and accounts for the majority of sequential optimizations. We then give an operational grainless semantics to the language, which gives us an operational notion of data-race-freedom. We show that our derived relaxed semantics has the DRF-guarantee. Our grainless semantics also bridges CSL and relaxed memory models naturally and allows us to prove the soundness of CSL in relaxed memory models. Our paper makes the following new contributions.

First, we propose a simple, operational and parameterized approach to formalizing memory models. We model the behaviors of a program as the behaviors of a set of related programs in the interleaving semantics. The idea is shown by the prototype rule.

$$\frac{(c, c'') \in \Lambda \quad \langle c'', \sigma \rangle \longmapsto \langle c', \sigma' \rangle}{[\Lambda] \, \langle c, \sigma \rangle \longmapsto \langle c', \sigma' \rangle}$$

Our relaxed semantics is parameterized over the relation Λ. At each step, the original program c is substituted with a related program c'', and then c'' executes one step following the normal interleaving semantics. Definition of the semantics is simple: the only difference between it and the standard interleaving semantics is this rule and a corresponding rule that handles the case that a program aborts.

Second, we give a particular instantiation of Λ — called program subsumption ($\preceq$) — which can relate a sequential segment of a thread between barriers with any other sequential segments that have the same or fewer observational behaviors. This gives programmers a simple and extensional view of relaxed memory models. The derived semantics is weaker than many existing memory models. It allows behaviors such as reordering of any two data-independent memory operations, write buffering with read bypassing, and those caused by the lack of cache coherence and store atomicity.

Third, our semantics gives us a simple way to prove the soundness of sequential program transformations in a relaxed memory model: now we only need to prove that the transformations preserve the subsumption relation used to instantiate Λ. Then the DRF-guarantee of our relaxed semantics gives us their soundness in concurrent settings for data-race-free programs. Furthermore, existing works on verification of sequential program transformations [3, 20, 30] have developed techniques to prove observational equivalence or simulation relations, which may be used to further derive the subsumption relation. Therefore our work makes it possible to incorporate these techniques into this framework and reuse the existing verification results.

Fourth, we give a grainless semantics to concurrent programs. The semantics is inspired by previous work on grainless trace semantics [25, 8], but it is operational instead of denotational. Since it permits only race-free programs to execute, the semantics gives us an operational formulation of data-race-freedom. As shown in Fig. 1 (b), it also bridges the sequential consistency semantics and our relaxed semantics, which greatly simplifies the proofs of the DRF-guarantee.

Last but not least, we finally give a formal proof of the folklore theorem that CSL is sound in relaxed memory models. As Fig. 1 (b) shows, we first prove that CSL guarantees the data-race-freedom and partial correctness of programs in our grainless semantics. This, combined with the DRF-guarantee of our relaxed semantics, gives us the soundness of CSL in the relaxed model.

2   The Language and Interleaving Semantics

$$
\begin{array}{lll}
(Expr) & e ::= n \mid x \mid e_1 + e_2 \mid -e \mid \ldots \\
(BExpr) & b ::= \textsf{true} \mid \textsf{false} \mid e_1 = e_2 \mid e_1 < e_2 \mid \ldots \\
(Comm) & c ::= x := e \mid x := [e] \mid [e] := e' \mid \textsf{skip} \mid x := \textsf{cons}(e_1, \ldots, e_n) \\
& \mid \textsf{dispose}(e) \mid c_1; c_2 \mid \textsf{if } b \textsf{ then } c_1 \textsf{ else } c_2 \mid \textsf{while } b \textsf{ do } c \\
& \mid \textsf{atomic } c \mid c_1 \parallel c_2
\end{array}
$$

The syntax of the language is shown above. Arithmetic expressions (e) and boolean expressions (b) are pure: they do not access memory. To simplify the presentation, we assume in this paper that parallel threads only share read-only variables, therefore evaluation of expressions would not be interfered by other threads. This allows us to focus on studying memory reads ($x := [e]$) and writes ($[e] := e'$). **cons** and **dispose** allocate and free memory respectively.

atomic c ensures that the execution of c is not interrupted by other threads. It can be viewed as a synchronization block in high-level languages. On the other hand, we can take a very low-level view and treat **atomic** as an annotation for hardware supported atomic operations with memory barriers. For instance, we can simulate a low-level compare-and-swap ($CAS(\ell, x, y)$) operation:

$$\textsf{atomic } \{ \ v := [\ell]; \ \textsf{if } v = x \textsf{ then } [\ell] := y \textsf{ else skip}; \ y := v \ \}$$

Higher-level synchronization primitives such as semaphores and mutexes can be implemented using this primitive construct. Also in this paper we only consider non-nested atomic blocks and we do not have parallel compositions in the block.

Before presenting the operational semantics of the language, we first define the runtime constructs in Fig. 2. Program states (σ) consist of heaps and stores. A heap (h) is a partial mapping from memory locations to integers. A store (s)

$$
\begin{array}{llll}
(Location) & \ell & ::= & n \ (natural \ number) \\
(Heap) & h & \in & Location \rightharpoonup_{\mathrm{fin}} Integer \qquad (State) \quad \sigma ::= (h, s) \\
(Store) & s & \in & Variable \rightarrow Integer \qquad\; (ThrdTree) \quad T ::= c \mid \langle\!\langle T, T \rangle\!\rangle c \\
\\
(LocSet) & rs, ws & \in & \mathcal{P}(Location) \qquad\qquad\quad (Footprint) \quad \delta ::= (rs, ws)
\end{array}
$$

$$
emp \stackrel{\mathrm{def}}{=} (\emptyset, \emptyset) \qquad\qquad\qquad\qquad \delta \cup \delta' \stackrel{\mathrm{def}}{=} (\delta.rs \cup \delta'.rs, \ \delta.ws \cup \delta'.ws)
$$

$$
\delta \subseteq \delta' \stackrel{\mathrm{def}}{=} (\delta.rs \subseteq (\delta'.rs \cup \delta'.ws)) \wedge (\delta.ws \subseteq \delta'.ws) \qquad \delta \subset \delta' \stackrel{\mathrm{def}}{=} (\delta \subseteq \delta') \wedge (\delta \neq \delta')
$$

Fig. 2. Runtime constructs and footprints

maps variables to integers. A thread tree (T) is either a command c, which can be viewed as a single thread; or two sub-trees running in parallel, with the parent node c to be executed after the two sub-trees both terminate.

$$
\begin{array}{lll}
(SeqContext) & \mathbf{E} & ::= \ [] \mid \mathbf{E}; c \\
(ThrdContext) & \mathbf{T} & ::= \ [] \mid \langle\!\langle \mathbf{T}, T \rangle\!\rangle c \mid \langle\!\langle T, \mathbf{T} \rangle\!\rangle c
\end{array}
$$

We give a contextual operational semantics for the language. The sequential context $(\mathbf{E})$ and thread context $(\mathbf{T})$ defined above show the places where the execution of primitive commands occurs. Sequential execution of threads is shown in Fig. 3. We use $[\![e]\!]_s$ to represent the evaluation of e with the store s. The definition is standard and is omitted here. The execution of a normal primitive command is modeled by the labeled transition $(\_ \xrightarrow{\ \mathbf{u}\ }{}_{\delta} \_)$. Here the footprint δ is defined in Fig. 2 as a pair (rs, ws), which records the memory locations that are read and written in this step. Recording the footprint allows us to discuss races between threads in the following sections. Since we assume threads only share read-only variables, accesses of variables do not cause races and we do not record variables in footprints. A step aborts if it accesses memory locations that are not in the domain of the heap.

The transition $(\_ \xrightarrow{\ \mathbf{o}\ }{}_{\delta} \_)$ models the execution of **cons** and **dispose**. We use the label $\mathbf{o}$ instead of $\mathbf{u}$ to distinguish them from other commands. They are at higher abstraction levels than other primitive commands that may have direct hardware implementations, but we decide to support them in our language because they are important high-level language constructs. Their implementations usually require synchronizations to be thread-safe, so we model them as built-in synchronized operations and they cannot be reordered in our relaxed semantics. In this paper we call them (along with atomic blocks and fork/join of threads) *ordered operations*. Remaining operations are called *unordered*.

We may omit the footprint δ and the labels $\mathbf{u}$ and $\mathbf{o}$ when they are not relevant. We also use R^* to represent the reflexive transitive closure of the relation R. For instance, we use $(\_ \xrightarrow{\ \ }{}_{\delta} \_)$ to represent the union of ordered and unordered transitions, and use $(\_ \longrightarrow \_)$ to ignore the footprint, whose reflexive transitive closure is represented by $(\_ \longrightarrow^* \_)$.

272 R. Ferreira, X. Feng, and Z. Shao

$$\langle \mathbf{E}[\, x := [e]\,], (h, s)\rangle \xrightarrow[(\{\ell\}, \emptyset)]{u} \langle \mathbf{E}[\mathbf{skip}], (h, s')\rangle \quad \text{if } [\![e]\!]_s = \ell,\ h(\ell) = n,\ s' = s[x \rightsquigarrow n]$$

$$\langle \mathbf{E}[\, x := [e]\,], (h, s)\rangle \xrightarrow[emp]{u} \text{abort} \quad \text{otherwise}$$

$$\langle \mathbf{E}[\, [e] := e'\,], (h, s)\rangle \xrightarrow[(\emptyset, \{\ell\})]{u} \langle \mathbf{E}[\mathbf{skip}], (h', s)\rangle \quad \text{if } [\![e]\!]_s = \ell,\ [\![e']\!]_s = n,\ \ell \in \mathrm{dom}(h),$$
$$\text{and } h' = h[\ell \rightsquigarrow n]$$

$$\langle \mathbf{E}[\, [e] := e'\,], (h, s)\rangle \xrightarrow[emp]{u} \text{abort} \quad \text{otherwise}$$

$$\langle \mathbf{E}[\, x := e\,], (h, s)\rangle \xrightarrow[emp]{u} \langle \mathbf{E}[\mathbf{skip}], (h, s')\rangle \quad \text{if } [\![e]\!]_s = n \text{ and } s' = s[x \rightsquigarrow n]$$

$$\langle \mathbf{E}[\, \mathbf{skip}; c\,], \sigma\rangle \xrightarrow[emp]{u} \langle \mathbf{E}[c], \sigma\rangle \quad \text{always}$$

$$\cdots \qquad \qquad \cdots$$

$$\langle \mathbf{E}[\, \mathbf{dispose}(e)\,], (h, s)\rangle \xrightarrow[(\emptyset, \{\ell\})]{o} \langle \mathbf{E}[\mathbf{skip}], (h', s)\rangle \quad \text{if } [\![e]\!]_s = \ell,\ \ell \in \mathrm{dom}(h),\ h' = h\backslash\{\ell\}$$

$$\langle \mathbf{E}[\, \mathbf{dispose}(e)\,], (h, s)\rangle \xrightarrow[emp]{o} \text{abort} \quad \text{otherwise}$$

$$\langle \mathbf{E}[\, x := \mathbf{cons}(e_1, \ldots, e_k)\,], (h, s)\rangle \xrightarrow[(\emptyset, ws)]{o} \langle \mathbf{E}[\mathbf{skip}], (h', s')\rangle$$
$$\text{if } ws = \{\ell, \ldots, \ell+k-1\},\ ws \cap \mathrm{dom}(h) = \emptyset,\ [\![e_i]\!]_s = n_i,$$
$$s' = s[x \rightsquigarrow \ell] \text{ and } h' = h[\ell \rightsquigarrow n_1, \ldots, \ell+k-1 \rightsquigarrow n_k]$$

$$\langle c, \sigma\rangle \xrightarrow{\delta} \langle c', \sigma'\rangle \quad \text{if } \langle c, \sigma\rangle \xrightarrow[\delta]{u} \langle c', \sigma'\rangle \text{ or } \langle c, \sigma\rangle \xrightarrow[\delta]{o} \langle c', \sigma'\rangle$$

$$\langle c, \sigma\rangle \xrightarrow{\delta} \text{abort} \quad \text{if } \langle c, \sigma\rangle \xrightarrow[\delta]{u} \text{abort or } \langle c, \sigma\rangle \xrightarrow[\delta]{o} \text{abort}$$

Fig. 3. Sequential footprint semantics

$$\langle \mathbf{T}[c], \sigma\rangle \longmapsto \langle \mathbf{T}[c'], \sigma'\rangle \quad \text{if } \langle c, \sigma\rangle \longrightarrow \langle c', \sigma'\rangle$$

$$\langle \mathbf{T}[c], \sigma\rangle \longmapsto \text{abort} \quad \text{if } \langle c, \sigma\rangle \longrightarrow \text{abort}$$

$$\langle \mathbf{T}[\mathbf{E}[\mathbf{atomic}\ c]], \sigma\rangle \longmapsto \langle \mathbf{T}[\mathbf{E}[\mathbf{skip}]], \sigma'\rangle \quad \text{if } \langle c, \sigma\rangle \longrightarrow^* \langle \mathbf{skip}, \sigma'\rangle$$

$$\langle \mathbf{T}[\mathbf{E}[\mathbf{atomic}\ c]], \sigma\rangle \longmapsto \text{abort} \quad \text{if } \langle c, \sigma\rangle \longrightarrow^* \text{abort}$$

$$\langle \mathbf{T}[\mathbf{E}[c_1 \parallel c_2]], \sigma\rangle \longmapsto \langle \mathbf{T}[\langle\!\langle c_1, c_2\rangle\!\rangle \mathbf{E}[\mathbf{skip}]], \sigma\rangle \quad \text{always}$$

$$\langle \mathbf{T}[\langle\!\langle \mathbf{skip}, \mathbf{skip}\rangle\!\rangle c], \sigma\rangle \longmapsto \langle \mathbf{T}[c], \sigma\rangle \quad \text{always}$$

Fig. 4. Interleaving semantics of concurrent programs

Figure 4 defines the interleaving semantics of concurrent programs. Following Vafeiadis and Parkinson [29], the execution of c in **atomic** c does not interleave with the environment. If c does not terminate, the thread gets stuck. Again, we assume there are no atomic blocks or parallel compositions in c.

Next we give a simple example to show the use of contexts and thread trees.

Example 1. Suppose $c = (c_1 \parallel c_2); c'$. Then we know $c = \mathbf{T}[\mathbf{E}[c_1 \parallel c_2]]$, where $\mathbf{T} = [\,]$ and $\mathbf{E} = [\,]; c'$. After one step, we reach the thread tree $\langle\!\langle c_1, c_2\rangle\!\rangle (\mathbf{skip}; c')$. Then the $\mathbf{T}'$ for the next step can be either $\langle\!\langle [\,], c_2\rangle\!\rangle (\mathbf{skip}; c')$ or $\langle\!\langle c_1, [\,]\rangle\!\rangle (\mathbf{skip}; c')$.

$$[\Lambda]\ \langle T, \sigma \rangle \longmapsto \langle T', \sigma' \rangle \quad \text{if}\ \exists T''.\ (T, T'') \in \Lambda \wedge \langle T'', \sigma \rangle \longmapsto \langle T', \sigma' \rangle$$

$$[\Lambda]\ \langle T, \sigma \rangle \longmapsto \text{abort} \qquad \text{if}\ \exists T'.\ (T, T') \in \Lambda \wedge \langle T', \sigma \rangle \longmapsto \text{abort}$$

Fig. 5. Semantics parameterized over Λ

3   Parameterized Relaxed Semantics

In this section, we present our parameterized operational semantics. Then we instantiate it with a relation between sequential programs to capture relaxed memory models and compiler optimizations.

3.1   Parameterized Semantics

Figure 5 shows the two new rules of our parameterized semantics. The stepping relation takes Λ as a parameter, which is a binary relation between thread trees:

$$\Lambda \in \mathcal{P}(\mathit{ThrdTree} \times \mathit{ThrdTree})$$

The semantics follows the interleaving semantics in Fig. 4, except that the current thread tree can be replaced at any given step by another thread tree related through the Λ relation. Λ is supposed to provide a set of thread trees that are equivalent to the current thread tree with some notion of equivalence. This Λ-based semantics chooses nondeterministically which command will execute.

Naturally, different instantiations of Λ yield different semantics. As one can see, this semantics is trivially equivalent to the interleaving semantics shown in Fig. 4 once Λ is instantiated with an identity relation. A more interesting relation to be used as an instantiation of Λ is presented in the following sections.

3.2   Command Subsumption

We define a command subsumption relation that

1. preserves synchronized operations of the code;
2. but permits the rewriting of non-synchronized sequential portions while preserving their *sequential* semantics.

The intuition is that programs should be well-synchronized to avoid unexpected behaviors in relaxed memory models. That is, accesses to shared memory should be performed through synchronized operations (**cons**, **dispose** and **atomic** c in our language), and non-synchronized (unordered) operations should only access thread-local or read-only memory (but note that the term "shared" and "local" are dynamic notions and their boundary does not have to be fixed). Therefore, the effect of a thread's non-synchronized code is not visible to other threads until the next synchronized point is reached. On the other hand, the behavior of the non-synchronized code will not be affected by other threads either since

$$\langle c, \sigma \rangle \xrightarrow[emp]{u}{}^0 \langle c, \sigma \rangle \qquad\qquad \text{always}$$

$$\langle c, \sigma \rangle \xrightarrow[\delta]{u}{}^{k+1} \langle c', \sigma' \rangle \qquad \text{if there exist } c'', \sigma'', \delta', \text{ and } \delta'' \text{ such that } \delta = \delta' \cup \delta'',$$
$$\langle c, \sigma \rangle \xrightarrow[\delta']{u} \langle c'', \sigma'' \rangle \text{ and } \langle c'', \sigma'' \rangle \xrightarrow[\delta'']{u}{}^k \langle c', \sigma' \rangle$$

$$\langle c, \sigma \rangle \quad \Downarrow_\delta \quad \langle c', \sigma' \rangle \qquad \text{if } \langle c, \sigma \rangle \xrightarrow[\delta]{u}{}^* \langle c', \sigma' \rangle, \ \neg(\langle c', \sigma' \rangle \xrightarrow{u} \text{abort}),$$
$$\text{and } \neg \exists c'', \sigma''.(\langle c', \sigma' \rangle \xrightarrow{u} \langle c'', \sigma'' \rangle)$$

$$\langle c, \sigma \rangle \quad \Downarrow \quad \langle c', \sigma' \rangle \qquad \text{if there exists } \delta \text{ such that } \langle c, \sigma \rangle \Downarrow_\delta \langle c', \sigma' \rangle$$

$$\langle c, \sigma \rangle \xrightarrow[emp]{}{}^0 \langle c, \sigma \rangle \qquad\qquad \text{always}$$

$$\langle c, \sigma \rangle \xrightarrow[\delta]{}{}^{k+1} \langle c', \sigma' \rangle \qquad \text{if there exist } c'', \sigma'', \delta', \text{ and } \delta'' \text{ such that } \delta = \delta' \cup \delta'',$$
$$\langle c, \sigma \rangle \xrightarrow[\delta']{} \langle c'', \sigma'' \rangle \text{ and } \langle c'', \sigma'' \rangle \xrightarrow[\delta'']{}{}^k \langle c', \sigma' \rangle$$

Fig. 6. Multi-step sequential transitions

the data it uses would not be updated by others. So we do not need to consider its interleaving with other threads.

The subsumption of c_1 by c_2 ($c_1 \preceq c_2$) is defined below. Here $(\_\xrightarrow[\delta]{u}{}^*\_)$ represents zero or multiple steps of unordered transitions, where δ is the union of the footprints of individual steps. $\langle c, \sigma \rangle \Downarrow \langle c', \sigma' \rangle$ is a big-step transition of unordered operations. From the definition shown in Fig. 6, we know c' must be either **skip**, or a command starting with an ordered operation.

Definition 3.1. $c_1 \preceq_0 c_2$ always holds; $c_1 \preceq_{k+1} c_2$ holds if and only if, for all $j \leq k$, the following are true:

1. If $\langle c_1, \sigma \rangle \xrightarrow{u}{}^*$ abort, then $\langle c_2, \sigma \rangle \xrightarrow{u}{}^*$ abort;
2. If $\langle c_1, \sigma \rangle \Downarrow \langle c_1', \sigma' \rangle$, then either $\langle c_2, \sigma \rangle \xrightarrow{u}{}^*$ abort, or there exists c_2' such that $\langle c_2, \sigma \rangle \Downarrow \langle c_2', \sigma' \rangle$ and the following constraints hold:
   (a) if $c_1' = \textbf{skip}$, then $c_2' = \textbf{skip}$;
   (b) if $c_1' = \mathbf{E}_1[c_1'' \| c_1''']$, there exist $\mathbf{E}_2$, c_2'' and c_2''' such that
      i. $c_2' = \mathbf{E}_2[c_2'' \| c_2''']$;
      ii. $c_1'' \preceq_j c_2''$ and $c_1''' \preceq_j c_2'''$;
      iii. $\mathbf{E}_1[\textbf{skip}] \preceq_j \mathbf{E}_2[\textbf{skip}]$;
   (c) if $c_1' = \mathbf{E}_1[\textbf{atomic } c_1'']$, there exist $\mathbf{E}_2$ and c_2'' such that
      i. $c_2' = \mathbf{E}_2[\textbf{atomic } c_2'']$;
      ii. $c_1'' \preceq_j c_2''$;
      iii. $\mathbf{E}_1[\textbf{skip}] \preceq_j \mathbf{E}_2[\textbf{skip}]$;
   (d) if $c_1' = \mathbf{E}_1[c_1'']$, where c_1'' is a **cons** or **dispose** command, there exist $\mathbf{E}_2$ and c_2'' such that
      i. for all σ, if $\langle c_1'', \sigma \rangle \xrightarrow{o}$ abort, then $\langle c_2'', \sigma \rangle \xrightarrow{o}$ abort;
      ii. for all σ and σ', if $\langle c_1'', \sigma \rangle \xrightarrow{o} \langle \textbf{skip}, \sigma' \rangle$, then $\langle c_2'', \sigma \rangle \xrightarrow{o} \langle \textbf{skip}, \sigma' \rangle$;
      iii. $\mathbf{E}_1[\textbf{skip}] \preceq_j \mathbf{E}_2[\textbf{skip}]$.

3. If $\langle c_1, \sigma \rangle \xrightarrow{\mathbf{u}}_{\delta_1}{}^* \langle c_1', \sigma' \rangle$, then either $\langle c_2, \sigma \rangle \xrightarrow{\mathbf{u}}{}^*$ abort, or there exist δ_2, c_2' and σ'' such that $\langle c_2, \sigma \rangle \xrightarrow{\mathbf{u}}_{\delta_2}{}^* \langle c_2', \sigma'' \rangle$ and $\delta_1 \subseteq \delta_2$;

We define $c_1 \preceq c_2$ as $\forall k.\ c_1 \preceq_k c_2$; and $c_1 \succeq c_2$ as $c_2 \preceq c_1$.   □

Informally, we say c_1 is subsumed by c_2 if for all input states — after performing a sequential big step — c_1 aborts only if c_2 aborts; or, if c_1 completes, then c_2 either aborts or takes a big step that ends in the same state. Also, if c_1 at the end of the big step terminates (**skip** case) or reaches a synchronization point (cases for thread fork and join, atomic blocks, **cons** and **dispose**), there must be a corresponding termination or synchronization point at the end of the big step taken by c_2 and the remaining parts (if any) of c_1 and c_2 still satisfy the relation. We use indices in the definition since $\mathbf{E}_1[\mathbf{skip}]$ in the cases 2(b), 2(c) and 2(d) might be "larger" than c_1. The last condition requires that the footprint of c_1 is not larger than that of c_2 if c_2 does not abort. The subset relation between footprints is defined in Fig. 2.

Properties of subsumption. Suppose c_1 and c_2 are sequential programs consisting of unordered operations only, and $c_1 \preceq c_2$. For any input state we have the following possibilities:

1. c_2 aborts and c_1 may have any behaviors;
2. c_1 and c_2 complete a big step and reach the same state;
3. c_1 diverges and c_2 may have any behaviors.

Here we intend to use c_2 to represent the original program and c_1 the one after optimizations (by compilers or hardware). By the three cases above we know c_1 preserves the partial correctness of c_2 [10] (to handle total correctness, an extra condition must be added to Definition 3.1 to ensure that normal termination is preserved by subsumption). The last condition in Definition 3.1 is also necessary to ensure the transformation from c_2 to c_1 does not introduce new races. We give examples in Sect. 4 to show the expressiveness of the subsumption relation and how it models behaviors of programs in relaxed memory models. More properties about the relation are shown by the following two lemmas.

Lemma 3.2. The relation $\preceq$ is reflexive and transitive.

Lemma 3.3. If $c_1 \preceq c_2$, then, for all contexts $\mathcal{C}$, $\mathcal{C}[c_1] \preceq \mathcal{C}[c_2]$.

Here $\mathcal{C}$ can be any context, i.e. a program with a hole in it. It does not have to be $\mathbf{E}$ or $\mathbf{T}$.

3.3   Relaxed Semantics

The subsumption relation can be lifted for thread trees.

Definition 3.4. We define the binary relation $\preceq_t$ for thread trees.

$$T_1 \preceq_t T_2 \stackrel{\text{def}}{=} \begin{cases} c_1 \preceq c_2 & \text{if } T_1 = c_1 \text{ and } T_2 = c_2 \\ c_1 \preceq c_2 \wedge T_1' \preceq_t T_2' & \text{if } T_1 = \langle\!\langle T_1', T_1'' \rangle\!\rangle c_1 \\ \wedge T_1'' \preceq_t T_2'' & \text{and } T_2 = \langle\!\langle T_2', T_2'' \rangle\!\rangle c_2 \end{cases}$$

We use $T_1 \succeq_t T_2$ to represent $T_2 \preceq_t T_1$.   □

We obtain a relaxed operational semantics by instantiating Λ of our parameterized semantics with this relation. The resulting stepping relation becomes

$$[\succeq_t] \; \langle T, \sigma \rangle \longmapsto \langle T', \sigma' \rangle \,.$$

At each step, this semantics performs a program transformation following the subsumption relation. This resembles a dynamic compiler that modifies the program as it executes.

On the other hand, as we show in Lemma 3.5, the execution according to this semantics is equivalent to performing one single initial program transformation and then executing the target program using the interleaving semantics. This resembles a static compiler that modifies the program prior to execution. Similarly, Lemma 3.6 shows the abort case.

Lemma 3.5. $[\succeq_t] \; \langle T, \sigma \rangle \longmapsto^* \langle \textbf{skip}, \sigma' \rangle$ iff there exists a T' such that $T \succeq_t T'$ and $\langle T', \sigma \rangle \longmapsto^* \langle \textbf{skip}, \sigma' \rangle$.

Lemma 3.6. $[\succeq_t] \; \langle T, \sigma \rangle \longmapsto^*$ abort iff there exists a T' such that $T \succeq_t T'$ and $\langle T', \sigma \rangle \longmapsto^*$ abort.

We will formulate and prove the DRF-guarantee of this relaxed semantics in Sect. 5, after we formally define data-race-freedom.

4   Examples

There are different aspects that characterize a particular memory model. In this section, we show how they are reflected in our semantics. The examples are shown with the following naming convention: v_1, v_2, v_3, etc, are thread-local variables that hold values; x, y, z, etc, are variables that hold memory addresses.

Data dependencies. At first glance, the definition of $\succeq$ is too restrictive since it quantifies over *all* input states. It does not allow

$$([x] := 1; v_1 := [y]) \succeq (v_1 := [y]; [x] := 1) \,,$$

where the data dependency of the two statements depends on the runtime values of x and y. However, the $\succeq$ relation allows the following transformation:

$$[x] := 1; v_1 := [y] \succeq \textbf{if } x = y \textbf{ then } ([x] := 1; v_1 := [x]) \textbf{ else } (v_1 := [y]; [x] := 1),$$

where we insert a dynamic test to see if x is an alias of y. So we do allow reordering of memory accesses that do not have data dependencies at runtime.

Memory reordering. It is easy to see that the $\succeq$ relation supports all four types of memory reordering (R,W $\rightarrow$ R,W). In the example below,

$$(v_1 := [x]; [y] := 1) \quad \| \quad (v_2 := [y]; [x] := 1) \ ,$$

we can get $v_1 = v_2 = 1$ if $x \neq y$. This can be achieved by reordering the commands in the second thread (not supported by Boudol and Petri [7]),

$$v_2 := [y]; [x] := 1 \succeq \textbf{if } x = y \textbf{ then } (v_2 := [x]; [x] := 1) \textbf{ else } ([x] := 1; v_2 := [y]).$$

Write atomicity. Write atomicity is not preserved by the $\succeq$ relation. In the classic cross-over example below,

$$([x] := 1; v_1 := [x]) \quad \| \quad ([x] := 2; v_2 := [x]) \ ,$$

we can get $v_1 = 2$ and $v_2 = 1$. This is achieved by adding a redundant write in the right hand side thread: $[x] := 2; v_2 := [x] \succeq [x] := 2; v_2 := [x]; [x] := 2$. This simulates the duration between the beginning and the end of the write. We may also store arbitrary values to memory before completing. For instance, the program below allows $v_1 = 33$ at the end.

$$v_1 := [x] \quad \| \quad [x] := 1$$

It happens with the following transformation of the right hand side thread:

$$[x] := 1 \succeq [x] := 33; [x] := 1,$$

which means the memory value is undefined until the write completes. This is commonly referred to as "out-of-thin-air" behavior. A similar behavior shows up when we have simultaneous writes to the same location:

$$(v_1 := 1; [x] := v_1) \quad \| \quad [x] := 2 \ .$$

In this case, the final value of $[x]$ could be arbitrary. It could be 3 if we do the following transformation of the left hand side thread:

$$v_1 := 1; [x] := v_1 \succeq [x] := 0; v_1 := [x]; v_1 := v_1 + 1; [x] := v_1 \ .$$

Strong barrier. In the relaxed semantics, we can enforce both atomicity and ordering by using **atomic** c. A memory fence MF can be implemented by **atomic skip**. The following examples show that MF is not sufficient to enforce program orders when there is no cache coherence. In the example below,

$$[x] := 1 \quad \| \quad [x] := 2 \quad \| \quad \begin{pmatrix} v_1 := [x]; \\ \text{MF}; \\ v_2 := [x] \end{pmatrix} \quad \| \quad \begin{pmatrix} v_3 := [x]; \\ \text{MF}; \\ v_4 := [x] \end{pmatrix}$$

We can get the outcome $v_1 = v_4 = 1$ and $v_2 = v_3 = 2$ by rewriting the leftmost thread: $[x] := 1 \succeq [x] := 1; [x] := 1.$

See also the independent-reads-independent-writes (IRIW) example:

$$[x] := 1 \quad \| \quad [y] := 1 \quad \| \quad \begin{pmatrix} v_1 := [x]; \\ \text{MF}; \\ v_2 := [y] \end{pmatrix} \quad \| \quad \begin{pmatrix} v_3 := [y]; \\ \text{MF}; \\ v_4 := [x] \end{pmatrix}$$

where the behavior $v_1 = v_3 = 1$ and $v_2 = v_4 = 0$ is permissible if we rewrite the leftmost thread through $[x] := 1 \succeq [x] := 1; [x] := 0; [x] := 1$.

Race-free programs. Race-free programs do not have unexpected behaviors in our semantics (see the DRF-guarantee in Sect. 5). In the example below:

$$\begin{pmatrix} v_1 := [x]; \\ \text{if } v_1 = 1 \text{ then } [y] := 1 \end{pmatrix} \quad \| \quad \begin{pmatrix} v_2 := [y]; \\ \text{if } v_2 = 1 \text{ then } [x] := 1 \end{pmatrix}$$

the only behavior allowed is $v_1 = v_2 = 0$. Because the two conditional statements cannot be reached (assuming $[x] = [y] = 0$ and $x \neq y$ initially), the program never issues a memory write. So the program is race-free. Also, transformations allowed by the $\succeq$ relation cannot introduce races by inserting redundant writes. This is guaranteed by the fact that the footprints of both threads are disjoint, and they cannot increase after transformations.

Compiler optimizations (and obfuscations). Redundant memory reads and writes can be introduced and eliminated, as shown by the following examples:

$$v_1 := [x]; v_2 := 1 \succeq v_1 := [x]; v_2 := [x]; v_2 := 1$$
$$v_1 := [x]; v_2 := [x] \succeq v_1 := [x]; v_2 := v_1$$
$$[x] := v_1 \succeq [x] := 1; [x] := v_1$$
$$[x] := 1; [x] := v_1 \succeq [x] := v_1$$

Furthermore, we can eliminate dead memory operations and reduce the memory footprint: $v_1 := [x]; v_1 := 1 \succeq v_1 := 1$. Note that the reverse is not true: $\neg(v_1 := 1 \succeq v_1 := [x]; v_1 := 1)$. A transformation cannot increase the footprint.

Now we can reproduce the prescient-write example:

$$(v_1 := [x]; [x] := 1) \quad \| \quad (v_2 := [x]; [x] := v_2)$$

where we could have $v_1 = v_2 = 1$ by rewriting the left hand side thread:

$$v_1 := [x]; [x] := 1 \succeq v_1 := [x]; [x] := 1; [x] := v_1; v_1 := [x]; [x] := 1.$$

Other optimizations, including instruction scheduling, register allocation, algebraic transformations and control transformations, can also be supported. More examples can be found in the technical report [15].

Total store ordering. We give another non-trivial instantiation of Λ in our parameterized semantics, which yields the Total Store Ordering (TSO) model implemented by the SPARCv8 architecture [28]. TSO allows write-to-read reordering. It enforces cache-coherence, but allows a thread to read its own writes earlier.

$$\mathbf{E}[\,[e_1] := e'; x := [e_2]\,] \succeq_{\text{TSO}} \mathbf{E}\left[\begin{array}{l} \text{if } (e_1 = e_2) \\ \text{then } (x := e';\,[e_1] := x) \\ \text{else } (x := [e_2];\,[e_1] := e') \end{array}\right]$$
$$\text{if } x \notin fv(e_1) \cup fv(e')$$

$$\mathbf{E}[\,[e] := e'_1; x := e'_2\,] \succeq_{\text{TSO}} \mathbf{E}[\,x := e'_2;\,[e] := e'_1\,] \qquad \text{if } x \notin fv(e) \cup fv(e'_1)$$

$$\mathbf{E}[\,[e] := e'; \mathbf{skip}\,] \succeq_{\text{TSO}} \mathbf{E}[\,\mathbf{skip};\,[e] := e'\,] \qquad \text{always}$$

$$\mathbf{E}[\,[e_1] := e'_1;\,[e_2] := e'_2\,] \succeq_{\text{TSO}} c' \qquad \begin{array}{l} \text{if } \exists c''.\ \mathbf{E}[\,[e_2] := e'_2\,] \succeq_{\text{TSO}} c'' \\ \wedge\ ([e_1] := e'_1; c'') \succeq_{\text{TSO}} c' \end{array}$$

$$\mathbf{E}\left[\left(\begin{array}{l} [e] := e'; \\ \text{if } b \text{ then } c_1 \text{ else } c_2 \end{array}\right)\right] \succeq_{\text{TSO}} \mathbf{E}\left[\left(\begin{array}{l} \text{if } b \text{ then } ([e] := e'; c_1) \\ \text{else } ([e] := e'; c_2) \end{array}\right)\right] \qquad \text{always}$$

$$\mathbf{E}[\,[e] := e'; \mathbf{while}\ b\ \mathbf{do}\ c\,] \succeq_{\text{TSO}} \mathbf{E}\left[\left(\begin{array}{l} \text{if } b \\ \text{then } ([e] := e'; c; \mathbf{while}\ b\ \mathbf{do}\ c) \\ \text{else } [e] := e' \end{array}\right)\right] \qquad \text{always}$$

$$c \succeq_{\text{TSO}} c \qquad \text{always}$$

Fig. 7. TSO

We define $\succeq_{\text{TSO}}$, an instantiation of Λ, in Fig. 7. The first rule shows the reordering of a write with a subsequent read. The **else** branch shows the reordering when there is no data dependency. The **then** branch allows a thread to read its own write earlier. Here $fv(e)$ is the set of free variables in e. The other rules (except the last one) show how to propagate the reordering to the subsequent code. Remember that the transformation may occur at any step during the execution in our parameterized semantics, so we only need to consider the statements starting with a write operation, and the write might be postponed indefinitely until an ordered operation is reached.

In real architectures, the reordering is caused by write buffering instead of swapping the two instructions. We do not model the write buffer here since our goal is not to faithfully model what happens in hardware. Instead, we just want to give an extensional model for programmers. To see the adequacy of our rules, we can view the right hand side of the first rule as a simplification of the following code, which simulates the write buffering [24] more directly:

local tmp, buf
in $tmp := e_1; buf := e';(\mathbf{if}\ tmp = e_2\ \mathbf{then}\ x := buf\ \mathbf{else}\ x := [e_2]);\ [tmp] := buf\,\mathbf{end}$

Here the local variable buf can be viewed as a write buffer. Also note that the side condition of this rule can be eliminated if we also simulate the hardware support of register renaming (like our use of tmp above).

Remark 1. $\succeq_{\text{TSO}}$ is a subset of $\succeq$.

Partial Store Ordering (PSO). In our technical report [15], we define $\succeq_{\text{PSO}}$, another instantiation of Λ that yields the PSO model [28]. It is defined by simply adding a couple of rules to $\succeq_{\text{TSO}}$ to support write-to-write reordering.

5   Grainless Semantics and DRF Guarantee

Following Reynolds [25] and Brookes [8], here we give a grainless semantics to our language, which is operational instead of being a trace-based denotational semantics. The semantics permits only data-race-free programs to execute, therefore it gives us a simple and operational formulation of data-race-freedom and allows us to prove the DRF-guarantee of our relaxed semantics.

5.1   Grainless Semantics

Below we first instrument thread trees with footprints for threads. Execution contexts $\widetilde{T}$ in the instrumented trees are defined similarly to T in Sect. 2.

$$(\mathit{ThrdTree}) \quad \widetilde{T} ::= (c, \delta) \mid \langle\!\langle \widetilde{T}, \widetilde{T} \rangle\!\rangle c$$

$$(\mathit{ThrdCtxt}) \quad \widetilde{\mathbf{T}} ::= [] \mid \langle\!\langle \widetilde{\mathbf{T}}, \widetilde{T} \rangle\!\rangle c \mid \langle\!\langle \widetilde{T}, \widetilde{\mathbf{T}} \rangle\!\rangle c$$

The footprint δ associated with each leaf node on $\widetilde{T}$ records the memory locations that are being accessed by this thread. To ensure the data-race-freedom, the footprint δ of the active thread at the context $\widetilde{\mathbf{T}}$ must be disjoint with the footprints of other threads. This requirement is defined in Fig. 8 as the wft (well-formed tree) condition. We also define $\lfloor T \rfloor$ to convert T to an instrumented thread tree with an initial footprint emp for each thread.

The grainless semantics is shown in Fig. 9, which refers to the sequential transitions defined in Figs. 3 and 6. In this semantics we execute unordered commands in a big step, as shown in the first rule (see Fig. 6 for the definition of $\langle c, \sigma \rangle \Downarrow_\delta \langle c', \sigma' \rangle$). It cannot be interrupted by other threads, therefore the environment cannot observe transitions of *the smallest granularity*. The footprint δ of this big step is recorded on the thread tree at the end, which means the transition has *duration* and the memory locations in δ are still in use (even though the state is changed to σ'). So when other threads execute, they cannot assume this step has finished and cannot issue conflicting memory operations.

cons and **dispose** (the third rule), atomic blocks (the sixth rule) and thread fork/join (the last two rules) are all *atomic* instead of being grainless. Comparing with the first rule, we can see the footprint at the end of the step is emp, showing that this step finishes and the memory locations in δ are no longer in use. Note the emp footprint also clears the footprint of the preceding unordered transition of this thread, therefore these atomic operations also serve as memory barriers that mark the end of the preceding unordered commands. The footprint on the left hand side is not used in these rules, so we use _ to omit it.

$$\delta \smile \delta' \stackrel{\mathrm{def}}{=} (\delta.ws \cap (\delta'.rs \cup \delta'.ws) = \emptyset) \wedge (\delta.rs \cap \delta'.ws = \emptyset)$$

$$\mathsf{wft}(\widetilde{\mathbf{T}}, \delta) \stackrel{\mathrm{def}}{=} \forall c, c', \delta', \widetilde{\mathbf{T}}'.\ (\widetilde{\mathbf{T}}[(c, \delta)] = \widetilde{\mathbf{T}}'[(c', \delta')]) \wedge (\widetilde{\mathbf{T}} \neq \widetilde{\mathbf{T}}') \to \delta \smile \delta'$$

$$\lfloor T \rfloor \stackrel{\mathrm{def}}{=} \begin{cases} (c, emp) & \text{if } T = c \\ \langle\!\langle \lfloor T_1 \rfloor, \lfloor T_2 \rfloor \rangle\!\rangle c & \text{if } T = \langle\!\langle T_1, T_2 \rangle\!\rangle c \end{cases}$$

Fig. 8. Auxiliary definitions

$$\langle \widetilde{T}[\,(c,\_)\,],\, \sigma \rangle \Longrightarrow \langle \widetilde{T}[\,(c',\delta)\,],\, \sigma' \rangle \qquad \text{if } \langle c, \sigma \rangle \Downarrow_\delta \langle c', \sigma' \rangle \text{ and } \mathsf{wft}(\widetilde{T}, \delta)$$

$$\langle \widetilde{T}[\,(c,\delta)\,],\, \sigma \rangle \Longrightarrow \langle \widetilde{T}[\,(c,\delta')\,],\, \sigma \rangle \qquad \text{if } \langle c, \sigma \rangle \xrightarrow[\delta']{u}{}^* \langle c', \sigma' \rangle,\ \delta \subset \delta',\ \mathsf{wft}(\widetilde{T}, \delta')$$

$$\langle \widetilde{T}[\,(c,\_)\,],\, \sigma \rangle \Longrightarrow \langle \widetilde{T}[\,(c',emp)\,],\, \sigma' \rangle \qquad \text{if } \langle c, \sigma \rangle \xrightarrow[\delta]{o} \langle c', \sigma' \rangle \text{ and } \mathsf{wft}(\widetilde{T}, \delta)$$

$$\langle \widetilde{T}[\,(c,\_)\,],\, \sigma \rangle \Longrightarrow \mathsf{race} \qquad \text{if } \langle c, \sigma \rangle \xrightarrow[\delta]{u}{}^* \langle c', \sigma' \rangle \text{ or } \langle c, \sigma \rangle \xrightarrow[\delta]{o} \langle c', \sigma' \rangle,$$
$$\text{and } \neg\,\mathsf{wft}(\widetilde{T}, \delta)$$

$$\langle \widetilde{T}[\,(c,\_)\,],\, \sigma \rangle \Longrightarrow \mathsf{abort} \qquad \text{if } \langle c, \sigma \rangle \xrightarrow{u}{}^* \mathsf{abort} \text{ or } \langle c, \sigma \rangle \xrightarrow{o} \mathsf{abort}$$

$$\langle \widetilde{T}[\,(\mathbf{E}[\,\mathbf{atomic}\ c\,],\_)\,],\, \sigma \rangle \Longrightarrow \langle \widetilde{T}[\,(\mathbf{E}[\,\mathbf{skip}\,],emp)\,],\, \sigma' \rangle \qquad \text{if } \langle c, \sigma \rangle \xrightarrow[\delta]{}{}^* \langle \mathbf{skip}, \sigma' \rangle$$
$$\text{and } \mathsf{wft}(\widetilde{T}, \delta)$$

$$\langle \widetilde{T}[\,(\mathbf{E}[\,\mathbf{atomic}\ c\,],\_)\,],\, \sigma \rangle \Longrightarrow \mathsf{race} \qquad \text{if } \langle c, \sigma \rangle \xrightarrow[\delta]{}{}^* \langle c', \sigma' \rangle$$
$$\text{and } \neg\,\mathsf{wft}(\widetilde{T}, \delta)$$

$$\langle \widetilde{T}[\,(\mathbf{E}[\,\mathbf{atomic}\ c\,],\_)\,],\, \sigma \rangle \Longrightarrow \mathsf{abort} \qquad \text{if } \langle c, \sigma \rangle \xrightarrow{}{}^* \mathsf{abort}$$

$$\langle \widetilde{T}[\,(\mathbf{E}[\,c_1 \,\|\, c_2\,],\_)\,],\, \sigma \rangle \Longrightarrow \langle \widetilde{T}[\,\langle\!\langle (c_1,emp),(c_2,emp)\rangle\!\rangle \mathbf{E}[\,\mathbf{skip}\,]\,],\, \sigma \rangle \qquad \text{always}$$

$$\langle \widetilde{T}\langle\!\langle (\mathbf{skip},\_),(\mathbf{skip},\_)\rangle\!\rangle c\,],\, \sigma \rangle \Longrightarrow \langle \widetilde{T}[\,(c,emp)\,],\, \sigma \rangle \qquad \text{always}$$

Fig. 9. Grainless semantics

In all these rules, we check the wft condition to ensure that each step does not issue memory operations that are in conflict with those ongoing ones made by other threads. If the check fails, we reach the special race configuration and the execution stops (the fourth and seventh rules).

The second rule, which has not been explained yet, allows an intermediate footprint δ' to be recorded on the thread tree before the big step transition of unordered commands finishes. This is necessary to characterize the following program as one with data-races:

$$(\mathbf{while}\ \mathsf{true}\ \mathbf{do}\ [x] := 3)\ \|\ (\mathbf{while}\ \mathsf{true}\ \mathbf{do}\ [x] := 4)$$

The first rule does not apply here because both threads diverge, but we can apply the second rule to record the write set $\{x\}$ on the thread tree and then apply the fourth rule to detect the race. Note that this rule does not change the command c or the state σ. If we ignore the footprint, it simply adds stuttering steps in the semantics. The side condition $\delta \subset \delta'$ (defined in Fig. 2) ensures the stuttering steps are not inserted arbitrarily. Here δ is either an intermediate footprint accessed earlier during this big-step transition, or the footprint accessed by the preceding transition of this thread. In the second case, the last step must be an atomic operation and δ must be *emp*.

Following Reynolds' principles for grainless semantics [25], both abort and race are viewed as bad program configurations. We distinguish race from abort to define data-race-freedom. A thread tree T is race-free if its execution never leads to race. By this definition, programs that abort may still be race-free. This allows us to talk about race-free but unsafe programs, as shown in Theorem 5.2.

Definition 5.1. $\langle T, \sigma \rangle$ racefree iff $\neg(\langle \lfloor T \rfloor, \sigma \rangle \Longrightarrow^*$ race$)$; T racefree iff, for all σ, $\langle T, \sigma \rangle$ racefree.

Example 2. Given the following programs,

(1) $[x] := 3$ $\|$ $[x] := 4$
(2) $[x] := 3$ $\|$ **atomic** $\{[x] := 4\}$
(3) $[x] := 3$ $\|$ **atomic** $\{$**while** true **do** $[x] := 4\}$
(4) **atomic** $\{[x] := 3\}$ $\|$ **atomic** $\{[x] := 4\}$

we know (4) is race-free, but (1), (2) and (3) are not.

5.2   DRF-Guarantee of the Relaxed Semantics

Theorem 5.2 formulates the DRF-guarantee of the relaxed semantics. It says a race-free program configuration has the same observable behaviors in both the relaxed semantics and the interleaving semantics: if it aborts in one semantics, it aborts in the other; if it never aborts (which means it is "safe"), it reaches the same set of final states in both settings. We need the premise in the second case because the subsumption relation allows us to transform an unsafe program into a safe one. Therefore a program that reaches $\langle \mathbf{skip}, \sigma' \rangle$ in the relaxed semantics may abort and never terminate at σ' in the interleaving semantics.

Theorem 5.2 (DRF-guarantee). If $\langle T, \sigma \rangle$ racefree, then

1. $[\succeq_t]$ $\langle T, \sigma \rangle \longmapsto^*$ abort iff $\langle T, \sigma \rangle \longmapsto^*$ abort.
2. If $\neg(\langle T, \sigma \rangle \longmapsto^*$ abort$)$, then
   $[\succeq_t]$ $\langle T, \sigma \rangle \longmapsto^* \langle \mathbf{skip}, \sigma' \rangle$ iff $\langle T, \sigma \rangle \longmapsto^* \langle \mathbf{skip}, \sigma' \rangle$.

The proof trivially follows from two important lemmas. Lemma 5.3 shows the equivalence between the interleaving semantics and the grainless semantics for race-free programs. Lemma 5.4 shows the equivalence between the grainless semantics and the relaxed semantics. Therefore, we can derive the DRF-guarantee using the grainless semantics as a bridge (see Fig. 1 (b)).

Lemma 5.3. If $\langle T, \sigma \rangle$ racefree, then

1. $\langle T, \sigma \rangle \longmapsto^*$ abort iff $\langle \lfloor T \rfloor, \sigma \rangle \Longrightarrow^*$ abort.
2. $\langle T, \sigma \rangle \longmapsto^* \langle \mathbf{skip}, \sigma' \rangle$ iff $\langle \lfloor T \rfloor, \sigma \rangle \Longrightarrow^* \langle (\mathbf{skip}, \_), \sigma' \rangle$.

Lemma 5.4. If $\langle T, \sigma \rangle$ racefree, then

1. $[\succeq_t]$ $\langle T, \sigma \rangle \longmapsto^*$ abort iff $\langle \lfloor T \rfloor, \sigma \rangle \Longrightarrow^*$ abort.
2. if $\neg(\langle T, \sigma \rangle \longmapsto^*$ abort$)$, then
   $[\succeq_t]$ $\langle T, \sigma \rangle \longmapsto^* \langle \mathbf{skip}, \sigma' \rangle$ iff $\langle \lfloor T \rfloor, \sigma \rangle \Longrightarrow^* \langle (\mathbf{skip}, \_), \sigma' \rangle$.

Details about the proofs can be found in the technical report [15].

$$\frac{\vdash \{p * I\} \, c \, \{q * I\}}{I \vdash \{p\} \, \mathbf{atomic} \; c \, \{q\}} \; \text{(ATOM)} \qquad \frac{I \vdash \{p_1\} \, c_1 \, \{q_1\} \quad I \vdash \{p_2\} \, c_2 \, \{q_2\}}{I \vdash \{p_1 * p_2\} \, c_1 \, \| \, c_2 \, \{q_1 * q_2\}} \; \text{(PAR)}$$

c_2 does not update free var. in p_1, c_1 and q_1, and conversely.

Fig. 10. Selected CSL Rules

6   Soundness of CSL

We prove the soundness of CSL in our relaxed semantics by first proving it is sound in the grainless semantics. The CSL we use here is mostly standard [23, 9]. It consists of sequential and concurrent rules. The sequential part $(\vdash \{p\} \, c \, \{q\})$ is standard sequential separation logic rules. The concurrent rules allow us to derive a judgment of the form $I \vdash \{p\} \, c \, \{q\}$. It informally says that the state can be split implicitly into a shared part and a local part; the local part can be accessed only by c; p and q are pre- and post-conditions for the local state; the shared part can be accessed by both c and its environment, but only in atomic blocks; accesses of the shared state must preserve its invariant I. Figure 10 shows two of the most important rules of CSL.

We define semantics of the judgment $I \models \{p\}c\{q\}$ below, based on the grainless semantics. The soundness of CSL rules is shown by Lemma 6.2.

Definition 6.1. $I \models \{p\}c\{q\}$ iff, for all σ and δ such that $\sigma \models I * p$ and $\sigma \models \delta \uplus I$, we have (1) $\neg (\langle (c, \delta), \sigma \rangle \Longrightarrow^* \mathbf{abort})$ and $\neg (\langle (c, \delta), \sigma \rangle \Longrightarrow^* \mathbf{race})$, and, (2) if $\langle (c, \delta), \sigma \rangle \Longrightarrow^* \langle (\mathbf{skip}, \_), \sigma' \rangle$, then $\sigma' \models I * q$.

Here $\sigma \models I * p$ means σ satisfies the assertion $I * p$, and $\sigma \models \delta \uplus I$ means the set of memory locations in δ is disjoint with the domain of the sub-heap (in σ) that satisfies I. The formal definitions are given in the technical report [15].

Lemma 6.2. If $I \vdash \{p\} \, c \, \{q\}$, then $I \models \{p\}c\{q\}$.

The proof of this lemma follows standard techniques, i.e. we need to first prove the locality [31, 10] of each primitive commands. We show details of the proofs in our technical report [15]. Next we give semantics to $I \vdash \{p\} \, c \, \{q\}$ based on our relaxed semantics, and show the soundness in Theorem 6.4.

Definition 6.3. $I \models_{[A]} \{p\}c\{q\}$ iff, for all σ such that $\sigma \models I * p$, we have (1) $\neg ([A] \, \langle c, \sigma \rangle \longmapsto^* \mathbf{abort})$, and, (2) if $[A] \, \langle c, \sigma \rangle \longmapsto^* \langle \mathbf{skip}, \sigma' \rangle$, then $\sigma' \models I * q$.

Theorem 6.4. If $I \vdash \{p\} \, c \, \{q\}$, then $I \models_{[\succeq_t]} \{p\}c\{q\}$.

Proof. Trivial by applying Lemmas 5.4 and 6.2. $\qquad \square$

Extensions of CSL. Bornat et al. [6] extended CSL with fractional permissions to distinguish exclusive total accesses and shared read-only accesses. We can prove CSL with fractional permissions is also sound with respect to the grainless semantics, but the model of heaps needs to be changed to a partial mapping from locations to a pair of values and permissions. The proof should be similar to the proof for standard CSL. We believe other extensions of CSL, such as CSL with storable locks [17, 18] and the combination of CSL with Rely-Guarantee reasoning [29, 13], can also be proved sound with respect to the grainless semantics. Then their soundness in our relaxed semantics can be derived easily from Lemma 5.4. We would like to verify our hypothesis in our future work.

7 Related Work and Conclusions

The literature on memory models is vast. We cannot give a detailed overview due to space constraints. Below we just discuss some closely related work.

The RAO model by Saraswat et al. [26] consists of a family of transformations (IM, CO, AU, LI, PR and DX). Unlike our subsumption relation which gives only an abstract and extensional formulation of semantics preservation between sequential threads, each of them defines a very specific class of transformations. We suspect that our model is weaker (not necessarily strictly weaker) than the RAO model. IM, CO and DX are obvious specializations of our subsumption relation with extra constraints. Although we only support intra-thread local transformations, we can define a more relaxed version of PR: $c \succeq$ if q then c' else c, assuming c' has the same behaviors with c if q holds over the initial state. AU enforces a specific scheduling. We allow all possible scheduling in our relaxed semantics. LI is an inter-thread transformation. It is unclear how it relates to our subsumption relation, but the examples [26] involving LI (e.g., the cross-over example) can be supported following the pattern with which we reproduce the prescient-write example in Sect. 4.

In this paper, we do not investigate the precise connection to the Java Memory Model (JMM [21]). Our semantics is operational and not based upon the happens-before model. We believe it provides a weaker memory model with the DRF-guarantee, and supports compiler optimizations that JMM does not, such as the one described by Cenciarelli et al. [11]. However, there are two key issues if we want to apply our model to Java, i.e. preventing the "out-of-thin-air" behaviors and supporting partial barriers. The first one can be addressed by adding constraints similar to Saraswat's DX-family transformations in our subsumption relation. The second one can be solved by allowing transformations to go beyond partial barriers. We will show the solution in an upcoming paper.

Boudol and Petri [7] presented an operational approach to relaxed memory models. Their weak semantics made explicit use of write buffers to simulate the effects of memory caching during execution, which was more concrete and constructive than most memory model descriptions. However, only a restricted set of reordering was observable in their semantics, while our semantics is much weaker and supports all four types of memory reordering. Also, since our formalization of memory models is based on program transformations, our semantics has better support of compiler optimizations. The connection between their semantics and program logics such as CSL is unclear either.

Sevcik [27] analyzed the impact of common optimizations in two relaxed memory models, establishing their validity and showing counter examples; some of our examples were inspired by his work. Gao and Sarkar [16] introduced Location Consistency (LC), probably the weakest memory model described in the literature; we stand by their view that memory models should be more relaxed and not based necessarily on cache consistence.

Conclusions. We present a simple operational semantics to formalize memory models. The semantics is parameterized on a binary relation over programs. By instantiating the parameter with a specific relation $\succeq_t$, we have obtained a memory model that is weaker than many existing ones. Since the relation is weaker than observational equivalence of sequential programs, this memory model also captures many sequential optimizations that usually preserve semantic equivalence. We then propose an operational grainless semantics, which allows us to define data-race-freedom and prove the DRF-guarantee of our relaxed memory model. We also proved the soundness of CSL in relaxed memory models, using the grainless semantics as a bridge between CSL and the relaxed semantics.

In our future work, we would like to extend our framework to support partial barriers. This can be achieved by extend the $\succeq$ relation with transformations that go beyond partial barriers. It is also interesting to formally verify the correctness of sequential optimization algorithms in a concurrent setting. Given this framework, it is sufficient to prove that the algorithms implement a subset of the $\succeq$ relation.

Acknowledgments. We thank anonymous referees for their comments on this paper. Rodrigo Ferreira and Zhong Shao are supported in part by NSF grants CCF-0811665, CNS-0915888, and CNS-0910670. Xinyu Feng is supported in part by National Natural Science Foundation of China (grant No. 90818019).

References

[1] Adve, S., Gharachorloo, K.: Shared memory consistency models: A tutorial. IEEE Computer 29(12), 66–76 (1996)

[2] Adve, S., Hill, M.: A unified formalization of four shared-memory models. IEEE Transactions on Parallel and Distributed Systems 4(6), 613–624 (1993)

[3] Benton, N.: Simple relational correctness proofs for static analyses and program transformations. In: 31st POPL, January 2004, pp. 14–25 (2004)

[4] Boehm, H., Adve, S.: The foundations of the C++ concurrency memory model. In: PLDI, Tucson, Arizona, June 2008, pp. 68–78 (2008)

[5] Boehm, H.-J.: Threads cannot be implemented as a library. In: PLDI, Chicago, June 2005, pp. 261–268 (2005)

[6] Bornat, R., Calcagno, C., O'Hearn, P., Parkinson, M.: Permission accounting in separation logic. In: 32nd POPL, January 2005, pp. 259–270 (2005)

[7] Boudol, G., Petri, G.: Relaxed memory models: an operational approach. In: 36th POPL, Savannah, Georgia, USA, January 2009, pp. 392–403 (2009)

[8] Brookes, S.: A grainless semantics for parallel programs with shared mutable data. Electronic Notes in Theoretical Computer Science 155, 277–307 (2006)

[9] Brookes, S.: A semantics for concurrent separation logic. Theoretical Comp. Sci. 375(1-3), 227–270 (2007)

[10] Calcagno, C., O'Hearn, P.W., Yang, H.: Local action and abstract separation logic. In: 22nd LICS, July 2007, pp. 366–378 (2007)
[11] Cenciarelli, P., Knapp, A., Sibilio, E.: The Java memory model: Operationally, denotationally, axiomatically. In: De Nicola, R. (ed.) ESOP 2007. LNCS, vol. 4421, pp. 331–346. Springer, Heidelberg (2007)
[12] Dijkstra, E.: Cooperating sequential processes. In: Genuys, F. (ed.) Programming Languages, pp. 43–112. Academic Press, London (1968)
[13] Feng, X.: Local rely-guarantee reasoning. In: 36th POPL, January 2009, pp. 315–327 (2009)
[14] Feng, X., Ferreira, R., Shao, Z.: On the relationship between concurrent separation logic and assume-guarantee reasoning. In: De Nicola, R. (ed.) ESOP 2007. LNCS, vol. 4421, pp. 173–188. Springer, Heidelberg (2007)
[15] Ferreira, R., Feng, X., Shao, Z.: Parameterized memory models and concurrent separation logic (extended version). Technical Report YALEU/DCS/TR-1422, Department of Computer Science, Yale University (2009), http://flint.cs.yale.edu/publications/rmm.html
[16] Gao, G., Sarkar, V.: Location consistency – a new memory model and cache consistency protocol. IEEE Transactions on Computers 49(8), 798–813 (2000)
[17] Gotsman, A., Berdine, J., Cook, B., Rinetzky, N., Sagiv, M.: Local reasoning for storable locks and threads. In: Shao, Z. (ed.) APLAS 2007. LNCS, vol. 4807, pp. 19–37. Springer, Heidelberg (2007)
[18] Hobor, A., Appel, A., Nardelli, F.: Oracle semantics for concurrent separation logic. In: Drossopoulou, S. (ed.) ESOP 2008. LNCS, vol. 4960, pp. 353–367. Springer, Heidelberg (2008)
[19] Lamport, L.: How to make a multiprocessor computer that correctly executes multiprocess programs. IEEE Transactions on Computers 28(9) (September 1979)
[20] Leroy, X.: Formal certification of a compiler back-end, or: Programming a compiler with a proof assistant. In: 33rd POPL, January 2006, pp. 42–54 (2006)
[21] Manson, J., Pugh, W., Adve, S.: The Java memory model. In: 32nd POPL, Long Beach, California, January 2005, pp. 378–391 (2005)
[22] Mosberger, D.: Memory consistency models. Operating Systems Review 27(1), 18–26 (1993)
[23] O'Hearn, P.: Resources, concurrency, and local reasoning. Theoretical Comp. Sci. 375(1-3), 271–307 (2007)
[24] Owens, S., Sarkar, S., Sewell, P.: A better x86 memory model: x86-TSO. In: 22nd TPHOLS, Munich, Germany, August 2009, pp. 391–407 (2009)
[25] Reynolds, J.: Toward a grainless semantics for shared-variable concurrency. In: Lodaya, K., Mahajan, M. (eds.) FSTTCS 2004. LNCS, vol. 3328, pp. 35–48. Springer, Heidelberg (2004)
[26] Saraswat, V., Jagadeesan, R., Michael, M., von Praun, C.: A theory of memory models. In: 12th PPoPP, San Jose (March 2007)
[27] Sevcik, J.: Program Transformations in Weak Memory Models. PhD thesis, School of Informatics, University of Edinburgh (2008)
[28] SPARC International Inc. The SPARC Architecture Manual, Version 8. Revision SAV080SI9308 (1992)
[29] Vafeiadis, V., Parkinson, M.: A marriage of rely/guarantee and separation logic. In: Caires, L., Vasconcelos, V.T. (eds.) CONCUR 2007. LNCS, vol. 4703, pp. 256–271. Springer, Heidelberg (2007)
[30] Yang, H.: Relational separation logic. Theoretical Computer Science 375(1-3), 308–334 (2007)
[31] Yang, H., O'Hearn, P.: A semantic basis for local reasoning. In: Nielsen, M., Engberg, U. (eds.) FOSSACS 2002. LNCS, vol. 2303, pp. 402–416. Springer, Heidelberg (2002)

Amortized Resource Analysis with Polynomial Potential

A Static Inference of Polynomial Bounds for Functional Programs

Jan Hoffmann* and Martin Hofmann

Ludwig-Maximilians-Universität München
{jan.hoffmann,martin.hofmann}@ifi.lmu.de

Abstract. In 2003, Hofmann and Jost introduced a type system that uses a potential-based amortized analysis to infer bounds on the resource consumption of (first-order) functional programs. This analysis has been successfully applied to many standard algorithms but is limited to bounds that are linear in the size of the input.

Here we extend this system to polynomial resource bounds. An automatic amortized analysis is used to infer these bounds for functional programs without further annotations if a maximal degree for the bounding polynomials is given. The analysis is generic in the resource and can obtain good bounds on heap-space, stack-space and time usage.

Keywords: Functional Programming, Static Analysis, Resource Consumption, Amortized Analysis.

1 Introduction

In this paper we study the problem of statically determining an upper bound on the resource usage of a given first-order functional program as a function of the size of its input.

As in an earlier work by Hofmann and Jost [1] we rely on the potential method of amortized analysis to take into account the interaction between the steps of a computation and thus obtain tighter bounds than by a mere addition of the worst case resource bounds of the individual steps. Furthermore, the use of potentials relieves one of the burden of having to manipulate symbolic expressions during the analysis by a priori fixing their format.

The main limitation of the system of Hofmann and Jost [1] is its restriction to linear resource bounds. While this restriction is often acceptable when accounting heap space, it is rather limiting when accounting time and other resources. This raises the question whether it is possible to effectively utilize the potential method to compute super-linear resource bounds. We address the problem in this work by using a potential-based amortized analysis to infer *polynomial resource bounds*.

---

* Supported by the DFG Graduiertenkolleg 1480 (PUMA).

A.D. Gordon (Ed.): ESOP 2010, LNCS 6012, pp. 287–306, 2010.
© Springer-Verlag Berlin Heidelberg 2010

The analysis system we present applies to functional first-order programs with integers, lists and recursion. It can also be extended to programs with tree-like data structures.

Our analysis of the programs is *fully automatic* and does not require type annotations. It is furthermore *generic in the resource* and provides good bounds on heap space, stack space, clock cycles (time) or other resources that might be of interest to a user.

The linear system [1,2] has been successfully applied in the domain of embedded systems [3]. We envisage that the present extension will also have applications there, in particular in situations where only a few functions exhibit super-linear resource consumption. For this, it is important that the system described here properly extends the linear one so that no expressive power is lost when moving to polynomials.

We give examples of typical programs with a polynomial resource behavior to which our extended system successfully applies. The examples have been implemented in a prototype of the system that is available online[1]. It can be directly used in a web browser to analyze and to evaluate user generated programs. We experimented with a variety of example programs such as

- quicksort, mergesort, insertionsort
- multiplication and division for bit-vectors of arbitrary length
- longest common subsequence via dynamic programming
- breadth-first traversal of a tree using a functional queue
- sieve of Eratosthenes

A comparison of the computed bounds with the actual resource costs showed that many bounds exactly match the measured worst-case time and heap-space behaviors of the functions (this is for instance the case for quicksort, insertionsort, pairs and triples). Plots of our experiments are available online and in the extended version of this article.

The main conceptual contribution of this paper lies in the transfer of the analysis method of Hofmann and Jost from linear to polynomial bounds. They used an *automatic amortized analysis* to infer first-order types that are annotated with information on the resource consumption. The analysis works basically like a standard type inference instrumented with linear constraints for the type annotations that can then be solved by linear programming. For this method to work it is essential that the occurring constraints are linear. Since one would expect an analysis for non-linear bounds to result in non-linear constraints it has been often assumed that amortized analysis is limited to linear bounds. That is maybe why the problem of an extension of amortized analysis to super-linear bounds has remained open for several years. The *amortized analysis with polynomial potential* we present is an elegant and powerful extension of the amortized analysis to polynomial bounds that naturally results in linear constraints.

The paper is organized as follows. In §2 we introduce the concept of amortized analysis and informally describe the novel technique that we introduce here. We

---

[1] http://raml.tcs.ifi.lmu.de

then, in §3, define the functional programming language RAML (Resource Aware ML) that is used to describe our system and give, in §4, the operational big-step semantics that define the resource consumption of RAML programs. In the sections 5 and 6 we define the type system for the resource aware types that are used in the analysis. §7 shows the analysis of example functions. §8 outlines how the typing of an sub-expressions can be improved in order to type complex expressions. The inference algorithm is presented in §9 and §10 gives an overview of the related work.

An extended version of this paper is available on the first authors web page. In addition, we show there how our system can be extended to trees and how it can be applied to infer sized types. Furthermore, it contains a compilation of the experimental results and more detailed versions of §7, §8 and §9.

2 Amortized Analysis: Examples and Intuition

Amortized analysis was initially introduced by Sleator and Tarjan [4] to analyze the efficiency of data structures. For a given data structure one is often interested in the costs of a sequence of operations whose costs vary depending on the state of the data structure. A method to analyze the cost of such a sequence is to introduce a non-negative potential of the data structure that can be used to pay (costly) operations. More precisely one defines the *amortized cost* of an operation as the sum of its actual cost and the (possibly negative) net gain of potential incurred by its invocation. The sum of the amortized costs taken over a sequence of operations plus the potential of the initial data structure then furnishes an upper bound on the actual cost of that sequence.

In 2003, Hofmann and Jost [1] applied amortized analysis to type systems in order to derive linear bounds on the heap-space usage of functional programs. The idea is to assign a linear potential to all data structures of variable length. This potential can then be used to "pay" for the resource consumption of functions that are applied to that data. Consider for example the function $attach:(int, L(int)) \rightarrow L(int, int)$ that takes an integer and a list of integers and returns a list of pairs of integers such that the first argument is attached to every element of the list. The expression $attach(1,[1,2,3,4])$ thus evaluates to $[(1,1),(1,2),(1,3),(1,4)]$. The function $attach$ can be implemented as follows.

$attach(x,l) = $ **match** l **with** $|$ nil $\rightarrow$ nil $|$ (y::ys) $\rightarrow$ (x,y)::(attach (x,ys))

To analyze the heap-space usage of $attach$ we suppose that we need one memory cell for both creating a new list element, and creating a new pair. The heap-space usage of an execution of $attach(x,l)$ is then $2n$ memory cells if n is the length of l. This fact can be expressed by the resource-annotated type

$$attach: (int, L^{(2)}(int)) \xrightarrow{0/0} L^{(0)}(int, int).$$

The intuitive meaning of this typing is the following: To evaluate $attach(x,l)$ one needs 0 memory cells and 2 memory cells per element in the list. After the execution there are 0 memory cells and 0 cells per element of the returned list left. We say that the list l has the potential $\Phi(l, 2) = 2 \cdot |l|$ and that $attach(x,l)$ has the potential 0. Another possible typing of $attach$ would be

$$attach: (int, L^{(4)}(int)) \xrightarrow{8/8} L^{(2)}(int, int).$$

This typing could be used for the inner occurrence of $attach$ to type an expression like $attach(x, attach(z, ys))$.

Surprisingly, it turned out that such resource-annotated types can be automatically inferred without requiring any type annotations [1]. Essentially, the inference is done by a conventional type checking that produces linear inequalities which can be solved with linear programming. Furthermore, it has been shown [2] that the same potential-based approach can be similarly applied to a wide range of resources such as time and stack space [5] as well as to polymorphic, higher-order programs [6].

Now consider the function $pairs: L(int) \rightarrow L(int, int)$ that computes the two-element sets of a given set (if one views the input list as a set). The expression $pairs([1,2,3,4])$ thus evaluates to the list $[(1,2),(1,3),(1,4),(2,3),(2,4),(3,4)]$. Below is an implementation of $pairs$.

pairs l = **match** l **with** | nil → nil
                   | (x :: xs) → append(attach(x,xs),pairs xs)

Since the size of $pairs(l)$ is quadratic in the size of l it is impossible to assign $pairs$ a type with linear potential analogous to $attach$. In the next sections we show how to extend the linear potential annotation in a way that allows us to type functions with a polynomial resource consumption while still being able to perform automatic type inference. The function $pairs$ could then be assigned the typing

$$pairs: \ L^{(0,4)}(int) \xrightarrow{0/0} L^{(1)}(int, int).$$

This means that a list l in an expression $pairs(l)$ has the potential $\Phi(l, (0, 4)) = 0 \cdot |l| + 4 \cdot \binom{|l|}{2}$ and thus the linear potential $4|l'|$ for every sub-list (suffix) l' of l. The function $append$ could get the type

$$append: (L^{(2)}(int, int), L^{(1)}(int, int)) \xrightarrow{0/0} L^{(1)}(int, int)$$

since the function consumes one heap-cell for every element in the first argument. That is why $pairs(l)$ consumes 3 heap-cells per element of every sub-list of l and we can attach the potential 1 to every element of the list $pairs(l)$.

In a nutshell, our approach is as follows. We start from an as yet unknown potential-function of the form $\sum p_i(n_i)$ with polynomials p_i of a given maximal degree k and n_i referring to the sizes of the parameters. We then derive linear constraints on the coefficients of the p_i by type-checking the program. We choose, and this is an important contribution, a representation of polynomials of degree k as sums $\sum_{i=0,...,k} a_i \binom{n}{i}$ with $a_i \geq 0$. Compared with the traditional representation $\sum a_i \cdot n^i$, $a_i \geq 0$, this has the following advantages.

1. Some naturally arising resource bounds such as $\sum_{i=1,...,n} i$ cannot be expressed as a polynomial with non-negative coefficients in the traditional representation. On the other hand it is true that $\binom{n}{2} = \sum_{i=1,...,n} i$.

2. It is the largest class C of non-negative, monotone polynomials such that $p \in C$ implies $f(n) = p(n + 1) - p(n) \in C$ (see §5). All three properties are clearly desirable. The latter one, in particular, expresses that the "spill" arising upon shortening a list by one falls itself into C.
3. The identity $\sum_{i=1,\ldots,k} a_i \binom{n+1}{i} = a_1 + \sum_{i=1,\ldots,k-1} a_{i+1} \binom{n}{i} + \sum_{i=1,\ldots,k} a_i \binom{n}{i}$ gives rise to a local typing rule for *cons match* which very naturally allows the typing of both recursive calls and other calls to subordinate functions.
4. The linear constraints arising from the type inference have a very simple form due to the above equation. In particular each constraint involves at most three variables.

A key notion in the polynomial system is the additive shift $\lhd$ of a type annotation which is defined through $\lhd(q_1, \ldots, q_k) = (q_1 + q_2, \ldots, q_{k-1} + q_k, q_k)$ to reflect the identity from item 3. It is for instance present in the typing $tail{:}L^{\vec{q}}(int) \xrightarrow{0/q_1} L^{\lhd(\vec{q})}(int)$ of the function *tail* that removes the first element from a list.

The idea behind the additive shift is that the potential resulting from the contraction $xs{:}L^{\lhd(\vec{q})}(int)$ of a list $(x{::}xs){:}L^{\vec{q}}(int)$ (usually in a pattern match) is used for three purposes: i) to pay the constant costs after and before the recursive calls (q_1), ii) to fund calls to auxiliary functions $((q_2, \ldots, q_n))$, and iii) to pay for the recursive calls $((q_1, \ldots, q_n))$. For instance, this pattern is present in the definition of the function *pairs*: In the pattern match, the type $xs{:}L^{(4,4)}(int)$ is assigned to the variable xs. The potential is then shared between the two occurrences of xs in the following expression by using $xs{:}L^{(4,0)}(int)$ to pay for *append* and *attach* (ii) and using $xs{:}L^{(0,4)}(int)$ to pay for the recursive call of *pairs* (iii); the constant costs (i) are zero in this example.

In this paper we restrict ourselves to bounds that are sums of univariate polynomials. Mixed bounds such as $m \cdot n$ must be over-approximated by polynomials like $m^2 + n^2$. This results in a particularly efficient inference algorithm since the number of constraints grows only linear in the maximal degree of the polynomials (see §9). We are nevertheless currently investigating an extension to arbitrary multivariate polynomials.

3   RAML – A Functional Programing Language

In this section we define the functional first-order language RAML (Resource Aware ML). RAML is similar to LF (linear functional language) from [1]. It enjoys an ML-style syntax, Booleans, integers, pairs, lists, recursion and pattern matching.

The differences between LF and RAML are irrelevant for the resource aware type analysis. On the one hand, we have added integers to formulate more realistic examples. On the other hand, we have abandoned the sum type since it is not used in the examples that are presented here. Additionally, for the sake of simplicity, we do not have a destructive match operation in RAML. The integration of both features into the system is straightforward and analogous to the method used in LF.

Below is the EBNF grammar for the *expressions of RAML*. We skip the standard definitions of integer constants $n \in \mathbb{Z}$ and variable identifiers $x \in \text{VID}$.

$$
\begin{aligned}
e ::=\ & ()\ |\ \mathit{True}\ |\ \mathit{False}\ |\ n\ |\ x \\
& |\ x_1\ \mathit{binop}\ x_2\ |\ f(x_1, \ldots, x_n) \\
& |\ \mathit{let}\ x = e_1\ \mathit{in}\ e_2 \\
& |\ \mathit{if}\ x\ \mathit{then}\ e_t\ \mathit{else}\ e_f \\
& |\ (x_1, x_2)\ |\ \mathit{match}\ x\ \mathit{with}\ (x_1, x_2) \to e \\
& |\ \mathit{nil}\ |\ \mathit{cons}(x_h, x_t)\ |\ \mathit{match}\ x\ \mathit{with}\ |\ \mathit{nil} \to e_1\ |\ \mathit{cons}(x_h, x_t) \to e_2 \\
\mathit{binop} ::=\ & +\ |\ -\ |\ *\ |\ \mathit{mod}\ |\ \mathit{div}\ |\ \mathit{and}\ |\ \mathit{or}
\end{aligned}
$$

For the resource analysis it is unimportant which ground operations are used in the definition of *binop*. In fact one can use here every function that has a constant worst-case resource consumption. In our case we assume that we have integers of a fixed length, say 32 bits, in our system to ensure this property of the integer operations.

In the examples we often write *(x::y)* instead of *cons(x,y)*.

We restrict our attention mainly to *list types* in this paper. However, we discuss extensions to other algebraic data types in an extended version of this article that is available on the web.

The expressions of RAML are in *let normal form*. This means that term formers are applied to variables only whenever possible. This simplifies typing rules and semantics considerably without hampering expressivity in any way.

Below we define the well-typed expressions of RAML by assigning a *simple type*, i.e. a usual ML type without resource annotations, to every well-typed expression. Simple types are zero-order and first-order types as given by the following grammars.

$$
A ::= \mathit{unit}\ |\ \mathit{bool}\ |\ \mathit{int}\ |\ L(A)\ |\ (A, A) \qquad F ::= (A, \ldots, A) \to A
$$

Let $\mathcal{A}_S$ be the set of simple zero-order types (A in the grammar) and let $\mathcal{F}_S$ be the set of simple first-order types (F in the grammar).

The typing rules for RAML expressions are given as an affine linear type system with a sharing rule that explicitly tracks multiple occurrences of variables. The type system thus imposes no linearity restrictions but gives finer information on occurrences of variables than a simple type system does.

A *typing context* is a partial, finite function $\Gamma : \text{VID} \to \mathcal{A}_S$ from variable identifiers to zero-order types. As usual Γ_1, Γ_2 denotes the union of the contexts Γ_1 and Γ_2 provided that $\text{dom}(\Gamma_1) \cap \text{dom}(\Gamma_2) = \emptyset$. We thus have the implicit side condition $\text{dom}(\Gamma_1) \cap \text{dom}(\Gamma_2) = \emptyset$ whenever Γ_1, Γ_2 occurs in a typing rule.

Let FID be a set of function identifiers. A *signature* $\Sigma : \text{FID} \to \mathcal{F}_S$ is a finite, partial mapping of function identifiers to first-order types.

The typing judgment $\Gamma \vdash_\Sigma e : A$ states that the expression e has type A under the signature Σ in the context Γ. Due to space restrictions we omit the typing rules that define the typing judgment. They are standard and identical with the resource-annotated typing rules T:CONST - T:SHARE from §6 if the resource annotations are omitted.

A *RAML program* is a tuple that consists of a signature Σ and a family of expressions with specified variable identifiers $(e_f, \vec{y}^f)_{f \in \text{dom}(\Sigma)}$ such that $y_1^f{:}A_1, \ldots, y_k^f{:}A_k \vdash_\Sigma e_f{:}A$ if $\Sigma(f) = (A_1, \ldots, A_k) \to A$.

In the example programs we write $f(y_1^f, \ldots, y_k^f) = e_f$ to indicate that the expression e_f and the variables $y_1^f, \ldots, y_k^f$ are associated with the function f.

4 Operational Semantics for RAML

In this section we define a big-step operational semantics for RAML which is instrumented with resource counters. It is parametric in the particular resource of interest and can be instantiated for different resources including time, heap space and stack size.

Preliminaries: Let Loc be an infinite set of *locations* modeling memory addresses on a heap. The set of RAML *values* Val is given by

$$v ::= l \mid b \mid n \mid \text{NULL} \mid (v, v)$$

Thus a value $v \in \text{Val}$ is either a location $l \in \text{Loc}$, a Boolean constant b, an integer n, a null value NULL or a pair of values (v_1, v_2).

A *heap* is a finite partial function $\mathcal{H} : \text{Loc} \to \text{Val}$ that maps locations to values. A *stack* is a finite partial mapping $\mathcal{V} : \text{VID} \to \text{Val}$ from variables to values.

The rules below define an evaluation judgment of the form $\mathcal{V}, \mathcal{H} \vdash^q_{q'} e \rightsquigarrow v, \mathcal{H}'$ expressing the following. If $q \in \mathbb{Q}^+$ is the value of the resource counter and if the stack $\mathcal{V}$ and the initial heap $\mathcal{H}$ are given then the expression e evaluates to the value v and the new heap $\mathcal{H}'$. Furthermore the resource counter is never negative during the evaluation and $q' \in \mathbb{Q}^+$ is the value of the resource counter after the evaluation. The actual resource consumption is then $\delta = q - q'$. Note that δ could be negative if resources become available during the execution of e.

There can exist two different evaluation judgments $\mathcal{V}, \mathcal{H} \vdash^q_{q'} e \rightsquigarrow v, \mathcal{H}'$ and $\mathcal{V}, \mathcal{H} \vdash^p_{p'} e \rightsquigarrow v, \mathcal{H}'$ for an expression e under the same heap $\mathcal{H}$ and stack $\mathcal{V}$. But then the resource consumption δ of e is identical in both cases and thus $\delta = q - q' = p - p'$. Since $q, q', p, p' \in \mathbb{Q}^+$ it follows also that $q, p \geq \delta$. Moreover it is an invariant of the rules that if $\mathcal{V}, \mathcal{H} \vdash^q_{q'} e \rightsquigarrow v, \mathcal{H}'$ then also $\mathcal{V}, \mathcal{H} \vdash^{q+a}_{q'+a} e \rightsquigarrow v, \mathcal{H}'$ for every $a \geq 0$. The execution steps below are formulated with respect to constants $K \in \mathbb{Q}$ that depend on the resource the user is interested in. For example one could set $K^{\text{pair}} = K^{\text{cons}} = 1$ and $K = 0$ for all other constants K to analyze the number of heap-cells that are used during the execution. The constants might also be negative if resources are restituted during an execution step. This is the case for stack space and also heap space if one were to include destructive pattern matching as in LF [1] which is omitted here for simplicity.

$$\frac{}{\mathcal{V}, \mathcal{H} \vdash^{q+K^{\text{unit}}}_{q} () \rightsquigarrow \text{NULL}, \mathcal{H}} \text{ (E:CONST-U)} \qquad \frac{b \in \{\text{True}, \text{False}\}}{\mathcal{V}, \mathcal{H} \vdash^{q+K^{\text{bool}}}_{q} b \rightsquigarrow b, \mathcal{H}} \text{ (E:CONST-B)}$$

$$\frac{n \in \mathbb{Z}}{\mathcal{V}, \mathcal{H} \vdash^{\frac{q+K^{\text{int}}}{q}} n \rightsquigarrow n, \mathcal{H}} \text{ (E:Const-I)} \qquad \frac{x \in \text{dom}(\mathcal{V})}{\mathcal{V}, \mathcal{H} \vdash^{\frac{q+K^{\text{var}}}{q}} x \rightsquigarrow \mathcal{V}(x), \mathcal{H}} \text{ (E:Var)}$$

$$\frac{\begin{array}{c} op \in \{+, -, *, mod, div, and, or\} \\ x_1, x_2 \in \text{dom}(\mathcal{V}) \qquad v = op(\mathcal{V}(x_1), \mathcal{V}(x_2)) \end{array}}{\mathcal{V}, \mathcal{H} \vdash^{\frac{q+K^{\text{op}}}{q}} x_1 \ op \ x_2 \rightsquigarrow v, \mathcal{H}} \text{ (E:BinOp)}$$

$$\frac{\begin{array}{c} \Sigma(f) = (A_1, \ldots, A_k) \to A \qquad \forall 1 \le i \le n : \mathcal{V}(x_i) = v_i \\ [y_1^f \mapsto v_1, \ldots, y_k^f \mapsto v_k], \mathcal{H} \vdash^{\frac{q-K_1^{\text{app}}}{q'+K_2^{\text{app}}}} e_f \rightsquigarrow v, \mathcal{H}' \end{array}}{\mathcal{V}, \mathcal{H} \vdash^{\frac{q}{q'}} f(x_1, \ldots, x_k) \rightsquigarrow v, \mathcal{H}'} \text{ (E:FunApp)}$$

$$\frac{\mathcal{V}, \mathcal{H} \vdash^{\frac{q_1-K_1^{\text{let}}}{q_2}} e_1 \rightsquigarrow v_1, \mathcal{H}_1 \qquad \mathcal{V}[x \mapsto v_1], \mathcal{H}_1 \vdash^{\frac{q_2-K_2^{\text{let}}}{q_3+K_3^{\text{let}}}} e_1 \rightsquigarrow v_2, \mathcal{H}_2}{\mathcal{V}, \mathcal{H} \vdash^{\frac{q_1}{q_3}} \text{let } x = e_1 \text{ in } e_2 \rightsquigarrow v_2, \mathcal{H}_2} \text{ (E:Let)}$$

$$\frac{\mathcal{V}(x) = \text{True} \qquad \mathcal{V}, \mathcal{H} \vdash^{\frac{q-K_1^{\text{conT}}}{q'+K_2^{\text{conT}}}} e_t \rightsquigarrow v, \mathcal{H}'}{\mathcal{V}, \mathcal{H} \vdash^{\frac{q}{q'}} \text{if } x \text{ then } e_t \text{ else } e_f \rightsquigarrow v, \mathcal{H}'} \text{ (E:Cond-T)}$$

$$\frac{\mathcal{V}(x) = \text{False} \qquad \mathcal{V}, \mathcal{H} \vdash^{\frac{q-K_1^{\text{conF}}}{q'+K_2^{\text{conF}}}} e_f \rightsquigarrow v, \mathcal{H}'}{\mathcal{V}, \mathcal{H} \vdash^{\frac{q}{q'}} \text{if } x \text{ then } e_t \text{ else } e_f \rightsquigarrow v, \mathcal{H}'} \text{ (E:Cond-F)}$$

$$\frac{x_1, x_2 \in \text{dom}(\mathcal{V}) \qquad v = (\mathcal{V}(x_1), \mathcal{V}(x_2)) \qquad l \notin \text{dom}(\mathcal{H})}{\mathcal{V}, \mathcal{H} \vdash^{\frac{q+K^{\text{pair}}}{q}} (x_1, x_2) \rightsquigarrow l, \mathcal{H}[l \mapsto v]} \text{ (E:Pair)}$$

$$\frac{\begin{array}{c} \mathcal{V}(x) = l \qquad \mathcal{H}(l) = (v_1, v_2) \\ \mathcal{H}, \mathcal{V}[x_1 \mapsto v_1, x_2 \mapsto v_2] \vdash^{\frac{q-K_1^{\text{matchP}}}{q'+K_2^{\text{matchP}}}} e \rightsquigarrow v, \mathcal{H}' \end{array}}{\mathcal{V}, \mathcal{H} \vdash^{\frac{q}{q'}} \text{match } x \text{ with } (x_1, x_2) \to e \rightsquigarrow v, \mathcal{H}'} \text{ (E:Match-P)}$$

$$\frac{}{\mathcal{V}, \mathcal{H} \vdash^{\frac{q+K^{\text{nil}}}{q}} \text{nil} \rightsquigarrow \text{NULL}, \mathcal{H}} \text{ (E:Nil)}$$

$$\frac{x_h, x_t \in \text{dom}(\mathcal{V}) \qquad v = (\mathcal{V}(x_1), \mathcal{V}(x_2)) \qquad l \notin \text{dom}(\mathcal{H})}{\mathcal{V}, \mathcal{H} \vdash^{\frac{q+K^{\text{cons}}}{q}} \text{cons}(x_h, x_t) \rightsquigarrow l, \mathcal{H}[l \mapsto v]} \text{ (E:Cons)}$$

$$\frac{\mathcal{V}(x) = \text{NULL} \qquad \mathcal{H}, \mathcal{V} \vdash^{\frac{q-K_1^{\text{matchN}}}{q'+K_2^{\text{matchN}}}} e_1 \rightsquigarrow v, \mathcal{H}'}{\mathcal{V}, \mathcal{H} \vdash^{\frac{q}{q'}} \text{match } x \text{ with } | \ \text{nil} \to e_1 \ | \ \text{cons}(x_h, x_t) \to e_2 \rightsquigarrow v, \mathcal{H}'} \text{ (E:Match-N)}$$

$$\frac{\begin{array}{c} \mathcal{V}(x) = l \qquad \mathcal{H}(l) = (v_h, v_t) \\ \mathcal{V}[x_h \mapsto v_h, x_t \mapsto v_t], \mathcal{H} \vdash^{\frac{q-K_1^{\text{matchC}}}{q'+K_2^{\text{matchC}}}} e_2 \rightsquigarrow v, \mathcal{H}' \end{array}}{\mathcal{V}, \mathcal{H} \vdash^{\frac{q}{q'}} \text{match } x \text{ with } | \ \text{nil} \to e_1 \ | \ \text{cons}(x_h, x_t) \to e_2 \rightsquigarrow v, \mathcal{H}'} \text{ (E:Match-C)}$$

Actual constants for stack-space, heap-space and clock-cycle consumption have been determined for the abstract machine of the language Hume [7] on the Renesas M32C/85U architecture. A list can be found in the literature [2].

5   Resource Annotations for Polynomial Bounds

Resource-annotated types are simple types where lists are annotated with non-negative vectors $\vec{p} \in \mathbb{Q}^n$. These vectors associate a potential with the list that can be used to pay for resource consumptions during an execution.

Recall the example functions *attach* and *pairs* that have been introduced in §2. We assigned the annotated type $attach: (int, L^{(2)}(int)) \xrightarrow{0/0} L^{(0)}(int, int)$ to the function to indicate that the evaluation of *attach(x,l)* consumes $2 \cdot |l|$ resource units.

The function *pairs* calls the function *attach* for every sub-list (suffix) of the input which leads to a quadratic resource consumption. This corresponds to a general pattern in the sense that many typical quadratic functions consume a linear amount of resources for every sub-lists (suffix) of an input just like a typical linear function that consumes a constant amount of resources per element in its input list. We reflect this resource behavior by assigning a type like *pairs*: $L^{(0,5)}(int) \xrightarrow{0/0} L^{(2)}(int, int)$. Informally, this type says: To evaluate *pairs(l)* one needs 0 resource units per element of l and 5 resource units per element of each sub-list of l. The result of the computation is a list of pairs of integers that has a potential of 2 resource units per element.

In general we define *resource-annotated zero-order types* A as follows.

$$A ::= unit \mid bool \mid int \mid L^{\vec{p}}(A) \mid (A, A)$$

Here $\vec{p}$ is a *resource annotation* for a list type which is defined as a k-tuple $\vec{p} = (p_1, \ldots, p_k) \in \mathbb{Q}^k$ with $p_i \geq 0$ and $k > 0$. Let $\mathcal{A}$ be the set of resource-annotated zero-order types.

For two resource annotations $\vec{p} = (p_1, \ldots, p_k)$ and $\vec{q} = (q_1, \ldots, q_l)$ we write $\vec{p} \leq \vec{q}$ if $k \leq l$ and $p_i \leq q_i$ for all $1 \leq i \leq k$. If $l \geq k$ then we define $\vec{p} + \vec{q} = (p_1 + q_1, \ldots, p_k + q_k, q_{k+1}, \ldots, q_l)$.

Let $\vec{p} = (p_1, \ldots, p_k)$ be an annotation for a list type. The *additive shift* of $\vec{p}$ is $\lhd(\vec{p}) = (p_1 + p_2, p_2 + p_3, \ldots, p_{k-1} + p_k, p_k)$.

Let $\mathcal{H}$ be a heap and A be a resource-annotated type and let v be a value matching type A in $\mathcal{H}$. The *potential* $\Phi_{\mathcal{H}}(v{:}A)$ is then defined as follows.

- $\Phi_{\mathcal{H}}(\text{NULL}{:}A) = 0$
- If $A \in \{unit, int, bool\}$ then $\Phi_{\mathcal{H}}(v{:}A) = 0$.
- If $A = (A_1, A_2)$ and $v = (v_1, v_2)$ is a pair then $\Phi_{\mathcal{H}}(v{:}A) = \Phi_{\mathcal{H}}(v_1{:}A_1) + \Phi_{\mathcal{H}}(v_2{:}A_2)$.
- If $A = L^{(p_1, \ldots, p_k)}(A')$ is a list type and $v = l$ is a location with $\mathcal{H}(l) = (v', l')$ then $\Phi_{\mathcal{H}}(l{:}A) = p_1 + \Phi_{\mathcal{H}}(v'{:}A') + \Phi_{\mathcal{H}}(l'{:} L^{\lhd(p_1, \ldots, p_k)}(A'))$.

In the following sections we will sometimes explain an idea by talking about the potential $\Phi(x{:}A)$ of a variable x with respect to an annotated type A. In such a case we mean in fact the potential $\Phi_{\mathcal{H}}(\mathcal{V}(x){:}A)$ with respect to a stack $\mathcal{V}$ and a heap $\mathcal{H}$ that we do not want to specify precisely.

If l_1 is a location that points to a list then we write $\mathcal{H}(l_1) = [v_1, \ldots, v_n]$ if $\mathcal{H}(l_i) = (v_i, l_{i+1})$ for $i = 1, \ldots, n$ and $l_{n+1} = \text{NULL}$. If $l_1 = \text{NULL}$ then we write $\mathcal{H}(l_1) = []$.

Let for example $\mathcal{H}$ be a heap and $\mathcal{H}(v) = [v_1 \ldots, v_n]$ an integer list. Then

- $\Phi_{\mathcal{H}}(l{:}L^{(p_1)}(\text{int})) = p_1 \cdot n$
- $\Phi_{\mathcal{H}}(l{:}L^{(0,p_2)}(\text{int})) = \sum_{i=1}^{n-1} p_2 \cdot i = p_2 \frac{n \cdot (n-1)}{2}$
- $\Phi_{\mathcal{H}}(l{:}L^{(0,0,p_3)}(\text{int})) = \sum_{i=1}^{n-1} p_3 \frac{i \cdot (i-1)}{2} = p_3 \frac{n \cdot (n-1) \cdot (n-2)}{6}$

The next lemma shows how to express the potential $\Phi_{\mathcal{H}}(v{:}A)$ of a value v with respect the heap $\mathcal{H}$ and a matching annotated type A in terms of polynomials in the lengths of the lists that are reachable from v. For a list annotation $\vec{p}$ and an integer n we define

$$\phi(n, \vec{p}) = \sum_{i=1}^{k} \binom{n}{i} p_i.$$

Lemma 1. *Let $\mathcal{H}$ be a heap such that $\mathcal{H}(l) = [v_1 \ldots, v_n]$ is a list of length n and let $\vec{p} = (p_1, \ldots, p_k)$ be an annotation for a list type. Then $\Phi_{\mathcal{H}}(l{:}L^{\vec{p}}(A)) = \phi(n, \vec{p}) + \sum_{i=1}^{n} \Phi_{\mathcal{H}}(v_i{:}A)$.*

The proof of Lemma 1 as well as the proofs of the following lemmas are given in the extended version of this article.

It is essential for the type system that ϕ is linear in the sense of the following lemma that follows directly from the definition of ϕ.

Lemma 2. *Let $n \in \mathbb{N}$, $\alpha \in \mathbb{Q}$ and let $\vec{p}, \vec{q}$ be resource annotations. Then $\phi(n, \vec{p}) + \phi(n, \vec{q}) = \phi(n, \vec{p} + \vec{q})$ and $\alpha \cdot \phi(n, \vec{p}) = \phi(n, \alpha \cdot \vec{p})$.*

As mentioned before it is a general pattern in functional programs to compute a task on a list recursively for the tail of the list and to use the result of the recursive call to compute the result of the function. In such a recursive function it is natural to assign a uniform potential to each sub-list (depending on its length) that occurs in a recursive call. In other words: one wants to use the potential of the input list to assign a uniform potential to every suffix of the list. With this view, the list potential $\alpha = \phi(n, (p_1, p_2, \cdots, p_k))$ can be read as follows: a recursive function on a list l of length n that has the potential α can use the potential $\phi(i, (p_2, \cdots, p_k))$ for the suffixes of l of length $1 \le i < n$ that occurs in the recursion. This intuition is proved by the following lemma.

Lemma 3. *Let $\vec{p} = (p_1, \ldots, p_k)$ be a resource annotation, let $n \in \mathbb{N}$ and define $\phi(n, ()) = 0$. Then $\phi(n, (p_1, \ldots, p_k)) = n \cdot p_1 + \sum_{i=1}^{n-1} \phi(i, (p_2, \ldots, p_k))$.*

Note that the binomial coefficients are a basis of the vector space of the polynomials. Here, however, we are only interested in non-negative linear combinations of binomial coefficients. These admit a natural characterization in terms of growth: for $f : \mathbb{N} \to \mathbb{N}$ define $(\Delta f)(n) = f(n+1) - f(n)$. Call f *hereditarily non-negative* if $\Delta^i f \ge 0$ for all $i \ge 0$. One can show that a polynomial p is hereditarily non-negative if and only if it can be written as a non-negative linear combination of binomial coefficients. To wit, the coefficient of $\binom{n}{i}$ in the representation of p is $(\Delta^i p)(0)$. The hereditarily non-negative polynomials are scalar multiples of unary *resource polynomials* [8] and thus are closed under sum, product, and composition. Note that they include all non-negative linear combinations of the polynomials $(x^i)_{i \in \mathbb{N}}$.

6   Type System

This section presents typing rules for the resource-annotated zero-order types .4 that have been defined in §5 and establishes their semantic soundness. Later in §8 we add another rule.

As in the case of the simple types, a *typing context* is a partial finite function $\Gamma : \mathrm{VID} \to \mathcal{A}$ from variable identifiers to annotated zero-order types. The potential of a typing context Γ with respect to a heap $\mathcal{H}$ and a stack $\mathcal{V}$ is

$$\Phi_{\mathcal{V},\mathcal{H}}(\Gamma) = \sum_{x \in \mathrm{dom}(\Gamma)} \Phi_{\mathcal{H}}(\mathcal{V}(x){:}\Gamma(x))$$

Sometimes we write just $\Phi(\Gamma)$ leaving stack and heap implicit.

The *resource-annotated first-order types* $\mathcal{F}$ are defined by

$$F ::= (A, \ldots, A) \xrightarrow{q/q'} A.$$

Here q, q' are rational numbers and A ranges over the resource-annotated zero-order types. Let $\mathcal{F}$ denote the set of resource-annotated first-order types.

A *resource-annotated signature* $\Sigma : \mathrm{FID} \to \mathcal{F}$ is a finite, partial mapping of function identifiers to resource-annotated first-order types. A *resource-annotated typing judgment* has the form $\Sigma; \Gamma \vdash^{q}_{q'} e{:}A$ where e is a RAML expression, $q, q' \in \mathbb{Q}^{+}$ are non-negative rational numbers, Σ is a resource-annotated signature, Γ is a resource-annotated context and A is a resource-annotated zero-order type. The intended meaning of this judgment is that if there are more than $q + \Phi(\Gamma)$ resource units available then this is sufficient to evaluate e and then there are more than $q' + \Phi(v{:}A)$ resource units left after the evaluation of e to a value v.

Similarly as for simple types, a RAML program with resource-annotated types is a tuple that consists of a resource-annotated signature Σ and a family of expressions with specified variable identifiers $(e_f, \vec{y}^f)_{f \in \mathrm{dom}(\Sigma)}$ such that for each e_f we have $\Sigma; y_1^f{:}A_1, \ldots, y_k^f{:}A_k \vdash^{q}_{q'} e_f{:}A$ if $\Sigma(f){=}(A_1, \ldots, A_k) \xrightarrow{q/q'} A$.

The following type rules are used to derive a resource-annotated type judgment for RAML expressions. Therein, we write $e[z/x]$ to denote the expression e with all free occurrences of the variable x replaced with the variable z.

$$\frac{}{\Sigma; \emptyset \vdash^{K^{\text{unit}}}_{0} ()\!:\!unit} \ (\text{T:Const-U}) \qquad \frac{n \in \mathbb{Z}}{\Sigma; \emptyset \vdash^{K^{\text{int}}}_{0} n : int} \ (\text{T:Const-I})$$

$$\frac{b \in \{True, False\}}{\Sigma; \emptyset \vdash^{K^{\text{bool}}}_{0} b\!:\!bool} \ (\text{T:Const-U}) \qquad \frac{}{\Sigma; x\!:\!A \vdash^{K^{\text{var}}}_{0} x : A} \ (\text{T:Var})$$

$$\frac{op \in \{+, -, *, mod, div\}}{\Sigma; x_1\!:\!int, x_2\!:\!int \vdash^{K^{\text{op}}}_{0} x_1 \ op \ x_2 : int} \ (\text{T:BinOp-I})$$

$$\frac{op \in \{or, and\}}{\Sigma; x_1\!:\!bool, x_2\!:\!bool \vdash^{K^{\text{op}}}_{0} x_1 \ op \ x_2 : bool} \ (\text{T:BinOp-B})$$

$$\frac{\Sigma(f) = (A_1, \ldots, A_k) \xrightarrow{q/q'} A \qquad \Gamma = x_1{:}A_1, \ldots, x_k{:}A_k}{\Sigma; \Gamma \vdash_{q' - K_2^{\mathrm{app}}}^{q + K_1^{\mathrm{app}}} f(x_1, \ldots, x_k) : A} \text{ (T:FunApp)}$$

$$\frac{\Sigma; \Gamma_1 \vdash_{p}^{q - K_1^{\mathrm{let}}} e_1 : A \qquad \Sigma; \Gamma_2, x{:}A \vdash_{q' + K_3^{\mathrm{let}}}^{p - K_2^{\mathrm{let}}} e_2 : B}{\Sigma; \Gamma_1, \Gamma_2 \vdash_{q'}^{q} \text{ let } x = e_1 \text{ in } e_2 : B} \text{ (T:Let)}$$

$$\frac{\Sigma; \Gamma \vdash_{q' + K_2^{\mathrm{conT}}}^{q - K_1^{\mathrm{conT}}} e_t : A \qquad \Sigma; \Gamma \vdash_{q' + K_2^{\mathrm{conF}}}^{q - K_1^{\mathrm{conF}}} e_f : A}{\Sigma; \Gamma, x{:}\mathrm{bool} \vdash_{q'}^{q} \text{ if } x \text{ then } e_t \text{ else } e_f : A} \text{ (T:Cond)}$$

$$\frac{}{\Sigma; x_1{:}A_1, x_2{:}A_2 \vdash_{0}^{K^{\mathrm{pair}}} (x_1, x_2) : (A_1, A_2)} \text{ (T:Pair)}$$

$$\frac{A = (A_1, A_2) \qquad \Sigma; \Gamma, x_1{:}A_1, x_2{:}A_2 \vdash_{q' + K_2^{\mathrm{matchP}}}^{q - K_1^{\mathrm{matchP}}} e : B}{\Sigma; \Gamma, x{:}A \vdash_{q'}^{q} \text{ match } x \text{ with } (x_1, x_2) \to e : B} \text{ (T:Match-P)}$$

$$\frac{A \in \mathcal{A}}{\Sigma; \emptyset \vdash_{0}^{K^{\mathrm{nil}}} \mathrm{nil}{:}L(A)} \text{ (T:Nil)}$$

$$\frac{\vec{p} = (p_1 \ldots p_k)}{\Sigma; x_h{:}A, x_t{:}L^{\lhd(\vec{p})}(A) \vdash_{0}^{p_1 + K^{\mathrm{cons}}} cons(x_h, x_t){:}L^{\vec{p}}(A)} \text{ (T:Cons)}$$

$$\frac{\vec{p} = (p_1, \ldots, p_k) \qquad \Sigma; \Gamma \vdash_{q' + K_2^{\mathrm{matchN}}}^{q - K_1^{\mathrm{matchN}}} e_1 : B}{\Sigma; \Gamma, x_h{:}A, x_t{:}L^{\lhd(\vec{p})}(A) \vdash_{q' + K_2^{\mathrm{matchC}}}^{q + p_1 - K_1^{\mathrm{matchC}}} e_2 : B} \\ \overline{\Sigma; \Gamma, x{:}L^{\vec{p}}(A) \vdash_{q'}^{q} \begin{array}{l} \text{match } x \text{ with } \mathrm{I} \text{ nil} \to e_1 \\ \mathrm{I} \text{ cons}(x_h, x_t) \to e_2 \end{array} : B} \text{ (T:Match-L)}$$

$$\frac{\Sigma; \Gamma, x{:}A_1, y{:}A_2 \vdash_{q'}^{q} e : B \qquad \curlyvee(A \mid A_1, A_2)}{\Sigma; \Gamma, z{:}A \vdash_{q'}^{q} e[z/x, z/y] : B} \text{ (T:Share)}$$

$$\frac{\Sigma; \Gamma, x{:}A \vdash_{q'}^{q} e : B \qquad A' <: A}{\Sigma; \Gamma, x{:}A' \vdash_{q'}^{q} e : B} \text{ (T:Super)} \qquad \frac{\Sigma; \Gamma \vdash_{q'}^{q} e : B \qquad B <: B'}{\Sigma; \Gamma \vdash_{q'}^{q} e : B'} \text{ (T:Sub)}$$

$$\frac{\Sigma; \Gamma \vdash_{p'}^{p} e : B \qquad q \geq p \qquad q - p \geq q' - p'}{\Sigma; \Gamma \vdash_{q'}^{q} e : B} \text{ (T:Relax)}$$

$$\frac{\Sigma; \Gamma \vdash_{q'}^{q} e : B \qquad x \in \mathrm{VID} \qquad A \in \mathcal{A}}{\Sigma; \Gamma, x{:}A \vdash_{q'}^{q} e : B} \text{ (T:Augment)}$$

The definitions of the relations $\curlyvee(. \mid ., .)$ and $<:$ are given below.

We describe the idea behind the type rules exemplary for T:Cons and T:Match. The rule T:Cons formalizes the fact that one has to pay for the resource consumption of the evaluation of $cons(x_h, x_t)$, i.e., basically the allocation of a new heap-cell that points to x_h and x_t. This is represented by the constant K^{cons} that depends on the resource that is studied. In addition one has to pay for the potential that is assigned to the new list of type $L^{\vec{p}}(A)$. We do so by requiring x_t to have the type $L^{\lhd(\vec{p})}(A)$ and to have p_1 resource units available. It corresponds exactly to the recursive definition of the potential function Φ and ensures that potential is neither gained nor lost.

Complementarily, the rule T:MATCH-L defines how to use the potential of a list to pay for resource consumptions. First, it matches the corresponding rules from the operational semantics E:MATCH-* in terms of resource consumption. It incorporates the fact that either e_1 or e_2 is evaluated. More interestingly, the "cons case" is inverse to the rule T:CONS and allows one to use the potential associated with a list. For one thing, p_1 resource units become available directly, for another the tail of the list is annotated with $\lhd(\vec{p})$ rather than $\vec{p}$, permitting e.g. a recursive call (requiring annotation $\vec{p}$) and an additional use of the tail with annotation $(p_2, p_3, \dots)$.

It is important that all the numerical constraints that result from rules T:CONS, T:MATCH-L and the other rules are *linear*. This is the reason why it is easy to verify the constraints and why one can use linear programming to infer type annotations that match the constraints.

The Subtyping Relation. Intuitively it is true that a zero-order type A is a subtype of a zero-order type B if and only if A and B have the same set of values, and for every value v the potential of $v{:}A$ is greater or equal than the potential of $v{:}B$. More formal, we define $<:$ to be the smallest relation such that

$$C <: C \text{ if } C \in \{\text{unit}, \text{bool}, \text{int}\}$$
$$(A_1, A_2) <: (B_1, B_2) \text{ if } A_1 <: B_1 \text{ and } A_2 <: B_2$$
$$L^{\vec{p}}(A) <: L^{\vec{q}}(B) \text{ if } A <: B \text{ and } \vec{p} \geq \vec{q}$$

The Sharing Relation. The sharing relation $\Upsilon(. \mid .,.)$ defines how the potential of a zero-order variable can be shared by multiple occurrences of that variable. We will have $\Upsilon(A \mid A_1, A_2)$ if and only if A, A_1 and A_2 are structural identical, i.e. have the same set of values, and for every value v the potential $\Phi(v{:}A)$ of $v{:}A$ is identical to the sum $\Phi(v{:}A_1) + \Phi(v{:}A_2)$ of the potentials of $v{:}A_1$ and $v{:}A_2$. So $\Upsilon(. \mid .,.)$ is the smallest relation such that

$$\Upsilon(C \mid C, C) \text{ if } C \in \{\text{unit}, \text{bool}, \text{int}\}$$
$$\Upsilon(L^{\vec{p}}(A) \mid L^{\vec{q}}(A_1), L^{\vec{r}}(A_2)) \text{ if } \Upsilon(A \mid A_1, A_2) \text{ and } \vec{p} = \vec{q} + \vec{r}$$
$$\Upsilon((A,B) \mid (A_1,B_1), (A_2,B_2)) \text{ if } \Upsilon(A \mid A_1, A_2) \text{ and } \Upsilon(B \mid B_1, B_2)$$

Soundness of the Analysis. The soundness theorem below states that a resource annotated type statement guarantees that an expression can be evaluated in the stated resource bounds and that at least the stated amount of resources is available after the evaluation.

Such a statement is only meaningful with respect to a well-formed stack and a well-formed heap. A stack $\mathcal{V}$ and a heap $\mathcal{H}$ are *well-formed* with respect to a context Γ if $\mathcal{V}(x)$ is a value matching the type $\Gamma(x)$ for every $x \in \text{dom}(\Gamma)$. We then write $\mathcal{H} \vDash \mathcal{V}{:}\Gamma$. It is not hard to show that if $\mathcal{H} \vDash \mathcal{V}{:}\Gamma$ and $\mathcal{V}, \mathcal{H} \vdash^{q}_{q'} e \rightsquigarrow v, \mathcal{H}'$ then also $\mathcal{H}' \vDash \mathcal{V} : \Gamma$.

Theorem 1 (Soundness). *Let Σ be the signature of a given RAML program and let e be an expression. Let $\mathcal{H} \vDash \mathcal{V}{:}\Gamma$ and let there exist some $u, u' \in \mathbb{Q}^{+}$ such that $\mathcal{V}, \mathcal{H} \vdash^{u}_{u'} e \rightsquigarrow v, \mathcal{H}'$. If $\Sigma; \Gamma \vdash^{p}_{p'} e{:}A$ and $q \geq \Phi_{\mathcal{V},\mathcal{H}}(\Gamma) + p + r$ for a $r \in \mathbb{Q}^{+}$ then there is a $q' \geq \Phi_{\mathcal{H}'}(v{:}A) + p' + r$ such that $\mathcal{V}, \mathcal{H} \vdash^{q}_{q'} e \rightsquigarrow v, \mathcal{H}'$.*

Theorem 1 is proved in the same way as the corresponding theorem in the system of [1]. The key ingredients that are used are the lemmas from §5.

7   Examples

We developed a prototype implementation and implemented a number of well-known, non-trivial algorithms that exhibit a super-linear resource consumption. These examples, as well as the prototype itself, are available online[2] and can be directly tested and modified in a web-browser. The prototype implementation can analyze the heap-space consumption and the number of evaluation steps. It is adequately documented easy to use. One can use it not only compute resource bounds but also to measure the actual resource consumption of a program. We invite everybody to experiment with it to explore the frontiers of our system.

The algorithms that we implemented include

- quicksort, mergesort, insertionsort
- multiplication and division for bit-vectors of arbitrary length
- longest common subsequence via dynamic programming
- breadth-first traversal of a tree using a functional queue
- sieve of Eratosthenes

A comparison of the measured resource costs with the computed bounds showed that the bounds match exactly the measured worst-case costs for many functions (e.g. quicksort, insertionsort, pairs and triples). The plots of the experiments can be found on the website and in the extended version of this article. Therein, we also present a somewhat artificial example (a version of dyadic vector product) that explores some boundaries of our system.

For simplicity we only provide examples for heap-space consumption in this section. We assume that one heap-cell is allocated whenever new data is created. Thus we set $K^{\text{pair}} = K^{\text{cons}} = 1$ and $K = 0$ for all other constants K.

For each function we give its annotated type and the type of the potential-carrying variables that appear in its definition. We distinguish different occurrences of the same variable by adding superscripts. To save space we omit some less interesting types and sometimes waive the let-normal form.

The types contain meta-variables p_1, c, d, q_3 ranging over non-negative rational numbers. Any instantiation of the former yields a correct typing.

---

[2] http://raml.tcs.ifi.lmu.de

7.1 Subsets of Size k

Our canonical example for polynomial heap-space consumption is the following problem: view a given list as a set and compute the subsets of size k for a given k. The size of the output is a polynomial of degree k.

Below we define the subset functions for $k = 2$ and $k = 3$ but one can also see how it works for $k > 3$. The function $attach(x,l)$ computes a list of pairs so that x is paired with every element in the list l. The function $pairs(l)$ computes a list of all (unordered) pairs that can be built from the elements of l and similarly the function $triples(l)$ computes a list of all (unordered) triples.

attach(x,l) = **match** l **with** | nil $\rightarrow$ nil | (y::ys)$\rightarrow$ **let** l' = attach(x,ys) **in** (x,y) ::l'

attach: $(int, L^{(p+2)}(int)) \xrightarrow{c/c} L^{(p)}(int, int)$, l:$L^{(p+2)}(int)$, ys:$L^{(p+2)}(int)$, l':$L^{(p)}(int, int)$

append(l,ys) = **match** l **with** | nil $\rightarrow$ ys | (x::xs) $\rightarrow$ **let** l' = append(xs,ys) **in** x::l'

append: $(L^{(p+1)}(A), L^{(p)}(A)) \xrightarrow{c/c} L^{(p)}(A)$
l:$L^{(p+1)}(A)$, ys:$L^{(p)}(A)$, xs:$L^{(p+1)}(A)$, l':$L^{(p)}(A)$

pairs(1) = **match** l **with** | nil $\rightarrow$ nil
| (x::xs) $\rightarrow$ **let** nps = attach(x,xs^1) **in**
let rps = pairs(xs^2) **in** append(nps,rps)

pairs: $L^{(0,p_2+3)}(int) \xrightarrow{c/c} L^{(p_2)}(int, int)$
l :$L^{(0,p_2+3)}(int)$,   xs^1:$L^{(p_2+3)}(int)$, rps:$L^{(p_2)}(int, int)$
xs:$L^{(p_2+3,p_2+3)}(int)$, xs^2:$L^{(0,p_2+3)}(int)$, nps:$L^{(p_2+1)}(int, int)$

triples(1) = **match** l **with** | nil $\rightarrow$ nil
| (x::xs) $\rightarrow$ **let** tps = pairs(xs^1) **in**
let nts = attach(x,tps) **in**
let rts = triples(xs^2) **in** append(nts,rts)

triples: $L^{(0,0,p_3+6)}(int) \xrightarrow{c/c} L^{(p_3)}(int, int, int)$
xs :$L^{(0,p_3+6,p_3+6)}(int)$, xs^2:$L^{(0,0,p_3+6)}(int)$,   nts:$L^{(p_3+1)}(int, int, int)$
xs^1:$L^{(0,p_3+6)}(int)$,   rts :$L^{(p_3)}(int, int, int)$, tps:$L^{(p_3+3)}(int, int)$

In the above functions it is the case that the type used for recursive calls is the same as the type of the function itself (monomorphic recursion). For example in the function *pairs* the type of *append(nps,rps)* and *rps* is identical. That is not the case in general. Suppose for example that one would swap the arguments of *append* in the last line of *pairs*:

pairs'(1) = **match** l **with** | nil $\rightarrow$ nil
| (x::xs) $\rightarrow$ **let** nps = attach(x,xs^1) **in**
let rps = pairs'(xs^2) **in** append(rps,nps)

pairs': $L^{(0,p_2+2,1)}(int) \xrightarrow{c/c} L^{(p_2)}(int, int)$
l :$L^{(0,p_2+2,1)}(int)$,   rps:$L^{(p_2+1)}(int, int)$, nps:$L^{(p_2)}(int, int)$
xs:$L^{(p_2+2,p_2+3,1)}(int)$, xs^2:$L^{(0,p_2+3,1)}(int)$, xs^1 :$L^{(p_2+2)}(int)$

The function *pairs'* is used resource polymorphically in its recursive call. That means that the resource annotation of the argument of *pairs'* differs from the annotation of the original argument. The soundness of polymorphic recursion is unproblematic and covered by our results; the inference of resource polymorphic is restricted to special cases. See §8 and §9 which cover the present example.

At a first glance it might be surprising that the heap-space consumption of *pairs'* is not quadratic but cubic. The reason is that the heap-space consumption of *append* is linear in the length of the first argument and *append* is called $|l|$ times. In the case of *pairs* the length of the first argument is about the length $|l|$ but in the case of *pairs'* the first argument is *rps* which is quadratic in $|l|$.

Note that a run-time analysis of *pairs* and *pairs'* would result in analogous types as above with different constants. That is to say the analysis of *pairs* would result in a quadratic bound while we would get a cubic bound for *pairs'*. But in contrast to the heap-space use, the run-time of *pairs'* would be cubic even in the presence of garbage collection or in an extended system that enjoys a destructive pattern matching. So this is a nice example where our system might help a programmer to produce more efficient code.

7.2   Longest Common Subsequence

A standard example of dynamic programming that can be found in many textbooks is the computation of the longest common subsequence (LCS) of two given lists (sequences). Given two sequences $a_1, \ldots, a_n$ and $b_1, \ldots, b_m$, one successively fills an $n \times m$ matrix (here a list of lists) A such that $A(i, j)$ contains the length of the LCS of $a_1, \ldots, a_i$ and $b_1, \ldots, b_j$. It is the case that

$$A(i,j) = \begin{cases} 0 & \text{if } i = 0 \text{ or } j = 0 \\ A(i-1, j-1) + 1 & \text{if } i, j > 0 \text{ and } a_i = b_j \\ \max(A(i, j-1), A(i-1, j)) & \text{if } i, j > 0 \text{ and } a_i \neq b_j \end{cases}$$

This algorithm can be analyzed in our system and is exemplary for similar algorithms that use dynamic programming.

tail'(1) = **match** l **with** | nil → nil | (x::xs) → xs

firstline(m) = **match** m **with** | nil → nil | (l::_) → l

```
lastvals (1) = match l with | nil       → (0,0)
                            | (a1 :: l') → match l' with | nil     → (a1,0)
                                                         | (a2 :: _) → (a1,a2)
```

tail'   : $L^p(int) \xrightarrow{c/c} L^p(int)$ firstline: $L^p(L^q(int)) \xrightarrow{c/c} L^q(int)$
lastvals: $L^p(int) \xrightarrow{c/c} (int, int)$

```
addcolumn(m,x,c) = match c with | nil → nil
    | (y :: ys) → let m' = addcolumn(tail'(m),x,ys) in
                  let (above,updiag) = lastvals( firstline (m')) in
                  let l1 = firstline (m) in
                  let ( left ,_) = lastvals (l1) in
                  let elem = if x = y then updiag+1 else max(above,left)
                  in ((elem :: l1 ):: m')
```

newline (y, lastline ,l) = **match** l **with** | nil → nil
   | (x::xs) → **let** nl = newline(y,tail'(lastline),xs) **in**
         let (left ,_) = lastvals (nl) **in**
         let (above,updiag) = lastvals(lastline) **in**
         let elem = **if** x = y **then** updiag+1 **else** max(above,left)
         in elem::nl

addline(m,y,xs) = **let** nl = newline(y, firstline (m),xs) **in** nl::m

addcolumn: $(L^p(L^q(int)), int, L^{p+q+2}(int)) \xrightarrow{c/c} L^p(L^q(int))$
newline: $(int, L^q(int), L^{q+1}(int)) \xrightarrow{c/c} L^q(int)$
addline: $(L^p(L^q(int)), int, L^{q+1}(int)) \xrightarrow{c+p+1/c} L^p(L^q(int))$

lcstable(l1 ,l2) = **match** l1 **with** | nil → nil
   | $(x::xs^1)$ → **match** l2^1 **with** | nil → nil
      | (y::ys) → **let** m = lcstable(xs^2,ys) **in**
         let m' = addline(m,y,xs^3) **in** addcolumn(m',x,l2^2)

lcstable: $(L^{(0,q+1)}(int), L^{(2p+q+3,p+q+2)}(int)) \xrightarrow{c/c} L^p(L^q(int))$
ys :$L^{(2p+q+3,p+q+2)}(int)$, xs^3:$L^{(q+1,0)}(int)$, m':$L^p(L^q(int))$,   l2^1:$L^{(p+1,p+q+2)}(int)$
xs^1:$L^{(q+1,q+1)}(int)$,   xs^2:$L^{(0,q+1)}(int)$, m :$L^p(L^q(int))$,   l2^2:$L^{(p+q+2)}(int)$

lcs(l1 ,l2) = **let** m = lcstable(l1 ,l2) **in**
         match m **with** | nil → 0 | ((len::_)::_) → len

lcs: $(L^{(0,1)}(int), L^{(3,2)}(int)) \xrightarrow{c/c} int$

8   Passing Non-linear Potential

An unsatisfying limitation of the type rules that have been presented in §6 is that
they fail to assign super-linear potential to the output of some basic functions
that can be typed with a linear output type. To overcome is limitation one can
use linear algebra to compute linear constraints that state how a super-linear
potential can be assigned to the output of a function, provided that a function
type with a linear output is given.

Due to the limited space we can only describe this idea by way of example. A
formal description and a type rule is given is the extended version of this paper.

Consider the function *append*. With the rules from §6 we are able to derive
a type of the form *append*: $(L^{(1)}(int), L^{(1)}(int)) \xrightarrow{0/0} L^{(1)}(int)$ if we use the *cost-free* resource metric in which all constants equal 0. Then it follows that the
length of the output is bounded by $n + m$ if n and m are the lengths of the
inputs of *append*. This information suffices to compute (once and for all) constraints for a super-linear output via linear algebra. In the (cost-free) quadratic
case we obtain for example *append*: $(L^{(p_1,p_2)}(int), L^{(q_1,q_2)}(int)) \xrightarrow{0/0} L^{(0,r_2)}(int)$
if $4p_1 \geq r_2, 4q_1 \geq r_2, p_2 \geq r_2$ and $q_2 \geq r_2$. Such a cost-free type can then
be additively combined with a typing of the function that was inferred with
respect to another resource-metric by adding the numbers in the type annotations. For example, for the heap metric from §7 we obtain the typing *append*:
$(L^{(4,12)}(int), L^{(3,12)}(int)) \xrightarrow{0/0} L^{(0,3)}(int)$.

9   Inference of Annotated Types

The type-inference algorithm for RAML works similar to the algorithm of Hofmann and Jost that has been developed for the linear system [1].

The basic algorithm does a classic type inference generating linear constraints for the annotations that are collected during the inference, and that can be solved later by linear programming. The only difference to the method of Hofmann and Jost is that we have to provide a maximal degree of the resource bounds in order to obtain a finite set of equations. If the degree is too low then the generated linear program is unsolvable. It can either be specified by the user or can be incremented successively after an unsuccessful analysis. In most cases it should be sufficient to run the analysis for instance twice, first with a maximal degree of, say, 5 and a second time with maximal degree 10.

In order to apply the technique that has been outlined in §8 we have to run the basic algorithm multiple times since we have to consider strongly connected components in the call graph one after another. More details are given in the extended version of this work.

The inference algorithm finds types for most example programs that we considered, including all programs in this paper. Nevertheless, it is not complete with respect to the declarative rules in the earlier sections. The reason is that it sometimes fails to infer a *resource-polymorphic* typing of a function, i.e., a typing in which the annotations of a recursive call differ from the annotations of the top-level function type. We are working on a more involved inference algorithm that is complete. However, we find that this algorithm exhibits some interesting ideas that should be explained in detail in separate work.

10   Conclusion and Related Work

We have extended amortized resource analysis for first-order functional programs from linear bounds to polynomial bounds. The main technical innovations of our paper are as follows: 1) the representations of resource bounds as non-negative linear combinations of binomial coefficients enabling a simple and local typing rule for pattern matching; 2) the derivation of constraints solvable by linear programming in spite of the super-linear bounds.

Most closely related is of course [1] which we extend with polynomial bounds. Other resource analyses that can in principle obtain polynomial bounds are approaches based on recurrences pioneered by Grobauer [9] and Flajolet [10]. In those systems, an a priori unknown resource bounding function is introduced for each function in the code; by a straightforward intraprocedural analysis a set of recurrence equations or inequations for these functions is then derived. A type-based extraction of such recurrences has been given in [11]. Even for relatively simple programs the resulting recurrences are quite complicated and difficult to solve with standard methods. In the COSTA project [12] progress has been made with the solution of those recurrences. Still, we find that amortization yields better results in cases where resource usage of intermediate functions depends on factors other than input size, e.g., sizes of partitions in QuickSort. Also compositions of functions seem to be better dealt with by amortization.

A successful method to estimate time bounds for C++ procedures with loops and recursion was recently developed by Gulwani et al. [13,14] in the SPEED project. They annotate programs with counters and use automatic invariant discovery between their values using off-the-shelf program analysis tools which are based on abstract interpretation. If the loops iterate over data-structures then the user needs to define numerical "quantitative functions" for the data-structures. In contrast our method is fully automatic. A methodological difference is that we infer (using linear programming) an abstract potential function which indirectly yields a resource-bounding function. As explained in the introduction the potential-based approach may be favorable in the presence of compositions and data scattered over different locations (partitions in QuickSort). Indeed, the examples from loc. cit. suggest that the two approaches are complementary in the sense that the method of Gulwani et al. works well for programs with little or no recursion but intricate interaction of linear arithmetic with loops. Our method, on the other hand, does not model the interaction of integer arithmetic with resource usage, but is particularly good for analyzing recursive programs involving inductive data types. As any type system, our approach is naturally compositional and lends itself to the smooth integration of components whose implementation is not available. Moreover, type derivations can be seen as certificates and can be automatically translated into formalized proofs in program logic [15]. However, we find the possibility of incorporating existing program analyses to be a particularly attractive feature of the SPEED approach. It would be interesting to investigate to what extent such analyses could also be harnessed for our method. Another pragmatic but interesting aspect is the use of slicing techniques to eliminate large code portions that do not contribute to the resource being analyzed.

Another related approach is the use of sized types [16,17,18,19] which provide a general framework to represent the size of the data in its type. Sized types are a very important concept and we also employ them indirectly. Our method adds a certain amount of data dependency and dispenses with the explicit manipulation of symbolic expressions in favour of numerical potential annotations. As we have demonstrated, there is a fruitful interaction between sized types and amortization.

Polynomial resource bounds have also been studied in [20]. Interestingly, the motivation of that paper is to extend amortized analysis to super-linear bounds; however loc. cit. only addresses the derivation of polynomial size bounds which is identified there as a necessary precursor to amortized analysis. Moreover, the analysis is restricted to functions whose exact growth rate is polynomial, and efficiency of inference remains unclear.

References

1. Hofmann, M., Jost, S.: Static Prediction of Heap Space Usage for First-Order Functional Programs. In: 30th ACM Symp. on Principles of Prog. Langs. (POPL 2003), pp. 185–197 (2003)

2. Jost, S., Loidl, H.W., Hammond, K., Scaife, N., Hofmann, M.: Carbon Credits for Resource-Bounded Computations using Amortised Analysis. In: Cavalcanti, A., Dams, D.R. (eds.) FM 2009. LNCS, vol. 5850, pp. 354–369. Springer, Heidelberg (2009)
3. Hammond, K., Dyckhoff, R., Ferdinand, C., Heckmann, R., Hofmann, M., Loidl, H.W., Michaelson, G., Sérot, J., Wallace, A.: The EmBounded Project: Automatic Prediction of Resource Bounds for Embedded Systems. Trends in Fun. Prog. 6 (2006)
4. Tarjan, R.E.: Amortized Computational Complexity. SIAM J. Algebraic Discrete Methods 6(2), 306–318 (1985)
5. Campbell, B.: Amortised Memory Analysis using the Depth of Data Structures. In: Castagna, G. (ed.) ESOP 2009. LNCS, vol. 5502, pp. 190–204. Springer, Heidelberg (2009)
6. Jost, S., Hammond, K., Loidl, H.W., Hofmann, M.: Static Determination of Quantitative Resource Usage for Higher-Order Programs. In: 37th ACM Symp. On Principles of Prog. Langs., POPL 2010 (to appear, 2010)
7. Hammond, K., Michaelson, G.: Hume: a Domain-Specific Language for Real-Time Embedded Systems. In: Pfenning, F., Smaragdakis, Y. (eds.) GPCE 2003. LNCS, vol. 2830, pp. 37–56. Springer, Heidelberg (2003)
8. Girard, J.Y., Scedrov, A., Scott, P.: Bounded Linear Logic. Theoret. Comput. Sci. 97(1), 1–66 (1992)
9. Grobauer, B.: Cost Recurrences for DML Programs. In: 6th Intl. Conf. on Funct. Prog. (ICFP 2001), pp. 253–264 (2001)
10. Flajolet, P., Salvy, B., Zimmermann, P.: Automatic Average-case Analysis of Algorithms. Theoret. Comput. Sci. 79(1), 37–109 (1991)
11. Crary, K., Weirich, S.: Resource Bound Certification. In: 27th ACM Symp. On Principles of Prog. Langs. (POPL 2000), pp. 184–198 (2000)
12. Albert, E., Arenas, P., Genaim, S., Puebla, G.: Automatic Inference of Upper Bounds for Recurrence Relations in Cost Analysis. In: Alpuente, M., Vidal, G. (eds.) SAS 2008. LNCS, vol. 5079, pp. 221–237. Springer, Heidelberg (2008)
13. Gulwani, S., Mehra, K.K., Chilimbi, T.M.: SPEED: Precise and Efficient Static Estimation of Program Computational Complexity. In: 36th ACM Symp. on Principles of Prog. Langs. (POPL 2009), pp. 127–139 (2009)
14. Gulavani, B.S., Gulwani, S.: A Numerical Abstract Domain Based on Expression Abstraction and Max Operator with Application in Timing Analysis. In: Gupta, A., Malik, S. (eds.) CAV 2008. LNCS, vol. 5123, pp. 370–384. Springer, Heidelberg (2008)
15. Beringer, L., Hofmann, M., Momigliano, A., Shkaravska, O.: Automatic Certification of Heap Consumption. In: Baader, F., Voronkov, A. (eds.) LPAR 2004. LNCS (LNAI), vol. 3452, pp. 347–362. Springer, Heidelberg (2005)
16. Hughes, J., Pareto, L., Sabry, A.: Proving the Correctness of Reactive Systems Using Sized Types. In: Symp. Princ. of Prog. Langs. (POPL 1996), pp. 410–423 (1996)
17. Hughes, J., Pareto, L.: Recursion and Dynamic Data-structures in Bounded Space: Towards Embedded ML Programming. In: 4th Intl. Conf. on Funct. Prog. (ICFP 1999), pp. 70–81 (1999)
18. Chin, W.N., Khoo, S.C.: Calculating Sized Types. High.-Ord. and Symb. Comp. 14(2-3), 261–300 (2001)
19. Chin, W.N., Khoo, S.C., Qin, S., Popeea, C., Nguyen, H.H.: Verifying Safety Policies with Size Properties and Alias Controls. In: Intl. Conf. on Software Eng. (ICSE 2005), pp. 186–195 (2005)
20. Shkaravska, O., van Kesteren, R., van Eekelen, M.C.: Polynomial Size Analysis of First-Order Functions. In: Della Rocca, S.R. (ed.) TLCA 2007. LNCS, vol. 4583, pp. 351–365. Springer, Heidelberg (2007)

Generative Operational Semantics
for Relaxed Memory Models*

Radha Jagadeesan, Corin Pitcher, and James Riely

School of Computing, DePaul University

Abstract. The specification of the Java Memory Model (JMM) is phrased in terms of acceptors of execution sequences rather than the standard generative view of operational semantics. This creates a mismatch with language-based techniques, such as simulation arguments and proofs of type safety.

We describe a semantics for the JMM using standard programming language techniques that captures its full expressivity. For data-race-free programs, our model coincides with the JMM. For lockless programs, our model is more expressive than the JMM. The stratification properties required to avoid causality cycles are derived, rather than mandated in the style of the JMM.

The JMM is arguably non-canonical in its treatment of the interaction of data races and locks as it fails to validate roach-motel reorderings and various peephole optimizations. Our model differs from the JMM in these cases. We develop a theory of simulation and use it to validate the legality of the above optimizations in any program context.

1 Introduction

In the context of shared memory imperative programs, Sequential Consistency (SC) (Lamport 1979) enforces a global total order on memory operations that includes the program order of each individual thread in the program. SC may be realized by a traditional interleaving semantics where shared memory is represented as a map from locations to values. It has been observed that SC disables compiler optimizations such as reordering of independent statements. Despite arguments that SC does not impair efficiency (Kamil et al. 2005), this observation and others have motivated a body of work on relaxed memory models; Adve and Gharachorloo (1996) provide a tutorial introduction with detailed bibliography.

A first (conceptual, if not chronological) step in generalizing SC is to consider the Data Race Free (DRF) models. Informally, a program is DRF if no execution of the program leads to a state in which a write happens concurrently with another operation on the same location. A DRF *model* requires that the programmer view of computation coincides with SC for programs that are DRF. The DRF viewpoint is most strongly reflected in languages such as C++, where any program with data races is deemed erroneous, with undefined semantics (Boehm and Adve 2008).

---

* We gratefully acknowledge conversations with Alan Jeffrey and referee comments on an earlier version of this paper. An extended version of this paper is available from the authors' homepages. Radha Jagadeesan and Corin Pitcher were supported by NSF 0916741. James Riely was supported by NSF Career 0347542.

A.D. Gordon (Ed.): ESOP 2010, LNCS 6012, pp. 307–326, 2010.
© Springer-Verlag Berlin Heidelberg 2010

Such an approach is at odds with the safety requirements of strongly typed languages that permit data races in well defined programs. Conceptually, this motivates the investigation of the Java Memory Model (JMM); see (Manson et al. 2005) for a detailed history. The JMM provides two key guarantees. First, it is a DRF model. Second, it disallows Thin Air Reads (no-TAR). In a configuration with multiple data races the JMM enforces a partial order on the resolution of these data races. Values that are written are justified by an execution of the program, and thus acyclicity of causality is maintained.

The formalization of the JMM is a technical tour-de-force. However, two criticisms are leveled at the JMM. First, the JMM is too complex. While simplicity is admittedly in the eyes of the beholder, some of the technical content of this criticism is that the JMM approach does not generate executions in the sense of traditional (structured) operational semantics (Saraswat 2004). Rather, it provides a means to test whether a given execution sequence is valid by providing criteria to establish the absence of causality cycles in the resolution of data races.

This is particularly problematic for standard tools-of-the-trade that often rely on a generative operational semantics. For example, proofs of type safety usually proceed by showing that each step of the execution of a program maintains the invariants provided in the type system. Similarly, (bi)simulation arguments proceed by showing that if two configurations are related by the candidate relation, and each takes an execution step(s), the resulting configurations are again related by the relation.

Second, the JMM impedes efficiency. As currently formalized, the JMM invalidates a variety of natural optimizations, such as reordering of independent statements (Cenciarelli et al. 2007). Sevcík and Aspinall (2008) show the incompatibility of JMM with roach-motel reordering (moving a read into the scope of a lock), redundant read after read elimination (reusing the results of a valid prior read) and some other peephole optimizations (such as eliminating a write that precedes another write to the same variable). As a result, the hotspot JVM has been non-compliant with the JMM (Sevcík 2008).

To address these issues, we describe a generative structured operational semantics for a concurrent object oriented language with a relaxed memory model. For DRF programs, our model coincides with the JMM. For lockless programs, our model allows every execution permitted by the JMM. Our model also allows executions that are forbidden by the JMM, but which are necessary to validate the peephole optimizations described above, such as redundant read after read elimination. For programs with both locks and data races, our model is better behaved than the JMM, for example, validating roach motel reorderings. Our model coincides with the JMM on the entire suite of causality test cases associated with the JMM (Pugh 2004).

We validate the utility of our operational semantics by establishing a theory of simulation. We use our study of simulation to validate several optimizations, including those mentioned above. Since simulation is a precongruence, our results show the legality of the transformations in any program context.

The rest of the paper is organized as follows. First, we discuss related work, then Section 3 provides an informal introduction to the basic ideas of the paper. The formalism follows in Section 4, with detailed examples in Section 5. We prove the DRF and lockless properties in Section 6. Section 7 defines simulation for a sub-language and shows the validity of some transformations.

2 Related Work

There is extensive research on memory models for hardware architectures, see (Steinke and Nutt 2004), (Luchangco 2001) and (Adve and Gharachorloo 1996) for surveys. This has led to research on (automated) verification of properties of memory models, e.g., see (Sarkar et al. 2009) for x86 and (Hangal et al. 2004) for Sparc TSO.

Our focus in this paper is on specifying the operational semantics for concurrent programming languages. The memory models for OpenMP (Bronevetsky and de Supinski 2007) and UPC (Yelick et al. 2004) deal with languages with weaker typing and pointer arithmetic and focus on synchronization primitives. These models may permit behaviors violating no-TAR (Boehm 2005). Saraswat (2004) provides a framework for operational semantics with relaxed memory models for typed languages. Saraswat et al. (2007) builds on this research and describes a collection of program transformations that are permitted in a relaxed memory model. In contrast to these papers, we capture the full expressiveness of the JMM for lockless programs, even while retaining DRF~ and no-TAR.

Our program of generative operational semantics using "true-concurrency" methods follows Cenciarelli et al. (2007) and Boudol and Petri (2009). While Cenciarelli et al. (2007) show that all their generated executions are permitted by the JMM, they do not discuss whether their theory is as expressive as the JMM. Boudol and Petri (2009) provide an operational model for write buffers and the ability for concurrent threads to snoop on the values in these buffers; causality test case 16 (Pugh 2004), discussed in Example 5, exemplifies the expressivity that is not captured.

In addition to eloquently articulating a collection of incisive examples, Aspinall and Sevcík (2007, 2008) formalize the Java DRF guarantee using theorem-provers and analyze several natural program transformations. Burckhardt et al. (2008) undertake the ambitious task of verifying concurrent programs in the presence of relaxed memory models, especially those associated with the CLR.

3 An Informal Introduction to Our Approach

We illustrate the key ideas underlying our approach using informal examples. We adopt the following notational conventions. Let x, y and z be thread-local variables. Let f and g be locations on the shared heap. Let l be a shared lock. Assume all heap locations and locks are initialized to 0. Locks are initially free and a lock's state increments on every action; thus even states are free and odd states are locked. Let s, t and u be thread identifiers. Write $s[M]$ for the thread with identifier s, executing statement M, and write the parallel composition of threads A and B as $A \mid B$.

In the SC view, each location in memory remembers only the last write to each location. Therefore an SC execution makes it impossible for t to read 2 and then 1 from f in the following program.

$$s[f=1; \ f=2; \ x=f;] \ \mid \ t[y=f; \ z=f;]. \qquad \text{(Program A)}$$

A relaxed memory model, such as the JMM, allows t to read 2 then 1 from f, even though the values are written by s in the reverse order. Rather than viewing memory as a map from locations to values, as in the SC model, we view memory as a sequence of *actions* which denote write and lock events; there are no read actions in our model. The action sequence generated by Program A is s[f=1] s[f=2]. A read can be assigned any value that is *visible*. In this case both values written by s are visible to the reads in t.

The order of statements in a program encodes the *program order* between actions of a single thread. A read can not see all of the values written by its own thread. In Program A, the read of f by s can only see 2, since 2 is written after 1 in s.

To model compiler and memory hierarchy effects, one may permit dynamic transformations to the action sequence generated by a single thread, as long as this does not introduce new behaviors. For example, it is permitted to rewrite s[f=1]s[f=2] to s[f=2], removing the value 1, which may be visible to concurrent threads. The converse transformation is not sound, however, since it introduces the value 1 out of thin-air.

Due to nondeterminism, the program s[f=1;] |t[g=1;] may result in either the sequence s[f=1]t[g=1] or the sequence t[g=1]s[f=1]. The program s[f=1;] |t[x=f; g=x;] may produce s[f=1]t[g=0] or s[f=1]t[g=1] or t[g=0]s[f=1]. However, it can *not* produce t[g=1]s[f=1] due to the data dependency between the two threads.

Synchronization makes the program order of a thread visible to other threads, potentially hiding previously visible values. For example, in any execution of the program

```
s[l.acquire(); f=1; f=2; l.release();] |
t[l.acquire(); x=f; y=f; l.release();]
```

the two reads of f in t must see the same value, and therefore $x = y$.

Lock actions must be recorded in the memory, since they affect visibility. We write lock actions as s[l:j], where j is an integer indicating the number of previous operations that have been performed on the lock. Thus, an even action corresponds to an acquire and an odd action to a release. In the example, if s executes first, we get the action sequence s[l:0]s[f=1]s[f=2]s[l:1]t[l:2]t[l:3]. Lock events in a memory induce a global *synchronization order*, which is used to define visibility.

Speculation. The approach sketched above can mimic the effects of write-buffers, cache-snooping and other non-SC executions. However it is insufficient to validate every behavior allowed by the JMM, such as the following (Manson et al. 2005, Fig 1).

$$s[x=g; f=1;] \mid t[y=f; g=2;] \qquad \text{(Program B)}$$

In any SC execution, at least one of the threads must read 0. The JMM allows the execution in which s reads 2 from g and t reads 1 from f, which can result from reordering independent statements in the two threads due to cache effects or optimization.

To accommodate such executions, we allow the execution to introduce *speculation*. Let A be the original pair of threads in Program B. Speculative execution reduces A to $(\top \Rightarrow A) \mathbin{[\!]} ((s\langle f=1\rangle t\langle g=2\rangle) \Rightarrow A)$, The reduction creates two copies of the original process, which are executed in separate universes with separate copies of the state. The left copy is called the *initial* process; the right, the *final* process. As indicated by the notation, the initial process may assume nothing, $\top$, whereas the final branch may assume the speculated writes, $s\langle f=1\rangle t\langle g=2\rangle$. A valid execution is one in which every speculation can be *finalized*, and therefore removed. When the speculation is removed, only the final process remains. The initial process is used only to justify the speculation. We rely on angelic nondeterminism to achieve a valid speculation, if possible.

The initial copy of Program B reads 0 in at least one of the threads and generates both writes. The final copy reads the speculative values and also generates both writes. Since the justifying writes are generated in both copies, the speculation can be finalized.

Unconstrained speculation can break both no-TAR and DRF. We constrain speculation so that it is *not self justifying*, but is *initial*, *consistent* and *timely*.

Self justifying computation allows a thread to see its own speculation, violating no-TAR. Consider the program $s[x=f; if(x==1)\{g=1;\} f=1;]$. To produce the write $s[g=1]$, one might speculate $s\langle f=1\rangle$. There is a later write which can justify the speculation. Our semantics forbids s from seeing its own speculation, however, thus ensuring that the conditional is false and g is not written.

Initiality requires that there is a computation that justifies the speculation without depending on the speculation. Consider the program $s[x=f; g=x;]$ | $t[y=g; f=y;]$ (Pugh 2004, §4). By speculating $s\langle g=1\rangle t\langle f=1\rangle$, both threads can read 1, violating no-TAR. The final process can produce the necessary writes $s[g=1]t[f=1]$, but the initial process can only write 0. Our semantics prevents the speculation from being finalized.

Consistency requires that the initial and final computations agree on certain actions. It is necessary for DRF. Consider the following program.

```
s[l.acquire(); x=f; if(x==0){f=1;} l.release();] |
t[l.acquire(); y=f; if(y==0){f=2;} l.release();] |      (Program C)
u[l.acquire(); z=f; g=z; l.release();]
```

The program is DRF. In an SC execution, it is not possible that f is 1 and g is 2 after execution. Using speculation $t\langle f=2\rangle$, however, the final process can achieve this result by scheduling order u, s, t, violating DRF. The initial process can produce the necessary write, but to do so it must schedule t before s. The inconsistent use of locks makes it impossible to finalize the speculation. Following the terminology of Manson et al. (2005), consistency prevents "bait" (in the initial process) and "switch" (in the final process), an intuition made precise in Example 6. Timeliness ensures that a speculation and its justifying write are in the same synchronization context. It is also necessary for DRF. Consider the following program.

```
s[l.acquire(); x=f; f=x+1; g=1; l.release();] |
t[l.acquire(); x=f; f=x+1; g=2; l.release();] |      (Program D)
u[l.acquire(); x=f; f=x+1; y=g; l.release();]
```

Again, the program is DRF. If s reads 0 from f, t reads 1 and u reads 2, then the order of the threads is determined. Clearly it is unacceptable in this case for u to read 1 from g. In the execution which runs s, then speculates $s\langle g=1\rangle$, then runs t and u, the memory after t runs is as follows.

$$s[1:0]s[f=1]s[g=1]s[1:1]s\langle g=1\rangle t[1:2]t[f=2]t[g=2]t[1:3]$$

The speculation $s\langle g=1 \rangle$ is "too late" with respect to its justifying write $s[g=1]$ since the intervening release $s[1:1]$ alters the synchronization context. In Section 5 we also discuss speculations which are "too early".

4   The Language

We develop the ideas of the previous section for an object oriented language with lock objects and thread parallelism. We do not explicitly treat volatile variables, final fields and several other features of the JMM. (From the synchronization perspective, a volatile write is similar to a lock release, a volatile read is similar to a lock acquire).

User Language. Let bt range over base type names, d over class names (including the reserved class Lock), f and g over field names, and m over method names (including the reserved method start). Types, T, include base types and classes ($T ::= bt \mid d$). Let $\vec{T}\ \vec{x}$ abbreviate $T_1\ x_1, \ldots, T_n\ x_n$. Class declarations, $\mathscr{D}$, are then given as usual ($\mathscr{D} ::= \text{class } d\{\vec{T}\ \vec{f}; \mathscr{M}\}$ where $\mathscr{M} ::= T\ m(\vec{T}\ \vec{x})\{M\}$). Fix a set of class declarations satisfying the well-formedness criteria of Igarashi et al. (2001). We assume, as there, an implicit constructor with arguments $\vec{T}\ \vec{f}$ for each class $d\{\vec{T}\ \vec{f}; \mathscr{M}\}$. Define the partial functions *fields* and *mbody* so that *fields*$(d) = \vec{T}\ \vec{f}$; if the field declarations of d are $\vec{T}\ \vec{f}$; and *mbody*$(d.m) = \lambda\vec{x}.M$ if class d contains method $T\ m(\vec{T}\ \vec{x})\{M\}$ for some T and $\vec{T}$. The abstraction $\lambda\vec{x}.M$ is written $\lambda.M$ when $\vec{x}$ is the empty sequence. A class d is *runnable* if *mbody*$(d.\text{run}) = \lambda.M$ for some M. Both *fields* and *mbody* are undefined on the reserved class Lock.

We assume disjoint sets of base values, $bv \in BV$, variables, x, y, and object names, p, q, s, t, ℓ. Base values include integers and the constants unit, true and false, with operators (such as ==, +, &&) ranged over by op. Variables include the reserved variable this. Each object name p is associated with a unique class $p.\text{class}$; a countable number of object names are associated with each class. By convention, we use name metavariables s, t for runnable objects and ℓ for lock objects. For any syntax category, let *fv* return the set of free variables and let *fn* return the set of free names.

A ground value is either an object name or a base value ($v, w, u ::= p \mid bv$). An open value may additionally be a variable ($V, W, U ::= p \mid bv \mid x$). The statement language is given in administrative normal form (Flanagan et al. 1993).

$$
\begin{aligned}
M, N ::= &\ \text{val } x = \{M\}\ N & \text{(Stack frame statement)} \\
\mid &\ \text{val } x = \text{new } d(\vec{V})\,;\ M & \text{(Creation statement)} \\
\mid &\ \text{val } x = W.m(\vec{V})\,;\ M & \text{(Method statement)} \\
\mid &\ \text{val } x = op(\vec{V})\,;\ M & \text{(Operator statement)} \\
\mid &\ \text{val } x = V.f\,;\ M & \text{(Field read statement)} \\
\mid &\ V.f = W\,;\ M & \text{(Field write statement)} \\
\mid &\ \text{if } (V)\ \{M\}\ \text{else } \{N\} & \text{(Conditional statement)} \\
\mid &\ \text{return } V\,; & \text{(Return statement)}
\end{aligned}
$$

As in Scala (Odersky et al. 2008), we use val to introduce local variables without requiring explicit type annotations. To make the examples shorter, we usually drop the val. We write $\uparrow V$ for "return V;" and $\uparrow(V,W)$ for "val x = new Pair(V,W); return x;", where x is fresh. In examples, we also use complex expressions, use infix notation for operators and drop occurrences of "return unit;". Thus, "y = a+b|c;" should is sugar for "val x = +(a,b); val y = +(x,c); return unit;", where x is fresh. We write "val $x = \cdots$; M" as "$\cdots$; M" if x does not occur free in M. We write "if(V){val $x = \cdots$; M} else {M}" as "if (V) {val $x = \cdots$;} M" if x does not occur free in M; this notation extends to field write statements, conditional statements and sequences of statements in the obvious way.

We expect that stack frame statements do not occur in the user language; they are introduced by the dynamics. The variable x is bound with scope M in all statements of the form "val $x = \cdots$; M". We identify syntax up to renaming of bound variables and names and write $M\{x := v\}$ for the capture avoiding substitution of v for x in M. We assume similar notation for substitution of names for names and for substitution over other syntax categories.

Actions and processes. Shared locations are assigned values via *actions*. Write, acquire and release actions are *committable* and so may be made visible at top-level. *Speculative* actions are introduced by the dynamics to explore possible future executions; they are not visible at top-level. The general class of actions include the evaluation context action $s[\![-]\!]$, belonging to thread s; this is used later to define justified reads and speculations.

$$
\begin{aligned}
\alpha, \beta &::= s[p.f{=}v] \mid s[\ell:j] &&\text{(Committable action)} \\
\phi, \psi &::= s\langle p.f{=}v\rangle &&\text{(Speculative action)} \\
\sigma, \tau &::= \alpha \mid \phi \mid s[\![-]\!] &&\text{(Actions)}
\end{aligned}
$$

Write and speculative actions identify the writing thread. The write action $s[p.f{=}v]$ indicates a write by s to location $p.f$ with value v. The speculative write $s\langle p.f{=}v\rangle$ allows threads other than s to subsequently read v from location $p.f$.

The meaning of a lock action $s[\ell:j]$ depends on the parity of the natural number j. When j is even, the lock is free and the corresponding action is an acquire. When j is odd, the lock is busy and the corresponding action is a release. We write $s[\text{acq } \ell:j]$ to indicate that j is even, and $s[\text{rel } \ell:j]$ to indicate that j is odd.

Let $thrd(\sigma)$ return the unique thread associated with an action. For all actions other than the evaluation context action, define loc to return the location of the action as $loc(s[p.f{=}v]) = loc(s\langle p.f{=}v\rangle) = p.f$ and $loc(s[\ell:j]) = \ell$. Similarly, define val as $val(s[p.f{=}v]) = val(s\langle p.f{=}v\rangle) = v$: and $val(s[\ell:j]) = j$. Write actions σ and τ *conflict* if $loc(\sigma) = loc(\tau)$; only two write actions can conflict.

The dynamics is defined using processes.

$$
\begin{aligned}
A,B ::= \;& \text{free } p &&\text{(Free object process)} \\
\mid\;& \text{runnable } p &&\text{(Runnable object process)} \\
\mid\;& \text{lock } \ell:j &&\text{(Lock process)} \\
\mid\;& s[M] &&\text{(Thread process)} \\
\mid\;& A \mid B &&\text{(Parallel process)} \\
\mid\;& (\nu p)A &&\text{(Scope restriction process)}
\end{aligned}
$$

$$| \; \alpha A \hspace{4cm} \text{(Action process)}$$
$$| \; \phi A \hspace{4cm} \text{(Guarded process)}$$
$$| \; \top \Rightarrow A \,[\!] \, \phi \Rightarrow B \hspace{2.5cm} \text{(Speculation process)}$$

The name p is bound with scope A in the process $(\nu p)A$. We identify processes up to renaming of bound names.

A *top-level* process contains no subterms that are guarded processes, ϕA, but may contain speculations. In speculation $\top \Rightarrow A \,[\!] \, \phi \Rightarrow B$, we refer to A as the *initial* process and to B as the *final* process. We write $\top \Rightarrow A \,[\!] \, \phi_1 \cdots \phi_n \Rightarrow B$ as shorthand for

$$\top \Rightarrow A \,[\!] \, \phi_1 \Rightarrow (\top \Rightarrow A \,[\!] \, \phi_2 \Rightarrow \cdots (\top \Rightarrow A \,[\!] \, \phi_n \Rightarrow B) \cdots).$$

An *initial process* has no free names or variables and contains a single thread. Initial processes have the form $(\nu s)\, s\,[M]$.

We assume several well-formedness criteria, which are true of initial processes and preserved by structural order and reduction. Let def return the *defined* names of a process; for example $def(\texttt{free } p) = def(\texttt{runnable } p) = def(p\,[M]) = def(\texttt{lock } p \!:\! j) = \{p\}$. Let $lockact(A)$ return the lock actions in A with thread identifiers removed; for example $lockact(s\,[\ell\!:\!i]A) = \{[\ell : i]\} \cup lockact(A)$. A process is *well-formed* if (1) in any subprocess $A\,|\,B$, $def(A) \cap def(B) = \emptyset$, (2) in any subprocess $A\,|\,B$, $lockact(A) \cap lockact(B) = \emptyset$, (3) in any action $s\,[\ell\!:\!i]$, $\ell.\texttt{class} = \texttt{Lock}$, (4) in any action $s\langle p.f{=}v\rangle$ or $s\,[p.f{=}v]$, $p.\texttt{class} \neq \texttt{Lock}$, and (5) in any subprocess $\top \Rightarrow A \,[\!] \, \phi \Rightarrow B$, $thrd(\phi) \in def(A)$. For the remainder of the paper, we consider only well-formed processes.

Evaluation contexts and justified reads. Evaluation contexts are defined as follows.

$$\mathbb{C} ::= [\!-\!] \mid A\,|\,\mathbb{C} \mid \mathbb{C}\,|\,A \mid (\nu p)\mathbb{C} \mid \alpha\mathbb{C} \mid \phi\mathbb{C}$$

The name p is *not* bound in evaluation context $(\nu p)\,\mathbb{C}$. There is no evaluation context for speculation processes; these are treated specially in the semantics.

We define the notion $\mathbb{C}$ *justifies read* $p.f{=}v$ *by* s to mean that context $\mathbb{C}$ contains a visible write $t\,[p.f{=}v]$ or speculation $t'\langle p.f{=}v\rangle$, where $t' \neq s$). The notion $\mathbb{C}$ *justifies speculation* ϕ is defined similarly.

To begin, define $act_s(\mathbb{C})$ to return the sequence of labeled actions occurring before the hole in $\mathbb{C}$.

$$act_s([\!-\!]) = s\,[\!-\!] \qquad act_s(A\,|\,\mathbb{C}) = act_s(\mathbb{C}) \qquad act_s(\alpha\mathbb{C}) = \alpha\,act_s(\mathbb{C})$$
$$act_s((\nu q)\,\mathbb{C}) = act_s(\mathbb{C}) \qquad act_s(\mathbb{C}\,|\,A) = act_s(\mathbb{C}) \qquad act_s(\phi\mathbb{C}) = \phi\,act_s(\mathbb{C})$$

Note that it is not possible for the hole to happen before any action. Given action sequence $\vec{\sigma}$ define *program order* ($<_{po}^{\vec{\sigma}}$) and *synchronizes-with* ($<_{sw}^{\vec{\sigma}}$) as follows.

$$i <_{po}^{\vec{\sigma}} j \quad \text{iff} \quad i < j \text{ and } thrd(\sigma_i) = thrd(\sigma_j)$$

$$i <_{sw}^{\vec{\sigma}} j \quad \text{iff} \quad \sigma_i = s\,[\texttt{rel } \ell\!:\!k] \text{ and } \sigma_j = t\,[\texttt{acq } \ell\!:\!k{+}1] \text{for some } s, t, \ell \text{ and odd } k$$

Note that $(<_{sw}^{\vec{\sigma}}) = \emptyset$ if $\vec{\sigma}$ contains no lock actions. Define *happens-before order* ($<_{hb}^{\vec{\sigma}}$) to be the transitive closure of the union of program order and synchronizes-with.

Definition 1 (Intervening write and justified read). We say that there is *no intervening write between i and k in $\vec{\sigma}$* if for every j such that σ_j is a write action and $i <^{\vec{\sigma}}_{hb} j <^{\vec{\sigma}}_{hb} k$, we have that $loc(\sigma_j) \neq loc(\sigma_i)$.

Let $\vec{\sigma} = acts_s(\mathbb{C})$. Let k be the index of $s[\![-]\!]$ in $\vec{\sigma}$. We say that $\mathbb{C}$ *justifies* read $p.f{=}v$ (by s) if there exists some i, with no intervening write between i and k in $\vec{\sigma}$, such that $\sigma_i = t[p.f{=}v]$, for some t (possibly equal to s), or $\sigma_i = t'\langle p.f{=}v\rangle$, for some $t' \neq s$.   □

For the purpose of reading, speculations are "transparent" in the sense that they do not obscure the prior writes. Both writes and speculations (of other threads) can be used to justify reads. Only writes can be used to justify speculations.

Definition 2 (Intervening release and justified speculation). We say that there is *no intervening release between i and k in $\vec{\sigma}$* if for every j such that σ_j is a release action and $i <^{\vec{\sigma}}_{hb} j <^{\vec{\sigma}}_{hb} k$, we have that $thrd(\sigma_j) \neq thrd(\sigma_i)$.

Let $\vec{\sigma} = acts_s(\mathbb{C})$. Let k be the index of $s[\![-]\!]$ in $\vec{\sigma}$. We say that $\mathbb{C}$ *justifies* speculation $s\langle p.f{=}v\rangle$ if there exists some i, with no intervening write nor intervening release between i and k in $\vec{\sigma}$, such that $\sigma_i = s[p.f{=}v]$.   □

The requirement that there be no intervening release between a write and the speculation that it justifies is motivated by Program D (Section 3). Since any synchronization edge originates from a release action, the absence of intervening releases ensures that a speculation and the write justifying it occupy the same position in the synchronization order and the happens-before relation.

Single-threaded action reordering and structural order. We define $\triangleright$ as a relation on single-threaded action sequences. That is $\vec{\sigma} \triangleright \vec{\tau}$ is defined only if $thrd(\vec{\sigma}) = thrd(\vec{\tau}) = \{s\}$, for some s.

Definition 3. Let $\triangleright$ be the least precongruence ($\vec{\sigma}\vec{\tau} \triangleright \vec{\sigma}'\vec{\tau}'$ whenever $\vec{\sigma} \triangleright \vec{\sigma}'$ and $\vec{\tau} \triangleright \vec{\tau}'$) on single-threaded action sequences that satisfies all instances of the following axiom schemata, where $\vec{\sigma} \bowtie \vec{\tau}$ abbreviates the axiom schemata $\vec{\sigma} \triangleright \vec{\tau}$ and $\vec{\tau} \triangleright \vec{\sigma}$.

(A-NONLOCK) If σ and τ are nonlock actions that do not conflict then $\sigma\tau \bowtie \tau\sigma$.
(A-ACQUIRE) If σ is a write and τ is an acquire then $\sigma\tau \triangleright \tau\sigma$.
(A-RELEASE) If σ is a release and τ is a write then $\sigma\tau \triangleright \tau\sigma$.
(A-ABSORPTION1) If σ is a write then $\sigma \triangleright \sigma\sigma$.
(A-ABSORPTION2) If σ and τ are conflicting writes then $\tau\sigma \triangleright \sigma$.
(A-ABSORPTION3) If σ, τ and τ' are conflicting writes then $\tau\tau'\sigma \bowtie \tau'\tau\sigma$.   □

If $\vec{\sigma} \triangleright \vec{\tau}$ then $\vec{\sigma}$ "simulates" $\vec{\tau}$; that is, all reads permitted by $\vec{\tau}$ are also permitted by $\vec{\sigma}$. This can be viewed as an adaptation of Lea's (2008) cookbook to our memory actions.

A-NONLOCK allows write actions and speculative actions in the same thread to commute. A-ACQUIRE and A-RELEASE permit enlarging the scope of locks. These rules are necessary to validate roach motel (Example 10). Were we to allow speculations to commute with lock actions, DRF would fail (Example 8).

In an SC model, later writes completely overwrite earlier writes to the same location. The absorption laws reflect approximations that are available in our relaxed memory model. The first rule allows identical writes to be copied. The second rule allows any

(S-PAR)	(S-FREE)	(S-NU-NU)	(S-PAR-PAR)
$\overline{A\mid A' \doteq A'\mid A}$	$\overline{A \doteq A\mid (\nu p)\,(\texttt{free }p)}$	$\overline{(\nu p)\,(\nu p')A \doteq (\nu p')\,(\nu p)A}$	$\overline{B\mid (A\mid A') \doteq (B\mid A)\mid A'}$

(S-PAR-PREFIX)	(S-PAR-NU) $p \notin fn(B)$	(S-PAR-SPECULATION) $thrd(\phi) \notin def(B)$
$\overline{B\mid (\sigma A) \geqq \sigma(B\mid A)}$	$\overline{B\mid ((\nu p)A) \doteq (\nu p)\,(B\mid A)}$	$\overline{B\mid (\top{\Rightarrow}A \,[\![\,\phi{\Rightarrow}A') \geqq \top{\Rightarrow}(B\mid A)\,[\![\,\phi{\Rightarrow}(B\mid A')}$

(S-NU-PREFIX) $p \notin fn(\sigma)$	(S-NU-SPECULATION) $p \notin fn(\phi)$
$\overline{(\nu p)\,\sigma A \doteq \sigma(\nu p)A}$	$\overline{(\nu p)\,(\top{\Rightarrow}A \,[\![\,\phi{\Rightarrow}A') \doteq \top{\Rightarrow}((\nu p)A)\,[\![\,\phi{\Rightarrow}((\nu p)A')}$

(S-PREFIX-PREFIX) $\sigma\tau \triangleright \tau\sigma$	(S-SPECULATION-PREFIX) $(thrd(\sigma) \neq thrd(\phi)) \vee (\phi\sigma \triangleright \sigma\phi)$
$\overline{\sigma\tau A \geqq \tau\sigma A}$	$\overline{\top{\Rightarrow}(\sigma A)\,[\![\,\phi{\Rightarrow}(\sigma A') \geqq \sigma(\top{\Rightarrow}A\,[\![\,\phi{\Rightarrow}A')}$

Fig. 1. Structural order $(A \geqq B)$

write to be eliminated when there is a subsequent "protecting" write to the same location. The third rule allows reordering behind a protecting write. Thus, we get:

Lemma 4. *If $\vec{\sigma}$ is a single-threaded sequence of write actions then $\vec{\sigma} \triangleright \vec{\sigma}\vec{\sigma}$.*

PROOF. Use the first absorption law to make multiple adjacent copies of each action. Use the remaining laws to rearrange them into the required order.   □

We define $A \geqq B$ to be the smallest precongruence on processes that satisfies the axioms in Figure 1 (where $A \doteq B$ abbreviates the two axioms $A \geqq B$ and $B \geqq A$). Many of the rules follow Milner (1991). We discuss the exceptions.

In order to allow speculation about objects that are not yet initialized, we separate object allocation and initialization. The structural rule S-FREE allows object names to be in scope before the corresponding call to the constructor.

The prefix and speculation rules are ordered so that parallel components can go under action prefixes and speculations, but can not come out. S-PAR-PREFIX effectively fixes the order of operations between threads once those operations become visible to other threads. The S-PREFIX-PREFIX and S-SPECULATION-PREFIX rules are induced by the single-threaded commutation rules. In the S-SPECULATION-PREFIX rule, the required order condition on actions holds for all the branches of speculation; so, it is appropriate to think of this as a "forall" speculation rule, in contrast to the "exists" speculation rule in the forthcoming reduction semantics.

The rules do not allow speculations to commute with each other; adding this rule would not affect contextual equivalence, but would affect the (finer) simulation relation introduced later, which is sensitive to the order of speculations.

In the remainder of the paper, let $\equiv$ denote the kernel of $\geqq$.

Reduction. Process reduction is defined as the least relation satisfying the rules and axioms given in Figure 2. $\twoheadrightarrow$ is the reflexive and transitive closure of $(\geqq) \cup (\rightarrow)$.

Again, many of the rules are standard. The built-in operators R-OPERATOR and the conditionals, R-IF-TRUE and R-IF-FALSE, carry no surprises. Method calls are implemented as usual by R-METHOD, R-FRAME and R-RETURN. The assumption of well-formedness guarantees that there is at most one thread for each object s, and therefore R-FRAME introduces no nondeterminism. Frames are deleted when a function returns.

(R-FRAME)
$$\frac{\mathbb{C}\left[\!\left[s\left[N\right]\right]\!\right] \to \mathbb{C}'\left[\!\left[s\left[N'\right]\right]\!\right]}{\begin{array}{l}\mathbb{C}\left[\!\left[s\left[\texttt{val } x = \{N\}M\right]\right]\!\right] \\ \to \mathbb{C}'\left[\!\left[s\left[\texttt{val } x = \{N'\}M\right]\right]\!\right]\end{array}}$$

(R-RETURN)
$$\frac{}{\begin{array}{l}\mathbb{C}\left[\!\left[s\left[\texttt{val } x = \{\texttt{return } v;\}M\right]\right]\!\right] \\ \to \mathbb{C}\left[\!\left[s\left[M\{x{:}=v\}\right]\right]\!\right]\end{array}}$$

(R-IF-TRUE)
$$\frac{}{\begin{array}{l}\mathbb{C}\left[\!\left[s\left[\texttt{if (true) } \{M\} \texttt{ else } \{N\}\right]\right]\!\right] \\ \to \mathbb{C}\left[\!\left[s\left[M\right]\right]\!\right]\end{array}}$$

(R-IF-FALSE)
$$\frac{}{\begin{array}{l}\mathbb{C}\left[\!\left[s\left[\texttt{if (false) } \{M\} \texttt{ else } \{N\}\right]\right]\!\right] \\ \to \mathbb{C}\left[\!\left[s\left[N\right]\right]\!\right]\end{array}}$$

(R-NEW)
$$\frac{p.\texttt{class} = d \quad \textit{fields}(d) = \vec{T}\,\vec{f}}{\begin{array}{l}\mathbb{C}\left[\!\left[\texttt{free } p \quad | \ s\left[\texttt{val } x = \texttt{new } d(\vec{v})\,; \ M\right]\right]\!\right] \\ \to \mathbb{C}\left[\!\left[\texttt{runnable } p \ | \ s\left[p.\vec{f}{=}\vec{v}\right] s\left[M\{x{:}=p\}\right]\right]\!\right]\end{array}}$$

(R-NEW-LOCK)
$$\frac{}{\begin{array}{l}\mathbb{C}\left[\!\left[\texttt{free } \ell \quad | \ s\left[\texttt{val } x = \texttt{new Lock}()\,; \ M\right]\right]\!\right] \\ \to \mathbb{C}\left[\!\left[\texttt{lock } \ell{:}0 \ | \ s\left[M\{x{:}=\ell\}\right]\right]\!\right]\end{array}}$$

(R-METHOD)
$$\frac{p.\texttt{class} = d \quad \textit{mbody}(d.m) = \lambda\vec{y}.N}{\begin{array}{l}\mathbb{C}\left[\!\left[s\left[\texttt{val } x = p.m(\vec{v})\,; \ M\right]\right]\!\right] \\ \to \mathbb{C}\left[\!\left[s\left[\texttt{val } x = \{N\{\texttt{this}{:}=p\}\{\vec{y}{:}=\vec{v}\}\}M\right]\right]\!\right]\end{array}}$$

(R-OPERATOR)
$$\frac{w \text{ is the result of applying } op \text{ to } \vec{v}}{\begin{array}{l}\mathbb{C}\left[\!\left[s\left[\texttt{val } x = op(\vec{v})\,; \ M\right]\right]\!\right] \\ \to \mathbb{C}\left[\!\left[s\left[M\{x{:}=w\}\right]\right]\!\right]\end{array}}$$

(R-METHOD-START)
$$\frac{p.\texttt{class} = d \quad \textit{mbody}(d.\texttt{run}) = \lambda\vec{y}.N}{\begin{array}{l}\mathbb{C}\left[\!\left[\texttt{free } \ell \ | \ \texttt{runnable } t \ | \ s\left[\texttt{val } x = t.\texttt{start}()\,; \ M\right]\right]\!\right] \\ \to \mathbb{C}\left[\!\left[t\left[\ell{:}1\right] t \left[N\{\texttt{this}{:}=t\}\right] \ | \ s\left[\ell{:}0\right] s\left[M\{x{:}=\texttt{unit}\}\right]\right]\!\right]\end{array}}$$

(R-METHOD-ACQUIRE)
$$j \text{ is even}$$
$$\frac{}{\begin{array}{l}\mathbb{C}\left[\!\left[\texttt{lock } \ell{:}j \quad | \ s\left[\texttt{val } x = \ell.\texttt{acquire}()\,; \ M\right]\right]\!\right] \\ \to \mathbb{C}\left[\!\left[\texttt{lock } \ell{:}j{+}1 \ | \ s\left[\ell{:}j\right] s\left[M\{x{:}=\texttt{unit}\}\right]\right]\!\right]\end{array}}$$

(R-METHOD-RELEASE)
$$j \text{ is odd}$$
$$\frac{}{\begin{array}{l}\mathbb{C}\left[\!\left[\texttt{lock } \ell{:}j \quad | \ s\left[\texttt{val } x = \ell.\texttt{release}()\,; \ M\right]\right]\!\right] \\ \to \mathbb{C}\left[\!\left[\texttt{lock } \ell{:}j{+}1 \ | \ s\left[\ell{:}j\right] s\left[M\{x{:}=\texttt{unit}\}\right]\right]\!\right]\end{array}}$$

(R-FIELD-WRITE)
$$\frac{}{\begin{array}{l}\mathbb{C}\left[\!\left[s\left[p.f = v;\ M\right]\right]\!\right] \\ \to \mathbb{C}\left[\!\left[s\left[p.f{=}v\right] s\left[M\right]\right]\!\right]\end{array}}$$

(R-SPECULATION-BEGIN)
$$\frac{\textit{thrd}(\phi) \in \textit{def}(A)}{\begin{array}{l}\mathbb{C}\left[\!\left[A\right]\!\right] \\ \to \mathbb{C}\left[\!\left[\top{\Rightarrow}A \ [\!] \ \phi{\Rightarrow}A\right]\!\right]\end{array}}$$

(R-SPECULATION-END)
$$\frac{\mathbb{C} \text{ justifies speculation } \phi}{\begin{array}{l}\mathbb{C}\left[\!\left[\top{\Rightarrow}A \ [\!] \ \phi{\Rightarrow}B\right]\!\right] \\ \to \mathbb{C}\left[\!\left[B\right]\!\right]\end{array}}$$

(R-FIELD-READ)
$$\frac{\mathbb{C} \text{ justifies read } p.f{=}v \text{ by } s}{\begin{array}{l}\mathbb{C}\left[\!\left[s\left[\texttt{val } x = p.f;\ M\right]\right]\!\right] \\ \to \mathbb{C}\left[\!\left[s\left[M\{x{:}=v\}\right]\right]\!\right]\end{array}}$$

(R-SPECULATION-CONTEXT1)
$$\frac{\mathbb{C}\left[\!\left[A\right]\!\right] \to \mathbb{C}\left[\!\left[A'\right]\!\right]}{\begin{array}{l}\mathbb{C}\left[\!\left[\top{\Rightarrow}A \ [\!] \ \phi{\Rightarrow}B\right]\!\right] \\ \to \mathbb{C}\left[\!\left[\top{\Rightarrow}A' \ [\!] \ \phi{\Rightarrow}B\right]\!\right]\end{array}}$$

(R-SPECULATION-CONTEXT2)
$$\frac{\mathbb{C}\left[\!\left[\phi B\right]\!\right] \to \mathbb{C}\left[\!\left[\phi B'\right]\!\right]}{\begin{array}{l}\mathbb{C}\left[\!\left[\top{\Rightarrow}A \ [\!] \ \phi{\Rightarrow}B\right]\!\right] \\ \to \mathbb{C}\left[\!\left[\top{\Rightarrow}A \ [\!] \ \phi{\Rightarrow}B'\right]\!\right]\end{array}}$$

Fig. 2. Reduction $(A \to B)$

The reserved methods `acquire` and `release` update the shared global counter associated with the appropriate lock object. As in Java, the reserved method `start` starts method `run` under the thread identity of the receiving object. As per Java semantics, this is a synchronization event, which we enforce using a fresh "dummy" lock.

Non-locks are initialized via R-NEW, consuming a free name of the appropriate class and initializing the fields using write actions by the initializing thread. We ignore types as much as possible, therefore all non-locks are runnable once initialized.

New lock creation is addressed separately in rule R-NEW-LOCK. The state of the lock is stored as an integer counter, which enforces sequential consistency on lock actions. Locks with even state may be acquired, and those with odd state released. (Both *fields* and *mbody* are undefined on the reserved class Lock.)

R-FIELD-WRITE describes field writes. This is a relaxed memory model, so the field writes become actions that float into the evaluation context, rather than updating a shared location. Field reads, as described in rule R-FIELD-READ, may take any value that is justified by the evaluation context. In a program with data races or locks, this could be nondeterministic.

Speculation can occur at any point, using R-SPECULATION-BEGIN. The initial branch has guard $\top$, indicating that this branch may make no additional assumptions. The final branch has a speculative action as its guard. The final branch may use the speculation to justify reads. R-SPECULATION-CONTEXT lets each branch of speculation evolve independently. This typically happens by using the structural rules of Figure 1 to bring parallel threads and locks into the speculation to enable computation. Results from an active speculation can only leak to the outside world via S-SPECULATION-PREFIX. If all branches produce an action, it can potentially float out into the surrounding environment. This is significant, since only actions that manage to make it outside of a speculation may be used to finalize it R-SPECULATION-END.

5 Examples

In the following examples, we assume an initialization thread which sets the initial state and starts the threads. We assume a single object p, with four fields, f, g, h, and e. To make the examples shorter, we elide the object name from field references, writing p.f as f. All fields are initially set to 0. (Further examples may be found in the extended version of this paper.)

Example 5 (Pugh (2004) §16). Consider the following variation of Program B from Section 3, which uses a single field: s[x=f;f=1;↑x] | t[y=f;f=2;↑y]. As in the JMM, the outcome s[↑2]|t[↑1] is possible. In our semantics, one may speculate s⟨f=1⟩ and t⟨f=2⟩, resulting in the following reduction.

$$\twoheadrightarrow\ \top \Rightarrow \qquad\qquad (s[x=f;f=1;↑x]\ |\ t[y=f;f=2;↑y])$$
$$[\!]\ s⟨f=1⟩t⟨f=2⟩ \Rightarrow (s[x=f;f=1;↑x]\ |\ t[y=f;f=2;↑y])$$

The read actions from each thread may now read any justifiable value. In the final branch, the value read may come from the speculation, as below.

$$\twoheadrightarrow\ \top \Rightarrow \qquad\qquad (s[f=1;↑0]\ |\ t[f=2;↑0])$$
$$[\!]\ s⟨f=1⟩t⟨f=2⟩ \Rightarrow (s[f=1;↑2]\ |\ t[f=2;↑1])$$

The write actions can then be performed. Because the same writes actions are performed in each branch, the write actions may leave the speculation using the structural order (S-PAR-PREFIX and S-SPECULATION-PREFIX).

```
⇸   ⊤⇒                    (s[f=1]s[↑0] | t[f=2]t[↑0])
    [] s⟨f=1⟩t⟨f=2⟩ ⇒ (s[f=1]s[↑2] | t[f=2]t[↑1])
≧  s[f=1]t[f=2](⊤⇒                    (s[↑0] | t[↑0])
                    [] s⟨f=1⟩t⟨f=2⟩ ⇒ (s[↑2] | t[↑1]) )
→  s[f=1]t[f=2](s[↑2] | t[↑1])
```

The speculation is justified, allowing us to use R-SPECULATION-END.   □

Most of the examples deal with integer fields because this is the typical style in the literature. Given that our semantics separates name binding from object initialization, as runtime systems do, dealing with object fields is no more complicated. For example, in s[x=f;f=new d();↑x] | t[y=f;f=new d();↑y] | free q | free r, reduction can proceed as above. In this case we speculate s⟨f=q⟩ and t⟨f=r⟩, resulting in s[f=q]t[f=r] (s[↑r] | t[↑q] | runnable q | runnable r)

Before getting negative, we present two more "positive" examples, which are consistent with the JMM. Example 6 discusses inlining. Example 7 discusses nested speculation. Inlining can reduce the number of concurrent reads available, but can also add flexibility in reordering writes if there are data or control dependencies between threads that prevent reordering.

Example 6 (Manson et al. (2005) figures 11 and 12).   Consider the following.

```
s[x=f; if(x==0){f=1;} y=f; g=y; ↑(x,y)] |
u[z=g; f=z; ↑z]
```

The outcome s[↑(1,1)]|u[↑1] is possible. Speculate s⟨g=1⟩ u⟨f=1⟩. The initial branch can produce s[f=1] s[g=1] u[f=1] in that order. Note that the write by u must follow the s's write to g, but is not dependent on the s's write to f. The semantics can therefore reorder the writes by s before making them visible to u, resulting in the sequence s[g=1] u[f=1] s[f=1]. The final branch can produce s[g=1] and u[f=1], in any order, but can not produce s[f=1]. We can therefore reach the following state.

```
   ⊤⇒            s[g=1]u[f=1]s[f=1](s[↑(0,1)]|u[↑1])
   [] s⟨g=1⟩u⟨f=1⟩ ⇒ (s[g=1]u[f=1](s[↑(1,1)]|u[↑1]))
→  s[g=1]u[f=1](⊤⇒      s[f=1](s[↑(0,1)]|u[↑1])
               [] s⟨g=1⟩u⟨f=1⟩ ⇒ (s[↑(1,1)]|u[↑1]))
→  s[g=1]u[f=1](s[↑(1,1)]|u[↑1])
```

Thus, the result is possible.

The situation changes, however, if we split thread s as follows. In this case, the result s[↑1]|t[↑1]|u[↑1] is impossible.

```
s[x=f; if(x==0){f=1;} ↑x] | t[y=f; g=y; ↑y] |
u[z=g; f=z; ↑z]
```

The dependency between s[f=1] and t[g=1] now crosses two threads, and therefore s[f=1] must be ordered before any subsequent actions. We reach the following state.

```
   ⊤⇒ s[f=1](s[↑0] | (t[g=1](t[↑1]|u[f=1]u[↑1])))
   [] ···
```

$\geqq$ $\top\Rightarrow$ $s[f=1]t[g=1]u[f=1](s[\uparrow 0]|t[\uparrow 1]|u[\uparrow 1])$
$[]\cdots\Rightarrow$ $t[g=1]u[f=1](s[\uparrow 1]|t[\uparrow 1]|u[\uparrow 1])$

In this case, however, we can not move the writes by t or u through to justify the speculation since they are blocked by $s[f=1]$ in the initial branch and this write can not be matched by the final branch. $\Box$

Example 7 (Pugh (2004) §11). Consider $s[x=h;e=x;y=f;g=y;\uparrow(x,y)]$ | $t[w=e;$ $z=g;h=z;f=1;\uparrow(w,z)]$. To get the result $s[\uparrow(1,1)]|t[\uparrow(1,1)]$,we first speculate $t\langle f=1\rangle s\langle g=1\rangle$, then $t\langle h=1\rangle$, and then $s\langle e=1\rangle$. These speculations result in a four-hole context.

$$\top\Rightarrow [\![-]\!]_1$$
$$[]\ t\langle f=1\rangle s\langle g=1\rangle \Rightarrow \top\Rightarrow [\![-]\!]_2$$
$$[]\ t\langle h=1\rangle \Rightarrow \top\Rightarrow [\![-]\!]_3$$
$$[]\ s\langle e=1\rangle \Rightarrow [\![-]\!]_4$$

Placing the term into this context creates four copies of the initial process, which we will refer to by number. Process 1 justifies the outer speculation, each subsequent process justifies the next speculation, and process 4 is the final process. To succeed, all processes must generate $t[f=1]$ and $s[g=1]$, processes 2–4 must generate $t[h=1]$, and processes 3 and 4 must generate $s[e=1]$.

Process 1 can perform the writes $t[h=0]t[f=1]$ and $s[e=0]s[g=1]$. The second write of s is only possible after the second write of t. The semantics can reorder the writes of t, keeping the first write private, and likewise for s. The other processes can reduce without any dependencies between threads and can therefore perform the same reordering. Thus we can get the following processes.

```
1: t[f=1]s[g=1](t[h=0]t[↑(0,0)]|s[e=0]s[↑(0,1)])
2: t[f=1]s[g=1]t[h=1](t[↑(0,1)]|s[e=0]s[↑(0,1)])
3: t[f=1]s[g=1]t[h=1]s[e=1](t[↑(0,1)]|s[↑(1,1)])
4: t[f=1]s[g=1]t[h=1]s[e=1](t[↑(1,1)]|s[↑(1,1)])
```

Using this stratification, the speculations can be discharged and the result is allowed.

The multiple nesting of speculations is necessary. While the write $s[e=1]$ is already possible in process 2, this write can only happen after the write to h in t. This dependency makes it impossible for process 2 to publish $s[g=1]$ without the necessarily preceding $t[h=1]$. This in turn prohibits the outer speculation from finalizing because process 1 can not match $t[h=1]$. $\Box$

The examples above demonstrate out-of-order reads, a hallmark of relaxed memory models. These examples argue informally that the model is "relaxed enough". We now revisit the examples given in Section 3, to argue that it is not "too relaxed".

The program $s[x=f;\ if(x==1)\{g=1;\}\ f=1;\ y=g;\ \uparrow y]$ should not be allowed to produce $s[\uparrow 1]$. Such *self justifying* executions are prevented by our semantics. Since only s can produce writes, only speculations by s can be finalized (via R-SPECULA-TION-END and Definition 2); yet reads by s can not be justified by its own speculations (Definition 1). Speculation is useless in single-threaded programs, as it should be.

Initiality prevents the program s[x=f;g=x;↑x] | t[y=g;f=y;↑y] from producing the outcome t[↑1]. The initial branch can not write anything but 0; therefore no useful speculations can be finalized via R-SPECULATION-END.

Consistency prevents Program C (Section 3) from producing the illegal execution reported there. S-SPECULATION-PREFIX prevents such executions by requiring that the initial and final branch of a speculation must execute the same actions in the *same order*. The actual requirement is slightly weaker, since S-SPECULATION-PAR and Definition 3 allow some reordering; but no reordering is allowed on lock actions.

Timeliness prevents Program D (Section 3) from producing the illegal execution reported there. This example motivates the "no intervening release" clause of Definition 2, which ensures that the speculation can not be finalized. Whereas Program D describes a speculation that occurs too late with respect to its justifying write, Example 8 discusses one that occurs too early.

Example 8. Consider the following program.

```
s[l.acquire(); x=f; f=x+1; g=1; l.release(); ↑x] |
u[l.acquire(); x=f; f=x+1; y=g; l.release(); ↑(x,y)]
```

Clearly s[↑1]|u[↑(0,1)] is unacceptable. If we attempt to get this result by first allowing u to acquire the lock, then speculating s⟨g=1⟩, we arrive at

```
u[1:0]
   T⇒        u[f=1]u[1:1]s[1:2]s[f=2]s[g=1]s[1:3](s[↑1]|u[↑(0,0)])
   ⟨] s⟨g=1⟩ ⇒u[f=1]u[1:1]s[1:2]s[f=2]s[g=1]s[1:3](s[↑1]|u[↑(0,1)]).
```

The actions of u can commute with the speculation since they belong to a different thread, but the actions of s can not, since s⟨g=1⟩s[1:2] ⋠ s[1:2]s⟨g=1⟩; clause A-ACQUIRE of Definition 3 applies to write actions, but not speculations. Thus the speculation can not be finalized.   □

The final two examples demonstrate areas where our model differs from the JMM. Example 9 shows that our model allows executions of lockless programs that are not allowed by the JMM. Example 10 shows that our model is incomparable to the JMM for programs with both locks and data races. In both cases, our model validates optimizations that are disallowed by the JMM. See Section 7 for more general results.

Example 9 (Sevcík (2008) §5.3.2). This example discusses redundant read after read elimination. Consider the following program.

```
s[x=f; g=x;] |
t[y=g; if(y==1){ z=g; f=z; } else {f=1;}; ↑y]
```

The outcome t[↑1] is allowed using the speculation s⟨g=1⟩. Both initial and final branches produce the actions t[f=1]s[g=1]. The same behavior is allowed, with the same speculation, if the boxed statement pair is replaced by "f=y;". Our semantics validates the transformation. The JMM disallows the behavior for the original program, but allows it for the transformed one (Sevcík 2008), thus invalidating the transformation.

Conversely, Sevcík (2008, §5.3.4) demonstrates a behavior that is allowed by the JMM, but invalidated by an irrelevant read introduction. Again, our semantics allows the behavior both before and after the transformation. (See the extended version of this paper.)   □

Example 10 (Sevcík (2008) §5.3.3). (Roach motel optimization). Consider whether the following program.

```
s[l.acquire(); f=2; l.release();] |
t[l.acquire(); f=1; l.release();] |
u[ x=f; l.acquire();
    y=h; if(x==2){g=1;} else {g=y;}
  l.release(); ↑(x,y)] |
v[z=g; h=z; ↑z]
```

The outcome u[↑(1,1)] | v[↑1] is possible using the speculation v⟨h=1⟩. The initial branch schedules as follows: s, u's initial read, t, u's acquire and write, v, then u's release. This allows the initial branch to reduce to the following.

```
s[l:0]s[f=2]s[l:1]t[l:2]t[f=1]t[l:3]
    u[l:4]u[g=1]v[h=1]u[l:5](u[↑(2,0)] | v[↑1])
```

The final branch performs the same schedule, except that t executes before u's initial read, with the speculation occurring after u's acquire. Using the false case of the conditional, it produces the same action sequence, but with the desired result.

This execution become impossible after reversing the order of the statements in the boxed term so that the lock is acquired before the read: "l.acquire(); x=f;". Now the actions of threads s, t and u are now totally ordered and therefore the relation of t and u's initial read must be consistent in the initial and final branches. If the initial branch reads 1 from f, then it must write v[h=0]. If the initial branch reads 2 from f, then the final branch must also read 2 and therefore can not produce the desired result.

Our semantics validates the transformation; the JMM does not. In a reversal of our results, the JMM disallows the first execution, but allows the second (Sevcík 2008).   □

6   Analysis

Informally, one can see that the speculation construct can not create thin air reads because it enjoys initiality (there is a computation justifying the speculation that does not use the speculation) and consistency (the only way in which results from an active speculation can leak to the outside world is via the S-SPECULATION-PREFIX rules). Thus, any speculation is validated by an execution consistent with the final execution.

Every valid JMM execution of a lockless program can be mimicked by the system in this paper. See the extended version of this paper for proof sketch. We now show that our semantics coincides with SC (and therefore with the JMM) for DRF programs. As shown by Example 10, our semantics is incomparable to the JMM for programs with both data-races and locks.

Our model does not record read actions. In order to define read-write data races, we use a modified reduction relation, which introduces a *read actions* into the process, notation $s \ulcorner p.f=v \urcorner$. A read write data race occurs whenever there is a race between a read and a write. Define $\mapsto$ as in Figure 2, but for the rule R-FIELD-READ, which becomes

$$\frac{\mathbb{C} \text{ justifies } s\langle p.f=v \rangle}{\mathbb{C} [\![s[\text{val } x = p.f;\ M]]\!] \mapsto \mathbb{C} [\![\ s \ulcorner p.f=v \urcorner\ s[M\{x:=v\}]]\!]}.$$

Define the partial function $act_s(A) = act_s(\mathbb{C})$, if $A = \mathbb{C}[\![s[M]]\!]$ for some $\mathbb{C}$ and M. We say that A has a *read-write data race* if $\vec{\sigma} = act_s(\mathbb{C})$ and there exists i and j such that $\sigma_i = t\ulcorner p.f=v \urcorner$ and $\sigma_j = s[p.f=w]$ such that $i \nprec_{hb}^{\vec{\sigma}} j$ and $j \nprec_{hb}^{\vec{\sigma}} i$. Define a *write-write data race* similarly.

A process A is *speculation-free* if it has no subterm that is a speculation process. Write $A_0 \to \cdots \to A_n$ to abbreviate $A_0 (\to \cup \geqq) \cdots (\to \cup \geqq) A_n$, and similarly for $\mapsto$. A reduction sequence $A_0 \to \cdots \to A_n$ is *top-level* if A_0 and A_n are speculation-free.

The speculation-free assumption on top-level processes is reasonable because user programs do not have speculations; speculations are only created by the operational semantics. Speculation transitions are redundant in read-write data race free reduction sequences.

Definition 11. Let A_i' be derived from A_i by replacing each speculation $(\top \Rightarrow A [\![\phi \Rightarrow B)$ by the final branch (B). By induction on n, such an A_i' exists for each A_i. A top-level reduction sequence $A_0 \mapsto \cdots \mapsto A_n$ is *read-write data race free*, if none of the A_i', so defined, has a read-write data race. □

Lemma 12. *Let the top-level reduction sequence $A_0 \to \cdots \to A_n$ be read-write data race free. Then, there is a reduction sequence $A_0 = B_0 \to \cdots \to B_n = A_n$, such that for all $j \in \{1,\ldots,n\}$, B_j is speculation-free.*
PROOF. See the extended version of this paper. □

For processes that are also write-write data race free, each read is matched by a unique write. Thus, the memory may be treated as a map from locations to values without any change to the possible reductions, ensuring that DRF programs can be executed in standard SC fashion.

7 Simulation

The goal of this section is to define a simulation relation that is a precongruence and that validates interesting examples. We are not concerned if the relation is finer than orders based on testing or contextual equivalence. For simplicity, we restrict our attention in this section to processes that do not contain name binders, object initialization or method calls other than `acquire` and `release`. For this class of processes, we impose the following additional well-formedness criterion: in any subprocess $\top \Rightarrow A [\![\phi \Rightarrow B$, $def(A) = def(B)$.

Intuitively, A simulates B if A and B have the same memory and whenever B reduces, then A can reduce to a matching process. The definition is complicated by the possible interleaving of actions and speculations, and the various ways that a context can interact with an environment. Rather than comparing memories, we compare *environment contexts*: $\mathbb{E} ::= [\![-]\!] \mid \alpha \mathbb{E} \mid \phi \mathbb{E} \mid s[\uparrow v] \mid \mathbb{E}$. The environment context $s[\uparrow v] \mid \mathbb{E}$ contains a placeholder for environment actions performed by thread s, in parallel with the rest of the context.

For a set of thread names S, the context $\mathbb{E}$ is *complete* iff for every $\sigma \in \mathbb{E}$ such that $s = thrd(\sigma) \notin S$, it is the case that $s[\uparrow v]$ occurs in $\mathbb{E}$ after σ.

In the remainder of this section, we use S to refer to the set of non-environment threads. Threads not in S can be used by the environment.

Definition 13. Given a set S of thread names and a binary relation $\mathscr{R}$ on well-formed processes, we define $S \vdash A \, \mathscr{F}(\mathscr{R}) \, B$ to hold iff the following conditions are satisfied.

(Threads) $def(A) = def(B)$ and $S \subseteq thrds(A)$ and for all $s \in thrds(A) \setminus S$, if $s[M]$ occurs in A or B then $M = \uparrow$ unit.

(Well-formed) For all $\mathbb{C}$, $\mathbb{C}[\![A]\!]$ is well-formed iff $\mathbb{C}[\![B]\!]$ is well-formed.

(Reduction) For all B', if $B \to B'$ then there exists A' such that $A \twoheadrightarrow A'$ and $S \vdash A' \, \mathscr{R} \, B'$.

(Structural order) For all B' if $B \geq B'$ then there exists A' such that $A \twoheadrightarrow A'$ and $S \vdash A' \, \mathscr{R} \, B'$.

(Equivalent top-level choices) For all B', ϕ, B'', if $B = \mathbb{E}[\![\top \Rightarrow B' \,[\!]\, \phi \Rightarrow B'']\!]$ then there exists A', ψ, A'' such that (1) $A = \mathbb{E}[\![\top \Rightarrow A' \,[\!]\, \psi \Rightarrow A'']\!]$, (2) $S \vdash \mathbb{E}[\![A']\!] \, \mathscr{R} \, \mathbb{E}[\![B']\!]$, and (3) $S \vdash \mathbb{E}[\![\phi A'']\!] \, \mathscr{R} \, \mathbb{E}[\![\psi B'']\!]$.

(Equivalent actions/guards/returns) For all $\mathbb{E}$, B' if $B = \mathbb{E}[\![B']\!]$ then there exists A' such that $A = \mathbb{E}[\![A']\!]$.

(Environment writes) For each $s \in thrds(A) \setminus S$ if B' is obtained from B by replacing every occurrence of $s[\uparrow\text{unit}]$ with $s[p.f{=}v]s[\uparrow\text{unit}]$ and similarly for A' obtained from A, then $S \vdash A' \, \mathscr{R} \, B'$.

(Top-level lock removal) For all $\vec{\sigma}$, B' and for all ℓ in the fixed set of lock names if $B = \vec{\sigma}(\text{lock } \ell{:}\,j\,|\,B')$ then there exists A' such that $A = \vec{\sigma}(\text{lock } \ell{:}\,j\,|\,A')$ and $S \vdash \vec{\sigma}A' \, \mathscr{R} \, \vec{\sigma}B'$.

(Top-level lock addition) For all ℓ in the fixed set of lock names if $(\text{lock } \ell{:}\,j\,|\,B)$ is well-formed then $S \vdash (\text{lock } \ell{:}\,j\,|\,A) \, \mathscr{R} \, (\text{lock } \ell{:}\,j\,|\,B)$.

(Environment locks) For each s in $thrds(A) \setminus S$ if
- the occurrences of lock $\ell{:}\,j\,|\,s[\uparrow\text{unit}]$ in B account for all occurrences of $s[\uparrow\text{unit}]$ in B, and
- B' is obtained from B by replacing all occurrences of lock $\ell{:}\,j\,|\,s[\uparrow\text{unit}]$ with lock $\ell{:}\,j{+}1\,|\,s[\ell{:}\,j]s[\uparrow\text{unit}]$,

then
- the occurrences of lock $\ell{:}\,j\,|\,s[\uparrow\text{unit}]$ in A account for all occurrences of $s[\uparrow\text{unit}]$ in A,
- A' is obtained from A by replacing all occurrences of lock $\ell{:}\,j\,|\,s[\uparrow\text{unit}]$ with lock $\ell{:}\,j{+}1\,|\,s[\ell{:}\,j]s[\uparrow\text{unit}]$, and
- $S \vdash A' \, \mathscr{R} \, B'$.

Define $S \vdash A \gtrsim B$ to be the largest relation such that $S \vdash A \gtrsim B$ implies $S \vdash A \, \mathscr{F}(\gtrsim) \, B$. Define the order $A \gtrsim B$ iff for all complete $\mathbb{E}$ such that $\mathbb{E}[\![A]\!]$ and $\mathbb{E}[\![B]\!]$ are well-formed, we have $thrds(A) \vdash \mathbb{E}[\![A]\!] \gtrsim \mathbb{E}[\![B]\!]$.

Consider terms M and N with no free variables but perhaps free names. Define the order $M \gtrsim N$ iff there exists t such that $t[M] \gtrsim t[N]$ The choice of t is irrelevant in this definition.   □

Proposition 14. $\gtrsim$ *is a precongruence on processes and on terms.*   □

We now use the theory of simulation to validate several optimizations. The first inequality shows that writes can be reordered. The second demonstrates roach motel reordering. The third demonstrates redundant read after read elimination. Since simulation is a precongruence, the transformations are valid in any program context.

Proposition 15. *The following inequivalences hold.*

$$p.f{=}1;p.g{=}1;\uparrow\text{unit} \gtrsim p.g{=}1;p.f{=}1;\uparrow\text{unit}$$
$$p.f{=}1;\ell.\text{acquire}();\uparrow\text{unit} \gtrsim \ell.\text{acquire}();p.f{=}1;\uparrow\text{unit}$$
$$\text{val } x{=}p.f;\text{val } y{=}p.f;M \gtrsim \text{val } x{=}p.f;M\{y{:=}x\}$$

PROOF. See the extended version of this paper.   □

8   Conclusion

This paper follows the research program of Cenciarelli et al. (2007) and Boudol and Petri (2009) in attempting to fit relaxed memory models into generative structured operational semantics. The technical novelty is manifest in the "speculation" construct. We show that the basic properties of the JMM hold in our setting. Our contributions advance the state-of-the-art in two ways. (1) We expand the expressivity of these methods to include full JMM behaviors for lockless programs and general object-oriented programs. (2) We describe simulation methods and precongruence results for the sublanguage that corresponds to the first-order imperative shared-memory computing.

Our treatment of programs with both data races and locks provides a technically robust variation on JMM ideas. For example, our methods validate expected roach-motel reordering laws and related peephole optimizations.

References

Adve, S.V., Gharachorloo, K.: Shared memory consistency models: A tutorial. Computer 29(12), 66–76 (1996)

Aspinall, D., Sevcík, J.: Formalising Java's data race free guarantee. In: Schneider, K., Brandt, J. (eds.) TPHOLs 2007. LNCS, vol. 4732, pp. 22–37. Springer, Heidelberg (2007)

Boehm, H.-J.: Threads cannot be implemented as a library. In: PLDI 2005, pp. 261–268. ACM, New York (2005)

Boehm, H.-J., Adve, S.V.: Foundations of the C++ concurrency memory model. In: PLDI 2008, pp. 68–78 (2008)

Boudol, G., Petri, G.: Relaxed memory models: an operational approach. In: POPL, pp. 392–403 (2009)

Bronevetsky, G., de Supinski, B.R.: Complete formal specification of the OpenMP memory model. Int. J. Parallel Program. 35(4), 335–392 (2007)

Burckhardt, S., Musuvath, M., Singh, V.: Verifying compiler transformations for concurrent programs. MSR-TR-2008-171 (2008)

Cenciarelli, P., Knapp, A., Sibilio, E.: The Java memory model: Operationally, denotationally, axiomatically. In: De Nicola, R. (ed.) ESOP 2007. LNCS, vol. 4421, pp. 331–346. Springer, Heidelberg (2007)

Flanagan, C., Sabry, A., Duba, B.F., Felleisen, M.: The essence of compiling with continuations. In: PLDI 1993, vol. 28(6), pp. 237–247. ACM Press, New York (1993)

Hangal, S., Vahia, D., Manovit, C., Lu, J.-Y.J.: TSOtool: A program for verifying memory systems using the memory consistency model. In: ISCA 2004, p. 114. IEEE, Los Alamitos (2004)

Igarashi, A., Pierce, B.C., Wadler, P.: Featherweight Java: a minimal core calculus for Java and GJ. ACM Trans. Programming Languages and Systems 23(3), 396–450 (2001)

Kamil, A., Su, J., Yelick, K.A.: Making sequential consistency practical in Titanium. In: SC, p. 15. IEEE, Los Alamitos (2005)

Lamport, L.: How to make a multiprocessor computer that correctly executes multiprocess program. IEEE Trans. Comput. 28(9), 690–691 (1979)

Lea, D.: The JSR-133 cookbook for compiler writers (2008), http://gee.cs.oswego.edu/dl/jmm/cookbook.html (Last modified: April 2008)

Luchangco, V.M.: Memory consistency models for high-performance distributed computing. PhD thesis, MIT (2001)

Manson, J., Pugh, W., Adve, S.V.: The Java memory model. In: POPL 2005, pp. 378–391. ACM Press, New York (2005)

Milner, R.: The polyadic pi-calculus: a tutorial. Technical report, Logic and Algebra of Specification (1991)

Odersky, M., Spoon, L., Venners, B.: Programming in Scala: A Comprehensive Step-by-step Guide. Artima (2008)

Pugh, W.: Causality test cases (2004), http://www.cs.umd.edu/~pugh/java/memoryModel/CausalityTestCases.html

Saraswat, V.A.: Concurrent constraint-based memory machines: A framework for Java memory models. In: Maher, M.J. (ed.) ASIAN 2004. LNCS, vol. 3321, pp. 494–508. Springer, Heidelberg (2004)

Saraswat, V.A., Jagadeesan, R., Michael, M.M., von Praun, C.: A theory of memory models. In: PPOPP, pp. 161–172. ACM, New York (2007)

Sarkar, S., Sewell, P., Nardelli, F.Z., Owens, S., Ridge, T., Braibant, T., Myreen, M.O., Alglave, J.: The semantics of x86-CC multiprocessor machine code. In: POPL, pp. 379–391 (2009)

Sevcík, J.: Program Transformations in Weak Memory Models. PhD thesis, Laboratory for Foundations of Computer Science, University of Edinburgh (2008)

Sevcík, J., Aspinall, D.: On validity of program transformations in the Java memory model. In: Vitek, J. (ed.) ECOOP 2008. LNCS, vol. 5142, pp. 27–51. Springer, Heidelberg (2008)

Steinke, R.C., Nutt, G.J.: A unified theory of shared memory consistency. J. ACM 51(5), 800–849 (2004)

Yelick, K., Bonachea, D., Wallace, C.: A proposal for a UPC memory consistency model, v1.1. Technical Report LBNL-54983, Lawrence Berkeley National Lab (2004)

Automating Security Mediation Placement

Dave King[1], Susmit Jha[2], Divya Muthukumaran[1],
Trent Jaeger[1], Somesh Jha[3], and Sanjit A. Seshia[2]

[1] Pennsylvania State University*
[2] University of California, Berkeley**
[3] University of Wisconsin

Abstract. We present a framework that automatically produces suggestions to resolve type errors in security-typed programs, enabling legacy
code to be retrofit with comprehensive security policy mediation. Resolving such type errors requires selecting a placement of *mediation
statements* that implement runtime security decisions, such as declassifiers and authorization checks. Manually placing mediation statements
in legacy code can be difficult, as there may be several, interacting type
errors. In this paper, we solve this problem by constructing a graph that
has the property that a vertex cut is equivalent to the points at which
mediation statements can be inserted to allow the program to satisfy the
type system. We build a framework that produces *suggestions* that are
minimum cuts of this graph, and the framework can be customized to
find suggestions that satisfy programmer requirements. Our framework
implementation for Java programs computes suggestions for 20,000 line
programs in less than 100 seconds, reduces the number of locations a
programmer must consider by 90%, and selects suggestions similar to
those proposed by expert programmers 80% of the time.

1 Introduction

Security-typed languages [20,22] use type systems that augment the types of
data with security labels to statically verify that a program satisfies a security
property based on a relationship among those labels. However, many programs
exhibit behavior that is not compatible with a static type system. For example,
we do not know whether a user accessing patient data in a medical data system
is assigned a doctor label or another label until runtime, requiring a runtime
authorization check.

To resolve these conflicts within the type system, programmers insert *mediation statements*, such as declassifiers or authorization checks, that ensure that
the runtime behavior of the program remains consistent with the security labels
expressed by the type system. Currently, the addition of mediation statements
is a manual task that requires examining a large amount of code and careful

---

* Research was supported by NSF grant CNS-0905343.
** Research was supported in part by NSF grants CNS-0627734 and CNS-0644436, and
an Alfred P. Sloan Research Fellowship.

A.D. Gordon (Ed.): ESOP 2010, LNCS 6012, pp. 327–344, 2010.

consideration to avoid errors. Automatic tools can identify missing mediation statements [8,20,32], but even after the errors have been identified, reaching a consensus on manual placement often takes a long time (e.g., for Jif programs [12] and the X Window Server [28]). Given a set of candidate mediation statements, they may not actually resolve all labeling conflicts, they may contain redundant statements, may significantly degrade performance, and they may violate the program's coding style.

In this paper, we present a method for automatic identification of mediation points in legacy programs that is based on a graph cut approach. A mediation point is a location where a mediation statement can be placed. We were inspired to investigate mediation point placement as a cut problem due to recent work assigning a quantitative measure of leaked information in a program by solving a maximum-flow graph problem [17]. By solving a cut problem, the dual of the maximum-flow problem, we present the programmer with options to insert mediation statements into the program. Our method outputs a set of *suggestions*: each suggestion is a set of locations for placing mediation statements that resolve a program's type system conflicts. We outline the properties required of the type system such that a cut of any information flow graph generated from a program using that type system is equivalent to a placement of mediation statements in the program. We use existing graph algorithms to output each equivalent cut of the graph, thereby providing the user with a set of legal placement suggestions to assess, reducing their effort significantly. We make the following contributions in this paper:

- We define a transformation from a set of information-flow constraints for a program into an information-flow graph, such that the corresponding information-flow graph has the property that every source-sink cut of the graph corresponds to a set of mediation points that completely resolve the program's illegal information flows.

- We develop a framework that computes *suggestions* for mediation points based on finding cuts of the information-flow graph. We describe how we modified the security-typed language Jif to output label constraints that could be converted into such an information-flow graph. We also describe how to cluster expressions to prevent many redundant suggestions from being output to the programmer.

- Our framework implementation computes suggestions for Java programs of more than 20K SLOC in less than 100 seconds. In addition, our results show that our suggestions reduce the number of locations that would be required for a programmer to examine given current tools for finding security-typed language errors by approximately 90%, and in programs originally written in a security-typed language, more than 80% of the selected mediation points were classified as similar to those placed by human programmers.

The graph-cut approach presented in this paper provides a framework for programmers to solve practical placement concerns, ensure that solutions resolve all conflicts, contain no redundant mediators, and can account for performance and style considerations.

Related Work: McCamant and Ernst [17] dynamically measure the quantitative information flow that a program leaks by solving a maximum flow problem. However, the corresponding minimum cut of the program's flow may not be the only suitable location to use as a mediation statement. Our work is aimed at providing a static mechanism for determining the mediation points that resolve the type system conflicts for a program. Programmers are currently using security-typed languages to build secure systems [2,13], but these systems have not been used to retrofit existing programs for security. There has also been a recent line of work in manually adding authorization checks to code in applications, such as Linux Security Modules [31], X Windows server [28] and dbus [29]. A variety of research aims to enforce type safety guarantees for C code [3,21], but we aim to resolve type errors. Program slicing [26] and type-based analyses [5] have been used to find information-flow errors. The principal advantage of our framework is that viewing the problem as graph cut enables us to find placements that achieve complete mediation that accounts for all of the errors in a single computation. However, the scope of work presented here applies to security types. Generalization is future work.

The remainder of the paper is structured as follows: In Section 2, we survey some problems related to placing mediation statements in code. We provide background about security type-checking in Section 3. In Section 4, we describe how to transform information-flow constraints into a graph that has the property that a cut of the graph is equivalent to a set of statements that mediate the corresponding program's illegal flows. In Section 5, we outline the design of our framework, which outputs mediation suggestions from this graph. In Section 6, we give the results of experiments, where we apply our tool to place mediators in eight different programs.

2   Overview

In this section, we introduce some of the challenges in placing mediation statements in program code. In security-typed languages, programmers specify security properties in code by annotating various security-relevant sources and sinks in the program with security labels from a lattice $\mathcal{L}$. These languages enforce *noninterference* [9]: a program satisfies noninterference if, at runtime, the computation of data with security label l is independent of data with security label l' if $l \not\leq l'$ in $\mathcal{L}$. Noninterference can be used to model both secrecy and integrity requirements, depending on the semantics of the labels in $\mathcal{L}$. A program satisfying noninterference is also said to satisfy *information-flow security*. Statically checking noninterference has two problems: (1) without a notion of declassification [24], programs can never violate $\mathcal{L}$, even when properly releasing data (e.g., releasing patient records to new doctors), and (2) without runtime authorization checks, we have no way to enforce $\mathcal{L}$ over labels whose security values may be instantiated at runtime, causing the program to unnecessarily violate noninterference. *Mediation statements* allow programs to execute flows between label l and incomparable labels l'.

To investigate issues in placing mediation statements in code, we introduce the example of `logrotate`, a program that rotates system logs into backup files. `logrotate` is trusted to maintain the security properties of the operating system: if the user configuring `logrotate` is not allowed to perform an action, then `logrotate` should not be allowed to perform that same action. In recent work [13], a version of `logrotate` has been written in the security-typed language Jif [20], a variant of Java. The Jif version of `logrotate` guarantees that the program satisfies information flow security. However, it also requires that the programmer insert mediation statements to allow information to flow from the `logrotate` configuration files to the logs being rotated. Without a mediation check, it is not clear whether or not `logrotate` violates the secrecy and integrity guarantees of the system: it is possible that it reveals configuration data through viewing the results of log rotation or that it compromises log data by allowing a user of `logrotate` to modify log file data that she does not have access to. We highlight three individual flows from the configuration file to the rotated logs in Figure 1. Each flow requires mediation.

- The number of logs to rotate before deleting the final log (`rotateCount`) is equal to the number of file rename operations performed.
- The filename specified by the configuration file is used to get a handle to the system file that `logrotate` renames through `oldName`. If an attacker can control this variable, then she can rotate logs containing evidence of attacks on the system.
- The filename specified by the configuration file is used to create the new name that a log file is renamed to, `newName`. If an attacker can control this variable, then she could cause a file to be overwritten.

The code in Figure 1 shows the logrotate code with mediation statements inserted. Each of the above flows has been mediated by adding a `mediate(e,lbl)` expression: if the label on the expression `e` is allowed to flow to `lbl`, then the expression has the value of `e` with the security label of `lbl`. Otherwise, the program throws a security exception and terminates. The placement given in the figure is not the only possible placement: for example, it would have also been possible to mediate the loop guard `i >= 0`, which would have disconnected the number of times the loop was executed from data labeled as {`config`}.

To place mediation statements that resolve these information flows, a programmer must first annotate the sources and sinks in the program with their security labels. Next, the programmer must examine each line of code contributing to errors that result. She can use automated methods to identify possible causes of information-flow errors [15]. Resolving these errors is currently a manual process and requires the error explanation analysis to be run multiple times to resolve each of the possible causes of an information-flow error. An automated solution would free the programmer from having to examine all the error explanations, requiring them only to determine whether the selected mediation points were suitable or not. Our method uses the results of a whole-program information-flow analysis to suggest a set of *mediation points*, locations in code where mediation statements can be inserted to resolve a program's labeling

```
1  label config, log_lbl, LogInfo[{config}]{config} log;
2  String{config} filename = log.getFilename(logNum);
3  int{config} rotateCount = log.getRotateCount();
4  File[{log_lbl}]{log_lbl} disposeFile =
5     Runtime.getFile(filename+"."+(rotateCount+1),log_lbl);
6  File[{log_lbl}]{log_lbl} newlogfile, oldlogfile = null;
7  // rename messages.n to messages.n + 1

8  for (int i =  mediate(rotateCount,log_lbl) ; i >= 0; i--) {

9     String newName = filename + "." + i;
10    String oldName = filename + "." + (i-1);

11    newlogfile = Runtime.getFile( mediate(newName,log_lbl) ,
12                                  log_lbl);

13    oldlogfile = Runtime.getFile( mediate(oldName,log_lbl) ,
14                                  log_lbl);
15    if (oldlogfile != null)
16       oldlogfile.renameTo(newlogfile);
17 }
```

Fig. 1. Example from `logrotate` that performs rotation of log files shown with mediation statements inserted

conflicts. The particular mediation mechanism required is application-specific, and so ultimately the programmer must decide for each selected mediation point what type of mediation statement should be inserted.

Often programmers have certain placement constraints with regards to where mediation statements should not be placed [24]. For example, class A is used for string formatting, while class B implements cryptographic operations on the contents of a string. Programmers might therefore prefer to perform a mediation statement in class B rather than class A so that security operations are performed in classes already used for security. Any automated system should be *customizable*, as requirements of this type for declassifier placement differ across applications and programmers.

3   Background on Information-Flow Checking

Security-typed languages [20,22] augment traditional compilers to allow programmers to specify the security properties of program data. Generally, these languages enforce noninterference in code by augmenting the type system with security types. There are two different categories of illegal information flow that noninterference disallows. *Explicit information flows* occur when high security data is written to a low output, such as writing a secret key to a socket. *Implicit information flows* occur when high security data otherwise affects a low observable result. For example, a password check that compares the hash of a guess against the hash of a password and reveals that information is an implicit flow of information. If h and l are high and low variables respectively, then the assignment l := h is an explicit flow of information, while the conditional if h then l := 1 is an implicit flow of information.

To prevent the programs from releasing secure information through an explicit information flow, types τ are annotated with labels l, and the type system forbids subtyping of the form $\tau\{l\} \preceq \tau\{l'\}$ if $l \not\preceq l'$. To prevent information from leaking through implicit flows, the type system maintains a label containing the security level of the program counter. This security label is equal to the join of all of the security labels that the execution of the current expression depends on. When an assignment is performed, the type system verifies that the variable being assigned to is greater than or equal to the program counter.

To enforce these security guarantees, type systems generate *information-flow constraints* from the program. Information-flow constraints contain both security labels l from the lattice $\mathcal{L}$ as well as label variables α representing the security level of program elements that have not been explicitly labeled. A security type system generates a set C of information-flow constraints corresponding to the information flows that a program permits [19]. If there exists a mapping ρ from label variables to security labels such that for each constraint $\xi \in C$, the substituted $\rho(\xi)$ holds, then C is *satisfiable*. A program with a satisfiable information-flow constraint set satisfies noninterference.

4   Constraint Methodology

In this section, we show how to generate information-flow constraints so that finding a set of mediation statements can be solved as a graph-cut problem. We introduce sIMP, a constraint-based type system for IMP, a simple imperative language [30]. The IMP language contains conditionals, variable assignment, and while loops, and is presented as a simple foundational language. The main technical distinction between the constraint-based type system presented here and standard type systems for information-flow security, such as the one presented by Volpano *et al.* [27], is that sIMP does not assume a total mapping from each variable to its security level. In the case where every variable is assigned a security level, there is no ambiguity as to where to place a mediation statement. In legacy code, it is unreasonable for the programmer to assign security semantics to each variable, meaning that the security level of an expression e is equal to the security level of every expression affecting e. A constraint-based type system models language expressions that have an undetermined security semantics: in sIMP, the security label of an expression e is associated with a unique label variable α_e.

In sIMP, a command c is information-flow secure if the set of information-flow constraints C that the type system assigns to c is satisfiable. Using a standard technique from the literature [6,7,11,25], we view the information-flow constraints C as a directed graph $\mathcal{G}_C$, which we refer to as *information-flow graph*. If C contains the constraint $\tau \leq a$ (where a is an atom: either a label variable or lattice element and τ is a join of atoms, see the formal definitions in the next section), then there is an edge from each atom in τ to a. The information-flow graph therefore contains a path between two nodes $n_1, n_2 \in \mathcal{G}_C$ if the value of the program element associated with n_1 can affect the value of the program element associated with n_2. We first show that for a two-point lattice consisting of $\top$ and $\bot$, the constraints generated by sIMP have the *cut-mediation equivalence* property, meaning that a set of mediation statements that resolve the illegal $(\top, \bot)$ flows in a sIMP program is equivalent to a $(\top, \bot)$ cut of the information-flow graph. We show how to generalize this approach for arbitrary lattices in Section 4.4.

4.1   A Constraint-Based Type System for Information Flow

We now introduce sIMP, a constraint-based type system for enforcing secure information flow in IMP. We begin by introducing the IMP language. IMP contains two distinct syntactic elements: commands and expressions. A command c can modify a global program state σ, while an expression e evaluates to an integer value n using variable bindings from σ. An example of an IMP command is $x := x + 1$: this updates the variable x to be equal to the current value of x added to 1. Commands c and expressions e in IMP have the following grammar[1]:

$$
\begin{array}{ll}
\text{Integers} & n ::= 0, 1, \ldots \\
\text{Variables} & v ::= x, y, \ldots \\
\text{Expressions } e & ::= n \mid v \mid e_1 + e_2 \\
\text{Commands } c & ::= \mathsf{skip} \mid c_1 \, ; \, c_2 \mid v := e \mid \\
& \quad\;\; \mathsf{if} \; e \; \mathsf{then} \; c_1 \; \mathsf{else} \; c_2 \mid \mathsf{while} \; e \; \mathsf{do} \; c
\end{array}
$$

Let σ be a memory, mapping variables to integer values. Evaluation in IMP has the judgment $\langle \sigma, c \rangle \to \sigma'$: under memory σ, command c produces memory σ'. Evaluating the above command under a memory that maps x to the integer 4 returns a memory mapping x to the integer 5. This is written $\langle \{x \mapsto 4\}, x := x + 1 \rangle \to \{x \mapsto 5\}$. The evaluation semantics for IMP are standard big-step semantics: as our focus is on static checking of the security properties of IMP commands, we omit its presentation.

Label Constraints: To enforce information-flow security on IMP, we define a *constraint-based type system* that determines *label constraints* from a command c and describes the flows that c enables in a security lattice $\mathcal{L}$. If a command c has a set of label constraints that is *satisfiable*, then for all flows that c enables from l_1 to l_2, $l_1 \le l_2$ in the lattice $\mathcal{L}$. If $l_1 \not\le l_2$, then this flow will require mediation before the program can be used as a component of a secure system. We now give the syntax of label expressions and constraints.

$$
\begin{array}{llll}
\text{Label Variables } \alpha & ::= \alpha, \beta, \ldots \in \mathcal{V} & \text{Security Labels } l & ::= l \in \mathcal{L} \\
\text{Atoms} & a ::= \alpha \mid l & \text{Label Joins} & \tau ::= a \mid a \sqcup \tau \\
\text{Constraints} & \xi ::= \tau \le a &&
\end{array}
$$

An atom a_i is a label expression that is either a label variable α or a label $l \in \mathcal{L}$. Label joins have the form $a_1 \sqcup \cdots \sqcup a_n \le a_0$. A label variable α states that an expression has not been explicitly been labeled by the programmer. A label l represents an expression that has a predefined security semantics defined by the lattice $\mathcal{L}$: for example, a key used for encryption that has been read from a file would be given a `Secret` security label that would prevent it from being leaked to security labels in the lattice that it dominates, including `Secret`.

---

[1] For simplicity, we omit presenting the semantics for handling Boolean values. This modification does not affect the security properties of sIMP.

We now give a security type system for IMP (sIMP) that enforces noninterference of high and low security data. Let Γ be a context assigning a security level to seed variables, which is a subset of the set of all program variables, and Δ be a context assigning to each program variable x a unique security variable α_x. To track implicit flows, the type system also keeps track of the current label of the program counter with the pc label. The constraint generation rules are as follows:

Expressions

$$\frac{\alpha_{n,p} \text{ fresh}}{\Gamma;\Delta \vdash (n)_p : \alpha_{n,p}, \emptyset}$$

$$\frac{x \in \text{dom}(\Gamma) \quad \alpha_{x,p} \text{ fresh}}{\Gamma;\Delta \vdash (x)_p : \alpha_{x,p}, \{\, \alpha_{x,p} \le \Delta(x), \Delta(x) \le \alpha_{x,p},\ \Gamma(x) \le \Delta(x), \Delta(x) \le \Gamma(x)\,\}}$$

$$\frac{x \notin \text{dom}(\Gamma) \quad \alpha_{x,p} \text{ fresh}}{\Gamma;\Delta \vdash (x)_p : \alpha_{x,p}, \{\alpha_{x,p} \le \Delta(x), \Delta(x) \le \alpha_{x,p}\}}$$

$$\frac{\Gamma;\Delta \vdash e_1 : \alpha_1, C_1 \quad \Gamma;\Delta \vdash e_2 : \alpha_2, C_2 \quad \alpha_{3,p} \text{ fresh}}{\Gamma;\Delta \vdash (e_1 + e_2)_p : \alpha_{3,p}, C_1 \cup C_2 \cup \{\alpha_1 \sqcup \alpha_2 \le \alpha_{3,p}\}}$$

$$\frac{\Gamma;\Delta \vdash e : \alpha_0, C \quad \alpha_{1,p} \text{ fresh}}{\Gamma;\Delta \vdash (\text{mediate}(e))_p : \alpha_{1,p}, C}$$

Commands

$$\frac{\Gamma;\Delta;pc \vdash \text{skip} : \emptyset \qquad \Gamma;\Delta;pc \vdash c_1 : C_1 \quad \Gamma;\Delta;pc \vdash c_2 : C_2}{\Gamma;\Delta;pc \vdash c_1 \,;\, c_2 : C_1 \cup C_2}$$

$$\frac{\Gamma;\Delta;pc \vdash v : \alpha_0, C_0 \quad \Gamma;\Delta \vdash e : \alpha_1, C_1}{\Gamma;\Delta;pc \vdash v := e : C_0 \cup C_1 \cup \{\alpha_1 \sqcup pc \le \Delta(v)\}}$$

$$\frac{\Gamma;\Delta \vdash e : \alpha_0, C_0 \quad \Gamma;\Delta;\alpha_{pc} \vdash c_1 : C_1 \quad \alpha_{pc} \text{ fresh} \quad \Gamma;\alpha_{pc} \vdash c_2 : C_2}{\Gamma;\Delta;pc \vdash \text{if } e \text{ then } c_1 \text{ else } c_2 : \begin{array}{l} C_0 \cup C_1 \cup C_2 \cup \\ \{pc \sqcup \alpha_0 \le \alpha_{pc}\} \end{array}}$$

$$\frac{\Gamma;\Delta \vdash e : \alpha_0, C_0 \quad \Gamma;\Delta;\alpha_{pc} \vdash c_1 : C_1 \quad \alpha_{pc} \text{ fresh}}{\Gamma;\Delta;pc \vdash \text{while } e \text{ do } c : C_0 \cup C_1 \cup \{pc \sqcup \alpha_0 \le \alpha_{pc}\}}$$

If the generated constraint set C for a command c is satisfiable, then when run, c will not cause any high-security data to affect low-security data. The type judgments presented in this figure are for both expressions e and commands c. An expression is assigned information-flow constraints C and a security variable α with the judgment $\Gamma;\Delta;pc \vdash e : \alpha, C$, while a command c is assigned information-flow constraints C with the judgment $\Gamma;\Delta;pc \vdash c : C$. We associate expressions e with a unique security variable α_e so that the vertices corresponding to a cut of the graph are uniquely identified with mediation points. In the type checking rules, we add a unique position tag p to refer to expressions e, allowing us to uniquely refer to subexpressions. We write $(e)_p$ to indicate that expression e has the position p (assumed to be taken from a unique set of positions). This is similar to converting a program to SSA form [4]. We refer to the label variable $\alpha_{e,p}$ as the *expression variable* for the expression-position pair (e, p). In the case where there is no loss of ambiguity, we refer to α_e as the expression variable for e.

Constraint Example: We now investigate the information-flow constraints associated with the main loop in Figure 1 by building the information-flow constraint set C. The constraints generated by this program represent the information flows through the program. Later in the section, we will show how these constraints induce an information-flow graph on the label variables and lattice elements.

Let $\alpha_{rc}, \alpha_{fn}, \alpha_{nn}, \alpha_{on}, \alpha_i, \alpha_{nlf}, \alpha_{olf}$ be the expression variables associated with the variables rotateCount, filename, newName, oldName, i, newlogfile, and oldlogfile, respectively. For a variable x, the label variable $\alpha_{x,n}$ represents the occurrence of x on line n. For all n such that x appears on line n, the constraint set contains the constraints $\alpha_x \leq \alpha_{x,n}$ and $\alpha_{x,n} \leq \alpha_x$ (the expression x on line n has the same security level as the variable α_x).

From the definitions at the beginning of the code, the constraint set C contains the constraints config $\leq \alpha_{rc}$ and config $\leq \alpha_{fn}$. The for loop introduces a new program counter variable α_{pc1} and the constraints $\alpha_{rc,8} \leq \alpha_i$ (from int i = rotateCount), $\alpha_{i,8} \leq \alpha_i$ (from the i-- statement), and $\alpha_i \leq \alpha_{pc1}$ (from the loop being executed until a condition on i is satisfied). The next two statements generate the constraints $\alpha_{i,9} \sqcup \alpha_{fn,9} \leq \alpha_{nn}$ and $\alpha_{i,10} \sqcup \alpha_{fn,10} \leq \alpha_{on}$. The call to Runtime.getFile requires that both the first argument passed and the value returned have the label of the second argument passed in. Therefore, the two calls to getFile generate the constraint set

$$\{ \; \alpha_{nn,11} \leq \text{log\_lbl}, \; \text{log\_lbl} \leq \alpha_{nlf},$$
$$\alpha_{on,13} \leq \text{log\_lbl}, \; \text{log\_lbl} \leq \alpha_{olf} \; \}$$

The if statement comparing oldlogfile to null creates a new program counter variable α_{pc2}, the constraint $\alpha_{pc1} \sqcup \alpha_{olf} \leq \alpha_{pc2}$. Finally, the call to renameTo generates the constraints $\alpha_{olf} \leq \alpha_{nlf}$, as the old log file must be able to flow to the new log file, and $\alpha_{pc2} \leq \alpha_{olf}$, $\alpha_{pc2} \leq \alpha_{nlf}$, as observing if one file has been renamed to another is an observable action that reveals information about the program counter.

4.2 Constraints as an Information-Flow Graph

We now define the information-flow graph as an alternative representation of an information-flow constraint set and show that a cut of the information-flow graph formed from a set of sIMP constraints C corresponds to a set of mediation points that make C satisfiable.

For the rest of this section, we assume that the lattice $\mathcal{L}$ has only two labels: $\top$ and $\bot$ with $\bot \leq \top$. We describe how to extend the cut-based approach to place declassifiers in a general security lattice in Section 4.4.

We now define a translation of an information-flow constraint set C into an information flow constraint graph $\mathcal{G}_C$, which contains dependency information for the label variables and labels that are described by C. Every label variable and lattice element that occurs in C is a vertex in $\mathcal{G}_C$. There is an edge between two vertices in $\mathcal{G}$ if the program permits a flow of information between the program elements that those vertices represent in the graph. For example, if

$\alpha \leq \beta \in C$, there are vertices for α and β in $\mathcal{G}_C$ and an edge between them, as the security level of α is constrained to be less than or equal to that of β.

Definition 1 (Information Flow Graph). *Let C be an information-flow constraint set. Let $\mathcal{G}_C$ be the graph with vertex set $V(\mathcal{G}_C) = \mathcal{V} \cup \mathcal{L}$ and, for atoms a, a', $(a, a') \in E(\mathcal{G}_C)$ if $\tau_0 \sqcup \cdots \sqcup a \sqcup \cdots \tau_n \leq a' \in C$.*

4.3 Correspondence of Graph Cuts and Mediation Points

We now show that a vertex cut of the information-flow graph containing only expression variables corresponds to a set of expressions that needs to be mediated. We will show that sIMP constraints have the property that a $(\top, \bot)$ cut of the information-flow graph $\mathcal{G}_C$ corresponds to a placement of mediation statements that fully resolves errors caused by the flows in the command c. We use the Rehof-Mogensen constraint solver [23], introduced in Section 3, in proving these claims.

The following lemma connects paths in the information-flow graph to the unsatisfiability of the constraints set C.

Lemma 2. *Let $\Gamma; \Delta \vdash c : C$. The set C is satisfiable if and only if there is no $(\top, \bot)$-path in $\mathcal{G}_C$.*

Proof. Please refer to the tech report [16] for the proof.

We define an *expression cut* as a $(\top, \bot)$ vertex cut of the information flow graph that only includes label variables of the form $\alpha_{e,p}$.

Definition 3. *Suppose $\Gamma; pc \vdash c : C$. An expression cut of (c, Γ) is a set of expression-position pairs $T = \{(e_0, p_0), \ldots, (e_n, p_n)\}$ such that the set $\{\alpha_{e_0, p_0}, \ldots, \alpha_{e_n, p_n}\}$ is a vertex $(\top, \bot)$ cut set of the graph $\mathcal{G}_C$.*

We now define the command $T(c)$, which is the command c with each expression e in the expression cut T replaced by mediate(e).

Definition 4. *Let T be a set of expression-position pairs (e_i, p_i). Let $T(c)$ represent the command with each e_i at position p_i replaced with mediate(e_i) at position p_i.*

We now show that expression cuts are exactly those sets of expressions which, when mediated, make the generated set of information-flow constraints C satisfiable.

Theorem 5 (Cut-Mediation Equivalence). *Let T be a set of expression-position pairs, $\Gamma \vdash c : C$, and $\Gamma \vdash T(c) : C'$. Suppose also that C is unsatisfiable. Then T is an expression cut of (c, Γ) if and only if C' is satisfiable.*

Proof. Please refer to the tech report [16] for the proof.

Cut Example: The logrotate program permits several flows between lattice labels config and log_lbl. To determine a set of mediation points from a cut of the graph, we allow vertices that correspond to the security values of expressions to be part of the cut. Every vertex cut of the graph that separates config from log_lbl and contains only vertices that correspond to expressions induces a set of mediation points placed in the code. For example, the vertices corresponding to rotateCount in line 8, oldName in line 13, and newName line 11 separates config from log_lbl, and corresponds to placing mediation statements mediating those expression in those lines.

4.4   Finding Mediation Points for General Lattices

We now describe the more general problem of finding a set of mediation points for an arbitrary lattice. We call this problem, *general lattice cut-mediation* (GLC). We will show that the GLC problem is an instance of the graph problem of *cut-conjunction* for directed graphs (DCC), which currently has unknown complexity [14]. Thus, we adopt an approximation strategy to solve GLC that employs the *hitting set* problem, which is known to be an NP-complete problem, but for which several good approximation algorithms exist.

Comparison to the *cut-conjunction* Problem: We first introduce the DCC problem. Let $G = (V, E)$ be a directed graph on vertex set V and edge set E. Let $\mathcal{P} \subseteq V \times V$ be an arbitrary family of pairs of vertices in G. A set of edges $E' \subseteq E$ is called a $\mathcal{P}$-cut if and only if none of the pairs of vertices in $\mathcal{P}$ are connected in $G' = (V, E \setminus E')$. The *cut-conjunction (CC)* problem is the following: given a graph $G = (V, E)$ and $\mathcal{P} \subseteq V \times V$ find a subset of edges $E' \subseteq E$ that is a minimal $\mathcal{P}$-cut. The cut-conjunction enumeration problem is to enumerate all minimal $\mathcal{P}$-cuts in a graph $G = (V, E)$. The *weighted cut-conjunction (WCC)* problem is the cut-conjunction problem, except that a function $f : E \to \mathbb{N}$ specifies edge weights, and the enumerated $\mathcal{P}$-cuts in G are required to have minimum weight.

Given an 0 security lattice $\mathcal{L}$ for a GLC problem, let $\mathcal{P}_{\mathcal{L}}$ be the set of all pairs of labels (l_1, l_2) such that $l_1 \nleq l_2$. The following lemma generalizes Lemma 2 to $\mathcal{P}_{\mathcal{L}}$-cuts.

Lemma 6. Let C be an unsatisfiable constraint set over a lattice $\mathcal{L}$ and $\mathcal{G}_C = (V, E)$ be the information-flow graph for C. Let $E' \subseteq E$ be a $\mathcal{P}_{\mathcal{L}}$-cut for $\mathcal{G}_C$ and $C_{E'}$ be the constraint set generated by the program where the expressions corresponding to the edges in E' have been mediated to $\bot$. The constraint set $C_{E'}$ is satisfiable.

The solution to the cut-conjunction problem for our constructed information-flow graph for a GLC problem then corresponds to the expressions that mediate all illegal flows through the program associated with the information-flow graph. However, the complexity of DCC is unknown [14], so we use an approximation in order to solve GLC.

Placement Algorithm for General Lattices: The algorithm we use to solve GLC consists of two steps: first, we solve the min-cut problem on a per-source

MEDIATIONPOINTS($\mathcal{G}_C, \mathcal{P}_\mathcal{L}$)

1   *Labels* $\leftarrow \{l \mid (l, l') \in \mathcal{P}_\mathcal{L}\}$, $\mathcal{X} \leftarrow \emptyset$
2   **for each** $l \in$ *Labels*
3        $T_l \leftarrow \{l' \mid (l, l') \in \mathcal{P}_\mathcal{L}\}$
4        $\mathcal{X}_l \leftarrow$ ALLMINIMUMCUTS($\mathcal{G}_C, l, T_l$)
5   $S \leftarrow$ MINGHS($\mathcal{X}_{l_0}, \ldots, \mathcal{X}_{l_{|Labels|}}$)
6   **return** EXPRESSIONSFROMEDGECUT(S)

Fig. 2. An algorithm for choosing a set of mediation points for a general lattice based on the generalized hitting set problem

basis, and then we use an algorithm that solves the *hitting set* problem to combine the results. This is an approximation of an optimal solution for the GLC problem, as the per-source cuts are local minima solutions. The hitting set problem is NP-complete, but there are known approximations [1,10].

An instance of the *hitting set (HS)* problem consists of a collection $\{S_1, S_2, \ldots, S_n\}$, where each S_i is a subset of T, and a positive integer $k \leq |T|$. The problem is to determine whether there is some subset H of T such that $|H| \leq k \wedge \forall i \ (H \cap S_i) \neq \emptyset$. We consider a generalized version of this problem where each of the elements in S_i is in turn a subset of T, i.e., S_i is a collection of sets. An instance of the *generalized hitting set (GHS)* problem consists of a set of collections $\{C_1, \cdots, C_n\}$ where each C_i is a collection of subsets of T (i.e., each $C_i = \{S_{i,1}, \cdots, S_{i,k_i}\}$ where $S_{i,j}$ is a subset of T) and a positive integer $k \leq |T|$. The problem is to determine whether there is a subset H of T such that $|H| \leq k$ and for all i such that $1 \leq i \leq n$ there exists a j such that $S_{i,j} \subseteq H$ (a set in the collection C_i is a subset of H. Let MINGHS($C_1, \ldots, C_n$) be a procedure that solves the hitting set problem. Figure 2 contains an algorithm for placing security mediators for a general lattice that relies on an external procedure for MINGHS to solve the hitting set problem. It is easy to see that if MEDIATIONPOINTS($\mathcal{G}_C, \mathcal{P}_\mathcal{L}$) = $\mathcal{X}$, for all $(l, l') \in \mathcal{P}_\mathcal{L}$, there is no path from l to l' in $\mathcal{G}_C \setminus \mathcal{X}$. Assume there is such a path from l to l': by the definition of a minimum vertex cut, this path intersects at least one vertex in S_l chosen from $\mathcal{X}_l$. This path cannot exist as each vertex in S_l was removed from $\mathcal{G}_C$. By Lemma 6, mediating the expressions specified in a $\mathcal{P}_\mathcal{L}$-cut results in a satisfiable constraint set.

The running time of this algorithm is primarily dependent on the size of the problem given to MINGHS. The number of cuts generated by ALLMINIMUMCUTS depends on the size of the lattice, and the size of the cuts depends on the complexity of the program.

5   Suggestion Framework

The information-flow graph construction in Section 4 constructs, from program code, a graph for which a cut is equivalent to a placement of mediation points. In this section, we discuss how to deploy this method in a framework that outputs sets of mediation points (i.e., *placement suggestions*) for Java programs.

Our tool outputs a set of *suggestions*, each of which is a set of points in the code that completely mediates the illegal information flows from a program. We built a framework that uses minimum graph cuts to select mediation points. The minimum cut of a graph corresponds to the minimum number of mediation points that need to be inserted into the program. While a minimum sized set of mediation points may not necessarily agree with programmer intent, we believe that a set of minimum size provides a good starting point for understanding how best to mediate the illegal flows in a program. If the programmer wishes to give incentive or decentive to select certain mediation points, then this can be accomplished by modifying the graph cut model.

The framework can be applied to any Java program whose language features are supported by the Jif compiler. The main feature of sIMP constraints is that mediating an expression e at position p removes any of the security information affecting the expression label variable $\alpha_{e,p}$. However, the unmodified constraints generated by the Jif compiler do not satisfy cut-mediation equivalence because the security labels that the compiler associates with an expression e are affected by both explicit and implicit security information. To make the Jif constraints satisfy cut-mediation equivalence, we modified the constraint generation procedure for every class of expression that could have a visible side effect, so that extra constraints to check implicit flows were included. These additional constraints ensure that information associated with an implicit flow is maintained if α_e is selected as part of a graph cut.

There may be many suggestions of minimum size that resolve the information flows for a given program, as a graph might have several minimum cuts. Therefore, most applications admit an infeasibly large number of minimum sets of mediation points, most of which are very similar. For example, let h be a high security integer variable. For the expression if h == 0 then l := 0, the expressions h and h == 0 are both part of the minimum set of mediation points. If our framework considers multiple expressions with equivalent security semantics as valid mediation points, the number of minimum cuts quickly becomes exponential in the number of vertices of the information-flow graph $\mathcal{G}_C$. To avoid enumerating an exponential number of mediation points to the programmer, we consider an expression e redundant if its value only flows to another expression e' in the information-flow graph. Suppose $\alpha_e, \alpha'_e \in \mathcal{G}_C$ and let l be a lattice label. If $\alpha_{e'}$ postdominates[2] α_e at exit node $T_l = \{l' \mid l \not\sqsubseteq l'\}$, do not consider α_e as a mediation point for l [18]. Because the definition of postdomination relies on the exit node, this must be done for each $l \in \mathcal{L}$. The process of removing postdominated expressions from the set of possible declassifiers is done before computing the maximum network flow between l and its associated super-sink T_l (Figure 2).

---

[2] Given a graph $G = (V, E)$, let $n, m \in V$, then m *postdominates* n if m is different from n and m is on every path from n to the end node.

Table 1. Runtime performance of our mediation placement algorithm. We separate Java programs (top) from Jif programs (bottom). Per application, we report the lines of code in the files analyzed, give the number of constraints solved, the number of minimum cut problems that our tool needed to solve, the average size of the information-flow graph for each label l, and the average number of mediation points from the minimum cut. We give the performance of our algorithm by reporting the two factors that had the most effect on running time: total time required to cluster the graphs before performing a minimum cut, and total time required to solve minimum cut problems. Finally, we give the total running time of the analysis.

Application	Code Lines	# of Constraints	Min Cut Probs.	Avg. Graph Vertices	Avg. Vertices per Min Cut	Cluster Time (s)	Cut Time (s)	Total Time (s)
JES	2,407	22,151	1	6,021.00	3.00	0.57	1.06	4.30
Java Card Purse	13,981	48,728	1	8,312.00	8.00	0.64	0.50	6.46
tinySQL	12,632	60,909	1	20,683.00	10.00	1.50	2.16	11.83
weirdx	22,308	239,521	2	92,802.00	88.00	15.54	21.61	83.74
logrotate	911	6,063	2	1,654.00	3.50	0.11	0.006	1.34
JPMail (reader)	3,934	8,438	59	3,151.29	3.31	3.88	0.46	13.37
JPMail (sender)	3,932	14,495	32	3,844.69	4.28	4.95	0.12	14.84
Mental Poker	1,578	13,344	1	3,553.00	4.00	0.25	0.24	2.21
Civitas (voter)	13,828	67,135	5	17,658.00	1.4	7.11	0.62	28.71

6   Experimental Results

In this section, we present the results of running our mediation point placement tool on program code on a variety of Java and Jif applications.

Experimental Setup: Our mediation placement algorithm is written in 1,001 lines of C++ code[3], and our experiments were run on a machine with a 2.3 GHz AMD Operton processor with 3 GB of memory. We used the Lemon graph libraries developed for scientific computing to calculate the minimum cut of a graph, but implemented our own dominator computation. We ran our analysis on eight separate applications as shown in Table 1: four Java applications for which mediation is added from scratch and four Jif applications in which the manually placed mediators are removed. The labeling and policy were determined per application. To generate the information-flow constraints, we used a context-insensitive, interprocedural label analysis. The mediation placement technique described in this paper is independent of the specific kind of label analysis, so long as that analysis has the cut-mediation equivalence in Theorem 5. An issue with every static analysis is the presence of false positives but our current analysis was sufficient for our examples; while we encountered some false positives, these were easily detected and removed. However, an improved analysis will be necessary in general.

Performance: Table 1 contains metrics about the performance of our system. We allow a programmer to specify a function as the starting point of the analysis. For example, the analysis of Civitas focused on six vote tallying methods.

---
[3] Our constraint-generation and mincut tools are available for download at http://siis.cse.psu.edu/jlift/jlift.html

Since code contains whitespace and comments, total number of constraints generated by the analysis (column 3) is a more accurate metric for the difficulty of the graph problem than file sizes (column 2). Two major factors affected the running time of our tool: Number of minimum-cut problems to be solved per program (column 4) and the number of mediation points returned as a solution to each minimum cut problem (column 6). The number of minimum cut problems is a multiplicative factor: because domination is a source-sink computation and different minimum-cut problems have different sources and sinks, clustering is performed once for each minimum-cut. Also, it took a longer time for the minimum cut algorithm to run for programs whose cuts had a higher number of vertices, as the Ford-Fulkerson method depends on finding augmenting paths to an existing cut. Our largest code example was an X Server written in Java that contained over 22,000 lines of code, corresponding to over 230,000 information flow constraints. It took 83 seconds for our suggestion method to complete when run on these constraints, returning 176 mediation points. A pattern in all of our experiments was the small size of the minimum cut relative to the size of the overall graph indicating that our suggestion algorithm should scale well on even larger programs.

Comparison To Previous Work: To evaluate how well our approach reduces the space of placement options, we compared our mediation placement algorithm to an existing mechanism for resolving information-flow errors for previously unmediated Java programs (JES, Java Card Purse, tinySQL and an X Server implementation called WeirdX). Recent work [15] proposed a tool to display complete and minimal *error traces* that show how an information-flow constraint becomes unsatisfiable, enabling a programmer to find suitable mediation sites. While this approach narrows down the points in the program that need to be examined, it only reports one error trace per failed information-flow constraint, requiring the programmer to run the analysis multiple times to resolve all of the errors per constraint. The results of comparing our tool to such error traces are given in Table 2. These results show that our tool reduces the number of locations by 90% or more for all but one case (Java Card Purse), which is nearly 90%.

Table 2. Comparison of selected mediation points to information-flow errors for each Java application. The second column gives the total number of candidate mediation points after clustering. The third column gives the number of mediation points highlighted by *error traces* in a prior work [15], while the fourth column gives the number of mediation points selected by our tool in all suggestions. Only tinySQL has multiple suggested min-cuts of the same size (48 of them).

Application	Mediation Points		
	Candidate	Error Trace	Min-Cut
JES	5,492	89	3
Java Card Purse	11,540	62	8
tinySQL	14,735	553	10
weirdx	133,356	1868	176

Quality of Placed Mediators: To investigate the quality of placed mediation points, we ran our tool on a number of applications (logrotate, JPMail, Mental Poker and Civitas) originally written in the security-typed language Jif. We define a similarity metric to compare automatically placed mediation points with the mediation points placed by the original application programmers. We classified each selected mediation point as either being *similar* or *not similar* and those classified as similar belonged to one of three categories: Mediation point that mediates the exact same data in the exact same location as the original (**Exact**), is in the same block of code as the original mediation point (**Same-Block**) and mediates the exact same value as the original (**SameData**). Our results in Table 3 show that in all the Jif applications, over 80% of the selected mediation points were placed in locations that matched one of our similarity metrics. The remaining 20% of mediation points that were placed by our tool generally were selected in a way to reduce the total number of mediation points, whereas the programmer had chose to insert more expressive mediation statements. This means that there are other factors used by expert programmers that need to be assessed in placement. Our framework supports programmer control through the adjustment of weights on the graph edges. We currently use this to enable programmers to prohibit locations (e.g., increase edge weights to ∞) or select locations (i.e., require them in every cut). A key issue appears to be if a programmer has a specific mediator in mind. Ensuring that a location is chosen only if it satisfies the functional requirements of a mediator or other programmer requirements are future work.

Table 3. Similarity Results. For each application, we give the number of mediation points that occur in at least one suggestion and the classification of these mediation points into one of four similarity categories. Additionally, we report the number of suggestion sets returned.

Application	Candidate Mediation Points	Total Mediation Points Suggested	Similarity Exact	Block	Data	Not	Suggestions (# of Sets)
logrotate	1,540	9	1	7	1	0	3
Mental Poker	3,569	7	3	0	1	3	4
JPMail (reader)	2,434	37	1	15	14	7	25
JPMail (sender)	3,976	74	2	52	19	1	23
Civitas (voter)	19,977	9	6	0	2	1	6

7   Conclusion

In this paper we have presented a framework to assist programmers in placing security mediation points. Our framework implements a method that constructs a graph $\mathcal{G}$ such that a minimum cut of $\mathcal{G}$ corresponds to a minimum placement of mediation points in the program. This framework reduced the number of expressions that need to be examined to resolve information-flow errors in four Java programs and placed mediation statements in locations similar to those placed by the original application programmers for four Jif programs. In the future, we plan to provide support for extracting functional requirements from programs that influence placements to improve accuracy.

References

1. Bar-Yehuda, R., Even, S.: A linear-time approximation algorithm for the weighted vertex cover problem. Journal of Algorithms 2(2), 198–203 (1981)
2. Clarkson, M.R., Chong, S., Myers, A.C.: Civitas: Toward a secure voting system. In: Proceedings of the 2008 IEEE Symposium on Security and Privacy, May 2008, pp. 354–368 (2008)
3. Criswell, J., Lenharth, A., Dhurjati, D., Adve, V.: Secure virtual architecture: a safe execution environment for commodity operating systems. SIGOPS Oper. Syst. Rev. 41(6), 351–366 (2007)
4. Cytron, R., Ferrante, J., Rosen, B.K., Wegman, M.N., Zadeck, F.K.: Efficiently computing static single assignment form and the control dependence graph. ACM Transactions on Programming Languages and Systems 13(4), 451–490 (1991)
5. Deng, Z., Smith, G.: Type inference and informative error reporting for secure information flow. In: ACM-SE 44: Proceedings of the 44th annual Southeast regional conference, pp. 543–548. ACM, New York (2006)
6. Fahndrich, M., Foster, J.S., Su, Z., Aiken, A.: Partial online cycle elimination in inclusion constraint graphs. In: Proceedings of PLDI 1998, pp. 85–96 (1998)
7. Flanagan, C., Flatt, M., Krishnamurthi, S., Weirich, S., Felleisen, M.: Catching bugs in the web of program invariants. SIGPLAN Not. 31(5), 23–32 (1996)
8. Fraser, T., Petroni Jr., N.L., Arbaugh, W.A.: Applying flow-sensitive CQUAL to verify minix authorization check placement. In: Proceedings of PLAS 2006, pp. 3–6. ACM, New York (2006)
9. Goguen, J.A., Meseguer, J.: Security policies and security models. In: Proceedings of the 1982 IEEE Symposium on Security and Privacy, April 1982, pp. 11–20 (1982)
10. Halperin, E.: Improved approximation algorithms for the vertex cover problem in graphs and hypergraphs. In: SODA 2000: Proceedings of the 11th Annual ACM-SIAM Symposium on Discrete Algorithms, pp. 329–337. Society for Industrial and Applied Mathematics (2000)
11. Heintze, N., Tardieu, O.: Ultra-fast aliasing analysis using CLA: A million lines of C code in a second. In: Proceedings of PLDI 2001, June 2001, pp. 254–263 (2001)
12. Hicks, B., Ahmadizadeh, K., McDaniel, P.: From languages to systems: Understanding practical application development in security-typed languages. In: ACSAC 2006: Proceedings of the 22nd Annual Computer Security Applications Conference, pp. 153–164. IEEE Computer Society, Los Alamitos (2006)
13. Hicks, B., Rueda, S., Jaeger, T., McDaniel, P.: From trusted to secure: Building and executing applications that enforce system security. In: Proceedings of the USENIX Annual Technical Conference, June 2007, pp. 1–14 (2007)
14. Khachiyan, L., Boros, E., Elbassioni, K., Gurvich, V., Makino, K.: Enumerating disjunctions and conjunctions of paths and cuts in reliability theory. Discrete Appl. Math. 155(2), 137–149 (2007)
15. King, D., Jaeger, T., Jha, S., Seshia, S.A.: Effective blame for information-flow violations. In: SIGSOFT 2008/FSE-16: Proceedings of the 16th ACM SIGSOFT International Symposium on Foundations of Software Engineering, pp. 250–260. ACM, New York (2008)

16. King, D., Jha, S., Muthukumaran, D., Jaeger, T., Jha, S., Seshia, S.: Automating Security Mediation Placement. Tech. Rep. NAS-TR-0123-2010, Network and Security Research Center, Department of Computer Science and Engineering, Pennsylvania State University, University Park, PA, USA (January 2010)
17. McCamant, S., Ernst, M.D.: Quantitative information flow as network flow capacity. In: Proceedings of PLDI 2008, pp. 193–205. ACM, New York (2008)
18. Muchnick, S.S.: Advanced Compiler Design and Implementation. Morgan Kaufmann, San Francisco (1997)
19. Myers, A., Liskov, B.: Complete, safe information flow with decentralized labels. In: Proceedings of the IEEE Symposium on Security & Privacy, May 1998, pp. 186–197 (1998)
20. Myers, A.C.: JFlow: Practical mostly-static information flow control. In: Proceedings of POPL 1999, January 1999, pp. 228–241 (1999)
21. Necula, G.C., Condit, J., Harren, M., McPeak, S., Weimer, W.: CCured: type-safe retrofitting of legacy software. ACM Transactions on Programming Languages and Systems 27(3), 477–526 (2005)
22. Pottier, F., Simonet, V.: Information flow inference for ML. In: Proceedings of POPL 2002, pp. 319–330. ACM Press, New York (2002)
23. Rehof, J., Mogensen, T.A.: Tractable constraints in finite semilattices. Science of Computer Programming 35(2-3), 191–221 (1999)
24. Sabelfeld, A., Sands, D.: Dimensions and principles of declassification. In: CSFW 2005: Proceedings of the 18th IEEE Workshop on Computer Security Foundations, pp. 255–269. IEEE Computer Society, Los Alamitos (2005)
25. Shapiro, M., Horwitz, S.: Fast and accurate flow-insensitive points-to analysis. In: Proceedings of POPL 1997, pp. 1–14. ACM, New York (1997)
26. Tip, F., Dinesh, T.B.: A slicing-based approach for locating type errors. ACM Trans. Softw. Eng. Methodol. 10(1), 5–55 (2001)
27. Volpano, D., Smith, G., Irvine, C.: A sound type system for secure flow analysis. Journal of Computer Security 4(3), 167–187 (1996)
28. Walsh, E.: Integrating X.Org with Security-Enhanced Linux. In: Proceedings of the Third Annual Security Enhanced Linux Symposium, March 2007, pp. 33–40 (2007)
29. Wheeler, D.A.: Software/dbus, http://www.freedesktop.org/wiki/Software/dbus
30. Winskel, G.: The Formal Semantics of Programming Languages: An Introduction. MIT Press, Cambridge (1993)
31. Wright, C., Cowan, C., Morris, J., Smalley, S., Kroah-Hartman, G.: Linux security modules: General security support for the linux kernel. In: Proceedings of the 11th USENIX Security Symposium, August 2002, pp. 17–31 (2002)
32. Zhang, X., Edwards, A., Jaeger, T.: Using CQUAL for static analysis of authorization hook placement. In: Proceedings of the 11th USENIX Security Symposium, August 2002, pp. 33–48 (2002)

TRX: A Formally Verified Parser Interpreter

Adam Koprowski and Henri Binsztok

MLstate, Paris, France

{Adam.Koprowski,Henri.Binsztok}@mlstate.com

Abstract. Parsing is an important problem in computer science and yet surprisingly little attention has been devoted to its formal verification. In this paper, we present TRX: a parser interpreter formally developed in the proof assistant Coq, capable of producing formally correct parsers. We are using parsing expression grammars (PEGs), a formalism essentially representing recursive descent parsing, which we consider an attractive alternative to context-free grammars (CFGs). From this formalization we can extract a parser for an arbitrary PEG grammar with the warranty of total correctness, i.e., the resulting parser is terminating and correct with respect to its grammar and the semantics of PEGs; both properties formally proven in Coq.

1 Introduction

Parsing is of major interest in computer science. Classically discovered by students as the first step in compilation, parsing is present in almost every program which performs data-manipulation.

For instance, the Web is built on parsers. The HyperText Transfer Protocol (HTTP) is a parsed dialog between the client, or browser, and the server. This protocol transfers pages in HyperText Markup Language (HTML), which is also parsed by the browser. When running web-applications, browsers interpret JavaScript programs which, again, begins with parsing. Data exchange between browser(s) and server(s) uses languages or formats like XML and JSON. Even inside the server, several components (for instance the trio made of the HTTP server Apache, the PHP interpreter and the MySQL database) often manipulate programs and data dynamically; all require parsers.

Parsing is not limited to compilation or the Web: securing data flow entering a network, signaling mobile communications, manipulating domain specific languages (DSL) all require a variety of parsers.

The most common approach to parsing is by means of *parser generators*, which take as input a grammar of some language and generate the source code of a parser for that language. They are usually based on regular expressions (REs) and context-free grammars (CFGs), the latter expressed in Backus-Naur Form (BNF) syntax. They typically are able to deal with some subclass of context-free languages, the popular subclasses including *LL(k)*, *LR(k)* and *LALR(k)* grammars. Such grammars are usually augmented with semantic actions that are used to produce a parse tree or an abstract syntax tree (AST) of the input.

A.D. Gordon (Ed.): ESOP 2010, LNCS 6012, pp. 345–365, 2010.

What about *correctness* of such parsers? Yacc is the most widely used parser generator and a mature program and yet [20] devotes a whole section ("Bugs in Yacc") to discuss common bugs in its distributions. Furthermore, the code generated by such tools often contains huge parsing tables making it near impossible for manual inspection and/or verification. In the recent article [17] about CompCert, an impressive project formally verifying a compiler for a large subset of C, the introduction starts with a question "Can you trust your compiler?". Nevertheless, the formal verification starts on the level of the AST and does not concern the parser [17, Figure 1]. Can you trust your parser?

Parsing expression grammars (PEGs) [14] are an alternative to CFGs, that have recently been gaining popularity. In contrast to CFGs they are unambiguous and allow easy integration of lexical analysis into the parsing phase. Their implementation is easy, as PEGs are essentially a declarative way of specifying recursive descent parsers [5]. With their backtracking and unlimited look-ahead capabilities they are expressive enough to cover all $LL(k)$ and $LR(k)$ languages as well as some non-context-free ones. However, recursive descent parsing of grammars that are not $LL(k)$ may require exponential time. A solution to that problem is to use memoization giving rise to *packrat parsing* and ensuring linear time complexity at the price of higher memory consumption [2,13,12]. It is not easy to support (indirect) left-recursive rules in PEGs, as they lead to non-terminating parsers [29].

In this paper we present TRX: a PEG-based parser interpreter *formally developed* in the proof assistant Coq [28,4]. As a result, expressing a grammar in Coq allows one, via its extraction capabilities [19], to obtain a parser for this grammar with *total correctness guarantees*. That means that the resulting parser is terminating and correct with respect to its grammar and the semantics of PEGs; both of those properties formally proved in Coq. Moreover every definition and theorem presented in this paper has been expressed and verified in Coq.

The contributions of this paper are:

- extension of PEGs with semantic actions,
- a Coq formalization of the theory of PEGs and
- a Coq development of TRX: a PEG interpreter allowing to obtain a parser with total correctness guarantees for an arbitrary PEG grammar.

The remainder of this paper is organized as follows. We introduce PEGs in Section 2 and in Section 3 we extend them with semantic actions. Section 4

$$
\begin{array}{llll}
\Delta ::= & \epsilon & \text{empty expr.} & | \; e_1/e_2 & \text{a } \textit{prioritized} \text{ choice } (e_1, e_2 \in \Delta) \\
& | \; [\cdot] & \text{any character} & | \; e* & \text{a} \geq 0 \textit{ greedy} \text{ repetition } (e \in \Delta) \\
& | \; [a] & \text{a terminal } (a \in \mathcal{V}_T) & | \; e+ & \text{a} \geq 1 \textit{ greedy} \text{ repetition } (e \in \Delta) \\
& | \; [\text{``}s\text{''}] & \text{a literal } (s \in \mathcal{S}) & | \; e? & \text{an optional expression } (e \in \Delta) \\
& | \; [a\text{--}z] & \text{a range } (a, z \in \mathcal{V}_T) & | \; !e & \text{a not-predicate } (e \in \Delta) \\
& | \; A & \text{a non-terminal } (A \in \mathcal{V}_N) & | \; \&e & \text{an and-predicate } (e \in \Delta) \\
& | \; e_1; e_2 & \text{a sequence } (e_1, e_2 \in \Delta) & &
\end{array}
$$

Fig. 1. Parsing expressions

describes a method for checking that there is no (indirect) left recursion in a grammar, a result ensuring that parsing will terminate. Section 5 reports on our experience with putting the ideas of preceding sections into practice and implementing a formally correct parser interpreter in Coq. Section 6 is devoted to a practical evaluation of this interpreter and contains a small case study of extracting an XML parser from it, presenting a benchmark of TRX against other parser generators and giving an account of our experience with extraction. We discuss related work in Section 7 and conclude in Section 8.

2 Parsing Expression Grammars (PEGs)

The content of this section is a different presentation of the ideas from [14]. For more details we refer to the original article. For a general overview of parsing we refer to, for instance, [1].

PEGs are a formalism for parsing that is an interesting alternative to CFGs. We will formally introduce them along with their semantics in Section 2.1. PEGs are gaining popularity recently due to their ease of implementation and some general desirable properties that we will sketch in Section 2.2, while comparing them to CFGs.

2.1 Definition of PEGs

Definition 1 (Parsing expressions). *We introduce a set of parsing expressions, Δ, over a finite set of terminals $\mathcal{V}_T$ and a finite set of non-terminals $\mathcal{V}_N$. We denote the set of strings as $\mathcal{S}$ and a string $s \in \mathcal{S}$ is a list of terminals $\mathcal{V}_T$. The inductive definition of Δ is given in Figure 1.*   ◇

Later on we will present the formal semantics but for now we informally describe the language expressed by all types of parsing expressions.

- *Empty expression* ϵ always succeeds without consuming any input.
- *Any-character* $[\cdot]$, a *terminal* $[a]$ and a *range* $[a - z]$ all consume a single terminal from the input but they expect it to be, respectively: an arbitrary terminal, precisely a and in the range between a and z.
- *Literal* $["s"]$ reads a string (*i.e.*, a sequence of terminals) s from the input.
- Parsing a *non-terminal* A amounts to parsing the expression defining A.
- A *sequence* $e_1; e_2$ expects an input conforming to e_1 followed by an input conforming to e_2.
- A *choice* e_1/e_2 expresses a *prioritized* choice between e_1 and e_2. This means that e_2 will be tried only if e_1 fails.
- A *zero-or-more (resp. one-or-more) repetition* $e*$ (*resp.* $e+$) consumes zero-or-more (*resp.* one-or-more) repetitions of e from the input. Those operators are *greedy*, *i.e.*, the longest match in the input, conforming to e will be consumed.
- An *and-predicate (resp. not-predicate)* $\&e$ (*resp.* $!e$) succeeds only if the input conforms to e (*resp.* does not conform to e) but does not consume any input.

We now define PEGs, which are essentially a finite set of non-terminals, also referred to as *productions*, with their corresponding parsing expressions.

Definition 2 (Parsing Expressions Grammar (PEG)). *A parsing expressions grammar (PEG), $\mathcal{G}$, is a tuple $(\mathcal{V}_T, \mathcal{V}_N, P_{exp}, v_{start})$, where:*

- $\mathcal{V}_T$ *is a finite set of terminals,*
- $\mathcal{V}_N$ *is a finite set of non-terminals,*
- P_{exp} *is the interpretation of the productions, i.e., $P_{exp} : \mathcal{V}_N \to \Delta$ and*
- v_{start} *is the start production, $v_{start} \in \mathcal{V}_N$.*   ◇

We will now present the formal semantics of PEGs. The semantics is given by means of tuples $(e, s) \overset{m}{\leadsto} r$, which indicate that parsing expression $e \in \Delta$ applied on a string $s \in \mathcal{S}$ gives, in m steps, the result r, where r is either $\bot$, denoting that parsing failed, or $\sqrt{s'}$, indicating that parsing succeeded and s' is what remains to be parsed. We will drop the m annotation whenever irrelevant.

$$\frac{}{(\epsilon, s) \overset{1}{\leadsto} \sqrt{s}} \qquad \frac{(P_{exp}(A), s) \overset{n}{\leadsto} r}{(A, s) \overset{n+1}{\leadsto} r} \qquad \frac{}{([\cdot], x :: xs) \overset{1}{\leadsto} \sqrt{xs}}$$

$$\frac{}{([\cdot], []) \overset{1}{\leadsto} \bot} \qquad \frac{}{([x], x :: xs) \overset{1}{\leadsto} \sqrt{xs}} \qquad \frac{}{([x], []) \overset{1}{\leadsto} \bot}$$

$$\frac{x \neq y}{([y], x :: xs) \overset{1}{\leadsto} \bot} \qquad \frac{(e, s) \overset{m}{\leadsto} \bot}{(!e, s) \overset{m+1}{\leadsto} \sqrt{s}} \qquad \frac{(e, s) \overset{m}{\leadsto} \sqrt{s'}}{(!e, s) \overset{m+1}{\leadsto} \bot}$$

$$\frac{(e_1, s) \overset{m}{\leadsto} \bot}{(e_1; e_2, s) \overset{m+1}{\leadsto} \bot} \qquad \frac{(e_1, s) \overset{m}{\leadsto} \sqrt{s'} \quad (e_2, s') \overset{n}{\leadsto} r}{(e_1; e_2, s) \overset{m+n+1}{\leadsto} r} \qquad \frac{(e_1, s) \overset{m}{\leadsto} \bot \quad (e_2, s) \overset{n}{\leadsto} r}{(e_1/e_2, s) \overset{m+n+1}{\leadsto} r}$$

$$\frac{(e_1, s) \overset{m}{\leadsto} \sqrt{s'}}{(e_1/e_2, s) \overset{m+1}{\leadsto} \sqrt{s'}} \qquad \frac{(e, s) \overset{m}{\leadsto} \sqrt{s'} \quad (e*, s') \overset{n}{\leadsto} \sqrt{s''}}{(e*, s) \overset{m+n+1}{\leadsto} \sqrt{s''}} \qquad \frac{(e, s) \overset{m}{\leadsto} \bot}{(e*, s) \overset{m+1}{\leadsto} \sqrt{s}}$$

Fig. 2. Formal semantics of PEGs

The complete semantics is presented in Figure 2. Please note that the following operators from Definition 1 can be derived and therefore are not included in the semantics:

$$[a\text{--}z] ::= [a] / \ldots / [z] \qquad\qquad e+ ::= e; e* \qquad\qquad \&e ::= !!e$$
$$["s"] ::= [s_0]; \ldots; [s_n] \qquad\qquad e? ::= e/\epsilon$$

2.2   CFGs vs PEGs

The main differences between PEGs and CFGs are the following:

- the choice operator, e_1/e_2, is *prioritized*, i.e., e_2 is tried only if e_1 fails;
- the repetition operators, $e*$ and $e+$, are *greedy*, which allows to easily express "longest-match" parsing, which is almost always desired;

– *syntactic predicates* [22], &e and !e, both of which consume no input and succeed if e, respectively, succeeds or fails. This effectively provides an *unlimited look-ahead* and, in combination with choice, limited *backtracking* capabilities.

An important consequence of the choice and repetition operators being deterministic (choice being prioritized and repetition greedy) is the fact that PEGs are *unambiguous*. We will see a formal proof of that in Theorem 32. This makes them unfit for processing natural languages, but is a much desired property when it comes to grammars for programming languages.

Another important consequence is ease of implementation. Efficient algorithms are known only for certain subclasses of CFGs and they tend to be rather complicated. PEGs are essentially a declarative way of specifying *recursive descent parsers* [5] and performing this type of parsing for PEGs is straightforward (more on that in Section 5). By using the technique of *packrat parsing* [2,13], *i.e.*, essentially adding memoization to the recursive descent parser, one obtains parsers with linear time complexity guarantees. The downside of this approach is high memory requirements: the worst-time space complexity of PEG parsing is linear in the size of the input, but with packrat parsing the constant of this correlation can be very high. For instance Ford reports on a factor of around 700 for a parser of Java [13].

CFGs work hand-in-hand with REs. The *lexical analysis*, breaking up the input into tokens, is performed with REs. Such tokens are subject to *syntactical analysis*, which is executed with CFGs. This split into two phases is not necessary with PEGs, as they make it possible to easily express both lexical and syntactical rules with a single formalism. We will see that in the following example.

Example 3 (PEG for simple mathematical expressions). Consider a PEG for simple mathematical expressions over 5 non-terminals: $V_N ::= \{$ws, number, term, factor, expr$\}$ with the following productions (P_{exp} function from Definition 2):

$$
\begin{aligned}
\text{ws} &::= ([\_] \ / \ [\backslash t])* \\
\text{number} &::= [0\text{–}9]+ \\
\text{term} &::= \text{ws number ws} \ / \ \text{ws} \ [(] \ \text{expr} \ [)] \ \text{ws} \\
\text{factor} &::= \text{term} \ [*] \ \text{factor} \ / \ \text{term} \\
\text{expr} &::= \text{factor} \ [+] \ \text{expr} \ / \ \text{factor}
\end{aligned}
$$

Please note that in this and all the following examples we write the sequence operator $e_1; e_2$ implicitly as $e_1 \ e_2$. The starting production is $v_{start} ::= $ expr.

First, let us note that lexical analysis is incorporated into this grammar by means of the ws production which consumes all white-space from the beginning of the input. Allowing white-space between "tokens" of the grammar comes down to placing the call to this production around the terminals of the grammar. If one does not like to clutter the grammar with those additional calls then a simple solution is to re-factor all terminals into separate productions, which consume not only the terminal itself but also all white-space around it.

Another important observation is that we made addition (and also multiplication) right-associative. If we were to make it, as usual, left-associative, by replacing the rule for expr with:

$$\texttt{expr} ::= \texttt{expr} \; [+] \; \texttt{factor} \; / \; \texttt{factor}$$

then we get a grammar that is left-recursive. Left-recursion (also indirect or mutual) is problematic as it leads to non-terminating parsers. We will come back to this issue in Section 4.   ◁

PEGs can also easily deal with some common idioms often encountered in practical grammars of programming languages, which pose a lot of difficulty for CFGs, such as modular way of handling reserved words of a language and a "dangling" else problem — for more details we refer to [12, Chapter 2.4].

3   Extending PEGs with Semantic Actions

3.1   XPEGs: Extended PEGs

In the previous section we introduced parsing expressions, which can be used to specify which strings belong to the grammar under consideration. However the role of a parser is not merely to recognize whether an input is correct or not but also, given a correct input, to compute its representation in some structured form. This is typically done by extending grammar expressions with *semantic values*, which are a representation of the result of parsing this expression on (some) input and by extending a grammar with *semantic actions*, which are functions used to produce and manipulate the semantic values. Typically a semantic value associated with an expression will be its parse tree so that parsing a correct input will give a *parse tree* of this input. For programming languages such parse tree would represent the AST of the language.

In order to deal with this extension we will replace the simple type of parsing expressions Δ with a family of types Δ_α, where the index α is a type of the semantic value associated with the expression. We also compositionally define default semantic values for all types of expressions and introduce a new construct: coercion, $e[\mapsto]f$, which converts a semantic value v associated with e to $f(v)$.

Borrowing notations from Coq we will use the following types:

- Type is the universe of types.
- True is the singleton type with a single value I.
- char is the type of machine characters. It corresponds to the type of terminals $\mathcal{V}_T$, which in concrete parsers will always be instantiated to char.
- list α is the type of lists of elements of α for any type α. Also string ::= list char.
- $\alpha_1 * \ldots * \alpha_n$ is the type of n-tuples of elements $(a_1, \ldots, a_n)$ with $a_1 \in \alpha_1, \ldots, a_n \in \alpha_n$ for any types $\alpha_1, \ldots, \alpha_n$. If v is an n-tuple then v_i is its i'th projection.
- option α is the type optionally holding a value of type α, with two constructors None and Some v with $v : \alpha$.

$$\frac{}{\epsilon \,:\, \Delta_{\text{True}}} \qquad \frac{}{[\cdot] \,:\, \Delta_{\text{char}}} \qquad \frac{a \in \mathcal{V}_T}{[a] \,:\, \Delta_{\text{char}}}$$

$$\frac{A \in \mathcal{V}_N}{A \,:\, \Delta_{\text{P}_{\text{type}}(A)}} \qquad \frac{e_1 \,:\, \Delta_\alpha \quad e_2 \,:\, \Delta_\beta}{e_1; e_2 \,:\, \Delta_{\alpha * \beta}} \qquad \frac{e_1 \,:\, \Delta_\alpha \quad e_2 \,:\, \Delta_\alpha}{e_1/e_2 \,:\, \Delta_\alpha}$$

$$\frac{e \,:\, \Delta_\alpha}{e* \,:\, \Delta_{\text{list}\,\alpha}} \qquad \frac{e \,:\, \Delta_\alpha}{!e \,:\, \Delta_{\text{True}}} \qquad \frac{e \,:\, \Delta_\alpha \quad f \,:\, \alpha \to \beta}{e[\mapsto]f \,:\, \Delta_\beta}$$

Fig. 3. Typing rules for parsing expressions with semantic actions

Definition 4 (Parsing expressions with semantic values). *We introduce a set of* parsing expressions with semantic values, Δ_α, *as an inductive family indexed by the type α of semantic values of an expression. The typing rules for Δ_α are given in Figure 3.* ◇

Note that for the choice operator e_1/e_2 the types of semantic values of e_1 and e_2 must match, which will sometimes require use of the coercion operator $e[\mapsto]f$.

Let us again see the derived operators and their types, as we need to insert few coercions:

$$\begin{aligned}
[a\text{--}z] \,:\, \Delta_{\text{char}} \quad &::= \quad [a] \;/\; \ldots \;/\; [z] \\
[\text{``}s\text{''}] \,:\, \Delta_{\text{string}} \quad &::= \quad [s_0]; \ldots; [s_n] \;[\mapsto]\; \text{tuple2str} \\
e+ \,:\, \Delta_{\text{list}\,\alpha} \quad &::= \quad e; e* \;[\mapsto]\; \lambda x . x_1 :: x_2 \\
e? \,:\, \Delta_{\text{option}\,\alpha} \quad &::= \quad e \;[\mapsto]\; \lambda x . \text{Some } x \\
& \qquad \;/\; \epsilon \;[\mapsto]\; \lambda x . \text{None} \\
\&e \,:\, \Delta_{\text{True}} \quad &::= \quad !!e
\end{aligned}$$

where $\text{tuple2str}(c_1, \ldots, c_n) = [c_1; \ldots; c_n]$.

The definition of an extended parsing expression grammar (XPEG) is as expected (compare with Definition 1).

Definition 5 (Extended Parsing Expressions Grammar (XPEG)). *An extended parsing expressions grammar (XPEG), $\mathcal{G}$, is a tuple $(\mathcal{V}_T, \mathcal{V}_N, \text{P}_{\text{type}}, \text{P}_{\text{exp}}, v_{\text{start}})$, where:*

- *$\mathcal{V}_T$ is a finite set of terminals,*
- *$\mathcal{V}_N$ is a finite set of non-terminals,*
- *$\text{P}_{\text{type}} : \mathcal{V}_N \to \text{Type}$ is a function that gives types of semantic values of all productions.*
- *P_{exp} is the interpretation of the productions of the grammar, i.e., $\text{P}_{\text{exp}} : \forall_{A:\mathcal{V}_N} \Delta_{\text{P}_{\text{type}}(A)}$ and*
- *v_{start} is the start production, $v_{\text{start}} \in \mathcal{V}_N$.* ◇

We extended the semantics of PEGs from Figure 2 to semantics of XPEGs in Figure 4.

$$(\epsilon, s) \overset{1}{\rightsquigarrow} \sqrt{}^I_s \qquad\qquad \frac{(P_{\exp}(A), s) \overset{m}{\rightsquigarrow} r}{(A, s) \overset{m+1}{\rightsquigarrow} r} \qquad\qquad ([\cdot], x :: xs) \overset{1}{\rightsquigarrow} \sqrt{}^x_{xs}$$

$$([\cdot], []) \overset{1}{\rightsquigarrow} \bot \qquad\qquad \frac{(e_1, s) \overset{m}{\rightsquigarrow} \bot \quad (e_2, s) \overset{n}{\rightsquigarrow} r}{(e_1/e_2, s) \overset{m+n+1}{\rightsquigarrow} r} \qquad\qquad \frac{(e_1, s) \overset{m}{\rightsquigarrow} \sqrt{}^v_{s'}}{(e_1/e_2, s) \overset{m+1}{\rightsquigarrow} \sqrt{}^v_{s'}}$$

$$([x], x :: xs) \overset{1}{\rightsquigarrow} \sqrt{}^x_{xs} \qquad\qquad ([x], []) \overset{1}{\rightsquigarrow} \bot \qquad\qquad \frac{x \neq y}{([y], x :: xs) \overset{1}{\rightsquigarrow} \bot}$$

$$\frac{(e_1, s) \overset{m}{\rightsquigarrow} \sqrt{}^{v_1}_{s'} \quad (e_2, s') \overset{n}{\rightsquigarrow} \bot}{(e_1; e_2, s) \overset{m+n+1}{\rightsquigarrow} \bot} \quad \frac{(e_1, s) \overset{m}{\rightsquigarrow} \sqrt{}^{v_1}_{s'} \quad (e_2, s') \overset{n}{\rightsquigarrow} \sqrt{}^{v_2}_{s'}}{(e_1; e_2, s) \overset{m+n+1}{\rightsquigarrow} \sqrt{}^{(v_1,v_2)}_{s''}} \quad \frac{(e_1, s) \overset{m}{\rightsquigarrow} \bot}{(e_1; e_2, s) \overset{m+1}{\rightsquigarrow} \bot}$$

$$\frac{(e, s) \overset{m}{\rightsquigarrow} \bot}{(e*, s) \overset{m+1}{\rightsquigarrow} \sqrt{}^{[]}_s} \qquad \frac{(e, s) \overset{m}{\rightsquigarrow} \sqrt{}^v_{s'} \quad (e*, s') \overset{n}{\rightsquigarrow} \sqrt{}^{vs}_{s''}}{(e*, s) \overset{m+n+1}{\rightsquigarrow} \sqrt{}^{v::vs}_{s''}} \qquad \frac{(e, s) \overset{m}{\rightsquigarrow} \bot}{(!e, s) \overset{m+1}{\rightsquigarrow} \sqrt{}^I_s}$$

$$\frac{(e, s) \overset{m}{\rightsquigarrow} \sqrt{}^v_{s'}}{(!e, s) \overset{m+1}{\rightsquigarrow} \bot} \qquad\qquad \frac{(e, s) \overset{m}{\rightsquigarrow} \sqrt{}^v_{s'}}{(e[\mapsto]f, s) \overset{m+1}{\rightsquigarrow} \sqrt{}^{f(v)}_{s'}} \qquad\qquad \frac{(e, s) \overset{m}{\rightsquigarrow} \bot}{(e[\mapsto]f, s) \overset{m+1}{\rightsquigarrow} \bot}$$

Fig. 4. Formal semantics of XPEGs with semantic actions

Example 6 (Simple mathematical expressions ctd.). Let us extend the grammar from Example 3 with semantic actions. The grammar expressed mathematical expressions and we attach semantic actions evaluating those expressions, hence obtaining a very simple calculator.

It often happens that we want to ignore the semantic value attached to an expression. This can be accomplished by coercing this value to I, which we will abbreviate by $e[\sharp] ::= e \; [\mapsto] \; \lambda x . I$.

```
      ws ::= ([.] / [\t])*        [♯]
  number ::= [0–9]+               [↦]  digListToNat
    term ::= ws number ws         [↦]  λx . x₂
         / ws [(| expr |)] ws     [↦]  λx . x₃
  factor ::= term [*] factor      [↦]  λx . x₁ * x₃
         / term
    expr ::= factor [+] expr      [↦]  λx . x₁ + x₃
         / factor
```

where digListToNat converts a list of digits to their decimal representation.

This grammar will associate, as expected, the semantical value 36 with the string "(1+2) * (3 * 4)". Of course in practice instead of evaluating the expression we would usually write semantic actions to build a parse tree of the expression for later processing.   ◁

3.2   Meta-properties of (X)PEGs

Now we will present some results concerning semantics of (X)PEGs. They are all variants of results obtained by Ford [14], only now we extend them to XPEGs.

First we prove that, as expected, the parsing only consumes a prefix of a string.

Theorem 31 *If* $(e, s) \overset{m}{\rightsquigarrow} \sqrt{}_{s'}^{v}$, *then* s' *is a suffix of* s.

Proof. Induction on the derivation of $(e, s) \overset{m}{\rightsquigarrow} \sqrt{}_{s'}^{v}$, using transitivity of the prefix property for sequence and repetition cases.   □

As mentioned earlier, (X)PEGs are unambiguous:

Theorem 32 *If* $(e, s) \overset{m_1}{\rightsquigarrow} r_1$ *and* $(e, s) \overset{m_2}{\rightsquigarrow} r_2$ *then* $m_1 = m_2$ *and* $r_1 = r_2$.

Proof. By complete induction on m_1. All cases immediate from the semantics of XPEGs.   □

We wrap up this section with a simple property about the repetition operator, that we will need later on. It states that the semantics of a repetition expression $e*$ is not defined if e succeeds without consuming any input.

Lemma 33 *If* $(e, s) \overset{m}{\rightsquigarrow} \sqrt{}_{s}^{v}$ *then* $(e*, s) \not\rightsquigarrow r$ *for all* r.

Proof. Assume $(e, s) \overset{m}{\rightsquigarrow} \sqrt{}_{s}^{v}$ and $(e*, s) \overset{n}{\rightsquigarrow} \sqrt{}_{s'}^{vs}$ for some n, vs and s' (we cannot have $(e*, s) \overset{n}{\rightsquigarrow} \bot$ as $e*$ never fails). By the first rule for repetition $(e*, s) \overset{m+n+1}{\rightsquigarrow} \sqrt{}_{s'}^{v::vs}$, which contradicts the second assumption by Theorem 32.   □

4   Well-Formedness of PEGs

We want to guarantee *total correctness* for generated parsers, meaning they must be *correct* (with respect to PEGs semantics) and *terminating*. In this section we focus on the latter problem. Throughout this section we assume a fixed PEG $\mathcal{G}$.

4.1   Termination Problem for XPEGs

Ensuring termination of a PEG parser essentially comes down to two problems:

- termination of all semantic actions in $\mathcal{G}$ and
- completeness of $\mathcal{G}$ with respect to PEGs semantics.

As for the first problem it means that all f functions used in coercion operators $e[\mapsto]f$ in $\mathcal{G}$, must be terminating. We are going to express PEGs completely in Coq (more that in Section 5) so for our application we get this property for free, as all Coq functions are total (hence terminating).

Concerning the latter problem, we must ensure that the grammar $\mathcal{G}$ under consideration is *complete*, *i.e.*, whether it either succeeds or fails on all input strings. The only potential source of incompleteness of $\mathcal{G}$ is (mutual) *left-recursion* in the grammar.

We already hinted at this problem in Example 3 with the rule:

$$\text{expr} ::= \text{expr} \; [+] \; \text{factor} \; / \; \text{factor}.$$

Recursive descent parsing of expressions with this rule would start with recursively calling a function to parse expression on the same input, obviously leading to an infinite loop. But not only direct left recursion must be avoided. In the following rule:

$$A ::= B \ / \ C \ !D \ A$$

a similar problem occurs provided that B may fail and C and D may succeed, the former without consuming any input.

While some techniques to deal with left-recursive PEGs have been developed recently [29], we choose to simply reject such grammars. In general it is undecidable whether a PEG grammar is complete, as it is undecidable whether the language generated by $\mathcal{G}$ is empty [14].

While in general checking grammar completeness is undecidable, we follow [14] to develop a simple syntactical check for *well-formedness* of a grammar, which implies its completeness. This check will reject left-recursive grammars even if the part with left-recursion is unreachable in the grammar, but from a practical point of view this is hardly a limitation.

4.2   PEG Analysis

We define the *expression set* of $\mathcal{G}$ as:

$$\mathrm{E}(\mathcal{G}) = \{e' \mid e' \sqsubseteq e, e \in \mathrm{P_{exp}}(A), A \in \mathcal{V}_N\}$$

where $\sqsubseteq$ is a (non-strict) sub-expression relation on parsing expressions.

We define three groups of properties over parsing expressions:

- "0": parsing expression can succeed without consuming any input,
- "> 0": parsing expression can succeed after consuming some input and
- "$\perp$": parsing expression can fail.

$$\frac{}{\epsilon \in \mathbb{P}_0} \quad \frac{}{[\cdot] \in \mathbb{P}_{>0}} \quad \frac{}{[\cdot] \in \mathbb{P}_\perp} \quad \frac{a \in \mathcal{V}_T}{[a] \in \mathbb{P}_{>0}} \quad \frac{a \in \mathcal{V}_T}{[a] \in \mathbb{P}_\perp} \quad \frac{e \in \mathbb{P}_\perp}{e* \in \mathbb{P}_0} \quad \frac{e \in \mathbb{P}_{>0}}{e* \in \mathbb{P}_{>0}}$$

$$\frac{\star \in \{0, > 0, \perp\} \quad A \in \mathcal{V}_N \quad \mathrm{P_{exp}}(A) \in \mathbb{P}_\star}{A \in \mathbb{P}_\star} \quad \frac{e_1 \in \mathbb{P}_\perp \vee (e_1 \in \mathbb{P}_{\geq 0} \wedge e_2 \in \mathbb{P}_\perp)}{e_1; e_2 \in \mathbb{P}_\perp}$$

$$\frac{(e_1 \in \mathbb{P}_{>0} \wedge e_2 \in \mathbb{P}_{\geq 0}) \vee (e_1 \in \mathbb{P}_{\geq 0} \wedge e_2 \in \mathbb{P}_{>0})}{e_1; e_2 \in \mathbb{P}_{>0}} \quad \frac{e_1 \in \mathbb{P}_0 \quad e_2 \in \mathbb{P}_0}{e_1; e_2 \in \mathbb{P}_0}$$

$$\frac{e_1 \in \mathbb{P}_0 \vee (e_1 \in \mathbb{P}_\perp \wedge e_2 \in \mathbb{P}_0)}{e_1/e_2 \in \mathbb{P}_0} \quad \frac{e_1 \in \mathbb{P}_\perp \quad e_2 \in \mathbb{P}_\perp}{e_1/e_2 \in \mathbb{P}_\perp}$$

$$\frac{e_1 \in \mathbb{P}_{>0} \vee (e_1 \in \mathbb{P}_\perp \wedge e_2 \in \mathbb{P}_{>0})}{e_1/e_2 \in \mathbb{P}_{>0}} \quad \frac{e \in \mathbb{P}_\perp}{!e \in \mathbb{P}_0} \quad \frac{e \in \mathbb{P}_{\geq 0}}{!e \in \mathbb{P}_\perp}$$

Fig. 5. Deriving grammar properties

We will write $e \in \mathbb{P}_0$ to indicate that the expression e has property "0" (similarly for $\mathbb{P}_{>0}$ and $\mathbb{P}_\perp$). We will also write $e \in \mathbb{P}_{\geq 0}$ to denote $e \in \mathbb{P}_0 \vee e \in \mathbb{P}_{>0}$. We define inference rules for deriving those properties in Figure 5.

We start with empty sets of properties and apply those inference rules over $E(\mathcal{G})$ until reaching a fix-point. The existence of the fix-point is ensured by the fact that we extend those property sets monotonically and they are bounded by the finite set $E(\mathcal{G})$. We summarize the semantics of those properties in the following lemma:

Lemma 41 ([14]) *For arbitrary $e \in \Delta$ and $s \in \mathcal{S}$:*

- *if $(e, s) \overset{n}{\leadsto} \sqrt{s}$ then $e \in \mathbb{P}_0$,*
- *if $(e, s) \overset{n}{\leadsto} \sqrt{s'}$ and $|s'| < |s|$ then $e \in \mathbb{P}_{>0}$ and*
- *if $(e, s) \overset{n}{\leadsto} \perp$ then $e \in \mathbb{P}_\perp$.*

Proof. Induction over n. All cases easy by the induction hypothesis and semantical rules of XPEGs, except for $e*$ which requires use of Lemma 33. □

4.3   PEG Well-Formedness

Using the semantics of those properties of parsing expression we can perform the completeness analysis of $\mathcal{G}$. We introduce a set of well-formed expressions WF and again iterate from an empty set by using derivation rules from Figure 6 over $E(\mathcal{G})$ until reaching a fix-point.

We say that $\mathcal{G}$ is well-formed if $E(\mathcal{G}) = WF$. We have the following result:

Theorem 42 ([14]) *If $\mathcal{G}$ is well-formed then it is complete.*

Proof. We will say that (e, s) is complete iff $\exists_{n,r} (e, s) \overset{n}{\leadsto} r$. So we have to prove that (e, s) is complete for all $e \in E(\mathcal{G})$ and all strings s. We proceed by induction over the length of the string s (IH$_{out}$), followed by induction on the depth of the derivation tree of $e \in WF$ (IH$_{in}$). So we have to prove correctness of a one step derivation of the well-formedness property (Figure 6) assuming that all expressions are total on shorter strings. The interesting cases are:

- For a sequence $e_1; e_2$ if $e_1; e_2 \in WF$ then $e_1 \in WF$, so (e_1, s) is complete by IH$_{in}$. If e_1 fails then $e_1; e_2$ fails. Otherwise $(e_1, s) \overset{n}{\leadsto} \sqrt{s'}^v$. If $s = s'$ then $e_1 \in \mathbb{P}_0$ (Lemma 41) and hence $e_2 \in WF$ and (e_2, s') is complete by IH$_{in}$. If $s \neq s'$ then $|s'| < |s|$ (Theorem 31) and (e_2, s') is complete by IH$_{out}$. Either way (e_2, s') is complete and we conclude by semantical rules for sequence.
- For a repetition $e*$, $e \in WF$ gives us completeness of (e, s) by IH$_{in}$. If e fails then we conclude by the base rule for repetition. Otherwise $(e*, s) \overset{n}{\leadsto} s'$ with $|s'| < |s|$ as $e \notin \mathbb{P}_0$. Hence we get completeness of $(e*, s')$ by IH$_{out}$ and we conclude with the inductive rule for repetition. □

$$\frac{A \in \mathcal{V}_N \quad P_{\mathrm{exp}}(A) \in \mathrm{WF}}{A \in \mathrm{WF}} \qquad \overline{\epsilon \in \mathrm{WF}} \qquad \overline{[\cdot] \in \mathrm{WF}} \qquad \frac{a \in \mathcal{V}_T}{[a] \in \mathrm{WF}} \qquad \frac{e \in \mathrm{WF}}{!e \in \mathrm{WF}}$$

$$\frac{e_1 \in \mathrm{WF} \quad e_1 \in \mathbb{P}_0 \Rightarrow e_2 \in \mathrm{WF}}{e_1; e_2 \in \mathrm{WF}} \qquad \frac{e_1 \in \mathrm{WF} \quad e_2 \in \mathrm{WF}}{e_1/e_2 \in \mathrm{WF}} \qquad \frac{e \in \mathrm{WF}, \quad e \notin \mathbb{P}_0}{e* \in \mathrm{WF}}$$

Fig. 6. Deriving well-formedness property for a PEG

5   Formally Verified XPEG Interpreter

In this Section we will present a Coq implementation of a parser interpreter. This task consists of formalizing the theory of the preceding sections and, based on this, writing an interpreter for well-formed XPEGs along with its correctness proofs. The development is too big to present it in detail here, but we will try to comment on its most interesting aspects.

We will describe how PEGs are expressed in Coq in Section 5.1, comment on the procedure for checking their well-formedness in Section 5.2 and describe the formal development of an XPEG interpreter in Section 5.3.

5.1   Specifying XPEGs in Coq

XPEGs in Coq are a simple reflection of Definition 5. They are specified over a finite enumeration of non-terminals (corresponding to $\mathcal{V}_N$) with their types (P_{type}):

> *Parameter prods : Enumeration.*
> *Parameter prods_type : prods → Type.*

We do not parameterize XPEGs by the set of terminals, as for that we simply use the existing *ascii* type of Coq, encoding standard ASCII characters. Building on that we define parsing expressions Δ_α, with the typing discipline from Figure 3 in an expected way. Finally the definitions of non-terminals (P_{exp}) and the starting production (v_{start}) become:

> *Parameter production : ∀ p : prods, PExp (prods_type p).*
> *Parameter start : prods.*

There are two observations that we would like to make at this point. First, by means of the above embedding of XPEGs in the logic of Coq, every such XPEG is well-defined (though not necessarily well-formed). In particular there can be no calls to undefined non-terminals and the conformance with the typing discipline from Figure 3 is taken care of by the type-checker of Coq.

Secondly, thanks to the use of Coq's mechanisms, such as notations and coercions, expressing an XPEG in Coq is still relatively easy as we will see in the following example.

Program Definition *production p* :=
  match *p* **return** *PExp (prod_type p)* **with**
  | *ws*   ⇒ (" " / "\t") [*]   [#]
  | *number* ⇒ ["0" -- "9"] [+]   [→] *digListToRat*
  | *term* ⇒ *ws*; *number*; *ws*   [→] (λv ⇒ *P2_3 v*)
         / *ws*; "("; *expr*; ")"; *ws* [→] (λv ⇒ *P3_5 v*)
  | *factor* ⇒ *term*; "*"; *factor* [→] (λv ⇒ *P1_3 v * P3_3 v*)
          / *term*
  | *expr* ⇒ *factor*; "+"; *expr*   [→] (λv ⇒ *P1_3 v + P3_3 v*)
         / *factor*
  end.

Fig. 7. A Coq version of the XPEG for mathematical expressions from Example 6

Example 7. Figure 7 presents a precise Coq rendering of the productions of the XPEG grammar from Example 6. It is not much more verbose than the original example. The most awkward part are the projections for tuples for which we use a family of functions $Pi\_n(v_1, \ldots, v_i, \ldots, v_n) ::= v_i$ ◁

5.2   Checking Well-Formedness of an XPEG

To check well-formedness of XPEGs we implement the procedure from Section 4. The main difficulty is that the function to compute XPEG properties, by iterating the derivation rules of Figure 5 until reaching a fix-point, is not structurally recursive. Similarly for the well-formedness check with rules from Figure 6. Fortunately the new Program feature of Coq makes specifying such functions much easier. We illustrate it on the well-formedness check (computing properties is analogous), which is realized with the following procedure:

Program Fixpoint *wf_compute* (*wf* : *WFset*)
    {**measure** (*wf_measure wf*)} : *WFset* :=
  let *wf'* := *wf_derive wf* **in**
  if *PES.equal wf wf'* **then** *wf* **else** *wf_compute wf'*.

where *WFset* is a set of well-formed expressions and *wf_derive* performs one-step derivation with the rules of Figure 6 over $E(\mathcal{G})$. The measure (into $\mathbb{N}$) is defined as:

$$wf\_measure ::= |E(\mathcal{G})| - |wf|$$

We can prove this procedure terminating, as the set of well-formed expressions is growing monotononically and is limited by $E(\mathcal{G})$:

$$wf \subseteq wf\_derive \; wf$$

$$wf \subseteq E(\mathcal{G}) \implies wf\_derive \; wf \subseteq E(\mathcal{G})$$

Please note that our formalized interpreter (more about it in the following section), and hence the analysis sketched above, is based on XPEGs, not on PEGs.

However, we still formalized simple parsing expressions, Definition 1 (though not their semantics, Figure 2), and the projection, defined as expected, from Δ_α to Δ.

This is because the well-formedness procedure needs to maintain a set of parsing expressions (*WFset* above) and for that we need a decidable equality over parsing expressions. Equality over Δ_α is not decidable, as, within coercion operator $e[\mapsto]f$ they contain arbitrary functions f, for which we cannot decide equality.

An alternative approach would be to consider *WFset* modulo an equivalence relation on parsing expressions coarser than the syntactic equality, which would ignore f components in $e[\mapsto]f$ coercions. We chose the former approach as developing the PEG analysis and well-formedness check over a non-dependently typed expressions Δ seemed to be easier than over Δ_α and the results carry over to this richer structure immediately.

5.3   A Formal Interpreter for XPEGs

For the development of a formal interpreter for XPEGs we used the *ascii* type of Coq for the set of terminals V_T. The string type from the standard library of Coq is isomorphic to lists of characters. In its place we just used a list of characters, in order to be able to re-use a rich set of available functions over lists.

The only difference in comparison with the theory presented in the preceding sections is that we implemented the range operator [*a-z*] as a primitive (so we had to extend the semantics of Figure 4 with this operator), as in practice it occurs frequently in parsers and implementing it with a choice over all the characters in the range is inefficient.

The interpreter is defined as a function with the following header:

> **Program Fixpoint** *parse* $(T : Type)$ $(e : PExp\ T \mid is\_gr\_exp\ e)$ $(s : string)$
> $\{\textbf{measure}\ (e, s)(\succ)\} : \{r : ParsingResult\ T \mid \exists\ n, [e, s] \Rightarrow [n, r]\}$

So this function takes three arguments (the first one implicit):

- T: a type of the result of parsing (α),
- e: a parsing expression of type T (Δ_α), which belongs to the grammar $\mathcal{G}$ (which in turn is checked beforehand to be well-formed) and
- s: a string to be parsed.

The last line in the above header describes the type of the result of this function, where $[e, s] \Rightarrow [n, r]$ is the expected encoding of the semantics from Figure 4 and corresponds to $(e, s) \overset{n}{\rightsquigarrow} r$. So the *parse* function produces the parsing result r (either $\bot$ or $\sqrt{\ }_s^v$, with $v : T$), such that $(e, s) \overset{n}{\rightsquigarrow} r$ for some n, *i.e.*, it is correct with respect to the semantic of XPEGs.

The body of the *parse* function performs pattern matching on expression e and interprets it according to the semantics from Figure 2.

This function is again not structurally recursive, but the recursive calls are decreasing with respect to the following $\succ$ relation on pairs of parsing expressions and strings:

$$(e_1, s_1) \succ (e_2, s_2) \iff \exists_{n_1, r_1, n_2, r_2} (e_1, s_1) \overset{n_1}{\rightsquigarrow} r_1 \wedge (e_2, s_2) \overset{n_2}{\rightsquigarrow} r_2 \wedge n_1 > n_2$$

So (e_1, s_1) is bigger than (e_2, s_2) in the order if its step-count in the semantics is bigger. The relation $\succ$ is clearly well-founded, due to the last conjunct with $>$, the well-founded order on $\mathbb{N}$. Since the semantics of $\mathcal{G}$ is complete (due to Theorem 42 and the check for well-formedness of $\mathcal{G}$ as described in Section 5.2) we can prove that all recursive calls are indeed decreasing with respect to $\succ$.

6   Extracting a Parser: Practical Evaluation

In the previous section we described a formal development of an XPEG interpreter in the proof assistant Coq. This should allow us for an arbitrary, well-formed XPEG $\mathcal{G}$, to specify it in Coq and, using Coq's extraction capabilities [19], to obtain a certified parser for $\mathcal{G}$. We are interested in code extraction from Coq, to ease practical use of TRX and to improve its performance. At the moment target languages for extraction from Coq are OCaml [18], Haskell [23] and Scheme [26]. We use the FSets [11] library, developed using Coq's modules and functors [7], which are not yet supported by extraction to Haskell or Scheme. However, there is an ongoing work on porting FSets to type classes [25], which are supported by extraction. In this section we will describe our experience with OCaml extraction on the example of an XML parser.

A well-known issue with extraction is the performance of obtained programs [8,19]. Often the root of this problem is the fact that many formalizations are not developed with extraction in mind and trying to extract a computational part of the proof can easily lead to disastrous performance [8]. On the other hand the CompCert project [17] is a well-known example of extracting a certified compiler with satisfactory performance from a Coq formalization.

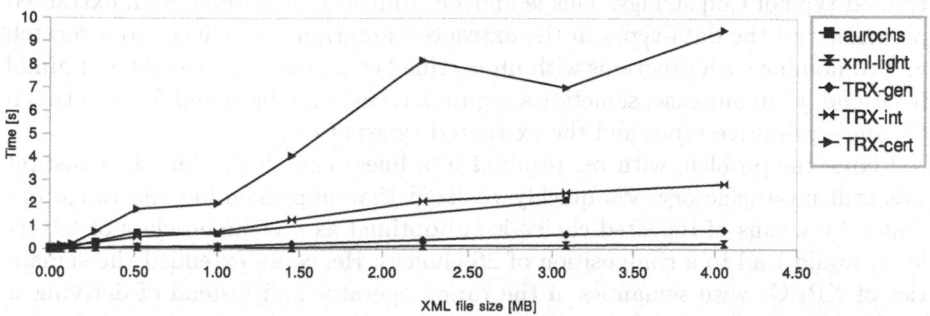

Fig. 8. Performance of certified TRX compared to a number of other tools

As most of TRX's formalization deals with grammar well-formedness, which should be discarded in the extracted code, we aimed at comparable performance for certified TRX and its non-certified counterpart. We found however that the first version's performance was unacceptable and required several improvements. In the remainder of this section, we will describe those improvements and compare certified TRX's performance with a few other tools.

For our benchmarking experiment, see Figure 8 on the following page, we used the following parsers, all of them OCaml-based to avoid differences coming from the use of different programming languages:

- TRX-cert: the certified TRX interpreter, which is the subject of this paper and is described in more detail in Section 5.
- TRX-int: a simple prototype with comparable functionality to TRX-cert, though developed manually. It does *not* produce a parse tree (just checks whether the input conforms to the grammar).
- TRX-gen: MLstate's own production-used PEG-based parser generator (for experiments we used its simple version without memoization).
- Aurochs [10]: the only PEG-based parser generator (apart from TRX) we are aware of that supports OCaml as the target language. It uses packrat parsing.
- xml-light [6]: a popular XML parser and printer for OCaml, internally using ocamllex for lexical analysis and ocamlyacc for syntactical analysis (based on $LALR(1)$ parsing).

6.1   Improving Performance of Certified TRX

The first extracted version of TRX-cert (not shown on Figure 8) parsed 32kB of XML in more than one minute. To our big surprise, performance was somewhere between quadratic and cubic with rather large constants. To our even bigger surprise, inspection of the code revealed that the *rev* function from Coq's standard library (from the module *Coq.Lists.List*) that reverses a list was the heart of the problem. The *rev* function is implemented using *append* to concatenate lists at every step, hence yielding quadratic time complexity.

We used this function to convert the input from OCaml strings to the extracted type of Coq strings. This is another difficulty of working with extracted programs: all the data-types in the extracted program are defined from scratch and combining such programs with un-certified code, even just to add a minimal front-end, as in our case, sometimes requires translating back and forth between OCaml's primitive types and the extracted types of Coq.

Fixing the problem with *rev* resulted in a linear complexity but the constant was still unsatisfactory. We quickly realized that implementing the range operator by means of repeated choice is suboptimal as a common class of letters [a–z] would lead to a composition of 26 choices. Hence we extended the semantics of XPEGs with semantics of the range operator and instead of deriving it implemented it "natively".

Yet another surprise was in store for us as the performance instead of improving got worse by approximately 30%. This time the problem was the fact that in Coq there is no predefined polymorphic comparison operator (as in OCaml) so for the range operation we had to implement comparison on characters. We did that by using the predefined function from the standard library converting a character to its ASCII code. And yet again we encountered a problem that the standard library is much better suited for reasoning than computing: this conversion function uses natural numbers in Peano representation. By re-implementing this function using natural numbers in binary notation (available in the standard library) we decreased the running time by a factor of 2.

Further profiling the OCaml program revealed that it spends 85% of its time performing garbage collection (GC). By tweaking the parameters of OCaml's GC, we obtained an important 3x gain, leading to TRX-cert's current performance shown in Figure 8. We believe a more careful inspection will reveal more potential sources of improvements, as there is still a gap between the performance that we reached now and the one of our prototype written by hand.

6.2 Performance Comparison

Figure 8 plots performance of the 5 aforementioned tools on a number of XML files (the biggest one of more than 4MB). For all PEG-based parsers, that is all tools except xml-light, we used the same PEG grammar (with minor tweaks due to differences in the tools). Few missing values for Aurochs are due to stack overflow errors.

The most interesting comparison is between TRX-cert and TRX-int. The latter was essentially a prototype of the former but developed manually, whereas TRX-cert is extracted from a formal Coq development. At the moment the certified version is approximately 2.5x slower, mso certainly there is room for improvement, especially given the fact that for the development of TRX-int we put emphasis on its simplicity (the actual interpreter is around 100 lines long) and not on efficiency.

The two main directions for improving performance seem to be:

– *Memoization* (packrat parsing): it does not help for simple grammars, as that of XML (TRX-gen with memoization is actually slower than without, due to the overhead of keeping the memoization table), but it does pay off for more complex grammars.
– *Code generation*: as witnessed by the difference between TRX-int and TRX-gen turning from interpretation to code generation can have a substantial impact on performance.

Admittedly XML is not the best test-case for TRX, due to its simple format, for which the expressive power offered by PEGs is an overkill. Parsing Java seems to be an established benchmark for PEGs [24,13,12,29]. One difficulty with the grammar of Java [15] is that it naturally contains left-recursive rules, most of which can be easily replaced with iteration, with the exception of a single definition [24], and for the moment TRX lacks the ability to handle left-recursive rules. Also obtaining reasonable (linear) performance for such a complicated grammar would require either packrat parsing or very careful crafting of the grammar. It is reported by Redziejowski [24] that "the resulting primitive parser shows an acceptable behavior, indicating that packrat parsing might be an overkill for practical languages", but is very sparse on details of what a reasonable performance is.

We would like to conclude this section with the observation that even though making such benchmarks is important it is often just one of many factors for choosing a proper tool for a given task. There are many applications which will never parse files exceeding $100kB$ and it is often irrelevant whether that will take $0.1s$. or $0.01s$. For some of those applications it may be much more relevant that the parsing is formally guaranteed to be correct. And at the moment TRX is the only tool that comes with such guarantees.

7   Related Work

Parsing is a well-studied and well-understood topic and the software for parsing, parser generators or libraries of parser combinators, is abundant. And yet there does seem to be hardly any work on *formally verified* parsing.

In Danielsson and Norell [9] a library of parser combinators (see Hutton [16]) with termination guarantees has been developed in the dependently typed functional programming language Agda [27]. The main difference in comparison with our work is that they provide a library of combinators, whereas we aim at parser generator for PEG grammars (though at the moment we only have an interpreter). The problem of termination is also handled differently: "[we] use dependent types to add information in the form of type indices to the parser type, and use these indices to ensure that left recursion is not possible" [9]. In many cases those type indices can be automatically inferred by Agda, however, if this is not possible they have to be provided by the user of the library, which requires some expertise and understanding of the underlying formal model. In our approach we proved correct a well-formedness checker for PEG grammars, making the termination analysis completely transparent to the user of TRX.

Ideas similar to Danielsson and Norell [9] were previously put forward, though just as a proof of concept, by McBride and McKinna [21].

Probably the closest work to ours is that of Barthwal and Norrish [3], where the authors developed an SLR parser in HOL. The main differences with our work are:

- PEGs are more expressive that SLR grammars, which are usually not adequate for real-world computer languages,
- as a consequence of using PEGs we can deal with lexical analysis, while it would have to be formalized and verified in a separate stage for the SLR approach.
- our parser is proven to be totally correct, *i.e.*, correct with respect to its specification and terminating on all possible inputs (which was actually far more difficult to establish than correctness), while the latter property does not hold for the work of Barthwal and Norrish.

- performance comparison with this work is not possible as the paper does not present any case-studies, benchmarks or examples, but the fact that "the DFA states are computed on the fly" [3] suggests that the performance was not the utmost goal of that work.

Finally there is the recent development of a packrat PEG parser in Coq by Wisnesky et al. [30], where the given PEG grammar is compiled into an imperative computation within the Ynot framework, that run over an arbitrary imperative character stream, returns a parsing result conforming with the specification of PEGs. Termination of such generated parsers is not guaranteed.

8 Conclusions and Future Work

In this paper we described a Coq formalization of the theory of PEGs and, based on it, a formal development of *TRX: a formally verified parser interpreter for PEGs*. This allows us to write a PEG, together with its semantic actions, in Coq and then to extract from it a *parser with total correctness guarantees*. That means that the parser will terminate on all inputs and produce parsing results correct with respect to the semantics of PEGs. Although TRX can still be improved (see future work discussion below), it is the first tool capable of generating provably correct parsers. Considering the importance of parsing, this result appears as a first step towards a general way to bring added quality and security to all kinds of software.

To extend our research, we identify the following subjects for future work:

1. A realistic *case study* of a practical language, such as Java, should be conducted to ensure scalability of this methodology and acceptable performance. This would also allow us to compare directly with other experiments of parsing Java with PEGs (see for instance Redziejowski [24] or Ford [12]). This would undoubtedly lead to some improvements to TRX making it easier to use.
2. In connection with the aforementioned case study the *performance* of our parser interpreter should be better understood and improved upon. One possibility here is implementation of packrat parsing, by means of implementing memoization in our interpreter [13].
3. Support for *error messages*, for instance following that of the PEG-based parser generator Puppy [12], should be added.
4. Another important aspect is that of left-recursive grammars, which occur naturally in practice. At the moment it is the responsibility of the user to eliminate left-recursion from a grammar. In the future, we plan to address this problem either by means of left-recursion elimination [12], *i.e.*, transforming a left-recursive grammar to an equivalent one where left-recursion does not occur (this is not an easy problem in presence of semantic actions, especially if one also wants to allow mutually left-recursive rules). Another possible approach is an extension to the memoization technique that allows dealing with left-recursive rules [29].

Acknowledgements. We would like to thank Matthieu Sozeau for his help with the new Program feature of Coq and the ESOP reviewers for valuable feedback.

References

1. Aho, A.V., Sethi, R., Ullman, J.D.: Compilers: Principles, Techniques, and Tools. Addison-Wesley, Reading (1986)
2. Aho, A.V., Ullman, J.D.: The Theory of Parsing, Translation and Compiling. Parsing, vol. I. Prentice-Hall, Englewood Cliffs (1972)
3. Barthwal, A., Norrish, M.: Verified, executable parsing. In: Castagna, G. (ed.) ESOP 2009. LNCS, vol. 5502, pp. 160–174. Springer, Heidelberg (2009)
4. Bertot, Y., Castéran, P.: Interactive Theorem Proving and Program Development. Coq'Art: The Calculus of Inductive Constructions. Texts in Theoretical Computer Science. Springer, Heidelberg (2004)
5. Burge, W.H.: Recursive Programming Techniques. Addison-Wesley, Reading (1975)
6. Cannasse, N.: Xml-light (2003), http://tech.motion-twin.com/xmllight.html
7. Chrzaszcz, J.: Implementing modules in the Coq system. In: Basin, D., Wolff, B. (eds.) TPHOLs 2003. LNCS, vol. 2758, pp. 270–286. Springer, Heidelberg (2003)
8. Cruz-Filipe, L., Letouzey, P.: A large-scale experiment in executing extracted programs. Electronic Notes in Theoretical Computer Science 151(1), 75–91 (2006)
9. Danielsson, N.A., Norell, U.: Structurally recursive descent parsing (2008), Draft, http://www.cs.nott.ac.uk/~nad/publications
10. Durak, B.: Aurochs (2009), http://aurochs.fr/
11. Filliâtre, J.-C., Letouzey, P.: Functors for proofs and programs. In: Schmidt, D. (ed.) ESOP 2004. LNCS, vol. 2986, pp. 370–384. Springer, Heidelberg (2004)
12. Ford, B.: Packrat parsing: a practical linear-time algorithm with backtracking. Master's thesis, Massachusetts Institute of Technology (2002)
13. Ford, B.: Packrat parsing: simple, powerful, lazy, linear time, functional pearl. In: ICFP 2002, pp. 36–47 (2002)
14. Ford, B.: Parsing expression grammars: a recognition-based syntactic foundation. In: POPL 2004, pp. 111–122 (2004)
15. Gosling, J., Joy, B., Steele, G., Bracha, G.: The Java language specification, 3rd edn. Addison-Wesley, Reading (2005)
16. Hutton, G.: Higher-order functions for parsing. The Journal of Functional Programming 2(3), 323–343 (1992)
17. Leroy, X.: Formal verification of a realistic compiler. Communications of the ACM 52(7), 107–115 (2009)
18. Leroy, X., et al.: Objective caml (1996), http://caml.inria.fr
19. Letouzey, P.: Extraction in Coq: An overview. In: Beckmann, A., Dimitracopoulos, C., Löwe, B. (eds.) CiE 2008. LNCS, vol. 5028, pp. 359–369. Springer, Heidelberg (2008)
20. Levine, J.R., Mason, T., Brown, D.: Lex & yacc. O'Reilly, Sebastopol (1992)
21. McBride, C., McKinna, J.: Seeing and doing. Presentation at the Workshop on Termination and Type Theory (2002)
22. Parr, T.J., Quong, R.W.: Adding semantic and syntactic predicates to LL(k): pred-LL(k). In: Fritzson, P.A. (ed.) CC 1994. LNCS, vol. 786, pp. 263–277. Springer, Heidelberg (1994)

23. Peyton-Jones, S., et al.: Haskell 98 language and libraries: The revised report (2002), http://haskell.org/
24. Redziejowski, R.R.: Parsing expression grammar as a primitive recursive-descent parser with backtracking. Fundamenta Informaticae 79(3-4), 513–524 (2007)
25. Sozeau, M., Oury, N.: First-class type classes. In: Mohamed, O.A., Muñoz, C., Tahar, S. (eds.) TPHOLs 2008. LNCS, vol. 5170, pp. 278–293. Springer, Heidelberg (2008)
26. Sussman, G.J., Steele Jr., G.L.: Scheme: A interpreter for extended lambda calculus. Higher-Order and Symbolic Computation 11(4), 405–439 (1998)
27. The Agda team. The Agda wiki (2008), http://wiki.portal.chalmers.se/agda/
28. The Coq Development Team. The Coq proof assistant: Reference manual, version 8.2, 1989–2009, http://coq.inria.fr
29. Warth, A., Douglass, J.R., Millstein, T.D.: Packrat parsers can support left recursion. In: PEPM 2008, pp. 103–110 (2008)
30. Wisnesky, R., Malecha, G., Morrisett, G.: Certified web services in Ynot. In: Proceedings of WWV 2009, pp. 5–19 (2009)

On the Expressive Power of Primitives for Compensation Handling*

Ivan Lanese[1], Cátia Vaz[2], and Carla Ferreira[3]

[1] Lab. Focus, Università di Bologna/INRIA, Italy
lanese@cs.unibo.it
[2] INESC-ID / DEETC, ISEL, Instituto Politécnico de Lisboa, Portugal
cvaz@cc.isel.ipl.pt
[3] CITI / Departamento de Informática, FCT, Universidade Nova de Lisboa, Portugal
carla.ferreira@di.fct.unl.pt

Abstract. Modern software systems have frequently to face unexpected events, reacting so to reach a consistent state. In the field of concurrent and mobile systems (e.g., for web services) the problem is usually tackled using long running transactions and compensations: activities programmed to recover partial executions of long running transactions. We compare the expressive power of different approaches to the specification of those compensations. We consider (i) *static recovery*, where the compensation is statically defined together with the transaction, (ii) *parallel recovery*, where the compensation is dynamically built as parallel composition of compensation elements and (iii) *general dynamic recovery*, where more refined ways of composing compensation elements are provided. We define an encoding of parallel recovery into static recovery enjoying nice compositionality properties, showing that the two approaches have the same expressive power. We also show that no such encoding of general dynamic recovery into static recovery is possible, i.e. general dynamic recovery is strictly more expressive.

1 Introduction

Modern software systems are complex and composed by different interacting components, commonly developed and managed separately. Also, they usually rely on communication infrastructures, such as the Internet or wireless networks, that are unreliable. Thus unexpected events can frequently arise during the execution of such applications: received data items may not have the desired structure, communication partners may disconnect, etc. In this context it is important to use suitable error handling techniques allowing the whole system to reach a correct state even if some of its components have failed.

In the field of concurrent and mobile systems (e.g., in the case of web services), this problem is usually tackled using the concept of long running transaction.

* Research supported by the Project FET-GC II IST-2005-16004 SENSORIA, FP7-231620 HATS and by FCT grant SFRH/BD/45572/2008.

A.D. Gordon (Ed.): ESOP 2010, LNCS 6012, pp. 366–386, 2010.

A long running transaction either succeeds, or a compensation is executed taking the system to a consistent state, possibly different from the one in which the transaction started. This weakens the constraint of ACID transactions from database theory, since it is difficult to guarantee ACID properties when transactions can last for a long time, and when some actions cannot be undone.

In the literature there are different proposals of primitives for long running transactions, from the Java try P catch e Q^1, where Q is in charge of managing exception e raised inside P, to the complex mechanisms of WS-BPEL [1] (the de-facto standard for web services composition), exploiting fault, termination and compensation handlers to deal with different error handling issues.

However, the relationships between the different proposals are not clear, and there has been little work trying to formally compare the expressive power of the proposed mechanisms. This problem is made hard by the fact that different primitives for long running transactions are realized on top of different underlying languages. Thus the different expressive power of the error handling primitives is hidden because of other differences between the underlying languages. Understanding the expressive power of different primitives is important for language design: primitives that do not add expressive power can be left out from the core language and implemented as macros when needed, primitives that add expressive power should be implemented in the core language.

This paper tackles this problem, by presenting a formal comparison of different approaches to long running transactions in a concurrent and mobile setting. To this end we add primitives for error handling, distilled from approaches in the literature, to the same underlying language, so to have a more clear comparison. We have chosen the simplest possible underlying language able to model concurrent and mobile systems: the π-calculus [2]. Then further work is required to apply the results to more complex calculi and real languages (see Section 6).

The approaches to error handling are far too many to be compared here, thus we concentrate on a main feature: whether the compensation code for a transaction is statically defined, or it is dynamically generated. *Static recovery* is for instance the approach of Java try-catch, and is the classic approach of interaction-based models [3–6]. For dynamic recovery we consider two different possibilities: in *parallel recovery* the compensation is incrementally built as parallel composition of simpler compensations, while in *general dynamic recovery* compensations can be both updated and replaced. Parallel recovery is commonly used [1, 7, 8] to execute compensations of subtransactions when a transaction fails, and it is the mechanism exploited by dcπ [9]. Most of the compensable flow approaches [7, 8, 10], where compensations of complex activities are built as compositions of compensations of their constituting activities, execute compensations of sequential activities in backward order. Compensations are always executed in backward order in *backward recovery* [11]. Backward recovery is the main instance of general dynamic recovery, which has been proposed in [12]. Backward recovery has also been applied to Java in [13].

---

[1] Actually, Java try-catch is designed for exception handling, but can be used also for programming long running transactions.

$$P, Q ::= \qquad \qquad \qquad \qquad \text{\pi-calculus processes}$$

$\pi ::=$	π-calculus prefixes	$\mathbf{0}$	(Inaction)
	$\bar{a}\langle v \rangle$ (Output prefix)	$\sum_{i \in I} \pi_i.P_i$	(Guarded choice)
	$a(x)$ (Input prefix)	$!\pi.P$	(Guarded replication)
		$P \mid Q$	(Parallel composition)
		$(\nu x)\, P$	(Restriction)

Fig. 1. π-calculus processes

This paper compares the expressive power of static recovery, parallel recovery and general dynamic recovery in the context of π-calculus. Our main results are:

- a compositional encoding of parallel recovery into static recovery;
- a separation result showing that no similar encoding exists from general dynamic recovery (neither from backward recovery) to static recovery.

We also discuss how these results can be applied to other calculi in the literature.

Structure of the work: Section 2 introduces the primitives for long running transactions. Section 3 discusses the conditions that a good encoding must satisfy. Sections 4 and 5 present the main technical results: the encoding of parallel recovery into static recovery, and the impossibility of encoding general dynamic recovery into static recovery. Finally, Section 6 discusses how to apply the results to calculi in the literature. Proofs can be found in [14].

2   Primitives for Compensations

2.1   Syntax

In this section we formalize in the framework of π-calculus [2] some primitives for static, parallel and general dynamic recovery. The relationships between these primitives and other primitives in the literature are discussed in Section 6.

To simplify the understanding and the comparisons, we define the three calculi corresponding to static, parallel and general dynamic recovery in an incremental way. The syntax of all our calculi relies on a countable set of names N, ranged over by lower case letters. We use x to denote a tuple $x_1, \cdots, x_n$ of such names, for some $n \geq 0$, and $\{x\}$ denotes the set of elements in the tuple. As already said, our calculi are built on top of π-calculus, whose syntax is in Fig. 1.

Prefixes in π-calculus can be either outputs $\bar{a}\langle v \rangle$ of a tuple of values v on channel a, or corresponding inputs $a(x)$. The π-calculus syntax includes the inactive process $\mathbf{0}$, guarded choice $\sum_{i \in I} \pi_i.P_i$, guarded replication $!\pi.P$, parallel composition $P \mid Q$ of processes P and Q, and restriction $(\nu x)\, P$ of name x inside P. We write $\bar{a}$ for $\bar{a}\langle v \rangle$ when v is empty, and a for $a(x)$ when x is empty. We also write (νx) for $(\nu x_1) \cdots (\nu x_n)$ when $x = x_1, \ldots, x_n$. The formal description of the semantics will be given in Section 2.2 (see also [2]).

The first, and simpler, extension that we present corresponds to static recovery. The syntax is presented in Fig. 2 (left). Static recovery can be realized by adding just two constructs: *transaction scope* and *protected block*. A transaction

$P, Q ::=$	*Static rec. processes*	$P, Q ::=$	*Compensable processes*
...	(π-calculus processes)	...	(Static rec. processes)
$\mid t[P,Q]$	(Transaction scope)	$\mid X$	(Process variable)
$\mid \langle P \rangle$	(Protected block)	$\mid \text{inst}\lfloor \lambda X.Q \rfloor.P$	(Compensation update)

Fig. 2. Static recovery and compensable processes

scope $t[P,Q]$ behaves as process P until an error is notified to it by an output $\overline{t}$ on the name t of the transaction. When such a notification is received, the body P of the transaction is killed and compensation Q is executed. Q is executed in a protected block, i.e. not influenced by successive external errors. Error notifications may be generated both from the body P and from external processes. Error notifications are simple output messages (without parameters). Thus one may have nondeterminism, since the same output may be caught either by an input or by a transaction scope. If such a behavior is not desired, it can be avoided by using a simple sorting system. We will not consider this issue. Protected block $\langle P \rangle$ behaves as P, but it is not killed in case of failure of an external transaction.

Compensable processes, which realize general dynamic recovery, extend static recovery processes. The main difference is that in compensable processes the body P of transaction $t[P,Q]$ can update the compensation Q. *Compensation update* is performed by a new operator $\text{inst}\lfloor \lambda X.Q' \rfloor.P'$, where function $\lambda X.Q'$ is the compensation update (X can occur inside Q'). Applying such a compensation update to compensation Q produces a new compensation $Q'\{Q/x\}$. Note that Q may not occur at all in the resulting compensation, and it may also occur more than once. For instance, $\lambda X.0$ deletes the current compensation. The syntax of compensable processes extends the one of static recovery processes with the compensation update operator and process variables (see Fig. 2 (right)).

We define for compensable processes the usual notions of free and bound names. Names in $\boldsymbol{x}$ are bound in $a(\boldsymbol{x}).P$, while x is bound in $(\nu\,x)\,P$. Other names are free. We denote with $\text{fn}(\bullet)$, $\text{bn}(\bullet)$ and $\text{n}(\bullet)$ the functions computing the sets of free, bound and all the names respectively. Also, variable X is bound in $\lambda X.Q$. Bound names and variables can be α-converted as usual. We consider only processes with no free variables. For simplicity we may drop trailing 0s.

Static recovery processes are a subcalculus of compensable processes where compensation update is never used. Also, if a compensation update has the form $\lambda X.Q \mid X$ where X does not occur in Q, then Q is added in parallel to the existing compensation. Thus parallel recovery can be seen as a particular case of compensable processes too. When speaking about parallel recovery we will write a compensation update $\lambda X.Q \mid X$ simply as Q.

Definition 1 (Classes of processes). Compensable processes $\mathcal{CP}$ *are defined by the syntax in Fig. 2 (right). Parallel recovery processes* $\mathcal{PP}$ *are compensable processes where all the compensation updates have the form* $\lambda X.Q \mid X$ *where* Q *is a process without free variables. Static recovery processes* $\mathcal{SP}$ *are compensable processes where the compensation update operator is never used.*

$$\text{extr}_n(0) = 0 \qquad \text{extr}_n(\langle P \rangle) = \langle P \rangle$$
$$\text{extr}_n(\textstyle\sum_{i \in I} \pi_i.P_i) = 0 \qquad \text{extr}_n(t\,[P,Q]) = \text{extr}_n(P) \mid \langle Q \rangle$$
$$\text{extr}_n(!\pi.P) = 0 \qquad \text{extr}_n(P \mid Q) = \text{extr}_n(P) \mid \text{extr}_n(Q)$$
$$\text{extr}_n(\text{inst}\lfloor \lambda X.Q \rfloor.P) = 0 \qquad \text{extr}_n((\nu\,x)\,P) = (\nu\,x)\,\text{extr}_n(P)$$

Fig. 3. Extraction function with nested failure

The main question that this paper wants to answer is whether the three classes of processes $\mathcal{CP}$, $\mathcal{PP}$ and $\mathcal{SP}$ have the same expressive power or not.

2.2 Operational Semantics

To define the operational semantics of compensable processes we need an auxiliary definition: when a transaction scope $t[P,Q]$ is killed, part of its body P has to be preserved, in particular the part composed of protected blocks.

The definition of function $\text{extr}(P)$ computing the part to be preserved depends on the meaning of transaction nesting. In the literature, two approaches are considered: according to the *nested failure* approach a subtransaction has to be killed when the transaction containing it is killed. This is for instance the approach of SAGAs calculi [8], WS-BPEL [1], and others. In the *non-nested failure* approach instead, subtransactions are unaffected by external failures (however the recovery of a transaction may include the explicit killing of its subtransactions). This is for instance the approach of Webπ [5]. We consider both the possibilities, since they just differ in the definition of function $\text{extr}(\bullet)$. Our results hold in both the cases. One can simulate the non-nested approach using the nested one by protecting each transaction using a protected block, while it is not clear whether the opposite simulation is possible. Clarifying this point is left for future work.

Definition 2 (Extraction function). *We denote the functions corresponding to nested and non-nested failure respectively as* $\text{extr}_n(\bullet)$ *and* $\text{extr}_{nn}(\bullet)$. *The function* $\text{extr}_n(\bullet)$ *is defined in Fig. 3. The definition of function* $\text{extr}_{nn}(\bullet)$ *is the same but for the clause for transaction scope, which becomes* $\text{extr}_{nn}(t\,[P,Q]) = t\,[P,Q]$.

There is no need to define $\text{extr}_n(X)$ or $\text{extr}_{nn}(X)$ since X can occur only inside the compensation update primitive.

We also need an auxiliary predicate $\text{noComp}(P)$ which is true iff P has no pending compensation update. This is needed since a compensation update is performed to reflect in the compensation some change in the state of the executing process, and it should never happen that the state has changed and the compensation update has not been performed. In other words, compensation update should have priority w.r.t. other transitions (see [15] for a discussion on this topic). Priority of compensation update is obtained by ensuring in the semantics that when an action (different from a compensation update) is performed, no compensation update is pending.

Definition 3 (noComp($\bullet$) predicate). *The predicate* $\text{noComp}(P)$ *that verifies the non-existence of pending compensation updates in P is defined in Fig. 4.*

$$\begin{array}{c} \text{noComp}(0) \\ \text{noComp}(\sum_{i \in I} \pi_i.P_i) \\ \text{noComp}(!\pi.P) \end{array} \qquad \begin{array}{l} \text{noComp}(\langle P \rangle) \text{ if noComp}(P) \\ \text{noComp}(t\,[P,Q]) \text{ if noComp}(P) \\ \text{noComp}(P \mid Q) \text{ if noComp}(P) \text{ and noComp}(Q) \\ \text{noComp}((\nu x)\,P) \text{ if noComp}(P) \end{array}$$

Fig. 4. No pending compensation update predicate

In particular, $\text{noComp}(P)$ is false if P is a compensation update primitive.

The operational semantics of compensable processes (and, implicitly, of static recovery and parallel recovery processes) is defined below. We use $a(v)$, $(w)\bar{a}\langle v \rangle$, τ, $(w)\lambda X.Q$ and τ_c as labels. The first three forms of labels are as in π-calculus (but outputs are also used for error notification, and inputs for receiving the notification), while the last two labels are for compensation update. In particular, $(w)\lambda X.Q$ requires a compensation update while τ_c is the corresponding internal action. This has to be distinguished from τ since it has priority. We write a for $a(v)$ and $\bar{a}$ for $\bar{a}\langle v \rangle$ if v is empty. We use t instead of a to emphasize that the name is used for error notification. Names in w are bound in $(w)\bar{a}\langle v \rangle$ and $(w)\lambda X.Q$. Other names are free. Functions $\text{fn}(\bullet)$, $\text{bn}(\bullet)$ and $\text{n}(\bullet)$ are extended accordingly. We drop the set of bound names (w) from labels if it is empty.

Definition 4 (Operational semantics). *The operational semantics with nested failure of compensable processes $\mathcal{CP}$ is the minimum labeled transition system (LTS) closed under the rules in Fig. 5 (symmetric rules are considered for (L-*PAR*) and (L-*CLOSE*)). The operational semantics with non-nested failure of compensable processes $\mathcal{CP}$ is the minimum LTS closed under the rules in Fig. 5 (symmetric rules are considered for (L-*PAR*) and (L-*CLOSE*)), but where function* $\text{extr}_\text{n}(\bullet)$ *is replaced by function* $\text{extr}_\text{nn}(\bullet)$.

The first seven rules and the ninth extend the corresponding π-calculus rules [2], the others define the behavior of transactions, compensations and protected blocks.

Auxiliary rules (P-OUT) and (P-IN) execute output and input prefixes respectively. The input rule guesses the received values v in the early style. Rules (L-CHOICE) and (L-REP) deal with guarded choice and replication respectively. Rule (L-PAR) allows one of the components of parallel composition to progress. If the performed action is not a compensation update, then the rule verifies that no compensation update is pending in the other component (last condition). Rule (L-RES) is the classic rule for restriction. Rule (L-OPEN) allows to extrude bound names. Rule (L-CLOSE) performs communication. If the output action contains some extruded names, restrictions for them are reintroduced.

Rule (L-SCOPE-OUT) allows the body P of a transaction scope to progress, provided that the performed action is not a compensation update. Rule (L-RECOVER-OUT) allows external processes to kill a transaction scope via an output $\bar{t}$. The resulting process is composed by two parts: the first one extracted from P, and the second one corresponding to compensation Q, which will be executed inside a protected block. The condition ensures that there are no pending compensation updates. Rule (L-RECOVER-IN) is similar to (L-RECOVER-OUT), but now the error notification comes from P. In this case condition

$$(\text{L-Choice})$$
$$\dfrac{\pi_j.P_j \xrightarrow{\alpha} P'_j \quad j \in I}{\sum_{i \in I} \pi_i.P_i \xrightarrow{\alpha} P'_j}$$

$$(\text{P-Out}) \qquad\qquad (\text{P-In})$$
$$\overline{a}\langle v\rangle.P \xrightarrow{\overline{a}\langle v\rangle} P \qquad\qquad a(x).P \xrightarrow{a(v)} P\{v/x\}$$

$$(\text{L-Par})$$
$$(\text{L-Rep}) \qquad\qquad \dfrac{P \xrightarrow{\alpha} P' \quad \mathsf{bn}(\alpha) \cap \mathsf{fn}(Q) = \emptyset}{\qquad\qquad} \qquad\qquad (\text{L-Res})$$
$$\dfrac{\pi.P \xrightarrow{\alpha} P'}{!\pi.P \xrightarrow{\alpha} P'|!\pi.P} \qquad \dfrac{\alpha \notin \{(w)\lambda X.R, \tau_c\} \Rightarrow \mathsf{noComp}(Q)}{P \mid Q \xrightarrow{\alpha} P' \mid Q} \qquad \dfrac{P \xrightarrow{\alpha} P' \quad x \notin \mathsf{n}(\alpha)}{(\nu x) P \xrightarrow{\alpha} (\nu x) P'}$$

$$(\text{L-Open}) \qquad\qquad\qquad\qquad\qquad (\text{L-Open2})$$
$$\dfrac{P \xrightarrow{(w)\overline{x}\langle v\rangle} P' \quad z \neq x \quad z \in \{v\} \setminus \{w\}}{(\nu z) P \xrightarrow{(zw)\overline{x}\langle v\rangle} P'} \qquad \dfrac{P \xrightarrow{(w)\lambda X.Q} P' \quad z \in \mathsf{fn}(Q) \setminus \{w\}}{(\nu z) P \xrightarrow{(zw)\lambda X.Q} P'}$$

$$(\text{L-Close})$$
$$\dfrac{P \xrightarrow{x(v)} P' \quad Q \xrightarrow{(z)\overline{x}\langle v\rangle} Q' \quad \{z\} \cap \mathsf{fn}(P) = \emptyset}{P \mid Q \xrightarrow{\tau} (\nu z)(P' \mid Q')}$$

$$(\text{L-Scope-close}) \qquad\qquad\qquad\qquad\qquad (\text{L-Recover-out})$$
$$\dfrac{P \xrightarrow{(z)\lambda X.R} P' \quad \{z\} \cap (\mathsf{fn}(Q) \cup \{t\}) = \emptyset}{t[P,Q] \xrightarrow{\tau_c} (\nu z)\, t[P', R\{Q/x\}]} \qquad \dfrac{\mathsf{noComp}(P)}{t[P,Q] \xrightarrow{t} \mathsf{extr_n}(P) \mid \langle Q\rangle}$$

$$(\text{L-Scope-out})$$
$$\dfrac{P \xrightarrow{\alpha} P' \quad \alpha \neq (z)\lambda X.Q \quad \mathsf{bn}(\alpha) \cap (\mathsf{fn}(Q) \cup \{t\}) = \emptyset}{t[P,Q] \xrightarrow{\alpha} t[P', Q]}$$

$$(\text{L-Recover-in}) \qquad\qquad\qquad\qquad\qquad\qquad (\text{L-Block})$$
$$\dfrac{P \xrightarrow{\overline{t}} P'}{t[P,Q] \xrightarrow{\tau} \mathsf{extr_n}(P') \mid \langle Q\rangle} \qquad \dfrac{(\text{L-Inst})}{\mathsf{inst}\lfloor \lambda X.Q\rfloor.P \xrightarrow{\lambda X.Q} P} \qquad \dfrac{P \xrightarrow{\alpha} P'}{\langle P\rangle \xrightarrow{\alpha} \langle P'\rangle}$$

Fig. 5. LTS for compensable processes

$\mathsf{noComp}(P)$ is redundant since it can be deduced from the derivation. Rule (L-Inst) requires a compensation update (note that the resulting internal action is τ_c) while rule (L-Open2) allows to extrude bound names occurring in it. Rule (L-Scope-close) updates the compensation of a transaction scope (the substitution should not capture free names). If the compensation update includes extruded names, restrictions for these names are reintroduced (similarly to rule (L-Close)). Finally, rule (L-Block) defines the behavior of protected blocks.

Example 1. We give here a few examples of transitions[2].

- Transaction scopes can compute: $\overline{a}\langle b\rangle \mid t[a(x).\overline{x}.0, Q] \xrightarrow{\tau} 0 \mid t[\overline{b}.0, Q]$
- Transaction scopes can be killed: $\overline{t} \mid t[\overline{a}.0, Q] \xrightarrow{\tau} \langle Q\rangle$
- Transaction scopes can commit suicide: $t[\overline{t}.0 \mid \overline{a}.0, Q] \xrightarrow{\tau} \langle Q\rangle$
- New compensations can be added in parallel:
  $t[\mathsf{inst}\lfloor \lambda X.P|X\rfloor.\overline{a}.0, Q] \xrightarrow{\tau_c} t[\overline{a}.0, P|Q]$

---

[2] To simplify the presentation we discard some garbage. This can be done using the notion of structural congruence in Definition 14.

- New compensations can be added at the beginning:
  $t[\mathsf{inst}\lfloor\lambda X.\overline{b}.X\rfloor.\overline{a}.0, Q] \xrightarrow{\tau_c} t[\overline{a}.0, \overline{b}.Q]$
- Compensations can be deleted: $t[\mathsf{inst}\lfloor\lambda X.0\rfloor.\overline{a}.0, Q] \xrightarrow{\tau_c} t[\overline{a}.0, 0]$

3   Conditions for Good Encodings

When discussing encodability/separation results, a main point is to decide which conditions an encoding has to satisfy in order to be considered a good means for language comparison. In the literature there are different proposals of such conditions [16–19]. The choice of the conditions determines the level of abstraction used when comparing the different languages. Since different expressiveness gaps are visible at different levels of abstraction, there are no universally good sets of conditions. Also, encodability results are stronger if stated at the low level of abstraction, i.e. with more strict conditions, while separation results are more general when proved at the high level of abstraction. However, it is important that related results are proved under the same conditions, thus defining a coherent picture of the expressiveness at the chosen level of abstraction. For these reasons we discuss below the conditions that we use throughout the paper, thus fixing our level of abstraction. We will consider stricter conditions too when proving encodability results, thus strengthening them.

There are two kinds of conditions: (i) syntactic conditions on the form of the translation, and (ii) conditions specifying the kind of behavior that the translation should preserve. We will base the latter on the concepts of divergence and should testing equivalence [20] (this choice will be discussed later).

Definition 5. *Process P diverges if there is an infinite sequence of actions τ or τ_c starting from P.*

Weak transitions are defined as follows: $\Longrightarrow$ is the reflexive and transitive closure of $\xrightarrow{\tau} \cup \xrightarrow{\tau_c}$, while $\stackrel{\alpha}{\Longrightarrow}$ is $\Longrightarrow\stackrel{\alpha}{\longrightarrow}\Longrightarrow$.

Definition 6 (Should testing). *Let P and O be processes and $\sqrt{}$ a special name occurring in O but not in P. We call O an observer. P should O iff for each P' such that $P \mid O \Longrightarrow P'$ we have $P' \stackrel{\sqrt{}}{\Longrightarrow}$. Two processes P and Q are should testing equivalent, written $P \simeq_{shd} Q$, if, for each observer O, P should O iff Q should O.*

We use should testing equivalence as our basic notion of process equivalence. However, we have to restrict its applicability. In fact, we are interested in how compensation update can be realized, but compensation update is only meaningful inside transaction scopes. Thus we have to restrict our attention to well formed processes, i.e. processes that will never feature a compensation update outside a transaction scope.

Definition 7 (Well formed processes). *Predicates $\mathsf{wf}(\bullet)$ and $\mathsf{wc}(\bullet)$ characterizing well formed processes and processes with well formed compensations are defined by mutual induction in Fig. 6.*

$$\text{wf}(\mathbf{0})$$
$$\text{wf}(\overline{a}\langle v\rangle.P) \text{ if } \text{wf}(P)$$
$$\text{wf}(a(x).P) \text{ if } \text{wf}(P)$$
$$\text{wf}((\nu x)\,P) \text{ if } \text{wf}(P)$$
$$\text{wf}(P \mid Q) \text{ if } \text{wf}(P) \wedge \text{wf}(Q)$$
$$\text{wf}(\langle P\rangle) \text{ if } \text{wf}(P)$$
$$\text{wf}(t[P,Q]) \text{ if } \text{wc}(P) \wedge \text{wf}(Q)$$
$$\text{wf}(X)$$

$$\text{wc}(\mathbf{0})$$
$$\text{wc}(\overline{a}\langle v\rangle.P) \text{ if } \text{wc}(P)$$
$$\text{wc}(a(x).P) \text{ if } \text{wc}(P)$$
$$\text{wc}(\text{inst}\lfloor \lambda X.R\rfloor.P) \text{ if } \text{wf}(R) \wedge \text{wc}(P)$$
$$\text{wc}((\nu x)\,P) \text{ if } \text{wc}(P)$$
$$\text{wc}(P \mid Q) \text{ if } \text{wc}(P) \wedge \text{wc}(Q)$$
$$\text{wc}(\langle P\rangle) \text{ if } \text{wf}(P)$$
$$\text{wc}(t[P,Q]) \text{ if } \text{wc}(P) \wedge \text{wf}(Q)$$
$$\text{wc}(X)$$

Fig. 6. Well formedness predicates

Next definition introduces n-ary contexts.

Definition 8. *An n-ary context $C[\bullet_1,\ldots,\bullet_n]$ is obtained by replacing in a process n occurrences of $\mathbf{0}$ with placeholders $\bullet_1,\ldots,\bullet_n$. Process $C[P_1,\ldots,P_n]$ is obtained by replacing inside $C[\bullet_1,\ldots,\bullet_n]$ each $\bullet_i$ with P_i.*

We describe below the conditions that we require for good encodings. Since we always deal with subcalculi of compensable processes we can use the notion of equivalence defined above for them, e.g. observers in should testing are compensable processes (not necessarily well-formed).

Definition 9 (Conditions for good encodings). *An encoding from a subcalculus C_1 of compensable processes to a subcalculus C_2 of compensable processes is a function $[\![\bullet]\!] : C_1 \to C_2$. Such an encoding is compositional if:*

1. *$[\![P \mid Q]\!] = [\![P]\!] \mid [\![Q]\!]$;*
2. *for each name substitution σ there is a name substitution σ' such that $[\![P\sigma]\!] = [\![P]\!]\sigma'$;*
3. *$[\![t\,[P,Q]]\!] = C_t[[\![P]\!],[\![Q]\!]]$, where $C_t[\bullet_1,\bullet_2]$ is a fixed binary context with parameter t.*

An encoding is correct *if for each well formed process P, P is should testing equivalent to $[\![P]\!]$. It is* divergence reflecting *if $[\![P]\!]$ diverges implies P diverges. An encoding is* good *if it is compositional, correct and divergence reflecting.*

The properties above have been taken from [19], where a general framework for proving encodability and separation results is presented, and then adapted to our setting. In particular, some of the conditions have been simplified since a few issues do not emerge in our work (e.g., since all the calculi are subcalculi of compensable processes). Condition 3, for instance, requires the transaction scope to be translated into a context in the target language, and such a condition is required for each operator in [19]. We have chosen should testing equivalence as correctness criterion. Roughly, it combines operational correspondence and success sensitiveness from [19]. Since we require also divergence reflection, using must testing [21] instead of should testing does not change our results [20].

As we already said, we will show that our encoding satisfies stricter conditions. In particular, we will replace the notion of correctness based on should testing equivalence with one based on weak bisimilarity (we have chosen should testing instead of must testing since weak bisimilarity implies should testing [20]).

Weak bisimilarity for compensable processes extends weak early π-calculus bisimilarity with features from higher-order bisimilarity [22], since compensation update is a form of higher-order communication.

Definition 10 (Weak bisimulation). *A weak bisimulation is a symmetric binary relation $\mathcal{R}$ such that $P\mathcal{R}Q$ implies:*

- *if $P \xrightarrow{\tau} P'$ or $P \xrightarrow{\tau_c} P'$ then there is Q' such that $Q \Longrightarrow Q'$ and $P'\mathcal{R}Q'$;*
- *if $P \xrightarrow{(z)\lambda X.R} P'$ and $\{z\} \cap \mathsf{fn}(Q) = \emptyset$ then there are S, Q' such that $Q \xRightarrow{(z)\lambda X.S} Q'$, $P'\mathcal{R}Q'$ and $R\{T/x\}\mathcal{R}S\{T/x\}$ for all processes T with no free variables;*
- *if $P \xrightarrow{\alpha} P'$ with $\alpha \neq \tau, (z)\lambda X.R$ and $\mathsf{bn}(\alpha) \cap \mathsf{fn}(Q) = \emptyset$, then there is Q' such that $Q \xRightarrow{\alpha} Q'$ and $P'\mathcal{R}Q'$;*
- *$\mathsf{extr}(P)\mathcal{R}\,\mathsf{extr}(Q)$.*

The function $\mathsf{extr}(\bullet)$ in the last condition should be instantiated to $\mathsf{extr_n}(\bullet)$ or $\mathsf{extr_{nn}}(\bullet)$ according to the chosen LTS semantics. Closure under the extraction function is required for having a compositional semantics (see [23]).

Definition 11. *Weak bisimilarity $\approx$ is the largest weak bisimulation.*

We will use the notion below as stronger form of correctness.

Definition 12. *An encoding is* bisimilarity preserving *if for each well formed process P, P is weakly bisimilar to $[\![P]\!]$.*

The lemma below proves that a bisimilarity preserving encoding is correct.

Lemma 3.1. *Let P and Q be processes. If $P \approx Q$ then $P \simeq_{shd} Q$.*

4   Parallel Recovery Can Be Implemented Using Static Recovery

In this section we compare the expressive power of parallel recovery and static recovery, considering both the cases of nested failure and non-nested failure. We present an encoding from parallel recovery to static recovery, showing that static recovery is as expressive as parallel recovery. The encoding respects the conditions of Definition 9 and Definition 12.

The encoding associates to each transaction scope a fresh name r. Compensations to be installed are left in the body of the transaction scope, protected by a protected block and guarded by an input on r. When the transaction scope is killed, an output on r, included in the static compensation, becomes enabled and can interact with the stored compensations, enabling them. Each of them also regenerates the output on r to enable further compensation elements.

$$(\nu r)\, t\, [\overline{book}.((\langle r.(\overline{unbook}|\overline{r})\rangle \mid \overline{pay}.\langle r.(\overline{refund}|\overline{r})\rangle), 0 \mid \overline{r}] \xrightarrow{\overline{book}}$$
$$(\nu r)\, t\, [(\langle r.(\overline{unbook}|\overline{r})\rangle \mid \overline{pay}.\langle r.(\overline{refund}|\overline{r})\rangle), 0 \mid \overline{r}] \xrightarrow{\overline{pay}}$$
$$(\nu r)\, t\, [\langle r.(\overline{unbook}|\overline{r})\rangle \mid \langle r.(\overline{refund}|\overline{r})\rangle), 0 \mid \overline{r}] \xrightarrow{t}$$
$$(\nu r)\, \langle r.(\overline{unbook}|\overline{r})\rangle \mid \langle r.(\overline{refund}|\overline{r})\rangle \mid \langle \overline{r}\rangle \xrightarrow{\tau}$$
$$(\nu r)\, \langle r.(\overline{unbook}|\overline{r})\rangle \mid \langle (\overline{refund}|\overline{r})\rangle \xrightarrow{\tau}$$
$$(\nu r)\, \langle \overline{unbook}|\overline{r}\rangle \mid \langle \overline{refund}\rangle \xrightarrow{\overline{unbook}}$$
$$(\nu r)\, \langle \overline{r}\rangle \mid \langle \overline{refund}\rangle \xrightarrow{\overline{refund}} (\nu r)\, \langle \overline{r}\rangle \mid \langle 0\rangle$$

Fig. 7. Sample execution

Definition 13 (From parallel to static recovery). *Let r be a fixed fresh name. The encoding $[\![\bullet]\!]_{p2s}$ from parallel recovery processes to static recovery processes is defined as:*

$$[\![t\,[P,Q]]\!]_{p2s} = (\nu r)\, t\, [[\![P]\!]_{p2s}, [\![Q]\!]_{p2s} \mid \overline{r}]$$
$$[\![\mathsf{inst}\lfloor \lambda X.Q \mid X\rfloor.P]\!]_{p2s} = [\![P]\!]_{p2s} \mid \langle r.([\![Q]\!]_{p2s} \mid \overline{r})\rangle$$

and maps all the other operators homomorphically to themselves.

Name r will be α-converted to different names inside different scopes.

Example 2. We apply here the translation to a simple example. Consider a transaction which books some hotel and then pays for it. In case of failure, the booking should be undone by sending a message $\overline{unbook}$, and the payment by sending a message $\overline{refund}$. For simplicity we do not consider the contents of the messages. The transaction can be modeled using parallel recovery processes as

$$t[\overline{book}.\,\mathsf{inst}\lfloor \overline{unbook}\rfloor.\overline{pay}.\,\mathsf{inst}\lfloor \overline{refund}\rfloor, 0]$$

Its translation is:

$$(\nu r)\, t[\overline{book}.((\langle r.(\overline{unbook}|\overline{r})\rangle \mid \overline{pay}.\langle r.(\overline{refund}|\overline{r})\rangle)), 0 \mid \overline{r}]$$

Figure 7 shows a sample execution, where the hotel is booked and payed, then the transaction scope is killed and the two items of compensation are executed.

It is easy to see that the encoding is compositional. Even more, it maps all the operators but transaction scope and compensation update homomorphically to themselves.

Remark 1. We have presented the encoding in the framework of synchronous π-calculus. The same encoding however can be used for CCS [24] and asynchronous π-calculus [25], extended with the primitives for transactions and compensations. In fact the encoding does not exploit name communication nor synchrony. We have presented it in the most general setting since it is easier to restrict the approach to CCS than to generalize an approach from CCS to π-calculus.

The rest of this section is devoted to prove that $[\![\bullet]\!]_{p2s}$ is a good, bisimilarity preserving encoding (see Definitions 9 and 12). We describe in detail the case of nested failure, the case of non-nested failure requires minimum changes.

Remark 2. If we drop the requirement of well formedness, bisimilarity preservation is no more satisfied, e.g. since

$$[\![\mathsf{inst}\lfloor \lambda X.Q \mid X \rfloor.P]\!]_{p2s} = [\![P]\!]_{p2s} \mid \langle r.([\![Q]\!]_{p2s} \mid \bar{r}) \rangle \xrightarrow{r}$$

while $\mathsf{inst}\lfloor \lambda X.Q \mid X \rfloor.P$ has no corresponding transition. Alternatively, one may require that actions on fresh names introduced by the translation, such as r here, are not observed by the behavioral equivalence.

While weak bisimilarity is preserved only for well formed processes, a strict relationship holds also between the behavior of a general process P and of its translation $[\![P]\!]_{p2s}$, as shown by Lemma 4.2 and Lemma 4.3. Roughly, the translation $\tilde{P}$ of a process P such that $P \xrightarrow{\alpha} P'$ evolves to some process $\tilde{P}'$ which is the translation of P'. However, this holds only up to some transformations deleting the garbage produced by the translation. To this end we exploit a *structural congruence* and an *auxiliary reduction relation*.

Definition 14 (Structural congruence). *Structural congruence on compensable processes is the minimum congruence $\equiv$ closed under the rules in Fig. 8.*

$$\mathbf{0} \mid P \equiv P \qquad P \mid Q \equiv Q \mid P \qquad (P \mid Q) \mid R \equiv P \mid (Q \mid R)$$

$$(\nu\, x)\, \mathbf{0} \equiv \mathbf{0} \qquad (\nu\, x)\, (\nu\, y)\, P \equiv (\nu\, y)\, (\nu\, x)\, P \qquad \langle\!\langle (\nu\, x)\, P \rangle\!\rangle \equiv (\nu\, x)\, \langle P \rangle \qquad (\nu\, x)\, \bar{x} \equiv \mathbf{0}$$

$$P \mid (\nu\, x)\, Q \equiv (\nu\, x)\, (P \mid Q) \quad \text{if } x \notin \mathsf{fn}(P)$$

$$t\, [(\nu\, x)\, P, Q] \equiv (\nu\, x)\, t\, [P, Q] \quad \text{if } t \neq x, \; x \notin \mathsf{fn}(Q)$$

$$\langle\!\langle P \rangle\!\rangle \equiv \langle P \rangle \qquad \langle P \mid Q \rangle \equiv \langle P \rangle \mid \langle Q \rangle \qquad \langle \mathbf{0} \rangle \equiv \mathbf{0}$$

Fig. 8. Structural congruence relation

Structural congruence includes standard rules from π-calculus, scope extrusion for the operators for transaction and compensation handling and a few rules capturing the properties of protected block. We also consider the simple garbage collection rule $(\nu\, x)\, \bar{x} \equiv \mathbf{0}$, since it simplifies our proofs.

Definition 15 (Auxiliary reduction relation). *The auxiliary reduction relation $\mapsto$ is the minimum congruence generated by the following rule:*

$$(\nu\, r)\, \langle \bar{r} \rangle \mid \prod_{i \in \{1,\ldots,n\}} \langle r.(Q_i \mid \bar{r}) \rangle \mapsto (\nu\, r)\, \langle \bar{r} \rangle \mid \prod_{i \in \{1,\ldots,n\}} \langle Q_i \rangle \quad \text{if } r \notin \mathsf{fn}(Q_i) \text{ for each } i \in \{1,\ldots,n\}.$$

The definition below introduces *possible translations*, which generalize the concept of translation. The idea is that each process in the set of possible translations of P behaves as P. Possible translations account for the different shapes that a dynamically created compensation can have, according to how it has been built as a composition of compensation items.

Definition 16 (Possible translations). *Let r be a fixed fresh name. Given a parallel recovery process P the set of its possible translations $\{|P|\}_{p2s}$ is defined by structural induction on P and then closed under the structural congruence and the auxiliary reduction relation. More precisely:*

- *if $P = t[R, Q]$ for each decomposition $Q \equiv \prod_{i \in \{0,\dots,n\}} Q_i$, each $\tilde{R} \in \{|R|\}_{p2s}$ and $\tilde{Q}_i \in \{|Q_i|\}_{p2s}$, we have that $(\nu\, r)\, t\left[\tilde{R} \mid \prod_{i \in \{1,\dots,n\}} \langle r.(\tilde{Q}_i \mid \bar{r}) \rangle, \tilde{Q}_0 \mid \bar{r}\right] \in \{|P|\}_{p2s}$;*
- *if $P = \mathsf{inst}\lfloor \lambda X.Q \mid X \rfloor.R$ for each $\tilde{Q} \in \{|Q|\}_{p2s}$ and each $\tilde{R} \in \{|R|\}_{p2s}$, we have that $\tilde{R} \mid \langle r.(\tilde{Q} \mid \bar{r}) \rangle \in \{|P|\}_{p2s}$;*
- *for each other n-ary operator op, if $P = \mathsf{op}(Q_1, \dots, Q_n)$ for each $\tilde{Q}_i \in \{|Q_i|\}_{p2s}$ we have that $\mathsf{op}(\tilde{Q}_1, \dots, \tilde{Q}_n) \in \{|P|\}_{p2s}$.*

Furthermore:

- *if $\tilde{P} \in \{|P|\}_{p2s}$ and $\tilde{P}' \equiv \tilde{P}$ then $\tilde{P}' \in \{|P|\}_{p2s}$;*
- *if $\tilde{P} \in \{|P|\}_{p2s}$ and $\tilde{P}' \mapsto \tilde{P}$ then $\tilde{P}' \in \{|P|\}_{p2s}$.*

The lemma below relates the possible translations of P and of $\mathsf{extr}_n(P)$.

Lemma 4.1. *Let $\tilde{P} \in \{|P|\}_{p2s}$. Then $\mathsf{extr}_n(\tilde{P}) \in \{|\mathsf{extr}_n(P)|\}_{p2s}$.*

The lemmas below relate the behavior of a process with the one of its possible translations. Namely, it will be shown that a possible translation evolves into a possible translation (this does not hold for translations). As already said, we write a compensation update $\lambda X.Q \mid X$ simply as Q.

Lemma 4.2. *Let P be a parallel recovery process and $\tilde{P} \in \{|P|\}_{p2s}$ one of its possible translations. If $P \xrightarrow{\alpha} P'$ then one of the following holds:*

1. *$\alpha \notin \{(z)Q, \tau_c\}$ and $\tilde{P} \xRightarrow{\alpha} \tilde{P}'$ with $\tilde{P}' \in \{|P'|\}_{p2s}$;*
2. *$\alpha = (z)Q$ and $\tilde{P} \Longrightarrow (\nu\, z)(\tilde{P}' \mid \langle r.(\tilde{Q} \mid \bar{r}) \rangle)$ where $\tilde{P}' \in \{|P'|\}_{p2s}$ and $\tilde{Q} \in \{|Q|\}_{p2s}$;*
3. *$\alpha = \tau_c$ and $\tilde{P} \Longrightarrow \tilde{P}'$ with $\tilde{P}' \in \{|P'|\}_{p2s}$.*

Proof. The proof is by structural induction on P, using a case analysis on the last applied rule.   □

The following lemma discusses the reverse implication.

Lemma 4.3. *Let P be a parallel recovery process such that $\mathsf{noComp}(P)$ and $\tilde{P} \in \{|P|\}_{p2s}$ one of its possible translations. If $\tilde{P} \xrightarrow{\alpha} \tilde{P}'$ with $\alpha \neq r$ then $P \xRightarrow{\alpha} P'$ with $\tilde{P}' \in \{|P'|\}_{p2s}$.*

Proof. The proof is by induction on the derivation of $\tilde{P} \in \{|P|\}_{p2s}$.   □

Theorem 4.1. *Let P be a well formed process. Then $P \approx [\![P]\!]_{p2s}$.*

Proof. First note that $[\![P]\!]_{p2s} \in \{|P|\}_{p2s}$. The proof is by coinduction. We have to show that the relation $\mathcal{R} = \{(P, \tilde{P}) \mid \mathsf{wf}(P) \wedge \tilde{P} \in \{|P|\}_{p2s}\}$ is a weak bisimulation. The proof exploits Lemmas 4.1, 4.2 and 4.3.   □

Corollary 1. $[\![\bullet]\!]_{p2s}$ *is a good encoding.*

5 General Dynamic Recovery Is More Expressive Than Static Recovery

In this section we compare the expressive power of general dynamic recovery and static recovery, showing that the former is more powerful. We also adapt our result to show that backward recovery is more powerful than static recovery.

The main idea is that with general dynamic recovery it is possible to check the order of execution of parallel actions by observing the compensations that they install, while this is not possible with static recovery. For instance, process $t[a.\operatorname{inst}\lfloor\lambda X.a'.0\rfloor \mid b.\operatorname{inst}\lfloor\lambda X.b'.0\rfloor, 0]$ can perform a computation with labels a, b, t, b' but no computation with labels b, a, t, b', i.e. whether b' is available or not depends on the order of execution of the parallel actions a and b. The proof of the separation result in Theorem 5.1 exploits similar arguments. The proof is based on the fact that the order of installation of compensations is not known statically because of the nondeterminism in the scheduling of parallel processes.

Before proving the theorem we need a few auxiliary notions and results.

Definition 17 (Enabling contexts). Enabling contexts $E[\bullet_1]$ are unary contexts generated by:
$$E[\bullet_1] ::= \bullet_1 \mid P|E[\bullet_1] \mid E[\bullet_1]|P \mid (\nu\, x)\, E[\bullet_1] \mid t[E[\bullet_1], Q] \mid \langle E[\bullet_1]\rangle$$

Definition 18. Given a process P the maximum choice degree $\operatorname{mcd}(P)$ of P is the maximum number of alternatives in a nondeterministic choice inside P. The maximum transaction nesting degree $\operatorname{mtd}(P)$ of P is the maximum level of nesting of transaction scopes inside P.

Next lemma shows that the maximum choice degree and the maximum transaction nesting degree of a process never increase during computations.

Lemma 5.1. If $P \xrightarrow{\alpha} P'$ then $\operatorname{mcd}(P') \le \operatorname{mcd}(P)$ and $\operatorname{mtd}(P') \le \operatorname{mtd}(P)$.

Next lemma exploits the definition above to determine structural properties of processes from their behavior.

Lemma 5.2. Let P be a static recovery process. Assume that $P \xrightarrow{a_i} P'_i$ for each $i \in \{1, \dots, n\}$. Assume that $n > c + t$ where c is the maximum choice degree of P and t is the maximum transaction nesting degree of P. Then there are an enabling context $E[\bullet_1]$, processes Q_1 and Q_2 and indexes j and k such that $P \Longrightarrow Q = E[Q_1|Q_2]$ with $Q_1 \xrightarrow{a_j} Q'_1$ and $Q_2 \xrightarrow{a_k} Q'_2$.

Proof. The proof is by structural induction on P.   □

We can finally prove the desired separation result.

Theorem 5.1. There is no good encoding $[\![\bullet]\!]_{g2s}$ of compensable processes into static recovery processes.

Proof. Suppose by contradiction that such an encoding exists. For each i let $P_i = a_i.\,\mathsf{inst}\lfloor \lambda Y_i.b_i.\mathbf{0}\rfloor.\mathbf{0}$. Consider the process $P = t[\prod_{i \in \{1,...,n\}} P_i, \mathbf{0}]$. Because of conditions 1 and 3 of compositional encodings, its encoding $[\![P]\!]_{g2s}$ should be of the form $C_t[\prod_{i \in \{1,...,n\}} [\![P_i]\!]_{g2s}, [\![\mathbf{0}]\!]_{g2s}]$, which we will denote as $\tilde{P}$. Note that P is well formed, thus $P \simeq_{shd} [\![P]\!]_{g2s}$. Let us consider the observers $O_{j,k} = \overline{a_j}.\overline{a_k}.t.\overline{b_k}.\sqrt{}$ and $O'_{j,k} = \overline{a_j}.\overline{a_k}.t.\overline{b_j}.\sqrt{}$. For each j, k note that P should $O_{j,k}$, while P should not $O'_{j,k}$. Also, given $O_j = \overline{a_j}.\sqrt{}$, P should O_j for each j. Thanks to correctness, $\tilde{P}$ has to pass the same tests. Test O_j can succeed only if $\tilde{P} \xrightarrow{a_j}$. Also, no action τ or τ_c should compromise the possibility of performing a_j for each j, since we are using should testing equivalence.

We show now by contradiction that $\tilde{P} \Longrightarrow Q$ for some Q such that $Q \xrightarrow{a_i} Q'_i$ for each $i \in \{1,\ldots,n\}$. We assume that such a Q does not exist and build an infinite computation composed by transitions τ and τ_c, contradicting divergence reflection. Since we assume Q does not exist, in particular, for some a_i there is no transition $\tilde{P} \xrightarrow{a_i}$. Thus since $\tilde{P} \xrightarrow{a_i}$ we have $\tilde{P} \xrightarrow{\tau}{}^+ Q_1 \xrightarrow{a_i}$ where $\xrightarrow{\tau}{}^+$ denotes a non empty sequence of transitions τ and τ_c. Also, Q_1 must still satisfy the tests. Since Q does not exist, there is also some a_j such that there is no transition $Q_1 \xrightarrow{a_j}$. Thus we can further extend the computation. By iterating the procedure we get an infinite sequence of transitions τ and τ_c. Since P does not diverge, and the encoding has to be divergence reflecting, we have a contradiction.

Now observe that thanks to condition 2 of compositional encoding all $[\![P_i]\!]_{g2s}$ are equal up to name substitution and thus have the same maximum choice degree and maximum transaction nesting degree. Thus the maximum choice degree c and maximum transaction nesting degree t of $\tilde{P}$ do not depend on n. In particular, we can choose $n > c + t$. Thanks to Lemma 5.1 the same relation holds also for Q. Thus we can apply Lemma 5.2 to prove that $Q = E[Q_1 | Q_2]$ with $Q_1 \xrightarrow{a_j} Q'_1$ and $Q_2 \xrightarrow{a_k} Q'_2$ for some enabling context $E[\bullet]$. We have $E[Q_1 | Q_2] \xrightarrow{a_j} E[Q'_1 | Q_2] \xrightarrow{a_k} E[Q'_1 | Q'_2]$ and $E[Q_1 | Q_2] \xrightarrow{a_k} E[Q_1 | Q'_2] \xrightarrow{a_j} E[Q'_1 | Q'_2]$. The final process $E[Q'_1 | Q'_2]$ is the same in both the cases.

These computations can be observed using observers $O_{j,k} = \overline{a_j}.\overline{a_k}.t.\overline{b_k}.\sqrt{}$ and $O'_{k,j} = \overline{a_k}.\overline{a_j}.t.\overline{b_k}.\sqrt{}$ above. $\tilde{P} \mid O \Longrightarrow E[Q'_1 | Q'_2] \mid t.\overline{b_k}.\sqrt{}$ for both $O = O_{j,k}$ and $O = O'_{k,j}$. From $\tilde{P}$ should $O_{j,k}$ we deduce $E[Q'_1 | Q'_2] \mid t.\overline{b_k}.\sqrt{} \xrightarrow{\sqrt{}}$, while from $\tilde{P}$ should not $O'_{k,j}$ we deduce that this computation cannot exist.

This is a contradiction, thus the encoding $[\![\bullet]\!]_{g2s}$ does not exist. □

The theorem above holds for both nested and non-nested failure.

Remark 3. We have presented this separation result in the framework of synchronous π-calculus. The same result however can be proved for CCS [24], extended with the primitives for transactions and compensations. In fact the used processes and observers are all CCS processes.

It is interesting to see how the result and the proof change if conditions for good encodings are modified, in particular as far as correctness is concerned. First note that requiring bisimilarity preservation instead of correctness weakens the result. However, this weaker result can be easily extended to asynchronous compensable processes, which are obtained by disallowing continuation after the output prefix, as done for π-calculus [25]. In particular, no compensation update can become enabled because of the execution of an output action.

Corollary 2. *There is no good bisimilarity preserving encoding $[\![\bullet]\!]_{g2s-a}$ of a-synchronous compensable processes into asynchronous static recovery processes.*

We have not been able to prove the result above without the condition of bisimilarity preservation, since it is difficult for asynchronous observers to force an order of execution for parallel actions.

Many approaches in the literature, such as [19], use as observers in the target language the encoding of the observers in the source language. In our case we can use the same observers since the target language is a sublanguage of the starting one. We can restate our results using the approach in [19], but we need some more conditions on the translation (e.g., preservation of the behavior of sequential CCS processes).

The theorem above concerns general dynamic recovery, however a similar result can be obtained for *backward recovery*. Backward recovery is easily defined in a calculus with sequential composition by requiring all the compensation updates to have the form $\lambda X.P; X$ where ; is sequential composition and X does not occur in P. It is easy to see that just having a very constrained form of backward recovery, where P is a single prefix, is enough to increase the expressive power beyond static recovery. This can be easily stated in our framework by allowing only compensation updates of the form $\lambda X.\pi.X$ where π is any prefix.

Corollary 3. *There is no good encoding $[\![\bullet]\!]_{b2s}$ of backward recovery processes into static recovery processes.*

Proof. It is enough to consider $P_i = a_i.\, \mathsf{inst}\lfloor \lambda Y_i.b_i.Y_i \rfloor.0$ instead of the process $P_i = a_i.\, \mathsf{inst}\lfloor \lambda Y_i.b_i.0 \rfloor.0$ in the proof of Theorem 5.1.   □

From the results of previous section we also deduce that both general dynamic recovery and backward recovery are more expressive than parallel recovery.

6   Applications and Related Works

We discuss here how to apply the results in sections 4 and 5 to other calculi and languages in the literature. The calculi more related to ours are the so-called interaction-based calculi [3–5, 9], which are obtained by adding primitives for compensation handling on top of concurrent calculi such as π-calculus [2] or Join [26]. These calculi differ on many design choices. The main differences are summarized in Table 1 and their impact on our results discussed below.

Dcπ. Dcπ [9] is a calculus with parallel recovery based on asynchronous π-calculus [25]. For this reason, compensation update is allowed only after input prefix. Actually, in dcπ, input prefix and compensation update are combined in an atomic primitive $a(x)\%Q.P$ that, after receiving values v on channel a, continues as $P\{v/x\}$ and adds $Q\{v/x\}$ in parallel to the current compensation. The same behavior can be obtained in parallel recovery processes by writing $a(x).\mathsf{inst}\lfloor\lambda X.Q \mid X\rfloor.P$, thanks to priority of compensation update. Thus dcπ can be seen as the asynchronous fragment of parallel recovery processes with nested failure where compensation update can occur only after input prefix. Both the encoding in Section 4 and the separation result for asynchronous calculi in Corollary 2 can be easily adapted to dcπ.

Webπ and Webπ$_\infty$. Webπ [5] is a calculus with static recovery based on asynchronous π-calculus [25]. It provides timed transactions, which add an orthogonal degree of expressive power. Its untimed fragment, Webπ$_\infty$ [23] instead corresponds exactly to the asynchronous fragment of static recovery with non-nested failure where all messages are inside protected blocks. The encoding in Section 4 can be adapted to both the calculi. The main change required is to implement protected block using a transaction scope with bound name. Also the separation result in Corollary 2 can be easily applied to the two calculi.

πt-calculus. The πt-calculus [3] is based on asynchronous π-calculus. When a component inside a transaction aborts, abortion or completion of parallel components is waited for. Then the compensation of the transaction (called failure manager) is executed, followed by the parallel composition of the compensations of the already terminated subtransactions. It is difficult to adapt our encoding to πt-calculus, since this will require to change the semantics of abortion allowing a transaction to abort even if it contains protected blocks. On the other hand the separation result in Corollary 2 can be applied, referred to an extension of the πt-calculus where the failure manager can be updated dynamically.

C-join. C-join [4] is a calculus with static recovery built on top of Join calculus [26]. However here transactions can be dynamically merged, and their

Table 1. Features of interaction-based calculi and languages

	underlying language	compens. definition	nested vs non-nested	protection operator	encoding applicable	separation res. applicable
dcπ	asynch. π	parallel	nested	yes	yes	asynch.
Webπ/Webπ$_\infty$	asynch. π	static	non-nested	implem.	yes	asynch.
πt	asynch. π	static	nested	no	no	asynch.
C-join	Join	static	nested	no	yes[a]	no
SOCK	-	dynamic	nested	implem.	yes	no
COWS	-	static	nested	yes	yes	no
Jolie	-	dynamic	nested	implem.	yes	no
WS-BPEL	-	static	nested	implem.	yes	no

[a] If a protection operator is added.

compensations are composed in parallel, thus obtaining some form of parallel recovery. Our encoding is not directly applicable since C-join has no protected block operator, but becomes applicable as soon as such an operator is introduced. As far as the separation result is concerned, join patterns are more powerful than π-calculus communication, and we conjecture that they can be used to implement general dynamic recovery.

Service oriented calculi. Many service oriented calculi have been recently proposed [27–32]. Long running transactions are an important aspect of service oriented computing thus many of these calculi include primitives for compensation handling. We discuss here the ones more related to our approach.

SOCK [28] is a language for composing service invocations and definitions using primitives from sequential languages and concurrent calculi. It has been extended with primitives for general dynamic recovery in [12]. Our encoding can be applied to SOCK using signals for mimicking CCS communication. Actually, in SOCK, the protected block is just used in the definition of the semantics, but it can be implemented too. Since SOCK has no restriction operator, fresh signal names should be statically generated, and the behavioral correspondence result should be restated along the lines of Remark 2. The separation result instead does not apply: SOCK services are stateful, and the state can be used to keep track of the order of execution of parallel activities. All the observations made for SOCK hold also for Jolie [33, 34], a service oriented language based on it.

COWS [30] communication is in the style of fusion calculus [35]. COWS has a kill primitive and a protected block. This allows to program static recovery (see [30]). Our encoding can be applied to program also parallel recovery. The separation result instead cannot be easily extended, since COWS communication and kill have priorities, thus allowing parallel processes to influence each other.

Other service oriented calculi include only mechanisms for exception handling [31] or notification of session failure [27, 32].

Compensable flow calculi. Calculi based on the compensable flow approach such as SAGAs calculi [8] or StAC [7], use backward recovery for sequential activities and parallel recovery for parallel ones. Thus our separation result does not apply. Also, since there is no communication, atomicity constraints are less strong. However we are not aware of good encodings of compensable flow calculi into static recovery calculi. For instance, the mapping in [6] of cCSP [10] into the conversation calculus [31] is not compositional.

WS-BPEL. WS-BPEL [1] is the de-facto standard for web services composition. Compensations are statically defined, and they are composed using backward recovery for sequential subtransactions, and parallel recovery for parallel ones. Our separation result does not apply because of the reasons discussed for SOCK and for compensable flow calculi. As far as the encoding is concerned, the same approach used for SOCK can be applied.

Future work. As we already discussed throughout the paper, many open issues concerning the expressive power of mechanisms for long running transactions remain. In fact this topic, while relevant, has been neglected until now: a few papers, such as [36, 37], study the expressive power of primitives for interruption, more than primitives for compensation as in our case. We think that the techniques presented in this paper can be successfully applied to answer some of the open issues. We refer in particular to the analysis of whether nested failure can be implemented using non-nested failure, and to the encodability of BPEL-style recovery into static recovery. We conjecture that this encoding is possible, thus BPEL-style recovery could be defined as a macro on top of static recovery. After those problems have been analyzed in a simple setting, additional work is required to transfer the results to other calculi/languages. Another important topic that deserves further investigation is the impact of communication primitives more powerful than π-calculus message passing, such as join patterns, on our separation result. It would also be interesting to generalize the techniques of this paper to deal with languages for adaptation [38], since dynamic compensations can be seen as an approach for adaptation of compensations.

Acknowledgments. We thank R. Bruni, F. Montesi, G. Zavattaro, F. Tiezzi and the anonymous reviewers for useful suggestions and comments.

References

1. Oasis: Web Services Business Process Execution Language Version 2.0 (2007), http://docs.oasis-open.org/wsbpel/2.0/OS/wsbpel-v2.0-OS.html
2. Milner, R., Parrow, J., Walker, J.: A calculus of mobile processes, I and II. Inf. Comput. 100(1), 1–40, 41–77 (1992)
3. Bocchi, L., Laneve, C., Zavattaro, G.: A calculus for long-running transactions. In: Najm, E., Nestmann, U., Stevens, P. (eds.) FMOODS 2003. LNCS, vol. 2884, pp. 124–138. Springer, Heidelberg (2003)
4. Bruni, R., Melgratti, H., Montanari, U.: Nested commits for mobile calculi: Extending join. In: Proc. of IFIP TCS 2004, pp. 563–576. Kluwer, Dordrecht (2004)
5. Laneve, C., Zavattaro, G.: Foundations of web transactions. In: Sassone, V. (ed.) FOSSACS 2005. LNCS, vol. 3441, pp. 282–298. Springer, Heidelberg (2005)
6. Caires, L., Ferreira, C., Vieira, H.: A process calculus analysis of compensations. In: Kaklamanis, C., Nielson, F. (eds.) TGC 2008. LNCS, vol. 5474, pp. 87–103. Springer, Heidelberg (2009)
7. Butler, M.J., Ferreira, C.: An operational semantics for StAC, a language for modelling long-running business transactions. In: De Nicola, R., Ferrari, G.-L., Meredith, G. (eds.) COORDINATION 2004. LNCS, vol. 2949, pp. 87–104. Springer, Heidelberg (2004)
8. Bruni, R., Melgratti, H., Montanari, U.: Theoretical foundations for compensations in flow composition languages. In: Proc. of POPL 2005, pp. 209–220. ACM Press, New York (2005)
9. Vaz, C., Ferreira, C., Ravara, A.: Dynamic recovering of long running transactions. In: Kaklamanis, C., Nielson, F. (eds.) TGC 2008. LNCS, vol. 5474, pp. 201–215. Springer, Heidelberg (2009)
10. Butler, M.J., Hoare, C., Ferreira, C.: A trace semantics for long-running transactions. In: Abdallah, A.E., Jones, C.B., Sanders, J.W. (eds.) Communicating Sequential Processes. LNCS, vol. 3525, pp. 133–150. Springer, Heidelberg (2005)

11. Garcia-Molina, H., et al.: Coordinating multi-transaction activities. Technical Report CS-TR-2412, University of Maryland, Dept. of Computer Science (1990)
12. Guidi, C., Lanese, I., Montesi, F., Zavattaro, G.: On the interplay between fault handling and request-response service invocations. In: Proc. of ACSD 2008, pp. 190–199. IEEE Computer Society Press, Los Alamitos (2008)
13. Weimer, W., Necula, G.: Finding and preventing run-time error handling mistakes. In: Proc. of OOPSLA 2004, pp. 419–431. ACM Press, New York (2004)
14. Lanese, I., Vaz, C., Ferreira, C.: On the expressive power of primitives for compensation handling, TR (2010),
    http://www.cs.unibo.it/~lanese/publications/fulltext/TR-ESOP2010.pdf
15. Guidi, C., Lanese, I., Montesi, F., Zavattaro, G.: Dynamic error handling in service oriented applications. Fundamenta Informaticae 95(1), 73–102 (2009)
16. Parrow, J.: Expressiveness of process algebras. In: Proc. of the LIX Colloquium on Emerging Trends in Concurrency Theory. ENTCS, vol. 209, pp. 173–186. Elsevier, Amsterdam (2008)
17. Palamidessi, C.: Comparing the expressive power of the synchronous and the asynchronous pi-calculus. In: Proc. of POPL 1997, pp. 256–265 (1997)
18. Nestmann, U.: What is a "good" encoding of guarded choice? Inf. Comput. 156(1-2), 287–319 (2000)
19. Gorla, D.: Towards a unified approach to encodability and separation results for process calculi. In: van Breugel, F., Chechik, M. (eds.) CONCUR 2008. LNCS, vol. 5201, pp. 492–507. Springer, Heidelberg (2008)
20. Rensink, A., Vogler, W.: Fair testing. Inf. Comput. 205(2), 125–198 (2007)
21. De Nicola, R., Hennessy, M.: Testing equivalences for processes. Theor. Comput. Sci. 34, 83–133 (1984)
22. Thomsen, B.: Calculi for Higher Order Communicating Systems. PhD thesis, Imperial College (1990)
23. Mazzara, M., Lanese, I.: Towards a unifying theory for web services composition. In: Bravetti, M., Núñez, M., Zavattaro, G. (eds.) WS-FM 2006. LNCS, vol. 4184, pp. 257–272. Springer, Heidelberg (2006)
24. Milner, R.: A Calculus of Communication Systems. LNCS, vol. 92. Springer, Heidelberg (1980)
25. Honda, K., Tokoro, M.: An object calculus for asynchronous communication. In: America, P. (ed.) ECOOP 1991. LNCS, vol. 512, pp. 133–147. Springer, Heidelberg (1991)
26. Fournet, C., Gonthier, G.: The reflexive CHAM and the join-calculus. In: Proc. of POPL 1996, pp. 372–385. ACM Press, New York (1996)
27. Boreale, M., Bruni, R., Caires, L., De Nicola, R., Lanese, I., Loreti, M., Martins, F., Montanari, U., Ravara, A., Sangiorgi, D., Vasconcelos, V., Zavattaro, G.: SCC: a Service Centered Calculus. In: Bravetti, M., Núñez, M., Zavattaro, G. (eds.) WS-FM 2006. LNCS, vol. 4184, pp. 38–57. Springer, Heidelberg (2006)
28. Guidi, C., Lucchi, R., Gorrieri, R., Busi, N., Zavattaro, G.: SOCK: a calculus for service oriented computing. In: Dan, A., Lamersdorf, W. (eds.) ICSOC 2006. LNCS, vol. 4294, pp. 327–338. Springer, Heidelberg (2006)
29. Lanese, I., Martins, F., Vasconcelos, V., Ravara, A.: Disciplining orchestration and conversation in service-oriented computing. In: Proc. of SEFM 2007, pp. 305–314. IEEE Computer Society Press, Los Alamitos (2007)
30. Lapadula, A., Pugliese, R., Tiezzi, F.: A calculus for orchestration of web services. In: De Nicola, R. (ed.) ESOP 2007. LNCS, vol. 4421, pp. 33–47. Springer, Heidelberg (2007)

31. Vieira, H., Caires, L., Seco, J.: The conversation calculus: A model of service-oriented computation. In: Drossopoulou, S. (ed.) ESOP 2008. LNCS, vol. 4960, pp. 269–283. Springer, Heidelberg (2008)
32. Boreale, M., Bruni, R., De Nicola, R., Loreti, M.: Sessions and pipelines for structured service programming. In: Barthe, G., de Boer, F.S. (eds.) FMOODS 2008. LNCS, vol. 5051, pp. 19–38. Springer, Heidelberg (2008)
33. Montesi, F., Guidi, C., Zavattaro, G.: Composing services with JOLIE. In: Proc. of ECOWS 2007, pp. 13–22. IEEE Computer Society Press, Los Alamitos (2007)
34. Jolie team: Jolie website (2009), http://www.jolie-lang.org/
35. Parrow, J., Victor, B.: The fusion calculus: Expressiveness and symmetry in mobile processes. In: Proc. of LICS 1998, pp. 176–185 (1998)
36. Aceto, L., Fokkink, W., Ingólfsdóttir, A., Nain, S.: Bisimilarity is not finitely based over bpa with interrupt. Theor. Comput. Sci. 366(1-2), 60–81 (2006)
37. Bravetti, M., Zavattaro, G.: On the expressive power of process interruption and compensation. Math. Stru. Comp. Sci. 19(3), 565–599 (2009)
38. Andersson, J., de Lemos, R., Malek, S., Weyns, D.: Modeling dimensions of self-adaptive software systems. In: Cheng, B.H.C., de Lemos, R., Giese, H., Inverardi, P., Magee, J. (eds.) Software Engineering for Self-Adaptive Systems. LNCS, vol. 5525, pp. 27–47. Springer, Heidelberg (2009)

Separating Shape Graphs

Vincent Laviron[1], Bor-Yuh Evan Chang[2], and Xavier Rival[1,3]

[1] École Normale Supérieure, Paris, France
[2] University of Colorado, Boulder, Colorado, USA
[3] INRIA Rocquencourt, France
laviron@di.ens.fr, bec@cs.colorado.edu, rival@di.ens.fr

Abstract. Detailed memory models that expose individual fields are necessary to precisely analyze code that makes use of low-level aspects such as, pointers to fields and untagged unions. Yet, higher-level representations that collect fields into records are often used because they are typically more convenient and efficient in modeling the program heap. In this paper, we present a shape graph representation of memory that exposes individual fields while largely retaining the convenience of an object-level model. This representation has a close connection to particular kinds of formulas in separation logic. Then, with this representation, we show how to extend the XISA shape analyzer for low-level aspects, including pointers to fields, C-style nested structures and unions, malloc and free, and array values, with minimal changes to the core algorithms (e.g., materialization and summarization).

1   Introduction

At the core of precise program analyzers, such as verification tools and shape analyses, is an abstract memory model that represents the program heap. The design of such representations for C code is particularly challenging because of a tension between keeping it simple and supporting low-level pointer manipulation.

Specifically, the level of detail exposed in an abstract memory model determines whether the analyzer can even reason about particular low-level aspects. For example, does the representation allow the addressing expression &(p->f$_1$.f$_2$) (i.e., taking the address of a nested structure or union field), while supporting basic field read expressions p->f easily?

To illustrate this tension, we show in Fig. 1, a simple, traditional shape graph (a) that represents the concrete memory shown in (b) as an informal box diagram. In this shape graph, each node corresponds to an object (i.e., a record of fields) and each edge stands for a points-to relation between objects. Historically, shape analyzers have focused on Java-like structures where memory can

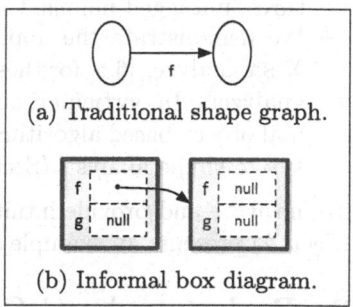

(a) Traditional shape graph.

(b) Informal box diagram.

Fig. 1. A shape graph for Java-like structures

A.D. Gordon (Ed.): ESOP 2010, LNCS 6012, pp. 387–406, 2010.
© Springer-Verlag Berlin Heidelberg 2010

be viewed as a simple collection of objects with field reads but no complex addressing expressions (e.g., [23,24,11]). Consequently, such a shape graph is convenient and widely used. For example, TVLA [24] uses three-valued logical structures to encode such shape graphs. In TVLA, the shape graph in Fig. 1a corresponds to the two-valued formula $f(u_1, u_2)$ over individuals u_1 and u_2. Similarly, in separation logic [22] and separation logic-based shape analyzers, we might represent the memory shown in Fig. 1b with the following formula: $u_1 \mapsto \{f\colon u_2, g\colon \text{null}\} \ * \ u_2 \mapsto \{f\colon \text{null}, g\colon \text{null}\}$ as, for example, in Berdine *et al.* [1]. This formula says that there are two disjoint records pointed to by u_1 and u_2, each with fields f and g, and where the f field of u_1 points to u_2 (and all other fields are null).

We see that something more detailed is needed to express, for example, a pointer to a field (i.e., &(p->f)). In particular, we must expose the individual fields (i.e., the components of a record) as shown informally in Fig. 2. However, if we simply take the components as the unit memory cells, then we lose the object-level structure. Such an object-level view is convenient for the common case with Java-like structures and necessary for the sound modeling of object-level properties, such as for analyzing uses of malloc and free.

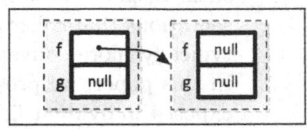

Fig. 2. Box diagram with exposed components

In this paper, we make the following contributions:

- We describe a graph-based memory representation that permits reasoning at the object level and the field level simultaneously. The key idea is to represent abstract memory cells with edges (rather than nodes as is traditional) and to view nodes as aggregates of their outgoing edges. This simple shift in view allows us to cleanly separate object-level properties from field-level ones. In particular, we show how this representation can be instantiated in different ways to express varying degrees of detail (Sect. 3).
- We present a particular instantiation of separating shape graphs to model low-level aspects of C, including pointer-to-field (i.e., &(p->f)), nested structures, untagged unions, C-style malloc-free, and array values (Sect. 4).
- We demonstrate the applicability of our representation by extending the XISA analyzer [6,5] for these low-level aspects of C, often unhandled in shape analyzers. In particular, our extension required minimal changes to the original object-based algorithms for materialization and summarization that are key to shape analysis (Sect. 5).

To motivate and provide intuition for separating shape graphs, the next section (Sect. 2) presents an example shape analysis with nested structures and unions.

2   Background and Overview

In separation logic, the record-level points-to relation is a standard abbreviation for separated points-to relations of components:

$$ e \mapsto \{f_1\colon e_1, \ldots, f_n\colon e_n\} \ \stackrel{\text{def}}{=} \ e \, @f_1 \mapsto e_1 * \cdots * e \, @f_n \mapsto e_n \qquad (\star) $$

where $e @ f$ is a field offset expression (i.e., the offset corresponding to field f from the base pointer given by expression e). By using formulas of the form on the right side, we essentially expose individual fields (referred by Parkinson as taking a field-splitting model of memory [21]).

For shape analysis of C code, we essentially want a representation that minimizes the need to convert back-and-forth between the left and right-hand sides of definition $(\star)$. In other words, we want a model that exposes individual fields and permits complex addressing expressions but maintains object-level structure. To begin, consider the graph shown in Fig. 3. A node denotes a value (e.g., a memory address, an integer, null) labeled by a *symbolic value*, which is an existen-

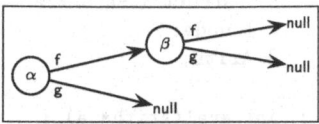

Fig. 3. A simple separating shape graph for the concrete memory in Fig. 1b

tially quantified variable. We use lowercase Greek letters $(\alpha, \beta, \gamma, \ldots)$ to range over symbolic values. An edge corresponds to a unit memory cell or a points-to relation at the component level (like on the right in definition $(\star)$ and Fig. 2); for instance, the edge between α and β says that at field f from address α, the contents of the cell is β. At the same time, if we ensure that all symbolic values correspond to base pointers of objects, we have a representation that also can be read as an object-level formula (like on the left in definition $(\star)$ and Fig. 1b) and looks fairly similar to the traditional shape graph in Fig. 1a. It is important to note that edges represent disjoint memory cells (like nodes in traditional shape graphs) but that nodes may correspond to the same concrete value (unlike in traditional shape graphs).

Thus far, we have a shape graph representation for Java-like structures as in our prior work [6,5] and similarly used by others (e.g., [1]). In this paper, we make the connection between such graphs and a restricted language of separation logic formulas explicit and take this view further to capture low-level aspects of C (see Sect. 3). In the remainder of this section, we provide intuition for our C-level model of memory with an example shown in Fig. 4. In particular, we consider the analysis of code for evaluating arithmetic expressions represented by a syntax tree (using the C-type `Arith`). These syntax trees feature several kinds of nodes (constants `cst`, unary operators `uni`, and binary operators `bin`) that are encoded with a union type. The `op` field is a tag, or discriminant, that indicates which branch of the union field `node` is being used.

Our shape analysis proceeds by abstract interpretation [10] computing sound local invariants at each program point (i.e., graphs that over-approximate the set of possible concrete memory states). In the figure, we show the local invariants inferred by our analysis boxed and right-justified at a number of program points. Like in our prior work [6,5], a thick edge, or a *checker edge*, represents a memory region summary (i.e., a set of points-to edges abstractly). Our abstract domain is parametric in inductive definitions that give rise to such summaries. These user-supplied inductive definitions come in the form of *invariant checkers*; that is, they can be viewed as code that traverses a data structure to check a run-time

```
      typedef struct Arith {
        char op;  // the tag: 0 for constants, 1 for unary −, 2 for +, 3 for *, ...
        union {
          struct { long long int value; } cst;  // a constant value
          struct { struct Arith* s; } uni;  // a unary operator
          struct { struct Arith* l; struct Arith* r; } bin;  // a binary operator
        } node;
      } Arith;
```

```
1     int eval(Arith* a) {
2
      Arith* c; Arith* n;
3     while (a->op != 0) {  // 0 stands for a constant
4       c = a;  // initialize the cursor
5       while (1) {  // traverse a branch until some
                     // simplification can be done
6
7         if (c->op == 1) {
            // 1 stands for unary negation
            n = c->node.uni.s;
8
            if (n->op == 0) {
9             // simplify
              c->op = 0; c->node.cst.value = - n->node.cst.value; free(n);
10
              break;
11          }
12          else { c = n; }
13        }
14        else { ... /* other cases for addition, multiplication, etc. */ ... }
15      }
16    }
17    return a->node.cst.value;
18  }
```

Fig. 4. An example analysis of a syntax tree operation using C-style unions

invariant. The first invariant at program point 2 indicates the pre-condition that a is a well-formed syntax tree given by the inductive checker arith. For now, we focus on the analysis (the formal definition of the arith checker will be given in Sect. 4.2). The loop invariant in the second loop at program point 6 expresses the fact that c points to a subtree of the syntax tree pointed to by a; specifically, there is a syntax tree *segment* between α and β described by a partial instance of checker arith, and separately, there is a completion of the tree from β.

The condition test on field op of c causes the analyzer to *unfold* the definition of arith for the syntax tree pointed to by c to produce the invariant at program point 8. Unfolding is a partial concretization or refinement step that *materializes* points-to edges, typically by considering cases. Here, the fact that $\gamma = 1$ (given by the guard that `c->op == 1`) leaves the one case where the uni branch of the union is active. Thus, we have two points-to edges materialized: one labeled with op for the op field of c and one labeled with node@uni@s for the subexpression pointer of the unary operator (i.e., `c->node.uni.s`). Data constraints, such as $\gamma = 1$, are captured by a *base abstract domain* that is also a parameter of our analysis; in our examples, we will note such constraints as necessary and assume that we are using a base domain that can capture them. Next, a similar unfolding happens at the syntax tree node pointed to by n (i.e., δ) to produce the invariant at program point 9. At this point, the structure below c is fully materialized, and the subsequent sequence of updates is reflected by modifications and deletions of points-to edges to produce the invariant at program point 10. The result of the outer evaluation loop is a syntax tree node for a constant corresponding to the inferred invariant at program point 17.

As alluded to earlier, the key challenge addressed in this paper is creating an analysis that is capable of reasoning about low-level C features, such as unions, while not unnecessarily complicating the analysis of higher-level, Java-like code. This challenge is highlighted in this example analysis. Focus again on the transition between points 9 and 10. On one hand, the view of the syntax tree node pointed to by c changes by writing through `node.cst.value` in the second statement, which is not evident in the state at point 9. Analyzing code with unions requires careful management of several such *views* of the same or overlapping memory cells (e.g., `c->node`) (Sect. 3.2); such views are accompanied by fields of varying *sizes* and thus necessitating delicate treatment of values and memory cells (Sect. 4). At the same time, the first statement updates the op tag, which is an ordinary field except for its role in discriminating the union. We want the modeling of this field to be largely independent of the complexities introduced by the union type (Sect. 3.1).

The most intricate aspect of most program analysis algorithms is the widening operator that extrapolates loop invariants—in our domain, it folds points-to edges into checker edges. Our algorithm is no exception but by encapsulating unions within a shape graph representation, our widening operator described in great detail in earlier papers [6,5] remains essentially unchanged (Sect. 4.3)

3   Separating Shape Graphs for Modeling Memory

In this section, we gradually evolve an abstract domain for shape analysis to model successively lower-level aspects. In particular, we want a domain that can be instantiated differently depending on the desired level of detail. For example, we may want to analyze code that relies on compiler implementation-specific details such as the size and packing of fields, or we may want to be compiler independent and reject certain low-level idioms. In Sect. 4, we formalize a particular instantiation with the lower-level aspects.

In Fig. 5, we show such an abstract domain using separating shape graphs. Separating shape graphs represent memories M, which consist of either an empty

memories	M ::=	**emp**	empty
		$\mid M_1 * M_2$	separate regions
		$\mid S$	region summary
		$\mid \alpha\,\ell \overset{q}{\mapsto} \beta\,r$	memory cell
summaries	S		
l-exprs, r-exprs	ℓ, r		
points-to properties	q		
variable environment	E ::=	$\cdot \mid E, x \mapsto \alpha$	static scope
value constraints	P	$\in \mathbb{P}^\sharp$	base domain
analysis state	A ::=	$\bot \mid \exists\vec{\alpha}.\,\langle E, M, P\rangle \mid A_1 \vee A_2$	disjunctive domain

Fig. 5. An abstract shape domain with separating shape graphs (M)

memory **emp** or separate regions $M_1 * M_2$ like in separation logic. Regions may be either a summary region S or a points-to relation. Summaries S abstract some configuration of points-to edges. They are necessary to capture an unbounded number of configurations needed by shape analysis. For example, in XISA [6,5], summaries consist of instances of inductive definitions and inductive segments derived from user-supplied checkers. However, because their exact form is unimportant here, we leave them unspecified. Instead, in this section, we focus on *fully unfolded separating shape graphs*, or *unfolded graphs* for short, that consist only of points-to edges.[1]

The rest of the analysis state is straightforward and mostly standard. We have an environment E that maps variables to their *addresses*, which allows us to model address-of-locals (i.e., &x), as in our prior work [6,5]. A base abstract domain $\mathbb{P}^\sharp$ tracks constraints on values (e.g., α, β). Overall, an analysis state is a finite disjunction of $\langle E, M, P\rangle$ tuples; we simply make explicit that symbolic values are existential variables at the analysis state-level. Recall from Sect. 2 that nodes correspond to values—typically base pointers of objects. The points-to relation $\alpha\,\ell \overset{q}{\mapsto} \beta\,r$ is an edge from α to β and represents a singleton memory cell (e.g., fields in the case of a field-splitting model for Java-like structures). The address expression ℓ and contents expression r allow for computing offsets from base values α and β, respectively. Finally, we allow edges to be decorated with properties q, which are used in the subsequent subsections. Note how memory layout properties (e.g., field size) can be captured on edges, while value properties (e.g., type of a value, range of an integer constant) refer to nodes. In particular, memory cells are modeled by *edges* not nodes as with traditional shape graphs.

To obtain separating shape graphs for Java-like structures (as in our prior work [6,5]), we simply define ℓ and r as shown inset. That is, we allow field offsets @f on the left but only base pointers on the right (ε indicates empty). Pictorially, we show

$$\begin{array}{l} \ell ::= \varepsilon \mid @f \\ r ::= \varepsilon \end{array}$$

an example separating shape graph (*ssg*) along with the corresponding separation logic formula (*sl*), two-valued structure (*2-val*), and informal box diagram (*boxes*) in the following:

---

[1] Unfolded graphs are analogous to TVLA's two-valued structures.

Example 1 (A Java-Like Structure with One Field).

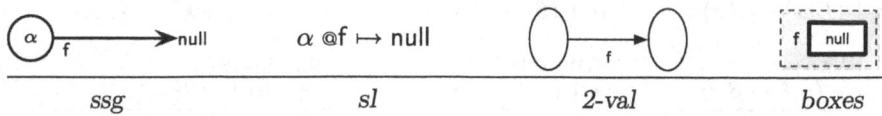

| ssg | sl | 2-val | boxes |

Kreiker *et al.* in a recent paper [18] present a "fine-grained semantics" in the context of TVLA using one node per component plus one node for the enclosing record in order to model pointer-to-field and nested structures. In Example 1, the two-valued structures we draw uses this one node per component model.[2] While the picture looks the same as Fig. 1a, the two-valued structure above represents an object with one field f not two objects.

In the subsequent sections, we consider low-level aspects of the C memory model. Note that we do not directly jump to a byte-level or assembly-level model, rather we want object-level notions like field names to coexist with lower-level aspects like numeric offsets. We first consider lowerings that are mostly compiler independent based solely on the semantics of C (Sect. 3.1) followed by those that are compiler dependent, such as field sizes (Sect. 3.2).

3.1   Compiler Independent Use of Aggregates

Internal Pointers. With individual fields exposed, the extension to internal pointers becomes clear. We simply need to allow field offset expressions on the right side of points-to in addition to the left side, instantiating ℓ and r as shown in the inset.

$$\ell ::= \varepsilon \mid @f$$
$$r ::= \ell$$

Example 2 (An Internal Pointer). A pointer to the g field of a structure is represented as follows:

$$\alpha @f \mapsto \beta @g$$
$$* \beta @g \mapsto \text{null}$$

| ssg | sl | 2-val | boxes |

Nested Structures. The base pointer of a nested structure is the field offset of its enclosing struct, so we need to allow for a path of field offsets with ℓ and r as defined in the inset. With nested structures, the contents or value of a field may be a record (i.e., another structure of subfields). Thus, in our representation, symbolic values may now take on record values $\{f_1 \colon \beta_1 \ r_1, \ldots, f_n \colon \beta_n \ r_n\}$ in addition to, for example, null and integers. As a consequence, we may need to

$$\ell ::= \varepsilon \mid \ell @f$$
$$r ::= \ell$$

---

[2] Note that in that paper, they also present a "coarse-grained semantics" that goes back to the one node per record model while retaining the ability to reference field pointers and nested structures. In addition to pointer-to-field and nested structures, we also consider untagged unions, field sizes, and array values in this paper.

VAR
$$\frac{(E(x) \mapsto \beta\, r) \in M}{x \downarrow (E(x) \mapsto \beta\, r)}$$

DEREF
$$\frac{e \Downarrow \beta\, r_1}{*e \downarrow (\beta\, r_1 \mapsto \gamma\, r_2)}$$

FIELDDEREF
$$\frac{e \Downarrow \beta\, r_1}{e{\to}f \downarrow (\beta\, r_1@f \mapsto \gamma\, r_2)}$$

RVAL
$$\frac{e \downarrow (\alpha\, \ell \mapsto \beta\, r)}{e \Downarrow \beta\, r}$$

ADDROF
$$\frac{e \downarrow (\alpha\, \ell \mapsto \beta\, r)}{\&e \Downarrow \alpha\, \ell}$$

FIELDOFFSET
$$\frac{e \downarrow (\alpha\, \ell \mapsto \beta\, r_1)}{e.f \downarrow (\alpha\, \ell@f \mapsto \gamma\, r_2)}$$

Fig. 6. Evaluation of program addressing expressions for structures

reduce between an edge containing a record and a set of edges of its components (essentially using definition (⋆) in Sect. 2).

Example 3 (Reduction for Nested Structures). Consider the following nested structure declaration: **typedef struct { struct { int i; int j; } t; } S;.** Then, the following is an example equivalence:

Thus far, we have been able to view all points-to edges as word-sized cells containing word-sized values. We now have irregularly-sized cells and values and thus want to ensure that updates at least respect cell size. We consider this issue further in Sect. 3.2.

Program Expression Evaluation. In an unfolded graph, pointer updates amount to the swinging of an edge. Such a destructive update is sound because of separation. To determine which edge to swing and how to update it, we traverse the graph starting from variables and following dereferences to find the edges corresponding the cell being written and the cells being read. To describe this traversal precisely, we define two judgments $e \downarrow_{E,M} (\alpha\, \ell \mapsto \beta\, r)$ and $e \Downarrow_{E,M} \beta\, r$ that evaluate a program expression e in an environment E and graph M to yield a cell and a value, respectively, in Fig. 6. These expressions allow dereferences of internal pointers, access of arbitrarily nested structures, and taking the address of any cell. To keep the rules concise, we elide the environment and graph parameters, as they are constant. Furthermore, we implicitly require that any edge appearing in the rules exists in the graph (though we show this side-condition explicitly in VAR as an example). The cell of a variable x is the one whose left side of points-to is the address given by the environment (VAR). Dereferences $*e$ and $e{\to}f$ follow an edge, that is, they get the value of their subexpression and find the edge whose left side of points-to is that value or that value plus the field offset, respectively (DEREF and FIELDDEREF). To find the value of an expression, we simply find the cell corresponding to the expression and yield the right side (i.e., the contents) (RVAL). The rule for the address-of operator $\&e$ (ADDROF) is more interesting in that its role as converting l-values into r-values is made evident. In particular, it makes sure the cell corresponding to e exists and then returns its address. Thus, l-expressions ℓ must be contained in r-expressions r to capture internal pointers, as addresses can be returned as values. The rule for the field offset expression $e.f$ (FIELDOFFSET) captures the shift from a points-to edge representing a record to edges for its components (see Example 3). Note that the cell evaluation judgment $e \downarrow (\alpha\,\ell \mapsto \beta\,r)$ is needed only for expressions $\&e$ and $e.f$ (i.e., the value evaluation judgment $e \Downarrow \beta\,r$ could be defined directly for x, $*e$, and $e{\rightarrow}f$ without it). Thus, in essence, the cell evaluation judgment captures the additional complexity of internal pointers (from $\&e$) and nested structures (from $e.f$). In fact, we include the FIELDDEREF rule even though the expression $e{\rightarrow}f$ is a synonym for $(*e).f$ as in C to emphasize this point. Now, the transfer function for an update can be captured extremely concisely with the following forward Hoare rule:

$$\frac{e \downarrow (\alpha\,\ell \mapsto \beta\,r) \qquad e' \Downarrow \beta'\,r'}{\{\alpha\,\ell \mapsto \beta\,r\}\ e := e'\ \{\alpha\,\ell \mapsto \beta'\,r'\}}$$

Note that this one rule captures updates to variables and fields given by arbitrary access paths involving '$*$', '.', and '$\&$' (but ignoring size constraints).

Analyzing C-Style Dynamic Memory Management. Intuitively, the transfer function for **free** should simply delete the outgoing points-to edges from the pointer being freed. However, according to C standard, **free** can only be called on pointers to the base address of an allocated block previously returned by **malloc**. For instance, in the code below, the pointer value &y cannot be passed to **free** because it was not returned by **malloc**:

```
S* x = (S*)malloc(sizeof(S)); S y = *x;
free(x) /* ok */; free(&y) /* fails */;
```

The address-of operator $\&e$ permits the creation of pointer values that are not necessarily returned by **malloc**. The analysis must therefore track the nodes that represent the base address of an allocated block along with those edges that make up the block. Such a "tag" for allocated blocks is an example of a property that naturally applies to nodes.

3.2   Compiler Dependencies Induced by Union Types

Thus far, we have focused on compiler independent modeling. However, one prevalent use of C is to access low-level features that are necessarily dependent on the compiler implementation. For example, a program may rely on sizes (e.g., int being 32-bits), address arithmetic, or a particular struct/object layout. In this section, we describe language features that are often used in a way dependent on the compiler implementation. Others have also realized that sometimes it is necessary to analyze code in a compiler-dependent manner (e.g., [20]).

Untagged Unions and Overlapping Cells. One such instance is dependence on multiple access paths mapping to the same memory location, which may occur

```
1  union {
2    struct { int f; int g; int h; } s;
3    long long l;
4  } x, y;
5  x.s.f = ...;
6  x.s.h = ...;
7  y.l = x.l;
```

(a) Union-manipulating code.   (b) An instance of the union type.

Fig. 7. An example to illustrate compiler dependence with C-style unions

with untagged unions in C. For example, consider the C code in Fig. 7. There are several questions that are compiler dependent. Will the write to `x.s.h` on line 6 modify `x.l`? Will the write on line 7 copy `x.s.f` and `x.s.g` to `y.s.f` and `y.s.g`? Should the read from `x.l` be allowed? Strictly according to the C specification, we might say no [16], but we might also want to analyze programs that use such assumptions. Furthermore, regardless of layout, a suitable representation must allow us to determine that the write to line 5 modifies `x.l` but not `x.s.g` and `x.s.h`. Note that the same kind of issues arise with type conversions and pointer arithmetic.

For such reasoning, we must expose byte-level offsets and field sizes. Offset expressions ℓ are now access paths p_{ath} as before (for compiler-independent accesses) or a path followed by a pair of a byte-level numeric offset o and an access path (for compiler-

$$\ell ::= p_{ath} \mid p_{ath} +o/p_{ath}$$
$$r ::= \ell$$
$$p_{ath} ::= \varepsilon \mid p_{ath}@f$$

dependent ones) as defined in the inset. The byte-level numeric offset is given by the compiler to correspond to the bundled access path. To expose field sizes, we annotate points-to edges with the size of the memory cell it represents as a compiler-provided integer sz (where necessary). We thus have edges of the following form: $\alpha \ \ell \mapsto \beta \ r$ or $\alpha \ \ell \overset{sz}{\mapsto} \beta \ r$. Note that this size information is a property of the memory cell and thus appears on the edge and not on the nodes.

These offset expressions allow us to express untagged unions directly. All fields of a union will have the same numeric offset but different access paths. Conceptually, with additional compiler-specific information about sizes, the analyzer can ensure that writes to any field will overwrite and remove the information about overlapping fields. Reading from a field that was not previously written can also be detected and either throw an error or rely on compiler dependent behaviors to interpret the data from the other field depending on the desired model. However, having a points-to edge for each union field would violate our representation invariant that all edges in the graph are separately conjoined. Union fields share the same concrete memory cells and thus are clearly not separate. What we want is some amount of local sharing (or use of non-separating conjunction) but we want to keep this additional complexity isolated.

To address this issue, we first introduce *memory region values* that correspond to memory regions on which there exists multiple views. In essence, to represent a union, the graph contains a points-to edge for the entire union and whose contents are points-to edges for the substructure. We notate a memory region value as follows: $[\,+o_1/p_{ath1} \overset{sz_1}{\mapsto} \gamma_1\ r_1\mid\cdots\mid +o_n/p_{ath_n} \overset{sz_n}{\mapsto} \gamma_n\ r_n\,]$.

Example 4 (Representing a Union). With memory region values, we represent an instance of the union type described in Fig. 7b (e.g., x) as follows:

$$\alpha \overset{12}{\mapsto} \beta \ \wedge \ \beta = [\,+0/\text{@s@f} \overset{4}{\mapsto} \gamma\mid +4/\text{@s@g} \overset{4}{\mapsto} \delta\mid +8/\text{@s@h} \overset{4}{\mapsto} \varepsilon\mid +0/\text{@l} \overset{8}{\mapsto} \eta\,]$$

Note the similarity of memory region values with record values for nested structures (Sect. 3.1). In particular, we can interpret memory region values as follows in separation logic:

$$\alpha\,\ell \overset{sz}{\mapsto} \beta \ \wedge \ \beta = [\,+o_1/p_{ath1} \overset{sz_1}{\mapsto} \beta_1\ r_1\mid\cdots\mid +o_n/p_{ath_n} \overset{sz_n}{\mapsto} \beta_n\ r_n\,]$$

$$\overset{\text{def}}{=} (\alpha\,\ell +o_1/p_{ath1} \overset{sz_1}{\mapsto} \beta_1\ r_1 * \textsf{true}) \ \wedge \ \cdots \ \wedge \ (\alpha\,\ell +o_n/p_{ath_n} \overset{sz_n}{\mapsto} \beta_n\ r_n * \textsf{true})$$

We write $\ell +o'/p_{ath}'$ for the concatenation of paths and offsets as appropriate (i.e., instantiating ℓ, we have two cases: $p_{ath} +o'/p_{ath}' \overset{\text{def}}{=} p_{ath} +o'/p_{ath}'$ and $+o/p_{ath} +o'/p_{ath}' \overset{\text{def}}{=} +(o+o')/p_{ath}\ p_{ath}'$ where $p_{ath}\ p_{ath}'$ is the concatenation of paths). Observe that the memory region edge (whose contents is a memory region value) encloses the complex sharing and can coexist with edges that do not have numeric offsets or even sizes. Also, note that with numeric offsets, it is tempting to compile away access paths into numeric offsets. However, doing so throws away useful object-level information.

At the same time, the above definition is not completely satisfactory from the point of view of representing unions entirely in the separating shape graph because of the use of non-separating conjunction ($\wedge$). Specifically, we desire a rule to push union edges of a memory region value into the graph (like for record values in Example 3). We observe that this use of non-separating conjunction is local to a node (i.e., it involves only outgoing points-to edges from α in the above). Thus, we simply need a mechanism to mark that a set of points-to edges from a node may share the same concrete memory cells (e.g., the edges on the right-side of the definition would be marked as such a set). The analyzer must then consider all of the points-to edges in the set simultaneously whenever one of them is updated. For example, the separating shape graph at program point 8 in Fig. 4 shows the edge labeled node@uni@s that is in fact one such shared edge. In the figure, we have elided other edges in its shared set; being more explicit, there are four edges in the set with the following addresses: β @node +0/@uni@s, β @node +0/@cst@value, β @node +0/@bin@l, and β @node +4/@bin@r. Note that one elegant way to keep track of which edges may share the same memory region is to apply the idea of fractional permissions [2,3]. Intuitively, reading from a union field requires only shared permission ($0 < permission < 1$) but writing to a union field requires exclusive permission ($permission = 1$) to ensure all other union fields are updated appropriately.

Compiler Independent Uses of Unions. Not all uses of unions depend on the compiler implementation like in Example 4. We may instead conservatively model that all branches of a union may overlap (e.g., x.s.h and x.l is not known to be disjoint). To do so, observe that the size and offsets need not correspond to sizes and offsets in bytes as long as they conservatively model overlap. For example, consider the following that conservatively approximates Example 4:

$$\alpha \overset{1}{\mapsto} \beta \;\land\; \beta = [\; +0/\text{@s@f} \overset{0.3}{\mapsto} \gamma \mid +0.3/\text{@s@g} \overset{0.3}{\mapsto} \delta \mid +0.6/\text{@s@h} \overset{0.4}{\mapsto} \varepsilon \mid +0/\text{@l} \overset{1}{\mapsto} \eta \;]$$

Here, we say $\alpha \mapsto \beta$ is of "unit size" and where the union fields s and l occupy the entire region; then, the structure fields within s divide up the region.

4   A C Memory Model as Separating Shape Graphs

In this section, we formalize a static analysis abstraction, instantiating the shape graphs introduced in Sect. 3, with explicit byte-level offsets and sizes.

A classical definition for memory states **Mem** is a finite map from values into values, that is, to let $\mathbf{Mem} = \mathbf{Val} \rightarrow_{\text{fin}} \mathbf{Val}$ where **Val** denotes machine values. However, this definition does not directly capture the properties we want to express and abstract. First, we need a detailed description of memory with fields, addresses, and sizes. Second, we need to account for memory management—we need to know for each byte, in which block it was allocated. Therefore, we adopt a lower-level and more precise definition here. Our definition is based on a notion of contiguous regions, that is, unbroken chunks of memory. A memory state is specified as a set of allocated regions, a subdivision of these chunks into fields, and a value mapping for each element of this subdivision. A contiguous region r is defined by its base address ba and its size in bytes sz. We use subscripts to indicate the region of a particular component (e.g., ba_r for the base address of region r). A region r then covers the range of addresses $R = [ba_r, ba_r + sz_r - 1]$. We say that regions r and r' are disjoint if and only if their ranges are disjoint (i.e., $R_r \cap R_{r'} = \emptyset$). A concrete memory state σ is a tuple (m, s, c) composed of the following:

- A *table of allocated memory chunks* m, which we model with a set of regions. These chunks represent allocation with **malloc** or on the stack.
- A *subdivision* s, which is a set of regions such that for all $r, r' \in s$, regions r and r' are disjoint, and for all $r \in s$, there exists an allocated memory chunk $k \in m$ such that $R_r \subseteq R_k$.
- A *content* function c, which consists of a function from s into content values such that for all regions $r = (ba_r, sz_r) \in s$ where $c(r)$ is defined, it denotes a value of sz_r bytes.

Two concrete memory states are equivalent if and only if their content functions describe the same address to byte mapping. In the following, we reason up to this equivalence and consider two equivalent memory states equal.

Figure 8a depicts an excerpt from a concrete store, which contains an Arith structure from Fig. 4 that represents the expression $-val$. Note that the Arith expression nodes do not have the same layout due to the union field in use. Each

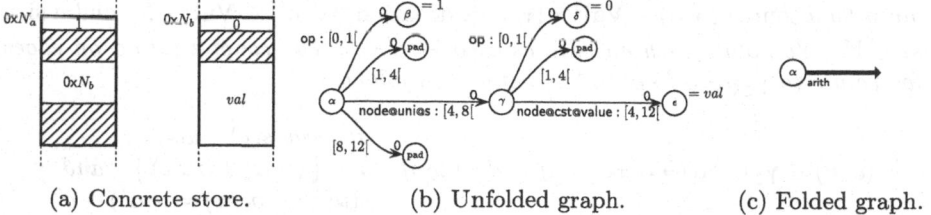

(a) Concrete store. (b) Unfolded graph. (c) Folded graph.

Fig. 8. Representation of an Arith object from Fig. 4

bold block corresponds to an allocated region (of size 12) and is partitioned into smaller regions that correspond to each field.

We can now describe the concretization of a separating shape graph $M \in \mathbb{M}^\sharp$ as a set of concrete stores σ. Recall from Fig. 5 that the analysis state contains an element $P \in \mathbb{P}^\sharp$ that tracks properties of values. For example, we may need numeric information (e.g., $\alpha = 42$) or to tag a value with its size (e.g., sizeof(β) = 8). To express the denotation of such an abstract element, we need to take into account the mapping of symbolic values $\alpha \in \mathbf{Val}^\sharp$ into values (e.g., addresses, integers, record values). This mapping is given by *valuations* $\nu : \mathbf{Val}^\sharp \rightarrow \mathbf{Val}$, which describes a physical mapping. Formally, the concretization is defined by

$$
\begin{aligned}
\gamma_{\mathbf{M}} : && \mathbb{M}^\sharp &\rightarrow \mathcal{P}(\mathbf{Mem} \times (\mathbf{Val}^\sharp \rightarrow \mathbf{Val})) \\
\gamma_{\mathbb{P}} : && \mathbb{P}^\sharp &\rightarrow \mathcal{P}(\mathbf{Val}^\sharp \rightarrow \mathbf{Val}) \\
\gamma : && \mathbb{D}^\sharp &\rightarrow \mathcal{P}(\mathbf{Mem}) \\
&\stackrel{\mathrm{def}}{=} (M, P) &\mapsto& \{ \sigma \in \mathbf{Mem} \mid \exists \nu.\ \nu \in \gamma_{\mathbb{P}}(P) \wedge (\sigma, \nu) \in \gamma_{\mathbf{M}}(M) \}
\end{aligned}
$$

where $\gamma_{\mathbf{M}}$ and $\gamma_{\mathbb{P}}$ are the concretization functions for separating graphs and elements of the base domain, respectively. The function γ is the concretization for the product domain $\mathbb{D}^\sharp$ of separating shape graphs and the base domain; note that the valuation ν connects the concretizations of the components M and P. In the following, we detail the main features of $\gamma_{\mathbf{M}}$, including how we concretize edges, disjoint regions, contiguous region summaries, and non-contiguous region summaries. We discuss these aspects in the context of the shape graphs in Fig. 8b and Fig. 8c that abstract the concrete store shown in Fig. 8a.

Concretizing Points-To Edges. A points-to edge models one memory cell with an address and contents. The address of the memory cell is represented by a base address—it's source node—and optionally an offset expression ℓ. Similarly, the contents of a memory is given by a base address—it's target node—and an optional offset. In the following, we use only byte-level offsets (i.e., $+o$), as symbolic access paths simply concretize to byte-level offsets in a compiler-dependent manner (e.g., @f lowers to $+$offset(f)). Similarly, we assume points-to edges have been annotated with the size of the cell they represent (e.g., by looking at field types in a compiler-dependent way).

Definition 1 (Concretization of Points-To Edges). *A* points-to edge *is given by a* source $(\alpha, o) \in \mathbf{Val}^{\sharp} \times \mathbb{N}$, *a* destination $(\alpha', o') \in \mathbf{Val}^{\sharp} \times \mathbb{N}$, *and a* size $sz \in \mathbb{N}$. *We notate such an edge as* $\alpha+o \overset{sz}{\mapsto} \alpha'+o'$. *The concretization on edges for points-to* $\gamma_{\mathcal{E}}(\alpha+o \overset{sz}{\mapsto} \alpha'+o')$ *is defined as follows:*

$$(\sigma, \nu) \in \gamma_{\mathcal{E}}(\alpha+o \overset{sz}{\mapsto} \alpha'+o') \quad \textit{if and only if} \quad \begin{array}{l} \sigma = (m, s, c) \quad \textit{and} \\ s = \{(\nu(\alpha) + o, sz)\} \quad \textit{and} \\ c(\nu(\alpha) + o, sz) = \nu(\alpha') + o' \end{array}$$

That is, the concrete memory is a single region with base address $\nu(\alpha) + o$ *and size* sz *with contents* $\nu(\alpha') + o'$. *Note that* ν *should interpret* α' *as an sz-bytes value (while we keep this implicit here, type and size information of values should be tracked in practice).*

Offsets o, o' are integers. Hence, this presentation allows for a straightforward handling of field-level pointer arithmetic. For instance in Fig. 8b, the edge drawn from α to γ is annotated with the range $[4, 8[$ and the target offset 0: it corresponds to a memory cell of size 4, with base address $\nu(\alpha) + 4$, and with contents $\nu(\gamma)$ and thus concretizes to part of the concrete store shown in Fig. 8a assuming $\nu(\alpha) = 0\mathrm{x}N_a$ and $\nu(\gamma) = 0\mathrm{x}N_b$.

Concretizing Disjoint Memory Chunks. Recall from Sect. 2 and Sect. 3 that in a separating shape graph, distinct edges stand for disjoint chunks of memory (assuming unions are represented as memory region values). Thus, the concretization of a graph is the union of the concretizations of each edge with a disjointness or separation constraint. This constraint is analogous to formulas in separation logic conjoined with $*$; however, to treat allocated memory explicitly, we give direct a formalization here. For the moment, assume that the graph M is fully unfolded (i.e., contains only points-to edges), then we define $\gamma_{\mathbf{M}}(M)$ as the set of all $(\sigma, \nu) \in \mathbf{Mem} \times (\mathbf{Val}^{\sharp} \to \mathbf{Val})$ where $\sigma = (m, s, c)$ and such that

- For each node α in graph M, if α is the base address of a memory region of size sz, then region $(\nu(\alpha), sz)$ belongs to m. In other words, the concrete memory state σ has an allocated region at $\nu(\alpha)$ of size sz.
- There exists a family of memory states $(\sigma_e)_{e \in M}$ such that

$$\sigma = *\{\sigma_e \mid e \in M\} \quad \text{and} \quad \sigma_e \in \gamma_{\mathcal{E}}(e) \text{ for all } e \in M$$

where we write $e \in M$ for an edge e in graph M and overload $\sigma_1 * \sigma_2$ on concrete states to mean the combining of disjoint memories σ_1 and σ_2. That is, memory state σ can be partitioned into a set of memory states that are the contributions of each of the edges of the graph.

A C **struct** consists of a set of contiguous cells. For instance, the concrete store presented in Fig. 8a is abstracted by the unfolded graph of Fig. 8b where each edge corresponds to a subregion of the concrete store. Note that to be completely explicit, some edges correspond to padding generated as part of the compiler-dependent lowering (no information is ever available about the content nodes).

In the remainder of this section, we consider the concretization of memory region values introduced in Sect. 3.2 to capture C-style unions (Sect. 4.1) and of inductive summaries (Sect. 4.2). Section 4.3 sums up the analysis operations using this instantiation of separating shape graphs.

4.1 Concretizing Contiguous Regions

Arrays and Points-To Edges over Non-Constant Ranges. Arrays correspond to contiguous sequences of bytes in memory, so sized points-to edges can be used to capture array values. For a fixed-length array, we can split it into a points-to edge for each cell, but we can also choose to represent it as one large cell and abstract its contents with a dedicated array domain (e.g., [12,13,15]) as part of $\mathbb{P}^\sharp$. With a slight extension to allow field sizes and offsets to be expressed symbolically (i.e., in terms of symbolic values), we can also model non-fixed-length arrays as one large region or some finite number of chunks. The base domain $\mathbb{P}^\sharp$ should express range and congruence constraints about that offset, like in Miné [20]. This representation is similar in purpose to iterated separating conjunction [22], but we generally want the entire contents to be modeled as a single value.

In certain cases, using one large cell may be desirable, as existing array abstractions can be re-used together with our shape abstraction. Thus, we can avoid a need to reason precisely about indexing expressions in the shape domain. At the same time, this choice potentially limits the interaction between the domains making it more difficult to analyze code that, for example, have an inductive structure using arrays of pointers.

Untagged Unions and Overlapping Regions. As alluded to Sect. 3.2, memory region values are key to capturing untagged unions or in general multiple regions for the same memory region.

Definition 2 (Concretization of Memory Region Values). *A multi-view points-to edge is a points-to to a memory region value, that is,* $\alpha + o \overset{sz}{\mapsto} \beta$ *and* $\beta = [\, o_1 \overset{sz_1}{\mapsto} \alpha'_1 \, o'_1 \mid \cdots \mid o_n \overset{sz_n}{\mapsto} \alpha'_n \, o'_n \,]$ *such that for all i such that* $1 \leq i \leq n$, $o_i + sz_i \leq sz$. *The concretization of such a family of edges is the set of pairs* (σ, ν) *such that* $\sigma = (m, s, c)$ *where* $s = \{\, (\nu(\alpha) + o, sz) \,\}$ *and* $\mathbf{read}(c, \nu(\alpha) + o + o_i, sz_i) = \nu(\alpha'_i) + o'_i$ *(for all i). The operation* $\mathbf{read}(c, v, sz)$ *stands for the sz-bytes value that can be read in contents c from address v. In other words, the concrete memory is a single region given by the points-to edge* $\alpha + o \overset{sz}{\mapsto} \beta$ *but whose contents are also described by each of the views of* β.

4.2 Summarizing Complex Regions Using Inductive Definitions

Recall that we summarize non-contiguous regions of unbounded size with *checker edges* that correspond to inductive structures. As in our prior work [6,5], we take advantage of user-supplied inductively-defined checkers c and generate summaries that correspond to complete and partial structures. In particular, a *checker edge* $(\alpha + o).c(\delta)$ is an instance of an inductive checker definition c, and a *segment edge* $(\alpha+o).c(\delta) \twoheadleftarrow (\alpha'+o').c'(\delta')$ is a partial derivation of checker c from $\alpha+o$ up to $\alpha'+o'$ and expecting checker c'.

We give here an *indirect* definition of the concretization of graphs containing summary edges: in a first step, we unfold shape graphs into fully unfolded shape graphs with no summary edges; in a second step, we concretize these using the previously defined concretization. This definition captures the same notion of inductively-defined regions as our previous definition [6,5], yet we take this indirect approach here since it extends more cleanly to the case where we take allocated regions into account. As a notation, we write $(M, P) \rightsquigarrow (M', P')$ to mean that the pair of graph and base domain element (M', P') can be obtained from (M, P) by unfolding one summary edge in M once. As inductive checkers include data constraints, unfolding updates both the graph and the base domain element.

Definition 3 (Concretization of a Graph with Summary Edges). *The concretization* $\gamma_{\mathbf{M}}(M)$ *is the set of pairs* (σ, ν) *such that* $(M, \top) \rightsquigarrow^* (M', P')$, M' *is fully unfolded,* $\sigma \in \gamma_{\mathbf{M}}(M')$, *and* $\nu \in \gamma_{\mathbb{P}}(P')$. *Note that we write* $\top$ *for the top element of the base domain (i.e., no data constraints) and* $\rightsquigarrow^*$ *for the reflexive-transitive closure of* $\rightsquigarrow$.

Returning to the syntax tree example from Fig. 4, a user-supplied checker for arith may specify that op serves as the discriminator:

```
t.arith() :=
    if (t.op = 0) then true
    else if (t.op = 1) then t.node.uni.s.arith()
    else if (t.op >= 2) then t.node.bin.l.arith() and t.node.bin.r.arith()
```

(i.e., 0 is for constants, 1 is a unary operator, and ≥ 2 are binary operators). This checker translates to the following low-level definition with compiler-specific offsets and sizes made explicit (which could be obtained from the C types):

$\pi.\mathbf{arith}() :=$
$\langle \pi@\mathtt{op} \xmapsto{1} \beta * \pi@\mathtt{node} \xmapsto{8} \gamma, \mathbf{alloc}(\pi, 12) \wedge \beta = 0 \wedge$
$\quad \gamma = [+0/@\mathtt{cst@value} \xmapsto{8} \delta_1 \mid +0/@\mathtt{uni@s} \xmapsto{4} \delta_2 \mid +0/@\mathtt{bin@l} \xmapsto{4} \delta_3 \mid +4/@\mathtt{bin@r} \xmapsto{4} \delta_4] \rangle$
$\vee \langle \pi@\mathtt{op} \xmapsto{1} \beta * \pi@\mathtt{node} \xmapsto{8} \gamma * \delta_2.\mathbf{arith}(), \mathbf{alloc}(\pi, 12) \wedge \beta = 1 \wedge \gamma = \ldots \rangle$
$\vee \langle \pi@\mathtt{op} \xmapsto{1} \beta * \pi@\mathtt{node} \xmapsto{8} \gamma * \delta_3.\mathbf{arith}() * \delta_4.\mathbf{arith}(), \mathbf{alloc}(\pi, 12) \wedge \beta \geq 2 \wedge \gamma = \ldots \rangle$

The predicate **alloc** expresses that a base address is an allocated region of a particular size. We note that Fig. 8b is one of the unfolded versions of Fig. 8c; that is, Fig. 8c abstracts the concrete store of Fig. 8a.

4.3   Shape Analysis for Compiler-Dependent C

Given a concrete operation $\Phi : \mathbf{Mem} \to \mathbf{Mem}$, the corresponding abstract transfer function $\Phi^\sharp : \mathbb{D}^\sharp \to \mathbb{D}^\sharp$ should be sound, that is, for all $D \in \mathbb{D}^\sharp$ and for all $\sigma \in \gamma(D)$, it is the case that $\Phi(\sigma) \in \gamma(\Phi^\sharp(D))$. In other words, performing the operation at the abstract level does not lose any concrete behavior.

Transfer Functions and Materialization. To reflect assignment statements and conditional guards, transfer functions evaluate expressions to cells and values using the rules given in Fig. 6 to determine which edges should be modified. However, in many cases, the edges corresponding to subexpressions are not readily available in shape graphs. They need to be materialized, that is, we need to concretize part of the summarized regions so that the appropriate points-to edges are revealed. Since materialization is a partial concretization operation, we now have two ways to materialize: for non-contiguous regions (Sect. 4.2) and for contiguous regions (Sect. 4.1). The former case corresponds to unfolding an inductive summary and is described in detail in our previous work [5]; the latter case corresponds to splitting a subpart of a points-to edge and is new to our framework. To describe this new materialization operation, we write $\mathbf{extract}_{[i,j[}(\alpha)$ for the operation that extracts bytes i to j from the value represented by α. Now, if $0 \le sz_0 < sz$, then the following pair of edges and constraints can be materialized from the edge $\alpha + o \overset{sz}{\mapsto} \alpha'$:

$$\alpha + o \overset{sz_0}{\mapsto} \alpha'_0 \; * \; \alpha + (o + s_0) \overset{sz - sz_0}{\mapsto} \alpha'_1$$
$$\text{where} \quad \alpha'_0 = \mathbf{extract}_{[0,s_0[}(\alpha') \quad \text{and} \quad \alpha'_1 = \mathbf{extract}_{[s_0,s[}(\alpha')$$

The two last constraints are represented (in a conservative way) in $\mathbb{P}^\sharp$. This rule allows, for example, to materialize a single array cell from a whole array value.

Memory Management Operators. To model a successful call to **malloc**, the analysis creates a fresh memory region value β tagged with the size of the allocated area; it then creates a points-to edge of that size to β. To analyze a call to **free**, we need to materialize the entire region to free based on the allocated-size predicate on the node. We then check that the region to free was indeed allocated before discarding the edges corresponding to the region. The pointer to the address of the freed block becomes dangling (i.e., all outgoing edges are removed). Parkinson [21] has also described this need to track allocated regions.

Widening. To enforce termination, we use a *widening* operator, which was extensively described in our prior work [6,5]. What is particularly interesting is that this operator requires minimal changes to accommodate the new kinds of edges introduced in this paper. Intuitively, the widening relies only on the graph structure, which is conserved by our extensions in this paper. It is sound (i.e., computes an over-approximation of concrete joins) and terminating (there is no infinite, non-converging sequence of widening iterates).

5   Implementation and Timing Results

We have extended the memory model of XISA to reflect the features introduced in Sect. 4, including support for nested structures, pointers to internal fields, numerical offsets and sizes, memory region values, and base address of allocated blocks (to check **malloc** and **free** in a sound manner). The overall structure of

Table 1. Benchmark results for verifying shape preservation. We show the size of the benchmark in lines of code (number of lines of the relevant function), the analysis time, the maximum number of disjuncts at any program point (Peak Disj.), and the maximum number of iterations at any point (Iter.).

Benchmark	Size (loc)	Time (sec)	Peak Disj. (num)	Iter. (num)
traversal	20	0.036	8	2
eval	70	0.060	24	2x2
remsub	37	0.116	8	2
distribute	41	0.144	14	2
move_neg_up	120	0.488	38	2

unfolding and folding (widening) algorithms remained largely unchanged; there were only small, local extensions to deal with the new annotations on points-to edges. Code that was analyzable by the previous XISA implementation is analyzable with this finer model. Support for arrays does not yet exist, primarily because it would require a more expressive numerical domain $\mathbb{P}^{\sharp}$ and extensions to the base domain interface.

Table 1 shows some implementation results that require this refined memory model. These examples are algorithms that traverse and/or modify in place a syntax tree structure like the one shown in Fig. 4. They evaluate or simplify arithmetic expressions (e.g., by distributivity) and delete or create new nodes as needed. In the table, we show analysis times, the maximum number of disjuncts at any program point, and the number of widening iterations needed in each loop (in the case of the "eval" example, we give numbers for each nested loops). The low values for number of iterations provides evidence that our widening operator enforces quick convergence while retaining precise results. We note that the peak number of disjuncts is rather high in the last example. This high number is due to the presence of nested if-statements that lead to successive unfolding of several levels of checker edges. Since we only try to collapse disjuncts at widening points, this implementation choice results in an exponential number of disjuncts in short code sections. Better heuristics to control the maximal number of disjuncts could improve performance, though we leave this to future work.

6   Related Work

The use of shape graphs for approximating unbounded structures dates back to at least Jones and Muchnick [17]. Their design and use have formed the basis of several steps in the development of shape analysis. Sagiv *et al.* [23] defined an early version of materialization with shape graphs that was subsequently refined in TVLA [24] with the perspective of "partial concretization" and the ability to simultaneously express both *may* and *must* relations between objects. A line of subsequent work has looked at compacting this representation (e.g., by merging similar graphs [19]). Traditionally, shape graphs have been applied on Java-like structures using the the "object-as-node" paradigm. Very recently, Kreiker *et al.* [18] have formulated an extended memory model in the TVLA framework to reason about pointers to nested structures. They describe shape graph models that capture nested structures and internal pointers using both "field-as-node" and "object-as-node" paradigms. In contrast, separating shape graphs take a "cell-as-edge" approach inspired by separation logic [22], which we use to separate object or value-level properties on nodes from field or component-level properties on edges.

There has also been a line of work that builds shape analyzers around formulas in separation logic (e.g., [11,14,6]). In the last few years, significant progress has been made in handling realistic C code. For example, Berdine *et al.* [1] handle composite data structures, such as lists of lists, and Yang *et al.* [26] have looked at a ≈10,000 line device driver. Nonetheless, the focus has been on Java-like structures (i.e., limited reasoning on internal pointers or layout dependent features). One exception is Calcagno *et al.* [4] that have described a low-level analyzer with pointer arithmetic inside memory blocks.

There are also program analyzers, such as Miné [20], that address many low-level aspects of C, including unions and pointer casts, but they are not typically concerned with dynamic memory allocation and unbounded structures as in shape analysis. Another class of tools focuses on being as concrete as possible potentially trading off some automation or exhaustiveness. We take a different angle where we want a representation that supports user-guided abstraction. The HAVOC tool [7] combines reachability predicates with pointer arithmetic reasoning and has been applied to verify low-level properties of system drivers [9]. Clarke *et al.* [8] give a low-level encoding of C features for model checking. Xie and Aiken [25] perform exact bit-level encoding with bounded symbolic execution.

7   Conclusion

In this paper, we propose separating shape graphs as an abstraction that can handle typical, high-level data types and low-level aspects of C in a compositional manner. From the analysis point of view, the main result is that existing algorithms for unfolding and widening of shape abstractions are mostly unaffected in this extended framework.

Acknowledgments. We thank Jörg Kreiker, Antoine Miné, Hongseok Yang, Matthew Parkinson and Peter O'Hearn for stimulating discussions.

References

1. Berdine, J., Calcagno, C., Cook, B., Distefano, D., O'Hearn, P.W., Wies, T., Yang, H.: Shape analysis for composite data structures. In: Damm, W., Hermanns, H. (eds.) CAV 2007. LNCS, vol. 4590, pp. 178–192. Springer, Heidelberg (2007)
2. Bornat, R., Calcagno, C., O'Hearn, P.W., Parkinson, M.J.: Permission accounting in separation logic. In: Principles of Program. Lang., POPL (2005)
3. Boyland, J.: Checking interference with fractional permissions. In: Cousot, R. (ed.) SAS 2003. LNCS, vol. 2694. Springer, Heidelberg (2003)

4. Calcagno, C., Distefano, D., O'Hearn, P.W., Yang, H.: Beyond reachability: Shape abstraction in the presence of pointer arithmetic. In: Static Analysis, SAS (2006)
5. Chang, B.-Y.E., Rival, X.: Relational inductive shape analysis. In: Principles of Program. Lang., POPL (2008)
6. Chang, B.-Y.E., Rival, X., Necula, G.C.: Shape analysis with structural invariant checkers. In: Riis Nielson, H., Filé, G. (eds.) SAS 2007. LNCS, vol. 4634, pp. 384–401. Springer, Heidelberg (2007)
7. Chatterjee, S., Lahiri, S.K., Qadeer, S., Rakamaric, Z.: A reachability predicate for analyzing low-level software. In: Grumberg, O., Huth, M. (eds.) TACAS 2007. LNCS, vol. 4424, pp. 19–33. Springer, Heidelberg (2007)
8. Clarke, E.M., Kroening, D., Lerda, F.: A tool for checking ANSI-C programs. In: Jensen, K., Podelski, A. (eds.) TACAS 2004. LNCS, vol. 2988, pp. 168–176. Springer, Heidelberg (2004)
9. Condit, J., Hackett, B., Lahiri, S.K., Qadeer, S.: Unifying type checking and property checking for low-level code. In: Principles of Program. Lang., POPL (2009)
10. Cousot, P., Cousot, R.: Abstract interpretation: A unified lattice model for static analysis of programs by construction or approximation of fixpoints. In: Principles of Program. Lang., POPL (1977)
11. Distefano, D., O'Hearn, P.W., Yang, H.: A local shape analysis based on separation logic. In: Hermanns, H., Palsberg, J. (eds.) TACAS 2006. LNCS, vol. 3920, pp. 287–302. Springer, Heidelberg (2006)
12. Gopan, D., Reps, T., Sagiv, M.: A framework for numeric analysis of array operations. In: Principles of Program. Lang., POPL (2005)
13. Gulwani, S., McCloskey, B., Tiwari, A.: Lifting abstract interpreters to quantified logical domains. In: Principles of Program. Lang., POPL (2008)
14. Guo, B., Vachharajani, N., August, D.I.: Shape analysis with inductive recursion synthesis. In: Program. Lang. Design and Implementation, PLDI (2007)
15. Halbwachs, N., Péron, M.: Discovering properties about arrays in simple programs. In: Program. Lang. Design and Implementation, PLDI (2008)
16. Harbison III, S., Steele Jr., G.: A Reference Manual. Prentice Hall, Englewood Cliffs (2002)
17. Jones, N.D., Muchnick, S.S.: Flow analysis and optimization of LISP-like structures. In: Program Flow Analysis: Theory and Applications, vol. 4 (1981)
18. Kreiker, J., Seidl, H., Vojdani, V.: Shape analysis of low-level overlapping structures. In: Verif., Model Checking, and Abstract Interp, VMCAI (2010)
19. Manevich, R., Sagiv, M., Ramalingam, G., Field, J.: Partially disjunctive heap abstraction. In: Giacobazzi, R. (ed.) SAS 2004. LNCS, vol. 3148, pp. 265–279. Springer, Heidelberg (2004)
20. Miné, A.: Field-sensitive value analysis of embedded c programs with union types and pointer arithmetics. In: Lang. Compilers Tools Embed. Syst., LCTES (2006)
21. Parkinson, M.: Local reasoning for Java. PhD thesis, U. of Cambridge (2005)
22. Reynolds, J.C.: Separation logic: A logic for shared mutable data structures. In: Logic in Computer Science, LICS (2002)
23. Sagiv, M., Reps, T., Wilhelm, R.: Solving shape-analysis problems in languages with destructive updating. ACM Trans. Program. Lang. Syst. 20(1) (1998)
24. Sagiv, M., Reps, T., Wilhelm, R.: Parametric shape analysis via 3-valued logic. ACM Trans. Program. Lang. Syst. 24(3) (2002)
25. Xie, Y., Aiken, A.: Scalable error detection using boolean satisfiability. In: Principles of Program. Lang., POPL (2005)
26. Yang, H., Lee, O., Berdine, J., Calcagno, C., Cook, B., Distefano, D., O'Hearn, P.W.: Scalable shape analysis for systems code. In: Gupta, A., Malik, S. (eds.) CAV 2008. LNCS, vol. 5123, pp. 385–398. Springer, Heidelberg (2008)

Deadlock-Free Channels and Locks

K. Rustan M. Leino[0], Peter Müller[1], and Jan Smans[2]

[0] Microsoft Research, Redmond, WA, USA
leino@microsoft.com
[1] ETH Zurich, Switzerland
peter.mueller@inf.ethz.ch
[2] KU Leuven, Belgium
jan.smans@cs.kuleuven.be

Abstract. The combination of message passing and locking to protect shared state is a useful concurrency pattern. However, programs that employ this pattern are susceptible to deadlock. That is, the execution may reach a state where each thread in a set waits for another thread in that set to release a lock or send a message.

This paper proposes a modular verification technique that prevents deadlocks in programs that use both message passing and locking. The approach prevents deadlocks by enforcing two rules: (0) a blocking receive is allowed only if another thread holds an obligation to send and (1) each thread must perform acquire and receive operations in accordance with a global order. The approach is proven sound and has been implemented in the Chalice program verifier.

0 Introduction

Concurrent threads of execution communicate and synchronize using various paradigms. One paradigm is to let threads have shared access to certain memory locations, but to insist that each thread accesses the shared memory only when holding a mutual-exclusion lock. Two familiar programming errors that can occur with this paradigm are forgetting to acquire a lock when accessing shared state and *deadlocks*, that is, not preventing situations where in a set of threads each is waiting to acquire a lock that some other thread in the set is currently holding. Another paradigm is to let threads synchronize by sending and receiving messages along channels. In a pure setting with channels, there are no shared memory locations and data is instead included in the messages. Deadlocks are possible programming errors in this setting, too. Here, a deadlock occurs when a set of threads each is waiting to receive a message from another thread in the set.

Because each of these two paradigms is especially natural for solving certain kinds of problems, there are also situations where one wants to use a combination of the paradigms. For example, consider a concurrently accessed binary tree protected by mutual-exclusion locks. An iterator of this data structure uses locks to read elements from the tree, but may choose to provide these elements to clients via channels, which are more suitable for that task. In the combined setting, a deadlock occurs when a set of threads each waits for another thread in that set to release a lock or send a message.

In this paper, we consider program verification in the combined setting. In particular, we present a technique for specifying programs in such a way that they can be verified

A.D. Gordon (Ed.): ESOP 2010, LNCS 6012, pp. 407–426, 2010.

to be free of deadlock. Our technique is *modular*, meaning that the verifier can be run on each part of a program separately. We consider multiple-writer, multiple-reader, copy-free channels with infinite slack, that is, with non-blocking sends. The channels are first class, meaning they can themselves be stored as shared data or passed along channels. We describe the work in the context of the prototype language and verifier Chalice.

This paper is structured as follows. Sec. 1 describes the existing features of the Chalice program verifier that are relevant to this paper. In Sec. 2 and 3, we extend Chalice with channels and show how deadlock can be avoided. The formal details of the verification technique together with a soundness proof are then given in Sec. 4 and 5.

1   Background on Chalice

Chalice [21,22] is a programming language and program verifier for concurrent programming. The language supports dynamically allocated objects and allows programs to include *contracts* (specifications). The verifier detects common bugs such as data races, null dereferences, violations of assertions and other contracts, and deadlocks. If a program passes the verifier, it is compiled (via C#) to executable code for the .NET platform. The executable code is free of contracts and ghost state, which the verifier confirmed to hold and which were used only to make the verification go through. In this section, we highlight Chalice's features that are relevant to this paper: permissions, locks, and deadlock prevention; see [22] for a full tutorial.

1.0   Permissions

Verification in Chalice centers around permissions and permission transfer. Conceptually, each activation record holds a set of permissions. A memory location can be read or written by an activation record only if it has permission to do so. In this paper, we do not distinguish between read and write permissions, but see [21]. We denote the permission to access the field f of an object o by **acc**(o.f). Our implementation provides *predicates* to abstract over permissions and to express permissions of whole object structures [22], but we omit them here for simplicity. Permissions are part of the ghost state used to reason about programs, but they are not represented in executable code.

The set of permissions held by an activation record can change over time. More specifically, when a new object is created, the creating activation record gains access to the fields of the new object. For example, when the method Main of Fig. 0 creates the object a, it gets permission to access a.balance, and thus it is allowed to set a.balance to 10 on the next line. In a similar fashion, Main receives permission to access b.balance when creating b. The fourth statement of Main is a method call: **call** b.SetBalance(20);. Execution of a method call starts by pushing a new activation record onto the stack. What permissions does this new activation record initially have? The answer to this question is determined by looking at the precondition (keyword **requires**) of SetBalance, which indicates that the caller must hold the permission to access **this**.balance. This permission transfers from the caller to the callee on entry to the method. In a similar fashion, the postcondition (keyword **ensures**) indicates what permissions transfer from the callee to the caller when the method returns. In our example, Main gives away its permission to access b.balance when it calls

```
class Account {
  var balance: int;

  invariant acc(this.balance);

  method SetBalance(a: int)
    requires acc(balance);
    ensures acc(balance) && balance == a;
  { balance := a; }

  method Transfer(from: Account, to: Account, amount: int)
    requires waitlevel << from.mu && from.mu << to.mu;
  {
    acquire from;
    acquire to;
    fork tok := to.SetBalance(to.balance + amount);
    call from.SetBalance(from.balance - amount);
    join tok;
    release to;
    release from;
  }

  method Main()
  {
    var a := new Account;
    a.balance := 10;
    var b := new Account;
    call b.SetBalance(20);
    share a above waitlevel; share b above a;
    call Transfer(a, b, 5);
  }
}
```

Fig. 0. A small Chalice program illustrating permissions, permission transfer, locks, and deadlock prevention

b.SetBalance(20). The activation record b.SetBalance(20) uses this permission to justify its update of b.balance, and then passes the permission back to the caller. That is, SetBalance effectively just borrows the permission from Main; in general, however, a method need not always return the permissions stipulated by its precondition.

If an activation record does not return the permissions that it may still hold at the end of the method, then those permissions are lost forever. In effect, this renders some fields inaccessible. We say that the method *leaks* the permissions, which is allowed.[1]

In addition to calls, Chalice supports **fork** statements. Just like an ordinary call, execution of a **fork** statement leads to the creation of a new activation record. However,

---

[1] The Chalice verifier has a -checkLeaks option that verifies the absence of leaking. An unused object can then be returned to the system, along with the permissions to its fields.

the new activation record is not pushed onto the current stack, but rather a new thread with its own stack is created and the callee is executed by the new thread. A **fork** operation is non-blocking. That is, the forking thread does not wait for the forkee to run to completion; instead, the forking and forked threads execute concurrently. Using a **join** statement, one thread can wait for another to complete. More specifically, **fork** returns a token, and a **join** on a token causes the joining thread to wait for the completion of the thread corresponding to the token. A token is allowed to be joined only once. Similarly to an ordinary call statement, the activation record that does the **fork** loses the permissions entailed by the precondition of the forkee, and the activation record that completes the corresponding **join** gains the permissions entailed by the postcondition. In our example, the forked activation record for SetBalance (in the method Transfer) obtains access permission to from.balance, and this permission is returned at the join statement.

Note that each **call** statement can be considered to be syntactic sugar for a **fork** statement immediately followed by a corresponding **join**.

Chalice enforces that when one thread holds full permission to a memory location, then no other thread can hold any permission to that memory location. This prevents race conditions and lets the verifier reason about data invariants in the presence of multiple threads.

1.1 Locks

The machinery introduced so far allows synchronization and permission transfer between threads only when threads are forked or joined. However, access to shared data such as a shared buffer requires various threads to obtain and relinquish permissions while the threads are running. Access to shared data can be synchronized using mutual-exclusion *locks*. In Chalice, a lock can hold access permissions, just like an activation record can. Therefore, a thread can pass permissions to another thread by first transferring them to a lock, which allows the other thread to obtain them from the lock.

An object in Chalice can be in one of three states: *not-a-lock*, *available*, and *held*. The object transitions between these states upon execution of a **share**, **acquire**, or **release** statement. A newly allocated object starts in the *not-a-lock* state, where it cannot be used as a lock. The **share** statement initializes a *not-a-lock* object as a lock and transitions the object to the *available* state. The **acquire** operation waits until the object is in the *available* state and then transitions it to the *held* state. The **release** operation transitions the object back to *available*.

A class can declare a *lock invariant* (keyword **invariant**), which indicates, for each lock corresponding to an instance of the class, what permissions are held by the lock when the lock is in the *available* state. For example, the **invariant** declaration in class Account of Fig. 0 indicates that the lock corresponding to an Account object o holds permission to the field o.balance. In other words, the lock o protects o.balance. When an activation record puts an object into the *available* state (by a **share** or **release** operation), it transfers the permissions entailed by the object's invariant to the lock. Conversely, the permissions held by the lock are transferred to an activation record when it completes an **acquire** operation on the lock.

So, when a thread wants to access a shared memory location, it uses an **acquire** operation to compete for the lock that protects the location. Upon successful acquisition of the lock, the permissions held by the lock are transferred to the acquiring thread. When the thread is done accessing the location, it uses the **release** operation to release the lock and transfer the permissions back into the lock. For example, the method Transfer in Fig. 0 locks the shared Account objects from and to to gain access to their balance fields.

Note that it is the mechanism of permissions that prevents data races. Lock acquisition is one way to obtain permissions, but the act of holding a lock does not by itself imply any rights to access memory.

1.2   Deadlock Prevention

To ensure mutual exclusion, the **acquire** operation suspends the execution of the acquiring thread until the requested lock can be given to that thread. A well-behaved program makes sure that other threads will eventually make such a lock available.

Chalice prevents deadlocks by breaking cycles among acquiring threads. This is done by letting a program associate each lock with a *wait level* and then checking that the program acquires the locks in strict ascending order. The wait levels are values from a set Mu, which is a dense partial order with a bottom element. Chalice uses $<<$ to denote the strict partial order on Mu. A program specifies the wait level of a lock using the **share** statement, which takes an optional **between** ... **and** ... clause. Alternatively, a clause **above** ... or **below** ... may be used if only one bound is given. By default, the **share** statement uses **above waitlevel**, where **waitlevel** denotes the highest lock currently held by the thread. For example, method Main in Fig. 0 shares a and b to make them available for locking. Since b is shared above a, a thread that holds b is not allowed to acquire a.

The wait level of an object is recorded in a ghost field called mu. In this paper, we assume mu to be immutable, that is, once a lock has been shared with a certain wait level, that level cannot change. Our previous work [21] permits dynamic lock re-ordering, which we omit here to focus on the essentials. Since mu is immutable, accesses to mu do not require any permissions. In Fig. 0, Transfer's precondition demands (0) that the current thread only hold locks whose wait level is strictly below from.mu and (1) that from's level lie below to's level.

2   Channels

A channel is an unbounded message buffer with two operations, **send** and **receive**. The former operation adds a message to the buffer, while the latter blocks until a message becomes available, removes that message from the buffer, and returns it to the receiving thread. A channel may declare a *message invariant* (keyword **where**), which constrains the messages sent over the channel and also specifies permissions that are transferred over the channel along with each message.

As an example, consider the program of Fig. 1. The first two lines declare a new channel type Ch with two parameters p0 and p1. These parameters indicate that each

412   K.R.M. Leino, P. Müller, and J. Smans

message for a Ch channel object consists of two Person objects. The **where** clause states that each message in a Ch channel carries the permissions for accessing the age field of the persons passed as parameters. In addition, it specifies that p0 must be at least 18 years old. The method Main creates two persons, cooper and dylan, sends a message on the channel ch, and finally receives a message on that channel. When an activation record sends a message, the permissions entailed by the **where** clause transfer from the sender to the message. Similarly, when a message is received, the permissions in the message transfer to the receiving activation record. The mechanism makes the channels *copy-less*, because only the object references among the message parameters, not the data fields accessed from those references, are sent over the channel.

```
channel Ch(p0: Person, p1: Person)
  where acc(p0.age) && acc(p1.age) && 18 <= p0.age;

class Person {
  var age: int;

  method Main() {
    var cooper := new Person; var dylan := new Person; cooper.age := 62;
    var ch := new Ch;
    send ch(cooper, dylan);
    // ...
    receive a, b := ch;
  }
}
```

Fig. 1. Declaration of a channel type Ch and a Main method that sends and receives

Note that, analogous to the semantics of pre- and postconditions and lock invariants, it is an error if at a **send** statement the sender lacks the permissions entailed by the message invariant or if the other constraints in the message invariant are not satisfied. For instance, if we omitted the update cooper.age := 62;, then the verifier would report that the last constraint in the **where** clause does not hold.

A program using channels can deadlock if a thread is blocked on a **receive** statement, waiting for a message that is never sent. For example, consider the following code snippet.

```
ch := new Ch;
receive a, b := ch; // deadlock
```

This program deadlocks, since the thread is blocked forever at the **receive** statement. To avoid such deadlocks, we impose the restriction that a thread may perform a **receive** statement only if there are sufficient messages in the channel or other threads hold obligations to send. We enforce the restriction as follows.

In addition to permissions, each activation record holds a number of credits. We denote the right to receive n messages ($0 \le n$) on channel ch by **credit**(ch, n). The obligation to send n messages on ch is denoted by **credit**(ch, -n). We sometimes refer to a negative credit as a debt. **credit** predicates can be used in specifications. Multiple occurrences of a **credit** predicate are equivalent to one predicate with the sum of the credits, that is, **credit**(ch,i) && **credit**(ch,j) is the same as **credit**(ch,i+j).

A **receive** statement is allowed only if the activation record holds at least one credit on the corresponding channel. Execution of a **receive** statement decreases the number of credits by one. Conversely, a **send** statement increases the number of credits by one. However, threads can always send messages without regard to the number of credits. While positive credits (permissions to receive) can be leaked at the end of method bodies, negative credits (obligations to send) must always be returned to the caller. These rules enforce the invariant that the total sum of the number of credits for a channel Ch never exceeds the number of items stored in the channel.

Just like permissions can be transferred between activation records (specified by **requires** and **ensures**), so can credits. For example, in the program in Fig. 2, the Main method transfers a debt to Producer. That is, Main decreases its balance for ch by -1, resulting in a positive balance for Main. Consequently, Producer starts with an obligation to send and Main has obtained permission to receive. Main then transfers a credit to Consumer, resulting in a 0 credit balance for Main.

Also, just like permissions can be stored in lock invariants and message invariants, so can *positive* credits. For example, every message with a non-negative x parameter in Fig. 2 entails a credit. Thus, in effect, Producer puts into each such message a promise that it will send yet another message, and this credit sent along the channel allows Consumer to "pay" for its next **receive** operation.

Storing negative credits in lock or message invariants is not allowed. Since a program need not acquire all available locks or receive all sent messages eventually, allowing negative credits here would be a way to hide debt. We enforce this requirement by a simple proof obligation for each lock and message invariant. Moreover, a **call** is allowed only if transferring the credits entailed by the precondition does not bring the caller into debt. This requirement is necessary to prevent a thread from creating a credit by a simple local method call. The callee could use the credit to receive, but the caller, which has the obligation to send and which executes in the same thread, would never continue its execution, and the program deadlocks. This restriction does not apply to **fork**, because there the forker will continue its execution and, thus, can live up to is obligation to send.

The credit accounting introduced so far handles channels with blocking receives and non-blocking sends. We can also support channels with finite slack (that is, blocking sends) by distinguishing between the receive credits described above and send credits. We omit a discussion of this extension because it does not reveal anything interesting.

In many languages, channels can be implemented using locks and condition variables. Channels have the advantage that each send operation earns a credit because it puts a message in the buffer. In contrast, a signal operation on a condition variable is lost when no thread is currently waiting on the condition variable. Therefore, one cannot decide locally whether a signal operation earned a credit or not. This difference makes it much harder to prove deadlock freedom for condition variables than for channels.

```
channel Ch(x: int) where 0 <= x ==> credit(this, 1);

class ProducerConsumer {
    method Produce(ch: Ch)
        requires credit(ch, -1);
    {
        var i := 0;
        while(i < 10)
            invariant 0 <= i && i <= 10 && credit(ch, -1);
        { send ch(i); i := i + 1; }

        send ch(-1);
    }

    method Consume(ch: Ch)
        requires credit(ch, 1) && waitlevel << ch.mu;
    {
        var x: int;
        receive x := ch;
        while(0 <= x)
            invariant waitlevel << ch.mu;
            invariant 0 <= x ==> credit(ch, 1);
        { receive x := ch; }
    }

    method Main() {
        var ch := new Ch;
        fork Produce(ch);
        fork Consume(ch);
    }
}
```

Fig. 2. Producer/Consumer example illustrating the use of channels. Operator ==> denotes short-circuit boolean implication. The loop invariant (keyword **invariant**) specifies what is given to each new iteration and what must be returned by each completed iteration.

3 Global Wait Order

The rules described in the previous section enforce the invariant that, for each receiving thread, either the corresponding channel contains a message or a thread holds the obligation to send. However, this invariant does not suffice to rule out deadlocks. A deadlock can still occur if execution reaches a state where a subset of the running threads is waiting for another thread in that set to send a message.

As an example, consider the program of Fig. 3. Both the main thread and the forkee block at their respective **receive** statements and wait forever for the other to send. A similar situation can occur when combining locks and channels. For example, the main thread in Fig. 4 waits for a message on channel ch, while the forkee waits for the main thread to release the lock. Note that both of these programs satisfy the rules described in the previous section. In particular, at each **receive** statement, the credits held by the activation record on the corresponding channel are strictly positive and no debt is leaked at the end of methods.

In the combined setting with locks and channels, we say a deadlock occurs if each of a set of threads is waiting for another thread in that set to either send a message or release a lock (or formally, if the graph corresponding to a configuration as defined in Definition 2 contains a cycle). We break cycles and prevent deadlocks in the combined setting by using a global wait order that includes locks and channels. Just as locks, channels have a wait level that is stored in the ghost field mu. For channels, the ghost field mu is set (using a **between** clause) when the channel is created. Receiving on a channel ch requires ch.mu to be larger than **waitlevel**. We redefine **waitlevel** as the larger of: the largest object whose lock is held by the thread and the largest channel for which the thread has an obligation to send.

The additional restrictions outlined above cause verification of the programs in Figs. 3 and 4 to fail. The first program does not verify (and cannot be made to verify by adding further specifications) because ch0.mu and ch1.mu cannot both be larger than the other. This means that either the **receive** statement in the main thread or in the forkee is disallowed, as the wait level of the corresponding channel does not lie above **waitlevel** of the respective thread. The second program does not verify because either the lock in the acquire statement in M or the channel of the **receive** statement in the main thread does not lie above **waitlevel** of the respective thread.

Besides **acquire** and **receive**, **join** is the third Chalice statement that might cause a thread to wait and is, thus, relevant for deadlock prevention. For instance, a thread might wait to receive a message before terminating while another thread joins the first thread before sending the awaited message. In this paper, we encode **join** statements via channels: Each method receives an extra parameter, a channel, and an obligation to send one message on that channel. Before forking, the forker must create a new channel

```
channel Ch() where true;

class Program {
  method M(ch0: Ch, ch1: Ch)
    requires ch0 != ch1;
    requires credit(ch0, 1) && credit(ch1, -1);
  { receive ch0; send ch1(); }

  method Main() {
    var ch0 := new Ch; var ch1 := new Ch;
    fork M(ch0, ch1);
    receive ch1; send ch0();
  }
}
```

Fig. 3. A program that deadlocks using just channels

```
channel Ch() where true;

class Program {
  method M(ch: Ch)
    requires credit(ch, -1);
  { acquire this; send ch(); release this; }

  method Main() {
    var ch := new Ch;
    acquire this;
    fork M(ch);
    receive ch;
    release this;
  }
}
```

Fig. 4. A program that deadlocks using channels and locks

above its wait level and pass it to the forkee. The forkee must send a message on that channel right before it terminates. A thread can then join another thread by receiving on the designated channel. The obligation to send on the designated channel increases the wait level of the forkee above the wait level of the forker, which prevents cyclic waiting. In this encoding, a **call** statement is encoded by a **fork** immediately followed by a **join**. This encoding simplifies the presentation of the proof rules and the soundness argument; programs may still contain **call** and **join** statements.

4   Verification

In this section, we make the informal rules described in previous sections precise. We define the proof rules for the most interesting statements by translating them into a pseudo-code language, whose weakest precondition semantics is obvious. In this translation, we use **assert** statements to denote proof obligations and **assume** statements to state assumptions that can be used to prove the assertions. We encode the heap as a two-dimensional array that maps object references and field names to values. The current heap is denoted by the global variable *Heap*. To avoid clutter, we omit null reference checking from the formalization. A program verifier can be built from these rules by writing the pseudo code in an intermediate verification language like Boogie [2]. In fact, the pseudo code we use is essentially Boogie 2, and this is how we implemented the Chalice verifier.

4.0   Encoding of Permissions and Credits

Conceptually, each activation record holds a number of permissions and credits. We track permissions during verification via a global variable $\mathcal{P}$. $\mathcal{P}$ is a two-dimensional map from object references and field names to permissions. For simplicity, we encode permissions as boolean values in this paper, but the Chalice verifier supports fractional permissions [21]. An activation record has access to o.f if and only if $\mathcal{P}[o, f]$ equals **true**.

In a similar fashion, we track credits via a global variable $\mathcal{C}$, a map from channel instances to integers. $\mathcal{C}[o]$ denotes the number of credits held by the current activation record for the channel o.

4.1 Encoding of Locks and Wait Levels

Our encoding introduces a thread-local variable λ, which yields the set of all objects whose locks are held by the thread of the current activation record.

The Chalice expression **waitlevel** is then encoded as the maximum of the wait levels of locks held by the current activation record and of channels for which the current activation record has an obligation to send:

$$\textbf{waitlevel} \quad \equiv \quad max(\{\ o.mu \mid o \in \lambda\ \} \cup \{\ c.mu \mid \mathcal{C}[c] < 0\ \})$$

For convenience, we will use **waitlevel** in the pseudo code below as an abbreviation for this encoding.

4.2 Encoding of Permission and Credit Transfer

In Chalice, permissions and credits often transfer from and to activation records. For each statement, the set of permissions and credits being transferred is described by an assertion. For example, when a message is sent, the permissions and credits described by the channel's **where** clause transfer from the activation record to the message. Similarly, when a lock is acquired, the permissions and credits described by the lock invariant transfer from the lock to the acquiring activation record. In our verification, we model permission and credit transfer via two operations, Inhale and Exhale. The former operation adds the permissions and credits described by an assertion to the activation record's $\mathcal{P}$ and $\mathcal{C}$, while the latter removes them.

The definitions for Inhale and Exhale are shown in Fig. 5. When an activation record obtains permission to access o.f by inhaling the permission, we assign an arbitrary value to $Heap[o.f]$ (keyword **havoc**) since other threads may have updated the location while it was not accessible to the current thread. Inhaling **credit**(ch, n) increases the number of credits for ch by n. Inhaling a conjunction P && Q corresponds to first inhaling P and afterwards inhaling Q. If the inhaled assertion is a pure boolean expression (that is, contains neither access nor credit predicates), we assume the expression holds.

Exhaling permission to access o.f corresponds to removing the permission. However, exhaling permissions is allowed only if the permission is present. Exhaling credits corresponds to decrementing the credit map. Exhaling a conjunction P && Q corresponds to first exhaling P and afterwards exhaling Q. Finally, exhaling a pure assertion corresponds to proving that the assertion holds.

$$\mathsf{Inhale}[\![\mathbf{acc(o.f)}]\!] \equiv$$
$$\mathbf{havoc}\ Heap[o,f];$$
$$\mathcal{P}[o,f]:=\mathbf{true};$$

$$\mathsf{Exhale}[\![\mathbf{acc(o.f)}]\!] \equiv$$
$$\mathbf{assert}\ \mathcal{P}[o,f]=\mathbf{true};$$
$$\mathcal{P}[o,f]:=\mathbf{false};$$

$$\mathsf{Inhale}[\![\mathbf{credit(ch,\ n)}]\!] \equiv$$
$$\mathcal{C}[ch]:=\mathcal{C}[ch]+n;$$

$$\mathsf{Exhale}[\![\mathbf{credit(ch,\ n)}]\!] \equiv$$
$$\mathcal{C}[ch]:=\mathcal{C}[ch]-n;$$

$$\mathsf{Inhale}[\![P\ \&\&\ Q]\!] \equiv$$
$$\mathsf{Inhale}[\![P]\!];$$
$$\mathsf{Inhale}[\![Q]\!];$$

$$\mathsf{Exhale}[\![P\ \&\&\ Q]\!] \equiv$$
$$\mathsf{Exhale}[\![P]\!];$$
$$\mathsf{Exhale}[\![Q]\!];$$

Otherwise :
$$\mathsf{Inhale}[\![E]\!] \equiv$$
$$\mathbf{assume}\ E;$$

Otherwise :
$$\mathsf{Exhale}[\![E]\!] \equiv$$
$$\mathbf{assert}\ E;$$

Fig. 5. Transfer of permissions and credits via Inhale and Exhale.

4.3 Encoding of Channel Operations

Channels support three operations: creation, sending, and receiving. The translation to pseudo code for each of these statements is shown in Fig. 6.

$$\mathtt{x} := \mathbf{new}\ \mathtt{Ch}\ \mathbf{between}\ \mathtt{1}\ \mathbf{and}\ \mathtt{u};\ \equiv$$
$$\mathbf{assert}\ l << u;$$
$$\mathbf{havoc}\ x;$$
$$\mathbf{assume}\ \mathcal{C}[x]=0;$$
$$\mathbf{assume}\ Heap[x,mu] << u;$$
$$\mathbf{assume}\ l << Heap[x,mu];$$

$$\mathbf{send}\ \mathtt{ch(x_1,\ldots,x_n)};\ \equiv$$
$$\mathcal{C}[ch] := \mathcal{C}[ch]+1;$$
$$\mathsf{Exhale}[\![W[ch/\mathbf{this},\ x_1/y_1,\ldots,x_n/y_n]]\!];$$

$$\mathbf{receive}\ \mathtt{x_1,\ldots,x_n} := \mathtt{ch};\ \equiv$$
$$\mathbf{assert\ waitlevel} << ch.mu;$$
$$\mathbf{assert}\ 0 < \mathcal{C}[ch];$$
$$\mathcal{C}[ch] := \mathcal{C}[ch]-1;$$
$$\mathsf{Inhale}[\![W[ch/\mathbf{this},\ x_1/y_1,\ldots,x_n/y_n]]\!];$$

Fig. 6. Translation to pseudo code for channel operations. For **new**, we omitted some details that encode that the new channel is different from all previously existing channels. For **send** and **receive**, ch is assumed to have type **channel** Ch(y_1: t_1, ..., y_n: t_n) **where** W.

A channel creation $\mathtt{x} := \mathbf{new}\ \mathtt{Ch}\ \mathbf{between}\ \mathtt{1}\ \mathbf{and}\ \mathtt{u}$; creates a new channel whose mu field lies between l and u.[2] To guarantee a wait level exists that lies between l and u, we first check that l is strictly smaller than u. Then, we assign an arbitrary channel identifier to x, such that the current thread has no credits for that channel x and such that $l << x.mu << u$.

The statement **send** ch(x_1, ..., x_n); adds a new message to the channel ch and earns a credit, which is reflected in the credit map of the sending activation record. The permissions and credits described by the **where** clause transfer from the activation record to the message (encoded by Exhale).

---

[2] For simplicity, we consider only a single lower and upper bound. However, our implementation supports an arbitrary number of bounds.

The statement **receive** x_1, ..., x_n := ch; removes a message from the channel ch. Receiving is allowed only if **waitlevel** is smaller than the wait level of ch and if the current activation record holds at least one credit for ch. Since receiving removes a message from the channel, the number of credits is decremented by one. The permissions and credits described by the **where** clause transfer from the message to the receiving activation record.

4.4 Encoding of Fork, Join, and Call

As described at the end of Sec. 3, we encode **join** statements via channels, and **call** statements via **fork** and **join**. In this encoding, we make the following modifications for each method m(p: T) **returns** (r: R) with precondition P and postcondition Q in a class C: (0) We declare a channel type Ch_m(t: C, p: T, r: R) **where** Q';. Q' is Q with t substituted for **this**. (1) We add a parameter j: Ch_m to m. (2) We add a precondition **credit**(j, -1) to m, which expresses that the method has an obligation to send a message on the join-channel j. (3) We add a precondition j.mu << u_i.mu for each channel expression u_i that occurs in a credit expression in m's precondition P. This precondition allows m to receive on the channels u_i even though it has a debt for channel j. (4) At the end of m's body, we place a send statement **send** j(**this**, p, r);. This send lives up to the obligation expressed by the precondition (2). (5) We remove the postcondition Q from m because all information, permissions, and credits are conveyed to the caller via the send operation (4).

We encode **fork** tok := x.m(y) as **var** tok := **new** Ch_m **above waitlevel** . **below** u_1, ..., u_n; **fork** x.m(y, tok);. That is, a **fork** passes a new channel instance to the forkee and transfers the permissions and credits described by the forkee's precondition P. The wait level of the join-channel lies above **waitlevel**, but below each channel u_i that occurs in a credit expression in m's precondition. This allows the forker to join the forkee and it allows the forkee to perform receive statements on the channels u_i. To allow the forkee to acquire locks, one also has to ensure that the wait level of the join-channel tok is below each lock that the forkee might want to acquire. Choosing such a level is possible, but we omit the details for simplicity.

We encode **join** z := tok; by receiving on the channel we passed to the thread when it was forked: **var** t: C; **var** p: T; **receive** t,p,z := tok;. This receive inhales the message invariant of Ch_m (that is, the joined thread's postcondition) and transfers permissions and credits accordingly.

We translate a call **call** z := x.m(y); into a fork immediately followed by a join: **fork** tok := x.m(y); **join** z := tok;, which are then further encoded as described above. This encoding automatically satisfies the rule that a call must not create a debt in the caller (see Sec. 2).

5 Deadlock Freedom

In this section, we prove that the verification technique described in the previous sections indeed prevents deadlocks. However, we provide only the key definitions and lemmas. For the full proof, we refer the reader to [23].

Note that our verification technique proves partial correctness, that is, it considers non-terminating methods to be correct. As a consequence, we do not prevent situations where a thread waits forever on another thread to send a message or release a lock, and that other thread ran into an infinite loop or recursion before executing the awaited operation. Proving termination of loops and recursion is an orthogonal issue.

5.0   Language

For the proof of deadlock freedom, we use a smaller programming language that omits all features that are not relevant for the proof such as permissions, classes, and the heap.

We prove soundness with respect to the language of Fig. 7. A program consists of a number of declarations and a main routine $\overline{s}$. A declaration is either a channel or a procedure. Each channel has a channel name, channel parameters, and a **where** clause. Each procedure has a procedure name, procedure parameters, a precondition, and a body. A statement is an object creation, a send or receive operation, a fork statement, an acquire statement, or a release statement. Finally, an assertion is either credit (of $+1$) or debt (of -1). Note that we do not distinguish objects and channels, and we use both terms interchangeably in the soundness proof.

$$
\begin{array}{rcl}
program & ::= & \overline{decl}\ \overline{s} \\
decl & ::= & channel \mid procedure \\
channel & ::= & \textbf{channel}\ C(\overline{x})\ \textbf{where}\ \overline{\phi}; \\
procedure & ::= & \textbf{procedure}\ m(\overline{x})\ \textbf{requires}\ \overline{\phi};\ \{\ \overline{s}\ \} \\
s & ::= & x := \textbf{new}\ C;\ \mid\ \textbf{send}\ x(\overline{x});\ \mid\ \textbf{receive}\ \overline{x} := x;\ \mid \\
& & \textbf{fork}\ m(\overline{x});\ \mid\ \textbf{acquire}\ x;\ \mid\ \textbf{release}\ x; \\
\phi & ::= & \textbf{credit}(x)\ \mid\ \textbf{debt}(x)
\end{array}
$$

Fig. 7. A small language with lockable channels

$\mathcal{O}$ is the set of object references, Mu the set of wait levels, and $\mathcal{X}$ the set of variables. The set Mu with the binary operator $<<$ forms a dense partial order. L is a function that maps each object reference to its wait level. We consider only channels whose **where** clause does not contain debt.

5.1   Execution Semantics

Definition 0 shows that threads can be in one of three states: *running, done,* and *aborted.* The job of the program verifier is to ensure that threads do not perform illegal operations and hence that no thread ends up in the *aborted* state. We say that a configuration is *aborting* if one or more threads is in the *aborted* state. A configuration is *final* if each thread is in the *done* state.

Definition 0. *A thread state* σ *is one of the following:*

- $\textbf{run}(\overline{s}, \Gamma)$, *indicating the thread is running with remaining statement* $\overline{s}$ *and environment* Γ. Γ *is a partial function from variable names to object references.*

– **done**, *indicating the thread has completed.*
– **aborted**, *indicating the thread has performed an illegal operation.*

Definition 1. *A configuration ψ is a pair consisting of:*

- Ω, *a partial function from object references to environment lists. Each environment in the list represents a message. Thus, $\Omega(o)$ denotes the list of messages inside channel o. We say that an object is* allocated *if $o \in \text{dom}(\Omega)$.*
- T, *a multiset of threads. Each thread is a triple $(\sigma, \kappa, \lambda)$. σ is a thread state, κ is a function from object references to integers, and λ is a set of object references. $\kappa(o)$ denotes the number of credits held by the thread and λ is the set of objects locked by the thread.*

Execution of programs is defined by the small-step relation $\rightarrow$ shown in Fig. 8. The rules of Fig. 8 contain premises marked dark gray and premises marked light gray. A premise marked dark gray indicates that threads must block and wait for the premise to become true. For example, a receive statement blocks until the corresponding channel contains a message (*i.e.*, $0 < \text{length}(\Omega(o))$). A premise marked light gray that does not hold indicates that the thread has performed an illegal operation and that the thread can transition to the aborted state. For example, a thread trying to execute a receive statement transfers to the aborted state if the number of credits ($\kappa(o)$) is not strictly positive.

As explained earlier, the job of the program verifier is to ensure that threads do not abort. In other words, the verifier must ensure that the premises marked light gray hold. As a consequence, these premises correspond to the assert statements in the pseudo code of Sec. 4.

$\text{def}(C)$ denotes the definition of channel C in the program. Each object has a corresponding type denoted by $\text{typeof}(o)$. $\text{credits}(\bar{\phi}, \Gamma)$ returns a function from object references to integers, where an entry for channel o indicates the credit associated with

$$\Gamma(x) = o \qquad \forall i \in \{1, \ldots, n\} \bullet \Gamma(x_i) = o_i$$
$$\text{typeof}(o) = C \qquad \text{def}(C) = \textbf{channel } C(y_1, \ldots, y_n) \textbf{ where } \bar{\phi};$$
$$\Gamma' = [\textbf{this} \mapsto o, y_1 \mapsto o_1, \ldots, y_n \mapsto o_n]$$
$$\kappa' = \text{credits}(\bar{\phi}, \Gamma') \qquad \kappa'' = \kappa[o \mapsto \kappa[o] + 1] - \kappa' \qquad \Omega' = \Omega[o \mapsto \Omega(o) + \Gamma']$$
$$\overline{(\Omega, \{(\textbf{run}(\textbf{send } x(x_1, \ldots, x_n); \ \bar{s}, \Gamma), \kappa, \lambda)\} \cup T) \rightarrow}$$
$$(\Omega', \{(\textbf{run}(\bar{s}, \Gamma), \kappa'', \lambda)\} \cup T)$$

$$\Gamma(x) = o$$
$$\text{typeof}(o) = C \qquad \text{def}(C) = \textbf{channel } C(y_1, \ldots, y_n) \textbf{ where } \bar{\phi}; \qquad 0 < \kappa(o)$$
$$\forall q \in \text{dom}(\Omega) \bullet (\kappa(q) < 0 \lor q \in \lambda) \Rightarrow \text{L}(q) << \text{L}(o) \qquad 0 < \text{length}(\Omega(o))$$
$$\Gamma' = \text{head}(\Omega(o)) \qquad \kappa' = \text{credits}(\bar{\phi}, \Gamma') \qquad \kappa'' = \kappa[o \mapsto \kappa[o] - 1] + \kappa'$$
$$\Omega' = \Omega[o \mapsto \text{tail}(\Omega)] \qquad \Gamma'' = \Gamma[x_1 \mapsto \Gamma'(y_1), \ldots, x_n \mapsto \Gamma'(y_n)]$$
$$\overline{(\Omega, \{(\textbf{run}(\textbf{receive } x_1, \ldots, x_n := x; \ \bar{s}, \Gamma), \kappa, \lambda)\} \cup T) \rightarrow}$$
$$(\Omega', \{(\textbf{run}(\bar{s}, \Gamma''), \kappa'', \lambda)\} \cup T)$$

Fig. 8. Execution semantics for well-formed programs (see [23] for all rules)

the assertion $\overline{\phi}$ for o. $f[a \mapsto b]$ denotes an update of the function f at a with b. If typeof$(o) = C$ and def$(C) = $ **channel** $C(\overline{y})$ **where** $\overline{\phi}$;, then $\Phi(o)$ denotes $\overline{\phi}$.

5.2 Properties

The key property we want to prove is Theorem 2: programs written in the language of Fig. 7 do not get stuck. The proof of this theorem relies on two other theorems, 0 and 1. Theorem 0 states that for each allocated channel c, the total number of credits for c (in activation records and messages) is at most the sum of the amount of debt for c and the number of messages inside c.

Theorem 0. *Suppose* $(\Omega, \{(\sigma_1, \kappa_1, \lambda_1), \ldots, (\sigma_n, \kappa_n, \lambda_n)\})$ *is a configuration reached by an execution of a well-formed program. Then for each channel* $o \in$ dom(Ω), *the following holds:*

$$0 \leq \text{length}(\Omega(o)) - ((\Sigma_{i \in \{1,\ldots,n\}} \kappa_i(o)) + (\Sigma_{q \in dom(\Omega), \Gamma \in \Omega(q)} \text{credits}(\Phi(q), \Gamma)(o)))$$

The proof runs by induction on the length of the execution and by case analysis on the step taken.

Each configuration ψ has a corresponding graph whose nodes are the threads in ψ. This graph contains an edge from thread f to t if f is waiting for t to send a message or to release a lock (see Definition 2). A *deadlock* occurs if the graph contains a cycle. Theorem 1 states that an edge in the graph between f and t implies that t's wait level is smaller than f's wait level. It follows from Theorem 1 that configurations reached by executions of well-formed programs are deadlock-free.

Definition 2. *Each configuration* $(\Omega, \{(\sigma_1, \kappa_1, \lambda_1), \ldots, (\sigma_n, \kappa_n, \lambda_n)\})$ *has a corresponding graph. The nodes in the graph are threads. The graph has an edge from* $(\sigma_f, \kappa_f, \lambda_f)$ *to* $(\sigma_t, \kappa_t, \lambda_t)$ *if one of the following holds:*

- *Thread f waits for t to send a message, that is,* σ_f *equals* **run**$(\text{receive } x; \overline{s}, \Gamma)$, $\kappa_t(\Gamma(x)) < 0$, *and* σ_f *cannot go to the aborted state.*
- *Thread f waits for t to release a lock, that is,* σ_f *equals* **run**$(\text{acquire } x; \overline{s}, \Gamma)$, $\Gamma(x) \in \lambda_t$, *and* σ_f *cannot go to the aborted state.*

Theorem 1. *Suppose the graph corresponding to a configuration in which no thread is aborted contains an edge from* $(\sigma_f, \kappa_f, \lambda_f)$ *to* $(\sigma_t, \kappa_t, \lambda_t)$. *Then the following holds:*

$$\max\{L(o)|\kappa_f(o) < 0 \vee o \in \lambda_f\} << \max\{L(o)|\kappa_t(o) < 0 \vee o \in \lambda_t\}$$

The proof runs by induction on the length of the execution and by case analysis on the step taken.

Theorem 2. *Suppose* ψ *is a non-final, non-aborting configuration. Then,* ψ *is not stuck.*

Proof. It follows from Theorem 1 that the graph contains a non-final thread t that has no outgoing edges. We have to consider three cases. If the first statement of t is not an acquire or a receive, then t can make progress. If t's first statement is a receive statement for channel o, then no other thread holds debt for o (otherwise t would have an outgoing edge). If $\kappa(o) \leqslant 0$, then the thread can make progress by aborting; otherwise, it follows from Theorem 0 that o contains at least one message and therefore that the thread can make progress. Finally, if the first statement is an acquire for object o, then no other thread holds o's lock (otherwise t would have an outgoing edge). Therefore, t can acquire o.

6 Related Work

Hoare's model of Communicating Sequential Processes (CSP) influentially set the style of languages that communicate over channels [13]. Channels in CSP have no slack, that is, they have no buffer capacity. This means that send and receive operations are executed in a synchronized fashion to form a rendezvous. The channels are named entities, not dynamically created values that can be stored in variables or passed along channels.

Newsqueak is a language that features channels and shared global variables [26]. Like CSP, Newsqueak uses zero-slack channels, but the channels are first class and can be passed around like other references to data structures in memory. After the rendezvous of a sender and receiver, the sender gets a chance to compute its message before it is communicated to the receiver. The language has support for atomic increment and decrement operations, but does not include built-in locking primitives.

The programming language Alef [35] and its successor Limbo [28] apply ideas of Newsqueak to larger programming-language designs. Limbo was designed and used for writing applications for the Inferno operating system. The languages include shared global variables, and locks are provided (Alef) or can be built from channels.

A language with channels that has had considerable success is Erlang [1], a functional language (hence, locks are irrelevant) used in a variety of applications.

Language support for mutual-exclusion locks is provided in several languages, including Modula-3, Java, and C#. Such languages may provide channels in a library, like ConcurrentLinkedQueue in Java's java.util.concurrent library.

The idea of using permissions to avoid data races was first formulated by Boyland [4] and has been adopted by concurrent separation logic [25]. Several researchers extended concurrent separation logic to handle dynamic thread creation [10,15,12], rely/guarantee [31,8], reentrant locking [11], and channels [14,27]. Our encoding of permissions in a first-order setting was inspired by implicit dynamic frames [29].

Enforcing the absence of deadlocks by checking that threads acquire locks in accordance with a global order is a well-known technique from operating systems and databases, and has been implemented in several verifiers [6,9,16,17] and static analyzers [20,3]. To the best of our knowledge, the only existing technique that prevents deadlocks in programs that use channels is Kobayashi's type system for the π-calculus [19]. A channel type in this type system consists of a message type and a usage. The usage describes the order of channel operations and associates an obligation and capability level with each of those operations. The notion of credits in our approach is similar to usages, while wait levels are similar to obligation and capability levels. Kobayashi's type system has two advantages with respect to our approach. First, fewer annotations are required as types can be inferred. Secondly, his approach can handle some programs that we cannot, such as encoding locks via channels. However, the type system has only been applied in the context of the π-calculus, while we integrate deadlock prevention into a verification system for an object-oriented language (which Kobayashi considers to be "useful and important" [18]).

Session types [32,7] are a technique for checking that channels are used in accordance with a predefined protocol. Recently, Villard et al. [34] have integrated the ideas from session types into separation logic. However, the focus of [32,7,34] lies in checking conformance of the code with the channel contract and in ensuring memory safety, i.e., that a memory location is not accessed after sending the corresponding permission over a channel. We do not specifically address protocol checking (though protocols can be encoded via ghost state), but we do check memory safety and in addition show how to enforce the absence of deadlocks.

Luecke et al. [24] and Vetter et al. [33] propose run-time deadlock detection algorithms for systems that use message passing. These algorithms may miss certain deadlocks. Moreover, run-time testing cannot guarantee the absence of deadlocks, since not all paths, thread interleavings, and input values can be considered.

Terauchi and Megacz [30] use ideas similar to those proposed in this paper in a static inference of channel buffer bounds. Their analysis uses a capability mapping per thread, a function from channel identifiers to natural numbers similar to our credit map, to track the number of messages that can be sent for each channel. Just as our credit map, the capability mapping is updated at send and receive statements. Another idea shared by both approaches is that capabilities can be transferred via channels. In particular, each channel type includes a capability mapping (similar to our **where** annotation) that describes what capabilities transfer along with messages on channels of that type.

The verification approach presented in this paper prevents non-termination caused by deadlock. However, infinite recursion and loops can still lead to non-terminating executions. For example, a thread may fail to acquire a lock because the thread holding the lock is stuck in an infinite loop. Proving termination of loops and recursion is a separate issue, which for instance can be solved using techniques like [5] and [0].

This paper builds on and extends our earlier work on the Chalice verifier [21]. In particular, we extend Chalice with channels, introduce credits, and insert channels into the wait order to prevent deadlocks involving blocking channel operations.

7   Conclusion

The key contribution of this paper is that it shows how to verify the absence of deadlocks in programs that combine channels and locking. In particular, deadlocks are prevented by enforcing two rules: (0) a blocking receive is allowed only if another thread holds the obligation to send and (1) receive and acquire operations must be done in accordance to a global wait order. The verification technique has been proven sound and was implemented in the Chalice program verifier. As future work, we plan to apply the presented methodology to classical concurrency examples and case studies from programs written in languages that support channels such as Scala and Go. Moreover, we are interested in combining our methodology with termination checking to guarantee that every obligation to send will eventually be fulfilled.

Acknowledgements

This research is partially funded by the Interuniversity Attraction Poles Programme Belgian State, Belgian Science Policy. We would like to thank Bart Jacobs and the anonymous referees for useful comments and feedback.

References

0. Albert, E., Arenas, P., Codish, M., Genaim, S., Puebla, G., Zanardini, D.: Termination analysis of Java bytecode. In: Barthe, G., de Boer, F.S. (eds.) FMOODS 2008. LNCS, vol. 5051, pp. 2–18. Springer, Heidelberg (2008)
1. Armstrong, J., Virding, R., Wikström, C., Williams, M.: Concurrent Programming in ERLANG, 2nd edn. Prentice Hall, Englewood Cliffs (1996)
2. Barnett, M., Chang, B.-Y.E., DeLine, R., Jacobs, B., Leino, K.R.M.: Boogie: A modular reusable verifier for object-oriented programs. In: de Boer, F.S., Bonsangue, M.M., Graf, S., de Roever, W.-P. (eds.) FMCO 2005. LNCS, vol. 4111, pp. 364–387. Springer, Heidelberg (2006)
3. Boyapati, C., Lee, R., Rinard, M.: Ownership types for safe programming: Preventing data races and deadlocks. In: OOPSLA. ACM, New York (2002)
4. Boyland, J.: Checking interference with fractional permissions. In: Cousot, R. (ed.) SAS 2003. LNCS, vol. 2694. Springer, Heidelberg (2003)
5. Cook, B., Podelski, A., Rybalchenko, A.: Termination proofs for systems code. In: PLDI. ACM, New York (2006)
6. Detlefs, D.L., Leino, K.R.M., Nelson, G., Saxe, J.B.: Extended static checking. Research Report 159, Compaq Systems Research Center (1998)
7. Fähndrich, M., Aiken, M., Hawblitzel, C., Hodson, O., Hunt, G., Larus, J.R., Levi, S.: Language support for fast and reliable message-based communication in Singularity OS. In: EuroSys (2006)
8. Feng, X.: Local rely-guarantee reasoning. In: POPL. ACM, New York (2009)
9. Flanagan, C., Leino, K.R.M., Lillibridge, M., Nelson, G., Saxe, J.B., Stata, R.: Extended static checking for Java. In: PLDI, ACM, New York (2002)
10. Gotsman, A., Berdine, J., Cook, B., Rinetzky, N., Sagiv, M.: Local reasoning for storable locks and threads. In: Shao, Z. (ed.) APLAS 2007. LNCS, vol. 4807, pp. 19–37. Springer, Heidelberg (2007)
11. Haack, C., Huisman, M., Hurlin, C.: Reasoning about Java's reentrant locks. In: Ramalingam, G. (ed.) APLAS 2008. LNCS, vol. 5356, pp. 171–187. Springer, Heidelberg (2008)
12. Haack, C., Hurlin, C.: Separation logic contracts for a Java-like language with fork/join. In: Meseguer, J., Roşu, G. (eds.) AMAST 2008. LNCS, vol. 5140, pp. 199–215. Springer, Heidelberg (2008)
13. Hoare, C.A.R.: Communicating sequential processes. Commun. ACM 21(8) (1978)
14. Hoare, T., O'Hearn, P.: Separation logic semantics for communicating processes. Electronic Notes on Theoretical Comput. Sci. 212 (2008)
15. Hobor, A., Appel, A.W., Nardelli, F.Z.: Oracle semantics for concurrent separation logic. In: Drossopoulou, S. (ed.) ESOP 2008. LNCS, vol. 4960, pp. 353–367. Springer, Heidelberg (2008)

16. Jacobs, B.: A Statically Verifiable Programming Model for Concurrent Object-Oriented Programs. PhD thesis, Katholieke Universiteit Leuven (2007)
17. Jacobs, B., Piessens, F.: The VeriFast program verifier. Technical Report CW-520, Department of Computer Science, Katholieke Universiteit Leuven (2008)
18. Kobayashi, N.: Type systems for concurrent programs. In: UNU/IIST 10th Anniversary Colloquium (2002)
19. Kobayashi, N.: A new type system for deadlock-free processes. In: Baier, C., Hermanns, H. (eds.) CONCUR 2006. LNCS, vol. 4137, pp. 233–247. Springer, Heidelberg (2006)
20. Korty, J.A.: Sema: A Lint-like tool for analyzing semaphore usage in a multithreaded UNIX kernel. In: Proceedings of the Winter 1989 USENIX Conference. USENIX Association (1989)
21. Leino, K.R.M., Müller, P.: A basis for verifying multi-threaded programs. In: Castagna, G. (ed.) ESOP 2009. LNCS, vol. 5502, pp. 378–393. Springer, Heidelberg (2009)
22. Leino, K.R.M., Müller, P., Smans, J.: Verification of concurrent programs with Chalice. In: Foundations of Security Analysis and Design V: FOSAD 2007/2008/2009 Tutorial Lectures. LNCS, vol. 5705. Springer, Heidelberg (2009)
23. Leino, K.R.M., Müller, P., Smans, J.: Deadlock-free channels and locks (extended version). Technical Report CW573, Department of Computer Science, K.U.Leuven (2010)
24. Luecke, G.R., Zou, Y., Coyle, J., Hoekstra, J., Kraeva, M.: Deadlock detection in MPI programs. Concurrency and Computation: Practice and Experience 14(11) (2002)
25. O'Hearn, P.W.: Resources, concurrency, and local reasoning. Theoretical Comput. Sci. 375(1-3) (2007)
26. Pike, R.: Newsqueak: A language for communicating with mice. Computing Science Technical Report 143, AT&T Bell Laboratories (1989)
27. Pym, D.J., Tofts, C.M.N.: A calculus and logic of resources and processes. Formal Aspects of Computing 18(4) (2006)
28. Ritchie, D.M.: The Limbo programming language. In: Inferno Programmer's Manual, vol. 2. Vita Nuova Holdings Ltd. (2000)
29. Smans, J., Jacobs, B., Piessens, F.: Implicit dynamic frames: Combining dynamic frames and separation logic. In: Drossopoulou, S. (ed.) ECOOP 2009 – Object-Oriented Programming. LNCS, vol. 5653, pp. 148–172. Springer, Heidelberg (2009)
30. Terauchi, T., Megacz, A.: Inferring channel buffer bounds via linear programming. In: Drossopoulou, S. (ed.) ESOP 2008. LNCS, vol. 4960. Springer, Heidelberg (2008)
31. Vafeiadis, V., Parkinson, M.: A marriage of rely/guarantee and separation logic. In: Caires, L., Vasconcelos, V.T. (eds.) CONCUR 2007. LNCS, vol. 4703, pp. 256–271. Springer, Heidelberg (2007)
32. Vasconcelos, V.T., Ravara, A., Gay, S.J.: Session types for functional multithreading. In: Gardner, P., Yoshida, N. (eds.) CONCUR 2004. LNCS, vol. 3170, pp. 497–511. Springer, Heidelberg (2004)
33. Vetter, J.S., de Supinski, B.R.: Dynamic software testing of MPI applications with umpire. In: Proceedings of the 2000 ACM/IEEE conference on Supercomputing. IEEE, Los Alamitos (2000)
34. Villard, J., Lozes, É., Calcagno, C.: Proving copyless message passing. In: Hu, Z. (ed.) APLAS 2009. LNCS, vol. 5904, pp. 194–209. Springer, Heidelberg (2009)
35. Winterbottom, P.: Alef language reference manual. In: Plan 9 Programmer's Manual: Volume Two. AT&T Bell Laboratories (1995)

Verifying a Compiler for Java Threads*

Andreas Lochbihler

Karlsruher Institut für Technologie (KIT), Karlsruhe, Germany
andreas.lochbihler@kit.edu

Abstract. A verified compiler is an integral part of every security infrastructure. Previous work has come up with formal semantics for sequential and concurrent variants of Java and has proven the correctness of compilers for the sequential part. This paper presents a rigorous formalisation (in the proof assistant Isabelle/HOL) of concurrent Java source and byte code together with an executable compiler and its correctness proof. It guarantees that the generated byte code shows exactly the same observable behaviour as the semantics for the multithreaded source code.

1 Introduction

In a recent "research highlights" article in CACM [14], the CompCert C compiler [13] by Leroy was praised as follows: "I think we are on the verge of a new paradigm for safety-critical systems, where we rely upon formal, machine checked verification, instead of human audits. Leroy's compiler is an impressive step toward this goal." And indeed, Leroy's work can be seen as a door opener, in particular because his verification includes various optimisations and generates assembler code for a real machine. However, concurrent programs call for formal methods even louder, because many bugs show up only in some interleavings of the threads' executions, which makes the bugs nearly impossible to find and reproduce. But so far, nobody has ever never included the compilation of thread primitives and multithreaded (imperative) programs.

In this paper, we present a compiler from a substantial subset of multithreaded Java source code to byte code and show semantic preservation w.r.t. interleaving semantics in the proof assistant Isabelle/HOL [23]. To our knowledge, this is the first verified compiler for a realistic concurrent language. The verification addresses the fundamental challenges of concurrency: nondeterministic interleaving and different granularity of atomic operations between source and byte code. At present, we ignore the Java Memory Model (JMM) and assume sequential consistency. Like Sun's javac compiler, ours does not optimise. Thus, we expect that the verification also works for the full JMM.

We show how to address nondeterminism by applying a bisimulation approach (Sec. 3) like in [24,27] to a compiler for a realistic concurrent language. We cope with interleaving by decomposing the correctness proof for the compiler into a correctness proof for individual threads. To that end, we introduce a generic

---

* This work is partially supported by DFG grant Sn 11/10-1.

A.D. Gordon (Ed.): ESOP 2010, LNCS 6012, pp. 427–447, 2010.

framework semantics which interleaves the individual threads and manages locks and wait sets. Since the observable behaviour includes all accesses to shared memory, method calls and synchronisation, we obtain a bisimulation for the multithreaded semantics from bisimulations for single threads. Bisimulation also solves the atomicity issue for us: unobservable steps may be decomposed into arbitrarily many unobservable steps, observable ones into multiple unobservable ones followed by an observable one.

We have based our work on the Jinja project [11], which contains formal semantics and a verified compiler for sequential Java. Our semantics JinjaThreads (Sec. 2) adds multithreading and concurrency primitives for arbitrary dynamic thread creation, synchronisation on monitors, the wait-notify mechanism and joining of threads. Our compiler (Sec. 4) may seem a straightforward extension of Jinja's, but its verification (Sec. 5) posed two fundamental challenges: In striking contrast to Jinja's big-step semantics and simulation-only proof, we had to (i) verify the compiler w.r.t. small-step interleaving semantics and (ii) show both directions of the bisimulation. Accordingly, our verification comprises 47kL of Isabelle code, whereas the original Jinja verification needed only 15kL. Finally, we discuss our design decisions that enabled the verification to succeed (Sec. 6).

Using Isabelle's code generator, we have mechanically extracted an executable implementation of our compiler in standard ML. It compiles source code programs in abstract syntax to byte code programs in abstract syntax. The full formalisation of JinjaThreads with all details is available online [19].

2   Jinja with Threads

In this section, we present the features of JinjaThreads that are relevant for our compiler verification. JinjaThreads is a complex model of Java that supports a broad spectrum of concepts, all of which must be correctly handled by the compiler all the way from source code to byte code: local variables, objects and fields, inheritance, dynamic dispatch and recursion, arrays and exception handling; for details see [11,18]. Here, we focus on Java's concurrency language features as specified in the Java Language Specification (JLS) [8, Ch. 17]: synchronisation via locks, the *wait-notify* mechanism, thread creation and joining. The interrupt mechanism is not modelled, but could be added at little cost to the formalisation. Fig. 1 illustrates the life cycle of a Java thread. After a thread has been spawned by invoking its *start* method, it keeps running (i) until it is *final*. If, however, it invokes the *wait* method on an object o, it temporarily releases its locks on o's monitor and is entered in o's wait set (ii). If another thread calls *notify* on o, a thread t is removed from o's wait set (iii), but t must reacquire its locks before it can continue to run.

Java source and byte code have the same thread and concurrency model, which is captured in our multithreaded semantics (Sec. 2.1). We use it as an interleaving semantics for all languages in JinjaThreads: source code J, (Sec. 2.3), byte code JVM (Sec. 2.4), and one intermediate language J_1 (Sec. 2.5).

2.1   The Framework Semantics

In this section, we present the multithreaded semantics for all JinjaThreads languages. To that end, we assume a small-step semantics for single threads, written $\langle x, h \rangle \xrightarrow{ta} \langle x', h' \rangle$, which contains all atomic execution steps for the individual threads. It takes a thread-local state x and the shared heap h: the result are a new thread-local state x' and heap h', and a thread action ta which spawns a new thread, locks a monitor, joins another thread, etc. For thread joining, we use the predicate *final* to identify thread states that have terminated. Then, the **framework semantics** *redT* takes such a semantics as a parameter to form the set of small-step reductions for the multithreaded case. Here, we only give a short summary of it, see [18] for full details.

A **multithreaded state** s consists of four components: (i) The **lock state** *locks s* stores for every monitor how many times it is locked by a thread, if at all. Locks are mutually exclusive. (ii) The **thread state** *thr s* stores for every thread t in s all information that is specific to it, i.e. the thread-local state x and the multiset *ln* of locks on monitors that this thread has temporarily released, e.g. when it was suspended to a wait set. (iii) The **shared memory** *shr s*. (iv) The **wait sets** *wset s*: a thread is in at most one wait set at a time.

A single thread t uses the thread action ta to query and update the state of the locks, threads and wait sets. Currently, the framework semantics provides the following **basic thread actions**: (i) Locking, unlocking, temporarily releasing, and testing whether it has (not) locked a monitor. (ii) Creating a new thread, testing whether a thread has been started, and joining a thread. (iii) Suspending to a wait set, notifying one (all) threads in a wait set. A **thread action (TA)** ta consists of multiple basic thread actions, written as a list ([] denotes the empty list). The whole list is checked and executed atomically. A call to the *wait* method, e.g., issues [HasLock l, Release l, Suspend w] to test whether the thread t has locked the monitor l, to temporarily release all locks on l, and to suspend itself to the wait set w. By composing TAs that affect multiple aspects of the multithreaded state from basic thread actions, we were able to keep the framework semantics flexible and the proofs about it simple.

The **framework semantics** *redT* has reductions (written $s \xrightarrow{t \triangleright ta} s'$) of two kinds. First, a reduction $\langle x, h \rangle \xrightarrow{ta} \langle x', h' \rangle$ of the thread t in s that is not in a wait set and has not temporarily released any locks (state (i) in Fig. 1). In that case, tests of the TA ta must hold in s. Then, *redT* atomically executes ta on s and updates t's local state to x' and the shared heap to h', which yields s'. Second, *redT* can choose a thread t in s that is not in a wait set, but has temporarily released some locks *ln* – state (iii) in Fig. 1. If t can reacquire all of them, *redT* assigns them to t again and resets *ln* to {} in s'. In that case, everything else remains unchanged from s to s'. A reduction $s \xrightarrow{t \triangleright ta} s'$ is unobservable (written is-mτ s (t, ta) s') iff it results from a τ-move of a thread (cf. Sec. 2.2). Note that a thread gets from (ii) to (iii) in Fig. 1 only if an *other* thread notifies it.

We also lift the *final* predicate to a multithreaded state s: s is **final** iff for all threads t in s, say *thr s t* = $\lfloor (x, ln) \rfloor$ ($\lfloor \_ \rfloor$ denotes definedness for a

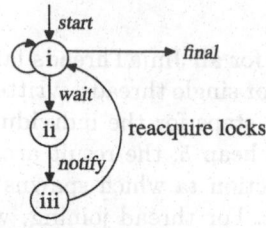

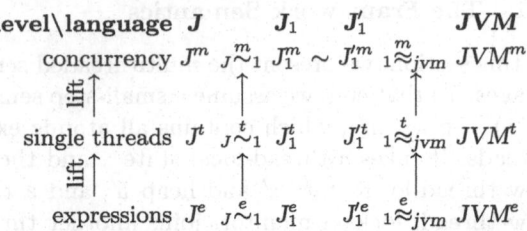

Fig. 1. Life cycle of a Java thread

Fig. 2. Composition of bisimulations for the correctness proof

partial function), t's local state x is *final* and t has not temporarily released any locks, i.e. $ln = \{\}$.

2.2 Concepts for All Languages in JinjaThreads

Each JinjaThreads language has three semantics levels, which Fig. 2 shows together with the delay bisimulations used in Sec. 5 for the verification. The expression level semantics, which is marked with ^{e}, contains all execution steps of a single thread except for method calls and returns. The semantics for a thread (marked ^{t}) lifts the expression level semantics to call stacks and adds method calls and returns. The multithreaded semantics (marked ^{m}) models the full behaviour for multithreaded programs. In all languages, this is the framework semantics instantiated with the call-stack semantics for single threads.

There are five kinds of **values**: booleans *Bool b*, integers *Intg i*, addresses *Addr a*, the null reference *Null*, and a dummy value *Unit*. Addresses reference objects or arrays on the heap, which is a map from addresses to heap objects. To avoid redundancies with the instruction for object creation in the formalisation, all system exceptions (like *NullPointer* and *IllegalMonitorState*) are preallocated on the heap. &_ denotes the address of a preallocated system exception.

In standard Java, only monitors – of which every object and array has exactly one – can be locked. Hence, addresses identify monitors in the framework instantiations. Since every monitor manages its own wait set, addresses also identify wait sets. JinjaThreads uses the same heap representation in all languages. Hence, every instantiation need only to specify the thread-local state.

All JinjaThreads languages use the same format for class and method declarations, only the method definitions depend on the language. Hence, a compiler *Comp* need to be specified only for method bodies. The generic function *compP* then uniformly applies *Comp* to all methods of all classes, i.e. the program P is compiled to *compP Comp P*. This generic approach ensures that compilation does not affect the class hierarchy and lookup functions for methods and fields.

JinjaThreads comes with standard well-formedness conditions (e.g. typeability, acyclic class hierarchy), see [11] for details. In the following, we will assume that all programs are well-formed.

JinjaThreads has two kinds of method calls: First, standard calls to methods that are implemented in the program P. Second, calls to methods that cannot be implemented in JinjaThreads syntax, e.g. native methods such as *wait*, *notify*, or *start* on *Thread* objects. We call them **external calls** and hardwire them in the semantics. Such a call executes atomically, written $P \vdash \langle a.M(vs), h \rangle \xrightarrow{ta}_{\rhd \text{ext}} \langle va, h' \rangle$ where a is the address of the object, M the method name and vs the list of parameter values. It returns va, which is either a normal value v or the address a of an exception, a thread action ta, and the new heap h'. Currently, the following native methods are provided: *wait*, *notify* and *notifyAll* implement the wait set mechanism for all objects and arrays; they simply translate the call into the TAs [*HasLock* a, *Release* a, *Suspend* a], [*HasLock* a, *Notify* a], and [*HasLock* a, *NotifyAll* a], resp., where a is the address of the object or array being called. For these methods, additional reductions with the TA [*HasNoLock* a] raise an *IllegalMonitorState* exception. The framework semantics selects the right reduction according to its lock status. Moreover, method *start* in class *Thread* spawns a new thread, or fails with an *IllegalThreadState* exception if the thread has already been started before. Finally, *join* joins the called thread. Via this mechanism, we could add more native methods and even model I/O easily.

Regarding the **observable behaviour**, we consider the following operations as observable moves: calling and returning from a method, locking and unlocking, creating objects and arrays and accessing data on the heap other than type information.[1] Since thread creation, joining and the wait-notify mechanism are implemented as external calls, all of them are, in particular, observable. Conversely, all control flow constructs, including exception throwing and handling, and local variable manipulation are only relevant to the thread that executes them, so these generate only τ-moves.

2.3 The Source Code Language J

In the source language J, everything is an expression with a return value: statements are treated as expressions that return *Unit*. An expression is *final* if it is either a value *Val* v (normal termination) or a thrown exception *throw* (*Addr a*), which we abbreviate as *Throw a*. For a program P, let $P \vdash \langle e,(h, xs) \rangle \xrightarrow{ta}_J \langle e',(h', xs') \rangle$ denote that the expression e executes in a single step to e' with TA ta, thereby changing the heap h to h' and the store for local variables from xs to xs'. J^e contains 84 reduction rules, but we only show those for synchronisation. For details on the syntax and the full sequential semantics, see [11,18].

Synchronisation in Java source code is done via the synchronized statement, which is specified in the JLS [8, Sec. 14.19]. The synchronized modifier for methods behaves as if its body was statement-synchronized on *this*, so we only need

---

[1] These observable moves strictly include all JMM inter-thread actions except for thread divergence actions. We omit the latter because the JMM is inconsistent for infinite executions [3]. Object creation, e.g., must be observable in our approach, because it changes the heap, but it is no inter-thread action: The JMM assumes that all objects have been preallocated, which is unrealistic for an actual semantics.

$$\frac{P \vdash \langle e,s \rangle \xrightarrow{ta}_J \langle e',s' \rangle}{P \vdash \langle sync(e)\ e_2,s \rangle \xrightarrow{ta}_J \langle sync(e')\ e_2,s' \rangle}\ \textbf{JS1}$$

$$P \vdash \langle sync(Throw\ a)\ e,s \rangle \xrightarrow{\ \ \downarrow\ \ }_J \langle Throw\ a,s \rangle\ \textbf{JS2}$$

$$P \vdash \langle sync(null)\ e,s \rangle \xrightarrow{\ \ \downarrow\ \ }_J \langle Throw\ \&NullPointer,s \rangle\ \textbf{JS3}$$

$$P \vdash \langle sync(addr\ a)\ e,s \rangle \xrightarrow{[Lock\ a]}_J \langle insync(a)\ e,s \rangle\ \textbf{JS4}$$

$$\frac{P \vdash \langle e,s \rangle \xrightarrow{ta}_J \langle e',s' \rangle}{P \vdash \langle insync(a)\ e,s \rangle \xrightarrow{ta}_J \langle insync(a)\ e',s' \rangle}\ \textbf{JS5}$$

$$P \vdash \langle insync(a)\ Val\ v,s \rangle \xrightarrow{[Unlock\ a]}_J \langle Val\ v,s \rangle\ \textbf{JS6}$$

$$P \vdash \langle insync(a)\ Throw\ ad,s \rangle \xrightarrow{[Unlock\ a]}_J \langle Throw\ ad,s \rangle\ \textbf{JS7}$$

Fig. 3. Source code reductions for the synchronized statement

to consider synchronized blocks in J. Fig. 3 shows the reduction rules for the synchronized statement $sync$: JS1 reduces the monitor subexpression. If it raises an exception, rule JS2 propagates it.[2] If the monitor subexpression evaluates to the $null$ value, a $NullPointer$ exception is thrown (JS3). If it reduces to some monitor address a, the thread can only reduce further (JS4) by acquiring a lock on a. To remember that the lock has been granted, the expression is rewritten to $insync(a)\ e$, a variant of the $sync$ expression that does not occur in programs. Then, the synchronized block's body is executed (JS5). If this terminates normally with a value v or with an exception at address ad, JS6 and JS7 release the lock on a and propagate the return value or exception.

J^e also includes all external calls into J^e, but it has no rule for standard method calls. It uses the predicate $is\text{-}ext\text{-}call$ to determine, based on type information, whether the call is external. Standard method calls are left to the semantics J^t, which lifts J^e to call stacks. The lifting is standard: as long as the frame's expression at the top of the call stack is not $final$, it is being reduced according to J^e. In case of a standard method call, J^t pushes a new call frame with the called method's body as expression on top of the stack. If the top frame's expression is $final$, the return value or thrown exception replaces the method call subexpression in the frame below. A thread in J^t is final iff the call stack contains only one expression, which is also $final$.

Originally, the JinjaThreads source code small-step semantics [18] did not model a call stack and dynamically inlined method calls in the expressions instead. But the compiler verification requires an explicit call stack, so we use this alternative semantics. We have also shown that they are strongly bisimilar: The strong bisimulation relates the call stack es to the expression e' iff folding es with method inlining equals e'.

---

[2] This is a typical example of how J^e handles exceptions: For every language construct, rules propagate thrown exceptions ($Throw\ a$) from subexpressions until a matching $try\text{-}catch$ block is reached or there are no surrounding expressions any more.

2.4   The Byte Code Language *JVM*

The byte code language and the JinjaThreads virtual machine (VM) model Java byte code and the Java VM according to the Java Virtual Machine Specification (JVMS) [16]. A thread-local state (xcp, frs) consists of an exception flag xcp ($\lfloor a \rfloor$ corresponds to *Throw a* in *J* and $\bot$ denotes none), and a stack *frs* of frames. A frame $fr = (stk, loc, C, M, pc)$ consists of the stack *stk*, an array *loc* for the parameters and local variables, the class *C* and method name *M* of the method, and the program counter *pc*. A state is *JVM-final* iff the frame stack is empty.

A method body (msl, mxs, ins, xt) consists of an instruction list *ins*, an exception table *xt*, the maximum stack length *msl* and the size *mxs* of the array for local variables. The exception table is a list of entries $(from, to, C, pc, d)$ where *C* is either a class name or the special value *Any*. The exception handler starting at index *pc* in *ins* expects *d* elements on the stack and handles exceptions that are raised by instructions in the interval $[from, to)$. If *C* is a class name, it handles only those that are a subclass of *C*; if *C* is *Any*, it handles all.

Regarding the JinjaThreads' instruction set, Java byte code instructions which only differ on their operand types (e.g. `iload` and `aload`) are combined in polymorphic ones (e.g. *Load*), but the instructions have not been simplified conceptually. Moreover, operations that directly manipulate the stack (e.g. `dup`) or the local variables like `iinc` are not part of the Jinja VM. Since they are all silent instructions, our silent instructions can easily simulate them.

The semantics of a single instruction is defined by the function *exec-instr*. Given the instruction, the heap and the frame stack, it produces a list of successor states together with the corresponding TAs. Like for *J*, we only explain method invocation, synchronisation and exception handling.

Method calls are very similar to *J*: the *Invoke* instruction decides via the predicate *is-ext-call* whether the call is external. If so, it uses the reductions from $P \vdash \langle a.M(vs), h \rangle \xrightarrow{ta} \triangleright_{ext} \langle va, h' \rangle$ to determine the successor states. Otherwise, it looks up the method in *P* and pushes a new call frame on top of the frame stack with the parameters and local variables correctly initialised.

The instructions *MEnter* and *MExit* for entering and exiting a monitor implement synchronisation. Both throw a *NullPointer* exception if the top stack element *v* is *null*. Otherwise, they increment the program counter and issue a *Lock* or *Unlock* action on the address *a* in *v*, resp. Additionally, *MExit* can also raise an *IllegalMonitorState* exception with the TA [*HasNoLock a*]. The latter possibility is to allow for unstructured locking, where unlocking may fail.

The function *exec P* $(xcp, h, fr \cdot frs)$ incorporates exception handling in the semantics: If no exception is flagged, this just executes the current instruction via *exec-instr*. Otherwise $(xcp = \lfloor a \rfloor)$, *a* is checked against the exception handlers for the program counter of *fr*: If one is found, the stack is trimmed to the length specified in the exception table, *a* is pushed onto the stack and the program counter is set to the start of the handler. Otherwise, *fr* is popped and *a* is rethrown at the *Invoke* statement in the previous call frame.

The VM model *exec* is aggressive: it assumes that there are always sufficiently many operands of the right types on the stack. If not, the result is undefined.

$$\frac{V < |xs_1| \qquad xs_1' = xs_1[V := Addr\ a]}{P \vdash \langle sync_V(addr\ a)\ e_1,\ (h,\ xs_1)\rangle \xrightarrow{[Lock\ a]}_{J_1} \langle insync_V(a)\ e_1,\ (h,\ xs_1')\rangle} \mathbf{J_1S4}$$

$$\frac{V < |xs_1| \qquad xs_{1[V]} = Addr\ a'}{P \vdash \langle insync_V(a)\ Throw\ ad,\ (h,\ xs_1)\rangle \xrightarrow{[Unlock\ a']}_{J_1} \langle Throw\ ad,\ (h,\ xs_1)\rangle} \mathbf{J_1S7}$$

$$\frac{V < |xs_1| \qquad xs_{1[V]} = Null}{P \vdash \langle insync_V(a)\ Val\ v,\ (h,\ xs_1)\rangle \xrightarrow{\ \Box\ }_{J_1'} \langle Throw\ \&NullPointer,\ (h,\ xs_1)\rangle} \mathbf{J_1'S8}$$

$$\frac{V < |xs_1| \qquad xs_{1[V]} = Addr\ a'}{P \vdash \langle insync_V\ (a)\ Val\ v,\ (h,\ xs_1)\rangle \xrightarrow{[HasNoLock\ a']}_{J_1'}}_{\langle Throw\ \&IllegalMonitorState,\ (h,\ xs_1)\rangle} \mathbf{J_1'S9}$$

Fig. 4. Example reduction rules for *sync* statements in J_1 and J_1'

JinjaThreads also contains a defensive VM, which performs such checks and raises a type error in case they fail. The byte code verifier, which is also part of JinjaThreads, ensures that for verified byte code programs and conform states, the type checks are always met and no type errors occur, i.e. aggressive and defensive VM agree. A separate proof shows (using a type compiler) that the byte code verifier accepts all programs generated by the JinjaThreads compiler [11].

In the compiler verification, we mostly use the defensive VM for the bisimulation proof. As before, we have three levels of semantics: JVM_d^e (JVM_a^e) contains all execution steps of the defensive (aggressive) VM that manipulate only the top frame on the call stack, i.e. all instructions except for *Invoke* and *Return*, including method-local exception handling. The single-threaded VM semantics JVM^t also includes the execution steps that JVM_d^e has omitted. Then, the multi-threaded VM JVM^m is again the framework semantics instantiated with JVM^t.

2.5   Local Variables in an Array: The Intermediate Language J_1

Our compiler operates in two stages: The first stage allocates local variables to array indices, the second generates the byte code instructions. The intermediate language J_1 stores local variable values in an array (like byte code does), but the expressions from the source code have not yet been replaced by instructions. Hence, local variables in J_1 are no longer identified by their name, but by an index in the array. A $sync_V(e_1)$ e_1' block is now annotated with a variable index V. Following the JVMS [16, Sec. 7.14], this variable will be used in the byte code to store the monitor address between the *MEnter* and *MExit* instructions that implement the monitor locking and unlocking. Since J_1 behaves like the byte code w.r.t. local variables, J_1 already uses this local variable for *sync* blocks.

We define a new semantics J_1^e for expressions (written $P \vdash \langle e_1,\ (h,\ xs_1)\rangle \xrightarrow{ta}_{J_1}$ $\langle e_1',\ (h',\ xs_1')\rangle$) with new rules for the expressions that operate on the variable array xs_1. In J_1^e, J_1S4 and J_1S7 (Fig. 4), e.g., replace JS4 and JS7. J_1S4 not only locks the monitor, but also stores its address in the variable array xs_1.

(The first premise ensures that the variable index does not exceed the size of the array.) Accordingly, $J_1 S7$ reads the monitor address for unlocking from the array.

Analogously to J, J_1^t lifts J_1^e to call stacks, which are again the thread-local states for the multithreaded semantics J_1^m. Like J^m and JVM^m, J_1^m is the framework semantics instantiated with J_1^t.

To be in line with the *MExit* semantics, we introduce a variant $J_1'^e$ of the J_1^e semantics. Apart from the reductions from J_1^e, it also includes in the unlocking for $sync_V$ blocks the cases where the entry V in xs_1 (written $xs_{1[V]}$) is *Null* or the thread does not hold the lock on the monitor at the address $xs_{1[V]}$. In these cases, it raises a *NullPointer* or *IllegalMonitorState* exception resp. $J_1' S8$ and $J_1' S9$ in Fig. 4 show these if the block has terminated normally with a value v. $J_1'^e$ contains analogous reductions for abnormal termination with an exception *Throw* a. As above, $J_1'^t$ lifts $J_1'^e$ to call stacks and $J_1'^m$ is the framework semantics instantiated with $J_1'^t$.

3   Semantic Preservation via Bisimulations

We now introduce the notion of semantic preservation (Sec. 3.1) and the bisimulation infrastructure (Sec. 3.2 and 3.3) for showing preservation for the compiler.

3.1   Semantic Preservation

Semantic preservation aims to show that semantic properties established on the source code also hold for the target code and vice versa. Such properties or specifications (e.g. a safety property like no null pointer exceptions) are typically modelled as predicates on the traces of observable behaviour, i.e. the observable steps of a program execution, or on the sets of possible traces (for nondeterministic programs). Thus, a correct compiler *Comp* must ensure that the (sets of) traces of the source program P and of the compiled program *Comp* P are equal.

Formally, *Comp* **preserves the semantics** of P iff the following holds: Let s_1 and s_2 be the initial states for P and *Comp* P, resp. For every execution of P that starts in s_1 and terminates in s_1', there must be an execution of *Comp* P from s_2 to s_2' such that both the executions' traces and the observable data in s_1' and s_2' (such as the result values or exceptional termination) are the same. Conversely, every terminating execution of *Comp* P from s_2 must be matched that way by one of P from s_1.

As multithreaded programs are inherently nondeterministic, both directions are essential. The compiled code must not miss any observable nondeterministic choice, neither may it introduce additional observable behaviour. Some atomic high-level statements are translated into a sequence of simple instructions, which allow more interleavings. A correct compiler must ensure that these new interleavings do not lead to new behaviours. Conversely, some constructs (like exception handling) are atomic in the compiled code, but require many steps in the source code semantics. Although the compiled code has less interleavings, no observable behaviour must be missed.

Regarding schedulers, semantic preservation is possibilistic: The source and compiled program may have different behaviour under a *fixed* scheduler whose strategy depends on unobservable steps. Under a round-robin scheduler, e.g., the number of unobservable steps between two observable ones influences the interleaving. Since a compiler changes this number, source and byte code may have different behaviours under this scheduler. In this sense, semantic preservation means: If there is a scheduler for P such that s_1 terminates in s'_1 with trace t, then there is also a scheduler for *Comp P* such that s_2 ends in s'_2 with trace t.

3.2   Simulation Properties

For semantic preservation, we must show trace equivalence for the source code and the compiled code. To do this, it is standard to show bisimilarity. The latter implies trace equivalence and can be shown by inspecting individual steps of execution instead of whole program executions. For the verification, we have chosen delay bisimilarity [20,1], as it is easy to obtain a delay bisimulation for multithreaded states from one for individual thread states (cf. Sec. 2.1). As it is transitive, we can decompose the compiler into smaller transformations and verify each on its own. Transitivity ensures that the overall compiler is correct, too.

Abstractly, programs define labelled transition systems whose states are the program states and whose labels constitute the observable behaviour. We write $s \xrightarrow{ta} s'$ for a single **transition** (move), i.e. execution step in the small-step semantics, from state s to state s' with label ta. A predicate $is\text{-}\tau\ s\ ta\ s'$ determines whether the transition $s \xrightarrow{ta} s'$ is unobservable. Such transitions are called silent or τ-**moves**. Since their labels are irrelevant, we don't keep track of them and write $s \xrightarrow{\tau} s'$ instead. Moreover, $\xrightarrow{\tau}{}^*$ denotes the reflexive and transitive closure of $\xrightarrow{\tau}$. A **visible** move consists of a finite sequence of τ-moves followed by an observable transition. In this paper, we will often have states, labels, reductions, and the like for two or more programs and semantics. We will index variables and arrows with numbers to assign them to one of the semantics, i.e. s_1, $\xrightarrow{}_1$, etc. for the first, s_2, $\xrightarrow{}_2$, etc. for the second and so on.

A relation $\sim$ on states is a **(delay) bisimulation** [20,1] iff (i) $s_1 \sim s_2$ for the initial states s_1 and s_2 and (ii) it satisfies the simulation diagrams in Fig. 5: Every τ-move is simulated by a finite (possibly empty) sequence of τ-moves, and observable moves are simulated by visible moves such that the resulting states are again $\sim$-related. Two programs (transition systems) are **(delay) bisimilar** iff there exists a delay bisimulation for them. A special case of delay bisimulation is **strong bisimulation** [21] where every move is simulated by exactly one move.

Note that the relational composition $\sim_1 \circ \sim_2$ of two delay bisimulations $\sim_1$ and $\sim_2$ is again a delay bisimulation [1], where $s_1 \sim_1 \circ \sim_2 s_3 \equiv \exists s_2.\ s_1 \sim_1 s_2 \wedge s_2 \sim_2 s_3$. Hence, delay bisimilarity is transitive.

A program execution $s_0 \xrightarrow{tas}{}^* s_n$ is a finite sequence of transitions $s_0 \xrightarrow{ta_1} s_1 \xrightarrow{ta_2} \ldots \xrightarrow{ta_n} s_n$ where tas is the list of all labels ta_i of observable steps $s_{i-1} \xrightarrow{ta_i} s_i$. To characterise complete executions for semantic preservation, we

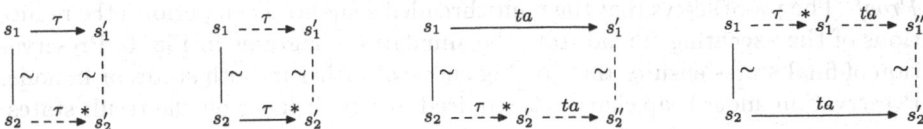

Fig. 5. Diagrams for delay bisimulation. Solid lines denote assumptions, dashed lines conclusions.

assume a predicate *final* that identifies terminal states. We say that a relation $\sim$ **preserves final states** iff final states are $\sim$-related to final states only. Delay bisimulations that preserve final states also preserve the semantics:

Lemma 1. *Let $\sim$ be a delay bisimulation that preserves final states and $s_1 \sim s_2$. If $s_1 \xrightarrow{tas} \!\!\!\triangleright_1^* s_1'$ such that $final_1\ s_1'$, then there exists an s_2' such that $s_2 \xrightarrow{tas} \!\!\!\triangleright_2^* s_2'$, $final_2\ s_2'$ and $s_1' \sim s_2'$. If $s_2 \xrightarrow{tas} \!\!\!\triangleright_2^* s_2'$ with $final_2\ s_2'$, then there exists an s_1' such that $s_1 \xrightarrow{tas} \!\!\!\triangleright_1^* s_1'$, $final_1\ s_1'$ and $s_1' \sim s_2'$.*

Proof. This lemma is shown by an easy induction on $s_1 \xrightarrow{tas} \!\!\!\triangleright_1^* s_1'$ and $s_2 \xrightarrow{tas} \!\!\!\triangleright_2^* s_2'$, resp., where the simulation properties from Fig. 5 are used in the inductive step.

3.3 Lifting for Bisimulations

The delay bisimulations for showing semantic preservation always relate multi-threaded states. As we use our framework semantics at all compilation stages, we uniformly lift delay bisimulations for single threads to multithreaded states. Thus, to show delay bisimilarity on the multithreaded level, it suffices to show delay bisimilarity for single threads plus some constraints that the lifting imposes:

First, we lift a relation $\sim$ on thread-local states and the shared memories for two instantiating semantics $\dashrightarrow_1$ and $\dashrightarrow_2$ to multithreaded states s_1 and s_2, denoted by $s_1 \sim_m s_2$: (i) The lock status and wait sets of s_1 and s_2 must be the same. (ii) All threads in s_1 also exist in s_2 and vice versa. (iii) For every thread t in s_1 and s_2, say $thr\ s_1\ t = \lfloor (x_1, ln_1) \rfloor$ and $thr\ s_2\ t = \lfloor (x_2, ln_2) \rfloor$, the temporarily released locks must be the same ($ln_1 = ln_2$) and the local states $\sim$-related: $(x_1, shr\ s_1) \sim (x_2, shr\ s_2)$. $\sim_m$ preserves final states iff $\sim$ does so.

Next, we show that the above definitions are sensible: if $\sim$ is a delay bisimulation, then so is $\sim_m$. However, this holds only if τ-moves are in fact not observable by other threads. To that end, we require that they neither execute any TAs, nor change the shared heap: $is\text{-}\tau\ (x, h)\ ta\ (x', h')$ implies $ta = []$ and $h = h'$ for all x, x', h, h', ta. Moreover, we must require that $\sim$ **is preserved by heap changes** by other executing threads: Let y_1 and y_2 be two thread-local states with $(y_1, h_1) \sim (y_2, h_2)$, each of which performs a visible move to (y_1', h_1') and (y_2', h_2') resp. such that $(y_1', h_1') \sim (y_2', h_2')$, i.e. the visible moves simulate each other. Then, whenever $(x_1, h_1) \sim (x_2, h_2)$ holds for the old heaps, $(x_1, h_1') \sim (x_2, h_2')$ must still hold for the new heaps.

Theorem 1. *Let $\sim$ be a delay bisimulation that is preserved by heap changes and preserves final states. Then $\sim_m$ is also a delay bisimulation.*

Proof. The proof shows that the multithreaded semantics can perform the reductions of the executing thread from the simulation diagrams in Fig. 5. Preservation of final states ensures that joining succeeds either in both states or in none. Preservation under heap changes is required to establish $\sim_m$ on the result states.

4   Compilation from Source Code to Byte Code

Jinja [11] already contains a nonoptimising compiler *J2JVM* from source code to byte code via the intermediate language J_1: *compE*₁ compiles *J* expressions to J_1 expressions. It allocates array indices to local variables and replaces all references to local variables in *e* by their indices. *compE*₂ and *compxE*₂ generate instruction sequences and exception tables for J_1 expressions. All of them are recursive on the expression structure. *compP*₁ lifts *compE*₁ to programs using *compP*, and so does *compP*₂ with *compE*₂ and *compxE*₂. The overall compiler *J2JVM* is the composition of *compP*₁ with *compP*₂. For JinjaThreads, we have extended *compE*₁, *compE*₂ and *compxE*₂ to handle *sync* expressions, which we present in this section. For details on the other constructs, see [11].

*compE*₁ assigns indices to variables in the following order: the *this* pointer, method parameters, local variables in the order of block nesting level. For *sync(e) e′* statements, *compE*₁ shifts local variables declared in *e′* by 1 and annotates *sync* with the index that it has freed this way.

The translation of a J_1 *sync*$_V(e_1)$ $e_1′$ expression to byte code must ensure that the monitor is unlocked even if an unhandled exception occurs in $e_1′$. An exception handler, which applies to all exceptions, needs to do this. Thus, the instructions for *sync*$_V(e_1)$ $e_1′$ are (where @ concatenates two lists):

*compE*₂ e_1 @ [*Store V, Load V, MEnter*] @ *compE*₂ $e_1′$ @ [*Load V, MExit, Goto* 4] @ [*Load V, MExit, Throw*]

First, the monitor expression e_1 is evaluated and the result (on the stack) is stored in *V*. *Load V* pushes the monitor address back onto the stack and *MEnter* locks the monitor. Then, the block is executed, the monitor address loaded again and the monitor unlocked. *Goto* 4 jumps to the instruction after the exception handler that follows. The handler also loads the monitor address, unlocks the monitor and rethrows the caught exception whose address is still on top of the stack. For the exception tables, *compxE*₂ (*sync*$_V(e_1)$ $e_1′$) appends to the exception tables for e_1 and $e_1′$ the entry (pc_1, pc_2, *Any*, pc_2 + 3, *d*) such that *compE*₂ $e_1′$ occupies the positions [pc_1, pc_2) in the instruction list and the *d* bottom values (of surrounding expressions) remain on the stack. Hence, this handler applies to any exception unless it is handled inside the body $e_1′$.

For example, consider the following method declaration, whose body is ([*f*], *sync(Var f) Var this.doIt(*[]))) in abstract syntax:

```
int foo(Object f) { synchronized(f) { return this.doIt(); } }
```

This compiles to [*Load* 1, *Store* 2, *Load* 2, *MEnter, Load* 0, *Invoke doIt* 0, *Load* 2, *MExit, Goto* 4, *Load* 2, *MExit, Throw, Return*] with exception table [(4, 6, *Any*, 9, 0)]. For realistic examples, see the formalisation online [19].

5   Correctness Proofs

In this section, we present the correctness proof for the compiler: a delay bisimulation between the source program P and the compiled program $J2JVM\ P$. Fig. 2 from Sec. 2 shows how we build it from smaller delay bisimulations: Between J and J_1 (Sec. 5.1), and between J_1' and JVM (Sec. 5.2), we present three delay bisimulations, one for each level (expressions, singlethreaded call stacks and multithreaded). The delay bisimulations for the call stack level lift the ones on the expression level to single threads and the multithreaded level is always $\sim_m$ from Sec. 3.3 instantiated with the ^{t} level. Finally, we show that J_1^m and $J_1'^m$ are equivalent for states of interest (Sec. 5.3). By transitivity, P and $J2JVM\ P$ are delay bisimilar, i.e. the compiler is correct (Thm. 2).

The delay bisimulation relations typically consist of two parts: (i) the actual relation between states of the two semantics and (ii) some well-formedness constraints on the states of either semantics (e.g. being typeable) required by the bisimulation proof. The latter restrict the set of "valid" states for which the bisimulation property holds. To increase proof automation, we have similarly split the bisimulation proofs: First, we show that simulating reductions exists under conditions (i) and (ii), and that the resulting states are again related in (i). Next, we show that the constraints in (ii) are preserved under reductions and that the initial states satisfy them.

5.1   Strong Bisimulation between J and J_1

J and J_1 only differ in the treatment of local variables. Hence, the thread features do not introduce anything essentially new for the verification. Still, transferring the old correctness proof (which uses the big step semantics) required several substantial changes: (i) We adapted the small step semantics J_1^e such that it is strongly bisimilar to J^e, whereas the old semantics would only allow delay bisimilarity. This way, we need not distinguish observable from silent moves, which greatly simplifies the inuctive cases in the proofs. (ii) The strong bisimulation $_J\sim_1$ between J^e and J_1^e must now relate not only initial and final states, but also all intermediate states. We require that both expressions are identical in structure except for variable names, which are resolved according to $compE_1$'s numbering scheme. In addition to the old well-formedness constraints (e.g. a definite assignment test), the monitor address in the local variables in J_1^e must agree with the monitor address in the $insync$ subexpression. (iii) We must now also show that small-step reductions preserve the well-formedness conditions.

Although the simulations are now much finer and must cover both directions, the old notions for the simulation proof [11] are still sufficient, i.e. the proofs do not pose any major difficulties. Establishing $_J\sim_1$ for the resulting states in the case for $sync_V(e)\ e'$ relies on V, the local monitor variable, not being accessed explicitly in the e', which the compiler numbering scheme guarantees.

5.2 Delay Bisimulation between J_1' and JVM

The translation from J_1 to JVM is the most complicated one. It flattens the tree structure of expressions to a linear list of instructions. Exception handlers are registered in exception tables. Synchronized blocks are implemented by $MEnter$ and $MExit$ instructions and an exception handler. Like between J and J_1, the key to correctness is delay bisimilarity on the expression level, on which we focus in this section. Calling and returning from methods works similarly in $J_1'^t$ and JVM^t, the laborious proof simply lifts delay bisimilarity. The multithreaded level is the framework semantics in both semantics. It is easy to show that the delay bisimulation for the thread level preserves final states and is preserved by heap changes. Thus, Thm. 1 from Sec. 3.3 yields delay bisimilarity for $J_1'^m$ and JVM^m.

For the expression level, we make with a detour via the aggressive VM JVM_a^e. We show that JVM_a^e simulates $J_1'^e$, but that $J_1'^e$ simulates JVM_d^e. Since the byte code verifier accepts all compiled programs, the defensive VM JVM_d^e simulates the aggressive JVM_a^e step by step. This detour saves us from showing type safety for $J_1'^e$. If we used JVM_d^e directly, only full run-time typeability of the $J_1'^e$ expression would ensure that the JVM_d^e does not halt because of a type error where $J_1'^e$ still continues to execute. Conversely, the aggressive VM performs fewer checks than $J_1'^e$, so $J_1'^e$ might get stuck when JVM_a^e continues with undefined behaviour. Hence, bisimilarity holds only for conformant byte code states.

Note that this detour only affects the semantics, not the delay bisimulation relation $_1\overset{e}{\approx}_{jvm}$. $P,e,h \vdash (e_1, xs_1) \; _1\overset{e}{\approx}_{jvm} (stk, loc, pc, xcp)$ relates a J_1^e state (e_1, xs_1) (expression and local variables) to a JVM^e state (stk, loc, pc, xcp) (stack, local variables, program counter, and exception flag) for a heap h that is the same for both. P only defines the class hierarchy, whereas the J_1 expression e compiles to the instruction list $compE_2\, e$ with exception table $compxE_2\, e$. The inductive definition for $_1\overset{e}{\approx}_{jvm}$ mirrors the $J_1'^e$ reduction rules and relates instruction positions and the stack in the compiled code to partially evaluated expressions.

Fig. 6 shows some representative rules from the inductive definition. The single rule B_1 for all expressions exploits that the last instruction in a compiled expression always puts its result value on top of the stack. Unfortunately, this does not translate to exceptions, because byte code does not propagate exceptions from subexpressions, but exception tables are used. Hence, $_1\overset{e}{\approx}_{jvm}$ contains separate exception propagation rules for all expressions, similar to B_2. Still, it abstracts from computed values and addresses of thrown exceptions and only requires that they are the same in both J_1^e and JVM^e. Moreover, rules like B_3 for all subexpressions of all expressions embed bisimilar states for the subexpression into the context of the larger expression, thereby shifting the stack and instruction pointer as necessary. Finally, the definition contains a rule for every byte code instruction and intermediate J_1^e state. For example, B_4 relates the J_1^e state which next acquires a monitor's lock to the intermediate JVM^e state after executing the $Store\, V$ instruction that saves the monitor address. Although J_1^e and JVM^e operate on the local variable array in the same way, they must not be equated in the bisimulation relation, because they differ in such intermediate states like in B_4, which J_1S4 skips.

$$P,e,h \vdash (Val\ v,\ xs)\ {}_1\!\approx^e_{jvm}\ ([v],\ xs,\ |compE_2\ e|,\ \bot)\ \mathbf{B}_1$$

$$\frac{P,e_1,h \vdash (Throw\ a,\ xs)\ {}_1\!\approx^e_{jvm}\ (stk,\ loc,\ pc,\ \lfloor a \rfloor)}{P,sync_V(e_1)\ e_2,h \vdash (Throw\ a,\ xs)\ {}_1\!\approx^e_{jvm}\ (stk,\ loc,\ pc,\ \lfloor a \rfloor)}\ \mathbf{B}_2$$

$$\frac{P,e_2,h \vdash (e,\ xs)\ {}_1\!\approx^e_{jvm}\ (stk,\ loc,\ pc,\ xcp)}{P,sync_V(e_1)\ e_2,h \vdash (insync_V(a)\ e,\ xs)\ {}_1\!\approx^e_{jvm}\ (stk,\ loc,\ 3+|compE_2\ e_1|+pc,\ xcp)}\ \mathbf{B}_3$$

$$P,sync_V(e_1)\ e_2,h \vdash (sync_V(Val\ v)\ e_2,\ xs)\ {}_1\!\approx^e_{jvm}\ ([],\ xs[V:=v],\ 1+|compE_2\ e_1|,\ \bot)\ \mathbf{B}_4$$

Fig. 6. Example introduction rules for the ${}_1\!\approx^e_{jvm}$ bisimulation relation

The simulation proofs heavily rely on this value passing scheme. The next lemma, which is shown by induction on ${}_1\!\approx^e_{jvm}$, says that for related states, if one of them denotes a result values or thrown expressions, then the other can produce the same outcome using only τ-moves.

Lemma 2. *Let* $P,e,h \vdash (e_1,\ xs_1)\ {}_1\!\approx^e_{jvm}\ (stk,\ loc,\ pc,\ xcp)$. *If* $e_1 = Val\ v$, *then* $(stk,\ loc,\ pc,\ xcp)$ *can silently execute to* $([v],\ xs_1,\ |compE_2\ e|,\ \bot)$. *If* $e_1 = Throw\ a$, *it can do so to* $([Addr\ a],\ xs_1,\ pc',\ \lfloor a \rfloor)$ *for some* pc'. *Conversely, if* $stk = [v]$ *and* $pc = |compE_2\ e|$, *then* $(e_1,\ xs_1)$ *can silently become* $(Val\ v,\ loc)$. *If* $xcp = \lfloor a \rfloor$, *then* $(e_1,\ xs_1)$ *can silently become* $(Throw\ a,\ loc)$.

Then, the simulation proofs consist of a huge induction on ${}_1\!\approx^e_{jvm}$ and case analysis of the execution steps. Control constructs like conditionals and loops, which are compiled to (conditional) jumps, are verified like in sequential settings.

5.3   Correctness of the Compiler

In Sec. 5.1 and 5.2, we have shown delay bisimilarity for the individual compiler stages, but w.r.t. two different semantics in the intermediate language J_1. To link J_1^m and $J_1'^m$ executions, we must show that the additional reductions in $J_1'^t$ due to e.g. $J_1'S8$ and $J_1'S9$ are never executed in $J_1'^m$, i.e. that the monitor exit instructions never raise *IllegalMonitorState* or *NullPointer* exceptions.

We prove that J_1^m and $J_1'^m$ are the same for a multithreaded state s_1, in which for every monitor a and thread t in s_1, the number of $insync_V(a)$ subexpressions of t equals the number of times t holds a in *locks* s_1 (written $\vdash s_1 \sqrt{}$). In such a state, $J_1'^m$ never picks $J_1'S9$ as the TA [*HasNoLock* a'] never holds. Since all J_1^m reductions preserve $\vdash s_1 \sqrt{}$, we add it as an additional well-formedness constraint to ${}_J\!\approx_1$. Similarly, $J_1'S8$ is never possible because ${}_J\!\approx_1$ (and thus ${}_J\!\approx_1^m$, too) does not allow *Null* being stored in the local variable for the monitor address. Thus, the augmented relation ${}_J\!\approx_1^m$ is also a delay bisimulation for J^m and $J_1'^m$.

We have shown all delay bisimulations from Fig. 2. By transitivity, J^m and JVM^m are delay bisimilar. In the initial state s_J in J, no monitor is locked, all wait sets are empty and there is only a single thread t whose expression is the body of some method M of class C in program P. For JVM, the initial state s_{jvm}

is the same as s_J except that t's local state is the call frame ([], loc, C, M, 0) and no exception is flagged. For an *mfinal* J^m state s, the function *mxcp* s extracts the correct exception flag for every thread in s, i.e. $\perp$ for normal termination and $\lfloor a \rfloor$ if the exception at address a caused the abrupt termination. Then, Lem. 1 from Sec. 3.2 gives the following main correctness theorem:

Theorem 2. *Let s_J execute to s'_J in J^m for P with trace tas such that mfinal s'_J. Then, s_{jvm} executes to mxcp s'_J in JVM^m for J2JVM P with trace tas. Conversely, if s_{jvm} executes to s'_{jvm} in JVM^m for J2JVM P with trace tas such that mfinal s'_{jvm}, then s'_{jvm} has the form mxcp s'_J and s_J executes to s'_J in J^m for P with trace tas.*

Proof. The full proof can be found online in the formalisation [19].

6   Discussion

Challenges due to concurrency. Verifying a compiler for a concurrent language adds three dimensions to compiler verification for sequential programs: (i) non-deterministic interleaving, (ii) different granularity of atomic operations between source and byte code, and (iii) memory models for optimisations. In JinjaThreads, we have addressed (i) and (ii).

For nondeterminism, bisimulation replaces the standard simulation approach for sequential programs, where only the compiled program simulates the source program. For bisimulation, it does not suffice to just show the other direction, but some subtleties arise: First, neither the source nor the compiled program may carry on if the other gets stuck, e.g. due to type errors. Our source code semantics is a small-step semantics, whereas the VM is an abstract state machine. Both naturally contain different type checks, only a full type system and type safety proof at every stage would ensure bisimilarity. By using both the aggressive and defensive VM in the simulation proofs, we only need a single type safety proof for byte code which ensures that both VMs are equivalent for verified byte code.

Second, the bisimulation must relate all states that are reachable from *either* initial state. Ordinary simulations do not have to relate intermediate states in the target code, which the source code skips, to any other state. This substantially increases the size of the bisimulation relation and consequently the number of cases the simulation proof has to consider. For $_1\overset{e}{\approx}_{jvm}$, Lem. 2 from Sec. 5.2 solves this problem for the numerous inductive steps in the simulation proof. For the base cases, we use similar lemmas for each expression, if necessary.

Our correctness result only mentions terminating executions, but a compiler should also preserve nontermination and deadlock. However, the standard (bi-)simulation approach with τ-moves cannot prove this because infinitely many consecutive τ-moves might be simulated by no moves at all, which is known as the *infinite stuttering problem*. Hence, our correctness result allows the byte code program to silently diverge even if all executions of the source program terminate, although this is not the case for our compiler. To prove this, we must strengthen the definition of delay bisimulation with an explicit notion of divergence like in [5], but we do not expect fundamental problems to arise from this.

Concerning (ii), several source code statements such as *sync* generate multiple byte code instructions. A single observable step in the source code program is decomposed into a number of silent steps and one observable step in between. Although it does not show up in the generated code, the number of atomic steps in the different semantics differs considerably. In particular, exceptions slowly propagate up in *J* whereas the VM directly jumps to the exception handler. The framework semantics, which we use at all stages, allows to decompose the multi-threaded case to single threaded, where shared memory accesses and synchronisation must be observable. Hence, we do not have to worry about interleavings and atomicity in the main correctness proofs themselves.

Java vs. JinjaThreads. JinjaThreads is a generalised subset of Java and Java byte code. In terms of concurrency, it models all Java features of the JLS except for time-dependent operations such as `Thread.sleep` and thread interruption. The latter could be easily added to the framework, but we cannot model the former because we have no notion of time. Other concurrency features like thread groups and the `java.util.concurrent` library are Sun's proprietary extensions, which we have not modelled. As to the sequential part, JinjaThreads inherits all features from Jinja: classes and objects, inheritance, dynamic dispatch, fields, arrays, exceptions, local variables, conditionals and loops, binary operators, etc. JinjaThreads models neither interfaces nor static fields and methods, but these are orthogonal to concurrency and could be added if desired. Thus, any Java program that uses only JinjaThreads features can be directly translated to JinjaThreads abstract syntax. JinjaThreads generalises Java in that it does not distinguish between statements and expressions to keep the formalisation simple. Unlike Java, e.g., the condition of a *while* loop may contain a *try catch* block.

For byte code, the situation is similar: all byte code instructions for the above features are modelled. The exception tables are slightly more general because for exception handling, the stack need only be trimmed to a specified size, but not completely cleared. For Jinja programs that respect the syntactic constraints of Java, our compiler only produces byte code that could be directly pretty-printed to Java byte code.

Although our formalisation completely ignores the memory model issue, it is still a sound model for real Java. For programs without data races in the sense of the JMM, the JMM guarantees sequential consistency [3], i.e. our interleaving semantics can reproduce all allowed executions. Hence, our results also apply to data race free Java programs. Moreover, our compiler is strictly nonoptimising; it just follows the recommendations in the JVMS [16, Ch. 7]. In fact, even Sun's `javac` compiler in Java 2 SE optimises only very little, but leaves this to the JIT compiler in the VM. Ševčík and Aspinall [25] showed that the JMM allows all program transformations that do not affect the JMM-observable behaviour. Since our compiler falls into this class, our verification will also work for the JMM.

Size of the formalisation. Currently, JinjaThreads consists of about 47k lines of Isabelle theories (without the a data flow analysis framework for the byte code verifer), but not everything is relevant to the compiler itself. The framework semantics has approx. 6k lines. About 4.3k lines provide general infrastructure for JinjaThreads. The semantics for J, J_1 and JVM, the byte code verifier and type safety proofs are 14k lines. 1k lines show that our J semantics is bisimilar to the original source code semantics which dynamically inlines method calls. The translation from J to J_1 is verified in about 3.4k lines, but the by far largest part is the bisimilarity proof for J_1 and JVM with more than 17k lines. Replaying all proofs (including type safety and the byte code verifier) in Isabelle2009 takes 52 minutes on an Intel DualCore 2.33GHz processor with 2GB memory.

In comparison, Jinja [11], on which JinjaThreads was based, has only 15k lines of Isabelle code (excluding the data flow analysis). The compiler verification in terms of the big-step semantics is much easier: about 3.2k lines. Hence, going from big-step to small-step and from sequential to multithreaded has blown up the amount of proofs to be done. In particular, semantic preservation in Jinja is only unidirectional from source code to byte code. Our proof scripts may be not optimal yet, and we expect that some improvements can be made, but the difference in size w.r.t. Jinja will remain immense.

7   Related Work

Formal semantics for Java. There are a lot of formal semantics for different subsets of sequential Java source code and byte code, e.g. [2,11,22]. As for concurrent Java, AtomicJava [7] by Flanagan et al. models most Java source code features except inheritance and exception handling. Stärk et al. [26] present a semantics for multithreaded source code based on abstract state machines, a pen-and-paper proof for type preservation, and a model of a sequential JVM. Liu and Moore's interpreter M5 [17] in ACL2 provides a monolithic multithreaded semantics for byte code, which also models class loading and initialisation. They aim at verifying JVM implementations w.r.t. the JVMS. Huisman and Petri's [10] detailed model of the JVMS in Coq features all byte code instructions, the wait/notify mechanism and thread interruption, but they do not report on any proofs with the semantics.

Like in our approach, Belblidia and Debabbi [4] have a semantics for threads in isolation and a second layer which manages the threads from which it receives thread actions, which they call labels. In contrast to ours, their single-thread semantics already takes care of the locks, which are stored in shared memory. Nor do they model the wait/notify mechanism or thread interruption. Also, they only give the byte code semantics, but do not report on any proofs with it.

Formally verified compilers. Compiler verification in general has been an active research topic for more than 40 years; see [6] for an annotated bibliography. Rittri [24] and Wand [27] first used bisimulations for compiler verification for a simple, parallel functional language. They showed that running the compiled code on a virtual machine is weakly bisimilar to the source code's denotational semantics.

Most closely related to our compiler is the one by Stärk et al. [26], but it handles only sequential Java source code. Also, they lack the formal rigour required for machine-checked proofs, as already pointed out in [11].

As for compiler verification for concurrent Java, Ševčík and Aspinall [25] report on verifying individual compiler optimisations w.r.t. the JMM. They show that the JMM does not allow as many as intended by its designers for programs with data races. However, their proofs are only on paper for a toy core language without almost all sequential Java features.

Leroy's CompCert project [13,14,15] has been the most remarkable landmark in mechanised compiler verification recently. He has verified a complete compilation tool chain from a subset of C source code to PowerPC assembly language in Coq. CompCert focuses on low-level details and language features such as memory layout, register allocation and instruction selection. Leroy also plans to extend CompCert to concurrency [15, Sec. 17.7]. He wants to show semantic preservation only for pseudo-sequential executions, where threads are rescheduled only at lock operations. By contrast, our approach directly covers all interleavings and all behaviours, since we use bisimulations instead of simulations. Hence, our proof also shows that the different granularity of atomicity in source code and byte code does not affect the possible behaviour of programs.

As part of the Verisoft project, Leinenbach [12] has verified a nonoptimising compiler from C0, a subset of C, directly to DLX assembler in Isabelle/HOL. Like CompCert, he focuses on low-level details and only proves a weak simulation theorem for sequential executions, but not for the backward direction.

8   Conclusion and Future Work

In the current paper, we presented the first verification of a compiler for multi-threaded Java to byte code. The proof technique is much more difficult than for sequential languages: (i) one must switch from big-step to small-step semantics in the source, target and intermediate languages, and (ii) one must show both directions of the required bisimulation to be semantics preserving. According to the more complex proof requirements, the verification required 47k lines of Isabelle formalisation compared to 15k lines for the sequential predecessor.

Our verified Java compiler is part of a larger project which aims to completely verify an infrastructure for language-based security [9,28]. Still, much remains to be done: Without a trusted VM, the guarantee of the verified compiler is vacuous. We are currently working together with the Isabelle team on mechanically extracting an executable VM from our formalisation. Moreover, our notion of bisimulation cannot distinguish a deadlocked program from a silently diverging one. Leroy's simulation property [15] might be a good starting point for a stronger notion. As the next step, we plan to add the JMM to our interleaving semantics. Using the techniques from [25], we expect to transfer our results to the JMM without meeting fundamental problems. This will further narrow the formalisation gap between Java and JinjaThreads. Finally, we are going to add the missing constructs from sequential Java to obtain a verified compiler for full Java. To automate the conversions, we are also working on a simple parser from Java source code to abstract syntax and a printer from byte code abstract syntax back to Java byte code.

Acknowledgements. We would like to thank G. Snelting, D. Wasserrab, D. Lohner, and C. Hammer for inspiring discussions about the formalisation and the anonymous reviewers for valuable comments on earlier drafts of this paper.

References

1. Aceto, L., van Glabbeek, R.J., Fokkink, W., Ingólfsdóttir, A.: Axiomatizing prefix iteration with silent steps. Information and Computation 127(1), 26–40 (1996)
2. Alves-Foss, J. (ed.): Formal Syntax and Semantics of Java. LNCS, vol. 1523. Springer, Heidelberg (1999)
3. Aspinall, D., Ševčík, J.: Formalising Java's data-race-free guarantee. In: Schneider, K., Brandt, J. (eds.) TPHOLs 2007. LNCS, vol. 4732, pp. 22–37. Springer, Heidelberg (2007)
4. Belblidia, N., Debbabi, M.: A dynamic operational semantics for JVML. Journal of Object Technology 6(3), 71–100 (2007)
5. Bergstra, J.A., Klop, J.W., Olderog, E.R.: Failures without chaos: a new process semantics for fair abstraction. In: IFIP 1987, Formal Description of Programming Concepts III, pp. 77–103. Elsevier Science Publishing, Amsterdam (1987)
6. Dave, M.A.: Compiler verification: a bibliography. SIGSOFT Software Engineering Notes 28(6), 2 (2003)
7. Flanagan, C., Freund, S.N., Lifshin, M., Qadeer, S.: Types for atomicity: Static checking and inference for Java. ACM TOPLAS 30(4), 1–53 (2008)
8. Gosling, J., Joy, B., Steele, G., Bracha, G.: The Java Language Specification, 3rd edn. Addison-Wesley, Reading (2005)
9. Hammer, C., Snelting, G.: Flow-sensitive, context-sensitive, and object-sensitive information flow control based on program dependence graphs. International Journal of Information Security 8(6), 399–422 (2009)
10. Huisman, M., Petri, G.: BicolanoMT: a formalization of multi-threaded Java at bytecode level. In: BYTECODE 2008. ENTCS (2008)
11. Klein, G., Nipkow, T.: A machine-checked model for a Java-like language, virtual machine and compiler. ACM TOPLAS 28, 619–695 (2006)
12. Leinenbach, D.: Compiler Verification in the Context of Pervasive System Verification. PhD thesis, Saarland University (2008)
13. Leroy, X.: Formal certification of a compiler backend or: Programming a compiler with a proof assistant. In: POPL 2006, pp. 42–54. ACM, New York (2006)
14. Leroy, X.: Formal verification of a realistic compiler. Communications of the ACM 52(7), 107–115 (2009)
15. Leroy, X.: A formally verified compiler back-end. Journal of Automated Reasoning 43(4), 363–446 (2009)
16. Lindholm, T., Yellin, F.: The Java Virtual Machine Specification, Second Edition. Addison-Wesley, Reading (1999)
17. Liu, H., Moore, J.S.: Executable JVM Model for Analytical Reasoning: A Study. In: IVME 2003, pp. 15–23 (2003)
18. Lochbihler, A.: Type safe nondeterminism - a formal semantics of Java threads. In: FOOL 2008 (2008)
19. Lochbihler, A.: Jinja with threads. In: The Archive of Formal Proofs (2009), http://afp.sf.net/devel-entries/JinjaThreads.shtml (Formal proof development)

20. Milner, R.: A modal characterisation of observable machine-behaviour. In: Astesiano, E., Böhm, C. (eds.) CAAP 1981. LNCS, vol. 112, pp. 25–34. Springer, Heidelberg (1981)

21. Milner, R.: Communication and Concurrency. Prentice Hall, Englewood Cliffs (1989)

22. Nipkow, T. (ed.): Special Issue on Java Bytecode Verification. Journal of Automated Reasoning, vol. 30(3-4). Springer, Heidelberg (2003)

23. Nipkow, T., Paulson, L.C., Wenzel, M.T. (eds.): Isabelle/HOL. LNCS, vol. 2283. Springer, Heidelberg (2002)

24. Rittri, M.: Proving the correctness of a virtual machine by a bisimulation. Licentiate thesis, Göteborg University (1988)

25. Ševčík, J., Aspinall, D.: On validity of program transformations in the Java memory model. In: Vitek, J. (ed.) ECOOP 2008. LNCS, vol. 5142, pp. 27–51. Springer, Heidelberg (2008)

26. Stärk, R.F., Schmid, J., Börger, E.: Java and the Java Virtual Machine. Springer, Heidelberg (2001)

27. Wand, M.: Compiler correctness for parallel languages. In: FPCA 1995, pp. 120–134. ACM, New York (1995)

28. Wasserrab, D., Lohner, D., Snelting, G.: On PDG-based noninterference and its modular proof. In: PLAS 2009, pp. 31–44. ACM, New York (2009)

A Grammar-Based Approach to Invertible Programs

Kazutaka Matsuda[1,2], Shin-Cheng Mu[1,3], Zhenjiang Hu[4],
and Masato Takeichi[1]

[1] University of Tokyo, Japan
[2] JSPS Research Fellow
[3] Academia Sinica, Taiwan
[4] National Institute of Informatics, Japan

Abstract. Program inversion has many applications such as in the implementation of serialization/deserialization and in providing support for redo/undo, and has been studied by many researchers. However, little attention has been paid to two problems: how to characterize programs that are easy or hard to invert and whether, for each class of programs, efficient inverses can be obtained. In this paper, we propose an inversion framework that we call *grammar-based inversion*, where a program is associated with an unambiguous grammar describing the range of the program. The complexity of the grammar indicates how hard it is to invert the program, while the complexity is related to how efficient an inverse can be obtained.

1 Introduction

The problem of *program inversion* — deriving a program computing f^{-1} from a program computing f, has been studied over decades [1, 7, 8, 11, 15–17, 25, 27, 30] and has many applications including providing support for undo/redo, deriving a deserializing program from a serializing program or vice versa, and serving as an auxiliary phase in other program transformations, such as bidirectionalization [21].

Every method of program inversion faces two challenges: how to handle a wide class of programs, and how to derive efficient inverses for them. Although it is possible to invert all the programs based on symbolic computation with search (e.g., [1]) as in logic programs, an inverse obtained this way could perform much worse than a handwritten inverse. Thus, an inversion method should restrict itself to a certain subclass of programs for which efficient inverses can be derived. It is certainly desirable for an inverter to handle a wider class of programs. Although often overlooked, it is also desirable for the criteria under which a program can be inverted by a particular inverter to be perspicuously specified. This is especially important when program inversion is used by other program transformations, and we have to convert the program into a form acceptable by the inverter.

A.D. Gordon (Ed.): ESOP 2010, LNCS 6012, pp. 448–467, 2010.

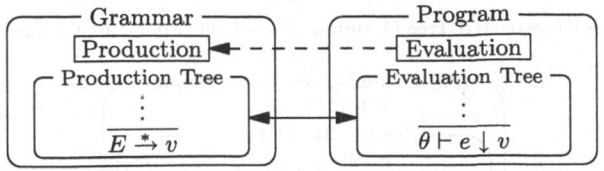

Fig. 1. Idea underlying our inversion: Inversion problem can be rephrased as "given expression e and value v, find environment θ under which e evaluates to v" (Sect. 2)

Two questions arise naturally: For what kind of programs, how efficient inverse programs can be obtained, and how difficult is the inversion process? Those who have worked on program inversion would agree that among the following programs, *double* is the easiest to invert, followed by *snoc*, and *reverse* is the most difficult of the three.

$$
\begin{array}{lll}
double(x) = \textbf{case } x \textbf{ of} & snoc(x,b) = \textbf{case } x \textbf{ of} &
\begin{array}{l}
reverse(x) = rev(x,[\,]) \\
rev(x,r) = \textbf{case } x \textbf{ of}
\end{array} \\
\quad \mathsf{Z} \;\rightarrow\; \mathsf{Z} & \quad [\,] \;\rightarrow\; [b] & \quad [\,] \quad\rightarrow\; r \\
\quad \mathsf{S}(y) \rightarrow \mathsf{S}(\mathsf{S}(double(y))), & \quad a:y \rightarrow a:snoc(y,b), & \quad a:y \rightarrow rev(y,a:r).
\end{array}
$$

A particular method may be able to handle some of these while it may fail on the others. It has not been clarified, however, whether this is merely due to the inadequacy of the method, or whether some problems are intrinsically hard. To the best of the authors' knowledge, there have been no formal classifications of invertible programs so far.

We propose a framework toward solving the classification problem, that we call *grammar-based inversion* in this paper, which is an adaptation of Yellin's inversion [30] for first-order functional programs. Our inversion is based on the correspondence between two proofs: a proof of $\exists x.\ f(x) = v$ for function f, and a proof of $v \in \mathsf{Range}(f)$ where $\mathsf{Range}(f)$ is described by a grammar. More concretely, as in Fig. 1, our inversion uses bijection between a proof for evaluation of a program (an evaluation tree) and a proof for production of a grammar (a production tree). From an output of the program (function), a production tree is obtained by parsing with the grammar. According to the correspondence, the production tree is then converted to an evaluation tree of the program. We also reconstruct the environment used in the evaluation with the evaluation tree, from which we recover the arguments to which the function was applied. The class of programs that can be inverted by the proposed approach is characterized by the complexity of grammars, as seen in Fig. 2. For example, to invert *double* and *snoc*, regular tree grammars (RTG) [6] is sufficient. To invert *reverse*, however, we need grammar beyond regular, such as (inside-out) context-free tree grammar [9]. While a more general grammar covers more programs, it also implies higher worst-case time complexity of parsing and, therefore, a less-efficient inverse. Grammar-based inversion has three main characteristics:

– A program is associated with a grammar, whose complexity characterizes how difficult it is to invert the program.

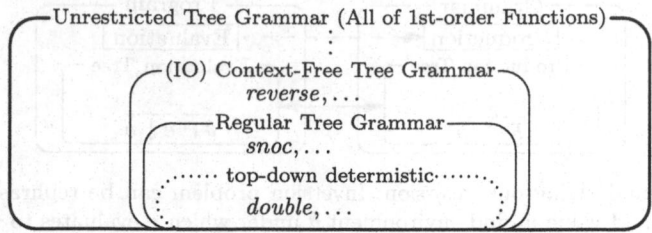

Fig. 2. Classification includes *double*, *snoc*, and *reverse*

- The derived inverse is efficiently evaluated by parsing the output with respect to the grammar.
- The correctness of the inversion is clearly expressed by bijection between two proofs.

We present grammar-based inversion with RTG as a case study in this paper. Invertible programs of grammar-based inversion using RTG cover *double* and *snoc* but not *reverse*. However, it will be explained in Sect. 5 that grammar-based inversion, being an extensible framework, can handle functions like *reverse*.

The main purpose of our work is *not* to invert as many programs as possible, or to obtain the most efficient inverses for certain programs. Instead, we aim at classifying programs by grammars that determine the worst-case time complexity of the derived inverses. Also note that we classify programs, not problems. That is, classification by grammar-based inversion is rather syntactic, not semantic.

This paper is organized as follows. Section 2 defines a small core language that we base our discussion on. Section 3 explains an informal account of grammar-based inversion using a small example. Section 4 presents a case study of grammar-based inversion using RTG in detail. Section 5 discusses grammar-based inversion in general. Section 6 describes an experiment that demonstrated the inverses obtained with our method are sufficiently efficient. Section 7 discusses related work. Section 8 concludes the paper and discusses some future directions.

Preliminaries. For function f, function g is called a *left inverse* of f if and only if $g(f(x)) = x$ for all x in the domain of f. For function f, function g is a *right inverse* of f if and only if $f(g(y)) = y$ for all y in the range of f. Both inverses are discussed in this paper. We only consider left/right inverses that are defined precisely on the range of f. Thus, the left inverse is always unique for injective function f. Unless otherwise noted, "inverse" and "invertible" in this paper refer to left inverses.

2   Core Language

To begin with, let us define a small core language to describe the programs to be inverted. The language is merely a first-order functional programming language with call-by-value semantics except for its slightly unusual evaluation rules.

$$prog ::= decl_1 \ldots decl_n$$
$$decl ::= f(x_1, \ldots, x_n) = e$$
$$e \quad ::= x \mid \mathsf{C}(e_1, \ldots, e_n) \mid f(e_1, \ldots, e_n) \mid \mathbf{case}\ x\ \mathbf{of}\ \{p_1 \to e_1; \ldots; p_n \to e_n\}$$
$$p \quad ::= x \mid \mathsf{C}(p_1, \ldots, p_n)$$

Fig. 3. Syntax of core language

Let Σ be a set of constructors each associated with an arity. The set of *values* are trees $\mathcal{T}_\Sigma$, inductively defined by: Let $\mathsf{C} \in \Sigma$ be an n-ary constructor, $\mathsf{C}(t_1, \ldots, t_n) \in \mathcal{T}_\Sigma$ if $t_1, \ldots, t_n \in \mathcal{T}_\Sigma$. Note that the definition implies that $\mathsf{C}()$ for nullary C is always in $\mathcal{T}_\Sigma$. For example, given an appropriate Σ, $\mathsf{Z}()$ and $\mathsf{S}(\mathsf{Z}())$ are both trees. For brevity, tree $\mathsf{C}()$ is written as C, and trees $\mathsf{Cons}(x, y)$ and Nil are written as $x : y$ and $[\,]$, respectively. In the later discussion, we assume set Σ containing all constructors in the examples.

A *program* is a set of definitions of first-order functions that take a tuple of values and return a value. The syntax of the language is formally described in Fig. 3. To simplify the presentation, the language does not have a **let** construct, and **case** always matches a variable against patterns. The restrictions do not affect the expressiveness of the language. The set of free variables in expression e is denoted by $\mathsf{vars}(e)$. For simplicity, we assume that the variables in p of **case**-alternative $p \to e$ are always fresh.

We call a program *nonerasing* if every variable in the LHS of a declaration also occurs in the corresponding RHS, and every variable in pattern p of **case**-alternative $p \to e$ occurs in e. If no variable in a program occurs more than once in the RHS, we call the program *affine*.

Substitution θ is a mapping from a finite domain of variables to values. Given pattern p, the value obtained by substituting variables in the domain of θ for corresponding values is denoted by $p\theta$. For set of variables X and substitution θ, domain restriction operator $-|_-$ is defined by $\theta|_X = \{x \mapsto \theta(x) \mid x \in X\}$. Partial operator $\uplus$ merges two substitutions if their domains are disjoint.

The semantics of the language is defined by the big-step call-by-value semantics given in Fig. 4. The semantics is rather standard, except that we eagerly remove unused variables in the environment by domain restriction, which will come in handy in our inversion later. To evaluate expression e, the rules in Fig. 4 are repeatedly applied and an *evaluation tree* (a derivation tree/a proof tree) is

$$\text{VAR:}\ \frac{\theta(x) = v}{\theta \vdash x \downarrow v} \qquad \text{CON:}\ \frac{\{\theta|_{\mathsf{vars}(e_i)} \vdash e_i \downarrow v_i\}_{i \in \{1, \ldots, n\}}}{\theta \vdash \mathsf{C}(e_1, \ldots, e_n) \downarrow \mathsf{C}(v_1, \ldots, v_n)}$$

$$\text{FUN:}\ \frac{\{\theta|_{\mathsf{vars}(e_i)} \vdash e_i \downarrow v_i\}_{i \in \{1, \ldots, n\}} \quad \{x_i \mapsto v_i \mid 1 \le i \le n\}|_{\mathsf{vars}(e')} \vdash e' \downarrow v}{\theta \vdash f(e_1, \ldots, e_n) \downarrow v}\ (\exists f(x_1, \ldots, x_n) = e')$$

$$\text{CASE:}\ \frac{\exists \sigma, i.\ p_i\sigma = \theta(x) \quad (\theta \uplus \sigma)|_{\mathsf{vars}(e_i)} \vdash e_i \downarrow v}{\theta \vdash \mathbf{case}\ x\ \mathbf{of}\ \{p_1 \to e_1; \ldots; p_n \to e_n\} \downarrow v}$$

Fig. 4. Big-step call-by-value semantics of core language

constructed. Evaluation tree $\mathcal{E}$ can be seen as a proof that e evaluates to some v under environment θ, which we denote by $\mathcal{E} : \theta \vdash e \downarrow v$. For simplicity, patterns in **case** are assumed to be non-overlapping, i.e., there is at most one pattern that matches any given input. Note that, given e and θ, evaluation tree $\mathcal{E} : \theta \vdash e \downarrow v$ is unique if it exists.

3   Grammar-Based Inversion: An Overview

Before going into details, we briefly overview grammar-based inversion.

3.1   Basic Idea Underlying Grammar-Based Inversion

Recall that, in Sect. 2, a program defines the semantics of expressions. Therefore, we can reduce program inversion to expression inversion as follows.

Problem (Expression Inversion). Given expression e in a program and value v, find environment (substitution) θ such that $\theta \vdash e \downarrow v$.

Given function f, it is reasonable to expect that any notion of a "correct" inversion should cover the entire range of f. That is, it should be complete in the sense that for all v, if there exists θ such that $\theta \vdash f(x) \downarrow v$, we are able to recover θ. This is apparently hard and inefficient for general f. Thus, we restrict ourselves to a method that is only complete for a chosen class of programs.

The goal of grammar-based inversion is to reconstruct the evaluation tree of $\theta \vdash e \downarrow v$, given e and v. This is as hard as only constructing the environment θ. Reconstruction is carried out in two steps: we first construct an approximation of evaluation by building a production tree with respect to a grammar induced by the program, then attempt to reconstruct environment θ from the production tree. Note that the grammar also approximates the range of the program. There is an overview of grammar-based inversion in Fig. 5.

3.2   Inverting *snoc* Step by Step

We demonstrate grammar-based inversion with the example of *snoc* in Sect. 1. The first step is to construct an unambiguous grammar whose production tree approximates an evaluation tree of *snoc*. One would prefer to construct a grammar belonging to a lower complexity class because the complexity is related to the efficiency of the derived inverse. It suffices to use a regular tree grammar (RTG) [6] for *snoc*. From a program, we derive an RTG such that:

- Each nonterminal E_e corresponds to expression e in the program.
- If expression e evaluates to e', we add production rule $E_e \rightarrow E_{e'}$.
- Constructors are converted to terminal symbols denoting themselves.
- Nonterminal E_x for variable-use expression x has production rule $E_x \rightarrow \top$, where $\top$ is a special symbol that will be explained later.

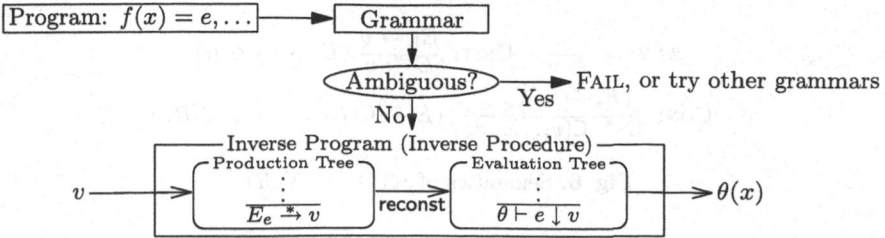

Fig. 5. An overview of grammar-based inversion

The conversion will be formalized in the next section. For example, *snoc* is converted to the (unambiguous) grammar below. Here, **case** x **of** $\{\ldots\}$ is an abbreviation for **case** x **of** $\{[\,] \to b:[\,]; \ a:y \to a:snoc(y,b)\}$, the unique RHS of *snoc*, the function we intend to invert.

$$E_{\textbf{case } x \textbf{ of } \{\ldots\}} \to E_{b:[\,]} \qquad E_{a:snoc(y,b)} \to E_a : E_{snoc(y,b)} \qquad E_b \to \top$$
$$E_{\textbf{case } x \textbf{ of } \{\ldots\}} \to E_{a:snoc(y,b)} \qquad E_{snoc(y,b)} \to E_{\textbf{case } x \textbf{ of } \{\ldots\}} \qquad E_{[\,]} \to [\,]$$
$$E_{b:[\,]} \qquad\quad \to E_b : E_{[\,]} \qquad E_a \qquad\qquad \to \top \qquad\qquad\qquad E_y \to \top$$

For the second step, given an output supposedly produced by *snoc*, we first try to parse it against the grammar, allowing $\top$ to match any value. For example, the production tree of $1:[\,]$, or the derivation/proof tree of production $E_{\textbf{case } x \textbf{ of } \{\ldots\}} \overset{*}{\to} 1:[\,]$, is:

$$\cfrac{\cfrac{\cfrac{\top \overset{*}{\to} 1}{E_b \overset{*}{\to} 1} \qquad E_{[\,]} \overset{*}{\to} [\,]}{E_{b:[\,]} \overset{*}{\to} 1:[\,]}}{E_{\textbf{case } x \textbf{ of } \{\ldots\}} \overset{*}{\to} 1:[\,]} \ .$$

From the production tree, we can reconstruct the following evaluation tree of $\theta \vdash snoc(x,b) \downarrow 1:[\,]$:

$$\cfrac{\cfrac{\cfrac{\{b \mapsto 1\}(b) = 1}{\{b \mapsto 1\} \vdash b \downarrow 1} \quad \overline{\emptyset \vdash [\,] \downarrow [\,]}}{\{b \mapsto 1\} \vdash [\,] \to b:[\,] \downarrow 1:[\,]} \quad \{b \mapsto 1, x \mapsto [\,]\}(x) = [\,]}{\{b \mapsto 1, x \mapsto [\,]\} \vdash \textbf{case } x \textbf{ of } \{[\,] \to b:[\,]; \ a:y \to a:snoc(y,b)\} \downarrow 1:[\,]} \ .$$

Each node of the obtained evaluation tree corresponds to a node in the production tree. $\top$ matches 1 in the topmost leaf of the production tree; therefore, the value of b is known to be 1 in the corresponding node in the evaluation tree. By completing the evaluation tree we have also recovered the initial environment, $\{b \mapsto 1, x \mapsto [\,]\}$, the result of inversion.

This reconstruction of evaluation trees from production trees is done by function **reconst** in Sect. 4. With **reconst**, our generated inverse program $snoc^{-1}$ has the form:

$$snoc^{-1}(v) = (\theta(x), \theta(b))$$
$$\textbf{where } (\mathcal{E} : \theta \vdash snoc(x,b) \downarrow v) = \textsf{reconst}(\mathcal{P})$$
$$\mathcal{P} \text{ is a production tree for } E_{\textbf{case } x \textbf{ of } \{\ldots\}} \overset{*}{\to} v.$$

$$\text{ANY: } \frac{}{\top \overset{*}{\to} v} \qquad \text{UNIT: } \frac{E_1 \overset{*}{\to} v}{E \overset{*}{\to} v} \ (E \to E_1 \in R)$$

$$\text{CON: } \frac{\{E_i \overset{*}{\to} v_i\}_{1 \leq i \leq n}}{E \overset{*}{\to} \mathsf{C}(v_1, \dots, v_n)} \ (E \to \mathsf{C}(E_1, \dots, E_n) \in R)$$

Fig. 6. Semantics of RTG (Σ, N, R)

Since the cost of parsing for RTGs is linear, the derived $snoc^{-1}$ runs in time that is linear to its input. It might seem that $snoc^{-1}$ entails a large overhead. The experiment discussed in Sect. 6 demonstrates that the overhead is acceptable.

4   Grammar-Based Inversion by Regular Tree Grammar

This section describes a case study of grammar-based inversion when we use RTG [6], one of the simplest tree grammars, which is relatively well understood; e.g., parsing for RTG can be efficiently performed done tree automaton and its variations [4, 6, 13, 24].

Definition 1 (RTG). *An RTG is a triple (Σ, N, R), where Σ is a set of constructors (terminals), N is a set of nonterminals, and R is a set of production rules in which each rule has either of the forms $E \to E_1$ or $E \to \mathsf{C}(E_1, \dots, E_n)$ with $E, E_1, \dots, E_n \in N$ and $\mathsf{C} \in \Sigma$ of arity n.*

Unlike conventional presentation, we define the semantics of a grammar in a "big-step" style as seen in Fig. 6. The rules in Fig. 6 are defined so that $E \overset{*}{\to} v$ means that value v is a normal form of E taking production rules to be rewriting rules. We assume that there exists special nonterminal $\top$ that can generate any value, and we treat $\top \overset{*}{\to} v$ as an axiom. Also note the above definition contains no start symbol. We sometimes write $\mathcal{P} : E \overset{*}{\to} v$ if $\mathcal{P}$ is a production tree (a derivation tree/a proof tree) for $E \overset{*}{\to} v$. We call a grammar *ambiguous* if, for some E and v, there is more than one production tree for $E \overset{*}{\to} v$. Otherwise, the grammar is *unambiguous*. Note that checking whether an RTG is ambiguous or not is known to be decidable [6].

4.1   Approximation of Evaluation Structure

We construct an RTG from a program so that each production rule in the grammar corresponds to an evaluation step of the program. The basic idea behind the construction has been explained in Sect. 3, and the formal rules are given in Fig. 7. The procedure itself is not new; it is almost the same as the type inference of regular expression types [19], and similar techniques have been adopted in the range inference of tree transducers (e.g., [10]).

To clarify the correspondence between a program and its derived grammar, we define a transformation, approx, from a proof of $\theta \vdash e \downarrow v$ to a proof of $E_e \overset{*}{\to} v$ in Fig. 8. Function approx defines the node-by-node correspondence between the two proofs. Formally, we have the following theorem.

$$
\begin{aligned}
x &\longrightarrow & E_x \to \top \\
C(e_1,\ldots,e_n) &\longrightarrow & E_{C(e_1,\ldots,e_n)} \to C(E_{e_1},\ldots,E_{e_n}) \\
f(e_1,\ldots,e_n) &\longrightarrow & E_{f(e_1,\ldots,e_n)} \to E_{e'} \quad \text{where } \exists(f(\ldots)=e')
\end{aligned}
$$

$$
\textbf{case } x \textbf{ of } \{p_1 \to e_1;\ldots;p_n \to e_n\} \longrightarrow
\begin{pmatrix}
E_{\textbf{case } x \textbf{ of } \{p_1 \to e_1;\ldots;p_n \to e_n\}} \to E_{e_1} \\
\vdots \\
E_{\textbf{case } x \textbf{ of } \{p_1 \to e_1;\ldots;p_n \to e_n\}} \to E_{e_n}
\end{pmatrix}
$$

Fig. 7. Construction of productions rules of RTG

$$
\mathsf{approx}\left(\frac{\theta(x) = v}{\theta \vdash x \downarrow v} \right)
$$

$$
= \frac{\top \xrightarrow{*} v}{E_x \xrightarrow{*} v}
$$

$$
\mathsf{approx}\left(\frac{\{\mathcal{E}_i : \theta|_{\mathsf{vars}(e_i)} \vdash e_i \downarrow v_i\}_{1 \le i \le n}}{\theta \vdash C(e_1,\ldots,e_n) \downarrow C(v_1,\ldots,v_n)} \right)
$$

$$
= \frac{\{\mathsf{approx}(\mathcal{E}_i)\}_{1 \le i \le n}}{E_{C(e_1,\ldots,e_n)} \xrightarrow{*} C(v_1,\ldots,v_n)}
$$

$$
\mathsf{approx}\left(\frac{\{\_ : \theta|_{\mathsf{vars}(e_i)} \vdash e_i \downarrow v_i\}_{1 \le i \le n} \quad \mathcal{E} : \{x_i \mapsto v_i \mid 1 \le i \le n\} \vdash e \downarrow v}{\theta \vdash f(e_1,\ldots,e_n) \downarrow v} \right)
$$

$$
= \frac{\mathsf{approx}(\mathcal{E})}{E_{f(e_1,\ldots,e_n)} \xrightarrow{*} v} \quad \text{where } \exists(f(x_1,\ldots,x_n) = e)
$$

$$
\mathsf{approx}\left(\frac{\exists \sigma, i. \ p_i\sigma = \theta(x) \quad \mathcal{E}_i : (\theta \uplus \sigma)|_{\mathsf{vars}(e_i)} \vdash e_i \downarrow v}{\theta \vdash \textbf{case } x \textbf{ of } \{p_1 \to e_1;\ldots;p_n \to e_n\} \downarrow v} \right)
$$

$$
= \frac{\mathsf{approx}(\mathcal{E}_i)}{E_{\textbf{case } x \textbf{ of } \{p_1 \to e_1;\ldots;p_n \to e_n\}} \xrightarrow{*} v}
$$

Fig. 8. Definition of approx

Theorem 1 (Approximation). *Given evaluation tree $\mathcal{E} : \theta \vdash e \downarrow v$, $\mathcal{P} = \mathsf{approx}(\mathcal{E})$ is a production tree for $E_e \xrightarrow{*} v$, i.e., $\mathcal{P} : E_e \xrightarrow{*} v$.* □

Since approx discards the evaluation trees of arguments at the third branch, approx is neither surjective nor injective: there may be production tree $\mathcal{P} : E_e \xrightarrow{*} v$ that does not correspond to any evaluation tree, i.e., $\forall \mathcal{E} : \theta \vdash e \downarrow v$. $\mathcal{P} \neq \mathsf{approx}(\mathcal{E})$, even if e evaluates to v under some environment. For example, consider the program

$$
\begin{aligned}
h(r) &= add(\mathsf{Z}, r) \\
add(x, r) &= \textbf{case } x \textbf{ of } \{\mathsf{Z} \to r; \ \mathsf{S}(y) \to \mathsf{S}(add(y,r))\}.
\end{aligned}
$$

Since h is injective, there is only one evaluation tree for $\{r \mapsto \mathsf{S}(\mathsf{Z})\} \vdash add(\mathsf{Z}, r) \downarrow \mathsf{S}(\mathsf{Z})$. From h we obtain the following grammar:

$$
\begin{aligned}
E_{add(\mathsf{Z},r)} &\to E_{\textbf{case } x \textbf{ of } \{\ldots\}} & E_{add(y,r)} &\to E_{\textbf{case } x \textbf{ of } \{\ldots\}} & E_y &\to \top. \\
E_{\textbf{case } x \textbf{ of } \{\ldots\}} &\to E_r & E_{\mathsf{Z}} &\to \mathsf{Z} \\
E_{\textbf{case } x \textbf{ of } \{\ldots\}} &\to \mathsf{S}(E_{add(y,r)}) & E_r &\to \top
\end{aligned}
$$

The reader may have found that there are two production trees for $E_{add(Z,r)} \xrightarrow{*} S(Z)$, and only one of these corresponds to the evaluation tree.

To deal with this situation, we propose two sufficient conditions to guarantee bijection between evaluation and production trees:

Condition (SUFF-LEFT)**:** The program is nonerasing and the derived grammar is unambiguous.

Condition (SUFF-RIGHT)**:** The program is affine and treeless (i.e., every argument of a function call must be a variable) [29].

Roughly speaking, (SUFF-LEFT) guarantees the injectivity of a program, while (SUFF-RIGHT) guarantees its surjectivity with respect to the range described by the grammar. With (SUFF-LEFT), for v of $\mathcal{E} : \theta \vdash e \downarrow v$, any $\mathcal{P} : E_e \xrightarrow{*} v$ must equal approx($\mathcal{E}$) since the grammar is unambiguous. With (SUFF-RIGHT), every $\mathcal{P} : E_e \xrightarrow{*} v$ must have a unique corresponding evaluation tree, $\mathcal{E} : \theta \vdash e \downarrow v$ (a direct consequence of [21]). As will be seen later, (SUFF-LEFT) is used to obtain left inverses, and (SUFF-RIGHT) is used to obtain right inverses.

4.2   Reconstructing Evaluation Trees

Our aim now is to construct an evaluation tree from a production tree, i.e., to construct the inverse of approx. Since the RHSs of approx are disjoint, inversion of approx is done in a straightforward way if we can recover the information lost in approx — the evaluation trees of arguments to each function call $f(e_1, \ldots, e_n)$. In other words, in reconstructing the evaluation tree of $f(e_1, \ldots, e_n) \downarrow v$ where f is defined by $f(x_1, \ldots, x_n) = e$, we must recover $\mathcal{E}_i$ of $\mathcal{E}_i : \theta_i \vdash e_i \downarrow \theta(x_i)$ from $\mathcal{E} : \theta \vdash e \downarrow v$. Luckily, this can be done. Assume that each e_i respectively evaluates to v_i. The values of v_i have been recovered by $v_i = \theta(x_i)$. Thus, evaluation tree $\mathcal{E}_i : \theta_i \vdash e_i \downarrow v_i$ is obtained by recursively rebuilding production tree $\mathcal{P}_i : E_{e_i} \xrightarrow{*} v_i$.

Formally, reconst defined in Fig. 9 reconstructs an evaluation tree from a production tree.[1] Function reconst is an inverse of approx obtained by swapping LHSs with RHSs except that invE recovers the lost information of approx, as explained in the previous paragraph. Operator $\uplus$ is extended to substitutions with overlapping domains: $\{x \mapsto 1\} \uplus \{x \mapsto 1\}$ yields $\{x \mapsto 1\}$, while $\{x \mapsto 1\} \uplus \{x \mapsto 2\}$ fails. Note that reconst is a partial function; e.g., $\uplus$ may fail.

Procedure invE in Fig. 9 appears to be nondeterministic since there might be more than one production tree. With constraints (SUFF-LEFT) and (SUFF-RIGHT), we ensure that there is at most one production tree and thus invE is deterministic.

---

[1] For simplicity, we assume that there is at most one possibility to choose p_i at the definition of reconst for **case**; e.g., we exclude **case** x **of** $\{Z \to Z; S(y) \to Z\}$. Note that a program containing such a **case**-expression does not satisfy (SUFF-LEFT). To invert such programs under (SUFF-RIGHT), it is sufficient to construct a nonterminal for each expression *occurrence* instead of the expression itself in constructing RTG.

$$\text{reconst}\left(\dfrac{\top \overset{*}{\rightarrow} v}{E_x \overset{*}{\rightarrow} v}\right)$$

$$= \dfrac{\{x \mapsto v\}(x) = v}{\{x \mapsto v\} \vdash x \downarrow v}$$

$$\text{reconst}\left(\dfrac{\{\mathcal{P}_i\}_{1 \leq i \leq n}}{E_{C(e_1,\ldots,e_n)} \overset{*}{\rightarrow} C(v_1,\ldots,v_n)}\right)$$

$$= \dfrac{\{\mathcal{E}_i : \theta_i \vdash e_i \downarrow v_i\}_{1 \leq i \leq n}}{\theta_1 \uplus \cdots \uplus \theta_n \vdash C(e_1,\ldots,e_n) \downarrow C(v_1,\ldots,v_n)} \quad \text{where } (\mathcal{E}_i : \theta_i \vdash e_i \downarrow v_i) = \text{reconst}(\mathcal{P}_i)$$

$$\text{reconst}\left(\dfrac{\mathcal{P} : E_e \overset{*}{\rightarrow} v}{E_{f(e_1,\ldots,e_n)} \overset{*}{\rightarrow} v}\right)$$

$$= \dfrac{\{\mathcal{E}_i : \theta_i \vdash e_i \downarrow v\}_{1 \leq i \leq n} \quad \mathcal{E} : \theta \vdash e \downarrow v}{\theta_1 \uplus \cdots \uplus \theta_n \vdash f(e_1,\ldots,e_n) \overset{*}{\rightarrow} v} \quad \text{where} \begin{array}{l} \exists f(x_1,\ldots,x_n) = e. \\ (\mathcal{E} : \theta \vdash e \downarrow v) = \text{reconst}(\mathcal{P}) \\ (\mathcal{E}_i : \theta_i \vdash e_i \downarrow v) = \text{invE}(e_i, \theta(x_i)) \end{array}$$

$$\text{reconst}\left(\dfrac{\mathcal{P}_i : E_{e_i} \overset{*}{\rightarrow} v}{E_{\text{case } x \text{ of } \{p_1 \rightarrow e_1; \ldots; p_n \rightarrow e_n\}} \overset{*}{\rightarrow} v}\right)$$

$$= \dfrac{\exists \sigma, i.\ p_i \sigma = \theta(x) \quad \mathcal{E} : \eta \vdash e_i \downarrow v}{\theta \vdash \text{case } x \text{ of } \{p_1 \rightarrow e_1; \ldots; p_n \rightarrow e_n\} \downarrow v} \quad \text{where} \begin{array}{l} (\mathcal{E}_i : \eta \vdash e_i \downarrow v) = \text{reconst}(\mathcal{P}_i) \\ \theta = \eta \uplus \{x \mapsto p_i \eta\} \\ \sigma = \eta|_{\text{vars}(p_i)} \end{array}$$

$\text{invE}(e, v) = \text{reconst}(\mathcal{P})$ where $\mathcal{P}$ is a production tree of $E_e \overset{*}{\rightarrow} v$.

Fig. 9. Definition of reconst

The following properties relate reconst and approx:

Theorem 2. *If* $\text{reconst}(\mathcal{P}) = (\mathcal{E} : \theta \vdash e \downarrow v)$, *then* $\mathcal{E}$ *is a proof of* $\theta \vdash e \downarrow v$.

Proof Sketch. Induction on $\mathcal{P}$. □

Theorem 3. *If* $\mathcal{E} = \text{reconst}(\mathcal{P})$, *then* $\text{approx}(\mathcal{E}) = \mathcal{P}$ *holds.*

Proof Sketch. Induction on $\mathcal{P}$. □

Lemma 1 (Correctness (Left)). *Assume that a program satisfies* (SUFF-LEFT). *Let* e *be an expression and* v *a value such that* $\exists \theta.\ \theta \vdash e \downarrow v$. *Then, for production tree* $\mathcal{P} : E_e \overset{*}{\rightarrow} v$, $\text{reconst}(\mathcal{P}) = (\mathcal{E} : \theta \vdash e \downarrow v)$ *holds.*

Proof Sketch. In this case, $\mathcal{P} = \text{approx}(\mathcal{E} : \theta \vdash e \downarrow v)$ holds for some $\mathcal{E}$ because of the unambiguity of the grammar. Then, by induction on the structure of $\mathcal{E}$, we prove $\text{reconst}(\text{approx}(\mathcal{E})) = \mathcal{E}$, which means $\text{reconst}(\mathcal{P})$ terminates and results in $\mathcal{E}$. The nonerasing property ensures that for each step of reconst, θ of $\theta \vdash e \downarrow v$ is defined for any variable occurring in e. □

Lemma 2 (Correctness (Right)). *Under* (SUFF-RIGHT), *for any production tree* $\mathcal{P} : E_e \overset{*}{\rightarrow} v$, $\text{reconst}(\mathcal{P}) = \mathcal{E} : \theta \vdash e \downarrow v$ *holds.*

Proof Sketch. In this case, since $\text{invE}(e, v)$ is always called with $e = x$, the call terminates and returns an evaluation tree of form $\{x \mapsto v\} \vdash x \downarrow v$. Thus, we conclude that under (SUFF-RIGHT), reconst always terminates. The rest of the proof is straightforward by induction on $\mathcal{P}$. Note that nonerasure does not matter here because we can assign any value to a variable that does not affect the output; leaving it as undefined is a correct solution.   □

From the lemmas above we can prove the following theorem.

Theorem 4 (Correctness of Grammar-based Inversion). *For a program with definition* $f(x_1, \ldots, x_n) = e$, *the program* f^{-1} *defined by*

$$f^{-1}(v) = (\theta(x_1), \ldots, \theta(x_n)) \text{ where } (\mathcal{E} : \theta \vdash e \downarrow v) = \mathsf{invE}(e, v)$$

satisfies the following two properties.

1. f^{-1} *is a left inverse of* f, *if* (SUFF-LEFT) *holds, and*
2. f^{-1} *is a right inverse of* f, *if* (SUFF-RIGHT) *holds.*   □

Note that *double* and *snoc* satisfy both (SUFF-LEFT) and (SUFF-RIGHT), while *reverse* satisfies neither of them. Program `runlength` used in the experiment to be discussed in Sect. 6 only satisfies (SUFF-LEFT).

Recall that in Sect. 1 we stated that we classify invertible programs instead of problems. We can give another definition of *reverse*, as shown in Fig. 10, from which the derived grammar is unambiguous. More precisely, *reverse'* satisfies (SUFF-LEFT) but not (SUFF-RIGHT). The definition of *reverse'*, while appearing tricky, is nothing but a nonerasing version of IO-swapped *reverse* [22]. Note that both *reverse* and *reverse'* run in time linear to the input size.

$reverse'(xs) = extract(call(shape(xs)))$
$shape(xs) = \textbf{case } xs \textbf{ of } \{[] \rightarrow \mathsf{Pair}(\mathsf{Z}, []); \; x : xs' \rightarrow inc(shape(xs'), x)\}$
$inc(r, x) = \textbf{case } r \textbf{ of } \{\mathsf{Pair}(n, xs) \rightarrow \mathsf{Pair}(\mathsf{S}(n), x : xs)\}$
$call(r) = \textbf{case } r \textbf{ of } \{\mathsf{Pair}(n, xs) \rightarrow revTABA(n, xs)\}$
$extract(r) = \textbf{case } r \textbf{ of } \{\mathsf{Pair}(xs, []) \rightarrow xs\}$
$revTABA(n, xs) = \textbf{case } n \textbf{ of } \{\mathsf{Z} \rightarrow \mathsf{Pair}(xs, []); \; \mathsf{S}(m) \rightarrow shift(revTABA(m, xs))\}$
$shift(r) = \textbf{case } r \textbf{ of } \{\mathsf{Pair}(x : xs, ys) \rightarrow \mathsf{Pair}(xs, x : ys)\}$

Fig. 10. Variant of *reverse* that is invertible with RTG

4.3   Properties

We discuss some properties of the inverses derived using grammar-based inversion with RTG.

Correspondence to Post Condition. Post conditions play important roles in many program inversion methods [8, 11, 16, 17]. Post condition P of e, which we write as $e\{P\}$, is a predicate on the state (i.e., values of all free variables) that is supposed to be true after e is executed. A *simple post condition* is a predicate on the value of e. Given a program, one may assign, for each function f, a post condition, post_f. The assignment is *valid* if we can assign a valid post condition to each sub-expression in the program in the way defined below:

Definition 2 (Simple Post Conditions). *Given a program and a post condition assignment for each function in the program, an assignment of post conditions to all sub-expressions is valid if*

- *every variable x is given a post condition, $P(\_) = \mathsf{True}$;*
- *each function call $f(\ldots)$ is assigned the post condition, post_f;*
- *$\mathsf{C}(e_1\{P_1\}, \ldots, e_n\{P_n\})\{P\}$ is valid if $\forall i.\ P_i(v_i) \Rightarrow P(\mathsf{C}(v_1, \ldots, v_n))$;*
- *$\mathbf{case}\_ \mathbf{of}\ \{p_1 \to e_1\{P_1\}; \ldots; p_n \to e_n\{P_n\}\}\{P\}$ is valid if $\exists i.\ P_i(v) \Rightarrow P(v)$;*
- *in a definition, $f(\ldots) = e\{P\}$, the right-hand side is assigned a post condition satisfying $P(v) \Rightarrow \mathsf{post}_f(v)$.*

Many approaches to program inversion rely on disjoint post conditions for each **case** expression. The expression **case** x **of** $\{p_1 \to e_1\{P_1\}; p_2 \to e_2\{P_2\}\}$, where P_1 and P_2 are disjoint, is inverted to a program that, given output v, tests which of $P_1(v)$ or $P_2(v)$ holds and performs, respectively, the inverse of e_1 or e_2. For non-simple post conditions, it is harder to check the validity of assignment and to test $P(v)$ in executing inverses. Human-assigned post conditions [8, 11, 17] without validity checks may be more expressive. In contrast, the post conditions in Glück and Kawabe [16] that support inference are basically simple. Note that, in functional language, post conditions can be seen as types satisfying the preservation (subject reduction) law.

The following theorem states that grammar-based inversion using RTG is equivalent to inversion using simple post conditions:

Theorem 5. *The RTG obtained from a program is unambiguous if and only if there exists a valid assignment of simple post conditions such that every* **case**-*expression in the program has an assignment*

$$\mathbf{case}\ x\ \mathbf{of}\ \{p_1 \to e_1\{P_1\}; \ldots; p_n \to e_n\{P_n\}\}$$

where $P_1 \ldots P_n$ are disjoint. That is, for any v, there is at most one P_i such that $P_i(v) = \mathsf{True}$.

Proof Sketch. In this case, for $e\{P\}$, we can prove $(\theta \vdash e \downarrow v) \Rightarrow P(v)$. Then, the "if" part is proved by showing the contraposition: if a grammar is ambiguous, then there exists such a **case**-expression. For grammars obtained with Fig. 7, we can prove that if a grammar is ambiguous, there exists E such that $E \to E_1 \xrightarrow{*} v$ and $E \to E_2 \xrightarrow{*} v$ for distinct E_1 and E_2, and such E must correspond to some **case**-expression. The "only if" part is proved by taking the P of $e\{P\}$ as $P(v) \equiv (\exists \mathcal{P}.\ \mathcal{P} : E_e \xrightarrow{*} v)$. □

It is thus a corollary that to invert more functions than those with grammar-based inversion with RTG, we must use more expressive post conditions that are harder to check, to infer, or to invert.

Efficiency. For RTG, the construction of a production tree for $E \xrightarrow{*} v$ takes time at worst proportional to the size of v [6]. It is remarkable that, thus, if a program is nonerasing, affine, and treeless, the derived inverse runs in $O(n)$, where n is the size of an input of the inverse. As a result, we can obtain linear time inverses for *double* and *snoc*. Being affine ensures that the domains of environments merged by $\uplus$ are always disjoint; thus, we do not need to spend time checking whether overlapping variables are equal. Being treeless means that arguments e_i of each function call $f(e_1, \ldots, e_n)$ are merely variables. Thus, all production tree constructions at $\mathsf{invE}(x, v)$ immediately match $\top$ with the given value in $O(1)$ time. In more general cases, the construction of production tree $\mathcal{P} : E_e \xrightarrow{*} v$ at $\mathsf{invE}(e, v)$ runs in time between $O(|\mathcal{P}|)$ and $O(|v|)$, where $|\mathcal{P}|$ and $|v|$ are the sizes of $\mathcal{P}$ and v, depending on the parsing method. For example, using guided tree automata for parsing [4], we can obtain a linear time inverse for *reverse'* in Fig. 10 because the lower complexity bound is achieved for each call of invE in the inverse. Generally, a derived inverse runs at worst in time that is proportional to the total size of "intermediate data" plus "duplicated data" in addition to the size of the output value. Note that a derived right inverse always takes time at worst linear to the size of its input because (SUFF-RIGHT) requires a program to be affine and treeless.

5   Grammar-Based Inversion in General

So far, we have discussed grammar-based inversion by RTG as a case study. In this section, we will give more general study on grammar-based inversion.

5.1   More Fine-Grained Classification

Recall that *double* and *snoc* are invertible by RTG. However, the difficulties of inversion differ in the two programs; *double* is easier to invert than *snoc*. Extra conditions for a grammar achieve more fine-grained classification. For example, the grammar of *double* is top-down deterministic (for $E \xrightarrow{*} \mathsf{C}(E_1, \ldots, E_n)$, the tuple $(E_1, \ldots, E_n)$ is unique to E and C) while that of *snoc* is not. If a top-down deterministic grammar has no rule $E \to E_1$ for E that has more than one production rule, swapping LHSs with RHSs results in a deterministic inverse. Even if such production rules exist, additional checking of the root of a value at **case** is sufficient to obtain a deterministic inverse.

5.2   Predefined Inverses as Axioms

Small parts of a program are sometimes very difficult to invert because they use mathematical properties, such as multiplication of prime numbers. In this case, treating them as language constructs with predefined inverses helps us to invert programs that contains them. For example, consider $mulPrime(x_1, x_2)$ that multiplies two primes x_1 and x_2 if $x_1 \leq x_2$. The semantics of function call $mulPrime(e_1, e_2)$ is defined by the predefined semantics $[\![mulPrime]\!]$ as

$$\frac{\{\theta \vdash e_i \downarrow v_i\}_{i=1,2} \quad [\![mulPrime]\!](v_1, v_2) = v \quad v_1 \leq v_2}{\theta \vdash mulPrime(e_1, e_2) \downarrow v} .$$

For the function, we prepare a special production rule, $E_{mulPrime(e_1,e_2)} \rightarrow Nat$, where Nat represents natural numbers, and then the corresponding reconst is defined in a straightforward way by using its predefined inverse $[\![mulPrime]\!]^{-1}$.

5.3   More Expressive Grammars

Using more expressive grammars enables us to invert more programs.

Inside-out (IO) context-free tree grammar (CFTG) [9] enables us to investigate accumulation parameters (parameters that are never pattern-matched in evaluation) in parsing. For example, the following IO CFTG can be obtained for *reverse*.

$$
\begin{array}{ll}
E_{rev(x,[\,])} \quad\quad \rightarrow E_{\mathbf{case}\ x\ \mathbf{of}\ \{...\}}([\,]) & E_{\mathbf{case}\ x\ \mathbf{of}\ \{...\}}(r) \rightarrow E_{rev(x,a:r)}(r) \\
E_{\mathbf{case}\ x\ \mathbf{of}\ \{...\}}(r) \rightarrow r & E_{rev(x,a:r)}(r) \quad\quad \rightarrow E_{\mathbf{case}\ x\ \mathbf{of}\ \{...\}}(a:r)
\end{array}
$$

In an RTG, non-terminals do not have parameters/arguments. Thus, as in Sect. 4, when we construct an RTG approximation of a program, we discard the arguments of functions. In an IO CFTG, non-terminals may have "accumulation parameters". Thus, we can similarly construct an IO-CFTG approximation of a program by discarding the arguments that are not accumulation parameters. Note that since approx changes according to the class of grammar, so does its inverse reconst. The change in reconst is straightforward in IO CFTG; similar to reconst for RTG, we re-parse to recover discarded evaluation trees of expressions occurring in non-accumulation parameters. Like (SUFF-LEFT), left-invertible programs are characterized by the unambiguity of the grammar, and like (SUFF-RIGHT), right-invertible programs are characterized by the syntactic condition that ensures that every production tree has a unique corresponding evaluation tree. Note that the class of right-invertible programs by IO CFTG contains the known class of tree transformations called deterministic linear macro tree transducers [10]. IO CFTG corresponds to the post conditions that can contain the variables of accumulation parameters.

For IO CFTG, it is known that checking whether or not $E \xrightarrow{*} v$ holds takes time polynomial to the size of v [3]. Unfortunately, there has been little discussion on "parsing" of IO CFTG because people have not found a use for the production trees. However, we believe that a variant of the CYK parser would yield polynomial-time parsing. Note that, similar to CFG in which a nonterminal generates a string and a string of length n contains n^2 substrings, in IO CFTG, a k-ary nonterminal generates a k-hole context (a value containing k holes to be filled) and a value of size n contains n^{k+1} k-hole contexts. Thus, we believe memoization as in CYK parsing should be applicable. For the example of *reverse*, we can obtain a linear-time inverse by using deterministic bottom-up push-down tree automata [28]. We also believe that it is possible to use a more expressive grammar, e.g., supporting equality check or synchronous production as in the tupled [20] function. For the string case, these features are adopted without violating the polynomial-time-parisible property [5]. Note that, even if the derived RTG is unambiguous, when a derived IO CFTG is can be parsed in linear time, the inverse derived by IO CFTG is sometimes more efficient than that derived by RTG. An inverse derived by IO CFTG calls invE no more than that derived by RTG; the inverse does not call invE for arguments occurring at accumulation-parameter positions of a function call because the evaluation has already been captured by the IO CFTG.

Note that ambiguity check for a grammar beyond regular, such as IO CFTG, is usually undecidable [18]. However, some automated systems or some restricted forms of programs can still guarantee the unambiguity of an expressive grammar in some cases. Investigations into appropriate ways to define "some" programs for which the ambiguity check of derived grammars are decidable would be important in future work.

6 Experiment

This section reports our automatic inversion system[2] using Haskell, and explains that the overhead of the derived inversion to the handwritten inverse is acceptable through an experiment with the implementation. The acceptably-small overhead revealed that our method is not only theoretically feasible but also useful for implementing a program inversion system for acceptably-efficient inverses. Note that to derive inverses as efficient as possible is not our main issue, but this is important because it is a general issue with program inversion.

6.1 Implementation

The prototype system implements grammar-based inversion with RTG (Sect. 4). The system takes a program, and then generates a Haskell program of the left inverse if (SUFF-LEFT) holds. Otherwise, the system generates a Haskell program, which becomes a right inverse of the program if (SUFF-RIGHT) holds.

For parsing, the implementation uses guided tree automata [4], allowing $\top$ to match any value. Since a guided tree automaton performs a top-down traversal before a bottom-up traversal, the special case for $\top$ is easy to implement. The derived inverse does not construct production or evaluation trees; they are eliminated by program fusion. Recall that what we need is only θ of $\theta \vdash e \downarrow v$ for given e and v. The implementation determinizes tree automata to reduce the overhead caused by nondeterminism of parsing. Although determinization costs $O(2^n)$, where n is the size of an automaton ($\simeq$ the size of a program), this cost is not severe for our purposes at least for the programs we tested in the experiments.

6.2 Comparison with Handwritten Inverses

For several programs, we compared the execution time of automatically-derived (left) inverses and handwritten (left) inverses for large inputs.[3] Three programs

---

[2] Available on: http://www.ipl.t.u-tokyo.ac.jp/~kztk/PaI/.
[3] We used a PC with an Intel Core2 E8400 (3 GHz) CPU and 2-GB memory, and used Haskell compiler GHC 6.8.2.

$runlength(x) = $ **case** x **of** $\{[] \to []; \; a : y \to step(runlength(y), a)\}$
$step(x, a) = $ **case** x **of** $\{ [] \qquad\qquad\qquad \to \mathsf{Pair}(a, zero()) : [];$
$\qquad\qquad\qquad\qquad \mathsf{Pair}(b, n) : y \to updateRL(eq(a, b), n, y) \}$
$updateRL(i, n, y) = $ **case** i **of** $\{ \mathsf{Right}(a) \to \mathsf{Pair}(a, inc(n)) : y;$
$\qquad\qquad\qquad\qquad\quad \mathsf{Left}(a, b) \to \mathsf{Pair}(a, zero()) : \mathsf{Pair}(b, n) : y \}$
...

Fig. 11. `runlength`: $eq(a, b)$ returns $\mathsf{Right}(a)$ if $a = b$, otherwise returns $\mathsf{Left}(a, b)$, and $zero()$ and $inc(x)$ are 0 and $+1$ on binary representation of numbers, respectively. Here $\mathsf{Pair}(a, n)$ means $inc(n)$-times successive occurrences of a.

Table 1. Results of experiment

Program	Inversion (s)	#Input	Automatically-Derived (s)	Handwritten (s)
snoc	< 0.05	≃ 8 millions	0.95	0.67
double	< 0.05	≃ 10 millions	0.23	0.11
runlength	0.3	≃ 9 millions	0.76	0.33

were investigated in the experiment: `snoc` and `double` implement *snoc* and *double* in Sect. 1, respectively, and `runlength` implements run-length encoding as in Fig. 11. Note that, for these three programs, the system can derive an inverse that has the same complexity as that of a handwritten inverse because construction of production tree $\mathcal{P} : E_e \xrightarrow{*} v$ at $\mathsf{invE}(e, v)$ runs in $O(|\mathcal{P}|)$.

All of these three programs satisfy (SUFF-LEFT). The results of the experiment are listed in Table 1. Each column represents the following: Program denotes the investigated program, Inversion denotes the elapsed time for inversion including code generation, #Input denotes the number of constructors occurring in the input tree, and Automatically-Derived and Handwritten denote the elapsed time of the automatically-derived inverse and the handwritten inverse, respectively. The size of input for each pair of automatically-derived and handwritten inverses was chosen to enable the elapsed time to compared in seconds, as long as there was no shortage of memory.

Inversion in Table 1 indicates that our implemented inversion runs very efficiently. Even though in `runlength` the inversion process took about 0.3 seconds, we found by extra profiling that more than half the time was spent for serialization that makes a textual code from an abstract syntax tree. Automatically-Derived and Handwritten in Table 1 indicate that the derived inverses run from a half to a third of the speed of the handwritten inverses. We believe that this small ratio would be acceptable. In addition, we expect that the ratio can scale because the ratios of small programs such as `snoc` and `double` are almost the same as that of a relatively involved program such as `runlength`.

7   Related Work

Many approaches to program inversion have been proposed [1, 7, 8, 11, 15–17, 25, 27, 30]. These methods are based on reverting the execution order of an input program, unlike our method. Of these, those by Yellin [30] and Glück and Kawabe [15] are the most closely related to ours.

Yellin [30] inverted string-to-string transformations written in a restricted class of attribute grammars. His idea is an extension of evaluation of synchronous grammars [2] — transformation by using two CFGs that share the same parse tree modulo permutation of children. We borrowed his basic idea of restoring the evaluation structure by parsing. Instead of CFG, we used tree grammars because functional programs describe tree transformations. Regarding of the class of invertible functions, with the restricted class of AG, one cannot deconstruct intermediate results, ruling out programs like runlength, i.e., those programs are not handled by his approach. His framework, on the other hand, is more suitable for programs defined using if-expressions, while we handle them indirectly as in the *eq* and *updateRL* in Fig. 11.

Glück and Kawabe [15] constructed inverse programs by reversing programs, before applying LR-parsing to the derived sequential programs to resolve nondeterminism. While our method and theirs are both "grammar-based", they place more emphasis on obtaining efficient inverses. Their method consists of the three steps: (1) convert a program to a program in their stack-based language, (2) apply LR-parsing to the stack-based program by taking the program to be CFG, and (3) generate a program in which the stack in LR-parsing is emulated by the stack of function call. Due to these three steps, they obtained the efficient inverses because the inverses that have no parsing overhead. However, what class of programs is invertible is less clear in theirs because all three steps affect invertibility. Steps 2 and 3 may fail, and Step 1 affects the later steps because, for non-linear recursive functions, the result of Step 1 differs if we choose a different evaluation order. Examples of functions discussed in this paper can be handled with their method, while many of the programs they handled would be invertible by grammar-based inversion with IO CFTG using a deterministic bottom-up push-down tree automaton [28], which is a counterpart of "LR-parsing" in CFTG. Theoretically, even with RTG, there exist programs that can be handled by ours but not theirs.

Many program inversion techniques rely on proof of injectivity. In many existing approaches, post conditions [8, 11, 16, 17] for branching statements/expressions are used for this purpose. In Nishida and Sakai [25], completion is used to check whether the obtained nondeterministic program is actually a function, which implies the injectivity of the original program [26]. In grammar-based inversion, we check injectivity by checking the unambiguity of grammar.

Another way to obtain inverse programs is, similarly to combinator-based bidirectional language [12], to construct programs using invertible combinators [23]; a program constructed in this way comes together with its inverse. Our method can be incorporated into such combinator-based frameworks both for providing basic invertible combinators and for gluing combinators as in Sect. 5.2. In their frameworks [12, 23], accumulative functions such as *reverse* cannot be represented directly but must be written as *reverse'* in Sect. 4. We believe that grammar-based inversion with grammar beyond RTG would enable us to invert more functions that are written in more natural forms.

Abramov and Glück [1] categorized inversion methods into *program inversion* and *inverse computation*. Program inversion takes a program and returns an inverse program while inverse computation takes a program and an output and computes the corresponding input. The two methods are different in two points: A minor difference is that program inversion performs code generation, but the main difference is the existence of partial evaluation; i.e., in program inversion the obtained inverse is specialized to the input program. Note that the two notions are not so different theoretically because generating a program that simply calls "eval" to the pair of an inverse computation and an input program achieves program inversion. Thus, it is important to discuss how much the inverse computation is specialized to the input program. In grammar-based inversion, the main chance of partial evaluation is when parsing the grammar. For a grammar derived statically for an input program, we can choose an appropriate parsing method according to the characteristics of the grammar.

The tree transducer [14] is a family of formal models of tree transformation. Instances of tree transducers vary in terms of expressive power and difficulty of inversion. We did not use tree transducers because, in all models of tree transducers we are aware of, a function may not perform case analysis on the output of another function, while many programs we are interested in (e.g. `runlength` in Fig. 11) are of the form $g(\ldots) = f(g(x))$ with an invertible f that looks into the result of g. We did, however, borrow many ideas from tree transducers, e.g., the grammar construction in Sect. 4.

8 Conclusion

We proposed grammar-based inversion, which is a framework for program inversion. Grammar-based inversion can describe how difficult inverting a program is through the complexity of the unambiguous grammar used for inversion. At the same time, the complexity of parsing determines the worst-case complexity of a derived inverse.

Grammar-based inversion gives us a new view of program inversion. With it, we can split program inversion into two problems: finding an unambiguous grammar that captures the evaluation structure of a program, and finding an efficient parsing method for the grammar. For example, so far, many inversion methods except Glück and Kawabe [15] have not handled functions containing accumulation parameters. A solution with grammar-based inversion for such functions is to use grammar such as IO CFTG that can capture the accumulation structure, and to find an efficient parsing method specialized to the grammar.

Although grammar-based inversion can derive a right inverse, this is not very useful because, in many applications, users do not want an arbitrary right inverse but *some* right inverse. That is, some right inverse is more preferable than other right inverses. For example, a right inverse achieving a high compression rate is preferable in LZSS compression where a compression procedure is a right inverse of decompression. Another interesting example is bidirectional transformation (e.g., [12]). In bidirectional transformation, function $f :: S \to V$ is coupled with its backward semantics $f_B :: (S, V) \to S$; if the result of f is changed from $f(s)$ to v, the change is put back on S as the change from s to $f_B(s, v)$. A simple example of bidirectional transformation is component extraction from a tuple, such as $fst(s_1, s_2) = s_1$ coupled with $fst_B((s_1, s_2), v) = (v, s_2)$. In bidirectional transformation, backward semantics f_B is a right inverse of its forward semantics f if the first argument of f_B is fixed. In such right inverses, a right inverse that achieves as small modification as possible is often preferable. It would be important to extend the framework to accept user-defined "preferable" measures to make grammar-based inversion more applicable.

Acknowledgments. We would like to thank Robert Glück, Keisuke Nakano, Kazuhiro Inaba, and Akimasa Morihata for their valuable comments on an earlier version of the paper. We are also grateful to the anonymous reviewers who gave us helpful advice to improve the paper. This work is partially supported by the Japan Society for the Promotion of Science, Grant-in-Aid for JSPS Fellows 20 · 9584 and Grant-in-Aid for Scientific Research (A) 19200002, and the Grand-Challenging Project on "Linguistic Foundation for Bidirectional Model Transformation" from National Institute of Informatics.

References

1. Abramov, S.M., Glück, R.: Principles of Inverse Computation and the Universal Resolving Algorithm. In: The Essence of Computation, pp. 269–295 (2002)
2. Aho, A.V., Ullman, J.D.: The Theory of Parsing, Translation, and Compiling. Prentice-Hall, Inc., Upper Saddle River (1972)
3. Asveld, P.R.J.: Time and Space Complexity of Inside-Out Macro Languages. Int. J. Comput. Math. 10(1), 3–14 (1981)
4. Biehl, M., Klarlund, N., Rauhe, T.: Algorithms for Guided Tree Automata. In: Raymond, D.R., Yu, S., Wood, D. (eds.) WIA 1996. LNCS, vol. 1260, pp. 6–25. Springer, Heidelberg (1997)
5. Boullier, P.: Range Concatenation Grammars. In: New Developments in Parsing Technology, pp. 269–289. Kluwer Academic Publishers, Norwell (2004)
6. Comon, H., Dauchet, M., Gilleron, R., Jacquemard, F., Lugiez, D., Tison, S., Tommasi, M.: Tree Automata Techniques and Applications, http://www.grappa.univ-lille3.fr/tata
7. Dershowitz, N., Mitra, S.: Jeopardy. In: Narendran, P., Rusinowitch, M. (eds.) RTA 1999. LNCS, vol. 1631, pp. 16–29. Springer, Heidelberg (1999)
8. Dijkstra, E.W.: Program Inversion. In: Gerhart, S.L., Pair, C., Pepper, P.A., Wössner, H., Dijkstra, E.W., Guttag, J.V., Owicki, S.S., Partsch, H., Bauer, F.L., Gries, D., Griffiths, M., Horning, J.J., Wirsing, M. (eds.) Program Construction. LNCS, vol. 69, pp. 54–57. Springer, Heidelberg (1979)
9. Engelfriet, J., Schmidt, E.M.: IO and OI. I. J. Comput. Syst. Sci. 15(3), 328–353 (1977)
10. Engelfriet, J., Vogler, H.: Macro Tree Transducers. J. Comput. Syst. Sci. 31(1), 71–146 (1985)
11. Eppstein, D.: A Heuristic Approach to Program Inversion. In: International Joint Conference on Artificial Intelligence (IJCAI 1985), pp. 219–221 (1985)

12. Foster, J.N., Greenwald, M.B., Moore, J.T., Pierce, B.C., Schmitt, A.: Combinators for Bidirectional Tree Transformations: A Linguistic Approach to the View-Update Problem. ACM Trans. Program. Lang. Syst. 29(3) (2007)
13. Frisch, A.: Regular Tree Language Recognition with Static Information. In: Lévy, J.J., Mayr, E.W., Mitchell, J.C. (eds.) Exploring New Frontiers of Theoretical Informatics, IFIP 18th World Computer Congress, TC1 3rd International Conference on Theoretical Computer Science (TCS 2004), pp. 661–674. Kluwer, Dordrecht (2004)
14. Fülöp, Z., Vogler, H.: Syntax-Directed Semantics: Formal Models Based on Tree Transducers. Springer, New York (1998)
15. Glück, R., Kawabe, M.: A Method for Automatic Program Inversion Based on LR(0) Parsing. Fundam. Inform. 66(4), 367–395 (2005)
16. Glück, R., Kawabe, M.: Revisiting an Automatic Program Inverter for Lisp. SIGPLAN Notices 40(5), 8–17 (2005)
17. Gries, D.: 21 Inverting Programs. In: The Science of Programming. Springer, Heidelberg (1981)
18. Hopcroft, J.E., Motwani, R., Ullman, J.D.: 7 Properties of Context-Free Languages. In: Introduction to Automata Theory, Languages, and Computation, 3rd edn. Addison-Wesley Longman Publishing Co., Inc., Amsterdam (2006)
19. Hosoya, H., Pierce, B.C.: XDuce: A Statically Typed XML Processing Language. ACM Trans. Internet Techn. 3(2), 117–148 (2003)
20. Hu, Z., Iwasaki, H., Takeichi, M., Takano, A.: Tupling Calculation Eliminates Multiple Data Traversals. In: ICFP 1997: Proceedings of the second ACM SIGPLAN International Conference on Functional Programming, pp. 164–175. ACM Press, New York (1997)
21. Matsuda, K., Hu, Z., Nakano, K., Hamana, M., Takeichi, M.: Bidirectionalization Transformation based on Automatic Derivation of View Complement Functions. In: ICFP 2007: Proceedings of the 12th ACM SIGPLAN International Conference on Functional Programming, pp. 47–58. ACM, New York (2007)
22. Morihata, A., Kakehi, K., Hu, Z., Takeichi, M.: Swapping Arguments and Results of Recursive Functions. In: Uustalu, T. (ed.) MPC 2006. LNCS, vol. 4014, pp. 379–396. Springer, Heidelberg (2006)
23. Mu, S.C., Hu, Z., Takeichi, M.: An Injective Language for Reversible Computation. In: Kozen, D. (ed.) MPC 2004. LNCS, vol. 3125, pp. 289–313. Springer, Heidelberg (2004)
24. Neumann, A., Seidl, H.: Locating Matches of Tree Patterns in Forests. In: Arvind, V., Sarukkai, S. (eds.) FST TCS 1998. LNCS, vol. 1530, pp. 134–146. Springer, Heidelberg (1998)
25. Nishida, N., Sakai, M.: Completion after Program Inversion of Injective Functions. Electr. Notes Theor. Comput. Sci. 237, 39–56 (2009)
26. Nishida, N., Sakai, M.: Proving Injectivity of Functions via Program Inversion in Term Rewriting. Accepted for FLOPS 2010. LNCS, vol. 6009. Springer, Heidelberg (2010)
27. Nishida, N., Sakai, M., Sakabe, T.: Partial Inversion of Constructor Term Rewriting Systems. In: Giesl, J. (ed.) RTA 2005. LNCS, vol. 3467, pp. 264–278. Springer, Heidelberg (2005)
28. Schimpf, K.M., Gallier, J.H.: Tree Pushdown Automata. J. Comput. Syst. Sci. 30(1), 25–40 (1985)
29. Wadler, P.: Deforestation: Transforming Programs to Eliminate Trees. Theor. Comput. Sci. 73(2), 231–248 (1990)
30. Yellin, D.M.: Attribute Grammar Inversion and Source-to-source Translation. LNCS, vol. 302. Springer, Heidelberg (1988)

Faulty Logic:
Reasoning about Fault Tolerant Programs

Matthew L. Meola and David Walker

Princeton University, Computer Science Department,
35 Olden Drive, 08540-5233 Princeton, New Jersey
{mmeola,dpw}@princeton.edu

Abstract. Transient faults are single-shot hardware errors caused by high energy particles from space, manufacturing defects, overheating, and other sources. Such faults can be devastating for security- and safety-critical systems. In order to mitigate these problems, software developers can add redundancy in various ways to their software systems. However, such redundancy is hard to reason about and corner cases are easy to miss, leaving these systems vulnerable. To solve this problem, we have developed a logic, based on Separation Logic, for reasoning about faults as resources. We show how to use this logic as a language of assertions and incorporate it into a Hoare Logic for verifying imperative programs. This Hoare Logic is parameterized by a formal fault model and it can be used to prove imperative programs correct with respect to that model. In addition to developing this basic verification platform, we have designed a modal operator that abstracts away the effects of individual faults, enabling modularization of proofs and greatly simplifying the reasoning involved. The logic is proved sound and studied through a number of examples, including a simplified version of the RSA Sign/Verify algorithm.

1 Introduction

Programmers almost always implement software under the assumption that the underlying hardware is completely reliable. This is the right choice – implementing software correctly is hard enough without worrying about hardware reliability. Nevertheless, there are a number of important situations in which a software engineer must face the fact that hardware faults can and do occur.

One such domain involves the implementation of cryptographic algorithms. For years, software engineers assumed that, while faults in these algorithms might occur, they would not reveal anything important about the embedded cryptographic secrets. However, in 1997, Boneh, DeMillo and Lipton [1] showed how a single fault in common implementations of RSA could be exploited to discover the underlying secret key. Moreover, since that time, other researchers have uncovered problems in DES, RC5 and AES. In related work, Govindavajhala and Appel showed how to exploit faults to break into a commercial Java virtual machine running completely type safe code [2]. There is currently a rich community dedicated to researching these threats and developing solutions. Bar-El's survey paper [3], provides an excellent overview of the area.

A.D. Gordon (Ed.): ESOP 2010, LNCS 6012, pp. 468–487, 2010.

In addition to worrying about faults in security-sensitive contexts, engineers must also consider their ramifications when fully optimizing systems for power and performance. For example, by decreasing hardware voltages one can save power at the expense of occasionally incurring faults, and by overclocking one can speed up performance, again at the expensive of the occasional erroneous result. Hedge and Shanbhag [4] illustrate the advantages of exploiting such tradeoffs in digital signal processing applications. Other contexts in which intermittent hardware faults have a significant overall impact may include safety-critical applications, avionics, satellites, supercomputers, and long-running simulations or experiments.

In situations such as these, conventional techniques for reasoning about programs are no longer sound. Consequently, we have begun to develop a new framework that will allow programmers to prove strong properties about their programs despite the presence of faults. Our framework involves a relatively simple and self-contained extension to a standard Hoare Logic for while programs. This extension allows programmers to reason about the faults that may or may not have happened to their programs in typical Hoare style. Transient faults appear explicitly as objects in the logic, and operators inspired by Separation Logic are used to count, limit, and contain the faults.

In summary, the main contributions of the paper are: the development of a logic for proving programs to be fault tolerant, the proof of soundness for this logic, parameterization of the logic by one of multiple fault models, illustration of logic's use through examples in multiple application areas, the proof that the logic supports the frame rule, the development of a modality that supports concise proofs, and a weakest precondition Hoare rule for the extension of Hoare Logic.

The rest of the paper is organized as follows. Section 3 discusses the programming language, including a new instruction, fault, which introduces the possibility of a fault at a specific program point. Section 4 extends standard Hoare Logic with the rule for fault. Section 5 demonstrates the complexity of dealing with fault functions explicitly in proofs and introduces a modality that abstracts away the explicit fault functions. Section 6 illustrates the application of the logic in security protocols, through a specification for a fault tolerant implementation of the RSA Sign/Verify protocol. Section 7 describes a compilation from programs and specifications in standard Hoare Logic into programs in our logic with fault tolerance achieved through triple modular redundancy. Related work is discussed in Section 8, and Section 9 concludes.

2   Modeling Faults

Before we can reason about faults, and indeed before programmers or hardware designers can protect against faults, there must be some kind of model for when and where faults can occur. Typical fault models dealt with in the literature are fairly simple, limiting faults to one or a few occurrences per program run. The most common models are the Single Event Upset (SEU) and Single Word Corruption (SWC) models. The SEU model allows a single bit flip in a single register in one run of the program, as seen in the work of Chang, Reis, and August; Shirvani, Saxena, and McCluskey; Bar-El, et al.; among others [3, 5, 6]. The SWC model allows arbitrary changes to a single register to occur once in the program, as seen in Bar-El, et al. and Shirvani, Saxena, and

McCluskey [3, 6]. The motivation behind these fault models is twofold: one, that the incidence of faults is rare enough that programmers may ignore the negligible chance of two occurring; and two, that the fault model defines a class of errors that is possible to protect against without extreme performance degradation. For this reason, we mainly focus on these two fault models. However, our logic supports other fault models, including those allowing up to two faults to occur during a single program run. Such a model is briefly examined in this paper.

3   The Programming Language

The programming language that we consider in this paper is the classic imperative language of while programs extended with a single pseudo-instruction that is used to specify where faults may occur within a program. For example, consider a simple loop:

```
x := 0;
while x != 0 do
    skip;
```

Here, the program variable x is assigned zero and the program loops endlessly, testing x for inequality with zero. To reason about the execution of the program in the presence of faults, the programmer or a static analysis inserts fault statements at appropriate program points. For example:

```
x := 0; fault x;
while x != 0 do
    { skip; fault x; }
```

This allows faults to occur at two points in the program. Intuitively, the statement fault x means that a fault *may occur* to program variable x at this point in the computation. Hence, by inserting the fault x statement between every pair of lines, the programmer considers the possibility that faults may occur at any point in the program.[1] Thus, the programming language and the logic to be introduced later in the paper are agnostic about where faults may occur in the program. This allows the programmer to focus on protecting critical sections of code.

If there are multiple program variables, each program variable must be mentioned separately. For example:

```
x := 0; fault x;
y := 0; fault y;
while (x != 0) and (y != 0) do
    { skip; fault x; fault y; }
```

---

[1] The reader may note that in any fault model where any occurring fault is arbitrary (such as the SWC model, or an n-word corruption model), it suffices to introduce a fault statement for a variable x immediately before each time the variable's value is read. This is also true for any fault model allowing at most one fault (including both the SWC and SEU models).

To abbreviate long sequences of fault statements, we normally write `fault x₁,...,xₙ;` in place of `fault x₁; ... fault xₙ;`.

The observant reader will also notice that there is no syntax for faults that may occur in the midst of a complex expression in a while loop bound, if statement, or right-hand side of an assignment. To consider such faults, the programmer must decompose the expressions into a series of statements:

```
x := 0; fault x;
y := 0; fault y;
flag1 := x != 0; fault flag1;
flag2 := y != 0; fault flag2;
flag1 := flag1 and flag2; fault flag1, flag2;
while flag1  do
    { skip; fault x, y, flag1, flag2;
      flag1 := x != 0; fault flag1;
      flag2 := y != 0; fault flag2;
      flag1 := flag1 and flag2; fault flag1, flag2;
    }
```

This example makes it clear that as programs get more complex, there is a proliferation of fault instructions. On the one hand, this proliferation reveals the inherent difficulty of reasoning about programs in a context with a rich fault model. On the other hand, it demonstrates that a production verification system should probably manage the insertion of fault instructions itself (e.g., by having the static analysis engine insert them automatically). In this paper, we leave the fault instructions in the syntax of the programming language because doing so makes the formal development particularly clear, modular, and self-contained. In a production environment, this language would correspond to an intermediate language or a language used with a proof assistant.

3.1 Syntax

A summary of the syntax of the language we use in the paper is presented in Figure 1. Here and throughout the rest of the paper, we let x range over program variable names, n range over integers and f range over computable functions from integers to integers. The specific set of integer and boolean expressions we choose for the language is unimportant and hence we will freely use other expressions in our examples as they require. Note that function variables do not appear in the source language itself. They are only used in expressions that appear in the program logic, to be described later.

3.2 Representation of Faults and Fault Models

When a `fault x` statement is executed, the value of x may change. Such changes can be represented by a function, f, on the integers. The function acts on the variable x, causing the new value, f x, to be stored there. For example, if the third bit of x is flipped, the function a bit flip function, written $\lambda y.y$ xor 2^2 as a lambda expression[2],

---

[2] Note that mathematical functions, not lambda expressions, are part of our logic, Lambda expressions are just used as a convenient representation.

$$
\begin{aligned}
&\text{integer vars} \quad x && \text{integers} \quad n\\
&\text{function vars} \ \phi && \text{functions} \quad f\\
&\text{function exps} \ G ::= \phi \mid f\\
&\text{integer exps} \quad E ::= x \mid n \mid E_1 + E_2 \mid E_1 \bmod E_2 \mid G\,E \mid e\\
&\text{boolean exps} \quad B ::= E_1 = E_2 \mid \text{not } B \mid B_1 \text{ and } B_2 \mid E_1 < E_2\\
&\text{statements} \quad S ::= \text{skip} \mid x := E \mid S_1; S_2 \mid \text{if } B \text{ then } S_1 \text{ else } S_2\\
&\qquad\qquad\qquad\quad \mid \ \text{while } B \text{ do } S \mid \text{fault } x
\end{aligned}
$$

Fig. 1. Syntax of Programs

will represent this fault. Similarly, if x is unchanged, the identity function will represent this trivial fault.

Over the course of a program run, we record the fault functions that have occurred in the *fault state* but not the variables that they applied to. This is because the effects of a fault spread wider than the initial variable affected and we are not doing any calculations of information flow to track the effects. Formally, fault states (F) are multi-sets and we use the notation $F_1 + F_2$ to denote multiset union of fault states. We also write $F_1 \subseteq F_2$ when F_1 is a sub-multiset of F_2. As an example, the fault state $\{\lambda x.x \text{ xor } 2^3\}$ represents a situation in which a single fault has occurred and that fault has toggled the 4th bit of the associated value. Over the course of a run, it is common for many trivial faults to occur and this will lead to an accumulation of identify functions in the fault state. For instance, the fault state $\{\lambda x.x \text{ xor } 2^3, \lambda x.x, \lambda x.x, \lambda x.x\}$ represents a situation in which only one true fault has occurred, but three additional trivial faults have been recorded in the fault state.[3]

A judgment $F \text{ ok}_m$ defines the fault states F that are allowed by the fault model m. Most of the rest of our development is independent of the particular choice of fault model except for the restrictions that the empty fault state must be valid and that validity must be preserved by subset ordering.

Definition 1 (Fault State Validity Criterion)

– $\{\} \text{ ok}_m$.
– *If* $F_1 \text{ ok}_m$ *and* $F_2 \subseteq F_1$ *then* $F_2 \text{ ok}_m$.

Using multisets of functions as our fault states is elegant and easy to work with and yet allows us to reason about several different interesting fault models. In this paper, we will work with the following three fault models, each of which maybe characterized according to its $F \text{ ok}_m$ relation, though the bulk of our work should extend to related models. The models are characterized by their $F \text{ ok}_m$ relations, each of which satisfies the Fault State Validity Criterion.

Definition 2 (SWC Fault Model). *The SWC fault model demands that* $F \text{ ok}_m$ *if and only if at most one function* f *drawn from* F *is not the identity function.*

Definition 3 (SEU Fault Model). *The SEU fault model demands that* $F \text{ ok}_m$ *if and only if at most one function* f *drawn from* F *is not the identity function and that non-identity function* f *has the form* $\lambda x.x \text{ xor } 2^k$ *for some* k.

---

[3] Allowing the fault state to accumulate many trivial faults helps simplify our operational semantics slightly.

Definition 4 (DWC Fault Model). *The DWC fault model demands that F* ok_m *if and only if at most two functions f and g drawn from F are not the identity function.*

3.3   Operational Semantics

A program state is a triple (F, V, Z) where F is the current fault state, V is the current environment and Z is either a statement S to execute or $-$, indicating execution is complete. We call states with the form $(F, V, -)$ *final states*. An environment is a finite partial map from variable names to integer values. We write $V(x)$ to denote the contents of the map at x and we write $V[x \mapsto n]$ to denote the map created by updating V at x with n.

The operational semantics of the language are presented in Figure 2. These rules depend upon a conventional denotational semantics (see, for example, Winskel, Chapter 5 [7]), which, given an environment, maps integer expressions to integers and boolean expressions to 0 (false) or 1 (true). We write the semantic functions $[\![E]\!]_V$ and $[\![B]\!]_V$ respectively.

The rules governing the standard statements (skip, assignment, if, and while) leave the fault state untouched and behave in the usual way. The operational rule for the fault statement non-deterministically chooses a fault function f that satisfies the given fault model, transforms the contents of the given variable, and adds f to the fault state. Note that f may be the identity function, meaning that a fault statement indicates a program point where a fault *may* occur as opposed to where a fault must occur.

$$\text{Eskip} \frac{}{(F, V, \texttt{skip}) \longmapsto (F, V, -)}$$

$$\text{Eassign} \frac{}{(F, V, x := E) \longmapsto (F, V[x \mapsto [\![E]\!]_V], -)}$$

$$\text{Eseq1} \frac{(F, V, S_1) \longmapsto (F', V', S_1')}{(F, V, S_1; S_2) \longmapsto (F', V', S_1'; S_2)}$$

$$\text{Eseq2} \frac{(F, V, S_1) \longmapsto (F', V', -)}{(F, V, S_1; S_2) \longmapsto (F', V', S_2)}$$

$$\text{Eif1} \frac{[\![B]\!]_V = 1}{(F, V, \texttt{if } B \texttt{ then } S_1 \texttt{ else } S_2) \longmapsto (F, V, S_1)}$$

$$\text{Eif2} \frac{[\![B]\!]_V = 0}{(F, V, \texttt{if } B \texttt{ then } S_1 \texttt{ else } S_2) \longmapsto (F, V, S_2)}$$

$$\text{Ewhile1} \frac{[\![B]\!]_V = 0}{(F, V, \texttt{while } B \texttt{ do } S) \longmapsto (F, V, -)}$$

$$\text{Ewhile2} \frac{[\![B]\!]_V = 1}{(F, V, \texttt{while } B \texttt{ do } S) \longmapsto (F, V, S; \texttt{while } B \texttt{ do } S)}$$

$$\text{Efault} \frac{F + \{f\} \, ok_m}{(F, V, \texttt{fault } x) \longmapsto (F + \{f\}, V[x \mapsto f(V(x))], -)}$$

Fig. 2. Operational Semantics of Programs

4   The Program Logic

Having described our programming language, we now present the programmer with the tools to reason about these programs. These tools consist of a basic Hoare Logic with extensions to allow reasoning about faults in program variables.

As a reminder, a Hoare triple is written $\{P\}S\{Q\}$. Following the rules of partial correctness, the Hoare triple means that, if P describes the program state immediately before S is executed and the execution of S terminates, then Q will describe the resulting program state.

Figure 3 contains inference rules and assertion language for a basic Hoare Logic, with a subscript m added for use in our logic. The subscript refers to the fault model considered in the Hoare triples. Note that the assignment rule works backwards. If some assertion P describes the program state after the assignment of E to x, then the same assertion with all occurrences of x replaced with E describes the state before the assignment.

$$\text{Hskip} \frac{}{\{P\}\texttt{skip}\{P\}_m}$$

$$\text{Hassign} \frac{}{\{P[E/x]\}\texttt{x := E}\{P\}_m}$$

$$\text{Hwhile} \frac{\{B\ \&\ P\}S\{P\}_m}{\{P\}\texttt{while } B \texttt{ do } S\{\neg B\ \&\ P\}_m}$$

$$\text{Hif} \frac{\{B\ \&\ P\}S_t\{Q\}_m \quad \{\neg B\ \&\ P\}S_e\{Q\}_m}{\{P\}\texttt{if } B \texttt{ then } S_t \texttt{ else } S_e\{Q\}_m}$$

$$\text{Hcons} \frac{P' \vDash_m P \quad \{P\}S\{Q\}_m \quad Q \vDash_m Q'}{\{P'\}S\{Q'\}_m}$$

$$\text{Hseq} \frac{\{P\}S_1\{Q\}_m \quad \{Q\}S_2\{R\}_m}{\{P\}S_1;S_2\{R\}_m}$$

$$P ::= \text{true} \mid \text{false} \mid \neg P \mid E = E \mid \forall x.P \mid \exists x.P \mid P \vee P \mid P\ \&\ P$$

Fig. 3. Inference Rules and Assertion Language for a basic Hoare Logic

4.1   A Straw Man Logic

Before describing our actual Hoare Logic, it is instructive to consider why a naive extension of our basic Hoare Logic does not work. Taking a cue from the assignment rule, we could generate a precondition from a postcondition by replacing the affected variable with the value it is assigned by the statement.

$$\text{Hfault} - \text{try1} \frac{}{\{P[f\ x/x]\}\texttt{fault } x\{P\}_m}$$

seems to be a plausible start, as the operational semantics say that the value of x changes to $f\ x$ for some function f. In order to consider all possible faults, we quantify over all possible functions on the integers:

$$\text{Hfault} - \text{try2} \frac{}{\{\forall \phi.\ P[\phi\ x/x]\}\mathtt{fault\ x}\{P\}_m}$$

Unfortunately, this rule does not integrate any properties of the fault model. This makes the rule quite useless, as the following example[4] using the SWC fault model, m, demonstrates:

Example 1

	{false}	
	$\{\forall \phi_1, \phi_2.\ \phi_1\ 3 = 3 \lor \phi_2\ 3 = 3\}_m$	(equivalent)
x = 3;	$\{\forall \phi_1, \phi_2.\ \phi_1\ x = 3 \lor \phi_2\ 3 = 3\}_m$	
y = 3;	$\{\forall \phi_1, \phi_2.\ \phi_1\ x = 3 \lor \phi_2\ y = 3\}_m$	
fault x,y;	$\{x = 3 \lor y = 3\}_m$	

Under the SWC fault model, at least one of the variables should equal 3 at the end, no matter what state the program begins in. However, the precondition we derive is equivalent to false and thus not true in any state. The problem is that our candidate Hoare rule does not allow us to apply any information about the fault model to the assertions. We need a way to describe the fault functions that can actually occur in the fault state.

4.2   A Useful Logic

The key insight is that we need a predicate hap f ("f happened") that says that a fault function is in the current fault state. hap f is true whenever the fault function f is the identity or is in the fault state. For example, hap $\lambda x.x$ describes any program state and hap f describes any state where f is in the fault state. This will allow us to reason about fault functions that are allowed in the current fault state.

In order to refer to the addition of fault functions to the state, rather than just their presence, we borrow $\multimap$ from Separation Logic [8, 9]. $P \multimap Q$ means that, in any state under which P holds, adding that state to the current state makes Q true. For example, hap $f \multimap Q$ implies that adding f to the current state makes Q true.

Using both $\multimap$ and hap, we can limit the range of fault functions to those that are allowed in the current fault state.

$$\text{Hfault} \frac{}{\{\forall \phi.\ \mathsf{hap}\ \phi \multimap P[\phi\ x/x]\}\mathtt{fault\ x}\{P\}_m}$$

This is the correct Hoare rule for fault x. Intuitively, it means that we know P after a fault statement if $P[f\ x/x]$ was true for any allowable fault function f beforehand.

Before we can use the fault rule to reason about the example from the previous section, we need a way to describe the values of fault functions. A simple approach

---

[4] In our examples, the left column contains code and the right column contains the corresponding assertions. A line of code, the precondition above and to the right, and the postcondition to the right together form a valid Hoare triple. Assertions one on top of the other with no code to the left indicate entailment. Using the sequence and consequence rules, a sequence of such entailments and Hoare triples results in a valid Hoare triple for the entire example.

suffices: we introduce predicates to say whether a function f is the identity ($\text{id } f$) or not ($\text{faulty } f$). For example, $\text{id } \lambda x.x$ & $\text{faulty } (\lambda x.x \text{ xor } 2^4)$ is always true.

Using the predicates $\text{id } f$, $\text{faulty } f$, and $\text{hap } f$, we can write down simple axioms that characterize our fault models. For instance, we can characterize the SWC fault model through the following axiom. This axiom uses Separation Logic's separating conjunction $P * Q$ to express the fact that both P and Q are true and that they describe disjoint subsets of the fault state.

$$\forall \phi_1, \phi_2. \text{ hap } \phi_1 * \text{hap } \phi_2 \twoheadrightarrow (\text{id } \phi_1 \vee \text{id } \phi_2)$$

This axiom says that, of any two fault functions in the fault state, at least one is the identity [5]. The separating conjunction in $\text{hap } \phi_1 * \text{hap } \phi_2$ guarantees that ϕ_1 and ϕ_2 do not refer to the same fault function instance in the fault state.

Using the proper Hoare rule for fault and this axiom about the SWC fault model, the example from the previous section works perfectly.

Example 2

```
            {true}_m
            {∀φ₂,φ₁. hap φ₂ * hap φ₁ -* id φ₁ ∨ id φ₂}_m    (by above property)
            {∀φ₂,φ₁. hap φ₂ * hap φ₁ -* φ₁ 3 = 3 ∨ φ₂ 3 = 3}_m
            {∀φ₂. hap φ₂ -* ∀φ₁. hap φ₁ -* φ₁ 3 = 3 ∨ φ₂ 3 = 3}_m
x = 3; y = 3; {∀φ₂. hap φ₂ -* ∀φ₁. hap φ₁ -* φ₁ x = 3 ∨ φ₂ y = 3}_m
fault x,y;   {x = 3 ∨ y = 3}_m
```

The SEU fault model allows for even more powerful properties, such as:

$$\forall f, x. f\, x \neq x (\text{mod } 3) \text{ iff faulty } f$$

which says that if there is a single bit flip in a variable (the only fault allowed in the SEU model), then difference between the changed variable and its original value is not divisible by 3, as it is a power of 2.

We use this property to prove that a simple example using an AN code is fault tolerant [5]. An AN code is a fault tolerant encoding of integers. To encode an integer encoded in base two, it is multiplied by a number that is relatively prime to two (in this case three). This way, any legal code word is a multiple of three. Any bit single flip will result in a number that is not a multiple of three and thus can be detected. What makes this code so useful is that it commutes with addition:

$$3 \cdot (a + b) = 3a + 3b.$$

This way, additions can be done efficiently on encoded numbers with regular hardware and the results can be checked for errors.

In Figure 4, we show that when using an AN code, only two independent copies of a computation are required to recover from a single bit flip fault, assuming no faults

---

[5] The reader may note that the two fault functions added to the fault state in the antecedent of this axiom are not "used" in the consequent. This is allowed, since, as can be seen in Section 4.3, our logic is an affine logic rather than a linear logic such as Separation Logic.

```
                  {x = n * y = n}_m
y = 3*y;          {x = n * y = 3n}_m
                  {∃g_1, g_2.hap g_1 * hap g_2 * y = g_2(3n) * x = g_1n})
while (y=3x)      {y = 3x & (∃g_1, g_2.hap g_1 * hap g_2 * y = g_2(3n) * x = g_1n)}_m
  do              {(y = 3x & y = 3n) ∨ (y = 3x & x = n)}_m
                  {y = 3n & x = n}
                  {∀g_3, g_4.hap g_3 * hap g_4 -* hap g_3 * hap g_4 * g_3y = g_3(3n) * g_4x = g_4n}_m
                  {∀g_3, g_4.hap g_3 * hap g_4 -* ∃g_1, g_2.hap g_1 * hap g_2*
                    g_3y = g_2(3n) * g_4x = g_1n}_m
  fault x,y;      {∃g_1, g_2.hap g_1 * hap g_2 * y = g_2(3n) * x = g_1n)}_m
                  {y ≠ 3x & (∃g_1, g_2.hap g_1 * hap g_2 * y = g_2(3n) * x = g_1n)}_m
                  {(y mod 3 = 0 & y = 3n) ∨ (y mod 3 ≠ 0 & x = n)}_m
if (y mod 3=0)    {y mod 3 = 0 & ((y mod 3 = 0 & y = 3n) ∨ (y mod 3 ≠ 0 & x = n))}_m
then              {y/3 = n}_m
  y = y/3;        {y = n}_m ⊢_m {y = n * y = n}_m
  x = y;          {x = n * y = n}_m
else              {y mod 3 ≠ 0 & ((y mod 3 = 0 & y = 3n) ∨ (y mod 3 ≠ 0 & x = n))}_m
                  {x = n}_m
                  {x = n * x = n}_m
  y = x;          {x = n * y = n}_m
                  {x = n * y = n}_m
```

Fig. 4. Proving a use of AN codes to be fault tolerant under the SEU fault model, m

during the recovery code. The example code simply sets the variable y to be three times its initial value (while x remains at the same initial value). It then loops, waiting for a fault. The code checks whether the fault occurred in x or y and sets the faulty variable from the unaffected one.

Note that this example uses the standard Separation Logic frame rule

$$\text{Hfaultframe} \frac{\{P\}\texttt{fault } \texttt{x}\{Q\}_m \quad \texttt{x} \notin fv(R)}{\{P * R\}\texttt{fault } \texttt{x}\{Q * R\}_m}$$

which we will prove later. The frame rule allows modular reasoning—if an unrelated assertion is separated from the one currently being considered, then it is unaffected. This is very useful in proofs of many fault tolerance properties including those involving independent redundant computations.

Our logic can also be used with a fault model allowing two arbitrary faults in a single program run. This results in an axiom very similar to that we had for the SWC model. The axiom appears below.

$$\forall \phi_1, \phi_2, \phi_3. \text{ hap } \phi_1 * \text{hap } \phi_2 * \text{hap } \phi_3 -* (\text{id } \phi_1 \vee \text{id } \phi_2 \vee \text{id } \phi_3)$$

Except for the addition of a third assignment and thus a third fault function, the example proceeds exactly like Example 1.

Example 3

$\{\text{true}\}_m$
$\{\forall \phi_3, \phi_2, \phi_1.\; \text{hap}\, \phi_3 * \text{hap}\, \phi_2 * \text{hap}\, \phi_1 \twoheadrightarrow \text{id}\, \phi_1 \vee \text{id}\, \phi_2 \vee \text{id}\, \phi_3\}_m$
(by the above axiom)
$\{\forall \phi_3, \phi_2, \phi_1.\; \text{hap}\, \phi_3 * \text{hap}\, \phi_2 * \text{hap}\, \phi_1 \twoheadrightarrow \phi_1 1 = 1 \vee \phi_2 1 = 1 \vee \phi_3 1 = 1\}_m$
$\{\forall \phi_3.\; \text{hap}\, \phi_3 \twoheadrightarrow \forall \phi_2.\; \text{hap}\, \phi_2 \twoheadrightarrow \forall \phi_1.\; \text{hap}\, \phi_1 \twoheadrightarrow \phi_1 1 = 1 \vee \phi_2 1 = 1 \vee \phi_3 1 = 1\}_m$
x=3 ; y=3 ; z=3 $\{\forall \phi_3.\; \text{hap}\, \phi_3 \twoheadrightarrow \forall \phi_2.\; \text{hap}\, \phi_2 \twoheadrightarrow \forall \phi_1.\; \text{hap}\, \phi_1 \twoheadrightarrow \phi_1 x = 1 \vee \phi_2 y = 1 \vee \phi_3 z = 1\}_m$
fault x,y,z $\{x = 1 \vee y = 1 \vee z = 1\}_m$

4.3   Formal Assertion Semantics

The assertions of our Hoare Logic are based on those of the Separation Logic of Ishtiaq, O'Hearn, and Reynolds [8, 9] with the current fault state taking on the role that the heap has in Separation Logic.

Assertion semantics are defined according to a judgment $F; V \vDash_m P$ between a fault model m, well-formed fault state, an environment, and an assertion. This judgment is defined in Figure 5. Note that these semantics depend on the definition of the well-formedness judgment $F\; \text{ok}_m$, which varies according to the fault model being considered. The novelty of these assertions lies in the interaction of the atomic assertions with the Separation Logic connectives $*$ and $\twoheadrightarrow$.

The fault state directly affects only the atomic assertion $\text{hap}\, f$, as the assertions $\text{faulty}\, f$ and $\text{id}\, f$ depend only on the function f, and the equality assertion between expressions depends on the environment but not the fault state. Furthermore, the logic is affine: the $\text{hap}\, f$ assertion uses up an occurrence of the function f in the fault state, but the function's appearance in the fault state does not *require* that it is used by a $\text{hap}\, f$. Thus the predicates describe a subset of all elements of the fault state (and possibly additional identity functions).

The purpose of the separating implications is to reason about adding fault functions to states. The separating conjunctions allow reasoning about fault functions that are distinct elements of the fault state. With $\twoheadrightarrow$ we can capture the notion of adding a fault function to the fault state. For example, $F; V \vDash_m \text{hap}\, f \twoheadrightarrow P$ says that P holds if f is added to the fault state (more precisely, in any fault state containing F plus a copy of f). Similarly, $*$ allows us to reason about multiple separate fault functions. The statement $F; V \vDash_m \text{hap}\, f * \text{hap}\, g \twoheadrightarrow \text{id}\, f \vee \text{id}\, g$ says that if two fault functions are added to the fault state, then at least one of them is the identity. This statement holds under the SWC fault model.

Unlike the heap contents in Separation Logic, fault functions do not refer to one another and there is no way to modify fault functions in our logic. As such, the complex descriptions of heap structure in Separation Logic have no analogue here. This is a good thing, as the large number of fault functions corresponding to possible faults are complex enough.

4.4   Properties

Let $\text{fv}(P)$ for a proposition P represent the free variables of P. Semantic entailment, $P \vDash_m Q$, holds between two formulae under the fault model m iff for all F and V such

$F; V \vDash_m P$

$F; V \vDash_m \forall x.\ P$ iff F ok$_m$ and for all n, $F; V \vDash_m P[n/x]$

$F; V \vDash_m \exists x.\ P$ iff F ok$_m$ and there exists n such that $F; V \vDash_m P[n/x]$

$F; V \vDash_m \forall \phi.\ P$ iff F ok$_m$ and for all f, $F; V \vDash_m P[f/\phi]$

$F; V \vDash_m \exists \phi.\ P$ iff F ok$_m$ and there exists f such that $F; V \vDash_m P[f/\phi]$

$F; V \vDash_m$ hap f iff F ok$_m$ and $f \in F$ or $f = \lambda x.x$

$F; V \vDash_m$ id f iff F ok$_m$ and $f = \lambda x.x$

$F; V \vDash_m$ faulty f iff F ok$_m$ and $f \neq \lambda x.x$

$F; V \vDash_m P_1 * P_2$ iff F ok$_m$ and there exist F_1 and F_2 such that
           $F = F_1 + F_2$, $F_1; V \vDash_m P_1$, and $F_2; V \vDash_m P_2$

$F; V \vDash_m P_1 \rightarrow P_2$ iff F ok$_m$ and for all F', if $F + F'$ ok$_m$ and $F'; V \vDash_m P_1$,
           then $F + F'; V \vDash_m P_2$

$F; V \vDash_m E_1 = E_2$ iff F ok$_m$ and $[\![E_1]\!]_V = [\![E_2]\!]_V$

$F; V \vDash_m P_1 \vee P_2$ iff F ok$_m$ and $F; V \vDash_m P_1$ or $F; V \vDash_m P_2$

$F; V \vDash_m P_1 \&\ P_2$ iff F ok$_m$ and $F; V \vDash_m P_1$ and $F; V \vDash_m P_2$

$F; V \vDash_m \neg P$ iff F ok$_m$ and $F; V \nvDash_m P$

$F; V \vDash_m$ true   iff F ok$_m$

$F; V \vDash_m$ false   iff never

Fig. 5. Assertion Semantics

that $fv(Q) \cup fv(P) \subseteq dom\ V$, $F; V \vDash_m Q$ whenever $F; V \vDash_m P$. The resulting logic has the following useful properties:

Proposition 1

- $*$ *is commutative and associative with unit* true.
- *If $P * Q$ holds, then so does P.*
- *$P \vee P$ is equivalent to P.*
- *If $P' \vDash_m P$ and $Q' \vDash_m Q$, then $P' * Q' \vDash_m P * Q$.*
- *In any state, if $\forall \phi_1, \phi_2.$ hap ϕ_1 $*$ hap ϕ_2 $\rightarrow$ P holds, then so does $\forall \phi_1.$ hap ϕ_1 $\rightarrow$ $\forall \phi_2.$ hap ϕ_2 $\rightarrow$ P.*
- faulty f, id f, *and equality of expressions are independent of well-formed fault states.*
- *If $F_1 + F_2$ ok$_m$ and $F_1, V \vDash_m P$, then $F_1 + F_2, V \vDash_m P$.*

Proof. Immediate using the semantics of assertions.

Lemma 1. *For all assertions P, fault states F, environments V, variables x, and expressions E, $F; V \vDash_m P[E/x]$ iff $F, V[x \mapsto E] \vDash_m P$.*

Proof. By induction on structure of P, simultaneously for the if and only if directions. This is necessary to get the inductive hypothesis in both directions for the $\rightarrow$ case.

Proposition 2. *The Hoare Logic fault rule, Hfault, is sound with respect to the assertion semantics.*

Proof. By induction on the derivation of $\{P\}$ fault $x\{Q\}_m$. Uses the above substitution lemma for the fault rule case.

Proposition 3. *The fault rule generates the weakest precondition, in the strong sense that for any F and V that do not entail the precondition, and any F' and V' such that* $(F, V, \texttt{fault } \texttt{x}) \longmapsto (F', V', -)$, *it is the case that F'; V' does not entail the postcondition.*

Proof. Easy proof from the definitions.

For every statment but the fault statement, the frame rule is standard. Here we verify that the frame rule holds for the fault statement as well.

Proposition 4. *The frame rule holds for the fault statement:*

$$\frac{\{P\}\texttt{fault } \texttt{x}\{Q\}_m}{\{P * R\}\texttt{fault } \texttt{x}\{Q * R\}_m} x \notin \text{fv}(R)$$

Proof. By induction on the derivation of $\{P\}\texttt{fault } \texttt{x}\{Q\}_m$.

5 Taming Proof Complexity

The large number of fault functions generated by the fault rule can make it difficult to manage proofs in the program logic. Even quite simple programs can require manipulation and reasoning about many fault functions. For example, the program in Figure 6 redundantly computes a single addition three times and compares the results. Even such a simple program generates a large and unwieldy precondition that includes nine different universally quantified variables. Fortunately, though the apparent complexity grows quickly, the reasoning itself is relatively simple. In this section, we show how to tame such complexity by introducing a new modal operator.

5.1 The Possibility Modality

To eliminate the need to deal with universally quantified fault functions directly, we have hidden them inside a modal operator $\bigcirc P$, read "maybe P" and meaning "P is true in the absence of faults." More precisely, $\bigcirc P$ says that either P is true, or a fault has occurred.

$$\bigcirc P \overset{\text{def}}{=} (\exists \phi. \text{ hap } \phi * \text{faulty } \phi) \vee P$$

The key property of $\bigcirc$ is its relation to the fault statement in our Hoare Logic. The modality $\bigcirc$ allows for a simple Hoare rule, as $\texttt{fault } \texttt{x}$ preserves $\bigcirc P$ for any P.

Proposition 5. $\{\bigcirc P\}\texttt{fault } \texttt{x}\{\bigcirc P\}_m$ *is valid for all P.*

Proof. This follows by proving that the precondition obtained by applying the Hfault rule to $\bigcirc P$ implies $\bigcirc P$. Uses substitution lemma 1.

By combining this Hoare rule with the frame rule for $\texttt{fault } \texttt{x}$, we obtained

$$\{\bigcirc P * Q\}\texttt{fault } \texttt{x}\{\bigcirc P * Q\}_m$$

$$\{a_0 = a \ \& \ a_1 = a \ \& \ a_2 = a \ \& \ b_0 = b \ \& \ b_1 = b \ \& \ b_2 = b\}_m$$

⋮ (sequence of entailments elided)

$$\{\forall \phi_{a_0}, \phi_{b_0}. \ \forall \phi_{a_1}, \phi_{b_1}. \ \forall \phi_{a_2}, \phi_{b_2}. \ \forall \phi_0, \phi_1, \phi_2. \ \mathsf{hap}\,(\phi_{a_1}) * \mathsf{hap}\,(\phi_{b_1})$$
$$* \mathsf{hap}\,(\phi_{a_2}) * \mathsf{hap}\,(\phi_{b_2}) * \mathsf{hap}\,(\phi_0) * \mathsf{hap}\,(\phi_1, \phi_2)) \twoheadrightarrow$$
$$(\phi_1(\phi_{a_1}a_1 + \phi_{b_1}b_1) = \phi_2(\phi_{a_2}a_2 + \phi_{b_2}b_2) \ \& \ \phi_1(\phi_{a_1}a_1 + \phi_{b_1}b_1) = a + b)\vee$$
$$(\phi_1(\phi_{a_1}a_1 + \phi_{b_1}b_1) \ne \phi_2(\phi_{a_2}a_2 + \phi_{b_2}b_2) \ \& \ \phi_0(\phi_{a_0}a_0 + \phi_{b_0}b_0) = a + b)\}_m$$

```
fault a0, b0;
a0 = a0 + b0;
fault a1, b1;

a1 = a1 + b1;        ⋮  (this is the complex part)
fault a2, b2;
a2 = a2 + b2;
fault a0, a1, a2;
```
$$\{(a_1 = a_2 \ \& \ a_1 = a + b) \vee (a_1 \ne a_2 \ \& \ a_0 = a + b)\}_m$$
```
if a1=a2

  then a0 = a1;       ⋮
  else skip;
```
$$\{a_0 = a + b\}_m$$

Fig. 6. An elided version of a complicated example with m = SWC fault model

whenever $x \notin \mathrm{fv}(Q)$. These $\bigcirc$-based Hoare rules for the `fault` statement do not contain any explicit fault functions, allowing us to ignore the fault functions in cases when the new rules apply.

Under the SWC fault model an additional and quite useful property holds:

Proposition 6. *Under the SEU fault model*

$$\bigcirc P * \bigcirc Q \vDash_m P \vee Q$$

and, in a generalized form:

$$\ast_{i=1}^{n} \bigcirc P_i \vDash_m \bigvee_{j=1}^{n} \&_{i=\{1,\dots,n\}\backslash\{j\}} P_i$$

Proof. By case analysis on whether and where a fault occurs.

This enables the easy derivation of useful postconditions to programs using modular redundancy. Using this rule with the Hoare rule involving $\bigcirc$, we can derive postconditions such as those of the form ⟨result is correct⟩ ∨ ⟨other result is correct⟩ where the two results come from modular computations.

With $\bigcirc$, the rough example from Section 5 is much simpler, as seen in Figure 7. Though still relatively long, this proof is quite simple and regular. There is not a single visible quantifier or fault function in the proof. What was formerly the most complex part of the proof now only has one simple assertion per line of code.

$$\{a_0 = a \ \& \ a_1 = a \ \& \ a_2 = a \ \& \ b_0 = b \ \& \ b_1 = b \ \& \ b_2 = b\}_m$$
$$\{a_0 + b_0 = a + b * a_1 + b_1 = a + b * a_2 + b_2 = a + b\}_m$$
$$\{\bigcirc a_0 + b_0 = a + b * \bigcirc a_1 + b_1 = a + b * \bigcirc a_2 + b_2 = a + b\}_m$$

```
fault a₀, b₀;     {Oa₀ + b₀ = a + b * Oa₁ + b₁ = a + b * Oa₂ + b₂ = a + b}ₘ
a₀ = a₀ + b₀;     {Oa₀ = a + b * Oa₁ + b₁ = a + b * Oa₂ + b₂ = a + b}ₘ
fault a₁, b₁;     {Oa₀ = a + b * Oa₁ + b₁ = a + b * Oa₂ + b₂ = a + b}ₘ
a₁ = a₁ + b₁;     {Oa₀ = a + b * Oa₁ = a + b * Oa₂ + b₂ = a + b}ₘ
fault a₂, b₂;     {Oa₀ = a + b * Oa₁ = a + b * Oa₂ + b₂ = a + b}ₘ
a₂ = a₂ + b₂;     {Oa₀ = a + b * Oa₁ = a + b * Oa₂ = a + b}ₘ
fault a₀, a₁, a₂; {Oa₀ = a + b * Oa₁ = a + b * Oa₂ = a + b}ₘ
```

$$P \stackrel{\text{def}}{=} \{(a_1 = a_2 \ \& \ a_1 = a + b) \vee (a_1 \neq a_2 \ \& \ a_0 = a + b)\}_m$$

```
if a₁=a₂
                  {a₁ = a₂ & P}ₘ
                  {a₁ = a + b}ₘ
  then a₀ = a₁;   {a₀ = a + b}ₘ
                  {a₁ ≠ a₂ & P}ₘ
                  {a₀ = a + b}ₘ
  else skip;      {a₀ = a + b}ₘ
                  {a₀ = a + b}ₘ
```

Fig. 7. The previous example, but smoother, $m = \text{SWC}$ fault model

6 RSA Sign/Verify

We now describe a more realistic example using the RSA Sign/Verify algorithm, one of many algorithms used to authenticate messages using digital signatures. RSA is a very widely used public key encryption system based on the difficulty of factoring a product of two large primes, $n = p \cdot q$. A public and private key, called e and d, respectively, are generated such that $e \cdot d \equiv 1 \bmod((p - 1) * (q - 1))$. When used for digital signatures, a signature is created by starting with a hash of the message and exponentiating it by raising it to the power given by the private key, modulo $p \cdot q$. The message and signature are then sent out. A recipient can *verify* the sender of the message by raising the signature to the power of the public key, modulo $p \cdot q$, and comparing this to the hash of the received message.

A common implementation of RSA uses the Chinese remainder theorem to speed up the exponentiation. The exponentiation is done twice, once modulo p and once modulo q. Then the results are multiplied by precalculated constants and added together. The same number of multiplications must be calculated, but the numbers are half the length in bits, so each multiplication takes about a quarter of the time. Thus there is an overall speedup of about 4.

However, Boneh and DeMilo showed that a single fault during execution of the Chinese remainder theorem algorithm for RSA not only fails validation, but can also compromise the secret key. As such, it is important to protect the algorithm with appropriate redundancy. One way to do so is to use a calculate-and-check form of fault tolerance where the check is simply the verify portion of the RSA algorithm. The verify step is also particularly fast, as the exponent used to decrypt the signature, e, is chosen so that it has a short bit length (commonly e is 65537, 17 bits long), enabling a very quick

$\{(\forall x, c \in V : c^e = x(\text{mod } n) \rightarrow c = x^d(\text{mod } n)) * d < 2^{512} * e < 2^{17} * \text{ev} = e * \text{nv} = p \cdot q * s2 = 1 * i2 = 17 * \text{mv2} = m * (\forall s_1, s_2, x.s_1 = x^{d_p} (\text{mod } p) * s_2 = x^{d_q} (\text{mod } q) \rightarrow a \cdot s_1 + b \cdot s_2 = x^d(\text{mod } p \cdot q)) * \text{av} = a * \text{bv} = b * \text{dvq} = d_q * \text{qv1} = q * \text{mvq} = m * d < 2^{17} * \text{sp} = 1 * \text{dvp} = d_p * \text{pv1} = p * \text{mvp} = m * \text{ip} := 511\}$

Calculate signature modulo p.
```
fault ip
while ip > -1
  fault sp, pv1
  sp := sp*sp (mod pv1)
  fault dvp, ip
  if dvp & (1 << ip) != 0:
    fault sp, mv, pv1
    sp := sp * mv (mod pv1)
  else:
    skip
  fault ip
  ip--
  fault ip
```

Calculate signature modulo q.
```
fault iq
while iq > -1
  fault sq, qv1
  sq := sq*sq (mod qv1)
  fault dvq, iq
  if dvq & (1 << iq) != 0:
    fault sq, mvq, qv1
    sq := sq * mvq (mod qv1)
  else:
    skip
  fault iq
  iq--
  fault iq
```

Combine results to get actual signature.
```
fault sp, av
tp := sp * av
fault sq, bv
tq := sq * bv
fault tp, tq
s := tp + tq
```

Check for errors by performing verify.
```
good := 1
fault s
out := s
fault i2
while i2 > -1:
  fault s2, nv2
  s2 := s2*s2 (mod nv2)
  fault ev2, i2
  fault ev2, i2
  if ev & (1<<i2) != 0:
    fault s2, out, nv2
    s2 := s2 * out (mod nv2)
  else:
    skip
  fault i2
  i2--
  fault i2 fault mv2, s2
if mv2 != s2:
  good := 0
else:
  skip
```

$$\{\text{good} = 0 \vee s = m^d(\text{mod } n)\}$$

Fig. 8. RSA Message Signing with Chinese Remainder Theorem, Fault Tolerant, SWC Fault Model

exponentiation. Using our system, we have proven the version of the RSA Sign/Verify algorithm appearing in Figure 8 fault tolerant with respect to the SWC Fault Model.

7 Certifying Compilation with Triple Modular Redundancy

In addition to being used as a standalone logic for proofs about fault tolerant programs, our logic can be used within the context of a certifying compiler to guarantee the compiler outputs fault tolerant code. To demonstrate this idea, we have developed a formal translation from ordinary, non-fault-tolerant Hoare triples, proven sound using conventional Hoare rules, into fault-tolerant Hoare triples proven sound with respect to the SWC fault model in our logic. The compiler achieves generic fault tolerance by adding triple modular redundancy to the program. In other words, each subexpression is recomputed three times and the results are compared to detect faults. Figure 9 presents the translation, which is composed of independent judgements for translating expressions ($B \rightsquigarrow B'$ for booleans and $E \rightsquigarrow (E_1, E_2, E_3)$ for integer expressions (there is one translated expression for each redundant computation)), statements ($S \rightsquigarrow S'$), and Hoare triples ($\{P\}S\{Q\}_m \rightsquigarrow \{P'\}S'\{Q'\}_m$). The top level translation of Hoare triples is performed according to the rule Ttriple, the program being translated according to the rules for translating statements and the precondition and postcondition being converted by the convert predicate.

The most interesting aspect of the translation is the coding of triple modular redundancy in our assertion logic: Given a standard assertion $P(x)$, which refers to some

Translation of Boolean and Integer Expressions:

$$\text{Tbool} \frac{}{B \rightsquigarrow \text{majority-vote}\,(B_1, B_2, B_3)} \quad \text{where } B_i \text{ is } B \text{ with an } i \text{ subscript added to each variable name.}$$

$$\text{Texpr} \frac{}{E \rightsquigarrow (E_1, E_2, E_3)} \quad \text{where } E_i \text{ is } E \text{ with an } i \text{ subscript added to each variable name.}$$

Translation of Imperative Statements:

$$\text{Twhile} \frac{B \rightsquigarrow B' \qquad S \rightsquigarrow S'}{\text{while } B \text{ do } S \rightsquigarrow \text{fault } fv(B')\ ;\ \text{while } B' \text{ do } (S'\ ;\ \text{fault } fv(B'))}$$

$$\text{Tseq} \frac{S \rightsquigarrow S' \qquad T \rightsquigarrow T'}{S\ ;\ T \rightsquigarrow S'\ ;\ T'}$$

$$\text{Tif} \frac{B \rightsquigarrow B' \qquad S \rightsquigarrow S' \qquad T \rightsquigarrow T'}{\text{if } B \text{ then } S \text{ else } T \rightsquigarrow \text{fault } fv(B')\ ;\ \text{if } B' \text{ then } S' \text{ else } T'}$$

$$\text{Tskip} \frac{}{\text{skip} \rightsquigarrow \text{skip}}$$

$$\text{Tasgn} \frac{E \rightsquigarrow (E_1, E_2, E_3)}{x := E \rightsquigarrow \text{fault } fv(E_1);\ x_1 := E_1;\ \text{fault } fv(E_2);\ x_2 := E_2;\ \text{fault } fv(E_3);\ x_3 := E_3}$$

Translation of Hoare triples:

Let convert$[P] \stackrel{\text{def}}{=} \exists x'.\ \bigcirc(x_1 = x') * \bigcirc(x_2 = x') * \bigcirc(x_3 = x') * P[x'/x]$ where x is the vector of program variables in P.

$$\text{Ttriple} \frac{S \rightsquigarrow S'}{\{P\}S\{Q\} \rightsquigarrow \{\text{convert}[P]\}S'\{\text{convert}[Q]\}_m}$$

Fig. 9. Translation from Program and Specification in standard Hoare logic to Triple Modular Redundant Program in our logic

(non-fault-tolerant) program variable x, the translated assertion will have the form $\exists x'. \bigcirc(x_1 = x') * \bigcirc(x_2 = x') * \bigcirc(x_3 = x') * P[x'/x]$. Intuitively, this assertion states that states that $P(x')$ will be true and x' may be equal to any one of three redundant versions of the original variable x, called x_1, x_2, and x_3. Additionally, when working in the SWC fault model, at most one of x_1, x_2, or x_3 will not be equal to x', allowing us to conclude at least two of the three assertions $P(x_1)$, $P(x_2)$ and $P(x_3)$ are true. By comparing x_1, x_2, and x_3 to each other, one can determine which (if any) variables are faulty and hence which predicates are true.

Proposition 7. *Given a valid standard Hoare triple as input, the translation produces a valid logic Hoare triple in our logic as output.*

8 Related Work

There are many existing methods for mitigating the effects of transient faults, using both hardware mechanisms, software mechanisms, and combinations of the two. For example, many solutions in software [10–13] require the compiler to duplicate computations and to insert comparisons to ensure that the two copies remain in agreement. Such techniques are usually evaluated experimentally using random fault injection, which shows that these solutions handle large classes of faults, but gives no hard and fast semantic guarantees about program behavior.

The SymPLFIED system [14] is a notable exception to the practice of random fault injection. SymPLFIED uses model checking to iterate through all possible hardware faults and to determine whether such faults can lead to catastrophic outcomes in the application being analyzed. SymPLIFIED has a significantly richer error model than the ones treated in this paper as it considers memory errors and control-flow errors. On the other hand, SymPLIFIED does not come with a program logic, like the one defined in this paper, that makes it possible to judge whether a program satisfies some general-purpose logical specification.

Another closely related line of research involves the development of type systems for checking fault tolerance properties. For example, the faulty lambda calculus, λ_{zap} [15], uses a type system to ensure its programs use triple modular redundancy properly. Elsman [16] shows how to extend that calculus with simplified error detection operations. More recent work applies these abstract, high-level ideas directly to assembly langauge [17, 18]. The main drawback of these type-based approaches is that each new fault tolerance scheme requires its own type system. In contrast, this paper proposes a more general logical framework for understanding how transient faults affect software behavior.

9 Conclusion

While development of most applications does not require reasoning about transient hardware faults, there are several domains in which such faults can cause substantial problems. One domain of particular interest is in the development of cryptographic algorithms where recent research has shown that even a single fault induced by an attacker is often sufficient to break the security of well-known algorithms such as RSA and DES.

This paper makes initial progress in the development of a framework for verifying such programs. It shows how to extend the operational semantics of a simple language of while programs with standard fault models and develops a variation of Separation Logic to reason about these programs and their faults. It also shows how to define and use a modal operator to simplify certain proofs of fault tolerance. Finally, the paper presents two illustrative applications of the logic: one involving a fault tolerant version of RSA and a second involving a compiler transformation that introduces triple modular redundancy.

Acknowledgments. The authors would like to acknowledge the help of Frances Perry in the early stages of the work presented in this paper. This research is funded in part by NSF award CNS-0627650. Any opinions, findings, and conclusions or recommendations expressed in this material are those of the author(s) and do not necessarily reflect the views of the NSF.

References

1. Boneh, D., DeMillo, R., Lipton, R.: On the importance of checking cryptographic protocols for faults. Journal of Cryptology 14(2), 101–119 (2001)
2. Govindavjhala, S., Appel, A.: Using memory errors to attack a virtual machine. In: Proceedings of the 2003 Symposium on Security and Privacy, May 2003, pp. 153–165 (2003)
3. Bar-El, H., Choukri, H., Naccache, D., Tunstall, M., Whelan, C.: The sorcerer's apprentice guide to fault attacks. Proceedings of the IEEE 94(2), 370–382 (2006)
4. Hegde, R., Shanbhag, N.R.: Energy-efficient signal processing via algorithmic noise-tolerance. In: ISLPED 1999: Proceedings of the 1999 international symposium on Low power electronics and design, pp. 30–35. ACM, New York (1999)
5. Chang, J., Reis, G.A., August, D.I.: Automatic instruction-level software-only recovery methods. In: Proceedings of the 2006 International Conference on Dependendable Systems and Networks (June 2006)
6. Shirvani, P.P., Saxena, N., McCluskey, E.J.: Software-implemented EDAC protection against SEUs. IEEE Transactions on Reliability 49, 273–284 (2000)
7. Winskel, G.: The Formal Semantics of Programming Languages. MIT Press, Cambridge (1996)
8. Ishtiaq, S., O'Hearn, P.: Bi as an assertion language for mutable data structures. In: Proceedings of the 28th ACM Symposium on Principles of Programming Languages, London, United Kingdom, January 2001, pp. 14–26 (2001)
9. Reynolds, J.C.: Separation logic: A logic for shared mutable data structures. In: Proceedings of the 17th Annual IEEE Symposium on Logic in Computer Science, pp. 55–74. IEEE Computer Society, Los Alamitos (2002)
10. Borin, E., Wang, C., Wu, Y., Araujo, G.: Software-based transparent and comprehensive control-flow error detection. In: CGO 2006: Proceedings of the International Symposium on Code Generation and Optimization, Washington, DC, USA, pp. 333–345. IEEE Computer Society, Los Alamitos (2006)
11. Oh, N., Shirvani, P.P., McCluskey, E.J.: Control-flow checking by software signatures 51(2), 111–122 (2002)

12. Reis, G.A., Chang, J., Vachharajani, N., Rangan, R., August, D.I.: SWIFT: Software implemented fault tolerance. In: Proceedings of the 3rd International Symposium on Code Generation and Optimization (March 2005)
13. Reis, G.A., Chang, J., Vachharajani, N., Rangan, R., August, D.I., Mukherjee, S.S.: Design and evaluation of hybrid fault-detection systems. In: Proceedings of the 32nd Annual International Symposium on Computer Architecture, June 2005, pp. 148–159 (2005)
14. Pattabiraman, K., Nakka, N., Kalbarczyk, Z., Iyer, R.: Symplfied: Symbolic program-level fault injection and error detection framework. In: International Conference on Dependable Systems and Networks (2008)
15. Walker, D., Mackey, L., Ligatti, J., Reis, G., August, D.I.: Static typing for a faulty lambda calculus. In: ACM International Conference on Functional Programming, Portland, Oregon (September 2006)
16. Elsman, M.: Fault-tolerant voting in a simply-typed lambda calculus. Technical Report ITU-TR-2007-99, IT University of Copenhagen, Rued Langgaards Vej 7, DK-2300 Copenhagen S, Denmark (June 2007)
17. Perry, F., Mackey, L., Reis, G.A., Ligatti, J., August, D.I., Walker, D.: Fault-tolerant typed assembly language. In: International Symposium on Programming Language Design and Implementation, PLDI (June 2007)
18. Perry, F., Walker, D.: Reasoning about control flow in the presence of transient faults. In: International Static Analysis Symposium (July 2008)

A Hoare Logic for the Coinductive Trace-Based Big-Step Semantics of While

Keiko Nakata and Tarmo Uustalu

Institute of Cybernetics at Tallinn University of Technology,
Akadeemia tee 21, EE-12618 Tallinn, Estonia
{keiko,tarmo}@cs.ioc.ee

Abstract. In search for a foundational framework for reasoning about observable behavior of programs that may not terminate, we have previously devised a trace-based big-step semantics for While. In this semantics, both traces and evaluation (relating initial states of program runs to traces they produce) are defined coinductively. On terminating runs, it agrees with the standard inductive state-based semantics. Here we present a Hoare logic counterpart of our coinductive trace-based semantics and prove it sound and complete. Our logic subsumes both the partial correctness Hoare logic and the total correctness Hoare logic: they are embeddable. Since we work with a constructive underlying logic, the range of expressible program properties has a rich structure; in particular, we can distinguish between termination and nondivergence, e.g., unbounded total search fails to be terminating but is nonetheless nondivergent. Our metatheory is entirely constructive as well, and we have formalized it in Coq.

1   Introduction

Standard big-step semantics and (partial correctness) Hoare logics do not support reasoning about nonterminating runs of programs. Essentially, they ignore them. But of course nonterminating runs are important. Not only need we often program a partially recursive function whose domain of definedness we cannot decide or is undecidable, e.g., an interpreter, but we also have to program functions that are inherently partially recursive. In programming with interactive input/output, for example, diverging runs are often what we really want.

In search for a foundational framework for reasoning about possibly nonterminating programs and intrigued by attempts in this direction in the literature, we have previously devised a big-step semantics for While based on traces [14]. In this semantics, traces are possibly infinite sequences of states that a program run goes through. They are defined coinductively, as is the evaluation relation, relating initial states of program runs to traces they produce. On terminating runs, this nonstandard semantics agrees with the standard, inductive state-based big-step semantics.

A.D. Gordon (Ed.): ESOP 2010, LNCS 6012, pp. 488–506, 2010.

In this paper, we put forward a Hoare logic to match this big-step semantics. In this new trace-based logic, program runs are reasoned about in terms of predicates on states and traces. More precisely, our Hoare triple $\{U\}\ s\ \{P\}$ is given by a statement s, a state predicate U (a condition on the initial state of a run of s) and a trace predicate P (a condition on the trace produced by the run). The interesting question is the choice of the language of assertions, i.e., the language in which we want to express these predicates. We would like to identify a suite of connectives for the assertion language with whom we achieve a sound and complete Hoare logic for a constructive underlying logic. We adopt a solution that is reminiscent of interval temporal logic [13,7] (with a chop-connective). The logic we propose is Spartan in terms of convenience of expression, but should well qualify as a foundational formalism into which more specialized applied logics can be translated.

The While language is total (as soon as we accept that traces of program runs can be infinite) and deterministic. This allows our logic to conservatively extend both the standard, state-based partial correctness Hoare logic as well as the standard, state-based total correctness Hoare logic. On the level of derivability alone this can be proved semantically by going through the soundness and completeness results. But we go one step further: we show that derivations in these two state-based logics are directly transformable into derivations in our logic. The transformations are relatively straightforward and do not require invention of new invariants or variants, demonstrating that our logic incurs no undue proof burden in comparison to the standard Hoare logics.

However, the power of our logic goes beyond that of the state-based partial and total correctness Hoare logics. The assertion language has access to traces. As suggested by its similarity to the assertion language of interval temporal logic, this allows us to specify liveness properties of diverging runs. We will demonstrate this extra expressiveness of our logic by a series of examples. Also, interpreted into a constructive underlying logic, our assertion language becomes quite discerning. In particular we can distinguish between termination and nondivergence, e.g., unbounded total[1] search fails to be terminating, but is nonetheless nondivergent.

We do not discuss this in the paper, but our logic can be adjusted to deal with exceptions and nondeterminism.

The paper is organized as follows. In Section 2, we present our trace-based big-step semantics. In Section 3, we proceed to the question of a corresponding Hoare logic. We explain our design considerations and then present our Hoare logic and the soundness and completeness proofs. In Section 4, we show the embeddings of the state-based partial and total correctness Hoare logics. In Section 5, we consider examples. In Section 6, we discuss the related work, to conclude in Section 7. We have formalized the development fully constructively in Coq version 8.1pl3 using the Ssreflect syntax extension library. The Coq development is available at http://cs.ioc.ee/~keiko/abyss.tgz.

---

[1] We should really say "nonpartial".

2 Big-Step Semantics

We start with our big-step semantics. This is defined in terms of states and traces. The notion of a state is standard. A state $\sigma \in state$ is an assignment of integer values to the variables. Traces $\tau \in trace$ are defined coinductively by the rules[2]

$$\frac{}{\langle \sigma \rangle \in trace} \qquad \frac{\tau \in trace}{\sigma :: \tau \in trace}$$

so a trace is a non-empty colist (possibly infinite sequence) of states. We also define bisimilarity of two traces, $\tau \approx \tau'$, coinductively by

$$\frac{}{\langle \sigma \rangle \approx \langle \sigma \rangle} \qquad \frac{\tau \approx \tau'}{\sigma :: \tau \approx \sigma :: \tau'}$$

Bisimilarity is straightforwardly seen to be an equivalence. We think of bisimilar traces as equal, i.e., type-theoretically we treat traces as a setoid with bisimilarity as the equivalence relation[3]. Accordingly, we have to make sure that all functions and predicates we define on traces are setoid functions and predicates (i.e., insensitive to bisimilarity). We define the initial state $hd\ \tau$ of a trace τ by case distinction by $hd\ \langle \sigma \rangle = \sigma, hd\ (\sigma :: \tau) = \sigma$. The function hd is a setoid function. We also define finiteness of a trace (with a particular final state) and infiniteness of a trace inductively resp. coinductively by

$$\frac{}{\langle \sigma \rangle \downarrow \sigma} \qquad \frac{\tau \downarrow \sigma'}{\sigma :: \tau \downarrow \sigma'} \qquad \frac{\tau^\uparrow}{(\sigma :: \tau)^\uparrow}$$

Finiteness and infiniteness are setoid predicates. It should be noticed that infiniteness is defined positively, not as negation of finiteness. Constructively, it is not the case that $\forall \tau. (\exists \sigma. \tau \downarrow \sigma) \vee \tau^\uparrow$, which amounts to asserting that finiteness is decidable. In particular, $\forall \tau. (\neg \exists \sigma. \tau \downarrow \sigma) \rightarrow \tau^\uparrow$ is constructively provable, but $\forall \tau. (\neg \tau^\uparrow) \rightarrow \exists \sigma. \tau \downarrow \sigma$ is not.

Evaluation $(s, \sigma) \Rightarrow \tau$, expressing that running a statement s from a state σ produces a trace τ, is defined coinductively by the rules in Figure 1. The rules for sequence and while implement the necessary sequencing with the help of extended evaluation $(s, \tau) \overset{*}{\Rightarrow} \tau'$, expressing that running a statement s from the last state (if it exists) of an already accumulated trace τ results in a total trace τ'. Extended evaluation is also defined coinductively, as the coinductive prefix closure of evaluation.

We look closer at the sequence rule. We want to conclude that $(s_0; s_1, \sigma) \Rightarrow \tau'$ from the premise $(s_0, \sigma) \Rightarrow \tau$. Classically, either the run of s_0 terminates, i.e., $\tau \downarrow \sigma'$ for some σ', or it diverges, i.e., $\tau^\uparrow$. In the first case, we would like to additionally use that τ is a finite prefix of τ' and that $(s_1, \sigma') \Rightarrow \tau''$, where τ''

---

[2] We mark coinductive definitions by double horizontal rules.

[3] Classically, strong bisimilarity is equality. But we work in an intensional type theory where strong bisimilarity of colists is weaker than equality (just as equality of two functions on all arguments is weaker than equality of these two functions).

$$\frac{}{(x := e, \sigma) \Rightarrow \sigma :: \langle \sigma[x \mapsto [\![e]\!]\sigma] \rangle} \quad \frac{}{(\text{skip}, \sigma) \Rightarrow \langle \sigma \rangle} \quad \frac{(s_0, \sigma) \Rightarrow \tau \quad (s_1, \tau) \overset{*}{\Rightarrow} \tau'}{(s_0; s_1, \sigma) \Rightarrow \tau'}$$

$$\frac{\sigma \models e \quad (s_t, \sigma :: \langle \sigma \rangle) \overset{*}{\Rightarrow} \tau}{(\text{if } e \text{ then } s_t \text{ else } s_f, \sigma) \Rightarrow \tau} \quad \frac{\sigma \not\models e \quad (s_f, \sigma :: \langle \sigma \rangle) \overset{*}{\Rightarrow} \tau}{(\text{if } e \text{ then } s_t \text{ else } s_f, \sigma) \Rightarrow \tau}$$

$$\frac{\sigma \models e \quad (s_t, \sigma :: \langle \sigma \rangle) \overset{*}{\Rightarrow} \tau \quad (\text{while } e \text{ do } s_t, \tau) \overset{*}{\Rightarrow} \tau'}{(\text{while } e \text{ do } s_t, \sigma) \Rightarrow \tau'} \quad \frac{\sigma \not\models e}{(\text{while } e \text{ do } s_t, \sigma) \Rightarrow \sigma :: \langle \sigma \rangle}$$

$$\frac{(s, \sigma) \Rightarrow \tau}{(s, \langle \sigma \rangle) \overset{*}{\Rightarrow} \tau} \quad \frac{(s, \tau) \overset{*}{\Rightarrow} \tau'}{(s, \sigma :: \tau) \overset{*}{\Rightarrow} \sigma :: \tau'}$$

Fig. 1. Big-step semantics

is the rest of τ'. In the second case, it should be case that $\tau \approx \tau'$. In both cases, the desirable condition is equivalent to $(s_1, \tau) \overset{*}{\Rightarrow} \tau'$, which is the second premise of our rule. The use of extended evaluation, defined as the coinductive (rather than inductive) prefix closure of evaluation, allows us to avoid the need to decide whether the run of s_0 terminates or not.

Evaluation is a setoid predicate. Moreover, for While, it is deterministic (up to bisimilarity, as is appropriate for our notion of trace equality).

Proposition 1. *For any* s, σ, τ *and* τ', *if* $(s, \sigma) \Rightarrow \tau$ *and* $(s, \sigma) \Rightarrow \tau'$, *then* $\tau \approx \tau'$.

In our definition, we have made a choice as regards to what grows the trace of a run. We have decided that assignments and testing of guards of if- and while-statements augment the trace by a state (but skip does not). This is good for several reasons. First, skip becomes a unit of sequential composition. Second, we get a notion of small steps that fully agrees with a very natural coinductive trace-based small-step semantics arising as a straightforward variation of the textbook inductive state-based small-step semantics.

Third, we obtain that any while-loop always progresses. For instance, in our semantics we can only derive (while true do skip, σ) $\Rightarrow \sigma :: \sigma :: \sigma :: \ldots$ (up to bisimilarity). Giving up insisting on progress in terms of growing the trace would introduce some semantic anomalies. For instance, we would not like to have (while true do skip, σ) $\Rightarrow \langle \sigma \rangle$, because an intuitively clearly infinite run would then be recorded in a finite trace, with the consequence that (while true do skip; $x := 17, \sigma$) $\Rightarrow \sigma :: \langle \sigma[x \mapsto 17] \rangle$ etc. But it also ensures that evaluation is total—as we should expect. Given that it also is deterministic, we can thus equivalently turn our relational big-step semantics into a functional one: the unique trace for a given statement and initial state is definable by corecursion. (For details, see our previous paper [14].)

The coinductive trace-based semantics agrees with the inductive state-based semantics.

Proposition 2. *For any s, σ, σ', existence of τ such that $(s, \sigma) \Rightarrow \tau$ and $\tau \downarrow \sigma'$ is equivalent to $(s, \sigma) \Rightarrow^{\mathrm{ind}} \sigma'$.*

We notice that the inductive state-based semantics is not total constructively—we cannot decide the halting problem.

3   Hoare Logic

We now proceed to the Hoare logic and its soundness and completeness proof. As we will base our consequence rule on semantic entailment rather than derivability in some fixed proof system, we sidestep the problem of its unavoidable incompleteness (due to the impossibility of complete axiomatization of any theory containing arithmetic). Regarding the choice of level of expressiveness of the assertion language, we deliberately keep the assertion language open, only making sure we have enough connectives to be able to express the strongest postcondition for any expressible precondition.

3.1   Assertion Language

Our assertions will be about states and traces, i.e., expressing state and trace predicates. A state predicate U is simply a predicate on states. From a trace predicate P, we require that it is a setoid predicate, i.e., it must be unable to distinguish bisimilar traces.

We introduce a number of connectives for our assertion language. All these connectives yield setoid predicates. The inference rules of the Hoare logic rely on the availability of these connectives. Indeed, it was an intriguing exercise for us to come up with connectives that would be simple but expressive enough practically and at the same time allow us to prove the Hoare logic sound and complete constructively. The semantic definitions of these connectives are given in Figure 2.[4]

The two most primitive state (resp. trace) predicates are true and false, which are respectively true and false for any state (resp. trace). We can also use the standard connectives $\neg, \wedge, \vee$ and quantifiers $\forall, \exists$ to build state and trace predicates. The context disambiguates the overloaded notations for these state and trace predicates.

For a state predicate U, the singleton $\langle U \rangle$ is a trace predicate that is true of singleton traces given by a state satisfying U. In particular $\langle \text{true} \rangle$ is true of any singleton trace.

For a state predicate U, the doubleton $\langle U \rangle^2$ is true of a doubleton trace whose two states are identical and satisfy U.

For a state predicate U, the update $U[x \mapsto e]$ is the strongest postcondition of the statement $x := e$ for the precondition U. It is true of a doubleton trace

---

[4] We use the symbol $\models$ for visual highlighting of predicates. We are not defining a single satisfaction relation $\models$ for some fixed language of predicates, but a number of individual state/trace predicates and operations on such predicates. Some of them are defined inductively, some coinductively, some definitions are not recursive at all.

$$\frac{}{\sigma \models \text{true}} \qquad \frac{\neg(\sigma \models U)}{\sigma \models \neg U} \qquad \frac{\sigma \models U \quad \sigma \models V}{\sigma \models U \wedge V} \quad \cdots$$

$$\frac{}{\tau \models \text{true}} \qquad \frac{\neg(\tau \models P)}{\tau \models \neg P} \qquad \frac{\tau \models P \quad \tau \models Q}{\tau \models P \wedge Q} \quad \cdots$$

$$\frac{\sigma \models U}{\langle \sigma \rangle \models \langle U \rangle} \qquad \frac{\tau \models P \quad \tau' \models_\tau Q}{\tau' \models P \ast\ast Q} \qquad \frac{\tau \models \langle \text{true} \rangle}{\tau \models P^\dagger} \qquad \frac{\tau \models P \quad \tau' \models_\tau P^\dagger}{\tau' \models P^\dagger}$$

$$\frac{\sigma \models U}{\sigma :: (\sigma[x \mapsto e]) \models U[x \mapsto e]} \qquad \frac{\sigma \models U}{\sigma :: \langle \sigma \rangle \models \langle U \rangle^2}$$

$$\frac{\tau \models P \quad \tau \downarrow \sigma}{\sigma \models Last\ P} \qquad \frac{\tau \downarrow \sigma}{\tau \models finite} \qquad \frac{\tau^\uparrow}{\tau \models infinite}$$

$$\frac{\langle \sigma \rangle \models Q}{\langle \sigma \rangle \models_{\langle \sigma \rangle} Q} \qquad \frac{\sigma :: \tau \models Q}{\sigma :: \tau \models_{\langle \sigma \rangle} Q} \qquad \frac{\tau' \models_\tau Q}{\sigma :: \tau' \models_{\sigma :: \tau} Q}$$

$$\frac{\forall \sigma\, (\sigma \models U \to \sigma \models V)}{U \models V} \qquad \frac{\forall \tau\, (\tau \models P \to \tau \models Q)}{P \models Q}$$

Fig. 2. Semantics of assertions

whose first state σ satisfies U and second state is obtained from the first by modifying the value of x to become $[\![e]\!]\,\sigma$.

For trace predicates P and Q, the chop $P \ast\ast Q$ is a trace predicate that is true, roughly speaking, of a trace τ' that has a prefix τ satisfying P, with the rest of τ' satisfying Q. But its definition is carefully crafted, so that Q is not checked, if τ is infinite (in which case necessarily $\tau \approx \tau'$), and this happens without case distinction on whether τ is finite. This effect is achieved with the premise $\tau' \models_\tau Q$. The relation $\tau' \models_\tau Q$ is defined coinductively. It traverses all of τ, making sure that it is a prefix of τ', and, upon possible exhaustion of τ in a finite number of steps, checks Q against the rest of τ'. This way the problem of deciding whether τ is finite is avoided, basically by postponing it, possibly infinitely.

Our chop operator is classically equivalent to the chop operator from interval temporal logic [13,7] (cf. also the separating conjunction of separating logic). Indeed, classically, $\tau' \models P \ast\ast Q$ holds iff

- either, for some finite prefix τ of τ', we have $\tau \models P$ and $\tau'' \models Q$, where τ'' is the rest of τ',
- or τ' is infinite and $\tau' \models P$.

This is how the semantics of chop is defined in interval temporal logic. But it involves upfront decision of whether P will be satisfied by a finite or an infinite prefix of τ'. Our definition is fine-tuned for constructive reasoning.

For a trace predicate P, its iteration $P^\dagger$ is a trace predicate that is true of a trace which is a concatenation of a possibly infinite sequence of traces, each of which satisfies P. It is reminiscent of the Kleene star operator. It is defined by coinduction and takes into account both infiniteness of some single iteration and infinite repetition.

For a trace predicate P, $Last\ P$ is a state predicate that is true of states that can be the last state of a finite trace satisfying P. Note that $Last\ P$ is defined inductively.

Proposition 3. *For any U, $\langle U \rangle$, $U[x \mapsto e]$, $\langle U \rangle^2$ are setoid predicates. For any setoid predicates P, Q, $P \ast\ast Q$ is a setoid predicate. For any setoid predicate P, $P^\dagger$ is a setoid predicate.*

A number of logical consequences and equivalences hold about these connectives. We have the trivial equivalence: $\langle \mathsf{true} \rangle \ast\ast P \Leftrightarrow P \Leftrightarrow P \ast\ast \langle \mathsf{true} \rangle$. The chop operator is associative: $(P \ast\ast Q) \ast\ast R \Leftrightarrow P \ast\ast (Q \ast\ast R)$. The iterator operator $P^\dagger$ repeats P either zero times or once followed by further repetitions: $P^\dagger \Leftrightarrow \langle \mathsf{true} \rangle \vee (P \ast\ast P^\dagger)$. A trace is infinite if and only if false holds for any last state: $infinite \Leftrightarrow \mathsf{true} \ast\ast \langle \mathsf{false} \rangle$. We have $P \ast\ast Last\ P \Leftrightarrow P$. We also have $Last\ (P \ast\ast Q) \models Last\ Q$, but the converse does not hold. If every trace satisfying P is infinite, i.e., if $P \models infinite$, then $Last\ P \Leftrightarrow \mathsf{false}$.

3.2   Inference Rules

The derivable judgements of the Hoare logic are given by the inductively interpreted inference rules in Figure 3. The proposition $\{U\}\ s\ \{P\}$ states derivability of the judgement. The intent is that $\{U\}\ s\ \{P\}$ should be derivable precisely when running a statement s from a initial state satisfying U is guaranteed to produce a trace satisfying P.

The rules for assignment and skip are self-explanatory.

The rule for sequence is defined in terms of the chop operator. The precondition V for the second statement s_1 is given by those states in which a run of the first statement s_0 may terminate. In particular, if $\{U\}\ s_0\ \{P\}$ and $P \models infinite$, i.e., s_0 is necessarily diverging for the precondition U, then we have $\{U\}\ s_0\ \{P \ast\ast \langle \mathsf{false} \rangle\}$. In this case, from the derivability of $\{\mathsf{false}\}\ s_1\ \{Q\}$ for any Q, we get $\{U\}\ s_0; s_1\ \{P \ast\ast Q\}$ for any Q. But this makes sense, since $P \ast\ast Q \Leftrightarrow P$ as soon as $P \models infinite$.

The rule for if-statement uses the doubleton operator in accordance with the operational semantics where we have chosen that testing the boolean guard grows the trace.

The rule for while-statement is inspired by the corresponding rule of the standard, state-based partial-correctness Hoare logic. It uses a loop invariant I. This is a state predicate that has to be true each time the boolean guard is about to be (re-)tested in a run of the loop. Accordingly, the precondition U should be stronger then I. Also, I must hold each time an iteration of s_t has finished, as enforced by having $P \ast\ast \langle I \rangle$ as the postcondition of s_t. The postcondition $\langle U \rangle^2 \ast\ast (P \ast\ast \langle I \rangle^2)^\dagger \ast\ast \langle \neg e \rangle$ of the loop consists of three parts. $\langle U \rangle^2$ accounts for

$$\frac{}{\{U\}\ x := e\ \{U[x \mapsto e]\}} \quad \frac{}{\{U\}\ \mathsf{skip}\ \{\langle U \rangle\}} \quad \frac{\{U\}\ s_0\ \{P ** \langle V \rangle\} \quad \{V\}\ s_1\ \{Q\}}{\{U\}\ s_0; s_1\ \{P ** Q\}}$$

$$\frac{\{e \wedge U\}\ s_t\ \{P\} \quad \{\neg e \wedge U\}\ s_f\ \{P\}}{\{U\}\ \mathsf{if}\ e\ \mathsf{then}\ s_t\ \mathsf{else}\ s_f\ \{\langle U \rangle^2 ** P\}}$$

$$\frac{U \models I \quad \{e \wedge I\}\ s_t\ \{P ** \langle I \rangle\}}{\{U\}\ \mathsf{while}\ e\ \mathsf{do}\ s_t\ \{\langle U \rangle^2 ** (P ** \langle I \rangle^2)^\dagger ** \langle \neg e \rangle\}}$$

$$\frac{U \models U' \quad \{U'\}\ s\ \{P'\} \quad P' \models P}{\{U\}\ s\ \{P\}} \quad \frac{\forall z.\{U\}\ s\ \{P\}}{\{\exists z.U\}\ s\ \{\exists z.P\}}$$

Fig. 3. Inference rules of Hoare logic

the first test of the guard; $(P ** \langle I \rangle^2)^\dagger$ accounts for iterations of the loop body in alternation with re-tests of the guard (notice that that we are again using the doubleton operator); $\langle \neg e \rangle$ accounts for the state in which the last test of the guard is finished.

We have chosen to introduce a separate rule for instantiating auxiliary variables. Alternatively, we might have stated the consequence rule in a more general form, as suggested by Kleymann [12]; yet the separation facilitates formalization in Coq.

The various logical consequences and equivalences about the connectives suggest also further alternative and equivalent formulations. For instance, we could replace the rule for the while-statement by

$$\frac{\{e \wedge I\}\ s_t\ \{P ** \langle I \rangle\}}{\{I\}\ \mathsf{while}\ e\ \mathsf{do}\ s_t\ \{\langle I \rangle^2 ** (P ** \langle I \rangle^2)^\dagger ** \langle \neg e \rangle\}}$$

if we strengthened the consequence rule to

$$\frac{U \models U' \quad \{U'\}\ s\ \{P'\} \quad \langle U' \rangle ** P' \models P}{\{U\}\ s\ \{P\}}$$

With our chosen rule for while, this strengthened version of consequence is admissible:

Lemma 1. *For any U, s and V, $\{U\}\ s\ \{P\}$ then $\{U\}\ s\ \{\langle U \rangle ** P\}$.*

We do not attempt to argue that our formulation is the best choice; yet we found that the present formulation is viable from the points-of-view of both the meta-theory and applicability of the logic.

3.3 Soundness

The soundness result states that any derivable Hoare triple is semantically valid.

Proposition 4 (Soundness). *For any s, U, P, σ, τ, if $\{U\}\ s\ \{P\}$ and $\sigma \models U$ and $(s, \sigma) \Rightarrow \tau$ and then $\tau \models P$.*

Proof. By induction on the derivation of $\{U\}\ s\ \{P\}$. We show the main cases of sequence and while.

- $s = s_0; s_1$: We are given as the induction hypotheses that, for any σ, τ, $(s_0, \sigma) \Rightarrow \tau$ and $\sigma \models U$ imply $\tau \models P **\langle V\rangle$, and that, for any σ, τ, $(s_1, \sigma) \Rightarrow \tau$ and $\sigma \models V$ imply $\tau \models Q$. We have to prove $\tau \models P ** Q$, given $\sigma \models U$ and $(s_0, \sigma) \Rightarrow \tau_0$ and $(s_1, \tau_0) \overset{*}{\Rightarrow} \tau_1$. By the induction hypothesis for s_0, we derive $h_0 : \tau_0 \models P$ and $\tau_0 \models_{\tau_0} \langle V\rangle$. We prove by coinduction an auxiliary lemma: for any $\tau, \tau', \tau \models_\tau \langle V\rangle$ and $(s_1, \tau) \overset{*}{\Rightarrow} \tau'$ give $\tau' \models_\tau Q$, using the induction hypothesis for s_1. The lemma gives us $h_1 : \tau_1 \models_{\tau_0} Q$. We can now close the case by h_0 and h_1.

- $s = \mathsf{while}\ e\ \mathsf{do}\ s_t$: We are given as the induction hypothesis that for any σ and τ, $\sigma \models I \wedge e$ and $(\sigma, s) \Rightarrow \tau$ imply $\tau \models P ** \langle I\rangle$. We have to prove $\tau \models \langle U\rangle^2 ** (P ** \langle I\rangle^2)^\dagger ** \langle\neg e\rangle$, given $U \models I$ and $\sigma \models U$ and $(\mathsf{while}\ e\ \mathsf{do}\ s_t, \sigma) \Rightarrow \tau$. We do so by proving the following conditions by mutual coinduction:

  • for any σ and τ, if $\sigma \models I$ and $(\mathsf{while}\ e\ \mathsf{do}\ s, \sigma) \Rightarrow \sigma :: \tau$, then $\tau \models (P ** \langle I\rangle^2)^\dagger ** \langle\neg e\rangle$

  • for any τ and τ', if $\tau \models_\tau \langle I\rangle$ and $(\mathsf{while}\ e\ \mathsf{do}\ s_t, \tau) \overset{*}{\Rightarrow} \tau'$, then $\tau' \models_\tau \langle I\rangle^2 ** (P ** \langle I\rangle^2)^\dagger ** \langle\neg e\rangle$.

3.4 Completeness

The completeness result states that any semantically valid Hoare triple is derivable. Following the standard approach (see, e.g., [17]) we define, for a given statement s and a given precondition U, a trace predicate $sp(s, U)$—the candidate strongest postcondition. Then we prove that $sp(s, U)$ is a postcondition according to the logic (i.e., $\{U\}\ s\ \{sp(s, U)\}$ is derivable) and that $sp(s, U)$ is semantically stronger than any other trace predicate that is a postcondition semantically. Completeness follows.

The trace predicate $sp(s, U)$ is defined by induction on s in Figure 4. The definition is mostly self-explanatory, as it mimics the inference rules of the logic, except that we need the loop-invariant $Inv(e, s, U)$. $Inv(e, s, U)$ characterizes the set of states that running $\mathsf{while}\ e\ \mathsf{do}\ s_t$ from a state satisfying U can reach at the boolean guard in finite steps.

For any s and U, the predicate $sp(s, U)$ is a monotone setoid predicate.

Lemma 2. *For any* s, U, τ, τ', *if* $\tau \models sp(s, U)$ *and* $\tau \approx \tau'$ *then* $\tau' \models sp(s, U)$.

Lemma 3. *For any* s, U, U', *if* $U \models U'$ *then* $sp(s, U) \models sp(s, U')$.

The following lemma states that any trace which satisfies $sp(s, U)$ has its first state satisfying U.

Lemma 4. *For any* s, U, τ, *if* $\tau \models sp(s, U)$ *then* $hd\ \tau \models U$.

The following lemma is central for the next two important lemmata, stating that *Last P* and $Inv(e, s, U)$ are adequate.

$$sp(x := e, U) = U[x \mapsto e]$$
$$sp(\mathbf{skip}, U) = \langle U \rangle$$
$$sp(s_0; s_1, U) = P ** sp(s_1, Last\ P)\ where\ P = sp(s_0, U)$$
$$sp(\mathbf{if}\ e\ \mathbf{then}\ s_t\ \mathbf{else}\ s_f, U) = \langle U \rangle^2 ** (sp(s_t, e \wedge U) \vee sp(s_f, \neg e \wedge U))$$
$$sp(\mathbf{while}\ e\ \mathbf{do}\ s, U) = \langle U \rangle^2 ** (sp(s, e \wedge I) ** \langle I \rangle^2)^\dagger ** \langle \neg e \rangle$$
$$where\ I = Inv(e, s, U)$$

$$\frac{\sigma \models U}{\sigma \models Inv(e, s, U)} \qquad \frac{V \models Inv(e, s, U) \quad \sigma \models Last\ ((\langle Inv(e, s, U) \wedge e \rangle ** sp(s, V))}{\sigma \models Inv(e, s, U)}$$

Fig. 4. Strongest postcondition

Lemma 5. *For any* τ, U, *if for any* σ, $\tau \downarrow \sigma$ *implies* $\sigma \models U$, *then* $\tau \models_\tau \langle U \rangle$.

Proof. By coinduction with case analysis on τ.

Lemma 6. *For any* P, $P \Leftrightarrow P ** \langle Last\ P \rangle$.

Proof. Suppose we are given $\tau \models P$. By the definition of $Last\ P$, we have for any σ, $\tau \downarrow \sigma$ implies $\sigma \models Last\ P$. We then deduce $\tau \models_\tau \langle Last\ P \rangle$ by Lemma 5, thus conclude $\tau \models P ** \langle Last\ P \rangle$.

Suppose we are given $\tau_0 \models P$ and $\tau_1 \models_{\tau_0} \langle Last\ P \rangle$. We prove the following condition by coinduction: for any U, τ, τ', $\tau' \models_\tau \langle U \rangle$ implies $\tau \approx \tau'$. Therefore we have $\tau_0 \approx \tau_1$, from which $\tau_1 \models P$ follows. (Recall that P is a setoid predicate.)

Lemma 7. *For any* s, e, U, τ, $sp(s, Inv(e, s, U) \wedge e) \Leftrightarrow sp(s, Inv(e, s, U) \wedge e) ** \langle Inv(e, s, U) \rangle$.

Proof. Suppose we are given $\tau \models sp(s, Inv(e, s, U) \wedge e)$. It suffices to prove $\tau \models_\tau \langle Inv(e, s, U) \rangle$. However, we have $\tau \models \langle Inv(e, s, U) \wedge e \rangle ** sp(s, Inv(e, s, U))$ by Lemma 3 and Lemma 4. By the definition of Inv, we have for any σ, $\tau \downarrow \sigma$ implies $\sigma \models Inv(e, s, U)$. Therefore we conclude $\tau \models_\tau \langle Inv(e, s, U) \rangle$ by Lemma 5. $sp(s, Inv(e, s, U) \wedge e) ** \langle Inv(e, s, U) \rangle \models sp(s, Inv(e, s, U) \wedge e)$ is proved similarly to Lemma 6.

We are now ready to establish that $sp(s, U)$ is a postcondition according to the Hoare logic.

Lemma 8. *For any* s, U, $\{U\}\ s\ \{sp(s, U)\}$.

Proof. By induction on s. We show the main case of while: $s = \mathbf{while}\ e\ \mathbf{do}\ s_t$. We are given as induction hypothesis that, for any U_0, $\{U_0\}\ s_t\ \{sp(s_t, U_0)\}$. We have to prove $\{U\}\ \mathbf{while}\ e\ \mathbf{do}\ s_t\ \{\langle U \rangle^2 ** (sp(s_t, e \wedge I) ** \langle I \rangle^2)^\dagger ** \langle \neg e \rangle\}$ where $I = Inv(e, s_t, U)$. It is sufficient to prove $\{e \wedge I\}\ s_t\ \{(sp(s_t, e \wedge I) ** \langle I \rangle)\}$, which follows from the induction hypothesis and Lemma 7.

Following the standard route, it should remain to prove the following condition: for any s, U, P, if for all σ, τ, $\sigma \models U$ and $(s, \sigma) \Rightarrow \tau$ imply $\tau \models P$, then $sp(s, U) \models P$.

This will be an immediate corollary from Lemma 4 and the following lemma, stating that any trace which satisfies $sp(s, U)$ is in fact produced by a run of s.

Lemma 9. *For any s, U, τ, if $\tau \models sp(s, U)$ then $(s, hd\ \tau) \Rightarrow \tau$.*

Proof. By induction on s. We show the main cases of sequence and while.

- $s = s_0; s_1$: We are given as the induction hypotheses that, for any $U', \tau', \tau' \models sp(s_0, U')$ (resp. $\tau' \models sp(s_1, U')$) implies $(s_0, hd\ \tau') \Rightarrow \tau'$ (resp. $(s_1, hd\ \tau') \Rightarrow \tau'$). We have to prove $(s_0; s_1, hd\ \tau) \Rightarrow \tau$, given $\tau \models sp(s_0; s_1, U)$, which unfolds into $\tau_0 \models sp(s_0, U)$ and $\tau \models_{\tau_0} sp(s_1, Last\ (sp(s_0, U)))$. By the induction hypothesis for s_0, we have $(s_0, hd\ \tau_0) \Rightarrow \tau_0$. Using the induction hypothesis for s_1, we prove by coinduction that, for any $\tau_1, \tau_2, \tau_2 \models_{\tau_1} sp(s_1, Last\ (sp(s_0, U)))$ implies $(s_1, \tau_1) \overset{*}{\Rightarrow} \tau_2$, thereby we close the case.
- $s = $ while e do s_t: We are given as the induction hypothesis that, for any $U', \tau', \tau' \models sp(s_t, U')$ implies $(s_t, hd\ \tau') \Rightarrow \tau'$. We have to prove (while e do $s_t, hd\ \tau) \Rightarrow \tau$, given $\tau \models \langle U \rangle^2 ** (sp(s, e \wedge I) ** \langle I \rangle^2)^\dagger ** \langle \neg e \rangle$ where $I = Inv(e, s, U)$. We do so by proving the following two conditions simultaneously by mutual coinduction:
  - for any τ, $\tau \models (sp(s, e \wedge I) ** \langle I \rangle^2)^\dagger ** \langle \neg e \rangle$ implies (while e do $s_t, hd\ \tau) \Rightarrow hd\ \tau :: \tau$,
  - for any τ and τ', $\tau' \models_\tau \langle I \rangle^2 ** (sp(s, e \wedge I) ** \langle I \rangle^2)^\dagger ** \langle \neg e \rangle$ implies (while e do $s_t, \tau) \overset{*}{\Rightarrow} \tau'$.

Corollary 1. *For any s, U, P, if for all σ, τ, $\sigma \models U$ and $(s, \sigma) \Rightarrow \tau$ imply $\tau \models P$, then $sp(s, U) \models P$.*

Completeness is proved as a corollary of the last two lemmata.

Proposition 5 (Completeness). *For any s, U, P, if for all σ, τ, $\sigma \models U$ and $(s, \sigma) \Rightarrow \tau$ imply $\tau \models P$, then $\{U\}\ s\ \{P\}$.*

Proof. Assume that for all σ, τ, $\sigma \models U$ and $(s, \sigma) \Rightarrow \tau$ imply $\tau \models P$. By Corollary 1, we have that $sp(s, U) \models P$. By Lemma 8, we have $\{U\}\ s\ \{sp(s, U)\}$. Applying consequence, we get $\{U\}\ s\ \{P\}$.

4   Relation to the Standard Partial and Total Correctness Hoare Logics

It is easy to see, by going through soundness and completeness results, that our trace-based Hoare logic is a conservative extension of the standard, state-based partial and total correctness Hoare logics. But more can be said. The derivations in these two logics are directly transformable into derivations in our logic, preserving their structure, without invention of new invariants or variants.

We formalize our claim in the next two propositions, whose direct proofs are algorithms for the transformations. Proposition 6 states that, if $\{U\}\ s\ \{V\}$ is a derivable partial correctness formula, then $\{U\}\ s\ \{\text{true} ** \langle V \rangle\}$ is derivable in our logic. The trace predicate $\text{true} ** \langle V \rangle$ indicates that V holds of any state that is reachable by traversing, in a finite number of steps, the whole trace τ produced by running s. Classically, this amounts to the condition of V being true of the last state of τ, if τ is finite and hence has one; if τ is infinite, then nothing is required. Proposition 7 states that, if $\{U\}\ s\ \{V\}$ is a derivable total correctness judgement, then $\{U\}\ s\ \{\text{finite} ** \langle V \rangle\}$ is derivable in our logic. The trace predicate $\text{finite} ** \langle V \rangle$ states that the trace τ produced by running s is finite and V holds of the last state of τ; the finiteness of τ guarantees the existence of the last state.

(For reference, the inference rules of the state-based logics appear in the Appendix.)

Proposition 6. *For any U, s and V, if $\{U\}\ s\ \{V\}$ is derivable in the partial correctness Hoare logic, then $\{U\}\ s\ \{\text{true} ** \langle V \rangle\}$.*

Proof. By induction on the Hoare logic derivation of $\{U\}\ s\ \{V\}$. We show the main case of while: $s \equiv \text{while } e \text{ do } s_t$. We are given as the induction hypothesis $\{e \wedge I\}\ s\ \{\text{true} ** \langle I \rangle\}$. We close the case by the derivation

$$\frac{\dfrac{\{e \wedge I\}\ s\ \{\text{true} ** \langle I \rangle\}}{\{I\}\ \text{while } e \text{ do } s_t\ \{\langle I \rangle^2 ** (\text{true} ** \langle I \rangle^2)^\dagger ** \langle \neg e \rangle\}}}{\{I\}\ \text{while } e \text{ do } s_t\ \{\text{true} ** \langle I \wedge \neg e \rangle\}}$$

For the embedding of total correctness derivations, we prove a slightly stronger statement to have the induction going through.

Proposition 7. *For any U, s and V, if $\{U\}\ s\ \{V\}$ is derivable in the total correctness Hoare logic, then for any U_0, $\{U \wedge U_0\}\ s\ \{\langle U_0 \rangle ** \text{finite} ** \langle V \rangle\}$.*

Proof. By induction on the Hoare logic derivation of $\{U\}\ s\ \{V\}$. We show the main case for while: $s \equiv \text{while } e \text{ do } s_t$. We are given as the induction hypothesis that for all $n : nat$ and U_0, $\{e \wedge I \wedge t = n \wedge U_0\}\ s_t\ \{\langle U_0 \rangle ** \text{finite} ** \langle I \wedge t < n \rangle\}$, Therefore we close the case by the derivation

$$\frac{\dfrac{\dfrac{\forall n.\{e \wedge I \wedge t = n\}\ s_t\ \{\langle t = n \rangle ** \text{finite} ** \langle I \wedge t < n \rangle\}}{\{\exists n.e \wedge I \wedge t = n\}\ s_t\ \{\exists n.\langle t = n \rangle ** \text{finite} ** \langle I \wedge t < n \rangle\}}}{\{e \wedge I\}\ s_t\ \{(\exists n.\langle t = n \rangle ** \text{finite} ** \langle t < n \rangle) ** \langle I \rangle\}}}{\dfrac{\{I \wedge U_0\}\ \text{while } e \text{ do } s_t}{\{I \wedge U_0\}\ \text{while } e \text{ do } s_t\ \{U_0 ** \text{finite} ** \langle I \wedge \neg e \rangle\}}\ \{\langle I \wedge U_0 \rangle^2 ** ((\exists n.\langle t = n \rangle ** \text{finite} ** \langle t < n \rangle) ** \langle I \rangle^2)^\dagger ** \langle \neg e \rangle\}}$$

5   Examples

Propositions 6 and 7 show that our trace-based logic is expressive enough to perform the same analyses that the state-based partial or total correctness Hoare logics can perform. However, the expressiveness of our logic goes beyond that of the partial and the total correctness Hoare logics. In this section, we demonstrate this by a series of examples. We adopt the usual notational convention that any occurrence of a variable in a state predicate represents the value of the variable in the state, e.g., a state predicate $x + y = 7$ abbreviates $\lambda\sigma.\ \sigma\,x + \sigma\,y = 7$.

5.1 Unbounded Total Search

Since we work in a constructive underlying logic, we can distinguish between termination of a run, *finite*, and nondivergence, *¬infinite*. For instance, any unbounded nonpartial search fails to be terminating but is nonetheless nondivergent.

This example is inspired by Markov's principle: $\neg\forall n.\ \neg B\,n \to \exists x.B\,n$ for any decidable predicate B on natural numbers, i.e., a predicate satisfying $\forall n.\ B\,n \lor \neg B\,n$. Markov's principle is a classical tautology, but is not valid constructively. This implies we cannot constructively prove a statement s that searches a natural number n satisfying B by successively checking whether $B\,0, B\,1, B\,2, \ldots$ to be terminating. In other words, we cannot constructively derive a total correctness judgement for s. The assumption $\neg\forall n.\ \neg B\,n$ only guarantees that B is not false everywhere, therefore the search cannot diverge; indeed, we can constructively prove that s is nondivergent in our logic.

We assume given a decidable predicate B on natural numbers and an axiom *B_noncontradictory*: $\neg\forall n.\ \neg B\,n$ stating that B is not false everywhere. Therefore running the statement

$$Search \equiv x := 0;\ \mathsf{while}\ \neg B\,x\ \mathsf{do}\ x := x + 1$$

cannot diverge: this would contradict *B_noncontradictory*. In Proposition 8 we prove that any trace produced by running s is nondivergent and $B\,x$ holds of the last state.

We define a predicate *cofinally* : $nat \to trace \to Prop$ coinductively as follows:

$$\frac{\sigma\,x = n \quad B\,n}{\sigma :: \langle\sigma\rangle \models cofinally\ n} \qquad \frac{\sigma\,x = n \quad \neg B\,n \quad \tau \models cofinally\ (n+1)}{\sigma :: \sigma :: \tau \models cofinally\ n}$$

cofinally is a setoid predicate.

A crucial observation is that, in the presence of *B_noncontradictory*, *cofinally* 0 is stronger than nondivergent:

Lemma 10. *cofinally* $0 \models \neg infinite$.

Proof. It is sufficient to prove that, for any τ, $\tau \models cofinally\ 0$ and $\tau \models infinite$ are contradictory. Suppose there is a trace τ such that $\tau \models cofinally\ 0$ and $\tau \models infinite$. Then by induction on n we can show that, for any n there is a trace τ' such that $\tau' \models cofinally\ n$ and $\tau' \models infinite$. But whenever the latter condition holds for some τ' and n, then $\neg B\,n$. Hence we also have $\forall n.\ \neg B\,n$. But this contradicts *B_noncontradictory*.

$$\frac{\{\neg B\,x\}\ x := x + 1\ \{(\neg B\,x)[x \mapsto x + 1]\}}{\{x = 0\}\ \text{while}\ \neg B\,x\ \text{do}\ x := x + 1}$$
$$\{\langle x = 0\rangle^2 \ast\!\ast\ ((\neg B\,x)[x \mapsto x + 1] \ast\!\ast\ \langle\text{true}\rangle^2)^\dagger \ast\!\ast\ \langle B\,x\rangle\}$$

$$\frac{\{\text{true}\}\ x := 0\ \{\text{true}[x \mapsto 0]\}\quad\{x = 0\}\ \text{while}\ \neg B\,x\ \text{do}\ x := x + 1\ \{\textit{cofinally }0\}}{\dfrac{\{\text{true}\}\ x := 0;\ \text{while}\ \neg B\,x\ \text{do}\ x := x + 1\ \{\text{true}[x \mapsto 0] \ast\!\ast\ \textit{cofinally }0\}}{\{\text{true}\}\ x := 0;\ \text{while}\ \neg B\,x\ \text{do}\ x := x + 1\ \{(\text{true} \ast\!\ast\ \langle B\,x\rangle) \wedge \neg\textit{infinite}\}}}$$

Fig. 5. Derivation of $\{\text{true}\}$ *Search* $\{(\text{true} \ast\!\ast\ \langle B\,x\rangle) \wedge \neg\textit{infinite}\}$

$$\frac{\{\text{true}\}\ x := x + 1\ \{\text{true}[x \mapsto x + 1]\}}{\{x = 0\}\ \text{while true do}\ x := x + 1}$$
$$\{\langle x = 0\rangle^2 \ast\!\ast\ (\text{true}[x \mapsto x + 1] \ast\!\ast\ \langle\text{true}\rangle^2)^\dagger \ast\!\ast\ \langle\text{false}\rangle\}$$

$$\frac{\{\text{true}\}\ x := 0\ \{\text{true}[x \mapsto 0]\}\quad\{x = 0\}\ \text{while true do}\ x := x + 1\ \{\textit{eventually } n\}}{\dfrac{\{\text{true}\}\ x := 0;\ \text{while true do}\ x := x + 1\ \{\text{true}[x \mapsto 0] \ast\!\ast\ \textit{eventually } n\}}{\{\text{true}\}\ x := 0;\ \text{while true do}\ x := x + 1\ \{\textit{finite} \ast\!\ast\ \langle x = n\rangle \ast\!\ast\ \text{true}\}}}$$

Fig. 6. Derivation of $\{\text{true}\}$ s $\{\textit{finite} \ast\!\ast\ \langle x = n\rangle \ast\!\ast\ \text{true}\}$

Proposition 8. $\{\text{true}\}$ *Search* $\{(\text{true} \ast\!\ast\ \langle B\,x\rangle) \wedge \neg\textit{infinite}\}$.

Proof. The derivation is given in Figure 5, with trivial applications of the consequence rule being omitted.

5.2 Liveness

As the similarity of our assertion language to the interval temporal logic suggests, we can specify and prove liveness properties. In Proposition 9, we prove that the statement

$$x := 0;\ \text{while true do}\ x := x + 1$$

eventually sets the value of x to n for any $n : nat$ at some point.

The example is simple but sufficient to demonstrate core techniques used to prove liveness properties of more practical examples. For instance, imagine that assignment to x involves a system call, with the assigned value as the argument. It is straightforward to enrich traces to record such special events, and we can then apply the same proof technique to prove the statement eventually performs the system call with n as the argument for any n.

We define inductively a predicate *eventually* : $nat \to trace \to Prop$ stating a state σ in which the value of x is n is eventually reachable by finitely traversing τ:

$$\frac{\sigma\,x = n}{\langle\sigma\rangle \models \textit{eventually } n}\qquad\frac{\sigma\,x = n}{\sigma :: \tau \models \textit{eventually } n}\qquad\frac{\tau \models \textit{eventually } n}{\sigma :: \tau \models \textit{eventually } n}$$

Proposition 9. *For any* n : *nat,* $\{true\}$ s $\{finite$ ** $\langle x = n \rangle$ ** $true\}$ *where* $s \equiv x := 0;$ while true do $x := x + 1.$

Proof. The derivation is given in Figure 6, with trivial applications of the consequence rule being omitted.

5.3   Weak Trace Equivalence

The last example is inspired by a notion of weak trace equivalence: two traces are weakly equivalent if they are bisimilar by identifying a finite number of consecutive identical states with a single state. It is conceivable that (strong) bisimilarity is too strong for some applications and one needs weak bisimilarity. For instance, we may want to prove that the observable behavior, such as the colist i/o events of a potentially diverging run, is bisimilar to a particular colist of i/o events. Then we must be able to collapse a finite number of non-observable internal steps. We definitely should not collapse an infinite number of internal steps, otherwise we would end up concluding that a statement performing an i/o operation after a diverging run, e.g., while true do skip; print *"hello"*, is observably equivalent to a statement immediately performing the same i/o operation, e.g., print *"hello"*.

In this subsection, we prove that the trace produced by running the statement

while true do $(y := x;$ (while $y \neq 0$ do $y := y - 1$); $x := x + 1$)

is weakly bisimilar to the ascending sequence of natural numbers $0 :: 1 :: 2 :: 3 ::$ ..., by projecting the value of x. The statement differs from that of the previous subsection in that it "stutters" for a finite but unbounded number of steps, i.e., while $y \neq 0$ do $y := y - 1$, before the next assignment to x happens.

This exercise is instructive in that we need to formalize weak trace equivalence in our constructive underlying logic. We do so by supplying an inductive predicate $\tau \overset{*}{\rightsquigarrow} \tau'$ stating that τ' is obtained from τ by dropping finitely many elements from the beginning, until the first state with a different value of x is encountered, and a coinductive predicate up $(n : nat) : trace \rightarrow Prop$, stating that τ is weakly bisimilar to the ascending sequence of natural numbers starting at n, by projecting the value of x. Formally:

$$\frac{\sigma\,x = hd\,\tau\,x \quad \tau \overset{*}{\rightsquigarrow} \tau'}{\sigma :: \tau \overset{*}{\rightsquigarrow} \tau'} \qquad \frac{\sigma\,x \neq hd\,\tau\,x \quad \tau \approx \tau'}{\sigma :: \tau \overset{*}{\rightsquigarrow} \tau'}$$

$$\frac{\sigma\,x = n \quad \sigma :: \tau \overset{*}{\rightsquigarrow} \tau' \quad \tau' \models up\,(n+1)}{\sigma :: \tau \models up\,n}$$

These definitions are tailored to our example. But a more general weak trace equivalence can be defined similarly. We note that our formulation is not the only one possible nor the most elegant. In particular, with a logic permitting mixing induction and coinduction [5], there is no need to separate the definition

$$\cfrac{\cfrac{\{y \neq 0\}\ y := y - 1\ \{(y \neq 0)[y \mapsto y - 1]\}}{\cfrac{\{y \geq 0\}\ \text{while}\ y \neq 0\ \text{do}\ y := y - 1}{\{\langle y \geq 0\rangle^2 ** ((y \neq 0)[y \mapsto y - 1] ** \langle \text{true}\rangle^2)^\dagger ** \langle y = 0\rangle\}}}{\{y \geq 0\}\ \text{while}\ y \neq 0\ \text{do}\ y := y - 1\ \{\langle x\rangle^*\}}}{}$$

$$\cfrac{\{x \geq 0\}\ y := x\ \{(x \geq 0)[y \mapsto x]\} \qquad \cfrac{\quad\ \cfrac{\{\text{true}\}\ x := x + 1\ \{\text{true}[x \mapsto x + 1]\}}{\{y \geq 0\}\ (\text{while}\ y \neq 0\ \text{do}\ y := y - 1); x := x + 1}}{\{\langle x\rangle^* ** \text{true}[x \mapsto x + 1]\}}}{\cfrac{\{x \geq 0\}\ y := x; (\text{while}\ y \neq 0\ \text{do}\ y := y - 1); x := x + 1\ \{\langle x\rangle^* ** \text{true}[x \mapsto x + 1]\}}{\cfrac{\{x = 0\}\ \text{while true do}\ (y := x; (\text{while}\ y \neq 0\ \text{do}\ y := y - 1); x := x + 1)}{\{\langle x = 0\rangle^2 ** (\langle x\rangle^* ** \text{true}[x \mapsto x + 1] ** \langle \text{true}\rangle^2)^\dagger ** \langle \text{false}\rangle\}}}{\{x = 0\}\ \text{while true do}\ (y := x; (\text{while}\ y \neq 0\ \text{do}\ y := y - 1); x := x + 1)\ \{up\ 0\}}}}{}$$

Fig. 7. Derivation of $\{\text{true}\}\ s\ \{up\ 0\}$

into an inductive part, $\tau \overset{*}{\leadsto} \tau'$, and a coinductive part, $up\ n$. Yet our formulation is amenable in our underlying logic, Coq.

We also use an auxiliary trace predicate $\langle x\rangle^*$ that is true of a finite trace in which the value of x does not change. It is defined inductively as follows:

$$\cfrac{}{\langle \sigma\rangle \models \langle x\rangle^*} \qquad \cfrac{\sigma\ x = hd\ \tau\ x \qquad \tau \models \langle x\rangle^*}{\sigma :: \tau \models \langle x\rangle^*}$$

Proposition 10. $\{x = 0\}\ s\ \{up\ 0\}$ where $s \equiv \text{while true do}\ (y := x; (\text{while}\ y \neq 0\ \text{do}\ y := y - 1); x := x + 1)$.

Proof. The derivation is given in Figure 7, with trivial applications of the consequence rule being omitted.

6 Related Work

Coinductive big-step semantics for nontermination have been considered by Leroy and Grall [10,11] (in the context of the CompCert project, which is a major demonstration of feasibility of certified compilation) and Cousot and Cousot [4]. Leroy and Grall investigate two approaches. The first, based on Cousot and Cousot [3], has different evaluation relations for terminating and diverges runs, one inductive (with finite traces), the other coinductive (with infinite traces). To conclude that any program either terminates or diverges, one needs the law of excluded middle (amounting to decidability of the halting problem), and, as a result, the small-step semantics cannot be proved sound wrt. the big-step semantics constructively. The other approach [1] uses a coinductively defined evaluation relation with possibly infinite traces, where while-loops are not ensured to be progressive in terms of growing traces (an infinite number of consecutive silent small steps may be collapsed).

Some other works on coinductive big-step semantics include Glesner [6] and Nestra [15,16]. In these it is accepted that a program evaluation can somehow

504 K. Nakata and T. Uustalu

continue after an infinite number of small steps. With Glesner, this seems to have been a curious unintended side-effect of the design, which she was experimenting with just for the interest of it. Nestra developed a nonstandard semantics with transfinite traces on purpose in order to obtain a soundness result for a widely used slicing transformation that is unsound standardly (can turn nonterminating runs into terminating runs).

Our trace-based coinductive big-step semantics [14] was heavily inspired by Capretta's [2] modelling of nontermination in a constructive setting similar to ours. Rather than using coinductive possibly infinite traces, he works with a coinductive notion of a possibly infinitely delayed (final) state. The categorical basis appears in Rutten's work [18]. But Rutten only studied the classical setting (any program terminates or not), where a delayed state collapses to a choice of between a state or a designated token signifying nontermination.

While Hoare logics for big-step semantics based on inductive, finite traces have been considered earlier (to reason about traces of terminating runs), Hoare or VDM-style logics for reasoning about properties of nonterminating runs seem not have been studied before, with one very interesting exception, see below. Neither do we in fact know about dynamic logic or KAT (Kleene algebra with tests) approaches that would have assertions about possibly infinite traces. Rather, nonterminating runs have been typically reasoned about in temporal logics like LTL and CTL* or in interval temporal logic [13,7]. These are however essentially different in spirit by their "exogeneity": assertions are made about traces in a transition system rather than traces of runs of a particular program. Notably, however, interval temporal logic has connectives similar to ours—in fact they were a source of inspiration for our design.

Hofmann and Pavlova [9] consider a VDM-style logic with finite trace assertions that are applied to all finite prefixes of the trace of a possibly nonterminating run of a program. This logic allows reasoning about safety, but not liveness. We expect that we should be able to embed a logic like this in ours.

7 Conclusions

We have presented a sound and complete Hoare logic for the coinductive trace-based big-step semantics of While. The logic naturally extends both the partial and total correctness Hoare logics. Its design may be exploratory at this stage—in the sense that one might wish to consider alternative choices of primitive connectives. But at any rate we would see our logic as a viable unifying foundational framework facilitating translations from more applied logics.

Acknowledgements. We are grateful to Martin Hofmann, Thierry Coquand and Adam Chlipala for discussions.

We acknowledge the support of the EU FP6 IST integrated project no. 15905 MOBIUS, the Estonian Centre of Excellence in Computer Science, EXCS, financed by the European Regional Development Fund, and the Estonian Science Foundation grant no. 6940.

References

1. Blazy, S., Leroy, X.: Mechanized semantics for the Clight subset of the C language. J. of Automated Reasoning 43(3), 263–288 (2009)
2. Capretta, V.: General recursion via coinductive types. Logical Methods in Computer Science 1(2), article 1 (2005)
3. Cousot, P., Cousot, R.: Inductive definitions, semantics and abstract interpretation. In: Conf. Record of 19th ACM SIGPLAN-SIGACT Symp. on Principles of Programming Languages, POPL 1992, Albuquerque, NM, January 1992, pp. 83–94. ACM Press, New York (1992)
4. Cousot, P., Cousot, R.: Bi-inductive structural semantics. Inform. and Comput. 207(2), 258–283 (2009)
5. Danielsson, N.A., Altenkirch, T.: Mixing induction and coinduction. Draft (2009), http://www.cs.nott.ac.uk/~nad/publications/
6. Glesner, S.: A proof calculus for natural semantics based on greatest fixed point semantics. In: Knoop, J., Necula, G.C., Zimmermann, W. (eds.) Proc. of 3rd Int. Wksh. on Compiler Optimization Meets Compiler Verification, COCV 2004, Barcelona, April 2004. Electron. Notes in Theor. Comput. Sci. vol. 132(1), pp. 73–93. Elsevier, Amsterdam (2004)
7. Halpern, J., Manna, Z., Moszkowski, B.: A hardware semantics based on temporal intervals. In: Díaz, J. (ed.) ICALP 1983. LNCS, vol. 154, pp. 278–291. Springer, Heidelberg (1983)
8. Hasuo, I., Jacobs, B., Sokolova, A.: Generic trace semantics via coinduction. Logical Methods in Computer Science 3(4), article 11 (2007)
9. Hofmann, M., Pavlova, M.: Elimination of ghost variables in program logics. In: Barthe, G., Fournet, C. (eds.) TGC 2007. LNCS, vol. 4912, pp. 1–20. Springer, Heidelberg (2008)
10. Leroy, X.: Coinductive big-step operational semantics. In: Sestoft, P. (ed.) ESOP 2006. LNCS, vol. 3924, pp. 54–68. Springer, Heidelberg (2006)
11. Leroy, X., Grall, H.: Coinductive big-step operational semantics. Inform. and Comput. 207(2), 285–305 (2009)
12. Kleymann, T.: Hoare logic and auxiliary variables. Formal Asp. Comput. 11(5), 541–566 (1999)
13. Moszkowski, B.: A temporal logic for reasoning about hardware. Computer 18(2), 10–19 (1985)
14. Nakata, K., Uustalu, T.: Trace-based coinductive operational semantics for While: big-step and small-step, relational and functional styles. In: Berghofer, S., Nipkow, T., Urban, C., Wenzel, M. (eds.) TPHOLs 2009. LNCS, vol. 5674, pp. 375–390. Springer, Heidelberg (2009)
15. Nestra, H.: Fractional semantics. In: Johnson, M., Vene, V. (eds.) AMAST 2006. LNCS, vol. 4019, pp. 278–292. Springer, Heidelberg (2006)
16. Nestra, H.: Transfinite semantics in the form of greatest fixpoint. J. of Logic and Algebr. Program. 78(7), 574–593 (2009)
17. Riis Nielson, H., Nielson, F.: Semantics with Applications: A Formal Introduction. Wiley, Chichester (1992)
18. Rutten, J.: A note on coinduction and weak bisimilarity for While programs. Theor. Inform. and Appl. 33(4-5), 393–400 (1999)

A   State-Based Partial Correctness and Total Correctness Hoare Logics

The figures below give the rules of the standard, state-based partial correctness and total correctness logics in the form used in Section 4.

$$\overline{\{U\}\ \mathsf{skip}\ \{U\}} \quad \overline{\{U[e/x]\}\ x := e\ \{U\}} \quad \frac{\{e \wedge U\}\ s_t\ \{V\} \quad \{\neg e \wedge U\}\ s_f\ \{V\}}{\{U\}\ \mathsf{if}\ e\ \mathsf{then}\ s_t\ \mathsf{else}\ s_f\ \{V\}}$$

$$\frac{\{e \wedge I\}\ s_t\ \{I\}}{\{I\}\ \mathsf{while}\ e\ \mathsf{do}\ s_t\ \{I \wedge \neg e\}} \quad \frac{U \models U' \quad \{U'\}\ s\ \{V'\} \quad V' \models V}{\{U\}\ s\ \{V\}}$$

Fig. 8. Inference rules of partial correctness Hoare logic

$$\overline{\{U\}\ \mathsf{skip}\ \{U\}} \quad \overline{\{U[e/x]\}\ x := e\ \{U\}} \quad \frac{\{e \wedge U\}\ s_t\ \{V\} \quad \{\neg e \wedge U\}\ s_f\ \{V\}}{\{U\}\ \mathsf{if}\ e\ \mathsf{then}\ s_t\ \mathsf{else}\ s_f\ \{V\}}$$

$$\frac{\forall n : nat\ \{e \wedge I \wedge t = n\}\ s_t\ \{I \wedge t < n\}}{\{I\}\ \mathsf{while}\ e\ \mathsf{do}\ s_t\ \{I \wedge \neg e\}} \quad \frac{U \models U' \quad \{U'\}\ s\ \{V'\} \quad V' \models V}{\{U\}\ s\ \{V\}}$$

Fig. 9. Inference rules of total correctness Hoare logic

A Universal Calculus for Stream Processing Languages

Robert Soulé[1], Martin Hirzel[2], Robert Grimm[1], Buğra Gedik[2],
Henrique Andrade[2], Vibhore Kumar[2], and Kun-Lung Wu[2]

[1] New York University
{soule,rgrimm}@cs.nyu.edu
[2] IBM Research
{hirzel,bgedik,hcma,vibhorek,klwu}@us.ibm.com

Abstract. Stream processing applications such as algorithmic trading, MPEG processing, and web content analysis are ubiquitous and essential to business and entertainment. Language designers have developed numerous domain-specific languages that are both tailored to the needs of their applications, and optimized for performance on their particular target platforms. Unfortunately, the goals of generality and performance are frequently at odds, and prior work on the formal semantics of stream processing languages does not capture the details necessary for reasoning about implementations. This paper presents Brooklet, a core calculus for stream processing that allows us to reason about how to map languages to platforms and how to optimize stream programs. We translate from three representative languages, CQL, StreamIt, and Sawzall, to Brooklet, and show that the translations are correct. We formalize three popular and vital optimizations, data-parallel computation, operator fusion, and operator re-ordering, and show under which conditions they are correct. Language designers can use Brooklet to specify exactly how new features or languages behave. Language implementors can use Brooklet to show exactly under which circumstances new optimizations are correct. In ongoing work, we are developing an intermediate language for streaming that is based on Brooklet. We are implementing our intermediate language on System S, IBM's high-performance streaming middleware.

1 Introduction

Stream processing applications are everywhere. In finance, algorithmic trading programs federate live data feeds from independent exchanges to execute trade orders. Media players decode fixed-rate, MPEG-formatted byte streams, when viewers watch video streamed over the internet and digital television networks, or from DVD and Blu-ray discs. Search engines use large compute clusters to analyze snapshots of the web streamed from disk to construct the indices that enable fast information retrieval.

Informally, all such *streaming applications* are similar in that they require moving large amounts of data through several computational steps. These three

A.D. Gordon (Ed.): ESOP 2010, LNCS 6012, pp. 507–528, 2010.

examples illustrate the diversity of requirements for stream processing with respect to, among other things, program topology, data rate, and distributed execution. This diversity has led language designers to develop numerous domain-specific languages [1,3,4,9,18,20,24,26,28] that are both tailored to the needs of their particular applications, and optimized for performance on their particular target runtimes. Three prominent examples are CQL, StreamIt, and Sawzall:

- CQL [1] and other StreamSQL dialects [24] are popularly used for algorithmic trading. CQL extends SQL's well studied relational operators with a notion of windows over infinite streams of data, and relies on classic query optimizations [1], such as moving a selection before a join.
- StreamIt [26], a synchronous data-flow language with stream abstractions, has been used for MPEG encoding and decoding [6]. The StreamIt compiler enforces static data transfer rates between user-defined operators with fixed topologies, and improves performance through operator fusion, fission, and pipelining [26].
- Sawzall [20], a scripting language for Google's MapReduce [5] platform, is used for web-related analysis. The MapReduce framework streams data items through multiple copies of user-defined *map* operators and then aggregates the results through *reduce* operators on a cluster of workstations. We view Sawzall as a streaming language in the broader sense, and address it in this paper to showcase the generality of our work.

These three examples by no means comprise an exhaustive list of stream programming languages, but they are representative of the design space. In each case, language designers made difficult choices when considering the trade-offs between performance, usability, and generality. For example, StreamIt sacrifices generality for performance by restricting data transfer to fixed rates.

When considering these trade-offs, it is essential that language designers understand both how a language maps to its target platform, and how to optimize stream programs with respect to that mapping. Unfortunately, while streaming systems are well studied [2,14,15,16], prior work on the formal semantics of stream processing languages does not capture the details necessary for reasoning about implementation techniques. This paper presents Brooklet, a core calculus for stream programming languages that universally models any streaming language, and facilitates reasoning about program implementation[1].

The challenge in defining a calculus is deciding what parts of a language constitute the core concepts that need to be modeled in the formal semantics, and what details can be abstracted away. The two goals of understanding how a language maps to a platform, and how to optimize stream programs with respect to that mapping, dictate the requirements. First, to understand how a language maps to an execution environment, we need to understand how the state embodied in its operational building blocks is implemented on a distributed platform. Therefore, Brooklet makes state explicit as a core concept. Second, to understand how to

---

[1] Brooklet is so named because it is the essence of a stream, and is unrelated to the Brook language [3].

optimize stream programs, we need to understand how to enable language-level determinism on top of the inherent implementation-level non-determinism of a distributed system. Therefore, Brooklet exposes non-determinism as another core concept. Exposing non-determinism makes the machinery for achieving global determinism explicit, such as when implementing synchronous data flow. On the other hand, modeling local deterministic computations is well-understood, so our semantics treat local computations as opaque functions. Since our semantics are small-step, this abstraction loses none of the fine-grained interleaving effects of the distributed computation.

In this paper we make the following contributions:

- We define a core calculus for stream processing that is universal, and facilitates reasoning about program implementation by modeling state and non-determinism as core concepts.
- We translate CQL, StreamIt, and Sawzall to Brooklet, demonstrating the comprehensiveness of our calculus. This translation also defines the first formal semantics for Sawzall.
- We use our calculus to show the conditions that enable three vital optimizations data-parallel computation, operator fusion, and operator re-ordering.

This sets a foundation for an implementation of Brooklet, which can serve as a common intermediate language for stream processing with a rigorous formal semantics. We are in the process of exploring this implementation on System S [9], IBM's high-performance streaming middleware.

2   Notation

Throughout the paper, an over-bar, as in $\bar{q}$, denotes a finite sequence $q_1, \ldots, q_n$, and the i-th element in that sequence is written q_i, where $1 \leq i \leq n$. The lowercase letter b is reserved for lists, and $\bullet$ is an empty list. A comma indicates *cons* or *append*, depending on the context; for example d, b is a list consed from the first item d and the remaining items b. A bag is a set with duplicates. The notation $\{e : condition\}$ denotes a bag comprehension: it specifies the bag of all e's where the *condition* is true. The symbol $\emptyset$ stands for both an empty set and an empty bag. If E is a store, then the substitution $[v \mapsto d]E$ denotes the store that maps name v to value d and is otherwise identical to E. Angle brackets identify a tuple. For example, $\langle \sigma, \tau \rangle$ is a tuple that contains the elements σ and τ. In inference rules, an expression of the form $d, b = b'$ performs pattern matching; it succeeds if the list b' is non-empty, in which case it binds d to the first element of b' and b to the remainder of b'. Pattern-matching also works on other meta-syntax, such as tuple construction. An underscore character _ indicates a wildcard, and matches anything. Semantics brackets such as $[\![P_b]\!]_z^p$ indicate translation. The subscripts b,c,s,z stand for Brooklet, CQL, StreamIt, and Sawzall, respectively.

3   Brooklet

A stream processing language is a language that hides the mechanics of stream processing; it notably has built-in support for moving data through computations

Brooklet syntax:

P_b ::= out in $\overline{op}$ *Brooklet program*
out ::= output $\overline{q}$;   *Output declaration*
in ::= input $\overline{q}$;   *Input declaration*
op ::= ($\overline{q}, \overline{v}$) ← f ($\overline{q}, \overline{v}$);   *Operator*
q ::= *id*   *Queue identifier*
v ::= $ *id*   *Variable identifier*
f ::= *id*   *Function identifier*

Brooklet example: IBM market maker.
```
output result;
input bids, asks;
(ibmBids)   ←  SelectIBM(bids);
(ibmAsks)   ←  SelectIBM(asks);
($lastAsk)  ←  Window(ibmAsks);
(ibmSales)  ←  SaleJoin(ibmBids,$lastAsk);
(result,$cnt) ←  Count(ibmSales,$cnt);
```

Brooklet semantics: $F_b \vdash \langle V, Q \rangle \longrightarrow \langle V', Q' \rangle$

$$d, b = Q(q_i)$$
$$op = (\_, \_) \leftarrow f(\overline{q}, \overline{v});$$
$$(\overline{b'}, \overline{d'}) = F_b(f)(d, i, V(\overline{v}))$$
$$V' = updateV(op, V, \overline{d'})$$
$$\frac{Q' = updateQ(op, Q, q_i, \overline{b'})}{F_b \vdash \langle V, Q \rangle \longrightarrow \langle V', Q' \rangle}\text{ (E-FireQueue)}$$

$$\frac{op = (\_, \overline{v}) \leftarrow f(\_, \_);}{updateV(op, V, \overline{d}) = [\overline{v} \mapsto \overline{d}]V}\text{ (E-UpdateV)}$$

$$op = (\overline{q}, \_) \leftarrow f(\_, \_);$$
$$d_f, b_f = Q(q_f)$$
$$Q'' = [\forall q_i \in \overline{q} : q_i \mapsto Q(q_i), b_i]Q'$$
$$\frac{Q' = [q_f \mapsto b_f]Q}{updateQ(op, Q, q_f, \overline{b}) = Q''}\text{ (E-UpdateQ)}$$

Fig. 1. Brooklet syntax and semantics

and for composing the computations with each other. Brooklet is a core calculus for such stream processing languages. It is designed to model any streaming language, and to facilitate reasoning about language implementation. To achieve these goals, Brooklet models state and non-determinism as core concepts, and abstracts away local deterministic computations.

3.1 Brooklet Program Example: IBM Market Maker

As an example of a streaming program, we consider a hypothetical application that trades IBM stock. Data arrives on two input streams, bids(symbol,price) and asks(symbol,price), and leaves on the result(cnt,symbol,price) output stream. Since the application is only interested in trading IBM stock, it filters out all other stock symbols from the input. The application then matches bid and ask prices from the filtered streams to make trades. To keep the example simple, we assume that each sale is for exactly one share. The Brooklet program in the bottom left corner of Fig. 1 produces a stream of trades of IBM stock, along with a count of the number of trades.

3.2 Brooklet Syntax

A Brooklet program defines a directed, possibly cyclic, graph of *operators* containing pure *functions* connected by FIFO *queues*. It uses *variables* to explicitly thread state through operators. Data items on a queue model network packets in transit. Data items in variables model stored state; since data items may be lists, a variable may store arbitrary amounts of historical data. The following line from the market maker application defines an operator:

```
(ibmSales)  ←  SaleJoin(ibmBids, $lastAsk);
```

The operator reads data from input queue ibmBids and variable $lastAsk. It passes that data as parameters to the pure function SaleJoin, and writes the result to the output queue ibmSales. Brooklet does not define the semantics of SaleJoin. Modeling local deterministic computations is well-understood [17,19], so Brooklet abstracts them away by encapsulating them in opaque functions. On the other hand, a Brooklet program does define explicit uses of state. In the example, the following line defines a window over the stream ibmAsks:

$$(\$lastAsk) \leftarrow Window(ibmAsks);$$

The window contains a single tuple corresponding to the most recent ask for an IBM stock, and the tuple is stored in the variable $lastAsk. Both the Window and SaleJoin operators access $lastAsk.

The Window operator writes data to $lastAsk, but does not use the data stored in the variable in its internal computations. Operators that incrementally update state must both read and write the same variable, such as in the Count operator:

$$(result, \$cnt) \leftarrow Count(ibmSales, \$cnt);$$

Queues that appear only as operator input, such as bids and asks, are program inputs, and queues that appear only as operator output, such as result, are program outputs. Brooklet's syntax uses the keywords input and output to declare a program's input and output queues. We say that a queue is *defined* if it is an operator output or a program input. We say that a queue is *used* if it is an operator input or a program output. Variables may be defined and used in several clauses, since they are intended to thread state through a streaming application. In contrast, each queue must be defined once and used once. This restriction facilitates using our semantics for proofs and optimizations. The complete Brooklet grammar appears in Fig. 1.

3.3 Brooklet Semantics

A program operates on data items from a domain $\mathcal{D}$, where a data item is a general term for anything that can be stored in queues or variables, including tuples, bags of tuples, lists, or entire relations from persistent storage. Queue contents are represented by lists of data items. We assume that the transport network is lossless and order-preserving but may have arbitrary delays, so queues support only *push*-to-back and *pop*-from-front operations.

3.3.1 Brooklet Execution Configuration

The function environment F_b maps function names to function implementations. This environment allows us to treat operator functions as opaque. For example, $F_b(\text{SelectIBM})$ would return a function that filters out data items whose stock symbol differs from IBM.

At any given time during program execution, the configuration of the Brooklet program is defined as a pair $\langle V, Q \rangle$, where V is a store that maps variable names to data items (in the market maker example, $cnt is initialized to zero and $lastAsk is initialized to the tuple $\langle \text{'IBM'}, \infty \rangle$), and Q is a store that maps queue names to lists of data items (initially, all queues except the input queues are empty).

3.3.2   Brooklet Execution Semantics

Computation proceeds in small steps. Each step fires Rule E-FireQueue from Fig. 1. To explain this rule, we illustrate each line rule one by one, starting with the following intermediate configuration of the market maker example:

$$V = [\text{\$lastAsk} \mapsto \langle\text{'IBM'}, 119\rangle, \text{\$cnt} \mapsto 0]$$

$$Q = \begin{bmatrix} \text{bids} \mapsto \bullet, \ \text{ibmBids} \mapsto (\langle\text{'IBM'}, 119\rangle, \langle\text{'IBM'}, 124\rangle), \\ \text{asks} \mapsto \bullet, \ \text{ibmAsks} \mapsto \bullet, \\ \text{ibmSales} \mapsto \bullet, \ \text{result} \mapsto \bullet \end{bmatrix}$$

$d, b = Q(q_i)$: Non-deterministically select a firing queue q_i. For a queue to be eligible as a firing queue, it must satisfy two conditions: it must be non-empty (because we are binding d, b to its head and tail), and it must appear as an input to some operator (because we are executing that operator's firing function). This step can select any queue satisfying these two conditions.

E.g., $q_i = \text{ibmBids}$, $d = \langle\text{'IBM'}, 119\rangle$, $b = (\langle\text{'IBM'}, 124\rangle)$.

$op = (\_, \_) \leftarrow f(\overline{q}, \overline{v})$; : Because of the single-use restriction, q_i uniquely identifies an operator.

E.g., $op = (\text{ibmSales}) \leftarrow \text{SaleJoin(ibmBids, \$lastAsk)};$.

$(\overline{b}', \overline{d}') = F_b(f)(d, i, V(\overline{v}))$: Use the function name to look up the corresponding function from the environment. The function parameters are the data item popped from q_i; the index i relative to the operator's input list; and the current values of the variables in the operator's input list. For each output queue, the function returns a list b'_j of data items to append, and for each output variable, the function returns a single data item d'_j to store.

E.g., $\overline{b}' = \big((\langle\text{'IBM'}, 119, 119\rangle)\big)$, $\overline{d}' = \bullet$,

$d = \langle\text{'IBM'}, 119\rangle$, $i = 1$, $V(\overline{v}) = \langle\text{'IBM'}, 119\rangle$.

$V' = updateV(op, V, \overline{d}')$: Update the variables using the output $\overline{d}'$.

E.g., in this example, $\overline{d}' = \bullet$, so $V' = V$.

$Q' = updateQ(op, Q, q_i, \overline{b}')$: Update the queues: remove the popped data item from the firing queue, and for each output queue, push the corresponding list of output data items. The example has only one output queue and datum.

$$\text{E.g., } Q' = \begin{bmatrix} \text{bids} \mapsto \bullet, & \text{ibmBids} \mapsto (\langle\text{'IBM'}, 124\rangle), \\ \text{asks} \mapsto \bullet, & \text{ibmAsks} \mapsto \bullet, \\ \text{ibmSales} \mapsto (\langle\text{'IBM'}, 119, 119\rangle), & \text{result} \mapsto \bullet \end{bmatrix}$$

3.4   Brooklet Execution Function

We denote a program's input $\langle V, Q\rangle$ as I_b and an output $\langle V', Q'\rangle$ as O_b. Given a function environment F_b, program P_b, and input I_b, the function $\rightarrow_b^* (F_b, P_b, I_b)$ yields the set of all final outputs. An execution yields a final output when no queue is eligible to fire. Due to non-determinism, the set may have more than one element. One possible output O_b of our running example is:

$$V = [\text{\$lastAsk} \mapsto \langle\text{'IBM'}, 119\rangle, \text{\$cnt} \mapsto 1]$$

$$Q = \begin{bmatrix} \texttt{bids} \mapsto \bullet, & \texttt{asks} \mapsto \bullet, \texttt{ibmSales} \mapsto \bullet, \\ \texttt{ibmBids} \mapsto \bullet, \texttt{ibmAsks} \mapsto \bullet, & \texttt{result} \mapsto (\langle 1, \text{'IBM'}, 119 \rangle) \end{bmatrix}$$

The example illustrates the finite case. But in some application domains, streams are conceptually infinite. To use our semantics in that case, we use a theoretical result from prior work: if a stream program is computable, then one can generalize from all finite prefixes of an infinite stream to the infinite case [11]. If $\rightarrow_b^*$ yields the same result for all finite inputs to two programs, then we consider these two programs equivalent even on infinite inputs.

3.5 Brooklet Summary

Brooklet is a core calculus for stream processing. We designed it to universally model any streaming language, and to facilitate reasoning about program implementation. Brooklet models state through explicit variables, thus making it clear where an implementation needs to store data. Brooklet captures inherent non-determinism by *not* specifying which queue to fire for each step, thus permitting all interleavings possible in a distributed implementation.

4 Language Mappings

We demonstrate Brooklet's generality by mapping three streaming languages CQL, StreamIt, and Sawzall to it. Each translation exposes implicit uses of state as explicit variables; exposes a mechanism for implementing global determinism on top of an inherently non-deterministic runtime; and abstracts away local deterministic computations with higher-order wrappers that statically bind the original function and dynamically adapt the runtime arguments (thus preserving small step semantics).

4.1 CQL and Stream-Relational Algebra

CQL, the Continuous Query Language, is a member of the StreamSQL family of languages. StreamSQL gives developers who are familiar with SQL's select-from-where syntax an incremental learning path to stream programming. This paper uses CQL to represent the entire StreamSQL family, because it has a clean design, has made significant impact [1], and has a formal semantics [2].

4.1.1 CQL Program Example: Bargain Finder
A CQL program P_c is a query that computes a stream or relation from other streams or relations. The following hypothetical example uses CQL for algorithmic trading:

```
select IStream(*) from quotes[Now], history
   where quotes.ask <= history.low and quotes.ticker == history.ticker
```

This program finds bargain quotes, whose ask price is lower than the historic low. The program has two inputs, a stream `quotes` and a time-varying relation `history`. A *stream* in CQL is a bag of time-tagged tuples. The same

Fig. 2. CQL semantics on Brooklet

CQL syntax:

$$P_c ::= P_{cr} \mid P_{cs} \qquad \textit{CQL program}$$
$$P_{cr} ::= \qquad\qquad\qquad \textit{(Relation query)}$$
$$RName \qquad\qquad \textit{Relation name}$$
$$\mid S2R(P_{cs}) \qquad\quad \textit{Stream to relation}$$
$$\mid R2R(\overline{P_{cr}}) \qquad\quad \textit{Relation to relation}$$
$$P_{cs} ::= \qquad\qquad\qquad \textit{(Stream query)}$$
$$SName \qquad\qquad \textit{Stream name}$$
$$\mid R2S(P_{cr}) \qquad\quad \textit{Relation to stream}$$
$$RName \mid SName ::= id \qquad \textit{Input name}$$
$$S2R \mid R2R \mid R2S ::= id \qquad \textit{Operator name}$$

CQL example: Bargain finder.
IStream(BargainJoin(Now(quotes), history))

CQL program translation: $[\![F_c, P_c]\!]^p_c = \langle F_b, P_b \rangle$

$$[\![F_c, SName]\!]^p_c = \emptyset, \text{output} \, SName; \text{input} \, SName; \bullet$$
$$(\mathrm{T}^p_c\text{-SNAME})$$

$$[\![F_c, RName]\!]^p_c = \emptyset, \text{output} \, RName; \text{input} \, RName; \bullet$$
$$(\mathrm{T}^p_c\text{-RNAME})$$

$$\frac{\begin{array}{c} F_b, \text{output } q_o; \text{ input } \overline{q}; \ \overline{op} = [\![F_c, P_{cs}]\!]^p_c \\ q'_o = freshId() \qquad v = freshId() \\ F'_b = [S2R \mapsto wrapS2R(F_c(S2R))]F_b \\ \overline{op}' = \overline{op}, (q'_o, v) \leftarrow S2R(q_o, v); \end{array}}{[\![F_c, S2R(P_{cs})]\!]^p_c = F'_b, \text{output } q'_o; \text{ input } \overline{q}; \ \overline{op}'}$$
$$(\mathrm{T}^p_c\text{-S2R})$$

$$\frac{\begin{array}{c} F_b, \text{output } q_o; \text{ input } \overline{q}; \ \overline{op} = [\![F_c, P_{cr}]\!]^p_c \\ q'_o = freshId() \qquad v = freshId() \\ F'_b = [R2S \mapsto wrapR2S(F_c(R2S))]F_b \\ \overline{op}' = \overline{op}, (q'_o, v) \leftarrow R2S(q_o, v); \end{array}}{[\![F_c, R2S(P_{cr})]\!]^p_c = F'_b, \text{output } q'_o; \text{ input } \overline{q}; \ \overline{op}'}$$
$$(\mathrm{T}^p_c\text{-R2S})$$

$$\frac{\begin{array}{c} \overline{F_b, \text{output } q_o; \text{ input } \overline{q}; \ \overline{op}} = [\![F_c, P_{cr}]\!]^p_c \\ n = |\overline{P_{cr}}| \qquad q'_o = freshId() \qquad \overline{q}' = \overline{q}_1, \ldots, \overline{q}_n \\ \forall i \in 1 \ldots n : v_i = freshId() \qquad \overline{op}' = \overline{op}_1, \ldots, \overline{op}_n \\ F'_b = [R2R \mapsto wrapR2R(F_c(R2R))](\cup \overline{F_b}) \\ \overline{op}'' = \overline{op}', (q'_o, \overline{v}) \leftarrow R2R(\overline{q_o}, \overline{v}); \end{array}}{[\![F_c, R2R(\overline{P_{cr}})]\!]^p_c = F'_b, \text{output } q'_o; \text{input } \overline{q}'; \overline{op}''}$$
$$(\mathrm{T}^p_c\text{-R2R})$$

CQL domains:

$$\tau \in \mathcal{T} \qquad\qquad\qquad\qquad\qquad Time$$
$$e \in \mathcal{TP} \qquad\qquad\qquad\qquad\qquad Tuple$$
$$\sigma \in \Sigma = \text{bag}(\mathcal{TP}) \quad \textit{Instantaneous relation}$$
$$r \in \mathcal{R} = \mathcal{T} \to \Sigma \quad \textit{Time-varying relation}$$
$$s \in \mathcal{S} = \text{bag}(\mathcal{TP} \times \mathcal{T}) \quad \textit{Time-varying stream}$$

CQL operator signatures:

$$S2R : S \times \mathcal{T} \to \Sigma$$
$$R2S : \Sigma \times \Sigma \to \Sigma$$
$$R2R : \Sigma^n \to \Sigma$$

CQL operator wrapper signatures:

$$S2R : (\Sigma \times \mathcal{T}) \times \{1\} \times S \to (\Sigma \times \mathcal{T}) \times S$$
$$R2S : (\Sigma \times \mathcal{T}) \times \{1\} \times \Sigma \to (\Sigma \times \mathcal{T}) \times \Sigma$$
$$R2R : (\Sigma \times \mathcal{T}) \times \{1 \ldots n\} \times (2^{\Sigma \times \mathcal{T}})^n$$
$$\to (\Sigma \times \mathcal{T}) \times (2^{\Sigma \times \mathcal{T}})^n$$

CQL operator wrappers:

$$\frac{\sigma, \tau = d_q \qquad s = d_v \\ s' = s \cup \{(e, \tau) : e \in \sigma\} \qquad \sigma' = f(s', \tau)}{wrapS2R(f)(d_q, \_, d_v) = \langle \sigma', \tau \rangle, s'}$$
$$(\mathrm{W}_c\text{-S2R})$$

$$\frac{\sigma, \tau = d_q \qquad \sigma' = d_v \qquad \sigma'' = f(\sigma, \sigma')}{wrapR2S(f)(d_q, \_, d_v) = \langle \sigma'', \tau \rangle, \sigma}$$
$$(\mathrm{W}_c\text{-R2S})$$

$$\frac{\sigma, \tau = d_q \qquad d'_i = d_i \cup \{\langle \sigma, \tau \rangle\} \\ \forall j \neq i \in 1 \ldots n : d'_j = d_j \\ \exists j \in 1 \ldots n : \nexists \sigma : \langle \sigma, \tau \rangle \in d_j}{wrapR2R(f)(d_q, i, \overline{d}) = \bullet, \overline{d}'}$$
$$(\mathrm{W}_c\text{-R2R-W{\scriptsize AIT}})$$

$$\frac{\sigma, \tau = d_q \qquad d'_i = d_i \cup \{\langle \sigma, \tau \rangle\} \\ \forall j \neq i \in 1 \ldots n : d'_j = d_j \\ \forall j \in 1 \ldots n : \sigma_j = aux(d_j, \tau)}{wrapR2R(f)(d_q, i, \overline{d}) = \langle f(\overline{\sigma}), \tau \rangle, \overline{d}'}$$
$$(\mathrm{W}_c\text{-R2R-R{\scriptsize EADY}})$$

$$\frac{\langle \sigma, \tau \rangle \in d}{aux(d, \tau) = \sigma}$$
$$(\mathrm{W}_c\text{-R2R-A{\scriptsize UX}})$$

information can be more conveniently represented as a mapping from time stamps to bags of tuples. CQL calls such a mapping a *time-varying relation*, and each individual bag of tuples an *instantaneous relation*. In the example, input history(ticker,low) is the time-varying relation r_h:

$$r_h = \Big[1 \mapsto \{\langle\text{'IBM'}, 119\rangle, \langle\text{'XYZ'}, 38\rangle\}, 2 \mapsto \{\langle\text{'IBM'}, 119\rangle, \langle\text{'XYZ'}, 35\rangle\} \Big]$$

The instantaneous relation $r_h(1)$ is $\{\langle\text{'IBM'}, 119\rangle, \langle\text{'XYZ'}, 38\rangle\}$. The CQL stream s_q represents the input quotes(ticker,ask):

$$s_q = \Big\{ \langle\langle\text{'IBM'}, 119\rangle, 1\rangle, \langle\langle\text{'IBM'}, 124\rangle, 1\rangle, \langle\langle\text{'XYZ'}, 35\rangle, 2\rangle, \langle\langle\text{'IBM'}, 119\rangle, 2\rangle \Big\}$$

The subquery quotes[Now] uses the window [Now] to turn the quotes stream into a time-varying relation r_q:

$$r_q = \Big[1 \mapsto \{\langle\text{'IBM'}, 119\rangle, \langle\text{'IBM'}, 124\rangle\}, 2 \mapsto \{\langle\text{'XYZ'}, 35\rangle, \langle\text{'IBM'}, 119\rangle\} \Big]$$

The next step of the query joins the quote relation r_q with the history relation r_h into a bargains relation r_b:

$$r_b = \Big[1 \mapsto \{\langle\text{'IBM'}, 119, 119\rangle\}, 2 \mapsto \{\langle\text{'XYZ'}, 35, 35\rangle, \langle\text{'IBM'}, 119, 119\rangle\}\Big]$$

Finally, the IStream operator monitors insertions into relation r_b and emits them as output stream s_o of time-tagged tuples:

$$s_o = \Big\{\langle\langle\text{'IBM'}, 119, 119\rangle, 1\rangle, \langle\langle\text{'XYZ'}, 35, 35\rangle, 2\rangle\Big\}$$

While CQL uses select-from-where syntax, the CQL semantics use an equivalent stream-relational algebra syntax (similar to relational algebra in databases):

```
IStream(BargainJoin(Now(quotes), history))
```

This algebraic notation makes the operator tree clearer. The leaves are stream name quotes and relation name history. CQL has three categories of operators. S2R operators turn a stream into a relation; e.g., Now(quotes) turns stream quotes into relation r_q. R2R operators turn one or more relations into a new relation; e.g., BargainJoin(r_q, r_h) turns relations r_q and r_h into the bargain relation r_b. Finally, R2S operators turn a relation into a stream; e.g., IStream(r_b) turns relation r_b into the stream of its insertions. CQL has no S2S operators, because they would be redundant. CQL's R2R operators coincide with traditional database relational algebra.

The CQL grammar is in Fig. 2. A CQL program P_c can be either a relation query P_{cr} or a stream query P_{cs}, and queries are either simple identifiers RName or SName, or composed using operators from the categories S2R, R2R, or R2S.

4.1.2   CQL Implementation Issues

Before we translate CQL to Brooklet, let us discuss the two issues of state and non-determinism in CQL.

CQL state. CQL represents global state explicitly as named relations, such as the history relation from our running example. But in addition, all three kinds of CQL operators implicitly maintain local state, referred to as "synopses" in [1]. An S2R operator maintains the state of a window on a stream to produce a relation. An R2S operator stores the previous state of the relation to compute the stream of differences. Finally, an R2R operator uses state to buffer data from whichever relation is available first, so it can be retrieved later to compute an output when data with matching time stamps is available for all relations.

CQL non-determinism. CQL is deterministic in the sense that the output of a program is fully determined by the times and values of its inputs [2]. Although a program can have independent inputs, for example, from a customer and from a stock exchange, any timing ambiguities outside the language are resolved by adding unambiguous time stamps. A CQL implementation might either assign time stamps upon receiving data, or use time stamps that are an inherent part of the input data, such as trading times. However, CQL implementations can permit non-determinism to exploit parallelism. For example, the implementation need not fully determine the order in which operators Now and BargainJoin process their data in BargainJoin(Now(quotes), history). They can run in parallel as long as BargainJoin always waits for its two inputs to have the same time stamp.

Translation to Brooklet will make all state explicit, and will clarify how the implementation enforces determinism.

4.1.3   CQL Translation Example

Given the CQL example program from Fig. 2, the translation to Brooklet is the program P_b:

```
output q_o;
input quotes, history;
(q_q, $v_n)        ← wrapNow(quotes, $v_n);
(q_b, $v_q, $v_h) ← wrapBargainJoin(q_q, history, $v_q, $v_h);
(q_o, $v_o)        ← wrapIStream(q_b, $v_o)
```

The leaves of the query tree serve as input queues; each subquery produces an intermediate queue, which the enclosing operator consumes; and the outermost query operator produces the program output queue. The translation to Brooklet makes the state of the operators explicit. The most interesting state is that of the wrapBargainJoin operator. Like each R2R operator, it has a function F_c(BargainJoin) that transforms one or more input instantaneous relations of the same time stamp to one output instantaneous relation. Brooklet models the choice of interleavings by allowing either queue q_q or history to fire independently. Hence, the Brooklet operator processes one data item each time either queue fires. Assume a data item arrives on the first queue q_q. If there is already a data item with the same time stamp in the variable v_h associated with the second queue, Brooklet performs the join, which may yield data items for the output queue q_b. Otherwise, it simply stores the data item in v_q for later.

4.1.4   CQL Translation

Fig. 2 shows the translation from CQL to Brooklet by recursion over the input program. Besides building up a program, the translation also builds up a function environment, which it populates with wrappers for the original functions. The translation introduces state, which the Brooklet wrappers maintain and consult to hand the right input to the wrapped CQL functions. Working in concert, the rules enforce a global convention: the execution sends exactly one instantaneous relation on every queue at every time stamp. Operators retain historical data in variables, e.g., to implement windows.

4.1.5   CQL Discussion

CQL is an SQL dialect for streaming [1]. Arasu and Widom specify big-step denotational semantics for CQL [2]. We show how to translate CQL to Brooklet, thus giving an alternative semantics. As we will show below, both semantics define equivalent input/output behavior for CQL programs. Translations from other languages can use similar techniques, i.e., make state explicit as variables; wrap computation in small-step firing functions; and define a global convention for how to achieve determinism.

4.2 StreamIt and Synchronous Data Flow

StreamIt [27,26] is a streaming language tailored for parallel implementations of applications such as MPEG decoding [6]. At its core, StreamIt is a synchronous data flow (SDF) language [16], which means that each time an operator fires, it consumes a fixed number of data items and produces a fixed number of data items. In the MPEG example, data items are pictures. StreamIt distinguishes between primitive and composite operators. A primitive operator (*filter* in StreamIt terminology) has optional local state. A composite operator is either a pipeline, a split-join, or a feedback loop. A pipeline puts operators in sequence, a split-join puts them in parallel, and a feedback loop puts them in a cycle. The topology of a StreamIt program is restricted to well-nested compositions of these. All StreamIt operators and programs have exactly one input and one output. We only focus on StreamIt's SDF core here, and encapsulate the local deterministic part of the computation in opaque pure functions, while keeping the parts of the computation that are relevant to streaming. We omit non-core features such as teleport messaging [6], which delivers control messages between operators and which could be modeled in Brooklet through shared variables.

4.2.1 StreamIt Program Example: MPEG Decoder
The following example StreamIt program P_s is based on a similar example by Drake et al. [6].

```
pipeline {
  splitjoin {
    split roundrobin;
    filter { work { tf ← FrequencyDecode(peek(1)); push(tf); pop(); }}
    filter { work { tm ← MotionVecDecode(peek(1)); push(tm); pop(); }}
    join roundrobin;
  }
  filter { s; work { s,tc ← MotionComp(s,peek(1)); push(tc); pop(); }}
}
```

It illustrates how the StreamIt language can be used to decode MPEG video. The example uses a pipeline and a split-join to compose three filters. Each filter has a work function, which peeks and pops from its predecessor stream, computes a temporary value, and pushes to its successor stream. In addition, the MotionComp filter also has an explicit state variable s for storing a reference picture between iterations. We omit the full syntax of StreamIt for space reasons; the interested reader can find it in Appendix B of the extended technical report[22].

4.2.2 StreamIt Implementation Issues
As before, we first discuss the intuition for the implementation before giving the details of the translation.

StreamIt state. Filters can have explicit state, such as s in the example. Furthermore, since Brooklet queues support only push and pop but not peek, the translation of StreamIt will have to buffer data items in a state variable until enough are available to satisfy the maximum peek() argument in the work function. Round-robin splitters also need a state variable with a *cursor* that determines where to send the next data item. A cursor is simply an index relative to the splitter. It keeps track of which queue is next in round-robin order. Round-robin joiners also need a cursor, plus a buffer for any data items that arrive out of turn.

StreamIt non-determinism. StreamIt, at the language level, is deterministic. Furthermore, since it is an SDF language, the number of data items peeked, popped, and pushed by each operator is constant. At the same time, StreamIt permits pipeline-, task-, and data-parallelism. This gives an implementation different scheduling choices, which Brooklet models by non-deterministically selecting a firing queue. Despite these non-deterministic choices, an implementation must ensure deterministic end-to-end behavior, which our translation makes explicit with buffering and synchronization.

4.2.3   StreamIt Translation Example

StreamIt program translation turns the StreamIt MPEG decoder P_s from earlier into a Brooklet program P_b:

```
output q_out;
input q_in;
(q_f, q_m, $sc)      ← wrapRRSplit-2(q_in, $sc);
(q_fd, $f)           ← wrapFilter-FrequencyDecode(q_f, $f);
(q_md, $m)           ← wrapFilter-MotionVecDecode(q_m, $m);
(q_d, $fd, $md, $jc) ← wrapRRJoin-2(q_fd, q_md, $fd, $md, $jc);
(q_out, $s, $mc)     ← wrapFilter-MotionComp(q_d, $s, $mc);
```

Each StreamIt filter becomes a Brooklet operator. StreamIt composite operators are reflected in Brooklet's operator topology. StreamIt's SplitJoin yields separate Brooklet split and join operators. The stateful filter MotionComp has two variables: $s models its explicit state s, and $mc models its implicit buffer.

4.2.4   StreamIt Translation

For space reasons, we give only a high-level overview of the StreamIt translation here (the details are in Appendix B of the extended technical report[22]). Similarly to CQL, there are recursive translation rules, one for each language construct. The base case is the translation of filters, and the recursive cases compose larger topologies for pipelines, split-joins, and feedback loops. Feedback loops turn into cyclic Brooklet topologies. The most interesting aspect are the helper rules for split and join, because they use explicit Brooklet state to achieve StreamIt determinism. Fig. 3 shows the rules. The input to the splitter is a queue q_a, and the output is a list of queues $\overline{q}$; conversely, the input to the joiner is a list of queues $\overline{q}'$, and the output is a single queue q_z. Both the splitter

StreamIt program xlation excerpt:

$$f = freshId()$$
$$v = freshId()$$
$$F_b = [f \mapsto wrapRRSplit(|\overline{q}|)]$$
$$op = (\overline{q}, v) \leftarrow f(q_a, v);$$

$$\overline{[\![F_s, \text{split roundrobin};, \overline{q}, q_a]\!]_s^p} = F_b, op$$
$$(\text{T}_s^p\text{-RR-SPLIT})$$

$$f = freshId()$$
$$\forall i \in 0 \ldots |\overline{q}'| : v_i = freshId()$$
$$F_b = [f \mapsto wrapRRJoin(|\overline{q}'|)]$$
$$op = (q_z, \overline{v}) \leftarrow f(\overline{q}', \overline{v});$$

$$\overline{[\![F_s, \text{join roundrobin};, q_z, \overline{q}']\!]_s^p} = F_b, op$$
$$(\text{T}_s^p\text{-RR-JOIN})$$

StreamIt operator wrappers excerpt:

$$c' = c + 1 \bmod N \qquad b_v = d_{in}$$
$$\forall i \in 1 \ldots N, i \neq c : b_i = \bullet$$

$$\overline{wrapRRSplit(N)(d_{in}, \_, c) = \overline{b}, c'}$$
$$(\text{W}_s\text{-RR-SPLIT})$$

$$d_i' = d_{in}, d_i \qquad \forall j \neq i \in 1 \ldots N : d_j' = d_j$$
$$d_c'', d_{out} = d_c' \qquad \forall j \neq c \in 1 \ldots N : d_j'' = d_j'$$
$$b_{out}, c', \overline{d}''' = wrapRRJoin(N)(\bullet, i, c + 1 \bmod N, \overline{d}'')$$

$$\overline{wrapRRJoin(N)(d_{in}, i, c, \overline{d}) = (b_{out}, d_{out}), c', \overline{d}'''}$$
$$(\text{W}_s\text{-RR-JOIN-READY})$$

$$\forall j \neq i \in 1 \ldots N : d_j' = d_j \qquad d_i' = d_{in}, d_i \qquad d_c = \bullet$$

$$\overline{wrapRRJoin(N)(d_{in}, i, c, \overline{d}) = \bullet, c, \overline{d}'}$$
$$(\text{W}_s\text{-RR-JOIN-WAIT})$$

Fig. 3. StreamIt round-robin split and join semantics on Brooklet

and the joiner maintain a cursor to keep track of the next queue in round-robin order. The joiner also stores one variable for each queue, to buffer data that arrives out-of-turn.

4.2.5 StreamIt Discussion

Our translation from StreamIt to Brooklet yields a program with maximum scheduling flexibility, allowing any interleavings as long as the end-to-end behavior matches the language semantics. This makes it amenable to distributed implementation. In contrast, StreamIt compilers [26] statically fix one schedule, which also determines where intermediate results are buffered. The buffering is implicit state, and StreamIt also has explicit state in filters. As we will see in Section 5, state affects the applicability of optimizations. Prior work on formal semantics for StreamIt does not model state [27]. By modeling state, our Brooklet translation facilitates reasoning about optimizations.

4.3 Sawzall and MapReduce

Sawzall [20] is a scripting language for MapReduce [5], which exploits cluster of workstations to analyze a massive but finite sequence of key/value pairs streamed from disk. In Sawzall, a stateless *map* operator transforms data one key/value pair at a time, feeding into a stateful *reduce* operator. The reduce operator works on separate keys separately, incrementally aggregating all values for a key into a single value. Although Sawzall programs are batch jobs, they use incremental operators to process large quantities of data in a single pass, and we therefore consider it a streaming language. Our translation provides the first formal semantics for Sawzall.

4.3.1 Sawzall Program Example: Query Log Analyzer

The example Sawzall program in Fig. 4 is based on a similar example in [20]. The program analyzes a query log to count queries per latitude and longitude, which can then be plotted on a world map. This program specifies one invocation of

Sawzall syntax:

$$
\begin{array}{lll}
P_z & ::= \overline{out\ in\ emit} & \text{Sawzall program}\\
out & ::= t : \text{table } f; & \text{Output aggregator}\\
in & ::= q : \text{input}; & \text{Input declaration}\\
emit & ::= \text{emit } t[f(q)] \leftarrow f(q); & \text{Emit statement}\\
q & ::= id & \text{Queue name}\\
f & ::= id & \text{Function name}\\
t & ::= id & \text{Table name}
\end{array}
$$

Sawzall example: Query log analyzer.
```
queryOrigins : table sum;
queryTargets : table sum;
logRecord : input;
emit queryOrigins[getOrigin(logRecord)]←1;
emit queryTargets[getTarget(logRecord)]←1;
```

Sawzall program xlation: $[\![F_z, P_z, R]\!]^p_z = \langle F_b, P_b \rangle$

$$
\overline{out}, q_{in}: \text{input};, \overline{emit} = P_z\\
\forall i \in 1 \dots R : q_i = freshId()\\
\forall i \in 1 \dots R : v_i = freshId()\\
f_{\text{Map}} = wrapMap(F_z, \overline{emit}, R)\\
f_{\text{Reduce}} = wrapReduce(F_z, \overline{out})\\
F_b = [\text{Map} \mapsto f_{\text{Map}}, \text{Reduce} \mapsto f_{\text{Reduce}}]\\
op_m = (\overline{q}) \leftarrow \text{Map}(q_{in})\\
\forall i \in 1 \dots R : op_i = (v_i) \leftarrow \text{Reduce}(q_i, v_i);\\
\overline{op'} = op_m, \overline{op}\\
\hline
[\![F_z, P_z, R]\!]^p_z = F_b, \text{output } \bullet; \text{input } q_{in}; \overline{op'}
$$
(T^p_z)

Sawzall domains:

$k_1 \in \mathcal{K}_1$	Input key	$k_2 \in \mathcal{K}_2$	Output key
$x_1 \in \mathcal{X}_1$	Input value	$x_2 \in \mathcal{X}_2$	Output value
$t \in \mathcal{T}$	Aggregate name	$O_z \in \mathcal{K}_2 \to \mathcal{X}_2$	Output table

Sawzall operator signatures:

$$
f_k : \mathcal{K}_1 \times \mathcal{X}_1 \to \mathcal{K}_2 \quad f_x : \mathcal{K}_1 \times \mathcal{X}_1 \to \mathcal{X}_2^*\\
f_a : \mathcal{X}_2 \times \mathcal{X}_2 \to \mathcal{X}_2
$$

Sawzall operator wrapper signatures:

$$
\text{Map} : (\mathcal{K}_1 \times \mathcal{X}_1) \times \{1\} \to (\mathcal{T} \times \mathcal{K}_2 \times \mathcal{X}_2)^*\\
\text{Reduce}: (\mathcal{T} \times \mathcal{K}_2 \times \mathcal{X}_2) \times \{1\} \times O_z \to O_z
$$

Sawzall operator wrappers:

$$
emit\ t[f_k(\_)] \leftarrow f_x(\_); = emit\\
\overline{b} = wrapMap(F_z, \overline{emit}, R)(d, 1)\\
k_1, x_1 = d \qquad k_2 = F_z(f_k)(k_1, x_1)\\
\overline{x_2} = F_z(f_x)(k_1, x_1) \qquad i = hash(k_2) \bmod R\\
b'_i = b_i, \langle t, k_2, x_{21} \rangle, \dots, \langle t, k_2, x_{2n} \rangle\\
\forall j \neq i \in 1 \dots R : b'_j = b_j\\
\hline
wrapMap(F_z, (emit, \overline{emit}), R)(d, \_) = \overline{b'}
$$
(W$_z$-MAP)

$$
\forall i \in 1 \dots R : b_i = \bullet\\
\hline
wrapMap(F_z, \bullet, R)(\_, \_) = \overline{b}
$$
(W$_z$-MAP-$\bullet$)

$$
t, k_2, x_2 = d_q \qquad t : \text{table } f_a[]; \in \overline{out}\\
k_2 \in d_v \qquad x'_2 = F_z(f_a)(x_2, d_v(k_2))\\
d'_v = [k_2 \mapsto x'_2]d_v\\
\hline
wrapReduce(F_z, \overline{out})(d_q, \_, d_v) = d'_v
$$
(W$_z$-REDUCE)

$$
t, k_2, x_2 = d_q \qquad t : \text{table } f_a[]; \in \overline{out}\\
k_2 \notin d_v \qquad d'_v = [k_2 \mapsto x_2]d_v\\
\hline
wrapReduce(F_z, \overline{out})(d_q, \_, d_v) = d'_v
$$
(W$_z$-REDUCE-$\emptyset$)

Fig. 4. Sawzall semantics on Brooklet

the map operator, and uses `table` clauses to specify `sum` as the reduce operator. The map operator transforms its input `logRecord` into two key/value pairs:

$$
\langle k, x \rangle = \langle \text{getOrigin}(\text{logRecord}), 1 \rangle\\
\langle k', x' \rangle = \langle \text{getTarget}(\text{logRecord}), 1 \rangle
$$

Here, `getOrigin` and `getTarget` are pure functions that compute the latitude and longitude of the host issuing the query and the host serving the result, respectively. The latitude and longitude together serve as the key into the tables. Since the number 1 serves as the value associated with the key, the `sum` aggregators end up counting query log entries by key. Fig. 4 shows the Sawzall grammar.

4.3.2 Sawzall Implementation Issues
Sawzall has stateful and non-deterministic implementations.

Sawzall state. The map operator is stateless, whereas the reduce operator is stateful, using state to incrementalize its aggregation. The implementation in Pike et al.'s paper [20] partitions the reducer key space into R parts, where R is a command-line argument upon job submission. There are multiple instances of the reduce operator, one per partition. Because reduction works independently per key, each instance of the reduce operator can maintain the state for its assigned part of the key space independently.

Sawzall non-determinism. At the language level, Sawzall is deterministic. Sawzall is designed for MapReduce, and the strength of MapReduce is that at the implementation level, it runs on a cluster of workstations for scalability. To exploit the parallelism of the cluster, at the implementation level, MapReduce makes non-deterministic dynamic scheduling decisions. Reducers can start while map is still in process, and different reducers can work in parallel with each other. Different mappers can also work in parallel; we will use Brooklet to address this optimization later in the paper, and describe a translation with a single map operator for now.

4.3.3   Sawzall Translation Example
Given the Sawzall program P_z from earlier, assuming $R = 4$ partitions, the Brooklet version P_b is:

```
output; /*no output queue, outputs are in variables*/
input q_log;
(q_1, q_2, q_3, q_4) ← Map(q_log); /*getOrigin/getTarget*/
($v_1) ← Reduce(q_1, $v_1);
($v_2) ← Reduce(q_2, $v_2);
($v_3) ← Reduce(q_3, $v_3);
($v_4) ← Reduce(q_4, $v_4);
```

There is one reduce operator for each of the R partitions. Each reducer performs the work for both aggregators (`queryOrigins` and `queryTargets`) from the original Sawzall program. The final reduction results are in variables $v_1 \ldots v_4$.

4.3.4   Sawzall Translation
Fig. 4 specifies the program translation, domains, and operator wrappers. There is only one program translation rule T_z^p. The translation $[\![F_z, P_z, R]\!]_z^p$ takes the Sawzall function environment, the Sawzall program, and the number of reducer partitions as arguments. All the $\overline{emit}$ statements become part of the single map operator. The map operator wrapper uses a hash function to scatter its output over the reducer key space for load balancing. All the $\overline{out}$ declarations become part of each of the reduce operators. Each reducer's variable stores the mapping from each key in that reducer's partition to the latest reduction result for that key. If the key is new, rule W_z-REDUCE-$\emptyset$ fires and registers x_2 as the initial value. At the end of the run, the results in the variables are deterministic, because aggregators are associative and reducers work on disjoint parts of the key space.

4.3.5   Sawzall Discussion
The Sawzall translation is simpler than that of CQL or StreamIt, because each translated program uses the same simple topology. The translation hard-codes the data parallelism for the reducers, but generates only one mapper, thus deferring data parallelism for mappers to a separate optimization step. There was no prior formal semantics for Sawzall, but Lämmel studies MapReduce and Sawzall by implementing an emulation in Haskell [15]. Now that we have seen how to

translate three languages, it is clear that it is possible to model additional streaming languages or language features on Brooklet. For example, Brooklet can serve as a basis for modeling teleport messaging [6].

4.4   Translation Correctness

We formulate correctness theorems for CQL and StreamIt with respect to their formal semantics [2,27]. The proofs are in an extended technical report [22]. We do not formulate a theorem for Sawzall, because it lacks formal semantics; our mapping to Brooklet provides the first formal semantics for Sawzall.

Theorem 1 (CQL translation correctness). *For all CQL function environments F_c, programs P_c, and inputs I_c, the results under CQL semantics are the same as the results under Brooklet semantics after translation $[\![F_c, P_c]\!]_c^p$.*

Theorem 2 (StreamIt translation correctness). *For all StreamIt function environments F_s, programs P_s, and inputs I_s, the results under StreamIt semantics are the same as the results under Brooklet semantics after translation $[\![F_s, P_s]\!]_s^p$.*

5   Optimizations

The previous section used our calculus to understand how a language maps to an execution platform. This section uses our calculus to specify how to use three vital optimizations: data-parallel computation, operator fusion, and operator reordering. Each optimization comes with a correctness theorem; for space reasons, we leave the proofs to an extended technical report [22].

5.1   Data Parallelism

If an operation is commutative across data items, then the order in which the data items are processed is irrelevant. MapReduce uses this observation to exploit the collective computing power of a cluster for analyzing extremely large data sets [5]. The input data set is partitioned, and copies of the map operator process the partitions in parallel. In general, the challenge in exploiting such *data parallelism* is determining if an operator commutes. Sawzall and StreamIt solve this challenge by restricting the programming model. In Brooklet, commutativity analysis can be performed with a simple code inspection. Since a pure function always commutes[2], and all state in Brooklet is explicit in an operator's signature, a sufficient condition for introducing data-parallelism is that an operator does not access variables. The transformation must ensure that the output data is combined in the same order that the input data was partitioned. Brooklet

---

[2] At least in the mathematical sense; in systems, floating point operations do not always commute.

can use the round-robin splitter and joiner described in the StreamIt translation for this purpose. Thus, the operator $(\text{out}) \leftarrow \text{wrapMap-LatLong}(q);$ can be parallelized with $N = 3$ copies like this:

```
(q1, q2, q3, $sc)          ← Split(q, $sc);
(q4)                       ← wrapMap-LatLong(q1);
(q5)                       ← wrapMap-LatLong(q2);
(q6)                       ← wrapMap-LatLong(q3);
(out, $v4, $v5, $v6, $jc)  ← Join(q4, q5, q6, $v4, $v5, $v6, $jc);
```

The following rule describes how to create the new program with N duplicates of the parallelized operator.

$$\frac{\begin{array}{c} op = (q_{out}) \leftarrow f(q_{in}); \\ \forall i \in 1 \ldots n : q_i = \mathit{freshId}() \qquad \forall i \in 1 \ldots n : q_i' = \mathit{freshId}() \\ F_b', op_s = [\![\emptyset, \text{split roundrobin}, \overline{q}, q_{in}]\!]_s^p \\ \forall i \in 1 \ldots n : op_i = (q_i') \leftarrow f(q_i); \\ F_b'', op_j = [\![\emptyset, \text{join roundrobin}, q_{out}, \overline{q}']\!]_s^p \end{array}}{\langle F_b, op \rangle \longrightarrow_{split}^{N} \langle F_b \cup F_b' \cup F_b'', op_s \; \overline{op} \; op_j \rangle} \quad (O_b\text{-SPLIT})$$

The precondition is that op does not refer to any state variables. The data parallelism optimization illustrates that Brooklet facilitates reasoning over shared state. The rules for round-robin split and join are in Fig. 3.

Making multiplexers explicit and fixing the degree of parallelism are important to faithfully model and reason about real-world systems. Possible implementation strategies for avoiding the limitation of a fixed degree of parallelism include using just-in-time compilation to do splitting online, or putting code on a larger number of machines and then in practice using only a subset as needed.

Theorem 3 (Correctness of O_b-Split). *For all function environments F_b, Brooklet programs P_b, and degrees of parallelism N, if rule O_b-SPLIT yields $\langle F_b, P_b \rangle \longrightarrow_{split}^{N} \langle F_b', P_b' \rangle$, then $\rightarrow_b^* (F_b, P_b, I_b) = \rightarrow_b^* (F_b', P_b', I_b)$ for all Brooklet inputs I_b.*

5.2 Operator Fusion

In practice, transmitting data between two operators can incur significant overhead. Data needs to be marshalled/unmarshalled, transferred over a network or written to a mutually accessible location, and buffered by the receiver, not to mention the expense of context switching. This overhead can be offset by *fusing* two operators into one. StreamIt applies this optimization to operators in a pipelined topology [26]. Operators may be fused if they meet two conditions. First, they appear in a simple pipeline. Brooklet makes this topology easy to validate because queues are defined and used exactly once. Second, the state used by the operators must not be modifiable anywhere else in the program. Again, because Brooklet requires an explicit declaration of all state, this condition can be verified with a simple code inspection. The following Brooklet program shows two steps in an MPEG decoder:

```
(q₁,$v1)   ←  ZigZag(qᵢₙ,$v1);
(qₒᵤₜ,$v2)  ←  IQuantization(q₁,$v2);
```

The fused equivalent of the program is:

$$(q_{out},\$v1,\$v2) \leftarrow$$
$$\texttt{Fused-ZigZag-IQuant}(q_{in},\$v1,\$v2);$$

The following rule formalizes this optimization:

$$\frac{\begin{array}{ll} op_1 = (q_1, v_1) \leftarrow f_1(q_{in}, v_1); & (\exists op' = (\_, v_1) \leftarrow f'(\_,\_)) \Rightarrow op' = op_1 \\ op_2 = (q_{out}, v_2) \leftarrow f_2(q_1, v_2); & (\exists op' = (\_, v_2) \leftarrow f'(\_,\_)) \Rightarrow op' = op_2 \\ f = freshId() \quad F'_b = [f \mapsto fusedOperator(F_b, f_1, f_2)]F_b \end{array}}{F_b, op_1 \; op_2 \longrightarrow F'_b, (q_{out}, v_1, v_2) \leftarrow f(q_{in}, v_1, v_2);} \text{(O}_b\text{-FUSE)}$$

The preconditions guard against other operators writing variables v_1 or v_2. The following rule defines the new internal function:

$$\frac{(d_{temp}, d'_1) = F_b(f_1)(d_{in}, 1, d_1) \qquad (d_{out}, d'_2) = F_b(f_2)(d_{temp}, 1, d_2)}{fusedOperator(F_b, f_1, f_2)(d_{in}, \_, d_1, d_2) = (d_{out}, d'_1, d'_2)} \text{(W}_b\text{-FUSE)}$$

In our example, this combines $F_b(\texttt{ZigZag})$ and $F_b(\texttt{IQuantization})$ into function $F'_b(\texttt{Fused-ZigZag-IQuant})$. The fusion optimization illustrates that Brooklet facilitates reasoning over topologies.

Theorem 4 (Correctness of O$_b$-Fuse). *For all function environments F_b and Brooklet programs P_b, if rule O$_b$-FUSE yields $\langle F_b, P_b \rangle \longrightarrow_{Fuse} \langle F'_b, P'_b \rangle$, then $\rightarrow^*_b (F_b, P_b, I_b) = \rightarrow^*_b (F'_b, P'_b, I_b)$ for all Brooklet inputs I_b.*

5.3   Reordering of Operators

A general rule of thumb for database query optimizations is that it is better to remove more tuples early in order to reduce downstream computations. The most popular example for this is hoisting a select operator, because a select reduces the tuple volume for operators it feeds into [1]. A select is said to *commute* with another operator if their output result is the same regardless of their execution order. The following program computes the commission on sales of IBM stock. The input is `sale(ticker, price)` and the output is `commission(ticker, cost)`. The commission is 2%.

```
output commission;
input sale;
(qt)         ←  BrokerCommission(sale);
(commission) ←  Select-IBM(qt);
```

The functions for the two operators are:

$$F_b(\texttt{BrokerCommission})(d, \_) = \text{let } \langle \texttt{ticker}, \texttt{price} \rangle = d \text{ in } \langle \texttt{ticker}, 0.02 \cdot \texttt{price} \rangle$$
$$F_b(\texttt{Select-IBM})(d, \_) = \text{let } \langle \texttt{ticker}, \texttt{cost} \rangle = d \text{ in if } \texttt{ticker} = \text{'IBM' then } d \text{ else•}$$

We can reorder the two operators for two reasons. First, the `BrokerCommission` operator is stateless, and therefore operates on each data item independently, so its semantics do not change when it sees a filtered stream of data item. Second, the Select-IBM operator only reads the ticker, and BrokerCommission forwards the ticker unmodified. In other words, Select-IBM does not rely on any data modified by BrokerCommission and vice versa. The optimized program is:

```
output commission;
input sale;
(qt) ← Select-IBM(sale);
(commission) ← BrokerCommission(qt);
```

The following rule encodes the optimization:

$$op_1 = (q_t) \leftarrow f_1(\overline{q}); \qquad op_2 = (q_{out}) \leftarrow f_2(q_t);$$
$$F_b(f_1)(d, i) = \text{let } \langle r, w \rangle = d \text{ in } \langle r, f_1(w, i) \rangle$$
$$F_b(f_2)(d, \_) = \text{let } \langle r, \_ \rangle = d \text{ in if } f_2(r) \text{ then } d \text{ else } \bullet$$
$$\forall i \in 1 \dots |\overline{q}| : q_i' = \mathit{freshId}()$$
$$\frac{op_1' = (q_{out}) \leftarrow f_1(\overline{q'}); \qquad \forall i \in 1 \dots |\overline{q}| : op_i = (q_i') \leftarrow f_2(q_i);}{F_b, op_1 \ op_2 \longrightarrow F_b, \overline{op} \ op_1'} \quad (O_b\text{-HoistSelect})$$

The first two preconditions restrict op_1 and op_2 to be stateless operators. The third precondition specifies that f_1 forwards a part r of the data item unmodified, and the fourth precondition specifies that f_2 is a select that only reads r, and forwards the entire data item unmodified. We have chosen in Brooklet to abstract away local deterministic computations into opaque functions, because their semantics are well-studied (e.g., [8,10,21]). We leverage this prior work by assuming that a static program analysis can determine the restrictions on the read and write sets of operator functions used for select hoisting.

Theorem 5 (Correctness of O_b-HoistSelect). *For all function environments F_b and Brooklet programs P_b, if $\langle F_b, P_b \rangle \longrightarrow_{HoistSelect} \langle F_b', P_b' \rangle$ by rule O_b-HoistSelect, then $\rightarrow_b^* (F_b, P_b, I_b) \Longrightarrow_b^* (F_b', P_b', I_b)$ for all Brooklet inputs I_b.*

5.4 Optimizations Summary

We have used our calculus to understand how a language can apply three vital optimizations. The concise and straightforward formalization of the optimizations validates the design of Brooklet. There are many other streaming optimizations, including, to name just a few, sharing redundant subqueries in CQL [1]; pre-aggregating data on the workers performing the map phase of MapReduce [5]; or eliminating spurious synchronization in StreamIt [26]. Furthermore, there are stronger variants of the optimizations we sketched; for example, it is sometimes possible to introduce data parallelism even for stateful operators. We believe that the examples in this section are a useful first step towards formalizing optimizations for stream processing languages.

6 Related Work

Our approach to defining a core minimal language that allows us to reason about correctness is inspired by Featherweight Java [13].

There has been extensive prior work in the semantics of stream processing. Stephens [23] provides a comprehensive survey, but it does not address recent language developments. Brooklet differs from prior work on streaming semantics because it models state and non-determinism as explicit core concepts. Kahn process networks [14], such as Unix pipes, assume deterministic execution. Synchronous data flow [16] models, such as StreamIt, assume fixed buffer sizes and static communication patterns. Hoare's communicating sequential process [12] assumes no buffering, and synchronous communication. Gurevich et al. [11] recently studied streaming systems, but focused on their more theoretical aspects.

The database literature often refers to streaming applications as "continuous queries" [4,25]. Surprisingly, there is little work from the database community on optimizations of queries with side effects. Two exceptions are a study of XQuery with side effects [10] and a study of object-oriented databases [7].

This paper uses CQL, Sawzall, and StreamIt as representative examples of streaming languages, but there are many more. Spade [9] is a streaming language for composing parallel and distributed flow graphs for System S, IBM's scalable data processing middleware. Pig Latin [18] is one of the languages designed to compose MapReduce or Hadoop jobs. DryadLinq [28] runs imperative code on local machines and uses integrated SQL to generate distributed queries.

7   Conclusion and Outlook

This paper presents Brooklet, a core calculus for stream processing. It represents stream processing applications as a graph of operators. Operators contain pure functions, thread all state through explicit variables, and trigger non-deterministically. Explicit state and non-deterministic execution are central concepts, capturing the reality of distributed implementations. We translate three representative languages, CQL, Sawzall, and StreamIt, to Brooklet, thus demonstrating its generality for language designers. We formalize three vital optimizations, data parallelism, operator fusion, and operator reordering, in Brooklet, thus demonstrating its usefulness for language implementors. Brooklet lays the ground work for a variety of future work, including formalization of additional languages, invention of new abstractions to expose and exploit parallelism, alternative translations for the languages we formalized, reverse translations from Brooklet back into source languages, type systems work, exploration of time or space resource constraints, investigations of progress, fairness, and dead-lock, static analyses for establishing optimization preconditions, and specifications of additional optimizations. Brooklet also provides the foundation for a common intermediate language for stream processing. In ongoing work, we are implementing the translations from CQL, Sawzall, and StreamIt to Brooklet, the optimizations from Brooklet to Brooklet, and a translation from Brooklet to C++. The implementation uses System S [9] as a high-performance streaming runtime, which manages all processes across a cluster and their communications. The long-term goal of our work is to establish Brooklet as both a formal and practical foundation for stream processing.

Acknowledgements

The authors would like to thank the anonymous reviewers for their comments and suggestions. We would also like to thank John Field, Rodric Rabbah, and Martin Vechev for their feedback on earlier versions of this paper, and Nagui Halim for his support of this project. This material is based upon work supported by the National Science Foundation under Grants No. CNS-0448349 and CNS-0615129.

References

1. Arasu, A., Babu, S., Widom, J.: The CQL continuous query language: Semantic foundations and query execution. VLDB Journal, 121–142 (2006)
2. Arasu, A., Widom, J.: A denotational semantics for continuous queries over streams and relations. In: SIGMOD Record, pp. 6–11 (2004)
3. Buck, I., Foley, T., Horn, D., Sugerman, J., Fatahalian, K., Houston, M., Hanrahan, P.: Brook for GPUs: Stream computing on graphics hardware. In: TOG, pp. 777–786 (2004)
4. Chen, J., DeWitt, D.J., Tian, F., Wang, Y.: NiagaraCQ: A scalable continuous query system for internet databases. In: SIGMOD, pp. 379–390 (2000)
5. Dean, J., Ghemawat, S.: MapReduce: Simplified data processing on large clusters. In: OSDI, pp. 137–150 (2004)
6. Drake, M., Hoffmann, H., Rabbah, R., Amarasinghe, S.: MPEG-2 decoding in a stream programming language. In: IPDPS, pp. 86–95 (2006)
7. Fegaras, L.: Optimizing queries with object updates. In: JIIS, pp. 219–242 (1999)
8. Ferrante, J., Ottenstein, K.J., Warren, J.D.: The program dependence graph and its use in optimization. In: TOPLAS, pp. 319–349 (1987)
9. Gedik, B., Andrade, H., Wu, K.-L., Yu, P.S., Doo, M.: SPADE: The System S declarative stream processing engine. In: SIGMOD, pp. 1123–1134 (2008)
10. Ghelli, G., Onose, N., Rose, K., Siméon, J.: XML query optimization in the presence of side effects. In: SIGMOD, pp. 339–352 (2008)
11. Gurevich, Y., Leinders, D., den Bussche, J.V.: A theory of stream queries. In: DBLP, pp. 153–168 (2007)
12. Hoare, C.A.R.: Communicating sequential processes. In: CACM, pp. 666–677 (1978)
13. Igarashi, A., Pierce, B., Wadler, P.: Featherweight Java - a minimal core calculus for Java and GJ. In: TOPLAS, pp. 132–146 (1999)
14. Kahn, G.: The semantics of a simple language for parallel programming. In: IFIP, pp. 471–475 (1974)
15. Lämmel, R.: Google's MapReduce Programming Model – Revisited. Science of Computer Programming Journal, 208–237 (2007)
16. Lee, E.A., Messerschmitt, D.G.: Synchronous data flow. In: Proc. IEEE, pp. 1235–1245 (1987)
17. Nielson, H.R., Nielson, F.: Semantics with applications: a formal introduction. John Wiley & Sons, Inc., Chichester (1992)
18. Olston, C., Reed, B., Srivastava, U., Kumar, R., Tomkins, A.: Pig Latin: A not-so-foreign language for data processing. In: SIGMOD, pp. 1099–1110 (2008)
19. Pierce, B.C.: Types and programming languages. MIT Press, Cambridge (2002)
20. Pike, R., Dorward, S., Griesemer, R., Quinlan, S.: Interpreting the data: Parallel analysis with Sawzall. In: Scientific Programming, pp. 277–298 (2005)

528 R. Soulé et al.

21. Rinard, M.C., Diniz, P.C.: Commutativity analysis: a new analysis framework for parallelizing compilers. In: PLDI, pp. 54–67 (1996)
22. Soulé, R., Hirzel, M., Grimm, R., Gedik, B., Andrade, H., Kumar, V., Wu, K.-L.: A unified semantics for stream processing languages (extended). Technical Report 2010-924, New York University (2010)
23. Stephens, R.: A survey of stream processing. In: Acta Inf., pp. 491–541 (1997)
24. The StreamBase dialect of StreamSQL, http://streamsql.org/
25. Terry, D., Goldberg, D., Nichols, D., Oki, B.: Continuous queries over append-only databases. In: SIGMOD, pp. 321–330 (1992)
26. Thies, W., Karczmarek, M., Amarasinghe, S.P.: StreamIt: A language for streaming applications. In: Horspool, R.N. (ed.) CC 2002. LNCS, vol. 2304, pp. 179–196. Springer, Heidelberg (2002)
27. Thies, W., Karczmarek, M., Gordon, M., Maze, D., Wong, J., Hoffman, H., Brown, M., Amarasinghe, S.: StreamIt: A compiler for streaming applications. In: MIT Laboratory for Computer Science Technical Memo LCS-TM-622 (2001)
28. Yu, Y., Isard, M., Fetterly, D., Budiu, M., Erlingsson, Ú., Gunda, P.K., Currey, J.: DryadLINQ: A system for general-purpose distributed data-parallel computing using a high-level language. In: OSDI, pp. 1–14 (2008)

Enforcing Stateful Authorization and Information Flow Policies in FINE

Nikhil Swamy[1], Juan Chen[1], and Ravi Chugh[2]

[1] Microsoft Research, Redmond
[2] University of California, San Diego
{nswamy,juanchen}@microsoft.com, rchugh@cs.ucsd.edu

Abstract. Proving software free of security bugs is hard. Languages that ensure that programs correctly enforce their security policies would help, but, to date, no security-typed language has the ability to verify the enforcement of the kinds of policies used in practice—dynamic, stateful policies which address a range of concerns including forms of access control and information flow tracking.

This paper presents FINE, a new source-level security-typed language that, through the use of a simple module system and dependent, refinement, and affine types, checks the enforcement of dynamic security policies applied to real software. FINE is proven sound. A prototype implementation of the compiler and several example programs are available from http://research.microsoft.com/fine.

1 Introduction

The security of a well-designed software system often revolves around the concept of a reference monitor, a security-critical kernel that mediates access to resources while enforcing a suitable policy. Reference monitors are expected to be compact and implemented in a form amenable to review. However, increasingly, reference monitors are tasked with enforcing complex policies that simultaneously address various aspects of security, mixing, for example, role- and history-based access control with information flow tracking. Policies are authored separately from the programs they govern, they are composed in non-trivial ways, and, as policies change over time, authorization decisions require reasoning about state. This makes it difficult to establish that a reference monitor enforces a policy correctly.

To illustrate the kinds of security concerns that arise in practice, consider the policy used by CONTINUE [14], a widely used program for managing academic conferences. CONTINUE's security policy is defined using Datalog-like rules in XACML. This policy stands separately from the implementation of the server program, making it hard to connect the policy to the program objects it governs. The policy is also particularly complex in that it makes extensive use of stateful features. For example, the conference management process is staged into a number of phases—in each phase, different policy rules apply. During the submission phase of a conference, authors may submit papers, but this right is revoked after the submission deadline is passed. In the bidding phase, papers are assigned to reviewers after accounting for conflicts of interest. During the rebuttal phase, reviews are disclosed to authors, but care must be taken to ensure that PC-confidential remarks and scores are not revealed. With such a complex policy to

A.D. Gordon (Ed.): ESOP 2010, LNCS 6012, pp. 529–549, 2010.

enforce, it is not surprising that the developers of CONTINUE report that almost all the interesting bugs they encountered were related to authorization in some form [7]. Policies used with other kinds of software, such as systems that manage medical records, applications that control the outsourcing of software development, and military systems, arguably have even more complex authorization requirements. Formally verifying that the reference monitors of such systems correctly enforce their policies would help alleviate concerns of security vulnerabilities.

This paper presents FINE, a new source-level security-typed programming language that can be used to implement programs like reference monitors and to check that these programs correctly enforce their security policies. FINE distinguishes itself from prior languages in this line, including FlowCaml [18], Jif [5], Fable [21], Aura [13], and RCF [1], primarily in its ability to express a combination of stateful authorization (none of the prior languages model state) and information flow (which is the focus of Flow-Caml and Jif, and can be encoded in Fable and Aura, but not, as far as we are aware, in RCF). The technical contribution of FINE is a new type system (§3) that uses dependent and refinement types to express authorization policies by including first-order logical formulas in the types of program expressions. FINE uses affine types, a weakening of linear types [24], to model changes to the state of an authorization policy. (Variables with an affine type can be used at most once.) The combination of affine and dependent types is subtle and can require tracking uses of affine assumptions in both types and terms. Our formulation keeps the metatheory simple by ensuring that affine variables never appear in types, while still allowing the state of a program to be refined by logical formulas. We also formalize a module system for FINE that provides a simple but strong information-hiding property—we exploit this property to model information flow.

Programming with these advanced typing constructs can impose a significant burden on the programmer. For this reason, languages like Fable and Aura position themselves as intermediate languages because verification depends on intricate security proofs too cumbersome for programmers to write down. Indeed, checking the 2000 lines of code in our benchmark programs produces nearly 200 proof obligations, a proof burden that would overwhelm most programmers. To alleviate this concern, FINE draws on the experience of languages like F7 (an implementation of RCF) and uses Z3 [6], an SMT solver, to automatically discharge proof obligations. The careful combination of refinement and affine types in FINE allows us to use a mature classical prover like Z3. Refinement formulas in FINE only involve the standard logical connectives, avoiding the need for still-experimental linear-logic provers.

We describe our experience using FINE to build several example programs (§4), including a model of the reference monitor of CONTINUE. The complete semantics of FINE, proofs of theorems, and additional examples appear in a technical report [20].

2 FINE, by Example

We begin by presenting FINE using several examples. Our first example is a simple form of password-based authentication. Next, we discuss permission-based access control enriched with information flow tracking. Finally, we show how to enforce stateful authorization policies by presenting code examples from our main case-study, a model of the CONTINUE conference management server.

2.1 Authentication, Access Control, and Information Flow

FINE's syntax is similar to languages in the ML family. In order to specify and enforce security policies, FINE programmers define modules that provide mediated access to security-sensitive resources. The module Authentication shown below mediates access to authentication routines.

Simple password authentication

```
1 module Authentication
2 type prin = U: string → prin | Admin: prin
3 private type cred :: prin → ⋆ = Auth: p:prin → cred p
4 val login: p:prin → string → option (cred p)
5 let login p pw = if (check_pwd_db p pw) then Some (Auth p) else None
```

The type prin is a standard variant type that represents principal names as either a string for the user's name, or the distinguished constant Admin. The type cred (line 3) is a dependent-type constructor with *kind* prin → ⋆, e.g., (cred Admin) is a legal type of kind ⋆ (the kind of normal types, distinguished from the kind of affine types, introduced in §2.2) and represents a credential for the Admin user. Values of the cred p type are constructed using the Auth data constructor. This constructor is given a dependent function type—the argument p is the name of the principal and is in scope to the right of the function arrow. By declaring cred **private**, the Authentication module indicates that its clients cannot directly use the Auth constructor. Instead, the only way a client module can obtain a credential is by calling the login function (given a dependent function type on line 4). The implementation of login (line 5) calls an external function (not shown) to check the password, and, if the password check succeeds, returns a credential for the user p. By indexing cred with the name of the principal which it authenticates, we can statically detect common security errors. For example, a client cannot use login to obtain a credential for U "Alice" and later pass it off as a credential for Admin—the type of the former, cred (U "Alice"), distinguishes it from the latter, which has type cred Admin.

We use Authentication to implement the FileRM module (shown on the next page), a reference monitor that mediates access to a file system. The policies implemented by reference monitors in FINE have two components: the types given to values exposed in the module's interface (e.g., the type of fread on line 7), and policy axioms introduced by the **assume** construct (e.g., **assume** AdminRW on line 6). A security review of a FINE module must confirm that the types and assumptions adequately capture the intent of a high-level policy. Importantly, client code need not be reviewed—typing ensures that clients comply with the reference monitor's security policy.

The FileRM module aims to provide a basic level of access protection on files by ensuring that principals that read and write to files have the requisite permissions. This basic protection is implemented by lines 1-7 of FileRM. The remainder of the module enriches the access control mechanism to track information flows so that, for example, users cannot reveal secrets by copying data from a secret file into a public file.

Permission-based access control and information flow on files

```
 1  module FileRM
 2  open Authentication (* Use non -private symbols from Authentication's namespace *)
 3  (* Propositions and assumptions for file permissions *)
 4  type CanRead:: prin → Sys.file → ⋆
 5  type CanWrite:: prin → Sys.file → ⋆
 6  assume AdminRW: forall f:Sys.file. CanRead Admin f && CanWrite Admin f
 7  val fread_simple: p:prin → cred p → {f:Sys.file | CanRead p f} → string
 8  (* Types and operators to track information flow *)
 9  type label = F : Sys.file → label | J : label → label → label
10  private type tracked :: ⋆ → label → ⋆ = L : α → p:label → tracked α p
11  val fmap: (α → β) → l:label → tracked α l → tracked β l
12  val tensor: l:label → m:label → tracked (α → β) l → tracked α m → tracked β (J l m)
13  (* Types and axioms for a partial order on labels *)
14  type CanFlow:: label → label → ⋆
15  assume Lattice: forall l:label, m1:label, m2:label. (CanFlow l l) &&
16     ((CanFlow l m1 && CanFlow l m2) ⇒ CanFlow l (J m1 m2)) &&
17     ((CanFlow m1 l && CanFlow m2 l) ⇒ CanFlow (J m1 m2) l)
18  assume Atomicflow: forall f:Sys.file, g:Sys.file.
19    (forall p:prin. CanRead p g ⇒ CanRead p f) ⇒ CanFlow (F f) (F g)
20  (* Secure wrappers for system calls *)
21  val fread: p:prin→ cred p→ f:{x:Sys.file | CanRead p x}→ tracked string (F f)
22  let fread p c f = L (Sys.fread f) (F f)
23  val fwrite: p:prin→ cred p→ f:{x:Sys.file | CanWrite p x}→
24               l:{y:label | CanFlow y (F f)} → tracked string l → unit
25  let fwrite p c f l (L s x) = Sys.fwrite f s
```

FileRM defines dependent-type constructors CanRead and CanWrite to describe access permissions. Permissions are granted using assumptions like AdminRW, which states that the Admin user has read- and write-permissions on all files. Client programs can use axioms like AdminRW to produce evidence of the propositions required to call functions like fread_simple, which wrap the underlying system calls. Client programs are assumed to not have direct access to these system calls—this can be established using standard systems techniques like sandboxing [25]. The type of fread_simple is used to enforce an access control policy. A caller of fread_simple is required to pass in a credential for a user p and a file handle f, where f has the refined type {x:Sys.file | CanRead p x} indicating that p has permission to read f.

We used fread_simple mainly to illustrate how refinement types can express simple authorization policies. When leaks due to information flows are a concern, FileRM would not include fread_simple in the API exposed to client programs. Clients would have to use fread instead, which augments fread_simple with information flow controls.

The encoding of information flow shown in FileRM is based on a model developed with the Fable calculus [21]. Information flow policies are specified and enforced by tagging sensitive data with *security labels* that record provenance. The type label (line 9) represents the provenance of data derived from one or more files, F x for data from file x, and J l1 l2 for data derived from the files in both l1 and l2. The dependent-type constructor tracked associates labels with data. For example, tracked string (F x) represents a string that originated from the file x. Importantly, tracked is defined as a private type. Client programs can only manipulate tracked values using functions that appear in the interface of FileRM, e.g., fmap, a functor that allows functions to be lifted into the tracked type and tensor, a combinator that treats the tracked type as an indexed applicative functor. Prior work on Fable showed that encodings of this style can be proved to correctly enforce security properties like noninterference.

Next, we define a type CanFlow and assumptions to describe a partial order on labels. The Lattice assumption states that the J constructor behaves as the least-upper-bound relation on a join semi-lattice and that flows are permissible from lower labels to higher ones. The Atomicflow assumption states that data can flow from a file f to a file g only if all principals that can read g can also read f. The types of fread and fwrite use these constructs to track information flow. The type of fread shows that the content of f is returned as a string tagged with its provenance, i.e., tracked string (F f). The type of fwrite requires that the string written to a file f has provenance l, where the refinement CanFlow y (F f) on the type of l requires it to only contain data visible to the readers of f.

Specific file permissions and a client program

```
 1  open Authentication, FileRM
 2  assume R_a: CanRead (U "Alice") "a.txt" &&
 3       (forall p:prin.CanRead p "a.txt" ⇒ p=U "Alice" || p=Admin)
 4  assume R_ab: CanRead (U "Alice") "ab.txt" && CanRead (U "Bob") "ab.txt" &&
 5       (forall p:prin.CanRead p "ab.txt" ⇒ p=U "Alice" || p=U "Bob" || p=Admin)
 6  val strcat: string → string → string
 7  let sudo (c:cred Admin) =
 8      let a, ab = fread Admin c "a.txt", fread Admin c "ab.txt" in
 9      let a_ab = tensor (F "a.txt") (F "ab.txt") (fmap strcat (F "a.txt") a) ab in
10          fwrite Admin c "a.txt" (J (F "a.txt") (F "ab.txt")) a_ab
```

Additional policy assumptions and client code. The code sample above includes axioms R_a and R_ab to define access permissions for some files. (We assume here that Sys.file and string are synonyms.) We also show a client program, sudo, which runs with the credentials of Admin, concatenates data from files a.txt and ab.txt, and writes the result to the file a.txt. In addition to Admin, the file a.txt is readable only by the user Alice and ab.txt only by Alice and Bob. Thus, sudo is secure since it writes to a.txt data that can be read by Alice and Admin. In contrast, if sudo were to write the result to ab.txt, the contents of a.txt are leaked to Bob, and this program should be detected as insecure.

At each call to fread, the solver appeals to AdminRW to show that Admin has read permission on the files. To concatenate tracked strings, we use the fmap and tensor operators from the FileRM API.[1] The type of a_ab is tracked string (J (F "a.txt") (F "ab.txt")). At line 10, we need to prove CanFlow (J (F "a.txt") (F "ab.txt")) (F "a.txt"), which is discharged automatically by Z3. Trying to write a_ab to ab.txt instead results in a type error.

---

[1] Our implementation currently lacks support for implicit parameters in function calls. Defining all label parameters to be implicit would produce more terse programs. For example, concatenation of tracked strings would read tensor (fmap strcat a) ab.

2.2   Stateful Authorization in the CONTINUE Conference Manager

We now present a more substantial example in FINE: a model of the CONTINUE conference management server. We first present a reference monitor ConfRM which mediates access to a database of paper submissions and reviews. Next, we show ConfPolicy, a set of policy axioms used to configure the reference monitor. Finally, we discuss ConfWeb, a web server processing requests and accessing the database via the reference monitor.

A model of stateful authorization. The design of the ConfRM reference monitor is based on a framework due to Dougherty et al. [7] for reasoning about the correctness of Datalog-style dynamic policies. This model specifies policies as inference rules that derive permissions from basic authorization attributes. For example, attributes may include assertions about a principal's role membership or the phase of the conference, and inference rules could grant permissions to principals depending on the current phase and role activations. Over time, whether due to a program's actions or due to external events, the set of authorization attributes can change. For example, to access a resource, a principal may alter the state of the authorization policy by activating a role; or, the PC chair can change the phase of the conference. In this state, the policy may grant a specific privilege to the principal, but a subsequent role deactivation revokes the privilege. Dougherty et al. show that this model captures many common policies and can be used to reason about policy correctness.

This model of stateful authorization can be represented directly in FINE. The type st represents the set of basic authorization attributes (line 10 in the listing on the next page). Attributes include values like Role (U "Alice") Author to represent a role activation, or values like Assigned r p to indicate that a paper p has been assigned to a reviewer r. The type perm represents permissions (the relations derived using inference rules from the basic authorization attributes). For example, Permit (U "Alice") (Submit p) represents a permission granted to an author. ConfRM also defines two propositions for stating invariants about the current state of the policy. Line 12 shows the type In, a proposition about list membership, e.g., In a s states that a is a member of the list s. We elide standard assumptions that axiomatize list membership, but show a simple recursive function check that decides list membership (line 13-15). The proposition Derivable s p (line 16) asserts that a permission p is derivable from the collection of authorization attributes s. We define two type abbreviations for refinements of the st type: rst<p> are those states in which p is derivable, and inst<a> are those states that include a.

For a flavor of refinement type checking, consider the check function. The essence of typing this function is proving that the true sub-expression can be given the type {b:bool | In a l}. We accomplish this by typing the value true in a context that records equalities between l and hd::tl (induced by the pattern match); an assumption that the expression (equals a hd) has the type {b:bool | b=true ⟺ a=hd} (by a type given to the built-in equals operator); an assumption that (equals a hd) evaluates to true (since we are typing the **then**-branch); and the axioms for list membership. We determine if the goal (In a l) is deducible from the assumptions by including the negation of the goal among the assumptions and requiring the solver to prove the resulting theory unsatisfiable.

Modeling state updates with affine types. The type constructor StateIs (line 19) addresses two concerns. A value of type StateIs s represents an assertion that s contains the current state of authorization facts. ConfRM uses this assertion to ensure the integrity of its authorization facts. StateIs is declared private, so untrusted clients cannot use the Sign constructor to forge StateIs assertions. Moreover, since the authorization state can change over time, FINE's type system provides a way to revoke StateIs assertions about stale states. For example, after a reviewer r has submitted a review for a paper p, we may add the fact Reviewed r p to the set of authorization facts s, revoke the assertion StateIs s, and use StateIs ((Reviewed r p)::s) instead.

A fragment of a reference monitor for a conference management server

```
 1  module ConfRM
 2  open Authentication
 3  type role = Author | Reviewer | Chair
 4  type phase = Submission | Reviewing | Meeting
 5  type paper = {id:int; title:string; author:prin; contents:string}
 6  type attr = Role : prin → role → attr | Assigned : prin → paper → attr
 7              | Phase : phase → attr | Reviewed : prin → paper → attr
 8  type action = Submit: paper → action | Review: paper → action
 9              | ReadScore: paper → action | CloseSub: action
10  type st = list attr
11  type perm = Permit : prin → action → perm
12  type In :: attr → st → ⋆
13  val check: a:attr → l:st → {b:bool | b=true ⇒ In a l}
14  let rec check a l = match l with [] → false
15                      | hd::tl → if equals a hd then true else check a tl
16  type Derivable :: st → perm → ⋆
17  type rst<p:perm> = {s:st | Derivable s p}
18  type inst<a:attr> = {s:st | In a s}
19  private type StateIs:: st → A = Sign: s:st → StateIs s
20  val submit: q:prin→ cred q→ p:paper→ s:rst<Permit q (Submit p)>→ StateIs s→ StateIs s
21  val review: r:prin → cred r → p:paper → q:string → s:rst<Permit r (Review p)> →
22              StateIs s → (s':inst<Reviewed r p> ∗ StateIs s')
23  val close_sub: c:prin → cred c → s:rst<Permit c CloseSub> →
24              StateIs s → (s':inst<Phase Reviewing> ∗ StateIs s')
```

FINE types are classified into two basic kinds: ⋆, the kind of normal types, and A, the kind of affine types. By declaring StateIs :: st → A we indicate that StateIs constructs an affine type from a value of type st. When the state of the authorization policy changes from s to t, ConfRM constructs a value Sign t to assert StateIs t, while destructing a StateIs s value to ensure that the assertion about the stale state s can never be used again.

An external API to the conference DB. Lines 20-24 show the types of functions exposed by ConfRM to clients. Using the refined state type rst<p>, the API ensures that each function is only called in states where the permission p is derivable. The submit function requires Permit q (Submit p) to be derivable in the state s. By returning StateIs s, the type of submit indicates that it does not change the authorization state. The review function allows a reviewer r to submit a review and then changes the authorization state to record the submission. The return type of review is a dependent pair consisting of a new list of authorization attributes s', and an assertion of type StateIs s' to indicate that s' is the new authorization state. The close_sub function has a similar type and allows the program chair to change the phase of the conference.

An example policy and a main event loop for the server

```
 1  module ConfPolicy : ConfRM
 2  let init:(s:st * StateIs s) = let a = [Role (U "Andy") Chair; ...] in (a, Sign a)
 3  assume C1: forall (q:prin), (p:paper), (s:st).
 4     In (Phase Submission) s && In (Role q Author) s ⇒ Derivable s (Permit q (Submit p))
 5  assume C2: forall (r:prin), (p:paper), (s:st).
 6     In (Phase Reviewing) s && In (Assigned r p) s ⇒ Derivable s (Permit r (Review p))
 7  assume ...
 8  (* Main event loop *)
 9  module ConfWeb
10  open Authentication, ConfRM, ConfPolicy
11  let rec loop s = match get_request() with
12   | Submit_paper q credq paper → let (a,tok) = s in
13      if (check (Phase Submission) a) and (check (Role q Author) a) then
14        let s1 = submit q credq paper a tok in
15        let _ = resp "Thanks for your submission!" in loop (a, s1)
16      else let _ = resp "Submissions are closed, or you are not an author." in loop (a,tok)
17   | Submit_review r credr paper review → ...
18  let _ = loop ConfPolicy.init
```

A sample policy. The module ConfPolicy above configures the ConfRM reference monitor with policy assumptions. At line 2, we show init, an initial collection of authorization attributes a, signed to attest that a is the authorization state. The Sign data constructor requires the privilege of ConfRM—FINE's module system grants this privilege to ConfPolicy using the notation **module** ConfPolicy : ConfRM, which allows ConfPolicy to use the private constructors of ConfRM. The assumptions C1-C2 show how permissions can be derived from authorization attributes—different conferences can use the same ConfRM but get different enforcement semantics by using different policy files.

An event loop to handle web requests. Finally, we show fragments from ConfWeb, a program that handles web requests to the conference management site. The main event loop of ConfWeb waits for a request (type elided). If principal q wishes to submit a paper, we check that the conference is in the Submission phase, and that q is registered in the role of an Author. We give the built-in boolean operator and the type $x:bool \rightarrow y:bool \rightarrow \{z:bool \mid z=true \Leftrightarrow x=true \&\& y=true\}$. We can use this type, the type of check, and assumption C1, to refine the type of the current state a in the **then**-branch to rst<Permit q (Submit paper)>.

2.3   Elements of FINE that Enable Stateful Programming

Before proceeding to a formal semantics for FINE, we discuss a number of elements in the design of FINE that facilitate, and in some cases simplify, stateful programming.

Non-affine state simplifies programming. Programming with affine types can be difficult, since affine variables can never be used more than once. Our approach of using an affine assertion StateIs s to track the current authorization state minimizes the difficulty. Importantly, the collection of authorization facts s is itself not affine and can be freely used several times, e.g., s is used in several calls to check. Non-affine state also enables writing functions like check, which, if s was affine, would destroy the state of the program. Only the affine token, tok:StateIs s, must be used with care, to ensure that it is not duplicated.

Non-affine refinements simplify automated proofs. Even ignoring the inability of prior languages to handle stateful policies, the proof terms required for our examples in languages like Fable or Aura would be extremely unwieldy. By ensuring that refinement formulas always apply to non-affine values, our proof system is kept tractable, allowing us to use Z3 to automatically discharge proof obligations. A naïve combination of dependent and affine types would allow refinements to apply to affine values, necessitating an embedding of linear logic in Z3. Our approach avoids this complication, while retaining the ability to refine the changing state of a program with logical formulas.

Affine types enable flexible mixing of stateful and pure code. Another approach to working with stateful policies could be to use an abstract monad. FINE's module system certainly supports programming in this style. However, affine types afford greater flexibility. For example, rather than monadically threading a monolithic store through the program, FINE programs can partition the state and pass only the relevant parts of the store to functions that need it. We use this idiom to good effect in one of our benchmark programs (FileAutomaton in §4), in which a bit of state representing the current state of a file is associated with the file handle rather than using a monolithic store to maintain the state of all file handles. Another benchmark, a model of an email client, uses affine types to model capabilities [15] that grant programs restricted access to certain sensitive stateful operations, such as sending emails.

3   Formalizing FINE

Our compiler translates FINE programs in type-preserving manner to .NET bytecode (CIL) [8]. Although we do not report on our type-preservation results in this paper, this design plays a significant role in various aspects of FINE's type system. This section formalizes FINE, presents a soundness result for the type system, and an information-hiding property for the module system. We begin by presenting a core syntax for FINE.

3.1   Core Syntax

Our formulation of FINE's module system is based on Grossman et al's [11] syntactic approach to type abstraction. In this formulation, module names correspond to "principals" and are ranged over by the meta-variables p, q, and r. Source expressions are annotated with the names of the modules to which they belong—in the form $\langle e \rangle_p$, the expression e delimited within brackets is privileged to use p's private types concretely. A principal constant is denoted p, and we include two distinguished principals: $\top$ includes the privileges of all other principals, and $\bot$ has no privileges. Values are partitioned into families corresponding to principals. A pre-value for code with p-privilege, u_p, is a variable or a fully-applied data constructor D. Values for p are either its pre-values, abstractions, or pre-values u_q for some other principal q, enclosed within brackets to denote that u_q carries q-privilege. The dynamic semantics of FINE (§3.3) tracks the privilege associated with an expression using these brackets and allows us to prove (§3.4) that programs without p-privilege treat p-values abstractly.

Core syntax of FINE

$p, q, r ::= \mathsf{p} \mid \top \mid \bot$	principals
$u_p ::= x \mid D\,\bar{\tau}\,\bar{v}_p$	pre p-values
$v_p ::= u_p \mid \lambda x{:}\tau.e \mid \Lambda\alpha{::}\kappa.e \mid \langle u_q \rangle_q$	p-values
$e ::= v_p \mid \mathsf{let}\ x = e_1\ \mathsf{in}\ e_2 \mid \mathsf{fix}\ f{:}\tau.e \mid v_p\,v_q \mid v_p\,\tau \mid \langle e \rangle_p$	terms
$\quad\quad \mathsf{match}\ v_p\ \mathsf{with}\ D\,\bar{\tau}\,\bar{x} \to e_1\ \mathsf{else}\ e_2$	
$\tau, \phi ::= \alpha \mid x{:}\tau \to \tau' \mid \forall\alpha{::}\kappa.\tau \mid \{x{:}\tau \mid \phi\} \mid !\tau \mid T \mid \tau\,\tau' \mid \tau\,v_p$	types
$\kappa ::= \star \mid \mathsf{A} \mid \star \to \kappa \mid \mathsf{A} \to \kappa \mid \tau \to \kappa$	kinds
$S ::= T{::}\kappa \mid D{:}(p, \tau) \mid p \sqsubseteq q \mid S, S' \mid \cdot$	signature
$\Gamma ::= \alpha{::}\kappa \mid x{:}(p, \tau) \mid v_p \doteq v'_p \mid \Gamma, \Gamma' \mid \cdot$	type env.

Expressions e are standard for a polymorphic lambda calculus. Types τ include dependent function types $x{:}\tau \to \tau'$, where x names the formal parameter and is bound in τ'. Polymorphic types $\forall\alpha{::}\kappa.\tau$ decorate the abstracted type variable α with its kind κ. Refinement types are written $\{x{:}\tau \mid \phi\}$, where ϕ is a type in which x is bound. An affine qualifier can be attached to a type using $!\tau$. Type constructors T can be applied to other types using $\tau\,\tau'$ or terms using $\tau\,v_p$. Note that type-level terms are always values, not expressions—this restriction explains our use of A-normal form [10] for the expression language. This form allows every intermediate result to be named and for these names to appear, potentially, as type indices. Types are partitioned into normal types (kind $\star$) and affine types (kind A). Type constructors T construct types of kind κ from normal types ($\star \to \kappa$), affine types ($\mathsf{A} \to \kappa$), or τ-typed terms ($\tau \to \kappa$). Although included in our implementation, for simplicity, our formalization omits dependent pairs.

Desugaring FINE **modules.** The type and data constructor declarations in a FINE module are desugared to a signature S. The type constructors of the Authentication module of §2.1, for example, are desugared to prin::$\star$ and cred::prin $\to \star$. Data constructors D are associated their type, as well as the privilege p required for their use. For example, the constructors of the prin type are U:($\bot$, string $\to$ prin) and Admin:($\bot$, prin), indicating that these may be used freely in unprivileged code. In contrast, being declared **private**, the constructor of the cred type is desugared to Auth : (Authentication, p:prin $\to$ cred p), indicating that it may only be used in code marked with the privilege of the Authentication module. Additionally, signatures use $p \sqsubseteq q$ to record a partial order among principals, with $\bot \sqsubseteq p \sqsubseteq \top$, for all p. We use this to represent sharing between modules, as achieved by the ConfPolicy : ConfRM declaration from §2.2. This is translated to the relation ConfRM $\sqsubseteq$ ConfPolicy, to indicate that ConfPolicy holds the privileges of ConfRM (and, in particular, can use ConfRM's private data constructors).

Desugaring formulas and assumptions. Refinement formulas and assumptions are represented using type and data constructors, respectively. For example, we use type constructors like And::$\star \to \star \to \star$ to represent the logical connectives. We model equality by specializing it to each type, e.g., Eq_bool::bool $\to$ bool $\to \star$. A polymorphic treatment of equality poses no fundamental difficulty, but we use a monomorphic treatment here for simplicity. Quantification is represented using the binders in dependent functions and pairs. For example, the AdminRW assumption from §2.1 is desugared to AdminRW : $(\bot$, f:file $\to$ And (CanRead Admin f) (CanWrite Admin f)). Note that assumptions are always public—we leave an exploration of private assumptions to future work.

Well-formedness conditions on data constructors. The soundness of FINE's type system relies on some restrictions on the use of data constructors D. We mention these restrictions briefly here, but space constraints leave their formalization and further discussion to a technical report [20]. First, we disallow partial application of data constructors as this complicates our translation to CIL. Next, we require the type of each data constructor to be of the form: $\forall \bar{\alpha}::\bar{\kappa}.x_1:\tau_1 \to \ldots \to x_n:\tau_n \to \tau$, i.e., we require any type arguments to precede any term arguments, although each term argument $x_i:\tau_i$ may itself contain quantifiers. This restriction is merely a convenience—it simplifies the shape of our pattern matching constructs. Finally, for each data constructor D with a type as shown above, we require $\bar{\alpha} \subseteq$ Free-type-variables(τ), i.e., every type argument must appear as an index on the constructed type τ. This is a more significant restriction and is necessary for showing that well-typed programs enjoy a type-erasure property.

3.2 Static Semantics

The static semantics makes use of a typing environment Γ, which binds type and term variables, and records the results of pattern matching tests using $v_p \doteq v'_p$. Variables x, like data constructors, are associated with a principal p representing the privilege required for their use.

Well-formedness of kinds: $S \vdash_i k$, and kinding of types: $S; \Gamma \vdash \tau :: \kappa$
Where, $i ::= \cdot \mid 1$, and $\star \leq \star$, $A \leq A$, $\star \leq A$

$$\frac{}{S \vdash \cdot \star} \qquad \frac{}{S \vdash_i A} \qquad \frac{S \vdash_i \kappa}{S \vdash_i \star \to \kappa} \qquad \frac{S \vdash_1 \kappa}{S \vdash_i A \to \kappa} \qquad \frac{S; \cdot \vdash \tau :: \star \quad S \vdash_i \kappa}{S \vdash_i \tau \to \kappa}$$

$$\frac{}{S; \Gamma \vdash \alpha :: \Gamma(\alpha)}\text{(K1)} \qquad \frac{}{S; \Gamma \vdash T :: S(T)}\text{(K2)} \qquad \frac{S; \Gamma \vdash \tau :: \star}{S; \Gamma \vdash !\tau :: A}\text{(K3)}$$

$$\frac{S; \Gamma, \alpha:\kappa \vdash \tau :: \kappa' \quad \kappa, \kappa' \in \{\star, A\}}{S; \Gamma \vdash \forall \alpha::\kappa.\tau :: \star}\text{(K4)} \qquad \frac{S; \Gamma \vdash \tau_1 :: \kappa \quad \kappa \leq \kappa' \quad S; \Gamma, x:(p, \tau_1) \vdash \tau_2 :: \kappa'}{S; \Gamma \vdash x:\tau_1 \to \tau_2 :: \star}\text{(K5)} \qquad \frac{S; \Gamma \vdash \tau_1 :: \kappa' \to \kappa \quad S; \Gamma \vdash \tau_2 :: \kappa'}{S; \Gamma \vdash \tau_1 \, \tau_2 :: \kappa}\text{(K6)}$$

$$\frac{S; \Gamma \vdash \tau_1 :: \tau \to \kappa \quad S; \Gamma; \cdot \vdash_\top v_p : \tau}{S; \Gamma \vdash \tau_1 \, v_p :: \kappa}\text{(K7)} \qquad \frac{S; \Gamma \vdash \tau :: \star \quad S; \Gamma, x:(p, \tau) \vdash \phi :: \star}{S; \Gamma \vdash \{x:\tau \mid \phi\} :: \star}\text{(K8)}$$

The first judgment $S \vdash_i \kappa$, shown above, defines a well-formedness relation on kinds. This judgment establishes two properties. First, types constructed from affine types must themselves be affine—this is standard [24]. Without this restriction, an affine value can be stored in a non-affine value and be used more than once. To enforce this property, we index the judgment using $i ::= \cdot \mid 1$, and when checking a kind $A \rightarrow \kappa$, we require κ to finally produce an A-kinded type. The second restriction, enforced by the first premise $(S; \cdot \vdash \tau :: \star)$ of the last rule, ensures that only non-affine values appear in a dependent type. Note that we omit higher kinds (e.g., $(\star \rightarrow \star) \rightarrow \star$) as these are not easily translated to CIL.

The judgment $S; \Gamma \vdash \tau :: \kappa$ states that τ has kind κ. Types inhabited by terms always have kind $\star$ or A. (K3) rules out "doubly-affine" types $(!!\tau)$. (K4) allows abstraction only over $\star$ and A-kinded types. (K5) requires that the type τ_1 of a function's parameter always have kind $\star$ or A and that functions with affine arguments produce affine results, both captured by an auxiliary relation on kinds, $\kappa \leq \kappa'$. (K7) checks the well-formedness of dependent types. As in Aura and RCF, we restrict type-level terms to values e.g., Eq_bool (true && false) false is not a well-formed type. This restriction reduces expressiveness by ruling out type-level computations, but greatly simplifies the compilation to CIL. The second premise of (K7) uses the typing judgment—we describe it shortly. (K8) only allows non-affine types τ to be refined by non-affine formulas ϕ.

Expression typing: $S; \Gamma; X \vdash_p e : \tau$

Where, $X ::= \cdot \mid x, X; \quad Q(X, \tau) = !\tau, Q(\cdot, \tau) = \tau; \quad$ and $?\tau$ denotes τ or $!\tau$

$$\frac{S(D) = (p, \tau)}{S; \Gamma; \cdot \vdash_p D : \tau}\text{(T1)} \quad \frac{\Gamma(x) = (p, \tau) \quad S; \Gamma \vdash \tau :: \star}{S; \Gamma; \cdot \vdash_p x : \tau}\text{(T2)} \quad \frac{\Gamma(x) = (p, \tau)}{S; \Gamma; x \vdash_p x : \tau}\text{(T3)}$$

$$\frac{q \sqsubseteq p \in S \quad S; \Gamma; X \vdash_q e : \tau}{S; \Gamma; X, X' \vdash_p e : \tau}\text{(T4)} \quad \frac{S; \Gamma \vdash \tau :: \star \quad S; \Gamma, f{:}(p, \tau); \cdot \vdash_p v_p : \tau}{S; \Gamma; \cdot \vdash_p \text{fix } f{:}\tau.v_p : \tau}\text{(T5)}$$

$$\frac{\begin{array}{c}S; \Gamma \vdash \tau_1 :: \kappa \quad \kappa \in \{\star, A\} \\ S; \Gamma, x{:}(p, \tau_1); X, x \vdash_p e : \tau_2\end{array}}{S; \Gamma; X \vdash_p \lambda x{:}\tau_1.e : Q(X, x{:}\tau_1 \rightarrow \tau_2)}\text{(T6)} \quad \frac{\begin{array}{c}\kappa \in \{\star, A\} \\ S; \Gamma, \alpha{::}\kappa; X \vdash_p e : \tau'\end{array}}{S; \Gamma; X \vdash_p \Lambda\alpha{::}\kappa.e : Q(X, \forall\alpha{::}\kappa.\tau')}\text{(T7)}$$

$$\frac{\begin{array}{c}S; \Gamma; X \vdash_p e_1 : \tau_1 \quad S; \Gamma \vdash \tau_2 :: \kappa \\ S; \Gamma, x{:}(p, \tau_1); X', x \vdash_p e_2 : \tau_2\end{array}}{S; \Gamma; X, X' \vdash_p \text{let } x = e_1 \text{ in } e_2 : \tau_2}\text{(T8)} \quad \frac{\begin{array}{c}S; \Gamma; X \vdash_p v_q : ?x{:}\tau_1 \rightarrow \tau_2 \\ S; \Gamma; X' \vdash_p v_r : \tau_1\end{array}}{S; \Gamma; X, X' \vdash_p v_q \, v_r : \tau_2[v_r/x]}\text{(T9)}$$

$$\frac{S; \Gamma; X \vdash_p v_q : ?\forall\alpha{::}\kappa.\tau \quad S; \Gamma \vdash \tau' :: \kappa}{S; \Gamma; X \vdash_p v_q \, \tau' : \tau[\tau'/\alpha]}\text{(T10)} \quad \frac{S; \Gamma; X \vdash_q e : \tau}{S; \Gamma; X \vdash_p \langle e \rangle_q : \tau}\text{(T11)}$$

$$\frac{\begin{array}{c}S; \Gamma; X \vdash_p v_q : \tau' \quad S; \Gamma, \bar{x}{:}(\bar{p}, \bar{\tau}_x); \bar{x} \vdash_p D \, \bar{\tau} \, \bar{x} : \tau'' \quad S; \Gamma \vdash \text{unify}(\tau', \tau'') : \bar{x} \doteq \bar{v} \\ S; \Gamma, \bar{x}{:}(\bar{p}, \bar{\tau}_x), \bar{x} \doteq \bar{v}, v_q \doteq D \, \bar{\tau} \, \bar{x}; X', \bar{x} \vdash_p e_1 : \tau \quad S; \Gamma; X' \vdash_p e_2 : \tau\end{array}}{S; \Gamma; X, X' \vdash_p \text{match } v_q \text{ with } D \, \bar{\tau} \, \bar{x} \rightarrow e_1 \text{ else } e_2 : \tau}\text{(T12)}$$

$$\frac{S; \Gamma; X \vdash_p v_q : \tau \quad S; \Gamma \vdash \tau :: \star}{S; \Gamma; X \vdash_p v_q : \{x{:}\tau \mid x = v_q\}}\text{(T13)} \quad \frac{S; \Gamma; X \vdash_q e : \tau' \quad S; \Gamma \vdash \tau' <: \tau}{S; \Gamma; X, X' \vdash_p e : \tau}\text{(T14)}$$

The typing judgment $S; \Gamma; X \vdash_p e : \tau$ above states that an expression e, when typed with the privilege of principal p in an environment Γ and signature S, has type τ. The set X records a subset of the variables in Γ, and each element of X represents a capability to use an assumption in Γ. The rule (T1) requires data constructors to be used only in code granted the appropriate privilege. In the second premise of (T12), we type check a pattern $D \bar{\tau} \bar{x}$ to ensure that data constructors are also destructed in a context with the appropriate privilege.

In (T2) we type a non-affine variable x by looking up its type in the environment and checking that the privilege of the context matches that of the variable. (T3) is similar, but additionally allows an affine variable to be used only when a capability for its use appears in X. Unlike linear typing, affine assumptions need not always be used. (T4) allows an arbitrary number of assumptions X' to be forgotten, and for e to be checked with a privilege q that is not greater than privilege p that it has been granted. An expression is granted privilege by enclosing it in angle brackets, as shown in (T11).

Returning to the second premise of (K7), we check a type-level term v_p with the privilege of $\top$. The intuition is that in well-typed programs, type-level terms have no operational significance and, as such, cannot violate information-hiding. We also check v_p in (K7) with an empty set of capabilities X. According to the well-formedness rule of kind $\tau \rightarrow \kappa$, no well-formed type constructors can be applied to an affine value, so a type-level term like v_p never uses an affine assumption.

In (T5), we require fixed variables f to be given a non-affine type, and for the recursive expression to not capture any affine assumptions. In (T6), we check that the type of the formal parameter is well-formed, and type check the body in an extended context. We record the privilege p of the program point at which the variable x was introduced to ensure that x is not destructed in unprivileged code in the function-body e. In the conclusion of (T6), we use the auxiliary function $Q(X, \tau)$, which attaches an affine qualifier to τ if the function captures any affine assumptions from its environment. (T7) is similar. Typing let-expressions is standard, with the addition that the second premise of (T8) ensures that the let-bound variable x does not escape its scope in the type τ_2. When typing an application $v_q \; v_r$ in (T9), we split the affine assumptions among the sub-terms. We allow v_q to be a possibly affine function type—the shorthand $?\tau$ captures this, and we use the same notation in (T10).

We illustrate pattern-matching using an example from FileRM. Consider matching a value v_q of type tracked string (F file) against a pattern L string x y. When checking the true-branch, we record several term equalities that capture the runtime behavior of pattern matching. These assumptions will be used by our theorem prover in discharging proofs of refinement formulas (via the type conversion relation, discussed shortly). In our example, one such equality assumption is, clearly, $v_q \doteq$ L string x y. However, with FINE's value-indexed types, we can also infer equalities for some of the pattern-bound variables. In particular, by unifying the type of the scrutinee, tracked string (F file), with the type of the pattern, tracked string y, we can infer $y \doteq$ F file.

In (T12), we split the affine assumptions between v_q and the branches. In the second premise, we type the pattern and in the third premise, unify the type of the scrutinee with the type of the pattern to compute equalities among the term indices—the definition of the unification judgment is standard and we omit it from our presentation. The fourth premise checks e_1 with the computed equality assumptions. The last premise checks e_2 with no additional assumptions. A variation in which e_2 is checked with a disequality **forall** $\bar{x}.v_q \neq D \; \bar{\tau} \; \bar{x}$ is also feasible. However, in practice, we use n-way exhaustive pattern matching (**match** x **with** P1 $\rightarrow$ e1 ... Pn $\rightarrow$ en) and derive disequalities by relying on axioms that discriminate data constructors, e.g., **forall** $D_1, D_2, \bar{x}_1, \bar{x}_2, \bar{\tau}_1, \bar{\tau}_2.D_1 \neq D_2 \Rightarrow D_1\bar{\tau}_1\bar{x}_1 \neq D_2\bar{\tau}_2\bar{x}_2$.

We use (T13) to give values a precise singleton type using an equality refinement. This is useful in bootstrapping the type conversion relation, used in the second premise of (T14), and defined below. Type conversion $S; \Gamma \vdash \tau <: \tau'$ is a reflexive, transitive relation without any structural rules, e.g., contra- and co-variant subtyping in function types. The type system of CIL uses nominal subtyping, and structural rules of this form are not easily translated. The rule (S3) is our interface to the solver—we discuss this with an example shortly. The rule (S4) treats a refined type as a subtype of the underlying type. Type conversion includes an equivalence relation on types $S; \Gamma \vdash \tau \cong \tau'$. In this judgment, (E5) allows a type-level term v_p to be equated with v'_p when an assumption $v_p \doteq v'_p$ appears in the context.

Type conversion: $S; \Gamma \vdash \tau <: \tau'$, $S; \Gamma \vdash \tau \cong \tau'$ and $S; \Gamma \vdash e \cong e'$
Where $S; \Gamma \models \phi$ is the first-order logic entailment relation

$$\frac{S; \Gamma \vdash \tau_1 \cong \tau_2}{S; \Gamma \vdash \tau_1 <: \tau_2}(S1) \qquad \frac{S; \Gamma \vdash \tau_1 <: \tau_2 \quad S; \Gamma \vdash \tau_2 <: \tau_3}{S; \Gamma \vdash \tau_1 <: \tau_3}(S2) \qquad \frac{S; \Gamma \vdash \tau <: \tau' \quad S; \Gamma, x:(p,\tau) \models \phi}{S; \Gamma \vdash \tau <: \{x:\tau' \mid \phi\}}(S3)$$

$$\frac{}{S; \Gamma \vdash \{x:\tau \mid \phi\} <: \tau}(S4) \qquad \frac{}{S; \Gamma \vdash \tau \cong \tau}(E1) \qquad \frac{}{S; \Gamma \vdash v_p \cong v_p}(E2)$$

$$\frac{S; \Gamma \vdash \tau_1 \cong \tau'_1 \quad S; \Gamma \vdash \tau_2 \cong \tau'_2}{S; \Gamma \vdash \tau_1 \tau_2 \cong \tau'_1 \tau'_2}(E3) \qquad \frac{S; \Gamma \vdash \tau_1 \cong \tau'_1 \quad S; \Gamma \vdash v_p \cong v'_p}{S; \Gamma \vdash \tau_1 v_p \cong \tau'_1 v'_p}(E4)$$

$$\frac{v_p \doteq v'_p \in \Gamma \vee v'_p \doteq v_p \in \Gamma}{S; \Gamma \vdash v_p \cong v'_p}(E5) \qquad \frac{\forall i,j \quad S; \Gamma \vdash \tau_i \cong \tau'_i \quad S; \Gamma \vdash v_j \cong v'_j}{S; \Gamma \vdash D \, \bar{\tau} \, \bar{v} \cong D \, \bar{\tau}' \, \bar{v}'}(E6)$$

The key rule in type conversion related to refinement typing is (S3). This rule allows a type τ to be promoted to a refined type $\{x:\tau' \mid \phi\}$ when τ is a subtype of τ', and when our solver can deduce the formula ϕ from the typing context. The entailment relation $S; \Gamma \models \phi$ is standard—we illustrate its behavior using an example from §2.2. When typing the main loop of ConfWeb, we are required to construct a derivation of the form $S; \Gamma \vdash s : \{x:st \mid \text{In } a \, x\}$, where (dropping principals for clarity) $\Gamma = s:st, a:attr, b:\{x:bool \mid x=true \Rightarrow \text{In } a \, s\}, b \doteq true$. We construct this derivation by using (T14) with (T13) in the first premise to derive $S; \Gamma \vdash s : \{x:st \mid x=s\}$, and a derivation of $S; \Gamma \vdash \{x:st \mid x=s\} <: \{x:st \mid \text{In } a \, x\}$ in the second premise. This latter derivation proceeds by using (S3), where we deduce $S; \Gamma, x:\{x:st \mid x=s\} \models \text{In } a \, x$ by using Z3 to show that the theory $(s:st, a:attr, b:bool, b=true \Rightarrow \text{In } a \, s, b=true, x:st, x=s, \text{not}(\text{In } a \, x))$ is unsatisfiable. Importantly, FINE's type system ensures that the theories we generate never contain any affine assumptions, thus eliminating the need for a linear logic prover.

3.3 Dynamic Semantics

The operational semantics of FINE is instrumented to account for two program properties. First, our semantics places affinely typed values in a memory M. Reads from the memory are destructive—this allows us to prove that in well-typed programs, affine values are never used more than once. The semantics also tracks the privilege of expressions by propagating brackets through reductions, which is useful in showing an information-hiding property for our module system. The main judgment is written $(M, e) \overset{p}{\leadsto} (M', e')$, and states that given an initial memory M an expression e steps to e' and updates the memory to M'. The p-superscript indicates that e steps while using the privilege of the principal p. The omitted rules include reductions for let-bindings, standard beta-reduction for type and term applications, unrolling of fixed points, and pattern matching.

Dynamic semantics (selected rules)

Where a memory $M ::= (x, v_p), M \mid \cdot$

$$\langle v_p \rangle_p \overset{p}{\leadsto} v_p \quad \text{(R1)} \qquad \langle \langle v_q \rangle_q \rangle_r \overset{p}{\leadsto} \langle v_q \rangle_q \quad \text{(R2)} \qquad \langle \lambda x{:}\tau.e \rangle_q \overset{p}{\leadsto} \lambda y{:}\tau.\langle e[\langle y \rangle_p / x] \rangle_q \quad \text{(R3)}$$

$$\frac{e \overset{q}{\leadsto} e'}{\langle e \rangle_q \overset{p}{\leadsto} \langle e' \rangle_q} \text{(R4)} \qquad \frac{S; \cdot; \cdot \vdash v_p : \tau \quad S; \cdot \vdash \tau :: \mathrm{A}}{M' = M, (x, v_q) \quad x \text{ fresh}}{M, v_p \overset{p}{\leadsto} M', x} \text{(R5)} \qquad \frac{M = M_1, (x, v_q), M_2}{M, x \overset{p}{\leadsto} (M_1, M_2), v_q} \text{(R6)}$$

Reduction rules that do not involve reading from or writing to memory are written $e \overset{p}{\leadsto} e'$. All the interesting rules that manage privileges and brackets fall into this fragment. Redundant brackets around p-values can be removed using (R1). However, not all nested brackets can be removed, as (R2) shows. In (R3), a λ-binder is extruded from a function with q-privilege so that it can be applied to a p-value. We have to be careful to enclose occurrences of the bound variable in e within p-brackets, to ensure that e treats its argument abstractly. Finally, (R4) allows evaluation to proceed under a bracket $\langle \cdot \rangle_q$ with q-privilege. The rules (R5) and (R6) model memory operations. The rule (R5) is applicable non-deterministically. It allocates a new location x for an affine value v_p into the memory M and replaces v_p with x. When a location x is in destruct position, (R6) reads a value v_p from M and deletes x.

Theorem 1 establishes the soundness of FINE through the standard progress and preservation lemmas. In the statement below, all free variables are implicitly universally quantified. Additionally, we say that a memory M is typeable with an environment $S; \Gamma$, if $S; \cdot; \cdot \vdash_p M(x) : \Gamma(x)$, for each location $x \in dom(M)$. In addition to showing that well-typed programs do not go wrong, our soundness result guarantees that affine values are destructed at most once—a result that shows that state changes are modeled accurately. The proof appears in our technical report [20].

Theorem 1 (Soundness): *For all well-formed signatures S; environments Γ; non-values e; and memories M typeable with $S; \Gamma$, the following statements are true:*

1) *If $S; \Gamma; dom(M) \vdash_p e : \tau$ then there exists M', e' such that $M, e \overset{p}{\leadsto} M', e'$.*
2) *If $S; \Gamma; X \vdash_p e : \tau$ and $M, e \overset{p}{\leadsto} M', e'$ for some p, M', e', and $X \subseteq dom(M)$; then, there exists Γ', X' such that $S; \Gamma'; X' \vdash_p e' : \tau$ and M' is typeable with $S; \Gamma'$. Furthermore, for $\Delta_X = (dom(M) \cup dom(M')) \setminus (dom(M) \cap dom(M'))$ if $dom(M') \supseteq dom(M)$ then $X' = X \cup \Delta_X$; otherwise $X' = X \setminus \Delta_X$.*

3.4 Reasoning about the Security of FINE Programs

FINE allows programmers to specify conditions for correct policy enforcement and the type system checks that these conditions are satisfied. But, the onus is on the programmer to get these specifications right. For example, in the FileRM module of §2.1, wrongly assuming **(forall** p:prin. CanRead p f $\Rightarrow$ CanRead p g) $\Rightarrow$ CanFlow (F f) (F g) (instead of the Atomicflow assumption) would destroy any meaningful confidentiality property intended for FileRM to enforce. Similarly, in the Authentication module, forgetting to declare the cred type **private** would allow adversaries to forge credentials. In neither case would FINE's type checker complain. However, the metatheory of FINE provides a useful set of primitives using which an expert can prove high-level security properties. In prior work on the Fable calculus, we adopted a similar approach and showed how the metatheory of Fable could be used to prove high-level security properties (e.g., noninterference) for encodings of information flow, provenance tracking, and role-based access control. We anticipate a similar strategy being effective for FINE. Additionally, in §4, we discuss how tools like model checkers can complement FINE and be used to establish that FINE programs correctly enforce high-level security goals.

In addition to type soundness, the metatheory of FINE yields two general purpose security properties—proofs appear in our technical report. The first, corresponding to a secrecy property, is value abstraction. The theorem below states that a program e without p-privilege cannot distinguish p-values. As a corollary, we can also derive an integrity property, namely that a program without p-privilege cannot manufacture a p-value to influence the behavior of code with p-privilege. Note that this theorem appeals only to the pure fragment of our reduction rules—affine typing plays no special role in value abstraction. Additionally, observe that this result applies to selective information sharing/hiding between multiple principals, as FINE's module system includes a lattice of principals ordered by the $p \sqsubseteq q$ relation. Finally, although this theorem applies to the abstraction of a single value from the p module exported at type τ, the program e can contain code from several principals.

Theorem 2 (Value abstraction): *For well-formed signatures S and non-values e, if e uses a p-value x but is well-typed without p-privilege, (i.e., $S; x{:}(p, \tau); x \vdash_q e : \tau'$ and $p \sqsubseteq q \notin S$) and, except for $\langle x \rangle_p$, e is free of r-brackets $\langle \cdot \rangle_r$, for any r where $p \sqsubseteq r \in S$; then, for any pair of τ-typed values v_p^1 and v_p^2, (i.e., $S; \cdot; \cdot \vdash_p v_p^i : \tau, i \in \{1, 2\}$) such that $e[v_p^1/x] \xrightarrow{q} e_1$, there exists e' such that $e_1 = e'[v_p^1/x]$ and $e[v_p^2/x] \xrightarrow{q} e'[v_p^2/x]$.*

4 Compiler Implementation and Application Experience

We have implemented a prototype compiler, currently approximately 20,000 lines of F# code extending a front-end and IL generation libraries derived from the F# compiler [23]. The type-preserving translation of FINE to CIL accounts for a significant fraction of the complexity. Our compiler currently generates .NET assemblies that allow FINE programs to easily interface with modules defined in F#. Interoperability with the rest of .NET allows us to write only security critical parts of an application in FINE, leaving the rest to other, more commonly used languages.

The table below shows several small reference monitors in FINE, their size, the number of proof obligations generated during type checking, and parsing and type checking time (on 3.2 GHz Pentium Core Duo desktop running Windows Vista). Most benchmarks contain dense security critical code, where nearly every function call demands proving refinement formulas. Our results show that using an external solver to discharge these proofs (as opposed to constructing them by hand as in Fable or Aura) is critical for practical programming. We expect the checking time to improve significantly as we move from naïve representations of typing environments (currently association lists) to more efficient data structures.

Name	LOC	# pf. obl.	parsing/type checker time (s)
AuthAC	34	1	0.28
FileRM	120	36	1.64
FileAutomaton	121	3	0.45
IFlow	127	22	0.84
HealthWeb	318	19	6.41
DynDKAL	336	34	1.26
Lookout	519	23	2.73
ConfRM and ConfWeb	647	57	4.01
ProofLib	9943	0	19.28
Total	2222 (+ 9943)	195	17.62 (+ 19.28)

4.1 Modeling CONTINUE

Our most substantial example is the modeling of the security policy of CONTINUE. CONTINUE's authors provided us with a specification of its policy, partly in natural language and partly as specification in the Alloy modeling language [12]. Starting from this specification, we implemented ConfRM to enforce a policy that contains 9 phases and 12 actions. Policy assumptions in ConfPolicy describe when each action is permissible, and a function exposed in the external interface of ConfRM (with a suitable refinement type on the state) mediates access to this action. In addition, each action corresponds to a particular web request handled by ConfWeb.

A significant fragment of the Alloy specification for CONTINUE is devoted to specifying validity conditions on the authorization state. For example, in any given state, validity requires the assignment of papers to reviewers to respect the conflict of interest constraints. We found it relatively straightforward to express several of these validity constraints, although our implementation has yet to cover all the features of CONTINUE's specification. One simplifying assumption we make is that there is a unique phase for the entire conference. In contrast, the Alloy specification associates a phase with each paper, and different papers can be in different phases at any given time. Extending our attr type to account for this complexity is possible, though we have yet to implement this.

Our experience with CONTINUE illustrates an important aspect of FINE. Tools like Alloy are useful for reasoning abstractly about policies and establishing that these correctly specify high-level security goals. However, the abstract analysis of policies in Alloy is disconnected from system implementations that are expected to enforce these policies. FINE, in contrast, does not attempt to validate policies, but provides assurance that system implementations properly enforce their policy specifications. We view these two approaches as complementary and expect their combination to be a potent tool for security analysis of system implementations. For example, the Alloy specification includes assertions to check that no sequence of actions allows a principal to read or write a review when there is a conflict of interest. We plan to investigate using the metatheory of FINE and the types of ConfRM, in conjunction with a tool like Alloy, to prove such facts of our implementation.

4.2 Other Benchmarks

The benchmark FileRM extends the example from §2.1 to account for confidentiality and integrity concerns when tracking information flow. Recall that in FileRM the lattice of security labels was derived from a specification of access control permissions using the Atomicflow assumption. To type check FileRM using Z3, we needed to rewrite the AtomicFlow assumption to the form shown below. To reason about formulas that use nested quantifiers, Z3 relies on a pattern-based instantiation mechanism that requires all bound variables (p in Atomicflow) to be guarded by non-equality predicates. Note that this is not a fundamental limitation of FINE. We are currently investigating the use of first-order solvers to reason directly about quantified formulas without this restriction. For example, a customized version of Coq's `firstorder` tactic can discharge proofs of the CanFlow proposition using the assumption AtomicFlow as shown in §2.1.

> **assume** CW:IsPrin Admin && IsPrin (U "Alice") && IsPrin (U "Bob") && ...
> **assume** AtomicFlow: **forall** f:file, g:file.
>   (**forall** p:prin. (IsPrin p && CanRead p g) $\Rightarrow$ CanRead p f) $\Rightarrow$ CanFlow (F f) (F g)

Of the other benchmarks, AuthAC is a small purely permission-based access control monitor for files combined with password-based authentication. FileAutomaton is a reference monitor that implements an automaton-like policy on files, where, through the use of dependent and affine types, a file handle is indexed with a value indicating its current state, e.g., Open, Closed etc. A similar idiom could be used in ConfRM to associate phases with papers, instead of a global phase for the entire conference. IFlow is an implementation of a traditional information flow policy using a three-point lattice of labels which does not require the nested quantifiers of FileRM. HealthWeb is a reference monitor for an application that manages a database of electronic medical records. It enforces a stateful authorization policy. DynDKAL is an interpreter for an authorization logic; it uses refinement types to ensure that instantiations of quantified assumptions in policies is performed correctly. Lookout is the core reference monitor of a plugin-based email client we have started to build. This program mixes stateful authorization in the style of ConfRM with information flow tracking in the style of FileRM.

Finally, ProofLib is an automatically generated program, our largest test case by far. This program makes no use of refinement types and is used as a utility by our type-preserving compiler to represent proof terms. We include it here to give the reader a sense of the cost of dependent type checking for larger programs.

5 Related Work and Conclusions

Several programming languages and proof assistants use dependent types, including Agda [17], Coq [2], and Epigram [16]. All of these systems can be used to verify full functional correctness of programs. However, to ensure logical consistency of the type system, these languages exclude arbitrary recursion, making them less applicable for general-purpose programming. Projects like YNot [4] and Guru [19] aim to mix effects like non-termination with dependently typed functional programming; YNot also supports programming with state in an imperative style. Restrictions in both languages ensure that proofs are pure, ensuring that logical consistency is preserved. All of these systems include automation and tactic languages, but programmers still need to construct interactive proofs for their code. In contrast, FINE targets weaker, security properties; forgoes logical consistency in favor of practical programming by including recursion; and automatically synthesizes proof terms using an SMT solver. FINE also provides affine types to allow the enforcement of state-modifying policies, which could be expressed in YNot, but not easily in the other languages.

Dependent types have also been used for security verification. Jif [5] uses a limited form of dependent typing to express dynamic information flow policies. Aura [13] is specialized for the enforcement of policies specified in a policy language based on an intuitionistic modal logic. This makes Aura less applicable to policies specified in other logics, e.g., the Datalog-based policy language of Dougherty et al. [7], and Aura cannot model stateful policies. Aura provides logical consistency by separating types from propositions and excluding arbitrary recursion in proof terms. However, proof terms in Aura are always programmer-provided. As such, Aura is positioned as an intermediate language, rather than a source-level language. Fable [21], is another intermediate language for security verification that uses dependent types. Fable uses a two-principal module system. FINE's module system generalizes Fable's, with support for a lattice of multiple principals. FINE is also related to λAIR [22], a calculus that targets the enforcement of declassification policies. λAIR's combination of affine and dependent types does not lend itself to integration with a solver and it was never implemented.

Refinement types in FINE are related to a similar construct in RCF [1]. Refinement formulas in RCF are drawn from an unsorted logic, rather than using dependent-type constructors, as we do. The lack of dependent type constructors in RCF makes it difficult to derive typeable proof terms, crucial to our goal of a type-preserving compiler for FINE. Additionally, without dependent type constructors, it appears impossible to enforce information flow policies in RCF, although RCF's implementation, F7, does include dependent type constructors. RCF also lacks support for stateful authorization policies, although recent work shows how stateful policies can be modeled in F7 using a refined state monad [3]. However, the soundness of this encoding relies on a trusted compilation of the program in a linear, store-passing style. FINE's type system also allows the use of refined state monads, but, as discussed in §2.3, affine types in FINE also admit other stateful programming idioms.

FINE is also related to hybrid-typed languages that use refinement types, like Sage [9]. Sage uses a trusted external solver to discharge proofs; we extract typeable proof terms from Z3 rather than trusting it. Another difference is that Sage automatically insert runtime checks when the solver fails to discharge a proof obligation. Failed runtime checks can cause subtle leaks of information, so automatic insertion of runtime checks is not yet a feature of FINE, where security is the primary concern—we plan to investigate adding support for automatic policy checking in the future.

Conclusions. This paper has presented FINE, a language for enforcing rich, stateful authorization and information flow policies. Our experience constructing several reference monitors provides initial evidence that programming in FINE is practical, due in part to the use of an automated solver to ease the proof burden, and that FINE can be used to check the enforcement of security policies commonly applied to software.

Acknowledgments. Thanks to Shriram Krishnamurthi for providing us with a specification of CONTINUE's policy; to Nikolaj Bjørner and Leonardo de Moura for help with Z3; to Karthik Bhargavan, Johannes Borgstroem, Cédric Fournet, and Andy Gordon for numerous discussions about this work.

References

1. Bengtson, J., Bhargavan, K., Fournet, C., Gordon, A.D., Maffeis, S.: Refinement types for secure implementations. In: CSF (2008)
2. Bertot, Y., Castéran, P.: Coq'Art: Interactive Theorem Proving and Program Development. Springer, Heidelberg (2004)
3. Borgstroem, J., Gordon, A., Pucella, R.: Roles, stacks, histories: A triple for hoare. Technical Report MSR-TR-2009-97, Microsoft Research (2009)
4. Chlipala, A., Malecha, G., Morrisett, G., Shinnar, A., Wisnesky, R.: Effective interactive proofs for higher-order imperative programs. In: ICFP (2009)
5. Chong, S., Myers, A.C., Nystrom, N., Zheng, L., Zdancewic, S.: Jif: Java + information flow (July 2006); Software release
6. de Moura, L., Bjørner, N.: Z3: An efficient SMT solver. In: Ramakrishnan, C.R., Rehof, J. (eds.) TACAS 2008. LNCS, vol. 4963, pp. 337–340. Springer, Heidelberg (2008)
7. Dougherty, D.J., Fisler, K., Krishnamurthi, S.: Specifying and reasoning about dynamic access-control policies. LNCS. Springer, Heidelberg (2006)
8. ECMA. Standard ECMA-335: Common language infrastructure (2006)
9. Flanagan, C.: Hybrid type checking. In: POPL. ACM, New York (2006)
10. Flanagan, C., Sabry, A., Duba, B.F., Felleisen, M.: The essence of compiling with continuations. In: PLDI. ACM, New York (1993)
11. Grossman, D., Morrisett, G., Zdancewic, S.: Syntactic type abstraction. ACM TOPLAS 22(6) (2000)
12. Jackson, D.: Alloy: a lightweight object modelling notation. TOSEM 11(2) (2002)
13. Jia, L., Vaughan, J., Mazurak, K., Zhao, J., Zarko, L., Schorr, J., Zdancewic, S.: Aura: A programming language for authorization and audit. In: ICFP (2008)
14. Krishnamurthi, S., Hopkins, P.W., Mccarthy, J., Graunke, P.T., Pettyjohn, G., Felleisen, M.: Implementation and use of the PLT Scheme web server. HOSC 20(4) (2007)
15. Levy, H.M.: Capability-Based Computer Systems. Butterworth-Heinemann, Butterworths (1984)
16. McBride, C., McKinna, J.: The view from the left. JFP 14(1) (2004)
17. Norell, U.: Towards a practical programming language based on dependent type theory. PhD thesis, Chalmers Institute of Technology (2007)
18. Simonet, V.: FlowCaml in a nutshell. In: Hutton, G. (ed.) APPSEM-II, pp. 152–165 (2003)
19. Stump, A., Deters, M., Petcher, A., Schiller, T., Simpson, T.: Verified programming in Guru. In: PLPV (2008)

20. Swamy, N., Chen, J., Chugh, R.: Enforcing stateful authorization and information flow policies in Fine. Technical Report MSR-TR-2009-164, Microsoft Research (2009)
21. Swamy, N., Corcoran, B.J., Hicks, M.: Fable: A language for enforcing user-defined security policies. In: S&P (2008)
22. Swamy, N., Hicks, M.: Verified enforcement of stateful information release policies. In: PLAS (2008)
23. Syme, D., Granicz, A., Cisternino, A.: Expert F#. Apress (2007)
24. Wadler, P.: Linear types can change the world. In: Prog. Concepts and Methods (1990)
25. Wahbe, R., Lucco, S., Anderson, T.E., Graham, S.L.: Efficient software-based fault isolation. In: SOSP (1993)

Stateful Contracts for Affine Types*

Jesse A. Tov and Riccardo Pucella

Northeastern University, Boston, MA 02115, USA
{tov,riccardo}@ccs.neu.edu

Abstract. Affine type systems manage resources by preventing some values from being used more than once. This offers expressiveness and performance benefits, but difficulty arises in interacting with components written in a conventional language whose type system provides no way to maintain the affine type system's aliasing invariants. We propose and implement a technique that uses behavioral contracts to mediate between code written in an affine language and code in a conventional typed language. We formalize our approach via a typed calculus with both affine-typed and conventionally-typed modules. We show how to preserve the guarantees of both type systems despite both languages being able to call into each other and exchange higher-order values.

1 Introduction

Substructural type systems augment conventional type systems with the ability to control the number and order of uses of a data structure or operation [20]. Linear type systems [1, 3, 11, 19], for example, ensure that values with linear type cannot be duplicated or dropped, but must be eliminated exactly once. Other substructural type systems refine these constraints. Affine type systems, which we consider here, prevent values from being duplicated but allow them to be dropped: a value of affine type may be used once or not at all.

Affine types are useful to support language features that rely on avoidance of aliasing. One example is session types [6], which are a method to represent and statically check communication protocols. Suppose that the type declared by

$$\textbf{type}_{\mathscr{A}}\ \textsf{prot} = (\textsf{int send} \rightarrow \textsf{string recv} \rightarrow \textsf{unit})\ \textsf{chan} \qquad (1)$$

represents a channel whose protocol allows us to to send an integer, then receive a string, and finally end the session. Further, suppose that *send* and *recv* consume a channel whose type allows sending or receiving, as appropriate, and return a channel whose type is advanced to the next step in the protocol. Then we might write a function that takes two such channels and runs their protocols in parallel:

$$
\begin{aligned}
&\textbf{let}_{\mathscr{A}}\ twice\ (c1: \textsf{prot},\ c2: \textsf{prot},\ z: \textsf{int}): \textsf{string} \otimes \textsf{string} = \\
&\quad \textbf{let}\ once\ (c: \textsf{prot})\ (\_: \textsf{unit}) = \\
&\qquad \textbf{let}\ c\quad = send\ c\ z\ \textbf{in} \\
&\qquad \textbf{let}\ (s,\ \_) = recv\ c\quad \textbf{in}\ s \\
&\quad \textbf{in}\ (once\ c1)\ |||\ (once\ c2)
\end{aligned}
\qquad (2)
$$

---

* Our prototype implementation and the full details of our soundness theorem may be found at http://www.ccs.neu.edu/~tov/pubs/affine-contracts/.

A.D. Gordon (Ed.): ESOP 2010, LNCS 6012, pp. 550–569, 2010.
© Springer-Verlag Berlin Heidelberg 2010

The protocol is followed correctly provided that *c1* and *c2* are *different* channels. Calling *twice*(*c*, *c*, 5), for instance, would violate the protocol. An affine type system can prevent this.

In addition to session types and other forms of typestate [15], substructural types have been used for memory management [8], for optimization of lazy languages [18], and to handle effects in pure languages [2]. Given this range of features, a programmer may wish to take advantage of substructural types in real-world programs. Writing real systems, however, often requires access to comprehensive libraries, which mainstream programming languages usually provide but experimental implementations often do not. The prospect of rewriting a large library to work in a substructural language strikes these authors as unappealing.

It is therefore compelling to allow conventional and substructural languages to interoperate. We envision complementary scenarios:

- A programmer wishes to import legacy code for use by affine-typed client code. Unfortunately, legacy code unaware of the substructural conditions may duplicate values received from the substructural language.
- A programmer wishes to export substructural library code for access from a conventional language. A client may duplicate values received from the library and resubmit them, causing aliasing that the library could not produce on its own and bypassing the substructural type system's guarantees.

Our Contributions. We present a novel approach to regulating the interaction between an affine language and a conventionally-typed language and implement a multi-language system having several notable features:

- The non-affine language may gain access to affine values and may apply affine-language functions.
- The non-affine type system is utterly standard, making no concessions to the affine type system.
- And yet, the composite system preserves the affine language's invariants.

We model the principal features of our implementation in a multi-language calculus that enjoys type soundness. In particular, the conventional language, although it has access to the affine language's functions and values, cannot be used to subvert the affine type system.

Our solution is to wrap each exchanged value in a software contract [4], which uses *one bit* of state to track when an affine value has been used. While this idea is simple, the details can be subtle.

Design Rationale and Background. Our multi-language system combines two sublanguages with different type systems. The 𝒞 ("conventional") language is based on the call-by-value, polymorphic λ calculus [7, 12] with algebraic datatypes and SML-style *abstype* [10]. The 𝒜 ("affine") language adds affine types and the ability to declare new abstract affine types, allowing us to implement affine abstractions such as session types and static read-write locks.

A program in our language consists of top-level module, value, and type definitions, each of which may be written in either of the two sublanguages. (In the example above (2), the subscripts on **type**$_{\mathscr{A}}$ and **let**$_{\mathscr{A}}$ indicate the $\mathscr{A}$ language.) Each language has access to modules written in the other language, although they view foreign types through a translation into the native type system. Affine modules are checked by an affine type system, and non-affine modules are checked by a conventional type system. Notably, non-functional affine types appear as abstract types to the conventional type system, which requires no special knowledge about affine types other than comparing them for equality.

In our introductory example, a protocol violation occurs only if the two arguments to *twice* are aliases for the same session-typed channel, which the $\mathscr{A}$ language type system prevents. Problems would arise if we could use the $\mathscr{C}$ language to subvert $\mathscr{A}$ language's type system non-aliasing invariants. To preserve the safety properties guaranteed by each individual type system and allow the two sublanguages to invoke one another and exchange values, we need to perform run-time checks in cases where the non-affine type system is too weak to express the affine type system's invariants. Because the affine type system can enforce all of the conventional type system's invariants, we may dispense with checks in the other direction.

For instance, the affine type system guarantees that an affine value created in an affine module will not be duplicated within the affine sublanguage. If, however, the value flows into a non-affine module, then static bets are off. In that case, we resort to a dynamic check that prevents the value from flowing back into an affine context more than once. Since our language is higher-order, we use a form of higher-order contract [4] to keep track of each module's obligations toward maintaining the affine invariants.

Our approach to integrating affine and conventional types borrows heavily from recent literature on multi-language interoperability [5, 13]. Our approach borrows from that of Typed Scheme [16, 17] and of Matthews and Findler [9], both of which use contracts to mediate between an untyped, Scheme-like language and a typed language.

2   Example: Taming the Berkeley Sockets API

The key feature of our system is the ability to write programs that safely mix code written in an affine-typed language and a conventionally-typed language. As an example, we develop a small networking library and application, using both of our sublanguages where appropriate.

The Berkeley sockets API is the standard C language interface to network communication [14]. Transmission Control Protocol (TCP), which provides reliable byte streams, is the standard transport layer protocol used by most internet applications (*e.g.*, SMTP, HTTP, and SSH). Setting up a TCP session using Berkeley sockets is a multi-step process (Fig. 1). A client must first create a communication end-point, called a *socket*, via the `socket` system call. It may optionally select a port to use with `bind`, and then it establishes a connection

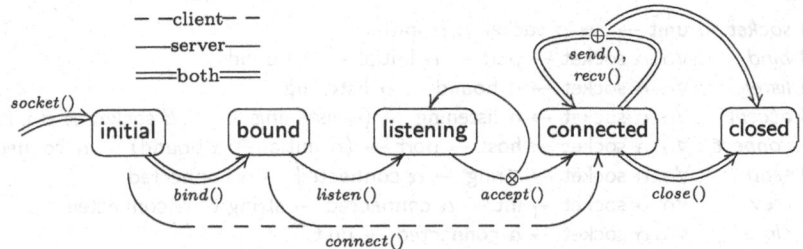

Fig. 1. States and transitions for TCP (simplified)

```
module 𝒞 Socket : sig
  type socket
  val socket : unit → socket          (* ∅ ⇒ initial *)
  val bind   : socket → port → unit   (* initial ⇒ bound *)
  val listen : socket → unit          (* bound ⇒ listening *)
  val accept : socket → socket        (* listening ⇒ connected ⊗ listening *)
  val send   : socket → string → bool (* connected ⇒ connected ⊕ closed *)
  ⋯ end
```

Fig. 2. Selected 𝒞 language socket operations, annotated with state transitions

with **connect**. Once a connection is established, the client may **send** and **recv** until either the client or the other side closes the connection.

For a server, the process is more involved: it begins with **socket** and **bind** as the client does, and then it calls **listen** to allow connection requests to begin queuing. The server calls **accept** to accept a connection request. When **accept** succeeds, it returns a *new* socket that is connected to a client, and the old, listening socket is available for further **accept** calls. (For simplicity, we omit error transitions, except for failure of **send** and **recv**.)

Our 𝒞 sublanguage provides the interface to sockets shown in Fig. 2. The socket operations are annotated with their pre- and post-conditions, but the implementation detects and signals state errors dynamically. For example, calling *listen* on a socket in state initial or calling *connect* on a socket that is already connected will raise an exception. If the other side hangs up, **send** and **recv** raise exceptions, but nothing in this interface prevents further communication attempts that are bound to fail.[1]

By reimplementing the sockets API in language 𝒜, we can use language 𝒜's type system to move the state transition information from comments into the type system itself. For example, we give *listen* in sublanguage 𝒜 the type

$$\forall\alpha.\ \alpha\ \text{socket} \to \alpha\ \text{bound} \to \alpha\ \text{listening}, \tag{3}$$

which means that given a socket and evidence that the socket is bound, *listen* changes the state to listening and returns evidence to that effect. These evidence

---

[1] This simplifies the Berkeley sockets API by omitting address families, protocols, half-closed sockets, non-blocking IO, etc., but the stateful essence remains.

val *socket*   : unit → ∃α. α socket ⊗ α initial
val *bind*   : ∀α. α socket → port → α initial → α bound
val *listen*   : ∀α. α socket → α bound → α listening
val *accept*   : ∀α. α socket → α listening → (α listening ⊗ ∃β. β socket ⊗ β initial)
val *connect* : ∀α. α socket → host → port → (α initial ⊕ α bound) → α connected
val *send*   : ∀α. α socket → string → α connected → α connected
val *recv*   : ∀α. α socket → int → α connected → string ⊗ α connected
val *close*   : ∀α. α socket → α connected → unit

Fig. 3. The $\mathscr{A}$ language sockets API

tokens are *capabilities*, and the type parameter on each capability ties it to the particular socket whose state it describes. These capabilities have affine type so that when *listen* consumes the bound capability, we cannot call *listen* again on the same socket.

We reimplement the sockets API in language $\mathscr{A}$ in terms of the language $\mathscr{C}$ operations. From the vantage of language $\mathscr{A}$, $\mathscr{C}$ function types are mapped to $\mathscr{A}$ function types, but the $\mathscr{C}$ type Socket.socket is mapped to an *opaque type* {Socket.socket}. Type constructor {·} delimits foreign types referenced from the other sublanguage.

We declare a new abstract type for sockets in language $\mathscr{A}$, along with a type to represent each of the states:

$$\begin{aligned}
\textbf{abstype}_{\mathscr{A}}\ &\alpha\ \text{socket} = \text{Sock of } \{\text{Socket.socket}\} \\
\textbf{and}\ &\alpha\ \text{initial} \quad \textbf{qualifier A} = \text{Initial} \\
\textbf{and}\ &\alpha\ \text{bound} \quad \textbf{qualifier A} = \text{Bound} \\
\textbf{and}\ &\alpha\ \text{listening} \quad \textbf{qualifier A} = \text{Listening} \\
\textbf{and}\ &\alpha\ \text{connected} \ \textbf{qualifier A} = \text{Connected} \\
\textbf{with}\ &\cdots\ (* \text{ operations detailed below } *)\ \cdots\ \textbf{end}
\end{aligned} \qquad (4)$$

Several aspects of this abstype declaration bear further explanation:

- Each type has a phantom parameter α, which is used to associate a socket with the type witnessing its state.
- The syntax **qualifier A** on each the state type declares that outside the abstraction boundary, values of those types will appear as affine. Code inside the abstype declaration sees that they are ordinary, non-affine data types.
- Because each of the capabilities has only one constructor with no values, they need not be represented at run time.

The $\mathscr{A}$ language sockets interface appears in Fig. 3. The $\mathscr{A}$ sockets implementation relies on delegating to $\mathscr{C}$ language functions. From within $\mathscr{A}$, $\mathscr{C}$ types are viewed through a simple translation: function types, quantified types, and a few base types such as int pass through transparently, whereas other types are wrapped opaquely as Socket.socket was above. Thus, the type of *Socket.socket*$_{\mathscr{C}}$

```
let𝒜 clientLoop[α] (sock: α socket) (f: string → string) (cap: α connected) =
  let rec loop (cap: α connected): unit =
    let (str, cap) = recv sock 1024 cap in
    let cap       = send sock (f str) cap in
    loop cap
  in try loop cap with SocketError _ → ()

let interface threadFork :> (unit ─ᵃ∘ unit) → {thread}𝒞 = threadFork𝒞

let rec𝒜 acceptLoop[α] (sock: α socket) (f: string → string) (cap: α listening): unit =
  let (cap, Pack(β, (clientsock, clientcap))) = accept sock cap in
  threadFork (fun () → clientLoop clientsock f clientcap);
  acceptLoop sock f cap

let𝒜 echoServe (port: int) (f: string → string) =
  let Pack(α, (sock, cap)) = socket () in
  let cap = bind sock port cap in
  let cap = listen sock cap in
  acceptLoop sock f cap
```

Fig. 4. An echo server in language 𝒜

becomes unit → {Socket.socket} when viewed from 𝒜. Each 𝒜 function is a minimal wrapper around its 𝒞 counterpart:

```
let𝒜 socket () =
  let sock = Socket.socket𝒞 () in
  in Pack(unit, (Sock[unit] sock, Initial[unit])) as ∃β. β socket ⊗ β initial

let𝒜 listen[α] (Sock sock as s: α socket) (_: α bound) =
  try Socket.listen𝒞 sock;
  Listening[α]
  with IOError msg → raise (StillBound (freezeBound s cap, msg))        (5)
```

For socket𝒜, we call Socket.socket𝒞 to create the new socket, which we wrap in the Sock constructor and pack into an existential with a new initial capability. (The type abstracted by the existential is immaterial; unit will do.) Function listen𝒜 calls its 𝒞 counterpart on the socket and returns a listening capability tied by α to the socket. On failure, the socket is still in state bound, so it raises an exception containing the bound capability. The remaining functions are equally straightforward, but when we're done, provided we got this trusted kernel correct, we have an 𝒜 library that enforces the correct ordering of socket operations.

Calling the various 𝒞 socket operations from 𝒜 is safe because none has a type that enables it to gain access to an 𝒜 language value. Other situations are not as simple. Figure 4 shows an implementation of an echo server in language 𝒜. (The working code is included with our prototype implementation on our web site.) The server sends back the data it receives from each client after passing it through an unspecified string → string function f. The main function echoServe creates a socket, binds it to the requested port, and begins to listen. The type system ensures that *echoServe* performs these operations in the right order, and because the capabilities have affine types, it disallows referring to any one of them more then once. Function *echoServe* calls *acceptLoop*, which blocks in *accept* waiting for clients. For each client, it spawns a thread to handle that client and continues waiting for another client. Spawning the thread is where the multi-language interaction becomes tricky.

As in other substructural type systems, $\mathscr{A}$ requires that a function be given a type whose usage (unlimited or affine) is at least as restrictive as any variable that it closes over. Thus far, we have seen only unlimited function types ($\rightarrow$), also written $\xrightarrow{u}$. Language $\mathscr{A}$ also has affine function types, written $\xrightarrow{a}$.

The new client capability *clientcap*, returned by *accept*, has affine type β connected. Because the thunk for the new thread, (**fun** () $\rightarrow$ *clientLoop clientsock f clientcap*), closes over *clientcap*, it has affine type as well: unit $\xrightarrow{a}$ unit. This causes a problem: To create a new thread, we must pass the thunk to the $\mathscr{C}$ function *threadFork$_\mathscr{C}$*, whose type as viewed from $\mathscr{A}$ is (unit $\rightarrow$ unit) $\rightarrow$ {thread}$_\mathscr{C}$. Such a type makes *no guarantee* about how many times *threadFork$_\mathscr{C}$* applies its argument. In order to pass the affine thunk to it, we assert that *threadFork$_\mathscr{C}$* has the desired behavior:

$$\textbf{let interface } threadFork :> (\text{unit} \xrightarrow{a} \text{unit}) \rightarrow \{\text{thread}\}_\mathscr{C} = threadFork_\mathscr{C} \quad (6)$$

This constitutes a checked assertion that the $\mathscr{C}$ value actually behaves according to the given $\mathscr{A}$ type. This gets the program past $\mathscr{A}$'s type checker, and if *threadFork$_\mathscr{C}$* attempts to apply its argument twice at run time, a dynamic check prevents it from doing so and signals an error.

The two sublanguages can interact in other ways:

– We may call *echoServe$_\mathscr{A}$* from the $\mathscr{C}$ language, passing it a $\mathscr{C}$ function for *f*. This is safe because function *f* has type string $\rightarrow$ string, and thus can never gain access to an affine value.
– We may use the $\mathscr{A}$ language sockets library from a $\mathscr{C}$ program:

$$\begin{aligned}
&\textbf{let}_\mathscr{C} \; sneaky \; () = \\
&\textbf{let } \text{Pack}(\alpha, (sock, cap1)) = socket_\mathscr{A} \; () \textbf{ in} \\
&\textbf{let } cap2 = connect_\mathscr{A} \; sock \; \texttt{"sneaky.example.org"} \; 25 \; cap1 \textbf{ in} \\
&\textbf{let } cap3 = connect_\mathscr{A} \; sock \; \texttt{"sneaky2.example.org"} \; 25 \; cap1 \textbf{ in} \\
&\cdots
\end{aligned} \quad (7)$$

This program passes $\mathscr{C}$'s type checker but is caught when it attempts to reuse the initial capability *cap1* at run time. This misbehavior is detected because *sneaky*'s interaction with $\mathscr{A}$ is mediated by a behavioral contract.

3   Implementing Stateful Contracts

In Findler and Felleisen's formulation [4], a contract is an agreement between two software components, or *parties*, about some property of a value. The *positive party* produces a value, which must satisfy the specified property. The *negative party* consumes the value and is held responsible for treating it appropriately. Contracts are concerned with catching violations of the property and blaming the guilty party, which may help locate the source of a bug. For first-order values the contract may be immediately checkable, but for functional values nontrivial properties are undecidable, so the check must wait until the negative party applies the function, at which point the negative party is responsible for providing a suitable argument and the positive party for producing a suitable result. Thus, for higher-order functions, checks are delayed until first-order values are reached.

In our language, the parties to contracts are modules, which must be in entirely one language or the other, and top-level functions, which we consider as singleton modules.

Contracts on first-order values check assertions about their arguments, and either return the argument or signal an error. Contracts on functions return functions that defer checking until first-order values are reached. The result of applying a contract should contextually approximate the argument. We represent a contract for a type α as a function taking two parties and a value of type α, and returning a value of the same type α:

$$\textbf{type } \alpha \text{ contract} = \textsf{party} \times \textsf{party} \to \alpha \to \alpha \tag{8}$$

A simple contract might assert something about a first-order value:

$$\begin{aligned} &\textbf{let } evenContract \ (neg: \textsf{party}, \ pos: \textsf{party}) \ (x: \textsf{int}) = \\ &\quad \textbf{if } isEven \ x \textbf{ then } x \textbf{ else } blame \ pos \end{aligned} \tag{9}$$

The contract is instantiated with the identities of the contracted parties, and then may be applied to a value. We may also construct contracts for functional values, given contracts for the domain and codomain:

$$\begin{aligned} &\textbf{let } makeFunctionContract[\alpha, \beta] \ (dom: \alpha \text{ contract}, \ codom: \beta \text{ contract}) \\ &\qquad\qquad\qquad\qquad (neg: \textsf{party}, \ pos: \textsf{party}) \ (f: \alpha \to \beta) = \\ &\quad \textbf{fun } (x: \alpha) \to codom \ (neg, \ pos) \ (f \ (dom \ (pos, \ neg) \ x)) \end{aligned} \tag{10}$$

When this contract is applied to a function, it can perform no checks immediately. Instead, it wraps the function so that, when the resulting function is applied, the domain contract is applied to the actual parameter and the codomain contract to the actual result.

We follow this approach closely, but with one small change—contracts for affine functions are stateful:

$$\begin{aligned} &\textbf{let } makeAffineFunContract[\alpha, \beta] \ (dom: \alpha \text{ contract}, \ codom: \beta \text{ contract}) \\ &\qquad\qquad\qquad\qquad (neg: \textsf{party}, \ pos: \textsf{party}) \ (f: \alpha \to \beta) = \\ &\quad \textbf{let } stillGood = \textbf{ref true in} \\ &\quad\quad \textbf{fun } (x: \alpha) \to \\ &\quad\quad\quad \textbf{if } ! \, stillGood \\ &\quad\quad\quad\quad \textbf{then } stillGood \leftarrow \textsf{false}; \\ &\quad\quad\quad\quad\quad\quad codom \ (neg, \ pos) \ (f \ (dom \ (pos, \ neg) \ x)) \\ &\quad\quad\quad\quad \textbf{else } blame \ neg \end{aligned} \tag{11}$$

This approach works for functions because we can wrap a function to modify its behavior. But what about for other affine values such as the socket capabilities in Sect. 2? We must consider how non-functional values move between the two sublanguages.

In order to understand the solution, we need to show in greater detail how types are mapped between the two sublanguages. (The rest of the type system appears in the next section.) We define mappings $(\cdot)^{\mathscr{A}}$ and $(\cdot)^{\mathscr{C}}$ from $\mathscr{C}$ types to $\mathscr{A}$ types and $\mathscr{A}$ types to $\mathscr{C}$ types, respectively. Base types such as int and bool, which may be duplicated without restriction in both languages, map to themselves:

$$(\mathcal{B})^{\mathscr{A}} = \mathcal{B} \qquad\qquad (\mathcal{B})^{\mathscr{C}} = \mathcal{B} \qquad (12)$$

Function types convert to function types. $\mathscr{C}$ function types go to unlimited functions in $\mathscr{A}$, and both unlimited and affine $\mathscr{A}$ functions collapse to ordinary ($\rightarrow$) functions in $\mathscr{C}$ (where q ranges over a and u):

$$(\tau_1 \rightarrow \tau_2)^{\mathscr{A}} = (\tau_2)^{\mathscr{A}} \xrightarrow{\ \mathsf{u}\ } (\tau_2)^{\mathscr{A}} \qquad (\sigma_1 \xrightarrow{\ \mathsf{q}\ } \sigma_2)^{\mathscr{C}} = (\sigma_1)^{\mathscr{C}} \rightarrow (\sigma_2)^{\mathscr{C}} \qquad (13)$$

Quantified types map to quantified types, but they require renaming because we distinguish type variables between the two languages. In particular, $\mathscr{A}$ language type variables carry usage qualifiers, which indicate whether they may be instantiated to any type or only to unlimited types. (All type variables in Sect. 2 were of the u kind.)

$$(\forall \alpha.\, \tau)^{\mathscr{A}} = \forall \beta^{\mathsf{u}}.\, (\tau_1[\{\beta^{\mathsf{u}}\}/\alpha])^{\mathscr{A}} \qquad (\forall \alpha^{\mathsf{q}}.\, \sigma)^{\mathscr{C}} = \forall \beta.\, (\sigma_1[\{\beta\}/\alpha^{\mathsf{q}}])^{\mathscr{C}} \qquad (14)$$

Finally, the remaining types are uninterpreted by the mapping, and merely enclosed in $\{\cdot\}$:

$$(\tau^o)^{\mathscr{A}} = \{\tau^o\},\text{ otherwise} \qquad (\sigma^o)^{\mathscr{C}} = \{\sigma^o\},\text{ otherwise} \qquad (15)$$

Values in this class of types are inert: they have no available operations other than passing them back to their native sublanguage, which removes the $\{\cdot\}$. (We take $\{\{\tau\}\}$ to be equivalent to τ.)

This mapping implies that all non-functional, affine types in $\mathscr{A}$ map to opaque types in $\mathscr{C}$.[2] Since all that the $\mathscr{C}$ language can do with values of opaque type is pass them back to $\mathscr{A}$, we are free to wrap such values when they flow into $\mathscr{C}$ and unwrap them when they return to $\mathscr{A}$. Specifically, when an affine value v passes into $\mathscr{C}$, we wrap it in a λ abstraction, **fun** (_: unit) $\rightarrow v$, and wrap that thunk with an affine function contract. If the wrapped value flows back into

---

[2] Opaque types may seem limiting, but Matthews and Findler [9] have shown that it is possible, in what they call the "lump embedding," for each sublanguage to marshal its opaque values for the other sublanguage as desired. In practice, this amounts to exporting a fold to the other sublanguage.

$$\mathscr{CA}[\![\text{int}]\!](n,p) = id$$
$$\mathscr{CA}[\![\sigma_1 \xrightarrow{u} \sigma_2]\!](n,p) = \text{makeFunctionContract } (\mathscr{AC}[\![\sigma_1]\!], \mathscr{CA}[\![\sigma_2]\!]) \; (n,\, p)$$
$$\mathscr{CA}[\![\sigma_1 \xrightarrow{a} \sigma_2]\!](n,p) = \text{makeAffineFunContract } (\mathscr{AC}[\![\sigma_1]\!], \mathscr{CA}[\![\sigma_2]\!]) \; (n,\, p)$$
$$\mathscr{CA}[\![\sigma^o]\!](n,p) = \textbf{fun } (v\colon \sigma^o) \to \text{makeAffineFunContract} \qquad (\textit{if } \sigma^o \textit{ is}$$
$$(\textit{id, id}) \; (n,\, p) \; (\textbf{fun } () \to v) \qquad \textit{affine})$$

$$\mathscr{AC}[\![\text{int}]\!](n,p) = id$$
$$\mathscr{AC}[\![\sigma_1 \xrightarrow{q} \sigma_2]\!](n,p) = \text{makeFunctionContract } (\mathscr{CA}[\![\sigma_1]\!], \mathscr{AC}[\![\sigma_2]\!]) \; (n,\, p)$$
$$\mathscr{AC}[\![\sigma^o]\!](n,p) = \textbf{fun } (v\colon \text{unit} \to \sigma^o) \to v \; () \qquad (\textit{if } \sigma^o \textit{ is affine})$$

Fig. 5. Type-directed generation of coercions

$\mathscr{A}$, we unwrap it by applying the thunk, which produces a contract error if we attempt unwrapping it more than once.

After type checking, our implementation translates $\mathscr{A}$ modules to $\mathscr{C}$ and wraps all interlanguage variable references with contracts that enforce the $\mathscr{A}$ language's view of the variable. In Fig. 5, we show several cases from a pair of metafunctions $\mathscr{AC}[\![\cdot]\!]$ and $\mathscr{CA}[\![\cdot]\!]$, which perform this wrapping. Metafunction $\mathscr{AC}[\![\cdot]\!]$ produces the coercion for references to $\mathscr{C}$ values from $\mathscr{A}$, and $\mathscr{CA}[\![\cdot]\!]$ is for references to $\mathscr{A}$ values from $\mathscr{C}$. Our formalization does not use this translation, but gives a semantics to the multi-language system directly.

4   Formalization

We model our language with a pair of calculi corresponding to the two sublanguages in the implementation. In this section, we first describe the two calculi independently, and then move on to explain how they interact.

To distinguish the two calculi, we typeset our affine calculus $\lambda^{\mathscr{A}}$ in a sans-serif font and our non-affine calculus $\lambda_{\mathscr{C}}$ in a **bold serif font**.

4.1   The Calculi $\lambda^{\mathscr{A}}$ and $\lambda_{\mathscr{C}}$

We model sublanguage $\mathscr{C}$ with calculus $\lambda_{\mathscr{C}}$, which is merely call-by-value System F [7] equipped with singleton modules, each of which for simplicity declares only one name bound to one value. The syntax of $\lambda_{\mathscr{C}}$ appears in Fig. 6, including module names, which are disjoint from variable names. We include integer literals, which serve as first-order values that should pass transparently into the affine subcalculus. A program comprises a mutually recursive collection of modules M and a main expression $\mathbf{e}$. We give only the semantics relevant to modules, as the rest is standard. The expression typing judgment has the form $\Delta; \Gamma \vdash^{M}_{\mathscr{C}} \mathbf{e} : \tau$, and it carries a module context M, which rule TC-MoD uses to type module expressions. To type a program, we must type each module with rule TM-C; note that the whole module context is available to each module, allowing for

$$
\begin{array}{ll}
variables & \mathbf{x}, \mathbf{y} \in Var_{\mathscr{C}} \\
type\ variables & \boldsymbol{\alpha}, \boldsymbol{\beta} \in TVar_{\mathscr{C}} \\
module\ names & \mathbf{f}, \mathbf{g} \in MVar_{\mathscr{C}}
\end{array}
$$

$$
\begin{array}{ll}
programs & \mathbf{P} ::= M\ \mathbf{e} \\
module\ contexts & M ::= \mathbf{m}_1 \ldots \mathbf{m}_k \\
modules & \mathbf{m} ::= \mathbf{module\ f} : \tau = \mathbf{v} \\
types & \tau ::= \forall \boldsymbol{\alpha}.\tau \mid \boldsymbol{\alpha} \\
& \mid \tau \to \tau \mid \mathbf{int} \\
expressions & \mathbf{e} ::= \mathbf{x} \mid \mathbf{f} \mid \mathbf{e}[\tau] \mid \mathbf{e}\,\mathbf{e} \\
& \mid \Lambda \boldsymbol{\alpha}.\mathbf{v} \mid \lceil z \rceil \mid \cdots
\end{array}
$$

TC-MOD
$$
\frac{\mathbf{module\ f} : \tau = \mathbf{v} \in M \qquad \cdot \vdash_{\mathscr{C}} \tau}{\Delta; \Gamma \vdash_{\mathscr{C}}^{M} \mathbf{f} : \tau}
$$

TM-C
$$
\frac{\cdot; \cdot \vdash_{\mathscr{C}}^{M} \mathbf{v} : \tau}{\vdash^{M} \mathbf{module\ f} : \tau = \mathbf{v}\ \text{okay}}
$$

C-MOD
$$
\frac{(\mathbf{module\ f} : \tau = \mathbf{v}) \in M}{\mathbf{f} \xmapsto{M} \mathbf{v}}
$$

Fig. 6. Selected syntax and semantics of $\lambda_{\mathscr{C}}$

recursion. Finally, C-MOD shows that module names reduce to the value of the module.

We model sublanguage $\mathscr{A}$ with calculus $\lambda^{\mathscr{A}}$, which extends $\lambda_{\mathscr{C}}$ with affine types. While $\lambda^{\mathscr{A}}$ includes all of $\lambda_{\mathscr{C}}$, we choose not to embed $\lambda_{\mathscr{C}}$ in $\lambda^{\mathscr{A}}$ to emphasize the generality of our approach, anticipating conventional language features that we do not know how to type in an affine language. The syntax of $\lambda^{\mathscr{A}}$ may be found in Fig. 7. Expressions are mostly conventional: values, which include λ and Λ abstractions, constants, and pairs; variables; application and type application; if expressions; pair construction; and pair elimination. Less conventionally, expressions also include *module names* ($\mathbf{f}$), which reduce to the value of the named module. We define the free variables of an expression in the usual way, but note that this includes only regular variables (*e.g.*, y), not module names (*e.g.*, g), which we assume are distinguished syntactically.

Types include integers, function types with qualifier q, universals, and the syntactically distinguished opaque types, which include type variables, products, and reference cells. Figure 8 defines a lattice on qualifiers, of which there are only two: u is bottom and a is top. A qualifier is assigned to each type, with the notation $|\sigma| = \mathsf{q}$. Integers are always assigned the unlimited qualifier u, whereas references always have the affine qualifier a. Function types and type variables are annotated with their qualifiers, and products get the stronger qualifier of either of their components. We define the qualifier of a value context Γ as well, to be the maximum qualifier of any type bound in it; in other words, Γ is affine if *any* variable is affine, but if none is then it is unlimited.

The subtyping relation appears in Fig. 8. It is reflexive and transitive, covariant on both pair components and function codomains, and contravariant on function domains, as usual. Subtyping arises from the qualifier lattice in two ways: an unlimited function may be used where an affine function is expected (but not vice versa), and a universal type whose bound variable has qualifier a may be instantiated by a type with qualifier u (but not vice versa).

Figure 8 defines context splitting, which is used by expression typing to distribute affine assumptions to only one use in a term, but unlimited variables to an unlimited number of mentions. When a value context must be split to type

$$
\begin{array}{rll}
\textit{variables} & \mathsf{x}, \mathsf{y} & \in \textit{Var}_{\mathscr{A}} \\
\textit{qualifiers} & \mathsf{q} & \in \{\mathsf{a}, \mathsf{u}\} \\
\textit{type variables} & \alpha^{\mathsf{q}}, \beta^{\mathsf{q}} & \in \textit{TVar}_{\mathscr{A}} \\
\textit{module names} & \mathsf{f}, \mathsf{g} & \in \textit{MVar}_{\mathscr{A}} \\[4pt]
\textit{modules} & \mathsf{m} ::= & \mathsf{module}\, \mathsf{f} : \sigma = \mathsf{v} \\
\textit{types} & \sigma ::= & \mathsf{int} \mid \sigma \xrightarrow{\mathsf{q}} \sigma \mid \forall \alpha^{\mathsf{q}}.\,\sigma \mid \sigma^{\circ} \\
\textit{opaque types} & \sigma^{\circ} ::= & \alpha \mid \sigma \otimes \sigma \mid \sigma\,\mathsf{ref} \\
\textit{expressions} & \mathsf{e} ::= & \mathsf{v} \mid \mathsf{x} \mid \mathsf{f} \mid \mathsf{e}\,\mathsf{e} \mid \mathsf{e}[\sigma] \mid \mathsf{if0}\,\mathsf{e}\,\mathsf{e}\,\mathsf{e} \\
& & \mid \langle \mathsf{e}, \mathsf{e} \rangle \mid \mathsf{let}\,\langle \mathsf{x}, \mathsf{x} \rangle = \mathsf{e}\,\mathsf{in}\,\mathsf{e} \\
\textit{values} & \mathsf{v} ::= & \mathsf{c} \mid \lambda \mathsf{x}{:}\sigma.\mathsf{e} \mid \Lambda \alpha^{\mathsf{q}}.\,\mathsf{v} \mid \langle \mathsf{v}, \mathsf{v} \rangle \\
\textit{constants} & \mathsf{c} ::= & \mathsf{new}[\sigma] \mid \mathsf{swap}[\sigma][\sigma] \mid \lceil z \rceil \mid - \mid (z{-}) \mid \cdots \\[4pt]
\textit{value contexts} & \Gamma ::= & \cdot \mid \Gamma, \mathsf{x}{:}\sigma \\
\textit{type contexts} & \Delta ::= & \cdot \mid \Delta, \alpha^{\mathsf{q}}
\end{array}
$$

Fig. 7. Syntax of $\lambda^{\mathscr{A}}$

$\boxed{\mathsf{q} \sqsubseteq \mathsf{q}}$, $\boxed{|\tau| = \mathsf{q}}$, $\boxed{|\Gamma| = \mathsf{q}}$

$$
\mathsf{u} \sqsubseteq \mathsf{q} \qquad \mathsf{q} \sqsubseteq \mathsf{a} \qquad |\mathsf{int}| = \mathsf{u} \qquad \left|\sigma_1 \xrightarrow{\mathsf{q}} \sigma_2\right| = \mathsf{q} \qquad |\forall \alpha^{\mathsf{q}}.\,\sigma| = |\sigma| \qquad |\alpha^{\mathsf{q}}| = \mathsf{q}
$$

$$
|\sigma_1 \otimes \sigma_2| = |\sigma_1| \sqcup |\sigma_2| \qquad\qquad |\sigma\,\mathsf{ref}\,| = \mathsf{a} \qquad\qquad |\Gamma| = \bigsqcup_{\mathsf{x} \in \mathrm{dom}(\Gamma)} |\Gamma(\mathsf{x})|
$$

$\boxed{\sigma <: \sigma}$

S-REFL

$$
\overline{\sigma <: \sigma}
$$

S-TRANS

$$
\frac{\sigma_1 <: \sigma_2 \qquad \sigma_2 <: \sigma_3}{\sigma_1 <: \sigma_3}
$$

S-PROD

$$
\frac{\sigma_1 <: \sigma_1' \qquad \sigma_2 <: \sigma_2'}{\sigma_1 \otimes \sigma_2 <: \sigma_1' \otimes \sigma_2'}
$$

S-ARROW

$$
\frac{\sigma_1' <: \sigma_1 \qquad \sigma_2 <: \sigma_2' \qquad \mathsf{q} \sqsubseteq \mathsf{q}'}{\sigma_1 \xrightarrow{\mathsf{q}} \sigma_2 <: \sigma_1' \xrightarrow{\mathsf{q}'} \sigma_2'}
$$

S-FORALL

$$
\frac{\mathsf{q}_2 \sqsubseteq \mathsf{q}_1 \qquad \sigma_1[\beta^{\mathsf{q}_2}/\alpha^{\mathsf{q}_1}] <: \sigma_2}{\forall \alpha^{\mathsf{q}_1}.\,\sigma_1 <: \forall \beta^{\mathsf{q}_2}.\,\sigma_2}
$$

$\boxed{\Gamma \boxplus \Gamma = \Gamma}$

$$
\overline{\cdot \boxplus \cdot = \cdot}
$$

$$
\frac{\Gamma_1 \boxplus \Gamma_2 = \Gamma_3 \qquad |\sigma| = \mathsf{a}}{\Gamma_1 \boxplus \Gamma_2, \mathsf{x}{:}\sigma = \Gamma_3, \mathsf{x}{:}\sigma} \qquad\qquad \frac{\Gamma_1 \boxplus \Gamma_2 = \Gamma_3 \qquad |\sigma| = \mathsf{a}}{\Gamma_1, \mathsf{x}{:}\sigma \boxplus \Gamma_2 = \Gamma_3, \mathsf{x}{:}\sigma}
$$

$$
\frac{\Gamma_1 \boxplus \Gamma_2 = \Gamma_3 \qquad |\sigma| = \mathsf{u}}{\Gamma_1, \mathsf{x}{:}\sigma \boxplus \Gamma_2, \mathsf{x}{:}\sigma = \Gamma_3, \mathsf{x}{:}\sigma}
$$

Fig. 8. Statics of $\lambda^{\mathscr{A}}$ (qualifiers, subtyping, contexts)

$$\boxed{\Delta; \Gamma \vdash^M_{\mathscr{A}} e : \sigma}$$

TA-Subsume
$$\dfrac{\Delta; \Gamma \vdash^M_{\mathscr{A}} e : \sigma \qquad \sigma <: \sigma'}{\Delta; \Gamma \vdash^M_{\mathscr{A}} e : \sigma'}$$

TA-Lam
$$\dfrac{\Delta; \Gamma, x : \sigma \vdash^M_{\mathscr{A}} e : \sigma' \qquad \Delta \vdash_{\mathscr{A}} \sigma \qquad |\Gamma|_{FV(\lambda x:\sigma.\,e)} = q}{\Delta; \Gamma \vdash^M_{\mathscr{A}} \lambda x{:}\sigma.\,e : \sigma \xrightarrow{q} \sigma'}$$

TA-TApp
$$\dfrac{\Delta; \Gamma \vdash^M_{\mathscr{A}} e : \forall \alpha^q.\,\sigma' \qquad \Delta \vdash_{\mathscr{A}} \sigma \qquad |\sigma| \sqsubseteq q}{\Delta; \Gamma \vdash^M_{\mathscr{A}} e[\sigma] : \sigma'[\sigma/\alpha^q]}$$

TA-App
$$\dfrac{\Delta; \Gamma_1 \vdash^M_{\mathscr{A}} e_1 : \sigma' \xrightarrow{q} \sigma \qquad \Delta; \Gamma_2 \vdash^M_{\mathscr{A}} e_2 : \sigma'}{\Delta; \Gamma_1 \boxplus \Gamma_2 \vdash^M_{\mathscr{A}} e_1\, e_2 : \sigma}$$

TA-Mod
$$\dfrac{module\ f : \sigma = v \in M \qquad \cdot \vdash_{\mathscr{A}} \sigma}{\Delta; \Gamma \vdash^M_{\mathscr{A}} f : \sigma}$$

TA-New
$$\dfrac{}{\Delta; \Gamma \vdash^M_{\mathscr{A}} new[\sigma] : \sigma \xrightarrow{u} \sigma\ ref}$$

TA-Swap
$$\dfrac{}{\Delta; \Gamma \vdash^M_{\mathscr{A}} swap[\sigma_1][\sigma_2] : (\sigma_1\ ref \otimes \sigma_2) \xrightarrow{u} (\sigma_1 \otimes \sigma_2\ ref)}$$

Fig. 9. Statics of $\lambda^{\mathscr{A}}$ (selected expressions)

$$
\begin{array}{rl}
locations & \ell \in Loc \\
values & v ::= \cdots \mid \ell \\
stores & s ::= \{\ell \mapsto v, \ldots, \ell \mapsto v\} \\
configurations & C ::= (s, e) \\
evaluation\ contexts & E ::= [\,]_{\mathscr{A}} \mid E[\sigma] \mid E\,e \mid v\,E \mid \langle E, e \rangle \mid \langle v, E \rangle \mid \cdots
\end{array}
$$

$$\boxed{C \longmapsto_M C}$$

(A-New) $$(s, new[\sigma]\,v) \xmapsto{\;\;} _M (s \uplus \{\ell \mapsto v\}, \ell)$$

(A-Swap) $$(s \uplus \{\ell \mapsto v_1\}, swap[\sigma_1][\sigma_2]\,\langle \ell, v_2 \rangle) \xmapsto{\;\;} _M (s \uplus \{\ell \mapsto v_2\}, \langle v_1, \ell \rangle)$$

Fig. 10. Dynamics of $\lambda^{\mathscr{A}}$ (selected rules)

two subexpressions, in an application expression, for example (Fig. 9), variables of affine type are made available to either the operator or operand, but not both.

Selected expression typing rules appear in Fig. 9. Rules TA-Lam and TA-App are the usual substructural rules for typing λ expressions and applications: for λ expressions, the qualifier q given to the resulting $\xrightarrow{q}$ type is the qualifier of the context Γ limited to the free variables of the expression; thus, the function is at least as restricted as any values it closes over. The type application rule TA-TApp requires that a type variable be at least as restrictive as any type with which it is instantiated.

Finally, rule TA-Swap takes a pair of a σ_1 reference and a σ_2, and returns a σ_1 and a σ_2 reference. From the operational semantics, a small selection of which appears in Fig. 10, it should be clear that swap swaps the σ_2 argument into the location and returns the value previously in the location. Since TA-Swap does

$$
\begin{array}{rcl}
\textit{programs} & P & ::= M\ e \\
\textit{module contexts} & M & ::= m_1 \ldots m_k \\
\textit{modules} & m & ::= \mathsf{m} \mid \mathbf{m} \\
& & \mid\ \mathbf{interface}\ f :> \sigma = g
\end{array}
\qquad
\begin{array}{rcl}
\lambda_{\mathscr{C}}\ \textit{expressions} & e & ::= \cdots \mid \mathsf{f}^{\mathsf{g}} \\
\lambda_{\mathscr{C}}\ \textit{types} & \tau & ::= \cdots \mid \{\sigma\} \\
\lambda^{\mathscr{A}}\ \textit{expressions} & e & ::= \cdots \mid \mathbf{f}^{\mathsf{g}} \\
\lambda^{\mathscr{A}}\ \textit{types} & \sigma & ::= \cdots \mid \{\tau\}
\end{array}
$$

Fig. 11. New syntax for $\lambda_{\mathscr{C}}^{\mathscr{A}}$

$$\boxed{\vdash P : \tau}\,,\ \boxed{\vdash^M m\ \mathrm{okay}}$$

PROG
$$\frac{\forall m \in M, \vdash^M m\ \mathrm{okay} \qquad \cdot ; \cdot \vdash_{\mathscr{C}}^M e : \tau}{\vdash M\ e : \tau}$$

TM-I
$$\frac{(\mathbf{module}\ g : (\sigma)^{\mathscr{C}} = v) \in M \qquad |\sigma| = \mathsf{u}}{\vdash^M \mathbf{interface}\ f :> \sigma = g\ \mathrm{okay}}$$

$$\boxed{\Delta; \Gamma \vdash_{\mathscr{C}}^M e : \tau}\,,\ \boxed{\Delta; \Gamma \vdash_{\mathscr{A}}^M e : \sigma}$$

TA-MODC
$$\frac{(\mathbf{module}\ f : \tau = v) \in M \qquad \cdot \vdash_{\mathscr{C}} \tau}{\Delta; \Gamma \vdash_{\mathscr{A}}^M f : (\tau)^{\mathscr{A}}}$$

TC-MODA
$$\frac{(\mathbf{module}\ f : \sigma = v) \in M \qquad \cdot \vdash_{\mathscr{A}} \sigma}{\Delta; \Gamma \vdash_{\mathscr{C}}^M f : (\sigma)^{\mathscr{C}}}$$

TA-MODI
$$\frac{(\mathbf{interface}\ f :> \sigma = g) \in M \qquad \cdot \vdash_{\mathscr{A}} \sigma}{\Delta; \Gamma \vdash_{\mathscr{A}}^M f : \sigma}$$

Fig. 12. New statics for $\lambda_{\mathscr{C}}^{\mathscr{A}}$

not require these two types to be the same, swap performs a *strong update*—
that is, it may change the type of the value residing in a reference cell. This is
why the qualifier given to references must be a: if a reference is aliased, then it
becomes possible to observe the type change in a way the destroys type safety.
This feature of the calculus is a stand-in for the variety of invariants that an
affine type system might enforce. In the mixed calculus, $\lambda_{\mathscr{C}}$ may gain access to
$\lambda^{\mathscr{A}}$ references. It has no operations available to read or write them, but it must
be prevented from passing an aliased reference cell back into $\lambda^{\mathscr{A}}$ where it can
cause trouble.

4.2 Mixing It up with $\lambda_{\mathscr{C}}^{\mathscr{A}}$

The primary aim of this work is to construct (type-safe) programs by mixing
modules written in an affine language and modules written in a non-affine language, and to have them interoperate as seamlessly as possible. We can then
model an affine program calling into a library written in a legacy language, or
a conventional program calling into code written in an affine language. In either case, we must ensure that the non-affine portions of the program do not
break the affine portions' invariants. As noted in Sect. 3, we accomplish this via
run-time checks in the style of higher-order contracts [4].

The additional syntax for mixed programs is in Fig. 11. The main expression in a mixed program is in subcalculus $\lambda_{\mathscr{C}}$. Modules now include $\lambda^{\mathscr{A}}$ modules, $\lambda_{\mathscr{C}}$ modules, and *interface* modules, which are used to assert a $\lambda^{\mathscr{A}}$ type about a $\lambda_{\mathscr{C}}$ module as we saw in Sect. 2.

We add to each subcalculus's expressions a production referring to modules from the other subcalculus. We decorate each such module name with the name of the module in which it appears (*e.g.*, $\mathbf{f^g}$ for a reference to $\lambda_{\mathscr{C}}$ module $\mathbf{f}$ from $\lambda^{\mathscr{A}}$ module $\mathbf{g}$) and use this name as the negative party in contracts regulating the intercalculus boundary, in order to assign blame.

Static Semantics. The type system for the mixed calculus is the union of the type systems for $\lambda^{\mathscr{A}}$ and $\lambda_{\mathscr{C}}$ (Figs. 6, 8, and 9), along with additional typing rules (Fig. 12) for $\lambda^{\mathscr{A}}$ module invocations in $\lambda_{\mathscr{C}}$ expressions and $\lambda_{\mathscr{C}}$ module invocations in $\lambda^{\mathscr{A}}$ expressions.

Rule TC-MODA (Fig. 12) types occurrences of $\lambda^{\mathscr{A}}$ module names in $\lambda_{\mathscr{C}}$ expressions. The rule uses the type conversion function $(\cdot)^{\mathscr{C}}$, defined in Sect. 3 (p. 558) to give a $\lambda_{\mathscr{C}}$ type to the $\lambda^{\mathscr{A}}$ module invocation. Because $\lambda^{\mathscr{A}}$ types are richer than $\lambda_{\mathscr{C}}$ types—$\lambda^{\mathscr{A}}$ function types carry extra information in the qualifier—the conversion loses information, which may need to be recovered through dynamic checks. For example, given a $\lambda^{\mathscr{A}}$ module $\mathbf{g}$ with type int $\xrightarrow{\mathsf{u}}$ int $\xrightarrow{\mathsf{a}}$ int, the conversion rule assigns it the $\lambda_{\mathscr{C}}$ type $\mathbf{int} \to \mathbf{int} \to \mathbf{int}$. Calculus $\lambda_{\mathscr{C}}$'s type system cannot enforce that the result of applying $\mathbf{g}$ be applied at most once, which will need to be checked at run time.

For a $\lambda_{\mathscr{C}}$ module with type τ invoked from a $\lambda^{\mathscr{A}}$ expression, we use the module at type $(\tau)^{\mathscr{A}}$. It would be reasonable for TA-MODC to give it any $\lambda^{\mathscr{A}}$ type in the pre-image of the $\lambda^{\mathscr{A}}$-to-$\lambda_{\mathscr{C}}$ mapping, but $(\cdot)^{\mathscr{A}}$ makes the most permissive, statically safe choice, which is to map all $\lambda_{\mathscr{C}}$ arrows $(\to)$ to the unlimited $\lambda^{\mathscr{A}}$ arrow $(\xrightarrow{\mathsf{u}})$. Consider:

- If $\mathbf{f}$: $\mathbf{int} \to \mathbf{int}$ in $\lambda_{\mathscr{C}}$, then int $\xrightarrow{\mathsf{u}}$ int is the right type in $\lambda^{\mathscr{A}}$. There is no reason to limit $\mathbf{f}$ to an affine function type, because $\lambda_{\mathscr{C}}$ does not impose that requirement, and subtyping allows us to use it at int $\xrightarrow{\mathsf{a}}$ int, if necessary.
- If $\mathbf{f}$: $(\mathbf{int} \to \mathbf{int}) \to \mathbf{int}$ in $\lambda_{\mathscr{C}}$, then (int $\xrightarrow{\mathsf{u}}$ int) $\xrightarrow{\mathsf{u}}$ int will allow the imported function to be passed unlimited functions but not affine functions. This is a safe choice, because $\lambda_{\mathscr{C}}$'s type system does not tell us whether $\mathbf{f}$ may call its argument more than once.

In the latter case, what if the programmer somehow knows that function $\mathbf{f}$ applies its argument at most once, as in the example of *threadFork$_{\mathscr{C}}$* (p. 556)? It should not violate $\lambda^{\mathscr{A}}$'s invariants to pass an affine function to *threadFork$_{\mathscr{C}}$*, but $\lambda^{\mathscr{A}}$ cannot know this. Therefore, rule TA-MODC gives $\lambda_{\mathscr{C}}$ modules a conservative $\lambda^{\mathscr{A}}$ type that requires no run-time checks. We can use an **interface** module to coerce a $\lambda_{\mathscr{C}}$ module's type τ to a more permissive $\lambda^{\mathscr{A}}$ type in the pre-image of τ, and this, too, requires a dynamic check.

Operational Semantics. We extend the syntax of our mixed language with several new forms (Fig. 13). Whereas our source syntax segregates the two subcalculi into separate modules, module invocation reduces to the body of the module, which leads expressions of both subcalculi to nest at run time. Rather than allow $\lambda^{\mathscr{A}}$ terms to appear directly in $\lambda_{\mathscr{C}}$, and vice versa, we need a way to cordon off terms from one calculus embedded in the other and to ensure that the interaction is well-behaved. We call these new expression forms *boundaries*.

The new run-time syntax includes both boundary expressions $^{\sigma}_{f}\mathrm{AC}_{g}(e)$ for embedding $\lambda_{\mathscr{C}}$ expressions in $\lambda^{\mathscr{A}}$ and boundary expressions $_{f}\mathbf{CA}^{\sigma}_{g}(e)$ for embedding $\lambda^{\mathscr{A}}$ expressions in $\lambda_{\mathscr{C}}$. Each of these forms has a superscript σ, written on the $\lambda^{\mathscr{A}}$ side, which represents a contract between the two modules that gave rise to the nested expression. Some contracts, for example int, are fully enforced by both type systems. Other contracts, such as int $\overset{a}{\multimap}$ int, require dynamic checks. The type system guarantees that such a function receives and returns only integers, but this type also imposes an obligation on the negative party to apply the function at most once, which the $\lambda_{\mathscr{C}}$ type system alone does not enforce.

The right subscript of a boundary is a module name in the inner subcalculus, representing the positive party to the contract: It promises that if the enclosed subexpression reduces to a value, then the value will obey contract σ. The left subscript is the negative party, which promises to treat the resulting value properly. In particular, if the contract is affine, then the negative party promises to use the resulting value at most once.

Boundaries first arise when a module in one calculus refers to a module in the other calculus. When the name of a $\lambda_{\mathscr{C}}$ module appears in a $\lambda^{\mathscr{A}}$ term, A-MODC wraps the module name with an AC boundary, using the $\lambda^{\mathscr{A}}$-conversion of the module's type τ as the contract. For interface modules, the contract is as declared by the interface, and the name of the interface is the positive party (A-MODI). From the other direction, a $\lambda^{\mathscr{A}}$ module invoked from a $\lambda_{\mathscr{C}}$ expression is wrapped in a **CA** boundary by rule C-MODA.

We add evaluation contexts for reduction under boundaries, which means it is now possible to construct a $\lambda_{\mathscr{C}}$ evaluation context with a $\lambda^{\mathscr{A}}$ hole, and vice versa. If the expression under a boundary reduces to a value, it is time to apply the boundary's contract to the value. There are three possibilities:

- Some values, such as integers, always satisfy the contract, so the boundary is discarded.
- Functional values and opaque affine values must have their checks deferred: functions until application time, and opaque values until they pass back into their original subcalculus. For deferred checks, we leave the value in a "sealed" boundary, $_{f}\mathbf{CA}[\ell]^{\sigma}_{g}(v)$ or $^{\sigma}_{f}\mathrm{AC}[\,]_{g}(\mathbf{v})$, which is itself a value form.
- When a previously sealed opaque value reaches a boundary back to its original subcalculus, both that boundary and the sealed boundary are discarded.

Rule C-WRAP implements contract application for $\lambda^{\mathscr{A}}$ values embedded in $\lambda_{\mathscr{C}}$ expressions, as indicated by metafunction *coerce*$_{\mathscr{C}}$. The first case of *coerce*$_{\mathscr{C}}$ handles immediate checks, and its second case unseals previously sealed $\lambda_{\mathscr{C}}$ values that have returned home. The second case of *coerce*$_{\mathscr{C}}$ seals and *blesses* a $\lambda^{\mathscr{A}}$ value, by allocating a location ℓ, to which it stores a distinguished value **blssd**; it adds this location to the boundary, which marks the sealed value as not yet

$$\lambda_{\mathscr{C}}\ terms\quad e ::= \cdots \mid \underset{f\,f}{\mathbf{CA}}^{\sigma}(e) \qquad\qquad \lambda^{\mathscr{A}}\ terms\quad e ::= \cdots \mid {}^{\sigma}\underset{f\,f}{\mathbf{AC}}(e)$$

$$\lambda_{\mathscr{C}}\ values\quad v ::= \cdots \mid \underset{f\,f}{\mathbf{CA}}[\ell]^{\sigma}(v) \qquad \lambda^{\mathscr{A}}\ values\quad v ::= \cdots \mid {}^{\sigma}\underset{f\,f}{\mathbf{AC}}[\,](v)$$

$$\lambda_{\mathscr{C}}\ eval.\ cxts.\ \mathbf{E} ::= \cdots \mid \underset{f\,f}{\mathbf{CA}}^{\sigma}(\mathbf{E}) \qquad \lambda^{\mathscr{A}}\ eval.\ cxts.\ \mathbf{E} ::= \cdots \mid {}^{\sigma}\underset{f\,f}{\mathbf{AC}}(\mathbf{E})$$

$$configurations\quad C ::= (s,e) \mid \mathbf{blame\,f}$$

$$answers\quad A ::= (s,v) \mid \mathbf{blame\,f}$$

$$stores\quad s ::= \{\} \mid s \uplus \{\ell \mapsto v\} \mid s \uplus \{\ell \mapsto v\}$$

$$(\text{C-MODA})\qquad (s, f^g) \underset{M}{\longmapsto} (s, \underset{g\,f}{\mathbf{CA}}^{\sigma}(f)) \qquad (\mathbf{module\,f}:\sigma = v) \in M$$

$$(\text{A-MODC})\qquad (s, f^g) \underset{M}{\longmapsto} (s, {}^{(\tau)^{\mathscr{A}}}\underset{g\,f}{\mathbf{AC}}(f)) \qquad (\mathbf{module\,f}:\tau = v) \in M$$

$$(\text{A-MODI})\qquad (s, f^g) \underset{M}{\longmapsto} (s, {}^{\sigma}\underset{g\,f}{\mathbf{AC}}(f')) \qquad (\mathbf{interface\,f} :> \sigma = f') \in M$$

$$(\text{C-WRAP})\qquad (s, \underset{f\,g}{\mathbf{CA}}^{\sigma}(v)) \underset{M}{\longmapsto} coerce_{\mathscr{C}}(s,\sigma,v,f,g)$$

$$(\text{A-WRAP})\qquad (s, {}^{\sigma}\underset{f\,g}{\mathbf{AC}}(v)) \underset{M}{\longmapsto} coerce_{\mathscr{A}}(s,\sigma,v,f,g)$$

$$(\text{C-}B\text{-A})\qquad (s, \underset{f\,g}{\mathbf{CA}}[\ell]^{\forall\alpha^q.\sigma}(v)[\tau]) \underset{M}{\longmapsto} check(s,\ell,|\sigma|,\underset{f\,g}{\mathbf{CA}}^{\sigma[(\tau)^{\mathscr{A}}/\alpha^q]}\!\left(v[(\tau)^{\mathscr{A}}]\right),f)$$

$$(\text{C-}\beta\text{-A})\qquad (s, \underset{f\,g}{\mathbf{CA}}[\ell]^{\sigma_1 \overset{q}{\multimap}\sigma_2}(v_1)\,v_2) \underset{M}{\longmapsto} check(s,\ell,q,\underset{f\,g}{\mathbf{CA}}^{\sigma_2}\!\left(v_1\ {}^{\sigma_1}\underset{g\,f}{\mathbf{AC}}(v_2)\right),f)$$

$$(\text{A-}B\text{-C})\qquad (s, {}^{\forall\alpha^q.\sigma}\underset{f\,g}{\mathbf{AC}}[\,](v)[\sigma_a]) \underset{M}{\longmapsto} (s, {}^{\sigma[\sigma_a/\alpha^q]}\underset{f\,g}{\mathbf{AC}}\left(v[(\sigma_a)^{\mathscr{C}}]\right))$$

$$(\text{A-}\beta\text{-C})\qquad (s, {}^{\sigma_1 \overset{q}{\multimap}\sigma_2}\underset{f\,g}{\mathbf{AC}}[\,](v_1)\,v_2) \underset{M}{\longmapsto} (s, {}^{\sigma_2}\underset{f\,g}{\mathbf{AC}}\left(v_1\ \underset{g\,f}{\mathbf{CA}}^{\sigma_1}(v_2)\right))$$

$$coerce_{\mathscr{C}}(s,\sigma,v,f,g) = \begin{cases} (s, \lceil z\rceil) & \text{if } v = \lceil z\rceil \\ (s, v') & \text{if } v = {}^{\{\tau^{\circ}\}}_{g'}\mathbf{AC}[\,]_{f'}(v') \\ (s \uplus \{\ell \mapsto \mathbf{blssd}\}, \underset{f\,g}{\mathbf{CA}}[\ell]^{\sigma}(v)) & \text{otherwise} \end{cases}$$

$$coerce_{\mathscr{A}}(s,\sigma,v,f,g) = \begin{cases} (s, \lceil z\rceil) & \text{if } v = \lceil z\rceil \\ check(s,\ell,|\sigma^{\circ}|,v',g') & \text{if } v = {}_{g'}\mathbf{CA}[\ell]^{\sigma^{\circ}}_{f'}(v') \\ (s, {}^{\sigma}\underset{f\,g}{\mathbf{AC}}[\,](v)) & \text{otherwise} \end{cases}$$

$$check(s,\ell,q,e,f) = \begin{cases} (s,e) & \text{if } q = u \\ (s' \uplus \{\ell \mapsto \mathbf{dfnct}\}, e) & \text{if } s = s' \uplus \{\ell \mapsto \mathbf{blssd}\} \\ (s, \mathbf{blame\,f}) & \text{otherwise} \end{cases}$$

Fig. 13. Dynamics of $\lambda_{\mathscr{C}}^{\mathscr{A}}$ (run-time syntax and reduction rules)

used. This corresponds directly to the reference cell allocated by *makeAffineFun-Contract* in Sect. 3.

Rule A-WRAP implements contracts for $\lambda_{\mathscr{C}}$ values in $\lambda^{\mathscr{A}}$ expressions. Metafunction *coerce$_{\mathscr{A}}$*'s first case is the same as *coerce$_{\mathscr{C}}$*'s, and the third case seals a value for deferred checking; it need not allocate a location to track the usage of a $\lambda_{\mathscr{C}}$ value. The third case unseals a previously sealed $\lambda^{\mathscr{A}}$ value on its way back to $\lambda^{\mathscr{A}}$, and this requires checking that an affine value has not been previously unsealed. This step is specified by metafunction *check*, which also has three cases. Unlimited values are unsealed with no check. If an affine value remains blessed, *check* updates the store to mark it "defunct" and returns the unsealed value. If, on the other hand, there is an attempt to unseal a defunct affine value, *check* blames the negative party. This is the key dynamic check that enforces the affine invariant for non-functional values.

Rules C-B-A, C-β-A, A-B-C, and A-β-C all handle sealed abstractions, which are unsealed when they are applied. For sealed $\lambda^{\mathscr{A}}$ abstractions, the seal location ℓ must be checked, to ensure that an affine function or type abstraction is not unsealed and applied more than once. This is the dynamic check that enforces the affine invariant for functions.

Type Soundness. The presence of strong updates means that aliasing a location can result in a program getting "stuck": if an aliased location is updated at a different type, reading from the alias produces a value of unexpected type. Calculus $\lambda^{\mathscr{A}}$'s type system prevents this, but adding $\lambda_{\mathscr{C}}$ means that a $\lambda^{\mathscr{A}}$ value may be aliased outside $\lambda^{\mathscr{A}}$. Our soundness criterion is that no program that gets stuck is assigned a type. In particular, all aliasing of affine values is either prevented by $\lambda^{\mathscr{A}}$'s type system or detected by a contract at run time.

In order to prove a Wright-Felleisen–style type soundness theorem [21], we identify precisely what property is preserved by subject reduction. We use an internal type system to track which portions of the store are reachable from $\lambda^{\mathscr{A}}$ values that have flowed into $\lambda_{\mathscr{C}}$. Under this type system, configurations enjoy standard progress and preservation, which allows us to state and prove a syntactic type soundness theorem using the internal type system's configuration typing judgment $\triangleright^M C : \tau$:

Theorem (Type Soundness). *If* $\vdash M$ e $:$ τ *and* $(\{\}, e) \longmapsto_M^* C$ *such that configuration* C *cannot take another step, then* C *is an answer with* $\triangleright^M C : \tau$.

Our full formalization, including complete definitions of the calculi and proofs, is available at http://www.ccs.neu.edu/~tov/pubs/affine-contracts/.

5   Conclusion

Our work is part of an ongoing program to investigate practical aspects of substructural type systems, and this paper describes one step in that program. Here, we have focused on the problem of interaction between substructural and non-substructural code, each governed by its own type system, and explored the use of higher-order contracts to prevent the conventional language from breaking the substructural language's invariants. Our answer to the problem at hand naturally raises more questions.

Exceptions. In a production language with a contract system, contract violations should not always terminate the program. Real programs may catch an exception and either try to mitigate the condition that caused it, try something easier instead, or report an error and go on with some other task. To ensure soundness, it suffices to prevent the questionable actions from occurring.

On one hand, we believe that ML-style exceptions should not provide too much difficulty in an affine setting. In our prototype, *try-with* expressions are multiplicative, in the sense that the type environment needs to be split between an expression and its exception handler, not given in whole to both.

On the other hand, we do not know how exceptions or any sort of blame might work in a linear setting—this is one reason why we chose an affine calculus. Terminating the program is problematic because of the implicit discarding of linear values, but catching an exception once part of a continuation containing linear values has been discarded seems even worse. Exceptions in linear languages remain an open question.

Linearity. Our work emphasizes contract-based interaction with affine type systems rather than linear type systems because it remains unclear to us what linear contracts ought to mean. We may want a conventional language to interoperate with a language that (at least sometimes) prohibits discarding values. However, unlike affine guarantees, which are safety properties, relevance guarantees—that a value is used at some point in the future—are a form of liveness property.

One approximation is to consider a contract representing a relevance guarantee to be violated if at any point we can determine that the contract necessarily will be violated. Detecting the violation of such a liveness property is undecidable in general, but tracing garbage collection approximates a liveness property very close to the one we desire. In an idealized semantics, we might garbage collect the store after each reduction step and signal a violation if the seal location of a not-yet-used linear value has become unreachable. In a real implementation, finalizers on linear values could detect discarding. If we detect a violation, we probably could do nothing to prevent it, but at worst we could file a bug report.

Our work suggests that adding substructural libraries to a conventional programming language such as ML does not require a particularly complicated implementation, and our results yield a realistic contract-based design.

Acknowledgments. We wish to thank Daniel Brown, Ryan Culpepper, Jed Davis, Matthias Felleisen, Alec Heller, Sam Tobin-Hochstadt, Aaron Turon, and the anonymous referees for their helpful comments, discussion, and corrections. This research was supported in part by AFOSR grant FA9550-09-1-0110.

References

1. Ahmed, A., Fluet, M., Morrisett, G.: L³: A linear language with locations. Tech. Rep. TR-24-04, Harvard University (2004)
2. Barendsen, E., Smetsers, S.: Uniqueness typing for functional languages with graph rewriting semantics. Mathematical Structures in Computer Science 6(6) (1996)
3. Benton, P.N.: A mixed linear and non-linear logic: Proofs, terms and models. In: Pacholski, L., Tiuryn, J. (eds.) CSL 1994. LNCS, vol. 933, pp. 121–135. Springer, Heidelberg (1995)
4. Findler, R.B., Felleisen, M.: Contracts for higher-order functions. In: ICFP 2002, pp. 48–59. ACM, New York (2002)
5. Flanagan, C.: Hybrid type checking. In: POPL 2006, vol. 41, pp. 245–256. ACM, New York (2006)
6. Gay, S.J., Hole, M.J.: Types and subtypes for client-server interactions. In: Swierstra, S.D. (ed.) ESOP 1999. LNCS, vol. 1576, pp. 74–90. Springer, Heidelberg (1999)
7. Girard, J.Y.: Interprétation fonctionelle et élimination des coupures de l'arithmétique d'ordre supérieur. Ph.D. thesis, Université Paris VI (1972)
8. Jim, T., Morrisett, G., Grossman, D., Hicks, M., Cheney, J., Wang, Y.: Cyclone: A safe dialect of C. In: Proc. USENIX Annual Technical Conference (2002)
9. Matthews, J., Findler, R.B.: Operational semantics for multi-language programs. In: POPL 2007, vol. 42, pp. 3–10. ACM, New York (2007)
10. Milner, R., Tofte, M., Harper, R., MacQueen, D.: The Definition of Standard ML, revised edn. MIT, Cambridge (1997)
11. Plotkin, G.: Type theory and recursion. In: LICS 1993, p. 374. IEEE Computer Society, Los Alamitos (1993)
12. Reynolds, J.C.: Towards a theory of type structure. In: Robinet, B. (ed.) Programming Symposium. LNCS, vol. 19, pp. 408–423. Springer, Heidelberg (1974)
13. Siek, J.G., Taha, W.: Gradual typing for functional languages. In: Workshop on Scheme and Functional Programming, pp. 81–92. ACM, New York (2006)
14. Stevens, W.R.: UNIX Network programming. Prentice-Hall, New Jersey (1990)
15. Strom, R., Yemini, S.: Typestate: A programming language concept for enhancing software reliability. IEEE Transactions on Software Engineering 12(1) (1986)
16. Tobin-Hochstadt, S., Felleisen, M.: Interlanguage migration: From scripts to programs. In: OOPSLA 2006, pp. 964–974. ACM, New York (2006)
17. Tobin-Hochstadt, S., Felleisen, M.: The design and implementation of Typed Scheme. In: POPL 2007, pp. 395–406. ACM, New York (2008)
18. Turner, D.N., Wadler, P., Mossin, C.: Once upon a type. In: FPCA 1995, pp. 1–11. ACM, New York (1995)
19. Wadler, P.: Linear types can change the world. In: Programming Concepts and Methods. In: Programming Concepts and Methods, pp. 347–359. North Holland, Amsterdam (1990)
20. Walker, D.: Substructural type systems. In: Pierce, B.C. (ed.) Advanced Topics in Types and Programming Languages, ch. 1, pp. 3–44. MIT, Cambridge (2005)
21. Wright, A.K., Felleisen, M.: A syntactic approach to type soundness. Information and Computation 115(1), 38–94 (1994)

CFA2: A Context-Free Approach
to Control-Flow Analysis

Dimitrios Vardoulakis and Olin Shivers

Northeastern University
{dimvar,shivers}@ccs.neu.edu

Abstract. In a functional language, the dominant control-flow mechanism is function call and return. Most higher-order flow analyses, including k-CFA, do not handle call and return well: they remember only a bounded number of pending calls because they approximate programs with control-flow graphs. Call/return mismatch introduces precision-degrading spurious control-flow paths and increases the analysis time.

We describe CFA2, the first flow analysis with precise call/return matching in the presence of higher-order functions and tail calls. We formulate CFA2 as an abstract interpretation of programs in continuation-passing style and describe a sound and complete summarization algorithm for our abstract semantics. A preliminary evaluation shows that CFA2 gives more accurate data-flow information than 0CFA and 1CFA.

1   Introduction

Higher-order functional programs can be analyzed using analyses such as the k-CFA family [1]. These algorithms approximate the valid control-flow paths through the program as the set of all paths through a finite graph of abstract machine states, where each state represents a program point plus some amount of abstracted environment and control context.

In fact, this is not a particularly tight approximation. The set of paths through a finite graph is a regular language. However, the execution traces produced by recursive function calls are strings in a *context-free language*. Approximating this control flow with regular-language techniques permits execution paths that do not properly match calls with returns. This is particularly harmful when analyzing higher-order languages, since flowing functional values down these spurious paths can give rise to further "phantom" control-flow structure, along which functional values can then flow, and so forth, in a destructive spiral that not only degrades precision but drives up the cost of the analysis.

Pushdown models of programs can match an unbounded number of calls and returns, tightening up the set of possible executions to strings in a context-free language. Such models have long been used for first-order languages. The functional approach of Sharir and Pnueli [2] computes transfer-functions for whole procedures by composing transfer-functions of their basic blocks. Then, at a call-node these functions are used to compute the data-flow value of the corresponding return-node directly. This "summary-based" technique has seen widespread

A.D. Gordon (Ed.): ESOP 2010, LNCS 6012, pp. 570–589, 2010.

use [3, 4]. Other pushdown models include Recursive State Machines [5] and Pushdown Systems [6].

In this paper, we propose CFA2, a pushdown model of higher-order programs. Our contributions can be summarized as follows:

- CFA2 is a flow analysis with precise call/return matching that can be used in the compilation of both typed and untyped languages. No existing analysis for functional languages enjoys all of these properties. k-CFA and its variants do not provide call/return matching (section 3.1). Rehof and Fähndrich's analysis [7] supports limited call/return matching and applies to typed languages only (section 7).
- CFA2 uses a stack and a heap for variable binding. Variable references are looked up in one or the other, depending on where they appear in the source code. As it turns out, most references in typical programs are read from the stack, which results in significant precision gains. Also, CFA2 can filter certain bindings off the stack to sharpen precision (section 4). k-CFA with abstract garbage collection [8] cannot infer that it is safe to remove these bindings. Last, the stack makes CFA2 resilient to syntax changes like η-expansion. It is well known that k-CFA is sensitive to such changes [9, 10].
- We formulate CFA2 as an abstract interpretation of programs in continuation-passing style (CPS). The abstract semantics uses a stack of unbounded height. Hence, the abstract state space is infinite, unlike k-CFA. To analyze the state space, we extend the tabulation algorithm of Reps et al. [3]. The resulting algorithm is a search-based variant of summarization that can handle higher-order functions and tail recursion. Currently, CFA2 does not handle first-class-control operators such as `call/cc` (section 5).
- We have implemented 0CFA, 1CFA and CFA2 in the Twobit Scheme compiler [11]. Our experimental results show that CFA2 is more precise than 0CFA and 1CFA. Also, CFA2 usually visits a smaller state space (section 6).

2 Preliminary Definitions and Notational Conventions

We begin with a description of our CPS language and its small-step semantics. For brevity, we develop the theory of CFA2 in the untyped λ-calculus. Primitive data, explicit recursion and side-effects can be easily added using standard techniques [1, ch. 3] [12, ch. 9]. Compilers that use CPS [13, 14] usually partition the terms in a program in two disjoint sets, the user and the continuation set, and treat user terms differently from continuation terms.

We adopt this partitioning for our language (Fig. 1). Variables, lambdas and calls are given labels from $ULab$ or $CLab$. Labels are pairwise distinct. User lambdas take a user argument and the current continuation; continuation lambdas take only a user argument. We apply an additional syntactic constraint: the only continuation variable that can appear free in the body of a user lambda $(\lambda_l (u\,k)\,call)$ is k. This simple constraint forbids first-class control [15]. Intuitively, we get such a program by CPS-converting a direct-style program without `call/cc`. We refer to this variant of CPS as "Restricted CPS" (RCPS).

$$
\begin{array}{rclcrcll}
v \in Var & = & UVar + CVar & \qquad & clam \in CLam & ::= & (\lambda_\gamma (u) \; call) \\
u \in UVar & = & \text{a set of identifiers} & & call \in Call & = & UCall + CCall \\
k \in CVar & = & \text{a set of identifiers} & & ucall \in UCall & ::= & (f \, e \, q)^l \\
\psi \in Lab & = & ULab + CLab & & ccall \in CCall & ::= & (q \, e)^\gamma \\
l \in ULab & = & \text{a set of labels} & & g \in Exp & = & UExp + CExp \\
\gamma \in CLab & = & \text{a set of labels} & & f, e \in UExp & = & ULam + UVar \\
lam \in Lam & = & ULam + CLam & & q \in CExp & = & CLam + CVar \\
ulam \in ULam & ::= & (\lambda_l (u \, k) \; call) & & pr \in Program & ::= & ULam
\end{array}
$$

Fig. 1. Partitioned CPS

We assume that all variables in a program have distinct names. Concrete syntax enclosed in $[\![\cdot]\!]$ denotes an item of abstract syntax. Functions with a '?' subscript are predicates, e.g., $Var_?(e)$ returns true if e is a variable and false otherwise. Labels can be split into disjoint sets according to the innermost user lambda that contains them. For example, in the following program, which has three user lambdas, these sets are $\{1, 6, 4, 8\}$, $\{2, 9, 5, 10\}$ and $\{3, 7\}$.

$$
\begin{aligned}
&(\lambda_1(\text{u1 k1}) \;\; _6((\lambda_2(\text{u2 k2}) \;\; _9((\lambda_5(\text{u5}) \;\; _{10}(\text{k2 u1})) \; \text{u2})) \\
&\qquad (\lambda_3(\text{u3 k3}) \;\; _7(\text{k3 u3})) \\
&\qquad (\lambda_4(\text{u4}) \;\; _8(\text{k1 u4}))))
\end{aligned}
$$

The "label to variable" map $LV(\psi)$ returns all the variables bound by any lambdas that belong in the same set as ψ, e.g., $LV(8) = \{\text{u1}, \text{k1}, \text{u4}\}$ and $LV(5) = \{\text{u2}, \text{k2}, \text{u5}\}$. We use this map to model stack behavior, because all the continuation lambdas that "belong" to a given user lambda λ_l get closed by extending λ_l's stack frame (cf. section 4). Notice that, for any ψ, $LV(\psi)$ contains exactly one continuation variable.

We use two notations for tuples, $(e_1, \ldots, e_n)$ and $\langle e_1, \ldots, e_n \rangle$, to avoid confusion when tuples are deeply nested. We use the latter for lists as well; ambiguities will be resolved by the context. Lists are also described by a head-tail notation, e.g., $3 :: \langle 1, 3, -47 \rangle$.

The semantics of RCPS appears in Fig. 2. Execution traces alternate between *Eval* and *Apply* states. At an *Eval* state, we evaluate the subexpressions of a call site before performing a call. At an *Apply* state, we perform the call.

The last component of each state is a *time*, which is a sequence of call sites. *Eval* to *Apply* transitions increment the time by recording the label of the corresponding call site. *Apply* to *Eval* transitions leave the time unchanged. Thus, the time t of a state reveals the call sites along the execution path to that state.

Times indicate points in the execution when variables are bound. The binding environment β is a partial function that maps variables to their binding times. The variable environment ve maps variable-time pairs to values. To find the value of a variable v, we look up the time v was put in β, and use that to search for the actual value in ve.

Let's look at the transitions more closely. At a *UEval* state with call site $(f \, e \, q)^l$, we evaluate f, e and q using the function $\mathcal{A}_{cs}$. Lambdas are paired up

$\varsigma \in State = Eval + Apply$
$\varsigma \in Eval = UEval + CEval$
$\varsigma \in UEval = UCall \times BEnv \times VEnv \times Time$
$\varsigma \in CEval = CCall \times BEnv \times VEnv \times Time$
$\varsigma \in Apply = UApply + CApply$
$\varsigma \in UApply = UClos \times UClos \times CClos \times$
$\quad\quad VEnv \times Time$

$\varsigma \in CApply = CClos \times UClos \times VEnv \times Time$
$Clos = UClos + CClos$
$d \in UClos = ULam \times BEnv$
$c \in CClos = (CLam \times BEnv) + halt$
$\beta \in BEnv = Var \rightharpoonup Time$
$ve \in VEnv = Var \times Time \rightharpoonup Clos$
$t \in Time = Lab^*$

$$\mathcal{A}_{cs}(g, \beta, ve) \triangleq \begin{cases} (g, \beta) & Lam_?(g) \\ ve(g, \beta(g)) & Var_?(g) \end{cases}$$

UEval to UApply:
$(\llbracket (f \, e \, q)^l \rrbracket, \beta, ve, t) \rightarrow (proc, d, c, ve, l :: t)$
$proc = \mathcal{A}_{cs}(f, \beta, ve)$
$d = \mathcal{A}_{cs}(e, \beta, ve)$
$c = \mathcal{A}_{cs}(q, \beta, ve)$

CEval to CApply:
$(\llbracket (q \, e)^\gamma \rrbracket, \beta, ve, t) \rightarrow (proc, d, ve, \gamma :: t)$
$proc = \mathcal{A}_{cs}(q, \beta, ve)$
$d = \mathcal{A}_{cs}(e, \beta, ve)$

UApply to Eval:
$(proc, d, c, ve, t) \rightarrow (call, \beta', ve', t)$
$proc = \langle \llbracket (\lambda_l (u \, k) \, call) \rrbracket, \beta \rangle$
$\beta' = \beta[u \mapsto t][k \mapsto t]$
$ve' = ve[(u, t) \mapsto d][(k, t) \mapsto c]$

CApply to Eval:
$(proc, d, ve, t) \rightarrow (call, \beta', ve', t)$
$proc = \langle \llbracket (\lambda_\gamma (u) \, call) \rrbracket, \beta \rangle$
$\beta' = \beta[u \mapsto t]$
$ve' = ve[(u, t) \mapsto d]$

Fig. 2. Concrete semantics and domains for Restricted CPS

with β to become closures, while variables are looked up in ve using β. We add the label l in front of the current time and transition to a $UApply$ state.

From $UApply$ to $Eval$, we bind the formals of a procedure $\langle \llbracket (\lambda_l (u \, k) \, call) \rrbracket, \beta \rangle$ to the arguments and jump to its body. The new binding environment β' is an extension of the procedure's environment, with u and k mapped to the current time. The new variable environment ve' maps (u, t) to the user argument d, and (k, t) to the continuation argument c.

The remaining two transitions are similar. We use $halt$ to denote the top-level continuation of a program pr. The initial state $\mathcal{I}(pr)$ is $((pr, \emptyset), input, halt, \emptyset, \langle \rangle)$, where $input$ is a closure of the form $\langle \llbracket (\lambda_l (u \, k) \, call) \rrbracket, \emptyset \rangle$. Note that the initial time is the empty sequence of call sites.

In the terminology of abstract interpretation, this semantics is called the *concrete* semantics. In order to find properties of a program at compile time, one needs to derive a computable approximation of the concrete semantics, called the *abstract* semantics. CFA2 and k-CFA are such approximations.

CPS-based compilers may or may not use a control stack for the final code. Steele's view, illustrated in the Rabbit compiler [13], is that argument evaluation pushes stack and function calls are GOTOs. Since arguments in CPS are not calls, argument evaluation is always trivial and Rabbit never needs to push stack. By this approach, every call in CPS is a tail call.

An alternative style was used in the Orbit compiler [14]. At every function call, Orbit pushes a frame for the arguments. By this approach, tail calls are only the calls where the continuation argument is a variable. These CPS call sites were in

```
(define (len l k)
  2(pair? l
    (λ3(test)
      4(if test
        (λ5()
          6(cdr l
            (λ7(rest)
              8(len rest
                (λ9(ans) 10(+ 1 ans k))))))
        (λ11() 12(k 0)))

  1(len '(3) halt)
```

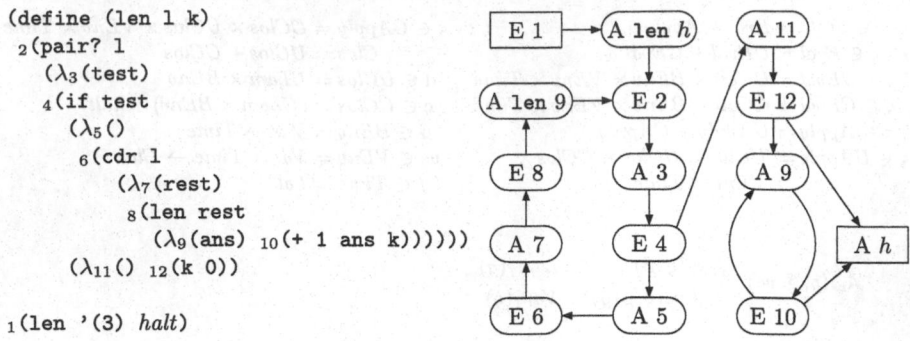

Fig. 3. 0CFA on len

tail position in the initial direct-style program. *CEval* states where the operator is a variable are calls to the current continuation with a return value. Orbit pops the stack at tail calls and before calling the current continuation.

We will see later that the abstract semantics of CFA2 uses a stack, like Orbit. However, CFA2 computes safe flow information which can be used by both aforementioned approaches. The workings of the abstract interpretation are independent of what style an implementor chooses for the final code.

3   Limitations of k-CFA

In this section, we discuss the main causes of imprecision and inefficiency in k-CFA. Our motivation in developing CFA2 is to create a higher-order flow analysis that overcomes these limitations.

We assume some familiarity with k-CFA, and abstract interpretation in general. Detailed descriptions on these topics can be found in [1,12]. We use Scheme syntax for our example programs.

3.1 k-CFA Does Not Match Calls and Returns

In order to make the state space of k-CFA finite, Shivers chose a mechanism similar to the call-strings of Sharir and Pnueli [2]. Thus, recursive programs introduce approximation by folding an unbounded number of recursive calls down to a fixed-size call-string. In effect, by applying k-CFA on a higher-order program, we turn it into a finite-state machine. Taken to the extreme, when k is zero, a function can return to any of its callers, not just the last one.

For example, consider the function that computes the length of a list, written in CPS (Fig. 3). 0CFA on len produces the graph in Fig. 3. *Eval* states (marked with "E") mention the corresponding call site. *Apply* states are marked with "A". *UApply* states mention the callee and the continuation argument. The continuation variable k is bound to either *halt* or λ_9. The cycle on the left is taken when the test is true, and it leads to a recursive call. The cycle on the right is taken by returning to λ_9 after a recursive call. Every path from the start to the end node is a valid 0CFA execution. In particular, we cannot exclude the path that recurs four times but applies λ_9 twice. By following such a path, the program will terminate with a *non-empty* stack. It is clear that k-CFA cannot help much with optimizations that require accurate calculation of the stack change between program states, such as stack allocation of closure environments.

Spurious flows caused by call/return mismatch affect traditional data-flow information as well. For instance, 0CFA-constant-propagation for the program below cannot spot that n2 is the constant 2, because 1 also flows to x and is mistakenly passed to the continuation λ_2. 1CFA helps in this example, but repeated η-expansion of the identity function can trick k-CFA for any k.

```
(let ((id (λ(x k) (k x))))
  (id 1 (λ₁(n1) (id 2 (λ₂(n2) (+ n1 n2 halt))))))
```

In a non-recursive program, a large enough k can provide accurate call/return matching, but this is not desirable because the analysis becomes intractably slow even when k is 1 [10]. Moreover, the ubiquity of recursion in higher-order programs calls for a static analysis that can match an unbounded number of calls and returns. This can be done if we approximate programs using pushdown models instead of finite-state machines.

3.2   The Environment Problem and Fake Rebinding

In higher-order languages, many bindings of the same variable can be simultaneously live. Determining at compile time whether two references to some variable will be bound in the same run-time environment is referred to as the *environment problem* [1]. For example, trace through the execution of the following direct-style code:

```
(let ((f (λ(x thunk) (if (integer? x) (thunk) (λ₁() x)))))
  (f 0 (f "foo" "bar")))
```

In the inner call to f, x is bound to "foo" and λ_1 is returned. We call f again; this time, x is an integer, so we jump through (thunk) to (λ_1() x), and reference x, which, despite the just-completed test, is *not* an integer: it is the earlier-bound string "foo". Thus, during abstract interpretation, it is generally *unsafe* to assume that a variable reference has some property just because an earlier reference had that property.

This has an unfortunate consequence: sometimes an earlier reference provides *safe* information about the reference at hand and k-CFA does not spot it:

```
(define (compose-same f x) ₂(f ₁(f x)))
```

In compose-same, both references to f are always bound at the same time. However, if multiple closures flow to f, k-CFA may call one closure at call site 1 and a different closure at call site 2. This flow never happens at run time.

CFA2 tackles this problem by treating references for a variable v differently from one another, depending on their location in the source code. If v appears in a static context where we know the current stack frame is its environment record, we can be precise. If v appears free in some possibly escaping lambda, we cannot predict its extent so we fall back to a conservative approximation.

3.3   Imprecision Increases the Running Time of the Analysis

It is known that k-CFA for $k > 0$ is not a cheap analysis, both in theory [10] and in practice [16]. Counterintuitively, imprecision in higher-order control-flow analyses can increase their running time: imprecision induces spurious control-flow paths, along which the analysis must then flow data, thus creating further spurious paths, and so on, in a vicious cycle which creates extra work whose only function is to degrade the precision of the analysis. This is why techniques that aggressively prune the search space, such as abstract garbage collection [8], not only increase the precision, but can also improve the speed of the analysis.

In the previous subsections, we saw examples of information known at compile time that k-CFA cannot exploit. CFA2 uses this information. The enhanced precision of CFA2 has a positive effect on its running time (cf. section 6).

4   The CFA2 Semantics

4.1   Abstract Semantics

The CFA2 semantics is an abstract interpreter that executes a program in RCPS, using a stack for variable binding and return-point information.

We describe the stack-management policy with an example. Assume that we run the len program of section 3. When calling (len '(3) *halt*) we push a frame $[1 \mapsto (3)][k \mapsto halt]$ on the stack. The test (pair? 1) is true, so we add the binding [test $\mapsto$ *true*] to the top frame and jump to the true branch. We take the cdr of 1 and add the binding [rest $\mapsto$ ()] to the top frame. We call len again, push a new frame for its arguments and jump to its body. This time the test is false, so we extend the top frame with [test $\mapsto$ *false*] and jump to the false branch. The call to k is a function return, so we pop a frame and pass 0 to λ_9. Call site 10 is also a function return, so we pop the remaining frame and pass 1 to the top-level continuation *halt*.

In general, we push a frame at function entries and pop at tail calls and at function returns. Results of intermediate computations are stored in the top frame. This policy enforces two invariants about the abstract interpreter. First, when executing inside a user function $(\lambda_l (u\ k)\ call)$, the domain of the top frame is a subset of $LV(l)$. Second, the frame below the top frame is the environment of the current continuation.

Each variable v in our example was looked up in the top frame, because each lookup happened while we were executing inside the lambda that binds v. This is not always the case; in the first snippet of section 3.2 there is a reference to x inside λ_1. When control reaches that reference, the top frame does not belong to the user lambda that binds x. CFA2 uses a *heap* to look up such references. The following definition makes these concepts precise.

$\widehat{UEval}$ to $\widehat{UApply}$:

$$([\![(f\, e\, q)^l]\!], st, h) \rightsquigarrow (ulam, \hat{d}, \hat{c}, st', h)$$

$ulam \in \mathcal{A}_u(f, st, h)$

$\hat{d} = \mathcal{A}_u(e, st, h)$

$\hat{c} = \mathcal{A}_k(q, st)$

$$st' = \begin{cases} pop(st) & Var_?(q) \\ st & Lam_?(q) \wedge (H_?(f) \vee Lam_?(f)) \\ setTop([f \mapsto \{ulam\}], st) & Lam_?(q) \wedge S_?(f) \end{cases}$$

$\widehat{UApply}$ to $\widehat{Eval}$:

$$([\![(\lambda_l (u\, k)\, call)]\!], \hat{d}, \hat{c}, st, h) \rightsquigarrow (call, st', h')$$

$st' = push([u \mapsto \hat{d}][k \mapsto \hat{c}], st)$

$$h' = \begin{cases} h \sqcup [u \mapsto \hat{d}] & H_?(u) \\ h & S_?(u) \end{cases}$$

$\widehat{CEval}$ to $\widehat{CApply}$:

$$([\![(q\, e)^\gamma]\!], st, h) \rightsquigarrow (clam, \hat{d}, st', h)$$

$clam = \mathcal{A}_k(q, st)$

$\hat{d} = \mathcal{A}_u(e, st, h)$

$$st' = \begin{cases} pop(st) & Var_?(q) \\ st & Lam_?(q) \end{cases}$$

$\widehat{CApply}$ to $\widehat{Eval}$:

$$([\![(\lambda_\gamma (u)\, call)]\!], \hat{d}, st, h) \rightsquigarrow (call, st', h')$$

$st' = setTop([u \mapsto \hat{d}], st)$

$$h' = \begin{cases} h \sqcup [u \mapsto \hat{d}] & H_?(u) \\ h & S_?(u) \end{cases}$$

$$\mathcal{A}_u(e, st, h) \triangleq \begin{cases} \{e\} & Lam_?(e) \\ st(e) & S_?(e) \\ h(e) & H_?(e) \end{cases}$$

$$\mathcal{A}_k(q, st) \triangleq \begin{cases} q & Lam_?(q) \\ st(q) & Var_?(q) \end{cases}$$

Abstract domains:

$\hat{\varsigma} \in \widehat{UEval} = UCall \times Stack \times Heap$

$\hat{\varsigma} \in \widehat{UApply} = ULam \times \widehat{UClos} \times \widehat{CClos} \times Stack \times Heap$

$\hat{\varsigma} \in \widehat{CEval} = CCall \times Stack \times Heap$

$\hat{\varsigma} \in \widehat{CApply} = \widehat{CClos} \times \widehat{UClos} \times Stack \times Heap$

$\hat{d} \in \widehat{UClos} = Pow(ULam)$

$\hat{c} \in \widehat{CClos} = CLam + halt$

$fr, tf \in Frame = (UVar \rightharpoonup \widehat{UClos}) \cup (CVar \rightharpoonup \widehat{CClos})$

$st \in Stack = Frame^*$

$h \in Heap = UVar \rightharpoonup \widehat{UClos}$

Stack operations:

$pop(tf :: st) \triangleq st$

$push(fr, st) \triangleq fr :: st$

$(tf :: st)(v) \triangleq tf(v)$

$setTop([u \mapsto \hat{d}], tf :: st) \triangleq tf[u \mapsto \hat{d}] :: st$

Fig. 4. Abstract semantics and relevant definitions

Definition 1 (Stack and heap references)

- Let ψ be a call site that refers to a variable v. The predicate $S_?(v)$ holds iff $v \in LV(\psi)$. We call v a **stack reference**.
- Let ψ be a call site that refers to a variable v. The predicate $H_?(v)$ holds iff $v \notin LV(\psi)$. We call v a **heap reference**.
- v is a **stack variable** iff all its references satisfy $S_?$.
- v is a **heap variable** iff some of its references satisfy $H_?$.

Put differently, if the innermost user lambda that contains ψ is the one that binds v, then v is a stack reference. In addition, if v is bound by a continuation lambda λ_γ, and the innermost user lambda that contains ψ also contains λ_γ, then v is a stack reference. Intuitively, only heap references may escape. We look up stack references in the top frame, and heap references in the heap. Stack lookups below the top frame never happen.

The CFA2 semantics appears in Fig. 4. An abstract value is either an abstract user closure (member of the set $\widehat{UClos}$) or an abstract continuation closure (member of $\widehat{CClos}$). An abstract user closure is a set of user lambdas. An abstract continuation closure is either a continuation lambda or *halt*. A frame is a map from variables to abstract values, and a stack is a sequence of frames. All stack operations except *push* are defined for non-empty stacks only. A heap is a map from variables to abstract values. It contains only user bindings because in RCPS every continuation variable is a stack variable.

On transition from a $\widehat{UEval}$ state $\hat{\varsigma}$ to a $\widehat{UApply}$ state $\hat{\varsigma}'$, we first evaluate f, e and q. We evaluate user terms using $\mathcal{A}_u$ and continuation terms using $\mathcal{A}_k$. We non-deterministically choose one of the lambdas that flow to f as the operator in $\hat{\varsigma}'$. The change to the stack depends on q and f. If q is a variable, the call is a tail call so we pop the stack (case 1). If q is a lambda, it evaluates to a new continuation closure whose environment is the top frame, hence we do not pop the stack (cases 2, 3). Moreover, if f is a lambda or a heap reference then we leave the stack unchanged. However, if f is a stack reference, we set f's value on the top frame to be $\{ulam\}$, possibly forgetting other lambdas that may flow to f. This "stack filtering" prevents fake rebinding (cf. section 3.2): when we return to $\hat{c}$, we may reach more stack references of f. These references and the current one are all bound at the same time. Since we are committing to *ulam* in this transition, these references must also be bound to *ulam*.

In the $\widehat{UApply}$-to-$\widehat{Eval}$ transition, we push a frame for the procedure's arguments. In addition, if u is a heap variable we must update its binding in the heap. The join operation $\sqcup$ is defined in the usual way.

In a $\widehat{CEval}$-to-$\widehat{CApply}$ transition, we are preparing for a call to a continuation so we must reset the stack to the stack of its birth. When q is a variable, the $\widehat{CEval}$ state is a function return and the continuation's environment is the second stack frame. Therefore, we pop a frame before calling *clam*. When q is a lambda, it is a newly created closure thus the stack does not change. Note that the transition is deterministic, unlike $\widehat{UEval}$-to-$\widehat{UApply}$. Since we always know which continuation we are about to call, call/return mismatch *never* happens. For instance, the function `len` may be called from many places in a program, so multiple continuations may flow to `k`. But, by retrieving `k`'s value from the stack, we always return to the correct continuation.

In the $\widehat{CApply}$-to-$\widehat{Eval}$ transition, our stack policy dictates that we extend the top frame with the binding for the continuation's parameter u. If u is a heap variable, we also update the heap.

$|([\![(h_1 \ldots h_n)^\psi]\!], \beta, ve, t)|_{ca} = ([\![(h_1 \ldots h_n)^\psi]\!], \; toStack(LV(\psi), \beta, ve), \; |ve|_{ca})$

$|(\langle[\![(\lambda_l(u\,k)\;call)]\!], \beta\rangle, d, c, ve, t)|_{ca} = ([\![(\lambda_l(u\,k)\;call)]\!], |d|_{ca}, |c|_{ca}, st, |ve|_{ca})$

where $st = \begin{cases} \langle\rangle & c = halt \\ toStack(LV(\gamma), \beta', ve) & c = ([\![(\lambda_\gamma(u')call')]\!], \beta') \end{cases}$

$|(\langle[\![(\lambda_\gamma(u)\;call)]\!], \beta\rangle, d, ve, t)|_{ca} = ([\![(\lambda_\gamma(u)\;call)]\!], |d|_{ca}, \; toStack(LV(\gamma), \beta, ve), |ve|_{ca})$

$|(halt, d, ve, t)|_{ca} = (halt, |d|_{ca}, \langle\rangle, |ve|_{ca})$

$|([\![(\lambda_l(u\,k)\;call)]\!], \beta)|_{ca} = \{[\![(\lambda_l(u\,k)\;call)]\!]\}$

$|([\![(\lambda_\gamma(u)\;call)]\!], \beta)|_{ca} = [\![(\lambda_\gamma(u)\;call)]\!]$

$|halt|_{ca} = halt$

$|ve|_{ca} = \{\, (u, \bigsqcup_t |ve(u,t)|_{ca}) \; : \; H_?(u)\}$

$toStack(\{u_1, \ldots, u_n, k\}, \beta, ve) \triangleq$

$\begin{cases} \langle[\overline{u_i \mapsto \hat{d}_i}][k \mapsto halt]\rangle & \hat{d}_i = |ve(u_i, \beta(u_i))|_{ca} \wedge \\ & halt = ve(k, \beta(k)) \\ [\overline{u_i \mapsto \hat{d}_i}][k \mapsto [\![(\lambda_\gamma(u)\;call)]\!]] :: toStack(LV(\gamma), \beta', ve) & \hat{d}_i = |ve(u_i, \beta(u_i))|_{ca} \wedge \\ & ([\![(\lambda_\gamma(u)\;call)]\!], \beta') = ve(k, \beta(k)) \end{cases}$

Fig. 5. From concrete states to abstract states

4.2 Correctness of CFA2

In this section, we show that the CFA2 semantics safely approximates the concrete semantics. First, we define a map $|\cdot|_{ca}$ from concrete to abstract states. Next, we show that if a state ς transitions to ς' in the concrete semantics, the abstract counterpart $|\varsigma|_{ca}$ of ς transitions to a state $\hat{\varsigma}'$ which approximates $|\varsigma'|_{ca}$. By proving this, we ensure that the possible behaviors of the abstract interpreter include the actual run-time behavior of the program.

The map $|\cdot|_{ca}$ appears in Fig. 5. The abstraction of an *Eval* state ς of the form $([\![(h_1 \ldots h_n)^\psi]\!], \beta, ve, t)$ is an $\widehat{Eval}$ state $\hat{\varsigma}$ with the same call site. Since ς does not have a stack, we must expose stack-related information hidden in β and ve. Assume that λ_l is the innermost user lambda that contains ψ. To reach ψ, control passed from a $\widehat{UApply}$ state $\hat{\varsigma}'$ over λ_l. According to our stack policy, the top frame must contain bindings for the formals of λ_l and any temporaries added along the path from $\hat{\varsigma}'$ to $\hat{\varsigma}$. Therefore, the domain of the top frame is a subset of $LV(l)$, i.e., a subset of $LV(\psi)$. For each user variable $u_i \in (LV(\psi) \cap \mathrm{dom}(\beta))$, the top frame contains $[u_i \mapsto |ve(u_i, \beta(u_i))|_{ca}]$. Let k be the sole continuation variable in $LV(\psi)$. If $ve(k, \beta(k))$ is $halt$ (the return continuation is the top-level continuation), the rest of the stack is empty. If $ve(k, \beta(k))$ is $([\![(\lambda_\gamma(u)\;call)]\!], \beta')$, the second frame is for the user lambda in which λ_γ was born, and so forth: proceeding through the stack, we add a frame for each live activation of a user lambda until we reach the top-level continuation.

The abstraction of a *UApply* state over $\langle [\![(\lambda_l \, (u \, k) \, call)]\!], \beta \rangle$ is a $\widehat{UApply}$ state $\hat{\varsigma}$ whose operator is $[\![(\lambda_l \, (u \, k) \, call)]\!]$. The stack of $\hat{\varsigma}$ is the stack in which the continuation argument was created, and we compute it using *toStack* as above.

Abstracting a *CApply* is similar to the *UApply* case, only now the top frame is the environment of the continuation operator. Note that the abstraction maps drop the time of the concrete states, since the abstract states do not use times.

We can now state our simulation theorem. The proof proceeds by case analysis on the concrete transition relation. The relation $\hat{\varsigma}_1 \sqsubseteq \hat{\varsigma}_2$ is a partial ordering on abstract states and can be read as "$\hat{\varsigma}_1$ is more precise than $\hat{\varsigma}_2$". The proof and the definition of $\sqsubseteq$ can be found in [17].

Theorem 1 (Simulation). *If* $\varsigma \to \varsigma'$ *and* $|\varsigma|_{ca} \sqsubseteq \hat{\varsigma}$, *then there exists* $\hat{\varsigma}'$ *such that* $\hat{\varsigma} \rightsquigarrow \hat{\varsigma}'$ *and* $|\varsigma'|_{ca} \sqsubseteq \hat{\varsigma}'$.

5   Computing CFA2

In the previous section we saw how CFA2 addresses the problems of k-CFA, but did not discuss how to explore its state space. Since the size of the stack is unbounded, the state space of CFA2 is infinite and the standard workset algorithms for k-CFA [1, 12] will diverge. For this reason, we have designed a new algorithm based on summarization, a dynamic-programming technique widely used in the interprocedural analysis of first-order programs [2, 3, 4] and in context-free language (CFL) reachability algorithms [18].

The difficulty with analyzing programs in a way that respects call/return matching is that the reachable program points from a point n do not depend solely on n, but on the stack contents as well. The intuition behind summarization is to flow facts from n with an *empty* stack to another point n' in the same procedure. We say that n' is *same-context reachable* from n. These facts are then suitably combined to get flow facts for the whole program.

Let's do the simplest data-flow analysis for the *first-order* program of Fig. 6, namely find which nodes are reachable from the entry of the main function. We will do so by using *path edges*, i.e., edges whose source is the entry of a procedure and target is some program point in the same procedure. Path edges represent intraprocedural paths, hence the name. We write n_f for the entry node and x_f for the exit node of a procedure f. Solid arrows are intraprocedural steps. Dotted arrows go from call nodes to the corresponding return nodes. Dashed arrows go from call nodes to entries and from exits to return nodes.

We first scan the program to identify the call sites of each procedure and then start the reachability analysis. Obviously, from 1 we can go to 2 and then to 3, so we record $\langle 1, 1 \rangle$, $\langle 1, 2 \rangle$ and $\langle 1, 3 \rangle$. Then 3 calls sum, so we jump to its body. Analysing sum produces $\langle 9, 9 \rangle$, $\langle 9, 10 \rangle$ and $\langle 9, 11 \rangle$. Node 11 is an exit reachable from 9, so each caller of sum can reach its corresponding return point. We keep track of this fact by recording the *summary* edges $\langle 3, 4 \rangle$ and $\langle 6, 7 \rangle$. Now 4 is reachable from 1, so we discover a new path edge $\langle 1, 4 \rangle$. We go on to discover $\langle 1, 5 \rangle$ and $\langle 1, 6 \rangle$. Reachability inside sum does not depend on its calling context,

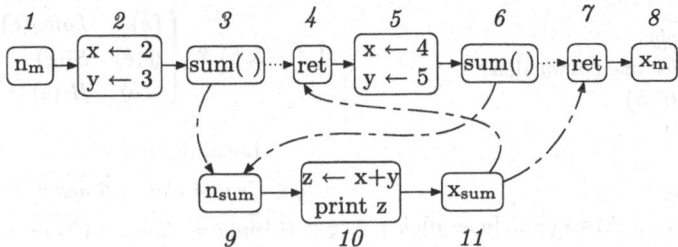

Fig. 6. Interprocedural flow-graph for a simple program

so from the summary edge $\langle 6, 7 \rangle$ we infer that we can reach 7, so we add $\langle 1, 7 \rangle$ to the set of path edges. Finally, we record $\langle 1, 8 \rangle$ which is the end of the program.

We cannot apply summarization to higher-order languages out of the box, because we do not know the call sites of a function by looking at a program's source code. We need a *search-based* variant of summarization, that records callers as it discovers them. Specifically, in the previous example we can record the call $\langle 3, 9 \rangle$ when we reach 3. On reaching 11, we record the summary edge $\langle 9, 11 \rangle$. To find possible return points for sum, we look at the set of callers. Since 3 calls 9, 11 can return to 4. Later, when we reach 6, we look at the set of summaries and see that sum reaches its exit, so 6 can reach 7. Note that our search-based variant of summarization uses entry-to-exit summaries instead of call-to-return summaries.

5.1 Local Semantics

Summarization-based algorithms operate on a finite set of program points. Hence, we cannot use (an infinite number of) abstract states as program points. For this reason, we introduce *local states* and define a map $|\cdot|_{al}$ from abstract to local states (Fig. 7). Intuitively, a local state is like an abstract state but with a single frame instead of a stack. Discarding the rest of the stack makes the local state space finite; keeping the top frame allows precise lookups for stack references.

Essentially, the local semantics describes executions that do not touch the rest of the stack (in other words, executions where functions do not return). Thus, a $\widetilde{CEval}$ state with call site $(k\,e)^\gamma$ has no successor in this semantics. Since functions do not call their continuations, the frames of local states contain only user bindings. Local steps are otherwise similar to abstract steps. The metavariable $\tilde{\varsigma}$ ranges over local states. We define the map $|\cdot|_{cl}$ from concrete to local states to be $|\cdot|_{al} \circ |\cdot|_{ca}$.

We can now see the emerging connection between local semantics and summarization: the local semantics is used for intraprocedural steps and function calls, and we discover return points by recording callers and summary edges.

Next, our algorithm needs to distinguish between different kinds of local states: entries, exits, calls, returns and inner states. CPS lends itself naturally to such a categorization:

$\widehat{UEval}$ to $\widehat{UApply}$:

$(\llbracket (f\,e\,q)^l \rrbracket, tf, h) \approx (ulam, \hat{d}, h)$

$ulam \in \hat{A}_u(f, tf, h)$

$\hat{d} = \hat{A}_u(e, tf, h)$

$\hat{A}_u(e, tf, h) \triangleq \begin{cases} \{e\} & Lam_?(e) \\ tf(e) & S_?(e) \\ h(e) & H_?(e) \end{cases}$

Local domains:

$\widehat{UApply}$ to $\widehat{Eval}$:

$(\llbracket (\lambda_l\,(u\,k)\,call) \rrbracket, \hat{d}, h) \approx (call, [u \mapsto \hat{d}], h')$

$h' = \begin{cases} h \sqcup [u \mapsto \hat{d}] & H_?(u) \\ h & S_?(u) \end{cases}$

$\tilde{\varsigma} \in \widehat{Eval} = Call \times \widehat{Stack} \times Heap$

$\tilde{\varsigma} \in \widehat{UApply} = ULam \times \widehat{UClos} \times Heap$

$\tilde{\varsigma} \in \widehat{CApply} = \widehat{CClos} \times \widehat{UClos} \times \widehat{Stack} \times Heap$

$\widehat{CEval}$ to $\widehat{CApply}$:

$(\llbracket (clam\,e)^\gamma \rrbracket, tf, h) \approx (clam, \hat{d}, tf, h)$

$\hat{d} = \hat{A}_u(e, tf, h)$

$\widehat{Frame} = UVar \rightharpoonup \widehat{UClos}$

$\widehat{Stack} = \widehat{Frame} + \langle\rangle$

Abstract to local maps:

$\widehat{CApply}$ to $\widehat{Eval}$:

$(\llbracket (\lambda_\gamma\,(u)\,call) \rrbracket, \hat{d}, tf, h) \approx (call, tf', h')$

$tf' = tf[u \mapsto \hat{d}]$

$h' = \begin{cases} h \sqcup [u \mapsto \hat{d}] & H_?(u) \\ h & S_?(u) \end{cases}$

$|(call, st, h)|_{al} = (call, |st|_{al}, h)$

$|(ulam, \hat{d}, \hat{c}, st, h)|_{al} = (ulam, \hat{d}, h)$

$|(\hat{c}, \hat{d}, st, h)|_{al} = (\hat{c}, \hat{d}, |st|_{al}, h)$

$|tf :: st'|_{al} = \{ (u, tf(u)) : UVar_?(u) \}$

$|\langle\rangle|_{al} = \langle\rangle$

Fig. 7. Local semantics

- A $\widehat{UApply}$ state corresponds to an **entry** node—control is about to enter the body of a function.
- A $\widehat{CEval}$ state where the operator is a variable is an **exit** node—a function is about to pass its result to its context.
- A $\widehat{UEval}$ state where the continuation argument is a variable is also an **exit**—at tail calls control does not return to the caller.
- A $\widehat{UEval}$ state where the continuation argument is a lambda is a **call**.
- A $\widehat{CEval}$ state where the operator is a lambda is an **inner** state.
- A $\widehat{CApply}$ state is a **return** if its predecessor is an exit, or an **inner** state if its predecessor is also an inner state. Our algorithm will not need to distinguish between the two kinds of $\widehat{CApply}$s; the difference is just conceptual.

Last, we generalize the notion of summary edges to handle tail recursion. In the following, we rewrite sum in a functional style and place it in a context where it gets called three times:

```
(let ((sum (λ(x y k) (+ x y (λ(z) ₁(print z k))))))
  ...₂(sum 2 3 (λ₃(u1) call₃))...
  ...₄(sum 4 5 (λ₅(u2) call₅))...
  ...((λ₆(n k2) ₇(sum n 1 k2)) 9 (λ₈(u3) call₈))...)
```

The first time (site 2), we record a summary edge from the entry of sum to its exit at call site 1, and return to λ_3. Then, at the second call (site 4) we use the summary edge to find that sum will pass its result to λ_5. The third call is a tail call, so no continuation is born at call site 7. Upon return from sum, we must be careful to pass the result to λ_8. Also, we must restore the environment of the call to λ_6, *not* the environment of the tail call. We achieve these by recording a "cross-procedure" summary edge from the entry of λ_6 to call site 1. This transitive nature of summaries is essential for tail recursion.

5.2 Summarization

The algorithm for CFA2 is shown in Fig. 8. It is a search-based summarization for higher-order programs with tail calls. Its goal is to compute which local states are reachable from the initial state of a program through paths that respect call/return matching.

An edge $(\tilde{\varsigma}_1, \tilde{\varsigma}_2)$ is an ordered pair of local states. We call $\tilde{\varsigma}_1$ the *source* and $\tilde{\varsigma}_2$ the *target* of the edge. The results of the analysis are stored in the set *Seen*. It contains path edges (from a procedure entry to a state in the same procedure) and summary edges (from an entry to a $\overline{CEval}$ exit, not necessarily in the same procedure). The target of an edge in *Seen* is reachable from the source and from the initial state (cf. theorem 2). Summaries are also stored in *Summary*.

The workset W contains path edges and summaries to be examined. *Final* records $\overline{CApply}$ states that call *halt* with a return value for the whole program. *Callers* contains triples $\langle \tilde{\varsigma}_1, \tilde{\varsigma}_2, \tilde{\varsigma}_3 \rangle$, where $\tilde{\varsigma}_1$ is an entry, $\tilde{\varsigma}_2$ is a call in the same procedure and $\tilde{\varsigma}_3$ is the entry of the callee. *TCallers* contains triples $\langle \tilde{\varsigma}_1, \tilde{\varsigma}_2, \tilde{\varsigma}_3 \rangle$, where $\tilde{\varsigma}_1$ is an entry, $\tilde{\varsigma}_2$ is a tail call in the same procedure and $\tilde{\varsigma}_3$ is the entry of the callee. The initial state $\tilde{\mathcal{I}}(pr)$ is defined as $|\mathcal{I}(pr)|_{cl}$. The helper function $succ(\tilde{\varsigma})$ returns the successor(s) of $\tilde{\varsigma}$ according to the local semantics.

At every iteration, we remove an edge $(\tilde{\varsigma}_1, \tilde{\varsigma}_2)$ from W and branch depending on $\tilde{\varsigma}_2$. If $\tilde{\varsigma}_2$ is an entry, a return or an inner state (line 6), then its successor $\tilde{\varsigma}_3$ is a state in the same procedure. Since $\tilde{\varsigma}_2$ is reachable from $\tilde{\varsigma}_1$, $\tilde{\varsigma}_3$ is also reachable from $\tilde{\varsigma}_1$. If we have not already recorded the edge $(\tilde{\varsigma}_1, \tilde{\varsigma}_3)$, we do it now (line 25).

If $\tilde{\varsigma}_2$ is a call (line 8) then $\tilde{\varsigma}_3$ is an entry of a new procedure, so we propagate $(\tilde{\varsigma}_3, \tilde{\varsigma}_3)$ instead of $(\tilde{\varsigma}_1, \tilde{\varsigma}_3)$ (line 10). Next, we record the call in *Callers*. If an exit $\tilde{\varsigma}_4$ is reachable from $\tilde{\varsigma}_3$, it should return its result to the continuation born at $\tilde{\varsigma}_2$ (line 12). The function Update is responsible for computing the return state. We find the return value $\hat{d}$ by evaluating the expression e_4 passed to the continuation (lines 29-30). Since we are returning to λ_{γ_2}, we must restore the environment of its creation which is tf_2 (possibly with stack filtering, line 31). The new state $\tilde{\varsigma}$ is the corresponding return node of $\tilde{\varsigma}_2$, so we propagate $(\tilde{\varsigma}_1, \tilde{\varsigma})$ (lines 32-33).

If $\tilde{\varsigma}_2$ is a $\overline{CEval}$ exit and $\tilde{\varsigma}_1$ is the initial state (lines 14-15), then $\tilde{\varsigma}_2$'s successor is a final state (lines 34-35). If $\tilde{\varsigma}_1$ is some other entry, we record the edge in *Summary* and pass the result of $\tilde{\varsigma}_2$ to the callers of $\tilde{\varsigma}_1$ (lines 17-18). Last, consider the case of a tail call $\tilde{\varsigma}_4$ to $\tilde{\varsigma}_1$ (line 19). No continuation is born at $\tilde{\varsigma}_4$. Thus, we must find where $\tilde{\varsigma}_3$ (the entry that led to the tail call) was called from.

```
01    Summary, Callers, TCallers, Final ⟵ ∅
02    Seen, W ⟵ {(Ĩ(pr), Ĩ(pr))}
03    while W ≠ ∅
04      remove (ς̃₁, ς̃₂) from W
05      switch ς̃₂
06        case ς̃₂ of Entry, CApply, Inner-CEval
07          for each ς̃₃ in succ(ς̃₂) Propagate(ς̃₁, ς̃₃)
08        case ς̃₂ of Call
09          for each ς̃₃ in succ(ς̃₂)
10            Propagate(ς̃₃, ς̃₃)
11            insert (ς̃₁, ς̃₂, ς̃₃) in Callers
12            for each (ς̃₃, ς̃₄) in Summary  Update(ς̃₁, ς̃₂, ς̃₃, ς̃₄)
13        case ς̃₂ of Exit-CEval
14          if ς̃₁ = Ĩ(pr) then
15            Final(ς̃₂)
16          else
17            insert (ς̃₁, ς̃₂) in Summary
18            for each (ς̃₃, ς̃₄, ς̃₁) in Callers  Update(ς̃₃, ς̃₄, ς̃₁, ς̃₂)
19            for each (ς̃₃, ς̃₄, ς̃₁) in TCallers Propagate(ς̃₃, ς̃₂)
20        case ς̃₂ of Exit-TC
21          for each ς̃₃ in succ(ς̃₂)
22            Propagate(ς̃₃, ς̃₃)
23            insert (ς̃₁, ς̃₂, ς̃₃) in TCallers
24            for each (ς̃₃, ς̃₄) in Summary Propagate(ς̃₁, ς̃₄)

      Propagate(ς̃₁, ς̃₂) ≜
25      if (ς̃₁, ς̃₂) not in Seen then insert (ς̃₁, ς̃₂) in Seen and W

      Update(ς̃₁, ς̃₂, ς̃₃, ς̃₄) ≜
26      ς̃₁ of the form  (⟦(λ_{l₁} (u₁ k₁) call₁)⟧ , d̂₁, h₁)
27      ς̃₂ of the form  (⟦(f e₂ (λ_{γ₂} (u₂) call₂))^{l₂}⟧, tf₂, h₂)
28      ς̃₃ of the form  (⟦(λ_{l₃} (u₃ k₃) call₃)⟧ , d̂₃, h₂)
29      ς̃₄ of the form  (⟦(k₄ e₄)^{γ₄}⟧, tf₄, h₄)
30      d̂ ⟵  Âᵤ(e₄, tf₄, h₄)
```

$$
31 \quad tf \longleftarrow \begin{cases} tf_2[f \mapsto \{⟦(λ_{l_3} (u_3 k_3) call_3)⟧\}] & S_?(f) \\ tf_2 & H_?(f) \lor Lam_?(f) \end{cases}
$$

```
32      ς̃ ⟵  (⟦(λ_{γ₂} (u₂) call₂)⟧, d̂, tf, h₄)
33      Propagate(ς̃₁, ς̃)

      Final(ς̃) ≜
34      ς̃ of the form  (⟦(k e)^γ⟧, tf, h)
35      insert (halt, Âᵤ(e, tf, h), ⟨⟩, h) in Final
```

Fig. 8. CFA2 workset algorithm

Then again, it is possible that all calls to $ς̃_3$ are tail calls, in which case we keep searching further back in the call chain to find a return point. We do this backward search by transitively adding a summary edge from $ς̃_3$ to $ς̃_2$ (line 25).

If $ς̃_2$ is a tail call (line 20), we find its successors and record the call in *TCallers* (lines 21-23). If a successor of $ς̃_2$ goes to an exit, we propagate a summary transitively (line 24).

The local state space is finite, so there is a finite number of path and summary edges. We record edges as seen when we insert them in W, which ensures that no edge is inserted in W twice. Therefore, the algorithm terminates.

We obviously cannot visit an infinite number of abstract states. To establish the soundness of our flow analysis, we show that if an abstract state $\hat{\varsigma}$ is reachable from the initial state, then the algorithm visits $|\hat{\varsigma}|_{al}$ (cf. theorem 2). For instance, CFA2 on len (cf. section 3) will tell us that we reach program point 10, *not* that we reach 10 with a stack of size 1, 2, 3 etc.

Soundness guarantees that the CFA2 algorithm does not miss any flows, but it could also compute flows that do not happen in the abstract semantics. For example, a sound but useless algorithm would add all pairs of local states in *Seen*. We establish the completeness of our algorithm by proving that every visited edge has a corresponding abstract flow (cf. theorem 3).

The theorems use two definitions. The first associates a state $\hat{\varsigma}$ with its *corresponding entry*, i.e., the entry of the procedure that contains $\hat{\varsigma}$. The second finds all entries that reach the corresponding entry of $\hat{\varsigma}$ through tail calls. We include the proofs of the theorems in [17].

Definition 2. *The Corresponding Entry* $CE_p(\hat{\varsigma})$ *of a state* $\hat{\varsigma}$ *in a path p is:*

- $\hat{\varsigma}$, *if* $\hat{\varsigma}$ *is an Entry*
- $\hat{\varsigma}_1$, *if* $\hat{\varsigma}$ *is not an Entry,* $\hat{\varsigma}_2$ *is not an Exit-CEval,*
  $p \equiv p_1 \leadsto \hat{\varsigma}_1 \leadsto^* \hat{\varsigma}_2 \leadsto \hat{\varsigma} \leadsto p_2$, *and* $CE_p(\hat{\varsigma}_2) = \hat{\varsigma}_1$
- $\hat{\varsigma}_1$, *if* $\hat{\varsigma}$ *is not an Entry,*
  $p \equiv p_1 \leadsto \hat{\varsigma}_1 \leadsto^+ \hat{\varsigma}_2 \leadsto \hat{\varsigma}_3 \leadsto^+ \hat{\varsigma}_4 \leadsto \hat{\varsigma} \leadsto p_2$, $\hat{\varsigma}_2$ *is a Call*
  and $\hat{\varsigma}_4$ *is an Exit-CEval,* $CE_p(\hat{\varsigma}_2) = \hat{\varsigma}_1$, *and* $\hat{\varsigma}_3 \in CE_p^*(\hat{\varsigma}_4)$

Definition 3. *For a state* $\hat{\varsigma}$ *and a path p,* $CE_p^*(\hat{\varsigma})$ *is the smallest set such that:*

- $CE_p(\hat{\varsigma}) \in CE_p^*(\hat{\varsigma})$
- $CE_p^*(\hat{\varsigma}_1) \subseteq CE_p^*(\hat{\varsigma})$, *when* $p \equiv p_1 \leadsto \hat{\varsigma}_1 \leadsto \hat{\varsigma}_2 \leadsto^* \hat{\varsigma} \leadsto p_2$,
  $\hat{\varsigma}_1$ *is a Tail Call,* $\hat{\varsigma}_2$ *is an Entry, and* $\hat{\varsigma}_2 = CE_p(\hat{\varsigma})$

Theorem 2 (Soundness). *If* $p \equiv \hat{\mathcal{I}}(pr) \leadsto^* \hat{\varsigma}$ *then, after summarization:*

- *if* $\hat{\varsigma}$ *is not a final state then* $(|CE_p(\hat{\varsigma})|_{al}, |\hat{\varsigma}|_{al}) \in Seen$
- *if* $\hat{\varsigma}$ *is a final state then* $|\hat{\varsigma}|_{al} \in Final$
- *if* $\hat{\varsigma}$ *is an Exit-CEval and* $\hat{\varsigma}' \in CE_p^*(\hat{\varsigma})$ *then* $(|\hat{\varsigma}'|_{al}, |\hat{\varsigma}|_{al}) \in Seen$

Theorem 3 (Completeness). *After summarization:*

- *For each* $(\tilde{\varsigma}_1, \tilde{\varsigma}_2)$ *in Seen, there exist* $\hat{\varsigma}_1$, $\hat{\varsigma}_2$ *and p such that*
  $p \equiv \hat{\mathcal{I}}(pr) \leadsto^* \hat{\varsigma}_1 \leadsto^* \hat{\varsigma}_2$ *and* $\tilde{\varsigma}_1 = |\hat{\varsigma}_1|_{al}$ *and* $\tilde{\varsigma}_2 = |\hat{\varsigma}_2|_{al}$ *and* $\hat{\varsigma}_1 \in CE_p^*(\hat{\varsigma}_2)$
- *For each* $\tilde{\varsigma}$ *in Final, there exist* $\hat{\varsigma}$ *and p such that*
  $p \equiv \hat{\mathcal{I}}(pr) \leadsto^+ \hat{\varsigma}$ *and* $\tilde{\varsigma} = |\hat{\varsigma}|_{al}$ *and* $\hat{\varsigma}$ *is a final state.*

6   Evaluation

We implemented CFA2, 0CFA and 1CFA for the Twobit Scheme compiler [11] and used them to do constant propagation and folding. In this section we report on some initial measurements and comparisons.

	$S_?$	$H_?$	0CFA		1CFA		CFA2	
			visited	constants	visited	constants	visited	constants
len	9	0	81	0	126	0	55	2
rev-iter	17	0	121	0	198	0	82	4
len-Y	15	4	199	0	356	0	131	2
tree-count	33	0	293	2	2856	6	183	10
ins-sort	33	5	509	0	1597	0	600	4
DFS	94	11	1337	8	6890	8	1719	16
flatten	37	0	1520	0	6865	0	478	5
sets	90	3	3915	0	54414	0	4251	4
church-nums	46	23	19130	0	19411	0	22671	0

Fig. 9. Benchmark results

We compared the effectiveness of the analyses on a small set of benchmarks (Fig. 9). We measured the number of stack and heap references in each program and the number of constants found by each analysis. We also recorded what goes in the workset in each analysis, i.e., the number of abstract states visited by 0CFA and 1CFA, and the number of path and summary edges visited by CFA2. The running time of an abstract interpretation is proportional to the amount of things inserted in the workset.

We chose programs that exhibit a variety of control-flow patterns. Len computes the length of a list recursively. Rev-iter reverses a list tail-recursively. Len-Y computes the length of a list using the Y-combinator instead of explicit recursion. Tree-count counts the nodes in a binary tree. Ins-sort sorts a list of numbers using insertion-sort. DFS does depth-first search of a graph. Flatten turns arbitrarily nested lists into a flat list. Sets defines the basic set operations and tests De Morgan's laws on sets of numbers. Church-nums tests distributivity of multiplication over addition for a few Church numerals.

CFA2 finds the most constants, followed by 1CFA. 0CFA is the least precise. CFA2 is also more efficient at exploring its abstract state space. In five out of nine cases, it visits fewer paths than 0CFA does states. The visited set of CFA2 can be up to 3.2 times smaller (flatten), and up to 1.3 times larger (DFS) than the visited set of 0CFA. 1CFA is less efficient than both 0CFA (9/9 cases) and CFA2 (8/9 cases). The visited set of 1CFA can be significantly larger than that of CFA2 in some cases (15.6 times in tree-count, 14.4 times in flatten, 12.8 times in sets).

Naturally, the number of stack references in a program is much higher than the number of heap references; most of the time, a variable is referenced only by the lambda that binds it. Thus, CFA2 uses the precise stack lookups more often than the imprecise heap lookups.

7 Related Work

We were particularly influenced by Chaudhuri's paper on subcubic algorithms for recursive state machines [4]. His clear and intuitive description of summarization helped us realize that we can use it to explore the state space of CFA2.

Reps et al. [3] used summarization to reduce certain data-flow problems for first-order languages to a graph-reachability problem. Our workset algorithm is a variant of their tabulation algorithm, extended for tail recursion and higher-order functions. The reader may have noticed that CFA2 essentially produces a pushdown system. Then, one may wonder why we designed a new algorithm instead of using an existing one like *post** [6, ch. 3]. The reason is that callers cannot be identified syntactically in higher-order languages. Hence, algorithms that analyze higher-order programs must be based on search. The tabulation algorithm can be changed to use search fairly naturally. It is unclear to us how to do that for *post**. In a way, CFA2 creates a pushdown system and analyzes it *at the same time*, much like what k-CFA does with control-flow graphs.

Melski and Reps [19] reduced Heintze's set-constraints [20] to an instance of CFL reachability, which they solve using summarization. Therefore, their solution has the same precision as 0CFA.

CFL reachability has also been used for points-to analysis of imperative higher-order languages. For instance, Sridharan and Bodík's points-to analysis for Java [21] uses CFL reachability to match writes and reads to object fields. Precise call/return matching is achieved only for programs without recursive methods. Hind's survey [22] discusses many other variants of points-to analysis.

Debray and Proebsting [23] used ideas from parsing theory to design an interprocedural analysis for first-order programs with tail calls. They describe control-flow with a context-free grammar. Then, the FOLLOW set of a procedure represents its possible return points. Our approach is different on the surface, but similar in spirit; we handle tail calls by computing summaries transitively.

Analyses that match an unbounded number of calls and returns have been neglected by the functional language community. The type-based flow analysis of Rehof and Fähndrich [7] is a notable exception. They encode flow information in a type system and then recast the type inference problem to an instance of CFL reachability. The type system uses let-polymorphism. As a result, it provides precise call/return matching for let- and letrec-bound variables but not for lambda-bound variables. For instance, if we lambda-bind id in our earlier example, their type system will not find n2 to be constant:

```
((λ(id) (let ((n1 (id 1))
              (n2 (id 2)))
          (+ n1 n2)))
 (λ(x) x))
```

CFA2 does not distinguish between let and lambda; in fact, the AST of Twobit contains no lets.

Midtgaard and Jensen [24] created a flow analysis for direct-style higher-order programs that keeps track of "return flow". They point out that continuations make return-point information explicit in CPS and show how to recover this information in direct-style. They do not address unbounded call/return matching.

Might and Shivers [8] proposed ΓCFA (abstract garbage collection) and μCFA (abstract counting) to increase precision in k-CFA. ΓCFA removes unreachable bindings from the variable environment; μCFA counts how many times a variable is bound during the analysis. The two techniques combined reduce spurious flows and improve environment information. Stack references in CFA2 have a similar effect, because different calls to the same function use different frames. However, we can use ΓCFA and μCFA to improve precision in the heap.

Recently, Kobayashi [25] proposed a way to statically verify properties of typed higher-order programs using model-checking. He models a program by a higher-order recursion scheme $\mathcal{G}$, expresses the property of interest in the modal μ-calculus and checks if the infinite tree generated by $\mathcal{G}$ satisfies the property. This technique can do flow analysis, since flow analysis can be encoded as a model-checking problem. The target language of this work is the simply-typed lambda calculus. Programs in a Turing-complete language must be approximated in the simply-typed lambda calculus in order to be model-checked.

8   Conclusions

In this paper we propose CFA2, a pushdown model of higher-order programs, and prove it correct. CFA2 provides precise call/return matching and has a better approach to variable binding than k-CFA. Our evaluation shows that CFA2 gives more accurate data-flow information than 0CFA and 1CFA.

CFA2 is monovariant in the heap. It can be easily extended with call-strings polyvariance, like k-CFA, to produce a family of analyses CFA2.0, CFA2.1 and so on. Then, any instance of CFA2.k would be strictly more precise than the corresponding instance of k-CFA. Another possibility is to add contours in the style of Agesen [26] or Wright and Jagannathan [9]. Note that CFA2 already has most of the above polyvariance "accidentally", because of the stack lookups.

We believe that pushdown models are a better tool for higher-order flow analysis than control-flow graphs, and are working on providing more empirical support to this thesis. We plan to use CFA2 for environment analysis and stack-related optimizations. We also plan to add support for `call/cc` in CFA2.

Acknowledgements. Thanks to Will Clinger and Felix Klock for help with Twobit, and to Manuel Fähndrich and Naoki Kobayashi for clarifications on their work. Comments from Bryan Chadwick, Matthias Felleisen, Felix Klock, Aaron Turon and the anonymous referees greatly improved the paper.

References

1. Shivers, O.: Control-Flow Analysis of Higher-Order Languages. PhD thesis, Carnegie-Mellon University (1991)
2. Sharir, M., Pnueli, A.: Two Approaches to Interprocedural Data Flow Analysis. In: Program Flow Analysis, Theory and Application. Prentice Hall, Englewood Cliffs (1981)
3. Reps, T.W., Horwitz, S., Sagiv, S.: Precise Interprocedural Dataflow Analysis via Graph Reachability. In: Principles of Programming Languages, pp. 49–61 (1995)
4. Chaudhuri, S.: Subcubic Algorithms for Recursive State Machines. In: Principles of Programming Languages, pp. 159–169 (2008)

5. Alur, R., Benedikt, M., Etessami, K., Godefroid, P., Reps, T.W., Yannakakis, M.: Analysis of Recursive State Machines. Transactions on Programming Languages and Systems 27(4), 786–818 (2005)
6. Schwoon, S.: Model-Checking Pushdown Systems. PhD thesis, Technische Universität München (2002)
7. Rehof, J., Fähndrich, M.: Type-Based Flow Analysis: From Polymorphic Subtyping to CFL-Reachability. In: Principles of Programming Languages, pp. 54–66 (2001)
8. Might, M., Shivers, O.: Improving Flow Analyses via ΓCFA: Abstract Garbage Collection and Counting. In: International Conference on Functional Programming, pp. 13–25 (2006)
9. Wright, A., Jagannathan, S.: Polymorphic Splitting: An Effective Polyvariant Flow Analysis. Trans. on Programming Languages and Systems 20(1), 166–207 (1998)
10. Van Horn, D., Mairson, H.G.: Deciding k-CFA is complete for EXPTIME. In: International Conference on Functional Programming, pp. 275–282 (2008)
11. Clinger, W.D., Hansen, L.T.: Lambda, the Ultimate Label or a Simple Optimizing Compiler for Scheme. In: LISP and Functional Programming, pp. 128–139 (1994)
12. Might, M.: Environment Analysis of Higher-Order Languages. PhD thesis, Georgia Institute of Technology (2007)
13. Steele, G.L.: Rabbit: A Compiler for Scheme. Master's thesis, MIT (1978)
14. Kranz, D.: ORBIT: An Optimizing Compiler for Scheme. PhD thesis, Yale University (1988)
15. Sabry, A., Felleisen, M.: Reasoning About Programs in Continuation-Passing Style. In: LISP and Functional Programming, pp. 288–298 (1992)
16. Shivers, O.: Higher-Order Control-Flow Analysis in Retrospect: Lessons Learned, Lessons Abandoned. In: Best of PLDI, pp. 257–269 (2004)
17. Vardoulakis, D., Shivers, O.: CFA2: a Context-Free Approach to Control-Flow Analysis. Technical Report NU-CCIS-10-01, Northeastern University (2010)
18. Yannakakis, M.: Graph-Theoretic Methods in Database Theory. In: Principles of Database Systems, pp. 230–242 (1990)
19. Melski, D., Reps, T.: Interconvertibility of a Class of Set Constraints and Context-Free-Language Reachability. Theoretical Comp. Sci. 248(1-2), 29–98 (2000)
20. Heintze, N.: Set-based program analysis. PhD thesis, Carnegie-Mellon Univ. (1992)
21. Sridharan, M., Bodík, R.: Refinement-based context-sensitive points-to analysis for java. In: Programming Language Design and Implementation, pp. 387–400 (2006)
22. Hind, M.: Pointer analysis: haven't we solved this problem yet? In: Program Analysis For Software Tools and Engineering, pp. 54–61 (2001)
23. Debray, S.K., Proebsting, T.A.: Interprocedural Control Flow Analysis of First-Order Programs with Tail-Call Optimization. Transactions on Programming Languages and Systems 19(4), 568–585 (1997)
24. Midtgaard, J., Jensen, T.: Control-flow analysis of function calls and returns by abstract interpretation. In: International Conference on Functional Programming, pp. 287–298 (2009)
25. Kobayashi, N.: Types and higher-order recursion schemes for verification of higher-order programs. In: Principles of Programming Languages, pp. 416–428 (2009)
26. Agesen, O.: The Cartesian Product Algorithm: Simple and Precise Type Inference of Parametric Polymorphism. In: European Conference on Object-Oriented Programming, pp. 2–26 (1995)

Weighted Dynamic Pushdown Networks

Alexander Wenner

Institut für Informatik, Fachbereich Mathematik und Informatik
Westfälische Wilhelms-Universität Münster
alexander.wenner@uni-muenster.de

Abstract. We develop a generic framework for the analysis of programs
with recursive procedures and dynamic process creation. To this end
we combine the approach of weighted pushdown systems (WPDS) with
the model of dynamic pushdown networks (DPN). The resulting model,
weighted dynamic pushdown networks (WDPN), describes processes running in parallel, each of them being able to perform pushdown actions,
that may spawn new processes as a side effect. As with WPDS, transitions are labelled by weights to carry additional information. Starting
from techniques for WPDS and DPN, we derive a method to determine
meet-over-all-paths values for the paths between regular sets of configurations of a WDPN. Using this method we are able to solve basic dataflow
analysis problems in a parallel context.

1 Introduction

The interest in writing parallel programs has increased in recent years. However parallel programming is notoriously difficult and error-prone. Thus static
analysis of parallel programs has become more and more important. The goal
of this paper is to present a generic framework for the analysis of parallel programs, especially in the presence of recursive procedures and dynamic process
creation. We base our framework on DPN [1] and WPDS [2]. DPN precisely
model procedures and process creation and have been studied for reachability
analyses. Since the analysis of recursive procedures and synchronisation is undecidable [3], DPNs do not model synchronisation between processes. However,
through the addition of weights we will be able to analyse some interaction between processes. WPDS extend pushdown systems (PDS) by labelling transitions
with weights and solving the generalised pushdown predecessor (GPP) problem,
which is the meet-over-all-paths solution for paths from a starting configuration
into a regular set of target configurations. The weights can be used to formulate
a wide range of analysis problems. The GPP problem formulation allows for a
specific query represented by a regular constraint on the shape of the call-stack,
in contrast to standard dataflow techniques, where typically all information at
the topmost program point is merged.

The main advantage of our framework is, that we extend this ability to formulate a query depending on a regular constraint on the shape of the call-stack
to queries depending on a regular constraint on the shape of the entire network.

A.D. Gordon (Ed.): ESOP 2010, LNCS 6012, pp. 590–609, 2010.

```
main:                init_worker:        worker:
1: call init_worker  5: spawn worker     7: write a
2: write a           6: return           8: return
3: use a
4: return
```

Fig. 1. Example program

Consider the pseudo program in Figure 1. It calls a procedure to initialise a worker process, that calculates a value which is then stored in the variable a. In parallel the main process uses the variable to store a value it needs in a following step. The program obviously contains a data race, since the worker can overwrite the value of a before the main process reads it. Our framework is now able to refine the analysis of such a data race by distinguishing the situation where the main process reaches the use and the worker process has completed his computation from the situation where the worker process has completed no or only some steps.

Up to this point our framework can solve the bitvector problems for DPNs formulated in [1], which is able to handle the same refinement described above. The automata based approach in [1] however requires multiple computations of predecessor sets, whereas our method only needs one step. The shortest path analysis from [2] is an example for an analysis with an infinite domain, which can not be formulated using the automata based techniques from [1], but can be easily handled by our framework. In [4] a different approach to generalize WPDS to parallel programs is presented, by introducing a context bound. This approach can handle more powerful analyses than our framework, but the introduction of a context bound leads to an underapproximation, whereas our approach handles unbounded context switches precisely.

A main result is, that our framework can handle all KILL/GEN analyses precisely in a uniform way. To the best of our knowledge no more general class of analyses is known, for which precise analysis for some class of parallel program is possible. In [5,6,7] KILL/GEN analyses have been considered for pcall type parallelism, which can not be used to accurately model the process creation of a DPN [1], which is the basis of our framework. In [8] KILL/GEN analyses were extended to a model similar to DPN, which can handle dynamic process creation. However in this approach all dataflow information reaching a program point is merged, regardless of the state of the rest of the network. As described above, our framework allows for a more distinct query, depending on the state of the whole network.

Approach. Analogous to WPDS we extend DPN to WDPN by annotating weights to transitions and study the GPP problem. Even though a WPDS is then simply a WDPN with one process, adapting the approach to solve the GPP problem from WPDS to WDPN is problematic. In general a path of a DPN is an interleaving of the transitions of arbitrary many parallel processes. Results from [1] show, that the set of paths connecting two regular sets of configurations can not be described in a way, where standard techniques like abstract interpretation [9] can be applied to compute the abstraction in the weight domain.

We avoid these problems by introducing a branching semantics for DPN similar to the tree semantics in [10]. Transitions of newly spawned processes are no longer mixed with the transitions of the creating process, but contained in their own branch. This results in executions which are tree shaped for single processes and form hedges, which contain a tree for each process, for configurations with multiple processes. The set of hedges connecting two regular sets of configurations can be described by a constraint system, adapting the approach for WPDS.

We introduce a weight domain to abstract these trees, and study the analogous branching GPP (BGPP) problem, which is the meet-over-all-hedges solution, for these branching WDPN (BWDPN). The solution of the BGPP problem can be obtained by abstract interpretation of the constraint system. We show, that if the weight domain of a WDPN and the extended weight domain of a BWDPN, based on the same DPN, are related, the solution for the GPP problem of the WDPN can be derived from the solution of the corresponding BGPP problem of the BWDPN.

We demonstrate how this framework of WDPN and BWDPN can be used to solve shortest path problems, bitvector analyses and the more general KILL/GEN analyses for programs with recursive procedures and dynamic thread creation.

Outline. The remainder of the paper is organised as follows: Section 2 presents the intuitive extension of WPDS to DPN called WDPN and defines the GPP. Section 3 introduces BWDPN. We formulate the BGPP problem and present the relation to the GPP problem. Section 4 presents applications and Section 5 introduces the approach to solve the BGPP problem for BWDPN.

2   Weighted Dynamic Pushdown Networks

A DPN [1] is a model for parallel programs with multiple processes and dynamic process creation. Each process is modeled as a PDS, where the rules are extended to allow creation of new processes. Formally a DPN is a tuple $\mathcal{M} = (P, \Gamma, \Delta)$, where P is a finite set of control states and Γ is a finite set of stack symbols, with $P \cap \Gamma = \emptyset$. Δ is a finite set of transition rules of the form:

$$p\gamma \hookrightarrow c \text{ with } p \in P, \gamma \in \Gamma, c \in (P\Gamma^*)^* P\Gamma^*.$$

The right side of a rule consists of the new control state and stacktop of the original process in the rightmost position and the control states and stacks of all processes spawned by this rule to the left. Configurations of a DPN are words from $\mathsf{Conf} = (P\Gamma^*)^*$. The empty configuration is written as ε. For the rest of the paper we fix a DPN $\mathcal{M} = (P, \Gamma, \Delta)$ and two regular sets $C_1, C_2 \subseteq \mathsf{Conf}$.

Example 1. The program in Figure 1 leads to a DPN with rules $r_1 = p\gamma_1 \hookrightarrow p\gamma_5\gamma_2$, $r_2 = p\gamma_5 \hookrightarrow p\gamma_7 p\gamma_6$, $r_3 = p\gamma_6 \hookrightarrow p$, $r_4 = p\gamma_2 \hookrightarrow p\gamma_3$, $r_5 = p\gamma_3 \hookrightarrow p\gamma_4$

and $r_6 = p\gamma_7 \hookrightarrow p\gamma_8$, where a stack symbol γ_i represents the control location at the beginning of line i of the program. The set of starting configurations for the analyses of our program described in the introduction would be $C_1 = \{p\gamma_1\}$ and the target sets would either be $C_2 = \{p\gamma_8 p\gamma_3\}$ if the spawned process makes all steps or $C_2' = \{p\gamma_7 p\gamma_3\}$ if it makes no steps.

Interleaving Semantics. An execution of the DPN $\mathcal{M}$ is represented by a path. A path is defined as a sequence of rules:

$$\rho = r_1 \dots r_n \text{ with } r_i \in \Delta.$$

The empty path is denoted by ε_ρ and Paths is the set of all paths. The execution of a path is modeled by the labelled transition relation $\longrightarrow \subseteq \text{Conf} \times \text{Paths} \times \text{Conf}$, similar to [1], with:

$$[\text{empty}] \; c \xrightarrow{\varepsilon_\rho} c \quad [\text{rule}] \; up\gamma v \xrightarrow{r\rho} c \text{ if } r = p\gamma \hookrightarrow c', uc'v \xrightarrow{\rho} c$$

Application of a rule replaces the control state and top symbol of one stack by the new control state and stacktop specified by the rule and inserts the newly created processes with their initial stacks, as defined by the rule, to the left. We call this the interleaving semantics of the DPN, since the rules of all processes are mixed up. We are interested in the set:

$$\text{Paths}(C_1, C_2) = \{\rho \in \text{Paths} \mid \exists c_1 \in C_1, c_2 \in C_2 \text{ with } c_1 \xrightarrow{\rho} c_2\},$$

of connecting paths from C_1 to C_2.

Example 2. The sets of connecting paths in our example are $\text{Paths}(C_1, C_2) = \{r_1 r_2 r_6 r_3 r_4, r_1 r_2 r_3 r_6 r_4, r_1 r_2 r_3 r_4 r_6\}$ and $\text{Paths}(C_1, C_2') = \{r_1 r_2 r_3 r_4\}$.

Weights. In order to abstract from the set of connecting paths to the aspects which are relevant to the analysis, we assign a weight to each transition of the DPN. The structure of the weight domain is captured by a complete idempotent semiring, which supports the necessary operators $\odot$ for concatenation of weights along a path and $\oplus$ for combination of weights of different paths. A complete idempotent semiring is a tuple $\mathcal{S} = (D, \oplus, \odot, 0, 1)$, where D is a set of elements with $0, 1 \in D$ and $\oplus, \odot$ are binary operators on D with:

- $(D, \oplus)$ is a commutative monoid with neutral element 0 and $\oplus$ is idempotent
- $(D, \odot)$ is a monoid with neutral element 1 and 0 annihilates $\odot$
- $(D, \sqsubseteq)$ is a complete lattice, where $\sqsubseteq$, with $d_1 \sqsubseteq d_2 :\Leftrightarrow d_1 \oplus d_2 = d_1$ for $d_1, d_2 \in D$, is the partial order induced by $\oplus$, i.e. $\oplus$ is the meet operator of the lattice $(D, \sqsubseteq)$ and 0 is the $\top$-element
- $\odot$ distributes over arbitrary $\oplus$, i.e. $\bigoplus D_1 \odot \bigoplus D_2 = \bigoplus \{d_1 \odot d_2 \mid d_i \in D_i\}$ for $D_1, D_2 \subseteq D$

We fix a semiring $\mathcal{S} = (D, \oplus, \odot, 0, 1)$. The weights are assigned to the transitions of the DPN $\mathcal{M}$ using a weight function $f : \Delta \to D$. The function depends on the current analysis, since it describes how the transitions of the DPN are connected to the analysed information represented by the semiring. We assume a given weight function f for the rest of the paper. The tuple $W = (\mathcal{M}, \mathcal{S}, f)$ is called a WDPN. Given the WDPN we define an abstraction function $\alpha :$ Paths $\to D$ for paths:

$$\text{[empty]} \; \alpha(\varepsilon_\rho) = 1 \quad \text{[rule]} \; \alpha(r\rho) = f(r) \odot \alpha(\rho)$$

Overloading it for sets of paths with $\alpha(M) = \bigoplus \{\alpha(\rho) \mid \rho \in M\}$, we can formulate the GPP problem for WDPN as computing:

$$\delta(C_1, C_2) = \alpha(\text{Paths}(C_1, C_2)).$$

3 Branching Weighted Dynamic Pushdown Networks

It follows from results in [1] that the set $\text{Paths}(C_1, C_2)$ can not be characterised as least solution of a constraint system which uses only operators to concatenate or interleave paths. Therefore we can not compute the solution for the GPP problem directly by an abstract interpretation [9] of such a constraint system. To avoid this problem we consider an alternative interpretation of an execution of a DPN in form of a tree or hedge, first introduced in [10]. We will later see, that set of connecting hedges can be assembled from sets of partial trees, which in turn can be characterised using a constraint system.

Branching Semantics. We recursively define the set Trees of execution trees, where Hedges = Trees* is the set of execution hedges.

$$\varepsilon_\tau \in \text{Trees} \quad r(\sigma\tau) \in \text{Trees} \; \text{ for } r \in \Delta, \sigma \in \text{Hedges}, \tau \in \text{Trees}$$

The empty tree ε_τ consisting of a single leaf node, representing a finished execution, is a tree. $r(\sigma\tau)$ is a tree with a root node labelled with a rule $r \in \Delta$, describing the first step of the execution, and an ordered list of subtrees $\sigma\tau \in$ Hedges, representing the executions σ of spawned processes and the rest of the execution τ of the spawning process. The order of the children corresponds to the order of processes on the right side of the rule r. ε_σ is the empty hedge.

The execution of a hedge is modeled by the labelled transition relation $\Longrightarrow \subseteq$ Conf $\times$ Hedges $\times$ Conf, with:

$$\text{[none]} \; \varepsilon \overset{\varepsilon_\sigma}{\Longrightarrow} \varepsilon \qquad \text{[tree]} \; cpw \overset{\sigma\tau}{\Longrightarrow} c'c'' \; \text{if } c \overset{\sigma}{\Longrightarrow} c' \text{ and } pw \overset{\tau}{\Longrightarrow} c''$$

$$\text{[empty]} \; pw \overset{\varepsilon_\tau}{\Longrightarrow} pw \qquad \text{[rule]} \; p\gamma w \overset{r(\sigma)}{\Longrightarrow} c \quad \text{if } r = p\gamma \hookrightarrow c', c'w \overset{\sigma}{\Longrightarrow} c$$

We call this the branching semantics of the DPN, since each process has its own branch in the execution. We are interested in the set

$$\text{Hedges}(C_1, C_2) = \{\sigma \in \text{Hedges} \mid \exists c_1 \in C_1, c_2 \in C_2 \text{ with } c_1 \overset{\sigma}{\Longrightarrow} c_2\},$$

of connecting hedges.

Example 3. The sets of connecting hedges for our example are $\mathsf{Hedges}(C_1, C_2) = \{r_1(r_2(r_6(\varepsilon_\tau)r_3(r_4(\varepsilon_\tau))))\}$ and $\mathsf{Hedges}(C_1, C_2') = \{r_1(r_2(\varepsilon_\tau r_3(r_4(\varepsilon_\tau))))\}$.

We define the ; operator to concatenate a hedge to the last tree of a hedge:

[hedge] $(\sigma\tau)\,;\sigma' = \sigma(\tau\,;\sigma')$ [empty] $\varepsilon_\tau\,;\sigma' = \sigma'$ [rule] $r(\sigma)\,;\sigma' = r(\sigma\,;\sigma')$

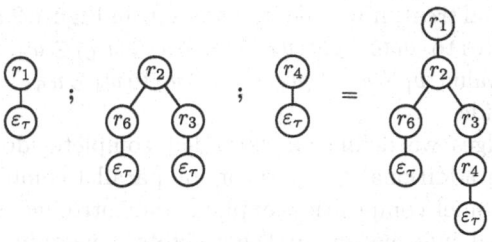

Fig. 2. Example for the concatenation of trees

Appending a hedge removes the rightmost leaf of the first hedge and adds the trees of the second hedge as new children. Thus, if you only consider concatenation of trees, it is simply concatenation along the rightmost branches. The reason for defining concatenation this way is, that we will later see, that we can assemble any execution tree for an initial process by concatenating trees from a finite number of classes. In the context of program analysis, these classes represent executions inside the body of a procedure. Figure 2 shows how we can assemble an execution of our example program by concatenating the call rule r_1, the execution inside the called `init_worker` procedure, containing the execution of the spawned process, and the rest of the execution of the `main` procedure. We extend concatenation of trees to concatenation of hedges to describe the construction of a new tree from a rule and a list of subtrees as concatenation of the tree with the rule as root node and the empty tree as only child and the hedge formed by the list of subtrees.

Interleaving vs. Branching. There is a strong connection between the interleaving and branching semantics of a DPN. A hedge represents of a set of paths, which can be constructed by interleaving the branches and trees of the hedge. Consider a function $\psi : 2^{\mathsf{Hedges}} \to 2^{\mathsf{Paths}}$ that computes the set of interleavings of a set of hedges, here $\|$ is used for the standard interleaving operator for paths:

[none] $\psi(\varepsilon_\sigma) = \{\varepsilon_\rho\}$ [tree] $\psi(\sigma\tau) = \psi(\sigma) \| \psi(\tau)$
[empty] $\psi(\varepsilon_\tau) = \{\varepsilon_\rho\}$ [rule] $\psi(r(\sigma)) = r\psi(\sigma)$

Results from [10] show, that:

Theorem 4. *We have:*

$$\mathsf{Paths}(C_1, C_2) = \psi(\mathsf{Hedges}(C_1, C_2)).$$

Extended Weights. The semiring structure used for WDPN is not suitable to abstract hedges. Especially with regard to the approach of combining an execution tree out of partial trees by concatenation. The semiring could be used to compute a weight for a given tree by computing the meet-over-all-interleavings, using the weights given by f for each rule. However in this case the operator $\odot$ is not useable as abstraction for concatenation of trees, since the interleaving of a concatenated tree would in general not be the same as the concatenation of the interleavings of the partial trees. If we take the trees from Figure 2 and set $f(r_i) = w_i$, the left side evaluates to $w_1 \odot w_2 \odot (w_6 \odot w_3 \oplus w_3 \odot w_6) \odot w_4$, which in general is different from the value $w_1 \odot w_2 \odot (w_6 \odot w_3 \odot w_4 \oplus w_3 \odot w_6 \odot w_4 \oplus w_3 \odot w_4 \odot w_6)$ of the right hand side.

To abstract hedges we define an extended complete idempotent semiring, which contains the additional $\bar{\otimes}$ operator for parallel combination of weights. By making the parallel composition explicit and introducing new weights, we can store additional information in the weights concerning parallel branches to delay the actual interleaving. An extended complete idempotent semiring $\mathcal{E} = (E, \bar{\oplus}, \bar{\odot}, \bar{\otimes}, \bar{0}, \bar{1})$ is a tuple, where E is a set of values and $\bar{\oplus}, \bar{\odot}, \bar{\otimes}$ are binary operators on E with:

- $(E, \bar{\oplus}, \bar{\odot}, \bar{0}, \bar{1})$ is a complete idempotent semiring
- $(E, \bar{\otimes})$ is a semigroup, $\bar{1} \bar{\otimes} e = e$ for $e \in E$ and $\bar{0}$ annihilates $\bar{\otimes}$
- $\bar{\otimes}$ distributes over arbitrary $\bar{\oplus}$, i.e. $\bar{\bigoplus} E_1 \bar{\otimes} \bar{\bigoplus} E_2 = \bar{\bigoplus}\{e_1 \bar{\otimes} e_2 \mid e_i \in E_i\}$
  for $E_1, E_2 \subseteq E$
- $(e_1 \bar{\otimes} e_2) \bar{\odot} e_3 = e_1 \bar{\otimes}(e_2 \bar{\odot} e_3)$, for $e_1, e_2, e_3 \in E$

The fourth property ensures, that ; is abstracted by $\bar{\odot}$, by always appending weights to the rightmost weight of a parallel combination. In this regard the $\bar{\otimes}$ operator differs from the abstract interleaving operator $\otimes$ introduced in [6]. The new operator is especially not commutative. This can also be seen in the fact, that $\bar{1}$ is only left identity for $\bar{\otimes}$, since a $\bar{1}$ in the right component can be altered by appending an additional weight.

We fix an extended semiring $\mathcal{E} = (E, \bar{\oplus}, \bar{\odot}, \bar{\otimes}, \bar{0}, \bar{1})$. As with WDPN we assume, that a weight function $\bar{f} : \Delta \to E$ is given. The tuple $\mathcal{B} = (\mathcal{M}, \mathcal{E}, \bar{f})$ is called a BWDPN. Given a BWDPN we define an abstraction function $\beta : \mathsf{Hedges} \to E$ for hedges:

$$
\begin{array}{llll}
[\text{none}] & \beta(\varepsilon_\sigma) = \bar{1} & [\text{tree}] & \beta(\sigma\tau) = \beta(\sigma) \bar{\otimes} \beta(\tau) \\
[\text{empty}] & \beta(\varepsilon_\tau) = \bar{1} & [\text{rule}] & \beta(r(\sigma)) = \bar{f}(r) \bar{\odot} \beta(\sigma)
\end{array}
$$

Overloading it for sets of hedges with $\beta(M) = \bar{\bigoplus}\{\beta(\sigma) \mid \sigma \in M\}$, we define the BGPP problem for BWDPN as computing:

$$\theta(C_1, C_2) = \beta(\mathsf{Hedges}(C_1, C_2)).$$

Weights vs. Extended Weights. At this point, we have formulated two problems. The GPP problem describes the meet-over-all-paths of the interleaving semantics, the BGPP problem describes the meet-over-all-hedges of the branching semantics. As mentioned in the beginning of this section, the solution to the GPP problem can not be computed directly. However we will later see, that the solution of the BGPP problem can be obtained by solving a constraint system. In the previous paragraph, we have seen, that we can not simply use the weight domain for the GPP problem as a weight domain for the corresponding BGPP problem. However Theorem 4 describes a strong relation between the set of reaching paths and the set of reaching hedges. A similar result can be shown for the solutions of the GPP and BGPP problems, if the semiring of the WDPN is related to the extended semiring of the BWDPN. We describe the necessary relation by an extension. An extension is a tuple $(\mathcal{S}, \mathcal{E}, \iota, \eta)$, containing embedding and projection functions $\iota : D \to E$ and $\eta : E \to D$, where for $d, d_i \in D, e, e_i \in E$ the following conditions hold:

- E is the smallest set with $\iota(D) \subseteq E$, closed under $\bar{\odot}, \bar{\otimes}$ and arbitrary $\bar{\oplus}$
- $\iota(0) = \bar{0}$, $\iota(1) = \bar{1}$ and $\eta(\iota(d)) = d$
- η distributes over arbitrary $\bar{\oplus}$, i.e. $\eta(\bar{\bigoplus}M) = \bigoplus\{\eta(e) \mid e \in M\}$ for $M \subseteq E$
- $\eta(e \bar{\otimes} \bar{1}) = \eta(e)$
- $\eta(e_1 \bar{\otimes} \dots \bar{\otimes} e_n) = \bigoplus_{i=1}^{n} d_i \odot \eta(e_1 \bar{\otimes} \dots \bar{\otimes} e_i' \bar{\otimes} \dots \bar{\otimes} e_n)$ for $e_i = \iota(d_i) \bar{\odot} e_i'$

The first three points ensure, that every weight of the original semiring has a corresponding weight in the extended semiring and in reverse every element of the extended semiring is a combination of embedded weights of the original semiring. The last two points ensure, that the combination of weights is mapped to the meet-over-all-interleavings of the weights they are constructed from. For the rest of the paper, we assume that the semiring $\mathcal{S}$ and the extended semiring $\mathcal{E}$ are connected by the extension $(\mathcal{S}, \mathcal{E}, \iota, \eta)$.

If $\bar{f}(r) = \iota(f(r))$, for all $r \in \Delta$, i.e. the analysis of the WDPN is embedded in the BWDPN, we can prove $\alpha(\psi(\sigma)) = \eta(\beta(\sigma))$ for all $\sigma \in$ Hedges by induction on σ. Consequently with Theorem 4:

Theorem 5. *It follows, that:*

$$\delta(C_1, C_2) = \eta(\theta(C_1, C_2)).$$

Construction of Extended Semiring and Extension. An example for an extended semiring $\mathcal{E}$ and extension $(\mathcal{E}, \mathcal{S}, \iota, \eta)$, which exists for any semiring $\mathcal{S}$, is the extended semiring of weighted hedges, i.e. hedges where nodes are labelled with a weight from the semiring $\mathcal{S}$. This abstraction contains nearly all information contained in the execution trees. An abstraction of an execution hedge is simply the hedge, where nodes previously annotated with r are now annotated with $f(r)$ and the empty tree is annotated with 1. Interior nodes labelled with the neutral element 1, which have no influence on the total weight of the tree, are removed.

We define the set of weighted trees WTrees recursively, where WHedges = WTrees$^+$ is the set of weighted hedges:

$$1 \in \text{WTrees} \quad w(\sigma) \in \text{WTrees} \ \text{ for } w \in D \setminus \{1\}, \sigma \in \text{WHedges}$$

1 is the empty weighted tree consisting of a single leaf node labelled with 1 and $w(\sigma)$ is a weighted tree with a root node labelled with w and children σ. 1 doubles as the initial empty weighted hedge, and we define $1\sigma = \sigma$.

The operations of the extended semiring are then mapped onto the corresponding weighted tree operations. We define $\sigma \otimes \sigma' = \sigma\sigma'$ and concatenation is concatenation of weighted hedges as with execution hedges:

$$[\text{hedge}]\ \sigma\tau \bar{\odot} \sigma' = \sigma(\tau \bar{\odot} \sigma')\quad [\text{empty}]\ 1 \bar{\odot} \sigma = \sigma \quad [\text{rule}]\ w(\sigma) \bar{\odot} \sigma' = w(\sigma \bar{\odot} \sigma')$$

Since there is no obvious way to compute a meet for two weighted hedges, we go to the powerset of WHedges. The extended semiring is given by $\mathcal{E} = (E, \bar{\oplus}, \bar{\odot}, \bar{\otimes}, \emptyset, \{1\})$, where $E = 2^{\text{WHedges}}$, $\bar{\oplus} = \cup$ and $\bar{\odot}, \bar{\otimes}$ are extended to sets.

The embedding of the corresponding extension $(\mathcal{S}, \mathcal{E}, \iota, \eta)$, transforms a weight into a corresponding set of weighted trees:

$$\iota(0) = \emptyset \quad \iota(1) = \{1\} \quad \iota(w) = \{w(1)\}$$

The projection back into the semiring then computes the value of all interleavings for a given weighted hedge:

$$\eta(1) = 1 \quad \eta(\sigma 1) = \eta(\sigma)$$
$$\eta(w_1(\sigma_1) \ldots w_n(\sigma_n)) = \bigoplus_{i=1}^{n} w_i \odot \eta(w_1(\sigma_1) \ldots \sigma_i \ldots w_n(\sigma_n))$$

η is extended to sets by $\eta(M) = \bigoplus\{\eta(\sigma) \mid \sigma \in M\}$ for $M \subseteq$ WHedges. It can be easily seen, that the definitions fulfill all the conditions for an extension between the semiring $\mathcal{S}$ and $\mathcal{E}$.

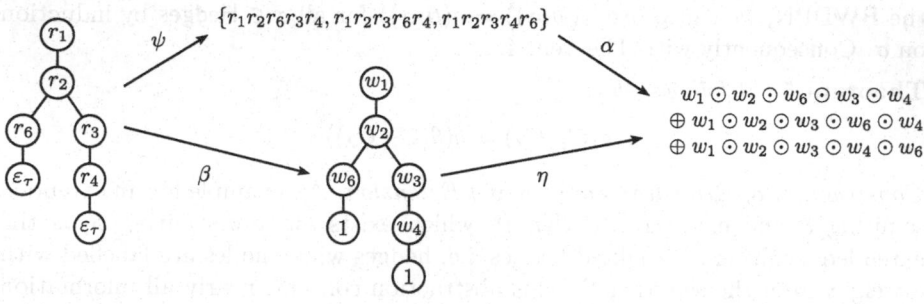

Fig. 3. Different abstractions provide the same result

Figure 3 shows, that in our example from Section 1, the abstraction, with $f(r_i) = w_i$, of the set of paths of the connecting hedges $\text{Hedges}(C_1, C_2)$ and the projection of the direct abstraction, with $\bar{f}(r_i) = \iota(w_i)$, of the same hedges lead to the same results, confirming the result of Theorem 5.

Howerver, since the size of the sets, trees and hedges is not bounded, this extended semiring is not efficient. In the next section we will explain, how in some cases a smaller representation for the weighted hedges can be found, that can be used to compute a solution for the BGPP problem.

4 Applications

Since the existence of an efficient extended semiring and a matching extension for a given semiring is not self-evident, we first give some examples of semirings, for which an efficient extended semiring and a corresponding extension can be constructed, before describing the approach to solve the BGPP problem in Section 5.

Starting form the weighted trees in the previous section, we can simplify the appearance of a tree by collapsing sequential parts of a tree using the $\odot$ operator of the semiring. To still be able to compute an interleaving of two collapsed branches, we assume an abstract interleaving operator $\otimes$. The existence of an abstract interleaving operator is again not self-evident, but is given for the applications described later in this section. Since a weighted tree can be a representation of a partial execution, we can not yet interleave the rightmost branch with any of the other branches, since it only represents part of the execution of the rightmost process. The solution to this problem is to precompute the total weight of the tree for all possible weights of appended weighted trees. Thus the extended weight representing a collapsed weighted tree is a function from D to D. Figure 4 visualizes the collapsing of the weighted hedge in our example into a function.

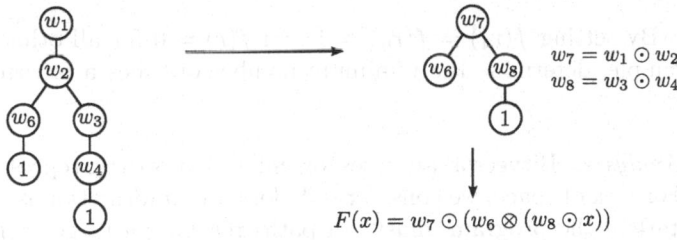

$$w_7 = w_1 \odot w_2$$
$$w_8 = w_3 \odot w_4$$

$$F(x) = w_7 \odot (w_6 \otimes (w_8 \odot x))$$

Fig. 4. Collapsing of a weighted tree

We set $E \subseteq \{F : D \to D\}$. The embedding of a weight $d \in D$ represents a tree with just a single node labelled by the embedded weight. Concatenation of another weighted tree leads to concatenation of d with the weight of the tree, hence $\iota(d) = F_d$, with $F_d(x) = d \odot x$. The projection is then a simple evaluation of the collapsed tree, where the empty weighted tree, with semiring weight 1 is appended, hence $\eta(F) = F(1)$. Concatenation of collapsed trees is then combination of the functions representing the trees $(F \bar{\odot} G)(x) = F(G(x))$ and the meet is the pointwise meet $(F \bar{\oplus} G)(x) = F(x) \oplus G(x)$. For interleaving, the left branch is evaluated at 1 to get the total weight of the left tree and the interleaving with all possible values for the right tree is precomputed, hence $(F \bar{\odot} G)(x) = F(1) \otimes G(x)$. Then E is the smallest set with $\iota(D) \subseteq E$, which is closed under $\bar{\odot}, \bar{\otimes}$ and arbitrary $\bar{\oplus}$.

Shortest Path Analysis. The shortest path analysis assigns a positive integer weight to all transitions. The weight of a path is the sum of the weights of the transitions occurring on the path. The goal is to find the weight of the path with the smallest weight. We use the semiring $\mathcal{S} = (\mathbb{N} \cup \{\infty\}, min, +, \infty, 0)$ introduced in [2]. Since $+$ is commutative and associative, the order in which transitions occur and are combined on a path is irrelevant. Thus $+$ can be used as the abstract interleaving operator $\otimes$.

If we apply the construction described above, we get an extended semiring $\mathcal{E} = (E, \bar{\oplus}, \bar{\odot}, \bar{\otimes}, F_\infty, F_0)$, with $\bar{\oplus}, \bar{\odot}$ and $\bar{\otimes}$ as described. Furthermore, we get an extension $(\mathcal{S}, \mathcal{E}, \iota, \eta)$, with $\iota(d)(x) = d + x$, for $d \in \mathbb{N} \cup \{\infty\}$ and η as described. Since E contains only the elements derived from elements in $\iota(D)$, it can be show that all elements $F \in E$ can be written as $F(x) = d_F + x$ with $d_F \in \mathbb{N} \cup \{\infty\}$. Then the operators of the extended semiring and extension can be reduced to the operators of the semiring as follows:

$$(F \bar{\odot} G)(x) = (d_F + d_G) + x \quad (F \bar{\oplus} G)(x) = min\{d_F, d_G\} + x$$
$$(F \bar{\otimes} G)(x) = (d_F + d_G) + x \quad \eta(F) \qquad = d_F$$

One can observe, that instead of the functional notation of $\mathcal{E}$, one can simply use $(\mathbb{N} \cup \{\infty\}, min, +, +, \infty, 0)$ as extended semiring. Using this construction, we can precisely compute the length of the shortest path connecting the starting and the target set in the DPN.

Example 6. By setting $f(r_4) = f(r_6) = 1$ and $f(r) = 0$ for all other rules, one can, for example, determine the minimum number of times **a** is written in our example.

Bitvector Analyses. Bitvector analyses examine a property represented by a single bit. For lack of space, we consider only forward, information is propagated from the start of the program, must, all paths reaching a target configuration must set the bit to 1, bitvector analyses. Backward, information is propagated from the end of the program, or may, it suffices, that one path reaching a target configuration sets the bit to 1, analyses can be handled similarly. The transitions of the DPN are annotated with transformers, that change the current state of the bit. We use the semiring $\mathcal{S} = (D, \oplus, \odot, \text{zero}, \text{id})$, where $D = \{\text{kill}, \text{id}, \text{gen}, \text{zero}\}$. Here **gen** represents the transformer setting the bit to 1, **id** is the identity and **kill** sets the bit to 0. The artificial weight **zero** is introduced to represent the zero element of the ring. For a forward analysis, $\odot$ is reversed functional combination extended to include **zero**. In case of a must analysis $\oplus$ is a meet operator inducing the ordering $\text{kill} \sqsubseteq \text{id} \sqsubseteq \text{gen} \sqsubseteq \text{zero}$. In [6] it was shown, that the operator $\otimes$, defined as $f \otimes g = (f \odot g) \oplus (g \odot f)$, is an abstract interleaving operator on the path level.

If we apply the construction described above, we get an extended semiring $\mathcal{E} = (E, \bar{\oplus}, \bar{\odot}, \bar{\otimes}, F_{\text{zero}}, F_{\text{id}})$, with $\bar{\oplus}, \bar{\odot}$ and $\bar{\otimes}$ as described, and an extension $(\mathcal{S}, \mathcal{E}, \iota, \eta)$. Since E is the smallest set containing $\iota(T)$ closed under $\bar{\oplus}, \bar{\odot}$ and $\bar{\otimes}$, it can be shown, that $E = \iota(D) \cup \{F_{\overline{\text{kill}}}\}$, with $F_{\overline{\text{kill}}}(x) = x \odot \text{kill}$, and $\eta(F_f) = f$ and $\eta(F_{\overline{\text{kill}}}) = \text{kill}$.

This is can be explained by the fact, that a kill occurring in a parallel has the most impact on the result if it is executed as last transition, where it can not be overwritten. Thus we need an additional weight, that describes exactly the effect, that once a kill has occurred as the result of a parallel process, it has to always be the last weight considered. The function $F_{\overline{\text{kill}}}$, describing a partial tree containing a kill as the result of a parallel branch, does exactly that.

In contrast to kill, id and gen influence an interleaving the most if they are considered as early as possible. In this case the weight of the parallel branch needs to be considered right after it was created. Thus parallel composition degenerates to sequential composition and no additional information needs to be stored.

Example 7. To determine, whether the value of a written in line 2 is always used in the calculation in line 3, we can use a forward must bitvector analysis. We set the weights for the transitions of the DPN to be $f(r_4) = $ gen, i.e. if we encounter the write at line 2, we set the bit to 1, $f(r_6) = $ kill, i.e. we set the bit to 0 if line 7 writes, and $f(r) = $ id for all other rules. If the resulting function sets the bit, we know, that the write in line 2 is always the last write to a before the use in line 3.

KILL/GEN. KILL/GEN analyses are a special kind of dataflow analysis, where dataflow facts are elements of a complete distributive lattice $(D, \sqcup)$, with least and greatest elements $\bot, \top$, and the set of transformers is restricted to $T = \{f : D \to D \mid \exists k, g \in D \text{ with } f(x) = (x \sqcap k_f) \sqcup g_f\}$. They can be used for bitvector analyses, but also encompass other analyses, like strong copy constant propagation [6].

We only consider forward KILL/GEN analyses, but backward analyses can be handled similarly. The semiring is $\mathcal{S} = (T \cup \{\text{zero}\}, \oplus, \odot, \text{zero}, \text{id})$, where zero is an artificial element representing the zero element of the ring and $\text{id}(x) = (x \sqcap \top) \sqcup \bot$. For elements $f, g \neq $ zero we then have $(f \oplus g)(x) = f(x) \sqcup g(x)$ and $(f \odot g)(x) = g(f(x))$. In [6] it was shown, that $f \otimes g = f \odot g \oplus g \odot f$ is an abstract interleaving operator.

Applying the construction described above, we arrive at an extended semiring $\mathcal{E} = (E, \bar{\oplus}, \bar{\odot}, \bar{\otimes}, F_{\text{zero}}, F_{\text{id}})$ and extension $(\mathcal{S}, \mathcal{E}, \iota, \eta)$. With $\iota(g)(f)(x) = f(g(x))$ it can be shown, that every element $F \in E \setminus \{F_{\text{zero}}\}$ can be written as $F(f)(x) = f(f_F(x)) \sqcup i_F$ with $f_F \in T, i_F \in D$. The operations on the extended semiring can then be reduced to operations of the semiring and underlying lattice as follows:

$$(F \bar{\odot} G)(f)(x) = f((f_F \odot f_G)(x)) \sqcup (i_F \sqcup i_G)$$
$$(F \bar{\oplus} G)(f)(x) = f((f_F \oplus f_G)(x)) \sqcup (i_F \sqcup i_G)$$
$$(F \bar{\otimes} G)(f)(x) = f(f_G(x \sqcap k_{f_F})) \sqcup (i_F \sqcup i_G \sqcup g_{f_F})$$
$$\eta(F)(x) \quad = f_F(x) \sqcup i_F$$

On the one hand the result for the interleaving operator can be seen as generalisation of the bitvector result. Parallel effects that improve the result are applied as early as possible, directly on the initial information and effects that worsen the result are applied as late as possible, after all information has been computed. On the other hand we arrive at a result similar to [8]. Here it was observed, that KILL/GEN analyses can be solved by separating paths directly reaching a program point from the possible interference of the environment. The same structure can be found in the extended weight domain, where a weight is described by a standard transformer, representing the reaching path, that is applied to the initial data and a lattice element, representing the possible interference, that is added at the end.

Example 8. To determine, which writes of a can be used in the calculation in line 3, we can use a forward KILL/GEN analysis over the lattice $(2^{\{2,7\}}, \subseteq)$. We set the weights for the transitions of the DPN to be $f(r_4) = \lambda x.\{2\}$, $f(r_6) = \lambda x.\{7\}$ and $f(r) = \lambda x.x$ for all other rules. If we apply the resulting function to the empty set, we get the set of writing locations whose value can be used in line 3.

5 Solving the BGPP Problem for BWDPN

Now consider an execution hedge in $\mathsf{Hedges}(C_1, C_2)$. Each tree of the hedge transforms a stack in a starting configuration $c_1 \in C_1$ into a configuration containing the transformed original stack and stacks of spawned processes, that is part of a target configuration $c_2 \in C_2$. Analogous to the approach in [2], we can split each tree into several parts along the rightmost branch. We differentiate between two main types of partial trees. The first type transforms an initial stacktop of the form $p\gamma$ into cp', meaning that the topmost stacksymbol is popped off the stack. The second type transforms $p\gamma$ into $cp'w$, with $w \in \Gamma^+$, pushing additional symbols on the stack. In both cases new process may be spawned and transformed, forming the configuration c to the left of the initial process. If we take an execution tree τ, we can observe, that the execution of the initial process can always be split into a sequence of pop transformation and a final push transformation.

If we now classify the partial trees by their initial stack $p\gamma$ and their result cp' or $cp'w$, we can assemble each execution tree out of these classes. Taking for example τ_1, τ_2 with $p_i\gamma_i \xRightarrow{\tau_i} c_i p_{i+1}$ and τ_3 with $p_3\gamma_3 \xRightarrow{\tau_3} p'w'$, we get an execution tree $\tau = \tau_1 ; \tau_2 ; \tau_3$ with $p_1\gamma_1\gamma_2\gamma_3 w \xRightarrow{\tau} c_1 c_2 c_3 p'w'w$.

Since the spawned processes and pushed stacksymbols of a partial tree are unbounded this is still an infinite number of classes. We exploit the fact, that we are only interested in the trees that reach a given regular set of configurations and assume the set is described by an automaton. The spawned processes and pushed stacksymbols of a partial tree will not be altered by a concatenated tree, it will only spawn and transform its own new processes and a push is the final phase of an execution. Consequently the spawned processes of a partial tree and the symbols pushed onto the stack have to be part of the final configuration. Since the configuration is part of a regular set we can describe these parts by two states of the automaton between which a part is accepted. Grouping the classes where the spawned processes and pushed stacksymbols are accepted by the same states together, we arrive at a finite number of classes.

To characterise these classes, we take a closer look at the saturation procedure introduced in [1] to compute the set of predecessor configurations of a given target set.

Regular Sets of Configurations. The saturation procedure requires special kinds of automata for representation of the target set. We use $\mathcal{M}$- and $\mathcal{M}^*$-automata, adapted from [1], as a compact representation for the target set. A $\mathcal{M}^*$-automaton is a finite automaton $\mathcal{A}^* = (S, P \cup \Gamma, \delta, \acute{s}, F)$ that satisfies the following additional conditions:

- $S^C, S^P \subseteq S$, where for all $s \in S^C, p \in P$ exists a unique and distinguished state $s_p \in S^P$
- $\delta = \delta^P \cup \delta^\Gamma$ where $\delta^P = \{(s, p, s_p) \mid s \in S^C, p \in P\}$ and $\delta^\Gamma \subseteq S \times (\Gamma \cup \{\varepsilon\}) \times S$
- $\mathcal{L}(\mathcal{A}) \subseteq \mathsf{Conf}$

A $\mathcal{M}$-automaton $\mathcal{A}$ is a $\mathcal{M}^*$-automaton, where the transition relation δ satisfies the stronger condition $\delta^\Gamma \subseteq S \times (\Gamma \cup \{\varepsilon\}) \times (S \setminus S^P)$ and $\acute{s} \in S \setminus S^P$. We write $s \xrightarrow{\lambda}_\delta s'$ for $(s, \lambda, s') \in \delta$ and $s \xrightarrow{c}{}^*_\delta s'$ for the reflexive transitive closure. $\mathcal{L}(\mathcal{A})$ is the language of the automaton. Each regular set of configurations can be described by an $\mathcal{M}$-automaton. For the rest of the paper we fix two $\mathcal{M}$-automata $\mathcal{A}_1 = (S_1, P \cup \Gamma, \delta_1, \acute{s}_1, F_1)$ and $\mathcal{A}_2 = (S_2, P \cup \Gamma, \delta_2, \acute{s}_2, F_2)$ with $\mathcal{L}(\mathcal{A}_1) = C_1$ and $\mathcal{L}(\mathcal{A}_2) = C_2$.

Characterising Trees and Hedges. The following saturation procedure, taken from [1], works by adding new transitions to the automaton $\mathcal{A}_2$, thus allowing more configurations to be accepted. The result is a $\mathcal{M}^*$-automaton $\mathcal{A}_2^* = (S_2, P \cup \Gamma, \bar{\delta}_2, \acute{s}_2, F_2)$, with $\bar{\delta}_2 = \delta_2^P \cup \bar{\delta}_2^\Gamma$, where $\bar{\delta}_2^\Gamma$ is the smallest set fulfilling the conditions:

[init] $t \in \bar{\delta}_2^\Gamma$ if $t \in \delta_2^\Gamma$

[step] $(s_p, \gamma, s') \in \bar{\delta}_2^\Gamma$ if $r = p\gamma \hookrightarrow c \in \Delta, s \in S^C, s \xrightarrow{c}{}^*_{\bar{\delta}_2} s'$

A transition is added, if there is a rule transforming the symbol into a configuration which is accepted by previously existing transitions. If these transitions were also added by the saturation, they themselves have a rules, which transform their symbols. If we follow this recursion and assemble the rules into a tree, we have a tree that transform the symbol of the newly added transition into a configuration that can be read using only transition of $\mathcal{A}_2$. Consequently all new configurations $\mathcal{L}(\mathcal{A}_2^*)$ which are accepted because of this transition, are predecessors of configurations in the original automaton. Additionally a new transition (s_p, γ, s') is a witness for the existence of a tree, that transforms $p\gamma$ into a configuration c which is accepted between the states s and s'. If $s' \in S^P$ then $c = c'p'$, since only P transitions reach states in S^P and the tree is a pop transformation as described above. If $s' \notin S^P$, we have $c = c'p'w'$ and the tree is a push transformation.

We later extend the saturation procedure to collect all of these trees for a transition by constructing a constraint system L over $(2^{\mathsf{Trees}}, \cup)$, similar to the grammar used to describe executions in [2]. The variables of the constraint system $\mathsf{L}[t]$ with $t \in \bar{\delta}_2^\Gamma$ can be seen as annotations to the transitions of the saturated automaton. The least solution of the constraint system then corresponds exactly to the classes of trees described above. We define a function $\pi_\mathsf{L} : S_2 \times \mathsf{Conf} \times S_2 \rightarrow 2^{\mathsf{Hedges}}$ that constructs a set of hedges for a configuration by reading the annotations from the automaton $\mathcal{A}_2^*$:

$$
\begin{aligned}
\text{[empty]} \quad & \pi_\mathsf{L}(s, \varepsilon, s) = \{\varepsilon_\sigma\} \\
\text{[epsilon]} \quad & \pi_\mathsf{L}(s, \varepsilon, s') = \bigcup \{\pi_\mathsf{L}(s, \varepsilon, s'') \mid s'' \xrightarrow{\varepsilon}_{\delta_2^\Gamma} s'\} \\
\text{[control]} \quad & \pi_\mathsf{L}(s, cp, s') = \bigcup \{\pi_\mathsf{L}(s, c, s'')\varepsilon_\tau \mid s'' \xrightarrow{p}_{\bar{\delta}_2^P} s'\} \\
& \qquad \cup \bigcup \{\pi_\mathsf{L}(s, cp, s'') \mid s'' \xrightarrow{\varepsilon}_{\delta_2^\Gamma} s'\} \\
\text{[stack]} \quad & \pi_\mathsf{L}(s, c\gamma, s') = \bigcup \{\pi_\mathsf{L}(s, c, s'') ; \mathsf{L}[(s'', \gamma, s')] \mid s'' \xrightarrow{\gamma}_{\bar{\delta}_2^\Gamma} s'\} \\
& \qquad \cup \bigcup \{\pi_\mathsf{L}(s, c\gamma, s'') \mid s'' \xrightarrow{\varepsilon}_{\delta_2^\Gamma} s'\}
\end{aligned}
$$

If we read a partial configuration c between two states of the saturated automaton, we can construct the set of hedges transforming the configuration into a partial configuration of the target set accepted between the same two states, using π_L.

We start with the set containing only the empty hedge and add a new empty tree, whenever we read a control state of the DPN. Consider for example now a configuration $p\gamma_1\gamma_2$. After reading p we are in a state s_p and the current set of hedges is $\{\varepsilon_\tau\}$. ε transitions do not contain any additional information and information is simply propagated trough. If we now read the next symbol in the saturated automaton, we can distinguish two cases for the next transition:

Either the transition is $(s_p, \gamma_1, s'_{p'})$. As observed above all trees annotated to this transition are pop transformations, applying them to $p\gamma_1\gamma_2$ ends in a configuration $cp'\gamma_2$, where $s \xrightarrow{c}{}^*_{\delta_2} s'$. The next transition for γ_2, is then $(s'_{p'}, \gamma_2, s'')$, which is annotated with trees transforming $p'\gamma_2$ into configurations c' with $s' \xrightarrow{c'}{}^*_{\delta_2} s''$. If we concatenate the trees, we get transformations of $p\gamma_1\gamma_2$ to cc', with $s \xrightarrow{cc'}{}^*_{\delta_2} s''$.

Or the transition is (s_p, γ_1, s'), with $s' \notin S^P$. As observed the trees annotated to this transition are push transformations. Starting from $p\gamma_1\gamma_2$, they lead to $cp'w'\gamma_2$, with $s \xrightarrow{cp'w'}{}^*_{\delta_2} s'$. Since we can accept the configuration as part of the target set, we have another transition (s', γ_2, s'') in the original automaton. The set of trees transforming the configuration $p\gamma_1\gamma_2$ is then simply the set of the first transition. To simplify the construction, we annotate transitions not starting in states in S^P, with the set only containing the empty tree, thus we can simply concatenate the annotated sets of all transitions in both cases.

This can be extended to a configuration with an arbitrary number of stack symbols. If we take a configuration $p_1 w_1 p_2 w_2$, we want to construct the set of hedges transforming the configuration. If we read the configuration left to right we construct the set of trees for the first stack a described above. If we now encounter a transition for a control state, a new initial empty tree is added to the end of the hedges. We can then construct the set of trees for second stack again as described above, since all concatenation operations now concern this new last tree of the hedges. This can be extended to a configuration with an arbitrary number of stacks.

Using these observations, we construct a set of constraints in a similar way the saturation procedure adds transitions to the automaton:

[init] $L[t] \supseteq \{\varepsilon_\tau\}$ if $t \in \delta_2^\Gamma$

[step] $L[(s_p, \gamma, s')] \supseteq \{r(\varepsilon_\tau)\}\,;\pi_L(s, c, s')$ if $r = p\gamma \hookrightarrow c \in \Delta, s \in S^C, s \xrightarrow{c}{}^*_{\delta_2} s'$

The trees are essentially constructed bottom up. Each transition starts with the set containing only the empty tree. If we add a new transition, we add all trees which can be constructed by the rule which lead to the addition, and all hedges, which are already known to transform the configuration reached by that rule.

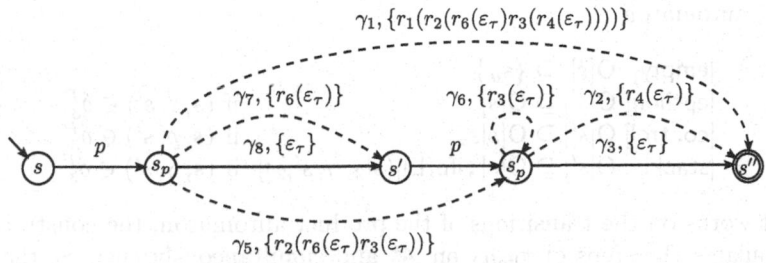

Fig. 5. Annotated automaton after saturation

Figure 5 shows part of the resulting automaton of the saturation procedure applied to the target C_2 set of our example and the least solution of the constraint system annotated to the transitions of the automaton. The initial automaton is displayed with solid arrows and transitions added by the saturation are dashed.

For the least solution lfp(L) of L we can prove, by induction on the structure of the trees τ:

Lemma 9. *For $s \in S_2^C, s' \in S_2, p \in P, \gamma \in \Gamma, (s_p, \gamma, s') \in \bar{\delta}_2^\Gamma$, we have:*

$$\mathsf{lfp}(\mathsf{L})[(s_p, \gamma, s')] = \{\tau \mid \exists c \in \mathsf{Conf} \text{ with } p\gamma \xRightarrow{\tau} c, s \xrightarrow{c}{}^*_{\delta_2} s'\},$$

and for $s \notin S_2^P, s' \in S_2, \gamma \in \Gamma, (s, \gamma, s') \in \bar{\delta}_2^\Gamma$, we get:

$$\mathsf{lfp}(\mathsf{L})[(s, \gamma, s')] = \{\varepsilon_\tau\}.$$

Thus the solution of the constraint system contains exactly the classes of trees we wanted to characterise. If we annotate the transitions of $\mathcal{A}_2^*$ with lfp(L), we can prove by induction on the length of the configurations c:

Lemma 10. *For $s, s' \in S_2, c \in \mathsf{Conf}$, we have:*

$$\pi_{\mathsf{lfp}(\mathsf{L})}(s, c, s') = \{\sigma \mid \exists c' \in \mathsf{Conf} \text{ with } c \xRightarrow{\sigma} c', s \xrightarrow{c'}{}^*_{\delta_2} s'\},$$

Hence we have $\mathsf{Hedges}(\{c\}, C_2) = \bigcup\{\pi_{\mathsf{lfp(L)}}(\dot{s}_2, c, s) \mid s \in F_2\}$ for a configuration $c \in \mathsf{Conf}$. We can describe the set of all reaching hedges from the single configuration c into the set C_2. We are now interested in the union of all these sets for configurations in C_1. It suffices to consider configurations in $C_1 \cap \mathcal{L}(\mathcal{A}_2^*)$, since all other configurations have an empty set of reaching hedges. Since the number of configurations can still be infinite and thus we can not evaluate $\pi_{\mathsf{lfp(L)}}$ for all these configurations, we construct a second constraint system O over $(\mathsf{Hedges}, \cup)$, that imitates the computation of $\pi_{\mathsf{lfp(L)}}$ by propagating sets of hedges along the transitions of an automaton and joining preliminary results at each state of the automaton.

Since we only want the result for configurations in $C_1 \cap \mathcal{L}(\mathcal{A}_2^*)$, we construct the constraint system for the product automaton $\mathcal{A}_3 = (S_3, P \cup \Gamma, \delta_3, \dot{s}_3, F_3)$ of $\mathcal{A}_1$ and $\mathcal{A}_2^*$, describing the intersection. For $s \in S_3$ we write $s|_i$, with $i \in \{1, 2\}$, to refer to the original state of automaton $\mathcal{A}_i$ that was used to form s in the product automaton.

$$
\begin{array}{lll}
[\text{empty}] & \mathsf{O}[\dot{s}] \supseteq \{\varepsilon_\sigma\} & \\
[\text{epsilon}] & \mathsf{O}[s'] \supseteq \mathsf{O}[s] & \text{if } (s, \varepsilon, s') \in \delta_3^\Gamma \\
[\text{control}] & \mathsf{O}[s'] \supseteq \mathsf{O}[s]\varepsilon_\tau & \text{if } (s, p, s') \in \delta_3^P \\
[\text{stack}] & \mathsf{O}[s'] \supseteq \mathsf{O}[s] \, ; \mathsf{lfp(L)}[(s|_2, \gamma, s'|_2)] & \text{if } (s, \gamma, s') \in \delta_3^\Gamma
\end{array}
$$

Since it works on the transitions of the product automaton, the constraint system emulates the steps of $\pi_{\mathsf{lfp(L)}}$ on $\mathcal{A}_2^*$ and simultaneously ensures, that each transition followed in $\mathcal{A}_2^*$ has a corresponding transition in $\mathcal{A}_1$. Thus it only works on configurations which are also in C_1.

It can then be shown, by induction on the length of the configuration c, that:

Lemma 11. *For $s \in S_3$, we get:*

$$
\mathsf{lfp(O)}[s] = \bigcup\{\pi_{\mathsf{lfp(L)}}(\dot{s}_3|_2, c, s|_2) \mid \dot{s}_3|_1 \xrightarrow{c}{}_{\delta_1}^* s|_1\},
$$

Consequently, the solution of the constraint system at the accepting states of the product automaton can be used to describe the set of all connecting hedges:

Theorem 12. *We get:*

$$
\mathsf{Hedges}(C_1, C_2) = \bigcup\{\mathsf{lfp(O)}[s] \mid s \in F_3\}.
$$

Abstraction. To compute the weight of the hedges, we construct a constraint system $\mathsf{L}^\#$, a function $\pi_{\mathsf{L}^\#}^\#$ and constraint system $\mathsf{O}^\#$ over the weight domain by replacing the operators and constants in the constraint system L, the function π_{L} and constraint system O, with the corresponding operators and constants according to the abstraction function β:

$$
\begin{array}{ll}
(2^{\mathsf{Hedges}}, \cup) \rightsquigarrow (E, \bar{\oplus}) & M \rightsquigarrow \beta(M) \\
M \, ; M' \rightsquigarrow \beta(M) \bar{\odot} \beta(M') & MM' \rightsquigarrow \beta(M) \bar{\otimes} \beta(M')
\end{array}
$$

Since the order in the abstract domain is dual to the ordering on sets of hedges, we compute the greatest fixpoint in the abstract domain. Using standard results from abstract interpretation [9], we get $\mathsf{gfp}(\mathsf{L}^\#) = \beta(\mathsf{lfp}(\mathsf{L}))$, $\pi^\#_{\mathsf{gfp}(\mathsf{L}^\#)} = \beta \circ \pi_{\mathsf{lfp}(\mathsf{L})}$ and $\mathsf{gfp}(\mathsf{O}^\#) = \beta(\mathsf{lfp}(\mathsf{O}))$ for the solutions of the constraint systems. With Theorem 12:

Theorem 13. *It follows, that:*

$$\theta(C_1, C_2) = \bigoplus \{\overline{\mathsf{gfp}(\mathsf{O}^\#)}[s] \mid s \in F_3\}.$$

Thus we can solve the BGPP problem by computing $\mathsf{gfp}(\mathsf{L}^\#)$ and $\mathsf{gfp}(\mathsf{O}^\#)$. Theorem 5 states, that we get the solution to the GPP problem by applying η.

Algorithm. Given a WDPN $(\mathcal{M}, \mathcal{S}, f)$ and two sets of configurations C_1, C_2, represented by $\mathcal{M}$-automata $\mathcal{A}_1, \mathcal{A}_2$, the complete algorithm to compute the solution of the GPP problem $\delta(C_1, C_2)$ consists of the following steps:

1. Find a suitable extended semiring $\mathcal{E}$ and extension $(\mathcal{S}, \mathcal{E}, \iota, \eta)$ and consider the BWDPN $(\mathcal{M}, \mathcal{E}, \bar{f})$, with $\bar{f}(r) = \iota(f(r))$.
2. Construct the automaton $\mathcal{A}_2^*$ using the saturation procedure. The saturation can be done in $O(|S_2|^3 |\Delta| \|\Delta\|)$ time, where $\|\Delta\|$ is the length of the longest right hand side of a rule in Δ. The size of the transition relation of the saturated automaton is in $O(|\delta_2| + |S_2|^2 |\Delta|)$.
3. Construct the abstract constraint system $\mathsf{L}^\#$ for $\mathcal{A}_2^*$ and solve it. The construction can be done during the saturation of the automaton. The size of the constraint system is in $O(|\delta_2| + |S_2|^{2\|\Delta\|}|\Delta|)$. The time needed to solve the constraint system depends on the solver and the height and complexity of the weight domain.
4. Compute the product automaton $\mathcal{A}_3$ from $\mathcal{A}_1$ and $\mathcal{A}_2^*$.
5. Construct the abstract constraint system $\mathsf{O}^\#$ for $\mathcal{A}_3$ and solve it. The construction can be done during the computation of the product automation. The size of the constraint system is equal to the size of the transition relation of the product automaton and thus in $O(|\delta_1|(|\delta_2| + |S_2|^2 |\Delta|))$.
6. Compute $\bigoplus \{\overline{\mathsf{gfp}(\mathsf{O}^\#)}[s] \mid s \in F_3\}$.
7. Apply η to get $\delta(C_1, C_2)$.

In total the algorithm is linear in the size of the program $|\Delta|$, exponential in the size of the rules $\|\Delta\|$ and polynomial in the number of states and transitions of the automata describing the starting and target sets of the query. Since all DPN can be transformed into DPN with only rules of the type $p\gamma \hookrightarrow p'$, $p\gamma \hookrightarrow p'\gamma'$, $p\gamma \hookrightarrow p'\gamma'\gamma''$ and $p\gamma \hookrightarrow p'\gamma'p''\gamma''$, where the number of rules increases by a constant factor, the size of the rules $\|\Delta\|$ can be considered fixed and small. Similarly the starting and target sets of a query are usually representable by small automata and thus we have an efficient algorithm. For the first two applications described in Section 4 the solution of the constraint system can be computed using standard fixpoint algorithms. Termination of the computation is guaranteed, since the domains do not contain infinite descending chains. For the KILL/GEN analyses we additionally require, that the underlying lattice has no infinite ascending chains, to ensure termination of the fixpoint iteration.

6   Conclusion

We presented the GPP problem for a WDPN, which is a model for parallel programs with dynamic process creation and recursive procedures. The GPP problem is a general problem formulation, which can, for example, be used to capture basic dataflow analysis problems. Since the GPP problem can not be solved directly, our approach is based on an alternative branching semantics for DPN. The resulting tree shaped executions can be characterised using a constraint system, which can then be solved over an abstract domain to get a solution for the BGPP problem for BWDPN. If the weight domains for the BWDPN and WDPN are connected through an extension, the solution for the GPP problem can be derived from the corresponding BGPP problem. We have shown how the results can be used to solve basic dataflow analysis problems like bitvector analyses or shortest path problems.

Future Work. Firstly, we are currently working on an implementation of the algorithm and different weight domains.

Another direction of research is the iterated application of our algorithm. One can observe, that the product automaton computed in Section 5 is again an $\mathcal{M}$-automaton, whose transitions are indirectly annotated by the solution of the constraint system. The idea is to take this automaton as the target set for a second computation, which is initialized with the annotation of the automaton. Similar techniques have been studied for DPN without weights [11] and WPDS [4] to realize context-bounded analyses.

To compute the BGPP solution we need to solve a constraint system over the extended semiring. In practice this requires the extended semiring to fulfill additional criteria for the computation to terminate, like finiteness or the descending chain condition. To deal with unbounded domains, widening [9] could be introduced. Additionally in recent work [12,13], new techniques have been presented to solve equations for more general types of semirings. We plan on examining, whether these can be applied to our extended semirings.

In addition the relation between a semiring and a corresponding extended semiring and extension needs to be studied further. Here especially conditions which guarantee the existence of an efficient construction are of interest. Or alternatively, whether there are ways to construct at least an efficient approximation.

Our main application of BWDPN up to now is solving the GPP problem for WDPN. BWDPN themselves can be interesting. One example are weight domains which rely on thread identity. The thread executing a specific transition can not be determined from an interleaved path, but is visible in an execution hedge. The acquisition structures studied in [10], to compute whether there exists a path connecting two regular sets of configurations w.r.t. a lock sensitive semantics, can for example be adapted into a weight domain for BWDPN. Furthermore we plan to investigate whether the approach to the analysis of synchronisation taken in [14] can be adapted to our framework and thus extended to dynamic process creation.

Acknowledgement. We thank Markus Müller-Olm and Peter Lammich for helpful discussions on the topic of dynamic pushdown networks.

References

1. Bouajjani, A., Müller-Olm, M., Touili, T.: Regular symbolic analysis of dynamic networks of pushdown systems. In: Abadi, M., de Alfaro, L. (eds.) CONCUR 2005. LNCS, vol. 3653, pp. 473–487. Springer, Heidelberg (2005)
2. Reps, T., Schwoon, S., Jha, S., Melski, D.: Weighted pushdown systems and their application to interprocedural dataflow analysis. Sci. Comput. Program. 58(1-2) (2005)
3. Ramalingam, G.: Context-sensitive synchronization-sensitive analysis is undecidable. ACM Trans. Program. Lang. Syst. 22(2) (2000)
4. Lal, A., Touili, T., Kidd, N., Reps, T.W.: Interprocedural analysis of concurrent programs under a context bound. In: Ramakrishnan, C.R., Rehof, J. (eds.) TACAS 2008. LNCS, vol. 4963, pp. 282–298. Springer, Heidelberg (2008)
5. Esparza, J., Podelski, A.: Efficient algorithms for *pre** and *post** on interprocedural parallel flow graphs. In: POPL. ACM, New York (2000)
6. Seidl, H., Steffen, B.: Constraint-based inter-procedural analysis of parallel programs. Nordic J. of Computing 7(4) (2000)
7. Knoop, J., Steffen, B., Vollmer, J.: Parallelism for free: efficient and optimal bitvector analyses for parallel programs. ACM Trans. Program. Lang. Syst. 18(3) (1996)
8. Lammich, P., Müller-Olm, M.: Precise fixpoint-based analysis of programs with thread-creation and procedures. In: Caires, L., Vasconcelos, V.T. (eds.) CONCUR 2007. LNCS, vol. 4703, pp. 287–302. Springer, Heidelberg (2007)
9. Cousot, P., Cousot, R.: Abstract interpretation: A unified lattice model for static analysis of programs by construction or approximation of fixpoints. In: POPL. ACM, New York (1977)
10. Lammich, P., Müller-Olm, M., Wenner, A.: Predecessor sets of dynamic pushdown networks with tree-regular constraints. In: Bouajjani, A., Maler, O. (eds.) Computer Aided Verification. LNCS, vol. 5643, pp. 525–539. Springer, Heidelberg (2009)
11. Bouajjani, A., Esparza, J., Schwoon, S., Strejček, J.: Reachability analysis of multithreaded software with asynchronous communication. In: Sarukkai, S., Sen, S. (eds.) FSTTCS 2005. LNCS, vol. 3821, pp. 348–359. Springer, Heidelberg (2005)
12. Esparza, J., Kiefer, S., Luttenberger, M.: Newton's method for ω-continuous semirings. In: Aceto, L., Damgård, I., Goldberg, L.A., Halldórsson, M.M., Ingólfsdóttir, A., Walukiewicz, I. (eds.) ICALP 2008, Part II. LNCS, vol. 5126, pp. 14–26. Springer, Heidelberg (2008)
13. Kühnrich, M., Schwoon, S., Srba, J., Kiefer, S.: Interprocedural dataflow analysis over weight domains with infinite descending chains. In: de Alfaro, L. (ed.) FOSSACS 2009. LNCS, vol. 5504, pp. 440–455. Springer, Heidelberg (2009)
14. Bouajjani, A., Esparza, J., Touili, T.: A generic approach to the static analysis of concurrent programs with procedures. In: POPL. ACM, New York (2003)

Explicit Stabilisation
for Modular Rely-Guarantee Reasoning

John Wickerson, Mike Dodds, and Matthew Parkinson

University of Cambridge Computer Laboratory

Abstract. We propose a new formalisation of stability for Rely-Guarantee, in which an assertion's stability is encoded into its syntactic form. This allows two advances in modular reasoning. Firstly, it enables Rely-Guarantee, for the first time, to verify concurrent libraries independently of their clients' environments. Secondly, in a sequential setting, it allows a module's internal interference to be hidden while verifying its clients. We demonstrate our approach by verifying, using RGSep, the Version 7 Unix memory manager, uncovering a twenty-year-old bug in the process.

1 Introduction

Reasoning about concurrent programs is hard because commands from different threads are interleaved non-deterministically. With many threads and many commands per thread, naïve reasoning soon succumbs to a combinatorial explosion. The Rely-Guarantee (RG) method [14] restores tractability through abstraction. In addition to the pre and postconditions inherited from Hoare logic [12], a command is specified by two relations between states: a *rely* R that specifies all the state transitions (or 'actions') the environment can cause, and a *guarantee* G that specifies all the actions of the command itself. (The environment is the set of concurrently-running threads.) The method conservatively assumes that between consecutive commands in a thread, any number of actions in R may occur. The truth of an assertion that holds after one command must be preserved by this 'interference', so that it may be safely assumed by the next command. Such an assertion is deemed *stable under* R.

Stability is traditionally enforced through side-conditions on proof rules. We propose (Sect. 3) a new formalisation in which stability is recorded within the syntactic form of the assertion itself. Just as 'explicit substitution' [1] added substitution to the syntax of λ-calculus terms, our work adds stabilisation to the syntax of RG assertions. We propose two new constructs: $\lfloor p \rfloor_R$ to denote the weakest assertion that is both stronger than p and stable under R, and dually, $\lceil p \rceil_R$ to denote the strongest stable assertion that is weaker than p.

The main benefit is in modularity, two forms of which we tease apart and tackle separately: verifying concurrent libraries independently of clients, and verifying clients of a (sequential) module independently of its implementation.

Verifying libraries independently of clients. RG is a compositional method: an entire program's proof depends only upon the proofs of its constituent commands.

A.D. Gordon (Ed.): ESOP 2010, LNCS 6012, pp. 610–629, 2010.

WEAKEN
$R', G' \vdash \{p'\} C \{q'\}$
$p \Rightarrow p' \qquad q' \Rightarrow q$
$R \subseteq R' \qquad G' \subseteq G$ PAR
$\dfrac{\qquad\qquad\qquad\qquad}{R, G \vdash \{p\} C \{q\}}$ $\dfrac{R \cup G_2, G_1 \vdash \{p_1\} C_1 \{q_1\} \qquad R \cup G_1, G_2 \vdash \{p_2\} C_2 \{q_2\}}{R, G_1 \cup G_2 \vdash \{p_1 \wedge p_2\} C_1 \parallel C_2 \{q_1 \wedge q_2\}}$

BASIC
$\dfrac{\vdash \{p\} c \{q\} \quad \overleftarrow{p} \cap c \subseteq G}{R, G \vdash \{p\} c \{q\}}$
$p \text{ stab } R \quad q \text{ stab } R$ SKIP $\dfrac{p \text{ stab } R}{R, G \vdash \{p\} \text{ skip} \{p\}}$ LOOP $\dfrac{R, G \vdash \{p\} C \{p\}}{R, G \vdash \{p\} C^+ \{p\}}$

Fig. 1. Selected RG proof rules (with stability checks)

Yet it is not modular: a command's proof cannot necessarily be re-used when the command features in a different program, because proofs are environment-specific. Thus, RG cannot verify libraries that are invoked in several different environments. Our solution (Sect. 4) has the library record stability requirements using $\lfloor \ \rfloor_R$ and $\lceil \ \rceil_R$, but leave the specification parametric in R. Each client then instantiates R appropriately and performs the stabilisation.

Verifying clients independently of module implementations. In Sect. 5, we bring explicit stabilisation to an RG-style logic that reasons about heap-manipulating programs: RGSep [20]. Because it divides the heap into both thread-local and shared regions, RGSep's notion of stability is more complex than that of ordinary RG; in particular, while only the shared heap is susceptible to interference, we shall see that the local heap can still affect stability arguments. Originally conceived for concurrency, RGSep is apt for verifying sequential modules too. Such a verification must consider every action by which a client can mutate the module's part of the heap. Our extension of explicit stabilisation to RGSep permits an INFOHIDING rule that allows this so-called 'internal interference' to be hidden while verifying clients. We demonstrate (Sect. 6) this approach by verifying – for the first time – the Version 7 Unix memory manager. In doing so, we uncover a bug that has lain dormant since 1979.

We begin with a short introduction to the RG proof system, followed by a brief account of the failure of traditional RG to provide a modular specification for even one of the most trivial library functions: increment.

2   Background: Rely-Guarantee Reasoning

RG specifications are of the form $R, G \vdash \{p\} C \{q\}$, where R and G are relations between states. Following [17], G shall be reflexive. This specification expresses that when C begins execution in a state satisfying the precondition p, in an environment whose interference is limited to the actions in the rely R, then any state transitions performed by C are within its guarantee G, and moreover, if the execution terminates, the final state satisfies the postcondition q.

Figure 1 presents a selection of the RG proof rules, which concern commands of the following simple parallel language:

$$C ::= \texttt{skip} \mid C\,;C \mid C \,\|\, C \mid C + C \mid C^+ \mid c$$

The $+$ operator chooses one of its operands to execute, while C^+ executes C at least once.[1] We consider only partial correctness, so these non-deterministic constructs for choice and looping suffice for encoding $\texttt{if}$ and $\texttt{while}$ commands. The language is parameterised on the set of basic commands c, which are relations that model atomic state transformations. We shall assume c includes $\texttt{assert}$ and $\texttt{assume}$ commands and variable assignment. See [21] for the complete set of proof rules and the formal semantics of our language.

The BASIC rule requires that c meets the sequential specification $\{p\}\,c\,\{q\}$, and that any action it performs is within its guarantee. It uses the notation $\overleftarrow{p} \stackrel{\text{def}}{=} \{(\sigma, \sigma') \mid \sigma \models p\}$. The pre and postconditions of the two 'ground' commands, c and $\texttt{skip}$, are required to be stable. Since the other commands are built inductively from these, their rules can assume any inherited assertions to be stable (or else derived from stable assertions by the WEAKEN rule). Stability checks are notated as follows:

Definition 1 (Stability). $p\,\text{stab}\,R \stackrel{\text{def}}{=} \forall \sigma, \sigma'. \sigma \models p \wedge R(\sigma, \sigma') \implies \sigma' \models p$.

The PAR rule marks the epitome of RG reasoning. When reasoning about commands composed in parallel, the rely of each command is extended to include the guarantee of the other. The composed command $C_1 \,\|\, C_2$ guarantees actions in either of its components' guarantees, and establishes both components' postconditions upon completion.

2.1   The Problem with Verifying Libraries

Consider a library function $\texttt{f()}$ that atomically increments a shared variable $\texttt{x}$. Its two clients, $\texttt{g()}$ and $\texttt{h()}$, invoke $\texttt{f()}$ in an empty environment and an environment that may increase $\texttt{x}$, respectively. Call this latter environment $R_{\texttt{x+}}$. The guarantee $G_{\texttt{x+}}$ additionally dictates that no variable other than $\texttt{x}$ changes.

Definition 2.

$$
\begin{aligned}
\texttt{f()} &\stackrel{\text{def}}{=} \texttt{x++} \\
\texttt{g()} &\stackrel{\text{def}}{=} \texttt{assume(x=3)}; \; \texttt{f()}; \; \texttt{assert(x=4)} \\
\texttt{h()} &\stackrel{\text{def}}{=} \texttt{assume(x=5)}; \; (\texttt{f()} \,\|\, \texttt{f()}); \; \texttt{assert(x}\geq\texttt{6)} \\
R_{\texttt{x+}} &\stackrel{\text{def}}{=} \{(\sigma, \sigma') \mid \sigma(\texttt{x}) \leq \sigma'(\texttt{x})\} \\
G_{\texttt{x+}} &\stackrel{\text{def}}{=} \{(\sigma, \sigma') \mid \sigma(\texttt{x}) \leq \sigma'(\texttt{x}) \wedge \forall v \neq \texttt{x}. \sigma(v) = \sigma'(v)\}
\end{aligned}
$$

Now, the proofs of $\texttt{g()}$ and $\texttt{h()}$ hinge, respectively, upon deriving the following two specifications for $\texttt{f()}$:

$$\emptyset, G_{\texttt{x+}} \vdash \{\texttt{x}=X\}\,\texttt{f()}\,\{\texttt{x}=X+1\} \qquad\qquad R_{\texttt{x+}}, G_{\texttt{x+}} \vdash \{\texttt{x}\geq X\}\,\texttt{f()}\,\{\texttt{x}\geq X+1\}$$

---

[1] Interestingly, a variant of the LOOP rule for reasoning about C^* commands would require a stability check on p, in case C^* should behave like $\texttt{skip}$. Our language uses C^+ so as to sidestep this check.

Both hold, yet no single 'most general' specification can derive them both. The first has the stronger postcondition but the smaller rely; the second is vice versa. This troublesome tradeoff can be blamed on stability: the larger the rely, the tougher the stability requirement, and thus, the weaker the postcondition.

In Sect. 4, we shall present a single specification for f() from which both of the above can be derived. Parameterised on an arbitrary rely R, it simply states that the postcondition needs weakening from x=X+1 just enough to become stable under R. Upon instantiating R to R_{x+}, to verify h(), the postcondition becomes x$\geq X$+1. And when R is $\emptyset$, for g()'s proof, no weakening is required.

3   Explicit Stabilisation

This section describes our formalisation of stability and applies it to the RG proof rules. The remaining sections develop two alternate proof systems: one (Sect. 4) that can specify libraries independently of clients, and another (Sects. 5 and 6) that lets a module hide from clients its internal interference.

We propose two new syntactic constructs: $\lfloor p \rfloor_R$ for the weakest assertion that is stronger than p and stable under R, and $\lceil p \rceil_R$ for the strongest assertion that is weaker than p and stable under R. That is, $\lfloor p \rfloor_R = \bigvee\{q \mid q \Rightarrow p \wedge q\ \text{stab}\ R\}$ and $\lceil p \rceil_R = \bigwedge\{q \mid q \Leftarrow p \wedge q\ \text{stab}\ R\}$.

Definition 3 (Semantics of $\lfloor p \rfloor_R$ and $\lceil p \rceil_R$). *The required properties are realised uniquely by the following constructions:*

$$\sigma \models \lfloor p \rfloor_R \overset{\text{def}}{\iff} \forall\sigma'. (\sigma,\sigma') \in R^* \implies \sigma' \models p$$

$$\sigma \models \lceil p \rceil_R \overset{\text{def}}{\iff} \exists\sigma'. (\sigma',\sigma) \in R^* \wedge \sigma' \models p.$$

Figure 2 presents the intuition behind our new operators. The nodes represent states; those that are filled satisfy some assertion p. The edges depict transitions of an arbitrary rely R. The states in $\lfloor p \rfloor_R$ are those from which any reachable state satisfies p. The states in $\lceil p \rceil_R$ are those reachable from a state in p.

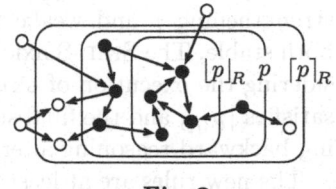

Fig. 2

Our operators can also be defined using Dijkstra's predicate transformer semantics [6]: $\lfloor p \rfloor_R$ is the weakest precondition of R^* given postcondition p, while $\lceil p \rceil_R$ is the strongest postcondition of R^* given precondition p.

Example. We stabilise x=0 and x$\neq$0 under R_{x+} (see Definition 2) like so:

$$\lfloor \text{x=0} \rfloor_{R_{x+}} \Leftrightarrow \text{false} \qquad \lceil \text{x=0} \rceil_{R_{x+}} \Leftrightarrow \text{x}\geq 0 \qquad \lfloor \text{x}\neq 0 \rfloor_{R_{x+}} \Leftrightarrow \text{x}> 0 \qquad \lceil \text{x}\neq 0 \rceil_{R_{x+}} \Leftrightarrow \text{true}$$

3.1   Properties of Explicit Stabilisation

Both $\lfloor\ \rfloor$ and $\lceil\ \rceil$ are monotonic with respect to $\Rightarrow$. They are related via the equivalence $\lfloor \neg p \rfloor_R \Leftrightarrow \neg \lceil p \rceil_{R^{-1}}$. Each has no effect on an already-stable operand, or when R is empty. Both true and false are stable, and conjunction and disjunction both preserve stability. The distributivity properties of $\lfloor \ \rfloor$ and $\lceil \ \rceil$ over $\land$ and $\lor$ are analogous to those of $\forall$ and $\exists$ respectively:

$$\lfloor p \land q \rfloor_R \Leftrightarrow \lfloor p \rfloor_R \land \lfloor q \rfloor_R \qquad\qquad \lfloor p \lor q \rfloor_R \Leftarrow \lfloor p \rfloor_R \lor \lfloor q \rfloor_R$$
$$\lceil p \land q \rceil_R \Rightarrow \lceil p \rceil_R \land \lceil q \rceil_R \qquad\qquad \lceil p \lor q \rceil_R \Leftrightarrow \lceil p \rceil_R \lor \lceil q \rceil_R$$

Several properties mirror those of the floor and ceiling functions in arithmetic, from which our syntax is borrowed. If $R \subseteq R'$, we have:

$$\lfloor \lfloor p \rfloor_R \rfloor_{R'} \Leftrightarrow \lfloor \lfloor p \rfloor_{R'} \rfloor_R \Leftrightarrow \lceil \lfloor p \rfloor_{R'} \rceil_R \Leftrightarrow \lfloor p \rfloor_{R'}$$
$$\lceil \lceil p \rceil_R \rceil_{R'} \Leftrightarrow \lceil \lceil p \rceil_{R'} \rceil_R \Leftrightarrow \lfloor \lceil p \rceil_{R'} \rfloor_R \Leftrightarrow \lceil p \rceil_{R'}$$

Finally, the following property reminds us of the trade-off mentioned in Sect. 2.1: that as the rely becomes more permissive, stability becomes harder to show:

$$R \subseteq R' \text{ implies } \lfloor p \rfloor_R \Leftarrow \lfloor p \rfloor_{R'} \text{ and } \lceil p \rceil_R \Rightarrow \lceil p \rceil_{R'}$$

3.2 Application to RG Proof Rules

We now describe how the RG proof rules (Fig. 1) can be adapted to use explicit stabilisation rather than side-conditions.

Figure 3 displays the replacements for the BA-SIC and SKIP rules; the others remain unchanged. The BASIC-S rule first derives p and q by considering c sequentially; that is, without concern for stability. A concurrent specification is obtained by strengthening p and weakening q until they are both stable. The SKIP-S axiom is justified by considering the execution of skip from an initial state satisfying p. This state also

BASIC-S
$$\frac{\vdash \{p\}\, c\, \{q\} \qquad \overline{p} \cap c \subseteq G}{R, G \vdash \{\lfloor p \rfloor_R\}\, c\, \{\lceil q \rceil_R\}}$$

SKIP-S
$$\frac{}{R, G \vdash \{p\}\, \text{skip}\, \{\lceil p \rceil_R\}}$$

Fig. 3. New RG proof rules (with stabilised assertions)

satisfies $\lceil p \rceil_R$, and the final state must too, since skip does nothing. The following backward-reasoning alternative is interderivable: $R, G \vdash \{\lfloor p \rfloor_R\}\, \text{skip}\, \{p\}$.

The new rules are at least as powerful as the originals, which can be obtained by restoring the stability checks and then removing the redundant stabilisations.

3.3 Aside: Simplification of Complex RG Proof Rules

We now highlight the elegance of explicit stabilisation by showing how it can simplify and generalise complex RG proof rules that rely subtly upon stability.

Coleman [5] proposes the following rule for reasoning about one-armed conditional statements whose test conditions are evaluated non-atomically in the presence of interference.

$$\frac{\text{StableExpr}(e_s, R) \quad R, G \vdash \{p \land e_s\}\, C\, \{q\} \quad \text{SingleUnstableVar}(e_u, R)}{\forall \sigma, \sigma'.\, \sigma \models p \land (\sigma, \sigma') \in R^* \land \sigma' \models \neg(e_s \land e_u) \Longrightarrow \sigma' \models q \quad \{\neg e_u, p, q\}\, \text{stab}\, R}{R, G \vdash \{p\}\, \text{if } e_u \land e_s \text{ then } C\, \{q\}}$$

Tests are pure, and comprise an unstable conjunct e_u and a 'stable' conjunct e_s that contains no variables that R can change (first premise). Crucially, only e_s can be assumed still to hold by C (second premise). By requiring e_u to involve only a single read of an unstable variable (third premise), we can treat it as a predicate of a single state – the state in which the read occurs – despite not knowing which state that is. Should the test fail, the postcondition must be met without evaluating C (fourth premise). That premise requires R to preserve the falsity of e_u (fifth premise) so as to ensure that the obligation to fulfil q cannot be bypassed by having the test evaluate to $\mathtt{false}$ but later become logically $\mathtt{true}$.

Now consider the following alternative rule, which uses explicit stabilisation.

$$\mathsf{SingleUnstableVar}(e, R) \qquad \{p, q\} \text{ stab } R \qquad \dfrac{R, G \vdash \{p \wedge \lceil e \rceil_R\} C_1 \{q\} \quad R, G \vdash \{p \wedge \lceil \neg e \rceil_R\} C_2 \{q\}}{R, G \vdash \{p\} \text{ if } e \text{ then } C_1 \text{ else } C_2 \{q\}}$$

Essentially, the execution of C_1 begins in a state that is reachable (by a sequence of environment actions) from one in which e evaluated to $\mathtt{true}$. Similarly, $\lceil \neg e \rceil_R$ describes a state reached from one where e did not hold. Stability checks on p and q remain only for compatibility with the rest of Coleman's system.

Thanks to explicit stabilisation, the new rule has fewer and simpler premises, plus it extends naturally to two-armed conditionals. Moreover, e need not be split into stable and unstable conjuncts, for our rule handles arbitrary test conditions.

4   Verifying Concurrent Library Code

Equipped with a notation for stabilising assertions, we revisit the challenge we set in Sect. 2.1: to verify concurrent library code using RG reasoning.

Recall our library function $\mathtt{f}()$ and its clients $\mathtt{g}()$ and $\mathtt{h}()$ from Definition 2. Using explicit stabilisation, we can derive the following specification, which is parametric in R (although its instantiation will be restricted, as described shortly).

$$R, G_{x+} \vdash \{\lceil \mathtt{x}=X \rceil_R\} \mathtt{f}() \{\lceil \mathtt{x}=X+1 \rceil_R\}$$

Observe that instantiating R to $\emptyset$ yields a specification suitable for proving $\mathtt{g}()$, while $\mathtt{h}()$ can be proved having set R to R_{x+}. We now present a proof system for such 'parametric specifications' and formally derive the above one for $\mathtt{f}()$.

In a parametric specification, the rely is replaced by a set of relies $\mathbb{R}$, and the pre and postconditions (denoted $\boldsymbol{p}$, $\boldsymbol{q}$, $\boldsymbol{r}$) become functions from relies to assertions. We shall use λ-calculus notation to describe such functions.

Definition 4. $\mathbb{R}, G \models_P \{\boldsymbol{p}\} C \{\boldsymbol{q}\} \overset{\text{def}}{\Longleftrightarrow} \forall R \in \mathbb{R}. R, G \models \{\boldsymbol{p}(R)\} C \{\boldsymbol{q}(R)\}$.

As the definition above shows, a parametric specification represents a family of specifications, one for each rely in $\mathbb{R}$. A selection of proof rules for parametric specifications are presented in Fig. 4; those not depicted are lifted in the obvious way. (See [21] for the full set.)

P-Weaken
$$\frac{\mathbb{R}', G' \vdash_\mathsf{P} \{p'\} C \{q'\} \quad p \Rightarrow_\mathbb{R} p' \quad q' \Rightarrow_\mathbb{R} q \quad \mathbb{R} \subseteq \mathbb{R}' \quad G' \subseteq G}{\mathbb{R}, G \vdash_\mathsf{P} \{p\} C \{q\}}$$

P-Par
$$\frac{\mathbb{R} \cup G_2, G_1 \vdash_\mathsf{P} \{p_1\} C_1 \{q_1\} \quad \mathbb{R} \cup G_1, G_2 \vdash_\mathsf{P} \{p_2\} C_2 \{q_2\}}{\mathbb{R}, G_1 \cup G_2 \vdash_\mathsf{P} \{p_1\ {}_{G_2}\|_{G_1}\ p_2\} C_1 \| C_2 \{q_1\ {}_{G_2}\|_{G_1}\ q_2\}}$$

P-Basic
$$\frac{\vdash \{p\} c \{q\} \quad \overline{p} \cap c \subseteq G}{\mathbb{U}, G \vdash_\mathsf{P} \{\lambda R. \lfloor p \rfloor_R\} c \{\lambda R. \lceil q \rceil_R\}}$$

P-Skip
$$\overline{\mathbb{U}, G \vdash_\mathsf{P} \{\lambda\_.p\} \ \mathtt{skip} \ \{\lambda R. \lceil p \rceil_R\}}$$

Abbreviations:

$$p_1 \Rightarrow_\mathbb{R} p_2 \ \overset{\text{def}}{=} \ \forall R \in \mathbb{R}.\, p_1(R) \Rightarrow p_2(R) \qquad \mathbb{R} \cup R \ \overset{\text{def}}{=} \ \{R' \cup R \mid R' \in \mathbb{R}\}$$
$$p_1\ {}_{R_1}\|_{R_2}\ p_2 \ \overset{\text{def}}{=} \ \lambda R.\, p_1(R \cup R_1) \wedge p_2(R \cup R_2) \qquad \mathbb{U} \ \overset{\text{def}}{=} \ \text{universal set of all relies}$$

Fig. 4. Selected proof rules for parametric specifications

$$\cfrac{\cfrac{\cfrac{\cfrac{\vdash \{p\} \, \mathtt{x{+}{+}} \, \{p[x-1/x]\}}{\vdash \{\lceil x{=}X \rceil_R\} \, \mathtt{x{+}{+}} \, \{\lceil x{=}X \rceil_R\,[x-1/x]\}} \ \text{Instantiate } p \text{ to } \lceil x{=}X \rceil_R}{\mathbb{U}, G_{x+} \vdash_\mathsf{P} \{\lambda R.\, \lceil x{=}X \rceil_R\} \, \mathtt{x{+}{+}} \, \{\lambda R.\, \lceil \lceil x{=}X \rceil_R [x-1/x] \rceil_R\}} \ \text{P-Basic}}{\mathtt{comm(x{+}{+})}, G_{x+} \vdash_\mathsf{P} \{\lambda R.\, \lceil x{=}X \rceil_R\} \, \mathtt{x{+}{+}} \, \{\lambda R.\, \lceil x{=}X{+}1 \rceil_R\}} \ \text{P-Weaken}} \ \text{Floyd's Assignment Axiom}$$

Fig. 5. Derivation of parametric specification for f()

The P-Par rule has grown considerably more complex. The reason is that at the fork and join of parallel commands, the rely changes. If the rely is R initially, then within the component commands the rely becomes either $R \cup G_2$ or $R \cup G_1$, and after joining, it reverts to R. Our rule simply reflects this progression.

The P-Basic and P-Skip rules both deduce specifications that feature the universal set of relies, which enables their use in *any* environment. The P-Weaken rule can then be used to shrink this set, typically removing the bigger relies. Doing so restricts a specification's reusability, but it enhances the applicability of the $\Rightarrow_\mathbb{R}$ relation that allows it to be simplified.

Theorem 5. *The proof rules of parametric stability are sound, that is:*

$$\mathbb{R}, G \vdash_\mathsf{P} \{p\} C \{q\} \implies \mathbb{R}, G \models_\mathsf{P} \{p\} C \{q\}$$

and they encode the proof rules of Fig. 1 (in which assertions do not contain explicit stabilisation), both completely and soundly, that is:

$$R, G \vdash \{p\} C \{q\} \implies \mathcal{P}(R), G \vdash_\mathsf{P} \{\lambda\_.p\} C \{\lambda\_.q\}$$
$$R, G \models \{p\} C \{q\} \impliedby \mathcal{P}(R), G \models_\mathsf{P} \{\lambda\_.p\} C \{\lambda\_.q\}$$

Here, the use of powersets lets the P-Weaken rule emulate the Weaken rule.

Figure 5 shows the derivation of our specification for f(). In applying the P-Basic rule, we utilised the identity $\lfloor \lceil x{=}X \rceil_R \rfloor_R \Leftrightarrow \lceil x{=}X \rceil_R$. The specification on the third line is the most general, as it allows the rely to be instantiated freely. Yet we do not stop there. We restrict the rely to the set comm(x++) of those that

$$\mathsf{comm}(\mathtt{x}{+}{+}), G_{\mathtt{x}+} \vdash_\mathsf{P} \{\lambda R.\ \lceil \mathtt{x}{=}X \rceil_R\}\ \mathtt{x}{+}{+}\ \{\lambda R.\ \lceil \lceil \mathtt{x}{=}X \rceil_R\ [\mathtt{x}{-}1/\mathtt{x}] \rceil_R\}$$

Set R to $\emptyset$ Set R to $R_{\mathtt{x}+}$

$$\emptyset, G_{\mathtt{x}+} \vdash \{\mathtt{x}{=}X\}\ \mathtt{f}()\ \{\mathtt{x}{=}X{+}1\} \qquad\qquad R_{\mathtt{x}+}, G_{\mathtt{x}+} \vdash \{\mathtt{x}{\geq}X\}\ \mathtt{f}()\ \{\mathtt{x}{\geq}X{+}1\}$$

Fig. 6. Instantiating the specification

'commute' with the $\mathtt{x}{+}{+}$ operation; that is, for which $\lceil p \rceil_R\ [\mathtt{x}{-}1/\mathtt{x}] \Leftrightarrow \lceil p[\mathtt{x}{-}1/\mathtt{x}] \rceil_R$ holds for all p. Using this property we can simplify the postcondition.

Figure 6 shows informally how the parametric specification can then be instantiated to two ordinary specifications, for use in proving the two clients $\mathtt{g}()$ and $\mathtt{h}()$. Really, this 'instantiation' is an application of the P-WEAKEN rule to restrict $\mathbb{R}$ to the singletons $\{\emptyset\}$ and $\{R_{\mathtt{x}+}\}$ respectively.[2]

In conclusion, we find that the 'most general' specifications that our parametric scheme can deduce are, though sometimes desirable, inhibited by their complexity. The specification on the third line of Fig. 5 contains two stabilisation operations in its postcondition – and this is for just a single basic command. A sequence of n basic commands, specified in a similar way, may contain up to $n + 1$ stabilisation operations in the postcondition (modelling the environmental interference before, between and after the commands). The complexity of the specification is thus comparable to the implementation it describes. Accordingly, it is crucial that our scheme allows specifications to be specialised to restricted sets of relies, and thence, simplified.

5 Explicit Stabilisation for RGSep

We now bring explicit stabilisation to RGSep [20], an RG-style logic that reasons about concurrent heap-manipulating programs by splitting the heap into shared and thread-local parts. The development in this section builds upon our application of explicit stabilisation to RG (Sect. 3), but we shall now leave behind the parametric specifications of Sect. 4.

Though designed for concurrency, we show (Sect. 5.3) how RGSep can be applied to sequential modules by reinterpreting the 'shared' heap as that part owned by the module (its so-called 'internal heap'). Our extension of RGSep with explicit stabilisation enables an INFOHIDING proof rule, by which a module can hide from clients the interference that affects its internal heap. We demonstrate our approach in Sect. 6, by verifying the Version 7 Unix memory manager.

5.1 Introduction to RGSep

RGSep extends ordinary RG reasoning with conceptual divisions of the heap into thread-local and shared parts. The rely and guarantee need specify only changes to the shared part, and thus become far more compact.

---

[2] Interestingly, although the relies $\emptyset$ and $R_{\mathtt{x}+}$ are both in $\mathsf{comm}(\mathtt{x}{+}{+})$, the same is not true of all those in $\mathcal{P}(R_{\mathtt{x}+})$: for instance, the rely that only increments $\mathtt{x}$ from 1 to 2.

$$P ::= e \overset{k}{\hookrightarrow} e \mid \mathsf{emp} \mid e = e \mid e > e \mid \mathsf{true} \mid \neg P \mid P \Rightarrow P \mid P * P \mid \exists x.\, P \mid \lfloor P \rfloor_R \mid \lceil P \rceil_R$$

where $k \in (0, 1]$ and e is a pure expression

$$h, i \models_{\mathsf{SL}} e_0 \overset{k}{\hookrightarrow} e_1 \quad \overset{\mathsf{def}}{\Longleftrightarrow} \quad h = \{ [\![e_0]\!]_i \overset{k}{\hookrightarrow} [\![e_1]\!]_i \}$$

$$h, i \models_{\mathsf{SL}} \mathsf{emp} \quad \overset{\mathsf{def}}{\Longleftrightarrow} \quad h = \emptyset$$

$$h, i \models_{\mathsf{SL}} P_0 * P_1 \quad \overset{\mathsf{def}}{\Longleftrightarrow} \quad \exists h_0, h_1.\, h_0 \bot h_1 \ \wedge \ h = h_0 \uplus h_1 \ \wedge \ h_0, i \models_{\mathsf{SL}} P_0 \ \wedge \ h_1, i \models_{\mathsf{SL}} P_1$$

$$h, i \models_{\mathsf{SL}} \lfloor P \rfloor_R \quad \overset{\mathsf{def}}{\Longleftrightarrow} \quad \forall h'.\, (h, h') \in R^* \Longrightarrow h', i \models_{\mathsf{SL}} P$$

$$h, i \models_{\mathsf{SL}} \lceil P \rceil_R \quad \overset{\mathsf{def}}{\Longleftrightarrow} \quad \exists h'.\, (h', h) \in R^* \ \wedge \ h', i \models_{\mathsf{SL}} P$$

where $h \bot h'$ means $\mathrm{dom}(h)$ and $\mathrm{dom}(h')$ are disjoint.

Fig. 7. Syntax and (selected) semantics of separation logic assertions

$$p ::= P \mid \boxed{P} \mid p * p \mid p \wedge p \mid p \vee p \mid \exists x.\, p \mid \forall x.\, p \mid \lfloor p \rfloor_R \mid \lceil p \rceil_R$$

$$l, s, i \models P \quad \overset{\mathsf{def}}{\Longleftrightarrow} \quad l, i \models_{\mathsf{SL}} P$$

$$l, s, i \models \boxed{P} \quad \overset{\mathsf{def}}{\Longleftrightarrow} \quad l = \emptyset \ \wedge \ s, i \models_{\mathsf{SL}} P$$

$$l, s, i \models p_0 * p_1 \quad \overset{\mathsf{def}}{\Longleftrightarrow} \quad \exists s_0, s_1.\, s_0 \bot s_1 \ \wedge \ s = s_0 \uplus s_1 \ \wedge \ l, s_0, i \models p_0 \ \wedge \ l, s_1, i \models p_1$$

$$l, s, i \models \lfloor p \rfloor_R \quad \overset{\mathsf{def}}{\Longleftrightarrow} \quad \forall s'.\, (s, s') \in (R \backslash l)^* \Longrightarrow l, s', i \models p$$

$$l, s, i \models \lceil p \rceil_R \quad \overset{\mathsf{def}}{\Longleftrightarrow} \quad \exists s'.\, (s', s) \in (R \backslash l)^* \ \wedge \ l, s', i \models p$$

Fig. 8. Syntax and (selected) semantics of RGSep assertions

RGSep inherits its ability to reason naturally about heap-manipulating programs from separation logic [13,18], the assertion language of which is presented in Fig. 7. States comprise a heap h mapping locations to values and a store i mapping variables to values. The $*$ operator attempts to split the heap using the $\uplus$ operator, such that the two (disjoint) parts respectively satisfy its two operands. We use the fractional permissions model [3], in which a heap may describe some locations only partially. For instance, the assertion $x \overset{1}{\mapsto} 3$ describes a heap comprising a single location x with value 3, and confers full (write) permission on that location. It may be split into several read-only permissions (e.g. $x \overset{.5}{\mapsto} 3 * x \overset{.5}{\mapsto} 3$) which may be shared between different threads. Threads communicate only via the heap, so the stabilisation operators can ignore the store.

Figure 8 presents the assertion language of RGSep, augmented with explicit stabilisation. The heap is split into disjoint local and shared regions, l and s, which are described by unboxed and boxed assertions respectively. The $*$ operator now splits only the local heap. The shared heap is never split, in order that all threads share the same view of it. For instance, if one thread's view of the overall state is described by $\boxed{P_s} * P_l$, and another's by $\boxed{Q_s} * Q_l$, then the $*$ operator combines them thus: $\boxed{P_s \wedge Q_s} * P_l * Q_l$.

Definition 6 (RGSep actions). *The action $P \rightsquigarrow Q$, defined $\{(s \uplus s_0, s' \uplus s_0) \mid \exists i.\, s, i \models_{\mathsf{SL}} P \ \wedge \ s', i \models_{\mathsf{SL}} Q\}$, replaces a part of the shared heap satisfying P with one satisfying Q.*

Definition 7 (Contextual actions). *The* contextual action $P \rightsquigarrow Q \mid F$, *defined* $\{(s \uplus s_F \uplus s_0, s' \uplus s_F \uplus s_0) \mid \exists i. \, s, i \models_{SL} P \, \wedge \, s', i \models_{SL} Q \, \wedge \, s_F, i \models_{SL} F\}$, *requires a separate (unaffected) part of the heap that satisfies F to catalyse it.*

5.2 RGSep and Stabilisation

Our semantics of $\lfloor p \rfloor_R$ and $\lceil p \rceil_R$ (Fig. 8) imposes the following restriction on R:

Definition 8 (Restricting the rely). $R \backslash l \overset{\text{def}}{=} \{(s, s') \in R \mid l \bot s \, \wedge \, l \bot s'\}$

The $R \backslash l$ operation removes from R impossible environmental actions that would make the shared heap overlap the current thread's local heap l.[3]

All of the properties detailed in Sect. 3.1 continue to hold. The following series of lemmas describe some additional RGSep-specific properties. Lemma 9 asserts that local assertions are vacuously stable.

Lemma 9 (Local assertions). $\lfloor P \rfloor_R \Leftrightarrow \lceil P \rceil_R \Leftrightarrow P$.

The next lemma says that we need not restrict the rely when stabilising a shared assertion. Such assertions imply that the local heap is empty (see Fig. 8), and thus unable to conflict with the shared heap.

Lemma 10 (Shared assertions). $\lfloor \boxed{P} \rfloor_R \Leftrightarrow \boxed{\lfloor P \rfloor_R}$ *and* $\lceil \boxed{P} \rceil_R \Leftrightarrow \boxed{\lceil P \rceil_R}$.

Finally, we describe the distributivity of the stabilisation operators over $*$.

Lemma 11 (Separately-conjoined assertions). $\lfloor p \rfloor_R * \lfloor q \rfloor_R \Rightarrow \lfloor p * q \rfloor_R$ *and* $\lceil p * q \rceil_R \Rightarrow \lceil p \rceil_R * \lceil q \rceil_R$.

Remark. Neither converse implication holds. Obtain a counterexample for the first from p as $\boxed{t \mapsto 0} * x \mapsto 0 \vee \boxed{t \mapsto 1} * y \mapsto 0$, q the same but with x and y swapped, and R as the single action $t \mapsto 0 \rightsquigarrow t \mapsto 1$. For the second, take p as $\boxed{\exists n. \, t \mapsto n \wedge n < 0}$, q as $\boxed{\exists n. \, t \mapsto n \wedge n > 0}$, and R able to increase t's value.

The proof rules of RGSep can be adapted to use explicit stabilisation. Figure 9 shows the replacement for RGSep's frame rule (see [21] for the complete set of new rules). The original rule required the frame r (which must not mention any local variables modified by C) to be stable under both R and G in case any shared heap it specifies is

FRAME-S

$$\frac{R, G \vdash \{p\} \, C \, \{q\} \qquad \text{fv}(r) \cap \text{mods}(C) = \emptyset}{R, G \vdash \{p * r\} \, C \, \{q * \lceil r \rceil_{R \cup G}\}}$$

Fig. 9. New frame rule

mutated by either the environment or C itself. In the new rule, this check becomes an explicit stabilisation on r in the postcondition. As in the SKIP-S rule (Fig. 3), the stabilisation could equally be done in the precondition instead.

---

[3] This approach slightly refines the presentation of stability in [19, Lem. 15], which did not consider such conflicts between shared and local heaps.

5.3   RGSep and Sequential Modules

This discussion lays the groundwork for the verification of a memory manager presented in Sect. 6. We shall assume a module comprises some state, including several heap locations, plus a collection of public routines that can manipulate this so-called 'internal heap'. A sequential module is one designed for single-threaded machines: its routines and all of its clients are sequential.

Sequential modules are analogous to the concurrent programs that RGSep was designed to verify. The RG method, of abstracting a command's environment by a rely, applies to both, albeit for different reasons. For concurrent programs, we must abstract the concurrently-running threads in order to avoid the combinatorial explosion that results from considering each possible interleaving of commands individually. For sequential modules, we must abstract clients' actions between module calls because we cannot know what clients will do. To verify sequential modules, we redeploy RGSep's 'shared' and 'thread-local' heaps to model the module's internal heap and, respectively, the heaps of its clients.

Consider a module M with several routines. A client first calls init(), which prepares part of M's state for this client, and may transfer ownership of some of M's heap cells. The return value x identifies subsequent calls in this sequence. The client then invokes some other routines of M – passing x as a parameter each time – before calling finalise(x) so that its parts of M's state can later be used for another client. We use 'client' here to refer to a sequence of calls parameterised on the same x.

The crux is to show that several interleaved clients can all interact with M safely. For instance: if one client executes x := init(), then another executes y := init() followed by a sequence of calls parameterised on y, can the first client be sure that M is still in a state of readiness for a sequence of calls parameterised on x, and that the intervening events have not affected its part of M's state?

This is actually a matter of stability: we are seeking to prove that the postcondition of x := init() is stable under an environment that can execute M's routines arbitrarily (excepting those parameterised on x). We need only consider an environment that calls M's routines: other activities do not affect M's internal state, so can be deemed local.

To define such an environment, we require x := init() to return a $token(\mathbf{x})$ predicate, to reside in the client's local heap. The predicate is *abstract* [16], which means that its definition is out of scope. Later module calls by this client (which we name $C_{\mathbf{x}}$) shall require the token's presence in its local heap, and the finalise(x) call shall confiscate it. The postcondition of x := init() is thus of the form $\boxed{P(\mathbf{x})} * token(\mathbf{x})$, where $P(\mathbf{x})$ describes an internal heap with a part initialised for $C_{\mathbf{x}}$. Let G be the set of RGSep actions by which M's routines can mutate its internal heap. Alone, $\boxed{P(\mathbf{x})}$ is not stable under G, for G includes actions that mutate $C_{\mathbf{x}}$'s part of the internal heap. Yet it becomes stable when combined with the local assertion $token(\mathbf{x})$. Why? Because the presence of the $token(\mathbf{x})$ in $C_{\mathbf{x}}$'s local state prohibits any *other* client having it and thus being able to continue the sequence of calls parameterised on x. It is vital that our refined notion of stability considers such conflicts between local and shared heaps

(Definition 8). Since stability occupies such a central role here, perhaps explicit stabilisation can be usefully applied? It can, in the following two ways.

Clarifying the stable parts of assertions. We have claimed $\boxed{P(\mathrm{x})} * token(\mathrm{x})$ to be a suitable – and stable – postcondition for init. Using explicit stabilisation, we now propose $\lfloor \boxed{P(\mathrm{x})} * token(\mathrm{x}) \rfloor_G$ instead. Strengthening the postcondition in this way *is* sound here, because the stabilisation has no effect on the already-stable assertion. Thus, the presence of $\lfloor \ \rfloor$ operators in the postcondition (and, dually, $\lceil \ \rceil$ in the precondition) serves to assert that their operands are stable. (In fact, $p \Leftrightarrow \lfloor p \rfloor_R$ exactly characterises those assertions that are stable under R.) We arrive at the following prototype specification:

$$G \vdash \{\lceil \boxed{P} \rceil_G\} \ \mathrm{x} := \mathtt{init}() \ \{\lfloor \boxed{P(\mathrm{x})} * token(\mathrm{x}) \rfloor_G * Q\}.$$

We omit here and henceforth the rely from specifications, there being only one thread. We retain the guarantee, whose abstraction of the module calls that the thread may make is utilised by the FRAME-S rule. The unparameterised P describes any valid internal heap of the module. See how the assertion Q, which describes cells that are transferred into the client's local heap, can be added outside the stabilised part: a client can mutate this part of the heap without concern for stability, the changes being purely local (see Lem. 9). Not all local changes can be treated so flippantly – indeed, the local assertion $token(\mathrm{x})$ is crucial to stability – but by delimiting the important assertions with the stabilisation syntax, we certify exactly which bits can and cannot be touched. Clients who obey this can be free of stability considerations, and instead rely on general properties of stabilisation, such as those detailed in Sect. 3.1.

Information hiding. Because the clients need not perform stabilisation, they need not even know the set of actions under which the assertions must be stable. That is, the definition of G can be kept internal to the module. This observation inspires the following proof rule.

$$\text{INFOHIDING} \quad \frac{\begin{array}{ll} \text{Module:} & (\Delta, G \vdash \{p_i\} \langle C_i \rangle \{q_i\})_{i=0}^n \\ \text{Client:} & \Delta' \subseteq \Delta \quad \Delta', (G \vdash \{p_i\} f_i \{q_i\})_{i=0}^n, G \vdash \{p\} C \{q\} \end{array}}{\text{Whole system:} \quad \vdash \{p\} \, \mathtt{let} \, (f_i{=}C_i)_{i=0}^n \, \mathtt{in} \, C \{q\}}$$

The rule concerns a sequential module comprising routines f_1 to f_n with implementations C_1 to C_n. The first line specifies each routine, in which G is the set of actions that clients of the module can perform. (In order to be able to access the module's internal heap, RGSep requires C_i to appear in angled brackets.) Δ denotes a set of predicate definitions, including the definition of *token* for instance. It also includes the definition of G, which we shall treat as an abstract predicate too. The second line specifies a client of the module, C. The Δ' it uses excludes the definitions of any predicates that are to remain abstract, and crucially, omits G's definition. Doing so makes the specification more reusable – even in the event that G changes – and hence more conducive to modular reasoning. Explicit stabilisation is vital here: the stabilisation operations in the p_i's and q_i's refer to a particular G in the module specifications, and an arbitrary G in the client specification.

Theorem 12. *The* INFOHIDING *rule is sound.*

Proof. The only departure from a typical rule for `let` commands is to remove G's definition from the client's specification, which logically strengthens one of the rule's assumptions.

6   Case Study: Verification of a Memory Manager

We now reify the concepts of Sect. 5 by verifying the Version 7 Unix memory manager. This illustrates both our extension of explicit stabilisation to RGSep, and the use of the INFOHIDING rule to hide a sequential module's internal interference from its clients. The verification itself is not only believed to be the first for this program; it also reveals a latent bug. The proof is one of safety: we prove neither termination nor that blocks are allocated in any particular fashion.

To begin, consider the following natural specifications, from [16], for `malloc` and `free`. Assume `malloc` cannot fail, and suppose a word is WORD bytes long.

$$\{\text{emp}\} \quad \text{x}:=\text{malloc}(\text{n} \times \text{WORD}) \quad \{token(\text{x},\text{n}) * \text{x}\mapsto\_ * \cdots * \text{x}+\text{n}-1\mapsto\_\}$$

$$\{\exists n.\, token(\text{x},n) * \text{x}\mapsto\_ * \cdots * \text{x}+n-1\mapsto\_\} \quad \text{free(x)} \quad \{\text{emp}\}$$

The `malloc` routine gives each client an abstract *token* predicate, which the client later uses to certify to `free` that the block being returned was truly allocated by `malloc` (`free`'s behaviour being undefined otherwise). These specifications could be realised naïvely by implementing $token(x,n)$ as $x-1\mapsto n$; that is, by storing the length of each block in the preceding cell.

Real memory managers are far more complex. The one we shall examine forms the cells that precede each block into a monotonically-increasing chain of pointers, linking all the allocated and free blocks. Such a manager must maintain in its internal heap the pointer chain, plus any free blocks, while the allocated blocks are conceptually held by each respective client. For a token, we can now afford only *half* of the cell preceding the block, because the manager must retain at least read-permission on this cell for later traversals of the pointer chain. Note that by creating the token from part of the existing datastructure, our proof avoids the need for auxiliary state.

The crux of the verification is to prove that a block allocated to a client remains allocated until, and only until, that client frees it; that is, it is not invalidated by other calls to `malloc` and `free`. Defining G as the set of actions of `malloc` and `free`, we are asking if `malloc`'s postcondition is stable under G.

It is easy to show that it is unaffected when these actions are applied to blocks other than the current one. And although the environment is *allowed* to apply these actions to the current block, it is actually *unable* to do so. Why? Because the current block cannot be accidentally re-allocated, since to do so would give

$$G \vdash \{\lceil \boxed{arena} \rceil_G\} \; \texttt{x:=malloc(n} \times \texttt{WORD)} \; \left\{ \begin{array}{c} \lfloor \boxed{arena} \rfloor_G * \lfloor arenatoken(\texttt{x},\texttt{n}) \rfloor_G \\ * \, \texttt{x} \mapsto_{-} * \cdots * \texttt{x+n}-1 \mapsto_{-} \end{array} \right\}$$

$$G \vdash \left\{ \begin{array}{c} \exists n. \lceil \boxed{arena} \rceil_G * \lceil arenatoken(\texttt{x},n) \rceil_G \\ * \, \texttt{x} \mapsto_{-} * \cdots * \texttt{x+n}-1 \mapsto_{-} \end{array} \right\} \; \texttt{free(x)} \; \{\lfloor \boxed{arena} \rfloor_G\}$$

Fig. 10. Specifications of `malloc` and `free`

$G \vdash \{\lceil \boxed{arena} \rceil_G\}$
    `x := malloc(2*WORD);`
3   $\{\lfloor \boxed{arena} \rfloor_G * \lfloor arenatoken(\texttt{x},2) \rfloor_G * \texttt{x} \mapsto_{-,-}\}$
   $\Longrightarrow \{\lceil \boxed{arena} \rceil_G * \lfloor arenatoken(\texttt{x},2) \rfloor_G * \texttt{x} \mapsto_{-,-}\}$
    `y := malloc(3*WORD);`
6   $\{\lfloor \boxed{arena} \rfloor_G * \lfloor arenatoken(\texttt{x},2) \rfloor_G * \texttt{x} \mapsto_{-,-} * \lfloor arenatoken(\texttt{y},3) \rfloor_G * \texttt{y} \mapsto_{-,-,-}\}$
    `[y+1] := 7;`
   $\{\lfloor \boxed{arena} \rfloor_G * \lfloor arenatoken(\texttt{x},2) \rfloor_G * \texttt{x} \mapsto_{-,-} * \lfloor arenatoken(\texttt{y},3) \rfloor_G * \texttt{y} \mapsto_{-,7,-}\}$
9   $\Longrightarrow \{\lceil \boxed{arena} \rceil_G * \lceil arenatoken(\texttt{x},2) \rceil_G * \texttt{x} \mapsto_{-,-} * \lfloor arenatoken(\texttt{y},3) \rfloor_G * \texttt{y} \mapsto_{-,7,-}\}$
    `free(x);`
   $\{\lfloor \boxed{arena} \rfloor_G * \lfloor arenatoken(\texttt{y},3) \rfloor_G * \texttt{y} \mapsto_{-,7,-}\}$

Fig. 11. Verification of a simple client

the client a duplicate token, which the $*$ operator forbids. And neither can it be accidentally freed, without yielding its token.

Using explicit stabilisation, here is a first attempt to specify `malloc`:

$$G \vdash \{\lceil \boxed{arena} \rceil_G\} \; \texttt{x:=malloc(n} \times \texttt{WORD)} \; \left\{ \begin{array}{c} \lfloor \boxed{arena(\texttt{x},\texttt{n})} * token(\texttt{x},\texttt{n}) \rfloor_G \\ * \, \texttt{x} \mapsto_{-} * \cdots * \texttt{x+n}-1 \mapsto_{-} \end{array} \right\}$$

The *arena* predicate asserts that the manager's internal heap is valid, while $arena(x,n)$ additionally asserts that the block at x is missing. Note that the stability of $\boxed{arena(x,n)}$ relies on the $token(x,n)$ predicate in the local heap.

This specification exposes too much of the manager's innards. We address this in the improved specifications in Fig. 10, by collapsing $\boxed{arena(x,n)} * token(x,n)$ into a single abstract predicate, $arenatoken(x,n)$. We also append the $\boxed{arena}$ predicate to both `malloc`'s postcondition and `free`'s precondition. Strictly, this is redundant, for $\boxed{arena}$ is entailed by $arenatoken$, but having `malloc`'s postcondition reestablish its precondition simplifies the verification of successive calls to `malloc` and allows the predicates to remain fully abstract.

Now consider the simple client in Fig. 11. Because the *content* of the block lies outside the scope of the stabilisation, the client can mutate it (line 7) without having to reconsider stability. The allocation of the block at y (line 5) does not affect the block at x: such a deduction is enabled by the FRAME-S rule of Fig. 9. (Although this rule imposes a stabilisation on the entire frame, we can leave this implicit for the local parts, by Lem. 9.) See how the use of explicit stabilisation allows the client's verifier to rely only on general properties of stabilisation: for instance, the deduction of the assertion on line 4 follows straight from $\lfloor p \rfloor_R \Rightarrow$

$p \Rightarrow \lceil p \rceil_R$. The definition of G is thus not needed by the client, so we can use our INFOHIDING rule to keep it internal to the module.

The rest of this section concerns the implementation (Sect. 6.1) and verification (Sect. 6.2) of the memory manager. The source code is provided in Appx. A; our full proof is in [21]. We omit an optimisation that tells `malloc` where to begin its search, because it contains a bug, which we explain in Sect. 6.3. Section 6.4 describes some peripheral details of the implementation and the verification.

6.1 Implementation of the Memory Manager

The memory manager controls the allocation and deallocation of blocks of main memory to and from client processes. The portion of memory it controls (shown in Fig. 12) contains both free and allocated blocks. The grey cells form a cyclic chain of pointers and the white blocks in between can be allocated to clients. Since blocks are word-

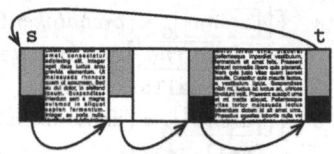

Fig. 12. An arena

aligned, the least significant bit in each pointer is redundant, and is hence employed to signal the availability of the following block. In the figure, black and white squares indicate that this so-called 'busy' bit is set and, respectively, unset. The module-level variables s and t respectively identify the first and last pointers in the arena. Because it is not followed by an allocatable block, the last pointer's busy bit is permanently set.

A client requests a block of n bytes by calling `malloc(n)`. For clarity of exposition we shall keep n a multiple of the word size, WORD. The routine traverses pointers until it finds a free block that is sufficiently large, returning the null pointer in the case of failure. It coalesces consecutive free blocks throughout the search. Should the block it finds be exactly the right size, a pointer to it is returned, and should it be too large, it is divided into two and a pointer to the first is returned. The client can later invoke `free(x)`, x being the address of the first cell in the block. Observe that `free` is not parameterised by the length of the block, because the length was recorded when `malloc` allocated it.

6.2 Details of the Verification

Figure 13 defines some auxiliary predicates used in the specifications and proof. $x \underset{u}{\to} y$ describes an unallocated block between x and y. Upon being allocated a block of size n with first cell x, the client is also given $token(x, n)$, which contains a half permission on the block's pointer; the manager retains the other half. We write $x \mapsto y_{busy}$ to mean that upon unsetting x's busy bit, it would contain the address of y. $x \frown y$ says that y is the special pointer at the end of the arena that points back to x, the start of the arena. $x \to y$ denotes a possibly-empty monotonically-increasing chain of pointers from x to y (including any unallocated blocks), the definition of which abbreviates $x \to x' * x' \twoheadrightarrow y$ to $x \to x' \twoheadrightarrow y$.

Figure 14 formalises the ways in which the internal heap of the module may be mutated by clients calling `malloc` and `free`. Only one routine can execute at

$$x_{\overrightarrow{u}}y \stackrel{\text{def}}{=} x<y \wedge x\mapsto y * (x+1)\mapsto_{-} * \cdots * (y-1)\mapsto_{-}$$

$$x_{\overrightarrow{a}}y \stackrel{\text{def}}{=} x<y \wedge x\overset{.5}{\mapsto} y_{\text{busy}}$$

$$x\,{}_{\shortmid}y \stackrel{\text{def}}{=} x_{\overrightarrow{u}}y \vee x_{\overrightarrow{a}}y$$

$$x^{\frown}y \stackrel{\text{def}}{=} x<y \wedge y\mapsto x_{\text{busy}}$$

$$x\rightarrow y \stackrel{\text{def}}{=} (\exists x'.\ x\rightarrow x'\twoheadrightarrow y) \vee (x{=}y \wedge \text{emp})$$

$$arena \stackrel{\text{def}}{=} s\twoheadrightarrow t * s^{\frown}t$$

$$arena(x,n) \stackrel{\text{def}}{=} s\twoheadrightarrow(x-1)_{\overrightarrow{a}}(x+n)\twoheadrightarrow t * s^{\frown}t$$

$$token(x,n) \stackrel{\text{def}}{=} (x-1)\overset{.5}{\mapsto}(x+n)_{\text{busy}}$$

$$arenatoken(x,n) \stackrel{\text{def}}{=} \boxed{arena(x,n)} * token(x,n)$$

Fig. 13. Predicates

Coalesce:	$a_{\overrightarrow{u}}b_{\overrightarrow{u}}c$	$\rightsquigarrow$	$a_{\overrightarrow{u}}c$	$\mid$ $s\twoheadrightarrow a$
AllocateEntire:	$a_{\overrightarrow{u}}b$	$\rightsquigarrow$	$a_{\overrightarrow{a}}b$	$\mid$ $s\twoheadrightarrow a$
AllocatePart:	$a_{\overrightarrow{u}}b$	$\rightsquigarrow$	$a_{\overrightarrow{a}}(b-n)_{\overrightarrow{u}}b$	$\mid$ $s\twoheadrightarrow a$
Free:	$a_{\overrightarrow{a}}b$	$\rightsquigarrow$	$a_{\overrightarrow{u}}b$	$\mid$ $s\twoheadrightarrow a$

Fig. 14. Main actions

once, so it would suffice to list a single action for each. We prefer to split them into several simple actions. The first coalesces two consecutive free blocks. The second allocates an entire block to a client, while the third allocates just the initial part. The fourth frees a block. The context $s\twoheadrightarrow a$ ensures that the blocks that are acted upon are really in the arena. G is the union of all these actions.

6.3 A (Faulty) Optimisation

The following bug was discovered during the verification process.

The manager maintains a global variable p (named allocp in the original source code) that, after a block is allocated, is pointed to the successive block, and after a block is freed, is pointed to that block. It serves to identify a good place for the next call to malloc to begin its search. The implementation does not update

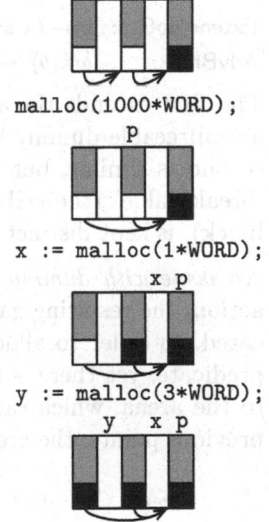

malloc(1000*WORD);

x := malloc(1*WORD);

y := malloc(3*WORD);

Fig. 15. The bug

p if allocation fails, however, and therein lies the bug: p *should* be updated in case the block to which it points has been coalesced with its predecessor, lest it be left pointing inside a block.

Figure 15 demonstrates how this bug could wreak havoc. Our contrived arena contains just two one-word blocks, both of which are free, and p initially points to the second. The first malloc call fails, but has the side-effect of leaving p inside the coalesced block. We then allocate a small block at x, before wrapping around to the start of the arena and allocating a larger block at y, thereby reaching a situation in which the contents of the smaller block is allocated twice.

The discovery of this bug was prompted by the failure of the invariant s↠p, which states that p identifies a valid pointer in the arena. We have successfully executed our exploit to confirm that the bug is real.

6.4   Other Issues

There are several other issues involved in the implementation and verification of the memory manager, which we explain now. These issues have been sidestepped so far in order to focus on the crucial parts of the verification.

Allocation failure.   To handle the case where `malloc` fails, its postcondition should be disjoined with the following assertion: $\lfloor \boxed{arena} \rfloor_{\mathsf{G}} * \mathbf{x}{=}0$.

Extending the arena.   Once the search for a block has exhausted the arena, `malloc` invokes `sbrk` to ask the system for another block of memory. This block will be located at an address above t because, in Version 7 Unix, memory allocated via `sbrk` is never returned. The following three actions should be added to G, to formalise these calls to `sbrk`:[4]

ExtendGap: $\&t{\mapsto}t * s{\frown}t * brk(b) \wedge b{>}t{+}1 \rightsquigarrow \&t{\mapsto}t' * t{-}_{\exists}b{-}_{\mathsf{U}}t' * s{\frown}t' * brk(t'{+}1)$
ExtendNoGap: $\&t{\mapsto}t * s{\frown}t * brk(t{+}1) \rightsquigarrow \&t{\mapsto}t' * t{-}_{\mathsf{U}}(t{+}1){-}_{\mathsf{U}}t' * s{\frown}t' * brk(t'{+}1)$
AdvBreak: $brk(b) \rightsquigarrow \exists n{>}0.\, brk(b{+}n)$

The first extends the arena with a new block, leaving a gap that is filled with an unfreeable dummy block to maintain the illusion of a contiguous arena. The second is similar, but without the gap. The third action, which advances the 'break value' (the cell at which the next successful call to `sbrk` will return a block), is kept distinct to reflect that it may be performed in other situations.

An issue with dummy blocks.   When the arena is extended via the ExtendGap action, the resulting gap is filled with a dummy block that is permanently allocated. In order to allocate such a block, we need to hand the caller the *token* predicate, yet there is no client in this situation. We thus add a `true` predicate to the arena, which can 'soak up' these spare tokens. Considering this and the previous points, the arena (see Fig. 13) can be more precisely defined as follows:

$$arena \stackrel{\text{def}}{=} \exists s,t,b.\, \mathsf{true} * \&s{\mapsto}s * \&t{\mapsto}t * s{\rightarrow}t * s{\frown}t * brk(b) \wedge t < b$$

7   Related Work

Explicit stabilisation arose out of 'mid stability' [19, §4.1], a variation of RG reasoning that places stability checks not on the pre and postconditions of basic commands, but at the points of sequential and parallel composition instead. This more strategic placement eliminates redundant checks, and also allows libraries

---

[4] We are now treating module-level variables more carefully: the variable t is modelled as a heap cell at address &t, thus allowing its value to be altered by these actions.

comprising just one basic command to be verified without considering stability. Our parametric proof system (Fig. 4) extends this to *all* library functions (and encodes mid stability soundly and completely).

RG-style reasoning has been used before to verify concurrent library code (e.g. [10]). The specifications of that approach involve a particular rely, whereas our parametric specifications do not require a particular rely to be instantiated.

RG has also furnished proofs of sequential modules before (e.g. [22]), but we believe ours to be the first that hides the module's internal interference. The INFOHIDING rule that enables this feat is related to the hypothetical frame rule [15]: the latter rule hides the module's *state* from the client, while ours hides the module's *interference*. Perhaps the hypothetical frame rule could be used to remove the $\boxed{arena}$ predicate from the verification given in Fig. 11, thus revealing to the client neither the module's state nor its internal interference.

SAGL [9], like RGSep, is a descendant of RG and separation logic, to which explicit stabilisation could also be applied. Local Rely-Guarantee (LRG) [8] is a third descendant that addresses an inherent flaw in the modularity of its siblings: that the shared heap must be globally known. It defines a ∗ operator over interference, which allows the shared heap to be split into portions that are shared between just a few threads. The application of explicit stabilisation to LRG could simplify the verification of clients that invoke multiple modules, for our approach currently handles only one.

Explicit stabilisation can be seen as a bridge between theory and implementation: tools, such as SmallfootRG [4], that automate RG-style reasoning may defer stability checks rather than perform them at the point of rule application, and explicit stabilisation can help to formalise this 'lazy' approach. We have not considered the implementation of stabilisation; this issue is explored in [2].

8 Conclusion

We have proposed explicit stabilisation as a new way to deal with stability in RG reasoning. The central idea is to record information about an assertion's stability into its syntactic form. The main benefits are in modular reasoning:

Library code can be verified independently of clients. In Sect. 4, we showed how an approach based upon explicit stabilisation enables RG reasoning to verify concurrent library code. Essentially, the stabilisation in the library's specification is evaluated so lazily that it actually becomes an obligation of the client.

Client code can be verified independently of a sequential module. We showed in Sect. 5 how the application of explicit stabilisation to RGSep gives rise to an INFOHIDING rule that allows a sequential module to hide its internal interference from its clients. Such information hiding is crucial for modular reasoning, because it allows the specification of a client to be reused, even despite changes to the specification of this internal interference. Section 6 demonstrated this reasoning by verifying a memory manager.

It would be interesting to investigate whether these two forms of modularity can be combined; that is, can we verify both a library and its clients, modularly, at the same time? It looks feasible. The specification for the library in Sect. 4 used explicit stabilisation with an arbitrary rely R, which became specific for each client in turn. Meanwhile, the specifications for the memory manager in Sect. 6 used explicit stabilisation with the specific G of the module, which was then generalised to an arbitrary G for the clients, so as to provide information hiding. Perhaps a combination of these approaches would parameterise on both the rely and the guarantee?

We also plan to apply explicit stabilisation to more advanced logics based on RG, such as LRG, Deny-Guarantee [7], and the logic of Gotsman et al. for proving liveness [11]. The notions of stability in such logics are becoming ever more demanding, so it is increasingly important to have a solid basis upon which to reason about stability. We believe explicit stabilisation provides such a basis.

Acknowledgements

The idea of parameterising RG specifications on the 'current rely' is due to Hongseok Yang. Richard Bornat introduced us to the malloc example. We also thank Joey Coleman, Xinyu Feng, Erica Fulbrook, Cliff Jones, Alexander Malkis, Tom Ridge and Viktor Vafeiadis for feedback and helpful discussions. This work was supported by EPSRC grant F019394/1. Parkinson is supported by a Royal Academy of Engineering/EPSRC fellowship.

References

1. Abadi, M., Cardelli, L., Curien, P.-L., Lévy, J.-J.: Explicit substitutions. In: POPL (1990)
2. Amjad, H., Bornat, R.: Towards automatic stability analysis for rely-guarantee proofs. In: Jones, N.D., Müller-Olm, M. (eds.) VMCAI 2009. LNCS, vol. 5403, pp. 14–28. Springer, Heidelberg (2009)
3. Bornat, R., Calcagno, C., O'Hearn, P., Parkinson, M.: Permission accounting in separation logic. In: POPL (2005)
4. Calcagno, C., Parkinson, M., Vafeiadis, V.: Modular safety checking for fine-grained concurrency. In: Riis Nielson, H., Filé, G. (eds.) SAS 2007. LNCS, vol. 4634, pp. 233–248. Springer, Heidelberg (2007)
5. Coleman, J.W.: Expression decomposition in a Rely/Guarantee context. In: Shankar, N., Woodcock, J. (eds.) VSTTE 2008. LNCS, vol. 5295, pp. 146–160. Springer, Heidelberg (2008)
6. Dijkstra, E.W.: A Discipline of Programming. Prentice Hall, Inc., Englewood Cliffs (1976)
7. Dodds, M., Feng, X., Parkinson, M., Vafeiadis, V.: Deny-Guarantee reasoning. In: Castagna, G. (ed.) ESOP 2009. LNCS, vol. 5502, pp. 363–377. Springer, Heidelberg (2009)
8. Feng, X.: Local rely-guarantee reasoning. In: POPL (2009)
9. Feng, X., Ferreira, R., Shao, Z.: On the relationship between concurrent separation logic and assume-guarantee reasoning. In: De Nicola, R. (ed.) ESOP 2007. LNCS, vol. 4421, pp. 173–188. Springer, Heidelberg (2007)
10. Flanagan, C., Freund, S.N., Qadeer, S., Seshia, S.A.: Modular verification of multithreaded programs. Theor. Comput. Sci. 338(1-3) (2005)

11. Gotsman, A., Cook, B., Parkinson, M., Vafeiadis, V.: Proving that non-blocking algorithms don't block. In: POPL (2009)
12. Hoare, C.A.R.: An axiomatic basis for computer programming. Commun. ACM 12(10) (1969)
13. Ishtiaq, S.S., O'Hearn, P.W.: BI as an assertion language for mutable data structures. In: POPL (2001)
14. Jones, C.B.: Development methods for computer programs including a notion of interference. PhD thesis, University of Oxford (1981)
15. O'Hearn, P.W., Yang, H., Reynolds, J.C.: Separation and information hiding. In: POPL (2004)
16. Parkinson, M., Bierman, G.: Separation logic and abstraction. In: POPL (2005)
17. Prensa Nieto, L.: The Rely-Guarantee method in Isabelle/HOL. In: Degano, P. (ed.) ESOP 2003. LNCS, vol. 2618, pp. 348–362. Springer, Heidelberg (2003)
18. Reynolds, J.C.: Separation logic: A logic for shared mutable data structures. In: LICS (2002)
19. Vafeiadis, V.: Modular fine-grained concurrency verification. PhD thesis, University of Cambridge (2007)
20. Vafeiadis, V., Parkinson, M.: A marriage of Rely/Guarantee and separation logic. In: Caires, L., Vasconcelos, V.T. (eds.) CONCUR 2007. LNCS, vol. 4703, pp. 256–271. Springer, Heidelberg (2007)
21. Wickerson, J., Dodds, M., Parkinson, M.: Explicit Stabilisation for Modular Rely-Guarantee Reasoning. Technical report, University of Cambridge (2010)
22. Yorsh, G., Skidanov, A., Reps, T., Sagiv, M.: Automatic assume/guarantee reasoning for heap-manipulating programs: Ongoing work. In: AIOOL (2005)

A   Source Code of Unix V7 Memory Manager

Abridged and corrected. Retrieved from the Unix Heritage Society.[5]

```
#define WORD sizeof(st)                         if(p>q) ;
#define BLOCK 1024                               else if(q!=t || p!=s) return 0;
#define testbusy(p) ((int)(p)&1)                 else if(++temp>1) break;
#define setbusy(p) (st *)((int)(p)|1)          }
#define clearbusy(p) (st *)((int)(p)&~1)       temp = ((nw+BLOCK/WORD)
struct store { struct store *ptr; };                   /(BLOCK/WORD))*(BLOCK/WORD);
typedef struct store st;                         q = (st *)sbrk(0);
static st s[2]; /*initial arena*/                if(q+temp < q) return 0;
// static struct store *allocp; (bug removed)    q = (st *)sbrk(temp*WORD);
static st *t;    /*arena top*/                   if((int)q == -1) return 0;
char* sbrk();                                    t->ptr = q;
char* malloc(unsigned nbytes) {                  if(q!=t+1) t->ptr = setbusy(t->ptr);
  register st *p, *q;                            t = q->ptr = q+temp-1;
  register nw; static temp;                      t->ptr = setbusy(s);
  // omitted: initialisation code             }
  nw = (nbytes+WORD+WORD-1)/WORD;             found:
  for(p=s; ; ) {                                 if(q>p+nw) ((st *)(p+nw))->ptr = p->ptr;
    for(temp=0; ; ) {                            p->ptr = setbusy(p+nw);
      if(!testbusy(p->ptr)) {                    return((char *)(p+1));
        while(!testbusy((q=p->ptr)->ptr))      }
          p->ptr = q->ptr;                     free(register char *ap) {
        if(q>=p+nw && p+nw>=p) goto found;       register st *p = ((st *)ap)-1;
      }                                          p->ptr = clearbusy(p->ptr);
      q = p; p = clearbusy(p->ptr);           }
```

---

[5] http://minnie.tuhs.org/UnixTree/V7/usr/src/libc/gen/malloc.c.html

Author Index

Adjé, Assalé   23
Aiken, Alex   246
Amtoft, Torben   43
Andrade, Henrique   507
Appel, Andrew W.   145
Askarov, Aslan   64
Atkey, Robert   85

Baillot, Patrick   104
Banerjee, Anindya   2
Bernardy, Jean-Philippe   125
Binsztok, Henri   345
Blazy, Sandrine   145
Boudol, Gérard   165

Chang, Bor-Yuh Evan   387
Chen, Juan   529
Chugh, Ravi   529
Claessen, Koen   125

Dal Lago, Ugo   205
Deshmukh, Jyotirmoy   226
Dillig, Isil   246
Dillig, Thomas   246
Dodds, Mike   610
D'Silva, Vijay   185

Feng, Xinyu   267
Ferreira, Carla   366
Ferreira, Rodrigo   267

Gaboardi, Marco   104
Gaubert, Stéphane   23
Gedik, Buğra   507
Goubault, Eric   23
Grimm, Robert   507

Hatcliff, John   43
Hirzel, Martin   507
Hoffmann, Jan   287
Hofmann, Martin   287
Hu, Zhenjiang   448

Jaeger, Trent   327
Jagadeesan, Radha   307
Jansson, Patrik   125

Jha, Somesh   327
Jha, Susmit   327

King, Dave   327
Koprowski, Adam   345
Kumar, Vibhore   507

Lanese, Ivan   366
Laviron, Vincent   387
Leino, K. Rustan M.   407
Lindley, Sam   1
Lochbihler, Andreas   427

Matsuda, Kazutaka   448
Meola, Matthew L.   468
Mogbil, Virgile   104
Müller, Peter   407
Mu, Shin-Cheng   448
Muthukumaran, Divya   327
Myers, Andrew   64

Nakata, Keiko   488
Naumann, David A.   2

Parkinson, Matthew   610
Petri, Gustavo   165
Pitcher, Corin   307
Pucella, Riccardo   550

Ramalingam, G.   226
Ranganath, Venkatesh-Prasad   226
Riely, James   307
Rival, Xavier   387
Robillard, Benoît   145
Rodríguez, Edwin   43

Schöpp, Ulrich   205
Seshia, Sanjit A.   327
Shao, Zhong   267
Shivers, Olin   570
Smans, Jan   407
Soulé, Robert   507
Swamy, Nikhil   529

Takeichi, Masato   448
Tov, Jesse A.   550

Uustalu, Tarmo   488

Vardoulakis, Dimitrios   570
Vaswani, Kapil   226
Vaz, Cátia   366

Wadler, Philip   1
Walker, David   468
Wenner, Alexander   590
Wickerson, John   610
Wu, Kun-Lung   507

Printed in the United States
By Bookmasters